Marketing Management

Knowledge and Skills

McGraw-Hill/Irwin Series in Marketing

Arens
Contemporary Advertising
Ninth Edition
Arnould, Price & Zinkhan
Consumers
Second Edition
Bearden, Ingram, & LaForge
Marketing: Principles & Perspectives
Fourth Edition
Belch & Belch
Advertising & Promotion: An Integrated Marketing Communications Approach
Sixth Edition
Bingham & Gomes
Business Marketing Management
Second Edition
Boyd, Walker, Mullins & Larreche
Marketing Management: A Strategic Decision-Making Approach
Fourth Edition
Cateora & Graham
International Marketing
Eleventh Edition
Cole & Mishler
Consumer and Business Credit Management
Eleventh Edition
Cravens & Piercy
Strategic Marketing
Seventh Edition
Cravens, Lamb & Crittenden
Strategic Marketing Management Cases
Seventh Edition
Crawford & Di Benedetto
New Products Management
Seventh Edition
Dolan
Marketing Management: Text and Cases
First Edition
Duncan
IMC: Using Advertising and Promotion to Build Brands
First Edition
Dwyer & Tanner
Business Marketing
Second Edition
Eisenmann
Internet Business Models: Text and Cases
First Edition
Etzel, Walker & Stanton
Marketing
Twelfth Edition
Forrest
Internet Marketing Intelligence
First Edition

Futrell
ABC's of Relationship Selling
Eighth Edition
Futrell
Fundamentals of Selling
Seventh Edition
Hair, Bush & Ortinau
Marketing Research
Second Edition
Hawkins, Best & Coney
Consumer Behavior
Ninth Edition
Johansson
Global Marketing
Third Edition
Johnston & Marshall
Churchill/Ford/Walker's Sales Force Management
Seventh Edition
Kerin, Hartley, & Rudelius
Marketing: The Core
First Edition
Kerin, Berkowitz, Hartley & Rudelius
Marketing
Seventh Edition
Lehmann & Winer
Analysis for Marketing Planning
Fifth Edition
Lehmann & Winer
Product Management
Third Edition
Levy & Weitz
Retailing Management
Fifth Edition
Mason & Perreault
The Marketing Game!
Third Edition
McDonald
Direct Marketing: An Integrated Approach
First Edition
Mohammed, Fisher, Jaworski & Cahill
Internet Marketing: Building Advantage in a Networked Economy
Second Edition
Monroe
Pricing
Third Edition
Pelton, Strutton & Lumpkin
Marketing Channels: A Relationship Management Approach
Second Edition
Peppers & Rogers
Managing Customer Relationships to Build Competitive Advantage
First Edition

Perreault & McCarthy
Basic Marketing: A Global Managerial Approach
Fourteenth Edition
Perreault & McCarthy
Essentials of Marketing: A Global Managerial Approach
Ninth Edition
Peter & Donnelly
A Preface to Marketing Management
Ninth Edition
Peter & Donnelly
Marketing Management: Knowledge and Skills
Seventh Edition
Peter & Olson
Consumer Behavior
Sixth Edition
Purvis & Burton
Which Ad Pulled Best?
Ninth Edition
Rayport & Jaworski
Introduction to e-Commerce
Second Edition
Rayport & Jaworski
e-Commerce
First Edition
Rayport & Jaworski
Cases in e-Commerce
First Edition
Richardson
Internet Marketing
First Edition
Roberts
Internet Marketing: Integrating Online and Offline Strategies
First Edition
Spiro, Stanton, Rich
Management of a Sales Force
Eleventh Edition
Stock & Lambert
Strategic Logistics Management
Fourth Edition
Ulrich & Eppinger
Product Design and Development
Second Edition
Walker, Boyd, Mullins & Larreche
Marketing Strategy: A Decision-Focused Approach
Fourth Edition
Weitz, Castleberry & Tanner
Selling: Building Partnerships
Fifth Edition
Zeithaml & Bitner
Services Marketing
Third Edition

Marketing Management

Knowledge and Skills

7th Edition

J. Paul Peter
University of Wisconsin–Madison

James H. Donnelly, Jr.
University of Kentucky

Boston Burr Ridge, IL Dubuque, IA Madison, WI New York
San Francisco St. Louis Bangkok Bogotá Caracas Kuala Lumpur
Lisbon London Madrid Mexico City Milan Montreal New Delhi
Santiago Seoul Singapore Sydney Taipei Toronto

Irwin

MARKETING MANAGEMENT: KNOWLEDGE AND SKILLS
Published by McGraw-Hill/Irwin, a business unit of The McGraw-Hill Companies, Inc., 1221 Avenue of the Americas, New York, NY, 10020. Copyright © 2004, 2001, 1998, 1995, 1992, 1989, 1986 by The McGraw-Hill Companies, Inc. All rights reserved. No part of this publication may be reproduced or distributed in any form or by any means, or stored in a database or retrieval system, without the prior written consent of The McGraw-Hill Companies, Inc., including, but not limited to, in any network or other electronic storage or transmission, or broadcast for distance learning.

Some ancillaries, including electronic and print components, may not be available to customers outside the United States.

This book is printed on acid-free paper.

domestic   1 2 3 4 5 6 7 8 9 0 DOW/DOW 0 9 8 7 6 5 4 3
international 1 2 3 4 5 6 7 8 9 0 DOW/DOW 0 9 8 7 6 5 4 3

ISBN 0-07-255217-4

Publisher: *John E. Biernat*
Executive editor: *Linda Schreiber*
Editorial Assistant: *Caroline McGillen*
Marketing manager: *Kim Kanakes*
Media producer: *Craig Atkins*
Senior project manager: *Jean Lou Hess*
Senior production supervisor: *Michael R. McCormick*
Director of design BR: *Keith J. McPherson*
Photo research coordinator: *Kathy Shive*
Photo researcher: *David A. Tietz*
Senior supplement producer: *Susan Lombardi*
Senior digital content specialist: *Brian Nacik*
Cover design: *JoAnne Schopler*
Cover Image: *© Getty Images, Javier Pierini*
Typeface: *10/12 New Baskerville*
Compositor: *Carlisle Communications, Ltd.*
Printer: *R. R. Donnelley*

Library of Congress Control Number: 2003102629

INTERNATIONAL EDITION ISBN 0-07-121505-0
Copyright © 2004. Exclusive rights by The McGraw-Hill Companies, Inc. for manufacture and export. This book cannot be re-exported from the country to which it is sold by McGraw-Hill. The International Edition is not available in North America.

www.mhhe.com

To Gayla, thank you for ten years.

Jim Donnelly

To Rose and Angie

J. Paul Peter

About the Authors

J. Paul Peter is the James R. McManus-Bascom Professor and Chair of the Marketing Department at the University of Wisconsin–Madison. He was a member of the faculty at Indiana State, Ohio State, and Washington University before joining the Wisconsin faculty in 1981. While at Ohio State, he was named Outstanding Marketing Professor by the students and has won the John R. Larson Teaching Award at Wisconsin. He has taught a variety of courses including Marketing Management, Marketing Strategy, Consumer Behavior, Marketing Research, and Marketing Theory, among others.

Professor Peter's research has appeared in the *Journal of Marketing,* the *Journal of Marketing Research,* the *Journal of Consumer Research,* the *Journal of Retailing,* and the *Academy of Management Journal,* among others. His article on construct validity won the prestigious William O'Dell Award from the *Journal of Marketing Research,* and he was a finalist for this award on two other occasions. He is an author or editor of over 30 books, including *A Preface to Marketing Management,* ninth edition; *Marketing Management: Knowledge and Skills,* seventh edition; *Consumer Behavior and Marketing Strategy,* seventh edition; *Strategic Management: Concepts and Applications,* third edition; and *Marketing: Creating Value for Customers,* second edition. He is one of the most cited authors in the marketing literature.

Professor Peter has served on the review boards of the *Journal of Marketing, Journal of Marketing Research, Journal of Consumer Research,* and *Journal of Business Research* and was measurement editor for *JMR* and professional publications editor for the American Marketing Association. He has taught in a variety of executive programs and consulted for several corporations as well as the Federal Trade Commission.

James H. Donnelly, Jr., is the Thomas C. Simons Professor in the Gatton College of Business and Economics at the University of Kentucky. In 1990 he received the first Chancellor's Award for Outstanding Teaching given at the University. Previously, he had twice received the UK Alumni Association's Great Teacher Award, an award one can only be eligible to receive every 10 years. He has also received two Outstanding Teacher awards from Beta Gamma Sigma, national business honorary. In 1992 he received an Acorn Award recognizing "those who shape the future" from the Kentucky Advocates for Higher Education. In 1995 he became one of six charter members elected to the American Bankers Association's Bank Marketing Hall of Fame. He has also received a "Distinguished Doctoral Graduate Award" from the University of Maryland.

During his career he has published in the *Journal of Marketing Research, Journal of Marketing, Journal of Retailing, Administrative Science Quarterly, Academy of Management Journal, Journal of Applied Psychology, Personnel Psychology, Journal of Business Research,* and *Operations Research* among others. He has served on the editorial review board of the *Journal of Marketing.* He is the author of more than a dozen books, which include widely adopted academic texts as well as professional books.

Professor Donnelly is very active in the banking industry where he currently serves on the board of directors of the Institute of Certified Bankers and the ABA's Marketing Network. He is also the academic dean of the ABA's School of Bank Marketing and Management.

Preface

From the outset, we have envisioned *Marketing Management: Knowledge and Skills* to be a complete student resource for marketing management education. Our vision for this, the seventh edition, remains the same. As the resources students and instructors need have changed, the book has changed. This edition is no exception. However, our overriding goal remains the same: to enhance students' *knowledge* of marketing management and to advance their *skills* in using this knowledge to develop and maintain successful marketing strategies.

THE SEVENTH EDITION

The basic structure of our text continues to evolve and has been expanded, particularly during this and the previous edition. Some important changes include the following:

1. Because the text chapters are an integral part of the book, they have been completely updated and revised in this edition. In fact, several chapter titles have been changed to reflect the new content. In addition, each chapter has been updated and contains additional references that students can use for writing projects and case presentations. Some specific content changes include a new What Is Marketing? discussion, new mission statement examples, and a reorganization and new discussion of organizational strategies; expanded coverage of the marketing research process with emphasis on both qualitative and quantitative research methods; a new section, Psychological Influences on Consumer Decision Making; a new section, Categories of Organizational Buyers; revised material on the effective use of cross-functional teams in product management, a new discussion of product mix and product line, and new material on the composition of new product teams; all new discussions of public relations and direct marketing, a new discussion of the promotion mix, an expanded discussion of integrated marketing communications, and a new discussion of push versus pull marketing; all new discussions of technology and the sales force and the evolution of personal selling; expanded coverage of electronic retailing with particular emphasis on the advantages and disadvantages for marketers; a new pricing model that emphasizes breaking down pricing decisions into a set of manageable stages; new material on quality service on the Internet; and an expanded discussion of organizing the multinational firm and global branding.

   A popular feature of the text chapters that has received very positive feedback from both students and teachers is the occasional "marketing highlight" that appears throughout. Not the usual "news items" found in other texts, this feature emphasizes important information and handy tools for analyzing marketing cases and problems. We have revised and replaced many in this edition.

2. A new section initiated with the previous edition includes 11 Internet exercises for those instructors wishing to add them to the skill development component of their course. These exercises have been revised and updated and were developed to relate specifically to the content of the text chapters. They are all strategic in

focus and allow students to relate the concepts in the text chapters to the challenges of marketing on the Internet.

3. The search for new cases is an unending one because finding relevant new cases is a challenge. But we have been fortunate to continue to locate truly outstanding new cases. We have added 17 new ones to this edition. Our emphasis continues to be on well-known companies whenever possible, including both domestic and global companies, high-tech companies, consumer and organizational products, small and large businesses, products and services, and manufacturers and channel members. Additional cases "Outback Goes International," Briggs & Stratton Corporation: Competing in the Outdoor Power Equipment Industry," and "Carnival Corporation: 1998" can be found on the website.

   We believe that many of the popular cases we retain in the book can truly be considered "classics." But whether set in 2002 or 1992, these "snapshots in time" enable students to analyze the situation within the time period the case was written and/or bring the situation up-to-date with their own research and analysis.

4. A new resource initiated in the previous edition and revised and updated in this edition is an annotated bibliography of the major online databases used in marketing. It is an up-to-date resource for students to use in the analysis of cases, the development of marketing plans, and the analysis of Internet exercises. It is included in Section IV immediately following the Internet exercises.

5. Some of the cases include in-class exercises that provide the instructor with additional means of enhancing student learning, participation, and team building.

6. A number of the cases include video instructions and discussion questions to enhance student interest, thinking, and analysis.

We have experimented over many years with various teaching philosophies. The structure of this book evolved and continues to evolve from these experiments. Currently, our six-stage learning approach includes (1) learning basic marketing principles, (2) learning approaches and tools for performing marketing analyses, (3) analyzing Internet exercises, (4) analyzing marketing management cases, (5) analyzing strategic marketing cases, and (6) developing marketing plans.

Our six-stage learning approach is the focus of the seven book sections. Each section has as its objective either *knowledge enhancement,* or *skill development,* or both. The framework and structure of our book is presented in the diagram on page ix, which will be used throughout the text to integrate various sections.

STAGE 1: LEARNING BASIC MARKETING PRINCIPLES

It is clearly necessary for students to learn and understand basic definitions, concepts, and marketing logic before they can apply them in the analysis of marketing problems or development of marketing plans. Section I of the book contains 13 chapters that present the essentials of marketing management. One problem we continually face in more advanced case-oriented courses is that most students have long ago discarded or sold their basic marketing texts. Consequently, when they are faced with case problems they have nothing to rely on but their memories. We believe this seriously detracts from the usefulness of case analysis. Thus, we include this section as a reference source for key marketing concepts. Our objective in this section is to focus on material that is relevant primarily for analyzing marketing problems and cases.

STAGE 2: LEARNING APPROACHES AND TOOLS FOR PROBLEM ANALYSIS

The second stage in our approach involves offering students basic tools and approaches for solving marketing problems. Section II, "Analyzing Marketing Problems and Cases," is a widely praised approach to analyzing, writing, and presenting case analyses. Section III, "Financial Analysis for Marketing Decisions," presents some important financial calculations that can be useful in evaluating the financial position of a firm and the financial impact of various marketing strategies. Section IV includes an annotated bibliography of some of the most widely used marketing databases. It will assist students in researching a particular industry or firm and can greatly improve the analysis of cases.

STAGE 3: ANALYZING INTERNET EXERCISES

As a way of introducing students to the challenges of case analysis, some instructors utilize Internet exercises. They find that these exercises are an especially useful way to integrate text material with case work. Accordingly, Section IV provides 11 such exercises. Other instructors, especially those with more advanced marketing students, find their students are fully prepared to tackle case analyses. For these instructors, this section is optional.

STAGE 4: ANALYZING MARKETING MANAGEMENT CASES

It has been our experience that few students have the confidence and experience necessary to analyze complex strategic marketing cases in their first exposure to this type of learning. We believe it is far better for them to apply their skills by analyzing cases for which traditional marketing principles can be applied somewhat directly before they attempt more challenging problems. Accordingly, Section V of the book has been expanded to include 32 marketing management cases, organized into six groups: market opportunity analysis, product strategy, promotion strategy, distribution strategy, pricing strategy, and social and ethical issues in marketing management. Within each group, cases are sequenced so that later cases contain more information and typically require higher levels of marketing management analysis skills than earlier ones.

STAGE 5: ANALYZING STRATEGIC MARKETING CASES

Once students have developed sufficient skills to provide thoughtful analyses of marketing management cases, they are prepared to tackle strategic marketing cases. These cases go beyond traditional marketing principles and focus on the role of marketing in cross-functional business or organization strategies. Section VI of our book contains 9 such cases. They are sequenced so that the latter cases contain more information and require higher skill levels to analyze them properly.

STAGE 6: DEVELOPING MARKETING PLANS

The final stage in our approach involves the development of an original marketing plan. We believe that after a two-course sequence in marketing management, students should be able to do one thing very well and should know that they can do it well: Students should be able to construct a quality marketing plan for any product or service. Section VII provides a framework for developing such a plan. Instructors can consult the *Instructors Manual* that accompanies this book for alternative ways to incorporate this stage into their course.

We have found that this six-stage process is very flexible and can easily be adapted to student needs and instructor objectives. For example, if the course is the first learning experience in marketing, then emphasis could be placed on the first four stages. If students progress well through these stages, then marketing management cases can be assigned on an individual or group basis.

If the course is for students with one or more previous courses in marketing or is the capstone marketing management course, then major attention should shift to stages 2 through 6. In this instance, Section I becomes a resource for review and reference and the course focuses more on skill development.

Finally, the text can be used for a two-course sequence in marketing management. The first course can emphasize stages 1 through 4 and the second can concentrate on stages 5 and 6.

Acknowledgments

Our appreciation and thanks go to all of the case and exercise writers who contributed their work to help others better educate marketing students. Each of the contributors' names and affiliations appear in the Contents and at the point in the book where their contribution appears.

Many thanks to the users who responded to our survey. Your responses were valuable because they were used in planning this edition and in making the hard choices involved in replacing cases, selecting new cases, and deciding on which of the "classic" cases remain. Again, thank you for your help.

We also want to acknowledge those colleagues who provided detailed reviews of previous editions:

Sammy G. Amin
Frostburg State University

Andrew Bergstein
Pennsylvania State University

V. Glenn Chappell
Meredith College

Henry Chen
University of West Florida

Newell Chiesl
Indiana State University

John Considine
LeMoyne College

Mike Dailey
University of Texas, Arlington

Randall Ewing
Ohio Northern University

Renee Foster
Delta State University

John Gauthier
Gateway Technical College

David Griffith
University of Oklahoma

Jack Healey
Golden State University

JoAnne S. Hooper
Western Carolina University

Benoy Joseph
Cleveland State University

Anne B. Lowery
University of Mobile

Gregory Martin
University of West Florida

Wendy Martin
Judson College

Mary K. McManamon
Lake Erie College

Donald J. Messmer
College of William & Mary

William F. Schoell
University of Southern Mississippi

Anusorn M. Singhapakdi
Old Henry Dominion University

Jean Shaneyfelt
Edicon Community College

John Shaw
Providence College

Charlotte Smedberg
Florida Metropolitan University System

Joseph R. Stasio
Merrimack College

Albert J. Taylor
Austin Peay State University

Kevin Webb
Drexel University

Dale Wilson
Michigan State University

We want to acknowledge these colleagues who provided valuable market feedback for this edition:

Denver D'Rozario
Howard University

Arun K. Jain
University at Buffalo

David Bourff
Boise State University

Patricia Duncan
Harris-Stowe State College

Paula Welch
Mansfield University

Wesley H. Jones
University of Indianapolis

Patricia Humphrey
Texas A&M University

Adel I. El-Ansary
University of North Florida

Daniel P. Chamberlin
Regent University

Thomas L. Parkinson
Moravian College

Dillard Tinsley
Austin State University

Carl Dresden
Coastal Carolina University

Carol Bruneau
University of Montana

R. Mark Smith
Campbell University

Joanne Trotter
Gwynedd-Mercy College

Pravat K. Choudhury
Howard University

Hatash Sachdev
Eastern Michigan University

Brad Brooks
Queens College

Jarrett Hudnall
Mississippi University for Women

Mark Young
Winona State University

Dr. Henry C.K. Chen
University of West Florida

Steven Lysonski
Marquette University

Hudson Nwakanma
Florida A&M University

Chris Samfilippo
University of Michigan—Dearborn

David J. Vachon
CSUN

Linda Schreiber, executive editor; Caroline McGillen, editorial assistant; Kimberly Kanakes, marketing manager; and Jean Lou Hess, senior project manager, provided the leadership required to bring the edition to print. Sarah Crago was invaluable in managing the survey of users. All of these professionals make it a pleasure to be Mc-Graw-Hill/Irwin authors.

Michael Knetter, Dean of the School of Business at the University of Wisconsin, and Devanthan Sudharshan, Dean of the Gatton College of Business and Economics at the University of Kentucky, support our efforts and we are very grateful to them.

Finally, thanks to Charles Heath of Xavier University and Geoffrey Gordon of Northern Illinois University who have contributed to this edition and its predecessors.

J. Paul Peter
James H. Donnelly, Jr.

Contents

SECTION ONE
ESSENTIALS OF MARKETING
MANAGEMENT   1

PART A
INTRODUCTION   1

1   Strategic Planning and the Marketing Management Process   2
   The Marketing Concept   2
   What Is Marketing?   3
   What Is Strategic Planning?   3
     Strategic Planning and Marketing Management   4
     The Strategic Planning Process   5
     The Complete Strategic Plan   13
   The Marketing Management Process   14
     Situation Analysis   14
     Marketing Planning   17
     Implementation and Control of the Marketing Plan   18
     Marketing Information Systems and Marketing Research   18
   The Strategic Plan, the Marketing Plan, and Other Functional Area Plans   19
   Conclusion   20
   Appendix
   Portfolio Models   22

PART B
MARKETING INFORMATION,
RESEARCH, AND UNDERSTANDING
THE TARGET MARKET   27

2   Marketing Research: Process and Systems for Decision Making   28
   The Role of Marketing Research   28
   The Marketing Research Process   29
     Purpose of the Research   29
     Plan of the Research   29
     Performance of the Research   34
     Processing of Research Data   34
     Preparation of the Research Report   36

     Limitations of the Research Process   37
   Marketing Information Systems   37
   Conclusion   39

3   Consumer Behavior   41
   Social Influences on Consumer Decision Making   41
     Culture and Subculture   43
     Social Class   43
     Reference Groups and Families   44
   Marketing Influences on Consumer Decision Making   44
     Product Influences   45
     Price Influences   45
     Promotion Influences   45
     Place Influences   45
   Situational Influences on Consumer Decision Making   45
   Psychological Influences on Consumer Decision Making   47
     Product Knowledge   47
     Product Involvement   47
   Consumer Decision Making   48
     Need Recognition   48
     Alternative Search   49
     Alternative Evaluation   50
     Purchase Decision   50
     Postpurchase Evaluation   52
   Conclusion   54
   Appendix
   Selected Consumer Behavior Data Sources   55

4   Business, Government, and Institutional Buying   56
   Categories of Organizational Buyers   56
     Producers   56
     Intermediaries   56
     Government Agencies   57
     Other Institutions   57
   The Organizational Buying Process   57
   Purchase-Type Influences on Organizational Buying   57
     Straight Rebuy   57
     Modified Rebuy   58
     New Task Purchase   58

Structural Influences on Organizational
Buying   58
  Purchasing Roles   59
  Organization-Specific Factors   59
  Purchasing Policies and Procedures   60
Behavioral Influences on Organizational
Buying   61
  Personal Motivations   61
  Role Perceptions   63
Stages in the Organizational Buying
Process   63
  Organizational Need   65
  Vendor Analysis   65
  Purchase Activities   65
  Postpurchase Evaluation   66
Conclusion   67

5   Market Segmentation   68
Delineate the Firm's Current Situation   68
Determine Consumer Needs and Wants   69
Divide Markets on Relevant Dimensions   69
  A Priori versus Post Hoc Segmentation   70
  Relevance of Segmentation Dimensions   70
  Bases for Segmentation   72
Develop Product Positioning   76
Decide Segmentation Strategy   78
Design Marketing Mix Strategy   79
Conclusion   80

PART C
THE MARKETING MIX   81

6   Product Strategy   82
Basic Issues in Product Management   82
  Product Definition   82
  Product Classification   83
  Product Quality and Value   84
  Product Mix and Product Line   85
  Branding and Brand Equity   88
  Packaging   90
Product Life Cycle   91
The Product Audit   92
  Deletions   92
  Product Improvement   94
Organizing for Product Management   94
Conclusion   96

**7   New Product Planning and
Development   98**
New Product Strategy   99
New Product Planning and Development
Process   102
  Idea Generation   102
  Idea Screening   104
  Project Planning   104
  Product Development   105
  Test Marketing   106
  Commercialization   106
  The Importance of Time   106
Causes of New Product Failure   106
  Need for Research   108
Conclusion   109

**8   Integrated Marketing Communications:
Advertising, Sales Promotion, Public
Relations, and Direct Marketing   111**
The Promotion Mix   111
Integrated Marketing Communications   113
Advertising: Planning and Strategy   114
  Objectives of Advertising   114
Advertising Decisions   116
  The Expenditure Question   116
  The Allocation Question   118
Sales Promotion   123
  Push versus Pull Marketing   123
  Trade Sales Promotions   123
  Consumer Promotions   124
  What Sales Promotion Can and Can't Do   124
Public Relations   126
Direct Marketing   126
Conclusion   127

Appendix
Major Federal Agencies Involved in Control of
Advertising   128

**9   Personal Selling, Relationship Building,
and Sales Management   129**
Importance of Personal Selling   129
The Sales Process   130
  Objectives of the Sales Force   130
  The Sales Relationship-Building Process   131
  People Who Support the Sales Force   136
Managing the Sales and Relationship-
Building Process   137
  The Sales Management Task   138

Controlling the Sales Force   139
Motivating and Compensating Performance   142
Conclusion   144

10   Distribution Strategy   145
The Need for Marketing Intermediaries   145
Classification of Marketing Intermediaries
and Functions   145
Channels of Distribution   146
Selecting Channels of Distribution   148
Specific Considerations   149
Managing a Channel of Distribution   152
Relationship Marketing in Channels   152
Vertical Marketing Systems   152
Wholesaling   154
Store and Nonstore Retailing   156
Store Retailing   156
Nonstore Retailing   157
Electronic Exchange   158
Conclusion   160

11   Pricing Strategy   162
Demand Influences on Pricing Decisions   162
Demographic Factors   162
Psychological Factors   162
Price Elasticity   164
Supply Influences on Pricing Decisions   164
Pricing Objectives   164
Cost Considerations in Pricing   164
Product Considerations in Pricing   166
Environmental Influences on Pricing
Decisions   167
Competition   167
Government Regulations   168
A General Pricing Model   168
Set Pricing Objectives   169
Evaluate Product-Price Relationships   170
Estimate Costs and Other Price Limitations   171
Analyze Profit Potential   171
Set Initial Price Structure   171
Change Price as Needed   171
Conclusion   172

PART D
MARKETING IN SPECIAL FIELDS   173

12   The Marketing of Services   174
Important Characteristics of Services   175
Intangibility   176

Inseparability   176
Perishability and Fluctuating Demand   178
Highly Differentiated Marketing Systems   178
Client Relationship   180
Providing Quality Services   180
Customer Satisfaction Measurement   182
The Importance of Internal Marketing   182
Overcoming the Obstacles in Service
Marketing   184
Limited View of Marketing   184
Limited Competition   184
Noncreative Management   185
No Obsolescence   185
The Service Challenge   186
Banking   186
Health Care   187
Insurance   187
Travel   187
Implications for Service Marketers   189
Conclusion   189

13   Global Marketing   190
Organizing for Global Marketing   191
Problems with Entering Foreign Markets   191
Organizing the Multinational Company   193
Programming for Global Marketing   195
Global Marketing Research   195
Global Product Strategy   198
Global Distribution Strategy   199
Global Pricing Strategy   200
*Global Advertising and Sales Promotion
Strategy   200*
Entry and Growth Strategies for Global
Marketing   202
Conclusion   204

SECTION TWO
**ANALYZING MARKETING PROBLEMS
AND CASES   205**

A Case Analysis Framework   206
1. Analyze and Record the Current Situation   207
*2. Analyze and Record Problems and Their Core
Elements   211*
*3. Formulate, Evaluate, and Record Alternative
Courses of Action   212*
*4. Select and Record the Chosen Alternative and
Implementation Details   212*

Pitfalls to Avoid in Case Analysis   213
Communicating Case Analyses   215
The Written Report   215
The Oral Presentation   217
Conclusion   217

SECTION THREE
FINANCIAL ANALYSIS FOR MARKETING DECISIONS   219

Financial Analysis   220
Break-Even Analysis   220
Net Present Value Analysis   222
Ratio Analysis   224
Conclusion   228

SECTION FOUR
INTERNET EXERCISES AND SOURCES OF MARKETING INFORMATION   229

PART A
INTERNET EXERCISES   231
Charles Heath: Xavier University

Exercise 1
Corporate Websites   232

Exercise 2
Online vs. Offline Retail Experiences   232

Exercise 3
Consumer Decision-Making Process   233

Exercise 4
Discovering Product Assortments Online   233

Exercise 5
Brand Equity on the Internet   234

Exercise 6
The Impact of Communities on Marketing   234

Exercise 7
Branding for Pure Plays   235

Exercise 8
Pricing Issues on the Internet   235

Exercise 9
Selecting the Internet as a Distribution Channel   236

Exercise 10
Internet Advertising   236

Exercise 11
The Adaptation of Services to the Internet   237

PART B
INTERNET SOURCES OF MARKETING INFORMATION   239
Charles Heath: Xavier University

SECTION FIVE
MARKETING MANAGEMENT CASES   245

CASE GROUP A
MARKET OPPORTUNITY ANALYSIS   247

Case 1
Abercrombie & Fitch   247

Jerry C. Olson: Pennsylvania State University

Case 2
McDonald's Corporation in the New Millennium   250

J. Paul Peter and Ashish Gokhale: University of Wisconsin–Madison

Case 3
Campus Calendar   257

William R. Wynd: Eastern Washington University

Case 4
3DV–LS: Assessing Market Opportunity in the Computer Visualization Market   261

Robin Habeger and Kay M. Palan: Iowa State University

Case 5
South Delaware Coors, Inc.   272

James E. Nelson and Eric J. Karson: University of Colorado

Case 6
Claritas Inc.: Using Compass and PRIZM   281

Valerie Walsh and J. Paul Peter: University of Wisconsin–Madison

CASE GROUP B
PRODUCT STRATEGY   294

Case 7
Starbucks   294

Ashish Gokhale and J. Paul Peter: University of Wisconsin–Madison

Case 8
Pfizer, Inc. Animal Health Products Industry Downturns and Marketing Strategy   298

Jakki J. Mohr and Sara Streeter: University of Montana

Case 9
Snacks to Go   309

JoAnn K. Linrud: Central Michigan University

Case 10
Salomon: The Monocoque Ski   326

Francis Bidault: International Management Development Institute

Case 11
Cannondale Corporation   343

Romuald A. Stone: Keller Graduate School of Management, and John E. Gamble: University of South Alabama

Case 12
Callaway Golf Company   372

John E. Gamble: University of South Alabama

CASE GROUP C
PROMOTION STRATEGY   406

Case 13
harley-davidson.com and the Global Motorcycle Industry   406

J. Paul Peter: University of Wisconsin–Madison

Case 14
Wind Technology   411

Ken Manning: University of South Carolina, and Jakki J. Mohr: University of Montana

Case 15
Lady Foot Locker: The Lobo Launch   417

Andrew J. Rohm: Northeastern University, David W. Rosenthal: Miami University, and Thomas C. Boyd: Cal State Fullerton

Case 16
Longevity Healthcare Systems, Inc.   436

Lawrence M. Lamont and Elizabeth W. Storey: both of Washington and Lee University

CASE GROUP D
DISTRIBUTION STRATEGY   451

Case 17
Amazon.com   451

J. Paul Peter: University of Wisconsin–
Madison

Case 18
Tupperware   454

J. Paul Peter: University of Wisconsin–
Madison

Case 19
Blockbuster Entertainment
Corporation   457

James A. Kidney: Southern Connecticut
State University

Case 20
Peapod in the Online Grocery Business   469

Alan B. Eisner and Nichole Belmont: Lubin
School of Business, Pace University

Case 21
eBay: King of the Online Auction
Industry   490

Lou Marino and Patrick Kreiser:
The University of Alabama

CASE GROUP E
PRICING STRATEGY   524

Case 22
Little Caesars   524

J. Paul Peter: University of Wisconsin–
Madison

Case 23
Schwinn Bicycles   526

J. Paul Peter: University of Wisconsin–
Madison

Case 24
Cowgirl Chocolates   529

John J. Lawrence, Linda J. Morris, and
Joseph J. Geiger: University of Idaho

Case 25
America Online (AOL)   543

Natalya V. Delcoure, Lawrence R. Jauch,
and John L. Scott: Northeast Louisiana
University

Case 26
Sun Microsystems: A High Growth, Loosely
Organized Giant in a Constrained,
Technology Intensive Environment   557

Walter E. Greene: University of Texas Pan
American, and William C. House: University
of Arkansas–Fayetteville

CASE GROUP F
SOCIAL AND ETHICAL ISSUES IN
MARKETING MANAGEMENT   568

Case 27
Notetakers Company: Selling Class Notes
and Instructional Notes to Students   568

S. J. Garner and Judy Spain: Eastern
Kentucky University

Case 28
Nintendo versus SEGA: Sex, Violence, and
Videogames   572

Romuald A. Stone: James Madison University

Case 29
E. & J. Gallo Winery   577

A. J. Strickland III and Daniel C. Thurman:
University of Alabama

Case 30
Sarah Norton and Wise Research   585

Ronald L. Coulter, D. Michael Fields, and
Mary K. Coulter: Southwest Missouri State
University, Rebecca J. Gordon-Runyan:
WRG Inc.

Case Thirty-One
Philip Morris Companies 598

Keith Robbins: George Mason University

Case Thirty-Two
Black Diamond Equipment, LTD. 612

Steven J. Maranville: University of St. Thomas, and Madeleine E. Pullman: Colorado State University

SECTION SIX
STRATEGIC MARKETING CASES 629

Case 1
Caterpillar Inc. 631

Sara L. Pitterle and J. Paul Peter: University of Wisconsin–Madison

Case 2
Harley-Davidson, Inc.—Motorcycle Division 644

J. Paul Peter: University of Wisconsin–Madison

Case 3
Nanophase Technologies Corporation 657

Lawrence M. Lamont: Washington and Lee University

Case 4
L. A. Gear, Inc. 676

A. J. Almaney, S. Green, S. Slotkin, and H. Speer: DePaul University

Case 5
Kikkoman Corporation in the Mid-1990s: Market Maturity, Diversification, and Globalization 697

Norihito Tanaka: Kanagawa University, Marilyn L. Taylor: University of Missouri at Kansas City, and Joyce A. Claterbos: University of Kansas

Case 6
Kentucky Fried Chicken and the Global Fast-Food Industry in 1998 722

Jeffrey A. Krug: University of Illinois at Urbana–Champaign

Case 7
The Black & Decker Corporation in 2000 746

John E. Gamble: University of South Alabama, and Arthur A. Thompson: University of Alabama

Case 8
Campbell Soup Company in 2000 769

John E. Gamble: University of South Alabama, and Arthur A. Thompson, Jr.: University of Alabama

Case 9
Dell Computer Corporation: Strategy and Challenges for the 21st Century 799

Arthur A. Thompson: University of Alabama: and John E. Gamble: University of South Alabama

SECTION SEVEN
DEVELOPING MARKETING PLANS 841

A Marketing Plan Framework 842
   Title Page 843
   Executive Summary 843
   Table of Contents 844
   Introduction 844
   Situational Analysis 844
   Marketing Planning 845
   Implementation and Control of the Marketing Plan 848
   Summary 848
   Appendix—Financial Analysis 849
   References 852
  Conclusion 852
Chapter Notes 853

Index 861

Section I

Essentials of Marketing Management

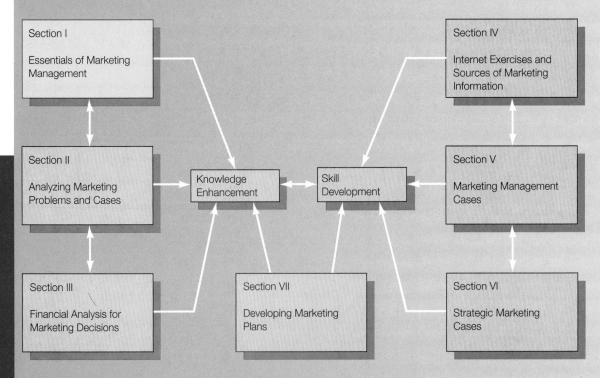

Section I
Essentials of Marketing Management

Section IV
Internet Exercises and Sources of Marketing Information

Section II
Analyzing Marketing Problems and Cases

Knowledge Enhancement

Skill Development

Section V
Marketing Management Cases

Section III
Financial Analysis for Marketing Decisions

Section VII
Developing Marketing Plans

Section VI
Strategic Marketing Cases

Introduction

Part A

1 Strategic Planning and the Marketing Management Process

1

Strategic Planning and the Marketing Management Process

The purpose of this introductory chapter is to present the marketing management process and outline what marketing managers must *manage* if they are to be effective. In doing so, it will also present a framework around which the remaining chapters are organized. Our first task is to review the organizational philosophy known as the marketing concept, since it underlies much of the thinking presented in this book. The remainder of this chapter will focus on the process of strategic planning and its relationship to the process of marketing planning.

THE MARKETING CONCEPT

Simply stated, the marketing concept means that *an organization should seek to make a profit by serving the needs of customer groups.* The concept is very straightforward and has a great deal of commonsense validity. Perhaps this is why it is often misunderstood, forgotten, or overlooked.

The purpose of the marketing concept is to rivet the attention of marketing managers on serving broad classes of customer needs (customer orientation), rather than on the firm's current products (production orientation) or on devising methods to attract customers to current products (selling orientation). Thus, effective marketing starts with the recognition of customer needs and then works backward to devise products and services to satisfy these needs. In this way, marketing managers can satisfy customers more efficiently in the present and anticipate changes in customer needs more accurately in the future. This means that organizations should focus on building long-term customer relationships in which the initial sale is viewed as a beginning step in the process, not as an end goal. As a result, the customer will be more satisfied and the firm will be more profitable.

The principal task of the marketing function operating under the marketing concept is not to manipulate customers to do what suits the interests of the firm, but rather to find effective and efficient means of making the business do what suits the interests of customers. This is not to say that all firms practice marketing in this way. Clearly, many firms still emphasize only production and sales. However, effective marketing, as defined in this text, requires that consumer needs come first in organizational decision making.

One qualification to this statement deals with the question of a conflict between consumer wants and societal needs and wants. For example, if society deems clean air and water as necessary for survival, this need may well take precedence over a consumer's want for goods and services that pollute the environment.

WHAT IS MARKETING?

Everyone reading this book has been a customer for most of their life. Last evening you stopped into a local supermarket to graze at the salad bar, pick up some bottled water and a bag of Fritos corn chips. While you were there, you snapped a $1.00 coupon for a new flavor salad dressing out of a dispenser and tasted some new breakfast potatoes being cooked in the back of the store. As you sat down at home to eat your salad, you answered the phone and someone suggested that you need to have your carpets cleaned. Later on in the evening you saw TV commercials for tires, soft drinks, athletic shoes, and the dangers of smoking and drinking during pregnancy. Today when you enrolled in a marketing course, you found that the instructor has decided that you must purchase this book. A friend has already purchased the book on the Internet. All of these activities involve marketing. And each of us knows something about marketing because it has been a part of our life since we had our first dollar to spend.

Since we are all involved in marketing, it may seem strange that one of the persistent problems in the field has been its definition.[1] The American Marketing Association defines marketing as "the process of planning and executing conception, pricing, promotion, and distribution of ideas, goods, and services to create exchanges that satisfy individual and organizational goals."[2] This definition takes into account all parties involved in the marketing effort: members of the producing organization, resellers of goods and services, and customers or clients. While the broadness of the definition allows the inclusion of nonbusiness exchange processes, the primary emphasis in this text is on marketing in the business environment. However, this emphasis is not meant to imply that marketing concepts, principles, and techniques cannot be fruitfully employed in other areas of exchange. In fact, some discussions of nonbusiness marketing take place later in the text.

WHAT IS STRATEGIC PLANNING?

Before a production manager, marketing manager, and personnel manager can develop plans for their individual departments, some larger plan or blueprint for the *entire* organization should exist. Otherwise, on what would the individual departmental plans be based?

In other words, there is a larger context for planning activities. Let us assume that we are dealing with a large business organization that has several business divisions and several product lines within each division (e.g., General Electric, Philip Morris). Before any marketing planning can be implemented by individual divisions or departments, a plan has to be developed for the entire organization.[3] This means that senior managers must look toward the future and evaluate their ability to shape their organization's destiny in the years and decades to come. The output of this process is objectives and strategies designed to give the organization a chance to compete effectively in the future. The objectives and strategies established at the top level provide the context for planning in each of the divisions and departments by divisional and departmental managers.

1. Companywide managerial awareness and appreciation of the consumer's role as it is related to the firm's existence, growth, and stability. As renowned management scholar Peter Drucker has noted, business enterprise is an organ of society; thus, its basic purpose lies outside the business itself. And the valid definition of business purpose is the creation of customers.

2. Active, companywide managerial awareness of, and concern with, interdepartmental implications of decisions and actions of an individual department. That is, the firm is viewed as a network of forces focused on meeting defined customer needs and comprising a system within which actions taken in one department or area frequently result in significant repercussions in other areas of the firm. Also, it is recognized that such actions may affect the company's equilibrium with its external environment, for example, its customers, its competitors.

3. Active, companywide managerial concern with innovation of products and services designed to solve selected consumer problems.

4. General managerial concern with the effect of new products and service introduction on the firm's profit position, both present and future, and recognition of the potential rewards that may accrue from new product planning, including profits and profit stability.

5. General managerial appreciation of the role of marketing intelligence and other fact-finding and reporting units, within and adjacent to the firm, in translating the general statements presented above into detailed statements of profitable market potentials, targets, and action. Implicit in this statement is not only an expansion of the traditional function and scope of formal marketing research, but also assimilation of other sources of marketing data, such as the firm's distribution system and its advertising agency counsel, into a potential marketing intelligence service.

6. Companywide managerial effort, based on participation and interaction of company officers, in establishing corporate and departmental objectives that are understood by and acceptable to these officers and that are consistent with enhancement of the firm's profit position.

Source: For an up-to-date discussion of the marketing concept, see Frederick E. Webster, Jr., "Defining the New Marketing Concept," *Marketing Management* 2, no. 4 (1994), pp. 22–31. For a classic discussion, see Robert L. King, "The Marketing Concept: Fact or Intelligent Platitude," *The Marketing Concept in Action*, Proceedings of the 47th National Conference (Chicago: American Marketing Association, 1964), p. 657.

Strategic Planning and Marketing Management

Some of the most successful business organizations are here today because many years ago they offered the right product at the right time to a rapidly growing market. The same can also be said for nonprofit and governmental organizations. Many of the critical decisions of the past were made without the benefit of strategic thinking or planning. Whether these decisions were based on wisdom or were just luck is not important; they worked for these organizations. However, a worse fate befell countless other organizations. Over three-quarters of the 100 largest U.S. corporations of 70 years ago have fallen from the list. These corporations at one time dominated their markets, controlled vast resources, and had the best-trained workers. In the end, they all made the same critical mistake. Their managements failed to recognize that business strategies need to reflect changing environments and emphasis must be placed on developing business systems that allow for continuous improvement. Instead, they attempted to carry on business as usual.

Present-day managers are increasingly recognizing that wisdom and innovation alone are no longer sufficient to guide the destinies of organizations, both large and small. These same managers also realize that the true mission of the organization is to provide value for three key constituencies: customers, employees, and investors. Without this type of outlook, no one, including shareholders, will profit in the long run.

Strategic planning includes all the activities that lead to the development of a clear organizational mission, organizational objectives, and appropriate strategies to achieve the objectives for the entire organization. The form of the process itself has come under criticism in some quarters for being too structured; however, strategic planning, if performed successfully, plays a key role in achieving an equilibrium between the short and the long term by balancing acceptable financial performance with preparation for inevitable changes in markets, technology, and competition, as well as in economic and political arenas. Managing principally for current cash flows, market share gains, and earnings trends can mortgage the firm's future. An intense focus on the near term can produce an aversion to risk that dooms a business to stagnation. Conversely, an overemphasis on the long run is just as inappropriate. Companies that overextend themselves betting on the future may penalize short-term profitability and other operating results to such an extent that the company is vulnerable to takeover and other threatening actions.

The strategic planning process is depicted in Figure 1–1. In the strategic planning process the organization gathers information about the changing elements of its environment. Managers from all functional areas in the organization assist in this information-gathering process. This information is useful in aiding the organization to adapt better to these changes through the process of strategic planning. The strategic plan(s)[4] and supporting plan are then implemented in the environment. The end results of this implementation are fed back as new information so that continuous adaptation and improvement can take place.

The Strategic Planning Process

The output of the strategic planning process is the development of a strategic plan. Figure 1-1 indicates four components of a strategic plan: mission, objectives, strategies, and portfolio plan. Let us carefully examine each one.

Organizational Mission

The organization's environment provides the resources that sustain the organization, whether it is a business, a college or university, or a government agency. In exchange for these resources, the organization must supply the environment with quality goods and services at an acceptable price. In other words, every organization exists to accomplish something in the larger environment and that purpose, vision, or mission usually is clear at the organization's inception. As time passes, however, the organization expands, and the environment and managerial personnel change. As a result, one or more things are likely to occur. First, the organization's original purpose may become irrelevant as the organization expands into new products, new markets, and even new industries. For example, Levi Strauss began as a manufacturer of work clothes. Second, the original mission may remain relevant, but managers begin to lose interest in it. Finally, changes in

FIGURE 1–1   **The Strategic Planning Process**

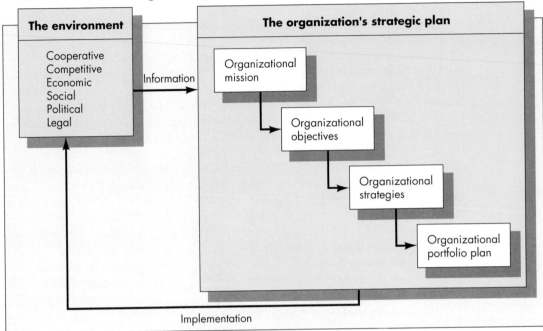

the environment may make the original mission inappropriate, as occurred with the March of Dimes when a cure was found for polio. The result of any or all three of these conditions is a "drifting" organization, without a clear mission, vision, or purpose to guide critical decisions. When this occurs, management must search for a purpose or emphatically restate and reinforce the original purpose.

The mission statement, or purpose, of an organization is the description of its reason for existence. It is the long-run vision of what the organization strives to be, the unique aim that differentiates the organization from similar ones and the means by which this differentiation will take place. In essence, the mission statement defines the direction in which the organization is heading and how it will succeed in reaching its desired goal. While some argue that vision and mission statements differ in their purpose, the perspective we will take is that both reflect the organization's attempt to guide behavior, create a culture, and inspire commitment.[5] However, it is more important that the mission statement comes from the heart and is practical, easy to identify with, and easy to remember so that it will provide direction and significance to all members of the organization regardless of their organizational level.

The basic questions that must be answered when an organization decides to examine and restate its mission are, What is our business? Who is the customer? What do customers value? and What will our business be?[6] The answers are, in a sense, the assumptions on which the organization is being run and from which future decisions will evolve. While such questions may seem simplistic, they are such difficult and critical ones that the major responsibility for answering them must lie with top management. In fact, the mission statement remains the most widely used management tool in business today. In developing a statement of mission, management must take into account three key elements: the organization's history, its distinctive competencies, and its environment.[7]

Organization	Mission
Health Publications	Our mission is to show people they can use the power of their bodies and minds to make their lives better. We say "You can do it" on every page of our books and magazines.
Local Bank	We will be the best bank in the state for medium-size businesses by 2010.
Skin Care Products	We will provide luxury skin care products with therapeutic qualities that make them worth their premium price.
Household Products	Our mission is offering simple household problem solutions.
Hotel Chain	Grow a worldwide lodging business using total quality management (TQM) principles to continuously improve preference and profitability. Our commitment is that *every guest leaves satisfied.*

1. *The organization's history.* Every organization—large or small, profit or nonprofit—has a history of objectives, accomplishments, mistakes, and policies. In formulating a mission, the critical characteristics and events of the past must be considered.

2. *The organization's distinctive competencies.* While there are many things an organization may be able to do, it should seek to do what it can do best. Distinctive competencies are things that an organization does well: so well in fact that they give it an advantage over similar organizations. For Honeywell, it's their ability to design, manufacture, and distribute a superior line of thermostats.[8] Similarly, Procter & Gamble's distinctive competency is its knowledge of the market for low-priced, repetitively purchased consumer products. No matter how appealing an opportunity may be, to gain advantage over competitors, the organization must formulate strategy based on distinctive competencies.

3. *The organization's environment.* The organization's environment dictates the opportunities, constraints, and threats that must be identified before a mission statement is developed. For example, managers in any industry that is affected by Internet technology breakthroughs should continually be asking, How will the changes in technology affect my customers' behavior and the means by which we need to conduct our business?

However, it is extremely difficult to write a useful and effective mission statement. It is not uncommon for an organization to spend one or two years developing a useful mission statement. When completed, an effective mission statement will be *focused on markets rather than products, achievable, motivating, and specific.*[9]

Focused on Markets Rather than Products   The customers or clients of an organization are critical in determining its mission. Traditionally, many organizations defined their business in terms of what they made ("our business is glass"), and in many cases they named the organization for the product or service (e.g., American Tobacco, Hormel Meats, National Cash Register, Harbor View Savings and Loan Association).

Many of these organizations have found that, when products and technologies become obsolete, their mission is no longer relevant and the name of the organization may no longer describe what it does. Thus, a more enduring way of defining the mission is needed. In recent years, therefore, a key feature of mission statements has been an *external* rather than *internal* focus. In other words, the mission statement should focus on the broad class of needs that the organization is seeking to satisfy (external focus), not on the physical product or service that the organization is offering at present (internal focus). These market-driven firms stand out in their ability to continuously anticipate market opportunities and respond before their competitors. This has been clearly stated by Peter Drucker:

> A business is not defined by the company's name, statutes, or articles of incorporation. It is defined by the want the customer satisfies when he buys a product or service. To satisfy the customer is the mission and purpose of every business. The question "What is our business?" can, therefore, be answered only by looking at the business from the outside, from the point of view of customer and market.[10]

While Drucker was referring to business organizations, the same necessity exists for both nonprofit and governmental organizations. That necessity is to state the mission in terms of serving a particular group of clients or customers and meeting a particular class of need.

Achievable   While the mission statement should stretch the organization toward more effective performance, it should, at the same time, be realistic and achievable. In other words, it should open a vision of new opportunities but should not lead the organization into unrealistic ventures far beyond its competencies.

Motivational   One of the side (but very important) benefits of a well-defined mission is the guidance it provides employees and managers working in geographically dispersed units and on independent tasks. It provides a shared sense of purpose outside the various activities taking place within the organization. Therefore, such end results as sales, patients cared for, students graduated, and reduction in violent crimes can then be viewed as the result of careful pursuit and accomplishment of the mission and not as the mission itself.

Specific   As we mentioned earlier, public relations should not be the primary purpose of a statement of mission. It must be specific to provide direction and guidelines to management when they are choosing between alternative courses of action. In other words, "to produce the highest-quality products at the lowest possible cost" sounds very good, but it does not provide direction for management.

Organizational Objectives

Organizational objectives are the end points of an organization's mission and are what it seeks through the ongoing, long-run operations of the organization. The organizational mission is distilled into a finer set of specific and achievable organizational objectives. These objectives must be *specific, measurable, action commitments* by which the mission of the organization is to be achieved.

As with the statement of mission, organizational objectives are more than good intentions. In fact, if formulated properly, they can accomplish the following:

1. They can be converted into specific action.
2. They will provide direction. That is, they can serve as a starting point for more specific and detailed objectives at lower levels in the organization. Each manager will then know how his or her objectives relate to those at higher levels.
3. They can establish long-run priorities for the organization.

FIGURE 1–2
Sample
Organizational
Objectives
(manufacturing firm)

Area of Performance	Possible Objective
1. Market standing	To make our brands number one in their field in terms of market share.
2. Innovations	To be a leader in introducing new products by spending no less than 7 percent of sales for research and development.
3. Productivity	To manufacture all products efficiently as measured by the productivity of the workforce.
4. Physical and financial resources	To protect and maintain all resources— equipment, buildings, inventory, and funds.
5. Profitability	To achieve an annual rate of return on investment of at least 15 percent.
6. Manager performance and responsibility	To identify critical areas of management depth and succession.
7. Worker performance and attitude	To maintain levels of employee satisfaction consistent with our own and similar industries.
8. Social responsibility	To respond appropriately whenever possible to societal expectations and environmental needs.

4. They can facilitate management control because they serve as standards against which overall organizational performance can be evaluated.

Organizational objectives are necessary in all areas that may influence the performance and long-run survival of the organization. As shown in Figure 1–2, objectives can be established in and across many areas of the organization. The list provided in Figure 1–2 is by no means exhaustive. For example, some organizations are specifying the primary objective as the attainment of a specific level of quality, either in the marketing of a product or the providing of a service. These organizations believe that objectives should reflect an organization's commitment to the customer rather than its own finances. Obviously, during the strategic planning process conflicts are likely to occur between various functional departments in the organization. The important point is that management must translate the organizational mission into specific objectives that support the realization of the mission. The objectives may flow directly from the mission or be considered subordinate necessities for carrying out the mission. As discussed earlier, the objectives are specific, measurable, action commitments on the part of the organization.

Organizational Strategies

Hopefully, when an organization has formulated its mission and developed its objectives, it knows where it wants to go. The next managerial task is to develop a "grand design" to get there. This grand design constitutes the organizational strategies. Strategy involves the choice of major directions the organization will take in pursuing its objectives. Toward this end, it is critical that strategies are consistent with goals and objectives and that top management ensures strategies are implemented effectively. As many as 60 percent of strategic plans have failed because the strategies in them were not well defined and, thus, were unable to be implemented effectively.[11] What follows is a discussion of various strategies organizations can pursue. We discuss three approaches: (1) strategies based on products and markets, (2) strategies based on competitive advantage, and (3) strategies based on value.

Marketing Highlight Potential Sources of Cross-Functional Conflict for Marketers

Functions	What They May Want to Deliver	What Marketers May Want Them to Deliver
Research and development	Basic research projects	Products that deliver customer value
	Product features	Customer benefits
	Few projects	Many new products
Production/operations	Long production runs	Short production runs
	Standardized products	Customized products
	No model changes	Frequent model changes
	Long lead times	Short lead times
	Standard orders	Customer orders
	No new products	Many new products
Finance	Rigid budgets	Flexible budgets
	Budgets based on return on investment	Budgets based on need to increase sales
	Low sales commissions	High sales commissions
Accounting	Standardized billing	Custom billing
	Strict payment terms	Flexible payment terms
	Strict credit standards	Flexible credit standards
Human resources	Trainable employees	Skilled employees
	Low salaries	High salaries

Source: G. A. Churchill, Jr. and J. Paul Peter, *Marketing: Creating Value for Customers* (Burr Ridge, IL: Irwin-McGraw-Hill, 1998), p. 15.

Organizational Strategies Based on Products and Markets One means to developing organizational strategies is to focus on the directions the organization can take in order to grow. Figure 1–3 presents the available strategic choices, which is known as a product-market matrix.[12] It indicates that an organization can grow by better managing what it is presently doing or by finding new things to do. In choosing one or both of these paths, it must also decide whether to concentrate on present customers or to seek new ones. Thus, according to Figure 1–3, there are only four paths an organization can take in order to grow.

Market Penetration Strategies These strategies focus primarily on increasing the sale of present products to present customers. For example:

- Encouraging present customers to use more of the product: "Orange Juice Isn't Just for Breakfast Anymore."
- Encouraging present customers to purchase more of the product: multiple packages of Pringles, instant winner sweepstakes at a fast-food restaurant.
- A university directs a fund-raising program at those graduates who already give the most money.

Tactics used to implement a market penetration strategy might include price reductions, advertising that stresses the many benefits of the product (e.g., "Milk Is a Natural"), packaging the product in different-sized packages, or making it available

FIGURE 1–3
Organizational
Growth Strategies

Products Markets	Present Products	New Products
Present customers	Market penetration	Product development
New customers	Market development	Diversification

at more locations. Other functional areas of the business could also be involved in implementing the strategy in addition to marketing. A production plan might be developed to produce the product more efficiently. This plan might include increased production runs, the substitution of preassembled components for individual product parts, or the automation of a process that previously was performed manually.

Market Development Strategies   Pursuing growth through market development, an organization would seek to find new customers for its present products. For example:

- Arm & Hammer continues to seek new uses for its baking soda.
- McDonald's continually seeks expansion into overseas markets.
- As the consumption of salt declined, a book appeared: "101 Things You Can Do with Salt Besides Eat It."

Market development strategies involve much, much more than simply getting the product to a new market. Before deciding on marketing techniques such as advertising and packaging, companies often find they must establish a clear position in the market, sometimes spending large sums of money simply to educate consumers as to why they should consider buying the product.

Product Development Strategies   Selecting one of the remaining two strategies means the organization will seek new things to do. With this particular strategy, the new products developed would be directed primarily to present customers. For example:

- Offering a different version of an existing product: mini-Oreos, Ritz with cheese.
- Offering a new-improved version of their product: Gillette's latest improvement in shaving technology.
- Offering a new way to use an existing product: Vaseline's Lip Therapy.

Diversification   This strategy can lead the organization into entirely new and even unrelated businesses. It involves seeking new products (often through acquisitions) for customers not currently being served. For example:

- Philip Morris, originally a manufacturer of cigarettes, is widely diversified in financial services, Post cereals, Sealtest dairy, and Kraft cheese, among others.
- Brown Foreman Distillers acquired Hartmann Luggage, and Sara Lee acquired Coach Leather Products.
- Some universities are establishing corporations to find commercial uses for faculty research.

Organizational Strategies Based on Competitive Advantage   Michael Porter developed a model for formulating organizational strategy that is applicable across a wide variety of industries.[13] The focus of the model is on devising means to gain competitive advantage. Competitive advantage is an ability to outperform competitors in providing something that the market values. Porter suggests that firms should first analyze their industry and then develop either a *cost leadership strategy* or a *strategy based on differentiation.* These general strategies can be used on marketwide bases or in a niche (segment) within the total market.

Using a cost leadership strategy, a firm would focus on being the low-cost company in their industry. They would stress efficiency and offer a standard, no-frills product. They could achieve this through efficiencies in production, product design, manufacturing, distribution, technology, or some other means. The important point is that to succeed, the organization must continually strive to be the cost leader in the industry or market segment it competes in. It must also offer products or services that are acceptable to customers when compared to the competition. Wal-Mart, Southwest Airlines, and Timex Group Ltd. are companies that have succeeded in using a cost leadership strategy.

Using a strategy based on differentiation, a firm seeks to be unique in its industry or market segment along particular dimensions that the customers value. These dimensions might pertain to design, quality, service, variety of offerings, brand name, or some other factor. The important point is that because of uniqueness of the product or service along one or more of these dimensions, the firm can charge a premium price. L. L. Bean, Rolex, Coca Cola, and Microsoft are companies that have succeeded using a differentiation strategy.

Organizational Strategies Based on Value   As competition increases, the concept of "customer value" has become critical for marketers as well as customers. It can be thought of as an extension of the marketing concept philosophy which focuses on developing and delivering superior value to customers as a way to achieve organizational objectives. Thus, it focuses not only on customer needs, but also on the question, How can we create value for them and still achieve our objectives?

It has become pretty clear that in today's competitive environment it is unlikely that a firm will succeed by trying to be all things to all people.[14] Thus, to succeed firms must seek to build long-term relationships with their customers by offering a unique value that only they can offer. It seems that many firms have succeeded by choosing to deliver superior customer value using one of three value strategies—best price, best product, or best service.

Dell Computers, Price/Costco, and Southwest Airlines are among the success stories of offering customers the best price. Rubbermaid, Nike, Starbucks, and Microsoft believe they offer the best products on the market. Airborne Express, Roadway, Cott Corporation, and Lands' End provide superior customer value by providing outstanding service.

Choosing an Appropriate Strategy

On what basis does an organization choose one (or all) of its strategies? Of extreme importance are the directions set by the mission statement. Management should select those strategies consistent with its mission and capitalize on the organization's distinctive competencies that will lead to a sustainable competitive advantage. A sustainable competitive advantage can be based on either the assets or skills of the organization. Technical superiority, low-cost production, customer service/product support, location, financial resources, continuing product innovation, and overall marketing skills are all examples of distinctive competencies that can lead to a sustainable competitive advantage. For example, Honda is known for providing quality automobiles at a reasonable price. Each succeeding generation of Honda automobiles has shown marked quality improvements over previous generations. Likewise, VF Corporation, manufacturer of Wrangler and Lee jeans, has formed "quick response" partnerships with both discounters and department stores to ensure the efficiency of product flow. The key to sustaining a competitive advantage is to continually focus and build on the assets and skills that will lead to long-term performance gains.

Organizational Portfolio Plan

The final phase of the strategic planning process is the formulation of the organizational portfolio plan. In reality, most organizations at a particular time are a portfolio of businesses, that is, product lines, divisions, schools. To illustrate, an appliance manufacturer may have several product lines (e.g., televisions, washers and dryers, refrigerators, stereos) as well as two divisions, consumer appliances and industrial appliances. A college or university will have numerous schools (e.g., education, business, law, architecture) and several programs within each school. Some widely diversified organizations such as Philip Morris are in numerous unrelated businesses, such as cigarettes, food products, land development, and industrial paper products.

Managing such groups of businesses is made a little easier if resources are plentiful, cash is plentiful, and each is experiencing growth and profits. Unfortunately, providing larger and larger budgets each year to all businesses is seldom feasible. Many are not experiencing growth, and profits and resources (financial and nonfinancial) are becoming more and more scarce. In such a situation, choices must be made, and some method is necessary to help management make the choices. Management must decide which businesses to build, maintain, or eliminate, or which new businesses to add. Indeed, much of the recent activity in corporate restructuring has centered on decisions relating to which groups of businesses management should focus on.

Obviously, the first step in this approach is to identify the various divisions, product lines, and so on that can be considered a "business." When identified, these are referred to as *strategic business units* (SBUs) and have the following characteristics:

- They have a distinct mission.
- They have their own competitors.
- They are a single business or collection of related businesses.
- They can be planned independently of the other businesses of the total organization.

Thus, depending on the type of organization, an SBU could be a single product, product line, or division; a college of business administration; or a state mental health agency. Once the organization has identified and classified all of its SBUs, some method must be established to determine how resources should be allocated among the various SBUs. These methods are known as *portfolio models*. For those readers interested, the appendix of this chapter presents two of the most popular portfolio models, the Boston Consulting Group model and the General Electric model.

The Complete Strategic Plan

Figure 1–1 indicates that at this point the strategic planning process is complete, and the organization has a time-phased blueprint that outlines its mission, objectives, and strategies. Completion of the strategic plan facilitates the development of marketing plans for each product, product line, or division of the organization. The marketing plan serves as a subset of the strategic plan in that it allows for detailed planning at a target market level. This important relationship between strategic planning and marketing planning is the subject of the final section of this chapter.

THE MARKETING MANAGEMENT PROCESS

Marketing management can be defined as "the process of planning and executing the conception, pricing, promotion, and distribution of goods, services, and ideas to create exchanges with target groups that satisfy customer and organizational objectives."[15] It should be noted that this definition is entirely consistent with the marketing concept, since it emphasizes the serving of target market needs as the key to achieving organizational objectives. The remainder of this section will be devoted to a discussion of the marketing management process according to the model in Figure 1–4.

Situation Analysis

With a clear understanding of organizational objectives and mission, the marketing manager must then analyze and monitor the position of the firm and, specifically, the marketing department, in terms of its past, present, and future situation. Of course, the future situation is of primary concern. However, analyses of past trends and the current situation are most useful for predicting the future situation.

The situation analysis can be divided into six major areas of concern: (1) the cooperative environment; (2) the competitive environment; (3) the economic environment; (4) the social environment; (5) the political environment; and (6) the legal environment. In analyzing each of these environments, the marketing executive must search both for opportunities and for constraints or threats to achieving objectives. Opportunities for profitable marketing often arise from changes in these environments that bring about new sets of needs to be satisfied. Constraints on marketing activities, such as limited supplies of scarce resources, also arise from these environments.

FIGURE 1–4
Strategic Planning and Marketing Planning

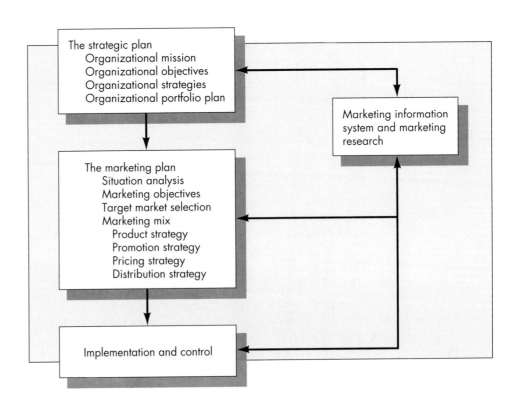

Marketing Highlight   Fifteen Guidelines for the Market-Driven Manager

1. Create customer focus throughout the business.
2. Listen to the customer.
3. Define and nurture your distinctive competence.
4. Define marketing as marketing intelligence.
5. Target customers precisely.
6. Manage for profitability, not sales volume.
7. Make customer value the guiding star.
8. Let the customer define quality.
9. Measure and manage customer expectations.
10. Build customer relationships and loyalty.
11. Define the business as a service business.
12. Commit to continuous improvement and innovation.
13. Manage culture along with strategy and structure.
14. Grow with partners and alliances.
15. Destroy marketing bureaucracy.

Source: Frederick E. Webster, Jr., "Executing the New Marketing Concept," *Marketing Management* 3, no. 1 (1994), pp. 8–16.

The Cooperative Environment   The cooperative environment includes all firms and individuals who have a vested interest in the firm accomplishing its objectives. Parties of primary interest to the marketing executive in this environment are (1) suppliers, (2) resellers, (3) other departments in the firm, and (4) subdepartments and employees of the marketing department. Opportunities in this environment are primarily related to methods of increasing efficiency. For example, a company might decide to switch from a competitive bid process of obtaining materials to a single source that is located near the company's plant. Likewise, members of the marketing, engineering, and manufacturing functions may use a teamwork approach to developing new products versus a sequential approach. Constraints consist of such things as unresolved conflicts and shortages of materials. For example, a company manager may believe that a distributor is doing an insufficient job of promoting and selling the product, or a marketing manager may feel that manufacturing is not taking the steps needed to produce a quality product.

The Competitive Environment   The competitive environment includes primarily other firms in the industry that rival the organization for both resources and sales. Opportunities in this environment include such things as (1) acquiring competing firms; (2) offering demonstrably better value to consumers and attracting them away from competitors; and (3) in some cases, driving competitors out of the industry. For example, one airline purchases another airline, a bank offers depositors a free checking account with no minimum balance requirements, or a grocery chain engages in an everyday low-price strategy that competitors can't meet. The primary constraints in these environments are the demand stimulation activities of competing firms and the number of consumers who cannot be lured away from competition.

The Economic Environment   The state of the macroeconomy and changes in it also bring about marketing opportunities and constraints. For example, such factors

Marketing Highlight   Key Issues in the Marketing Planning Process That Need to Be Addressed

Speed of the Process. There is the problem of either being so slow that the process seems to go on forever or so fast that there is an extreme burst of activity to rush out a plan.

Amount of Data Collected. Sufficient data are needed to properly estimate customer needs and competitive trends. However, the law of diminishing returns quickly sets in on the data-collection process.

Responsibility for Developing the Plan. If planning is delegated to professional planners, valuable line management input may be ignored. If the process is left to line managers, planning may be relegated to secondary status.

Structure. Many executives believe the most important part of planning is not the plan itself but the structure of thought about the strategic issues facing the business. However, the structure should not take precedence over the content so that planning becomes merely filling out forms or crunching numbers.

Length of the Plan. The length of a marketing plan must be balanced between being so long it is ignored by both staff and line managers and so brief that it ignores key details.

Frequency of Planning. Too frequent reevaluation of strategies can lead to erratic firm behavior. However, when plans are not revised frequently enough, the business may not adapt quickly enough to environmental changes and thus suffer a deterioration in its competitive position.

Number of Alternative Strategies Considered. Discussing too few alternatives raises the likelihood of failure, whereas discussing too many increases the time and cost of the planning effort.

Cross-Functional Acceptance. A common mistake is to view the plan as the proprietary possession of marketing. Successful implementation requires a broad consensus including other functional areas.

Using the Plan as a Sales Document. A major but often overlooked purpose of a plan and its presentation is to generate funds from either internal or external sources. Therefore, the better the plan, the better the chance of gaining desired funding.

Source: Donald R. Lehmann and Russell S. Winer, *Analysis for Marketing Planning,* 4th ed., chap. 1. © Richard D. Irwin, Inc., 1997.

as high inflation and unemployment levels can limit the size of the market that can afford to purchase a firm's top-of-the-line product. At the same time, these factors may offer a profitable opportunity to develop rental services for such products or to develop less-expensive models of the product. In addition, changes in technology can provide significant threats and opportunities. For example, in the communications industry, technology has developed to a level where it is now possible to provide cable television using phone lines. Obviously such a system poses a severe threat to the existence of the cable industry as it exists today.

The Social Environment   This environment includes general cultural and social traditions, norms, and attitudes. While these values change slowly, such changes often bring about the need for new products and services. For example, a change in values concerning the desirability of large families brought about an opportunity to market better methods of birth control. On the other hand, cultural and social values also place constraints on marketing activities. As a rule, business practices that are contrary to social values become political issues, which are often resolved by legal constraints. For example, public demand for a cleaner environment has caused the government to require that automobile manufacturers' products meet certain average gas mileage and emission standards.

The Political Environment   The political environment includes the attitudes and reactions of the general public, social and business critics, and other organizations, such as the Better Business Bureau. Dissatisfaction with such business and marketing practices as unsafe products, products that waste resources, and unethical sales procedures can have adverse effects on corporation image and customer loyalty. However, adapting business and marketing practices to these attitudes can be an opportunity. For example, these attitudes have brought about markets for such products as unbreakable children's toys, high-efficiency air conditioners, and more economical automobiles.

The Legal Environment   This environment includes a host of federal, state, and local legislation directed at protecting both business competition and consumer rights. In past years, legislation reflected social and political attitudes and has been primarily directed at constraining business practices. Such legislation usually acts as a constraint on business behavior, but again can be viewed as providing opportunities for marketing safer and more efficient products. In recent years, there has been less emphasis on creating new laws for constraining business practices. As an example, deregulation has become more common as evidenced by recent events in the airlines, financial services, and telecommunications industries.

Marketing Planning

In the previous sections it was emphasized that (1) marketing activities must be aligned with organizational objectives and (2) marketing opportunities are often found by systematically analyzing situational environments. Once an opportunity is recognized, the marketing executive must then plan an appropriate strategy for taking advantage of the opportunity. This process can be viewed in terms of three interrelated tasks: (1) establishing marketing objectives, (2) selecting the target market, and (3) developing the marketing mix.

Establishing Objectives   Marketing objectives usually are derived from organizational objectives; in some cases where the firm is totally marketing-oriented, the two are identical. In either case, objectives must be specified and performance in achieving them should be measurable. Marketing objectives are usually stated as standards of performance (e.g., a certain percentage of market share or sales volume) or as tasks to be achieved by given dates. While such objectives are useful, the marketing concept emphasizes that profits rather than sales should be the overriding objective of the firm and marketing department. In any case, these objectives provide the framework for the marketing plan.

Selecting the Target Market   The success of any marketing plan hinges on how well it can identify customer needs and organize its resources to satisfy them profitably. Thus, a crucial element of the marketing plan is selecting the groups or segments of potential customers the firm is going to serve with each of its products. Four important questions must be answered:

1. What do customers want or need?
2. What must be done to satisfy these wants or needs?
3. What is the size of the market?
4. What is its growth profile?

Present target markets and potential target markets are then ranked according to (*a*) profitability; (*b*) present and future sales volume; and (*c*) the match between what it takes to appeal successfully to the segment and the organization's capabilities. Those that appear to offer the greatest potential are selected. One cautionary note on this process involves the importance of not neglecting present customers when developing market share and sales strategies. In a recent study, it was found that for every 10 companies that develop strategies aimed at increasing the number of first-time customers, only 4 made any serious effort to develop strategies geared toward retaining present customers and increasing their purchases.[16] Chapters 3, 4, and 5 are devoted to discussing consumer behavior, industrial buyers, and market segmentation.

Developing the Marketing Mix   The marketing mix is the set of controllable variables that must be managed to satisfy the target market and achieve organizational objectives. These controllable variables are usually classified according to four major decision areas: product, price, promotion, and place (or channels of distribution). The importance of these decision areas cannot be overstated, and in fact, the major portion of this text is devoted to analyzing them. Chapters 6 and 7 are devoted to product and new product strategies; Chapters 8 and 9 to promotion strategies in terms of both nonpersonal and personal selling; Chapter 10 to distribution strategies; and Chapter 11 to pricing strategies. In addition, marketing mix variables are the focus of analysis in two chapters on marketing in special fields, that is, the marketing of services (Chapter 12) and international marketing (Chapter 13). Thus, it should be clear to the reader that the marketing mix is the core of the marketing management process.

The output of the foregoing process is the marketing plan. It is a formal statement of decisions that have been made on marketing activities; it is a blueprint of the objectives, strategies, and tasks to be performed.

Implementation and Control of the Marketing Plan

Implementing the marketing plan involves putting the plan into action and performing marketing tasks according to the predefined schedule. Even the most carefully developed plans often cannot be executed with perfect timing. Thus, the marketing executive must closely monitor and coordinate implementation of the plan. In some cases, adjustments may have to be made in the basic plan because of changes in any of the situational environments. For example, competitors may introduce a new product. In this event, it may be desirable to speed up or delay implementation of the plan. In almost all cases, some minor adjustments or fine tuning will be necessary in implementation.

Controlling the marketing plan involves three basic steps. First, the results of the implemented marketing plan are measured. Second, these results are compared with objectives. Third, decisions are made on whether the plan is achieving objectives. If serious deviations exist between actual and planned results, adjustments may have to be made to redirect the plan toward achieving objectives.

Marketing Information Systems and Marketing Research

Throughout the marketing management process, current, reliable, and valid information is needed to make effective marketing decisions. Providing this information is the task of the marketing information system and marketing research. These topics are discussed in detail in Chapter 2.

Poorly Stated Objectives	Well Stated Objectives
Our objective is to be a leader in the industry in terms of new product development.	Our objective is to spend 12 percent of sales revenue between 2001 and 2002 on research and development in an effort to introduce at least five new products in 2002.
Our objective is to maximize profits.	Our objective is to achieve a 10 percent return on investment during 2001, with a payback on new investments of no longer than four years.
Our objective is to better serve customers.	Our objective is to obtain customer satisfaction ratings of at least 90 percent on the 2001 annual customer satisfaction survey, and to retain at least 85 percent of our 2001 customers as repeat purchasers in 2002.
Our objective is to be the best that we can be.	Our objective is to increase market share from 30 percent to 40 percent in 2001 by increasing promotional expenditures by 14 percent.

Source: Charles W. Lamb, Jr., Joseph F. Hair, Jr., and Carl McDaniel, *Marketing*, 6th ed. (Cincinnati, OH: South-Western Publishing Co., 2002), p. 35.

THE STRATEGIC PLAN, THE MARKETING PLAN, AND OTHER FUNCTIONAL AREA PLANS

Strategic planning is clearly a top management responsibility. In recent years, however, there has been an increasing shift toward more active participation by marketing managers in strategic analysis and planning. This is because, in reality, nearly all strategic planning questions have marketing implications. In fact, the two major strategic planning questions—What products should we make? and What markets should we serve?—are clearly marketing questions. Thus, marketing executives are involved in the strategic planning process in at least two important ways: (1) they influence the process by providing important inputs in the form of information and suggestions relating to customers, products, and middlemen; and (2) they must always be aware of what the process of stategic planning involves as well as the results because everything they do, the marketing objectives and strategies they develop, must be derived from the strategic plan. In fact, the planning done in all functional areas of the organization should be derived from the strategic plan.

In well-managed organizations, therefore, a direct relationship exists between strategic planning and the planning done by managers at all levels. The focus and time perspectives will, of course, differ. Figure 1–5 illustrates the cross-functional perspective of strategic planning. It indicates very clearly that all functional area plans should be derived from the strategic plan while at the same time contributing to the achievement of it.

FIGURE 1–5   **The Cross-Functional Perspective in Planning**

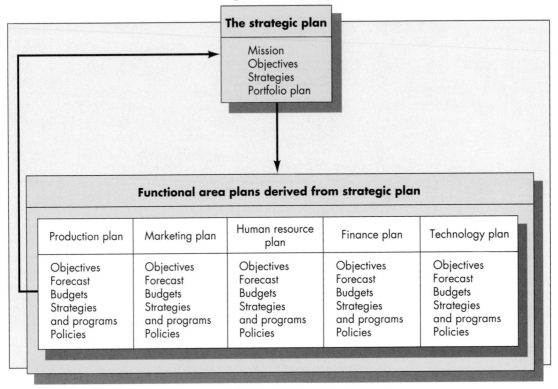

If done properly, strategic planning results in a clearly defined blueprint for management action in all functional areas of the organization. Figure 1–6 clearly illustrates this blueprint using only one organizational objective and two strategies from the strategic plan (above the dotted line) and illustrating how these are translated into elements of the marketing department plan and the production department plan (below the dotted line). Note that in Figure 1–6, all objectives and strategies are related to other objectives and strategies at higher and lower levels in the organization: that is, a hierarchy of objectives and strategies exists. We have illustrated only two possible marketing objectives and two possible production objectives. Obviously, many others could be developed, but our purpose is to illustrate the cross-functional nature of strategic planning and how objectives and strategies from the strategic plan must be translated into objectives and strategies for all functional areas including marketing.

CONCLUSION

This chapter has described the marketing management process in the context of the organization's overall strategic plan. Clearly, marketers must understand their cross-functional role in joining the marketing vision for the organization with the financial goals and manufacturing capabilities of the organization. The greater this ability, the better the likelihood is that the organization will be able to achieve and sustain a competitive advantage, the ultimate purpose of the strategic planning process.

At this point it would be useful to review Figures 1–4, 1–5, and 1–6 as well as the book's Table of Contents. This review will enable you to better relate the content and progression of the material to follow to the marketing management process.

FIGURE 1–6   **A Blueprint for Management Action: Relating the Marketing Plan to the Strategic Plan and the Production Plan**

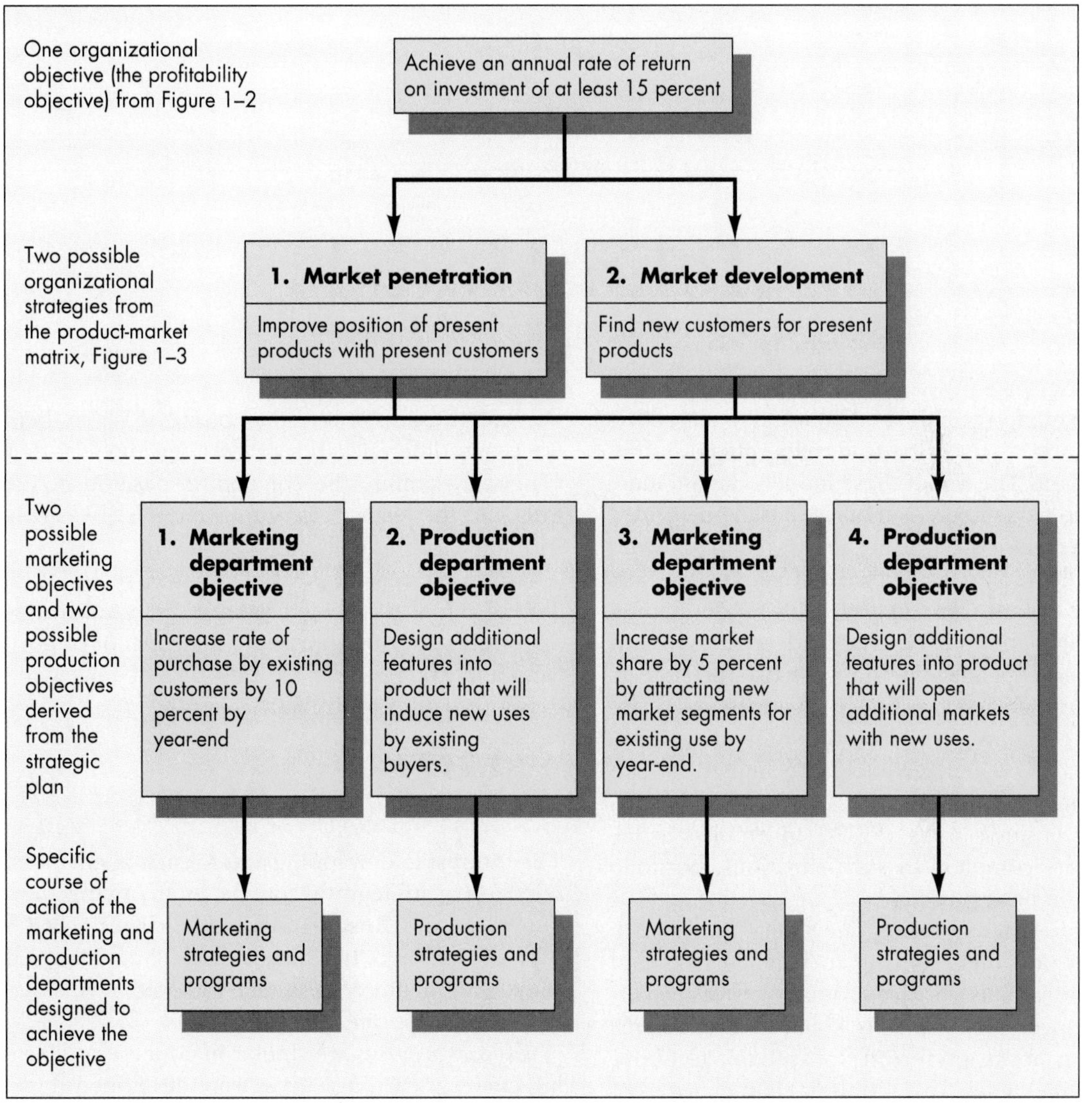

One organizational objective (the profitability objective) from Figure 1–2

> Achieve an annual rate of return on investment of at least 15 percent

Two possible organizational strategies from the product-market matrix, Figure 1–3

1. Market penetration
Improve position of present products with present customers

2. Market development
Find new customers for present products

Two possible marketing objectives and two possible production objectives derived from the strategic plan

1. Marketing department objective
Increase rate of purchase by existing customers by 10 percent by year-end

2. Production department objective
Design additional features into product that will induce new uses by existing buyers.

3. Marketing department objective
Increase market share by 5 percent by attracting new market segments for existing use by year-end.

4. Production department objective
Design additional features into product that will open additional markets with new uses.

Specific course of action of the marketing and production departments designed to achieve the objective

Marketing strategies and programs

Production strategies and programs

Marketing strategies and programs

Production strategies and programs

Additional Readings

Ambler, Tim. "What Does Marketing Success Look Like?" *Marketing Management,* Spring 2001, pp. 12–19.

Fredericks, Joan O.; Ronald R. Hurd; and James M. Salter II. "Connecting Customer Loyalty to Financial Results." *Marketing Management,* Spring 2001, pp. 26–33.

Iacobucci, Dawn. ed. *Kellogg on Marketing.* New York: John Wiley and Sons, 2001.

Lusch, Robert F. "Creating Long-Term Marketing Health." *Marketing Management,* Spring 2000, pp. 17–24.

Matanovich, Timothy. "Value Measures in the Executive Suite." *Marketing Management,* Spring 2000, pp. 35–41.

Reichheld, Frederick F. *The Loyalty Effect.* Boston: HBS Press, 1996.

Slywotzky, Adrian J. *Value Migration: How to Think Several Moves Ahead of the Competition.* Boston: HBS Press, 1996.

Appendix

Portfolio Models

Portfolio models remain a valuable aid to marketing managers in their efforts to develop effective marketing plans. The use of these models can aid managers who face situations that can best be described as "more products, less time, and less money." More specifically, (1) as the number of products a firm produces expands, the time available for developing marketing plans for each product decreases; (2) at a strategic level, management must make resource allocation decisions across lines of products and, in diversified organizations, across different lines of business; and (3) when resources are limited (which they usually are), the process of deciding which strategic business units (SBUs) to emphasize becomes very complex. In such situations, portfolio models can be very useful.

Portfolio analysis is not a new idea. Banks manage loan portfolios seeking to balance risks and yields. Individuals who are serious investors usually have a portfolio of various kinds of investments (common stocks, preferred stocks, bank accounts, and the like), each with different characteristics of risk, growth, and rate of return. The investor seeks to manage the portfolio to maximize whatever objectives he or she might have. Applying this same idea, most organizations have a wide range of products, product lines, and businesses, each with different growth rates and returns. Similar to the investor, managers should seek a desirable balance among alternative SBUs. Specifically, management should seek to develop a business portfolio that will ensure long-run profits and cash flow.

Portfolio models can be used to classify SBUs to determine the future cash contributions that can be expected from each SBU as well as the future resources that each will require. Remember, depending on the organization, an SBU could be a single product, product line, division, or a distinct business. While there are many different types of portfolio models, they generally examine the competitive position of the SBU and the chances for improving the SBU's contribution to profitability and cash flow.

There are several portfolio analysis techniques. Two of the most widely used are discussed in this appendix. To truly appreciate the concept of portfolio analysis, however, we must briefly review the development of portfolio theory.

A REVIEW OF PORTFOLIO THEORY

The interest in developing aids for managers in the selection of strategy was spurred by an organization known as the Boston Consulting Group (BCG) over 25 years ago. Its ideas, which will be discussed shortly, and many of those that followed were based on the concept of experience curves.

Experience curves are similar in concept to learning curves. Learning curves were developed to express the idea that the number of labor hours it takes to produce one unit of a particular product declines in a predictable manner as the number of units produced increases. Hence, an accurate estimation of how long it takes to produce the 100th unit is possible if the production times for the 1st and 10th units are known.

The concept of experience curves was derived from the concept of learning curves. Experience curves were first widely discussed in the ongoing Profit Impact of Marketing Strategies (PIMS) study conducted by the Strategic Planning Institute. The PIMS project studies 150 firms with more than 1,000 individual business units. Its major focus is on determining which environmental and internal firm variables influence the firm's return on investment (ROI) and cash flow. The researchers have concluded that seven categories of variables appear to influence the return on investment: (1) competitive position, (2) industry/market environment, (3) budget allocation, (4) capital structure, (5) production processes, (6) company characteristics, and (7) "change action" factors.[17]

The experience curve includes all costs associated with a product and implies that the per-unit costs of a product should fall, due to cumulative experience, as production volume increases. In a given industry, therefore, the producer with the largest volume and corresponding market share should have the lowest marginal cost. This leader in market share should be able to underprice competitors, discourage entry into the market by potential competitors, and, as a result, achieve an acceptable return on investment. The linkage of experience to cost to price to market share to ROI is exhibited in Figure A–1. The Boston Consulting Group's view of the experience curve led the members to develop what has become known as the BCG Portfolio Model.

THE BCG MODEL

The BCG is based on the assumption that profitability and cash flow will be closely related to sales volume. Thus, in this model, SBUs are classified according to their relative market share and the growth rate of the market the SBU is in. Using these dimensions, products are either classified as stars, cash cows, dogs, or question marks. The BCG model is presented in Figure A–2.

- *Stars* are SBUs with a high share of a high-growth market. Because high-growth markets attract competition, such SBUs are usually cash users because they are growing and because the firm needs to protect their market share position.

- *Cash cows* are often market leaders, but the market they are in is not growing rapidly. Because these SBUs have a high share of a low-growth market, they are cash generators for the firm.

- *Dogs* are SBUs that have a low share of a low-growth market. If the SBU has a very loyal group of customers, it may be a source of profits and cash. Usually, dogs are not large sources of cash.

- Question marks are SBUs with a low share of a high-growth market. They have great potential but require great resources if the firm is to successfully build market share.

As you can see, a firm with 10 SBUs will usually have a portfolio that includes some of each of the above. Having developed this analysis, management must determine what role each SBU should assume. Four basic objectives are possible:

1. *Build share.* This objective sacrifices immediate earnings to improve market share. It is appropriate for promising question marks whose share has to grow if they are ever to become stars.

2. *Hold share.* This objective seeks to preserve the SBU's market share. It is very appropriate for strong cash cows to ensure that they can continue to yield a large cash flow.

FIGURE A–1   Experience Curve and Resulting Profit

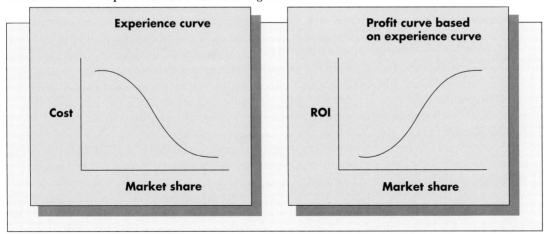

FIGURE A–2
**The Boston
Consulting Group
Portfolio Model**

Relative Market Share

	High	Low
High	Stars	Question marks
Low	Cash cows	Dogs

**Market
Growth
Rate**

3. *Harvest.* Here, the objective seeks to increase the product's short-term cash flow without concern for the long-run impact. It allows market share to decline in order to maximize earnings and cash flow. It is an appropriate objective for weak cash cows, weak question marks, and dogs.

4. *Divest.* This objective involves selling or divesting the SBU because better investment opportunities exist elsewhere. It is very appropriate for dogs and those question marks the firm cannot afford to finance for growth.

There have been several major criticisms of the BCG Portfolio Model, revolving around its focus on market share and market growth as the primary indicators of preference. First, the BCG model assumes market growth is uncontrollable.[18] As a result, managers can become preoccupied with setting market share objectives instead of trying to grow the market. Second, assumptions regarding market share as a critical factor affecting firm performance may not hold true, especially in international markets.[19] Third, the BCG model assumes that the major source of SBU financing comes from internal means. Fourth, the BCG matrix does not take into account any interdependencies that may exist between SBUs, such as shared distribution.[20] Fifth, the BCG matrix does not take into account any measures of profits and customer satisfaction.[21] Sixth, and perhaps most important, the thrust of the BCG matrix is based on the underlying assumption that corporate strategy begins with an analysis of competitive position. By its very nature, a strategy developed entirely on com-

petitive analysis will always be a reactive one.[22] While the above criticisms are certainly valid ones, managers (especially of large firms) across all industries continue to find the BCG matrix useful in assessing the strategic position of SBUs.[23]

THE GENERAL ELECTRIC MODEL

Although the BCG model can be useful, it does assume that market share is the sole determinant of an SBU's profitability. Also, in projecting market growth rates, a manager should carefully analyze the factors that influence sales and any opportunities for influencing industry sales.

Some firms have developed alternative portfolio models to incorporate more information about market opportunities and competitive positions. The GE model is one of these. The GE model emphasizes all the potential sources of strength, not just market share, and all of the factors that influence the long-term attractiveness of a market, not just its growth rate. As Figure A–3 indicates, all SBUs are classified according to *business strength* and *industry attractiveness.* Figure A–4 presents a list of items that can be used to position SBUs in the matrix.

Industry attractiveness is a composite index made up of such factors as those listed in Figure A–4. For example: *market size*—the larger the market, the more attractive it will be; *market growth*—high-growth markets are more attractive than low-growth markets; *profitability*—high-profit-margin markets are more attractive than low-profit-margin industries.

FIGURE A–3
The General Electric
Portfolio Model

Business Strength

		Strong	Average	Weak
	High	A	A	B
Industry Attractiveness	Medium	A	B	C
	Low	B	C	C

FIGURE A–4
Components of Industry Attractiveness and Business Strength at GE

Industry Attractiveness	Business Strength

Market size
Market growth
Profitability
Cyclicality
Ability to recover from inflation
World scope
	Market position
	  Domestic market share
	  World market share
	  Share growth
	  Share compared with leading competitor
	
	Competitive strengths
	  Quality leadership
	  Technology
	  Marketing
	  Relative profitability

Business strength is a composite index made up of such factors as those listed in Figure A–4. For example: *market share*—the higher the SBU's share of market, the greater its business strength; *quality leadership*—the higher the SBU's quality compared to competitors, the greater its business strength; *share compared with leading competitor*—the closer the SBU's share to the market leader, the greater its business strength.

Once the SBUs are classified, they are placed on the grid (Figure A–3). Priority "A" SBUs (often called *the green zone*) are those in the three cells at the upper left, indicating that these are SBUs high in both industry attractiveness and business strength, and that the firm should "build share."

Priority "B" SBUs (often called *the yellow zone*) are those medium in both industry attractiveness and business strength. The firm will usually decide to "hold share" on these SBUs. Priority "C" SBUs are those in the three cells at the lower right (often called the *red zone*). These SBUs are low in both industry attractiveness and business strength. The firm will usually decide to harvest or divest these SBUs.

Whether the BCG model, the GE model, or a variation of these models is used, some analyses must be made of the firm's current portfolio of SBUs as part of any strategic planning effort. Marketing must get its direction from the organization's strategic plan.

Marketing Information, Research, and Understanding the Target Market

Part B

2 Marketing Research: Process and Systems for Decision Making

3 Consumer Behavior

4 Business, Government, and Institutional Buying

5 Market Segmentation

Section I Essentials of Marketing Management

2

Marketing Research: Process and Systems for Decision Making

Marketing managers require current, reliable, useful information to make effective decisions. In today's highly competitive global economy, marketers need to exploit opportunities and avoid mistakes if they are to survive and be profitable. Not only is sound marketing research needed, but also a system that gets current, valid information to the marketing decision maker in a timely manner.

This chapter is concerned with the marketing research process and information systems for decision making. It begins by discussing the marketing research process that is used to develop useful information for decision making. Then, marketing information systems are briefly discussed. The chapter is intended to provide a detailed introduction to many of the important topics in the area, but it does not provide a complete explanation of the plethora of marketing research topics.

THE ROLE OF MARKETING RESEARCH

Marketing research is the process by which information about the environment is generated, analyzed, and interpreted for use in marketing decision making.[1] It cannot be overstated that *marketing research is an aid to decision making and not a substitute for it.* In other words, marketing research does not make decisions, but it can substantially increase the chances that good decisions are made. Unfortunately, too many marketing managers view research reports as the final answer to their problems; whatever the research indicates is taken as the appropriate course of action. Instead, marketing managers should recognize that (1) even the most carefully executed research can be fraught with errors; (2) marketing research does not forecast with certainty what will happen in the future; and (3) they should make decisions in light of their own knowledge and experience since no marketing research study includes all of the factors that could influence the success of a strategy.

Although marketing research does not make decisions, it can reduce the risks associated with managing marketing strategies. For example, it can reduce the risk of introducing new products by evaluating consumer acceptance of them prior to full-scale introduction. Marketing research is also vital for investigating the effects of various marketing strategies after they have been implemented. For example, marketing research can examine the effects of a change in any element of the marketing mix on customer perception and behavior.

At one time, marketing researchers were primarily engaged in the technical aspects of research, but were not heavily involved in the strategic use of research findings. Today, however, many marketing researchers work hand-in-hand with marketing managers throughout the research process and have responsibility for making strategic recommendations based on the research.

THE MARKETING RESEARCH PROCESS

Marketing research can be viewed as systematic processes for obtaining information to aid in decision making. There are many types of marketing research, and the framework illustrated in Figure 2–1 represents a general approach to the process. Each element of this process is discussed next.

Purpose of the Research

The first step in the research process is to determine explicitly why the research is needed and what it is to accomplish. This may be much more difficult than it sounds. Quite often a situation or problem is recognized as needing research, yet the nature of the problem is not clear or well defined nor is the appropriate type of research evident. Thus, managers and researchers need to discuss and clarify the current situation and develop a clear understanding of the problem. At the end of this stage, managers and researchers should agree on (1) the current situation involving the problem to be researched, (2) the nature of the problem, and (3) the specific question or questions the research is designed to investigate. This step is crucial since it influences the type of research to be conducted and the research design.

Plan of the Research

Once the specific research question or questions have been agreed upon, a research plan can be developed. A research plan spells out the nature of the research to be

FIGURE 2–1
The Five Ps of the Research Process

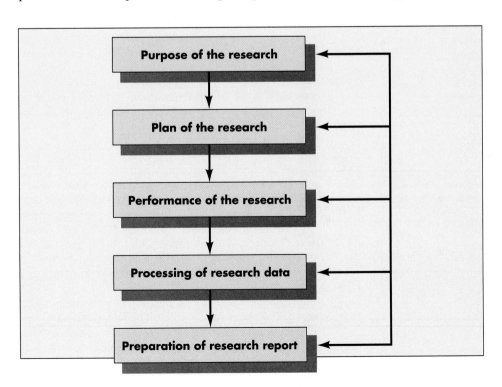

conducted and includes an explanation of such things as the sample design, measures, and analysis techniques to be used. Figure 2–2 presents a sample research plan. Three critical issues that influence the research plan are (1) whether primary or secondary data are needed, (2) whether qualitative or quantitative research is needed, and (3) whether the company will do its own research or contract with a marketing research specialist.

Primary versus Secondary Data

Given the information needed and budget constraints, a decision must be made as to whether primary data, secondary data, or some combination of the two is needed. *Primary data* are data collected specifically for the research problem under investigation; *secondary data* are those that have previously been collected for other purposes but can be used for the problem at hand. For example, if a company wanted to know why users of a competitive brand didn't prefer its brand, it may have to collect primary data to find out. On the other hand, if a company wanted to know the population size of key global markets that it might enter, it could find this information from secondary sources. Secondary information has the advantage of usually being cheaper than primary data, although it is not always available for strategy-specific research questions.

There are many sources of secondary data for use in marketing research. Research services such as A.C. Nielsen Co, Arbitron Co., IMS International, and Information Resources, Inc., sell a variety of useful data to companies. Business and industry pub-

FIGURE 2–2
Sample Sections of a Research Plan

I. Tentative projective title

II. Statement of the problem
One or two sentences describing the general problem under consideration.

III. Define and delimit the problem
Here the writer states the purpose(s) and scope of the problem. *Purpose* refers to goals or objectives. Closely related to this is *justification*. Sometimes this is a separate step, depending on the urgency of the task. *Scope* refers to the limits of the research effort; in other words, what *is* and *is not* going to be investigated. Here is the point where the researcher spells out the various hypotheses to be investigated or the questions to be answered.

IV. Outline
Generally, this is a tentative framework for the entire project. It should be flexible enough to accommodate unforeseen difficulties, show statistical tables in outline form, and also show planned graphs.

V. Method and data sources
The types of data to be sought (primary, secondary) are briefly identified. A brief explanation of how the necessary information or data will be gathered (e.g., surveys, experiments, library sources) is given. *Sources* refer to the actual depositories for the information, whether from government publications, company records, actual people, and so forth. If measurements are involved, such as consumers' attitudes, the techniques for making such measurements are stated. The relevance of all techniques (qualitative and quantitative) should be discussed. The nature of the problem will probably indicate the types of techniques to be employed, such as factor analysis, depth interviews, or focus groups.

VI. Sample design
This provides a description of the population to be studied and how it will be defined. The researcher specifies the population, states the desired sample size, and discusses how nonresponse and missing data are to be handled. If a nonrandom sample is to be used, the justification and type of sampling strategy to be employed, such as convenience sample, are stated.

FIGURE 2–2
(continued)

> **VII. Data collection forms**
> The forms to be employed in gathering the data are discussed here. For surveys, this involves either a questionnaire or an interview schedule. For other research, the forms could include inventory forms, psychological tests, and so forth. The plan should state how these instruments have been or will be validated, and the reader should be given any evidence of their reliability and validity.
>
> **VIII. Personnel requirements**
> This provides a complete list of all personnel who will be required, indicating exact jobs, time duration, and expected rate of pay. Assignments should be made indicating each person's responsibility and authority.
>
> **IX. Phases of the study with a time schedule**
> This is a detailed outline of the plan to complete the study. The study should be divided into workable pieces. Then, considering the persons involved in each phase, their qualifications and experience, and so forth, the time for the job is estimated. Some jobs may overlap. This plan will help in estimating the time required.
>   Illustration:
>   1. Preliminary investigation—two weeks.
>   2. Final test of questionnaire—one week.
>   3. Sample selection—one week.
>   4. Mail questionnaires, field follow-up, and so forth—two months.
>   5. Additional tasks.
>
> **X. Analysis plans**
> This is a discussion of editing and proofreading of questionnaires, coding instructions, and the type of data analysis. An outline of some of the major tables that will appear in the report should be presented.
>
> **XI. Cost estimate for doing the study**
> Personnel requirements are combined with time on different phases to estimate total personnel costs. Estimates on travel, materials, supplies, drafting, computer charges, and printing and mailing costs must also be included. If an overhead charge is required, it should be calculated and added to the subtotal of the above items.

lications such as the *Million Dollar Directory* or the *Encyclopedia of Associations* provide useful information for decision making, as do government reports such as *Statistical Abstracts of the United States* or the *Survey of Current Business.* Trade groups such as the American Medical Association or the National Association of Retail Dealers of America can also be contacted for information relevant to their industries.[2]

Qualitative versus Quantitative Research

Given a research question, a decision must be made whether qualitative or quantitative research would be a better approach. Qualitative research typically involves face-to-face interviews with respondents designed to develop a better understanding of what they think and feel concerning a research topic, such as a brand name, a product, a package, or an advertisement. The two most common types of qualitative research in marketing are focus groups and long interviews. *Focus groups* involve discussions among a small number of individuals led by an interviewer; they are designed to generate insights and ideas. *Long interviews* are conducted by an interviewer with a single respondent for several hours. They are designed to find out such things as the meanings various products or brands have for an individual or how a product influences a person's life.

Quantitative research involves more systematic procedures designed to obtain and analyze numerical data. Four common types of quantitative research in marketing are observation, surveys, experiments, and mathematical modeling.

Marketing Highlight   Digging Deeper into Consumers' Minds and Lives

Market researchers use a variety of techniques to learn about consumers. For example, focus groups, surveys, experiments, and scanner data studies have long helped marketers develop more effective strategies. However, a recent trend in market research is to dig deeper into consumers' minds and lives using a variety of anthropological techniques to better understand the deeper meaning of products and brands. Catherine DeThorne, director of planning at ad agency Leo Burnett, calls these techniques "getting in under the radar." Below is a sample of some of the types of research companies are doing.

- As Mary Flimin chops onions for risotto late one afternoon, a pair of video cameras and two market researchers stationed in a corner are recording her every move. Meg Armstrong and Joel Johnson, who represent a cookware company, want to see how a gourmet like Flimin cooks and what she likes. Hours later, Armstrong and Johnson review their observations. Even though Flimin said she often makes cakes and bakes with fresh fruit, Armstrong notes that "her baking dishes are stashed in the boondocks, so she doesn't bake much." This insight could not be captured by typical methods that rely on consumers to tell researchers what they do.

- Thomson Electronics hired E-lab to perform a study to find out how consumers mix listening to music with their daily lives. E-lab did a "beeper" study in which participants were instructed to write down what they were doing when they were paged. Participants recorded where they were; what music, if any, was playing; who picked it; and their mood. Researchers also tailed people around their homes, noting where they kept their stereo and how their music collections were organized. The company was trying to find out how often people sit down to enjoy a CD as opposed to using it for background music. This information would help Thomson Electronics in its new product decisions.

- Traditional focus groups often involve meetings among strangers which could inhibit consumers from saying what they really feel. To overcome this problem, ad agency Leo Burnett set up a meeting with six professional female friends in their 30s and 40s at a coffeehouse called Urban Blend. While enjoying wine and crudités, the women discussed a Wells Fargo ad that touts its investments to women-owned businesses. In one session, the women agreed that they would invest their money with this company if it were around the area. However, in another session later, some younger women felt the ad was pandering to them. Both of these insights are useful for the agency, since it han-

Observational research involves watching people and recording relevant facts and behaviors. For example, retail stores may use observational research to determine what patterns customers use in walking through stores, how much time they spend in various parts of the store, and how many items of merchandise they examine. This information can be used to design store layouts more effectively. Similarly, many retail marketers do traffic counts at various intersections to help determine the best locations for stores.

Survey research involves the collection of data by means of a questionnaire either by mail, phone, or in person. Surveys are commonly used in marketing research to

dles advertising for the New York Stock Exchange and Morgan Stanley Dean Witter. Both sets of opinions will be considered when the agency creates ads targeted to either group.

- Before a Miramax movie opens in theaters, the previews are usually screened by psychiatrist Russ Ferstandig using groups of moviegoers from around the country. As people watch the previews and answer Ferstandig's questions, he watches their body language. Based on what he hears and sees, he may recommend that the Disney unit change previews to make them more compelling to audiences. He might suggest a short pause to let people catch up with a message or a change in wording in a preview, such as taking out the word *comedy* in describing the movie, *An Ideal Husband.*

- The MacManus Group uses a TV talk show format called "Just Ask a Woman" to encourage research participants to speak up in groups. In a project for Continental Airlines, 19 female business travelers gathered in a Manhattan loft set up like a talk show set. Cameras rolled, and two women with microphones encouraged the participants to stand up and share frustrations they encountered on the road—from bad airplane food to inefficient rental car services. It was as if Sally Jessy Raphael were on the set. As soon as the lights and cameras came on, the participants seemed to vie for the microphone.

- At Norman Thomas High School in Manhattan, Inez Cintron, 14, chats exuberantly with her girlfriends between classes. The topics: singer Lauryn Hill, Old Navy clothes, and the NBC hit *Friends.* Tru Pettigrew, a 30-year-old researcher for a company called Triple Dot, leans close. The trend hunter has dropped by the public high school to glean intelligence for Eastpak. He listens to the girls mix Spanish phrases into their English chatter—something new to Pettigrew that may result in Eastpak ads with "Spanglish." Pettigrew also is interested to hear that the teens, who preferred rival Jansport's packs, buy as many as eight backpacks to mix with their wardrobes. "That's a key piece of information," he says later.

Not everyone is cheering these modern market research methods. "It's kind of pathetic that people are willing to be subjects in order to help marketers get inside a certain group's head and sell, sell, sell," says Michael Jacobson of the Center for Science in the Public Interest. However, respondents are often paid—at least $100 by E-lab—for participating and are free to choose whether or not they want to be in the study.

Source: Melanie Wells, "New Ways to Get Into Our Heads," *USA Today,* March 2, 1999, pp. B1, B2.

investigate customer beliefs, attitudes, satisfaction, and many other issues. Mail surveys are useful for reaching widely dispersed markets but take more time to get responses than telephone surveys; personal surveys involving structured questions are useful but expensive.

Experimental research involves manipulating one variable and examining its impact on other variables. For example, the price of a product in one test store could be changed while left the same in other stores. By comparing sales in the test store with those in other stores, evidence can be obtained about the likely impact of a price change in the overall market. Experiments are useful for getting a better idea of the causal relationships among variables, but they are often difficult to design and administer effectively in natural settings. Thus, many marketing research experiments are conducted in laboratories or simulated stores to carefully control other variables that could impact results.

Mathematical modeling research often involves secondary data, such as scanner data collected and stored in computer files from retail checkout counters. This approach involves the development of equations to model relationships among variables and uses econometric and statistical techniques to investigate the impact of various strategies and tactics on sales and brand choices. Math modeling is useful because it provides an efficient way to study problems with extremely large secondary data sets.

Which of these types of research is best for particular research questions requires considerable knowledge of each of them. Often, qualitative research is used in early stages of investigating a topic to get more information and insight about it. Then, quantitative approaches are used to investigate the degree to which the insights hold across a larger sample or population.

Company versus Contract Research

Most large consumer goods companies have marketing research departments that can perform a variety of types of research. However, there are many marketing research firms, advertising agencies, and consulting companies that do marketing research on a contract basis. Some marketing research suppliers have special expertise in a particular type of research that makes them a better choice than doing the research internally. A decision has to be made as to whether the marketing research department has the ability to do a particular type of research itself or whether all or part of the research should be contracted with a research supplier. In either case, schedules for task completion, the exact responsibilities of all involved parties, and cost need to be considered.

Performance of the Research

Performance of the research involves preparing for data collection and actually collecting them. The tasks at this stage obviously depend on the type of research that has been selected and the type of data needed. If secondary data are to be used, they must be located, prepared for analysis, and possibly paid for. If primary data are to be collected, then observational forms, questionnaires, or other types of measures must be designed, pretested, and validated. Samples must be drawn and interviews must be scheduled or preparations must be made for mailing or phoning selected individuals.

In terms of actual data collection, a cardinal rule is to obtain and record the maximal amount of useful information, subject to the constraints of time, money, and respondent privacy. Failure to obtain and record data clearly can obviously lead to a poor research study, while failure to consider the rights of respondents raises both practical and ethical problems. Thus, both the objectives and constraints of data collection must be closely monitored.

Processing of Research Data

Processing research data includes the preparation of data for analysis and the actual analysis of them. Preparations include such things as editing and structuring data and coding them for analysis. Data sets should be clearly labeled to ensure they are not misinterpreted or misplaced.

The appropriate analysis techniques for collected data depend on the nature of the research question and the design of the research. Qualitative research data consist of interview records that are content analyzed for ideas or themes. Quantitative research

Marketing Highlight   Types of Questions
that Marketing Research Can Help Answer

I. Planning

A. What types of people buy our product? Where do they live? How much do they earn? How many of them are there?

B. Is the market for our product increasing or decreasing? Are there promising markets that we have not yet reached?

C. Are there markets for our products in other countries?

II. Problem solving

A. Product

1. Which, of various product designs, is likely to be the most successful?

2. What kind of packaging should we use?

B. Price

1. What prices should we charge for our products?

2. As production costs decline, should we lower our prices or try to develop a higher-quality product?

C. Place

1. Where, and by whom, should our product be sold?

2. What kinds of incentives should we offer to induce the trade to push our product?

D. Promotion

1. How effective is our advertising? Are the right people seeing it? How does it compare with the competition's advertising?

2. What kinds of sales promotional devices—coupons, contests, rebates, and so forth—should we employ?

3. What combination of media—newspapers, radio, television, magazines and Internet—should we use?

III. Control

A. What is our market share overall? In each geographic area? By each customer type?

B. Are customers satisfied with our product? How is our record for service? Are there many returns?

C. How does the public perceive our company? What is our reputation with the trade?

Source: Table from Gilbert A. Churchill, Jr. and Dawn Iacobucci, *Marketing Research: Methodological Foundations,* 8th ed. © 2002, Fort Worth, TX, Dryden Press. Reproduced by permission of the publisher.

data may be analyzed in a variety of ways depending on the objectives of the research. Figure 2–3 lists a number of data analysis methods used in marketing research.

A critical part of this stage is interpreting and assessing the research results. Seldom, if ever, do marketing research studies obtain findings that are totally unambiguous. Usually, relationships among variables or differences between groups are small to moderate, and judgment and insight are needed to draw appropriate inferences and conclusions. Marketing researchers should always double-check their analysis and avoid overstating the strength of their findings. The implications for developing or changing a marketing strategy should be carefully thought out and tempered with judgment about the overall quality of the study.

FIGURE 2–3   **Some Statistical Techniques Used in Marketing Research**

Marketing researchers use many statistical techniques to analyze data and obtain insights for strategy. In many cases, researchers are interested in investigating the impact of one or more variables (called *independent variables* or *predictor variables*) on another variable (called the *dependent variable* or *criterion variable*). In other types of marketing research, the goals are to investigate differences between groups of consumers on various measures or to group variables or people into smaller sets. Below are brief descriptions of a number of statistical techniques used in the field. More information on these techniques can be found in the texts listed in the Additional Readings for this chapter.

Analysis of variance (ANOVA). A statistical procedure for examining whether different samples came from populations with equal means. This procedure is commonly used to compare the average or mean scores for different groups in experiments to determine the impact of a particular variable.

Conjoint analysis. A statistical technique in which respondents' valuations of attributes are inferred from the preferences they express for various combinations of these attributes. This technique is commonly used to determine the most important attributes to build into new products or to enhance in existing products.

Cluster analysis. A body of statistical techniques concerned with developing empirical groupings of objects based on a set of measures. These techniques are used in market segmentation to form groups of similar people that could be treated as target markets.

Correlation analysis. A statistical technique that determines the linear relationship between two variables. Correlations range from +1.0, for a perfect positive linear relationship, to 0.0, no linear relationship, to –1.0, a perfect negative linear relationship.

Cross tabulation. A technique that involves counting the number of cases (usually people) that falls into each of several categories when the categories are based on two or more variables considered at the same time. For example, a cross tabulation may compare the number of cars owned in different income groups to investigate the effects of income on car ownership.

Discriminant analysis. A statistical technique used to model the relationships between a criterion and a set of predictor variables. The criterion variable is a category (such as buyers and nonbuyers) in this procedure.

Factor analysis. A body of statistical techniques concerned with the study of interrelationships among a set of variables. It is commonly used to reduce a large set of variables into a smaller set of factors that can be meaningfully interpreted.

Multidimensional scaling. An approach in which people's perceptions of the similarity of objects and their preferences among them are measured and plotted in a multidimensional space.

Regression analysis. A statistical technique used to derive an equation that relates a single criterion variable to one or more predictor variables. It is commonly used in many types of marketing research that investigate the impact of various strategic elements on such things as sales, profits, overall customer satisfaction, and purchase intentions.

Source: Based on definitions in Gilbert A. Churchill, Jr. and Dawn Iacobucci, *Marketing Research: Methodological Foundations,* 8th ed. (Fort Worth, TX: Dryden Press, 2002); and Peter D. Bennett, ed., *Dictionary of Marketing Terms,* 2nd ed. (Chicago: American Marketing Association, 1995).

Preparation of the Research Report

The research report is a complete statement of everything done in a research project and includes a write-up of each of the previous stages as well as the strategic recommendations from the research. The limitations of the research should be carefully noted. Figure 2–4 illustrates the types of questions marketing researchers and managers should discuss prior to submitting the final research report.

Research reports should be clear and unambiguous with respect to what was done and what recommendations are made. Often research reports must trade off the apparent precision of scientific jargon for everyday language that managers can understand. Researchers should work closely with managers to ensure that the study and its limitations are fully understood.

FIGURE 2–4
Eight Criteria for Evaluating Marketing Research Reports

1. Was the type of research appropriate for the research questions?
2. Was the research well designed?
   a. Was the sample studied appropriate for the research questions?
   b. Were measures well developed, pretested, and validated?
   c. Were the data analysis techniques the best ones for the study?
3. Was there adequate supervision of data collection, editing, and coding?
4. Was the analysis conducted according to standards accepted in the field?
5. Do the findings make sense given the research question and design, and were they considered in light of previous knowledge and experience?
6. Are the limitations of the study recognized and explained in detail?
7. Are the conclusions appropriately drawn or are they over- or understated?
8. Are the recommendations for marketing strategy clear and appropriate?

Limitations of the Research Process

Although the foregoing discussion presented the research process as a set of simple stages, this does not mean that conducting quality marketing research is a simple task. There are many problems and difficulties that must be overcome if a research study is to provide valuable information for decision making.[3] For example, consider the difficulties in one type of marketing research, *test marketing*.

The major goal of most test marketing is to measure new product sales on a limited basis where competitive retaliation and other factors are allowed to operate freely. In this way, future sales potential can often be estimated reasonably well. Listed below are a number of problems that could invalidate test marketing study results.

1. Test market areas are not representative of the market in general in terms of population characteristics, competition, and distribution outlets.
2. Sample size and design are incorrectly formulated because of budget constraints.
3. Pretest measurements of competitive brand sales are not made or are inaccurate, limiting the meaningfulness of market share estimates.
4. Test stores do not give complete support to the study such that certain package sizes may not be carried or prices may not be held constant during the test period.
5. Test market products are advertised or promoted beyond a profitable level for the market in general.
6. The effects of factors that influence sales, such as the sales force, season, weather conditions, competitive retaliation, shelf space, and so forth, are ignored in the research.
7. The test market period is too short to determine whether the product will be repurchased by customers.

A list of such problems could be developed for any type of marketing research. However, careful research planning, coordination, implementation, and control can help reduce such problems and increase the value of research for decision making.

MARKETING INFORMATION SYSTEMS

Most marketers use computer-based systems to help them gather, sort, store, and distribute information for marketing decisions.[4] A popular form of marketing information system is the marketing decision support system, which is a coordinated collection of data, tools, and techniques involving both computer hardware and

Marketing Highlight   Ethical Responsibilities of Marketing Researchers

Marketing researchers have ethical responsibilities to the respondents who provide them primary data, clients for whom they work, and subordinates who work under them. Below are a number of ethical responsibilities to these groups.

RESPONSIBILITIES TO RESPONDENTS

1. *Preserving respondent anonymity.* Marketing researchers should ensure that respondents' identities are safe from invasion of privacy.
2. *Avoiding mental stress for respondents.* Marketing researchers should minimize the mental stress placed on respondents.
3. *Avoiding questions detrimental to respondents.* Marketing researchers should avoid asking questions for which the answers conflict with the self-interest of the respondents.
4. *Avoiding the use of dangerous equipment or techniques.* Physical or reputational harm to respondents based on their participation in marketing research should not occur. Respondents should be informed of any other than minimal risks involved in the research and be free to self-determine their participation.
5. *Avoiding deception of respondents.* Respondents should not be deceived about the purpose of the study in most cases. Many consider deception acceptable in research where it is needed to obtain valid results, there is minimal risk to respondents, and respondents are debriefed explaining the real purpose of the study.
6. *Avoiding coercion of respondents.* Marketing researchers should avoid coercing or harassing people to try to get them to agree to be interviewed or fill out questionnaires.

software by which marketers gather and interpret relevant information for decision making. These systems require three types of software:

1. Database management software for sorting and retrieving data from internal and external sources.
2. Model base management software that contains routines for manipulating data in ways that are useful for marketing decision making.
3. A dialog system that permits marketers to explore databases and use models to produce information to address their decision-making needs.

Marketing decision support systems are designed to handle information from both internal and external sources. Internal information includes such things as sales records, which can be divided by territory, package size, brand, price, order size, or salesperson; inventory data that can indicate how rapidly various products are selling; or expenditure data on such things as advertising, personal selling, or packaging. Internal information is particularly important for investigating the efficiency and effectiveness of various marketing strategies.

RESPONSIBILITIES TO CLIENTS

1. *Providing confidentiality.* Marketing researchers are obliged not to reveal information about a client to competitors and should carefully consider when a company should be identified as a client.
2. *Providing technical integrity.* Marketing researchers are obliged to design efficient studies without undue expense or complexity and accurately report results.
3. *Providing administrative integrity.* Marketing researchers are obliged to price their work fairly without hidden charges.
4. *Providing guidance on research usage.* Marketing researchers are obliged to promote the correct usage of research and to prevent the misuse of findings.

RESPONSIBILITIES TO SUBORDINATE EMPLOYEES

1. *Creating an ethical work environment.* Marketing research managers are obliged to create an ethical work environment where unethical behavior is not encouraged or overlooked.
2. *Avoiding opportunities for unethical behavior.* Marketing research managers are obliged to avoid placing subordinates in situations where unethical behavior could be concealed but rewarded.

Source: Based on Gilbert A. Churchill, Jr. and Dawn Iacobucci, *Marketing Research: Methodological Foundations,* 8th ed. (Fort Worth, TX: Dryden Press, 2002), p. 47.

External information is gathered from outside the organization and concerns changes in the environment that could influence marketing strategies. External information is needed concerning changes in global economies and societies, competitors, customers, and technology. Figure 2–5 lists a sample of sources of external information that could help global marketers make better decisions. Of course, information from marketing research studies conducted by an organization is also put into marketing information systems to improve marketing strategy development.

CONCLUSION

This chapter emphasized the importance of marketing research for making sound marketing strategy decisions. The chapter discussed marketing research as a process involving several stages, which include determining the purpose of the research, designing the plan for the research, performing the research, processing the research data, and preparing the research report. Then, marketing information systems were discussed and one type, the marketing decision support system, was explained. Such systems provide decision makers with the right information, at the right time, in the right way, to make sound marketing decisions.

FIGURE 2–5   **Global Information Sources for Marketing Information Systems**

Information Source	Types of Data
The Export Connection, a national trade databank service of the U.S. Department of Commerce (Washington, DC)	Monthly series of CD-ROM discs containing data from 15 U.S. government agencies, including marketing research reports, information about specific countries and their economies, and a listing of foreign importers of U.S. products
Global Market Surveys	Detailed surveys for given industries such as graphics, computers, medical equipment, industrial equipment
Dun & Bradstreet's *Principal International Business*	Names, addresses, number of employees, products produced, and chief executive officer, up to 6 SIC classifications (4-digit) for each organization; over 144,000 business units classified by 4-digit SIC and alphabetical order
Moody's International Manual	Company histories, descriptions of business, financial statistics, management personnel
Overseas Business Reports	Monthly reports provide information for marketing to specific countries (e.g., "Marketing in Pakistan," "Marketing in Nigeria")
The Exporter's Guide to Federal Resources for Small Business (Washington, DC: U.S. Government Printing Office)	Reference guide to export assistance available from the U.S. government
Automated Trade Locator Assistance System (district offices of the Small Business Administration)	Results of current marketing research about world markets
Small Business Foundation of America, export opportunity hotline: 800-243-7232	Answers to questions from small businesses interested in exporting
Hotline sponsored by AT&T and seven other organizations: 800-USA-XPORT	Free exporter's kit and data on 50 industries and 78 countries
International trade fairs (sponsored by many industry organizations and national governments, including the U.S. Small Business Administration)	Products and needs of existing and potential buyers and competitors from around the world

Source: Gilbert A. Churchill, Jr. and J. Paul Peter, *Marketing: Creating Value for Customers,* 2nd ed. (Burr Ridge, IL: Irwin/McGraw-Hill, 1998), p. 135.

Additional Readings

Aaker, David A.; V. Kumar; and George S. Day. *Marketing Research.* 6th ed. New York: John Wiley, 1998.

Burns, Alvin C., and Ronald F. Bush. *Marketing Research.* 2nd ed. Englewood Cliffs, NJ: Prentice Hall, 1998.

Churchill, Gilbert A., Jr. *Basic Marketing Research.* 4th ed. Fort Worth, TX: Dryden Press, 2001.

———— and Dawn Iacobucci. *Marketing Research: Methodological Foundations.* 8th ed. Fort Worth, TX: Dryden Press, 2002.

Lehmann, Donald R.; Sunil Gupta; and Joel H. Steckel. *Marketing Research.* Reading, MA: Addison-Wesley, 1998.

O'Brien, James A. *Management Information Systems.* Homewood, IL: Richard D. Irwin, 1998.

Sudman, Seymour, and Edward Blair. *Marketing Research: A Problem-Solving Approach.* Boston: Irwin/McGraw-Hill, 1998.

Zikmund, William G. *Exploring Marketing Research.* 6th ed. Fort Worth, TX: Dryden Press, 1997.

Chapter 3

Consumer Behavior

The marketing concept emphasizes that profitable marketing begins with the discovery and understanding of consumer needs and then develops a marketing mix to satisfy these needs. Thus, an understanding of consumers and their needs and purchasing behavior is integral to successful marketing. Unfortunately, there is no single theory of consumer behavior that can totally explain why consumers behave as they do. Instead, there are numerous theories, models, and concepts making up the field. In addition, the majority of these notions have been borrowed from a variety of other disciplines, such as sociology, psychology, anthropology, and economics, and must be integrated to understand consumer behavior.

In this chapter, consumer behavior will be examined in terms of the model in Figure 3–1. The chapter begins by reviewing social, marketing, and situational influences on consumer decision making. These provide information that can influence consumers' thoughts and feelings about purchasing various products and brands. The degree to which this information influences consumers' decisions depends on a number of psychological influences. Two of the most important of these are product knowledge and product involvement, which will then be discussed. The chapter concludes by discussing the consumer decision-making process.

SOCIAL INFLUENCES ON CONSUMER DECISION MAKING

Behavioral scientists have become increasingly aware of the powerful effects of the social environment and personal interactions on human behavior. In terms of consumer behavior, culture, social class, and reference group influences have been related to purchase and consumption decisions. It should be noted that these influences can have both direct and indirect effects on the buying process. By direct

FIGURE 3–1

An Overview of the Buying Process

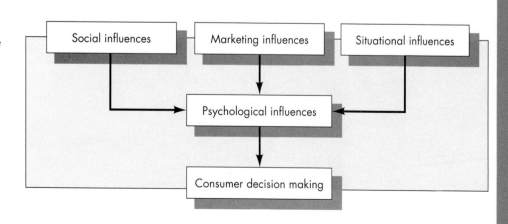

Marketing Highlight A Summary of American Cultural Values

Value	General Features	Relevance to Marketing
Achievement and success activity	Hard work is good; success flows from hard work Keeping busy is healthy and natural	Acts as a justification for acquisition of goods ("You deserve it") Stimulates interest in products that are time-savers and enhance leisure time
Efficiency and practicality	Admiration of things that solve problems (e.g., save time and effort) People can improve themselves; tomorrow should be better than today	Stimulates purchase of products that function well and save time Stimulates desire for new products that fulfill unsatisfied needs; ready acceptance of products that claim to be "new" or "improved"
Material comfort	"The good life"	Fosters acceptance of convenience and luxury products that make life more enjoyable
Individualism	Being oneself (e.g., self-reliance, self-interest, self-esteem)	Stimulates acceptance of customized or unique products that enable a person to "express his or her own personality"
Freedom	Freedom of choice	Fosters interest in wide product lines and differentiated products
External conformity	Uniformity of observable behavior; desire for acceptance	Stimulates interest in products that are used or owned by others in the same social group
Humanitarianism	Caring for others, particularly the underdog	Stimulates patronage of firms that compete with market leaders
Youthfulness	A state of mind that stresses being "young at heart" and having a youthful appearance	Stimulates acceptance of products that provide the illusion of maintaining or fostering youthfulness
Fitness and health	Caring about one's body, including the desire to be physically fit and healthy	Stimulates acceptance of food products, activities, and equipment perceived to maintain or increase physical fitness

Source: Leon G. Schiffman and Leslie Lazar Kanuck, *Consumer Behavior,* 6th ed., p. 437 © 1997. Reprinted by permission of Prentice Hall, Inc., Upper Saddle River, NJ.

effects we mean direct communication between the individual and other members of society concerning a particular decision. By indirect effects we mean the influence of society on an individual's basic values and attitudes as well as the important role that groups play in structuring an individual's personality.

Culture and Subculture

Culture is one of the most basic influences on an individual's needs, wants, and behavior, since all facets of life are carried out against the background of the society in which an individual lives. Cultural antecedents affect everyday behavior, and there is empirical support for the notion that culture is a determinant of certain aspects of consumer behavior.

Cultural values are transmitted through three basic organizations: the family, religious organizations, and educational institutions; and in today's society, educational institutions are playing an increasingly greater role in this regard. Marketing managers should adapt the marketing mix to cultural values and constantly monitor value changes and differences in both domestic and global markets. To illustrate, one of the changing values in America is the increasing emphasis on achievement and career success. This change in values has been recognized by many business firms that have expanded their emphasis on timesaving, convenience-oriented products.

In large nations such as the United States, the population is bound to lose a significant amount of its homogeneity, and thus subcultures arise. In other words, there are subcultures in the American culture where people have more frequent interactions than with the population at large and thus tend to think and act alike in some respects. Subcultures are based on such things as geographic areas, religions, nationalities, ethnic groups, and age. Many subcultural barriers are decreasing because of mass communication, mass transit, and a decline in the influence of religious values. However, age groups, such as the teen market, baby boomers, and the mature market, have become increasingly important for marketing strategy. For example, since baby boomers (those born between 1946 and 1962) make up about a third of the U.S. population and soon will account for about half of discretionary spending, many marketers are repositioning products to serve them. Snickers candy bars, for instance, used to be promoted to children as a treat but are now promoted to adults as a wholesome, between-meals snack.

Social Class

While many people like to think of America as a land of equality, a class structure can be observed. Social classes develop on the basis of such things as wealth, skill, and power. The single best indicator of social class is occupation. However, interest at this point is in the influence of social class on the individual's behavior. What is important here is that different social classes tend to have different attitudinal configurations and values, which influence the behavior of individual members. For marketing purposes, four different social classes have been identified.[1]

Upper Americans comprise 14 percent of the population and are differentiated mainly by having high incomes. This class remains the group in which quality merchandise is most prized and prestige brands are commonly sought. Spending with good taste is a priority as are products such as theater, books, investments in art, European travel, household help, club memberships for tennis, golf, and swimming, and prestige schooling for children.

The *middle class* comprises 34 percent of the population, and these consumers want to do the right thing and buy what is popular. They are concerned with fashion and buying what experts in the media recommend. Increased earnings have led to spending on more "worthwhile experiences" for children, including winter ski trips, college education, and shopping for better brands of clothes at more expensive stores. Appearance of the home is important. This group emulates the upper Americans, which distinguishes it from the working class.

The *working class* comprises 38 percent of the population and are "family folk" who depend heavily on relatives for economic and emotional support. The emphasis on family ties is only one sign of how much more limited and different working-class horizons are socially, psychologically, and geographically compared to those of the middle class. For them, "keeping up with the times" focuses on the mechanical and recreational, and thus, ease of labor and leisure is what they continue to pursue.

Lower Americans comprise 16 percent of the population and are as diverse in values and consumption goals as are other social levels. Some members of this group are prone to every form of instant gratification known to humankind when the money is available. However, others are dedicated to resisting worldly temptations as they struggle toward what some believe will be a "heavenly reward" for their earthly sacrifices.

For the marketing manager, social class offers some insights into consumer behavior and is potentially useful as a market segmentation variable. However, there is considerable controversy as to whether social class is superior to income for the purpose of market segmentation.

Reference Groups and Families

Groups that an individual looks to (uses as a reference) when forming attitudes and opinions are described as reference groups.[2] Primary reference groups include family and close friends, while secondary reference groups include fraternal organizations and professional associations. A buyer may also consult a single individual about decisions, and this individual would be considered a reference individual.

A person normally has several reference groups or reference individuals for various subjects or different decisions. For example, a woman may consult one reference group when she is purchasing a car and a different reference group for lingerie. In other words, the nature of the product and the role the individual is playing during the purchasing process influence which reference group will be consulted. Reference group influence is generally considered to be stronger for products that are "public" or conspicuous—that is, products that other people see the individual using, such as clothes or automobiles.

As noted, the family is generally recognized to be an important reference group, and it has been suggested that the household, rather than the individual, is the relevant unit for studying consumer behavior.[3] This is because within a household the purchaser of goods and services is not always the user of these goods and services. Thus, it is important for marketing managers to determine not only who makes the actual purchase but also who makes the decision to purchase. In addition, it has been recognized that the needs, income, assets, debts, and expenditure patterns change over the course of what is called the *family life cycle*. The family life cycle can be divided into a number of stages ranging from single, to married, to married with children of different age groups, to older couples, to solitary survivors. It may also include divorced people, both with and without children. Because the life cycle combines trends in earning power with demands placed on income, it is a useful way of classifying and segmenting individuals and families.[4]

MARKETING INFLUENCES ON CONSUMER DECISION MAKING

Marketing strategies are often designed to influence consumer decision making and lead to profitable exchanges. Each element of the marketing mix (product, price, promotion, place) can affect consumers in various ways.

Product Influences

Many attributes of a company's products, including brand name, quality, newness, and complexity, can affect consumer behavior. The physical appearance of the product, packaging, and labeling information can also influence whether consumers notice a product in-store, examine it, and purchase it. One of the key tasks of marketers is to differentiate their products from those of competitors and create consumer perceptions that the product is worth purchasing.

Price Influences

The price of products and services often influences whether consumers will purchase them at all and, if so, which competitive offering is selected. Stores, such as Wal-Mart, that are perceived to charge the lowest prices attract many consumers based on this fact alone. For some offerings, higher prices may not deter purchase because consumers believe that the products or services are higher quality or are more prestigious. However, many of today's value-conscious consumers may buy products more on the basis of price than other attributes.

Promotion Influences

Advertising, sales promotions, salespeople, and publicity can influence what consumers think about products, what emotions they experience in purchasing and using them, and what behaviors they perform, including shopping in particular stores and purchasing specific brands. Since consumers receive so much information from marketers and screen out a good deal of it, it is important for marketers to devise communications that (1) offer consistent messages about their products and (2) are placed in media that consumers in the target market are likely to use. Marketing communications play a critical role in informing consumers about products and services, including where they can be purchased, and in creating favorable images and perceptions.

Place Influences

The marketer's strategy for distributing products can influence consumers in several ways. First, products that are convenient to buy in a variety of stores increase the chances of consumers finding and buying them. When consumers are seeking low-involvement products, they are unlikely to engage in extensive search, so ready availability is important. Second, products sold in exclusive outlets, such as Nordstrom, may be perceived by consumers as higher quality. In fact, one of the ways marketers create brand equity, that is, favorable consumer perceptions of brands, is by selling them in prestigious outlets. Third, offering products by nonstore methods, such as on the Internet or in catalogs, can create consumer perceptions that the products are innovative, exclusive, or tailored for specific target markets.

SITUATIONAL INFLUENCES ON CONSUMER DECISION MAKING

Situational influences can be defined as all those factors particular to a time and place of observation that have a demonstrable and systematic effect on current behavior. In terms of purchasing situations, five groups of situational influences have been identified.[5] These influences may be perceived either consciously or subconsciously and may have considerable effect on product and brand choice.

1. *Physical features* are the most readily apparent features of a situation. These features include geographical and institutional location, decor, sounds, aromas, lighting, weather, and visible configurations of merchandise or other material surrounding the stimulus object.

Marketing Highlight   Adapting Marketing Strategies for Global Consumers

In formulating global marketing strategies, marketers must be keenly aware that consumers in different countries and parts of the world may have different cultural values, living conditions, and ways of purchasing and using products. Failure to do so may lead to strategies that are ineffective, as discussed in the example below.

In the late 1980s, the U.S. market for refrigerators and other major appliances was mature. But in Western Europe barely 20 percent of households had clothes dryers, versus some 70 percent in the United States. In Europe, there are dozens of appliance makers, nearly all ripe for consolidation, whereas in the United States there are four producers that control 90 percent of the market. Europe, then, should have been a golden opportunity for U.S. appliance makers Whirlpool Corp. and Maytag.

In 1989, archrivals Whirlpool Corp. and Maytag leaped across the Atlantic. Maytag bought Britain's Hoover for about $320 million, and Whirlpool paid $960 million for the appliance unit of Dutch electronics giant Phillips and spent another $500 million to retool its plants.

But the invasion fizzled. In 1995, Maytag sold its European operations to an Italian appliance maker, booking a $135 million loss. Whirlpool continued in the market, but experienced flat sales and declining earnings per share. Where did these companies go wrong?

In part, these companies misjudged European consumers. American consumers often want the lowest price, and when appliances wear out, they buy new ones. However, many Europeans still think of appliances as investments. They will pay more and expect to get more in finish, durability, and appearance. Also, American households will often put their washer/dryer in the garage or basement or tuck it away in a closet, where noise and appearance don't matter. However, many Europeans live in smaller houses and often put their laundry equipment in their kitchens, where noise and looks matter greatly.

Apparently, the failure to properly analyze consumers in European markets led to market entry strategies that were unsuccessful. While there were many factors that made the market an attractive opportunity, failure to properly analyze consumer behavior led to a huge loss for Maytag and a marginal position for Whirlpool in European markets.

Source: Adapted from Marcia Berss, "Whirlpool's Bloody Nose," *Forbes*, March 11, 1996, pp. 90–91.

2. *Social features* provide additional depth to a description of a situation. Other persons present, their characteristics, their apparent roles and interpersonal interactions are potentially relevant examples.

3. *Time* is a dimension of situations that may be specified in units ranging from time of day to season of the year. Time also may be measured relative to some past or future event for the situational participant. This allows such conceptions as time since last purchase, time since or until meals or paydays, and time constraints imposed by prior or standing commitments.

4. *Task features* of a situation include an intent or requirement to select, shop for, or obtain information about a general or specific purchase. In addition, task may reflect different buyer and user roles anticipated by the individual. For instance, a person shopping for a small appliance as a wedding gift for a friend is in a different situation than when shopping for a small appliance for personal use.

5. *Current conditions* make up a final feature that characterizes a situation. These are momentary moods (such as acute anxiety, pleasantness, hostility, and excitation) or momentary conditions (such as cash on hand, fatigue, and illness) rather than chronic individual traits. These conditions are further stipulated to be immediately antecedent to the current situation to distinguish the states the individual brings to

the situation from states of the individual resulting from the situation. For instance, people may select a certain motion picture because they feel depressed (an antecedent state and a part of the choice situation), but the fact that the movie causes them to feel happier is a response to the consumption situation. This altered state then may become antecedent for behavior in the next choice situation encountered, such as passing a street vendor on the way out of the theater.

PSYCHOLOGICAL INFLUENCES ON CONSUMER DECISION MAKING

Information from group, marketing, and situational influences affects what consumers think and feel about particular products and brands. However, there are a number of psychological factors that influence how this information is interpreted and used and how it impacts the consumer decision-making process. Two of the most important psychological factors are product knowledge and product involvement.[6]

Product Knowledge

Product knowledge refers to the amount of information a consumer has stored in her or his memory about particular product classes, product forms, brands, models, and ways to purchase them. For example, a consumer may know a lot about coffee (product class), ground versus instant coffee (product form), Folgers versus Maxwell House (brand), and various package sizes (models) and stores that sell it (ways to purchase).

Group, marketing, and situational influences determine the initial level of product knowledge as well as changes in it. For example, a consumer may hear about a new Starbucks opening up from a friend (group influence), see an ad for it in the newspaper (marketing influence), or see the coffee shop on the way to work (situational influence). Any of these increase the amount of product knowledge, in this case, a new source for purchasing the product.

The initial level of product knowledge may influence how much information is sought when deciding to make a purchase. For example, if a consumer already believes that Folgers is the best-tasting coffee, knows where to buy it, and knows how much it costs, little additional information may be sought.

Finally, product knowledge influences how quickly a consumer goes through the decision-making process. For example, when purchasing a new product for which the consumer has little product knowledge, extensive information may be sought and more time may be devoted to the decision.

Product Involvement

Product involvement refers to a consumer's perception of the importance or personal relevance of an item. For example, Harley-Davidson motorcycle owners are generally highly involved in the purchase and use of the product, brand, and accessories. However, a consumer buying a new toothbrush would likely view this as a low-involvement purchase.

Product involvement influences consumer decision making in two ways. First, if the purchase is for a high-involvement product, consumers are likely to develop a high degree of product knowledge so that they can be confident that the item they purchase is just right for them. Second, a high degree of product involvement encourages extensive decision making by consumers, which likely increases the time it takes to go through the decision-making process.

CONSUMER DECISION MAKING

The process by which consumers make decisions to purchase various products and brands is shown in Figure 3–2. In general, consumers recognize a need for a product, search for information about alternatives to meet the need, evaluate the information, make purchases, and evaluate the decision after the purchase. There are three types of decision making, which vary in terms of how complex or expensive a product is and how involved a consumer is in purchasing it.

Extensive decision making requires the most time and effort since the purchase involves a highly complex or expensive product that is important to the consumer. For example, the purchase of a car, house, or computer often involves considerable time and effort comparing alternatives and deciding on the right one. In terms of the number of purchases a consumer makes, extensive decision making is relatively rare, but it is critical for marketers of highly complex or expensive products to understand that consumers are willing to process considerable information to make the best choice. Thus, marketers should provide consumer factual information that highlights competitive advantages for such high-involvement products.

Limited decision making is more moderate but still involves some time and effort searching for and comparing alternatives. For example, when buying shirts or shorts, consumers may shop several stores and compare a number of different brands and styles. Marketers of products for which consumers usually do limited decision making often use eye-catching advertising and in-store displays to make consumers aware of their products and encourage consumers to consider buying them.

Routine decision making is the most common type and the way consumers purchase most packaged goods. Such products are simple, inexpensive, and familiar, and consumers often have developed favorite brands that they purchase without much deliberation. For example, consumers often make habitual purchases of soft drinks, candy bars, or canned soup without carefully comparing the relative merits of different brands. Marketers of such products need to have them readily available for purchase in a variety of outlets and price them competitively if price is an important criterion to consumers. Marketers of these low-involvement products often use celebrity spokespeople and other non-product-related cues to encourage purchases.

Need Recognition

The starting point in the buying process is the recognition of an unsatisfied need by the consumer. Any number of either internal or external stimuli may activate needs or wants and recognition of them. Internal stimuli are such things as feeling hungry and wanting some food, feeling a headache coming on and wanting some Excedrin,

FIGURE 3–2   The Consumer Decision-Making Process

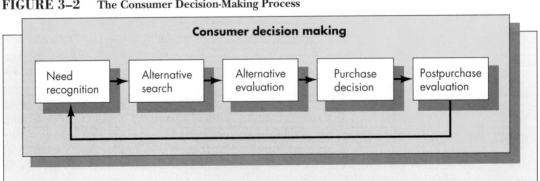

or feeling bored and looking for a movie to go to. External stimuli are such things as seeing a McDonald's sign and then feeling hungry or seeing a sale sign for winter parkas and remembering that last year's coat is worn out.

It is the task of marketing managers to find out what needs and wants a particular product can and does satisfy and what unsatisfied needs and wants consumers have for which a new product could be developed. In order to do so, marketing managers should understand what types of needs consumers may have. A well-known classification of needs was developed many years ago by Abraham Maslow and includes five types.[7] Maslow's view is that lower-level needs, starting with physiological and safety, must be attended to before higher-level needs can be satisfied. Maslow's hierarchy is described below.

Physiological needs. This category consists of the primary needs of the human body, such as food, water, and sex. Physiological needs will dominate when all needs are unsatisfied. In such a case, none of the other needs will serve as a basis for motivation.

Safety needs. With the physiological needs met, the next higher level assumes importance. Safety needs consist of such things as protection from physical harm, ill health, economic disaster, and avoidance of the unexpected.

Belongingness and love needs. These needs are related to the social and gregarious nature of humans and the need for companionship. This level in the hierarchy is the point of departure from the physical or quasi-physical needs of the two previous levels. Nonsatisfaction of this level of need may affect the mental health of the individual.

Esteem needs. These needs consist of both the need for the self-awareness of importance to others (self-esteem) and actual esteem from others. Satisfaction of these needs leads to feelings of self-confidence and prestige.

Self-actualization needs. This need can be defined as the desire to become more and more what one is, to become everything one is capable of becoming. This means that the individual will fully realize the potentialities of given talents and capabilities. Maslow assumes that satisfaction of these needs is only possible after the satisfaction of all the needs lower in the hierarchy.

While the hierarchical arrangement of Maslow presents a convenient explanation, it is probably more realistic to assume that the various need categories overlap. Thus, in affluent societies, many products may satisfy more than one of these needs. For example, gourmet foods may satisfy both the basic physiological need of hunger as well as esteem and status needs for those who serve gourmet foods to their guests.

Alternative Search

Once a need is recognized, the individual then searches for alternatives for satisfying the need. There are five basic sources from which the individual can collect information for a particular purchase decision.

1. *Internal sources.* In most cases the individual has had some previous experience in dealing with a particular need. Thus, the individual will usually "search" through whatever stored information and experience is in his or her mind for dealing with the need. If a previously acceptable product for satisfying the need is remembered, the individual may purchase with little or no additional information search or evaluation. This is quite common for routine or habitual purchases.

2. *Group sources.* A common source of information for purchase decisions comes from communication with other people, such as family, friends, neighbors, and acquaintances. Generally, some of these (i.e., relevant others) are selected that the individual views as having particular expertise for the purchase decision. Although it may be quite difficult for the marketing manager to determine the exact nature of this source of information, group sources of information often are considered to be the most powerful influence on purchase decisions.

3. *Marketing sources.* Marketing sources of information include such factors as advertising, salespeople, dealers, packaging, and displays. Generally, this is the primary source of information about a particular product. These sources of information will be discussed in detail in the promotion chapters of this text.

4. *Public sources.* Public sources of information include publicity, such as a newspaper article about the product, and independent ratings of the product, such as *Consumer Reports.* Here product quality is a highly important marketing management consideration, since such articles and reports often discuss such features as dependability and service requirements.

5. *Experiential sources.* Experiential sources refer to handling, examining, and perhaps trying the product while shopping. This usually requires an actual shopping trip by the individual and may be the final source consulted before purchase.

Information collected from these sources is then processed by the consumer.[8] However, the exact nature of how individuals process information to form evaluations of products is not fully understood. In general, information processing is viewed as a four-step process in which the individual is (1) exposed to information, (2) becomes attentive to the information, (3) understands the information, and (4) retains the information.[9]

Alternative Evaluation

During the process of collecting information or, in some cases, after information is acquired, the consumer evaluates alternatives on the basis of what he or she has learned. One approach to describing the evaluation process is as follows:

1. The consumer has information about a number of brands in a product class.
2. The consumer perceives that at least some of the brands in a product class are viable alternatives for satisfying a recognized need.
3. Each of these brands has a set of attributes (color, quality, size, and so forth).
4. A set of these attributes is relevant to the consumer, and the consumer perceives that different brands vary in how much of each attribute they possess.
5. The brand that is perceived as offering the greatest number of desired attributes in the desired amounts and desired order will be the brand the consumer will like best.
6. The brand the consumer likes best is the brand the consumer will intend to purchase.[10]

Purchase Decision

If no other factors intervene after the consumer has decided on the brand that is intended for purchase, the actual purchase is a common result of search and evaluation. Actually, a purchase involves many decisions, which include product type, brand, model, dealer selection, and method of payment, among other factors. In addition, rather than purchasing, the consumer may make a decision to modify, postpone, or avoid purchase based on an inhibitor to purchase or a perceived risk.

The marketing profession has long recognized the need to uphold its integrity, honor, and dignity. Part of this obligation is to treat customers fairly and honestly. In the American Marketing Association Code of Ethics, a number of issues are concerned with this obligation. Below is a list of some of the Code of Ethics responsibilities that bear directly or indirectly on exchanges with consumers and organizational buyers.

PRODUCT DEVELOPMENT AND MANAGEMENT AREA

Products and services offered should be safe and fit for their intended use.

All substantial risks associated with product or service usage should be disclosed.

Product component substitutions that might materially change the product or impact the buyer's decision should be disclosed.

Extra-cost added features should be identified.

PROMOTION AREA

Communication about offered products and services should not be deceptive.

False and misleading advertising should be avoided.

High-pressure manipulation or misleading sales tactics should be avoided.

Sales promotions that use deception or manipulation should be avoided.

DISTRIBUTION AREA

The availability of a product should not be manipulated for the purpose of exploitation.

Coercion in the marketing channel should not be used.

Undue influence over the resellers' choice to handle products should be avoided.

PRICING AREA

Pricing fixing should not be practiced.

Predatory pricing should not be practiced.

The full price associated with any purchase should be disclosed.

Source: Adapted from the American Marketing Association Code of Ethics.

Traditional risk theorists believe that consumers tend to make risk-minimizing decisions based on their *perceived* definition of the particular purchase. The perception of risk is based upon the possible consequences and uncertainties involved. Consequences may range from economic loss, to embarrassment if a new food product does not turn out well, to actual physical harm. Perceived risk may be either functional (related to financial and performance considerations) or psychosocial (related to whether the product will further one's self- or reference group image). The amount of risk a consumer perceives in a particular product depends on such things as the price of the product and whether other people will see the individual using it.

The perceived risk literature emphasizes that consumers generally try to reduce risk in their decision making. This can be done by either reducing the possible negative consequences or by reducing the uncertainty. The possible consequences of a purchase might be minimized by purchasing in small quantities or by lowering the individual's aspiration level to expect less in the way of results from the product. However, this cannot always be done. Thus, reducing risk by attempting to increase the certainty of the purchase outcome may be the more widely used strategy. This can be done by seeking additional information regarding the proposed purchase. In general, the more information the consumer collects prior to purchase, the less likely postpurchase dissonance is to occur.

Postpurchase Evaluation

In general, if the individual finds that a certain response achieves a desired goal or satisfies a need, the success of this cue-response pattern will be remembered. The probability of responding in a like manner to the same or similar situation in the future is increased. In other words, the response has a higher probability of being repeated when the need and cue appear together again, and thus it can be said that learning has taken place. Frequent reinforcement increases the habit potential of the particular response. Likewise, if a response does not satisfy the need adequately, the probability that the same response will be repeated is reduced.

For some marketers this means that if an individual finds a particular product fulfills the need for which it was purchased, the probability is high that the individual will repurchase the product the next time the need arises. The firm's promotional efforts often act as the cue. If an individual repeatedly purchases a product with favorable results, loyalty may develop toward the particular product or brand. This loyalty can result in habitual purchases, and such habits are often extremely difficult for competing firms to alter.

Although many studies in the area of buyer behavior center on the buyer's attitudes, motives, and behavior before and during the purchase decision, emphasis has also been given to study of behavior after the purchase. Specifically, studies have been undertaken to investigate postpurchase dissonance, as well as postpurchase satisfaction.

The occurrence of postdecision dissonance is related to the concept of *cognitive dissonance*. This theory states that there is often a lack of consistency or harmony among an individual's various cognitions, or attitudes and beliefs, after a decision has been made—that is, the individual has doubts and second thoughts about the choice made. Further, it is more likely that the intensity of the anxiety will be greater when any of the following conditions exist:

1. The decision is an important one psychologically or financially, or both.
2. There are a number of forgone alternatives.
3. The forgone alternatives have many favorable features.

Marketing Highlight   Factors Affecting Information Search by Consumers

Influencing Factor	Increasing the Influencing Factor Causes the Search to:
I. Market characteristics	
A. Number of alternatives	Increase
B. Price range	Increase
C. Store concentration	Increase
D. Information availability	Increase
1. Advertising	
2. Point-of-purchase	
3. Sales personnel	
4. Packaging	
5. Experienced consumers	
6. Independent sources	
II. Product characteristics	
A. Price	Increase
B. Differentiation	Increase
C. Positive products	Increase
III. Consumer characteristics	
A. Learning and experience	Decrease
B. Shopping orientation	Mixed
C. Social status	Increase
D. Age, gender, and household life cycle	Mixed
E. Product involvement	Mixed
F. Perceived risk	Increase
IV. Situational characteristics	
A. Time availability	Increase
B. Purchase for self	Decrease
C. Pleasant surroundings	Increase
D. Social surroundings	Mixed
E. Physical/mental energy	Increase

Source: Del I. Hawkins, Kenneth A. Coney, and Roger Best, Jr., *Consumer Behavior: Implications for Marketing Strategy*, 8th ed. (Burr Ridge, IL: Irwin/McGraw-Hill, 2001), p. 544.

These factors can relate to many buying decisions. For example, postpurchase dissonance might be expected to be present among many purchasers of such products as automobiles, major appliances, and homes. In these cases, the decision to purchase is usually an important one both financially and psychologically, and there are usually a number of favorable alternatives available.

These findings have much relevance for marketers. In a buying situation, when a purchaser becomes dissonant it is reasonable to predict such a person would be highly receptive to advertising and sales promotion that support the purchase decision. Such communication presents favorable aspects of the product and can be useful in reinforcing the buyer's wish to believe that a wise purchase decision was made. For example, purchasers of major appliances or automobiles might be given a phone call or sent a letter reassuring them that they have made a wise purchase.

As noted, researchers have also studied postpurchase consumer satisfaction. Much of this work has been based on what is called the *disconfirmation paradigm*. Basically, this approach views satisfaction with products and brands as a result of two other variables. The first variable is the expectations a consumer has about a product before purchase. These expectations concern the beliefs the consumer has about the product's performance.

The second variable is the difference between expectations and postpurchase perceptions of how the product actually performed. If the product performed as well as expected or better than expected, the consumer will be satisfied with the product. If the product performed worse than expected, the consumer will be dissatisfied with it.

One implication of this view for marketers is that care must be taken not to raise prepurchase expectations to such a level that the product cannot possibly meet them. Rather, it is important to create positive expectations consistent with the product's likely performance.[11]

CONCLUSION

This chapter presented an overview of consumer behavior. Social, marketing, and situational influences on consumer decision making were discussed first followed by a discussion of two important psychological factors, product knowledge and product involvement. Consumer decision making, which can be extensive, limited, or routine, was viewed as a series of stages: need recognition, alternative search, alternative evaluation, purchase decision, and postpurchase evaluation. Clearly, understanding consumer behavior is a prerequisite for developing successful marketing strategies.

Additional Readings

Assael, Henry. *Consumer Behavior and Marketing Action*. 6th ed. Cincinnati, OH: South-Western College Publishing, 1998.

Engel, James F.; Roger D. Blackwell; and Paul W. Miniard. *Consumer Behavior*. 8th ed. Fort Worth, TX: Dryden Press, 1995.

Hawkins, Del; Kenneth A. Coney; and Roger Best, Jr. *Consumer Behavior: Building Marketing Strategy*. 8th ed. Burr Ridge, IL: Irwin/McGraw-Hill, 2001.

Hoyer, Wayne D., and Deborah J. MacInnis. *Consumer Behavior*. Boston: Houghton Mifflin, 1997.

Kardes, Frank R. *Consumer Behavior and Managerial Decision Making*. Reading, MA: Addison-Wesley, 1999.

Mowen, John C., and Michael Minor. *Consumer Behavior*. 5th ed. New York: Macmillan Publishing, 1998.

Peter, J. Paul, and Jerry C. Olson. *Consumer Behavior and Marketing Strategy*. 6th ed. Burr Ridge, IL: Irwin/McGraw-Hill, 2002.

Schiffman, Leon G., and Leslie Kanuck. *Consumer Behavior*. 7th ed. Englewood Cliffs, NJ: Prentice Hall, 2000.

Solomon, Michael R. *Consumer Behavior*. 4th ed. Boston: Allyn & Bacon, 1999.

Wells, William D., and David Prensky. *Consumer Behavior*. New York: John Wiley & Sons, 1996.

Appendix

Selected Consumer Behavior Data Sources

1. Demographic Information
   U.S. Census of Population,
   http://www.census.gov.
   Marketing Information Guide.
   A Guide to Consumer Markets.
   State and city government publications.
   Media (newspapers, magazines, television, and radio stations) make demographic data about their readers or audiences available.

2. Consumer Research Findings
   Advances in Consumer Research
   American Demographics
   Journal of the Academy of Marketing Science
   Journal of Advertising
   Journal of Advertising Research
   Journal of Applied Psychology
   Journal of Consumer Psychology
   Journal of Consumer Research
   Journal of Marketing
   Journal of Marketing Research
   Marketing Science

3. Marketing Applications
   Advertising Age
   Business Week
   Forbes
   Fortune
   Marketing Communications
   Nation's Business
   Sales & Marketing Management

4

Business, Government, and Institutional Buying

In the previous chapter we discussed consumer behavior and the decision-making process used to purchase products and services. However, final consumers are not the only purchasers of products and services. Rather, businesses, government agencies, and other institutions buy products and services to maintain their organizations and achieve their organizational objectives. These organizations are major customers for many marketers. In this chapter we discuss the nature of these organizations and offer a general model of the buying process for them. The chapter begins by discussing four categories of organizational buyers and then presents an overview of the organizational buying process.

CATEGORIES OF ORGANIZATIONAL BUYERS

There are four major categories of organizational buyers that include producers, intermediaries, government agencies, and other institutions. Taken collectively, marketing to producers and intermediaries is called *business-to-business* or *b2b marketing*. Business-to-business marketing has become a topic of increasing interest because it is the major area where Internet marketing has been done profitably.

Producers

These organizational buyers consist of businesses that buy goods and services in order to produce other goods and services for sale. For example, Dell Computer buys computer chips from Intel in order to make computers to be sold to consumers and other organizations. Producers are engaged in many different industries, ranging from agriculture to manufacturing, from construction to finance. Together they constitute the largest segment of organizational buyers. Producers of goods tend to be larger and more geographically concentrated than producers of services.

Intermediaries

Marketing intermediaries or resellers purchase products to resell at a profit. This group includes a number of types of resellers such as wholesalers (Grainger) and retailers (Wal-Mart) who buy products from manufacturers and distribute them to consumers and other organizational buyers. Intermediaries also purchase products and services to run their own businesses, such as office supplies and maintenance services. Given their importance to marketing, intermediaries will be discussed in detail in Chapter 10.

Government Agencies

In the United States, government agencies operate at the federal, state, and local levels; there are over 86,000 governmental agencies in this country that purchase machinery, equipment, facilities, supplies, and services. Government influence agencies account for trillions of dollars worth of buying, and over half of this amount represents purchases by the federal government, making it the world's biggest customer. The governments of other countries also are huge customers for marketers. Marketing to government agencies can be complex since they often have strict purchasing policies and regulations.

Other Institutions

Besides businesses and government agencies, marketers also sell products and services to a variety of other institutions, such as hospitals, museums, universities, nursing homes, and churches. Many of these are nonprofit organizations that purchase products and services to maintain their operations and serve their clientele.

THE ORGANIZATIONAL BUYING PROCESS

Regardless of the type of organization, a buying process is needed to ensure that products and services are purchased and received in a timely and efficient manner. In general, organizations develop a buying process to serve their purchasing needs. Figure 4–1 presents a model of organizational buying that represents some of the common influences and stages in the process.

PURCHASE-TYPE INFLUENCES ON ORGANIZATIONAL BUYING

A major consideration that affects the organizational buying process is the complexity of the purchase that is to be made. Three types of organizational purchase based on their degree of complexity include the straight rebuy, modified rebuy, and new task purchase.[1]

Straight Rebuy

The simplest and most common type of purchase is called a *straight rebuy*. This type of purchase involves routinely reordering from the same supplier a product that has

FIGURE 4–1   A Model of the Organizational Buying Process

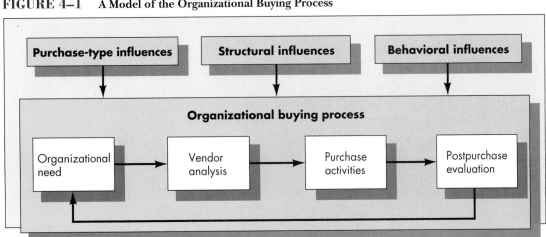

been purchased in the past. Organizations use a straight rebuy when they are experienced at buying the product, have an ongoing need for it, and have regular suppliers of it. In many cases, organizations have computer systems that automatically reorder certain commonly used products. Organizations use this simple approach to purchasing because it is fast and requires relatively few employees.

Straight rebuys are common among organizations that practice *just-in-time inventory*, which is a system of replenishing parts or goods for resale just before they are needed. Such buyers do not have time to hunt around for potential suppliers and solicit bids. Instead they regularly place their orders with a supplier whose quality and timely delivery can be counted on. If a supplier delivers items that are late or of unacceptable quality, these buyers will not have a reserve in inventory to draw on. Therefore, organizations that use just-in-time inventory tend to favor suppliers with a strong commitment to quality.

To retain customers who use straight rebuys, the marketer needs to maintain high-quality products and reliable service so that the customers will continue to be satisfied with their purchases.

Modified Rebuy

When some aspects of the buying situation are unfamiliar, the organization will use a *modified rebuy*. This type of purchase involves considering a limited number of alternatives before making a selection. Organizational buyers follow this approach rather than a straight rebuy when a routine purchase changes in some way; for example, a supplier discontinues a product or stops satisfying the customer, the price of a usual product rises, or a new product becomes available to meet the same need.

In such situations, the organizational buyer considers the new information and decides what changes to make. If the change proves satisfactory and the product is one needed routinely, the buyer may then make it a straight rebuy. Marketers seek to win new organizational customers by giving them reasons to change from a straight rebuy to a modified rebuy in which the marketer's products are considered.

New Task Purchase

Organizations purchase some products only occasionally, especially in the case of large investments such as machinery, equipment, and real estate. In these cases, the organization may use a *new task purchase*. This type of purchase involves an extensive search for information and a formal decision process.

New task purchases are most often used for big-ticket items, so the cost of a mistake is great. Therefore, a new task purchase is time consuming and involves a relatively large number of decision makers, who may consider many alternatives. This is the type of purchase decision that is most likely to involve joint decision making because many kinds of expertise are required to make the best decision.

A new task purchase is an opportunity for the marketer to learn about the needs of the organizations in its target market and to discuss ways to meet organizational needs, such as through the use of new products and technology. Figure 4–2 summarizes the differences in the three types of purchases.

STRUCTURAL INFLUENCES ON ORGANIZATIONAL BUYING

The term *structural influences* refers to the design of the organizational environment and how it affects the purchasing process. Three important structural influences on organizational buying are purchasing roles, organization-specific factors, and purchasing policies and procedures.

FIGURE 4–2 **Differences in Types of Organizational Purchases**

Purchase Type	Complexity	Time Frame	Number of Suppliers	Applications
Straight rebuy	Simple	Short	One	Frequently purchased, routine products, such as printer paper and toner
Modified rebuy	Moderate	Medium	Few	Routine purchase that has changed in some way, such as air travel (new fares, flights, destinations)
New task purchase	Complex	Long	Many	Expensive, seldom-purchased products, such as a new location for a department store

Purchasing Roles

It is common in organizational buying for purchases to be made cross-functionally with representatives from different functional departments playing various roles in the process. Taken collectively, these are called *the buying center* and include the following roles:

1. *Initiators,* who start the purchasing process by recognizing a need or problem in the organization. For example, an executive might see a need for faster computers.
2. *Users,* who are the people in the organization who actually use the product, for example, an assistant who would use a new word processor.
3. *Influencers,* who affect the buying decision, usually by helping define the specifications for what is bought. For example, an information systems manager would be a key influencer in the purchase of a new computer system.
4. *Buyers,* who have the formal authority and responsibility to select the supplier and negotiate the terms of the contract. For example, in the purchase of a computer system, the *purchasing agent* would likely perform this role.
5. *Deciders,* who have the formal or informal power to select or approve the supplier that receives the contract. For important technical purchases, deciders may come from R&D, engineering, or quality control.
6. *Gatekeepers,* who control the flow of information in the buying center. Purchasing personnel, technical experts, and assistants can all keep marketers and their information from reaching people performing the other four roles.[2]

When several persons are involved in the organizational purchase decision, marketers may need to use a variety of means to reach each individual or group. Fortunately, it is often easy to find which individuals in organizations are involved in a purchase because such information is provided to suppliers. Organizations do this because it makes suppliers more knowledgeable about purchasing practices, thus making the purchasing process more efficient.[3] Also, a number of firms have developed closer channel relationships that facilitate these transactions, as discussed in Chapter 10.

Organization-Specific Factors

There are three primary organization-specific factors that influence the purchasing process: orientation, size, and degree of centralization. First, in terms of orientation, the dominant function in an organization may control purchasing decisions. For

Marketing Highlight   Key Differences in Marketing to Organizational Buyers

How Marketing to Organizational Buyers Differs	Example
More variation in buyer-seller relationships	Relationships can be deep and involve several layers of the industry: BASF partners with Gaskell and GM, for example.
Shorter distribution channels	BASF sells fibers *direct* to DuPont for the manufacture of carpet; through distributors to smaller companies—consumer goods sold through distributors, wholesalers, and retailers.
Greater emphasis on personal selling	BASF salespeople work directly with fire departments to sell the latest fire-fighting chemicals and ensure that they are used properly.
Greater Web integration	BASF uses its *cc-markets* website to create a communication space with special customers.
Unique promotional strategies	BASF exhibits at trade shows like Powder Coatings Europe, a show held every January in Amsterdam.

Source: F. Robert Dwyer and John F. Tanner, *Business Marketing,* 2nd ed. (Burr Ridge, IL: McGraw-Hill/Irwin, 2002), p. 11.

example, if the organization is technology oriented, it is likely to be dominated by engineering personnel, and buying decisions will be made by them. Similarly, if the organization is production oriented, production personnel may dominate buying decisions.

Second, the size of the organization may influence the purchasing process. If the organization is large, it will likely have a high degree of joint decision making for other than straight rebuys. Smaller organizations are likely to have more autonomous decision making.

Finally, the degree of centralization of an organization influences whether decisions are made individually or jointly with others. Organizations that are highly centralized are less likely to have joint decision making. Thus, a privately owned, small company with technology or production orientations will tend toward autonomous decision making, while a large-scale, public corporation with considerable decentralization will tend to have greater joint decision making.

Purchasing Policies and Procedures

Organizations typically develop a number of policies and procedures for various types of purchases. These policies and procedures are designed to ensure that the appropriate products and services are purchased efficiently and that responsibility for buying is assigned appropriately. Often a purchasing department will be assigned the task of centralized buying for the whole organization, and individuals within this department will have authority to purchase particular types of products and services in a given price range.

A current trend in many organizations is *sole sourcing,* in which all of a particular type of product is purchased from a single supplier. Sole sourcing has become more popular because organizational buyers have become more concerned with quality and timely delivery and less likely to purchase only on the basis of price. Sole sourcing is advantageous for suppliers because it provides them with predictable and profitable demand and allows them to build long-term relationships with organizational buyers. It is advantageous for organizational buyers because it not only increases timely delivery and quality of supplies but also allows the buyers to work more closely with suppliers to develop superior products that meet their needs and those of their customers. The use of sole sourcing also simplifies the buying process and can make what were formerly modified rebuys into simpler straight rebuys.

Of course, many organizational purchases are more complicated and require policies and procedures to direct the buying process. In many cases, organizations will develop a list of approved vendors from which buyers have authorization to purchase particular products. The buyer's responsibility is to select the vendor that will provide the appropriate levels of quality and service at the lowest cost. These policies and procedures also specify what positions in the purchasing department or buying center have authority to make purchases of different types and dollar amounts.

For large one-time projects, such as the construction of a building, organizations may seek competitive bids for part or all of the project. The development of policies and procedures for handling such purchases is usually complex and involves a number of criteria and committees.

BEHAVIORAL INFLUENCES ON ORGANIZATIONAL BUYING

Organizational buyers are influenced by a variety of psychological and social factors. We will discuss two of these, personal motivations and role perceptions.

Personal Motivations

Organizational buyers are, of course, subject to the same personal motives or motivational forces as other individuals. Although these buyers may emphasize nonpersonal motives in their buying activities, it has been found that organizational buyers often are influenced by such personal factors as friendship, professional pride, fear and uncertainty (risk), trust, and personal ambitions in their buying activities.

For example, professional pride often expresses itself through efforts to attain status in the firm. One way to achieve this might be to initiate or influence the purchase of goods that will demonstrate a buyer's value to the organization. If new materials, equipment, or components result in cost savings or increased profits, the individuals initiating the changes have demonstrated their value at the same time. Fear and uncertainty are strong motivational forces on organizational buyers, and reduction of risk is often important to them. This can have a strong influence on purchase behavior. Marketers should understand the relative strength of personal gain versus risk-reducing motives and emphasize the more important motives when dealing with buyers.

Thus, in examining buyer motivations, it is necessary to consider both personal and nonpersonal motivational forces and to recognize that the relative importance of each is not a fixed quantity. It will vary with the nature of the product, the climate within the organization, and the relative strength of the two forces in the particular buyer.

Marketing Highlight   Twenty Potential Decisions
Facing Organizational Buyers

1. Is the need or problem pressing enough that it must be acted upon now? If not, how long can action be deferred?

2. What types of products or services could conceivably be used to solve our need or problem?

3. Should we make the item ourselves?

4. Must a new product be designed, or has a vendor already developed an acceptable product?

5. Should a value analysis be performed?

6. What is the highest price we can afford to pay?

7. What trade-offs are we prepared to make between price and other product/vendor attributes?

8. Which information sources will we rely on?

9. How many vendors should be considered?

10. Which attributes will be stressed in evaluating vendors?

11. Should bids be solicited?

12. Should the item be leased or purchased outright?

13. How far can a given vendor be pushed in negotiations? On what issues will that vendor bend the most?

14. How much inventory should a vendor be willing to keep on hand?

15. Should we split our order among several vendors?

16. Is a long-term contract in our interest?

17. What contractual guarantees will we require?

18. How shall we establish our order routine?

19. After the purchase, how will vendor performance be evaluated?

20. How will we deal with inadequate product or vendor performance?

Source: Michael H. Morris, Leyland F. Pitt, and Earl D. Honeycutt, Jr., *Business-to-Business Marketing,* 3rd ed. (Thousand Oaks, CA: Sage Publications, 2001), p. 74.

Role Perceptions

A final factor that influences organizational buyers is their own perception of their role. The manner in which individuals behave depends on their perception of their role, their commitment to what they believe is expected of their role, the "maturity" of the role type, and the extent to which the institution is committed to the role type.

Different buyers will have different degrees of commitment to their buying role, which will cause variations in role behavior from one buyer to the next. By *commitment* we mean willingness to perform their job in the manner expected by the organization. For example, some buyers seek to take charge in their role as buyer and have little commitment to company expectations. The implication for marketers is that such buyers expect, even demand, that they be kept constantly advised of all new developments to enable them to more effectively shape their own role. On the other hand, other buyers may have no interest in prescribing their role activities and accept their role as given to them. Such a buyer is most concerned with merely implementing prescribed company activities and buying policies with sanctioned products. Thus, some buyers will be highly committed to play the role the firm dictates (i.e., the formal organization's perception of their role), while others might be extremely innovative and uncommitted to the expected role performance. Obviously, roles may be heavily influenced by the organizational climate existing in the particular organization.[4]

Organizations can be divided into three groups based on differences in degree of employee commitment. These groups include innovative, adaptive, and lethargic firms. In *innovative firms,* individuals approach their occupational roles with a weak commitment to expected norms of behavior. In an *adaptive organization,* there is a moderate commitment. In a *lethargic organization,* individuals express a strong commitment to traditionally accepted behavior and behave accordingly. Thus, a buyer in a lethargic firm would probably be less innovative in order to maintain acceptance and status within the organization and would keep conflict within the firm to a minimum.

Buyers' perception of their role may differ from the perception of their role held by others in the organization. This difference can result in variance in perception of the actual purchase responsibility held by the buyer. One study involving purchasing agents revealed that, in every firm included in the study, the purchasing agents believed they had more responsibility and control over certain decisions than the other influential purchase decision makers in the firm perceived them as having. The decisions were (1) design of the product, (2) cost of the product, (3) performance life, (4) naming of the specific supplier, (5) assessing the amount of engineering help available from the supplier, and (6) reduction of rejects. This variance in role perception held true regardless of the size of the firm or the significance of the item purchased to the overall success of the firm. It is important, therefore, that the marketer be aware that such perceptual differences may exist and to determine as accurately as possible the amount of control and responsibility over purchasing decisions held by each purchase decision influencer in the firm.

STAGES IN THE ORGANIZATIONAL BUYING PROCESS

As with consumer buying, most organizational purchases are made in response to a particular need or problem. Ideally, the products or services purchased will meet the organizational need and improve the organization's efficiency, effectiveness, and profits. The organizational buying process can be analyzed as a series of four stages: organizational need, vendor analysis, purchase activities, and postpurchase evaluation.

Marketing Highlight Code of Ethics for Organizational Buyers

1. Avoid the intent and appearance of unethical or compromising practice in relationships, actions, and communications.

2. Demonstrate loyalty to the employer by diligently following the lawful instructions of the employer, using reasonable care and only the authority granted.

3. Refrain from any private or professional business activity that would create a conflict between personal interests and the interests of the employer.

4. Refrain from soliciting or accepting money, loans, credits, or prejudicial discounts and the acceptance of gifts, entertainment, favors, or services from past or potential suppliers that might influence or appear to influence purchasing decisions.

5. Handle confidential or proprietary information belonging to employers or suppliers with due care and proper consideration of ethical and legal ramifications and government regulations.

6. Promote positive supplier relationships through courtesy and impartiality throughout all phases of the purchasing cycle.

7. Refrain from reciprocal agreements that restrain competition.

8. Know and obey the letter and spirit of laws governing the purchasing function, and remain alert to the legal ramifications of purchasing decisions.

9. Encourage all segments of society to participate by demonstrating support for small, disadvantaged, and minority-owned businesses.

10. Discourage purchasing's involvement in employer-sponsored programs of personal purchases that are not business related.

11. Enhance the proficiency and stature of the purchasing profession by acquiring and maintaining current technical knowledge and the highest standards of ethical behavior.

12. Conduct international purchasing in accordance with the laws, customs, and practices of foreign countries, consistent with U.S. laws, your organization's policies, and these Ethical Standards and Guidelines.

Source: National Association of Purchasing Managers as reported in F. Robert Dwyer and John F. Tanner, *Business Marketing,* 2nd ed. (Burr Ridge, IL: McGraw-Hill/Irwin, 2002), p. 88.

Organizational Need

Organizations have many needs for products and services to help them survive and meet their objectives. For example, a manufacturer may need to purchase new machinery to increase its production capacity and meet demand; a retailer may need to purchase services from a marketing research firm to better understand its market; a government agency may need to purchase faster computers to keep up with growing demand for its services; a hospital may need to purchase more comfortable beds for its patients. Recognizing these needs, and a willingness and ability to meet them, often results in organizational purchases. For straight rebuys, the purchase process may involve little more than a phone call or a few clicks on a computer to order products and arrange payment and delivery. For modified rebuys or new task purchases, the process may be much more complex.

Vendor Analysis

Organizational buyers must search for, locate, and evaluate vendors of products and services to meet their needs. Searching for and locating vendors is often easy since they frequently make sales calls on organizations that might need their products. Vendors also advertise in trade magazines or on the Internet and have displays at industry trade shows to increase their visibility to organizational buyers. For products and services that the organization has previously purchased, a list of approved vendors may have already been developed by the organization.

Organizational buyers often use a vendor analysis to evaluate possible suppliers. A *vendor analysis* is the process by which buyers rate each potential supplier on various performance measures such as product quality, on-time delivery, price, payment terms, and use of modern technology. Figure 4–3 presents a sample vendor analysis form that lists a number of purchase criteria and the weights one organization used to compare potential suppliers.

A formal vendor analysis can be used for at least three purposes. First, it can be used to develop a list of approved vendors, all of which provide acceptable levels of products and services. Organizational buyers can then select any company on the list, simplifying the purchase process. Second, a vendor analysis could be used to compare competing vendors; the buyers then select the best one on the basis of the ratings. This could help the organization pare down vendors to a single supplier for which a long-term, sole-sourcing relationship could be developed. Third, a vendor analysis can be done both before and after purchases to compare performance on evaluation criteria and evaluate the process of vendor selection.

Purchase Activities

Straight rebuys may involve a quick order to an approved vendor or sole-source supplier. However, other types of organizational purchases can involve long time periods with extensive negotiations on price and terms and formal contracts stating quality, delivery, and service criteria. The complexity of the product or service, the number of suppliers available, the importance of the product to the buying organization, and pricing all influence the number of purchase activities to be performed and their difficulty. For example, an airline buying a fleet of jumbo jets or a car rental agency buying a fleet of cars may take months or years to negotiate and make purchases. While such buyers may have considerable leverage in negotiating, it should be remembered that these organizations need the products just as badly as the sellers need to sell them. Thus, there is often more collaboration among organizational buyers and sellers than in the consumer market.

FIGURE 4–3   **Sample Vendor Analysis Form**

	5 Excellent	4 Good	3 Satisfactory	2 Fair	1 Poor	0 N/A

Supplier Name: _____   Type of Product: _____

Shipping Location: _____   Annual Sales Dollars: _____

	5 **Excellent**	**4** **Good**	**3** **Satisfactory**	**2** **Fair**	**1** **Poor**	**0** **N/A**
Quality (45%)						
Defect rates	—	—	—	—	—	—
Quality of sample	—	—	—	—	—	—
Conformance with quality program	—	—	—	—	—	—
Responsiveness to quality problems	—	—	—	—	—	—
Overall quality	—	—	—	—	—	—
Delivery (25%)						
Avoidance of late shipments	—	—	—	—	—	—
Ability to expand production	—	—	—	—	—	—
Performance in sample delivery	—	—	—	—	—	—
Response to changes in order size	—	—	—	—	—	—
Overall delivery	—	—	—	—	—	—
Price (20%)						
Price competitiveness	—	—	—	—	—	—
Payment terms	—	—	—	—	—	—
Absorption of costs	—	—	—	—	—	—
Submission of cost savings plans	—	—	—	—	—	—
Overall price	—	—	—	—	—	—
Technology (10%)						
State-of-the-art components	—	—	—	—	—	—
Sharing research & development capability	—	—	—	—	—	—
Ability and willingness to help with design	—	—	—	—	—	—
Responsiveness to engineering problems	—	—	—	—	—	—
Overall technology	—	—	—	—	—	—

Buyer: _____   Date: _____

Comments: _____

Source: Gilbert A. Churchill, Jr. and J. Paul Peter, *Marketing: Creating Value for Customers,* 2nd ed. (Burr Ridge, IL: Irwin/McGraw-Hill, 1998), p. 186.

Postpurchase Evaluation

Organizational buyers must evaluate both the vendors and the products they purchase to determine whether the products are acceptable for future purchases or whether other sources of supply should be found. A comparison of the performance of the vendor and products with the criteria listed on the prior vendor analysis can be useful for this purpose. If the purchase process goes smoothly and products meet price and quality criteria, then the vendor may be put on the approved list or perhaps further negotiations can be made to sole-source with the supplier.

One problem in judging the acceptability of suppliers and products is that different functional areas may have different evaluation criteria. Figure 4–4 presents

FIGURE 4–4
Functional Areas and Their Key Concerns in Organizational Buying

Functional Areas	Key Concerns
Design and development engineering	Name reputation of vendor; ability of vendors to meet design specifications
Production	Delivery and reliability of purchases such that interruption of production schedules is minimized
Sales/marketing	Impact of purchased items on marketability of the company's products
Maintenance	Degree to which purchased items are compatible with existing facilities and equipment; maintenance service offered by vendor; installation arrangements offered by vendor
Finance/accounting	Effects of purchases on cash flow, balance sheet, and income statement positions; variances in costs of materials over estimates; feasibility of make-or-buy and lease options to purchasing
Purchasing	Obtaining lowest possible price at acceptable quality levels; maintaining good relations with vendors
Quality control	Assurance that purchased items meet prescribed specifications and tolerances, governmental regulations, and customer requirements

Source: Michael H. Morris, Leyland F. Pitt, and Earl D. Honeycutt, Jr. *Business-to-Business Marketing*, 3rd ed. (Thousand Oaks, CA: Sage Publications, 2001), p. 66.

several functional areas of a manufacturing company and their common concerns in purchasing. Clearly, these concerns should be considered both prior to purchasing from a particular supplier and after purchase to ensure that every area's needs are being met as well as possible.

CONCLUSION

Organizational buyers include individuals involved in purchasing products and services for businesses, government agencies, and other institutions and agencies. The organizational buying process is influenced by whether the purchase is a straight rebuy, modified rebuy, or new task purchase. It is also influenced by people in various purchasing roles, the orientation, size, and degree of centralization of the organization, the organization's purchasing policies and procedures, and individuals' motivations and perceived roles. The organizational buying process can be viewed as a series of four stages ranging from organizational need, to vendor analysis, to purchase activities, to postpurchase evaluation. It is important for companies marketing to organizations to understand the influences and process by which organizations buy products and services so that their needs can be met fully and profitably.

Additional Readings

Anderson, James C., and James A. Narus. *Business Market Management*. Upper Saddle River, NJ: Prentice Hall, 1999.

Dwyer, F. Robert, and John F. Tanner. *Business Marketing*. 2nd ed. Burr Ridge, IL: McGraw-Hill/Irwin, 2002.

Morris, Michael H; Leyland F. Pitt; and Earl D. Honeycutt. *Business-to-Business Marketing*. 3rd ed. Thousand Oaks, CA: Sage Publications, 2001.

Reid, David A., and Richard E. Plank. "Business Marketing Comes of Age: A Comprehensive Review of the Literature." *Journal of Business-to-Business Marketing* 7(213), 2000, pp. 9–185.

Chapter 5

Market Segmentation

Market segmentation is one of the most important concepts in marketing. In fact, a primary reason for studying consumer and organizational buyer behavior is to provide bases for effective segmentation, and a large portion of marketing research is concerned with segmentation. From a marketing management point of view, selection of the appropriate target market is paramount to developing successful marketing programs.

The logic of market segmentation is quite simple and is based on the idea that a single product item can seldom meet the needs and wants of *all* consumers. Typically, consumers vary as to their needs, wants, and preferences for products and services, and successful marketers adapt their marketing programs to fulfill these preference patterns. For example, even a simple product like chewing gum has multiple flavors, package sizes, sugar contents, calories, consistencies (e.g., liquid centers), and colors to meet the preferences of various consumers. While a single product item cannot meet the needs of all consumers, it can almost always serve more than one consumer. Thus, there are usually *groups of consumers* who can be served well by a single item. If a particular group can be served *profitably* by a firm, it is a viable market segment. In other words, the firm should develop a marketing mix to serve the group or market segment.

In this chapter we consider the process of market segmentation. We define *market segmentation* as the process of dividing a market into groups of similar consumers and selecting the most appropriate group(s) for the firm to serve. The group or market segment that a company selects to focus on is called a *target market.* We break down the process of market segmentation into six steps, as shown in Figure 5–1. While we recognize that the order of these steps may vary, depending on the firm and situation, there are few if any times when market segmentation analysis can be ignored. In fact, even if the final decision is to "mass market" and not segment at all, this decision should be reached only *after* a market segmentation analysis has been conducted. Thus, market segmentation analysis is a cornerstone of sound marketing planning and decision making.

DELINEATE THE FIRM'S CURRENT SITUATION

As emphasized in Chapter 1, a firm must do a complete situational analysis when embarking on a new or modified marketing program. At the marketing planning level, such an analysis aids in determining objectives, opportunities, and constraints to be considered when selecting target markets and developing marketing mixes. In addition, marketing managers must have a clear idea of the amount of financial and other resources that will be available for developing and executing a marketing plan. Thus, the inclusion of this first step in the market segmentation process is intended to be a reminder of tasks to be performed prior to marketing planning.

FIGURE 5–1
A Model of the
Market Segmentation
Process

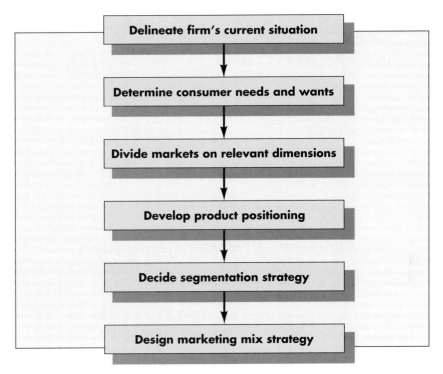

Delineate firm's current situation

↓

Determine consumer needs and wants

↓

Divide markets on relevant dimensions

↓

Develop product positioning

↓

Decide segmentation strategy

↓

Design marketing mix strategy

DETERMINE CONSUMER NEEDS AND WANTS

As emphasized throughout this text, successful marketing strategies depend on discovering and satisfying consumer needs and wants. In some cases, this idea is quite operational. To illustrate, suppose a firm has a good deal of venture capital and is seeking to diversify its interest into new markets. A firm in this situation may seek to discover a broad variety of unsatisfied needs. However, in most situations, the industry in which the firm operates specifies the boundaries of a firm's need satisfaction activities. For example, a firm in the communication industry may seek more efficient methods for serving consumers' long-distance telephone needs.

As a practical matter, new technology often brings about an investigation of consumer needs and wants for new or modified products and services. In these situations, the firm is seeking the group of consumers whose needs could best be satisfied by the new or modified product. Further, at a strategic level, consumer needs and wants usually are translated into more operational concepts. For instance, consumer attitudes, preferences, and benefits sought, which are determined through marketing research, are commonly used for segmentation purposes.

DIVIDE MARKETS ON RELEVANT DIMENSIONS

In a narrow sense, this step is often considered to be the whole of market segmentation (i.e., consumers are grouped on the basis of one or more similarities and treated as a homogeneous segment of a heterogeneous total market). There are three important questions to be considered here:

1. Should the segmentation be a priori or post hoc?
2. How does one determine the relevant dimensions or bases to use for segmentation?
3. What are some bases for segmenting consumer and organizational buyer markets?

Forrester Research Inc. and NPD Group conducted marketing research to determine the profiles of customers in the market for high-tech products. The study polled 131,000 people about their motivations, buying habits, and financial ability to purchase high-tech products. The study identified the 10 market segments described on the facing page. Marketers of high-tech products could use these to select the best target markets for their offerings.

A Priori versus Post Hoc Segmentation

Real-world segmentation has followed one of two general patterns. An *a priori segmentation* approach is one in which the marketing manager has decided on the appropriate basis for segmentation in advance of doing any research on a market. For example, a manager may decide that a market should be divided on the basis of whether people are nonusers, light users, or heavy users of a particular product. Segmentation research is then conducted to determine the size of each of these groups and their demographic or psychographic profiles.

Post hoc segmentation is an approach in which people are grouped into segments on the basis of research findings. For example, people interviewed concerning their attitudes or benefits sought in a particular product category are grouped according to their responses. The size of each of these groups and their demographic and psychographic profiles are then determined.

Both of these approaches are valuable, and the question of which to use depends in part on how well the firm knows the market for a particular product class. If through previous research and experience a marketing manager has successfully isolated a number of key market dimensions, then an a priori approach based on them may provide more useful information. In the case of segmentation for entirely new products, a post hoc approach may be useful for determining key market dimensions. However, even when using a post hoc approach, some consideration must be given to the variables to be included in the research design. Thus, some consideration must be given to the relevant segmentation dimensions regardless of which approach is used.

Relevance of Segmentation Dimensions

Unfortunately, there is no simple solution for determining the relevant dimensions for segmenting markets. Certainly, managerial expertise and experience are needed for selecting the appropriate dimensions or bases on which to segment particular markets. In most cases, however, at least some initial dimensions can be determined from previous research, purchase trends, and managerial judgment. For instance, suppose we wish to segment the market for all-terrain vehicles. Clearly, several dimensions come to mind for initial consideration, including sex (male), age (18 to 35 years), lifestyle (outdoorsman), and income level (perhaps $30,000 to $80,000). At a minimum, these variables should be included in subsequent segmentation research. Of course, the most market-oriented approach to segmentation is on the basis of what benefits the potential consumer is seeking. Thus, consideration and research of sought benefits are a strongly recommended approach in the marketing literature. This approach will be considered in some detail in the following section.

Marketing Highlight Market Segments for High-Tech Products (continued)

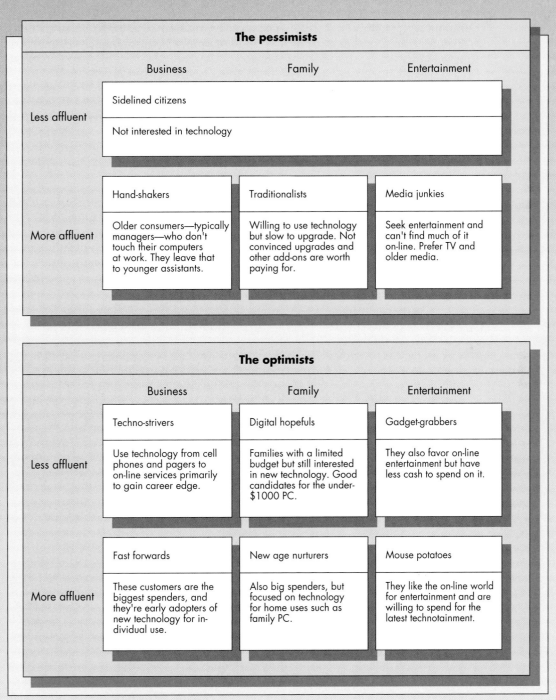

The pessimists

	Business	Family	Entertainment
Less affluent	Sidelined citizens		
	Not interested in technology		
More affluent	**Hand-shakers** — Older consumers—typically managers—who don't touch their computers at work. They leave that to younger assistants.	**Traditionalists** — Willing to use technology but slow to upgrade. Not convinced upgrades and other add-ons are worth paying for.	**Media junkies** — Seek entertainment and can't find much of it on-line. Prefer TV and older media.

The optimists

	Business	Family	Entertainment
Less affluent	**Techno-strivers** — Use technology from cell phones and pagers to on-line services primarily to gain career edge.	**Digital hopefuls** — Families with a limited budget but still interested in new technology. Good candidates for the under-$1000 PC.	**Gadget-grabbers** — They also favor on-line entertainment but have less cash to spend on it.
More affluent	**Fast forwards** — These customers are the biggest spenders, and they're early adopters of new technology for individual use.	**New age nurturers** — Also big spenders, but focused on technology for home uses such as family PC.	**Mouse potatoes** — They like the on-line world for entertainment and are willing to spend for the latest technotainment.

Source: Jakki Mohr, *Marketing of High-Technology Products and Innovations* (Upper Saddle River, NJ: Prentice Hall, 2001), p. 135, and adapted from Paul Judge, "Are Tech Buyers Different?" *Business Week,* January 26, 1998, pp. 64–66.

Bases for Segmentation

A number of useful bases for segmenting consumer and organizational markets are presented in Figure 5–2. This is by no means a complete list of possible segmentation variables but represents some useful bases and categories. Two commonly used approaches for segmenting markets include benefit segmentation and psychographic segmentation. We will discuss these two in some detail. We will also discuss geodemographic segmentation, a recent development with a number of advantages for marketers.

Benefit Segmentation

The belief underlying this segmentation approach is that the benefits that people are seeking in consuming a given product are the basic reasons for the existence of true market segments.[1] Thus, this approach attempts to measure consumer value systems and consumer perceptions of various brands in a product class. To illustrate, the classic example of a benefit segmentation was provided by Russell Haley and concerned the toothpaste market. Haley identified five basic segments, which are presented in Figure 5–3. Haley argued that this segmentation could be very useful for selecting advertising copy, media, commercial length, packaging, and new product design. For example, colorful packages might be appropriate for the sensory segment, perhaps aqua (to indicate fluoride) for the worrier group, and gleaming white for the social segment because of this segment's interest in white teeth.

FIGURE 5–2   **Useful Segmentation Bases for Consumer and Organizational Buyer Markets**

	Consumer Markets	
Segmentation Base	**Examples of Market Segments**	
Geographic:		
Continents	Africa, Asia, Europe, North America, South America	
Global regions	Southeast Asia, Mediterranean, Caribbean	
Countries	China, Canada, France, United States, Brazil	
Country regions	Pacific Northwest, Middle Atlantic, Midwest	
City, county, or SMSA size	Under 5,000 people, 5,000–19,999, 20,000–49,999, 50,000+	
Population density	Urban, suburban, rural	
Climate	Tropical, temperate, cold	
Demographic:		
Age	Under 6 years old, 6–12, 13–19, 20–29, 30–39, 40–49, 50+	
Gender	Male, female	
Family size	1–2 persons, 3–4 persons, more than 4 persons	
Family life cycle	Single, young married, married with children, sole survivor	
Income	Under $10,000 per year, $10,000–$19,999, $20,000–$29,999, $30,000–$39,999, $40,000–$49,999, $50,000+	
Education	Grade school or less, some high school, graduated from high school, some college, graduated from college, some graduate work, graduate degree	
Marital status	Single, married, divorced, widowed	
Social:		
Culture	American, Hispanic, African, Asian, European	
Subculture		
Religion	Jewish, Catholic, Muslim, Mormon, Buddhist	
Race	European American, Asian American, African American, Hispanic American	
Nationality	French, Malaysian, Australian, Canadian, Japanese	
Social class	Upper class, middle class, working class, lower class	

FIGURE 5–2   (continued)

Consumer Markets	
Segmentation Base	**Examples of Market Segments**
Thoughts and feelings:	
Knowledge	Expert, novice
Involvement	High, medium, low
Attitude	Positive, neutral, negative
Benefits sought	Convenience, economy, prestige
Innovativeness	Innovator, early adopter, early majority, late majority, laggards, nonadopter
Readiness stage	Unaware, aware, interested, desirous, plan to purchase
Perceived risk	High, moderate, low
Behavior:	
Media usage	Newspaper, magazine, TV, Internet
Specific media usage	*Sports Illustrated, Life, Cosmopolitan*
Payment method	Cash, Visa, MasterCard, American Express, check
Loyalty status	None, some, total
Usage rate	Light, medium, heavy
User status	Nonuser, ex-user, current user, potential user
Usage situation	Work, home, vacation, commuting
Combined approaches:	
Psychographics	Achievers, strivers, strugglers
Person/situation	College students for lunch, executives for business dinner
Geodemography	Blue Blood Estates, Towns and Gowns, Hispanic Mix
Organizational Buyer Markets	
Segmentation Base	**Examples of Market Segments**
Source loyalty	Purchases product from one, two, three, four, or more suppliers
Company size	Small, medium, large relative to industry
Purchase quantity	Small, medium, large account
Product application	Production, maintenance, product component
Organization type	Manufacturer, retailer, government agency, hospital
Location	North, south, east, west sales territory
Purchase status	New customer, occasional purchaser, frequent purchaser, nonpurchaser
Attribute importance	Price, service, reliability of supply

FIGURE 5–3   Toothpaste Market Benefit Segments

	Sensory Segment	Sociable Segment	Worrier Segment	Independent Segment
Principal benefit sought	Flavor and product appearance	Brightness of teeth	Decay prevention	Price
Demographic strengths	Children	Teens, young people	Large families	Men
Special behavioral characteristics	Users of spearmint-flavored toothpaste	Smokers	Heavy users	Heavy users
Brands disproportionately favored	Colgate	Macleans, Ultra Brite	Crest	Cheapest brand
Lifestyle characteristics	Hedonistic	Active	Conservative	Value-oriented

Source: Adapted from Russell I. Haley, "Benefit Segmentation: A Decision-Oriented Research Tool," *Journal of Marketing,* July 1968, pp. 30–35.

Marketing Highlight   Want to Know Your VALS Category?
Check It Out on the Internet

You can find your VALS classification by filling out a questionnaire on the Internet. The Web address is http://future.sri.com/vals/valshome.html. The questionnaire takes about 10 minutes to complete, and your lifestyle will take about 10 seconds to compute. You will get a report that includes both your primary and secondary VALS type. The VALS Web site has a lot of information describing the program and different types of VALS segments.

Calantone and Sawyer also used a benefit segmentation approach to segment the market for bank services.[2] Their research was concerned with the question of whether benefit segments remain stable across time. While they found some stability in segments, there were some differences in attribute importance, size, and demographics at different times. Thus, they argue for ongoing benefit segmentation research to keep track of any changes in a market that might affect marketing strategy.

Benefit segmentation is clearly a market-oriented approach to segmentation that seeks to identify consumer needs and wants and to satisfy them by providing products and services with the desired benefits. It is clearly very consistent with the approach to marketing suggested by the marketing concept.

Psychographic Segmentation

Whereas benefit segmentation focuses on the benefits sought by the consumer, psychographic segmentation focuses on the personal attributes of the consumer. The psychographic or lifestyle approach typically follows a post hoc model of segmentation. Generally, a large number of questions are asked concerning consumers' activities, interests, and opinions, and then consumers are grouped together empirically based on their responses. Although questions have been raised about the validity of this segmentation approach, it provides much useful information about markets.[3]

A well-known psychographic segmentation was developed at SRI International in California. The original segmentation divided consumers in the United States into nine groups and was called VALS™, which stands for "values and lifestyles." However, while this segmentation was commercially successful, it tended to place the majority of consumers into only one or two groups, and SRI felt it needed to be updated to reflect changes in society. Thus, SRI developed a new typology called VALS 2™.[4]

VALS 2 is based on two national surveys of 2,500 consumers who responded to 43 lifestyle questions. The first survey developed the segmentation, and the second validated it and linked it to buying and media behavior. The questionnaire asked consumers to respond to whether they agreed or disagreed with statements such as "My idea of fun at a national park would be to stay at an expensive lodge and dress up for dinner" and "I could stand to skin a dead animal." Consumers were then clustered into eight groups, shown and described in Figure 5–4.

The VALS 2 groups are arranged in a rectangle and are based on two dimensions. The vertical dimension represents resources, which include income, education, self-confidence, health, eagerness to buy, intelligence, and energy level. The horizontal dimension represents self-orientations and includes three different types. *Principle-oriented consumers* are guided by their views of how the world is or should be; *status-oriented consumers* by the action and opinions of others; and *action-oriented consumers* by a desire for social or physical activity, variety, and risk taking.

FIGURE 5–4
VALS 2 Eight
American Lifestyles

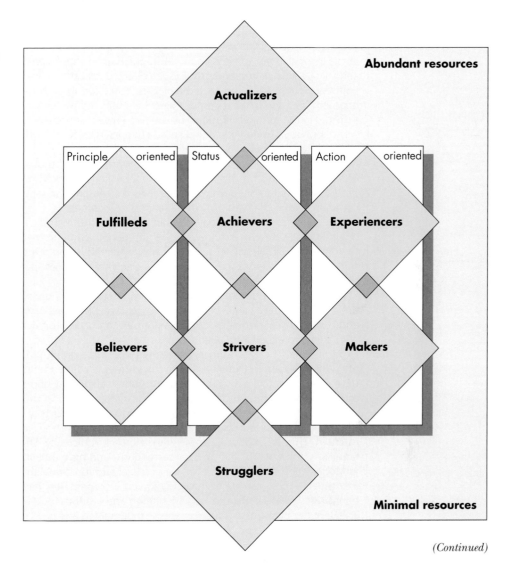

(Continued)

Each of the VALS 2 groups represents from 9 to 17 percent of the U.S. adult population. Marketers can buy VALS 2 information for a variety of products and can have it tied to a number of other consumer databases.

Geodemographic Segmentation

One problem with many segmentation approaches is that while they identify types or categories of consumers, they do not identify specific individuals or households within a market. *Geodemographic segmentation* does identify specific households in a market by focusing on local neighborhood geography (such as zip codes) to create classifications of actual, addressable, mappable neighborhoods where people live and shop. One geodemographic system created by Claritas, Inc., is called PRIZM, which stands for Potential Ranking Index by Zip Markets. This system classifies every U.S. neighborhood into one of 62 distinct types or clusters of consumers. Each PRIZM cluster is based on zip codes, demographic information from the U.S. census, and information on product usage, media usage, and lifestyle preferences to create profiles of the people who live in specific neighborhoods. Figure 5–5 shows a sample cluster profile. The PRIZM system includes maps of different areas that rank neighborhoods on their potential to purchase specific products or services.

FIGURE 5–4
(continued)

Actualizers. These consumers have the highest incomes and such high self-esteem and abundant resources that they can indulge in any or all self-orientations. They are located above the rectangle. Image is important to them as an expression of taste, independence, and character. Their consumer choices are directed toward the finer things in life.

Fulfilleds. These consumers are the high-resource group of those who are principle oriented. They are mature, responsible, well-educated professionals. Their leisure activities center on their homes, but they are well-informed about what goes on in the world and open to new ideas and social change. They have high incomes but are practical consumers.

Believers. These consumers are the low-resource group of those who are principle oriented. They are conservative and predictable consumers who favor American products and established brands. Their lives are centered on family, church, community, and the nation. They have modest incomes.

Achievers. These consumers are the high-resource group of those who are status oriented. They are successful, work-oriented people who get their satisfaction from their jobs and families. They are politically conservative and respect authority and the status quo. They favor established products and services that show off their success to their peers.

Strivers. These consumers are the low-resource group of those who are status oriented. They have values very similar to achievers but have fewer economic, social, and psychological resources. Style is extremely important to them as they strive to emulate people they admire and wish to be like.

Experiencers. These consumers are the high-resource group of those who are action oriented. They are the youngest of all the segments with a median age of 25. They have a lot of energy, which they pour into physical exercise and social activities. They are avid consumers, spending heavily on clothing, fast foods, music, and other youthful favorites—with particular emphasis on new products and services.

Makers. These consumers are the low-resource group of those who are action oriented. They are practical people who value self-sufficiency. They are focused on the familiar—family, work, and physical recreation—and have little interest in the broader world. As consumers, they appreciate practical and functional products.

Strugglers. These consumers have the lowest incomes. They have too few resources to be included in any consumer self-orientation and are thus located below the rectangle. They are the oldest of all the segments with a median age of 61. Within their limited means, they tend to be brand-loyal consumers.

Source: Martha Farnsworth Riche, "Psychographics for the 1990s," *American Demographics,* July 1989, pp. 24–26ff.

The PRIZM system is based on the assumptions that consumers in particular neighborhoods are similar in many respects and that the best prospects are those who actually use a product or other consumers like them. Marketers use PRIZM to better understand consumers in various markets, what they're like, where they live, and how to reach them. These data help marketers with target market selection, direct-marketing campaigns, site selection, media selection, and analysis of sales potential in various areas.

DEVELOP PRODUCT POSITIONING

By this time, the firm should have a good idea of the basic segments of the market that could potentially be satisfied with its product. The current step is concerned with positioning the product favorably in the minds of customers relative to competitive products. There are several different positioning strategies that can be used. First, products can be positioned by focusing on their superiority to competitive products based on one or more attributes. For example, a car could be positioned as less expensive

FIGURE 5–5
Claritas PRIZM Cluster 36—Towns and Gowns

The "towns and gowns" cluster describes most of our college towns and university campus neighborhoods. With a typical mix of half locals (towns) and half students (gowns), it is wholly unique, with thousands of penniless 18- to 24-year-old kids, plus highly educated professionals, all with a taste for prestige products beyond their evident means.

Predominant Characteristics

• Households (% U.S.):	1,290,200 (1.4%)
• Population:	3,542,500
• Demographic caption:	College-town singles
• Ethnic diversity:	Dominant white, high Asian
• Family type:	Singles
• Predominant age ranges:	Under 24, 25–34
• Education:	College graduates
• Employment level:	White collar/service
• Housing type:	Renters/multiunit 10+
• Density percentile:	58 (1 = sparse, 99 = dense)

More Likely to:

Lifestyle	Products and Services
Go to college football games	Have a personal education loan
Play racquetball	Use an ATM card
Go skiing	Own a Honda
Play billiards/pool	Buy 3+ pairs of jeans annually
Use cigarette rolling paper	Drink Coca-Cola Classic
Use a charter/tour bus	Eat Kraft Macaroni and Cheese

Radio/TV	Print
Watch VH1	Read *Self*
Listen to alternative rock music	Read newspaper comics section
Watch "Jeopardy"	Read *Rolling Stone*
Listen to variety radio	Read *GQ*
Watch "The Simpsons"	

Source: Valarie Walsh and J. Paul Peter, "Claritas Inc.: Using Compass and PRIZM," in *Marketing Management: Knowledge and Skills,* 6th ed., eds. J. Paul Peter and James H. Donnelly, Jr. (Burr Ridge, IL: Irwin/McGraw-Hill, 2001), p. 284.

(Hyundai), safer (Volvo), higher quality (Toyota), or more prestigious (Lexus) than other cars. Second, products can be positioned by use or application. For example, Campbell's soup is positioned not only as a lunch item but also for use as a sauce or dip or as an ingredient in main dishes. Third, products can be positioned in terms of particular types of product users. For example, sales for Johnson's Baby Shampoo increased dramatically after the company positioned the product not only for babies but also for active adults who need to wash their hair frequently. Fourth, products can be positioned relative to a product class. For example, Caress soap was positioned by Lever Brothers as a bath oil product rather than as a soap. Finally, products can be positioned directly against particular competitors. For example, Coke and Pepsi and McDonald's and Burger King commonly position directly against each other on various criteria, such as taste. The classic example of positioning is of this last type: Seven-Up positioned itself as a tasty alternative to the dominant soft drink, colas.

One way to investigate how to position a product is by using a *positioning map,* which is a visual depiction of customer perceptions of competitive products, brands, or models. It is constructed by surveying customers about various product attributes and developing dimensions and a graph indicating the relative position of competitors.

FIGURE 5–6
Positioning Map for
Automobiles

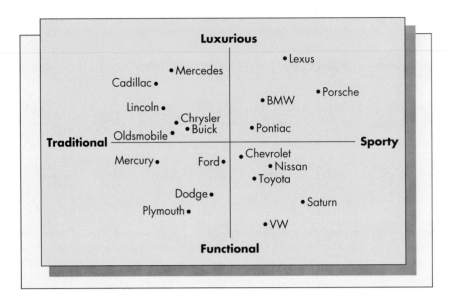

Source: Gilbert A. Churchill, Jr. and J. Paul Peter, *Marketing: Creating Value for Customers,* 2nd ed. (Burr Ridge, IL: Irwin/McGraw-Hill, 1998), p. 221.

Figure 5–6 presents a sample positioning map for automobiles that offers marketers a way of assessing whether their brands are positioned appropriately. For example, if Chrysler or Buick wants to be positioned in the minds of consumers as serious competitors to Lexus, then their strategies need to be changed to move up on this dimension. After the new strategies are implemented, a new positioning map could be developed to see if the brands moved up as desired.

Some experts argue that different positioning strategies should be used depending on whether the firm is a market leader or follower and that followers usually should not attempt to position directly against the industry leader.[5] The main point here is that in segmenting markets, some segments might have to be forgone because a market-leading competitive product already dominates in sales and in the minds of customers. Thus, a smaller or less desirable target market may have to be selected since competing with market leaders is costly and not often successful.

DECIDE SEGMENTATION STRATEGY

The firm is now ready to select its segmentation strategy. There are four basic alternatives. First, the firm may decide not to enter the market. For example, analysis to this stage may reveal there is no viable market niche for the firm's offering. Second, the firm may decide not to segment but to be a mass marketer. There are at least three situations when this may be the appropriate decision for the firm:

1. The market is so small that marketing to a portion of it is not profitable.
2. Heavy users make up such a large proportion of the sales volume that they are the only relevant target.
3. The brand is the dominant brand in the market, and targeting to a few segments would not benefit sales and profits.

Third, the firm may decide to market to one segment. And fourth, the firm may decide to market to more than one segment and design a separate marketing mix for each. In any case, the firm must have some criteria on which to base its segmentation

FIGURE 5–7
Selecting Target Markets: Some Questions Marketing Managers Should Answer

In order to select the best target markets, marketing managers must evaluate market segments on a number of dimensions. Below is a list of questions managers should answer before selecting target markets.

Measurability Questions

1. What are the appropriate bases for segmenting this market and are these bases readily measurable?
2. Are secondary data available on these bases so that the market segment can be identified and measured inexpensively?
3. If primary data are needed, is there sufficient return on investment to do the research?
4. Are specific names and addresses of people in this market segment needed or is general knowledge of their existence, number, and geographic location sufficient?
5. Can purchases of people in this market segment be readily measured and tracked?

Meaningfulness Questions

1. How many people are in this market segment and how frequently will they purchase our product?
2. What market share can we expect in this segment?
3. What is the growth potential of this segment?
4. How strong is competition for this market segment and how is it likely to change in the future?
5. How satisfied are customers in this market segment with current product offerings?

Marketability Questions

1. Can this market segment be reached with our current channels of distribution?
2. If new channels are needed, can we establish them efficiently?
3. What specific promotion media do these people read, listen to, or watch?
4. Can we afford to promote to these people in the appropriate media to reach them?
5. Are people in this market segment willing to pay a price that is profitable for the company?
6. Can we produce a product for this market segment and do so profitably?

strategy decisions. Three important criteria on which to base such decisions are that a viable segment must be (1) measurable, (2) meaningful, and (3) marketable.

1. *Measurable.* For a segment to be selected, the firm must be capable of measuring its size and characteristics. For instance, one of the difficulties with segmenting on the basis of social class is that the concept and its divisions are not clearly defined and measured. Alternatively, income is a much easier concept to measure.
2. *Meaningful.* A meaningful segment is one that is large enough to have sufficient sales and growth potential to offer long-run profits for the firm.
3. *Marketable.* A marketable segment is one that can be reached and served by the firm in an efficient manner.

Figure 5–7 offers a list of questions marketing managers should answer when deciding whether a market segment meets these criteria. Segments that do so are viable target markets for the firm's offering. The firm must now give further attention to completing its marketing mix.

DESIGN MARKETING MIX STRATEGY

The firm is now in a position to complete its marketing plan by finalizing the marketing mix or mixes to be used for each segment. Clearly, selection of the target market and designing the marketing mix go hand in hand, and thus many marketing mix

Dividing markets into segments and then selecting the best ones to serve is one of the cornerstones of sound marketing practice. However, there are situations when target marketing has been criticized as being unethical.

- R. J. Reynolds Tobacco Company planned to target African American consumers with a new brand of menthol cigarettes, Uptown. This brand was to be advertised with suggestions of glamour, high fashion, and night life. After criticism for targeting a vulnerable population, the company canceled plans for the brand.

- RJR planned to target white, 18- to 24-year-old "virile" females with a new cigarette brand, Dakota. It was criticized for targeting young, poorly educated, blue-collar women; and although it expanded the market to include males, Dakota failed in test markets and was withdrawn.

- Heileman Brewing Company planned to market a new brand of malt liquor called PowerMaster. Malt liquor is disproportionately consumed by African Americans and in low-income neighborhoods. Criticism of this strategy led the brand to be withdrawn.

One study suggests that whether targeting a group of consumers is unethical depends on two dimensions. The first is the degree to which the product can harm the consumers, and the second is the vulnerability of the group. Thus, to market harmful products to vulnerable target markets is likely to be considered unethical and could result in boycotts, negative word of mouth, and possibly litigation or legislation.

Source: N. Craig Smith and Elizabeth Cooper-Martin, "Ethics and Target Marketing: The Role of Product Harm and Consumer Vulnerability," *Journal of Marketing,* July 1997, pp. 1–20.

decisions should have already been carefully considered. To illustrate, the target market selected may be price sensitive, so some consideration has already been given to price levels, and clearly product positioning has many implications for promotion and channel decisions. Thus, while we place marketing mix design at the end of the model, many of these decisions are made in *conjunction* with target market selection. In the next six chapters of this text, marketing mix decisions will be discussed in detail.

CONCLUSION

The purpose of this chapter was to provide an overview of market segmentation. Market segmentation was defined as the process of dividing a market into groups of similar consumers and selecting the most appropriate group(s) for the firm to serve. Market segmentation was analyzed as a six-stage process: (1) to delineate the firm's current situation, (2) to determine consumer needs and wants, (3) to divide the market on relevant dimensions, (4) to develop product positioning, (5) to decide segmentation strategy, and (6) to design marketing mix strategy.

Additional Readings

Dickson, Peter R., and James L. Ginter. "Market Segmentation, Product Differentiation, and Marketing Strategy." *Journal of Marketing,* April 1987, pp. 1–10.

Green, Paul E., and Abba M. Krieger. "Segmenting Markets with Conjoint Analysis." *Journal of Marketing,* October 1991, pp. 20–31.

Myers, James H. *Segmentation and Positioning for Strategic Marketing Decisions.* Chicago: American Marketing Association, 1996.

The Marketing Mix

Part C

6 Product Strategy

7 New Product Planning and Development

8 Integrated Marketing Communications: Advertising, Sales Promotion, Public Relations, and Direct Marketing

9 Personal Selling, Relationship Building, and Sales Management

10 Distribution Strategy

11 Pricing Strategy

Section I Essentials of Marketing Management

Chapter 6

Product Strategy

Product strategy is a critical element of marketing and business strategy, since it is through the sale of products and services that companies survive and grow. This chapter discusses four important areas of concern in developing product strategies. First, some basic issues are discussed, including product definition, product classification, product quality and value, product mix and product line, branding and brand equity, and packaging. Second, the product life cycle and its implications for product strategy are explained. Third, the product audit is reviewed, and finally, three ways to organize for product management are outlined. These include the marketing manager system, brand manager system, and cross-functional teams.

BASIC ISSUES IN PRODUCT MANAGEMENT

Successful marketing depends on understanding the nature of products and basic decision areas in product management. In this section, we discuss the definition and classification of products, the importance of product quality and value, and the nature of a product mix and product lines. Also considered is the role of branding and packaging.

Product Definition

The way in which the product variable is defined can have important implications for the survival, profitability, and long-run growth of the firm. For example, the same product can be viewed at least three different ways. First, it can be viewed in terms of the *tangible product*—the physical entity or service that is offered to the buyer. Second, it can be viewed in terms of the *extended product*—the tangible product along with the whole cluster of services that accompany it. For example, a manufacturer of computer software may offer a 24-hour hotline to answer questions users may have or to offer free or reduced-cost software updates, free replacement of damaged software, and a subscription to a newsletter that documents new applications of the software. Third, it can be viewed in terms of the *generic product*—the essential benefits the buyer expects to receive from the product. For example, many personal care products bring to the purchaser feelings of self-enhancement and security in addition to the tangible benefits they offer.

From the standpoint of the marketing manager, to define the product solely in terms of the tangible product is to fall into the error of "marketing myopia." Executives who are guilty of committing this error define their company's product too narrowly, since they overemphasize the physical object itself. The classic example of this mistake can be found in railroad passenger service. Although no amount of product improvement could have staved off its decline, if the industry had defined itself as being in the transportation business, rather than the railroad business, it might still be

1. An audit of the firm's actual and potential resources
   a. Financial strength
   b. Access to raw materials
   c. Plant and equipment
   d. Operating personnel
   e. Management
   f. Engineering and technical skills
   g. Patents and licenses
2. Approaches to current markets
   a. More of the same products
   b. Variations of present products in terms of grades, sizes, and packages
   c. New products to replace or supplement current lines
   d. Product deletions
3. Approaches to new or potential markets
   a. Geographical expansion of domestic sales
   b. New socioeconomic or ethnic groups
   c. Overseas markets
   d. New uses of present products
   e. Complementary goods
   f. Mergers and acquisitions
4. State of competition
   a. New entries into the industry
   b. Product imitation
   c. Competitive mergers or acquisitions

profitable today. On the positive side, toothpaste manufacturers have been willing to exercise flexibility in defining their product. For years toothpaste was an oral hygiene product where emphasis was placed solely on fighting tooth decay and bad breath (e.g., Crest with fluoride). More recently, many manufacturers have recognized the need to market toothpaste as a cosmetic item (to clean teeth of stains), as a defense against gum disease (to reduce the buildup of tartar above the gumline), as an aid for denture wearers, and as a breath freshener. As a result, special purpose brands have been designed to serve these particular needs, such as Ultra Brite, Close-Up, Aqua-Fresh, Aim, Dental Care, and the wide variety of baking soda, tartar-control formula, and gel toothpastes offered under existing brand names.

In line with the marketing concept philosophy, a reasonable definition of product is that it is *the sum of the physical, psychological, and sociological satisfactions the buyer derives from purchase, ownership, and consumption.* From this standpoint, products are customer-satisfying objects that include such things as accessories, packaging, and service.

Product Classification

A product classification scheme can be useful to the marketing manager as an analytical device to assist in planning marketing strategy and programs. A basic assumption underlying such classifications is that products with common attributes can be marketed in a similar fashion. In general, products are classed according to two basic criteria: (1) end use or market, and (2) degree of processing or physical transformation.

1. *Agricultural products and raw materials.* These are goods grown or extracted from the land or sea, such as iron ore, wheat, and sand. In general, these products are fairly homogeneous, sold in large volume, and have low value per unit or in bulk weight.

2. *Organizational goods.* Such products are purchased by business firms for the purpose of producing other goods or for running the business. This category includes the following:

   a. Raw materials and semifinished goods.

   b. Major and minor equipment, such as basic machinery, tools, and other processing facilities.

   c. Parts or components, which become an integral element of some other finished good.

   d. Supplies or items used to operate the business but that do not become part of the final product.

3. *Consumer goods.* Consumer goods can be divided into three classes:

   a. Convenience goods, such as food, which are purchased frequently with minimum effort. Impulse goods would also fall into this category.

   b. Shopping goods, such as appliances, which are purchased after some time and energy are spent comparing the various offerings.

   c. Specialty goods, which are unique in some way so the consumer will make a special purchase effort to obtain them.

In general, the buying motive, buying habits, and character of the market are different for organizational goods vis-à-vis consumer goods. A primary purchasing motive for organizational goods is, of course, profit. As mentioned in a previous chapter, organizational goods are usually purchased as means to an end and not as an end in themselves. This is another way of saying that the demand for organizational goods is a derived demand. Organizational goods are often purchased directly from the original source with few middlemen, because many of these goods can be bought in large quantities; they have high unit value; technical advice on installation and use is required; and the product is ordered according to the user's specifications. Many organizational goods are subject to multiple-purchase influence, and a long period of negotiation is often required.

The market for organizational goods has certain attributes that distinguish it from the consumer goods market. Much of the market is concentrated geographically, as in the case of steel, auto, or shoe manufacturing. For certain products there are a limited number of buyers; this is known as a *vertical market,* which means that (1) it is narrow, because customers are restricted to a few industries; and (2) it is deep, in that a large percentage of the producers in the market use the product. Some products, such as desktop computers, have a *horizontal market,* which means that the goods are purchased by all types of firms in many different industries. In general, buyers of organizational goods are reasonably well informed. As noted previously, heavy reliance is often placed on price, quality control, and reliability of supply source.

In terms of consumer products, many marketing scholars have found the convenience, shopping, and specialty classification inadequate and have attempted either to refine it or to derive an entirely new typology. None of these attempts appears to have met with complete success. Perhaps there is no best way to deal with this problem. From the standpoint of the marketing manager, product classification is useful to the extent that it assists in providing guidelines for developing an appropriate marketing mix. For example, convenience goods generally require broadcast promotion and long channels of distribution as opposed to shopping goods, which generally require more targeted promotion and somewhat shorter channels of distribution.

Product Quality and Value

Quality can be defined as the degree of excellence or superiority that an organization's product possesses.[1] Quality can encompass both the tangible and intangible aspects of a firm's products or services. In a technical sense, quality can refer to physical traits such as features, performance, reliability, durability, aesthetics, serviceability, and conformance to specifications. Although quality can be evaluated from many perspectives, the customer is the key perceiver of quality because his or her purchase decision determines the success of the organization's product or service and often the fate of the organization itself.

Many organizations have formalized their interest in providing quality products by undertaking total quality management (TQM) programs. TQM is an organizationwide commitment to satisfying customers by continuously improving every business process involved in delivering products or services. Instead of merely correcting defects when they occur, organizations that practice TQM train and commit employees to continually look for ways to do things better so defects and problems don't arise in the first place. The result of this process is higher-quality products being produced at a lower cost. Indeed, the emphasis on quality has risen to such a level that over 70 countries have adopted the ISO 9000 quality system of standards, a standardized approach for evaluating a supplier's quality system, which can be applied to virtually any business.[2]

The term quality is often confused with the concept of value. Value encompasses not only quality but also price. *Value* can be defined as what the customer gets in exchange for what the customer gives. In other words, a customer, in most cases, receives a product in exchange for having paid the supplier for the product. A customer's perception of the value associated with a product is generally based both on the degree to which the product meets his or her specifications and the price that the customer will have to pay to acquire the product. Some organizations are beginning to shift their primary focus from one that solely emphasizes quality to one that also equally encompasses the customer's viewpoint of the price/quality trade-off. Organizations that are successful at this process derive their competitive advantage from the provision of customer value. In other words, they offer goods and services that meet or exceed customer needs at a fair price. Recall that Chapter 1 described various strategies based on value.

Product Mix and Product Line

A firm's *product mix* is the full set of products offered for sale by the organization; A product mix may consist of several *product lines,* or groups of products that share common characteristics, distribution channels, customers, or uses. A firm's product mix is described by its width and depth. *Width* of the product mix refers to the number of product lines handled by the organization. For example, one division of General Mills has a widespread mix consisting of five different product lines; ready-to-eat cereals, convenience foods, snack foods, baking products, and dairy products. *Depth* refers to the average number of products in each line. In its ready-to-eat cereals line, General Mills has eight different products. It has five different products in its line of convenience foods. Thus, the organization has a wide product mix and deep product lines.

An integral component of product line planning revolves around the question of how many product variants should be included in the line.[3] Manufacturing costs are usually minimized through large-volume production runs, and distribution costs tend to be lower if only one product is sold, stocked, and serviced. At a given level of sales, profits will usually be highest if those sales have been achieved with a single product. However, many product variants are offered by many firms.

There are three reasons organizations offer varying products within a given product line. First, potential customers rarely agree on a single set of specifications regarding their "ideal product," differing greatly in the importance and value they place on specific attributes. For example, in the laundry detergent market, there is

Marketing Highlight

A. CLASSES OF CONSUMER GOODS—SOME CHARACTERISTICS AND MARKETING CONSIDERATIONS

Characteristics and Marketing Considerations	Type of Product		
	Convenience	Shopping	Specialty
Characteristics			
Time and effort devoted by consumer to shopping	Very little	Considerable	Cannot generalize; consumer may go to nearby store and buy with minimum effort or may have to go to distant store and spend much time and effort
Time spent planning the purchase	Very little	Considerable	Considerable
How soon want is satisfied after it arises	Immediately	Relatively long time	Relatively long time
Are price and quality compared?	No	Yes	No
Price	Usually low	High	High
Frequency of purchase	Usually frequent	Infrequent	Infrequent
Importance	Unimportant	Often very important	Cannot generalize
Marketing considerations			
Length of channel	Long	Short	Short to very short
Importance of retailer	Any single store is relatively unimportant	Important	Very important
Number of outlets	As many as possible	Few	Few; often only one in a market
Stock turnover	High	Lower	Lower
Gross margin	Low	High	High
Responsibility for advertising	Producer	Retailer	Joint responsibility
Importance of point-of-purchase display	Very important	Less important	Less important
Brand or store name important	Brand name	Store name	Both
Importance of packaging	Very important	Less important	Less important

Source: Michael J. Etzel, Bruce J. Walker, and William J. Stanton, *Fundamentals of Marketing*, 11th ed. © 1997, New York, McGraw-Hill, Inc., pp. 195, 198. Reproduced by permission of The McGraw-Hill Companies.

a marked split between preferences for powder versus liquid detergent. Second, customers prefer variety. For example, a person may like Italian food but does not want to only eat spaghetti. Therefore, an Italian restaurant will offer the customer a wide variety of Italian dishes to choose from. Third, the dynamics of competition lead to multiproduct lines. As competitors seek to increase market share, they find it advantageous to introduce new products that subsegment an existing market segment by offering benefits more precisely tailored to the specific needs of a portion of that

Marketing Highlight   (continued)

B. CLASSES OF ORGANIZATIONAL PRODUCTS—SOME CHARACTERISTICS AND MARKETING CONSIDERATIONS

Characteristics and Marketing Considerations	Type of Product				
	Raw Materials	Fabricating Parts and Materials	Installations	Accessory Equipment	Operating Supplies
Example	Iron ore	Engine blocks	Blast furnaces	Storage racks	Paper clips
Characteristics					
Unit price	Very low	Low	Very high	Medium	Low
Length of life	Very short	Depends on final product	Very long	Long	Short
Quantities purchased	Large	Large	Very small	Small	Small
Frequency of purchase	Frequent delivery; long-term purchase contract	Infrequent purchase, but frequent delivery	Very infrequent	Medium frequency	Frequent
Standardization of competitive products	Very much; grading is important	Very much	Very little; custom made	Little	Much
Quantity of supply	Limited; supply can be increased slowly or not at all	Usually no problem	No problem	Usually no problem	Usually no problem
Marketing considerations					
Nature of channel	Short; no middlemen	Short; middlemen for small buyers	Short; no middlemen	Middlemen used	Middlemen used
Negotiation period	Hard to generalize	Medium	Long	Medium	Short
Price competition	Important	Important	Not important	Not main factor	Important
Presale/postsale service	Not important	Important	Very important	Important	Very little
Promotional activity	Very little	Moderate	Sales people very important	Important	Not too important
Brand preference	None	Generally low	High	High	Low
Advance buying contract	Important; long-term contracts used	Important; long-term contracts used	Not usually used	Not usually used	Not usually used

segment. For example, Procter & Gamble offers Jif peanut butter in a low-salt version to target a specific subsegment of the peanut butter market.

All too often, organizations pursue product line additions with little regard for consequences.[4] However, in reaching a decision on product line additions, organizations need to evaluate whether (1) total profits will decrease or (2) the quality/value associated with current products will suffer. If the answer to either of the above is yes, then the organization should not proceed with the addition. Closely related to product line additions are issues associated with branding. These are covered next.

Branding and Brand Equity

For some organizations, the primary focus of strategy development is placed on brand building, developing, and nurturing activities.[5] Factors that serve to increase the strength of a brand include[6] (1) product quality when products do what they do very well (e.g., Windex and Easy-Off); (2) consistent advertising and other marketing communications in which brands tell their story often and well (e.g., Pepsi and Visa); (3) distribution intensity whereby customers see the brand wherever they shop (e.g., Marlboro); and (4) brand personality where the brand stands for something (e.g., Disney). The strength of the Coca-Cola brand, for example, is widely attributed to its universal availability, universal awareness, and trademark protection, which came as a result of strategic actions taken by the parent organization.[7]

The brand name is perhaps the single most important element on the package, serving as a unique identifier. Specifically, a *brand* is a name, term, design, symbol, or any other feature that identifies one seller's good or service as distinct from those of other sellers. The legal term for brand is *trademark*.[8] A good brand name can evoke feelings of trust, confidence, security, strength, and many other desirable characteristics.[9] To illustrate, consider the case of Bayer aspirin. Bayer can be sold at up to two times the price of generic aspirin due to the strength of its brand image.

Many companies make use of manufacturer branding strategies in carrying out market and product development strategies. The *line extension* approach uses a brand name to facilitate entry into a new market segment (e.g., Diet Coke and Liquid Tide). An alternative to line extension is brand extension. In *brand extension,* a current brand name is used to enter a completely different product class (e.g., Jello pudding pops, Ivory shampoo).[10]

A third form of branding is *franchise extension* or *family branding,* whereby a company attaches the corporate name to a product either to enter a new market segment or a different product class (e.g., Honda lawnmower, Toyota Lexus). A final type of branding strategy that is becoming more and more common is dual branding. A *dual branding* (also known as joint or cobranding) strategy is one in which two or more branded products are integrated (e.g., Bacardi rum and Coca-Cola, Long John Silver's and A&W Root Beer, Archway cookies and Kellogg cereal, US Airways and Nationsbank Visa). The logic behind this strategy is that if one brand name on a product gives a certain signal of quality, then the presence of a second brand name on the product should result in a signal that is at least as powerful as, if not more powerful than, the signal in the case of the single brand name. Each of the preceeding four approaches is an attempt by companies to gain a competitive advantage by making use of its or others' established reputation, or both.

Companies may also choose to assign different brand names to each product. This is known as *multibranding* strategy. By doing so, the firm makes a conscious decision to allow the product to succeed or fail on its own merits. Major advantages of using multiple brand names are that (1) the firm can distance products from other offerings it markets; (2) the image of one product (or set of products) is not associated with other products the company markets; (3) the product(s) can be targeted at a specific market segment; and (4) should the product(s) fail, the probability of failure impacting on other company products is minimized. For example, many consumers are unaware that Dreft, Tide, Oxydol, Bold, Cheer, and Dash laundry detergents are all marketed by Procter & Gamble. The major disadvantage of this strategy is that because new names are assigned, there is no consumer brand awareness and significant amounts of money must be spent familiarizing customers with new brands.

Increasingly, companies are finding that brand names are one of the most valuable assets they possess. Successful extensions of an existing brand can lead to additional loyalty and associated profits. Conversely, a wrong extension can cause damaging associations, as perceptions linked to the brand name are transferred back from one product to the other.[11] *Brand equity* can be viewed as the set of assets (or liabilities) linked to the brand that add (or subtract) value.[12] The value of these assets is dependent upon the consequences or results of the marketplace's relationship with a brand. Figure 6–1 lists the elements of brand equity. Brand equity is determined by the consumer and is the culmination of the consumer's assessment of the product, the company that manufactures and markets the product, and all other variables that impact on the product between manufacture and consumer consumption.

Before leaving the topic of manufacturer brands, it is important to note that, as with consumer products, organizational products also can possess brand equity. However, several differences do exist between the two sectors.[13] First, organizational products are usually branded with firm names. As a result, loyalty (or disloyalty) to

FIGURE 6–1
Elements of Brand Equity

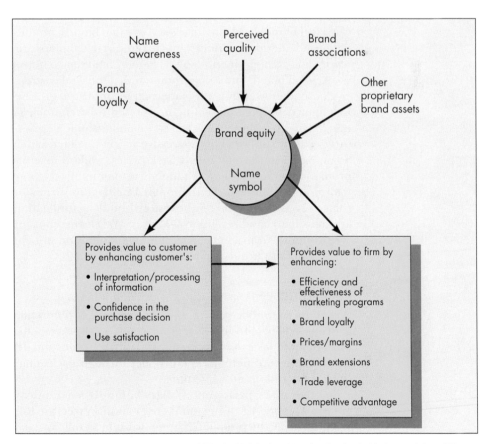

Source: David A. Aaker, *Managing Brand Equity.* © 1991, New York, by David A. Aaker. Reprinted with the permission of The Free Press, a division of Simon & Schuster.

the brand tends to be of a more global nature, extending across all the firm's product lines. Second, because firm versus brand loyalty exists, attempts to position new products in a manner differing from existing products may prove to be difficult, if not impossible. Finally, loyalty to organizational products encompasses not only the firm and its products but also the distribution channel members employed to distribute the product. Therefore, attempts to establish or change brand image must also take into account distributor image.

As a related branding strategy, many retail firms produce or market their products under a so-called private label. For example, Kmart has phased in its own store-brand products to compete with the national brands. There's Nature's Classics, a line of fancy snacks and cookies; Oral Pure, a line of dental care products; Prevail house cleaners; B.E., a Gap-style line of weekend wear; and Benchmark, a line of "made in the U.S.A." tools. Such a strategy is highly important in industries where middlemen have gained control over distribution to the consumer. The growth of the large discount and specialty stores, such as Kmart, Wal-Mart, Target, The Gap, Limited, and others, has accelerated the development of private brands. If a manufacturer refuses to supply certain middlemen with private branded merchandise, the alternative is for these middlemen to go into the manufacturing business, as in the case of Kroger supermarkets.

Private label products differ markedly from so-called generic products that sport labels such as "beer," "cigarettes," and "potato chips." Today's house brands are packaged in distinctively upscale containers. The quality of the products used as house brands equals and sometimes exceeds those offered by name brands. While generic products were positioned as a means for consumers to struggle through recessionary times, private label brands are being marketed as value brands, products that are equivalent to national brands but are priced much lower. Private brands are rapidly growing in popularity. For example, it only took JC Penney five years to nurture its private label jeans, the Arizona brand, into a powerhouse with annual sales surpassing $500 million.

Consolidation within the supermarket industry, growth of super centers, and heightened product marketing are poised to strengthen private brands even further.[14] However, these gains will not come without a fight from national manufacturers who are undertaking aggressive actions to defend their brands' market share. Some have significantly rolled back prices, while others have instituted increased promotional campaigns. The ultimate winner in this ongoing battle between private (store) and manufacturer (national) brands, not surprisingly, should be the consumer who is able to play off these store brands against national brands. By shopping at a mass merchandiser like Wal-Mart or Walgreens, consumers are exposed to and able to choose from a wide array of both national and store brands, thus giving them the best of both worlds: value and variety.

Packaging

Distinctive or unique packaging is one method of differentiating a relatively homogeneous product. To illustrate, shelf-stable microwave dinners, pumps rather than tubes of toothpaste or bars of soap, and different sizes and designs of tissue packages are attempts to differentiate a product through packaging changes and to satisfy consumer needs at the same time.

In other cases, packaging changes have succeeded in creating new attributes of value in a brand. A growing number of manufacturers are using green labels or packaging their products totally in green wrap to signify low- or no-fat content.[15] Frito-Lay, Quaker Oats, ConAgra, Keebler, Pepperidge Farm, Nabisco, and Sunshine Biscuits are all examples of companies involved in this endeavor.

Finally, packaging changes can make products urgently salable to a targeted segment. For example, the products in the Gillette Series grooming line, including shave cream, razors, aftershave, and skin conditioner, come in ribbed, rounded, metallic-gray shapes, looking at once vaguely sexual and like precision engineering.[16]

Marketing managers must consider both the consumer and costs in making packaging decisions. On one hand, the package must be capable of protecting the product through the channel of distribution to the consumer. In addition, it is desirable for packages to have a convenient size and be easy to open for the consumer. For example, single-serving soups and zip-lock packaging in cereal boxes are attempts by manufacturers to serve consumers better. Hopefully, the package is also attractive and informative, capable of being used as a competitive weapon to project a product's image. However, maximizing these objectives may increase the cost of the product to such an extent that consumers are no longer willing to purchase it. Thus, the marketing manager must determine the optimal protection, convenience, positioning, and promotional strengths of packages, subject to cost constraints.

PRODUCT LIFE CYCLE

A firm's product strategy must take into account the fact that products have a life cycle. Figure 6–2 illustrates this life-cycle concept. Products are introduced, grow, mature, and decline. This cycle varies according to industry, product, technology, and market. Marketing executives need to be aware of the life-cycle concept because it can be a valuable aid in developing marketing strategies.

During the introduction phase of the cycle, there are usually high production and marketing costs, and since sales are only beginning to materialize, profits are low or nonexistent. Profits increase and are positively correlated with sales during the growth stage as the market begins trying and adopting the product. As the product matures, profits for the initiating firm do not keep pace with sales because of

FIGURE 6–2
The Product Life Cycle

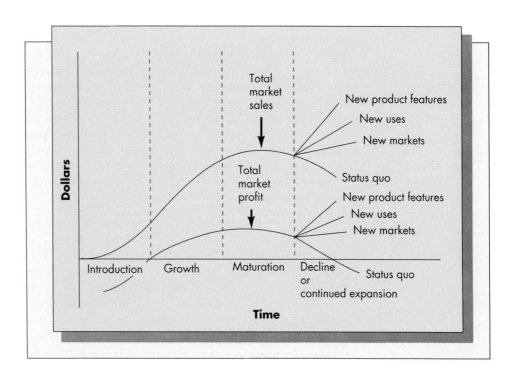

competition. Here the seller may be forced to "remarket" the product, which may involve making price concessions, increasing product quality, or expanding outlays on advertising and sales promotion just to maintain market share. At some point sales decline, and the seller must decide whether to (1) drop the product, (2) alter the product, (3) seek new uses for the product, (4) seek new markets, or (5) continue with more of the same.

The usefulness of the product life-cycle concept is primarily that it forces management to take a long-range view of marketing planning. In doing so, it should become clear that shifts in phases of the life cycle correspond to changes in the market situation, competition, and demand. Thus, the astute marketing manager should recognize the necessity of altering the marketing mix to meet these changing conditions. It is possible for managers to undertake strategies that, in effect, can lead to a revitalized product life cycle. For example, past advancements in technology led to the replacement of rotary dial telephones by touch-tone, push-button phones. Today, newer technology is allowing the cordless and cellular phone to replace the traditional touch-tone, push-button phone. When applied with sound judgment, the life-cycle concept can aid in forecasting, pricing, advertising, product planning, and other aspects of marketing management. However, the marketing manager must also recognize that the life cycle is purely a tool for assisting in strategy development and not let the life cycle dictate strategy development.[17]

THE PRODUCT AUDIT

The product audit is a marketing management technique whereby the company's current product offerings are reviewed to ascertain whether each product should be continued as is, improved, modified, or deleted. The audit is a task that should be carried out at regular intervals as a matter of policy. Product audits are the responsibility of the product manager unless specifically delegated to someone else.

Deletions

In today's environment, there are a growing number of products being introduced each year that are competing for limited shelf space. This growth is primarily due to (1) new knowledge being applied faster, and (2) the decrease in time between product introductions (by a given organization).[18] In addition, companies are not consistently removing products from the market at the same time they are introducing new products. The result is a situation in which too many products are fighting for too little shelf space. One of the main purposes of the product audit is to detect sick products and then bury them. Rather than let the retailer or distributor decide which products should remain, organizations themselves should take the lead in developing criteria for deciding which products should stay and which should be deleted. Some of the more obvious factors to be considered are

Sales trends. How have sales moved over time? What has happened to market share? Why have sales declined? What changes in sales have occurred in competitive products both in our line and in those of other manufacturers?

Profit contribution. What has been the profit contribution of this product to the company? If profits have declined, how are these tied to price? Have selling, promotion, and distribution costs risen out of proportion to sales? Does the product require excessive management time and effort?

Product life cycle. Has the product reached a level of maturity and saturation in the market? Has new technology been developed that poses a threat to the product?

**Marketing Highlight   Marketing Strategy Implications
of the Product Life Cycle**

Strategy Dimension	Life-Cycle Stage			
	Introduction	**Growth**	**Maturity**	**Decline**
Basic objectives	Establish a market for product type; persuade early adopters to buy	Build sales and market share; develop preference for brand	Defend brand's share of market; seek growth by luring customers from competitors	Limit costs or seek ways to revive sales and profits
Product	Provide high quality; select a good brand; get patent or trademark protection	Provide high quality; add services to enhance value	Improve quality; add features to distinguish brand from competitors' brands	Continue providing high quality to maintain brand's reputation; seek ways to make the product new again
Pricing	Often high to recover development costs; sometimes low to build demand rapidly	Somewhat high because of heavy demand	Low, reflecting heavy competition	Low to sell off remaining inventory or high to serve a niche market
Channels	Limited number of channels	Greater number of channels to meet demand	Greater number of channels and more incentives to resellers	Limited number of channels
Communication	Aimed at early adopters; messages designed to educate about product type; incentives such as samples and coupons to induce trial	Aimed at wider audience; messages focus on brand benefits; for consumer products, emphasis on advertising	Messages focus on differentiating brand from its competitors' brands; heavy use of incentives such as coupons to induce buyers to switch brands	Minimal, to keep costs down

Source: Gilbert A. Churchill, Jr., and J. Paul Peter, *Marketing: Creating Value for Customers,* rev. ed. (Burr Ridge, IL: Richard D. Irwin, 1998), p. 238.

Are there more effective substitutes on the market? Has the product outgrown its usefulness? Can the resources used on this product be put to better use?

Customer migration patterns. If the product is deleted, will customers of this product switch to other substitute products marketed by our firm? In total, will profits associated with our line increase due to favorable switching patterns?

The above factors should be used as guidelines for making the final decision to delete a product. Deletion decisions are very difficult to make because of their potential impact on customers and the firm. For example, eliminating a product may force a company to lay off some employees. There are other factors to consider, such as keeping consumers supplied with replacement parts and repair service and maintaining the goodwill of distributors who have an inventory of the product. The deletion plan should provide for clearing out of stock in question.

Product Improvement

One of the other important objectives of the audit is to ascertain whether to alter the product in some way or to leave things as they are. Altering the product means changing one or more of its attributes or marketing dimensions. *Attributes* refer mainly to product features, design, package, and so forth. *Marketing dimensions* refer to such things as price, promotion strategy, and channels of distribution.

It is possible to look at the product audit as a management device for controlling the product strategy. Here, control means feedback on product performance and corrective action in the form of product improvement. Product improvement is a top-level management decision, but the information needed to make the improvement decision may come from the consumer or the middlemen. Suggestions are often made by advertising agencies or consultants. Reports by the sales force should be structured in a way to provide management with certain types of product information; in fact, these reports can be the firm's most valuable product improvement tool. Implementing a product improvement decision will often require the coordinated efforts of several specialists, plus some research. For example, product design improvement decisions involve engineering, manufacturing, accounting, and marketing. When a firm becomes aware that a product's design can be improved, it is not always clear how consumers will react to the various alterations. To illustrate, in blind taste tests, the Coca-Cola Company found that consumers overwhelmingly preferred the taste of a reformulated, sweeter new Coke over old Coke. However, when placed on the market in labeled containers, new Coke turned out to be a failure due to consumers' emotional attachments to the classic Coke. Consequently, it is advisable to conduct some market tests in realistic settings.

A discussion of product improvement would not be complete without taking into account the benefits associated with benchmarking, especially as they relate to the notion of the extended product, the tangible product along with the whole cluster of services that accompany it.[19] The formal definition of *benchmarking* is the continuous process of measuring products, services, and practices against those of the toughest competitors or companies renowned as leaders. In other words, benchmarking involves learning about best practices from best-performing companies—how they are achieving strong performance. It is an effective tool being used by organizations to improve on existing products, activities, functions, or processes. Major corporations such as IBM, AT&T, DuPont, Ford, Eastman Kodak, Miliken, Motorola, and Xerox all have numerous benchmarking studies in progress. For example, IBM has already performed more than 500 benchmarking studies. Benchmarking can assist companies in many product improvement efforts, including (1) boosting product quality, (2) developing more user-friendly products, (3) improving customer order-processing activities, and (4) shortening delivery lead times. In the case of benchmarking, companies can achieve great success by copying others. Thus, by its very nature, benchmarking becomes an essential element in the ongoing product auditing process.

ORGANIZING FOR PRODUCT MANAGEMENT

Whether managing existing products or developing new products (the subject of the next chapter), organizations that are successful have one factor in common: they actively manage both types. Obviously, if a firm has but one product it gets every-

Marketing Highlight   Advantages of Rejuvenating a Product

Instead of abandoning or harvesting an older, mature product, many companies are looking instead to rejuvenate that product and extend its life cycle. The advantages of product rejuvenation include the following:

Less risk. Past experience in all phases of the product's life cycle permits the company to focus on improving business practices instead of formulating completely new, untested methods.

Lower costs. Most, if not all, of the product's start-up costs are now avoided. Plus, prior experience in both marketing and producing the product makes spending more efficient.

Less time. Because the beginning stages of product development have already occurred, the time involved in rejuvenating a product is significantly less than a new venture.

Cheaper market share. The money new products need to invest to create initial brand recognition as well as the lower costs mentioned above can be saved, used to enhance the product offering, or enable the product to be offered at a lower price.

Higher profits. Efficiency, brand recognition, superior product quality, and the ability to have a narrow focus all contribute to lower costs or increased sales, or both, thus increasing the potential for higher profits.

Source: Conrad Berenson and Iris Mohr-Jackson, "Product Rejuvenation: A Less Risky Alternative to Product Innovation," *Business Horizons,* November–December 1994, pp. 51–57. © 1994 by the Foundation for the School of Business at Indiana University. Used with permission.

one's attention. But as the number of products grow and the need to develop new products becomes evident, some rational management system is necessary.

Under a *marketing-manager system,* one person is responsible for overseeing an entire product line with all of the functional areas of marketing such as research, advertising, sales promotion, sales, and product planning. This type of system is popular in organizations with a line or lines of similar products or one dominant product line. Sometimes referred to as category management, the marketing manager system is seen as being superior to a brand manager system because one manager oversees all brands within a particular line, thus avoiding brand competition. Organizations such as PepsiCo, Purex, Eastman Kodak, and Levi Strauss use some form of marketing manager system.

Under a *brand manager system,* there is a manager who focuses on a single product or a very small group of new and existing products. Typically, this person is responsible for everything from marketing research and package design to advertising. Often called a product management system, the brand manager system has been criticized on several dimensions. First, brand managers often have difficulty because they do not have authority commensurate with their responsibilities. Second, they often pay inadequate attention to new products. Finally, they are often more concerned with their own brand's profitability than with the profitability of all of the organization's brands. These criticisms are not aimed at people but at the system itself, which may force brand managers into the above behaviors. Despite its drawbacks, organizations such as RJR Nabisco and Black & Decker have used that system.

Successful *new* products often come from organizations that try to bring all of the capabilities of the organization to bear on the problems of customers. Obviously, this requires the cooperation of all of the various functional departments in the organization. Thus, the use of *cross-functional teams* has become an important way to manage the development of new products. A *venture team* is a popular method used in such

FIGURE 6–3
Some Requirements for the Effective Use of Cross-Functional Teams in Product Management and New Product Development

A growing number of organizations have begun using cross-functional teams for product management and new product development. Having representatives from various departments clearly has its advantages, but most important, effective teams must have the nurture and support of management. Some requirements for effective teams are

1. *Commitment of top management and provision of clear goals.* Organizations that successfully use cross-functional teams in product management or development have managers who are deeply committed to the team concept. As a result, high-performance teams have a clear understanding of the product management and development goals of the organization. The importance of these goals encourages individuals to defer their own functional or departmental concerns to team goals.
2. *Trust among members.* For cross-functional teams to work, a high level of trust must exist among members. The climate of trust within a team seems to be highly dependent on members' perception of management's trust of the group as a whole.
3. *Cross-functional cooperation.* If a team is to take responsibility and assume the risk of product development, its members will need detailed information about the overall operation of the organization. It often requires that functional units be willing to share information that previously was not shared with other departments.
4. *Time and training.* Effective cross-functional teams need time to mature. They require massive planning and intense and prompt access to resources, financial and other. Because members have to put aside functional and departmental loyalties and concerns, training is usually necessary.

organizations as Xerox, Polaroid, Exxon, IBM, Monsanto, and Motorola. A venture team is a cross-functional team responsible for all the tasks involved in the development of a new product. Once the new product is already launched, the team may turn over responsibility for managing the product to a brand manager or product manager or it may manage the new product as a separate business.

The use of cross-functional teams in product management and new product development is increasing for a very simple reason: organizations need the contributions of all functions and therefore require their cooperation. Cross-functional teams operate independently of the organization's functional departments but include members from each function. A team might include a member from engineering, marketing, finance, service, and designers. Some organizations even include important outsiders (e.g., parts suppliers) on cross-functional teams. Figure 6–3 presents some important prerequisites for the use of cross-functional teams in managing existing products and developing new products.

CONCLUSION

This chapter has been concerned with a central element of marketing management—product strategy. The first part of the chapter discussed some basic issues in product strategy, including product definition and classification, product quality and value, product mix and product lines, branding and brand equity, and packaging. The product life cycle was discussed as well as the product audit. Finally, three methods of organizing for product management were presented. Although product considerations are extremely important, remember that the product is only one element of the marketing mix. Focusing on product decisions alone, without consideration of the other marketing mix variables, would be an ineffective approach to marketing strategy.

Additional Readings

Chaudhuri, Arjun, and Morris B. Holbrook. "The Chain of Effects from Brand Trust and Brand Affect to Brand Performance: The Role of Brand Loyalty." *Journal of Marketing*, April 2001, pp. 81–93.

Chiagouris, Larry, and Brant Wansley. "Branding on the Internet." *Marketing Management*, Summer 2000, pp. 34–39.

Keller, Kevin Lane. *Strategic Brand Management: Building, Measuring, and Managing Brand Equity.* Upper Saddle River, NJ: Prentice Hall, 1998.

Lehman, Donald R., and Russell S. Winer. *Product Management.* Burr Ridge, IL: McGraw-Hill/Irwin, 2001.

Marconi, Joe. *The Brand Marketing Book: Creating, Managing, and Extending the Value of Your Brand.* Lincolnwood, IL: American Marketing Association and NTC Business Books, 2000.

Shultz, Don E. "Understanding and Measuring Brand Equity." *Marketing Management*, Spring 2000, pp. 8–9.

Ward, Scott; Larry Light; and Jonathan Goldstine. "What High-Tech Managers Need to Know about Brands." *Howard Business Review*, July–August 1999, pp. 85–95.

New Product Planning and Development

New products are a vital part of a firm's competitive growth strategy. Leaders of successful firms know that it is not enough to develop new products on a sporadic basis. What counts is a climate of product development that leads to one triumph after another. It is commonplace for major companies to have 50 percent or more of their current sales in products introduced within the last 10 years. For example, the 3M Company derives 30 percent of its revenues from products less than four years old.[1]

Some additional facts about new products are:

- Many new products are failures. Estimates of new product failures range from 33 percent to 90 percent, depending on industry.
- New product sales grow far more rapidly than sales of current products, potentially providing a surprisingly large boost to a company's growth rate.
- Companies vary widely in the effectiveness of their new product programs.
- A major obstacle to effectively predicting new product demand is limited vision.
- Common elements appear in the management practices that generally distinguish the relative degree of efficiency and success between companies.

In one recent year, almost 22,000 products were introduced in supermarkets, drugstores, mass merchandisers, and health food stores.[2] Of these, only a small percentage (less than 20 percent) met sales goals. The cost of introducing a new brand in some consumer markets can range from $50 million to hundreds of millions of dollars. In addition to the outlay cost of product failures, there are also opportunity costs. These opportunity costs refer not only to the alternative uses of funds spent on product failures but also to the time spent in unprofitable product development.

Product development can take many years. For example, Hills Brothers (now owned by Nestlé) spent 22 years in developing its instant coffee, while it took General Foods (now owned by Philip Morris) 10 years to develop Maxim. However, the success of one new product is no guarantee that the way will be paved for additional and successful low-cost brand extensions. For example, on the positive side, Gillette was able to leverage the research and monies spent on the original Sensor to successfully develop and launch the Sensor razor for women and the Sensor Excel razor. On the negative side, Maxwell House (Philip Morris), Folgers (Procter & Gamble), and Nestlé are still struggling to develop commercially successful lines of fresh whole bean coffee, having been beaten to the punch by smaller companies such as Starbucks, Millstone Coffee, Inc., and Brothers Gourmet Coffees.[3]

Good management, with heavy emphasis on planning, organization, and interaction among the various functional units (e.g., marketing, manufacturing,

Marketing Highlight Three Common Misconceptions about the New Product Development Process

Since successful new product development is of vital importance to an organization, corporations are searching for numerous methods to improve the NPD process. However, in the mad rush, managers can overlook their greatest ally, common sense. What follows are three misconceptions that are commonly held by managers involved in the new product development process.

1. *It worked there; it will work here.* What works well at one company may not be as easily transferable with equal success to another company. There is no one common formula to the new product development process.

2. *It worked once; it will work again.* There will be peaks and valleys in every new product development process. Failure, as well as success, should be viewed as a common outcome.

3. *The cart can come before the horse.* Successful implementation of a means to improve the new product development process is heavily dependent on assumed conditions already existing within the corporation. Before the process can be improved, other organizational changes may have to be implemented.

Source: Adapted from Geoffrey Gordon, Douglas Ayers, Nessim Hanna, and Rick Ridnour, "The Product Development Process: Three Misconceptions which Can Derail Even the 'Best-Laid' Plans," *Journal of Product and Brand Management* 4, no. 1 (1995), pp. 7–17.

engineering, R&D), seems to be the key factor contributing to a firm's success in launching new products. The primary reason found for new product failure is an inability on the part of the selling company to match up its offerings to the needs of the customer. This inability to satisfy customer needs can be attributed to three main sources: inadequacy of upfront intelligence efforts, failure on the part of the company to stick close to what the company does best, and the inability to provide better value than competing products and technologies.

NEW PRODUCT STRATEGY

In developing new products, the first question a marketing manager must ask is, In how many ways can a product be new? C. Merle Crawford and Anthony DiBenedetto developed a definition of new products based on the following five different categories:[4]

1. *New-to-the-world products.* Products that are inventions, for example, Polaroid camera, the first car, rayon, the laser printer, in-line skates.

2. *New category entries.* Products that take a firm into a category new to it, but that are not new to the world, for example, P&G's first shampoo, Hallmark gift items, AT&T's Universal Card.

3. *Additions to product lines.* Products that are line extensions, flankers, and so on, to the firm's current markets, for example, Tide Liquid detergent, Bud Light, Apple's Power Mac.

4. *Product improvements.* Current products made better; virtually every product on the market has been improved, often many times.

5. *Repositionings.* Products that are retargeted for a new use or application; a classic case is Arm & Hammer baking soda, which was repositioned several times as drain deodorant, refrigerator freshener, toothpaste, deodorant, and so on.

The new product categories listed above raise the issue of imitation products, strictly me-too or improved versions of existing products. If a firm introduces a form of dry beer that is new to them but is identical or similar to those on the market, is it a new product? The answer is yes, as it is new to the firm. Managers should not get the idea that to imitate is bad and to innovate is good, for most of the best-selling products on the market today are improvements over another company's original invention. The best strategy is the one that will maximize company goals. It should be noted that Crawford and DiBenedetto's categories don't encompass variations such as, new to a country, new channel of distribution, packaging improvement, and different resources or method of manufacture, which they consider to be variations of the five categories, especially as these variations relate to additions to product lines.

A second broader approach to the new product question is the one developed by H. Igor Ansoff in the form of growth vectors.[5] This is the matrix first introduced in Chapter 1 that indicates the direction in which the organization is moving with respect to its current products and markets. It is shown again in Figure 7–1.

Market penetration denotes a growth direction through the increase in market share for present product markets. *Product development* refers to creating new products to replace existing ones. Firms using either market penetration or product development strategies are attempting to capitalize on existing markets and combat competitive entry and/or further market incursions. *Market development* refers to finding new customers for existing products. *Diversification* refers to developing new products and cultivating new markets. Firms using market development and diversification strategies are seeking to establish footholds in new markets or preempt competition in emerging market segments.

As shown in Figure 7–1, market penetration and market development strategies use present products. A goal of these types of strategies is to either increase frequency of consumption or increase the number of customers using the firm's product(s). A strategic focus is placed on altering the breadth and depth of the firm's existing product lines. Product development and diversification can be characterized as product mix strategies. New products, as defined in the growth vector matrix, usually require the firm to make significant investments in research and development and may require major changes in its organizational structure. Firms are not confined to pursuing a single direction. For example, Miller Brewing Co. has decided four key strategies should dictate its activities for the next decade, including (1) building its premium-brand franchises through investment spending, (2) continuing to develop value-added new products with clear consumer benefits, (3) leveraging local markets to build its brand franchise, and (4) building business globally.[6] Success for Miller depends on pursuing strategies that encompass all areas of the growth vector matrix.

It has already been stated that new products are the lifeblood of successful business firms. Thus, the critical product policy question is not whether to develop new

FIGURE 7–1
Growth Vector
Components

Markets	Products	
	Present	New
Present	Market penetration	Product development
New	Market development	Diversification

1. *Product superiority/quality.* The competitive advantage the product has by virtue of features, benefits, quality, uniqueness, and so on.

2. *Economic advantage to user.* The product's quality for the customer's money.

3. *Overall company/project fit.* The product's synergy with the company—marketing, managerial, business fit.

4. *Technological compatibility.* The product's technological synergy with the company—R&D, engineering, production fit.

5. *Familiarity to the company.* How familiar or "close to home" the product is to the company's current products and markets (as opposed to being targeted at new customers or markets).

6. *Market need, growth, and size.* The magnitude of the market opportunity.

7. *Competitive situation.* How easy the market is to penetrate from a competitive standpoint.

8. *Defined opportunity.* Whether the product has a well-defined category and established market to enter.

9. *Market-driven process.* The new product process is well planned and executed, receiving adequate resources suited to the customer's needs, wants, and buying behavior.

10. *Customer service.* The product is supported by friendly, courteous, prompt, and efficient customer service.

Source: Based on research conducted by Robert G. Cooper, "What Distinguishes the Top Performing New Products in Financial Services," *Journal of Product Innovation Management,* September 1994, pp. 281–99; and "The NewProd System: The Industry Experience," *Journal of Product Innovation Management,* June 1992, pp. 113–27.

products but in what direction to move. One way of dealing with this problem is to formulate standards or norms that new products must meet if they are to be considered candidates for launching. In other words, as part of its new product policy, management must ask itself the basic question, What is the potential contribution of each anticipated new product to the company?

Each company must answer this question in accordance with its long-term goals, corporate mission, resources, and so forth. Unfortunately, some of the reasons commonly given to justify the launching of new products are so general that they become meaningless. Phrases such as *additional profits, increased growth,* or *cyclical stability* must be translated into more specific objectives. For example, one objective may be to reduce manufacturing overhead costs by using plant capacity better. This may be accomplished by using the new product as an off-season filler. Naturally, the new product proposal would also have to include production and accounting data to back up this cost argument.

In every new product proposal some attention must be given to the ultimate economic contribution of each new product candidate. If the argument is that a certain type of product is needed to keep up with competition or to establish leadership in the market, it is fair to ask, Why? To put the question another way, top management can ask: What will be the effect on the firm's long-run profit picture if we do not develop and launch this or that new product? Policy-making criteria on new products should specify (1) a working definition of the profit concept acceptable to top management, (2) a minimum level or floor of profits, (3) the availability and cost of capital to develop a new product, and (4) a specified time period in which the new product must recoup its operating costs and begin contributing to profits.

It is critical that firms not become solely preoccupied with a short-term focus on earnings associated with new products. For example, in some industrial markets, there has been found to be a 20-year spread between the development and widespread adoption of products, on average. Indeed, an advantage that some Japanese firms appear to possess is that their management is free from the pressure of steady improvement in earnings per share that plagues American managers who emphasize short-term profits. Japanese managers believe that market share will lead to customer loyalty, which in turn will lead to profits generated from repeat purchases. Through a continual introduction of new products, firms will succeed in building share. This share growth will then ultimately result in earnings growth and profitability that will be supported by the stock market in terms of higher share prices over the long term.

NEW PRODUCT PLANNING AND DEVELOPMENT PROCESS

Ideally, products that generate a maximum dollar profit with a minimum amount of risk should be developed and marketed. However, it is very difficult for planners to implement this idea because of the number and nature of the variables involved. What is needed is a systematic, formalized process for new product planning. Although such a process does not provide management with any magic answers, it can increase the probability of new product success. Initially, the firm must establish some new product policy guidelines that include the product fields of primary interest, organizational responsibilities for managing the various stages in new product development, and criteria for making go-ahead decisions. After these guidelines are established, a process such as the one shown in Figure 7–2 should be useful in new product development.

Idea Generation

Every product starts as an idea. But all new product ideas do not have equal merit or potential for economic or commercial success. Some estimates indicate that as many as 60 or 70 ideas are necessary to yield one successful product. This is an average figure, but it serves to illustrate that new product ideas have a high mortality rate. In terms of money, almost three-fourths of all the dollars of new product expense go to unsuccessful products.

The problem at this stage is to ensure that all new product ideas available to the company at least have a chance to be heard and evaluated. Ideas are the raw materials for product development, and the whole planning process depends on the quality of the idea generation and screening process. Since idea generation is the least costly stage in the new product development process (in terms of investment in funds, time, personnel, and escalation of commitment), it makes sense that an emphasis be placed first on recognizing available sources of new product ideas and then on funneling these ideas to appropriate decision makers for screening.

Top management support is critical to providing an atmosphere that stimulates new product activity. Many times, great ideas come from some very unusual sources. A top management structure that is unwilling to take risks will avoid radical, new product and other innovation activities and instead concentrate solely on minor ar-

FIGURE 7–2
The New Product Development Process

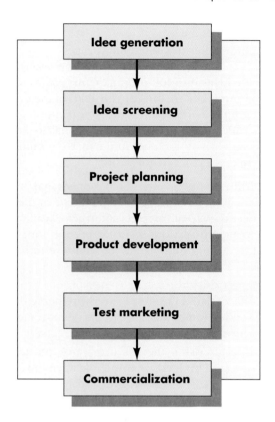

eas of improvement such as line extensions. To facilitate top management support, it is essential that new product development be focused on meeting market needs.

Both technology push and market pull research activities play an important role in new product ideas and development. By taking a broad view of customer needs and wants, basic and applied research (technology push) can lead to ideas that will yield high profits to the firm. For example, Compaq bet millions (and won) on PC network servers in the early 1990s even though business customers said they would never abandon their mainframes. In a similar vein, Chrysler forged ahead with the original minivan despite research showing people disliked the odd-looking vehicle.[7] Marketing, on the other hand, is more responsible for gathering and disseminating information gained from customers and other contacts. This information relates mainly to specific features and functions of the product that can be improved upon or market needs that current products are not satisfying (market pull). For example, product ideas at Rubbermaid often come from employees roaming the aisles at hardware stores and conversations with family and friends.[8] Both technology push and market pull approaches are essential to the generation of new product ideas.

Some firms use mechanisms such as "out-rotation," outsider involvement, and rewards to foster cooperation between design engineers and marketers.[9] Out-rotation involves placing employees in positions that require direct contact with customers, competitors, and other key outside groups. For example, Hewlett-Packard regularly rotates design engineers to retail sales positions on a temporary basis. Other organizations actively involve "outsiders" in planning or reward engineers for making external customer contacts. Regardless of method used, the primary lesson is to keep the communications flow going in all directions throughout the organization.

Idea Screening

The primary function of the idea screening process is twofold: first, to eliminate ideas for new products that could not be profitably marketed by the firm, and second, to expand viable ideas into full product concepts. New product ideas may be eliminated either because they are outside the fields of the firm's interest or because the firm does not have the necessary resources or technology to produce the product at a profit. Generally speaking, the organization has to consider three categories of risk (and its associated risk tolerance) in the idea screening phase prior to reaching a decision. These three risk categories are:[10]

1. *Strategic risk.* Strategic risk involves the risk of not matching the role or purpose of a new product with a specific strategic need or issue of the organization. If an organization feels it necessary to develop certain types of radical innovations or products new to the company in order to carry out long-term strategies, then management must be willing to dedicate necessary resources and time to pursue these type projects.

2. *Market risk.* Market risk is the risk that a new product won't meet a market need in a value-added, differentiated way. As products are being developed, customer requirements change and new technologies evolve. Management must be willing and able to shift its new product efforts to keep pace with change.

3. *Internal risk.* Internal risk is the risk that a new product won't be developed within the desired time and budget. Up front, management must decide the level of commitment it will extend in terms of time and budgetary expenditures to adequately ensure the completion of specific projects. Concurrently, progress goals must be established so that "proceed" or "do not proceed" decisions can be reached regarding continuation of projects.

In evaluating these risks, firms should not act too hastily in discounting new product ideas solely because of a lack of resources or expertise. Instead, firms should consider forming joint or strategic alliances with other firms. A strategic alliance is a long-term partnership between two organizations designed to accomplish the strategic goals of both parties. Potential benefits to be gained from alliances include (1) increased access to technology, funding, and information, (2) market expansion and greater penetration of current markets, and (3) de-escalated competitive rivalries. Motorola is a company that has prospered by forming numerous joint ventures with both American and foreign companies.[11]

Ideas that appear to have adequate profit potential and offer the firm a competitive advantage in the market should be accepted for further study.

Project Planning

This stage of the process involves several steps. It is here that the new product proposal is evaluated further and responsibility for the project is assigned to a project team. The proposal is analyzed in terms of production, marketing, financial, and competitive factors. A development budget is established, and some preliminary marketing and technical research is undertaken. The product is actually designed in a rough form. Alternative product features and component specifications are outlined. Finally, a project plan is written up, which includes estimates of future development, production, and marketing costs along with capital requirements and manpower needs. A schedule or timetable is also included. Finally, the project proposal is given to top management for a go or no-go decision.

Various alternatives exist for creating and managing the project teams. Two of the better-known methods are the establishment of a *skunkworks,* whereby a project

Marketing Highlight   Some Sources of New Product Ideas

1. Customers
   a. Customer requests
   b. Customer complaints/compliments
   c. Market surveys
   d. Focus groups
2. Competitors
   a. Monitoring competitors' developments
   b. Monitoring testing of competitors' products
   c. Monitoring industry movements
3. Distribution channels
   a. Suppliers
   b. Distributors
   c. Retailers
   d. Trade shows

4. Research and engineering
   a. Product testing
   b. Product endorsement
   c. Brainstorming meetings
   d. Accidental discovery
5. Other internal sources
   a. Management
   b. Sales force
   c. Employee suggestions
   d. Innovation group meetings
   e. Stockholders
6. Other external sources
   a. Consultants
   b. Academic journals
   c. Periodicals and other press

team can work in relative privacy away from the rest of the organization, and a *rugby* or *relay approach,* whereby groups in different areas of the company are simultaneously working on the project.[12] The common tie that binds these and other successful approaches together is the degree of interaction that develops among the marketing, engineering, production, and other critical staff. The earlier in the process that interactive, cooperative efforts begin, the higher the likelihood is that development efforts will be successful. A key component contributing to the success of many companies' product development efforts relates to the emphasis placed on creating *cross-functional teams* early in the development process. Both of the above methods use cross-functional teams. Members from many different departments come together to jointly establish new product development goals and priorities and to develop new product development schedules. Frequently, marketing and/or sales personnel are called in to lead these teams.[13]

Product Development

At this juncture, the product idea has been evaluated from the standpoint of engineering, manufacturing, finance, and marketing. If it has met all expectations, it is considered a candidate for further research and testing. In the laboratory, the product is converted into a finished good and tested. A development report to management is prepared that spells out in fine detail: (1) results of the studies by the engineering department, (2) required plan design,(3) production facilities design, (4) tooling requirements, (5) marketing test plan; (6) financial program survey, and (7) estimated release date.[14]

Test Marketing

Up until now the product has been a company secret. Now management goes outside the company and submits the product candidate for customer approval. Test market programs are conducted in line with the general plans for launching the product. Test marketing is a controlled experiment in a limited geographical area to test the new product or in some cases certain aspects of the marketing strategy, such as packaging or advertising.

The main goal of a test market is to evaluate and adjust, as necessary, the general marketing strategy to be used and the appropriate marketing mix. Additionally, producers can use the early interaction with buyers, occurring in test markets, to begin exploration of issues related to the next generation of product development.[15] Especially in cases where new technologies and markets are emerging, firms can benefit greatly from knowledge gained in test markets. Throughout the test market process, findings are being analyzed and forecasts of volume developed. In summary, a well-done test market procedure can reduce the risks that include not only lost marketing and sales dollars but also capital—the expense of installing production lines or building a new factory. Upon completion of a successful test market phase, the marketing plan can be finalized and the product prepared for launch.

Commercialization

This is the launching step where the firm commits to introducing the product into the marketplace. During this stage, heavy emphasis is placed on the organization structure and management talent needed to implement the marketing strategy. Emphasis is also given to following up on such things as bugs in the design, production costs, quality control, and inventory requirements. Procedures and responsibility for evaluating the success of the new product by comparison with projections are also finalized.

The Importance of Time

Over the course of the last five years, companies have placed an increasing emphasis on shortening their products' time to market. *Time to market* can be defined as the elapsed time between product definition and product availability. It has been well documented that companies that are first in bringing their products to market enjoy a competitive advantage both in terms of profits and market share.[16] Successful time-based innovations can be attributed to the use of short production runs, whereby products can be improved on an incremental basis, and the use of cross-functional teams, decentralized work scheduling and monitoring, and a responsive system for gathering and analyzing customer feedback.

Several U.S. companies, including Procter & Gamble, have taken steps to speed up the new product development cycle by giving managers, at the product class and brand family level, more decision-making power. Increasingly, companies are bypassing time-consuming regional test markets, when feasible, in favor of national launches. It is becoming important, more than ever, that firms do a successful job of developing new products right the first time. To accomplish this, companies must have the right people with the right skills and talents in key positions within the new product framework.

CAUSES OF NEW PRODUCT FAILURE

Many new products with satisfactory potential have failed to make the grade. Many of the reasons for new product failure relate to execution and control problems. What follows is a brief list of some of the more important causes of new product failures after the products have been carefully screened, developed, and marketed.[17]

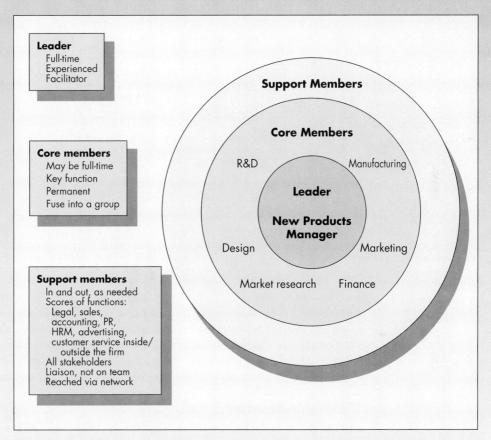

Source: C. Merle Crawford, *New Products Management*, 5th ed. (Burr Ridge, IL: Irwin, 1997), p. 31.

1. No competitive point of difference, unexpected reactions from competitors, or both.
2. Poor positioning.
3. Poor quality of product.
4. Nondelivery of promised benefits of product.
5. Too little marketing support.
6. Poor perceived price/quality (value) relationship.
7. Faulty estimates of market potential and other marketing research mistakes.
8. Faulty estimates of production and marketing costs.
9. Improper channels of distribution selected.
10. Rapid change in the market (economy) after the product was introduced.

Some of these problems are beyond the control of management; but it is clear that successful new product planning requires large amounts of reliable information in diverse areas. Each department assigned functional responsibility for product development automatically becomes an input to the information system needed by the

FINANCIAL CRITERIA

Return on investment (ROI)

Various profit margin measures

Sales and sales growth

Various profit measures

Payback and payback period

Internal rate of return (IRR)

Return on assets (ROA)

Return on equity (ROE)

Breakeven and breakeven point

Share and market share

Return on sales

Net present value (NPV)

NONFINANCIAL CRITERIA

Performance of new products

Market share achieved

Satisfaction of customer needs

Other market-related benefits

Strategic issues/fit/synergy

Technical aspects of production

Uniqueness of the new products

Source: Albert L. Page, "Assessing New Product Development Practices and Performance: Establishing Crucial Norms," *Journal of Product Innovation Management,* September 1993, pp. 273–90. 1993 by Elsevier Science Inc. Reprinted by permission of the publisher.

new product decision maker. For example, when a firm is developing a new product, it is wise for both engineers and marketers to consider both the kind of market to be entered (e.g., consumer, organizational, international) and specific target segments. These decisions will be of paramount influence on the design and cost of the finished good, which will, of course, directly influence price, sales, and profits.

Need for Research

In many respects it can be argued that the keystone activity of any new product planning system is research—not just marketing research, but technical research as well. Regardless of the way in which the new product planning function is organized in the company, new product development decisions by top management require data that provide a base for making more intelligent choices. New product project reports ought to be more than a collection of "expert" opinions. Top management has a responsibility to ask certain questions, and the new product planning team has an obligation to generate answers to these questions based on research that provides marketing, economic, engineering, and production information. This need will be more clearly understood if some of the specific questions commonly raised in evaluating product ideas are examined:

1. What is the anticipated market demand over time? Are the potential applications for the product restricted?

2. Can the item be patented? Are there any antitrust problems?

3. Can the product be sold through present channels and sales force? What will be the number of new salespersons needed? What additional sales training will be required?

4. At different volume levels, what will be the unit manufacturing costs?

5. What is the most appropriate package to use in terms of color, material, design, and so forth?

Marketing Highlight   Why Cross-Functional Product Development Teams Can Work

When specialized knowledge is needed to satisfy the needs of customers, cross-functional teams can greatly improve product development success. Such teams bring together complementary skills in one of three areas: technical or functional expertise, problem-solving and decision-making skills, and interpersonal skills.

1. *Technical or functional skills.* It would make little sense for a marketer to design technical specifications for a new type of cellular phone. Likewise, it would make little sense for an engineer to try to guess what features consumers find most important in choosing what type of phone to purchase. In this case, a product development group that consists solely of marketers or engineers would be less likely to succeed than a cross-functional team using the complementary skills of both.

2. *Problem-solving and decision-making skills.* Cross-functional teams possess the ability to identify problems and opportunities the entire organization faces, identify feasible new product alternatives, and make

the necessary choices quicker. Most industrial functional units are not able to perform all of these tasks effectively. However, it is likely that the necessary skills are present in a well-chosen cross-functional team and that these skills can be used in the organization's best interests.

3. *Interpersonal skills.* Common understanding and knowledge of problems faced and decisions needed for effective product development cannot arise without effective communication and constructive conflict. What is needed is risk-taking, helpful criticism, objectivity, active listening, support, and recognition of the interests and achievements of others. An effective, cross-functional team is made up of members who, in total, possess all of these skills. Individual members, at various times, will be called on to use their interpersonal skill to move the team forward. The use of the complementary interpersonal skills of team members can lead to extraordinary results for organizations.

6. What is the estimated return on investment?
7. What is the appropriate pricing strategy?

While this list is not intended to be exhaustive, it serves to illustrate the serious need for reliable information. Note also that some of the essential facts required to answer these questions can be obtained only through time-consuming and expensive marketing research studies. Other data can be generated in the engineering laboratories or pulled from accounting records. Certain types of information must be based on assumptions, which may or may not hold true, and on expectations about what will happen in the future, as in the case of anticipated competitive reaction or the projected level of sales.

CONCLUSION

This chapter has focused on the nature of new product planning and development. Attention has been given to the management process required to have an effective program for new product development. It should be obvious that this is one of the most important and difficult aspects of marketing management. The problem is so complex that, unless management develops a plan for dealing with the problem, it is likely to operate at a severe competitive disadvantage in the marketplace.

Additional Readings

Butscher, Stephen A., and Michael Laker. "Market Driven Product Development." *Marketing Management*, Summer 2000, pp. 48–53.

Crawford, C. Merle, and Anthony DeBenedetto. *New Products Management*. Burr Ridge, IL: McGraw-Hill/Irwin, 2001.

Jain, Dipak. "Managing New Product Development for Strategic Competitive Advantage." In *Kellogg on Marketing*, ed. Dawn Iacobucci. New York: John Wiley, 2001.

Kuczmarski, Thomas D. "Measuring Your Return on Innovation." *Marketing Management*, Spring 2000, pp. 25–34.

Sheehy, Barry; Bracey Hyler; and Rick Frazier. *Winning the Race for Value*. New York: AMACON, 2000.

Shikhar, Sarun, and Vijay Mahajan. "The Effect of Reward Structure on the Performance of Cross-Functional Product Development Teams." *Journal of Marketing*, April 2001, pp. 35–53.

Sobek, Durwood K., II; Jeffrey K. Liker; and Allen C. Ward. "Another Look at How Toyota Integrates Product Development." *Harvard Business Review*, July–August 1998, pp. 36–48.

8

Integrated Marketing Communications: Advertising, Sales Promotion, Public Relations, and Direct Marketing

Communicating with customers will be the broad subject of the next two chapters which focus on various elements of promotion. To simplify our discussion, the topic has been divided into two basic categories, nonpersonal communication (Chapter 8) and personal communication (Chapter 9). This chapter also discusses the necessity to integrate the various elements of marketing communication.

THE PROMOTION MIX

The promotion mix concept refers to the combination and types of nonpersonal and personal communication the organization puts forth during a specified period.[1] There are five elements of the promotion mix, four of which are nonpersonal forms of communication (advertising, sales promotion, public relations, and direct marketing), and one, personal selling, which is a personal form of communication. Let's briefly examine each one.

1. *Advertising* is a paid form of nonpersonal communications about an organization, its products, or its activities that is transmitted through a mass medium to a target audience. The mass medium might be television, radio, newspapers, magazines, outdoor displays, car cards, or directories.

2. *Sales promotion* is an activity or material that offers customers, sales personnel, or resellers a direct inducement for purchasing a product. This inducement, which adds value to or incentive for the product, might take the form of a coupon, sweepstakes, refund, or display.

FIGURE 8–1
Some Strengths and
Weaknesses of the
Major Promotion
Elements

Element	Strengths	Weaknesses
Advertising	Efficient for reaching many buyers simultaneously; effective way to create image of the brand; flexible; variety of media to choose from	Reaches many people who are not potential buyers; ads are subject to much criticism; exposure time is usually short; people tend to screen out advertisements; total cost may be high
Personal selling	Salespeople can be persuasive and influential; two-way communication allows for questions and other feedback; message can be targeted to specific individuals	Cost per contact is high; salespeople may be hard to recruit and motivate; presentation skills may vary among salespeople
Sales promotion	Supports short-term price reductions designed to stimulate demand; variety of sales promotion tools available; effective in changing short-term behavior; easy to link to other communications	Risks inducing brand-loyal customers to stock up while not influencing others; impact may be limited to short term; price-related sales promotion may hurt brand image; easy for competitors to copy
Public relations	Total cost may be low; media-generated messages seen as more credible than marketer-sponsored messages	Media may not cooperate; heavy competition for media attention; marketer has little control over message
Direct marketing	Message can be customized and prepared quickly; can facilitate a relationship with customer	Managing and maintaining up-to-date database can be costly; often low customer response

3. *Public relations* is a nonpersonal form of communication that seeks to influence the attitudes, feelings, and opinions of customers, noncustomers, stockholders, suppliers, employees, and political bodies about the organization. A popular form is *publicity*, which is a nonpaid form of nonpersonal communication about the organization and its products that is transmitted through a mass medium in the form of a news story. Obviously, marketers seek positive publicity.

4. *Direct marketing* uses direct forms of communication with customers. It can take the form of direct mail, online marketing, catalogs, telemarketing, and direct response advertising. Similar to personal selling, it may consist of an interactive dialog between the marketer and the customer. Its objective is to generate orders, visits to retail outlets, or requests for further information. Obviously, personal selling is a form of direct marketing, but because it is a very personal form of communication, we place it in its own category.

5. *Personal selling* is face-to-face communication with potential buyers to inform them about and persuade them to buy an organization's product. It will be examined in detail in the next chapter.

Obviously, marketers strive for the right mix of promotional elements to ensure that their product is well received. For example, if the product is a new soft drink, promotional effort is likely to rely more on advertising, sales promotion, and public relations (publicity) in order to (1) make potential buyers aware of the product, (2) inform these buyers about the benefits of the product, (3) convince buyers of the product's value, and (4) entice buyers to purchase the product. If the product is more established but the objective is to stabilize sales during a nonpeak season, the promotion mix will likely contain short-run incentives (sales promotions) for people to buy the product immediately. Finally, if the product is a new complex technology which requires a great deal of explanation, the promotional mix will likely focus heavily on personal selling so that potential buyers can have their questions answered.

As seen by the previous examples, a firm's promotion mix is likely to change over time. The mix will need continual altering and adapting to reflect changes in the market, competition, the product's life cycle, and the adoption of new strategies. In essence, the firm should take into account three basic factors when devising its promotion mix: (1) the role of promotion in the overall marketing mix, (2) the nature of the product, and (3) the nature of the market. Figure 8–1 provides an overview of the major strengths and weaknesses associated with the elements of the promotion mix.

INTEGRATED MARKETING COMMUNICATIONS

In many organizations, elements of the promotion mix are often managed by specialists in different parts of the organization or, in some cases, outside the organization when an advertising agency is used. For example, advertising plans might be done jointly by the advertising department and the advertising agency; plans for the sales force might be done by managers of the sales force; and sales promotions might be developed independently of the advertising and sales plans. Thus, it is not surprising that the concept of *integrated marketing communications* has evolved in recent years.

The idea of integrated marketing communications is easy to understand and certainly has a great deal of commonsense validity. But like so many concepts in marketing, it is difficult to implement. The goal of integrated marketing communications is to develop marketing communications programs that coordinate and integrate all elements of promotion—advertising, sales promotion, personal selling, and publicity—so that the organization presents a consistent message. Integrated marketing communication seeks to manage all sources of brand or company contacts with existing and potential customers. Marketing Highlight 8–1 presents the critical aspects of integrated marketing communications and how they differ from the way traditional marketing communications efforts have been managed.

The concept of integrated marketing communication is illustrated in Figure 8–2 on page 115. It is generally agreed upon that potential buyers generally go through a process of (1) *awareness* of the product or service, (2) *comprehension* of what it can do and its important features, (3) *conviction* that it has value for them, and (4) *ordering* on the part of a sufficient number of potential buyers. Consequently, the firm's marketing communication tools must encourage and allow the potential buyer to experience the various stages. Figure 8–2 illustrates the role of various marketing communication tools for a hypothetical product.

The goal of integrated marketing communication is an important one, and many believe it is critical for success in today's crowded marketplace. As with many management concepts, implementation is slower than many would like to see. Internal "turf" battles within organizations and the reluctance of some advertising agencies to willingly broaden their role beyond advertising are two factors that are hindering the successful implementation of integrated marketing communication.

Marketing Highlight   Some Differences between Traditional Marketing Communication Efforts and Integrated Marketing Communications

There is wide agreement about the importance of integrating marketing communication efforts. While organizations differ on just how fully integrated their efforts are, it is clear that integrated marketing communications is an idea whose time has come. The following are some important differences between a traditional approach to marketing communications and an integrated approach.

Traditional Approach	Integrated Approach
Focus on:	Focus on:
1. Making transactions	1. Building and nourishing relationships
2. Customers	2. All stakeholders in the organization
3. Independent brand messages	3. Strategic consistency on brand messages
4. Mass media—monologue with customers	4. Interactivity—dialogue with customers
5. Product claims	5. Corporate mission marketing
6. Adjusting prior year's plan	6. Zero-based campaign planning
7. Functional department planning and monitoring	7. Cross-functional planning and monitoring
8. Communication specialists	8. Creating core competencies
9. Mass marketing and customer acquisition	9. Building and managing databases to retain customers
10. Stable of agencies	10. One communication management agency

Source: Adapted from Tom Duncan and Sandra Moriarity, *Driving Brand Value: Using Integrated Marketing to Manage Profitable Stakeholder Relationships* (New York: McGraw-Hill, 1997), pp. 16–19.

ADVERTISING: PLANNING AND STRATEGY

Advertising seeks to promote the seller's product by means of printed and electronic media. This is justified on the grounds that messages can reach large numbers of people and make them aware, persuade, and remind them about the firm's offerings.

From a marketing management perspective, advertising is an important strategic device for maintaining a competitive advantage in the marketplace. Advertising budgets represent a large and growing element in the cost of goods and services. In a year it is possible for large multiproduct firms to spend $1.5 to $2 billion advertising their products, and it is common to spend $74 to $100 million on one individual brand. Clearly, advertising must be carefully planned.

Objectives of Advertising

There are at least three different viewpoints taken in attempts to evaluate the contribution of advertising to the economic health of the firm. The generalist viewpoint is primarily concerned with sales, profits, return on investment, and so forth. At the other extreme, the specialist viewpoint is represented by advertising experts who are primarily concerned with measuring the effects of specific ads or campaigns; here primary attention is given to organizations that offer services which measure different as-

FIGURE 8–2

How Various Promotion Tools Might Contribute to the Purchase of a Hypothetical Product

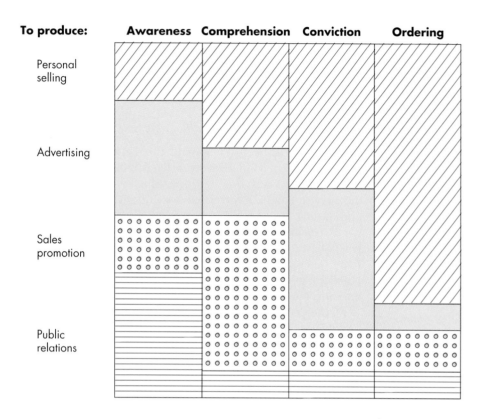

pects of the effects of advertising such as the Nielsen Index, Starch Reports, Arbitron Index, and Simmons Reports. A middle view, one that might be classified as more of a marketing management approach, understands and appreciates the other two viewpoints but, in addition, sees advertising as a competitive weapon. Emphasis in this approach is given to the strategic aspects of the advertising function.[2]

Building on what was said earlier, objectives for advertising can be assigned that focus on creating *awareness,* aiding *comprehension,* developing *conviction,* and encouraging *ordering.* Within each category, more specific objectives can be developed that take into account time and degree of success desired. Obviously, compared to the large number of people that advertising makes aware of the product or service, the number actually motivated to purchase is usually quite small.

In the long run and often in the short run, advertising is justified on the basis of the revenue it produces. Revenue in this case may refer to either sales or profits. Economic theory assumes that firms are profit maximizers, and the advertising outlays should be increased in every market and medium up to the point where the additional cost of gaining more business equals the incremental profits. Since most business firms do not have the data required to use the marginal analysis approach, they usually employ less sophisticated decision-making models. There is also evidence to show that many managers advertise to maximize sales on the assumption that higher sales mean more profits (which may or may not be true).

The point to be made here is that the ultimate objective of the business advertiser is to make sales and profits. To achieve this objective, the actions taken by customers must encompass purchase and continued repurchases of the advertised product. Toward this end, an approach to advertising is needed that provides for intelligent decision making. This approach must recognize the need for measuring the results of advertising, and these measurements must be as valid and reliable as possible. Marketing managers must also be aware that advertising not only complements other forms of communication but is subject to the law of diminishing returns. This means that for any advertised product, it can be assumed a point is eventually reached at which additional advertising produces little or no additional sales.

ADVERTISING DECISIONS

In line with what has just been said, the marketing manager must make two key decisions. The first decision deals with determining the size of the advertising budget, and the second deals with how the advertising budget should be allocated. Although these decisions are highly interrelated, we deal with them separately to achieve a better understanding of the problems involved. Today's most successful brands of consumer goods were built by heavy advertising and marketing investment long ago. Many marketers have lost sight of the connection between advertising spending and market share. They practice the art of discounting: cutting ad budgets to fund price promotions or fatten quarterly earnings. Companies employing these tactics may benefit in the short term but may be at a severe competitive disadvantage in the long term.

Marketers at some companies, however, know that brand equity and consumer preference for brands drive market share. They understand the balance of advertising and promotion expenditures needed to build brands and gain share, market by market, regardless of growth trends in the product categories where they compete. For example, Procter & Gamble has built its Jif and Folger's brands from single-digit shares to being among category leaders. In peanut butter and coffee, P&G invests more in advertising and less in discounting than its major competitors. What P&G and other smart marketers such as Kellogg, General Mills, Coke, and PepsiCo hold in common is an awareness of a key factor in advertising: consistent investment spending. They do not raid their ad budgets to increase earnings for a few quarters, nor do they view advertising as a discretionary cost.

The Expenditure Question

Most firms determine how much to spend on advertising by one of the following methods:

Percent of Sales

This is one of the most popular rule-of-thumb methods, and its appeal is found in its simplicity. The firm simply takes a percentage figure and applies it to either past or future sales. For example, suppose next year's sales are estimated to be $1 million. Using a 2-percent-of-sales criterion, the ad budget would be $20,000. This approach is usually justified by its advocates in terms of the following argument: (1) advertising is needed to generate sales; (2) a number of cents, that is, the percentage used, out of each dollar of sales should be devoted to advertising in order to generate needed sales; and (3) the percentage is easily adjusted and can be readily understood by other executives. The percent-of-sales approach is popular in retailing.

Per-Unit Expenditure

Closely related to the above technique is one in which a fixed monetary amount is spent on advertising for each unit of the product expected to be sold. This method is popular with higher priced merchandise, such as automobiles or appliances. For instance, if a company is marketing color televisions priced at $500, it may decide that it should spend $30 per set on advertising. Since this $30 is a fixed amount for each unit, this method amounts to the same thing as the percent-of-sales method. The big dif-

Marketing Highlight   Developing Advertising Objectives: Nine Questions

1. Does the advertising aim at *immediate sales*? If so, objectives might be:

   - Perform the complete selling function.
   - Close sales to prospects already partly sold.
   - Announce a special reason for buying now (price, premium, and so forth).
   - Remind people to buy.
   - Tie in with special buying event.
   - Stimulate impulse sales.

2. Does the advertising aim at *near-term sales*? If so, objectives might be:

   - Create awareness.
   - Enhance brand image.
   - Implant information or attitude.
   - Combat or offset competitive claims.
   - Correct false impressions, misinformation.
   - Build familiarity and easy recognition.

3. Does the advertising aim at building a *long-range consumer franchise*? If so, objectives might be:

   - Build confidence in company and brand.
   - Build customer demand.
   - Select preferred distributors and dealers.
   - Secure universal distribution.
   - Establish a "reputation platform" for launching new brands or product lines.
   - Establish brand recognition and acceptance.

4. Does the advertising aim at helping *increase sales*? If so, objectives would be:

   - Hold present customers.
   - Convert other users to advertiser's brand.
   - Cause people to specify advertiser's brand.
   - Convert nonusers to users.
   - Make steady customers out of occasional ones.
   - Advertise new uses.
   - Persuade customers to buy larger sizes or multiple units.
   - Remind users to buy.
   - Encourage greater frequency or quantity of use.

5. Does the advertising aim at some specific step that leads to a sale? If so, objectives might be:

   - Persuade prospect to write for descriptive literature, return a coupon, enter a contest.
   - Persuade prospect to visit a showroom, ask for a demonstration.
   - Induce prospect to sample the product (trial offer).

6. How important are supplementary benefits of advertising? Objectives would be:

   - Help salespeople open new accounts.
   - Help salespeople get larger orders from wholesalers and retailers.
   - Help salespeople get preferred display space.
   - Give salespeople an entrée.
   - Build morale of sales force.
   - Impress the trade.

7. Should the advertising impart information needed to consummate sales and build customer satisfaction? If so, objectives may be to use:

   - "Where to buy it" advertising.
   - "How to use it" advertising.
   - New models, features, package.
   - New prices.
   - Special terms, trade-in offers, and so forth.
   - New policies (such as guarantees).

8. Should advertising build confidence and goodwill for the corporation? Targets may include:

   - Customers and potential customers.
   - The trade (distributors, dealers, retail people).
   - Employees and potential employees.
   - The financial community.
   - The public at large.

9. What kind of images does the company wish to build?

   - Product quality, dependability.
   - Service.
   - Family resemblance of diversified products.
   - Corporate citizenship.
   - Growth, progressiveness, technical leadership.

Source: William Arens, *Contemporary Advertising,* 7th ed. (Burr Ridge, IL: Irwin/McGraw-Hill, 1999), p. R18.

ference is in the rationale used to justify each of the methods. The per-unit expenditure method attempts to determine the retail price by using production costs as a base. Here the seller realizes that a reasonably competitive price must be established for the product in question and attempts to cost out the gross margin. All this means is that, if the suggested retail price is to be $500 and manufacturing costs are $250, there is a gross margin of $250 available to cover certain expenses, such as transportation, personal selling, advertising, and dealer profit. Some of these expense items are flexible, such as advertising, while others are nearly fixed, as in the case of transportation. The basic problem with this method and the percentage-of-sales method is that they view advertising as a function of sales, rather than sales as a function of advertising.

All You Can Afford

Here the advertising budget is established as a predetermined share of profits or financial resources. The availability of current revenues sets the upper limit of the ad budget. The only advantage to this approach is that it sets reasonable limits on the expenditures for advertising. However, from the standpoint of sound marketing practice, this method is undesirable because there is no necessary connection between liquidity and advertising opportunity. Any firm that limits its advertising outlays to the amount of available funds will probably miss opportunities for increasing sales and profits.

Competitive Parity

This approach is often used in conjunction with other approaches, such as the percent-of-sales method. The basic philosophy underlying this approach is that advertising is defensive. Advertising budgets are based on those of competitors or other members of the industry. From a strategy standpoint, this is a "followership" technique and assumes that the other firms in the industry know what they are doing and have similar goals. Competitive parity is not a preferred method, although some executives feel it is a safe approach. This may or may not be true depending in part on the relative market share of competing firms and their growth objectives.

The Research Approach

Here the advertising budget is argued for and presented on the basis of research findings. Advertising media are studied in terms of their productivity by the use of media reports and research studies. Costs are also estimated and compared with study results. A typical experiment is one in which three or more test markets are selected. The first test market is used as a control, either with no advertising or with normal levels of advertising. Advertising with various levels of intensity are used in the other markets, and comparisons are made to see what effect different levels of intensity have. The marketing manager then evaluates the costs and benefits of the different approaches and intensity levels to determine the overall budget. Although the research approach is generally more expensive than some other models, it is a more rational approach to the expenditure decision.

The Task Approach

Well-planned advertising programs usually make use of the task approach, which initially formulates the advertising goals and defines the tasks to accomplish these goals. Once this is done, management determines how much it will cost to accomplish each task and adds up the total. This approach is often in conjunction with the research approach.

The Allocation Question

This question deals with the problem of deciding on the most effective way of spending advertising dollars. A general answer to the question is that management's

Marketing Highlight Preparing the Advertising Campaign: The Eight-M Formula

Effective advertising should follow a plan. There is no one best way to go about planning an advertising campaign, but in general, marketers should have good answers to the following eight questions:

1. *The management question:* Who will manage the advertising program?

2. *The money question:* How much should be spent on advertising as opposed to other forms of communication?

3. *The market question:* To whom should the advertising be directed?

4. *The message question:* What should the ads say about the product?

5. *The media question:* What types and combinations of media should be used?

6. *The macroscheduling question:* How long should the advertising campaign be in effect before changing ads or themes?

7. *The microscheduling question:* At what times and dates would it be best for ads to appear during the course of the campaign?

8. *The measurement question:* How will the effectiveness of the advertising campaign be measured and how will the campaign be evaluated and controlled?

choice of strategies and objectives determines the media and appeals to be used. In other words, the firm's or product division's overall marketing plan will function as a general guideline for answering the allocation question.

From a practical standpoint, however, the allocation question can be framed in terms of message and media decisions. A successful ad campaign has two related tasks: (1) say the right things in the ads themselves, and (2) use the appropriate media in the right amounts at the right time to reach the target market.

Message Strategy

The advertising process involves creating messages with words, ideas, sounds, and other forms of audiovisual stimuli that are designed to affect consumer (or distributor) behavior. It follows that much of advertising is a communication process. To be effective, the advertising message should meet two general criteria: (1) it should take into account the basic principles of communication, and (2) it should be predicated upon a good theory of consumer motivation and behavior.

The basic communication process involves three elements: (1) the sender or source of the communication, (2) the communication or message, and (3) the receiver or audience. Advertising agencies are considered experts in the communications field and are employed by most large firms to create meaningful messages and assist in their dissemination. Translating the product idea or marketing message into an effective ad is termed *encoding*. In advertising, the goal of encoding is to generate ads that are understood by the audience. For this to occur, the audience must be able to *decode* the message in the ad so that the perceived content of the message is the same as the intended content of the message. From a practical standpoint, all this means is that advertising messages must be sent to consumers in an understandable and meaningful way.

Advertising messages, of course, must be transmitted and carried by particular communication channels commonly known as advertising media. These media or channels vary in efficiency, selectivity, and cost. Some channels are preferred to others because they have less "noise," and thus messages are more easily received and understood. For example, a particular newspaper ad must compete with other ads, pictures, or stories on the same page. In the case of radio or TV, while only one firm's message is usually broadcast at a time, there are other distractions (noise) that can hamper clear communications, such as driving while listening to the radio.

The relationship between advertising and consumer behavior is quite obvious. For many products and services, advertising is an influence that may affect the consumer's decision to purchase a particular product or brand. It is clear that consumers are subjected to many selling influences, and the question arises about how important advertising is or can be. Here is where the advertising expert must operate on some theory of consumer behavior. The reader will recall from the discussion of consumer behavior that the buyer was viewed as progressing through various stages from an unsatisfied need through and beyond a purchase decision. The end goal of an advertisement and its associated campaign is to move the buyer to a decision to purchase the advertised brand. By doing so, the advertisement will have succeeded in moving the consumer to the trial and repeat purchase stage of the consumer behavior process, which is the end goal of advertising strategy.

The planning of an advertising campaign and the creation of persuasive messages require a mixture of marketing skill and creative know-how. Relative to the dimension of marketing skills, there are some important pieces of marketing information needed before launching an ad campaign. Most of this information must be generated by the firm and kept up-to-date. Listed below are some of the critical types of information an advertiser should have.

1. *Who* the firm's customers and potential customers are; their demographic, economic, and psychological characteristics; and any other factors affecting their likelihood of buying.
2. *How many* such customers there are.
3. *How much* of the firm's type and brand of product they are currently buying and can reasonably be expected to buy in the short-term and long-term future.
4. *Which* individuals, other than customers and potential customers, *influence* purchasing decisions.
5. *Where* they buy the firm's brand of product.
6. *When* they buy, and frequency of purchase.
7. *Which* competitive brands they buy and frequency of purchase.
8. *How* they use the product.
9. *Why* they buy particular types and brands of products.

Media Mix

Media selection is no easy task. To start with, there are numerous types and combinations of media to choose from. Marketing Highlight 8–4 presents a brief summary of the advantages and disadvantages of some of the major advertising media.

In the advertising industry, a common measure of efficiency or productivity is cost per thousand, or CPMs. This figure generally refers to the dollar cost of reaching 1,000 prospects, and its chief advantage lies in its simplicity and allowance for a common base of comparison between differing media types. The major disadvantage of the use of CPMs also relates to its simplicity. For example, the same commercial placed in two different television programs, having the same viewership and the same audience profile, may very well generate different responses depending

Marketing Highlight Some Relative Merits of Major Advertising Media

NEWSPAPERS

Advantages

1. Flexible and timely.
2. Intense coverage of local markets.
3. Broad acceptance and use.
4. High believability of printed word.

Disadvantages

1. Short life.
2. Read hastily.
3. Small "pass-along" audience.

RADIO

Advantages

1. Mass use (over 25 million radios sold annually).
2. Audience selectivity via station format.
3. Low cost (per unit of time).
4. Geographic flexibility.

Disadvantages

1. Audio presentation only.
2. Less attention than TV.
3. Chaotic buying (nonstandardized rate structures).
4. Short life.

OUTDOOR

Advantages

1. Flexible.
2. Relative absence of competing advertisements.
3. Repeat exposure.
4. Relatively inexpensive.

Disadvantages

1. Creative limitations.
2. Many distractions for viewer.
3. Public attack (ecological implications).
4. No selectivity of audience.

TELEVISION

Advantages

1. Combination of sight, sound, and motion.
2. Appeals to senses.
3. Mass audience coverage.
4. Psychology of attention.

Disadvantages

1. Nonselectivity of audience.
2. Fleeting impressions.
3. Short life.
4. Expensive.

MAGAZINES

Advantages

1. High geographic and demographic selectivity.
2. Psychology of attention.
3. Quality of reproduction.
4. Pass-along readership.

Disadvantages

1. Long closing periods (6 to 8 weeks prior to publication).
2. Some waste circulation.
3. No guarantee of position (unless premium is paid).

DIRECT MAIL

Advantages

1. Audience selectivity.
2. Flexible.
3. No competition from competing advertisements.
4. Personalized.

Disadvantages

1. Relatively high cost.
2. Consumers often pay little attention and throw it away.

INTERNET

Advantages

1. Interactive.
2. Low cost per exposure.
3. Ads can be placed in interest sections.
4. Timely.
5. High information content possible.
6. New favorable medium.

Disadvantages

1. Low attention getting.
2. Short message life.
3. Reader selects exposure.
4. May be perceived as intruding.
5. Subject to download speeds.

Marketing Highlight   Procedures for Evaluating Advertising Programs and Some Services Using the Procedures

PROCEDURES FOR EVALUATING SPECIFIC ADVERTISEMENTS

1. *Recognition tests.* Estimate the percentage of people claiming to have read a magazine who recognize the ad when it is shown to them (e.g., Starch Message Report Service).

2. *Recall tests.* Estimate the percentage of people claiming to have read a magazine who can (unaided) recall the ad and its contents (e.g., Gallup and Robinson Impact Service, various services for TV ads as well).

3. *Opinion tests.* Potential audience members are asked to rank alternative advertisements as most interesting, most believable, best liked.

4. *Theater tests.* Theater audience is asked for brand preferences before and after an ad is shown in context of a TV show (e.g., Schwerin TV Testing Service).

PROCEDURES FOR EVALUATING SPECIFIC ADVERTISING OBJECTIVES

1. *Awareness.* Potential buyers are asked to indicate brands that come to mind in a product category. A message used in an ad campaign is given and buyers are asked to identify the brand that was advertised using that message.

2. *Attitude.* Potential buyers are asked to rate competing or individual brands on determinant attributes, benefits, characterizations using rating scales.

PROCEDURES FOR EVALUATING MOTIVATIONAL IMPACT

1. *Intention to buy.* Potential buyers are asked to indicate the likelihood they will buy a brand (on a scale from "definitely will not" to "definitely will").

2. *Market test.* Sales changes in different markets are monitored to compare the effects of different messages, budget levels.

Source: Joseph Guiltinan and Gordon Paul, *Marketing Management,* 6th ed., © 1997, New York, McGraw-Hill, Inc., p. 274. Reproduced by permission of The McGraw-Hill Companies.

on the level of viewer involvement. This "positive effects" theory states that the more the viewers are involved in a television program, the stronger they will respond to commercials. In essence, involving programs produce engaged respondents who demonstrate more favorable responses to advertising messages.

Generally, such measures as circulation, audience size, and sets in use per commercial minute are used in the calculation. Of course, different relative rankings of media can occur, depending on the measure used. A related problem deals with what is meant by "effectively reaching" the prospect.[3] *Reach*, in general, is the number of different targeted audience members exposed at least once to the advertiser's message within a predetermined time frame. Just as important as the number of different people exposed (reach) is the number of times, on average, that they are exposed to an advertisement within a given time period. This rate of exposure is called *average frequency.* Since marketers all have budget constraints, they must decide whether to increase reach at the expense of average frequency or average frequency at the expense of reach. In essence, the marketer's dilemma is to develop a media schedule that both (1) exposes a sufficient number of targeted customers (reach) to the firm's product and (2) exposes them enough times (average frequency) to the product to produce the desired effect. The desired effect can come in the form of reaching goals associated with any or all of the categories of advertising objectives (prospect becomes aware of the product, takes action, etc.) covered earlier in the chapter.

SALES PROMOTION

Over the past two decades, the popularity of sales promotion has been increasing. Two reasons for this increased popularity are undoubtedly the increased pressure on management for short-term results and the emergence of new purchase tracking technology. For example, many supermarket cash registers are now equipped with a device that dispenses coupons to a customer at the point of purchase. The type, variety, and cash amount of the coupon will vary from customer to customer based on their purchases. In essence, it is now possible for the Coca-Cola Company to dispense coupons to only those customers who purchase Pepsi Cola, thus avoiding spending promotional dollars on already-loyal Coke drinkers. Figure 8–3 presents some popular targets of sales promotion and the methods used.

Push versus Pull Marketing

Push and pull marketing strategies comprise the two options available to marketers interested in getting their product into the hands of customers. *Push strategies* involve aiming promotional efforts at distributors, retailers, and sales personnel to gain their cooperation in ordering, stocking, and accelerating the sales of a product. For example, a local rock band may visit local DJs seeking air play for their record, offer distributors special prices to carry the CD, and offer retailers special allowances for putting up posters or special counter displays. These activities, which are usually in the form of price allowances, distribution allowances, and advertising dollar allowances, are designed to "push" the CD toward the customer.[4]

Pull strategies involve aiming promotional efforts directly at customers to encourage them to ask the retailer for the product. In the past few years drug manufacturers have begun to advertise prescription drugs directly to consumers. Customers are encouraged to "Ask Your Doctor" about Viagra or Claritan. These activities, which can include advertising and sales promotion, are designed to "pull" a product through the channel from manufacturer to buyer.

Trade Sales Promotions

Trade promotions are those promotions aimed at distributors and retailers of products who make up the distribution channel. The major objectives of trade promotions are to (1) convince retailers to carry the manufacturer's products, (2) reduce the

FIGURE 8–3   **Example of Sales Promotion Activities**

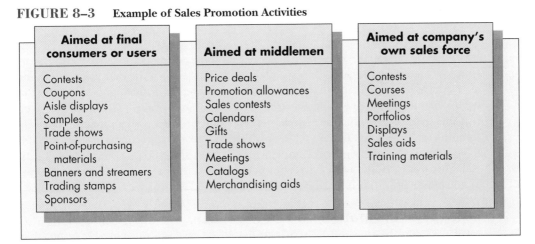

Aimed at final consumers or users	Aimed at middlemen	Aimed at company's own sales force
Contests	Price deals	Contests
Coupons	Promotion allowances	Courses
Aisle displays	Sales contests	Meetings
Samples	Calendars	Portfolios
Trade shows	Gifts	Displays
Point-of-purchasing materials	Trade shows	Sales aids
Banners and streamers	Meetings	Training materials
Trading stamps	Catalogs	
Sponsors	Merchandising aids	

Source: William D. Perreault, Jr. and E. Jerome McCarthy, *Basic Marketing: A Global Managerial Approach,* 12th ed. Irwin/McGraw-Hill, 1999, Chap. 14.

Marketing Highlight   Some Objectives of Sales Promotion

WHEN DIRECTED AT CONSUMERS

1. To obtain the trial of a product.
2. To introduce a new or improved product.
3. To encourage repeat or greater usage by current users.
4. To bring more customers into retail stores.
5. To increase the total number of users of an established product.

WHEN DIRECTED AT SALESPEOPLE

1. To motivate the sales force.
2. To educate the sales force about product improvements.
3. To stabilize a fluctuating sales pattern.

WHEN DIRECTED AT RESELLERS

1. To increase reseller inventories.
2. To obtain displays and other support for products.
3. To improve product distribution.
4. To obtain more and better shelf space.

Source: Steven J. Skinner, *Marketing*, 2nd ed., p. 673. © 1994 by Houghton Mifflin Company. Adapted with permission.

manufacturer's and increase the distributor's or retailer's inventories, (3) support advertising and consumer sales promotions, (4) encourage retailers to either give the product more favorable shelf space or place more emphasis on selling the product, and (5) serve as a reward for past sales efforts.

Promotions built around price discounts and advertising or other allowances are likely to have higher distributor/retailer participation levels than other type promotions because there is a direct economic incentive attached to the promotion.[5] The importance attached to individual types of promotions may vary by the size of distributor/retailer. For example, small retailers do not consider contests, sweepstakes, and sales quotas as being important to their decision to participate in promotions; getting the full benefit of such promotions is difficult due to their size. Marketers must keep in mind that not all distributors or retailers will have the same reaction to promotions offered. Differences in attitudes need to be carefully considered by the manufacturer when designing and implementing trade promotion programs.

Consumer Promotions

Consumer promotions can fulfill several distinct objectives for the manufacturer. Some of the more commonly sought-after objectives include: (1) inducing the consumer to try the product, (2) rewarding the consumer for brand loyalty, (3) encouraging the consumer to trade up or purchase larger sizes of a product, (4) stimulating the consumer to make repeat purchases of the product, (5) reacting to competitor efforts, and (6) reinforcing and serving as a complement to advertising and personal selling efforts.

Figure 8–4 presents a brief description of some of the most commonly used forms of consumer promotion activities.

What Sales Promotion Can and Can't Do

Advocates of sales promotion often point to its growing popularity as a justification for the argument that we don't need advertising; sales promotion itself will suffice.

FIGURE 8–4
Some Commonly Used Forms of Consumer Promotions

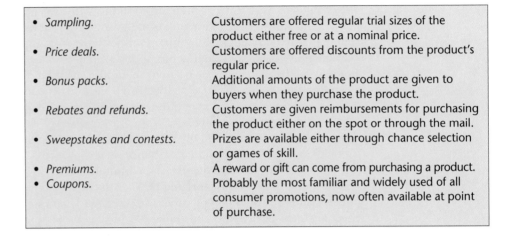

• *Sampling.*	Customers are offered regular trial sizes of the product either free or at a nominal price.
• *Price deals.*	Customers are offered discounts from the product's regular price.
• *Bonus packs.*	Additional amounts of the product are given to buyers when they purchase the product.
• *Rebates and refunds.*	Customers are given reimbursements for purchasing the product either on the spot or through the mail.
• *Sweepstakes and contests.*	Prizes are available either through chance selection or games of skill.
• *Premiums.*	A reward or gift can come from purchasing a product.
• *Coupons.*	Probably the most familiar and widely used of all consumer promotions, now often available at point of purchase.

FIGURE 8–5   The Sales Promotion Dilemma

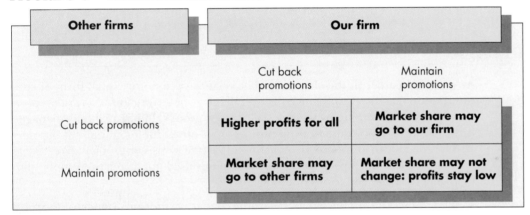

Source: George E. Belch and Michael A. Belch, *Introduction to Advertising and Promotion: An Integrated Communications Perspective*, 4th ed. (Burr Ridge, IL: Irwin/McGraw-Hill, 1998), p. 509.

Marketers should bear in mind that sales promotion is only one part of a well-constructed integrated marketing communications program. While proven to be effective in achieving the objectives listed in the previous sections, there are several compelling reasons why sales promotion should not be used as the sole promotional tool. These reasons include sales promotion's inability to (1) generate long-term buyer commitment to a brand in many cases, (2) change, except on a temporary basis, declining sales of a product, (3) convince buyers to purchase an otherwise unacceptable product, and (4) make up for a lack of advertising or sales support for a product. In addition, promotions can often fuel the flames of competitive retaliation far more than other marketing activities. When the competition gets drawn into the promotion war, the effect can be a significant slowing of the sharp sales increases predicted by the initiator of the promotion. Worse yet, promotions can often devalue the image of the promoted brand in the consumer's eyes.

The dilemma faced by marketers, as shown in Figure 8–5, is how to cut back on sales promotions without losing market share to competitors. In an effort to overcome this problem, some consumer products companies are instituting new pricing policies to try to cut back on the amount of sales promotions used. For example, Procter & Gamble and General Mills have instituted everyday low-price strategies for many of their products. The intent of this type of policy is to give retailers a lower list price in exchange for the cutting of trade promotions. While the net cost of the product to retailers remains unchanged, retailers are losing promotional dollars that they controlled. In many situations, although trade allowances are supposed to be used for encouraging retail sales, it is not uncommon for retailers to take a portion of the trade allowance money as profit. The rationale behind companies' (such as Procter & Gamble and General Mills) efforts to cut back on trade and other promotions is to (1) not force brand-loyal customers to pay unusually high prices when a product isn't on special, (2) allow consumers to benefit from a lower average shelf price since retailers will no longer have discretion over the use of allowance dollars, and (3) improve efficiencies in manufacturing and distribution systems because retailers will lose the incentive to do heavy forward buying of discounted items.

In addition to developing pricing policies to cut back on short-term promotions, some consumer products companies are starting to institute *frequency marketing programs* in which they reward consumers for purchases of products or services over a sustained period of time.[6] These programs are not technically considered sales promotions due to their ongoing nature. Frequency marketing originated in 1981 when American Airlines launched its frequent-flyer program with the intention of securing the loyalty of business travelers.

PUBLIC RELATIONS

As we noted earlier in the chapter, public relations is a nonpersonal form of communication that tries to influence the overall image of the organization and its products and services among its various stakeholder groups. Public relations managers prefer to focus on communicating positive news about the organization, but must also be available to minimize the negative impacts of a crisis or problem. We have already noted that the most popular and frequently used public relations tool is publicity. There are several forms of publicity:

1. *News release.* An announcement regarding changes in the organization or the product line, sometimes called a *press release.* The objective is to inform members of the media of a newsworthy event in the hope that they will convert it into a story.
2. *News conference.* A meeting held for representatives of the media so that the organization can announce major news events such as new products, technologies, mergers, acquisitions, and special events, or, in the case of a crisis or problem, present its position and plans for dealing with the situation.
3. *Sponsorship.* Providing support for and associating the organization's name with events, programs, or even people such as amateur athletes or teams. Besides publicity, sponsorship can also include advertising and sales promotion activities. Many organizations sponsor sporting events, art festivals, and public radio and television programs.
4. *Public service announcements.* Many nonprofit organizations rely on the media to donate time for advertising for contributions and donors. Many nonprofit organizations cannot afford the cost of advertising or in some cases are prohibited from doing so.

DIRECT MARKETING

We already know that with direct marketing, the organization communicates directly with customers either online, through direct mail, catalogs, direct response advertising, or personal selling (the subject of the next chapter).

Direct marketing methods are certainly not new. In fact, several of them will be discussed later in the book as methods of nonstore retailing. What is new is the ability to design and use them more efficiently and effectively because of the availability of computers and databases. Technology has clearly been the catalyst in the tremendous growth in direct marketing activities in the last decade. Because of technology, it is now possible for marketers to customize communication efforts and literally create one-to-one connections and dialogues with customers. This would be especially true for those organizations that have successfully implemented an integrated marketing communications program.

Another obvious catalyst for growth in direct marketing has been the increased use of the Internet by consumers for purchasing many types of products. And the projected growth rates for online expenditures continue to rise. As growth continues in the number of households with Internet access and in the number of businesses with websites and product or service offerings via the Internet, it will likely fuel even greater growth in direct marketing.

For the American consumer facing a "poverty of time," direct marketing offers many benefits. In addition to saving time, consumers often save money, get better service, and enjoy increased privacy; many even find it entertaining. For the marketer, sales revenues are the obvious benefit but not the only one. Direct marketing activities are often very effective in generating sales leads when a customer asks for more information about a product or service and can also increase store traffic when potential buyers are encouraged to visit a dealership or retail store.

CONCLUSION

This chapter has been concerned with integrated marketing communications. Remember that advertising and sales promotion are only two of the ways by which sellers can affect the demand for their product. Advertising and sales promotion are only part of the firm's promotion mix, and in turn, the promotion mix is only part of the overall marketing mix. Thus, advertising and sales promotion begin with the marketing plan and not with the advertising and sales promotion plans. Ignoring this point can produce ineffective and expensive promotional programs because of a lack of coordination with other elements of the marketing mix.

Additional Readings

Bishop, Bill. *Strategic Marketing in the Digital Age.* Lincolnwood, IL: American Marketing Association and NTC Business Books, 1998.

Duncan, Tom, and Sandra Moriority. *Driving Brand Value: Using Integrated Marketing to Manage Profitable Stakeholder Relationships.* New York: McGraw-Hill, 1997.

Krishnamurthy, Sandeep. "Solving the Internet Advertising Puzzle." *Marketing Management,* Fall 2000, pp. 34–39.

McArthur, D.N., and T. Griffin. "A Marketing Management View of Integrated Marketing Communications." *Journal of Advertising Research,* September–October 1997, pp. 19–26.

Peterman, John. "The Rise and Fall of the J. Peterman Company." *Howard Business Review,* September–October 1999, pp. 58–66.

Sternthal, Brian. "Advertising Strategy." In *Kellogg on Marketing,* ed. Dawn Iacobucci. New York: John Wiley, 2001, pp. 215–246.

Appendix

Major Federal Agencies Involved in Control of Advertising

Agency	Function
Federal Trade Commission	Regulates commerce between states; controls unfair business practices; takes action on false and deceptive advertising; most important agency in regulation of advertising and promotion.
Food and Drug Administration	Regulatory division of the Department of Health, Education, and Welfare; controls marketing of food, drugs, cosmetics, medical devices, and potentially hazardous consumer products.
Federal Communications Commission	Regulates advertising indirectly, primarily through the power to grant or withdraw broadcasting licenses.
Postal Service	Regulates material that goes through the mails, primarily in areas of obscenity, lottery, and fraud.
Alcohol and Tobacco Tax Division	Part of the Treasury Department; has broad powers to regulate deceptive and misleading advertising of liquor and tobacco.
Grain Division	Unit of the Department of Agriculture responsible for policing seed advertising.
Securities and Exchange Commission	Regulates advertising of securities.

Information Source	Description
Patent Office	Regulates registration of trademarks.
Library of Congress	Controls protection of copyrights.
Department of Justice	Enforces all federal laws through prosecuting cases referred to it by other government agencies.

9

Personal Selling, Relationship Building, and Sales Management

Personal selling, unlike advertising or sales promotion, involves direct relationships between the seller and the prospect or customer. In a formal sense, personal selling can be defined as a two-way flow of communication between a potential buyer and a salesperson that is designed to accomplish at least three tasks: (1) identify the potential buyer's needs; (2) match those needs to one or more of the firm's products or services; and (3) on the basis of this match, convince the buyer to purchase the product.[1] The personal selling element of the promotion mix can encompass diverse forms of direct interaction between a salesperson and a potential buyer, including face-to-face, telephone, written, and computer communication. The behavioral scientist would most likely characterize personal selling as a type of personal influence. Operationally, it is a complex communication process, one still not fully understood by marketers.

IMPORTANCE OF PERSONAL SELLING

The importance of the personal selling function depends partially on the nature of the product. As a general rule, goods that are new and different, technically complex, or expensive require more personal selling effort. The salesperson plays a key role in providing the consumer with information about such products to reduce the risks involved in purchase and use. Insurance, for example, is a complex and technical product that often needs significant amounts of personal selling. In addition, many organizational products cannot be presold, and the salesperson has a key role to play in finalizing the sale.

It is important to remember that, for many companies, the salesperson represents the customer's main link to the firm. In fact, to some, the salesperson is the company. Therefore, it is imperative that the company take advantage of this unique link. Through the efforts of the successful salesperson, a company can build relationships with customers that continue long beyond the initial sale. It is the salesperson who serves as the conduit through which information regarding product flaws, improvements, applications, or new uses can pass from the customer to the marketing department. To illustrate the importance of using salespeople as an information resource, consider this fact: In some industries, customer information serves as a major source for up to 90 percent of new product and process ideas. Along with techniques described in the previous chapter, personal selling provides the push needed to get middlemen to carry new products, increase their amount of goods purchased, and devote more effort in merchandising a product or brand.

In summary, personal selling is an integral part of the marketing system, fulfilling two vital duties (in addition to the core sales task itself): one for customers and one for companies.[2] First, the salesperson dispenses knowledge to buyers. Lacking relevant information, customers are likely to make poor buying decisions. For example, computer users would not learn about new equipment and new programming techniques without the assistance of computer sales representatives. Doctors would have difficulty finding out about new drugs and procedures were it not for pharmaceutical salespeople. Second, salespeople act as a source of marketing intelligence for management. Marketing success depends on satisfying customer needs. If present products don't fulfill customer needs, then profitable opportunities may exist for new or improved products. If problems with a company's product exist, then management must be quickly apprised of the fact. In either situation, salespeople are in the best position to act as the intermediary through which valuable information can be passed back and forth between product providers and buyers.

THE SALES PROCESS

Personal selling is as much an art as it is a science. The word *art* is used to describe that portion of the selling process that is highly creative in nature and difficult to explain. This does not mean there is little control over the personal selling element in the promotion mix. It does imply that, all other things equal, the trained salesperson can outsell the untrained one.

Before management selects and trains salespeople, it should have an understanding of the sales process. Obviously, the sales process will differ according to the size of the company, the nature of the product, the market, and so forth, but there are some elements common to almost all selling situations that should be understood. For the purposes of this text, the term *sales process* refers to two basic factors: (1) the objectives the salesperson is trying to achieve while engaged in selling activities; and (2) the sequence of stages or steps the salesperson should follow in trying to achieve the specific objectives (the relationship-building process).

Objectives of the Sales Force

Much like the concepts covered in the previous chapter, personal selling can be viewed as a strategic means to gain competitive advantage in the marketplace. For example, most organizations include service representatives as part of their sales team to ensure that customer concerns with present products are addressed and remedied at the same time new business is being solicited.

In a similar manner, marketing management understands that, while ultimately personal selling must be justified on the basis of the revenue and profits it produces, there are other categories of objectives generally assigned to the personal selling function as part of the overall promotion mix.[3] These objectives are:

1. *Information provision.* Especially in the case of new products or customers, the salesperson needs to fully explain all attributes of the product or service, answer any questions, and probe for additional questions.

Marketing Highlight   Information the Sales Force Can Obtain from Organizational Customers

a. Problems with current products.

b. Cost-reduction needs of customer.

c. Unmet needs or wishes of customer.

d. Superior features of competitive products.

e. Changes in technology/industry standards.

f. Additions needed for service(s) accompanying the product.

g. Changes in the regulatory environment.

h. Other manufacturers' (competitors') products currently used by customer.

i. Customer's level of satisfaction with products currently used.

j. Product features evaluated by customers in choosing another manufacturer's product.

k. Customer's ideal products according to relevant choice criteria.

l. Customer's criteria for rating products.

m. Customer's order of preference for competing products.

n. Customer's likely demand for products in the future.

Source: Adapted from Geoffrey Gordon, Denise Schoenbachler, Peter Kaminski, and Kimberly Brouchous, "The Use of the Sales Force in the Opportunity Identification Phase of the New Product Development Process," *Journal of Business and Industrial Marketing* 12, no. 1 (1997), pp. 33–48.

2. *Persuasion.* Once the initial product or service information is provided, the salesperson needs to focus on the following objectives:
   - Clearly distinguish attributes of the firm's products or services from those of competitors.
   - Maximize the number of sales as a percent of presentations.
   - Convert undecided customers into first-time buyers.
   - Convert first-time customers into repeat purchasers.
   - Sell additional or complementary items to repeat customers.
   - Tend to the needs of dissatisfied customers.

3. *After-sale service.* Whether the sale represents a first-time or repeat purchase, the salesperson needs to ensure the following objectives are met:
   - Delivery or installation of the product or service that meets or exceeds customer expectations.
   - Immediate follow-up calls and visits to address unresolved or new concerns.
   - Reassurance of product or service superiority through demonstrable actions.

The Sales Relationship-Building Process

For many years, the traditional approach to selling emphasized the first-time sale of a product or service as the culmination of the sales process. As emphasized in Chapter 1, the marketing concept and accompanying approach to personal selling view the initial sale as merely the first step in a long-term relationship-building process, not as the end goal. As we shall see later in this chapter, long-term relationships between the buyer and seller can be considered partnerships because the buyer and seller have an ongoing, mutually beneficial affiliation, with each party having concern for the other party's well-being.[4] The relationship-building process is designed to meet the objectives listed in the previous section and contains six sequential stages (Figure 9–1). These stages are (1) prospecting, (2) planning the sales call, (3) presentation, (4) responding to objections, (5) obtaining commitment/closing the sale, and (6) building a long-term relationship. What follows is a brief description of each of the stages.

Prospecting

The process of locating potential customers is called *prospecting*. The prospecting activity is critical to the success of organizations in maintaining or increasing sales volume. Continual prospecting is necessary for several reasons, including the fact that customers (1) switch to other suppliers, (2) move out of the organization's market area, (3) go out of business because of bankruptcy, (4) are acquired by another firm, or (5) have only a one-time need for the product or service. In addition, the organization's buying contracts with present customers may be replaced and organizations who wish to grow must increase their customer base. Prospecting in some fields is more important than in others. For example, a stockbroker, real estate agent, or partner in an accounting firm with no effective prospecting plan usually doesn't last long in the business. In these positions, it may take as many as 100 contacts to gain 10 prospects who will listen to presentations from which one to two sales may result.

FIGURE 9–1
The Sales Relationship-Building Process

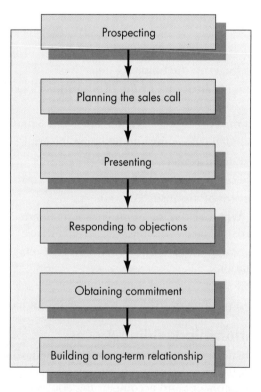

Source: Adapted from material discussed in Barton A. Weitz, Stephen B. Castleberry, and John F. Tanner, *Selling: Building Partnerships,* 4th ed. (Burr Ridge, IL: Irwin/McGraw-Hill, 2001), p. 185.

On the other hand, a Procter & Gamble sales representative in a certain geographic area would likely know all the potential retailers for Crest toothpaste.

The prospecting process usually involves two major activities that are undertaken on a continual, concurrent basis. First, prospects must be located. When names and addresses of prospects are not available, as is usually the case when firms enter new markets or a new salesperson is hired, they can be generated by randomly calling on businesses or households or by employing mass appeals (through advertising). This process is called *random lead generation* and usually requires a high number of contacts to gain a sale. A *lead* is a potential prospect that may or may not have the potential to be a true prospect, a candidate, to whom a sale could be made.

For most professional, experienced salespeople, a more systematic approach to generating leads from predetermined target markets is used. This approach, aptly named *selected-lead searching*, uses existing contacts and knowledge to generate new prospects. In general, the best source of prospects is referrals from satisfied customers. The more satisfied one's customers are, the higher the quality of leads a salesperson will receive from them. Marketing highlight 9–2 lists some common sources of leads and how they are used to generate new contacts.

The second step in the prospecting process involves screening. Once leads are generated, the salesperson must determine whether the prospect is a true prospect. This qualifying process usually entails gathering information, which leads to answering five questions:

1. Does the lead have a want or need that can be satisfied by the purchase of the firm's products or services?
2. Does the lead have the ability to pay?
3. Does the lead have the authority to pay?
4. Can the lead be approached favorably?
5. Is the lead eligible to buy?

Depending on the analysis of answers to these questions, the determination of whether a lead is a true prospect can be made. In seeking and qualifying leads, it is important to recognize that responsibility for these activities should not be totally assumed by individual salespeople. Rather, companies should develop a consistent, organized program, recognizing that the job of developing prospects belongs to the entire company, not just the sales force.

Planning the Sales Call

Salespeople will readily admit that their number one problem is getting through the door for an appointment with a prospect. Customers have become sophisticated in their buying strategies. Consequently, salespeople have to be equally sophisticated in developing their selling strategies.

While a full discussion on the topic of planning sales calls is beyond the scope of this text, what follows are brief descriptions of some key areas of knowledge salespeople should possess prior to embarking on sales calls.

1. They should have thorough knowledge of the company they represent, including its past history. This includes the philosophy of management as well as the firm's basic operating policies.
2. They should have thorough knowledge of their products and/or product lines. This is particularly true when selling organizational products. When selling very technical products, many firms require their salespeople to have training as engineers.

Marketing Highlight   Common Sources of Sales Leads

Source	How Used
Satisfied customers	Current and previous customers are contacted for additional business and leads.
Endless chain	Salesperson attempts to secure at least one additional lead from each person he or she interviews.
Center of influence	Salesperson cultivates well-known, influential people in the territory who are willing to supply lead information.
Promotional activities	Salesperson ties into the company's direct mail, telemarketing, and trade shows to secure and qualify leads.
Lists and directories	Salesperson uses secondary data sources, which can be free or fee-based.
Canvassing	Salesperson tries to generate leads by calling on totally unfamiliar organizations.
Spotters	Salesperson pays someone for lead information.
Telemarketing	Salesperson uses phone and/or telemarketing staff to generate leads.
Sales letters	Salesperson writes personal letters to potential leads.
Other sources	Salesperson uses noncompeting salespeople, people in his or her own firm, social clubs, and so forth, to secure lead information.

Source: Adapted from material discussed in Barton A. Weitz, Stephen B. Castleberry, and John F. Tanner, *Selling: Building Partnerships,* 4th ed. (Burr Ridge, IL: Irwin/McGraw-Hill, 2001), p. 189.

3. They should have good working knowledge of competitors' products. This is a vital requirement because the successful salesperson will have to know the strengths and weaknesses of those products that are in competition for market share.

4. They should have in-depth knowledge of the market for their merchandise. *The market* here refers not only to a particular sales territory but also to the general market, including the economic factors that affect the demand for their goods.

5. They should have accurate knowledge of the buyer or the prospect to whom they are selling. Under the marketing concept, knowledge of the customer is a vital requirement.

Presenting

Successful salespeople have learned the importance of making a good impression. One of the most important ways of improving the buyer's impression is for the salesperson to be well prepared in the knowledge areas discussed above. Some salespeople actually develop a checklist of things to take to the presentation so that nothing is forgotten. Just as important is the development of good interpersonal skills; they are a key ingredient of effective selling. Salespeople who can adapt their selling style to individual buyer needs and styles have a much stronger overall performance than less-flexible counterparts.

Responding to Objections

To assume the buyer will passively listen and positively respond to a sales presentation by placing an immediate order would be unrealistic. Salespeople can expect to hear objections (issues or concerns raised by the buyer) at any time during the presentation and subsequent relationship. Objections can be raised when the salesperson attempts to secure appointments, during the presentation, when the salesperson attempts to obtain commitment, or during the after-sale follow-up.

	Production	Sales	Marketing	Partnering
Time Period	Before 1930	1930 to 1960	1960 to 1990	After 1990
Objective	Making sales	Making sales	Satisfying customer needs	Building relationships
Orientation	Short-term seller needs	Short-term seller needs	Short-term customer needs	Long-term customer and seller needs
Role of Salesperson	Provider	Persuader	Problem solver	Value creator
Activities of Salespeople	Taking orders, delivering goods	Aggressively convincing buyers to buy products	Matching available offerings to buyer needs	Creating new alternatives, matching buyer needs with seller capabilities

Source: Barton A. Weitz, Stephen B. Castleberry, and John F. Tanner, *Selling: Building Relationships,* 4th ed. (Burr Ridge, IL: McGraw-Hill/Irwin, 2001) p. 33.

When sales prospects raise an objection, it is a sign that they are not ready to buy and need an acceptable response to the objection before the buying decision can be made. In response to an objection, the salesperson should not challenge the respondent. Rather, the salesperson's objective should be to present the necessary information so that the prospect is able to make intelligent decisions based on that information.

Obtaining Commitment

At some point, if all objections have been resolved, the salesperson must ask for commitment. It's a rare moment when a customer will ask to buy. Consequently, knowing how and when to close a sale is one of a salesperson's most indispensable skills.

It should be noted that not all sales calls end in commitment, a successful closing. If commitment is not obtained, salespeople should analyze the reasons and determine if (1) more sales calls are necessary to obtain commitment; or (2) currently, there just does not exist a good match between customer needs and seller offerings. If the salesperson determines more calls are necessary, then he or she should leave the meeting with a clear action plan, which is agreeable to the customer, for the next visit.

Building a Long-Term Relationship

Focusing on building and maintaining long-term relationships with customers has become an important goal for salespeople. As marketers realize that it can take five times as much to acquire a new customer than to service an existing one, the importance of customer retention and relationship building has become very clear.[5] Terry Vavra focuses on the value of current customers to the organization and has developed the concept of *aftermarketing,* which focuses the organization's attention on providing continuing satisfaction and reinforcement to individuals or organizations that are past or current customers. The goal of aftermarketing is to build lasting relationships with customers.[6] Successful aftermarketing efforts require that many specific activities be undertaken by the salesperson and others in the organization. These activities include:

1. Establishing and maintaining a customer information file.
2. Monitoring order processing.
3. Ensuring initial proper use of the purchased product or service.
4. Providing ongoing guidance and suggestions.
5. Analyzing customer feedback and responding quickly to customer questions and complaints.
6. Continually conducting customer satisfaction research and responding to it.

As seen by the preceeding discussion, there are no magic secrets of successful selling. The difference between good salespeople and mediocre ones is often the result of training plus experience. Training is no substitute for experience; the two complement each other. The difficulty with trying to discuss the selling job in terms of basic principles is that experienced, successful salespeople will always be able to find exceptions to these principles.

Relationships Can Lead to Partnerships

When the interaction between a salesperson and a customer does not end with the sale, the beginnings of a relationship are present. Many salespeople are finding that building relationships and even partnering with customers is becoming increasingly important.

When a buyer and a salesperson have a close personal relationship, they both begin to rely on each other and communicate honestly. When each has a problem, they work together to solve it. Such market relationships are known as *functional relationships.* An important trust begins to exist between each party. As with any relationship, each often gives and takes when the situation calls for it in order to keep the relationship intact. The reader may have such a relationship with a long-term medical or dental practitioner or hair cutter.

When organizations move beyond functional relationships, they develop *strategic partnerships,* or *strategic alliances.* These are long-term, formal relationships in which both parties make significant commitments and investments in each other in order to pursue mutual goals and to improve the profitability of each other. While a functional relationship is based on trust, a strategic partnership or alliance moves beyond trust. The partners in the relationship actually invest in each other. Obviously, the reasons for forming strategic partnerships vary. Some do it to create joint opportunities (banks, insurance companies, and brokerage firms), to gain access to new markets (United Parcel Service of America and Mail Boxes Etc.), to develop new technology or exploit joint opportunities (IBM and Apple), or to gain a marketing advantage over competitors (United Airlines and Starbucks Coffee, American Airlines and Career Track).

People Who Support the Sales Force

In many instances, sales personnel will require some assistance at various stages of the sales process. These support personnel do not seek the order. Their purpose is to focus on the long-term relationship and increase the likelihood of sales in the long run.

Marketing Highlight   Why Cross-Functional Sales Teams Are Growing in Popularity

1. *Improved sales productivity.* When the product or system being purchased is for the whole organization, different specialists handle different parts of the job. This usually results in a more effective and efficient sales process.

2. *More flexibility and quicker decisions.* To thrive in today's increasingly competitive markets, buying organizations often require selling organizations to produce small runs of tailored products on a very tight schedule. Cross-functional sales teams enable sellers to be more flexible because all functional units are involved in the sales process, which also enables the seller to make quicker decisions in response to buyer demands.

3. *Better decisions.* In most cases, the use of cross-functional teams composed of individuals with varied backgrounds in the company will lead to more innovative forms of thought and superior decisions than would be the case of an individual acting alone. Improved decisions would benefit both the buyer and the seller.

4. *Increased customer satisfaction.* The ultimate measure of the success of cross-functional sales teams comes with increased customer satisfaction, cemented relationships, and repeat business. The energy, flexibility, and commitment associated with cross-functional sales teams have led many organizations to adopt the approach.

Missionary salespeople are used in certain industries such as pharmaceuticals to focus solely on promotion of existing products and introduction of new products. They may call on physicians to convince them to prescribe a new drug or on pharmacies to convince them to promote a new cold remedy with a large display during the cold and flu season.

A *technical sales specialist* supports the sales staff by providing training or other technical assistance to the prospect. This individual may follow up an expression of interest to the salesperson from a prospect, especially when the product is to be used to solve certain technical problems of the buyer. Some organizations will provide training to the front-line staff of the buying organization who will be expected to sell the product to their customers.

Finally, when the product is extremely high priced and is being sold to the whole organization, *cross-functional sales teams* are often used. Since products increase in technical complexity, and specialized knowledge is required by units of the buying organization before a buying decision can be made, team selling has increased in popularity. For example, a manufacturer's sales team might be made up of people from sales, engineering, customer service, and finance, depending on the needs of the customer. A bank's sales team might consist of people from the commercial lending, investments, small business, and trust departments.

MANAGING THE SALES AND RELATIONSHIP-BUILDING PROCESS

Every personal sale can be divided into two parts: the part done by the salespeople and the part done for the salespeople by the company. For example, from the standpoint of the product, the company should provide the salesperson with a product skillfully designed, thoroughly tested, attractively packaged, adequately advertised, and priced to compare favorably with competitive products. Salespeople have the responsibility of being thoroughly acquainted with the product, its selling features, and points of superiority, and a sincere belief in the value of the product. From a sales management standpoint, the company's part of the sale involves the following:

1. Efficient and effective sales tools, including continuous sales training, promotional literature, samples, trade shows, product information, and adequate advertising.
2. An efficient delivery and reorder system to ensure that customers will receive the merchandise as promised.
3. An equitable compensation plan that rewards performance, motivates the salesperson, and promotes company loyalty. It should also reimburse the salesperson for all reasonable expenses incurred while doing the job.
4. Adequate supervision and evaluation of performance as a means of helping salespeople do a better job not only for the company but for themselves as well.

The Sales Management Task

Sales managers are line officers whose primary responsibility is establishing and maintaining an active sales organization. In terms of authority, they usually have equivalent rank to that of other marketing executives who manage aspects of the marketing program, such as advertising, product planning, or logistics. The sales organization may have separate departments and department heads to perform specialized tasks, such as training, personnel, promotion, and forecasting. Figure 9–2 is an example of such a sales organization.

In other cases, a general marketing manager may have product managers or directors reporting to them. This is common in cases where the firm sells numerous products and each product or product line is handled by a separate manager. Another common arrangement is to have sales managers assigned to specific geographic regions or customer groups. This type of specialization enables the sales force to operate more efficiently and effectively by avoiding overlaps.

Toward this end, more and more organizations are embracing the concept of national account management programs. National account management programs allow firms to identify and target their largest and most important customer accounts and provide these accounts with special treatment in order processing and service.[7]

FIGURE 9–2   **An Example of a Sales Organization**

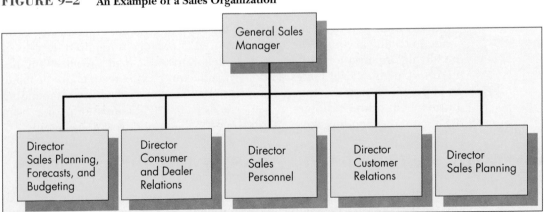

Specific sales personnel are assigned to handle each national account regardless of the geographic location where individual offices and facilities of the account may reside. National accounts differ from traditional customers in that they tend to have more centralized purchasing processes and purchase a much larger volume of products. National account management programs provide a number of benefits for both the selling organization and the customer. For the selling firm, there is the potential to develop better, closer relationships with the customer, which can give the firm a competitive advantage through increased profit margins, increased communication between the buying and selling firm, and maintenance of a stable customer base among a firm's national accounts. From the customer's perspective two benefits are that fewer mistakes are likely to occur during processing and servicing orders due to fewer points of contact with the selling firm, and customer needs can be addressed more immediately than if they were processed through more traditional channels.

Controlling the Sales Force

There are two obvious reasons why it is critical that the sales force be properly controlled. First, personal selling can be the largest marketing expense component in the final price of the product. Second, unless the sales force is somehow directed, motivated, and audited on a continual basis, it is likely to be less efficient than it is capable of being. Controlling the sales force involves four key functions: (1) forecasting sales, (2) establishing sales territories and quotas, (3) analyzing expenses, and (4) motivating and compensating performance.

Forecasting Sales

Sales planning begins with a forecast of sales for some future period or periods. From a practical standpoint, these forecasts are made on a short-term basis of a year or less, although long-range forecasts of one to five years are made for purposes other than managing the sales force, such as financing, production, and development. Generally speaking, forecasting is the marketing manager's responsibility. In large firms, because of the complexity of the task, it is usually delegated to a specialized unit, such as the marketing research department. Forecast data should be integrated into the firm's marketing information system for use by sales managers and other executives. For many companies, the sales forecast is the key instrument in the planning and control of operations.

The *sales forecast* is an estimate of how much of the company's output, either in dollars or in units, can be sold during a specified future period under a proposed marketing plan and under an assumed set of economic conditions. A sales forecast has several important uses: (1) it is used to establish sales quotas; (2) it is used to plan personal selling efforts as well as other types of promotional activities in the marketing mix; (3) it is used to budget selling expenses; and (4) it is used to plan and coordinate production, logistics, inventories, personnel, and so forth.

Sales forecasting has become very sophisticated in recent years, especially with the increased availability of computer software. It should be mentioned, however, that a forecast is never a substitute for sound business judgment. At the present time there is no single method of sales forecasting known that gives uniformly accurate results with infallible precision. Outlined below are some commonly used sales forecasting methods.[8]

1. *Jury of executive opinion method.* This combines and averages the views of top management representing marketing, production, finance, purchasing, and administration.

2. *Sales force composite method.* This is similar to the first method in that it obtains the combined views of the sales force about the future outlook for sales. In some

companies all salespeople, or district managers, submit estimates of the future sales in their territory or district.

3. *Customer expectations method.* This approach involves asking customers or product users about the quantity they expect to purchase.

4. *Time-series analysis.* This approach involves analyzing past sales data and the impact of factors that influence sales (long-term growth trends, cyclical fluctuations, seasonal variations).

5. *Correlation analysis.* This involves measuring the relationship between the dependent variable, sales, and one or more independent variables that can explain increases or decreases in sales volumes.

6. *Other quantitative techniques.* Numerous statistical and mathematical techniques can be used to predict or estimate future sales. Two of the more important techniques are (*a*) growth functions, which are mathematical expressions specifying the relationship between demand and time; and (*b*) simulation models, where a statistical model of the industry is developed and programmed to compute values for the key parameters of the model.

Establishing Sales Territories and Quotas

The establishment of sales territories and sales quotas represents management's need to match personal selling effort with sales potential (or opportunity). Soundly designed sales territories can improve how the market is served.[9] It is much easier to pinpoint customers and prospects and to determine who should call on them when the market is geographically divided than when the market is considered a large aggregate of potential accounts. The geographic segments should represent small clusters of customers or prospects within some physical proximity. Implied here is the notion that there are some distinct economic advantages to dividing the market into smaller segments. Salespeople restricted to a geographic area are likely to get more sales in the territory. Instead of simply servicing the "easy" and larger accounts, they are prone to develop small accounts. Of course, there are criteria other than geography for establishing territories. One important criterion is product specialization. In this case, salespeople are specialists relative to particular product or customer situations.

The question of managing sales territories cannot be discussed meaningfully without saying something about sales quotas. In general, quotas represent goals assigned to salespeople. As such, quotas provide three main benefits. First, they provide incentives for salespeople. For example, the definite objective of selling $500,000 worth of computer equipment is more motivating to most salespeople than the indefinite charge to go out and sell computer equipment. Sales bonuses and commissions based on quotas can also be motivational. Second, quotas provide a quantitative standard against which the performance of individual sales representatives or other marketing units can be measured. They allow management to pinpoint individuals and units that are performing above average and those experiencing difficulty. Third, quotas can be used not only to evaluate salespersons' performances but also to evaluate and control their efforts. As part of their job, salespeople are expected to engage in various activities besides calling on established accounts. These activities might include calling on new accounts, collecting past-due accounts, and planning and developing sales presentations. Activity quotas allow the company to monitor whether salespeople are engaging in these activities to the extent desired.

Sales quotas represent specific sales goals assigned to each territory or unit over a designated time period. The most common method of establishing quotas for territories is to relate sales to forecasted sales potential. For example, if the Ajax Drug Company's territory M has an estimated industry sales potential for a particular product of $400,000 for the year, the quota might be set at 25 percent of that po-

Marketing Highlight   Technology and the Sales Force

In today's information-driven business environment, companies are looking to their sales force as a vital souce of customer information. The image of salespeople carrying a sample case and making random sales calls is quickly fading. Today's salesperson uses technology to gather information about and communicate with prospects and customers. They also use it internally to bring the resources of their organization together to solve the problems of customers. Following are the percentage of sales forces surveyed that use a particular form of technology and some of the tangible and intangible benefits companies are experiencing from technology.

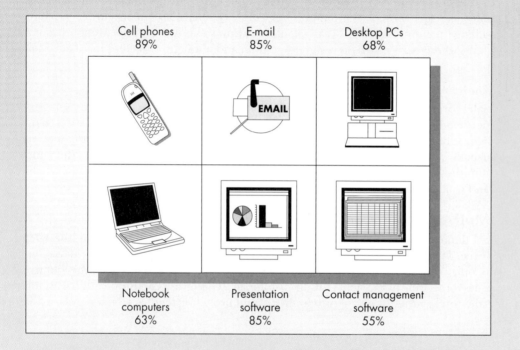

Cell phones 89%	E-mail 85%	Desktop PCs 68%
Notebook computers 63%	Presentation software 85%	Contact management software 55%

Tangible Benefits

- Better business results.
- Increased time spent with customer/clients.
- Increased customer satisfaction.
- Increased number of promising prospects.
- Consistent and prompt follow-up correspondence.
- Increased revenue per salesperson.
- Improved customer service.
- Better time management by salespeople and managers.
- Improved internal communication.

Intangible Benefits

- Improved employee motivation and satisfaction.
- Better-trained salespeople and marketing personnel.
- More recent and pertinent information with easier access.
- Improved responsiveness to customer and prospect needs.
- Smoother organizational change.
- Improved control and understanding of selling expenses.

Source: The results of sales forces surveyed is from Ginger Conlan, "Plug and Play," *Sales and Marketing Management,* December 1998, pp. 64–66. Adapted from Barton A. Weitz, Stephen B. Castleberry, and John F. Tanner, *Selling: Building Partnerships,* 4th ed. (Burr Ridge, IL: Irwin/McGraw-Hill, 2001), p. 4.

tential, or $100,000. The 25 percent figure represents the market share Ajax esti-mates to be a reasonable target. This $100,000 quota may represent an increase of $20,000 in sales over last year (assuming constant prices) that is expected from new business.

In establishing sales quotas for its individual territories or sales personnel, man-agement needs to take into account three key factors. First, all territories will not have equal potential and, therefore, compensation must be adjusted accordingly. Second, all salespeople will not have equal ability, and assignments may have to be made accordingly. Third, the sales task in each territory may differ from time period to time period. For instance, the nature of some territories may require that sales-people spend more time seeking new accounts, rather than servicing established ac-counts, especially in the case of so-called new territories. The point to be made here is that quotas can vary, not only by territory but also by assigned tasks. The effective sales manager should assign quotas not only for dollar sales but also for each major selling function. Figure 9–3 is an example of how this is done for the Medi-test Com-pany, where each activity is assigned a quota and a weight reflecting its relative im-portance.

Analyzing Expenses

Sales forecasts should include a sales expense budget. In some companies, sales ex-pense budgets are developed from the bottom up. Each territorial or district man-ager submits estimates of expenses and forecasted sales quotas. These estimates are usually prepared for a period of a year and then broken down into quarters and months. The sales manager then reviews the budget requests from the field offices and from staff departments.

Motivating and Compensating Performance

An important task for the sales manager is motivating and compensating the sales force. These two tasks are major determinants of sales force productivity. Managing people is always a challenge and involves personal interaction with members of the sales force, time in the field visiting customers, free-flowing communication with the sales force, either by e-mail or telephone, and providing feedback on a regular basis

FIGURE 9–3   Medi-test Company Sales Activity Evaluation

Territory: Southern Salesperson: Marsha Smith					
Functions	(1) Quota	(2) Actual	(3) Percent (2 ÷ 1)	(4) Weight	(5) Score (3 × 4)
Sales volume					
Old business	$380,000	$300,000	79	0.7	55.7
New business	$ 20,000	$ 20,000	100	0.5	50.0
Calls on prospects					
Doctors	20	15	75	0.2	15.0
Druggists	80	60	75	0.2	15.0
Wholesalers	15	15	100	0.2	20.0
Hospitals	10	10	100	0.2	20.0
				2.0	175.7

Performance index = 175.7

Marketing Highlight   **Effort- and Results-Oriented Measures for Evaluating Salespeople**

EFFORT-ORIENTED MEASURES

1. Number of sales calls made.
2. Number of MRO (maintenance-repairs-operations) calls made.
3. Number of complaints handled.
4. Number of checks on reseller stocks.
5. Uncontrollable lost job time.
6. Number of inquiries followed up.
7. Number of demonstrations completed.

RESULTS-ORIENTED MEASURES

1. Sales volume (total or by product or model).
2. Sales volume as a percentage of quota.
3. Sales profitability (dollar gross margin or contribution).
4. Number of new accounts.
5. Number of stockouts.
6. Number of distributors participating in programs.
7. Number of lost accounts.
8. Percentage volume increase in key accounts.
9. Number of customer complaints.
10. Distributor sales-inventory ratios.

Source: Adapted from Thomas N. Ingram, Raymond W. Laforge, and Charles H. Schwepker, Jr., *Sales Management: Analysis and Decision Making,* 3d ed. (Fort Worth, TX: The Dryden Press, 1997), chap. 15; and Thayer C. Taylor, "SFA: The Newest Orthodoxy," *Sales and Marketing Management,* February 1993, pp. 26–28.

as well as coaching and developing incentive programs through which job promotions or increased earnings can be achieved.[10]

There are two basic types of compensation: salary and commission. *Salary* usually refers to a specific amount of monetary compensation at an agreed rate for definite time periods. *Commission* is usually monetary compensation provided for each unit of sales and expressed as a percentage of sales. The base on which commissions are computed may be volume of sales in units of product, gross sales in dollars, net sales after returns, sales volume in excess of a quota, or net profits. Very often, several compensation approaches are combined. For example, a salesperson might be paid a base salary, a commission on sales exceeding a volume figure, and a percentage share of the company's profits for that year.

In addition to straight dollar compensation, there are numerous other forms of incentives that can be used to motivate the sales force. Some of these types of incentives and their potential performance outcomes are listed in Figure 9–4.

FIGURE 9–4
Types of Incentives and Their Possible Performance Outcomes

Types of Incentives

- Positive feedback on salesperson performance evaluation
- Company praise (e.g., recognition in a newsletter)
- Bonus (e.g., cash, merchandise, or travel allowances)
- Salary increase
- Pay for performance for specific new product idea
- Paid educational allowance
- Earned time off
- Fringe benefits
- Stock options
- Vested retirement plan
- Profit sharing

Performance Outcomes

- Sell a greater dollar volume
- Increase sales of more profitable products
- Push new products
- Push selected items at designated seasons
- Achieve a higher degree of market penetration by products, kinds of customers, or territories
- Increase the number of calls made
- Secure large average orders
- Secure new customers
- Service and maintain existing business
- Reduce turnover of customers
- Achieve full-line (balanced) selling
- Reduce direct selling costs
- Submit reports and other data promptly

Source: Some of the material was adapted from Gilbert A. Churchill Jr., Neil M. Ford, and Orville C. Walker, *Sales Force Management*, 5th ed. (Burr Ridge, IL: Irwin/McGraw-Hill, 1997), p. 490.

CONCLUSION

This chapter has attempted to outline and explain the personal selling aspect of the promotion mix. An emphasis was placed on describing the importance of the relationship-building aspect of the personal selling process. For organizations that wish to continue to grow and prosper, personal selling plays an integral part in the marketing of products and services. As long as production continues to expand through the development of new and highly technical products, personal selling will continue to be an important part of marketing strategy.

Additional Readings

Crosby, Lawrence A., and Sheree L. Johnson. "Customer Relationship Management." *Marketing Management*, Fall 2000, pp. 4–5.

Fram, Eugene H., and Michael S. McCarthy. "For the Sales Function, Is E-Commerce Friend or Foe." *Marketing Management*, Fall 2000, pp. 24–33.

Kissan, Joseph. "On the Optimality of Delegating Price Authority to the Sales Force." *Journal of Marketing*, January 2001, pp. 62–70.

Lemon, Katherine N., Roland T. Rust, and Valarie Zeithaml. "What Drives Customer Loyalty." *Marketing Management*, Spring 2001, pp. 20–25.

Vavra, Terry G. *Aftermarketing.* Burr Ridge, IL: McGraw-Hill, 1995.

Weitz, Barton A., Stephen B. Castleberry, and John F. Tanner, Jr. *Selling: Building Relationships.* 4th ed. Burr Ridge, IL: McGraw-Hill/Irwin, 2001.

Chapter

10

Distribution Strategy

Channel of distribution decisions involve numerous interrelated variables that must be integrated into the total marketing mix. Because of the time and money required to set up an efficient channel, and since channels are often hard to change once they are set up, these decisions are critical to the success of the firm.

This chapter is concerned with the development and management of channels of distribution and the process of goods distribution in complex, highly competitive, and specialized economies. It should be noted at the outset that channels of distribution provide the ultimate consumer or organizational buyer with time, place, and possession utility. Thus, an efficient channel is one that delivers the product when and where it is wanted at a minimum total cost.

THE NEED FOR MARKETING INTERMEDIARIES

A *channel of distribution* is the combination of institutions through which a seller markets products to the user or ultimate consumer. The need for other institutions or intermediaries in the delivery of goods is sometimes questioned, particularly since the profits they make are viewed as adding to the cost of the product. However, this reasoning is generally fallacious, since producers use marketing intermediaries because the intermediary can perform functions more cheaply and more efficiently than the producer can. This notion of efficiency is critical when the characteristics of advanced economies are considered.

For example, the U.S. economy is characterized by heterogeneity in terms of both supply and demand. In terms of numbers alone, there are nearly 7 million establishments comprising the supply segment of the economy, and there are over 200 million households making up the demand side. Clearly, if each of these units had to deal on a one-to-one basis to obtain needed goods and services, and there were no intermediaries to collect and disperse assortments of goods, the system would be totally inefficient. Thus, the primary role of intermediaries is to bring supply and demand together in an efficient and orderly fashion.

CLASSIFICATION OF MARKETING INTERMEDIARIES AND FUNCTIONS

There are a great many types of marketing intermediaries, many of which are so specialized by function and industry that they need not be discussed here. Figure 10–1 presents the major types of marketing intermediaries common to many industries.

FIGURE 10–1

Major Types of Marketing Intermediaries

Middleman—an independent business concern that operates as a link between producers and ultimate consumers or organizational buyers.

Merchant middleman—a middleman who buys the goods outright and takes title to them.

Agent—a business unit that negotiates purchases, sales, or both but does not take title to the goods in which it deals.

Wholesaler—a merchant establishment operated by a concern that is primarily engaged in buying, taking title to, usually storing and physically handling goods in large quantities, and reselling the goods (usually in smaller quantities) to retailers or to organizational buyers.

Retailer—a merchant middleman who is engaged primarily in selling to ultimate consumers.

Broker—a middleman who serves as a go-between for the buyer or seller. The broker assumes no title risks, does not usually have physical custody of products, and is not looked upon as a permanent representative of either the buyer or the seller.

Manufacturers' agent—an agent who generally operates on an extended contractual basis, often sells within an exclusive territory, handles noncompeting but related lines of goods, and possesses limited authority with regard to prices and terms of sale.

Distributor—a wholesale middleman especially in lines where selective or exclusive distribution is common at the wholesaler level in which the manufacturer expects strong promotional support; often a synonym for wholesaler.

Jobber—a middleman who buys from manufacturers and sells to retailers; a wholesaler.

Facilitating agent—a business firm that assists in the performance of distribution tasks other than buying, selling, and transferring title (i.e., transportation companies, warehouses, etc.)

Source: Based on Peter D. Bennett, ed., *Dictionary of Marketing Times,* 2d ed. (Chicago: American Marketing Association, 1995).

Although there is some overlap in this classification, these categories are based on the marketing functions performed. That is, various intermediaries perform different marketing functions and to different degrees. Figure 10–2 is a listing of the more common marketing functions performed in the channel.

It should be remembered that whether or not a manufacturer uses intermediaries to perform these functions, the functions have to be performed by someone. In other words, the managerial question is not whether to perform the functions, but who will perform them and to what degree.

CHANNELS OF DISTRIBUTION

As previously noted, a channel of distribution is the combination of institutions through which a seller markets products to the user or ultimate consumer. Some of these links assume the risks of ownership; others do not. The conventional channel of distribution patterns for consumer goods markets are shown in Figure 10–3.

Some manufacturers use a *direct channel,* selling directly to a market. For example, Gateway 2000 sells computers through the mail without the use of other intermediaries. Using a direct channel, called *direct marketing,* increased in popularity as marketers found that products could be sold directly using a variety of methods. These include direct mail, telemarketing, direct-action advertising, catalog selling, cable selling, online selling, and direct selling through demonstrations at home or place of work. These will be discussed in more detail later in this chapter.

FIGURE 10–2
Marketing Functions Performed in Channels of Distribution

Buying—purchasing products from sellers for use or for resale.
Selling—the personal or impersonal process whereby the salesperson ascertains, activates, and satisfies the needs of the buyer to the mutual continuous benefit of both buyer and seller.
Sorting—a function performed by intermediaries to bridge the discrepancy between the assortment of goods and services generated by the producer and the assortment demanded by the consumer. This function includes four distinct processes: sorting out, accumulation, allocation, and assorting.
Sorting out—a sorting process that breaks down a heterogeneous supply into separate stocks that are relatively homogeneous.
Accumulation—a sorting process that brings similar stocks from a number of sources together into a larger homogeneous supply.
Allocation—a sorting process that consists of breaking a homogeneous supply down into smaller and smaller lots.
Assorting—a sorting process that consists of building an assortment of products for use in association with each other.
Concentration—the process of bringing goods from various places together in one place.
Financing—providing credit or funds to facilitate a transaction.
Storage—maintaining inventories and protecting products to provide better customer service.
Grading—the classifying of a product by examining its quality. It is often done with a program of grade labeling, though individual firms can grade their own products by a private system if they wish, for example, good, better, best.
Transportation—a marketing function that adds time and place utility to the product by moving it from where it is made to where it is purchased and used. It includes all intermediate steps in the process.
Risk-taking—taking on business risks involved in transporting and owning products.
Marketing research—collecting information concerning such things as market conditions, expected sales, consumer trends, and competitive forces.

Source: Based on Peter D. Bennett, ed., *Dictionary of Marketing Terms*, 2d ed. (Chicago: American Marketing Association, 1995).

FIGURE 10–3   Conventional Channels of Distribution of Consumer Goods

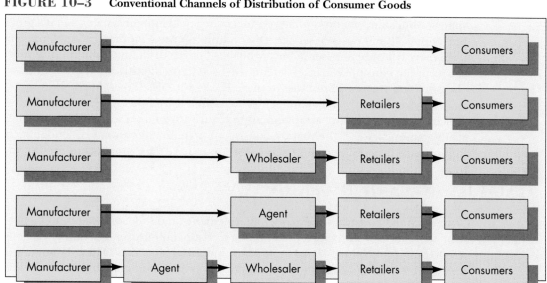

FIGURE 10–4   **Conventional Channels of Distribution for Organizational Goods**

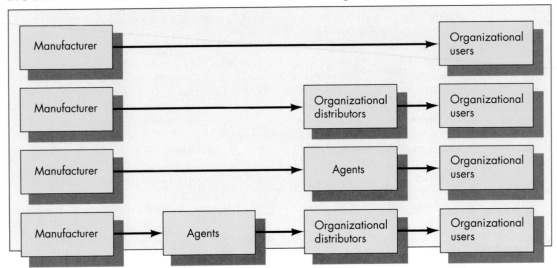

In other cases, one or more intermediaries may be used in the distribution process. For example, Hewlett-Packard sells its computers and printers through retailers such as Best Buy and Office Max. A common channel for consumer goods is one in which the manufacturer sells through wholesalers and retailers. For instance, a cold remedy manufacturer may sell to drug wholesalers who, in turn, sell a vast array of drug products to various retail outlets. Small manufacturers may also use agents, since they do not have sufficient capital for their own sales forces. Agents are commonly used intermediaries in the jewelry industry. The final channel in Figure 10–3 is used primarily when small wholesalers and retailers are involved. Channels with one or more intermediaries are referred to as *indirect channels.*

In contrast to consumer products, the direct channel is often used in the distribution of organizational goods. The reason for this stems from the structure of most organizational markets, which often have relatively few but extremely large customers. Also, many organizational products, such as computer systems, need a great deal of presale and postsale service. Distributors are used in organizational markets when there is a large number of buyers but each purchases a small amount of a product. As in the consumer market, agents are used in organizational markets in cases where manufacturers do not wish to have their own sales forces. Such an arrangement may be used by small manufacturers or when the market is geographically dispersed. The final channel arrangement in Figure 10–4 may also be used by a small manufacturer or when the market consists of many small customers. Under such conditions, it may not be economical for sellers to have their own sales organization.

SELECTING CHANNELS OF DISTRIBUTION

Given the numerous types of channel intermediaries and functions that must be performed, the task of selecting and designing a channel of distribution may at first appear to be overwhelming. However, in many industries, channels of distribution have developed over many years and have become somewhat traditional. In such cases, the producer may be limited to this type of channel to operate in the industry. This is not to say that a traditional channel is always the most efficient and that there are no op-

FIGURE 10–5   General Considerations in Channel Planning

1. **Customer characteristics**
   a. Number
   b. Geographic dispersion
   c. Preferred channels and outlets for purchase
   d. Purchasing patterns
   e. Use of new channels (e.g., online purchasing)
2. **Product characteristics**
   a. Unit value
   b. Perishability
   c. Bulkiness
   d. Degree of standardization
   e. Installation and maintenance services required
3. **Intermediary characteristics**
   a. Availability
   b. Willingness to accept product or product line
   c. Geographic market served
   d. Marketing functions performed
   e. Potential for conflict
   f. Potential for long-term relationship
   g. Competitive products sold
   h. Financial condition
   i. Other strengths and weaknesses
4. **Competitor characteristics**
   a. Number
   b. Relative size and market share

   c. Distribution channels and strategy
   d. Financial condition and estimated marketing budget
   e. Size of product mix and product lines
   f. Overall marketing strategy employed
   g. Other strengths and weaknesses
5. **Company characteristics**
   a. Relative size and market share
   b. Financial condition and marketing budget
   c. Size of product mix and product lines
   d. Marketing strategy employed
   e. Marketing objectives
   f. Past channel experience
   g. Marketing functions willing to perform
   h. Other strengths and weaknesses
6. **Environmental characteristics**
   a. Economic conditions
   b. Legal regulations and restrictions
   c. Political issues
   d. Global and domestic cultural differences and changes
   e. Technological changes
   f. Other opportunities and threats

portunities for innovation. But the fact that such a channel is widely accepted in the industry suggests it is highly efficient. A primary constraint in these cases and in cases where no traditional channel exists is that of *availability* of the various types of middlemen. All too often in the early stages of channel design, executives map out elaborate channel networks only to find out later that no such independent intermediaries exist for the firm's product in selected geographic areas. Even if they do exist, they may not be willing to accept the seller's products. In general, there are six basic considerations in the initial development of channel strategy. These are outlined in Figure 10–5.

It should be noted that for a particular product any one of these characteristics greatly influences choice of channels. To illustrate, highly perishable products generally require direct channels, or a firm with little financial strength may require intermediaries to perform almost all of the marketing functions.

Specific Considerations

The above characteristics play an important part in framing the channel selection decision. Based on them, the choice of channels can be further refined in terms of (1) distribution coverage required, (2) degree of control desired, (3) total distribution cost, and (4) channel flexibility.

Distribution Coverage Required

Because of the characteristics of the product, the environment needed to sell the product, and the needs and expectations of the potential buyer, products will vary in the intensity of distribution coverage they require. Distribution coverage can be viewed along a continuum ranging from intensive to selective to exclusive distribution.

Intensive Distribution   Here the manufacturer attempts to gain exposure through as many wholesalers and retailers as possible. Most convenience goods require intensive distribution based on the characteristics of the product (low unit value) and the needs and expectations of the buyer (high frequency of purchase and convenience).

Selective Distribution   Here the manufacturer limits the use of intermediaries to the ones believed to be the best available in a geographic area. This may be based on the service organization available, the sales organization, or the reputation of the intermediary. Thus, appliances, home furnishings, and better clothing are usually distributed selectively. For appliances, the intermediary's service organization could be a key factor, while for better clothing and home furnishings, the intermediary's reputation would be an important consideration.

Exclusive Distribution   Here the manufacturer severely limits distribution, and intermediaries are provided exclusive rights within a particular territory. The characteristics of the product are a determining factor here. Where the product requires certain specialized selling effort or investment in unique facilities or large inventories, this arrangement is usually selected. Retail paint stores are an example of such a distribution arrangement.

Degree of Control Desired

In selecting channels of distribution, the seller must make decisions concerning the degree of control desired over the marketing of the firm's products. Some manufacturers prefer to keep as much control over their products as possible. Ordinarily, the degree of control achieved by the seller is proportionate to the directness of the channel. One Eastern brewery, for instance, owns its own fleet of trucks and operates a wholly owned delivery system direct to grocery and liquor stores. Its market is very concentrated geographically, with many small buyers, so such a system is economically feasible. However, all other brewers in the area sell through distributors.

When more indirect channels are used, the manufacturer must surrender some control over the marketing of the firm's product. However, attempts are commonly made to maintain a degree of control through some other indirect means, such as sharing promotional expenditures, providing sales training, or other operational aids, such as accounting systems, inventory systems, or marketing research data on the dealer's trading area.

Total Distribution Cost

The total distribution cost concept has developed out of the more general topic of systems theory. The concept suggests that a channel of distribution should be viewed as a total system composed of interdependent subsystems, and that the objective of the system (channel) manager should be to optimize total system performance. In terms of distribution costs, it generally is assumed that the total system should be designed to minimize costs, other things being equal. The following is a representative list of the major distribution costs to be minimized.

1. Transportation
2. Order processing
3. Cost of lost business (an opportunity cost due to inability to meet customer demand)
4. Inventory carrying costs, including
    a. Storage-space charges
    b. Cost of capital invested
    c. Taxes

Marketing Highlight   Manufacturers and Intermediaries: A Perfect Working Relationship

THE PERFECT INTERMEDIARY

1. Has access to the market that the manufacturer wants to reach.
2. Carries adequate stocks of the manufacturer's products and a satisfactory assortment of other products.
3. Has an effective promotional program—advertising, personal selling, and product displays. Promotional demands placed on the manufacturer are in line with what the manufacturer intends to do.
4. Provides services to customers—credit, delivery, installation, and product repair— and honors the product warranty conditions.
5. Pays its bills on time and has capable management.

THE PERFECT MANUFACTURER

1. Provides a desirable assortment of products—well designed, properly priced, attractively packaged, and delivered on time and in adequate quantities.
2. Builds product demand for these products by advertising them.
3. Furnishes promotional assistance to its middlemen.
4. Provides managerial assistance for its middlemen.
5. Honors product warranties and provides repair and installation service.

THE PERFECT COMBINATION

1. Probably doesn't exist.

Source: Adapted from William J. Stanton, Michael J. Etzel, and Bruce J. Walker, *Fundamentals of Marketing,* 9th ed. © New York, McGraw-Hill, 1991, p. 305. Reproduced by permission of the McGraw-Hill Companies.

    d. Insurance
    e. Obsolescence and deterioration
5. Packaging
6. Materials handling

The important qualification to the total-cost concept is the statement "other things being equal." The purpose of the total-cost concept is to emphasize total system performance to avoid suboptimization. However, other important factors must be considered, not the least of which are level of customer service, sales, profits, and interface with the total marketing mix.

Channel Flexibility

A final consideration relates to the ability of the manufacturer to adapt to changing conditions. To illustrate, much of the population have moved from inner cities to suburbs and thus make most of their purchases in shopping centers and malls. If a manufacturer had long-term, exclusive dealership with retailers in the inner city, the ability to adapt to this population shift could have been severely limited.

MANAGING A CHANNEL OF DISTRIBUTION

Once the seller has decided on the type of channel structure to use and selected the individual members, the entire coalition should operate as a total system. From a behavioral perspective, the system can be viewed as a social system since each member interacts with the others, each member plays a role vis-à-vis the others, and each has certain expectations of the other. Thus, the behavioral perspective views a channel of distribution as more than a series of markets or participants extending from production to consumption.

Relationship Marketing in Channels

For many years in theory and practice, marketing has taken a competitive view of channels of distribution. In other words, since channel members had different goals and strategies, it was believed that the major focus should be on concepts such as power and conflict. Research interests focused on issues concerning bases of power, antecedents and consequences of conflict, and conflict resolution.

More recently, however, a new view of channels has developed. Perhaps because of the success of Japanese companies in the 1980s, it was recognized that much could be gained by developing long-term commitments and harmony among channel members. This view is called *relationship marketing*, which can be defined as "marketing with the conscious aim to develop and manage long-term and/or trusting relationships with customers, distributors, suppliers, or other parties in the marketing environment."[1]

It is well documented in the marketing literature that long-term relationships throughout the channel often lead to higher-quality products with lower costs. These benefits may account for the increased use of vertical marketing systems.[2]

Vertical Marketing Systems

To this point in the chapter the discussion has focused primarily on conventional channels of distribution. In conventional channels, each firm is relatively independent of the other members in the channel. However, one of the important developments in channel management in recent years is the increasing use of vertical marketing systems.

Vertical marketing systems are channels in which members are more dependent on one another and develop long-term working relationships in order to improve the efficiency and effectiveness of the system. Figure 10–6 shows the major types of vertical marketing systems, which include administered, contractual, and corporate systems.[3]

Administered Systems

Administered vertical marketing systems are the most similar to conventional channels. However, in these systems there is a higher degree of interorganizational planning and management than in a conventional channel. The dependence in these

FIGURE 10–6
Major Types of Vertical Marketing Systems

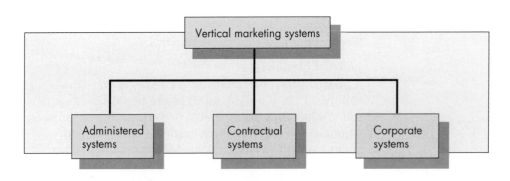

Marketing Highlight   Franchising: An Alternative to Conventional Channels of Distribution

A franchise is a means by which a producer of products or services achieves a direct channel of distribution without wholly owning or managing the physical facilities in the market. In effect, the franchisor provides the franchisee with the franchisor's knowledge, manufacturing, and marketing techniques for a financial return.

INGREDIENTS OF A FRANCHISED BUSINESS

Six key ingredients should be included within a well-balanced franchise offered to a franchisee. These are given in order of importance.

- *Technical knowledge* in its practical form is supplied through an intensive course of study.
- *Managerial techniques* based on proven and time-tested programs are imparted to the franchisee on a continuing basis, even after the business has been started or taken over by the franchisee.
- *Commercial knowledge* involving prescribed methods of buying and selling is explained and codified. Most products to be obtained, processed, and sold to the franchisee are supplied by the franchisor.
- *Financial instruction* on managing funds and accounts is given to the franchisee during the indoctrination period.
- *Accounting controls* are set up by the franchisor for the franchisee.
- *Protective safeguards* are included in the intensive training of the franchisee for employees and customers, including the quality of the product, as well as the safeguards for assets through adequate insurance controls.

ELEMENTS OF AN IDEAL FRANCHISE PROGRAM

- *High gross margin.* In order for the franchisee to be able to afford a high franchise fee (which the franchisor needs), it is necessary to operate on a high gross margin percentage. This explains the widespread application of franchising in the food and service industries.
- *In-store value added.* Franchising works best in those product categories where the product is at least partially processed in the store. Such environments require constant on-site supervision—a chronic problem for company-owned stores using a hired manager. Owners simply are willing to work harder over longer hours.
- *Secret processes.* Concepts, formulas, or products that the franchisee can't duplicate without joining the franchise program.
- *Real estate profits.* The franchisor uses income from ownership of property as a significant revenue source.
- *Simplicity.* The most successful franchises have been those that operate on automatic pilot: All the key decisions have been thought through, and the owner merely implements the decisions.

Source: Partially adapted from Philip D. White and Albert D. Bates, "Franchising Will Remain Retailing Fixture, but Its Salad Days Have Long Since Gone," *Marketing News*, February 17, 1984, p. 14; and Scott Shane and Chester Spell, "Factors for New Franchise Success," *Sloan Management Review*, Spring 1998, pp. 43–50.

systems can result from the existence of a strong channel leader such that other channel members work closely with this company in order to maintain a long-term relationship. While any level of channel member may be the leader of an administered system, Wal-Mart, Kmart, and Sears are excellent examples of retailers that have established administered systems with many of their suppliers.

Contractual Systems

Contractual vertical marketing systems involve independent production and distribution companies entering into formal contracts to perform designated marketing functions. Three major types of contractual vertical marketing systems are the retail cooperative organization, wholesaler-sponsored voluntary chain, and various franchising programs.

In a retail cooperative organization, a group of independent retailers unite and agree to pool buying and managerial resources to improve competitive position. In a wholesaler-sponsored voluntary chain, a wholesaler contracts with a number of retailers and performs channel functions for them. Usually, retailers agree to concentrate a major portion of their purchasing with the sponsoring wholesaler and to sell advertised products at the same price. The most visible type of contractual vertical marketing systems involves a variety of franchise programs. Franchises involve a parent company (the franchisor) and an independent firm (the franchisee) entering into a contractual relationship to set up and operate a business in a particular way. Many products and services reach consumers through franchise systems, including automobiles (Ford), gasoline (Mobil), hotels and motels (Holiday Inn), restaurants (McDonald's), car rentals (Avis), and soft drinks (Pepsi). In fact, some analysts predict that within the next 10 years, franchises will account for 50 percent of all retail sales.

Corporate Systems

Corporate vertical marketing systems involve single ownership of two or more levels of a channel. When a manufacturer purchases wholesalers or retailers, it is called *forward integration*. When wholesalers or retailers purchase channel members above them, it is called *backward integration*. Firms may choose to develop corporate vertical marketing systems in order to compete more effectively with other marketing systems, to obtain scale economies, and to increase channel cooperation and avoid channel conflict.

WHOLESALING

As noted, wholesalers are merchants that are primarily engaged in buying, taking title to, usually storing and physically handling goods in large quantities, and reselling the goods (usually in smaller quantities) to retailers or to industrial or business users.[4] Wholesalers are also called *distributors* in some industries, particularly when they have exclusive distribution rights, such as in the beer industry. Other wholesalers that do not take title to goods are called *agents, brokers,* or *manufacturers' representatives* in various industries. There are over 520,000 wholesalers in the United States.

Wholesalers create value for suppliers, retailers, and users of goods by performing distribution functions efficiently and effectively. They may transport and warehouse goods, exhibit them at trade shows, and offer advice to retailers concerning which lines of products are selling best in other areas. Producers use wholesalers to reach large markets and extend geographic coverage for their goods. Wholesalers may lower the costs for other channel members by efficiently carrying out such activities as physically moving goods to convenient locations, assuming the risk of managing large inventories of diverse products, and delivering products as needed to replenish retail shelves.

While producers may actively seek out wholesalers for their goods, wholesalers also try to attract producers to use their services. To do so, they may offer to perform all the distribution functions or tailor their services to include only the functions that producers do not have the ability to perform effectively. Naturally, wholesalers especially seek producers of major brands for which sales and profit potential are likely to be the greatest. Wholesalers may compete with other wholesalers to attract producers by offering lower costs for the functions they perform. Wholesalers with excellent track records that do not carry directly competing products and brands, that have appropriate locations and facilities, and that have relationships with major retail customers

BENEFITS FOR MANUFACTURERS

- Provides the ability to reach diverse geographic markets cost effectively.
- Provides information about retailers and end users in various markets.
- Reduces costs through greater efficiency and effectiveness in distribution functions performed.
- Reduces potential losses by assuming risks and offering expertise.

BENEFITS FOR RETAILERS

- Provides potentially profitable products otherwise unavailable for resale in retail area.
- Provides information about industries, manufacturers, and other retailers.
- Reduces costs by providing an assortment of goods from different manufacturers.
- Reduces costs through greater efficiency in distribution functions performed.

BENEFITS FOR END USERS

- Increases the product alternatives available in local markets.
- Reduces retail prices by the efficiency and effectiveness contributed to the channel.
- Improves product selection by providing information to retailers about the best products to offer end users.

can more easily attract manufacturers of successful products. Also, wholesalers that serve large markets may be more attractive since producers may be able to reduce the number of wholesalers they deal with and thereby lower their costs. Long-term, profitable producer-wholesaler relationships are enhanced by trust, doing a good job for one another, and open communication about problems and opportunities.

Wholesalers also need to attract retailers and organizational customers to buy from them. In many cases, wholesalers have exclusive contracts to distribute products in a particular trading area. For popular products and brands with large market shares, the wholesaler's task is simplified because retailers want to carry them. For example, distributors of Coke and Pepsi can attract retailers easily because the products sell so well and consumers expect to find them in many retail outlets. Retail supermarkets and convenience stores would be at a competitive disadvantage without these brands.

However, for new or small market-share products and brands, particularly those of less well known manufacturers, wholesalers may have to do considerable marketing to get retailers to stock them. Wholesalers may get placement for such products and brands in retail stores because they have previously developed strong long-term working relationships with them. Alternatively, wholesalers may have to carefully explain the marketing plan for the product, why it should be successful, and why carrying the product will benefit the retailer.

While there are still many successful wholesalers, the share of products sold by them is likely to continue to decrease. This is because large retail chains like Wal-Mart have gained such market power that they can buy directly from manufacturers and bypass wholesalers altogether. The survival of wholesalers depends on their ability to meet the needs of both manufacturers and retailers by performing distribution functions more efficiently and effectively than a channel designed without them.

STORE AND NONSTORE RETAILING

As noted, retailers are merchants that are primarily engaged in selling to ultimate consumers. The more than 1.5 million retailers in the United States can be classified in many ways. For example, they are broken down in the North American Industry Classification System (NAICS) codes into eight general categories and a number of subcategories based on the types of merchandise they sell.[5]

Marketers have a number of decisions to make to determine the best way to retail their products. For example, decisions have to be made as to whether to use stores to sell merchandise, and if so, whether to sell through company-owned stores, franchised outlets, or independent stores or chains. Decisions have to be made as to whether to sell through nonstore methods, such as the Internet, and if so, which methods of nonstore retailing should be used. Each of these decisions brings about a number of others such as what types of stores to use, how many of them, what locations should be selected, and what specific types of nonstore retailing to use.

Store Retailing

Over 90 percent of retail purchases are made through stores, which makes them an appropriate retail method for most types of products and services. Retailers vary not only in the types of merchandise they carry but also in the breadth and depth of their product assortments and the amount of service they provide. In general, *mass merchandisers* carry broad product assortments and compete on two bases. Supermarkets (Kroger), department stores (Marshall Fields), and catalog showrooms (Service Merchandise) compete with other retailers on the basis of offering a good selection in a number of different product categories, whereas superstores (Cub Foods), hypermarkets (Bigg's), discount stores (Wal-Mart), warehouse stores (Price Club), variety stores (Woolworth), and off-price retailers (T. J. Maxx) compete more on the basis of offering lower prices on products in their large assortments. Manufacturers of many types of consumer goods must get distribution in one or more types of mass merchandisers to be successful.

Specialty stores handle deep assortments in a limited number of product categories. Specialty stores include limited-line stores that offer a large assortment of a few related product lines (The Gap), single-line stores that emphasize a single product (Batteries Plus), and category killers (Circuit City), which are large, low-priced limited-line retail chains that attempt to dominate a particular product category. If a product type is sold primarily through specialty stores and sales are concentrated in category killer chains, manufacturers may have to sell through them to reach customers.

Convenience stores (7-Eleven) are retailers whose primary advantage to consumers is location convenience, close-in parking, and easy entry and exit. They stock products that consumers want to buy in a hurry, such as milk or soft drinks, and charge higher prices for the purchase convenience. They are an important retail outlet for many types of convenience goods.

In selecting the types of stores and specific stores and chains to resell their products, manufacturers (and wholesalers) have a variety of factors to consider. They want stores and chains that reach their target market and have good reputations with consumers. They want stores and chains that handle distribution functions efficiently and effectively, order large quantities, pay invoices quickly, display their merchandise well, and allow them to make good profits. Selling products in the right stores and chains increases sales, and selling in prestigious stores can increase the equity of a brand and the price that can be charged. The locations of retail stores, the types of people who shop at them, and the professionalism of the salespeople and clerks who work in them all affect the success of the stores and the products they sell. In addition to the merchandise offered, store advertising, and price levels, the characteristics of the store itself—including layout, colors, smells, noises, lights, signs, and shelf space and displays—influence the success of both the stores and the products they offer.

Nonstore Retailing

Although stores dominate sales for most products, there are still opportunities to market products successfully in other ways. Five nonstore methods of retailing include catalogs and direct mail, vending machines, television home shopping, direct sales, and electronic exchanges.[6]

Catalogs and Direct Mail

As shown in Figure 10–7, catalogs and direct mail dominate nonstore retailing. The advantages of this type of nonstore retailing for marketers are that consumers can be targeted effectively and reached in their homes or at work, overhead costs are decreased, and assortments of specialty merchandise can be presented with attractive pictures and in-depth descriptions of features and benefits. Catalogs can also remain in homes or offices for a lengthy time period, making available potential sales. Catalogs can offer specialty products for unique

FIGURE 10–7
Annual Nonstore Retail Sales, 2000

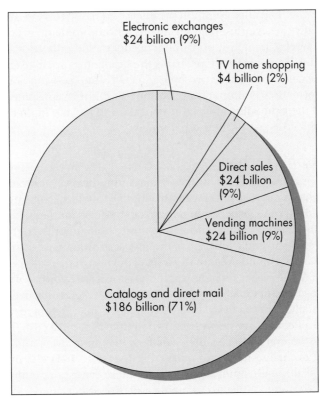

Source: Michael Levy and Barton A. Weitz, *Retail Management*, 4th ed. (Burr Ridge, IL: Irwin/McGraw-Hill, 2001), p. 78.

markets that are geographically dispersed in a cost-effective manner. Although consumers cannot experience products directly as they can in stores, catalog retailers with reputations for quality and generous return policies can reduce consumers' risks. For example, Levenger, which sells pens, desks, and "other tools for serious readers," sends consumers a postage-paid label to return unwanted merchandise. Many consumers enjoy the time savings of catalog shopping and are willing to pay higher prices to use it.

Vending Machines

Vending machines are a relatively limited method of retail merchandising, and most vending machine sales are for beverages, food, and candy. The advantages for marketers include: They are available for sales 24 hours a day, can be placed in a variety of high-traffic locations, and can charge higher prices. While uses of vending machines for such things as airline insurance and concert and game tickets are not unusual, this method has limited potential for most products.

Television Home Shopping

Television home shopping includes cable channels dedicated to shopping, infomercials, and direct-response advertising shown on cable and broadcast networks. Home Shopping Network and QVC are the leaders in this market, and the major products sold are inexpensive jewelry, apparel, cosmetics, and exercise equipment. While this method allows better visual display than catalogs, potential customers must be watching at the time the merchandise is offered; if not, they have no way of knowing about the product or purchasing it.

Direct Sales

Direct sales are made by salespeople to consumers in their homes or offices or by telephone. The most common products purchased this way are cosmetics, fragrances, decorative accessories, vacuum cleaners, home appliances, cooking utensils, kitchenware, jewelry, food and nutritional products, and educational materials. Avon, Mary Kay, and Tupperware are probably the best-known retail users of this channel. Salespeople can demonstrate products effectively and provide detailed feature and benefit information. A limitation of this method is that consumers are often too busy to spend their time this way and do not want to pay the higher prices needed to cover the high costs of this method of retailing.

Electronic Exchange

Electronic exchanges or Internet marketing involves customers collecting information, shopping, and purchasing from websites on the Internet. Electronic exchange has had its greatest success in business-to-business marketing, although it accounts for only about 10 percent of business-to-business commerce. In the business-to-consumer market, electronic exchange is the fastest growing type of nonstore retailing. However, sales in this market are still a small portion of the sales in traditional retail stores. In fact, Wal-Mart's sales in its traditional stores are far greater than the total of all business-to-consumer exchanges on the Internet taken collectively.

Initially, many analysts thought that electronic exchange would become a leading source of commerce because of its potential to reduce costs for marketers and prices for customers. However, these analysts may have overestimated the ability of electronic exchange to do so; marketing functions in a channel still have to be performed although, admittedly, some of them can be done more efficiently using this method. For example, order taking and processing can be done more efficiently and accurately by electronic means.

Marketing Highlight   Recommendations for Developing Successful Commercial Websites

Because electronic commerce is expected to grow dramatically, many companies are spending heavily to develop effective websites. One study found that 32 percent of the companies it polled were spending from $500,000 to over $5 million to create a commerce-based website. Like most marketing strategies, designing successful websites requires careful analysis of consumers. Below are five recommendations for designing websites that consumers will be able to use efficiently and effectively.

1. Make sure the site has contact information that is accurate and complete. Many websites lack basics such as postal address, phone and fax numbers, and e-mail addresses. Don't hide this stuff five levels deep in a back corner; make it easy to find.

2. Don't make factual information, such as product updates and prices, hard to come by. Someone other than the Webmaster should be responsible for tracking this information and keeping it up-to-date.

3. Make sure users can find the site with straightforward key words. Make it simple to find the site via the various search engines. Work on improving the search function on the site itself.

4. Make it just as easy for consumers to exit the site as it is for them to find and use it. The layout and design of the site should be fairly obvious to viewers no matter where they land inside.

5. Create a good table of contents and index. Most consumers do not want to start at the front door and proceed in an orderly fashion through the entire site. Keep the number of screens and subscreens for contents and site organization down to a bare minimum. Put links both to the table of contents and to an index on the front page so that consumers can find them quickly.

To find more information about site usability, see the Alertbox written by Jakob Nielsen of SunSoft (www.useit.com/alertbox/) or read *Understanding Electronic Commerce* by David Kosiur available through www.Amazon.com.

Sources: Adapted from Mark Halper, "So Does Your Web Site Pay?" *Forbes ASAP,* August 25, 1997, pp. 117–18; and David Strom, "Five Steps for Site Success," *Forbes ASAP,* August 25, 1997, p. 118.

Figure 10–8 lists some of the advantages and disadvantages of the electronic exchange for marketers. In examining this figure, it is important to recognize that there are some differences in the advantages and disadvantages depending on whether the marketer is a small, entrepreneurial venture or a large, established company. Since electronic exchange offers low-entry barriers, this is an advantage for a small company that wants to get into a market and compete for business with less capital. However, for large, established companies, this is less of an advantage since they have the capital to invest; low-entry barriers create more competition for them from smaller companies.

Similarly, large companies with established names and brand equity can more easily market products that customers would ordinarily want to examine before purchase (touch-and-feel products) than can smaller companies with less brand equity. For example, companies like Lands' End, JCPenney, and Wal-Mart are more successful in

FIGURE 10–8
Electronic
Commerce:
Advantages and
Disadvantages for
Marketers

Advantages for Marketers

Reduces the need for stores, paper catalogs, and salespeople; can be cost efficient

Allows good visual presentation and full description of product features and benefits

Allows vast assortments of products to be offered efficiently

Allows strategic elements, such as product offerings, prices, and promotion appeals to be changed quickly

Allows products to be offered globally in an efficient manner

Allows products to be offered 24 hours a day, 365 days a year

Fosters the development of one-on-one, interactive relationships with customers

Provides an efficient means for developing a customer database and doing online marketing research

Disadvantages for Marketers

Strong price competition often squeezes profit margins

Low entry barriers led some e-marketers to overemphasize order-taking and not develop sufficient infrastructure for order fulfillment

Customers must go to the website rather than having marketers seek them out via salespeople and advertising; advertising their websites is prohibitively expensive for many small e-marketers

Limits the market to customers who are willing and able to purchase electronically; many countries still have a small population of computer-literate people

Not as good for selling touch-and-feel products as opposed to look-and-buy products unless there is strong brand/store/site equity (Dell computers/Wal-Mart/Amazon.com) or the products are homogeneous (books, CDs, plane tickets, etc.)

Often less effective and efficient in business-to-consumer markets than in business-to-business markets

attracting customers electronically because customers know the companies and their offerings better and perceive less risk in purchasing from them than from a new or unknown electronic marketer. This does not mean that newer companies that sell only by electronic means cannot compete for business. Companies like Amazon.com and Priceline.com have created well-known websites and have generated considerable sales. However, as with most dot.com businesses, it has been difficult for them to generate profits.

In sum, while electronic exchange has not met the growth expectations of many marketers, it is an established alternative for marketing some products and services. It does provide customers with a wealth of product information and product assortments that are readily available. Many electronic marketers will have to find ways to deliver superior customer value in order to become profitable and survive in the long run.[7]

CONCLUSION

This chapter introduced the distribution of goods and services in a complex, highly competitive, highly specialized economy. It emphasized the vital need for marketing intermediaries to bring about exchanges between buyers and sellers in a reasonably efficient manner. The chapter examined various types of intermediaries and the distribution functions they perform as well as topics in the selection and management of distribution channels. Finally, both wholesaling and store and nonstore retailing were discussed.

Additional Readings

Berman, Barry. *Marketing Channels.* New York: Wiley, 1996.

Bowersox, Donald J., and M. Bixby Cooper. *Strategic Marketing Channel Management.* New York: McGraw-Hill, 1992.

Chopra, Sunil, and Peter Meindl. *Supply Chain Management.* Upper Saddle River, NJ: Prentice Hall, 2001.

Coughlin, Anne T.; Erin Anderson; Louis W. Stern; and Adel I. El-Ansary. *Marketing Channels.* 6th ed. Upper Saddle River, NJ: Prentice Hall, 2001.

Lambert, Douglas M.; James R. Stock; and Lisa M. Ellram. *Fundamentals of Logistics Management.* Burr Ridge, IL: Irwin/McGraw-Hill, 1998.

Levy, Michael, and Burton A. Weitz. *Retailing Management.* 4th ed. Burr Ridge, IL: Irwin/McGraw-Hill, 2001.

Pelton, Lou E.; David Strutton; and James R. Lumpkin. *Marketing Channels: A Relationship Management Approach.* Burr Ridge, IL: Irwin, 1997.

Rosenbloom, Bert. *Marketing Channels: A Management View.* 6th ed. Fort Worth: Dryden Press, 1999.

Woods, John A., and Edward J. Marien. *The Supply Chain Yearbook.* New York: McGraw-Hill, 2001.

Chapter

11

Pricing Strategy

One of the most important and complex decisions a firm has to make relates to pricing its products or services. If consumers or organizational buyers perceive a price to be too high, they may purchase competitive brands or substitute products, leading to a loss of sales and profits for the firm. If the price is too low, sales might increase, but profitability may suffer. Thus, pricing decisions must be given careful consideration when a firm is introducing a new product or planning a short- or long-term price change.

This chapter discusses demand, supply, and environmental influences that affect pricing decisions and emphasizes that all three must be considered for effective pricing. However, as will be discussed in the chapter, many firms price their products without explicitly considering all of these influences.

DEMAND INFLUENCES ON PRICING DECISIONS

Demand influences on pricing decisions concern primarily the nature of the target market and expected reactions of consumers to a given price or change in price. There are three primary considerations here: demographic factors, psychological factors, and price elasticity.

Demographic Factors

In the initial selection of the target market that a firm intends to serve, a number of demographic factors are usually considered. Demographic factors that are particularly important for pricing decisions include the following:

1. Number of potential buyers, and their age, education, and gender.
2. Location of potential buyers.
3. Position of potential buyers (organizational buyers or final consumers).
4. Expected consumption rates of potential buyers.
5. Economic strength of potential buyers.

These factors help determine market potential and are useful for estimating expected sales at various price levels.

Psychological Factors

Psychological factors related to pricing concern primarily how consumers will perceive various prices or price changes. For example, marketing managers should be concerned with such questions as

1. Will potential buyers use price as an indicator of product quality?
2. Will potential buyers be favorably attracted by odd pricing?

Marketing Highlight   Effects on Profitability for Small Changes in Price

Small changes in the price received by marketers can lead to large differences in net income. For example, at Coca-Cola, a 1 percent improvement in the price received for its products would result in a net income boost of 6.4 percent; at Fuji Photo, 16.7 percent; at Nestlé, 17.5 percent; at Ford, 26 percent; and at Philips, 28.7 percent. In some companies, a 1 percent improvement in the price received would be the difference between a profit and a significant loss. Given the cost structure of large corporations, a 1 percent boost in realized price yields an average net income gain of 12 percent. In short, when setting pricing objectives and developing pricing strategies, it's worth the effort to do pricing research to see what prices consumers are willing to pay and still feel they are receiving good value.

Source: Based on Robert J. Dolan and Hermann Simon, *Power Pricing: How Managing Price Transforms the Bottom Line* (New York: Free Press, 1996), p. 4.

3. Will potential buyers perceive the price as too high relative to the service the product gives them?
4. Are potential buyers prestige oriented and therefore willing to pay higher prices to fulfill this need?
5. How much will potential buyers be willing to pay for the product?

While psychological factors have a significant effect on the success of a pricing strategy and ultimately on marketing strategy, answers to the above questions may require considerable marketing research. In fact, a review of buyers' subjective perceptions of price concluded that very little is known about how price affects buyers' perceptions of alternative purchase offers and how these perceptions affect purchase response.[1] However, some tentative generalizations about how buyers perceive price have been formulated. For example, research has found that persons who choose high-priced items usually perceive large quality variations within product categories and see the consequences of a poor choice as being undesirable. They believe that quality is related to price and see themselves as good judges of product quality. In general, the reverse is true for persons who select low-priced items in the same product categories. Thus, although information on psychological factors involved in purchasing may be difficult to obtain, marketing managers must at least consider the effects of such factors on their desired target market and marketing strategy.[2]

There are three types of psychological pricing strategies. First there is *prestige pricing*, in which a high price is charged to create a signal that the product is exceptionally fine. Prestige pricing is commonly used for some brands of cars, clothing, perfume, jewelry, cosmetics, wine and liquor, and crystal and china. Second, there is *odd pricing*, or odd-even pricing, in which prices are set a few dollars or a few cents below a round number. For example, Frito-Lay's potato chips are priced at 69 cents a bag rather than 70 cents to encourage consumers to think of them as less expensive (60 some-odd cents) rather than 70 cents. Hertz economy cars are rented for $129 rather than $130 to appear less expensive. Third, there is *bundle pricing*, in which several products are sold together at a single price to suggest a good value. For example, travel agencies offer vacation packages that include travel, accommodations, and entertainment at a single price to connote value and convenience for customers.

Price Elasticity

Both demographic and psychological factors affect price elasticity. Price elasticity is a measure of consumers' price sensitivity, which is estimated by dividing relative changes in the quantity sold by the relative changes in price:

$$e = \frac{\text{Percent change in quantity demanded}}{\text{Percent change in price}}$$

Although difficult to measure, there are two basic methods commonly used to estimate price elasticity. First, price elasticity can be estimated from historical data or from price/quantity data across different sales districts. Second, price elasticity can be estimated by sampling a group of consumers from the target market and polling them concerning various price/quantity relationships. Both of these approaches provide estimates of price elasticity; but the former approach is limited to the consideration of price changes, whereas the latter is often expensive and there is some question as to the validity of subjects' responses. However, even a crude estimate of price elasticity is a useful input to pricing decisions.[3]

SUPPLY INFLUENCES ON PRICING DECISIONS

For the purpose of this text, supply influences on pricing decisions can be discussed in terms of three basic factors. These factors relate to the objectives, costs, and nature of the product.

Pricing Objectives

Pricing objectives should be derived from overall marketing objectives, which in turn should be derived from corporate objectives. Since it is traditionally assumed that business firms operate to maximize profits in the long run, it is often thought that the basic pricing objective is solely concerned with long-run profits. However, the profit maximization norm does not provide the operating marketing manager with a single, unequivocal guideline for selecting prices. In addition, the marketing manager does not have perfect cost, revenue, and market information to be able to evaluate whether or not this objective is being reached. In practice, then, many other objectives are employed as guidelines for pricing decisions. In some cases, these objectives may be considered as operational approaches to achieve long-run profit maximization.

Research has found that the most common pricing objectives are (1) pricing to achieve a target return on investment, (2) stabilization of price and margin, (3) pricing to achieve a target market share, and (4) pricing to meet or prevent competition.

Cost Considerations in Pricing

The price of a product usually must cover costs of production, promotion, and distribution, plus a profit for the offering to be of value to the firm. In addition, when products are priced on the basis of costs plus a fair profit, there is an implicit assumption that this sum represents the economic value of the product in the marketplace.

Cost-oriented pricing is the most common approach in practice, and there are at least three basic variations: markup pricing, cost-plus pricing, and rate-of-return pricing. *Markup pricing* is commonly used in retailing, where a percentage is added to the retailer's invoice price to determine the final selling price. Closely related to markup pricing is *cost-plus pricing,* where the costs of producing a product or completing a project are totaled and a profit amount or percentage is added on. Cost-plus pricing is most often used to describe the pricing of jobs that are nonroutine and difficult to "cost" in advance, such as construction and military weapon development.

Marketing Highlight   Retail Pricing Strategies: EDLP or High/Low?

There are two common pricing strategies at the retail level: EDLP, which stands for "everyday low pricing," and high/low, which means that the retailer charges prices that are sometimes above competitors' but promotes frequent sales that lower prices below them. Four of the most successful U.S. retailers—Home Depot, Wal-Mart, Office Depot, and Toys 'R' Us—have adopted EDLP, while many fashion, grocery, and drug stores use high/low. Below is a list of the advantages of each of these pricing strategies.

ADVANTAGES OF EDLP

1. *Reduces price wars*—If consumers believe that the store's prices are low, the retailer can avoid getting into price wars with competitors.
2. *Reduces advertising*—Since prices are relatively stable using EDLP, weekly advertisements promoting sales are unnecessary.
3. *Improves customer service*—Since customer flow is more steady without sales-stimulating throngs of shoppers, in-store salespeople and clerks can spend more time with each customer.
4. *Reduces stockouts and improves inventory management*—Since large variations in demand created by sales are eliminated, necessary inventory can be kept on the shelf to avoid stockouts; inventory ordering, delivery, and handling are more efficient.
5. *Increases overall profit margins*—Even though prices are generally lower using EDLP, overall profit margins can increase since merchandise is no longer sold at large price reductions and some costs are reduced.

ADVANTAGES OF HIGH/LOW

1. *Helps segment the market*—Since different groups of customers are willing to pay different prices for products, high/low allows stores to receive higher prices from the first people to buy and still serve hard-core bargain hunters at the end of the fashion cycle.
2. *Creates excitement*—Sales can draw crowds and create an exciting buying experience for shoppers. This exciting experience may bring shoppers back for other sales.
3. *Moves merchandise*—Frequent sales enable retailers to move merchandise, even though profits are lower on sale merchandise.
4. *Emphasizes product quality and store service*—The high initial price sends a signal to customers that a product is high quality or the store provides excellent service, or both.
5. *Is easier to use*—Most retailers have a difficult time using EDLP since they must convince customers that the store's prices are relatively low on most products. High/low, on the other hand, offers customers a means of assessing how low prices are since the original and sale prices are readily available and can be compared.

Source: Based on Michael Levy and Barton A. Weitz, *Retailing Management,* 4th ed. (Burr Ridge, IL: Irwin/McGraw-Hill, 2001), pp. 457–8.

Rate-of-return or *target pricing* is commonly used by manufacturers. In this method, price is determined by adding a desired rate of return on investment to total costs. Generally, a break-even analysis is performed for expected production and sales levels and a rate of return is added on. For example, suppose a firm estimated production and sales to be 75,000 units at a total cost of $300,000. If the firm desired a before-tax return of 20 percent, the selling price would be (300,000 + 0.20 × 300,000) ÷ 75,000 = $4.80.

Cost-oriented approaches to pricing have the advantage of simplicity, and many practitioners believe that they generally yield a good price decision. However, such approaches have been criticized for two basic reasons. First, cost approaches give little or no consideration to demand factors. For example, the price determined by markup or cost-plus methods has no necessary relationship to what people will be willing to pay for the product. In the case of rate-of-return pricing, little emphasis is placed on estimating sales volume. Even if it were, rate-of-return pricing involves circular reasoning, since unit cost depends on sales volume but sales volume depends on selling price. Second, cost approaches fail to reflect competition adequately. Only in industries where all firms use this approach and have similar costs and markups can this approach yield similar prices and minimize price competition. Thus, in many industries, cost-oriented pricing could lead to severe price competition, which could eliminate smaller firms. Therefore, although costs are a highly important consideration in price decisions, numerous other factors need to be examined.

Product Considerations in Pricing

Although numerous product characteristics can affect pricing, three of the most important are (1) perishability, (2) distinctiveness, and (3) stage in the product life cycle.

Perishability

Goods that are very perishable in a physical sense must be priced to promote sales without costly delays. Foodstuffs and certain types of raw materials tend to be in this category. Products can be considered perishable in two other senses. High fashion, fad, and seasonal products are perishable not in the sense that the product deteriorates but that demand for the product is confined to a specific time period. Perishability also relates to consumption rate, which means that some products are consumed very slowly, as in the case of consumer durables. Two important pricing considerations here are that (1) such goods tend to be expensive because large amounts of service are purchased at one time; and (2) the customer has a certain amount of discretionary time available in making replacement purchase decisions.

Distinctiveness

Products can be classified in terms of how distinctive they are. Homogeneous goods are perfect substitutes for each other, as in the case of bulk wheat or whole milk, while most manufactured goods can be differentiated on the basis of certain features, such as package, trademark, engineering design, and chemical features. Thus, few consumer goods are perfectly homogeneous, and one of the primary marketing objectives of most firms is to make their products and brands distinctive in the minds of buyers. Large sums of money are often invested to accomplish this task, and one of the payoffs for such investments is the seller's ability to charge higher prices for distinctive products.

Life Cycle

The stage of the life cycle that a product is in can have important pricing implications. With regard to the life cycle, two approaches to pricing are skimming and penetration price policies. A *skimming* policy is one in which the seller charges a relatively high price

The following formulas are used to calculate break-even points in units and in dollars:

$$BEP_{(in\ units)} = \frac{FC}{(SP - VC)}$$

$$BEP_{(in\ dollars)} = \frac{FC}{1 - (VC/SP)}$$

where

   FC = Fixed cost
   VC = Variable cost
   SP = Selling price

If, as is generally the case, a firm wants to know how many units or sales dollars are necessary to generate a given amount of profit, profit (P) is simply added to fixed costs in the formulas. In addition, if the firm has estimates of expected sales and fixed and variable costs, the selling price can be solved for. (A more detailed discussion of break-even analysis is provided in the financial analysis section of this book.)

on a new product. Generally, this policy is used when the firm has a temporary monopoly and when demand for the product is price inelastic. In later stages of the life cycle, as competition moves in and other market factors change, the price may then be lowered. Digital watches and calculators are examples of this. A *penetration* policy is one in which the seller charges a relatively low price on a new product. Generally, this policy is used when the firm expects competition to move in rapidly and when demand for the product is, at least in the short run, price elastic. This policy is also used to obtain large economies of scale and as a major instrument for rapid creation of a mass market. A low price and profit margin may also discourage competition. In later stages of the life cycle, the price may have to be altered to meet changes in the market.

ENVIRONMENTAL INFLUENCES ON PRICING DECISIONS

Environmental influences on pricing include variables that are uncontrollable by the marketing manager. Two of the most important of these are competition and government regulation.

Competition

In setting or changing prices, the firm must consider its competition and how competition will react to the price of the product. Initially, consideration must be given to such factors as:

1. Number of competitors.
2. Size of competitors.
3. Location of competitors.

4. Conditions of entry into the industry.

5. Degree of vertical integration of competitors.

6. Number of products sold by competitors.

7. Cost structure of competitors.

8. Historical reaction of competitors to price changes.

These factors help determine whether the firm's selling price should be at, below, or above competition. Pricing a product at competition (i.e., the average price charged by the industry) is called *going-rate pricing* and is popular for homogeneous products, since this approach represents the collective wisdom of the industry and is not disruptive of industry harmony. An example of pricing below competition can be found in *sealed-bid pricing*, where the firm is bidding directly against competition for project contracts. Although cost and profits are initially calculated, the firm attempts to bid below competitors to obtain the job contract. A firm may price above competition because it has a superior product or because the firm is the price leader in the industry.

Government Regulations

Prices of certain goods and services are regulated by state and federal governments. Public utilities are examples of state regulation of prices. However, for most marketing managers, federal laws that make certain pricing practices illegal are of primary consideration in pricing decisions. The list below is a summary of some of the more important legal constraints on pricing. Of course, since most marketing managers are not trained as lawyers, they usually seek legal counsel when developing pricing strategies to ensure conformity to state and federal legislation.

1. Price fixing is illegal per se. Sellers must not make any agreements with competitors or distributors concerning the final price of the goods. The Sherman Antitrust Act is the primary device used to outlaw horizontal price fixing. Section 5 of the Federal Trade Commission Act has been used to outlaw price fixing as an unfair business practice.

2. Deceptive pricing practices are outlawed under Section 5 of the Federal Trade Commission Act. An example of deceptive pricing would be to mark merchandise with an exceptionally high price and then claim that the lower selling price actually used represents a legitimate price reduction.

3. Price discrimination that lessens competition or is deemed injurious to it is outlawed by the Robinson-Patman Act (which amends Section 2 of the Clayton Act). Price discrimination is not illegal per se, but sellers cannot charge competing buyers different prices for essentially the same products if the effect of such sales is injurious to competition. Price differentials can be legally justified on certain grounds, especially if the price differences reflect cost differences. This is particularly true of quantity discounts.

4. Promotional pricing, such as cooperative advertising, and price deals are not illegal per se; but if a seller grants advertising allowances, merchandising service, free goods, or special promotional discounts to customers, it must do so on proportionately equal terms. Sections 2(d) and 2(e) of the Robinson-Patman Act are designed to regulate such practices so that price reductions cannot be granted to some customers under the guise of promotional allowances.[4]

A GENERAL PRICING MODEL

It should be clear that effective pricing decisions involve considerations of many factors, and different industries may have different pricing practices. Although no sin-

FIGURE 11–1
A General Pricing Model

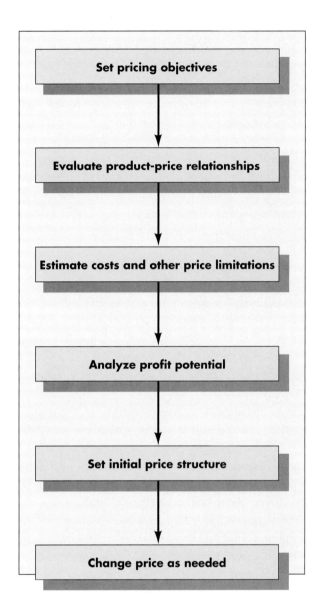

gle model will fit all pricing decisions, Figure 11–1 presents a general model for developing prices for products and services.[5] While all pricing decisions cannot be made strictly on the basis of this model, it does break pricing strategy into a set of manageable stages that are integrated into the overall marketing strategy.

Set Pricing Objectives

Given a product or service designed for a specific target market, the pricing process begins with a clear statement of the pricing objectives. These objectives guide the pricing strategy and should be designed to support the overall marketing strategy. Because pricing strategy has a direct bearing on demand for a product and the profit obtained, efforts to set prices must be coordinated with other functional areas. For example, production will have to be able to meet demand at a given price, and finance will have to manage funds flowing in and out of the organization at predicted levels of production.

Marketing Highlight   Eight Tips for Improving a Company's Pricing Strategy

1. *Base pricing strategies on sound research.* Although a recent study found that few companies do serious pricing research, it is a must for sound pricing strategies. Research is needed to understand the factors that influence supply and demand.

2. *Continuously monitor pricing decisions.* Pricing should be treated as a process of developing prices and changing them as needed rather than an annual budgeting exercise. Price decisions define an organization's value image in the eyes of customers and competitors.

3. *Recognize that buyers may have difficulty in computing price differences.* Buyers do not constantly monitor the prices of many products and will not necessarily quickly recognize the value in a price deal.

4. *Recognize that customers evaluate prices comparatively.* Behavioral pricing research suggests that customers compare prices and price deals relative to internal or external reference prices rather than just evaluating them in an absolute sense. An internal reference price is the price a customer has in mind for a product and an external reference price is one the customer has seen in advertising, a catalog, or on a store sign or price tag.

5. *Recognize that buyers typically have a range of acceptable prices.* Buyers often have an upper and lower threshold or range of acceptable prices rather than only one acceptable price they are willing to pay.

6. *Understand the importance of relative price to buyers.* The relative price of a product compared to competitive offerings or to what a buyer previously paid for it may be more important than the absolute price asked.

7. *Understand the importance of price information.* Price information can affect preferences and choices for different models in a product line or for competitive offerings, particularly when buyers cannot easily evaluate product quality.

8. *Recognize that price elasticities vary.* Price elasticities vary according to the direction of a price change, and buyers are generally more sensitive to price increases than to price decreases. Thus, it is easier to lose sales to current customers by increasing prices than it is to gain sales from new buyers by reducing them.

Source: Based on Kent B. Monroe and Jennifer L. Cox, "Pricing Practices That Endanger Profits," *Marketing Management,* September/October 2001, pp. 42–46.

Evaluate Product-Price Relationships

As noted, the distinctiveness, perishability, and stage of the life cycle a product is in all affect pricing. In addition, marketers need to consider what value the product has for customers and how price will influence product positioning. There are three basic value positions. First, a product could be priced relatively high for a product class because it offers value in the form of high quality, special features, or prestige. Second, a product could be priced at about average for the product class because it offers value in the form of good quality for a reasonable price. Third, a product could be priced relatively low for a product class because it offers value in the form of acceptable quality at a low price. A Porsche or Nike Air Jordans are examples of the first type of value; a Honda Accord or Keds tennis shoes are examples of the second; and Hyundai cars and private label canvas shoes are examples of the third. Setting prices so that targeted customers will perceive products to offer greater value than competitive offerings is called *value pricing*.

In addition, research is needed to estimate how much of a particular product the target market will purchase at various price levels—price elasticity. This estimate provides valuable information about what the target market thinks about the product and what it is worth to them.

Estimate Costs and Other Price Limitations

The costs to produce and market products provide a lower bound for pricing decisions and a baseline from which to compute profit potential. If a product cannot be produced and marketed at a price to cover its costs and provide reasonable profits in the long run, then it should not be produced in its designed form. One possibility is to redesign the product so that its costs are lower. In fact, some companies first determine the price customers are willing to pay for a product and then design it so that it can be produced and marketed at a cost that allows targeted profits.

Other price limitations that need to be considered are government regulations and the prices that are charged by competitors for similar and substitute products. Also, likely competitive reactions that could influence the price of a new product or a price change in an existing one need to be considered.

Analyze Profit Potential

Analysis in the preceding stages should result in a range of prices that could be charged. Marketers must then estimate the likely profit in pricing at levels in this range. At this stage, it is important to recognize that it may be necessary to offer channel members quantity discounts, promotional allowances, and slotting allowances to encourage them to actively market the product. *Quantity discounts* are discounts for purchasing a large number of units. *Promotional allowances* are often in the form of price reductions in exchange for the channel member performing various promotional activities, such as featuring the product in store advertising or on in-store displays. *Slotting allowances* are payments to retailers to get them to stock items on their shelves. All of these can increase sales but also add marketing cost to the manufacturer and affect profits.

Set Initial Price Structure

Since all of the supply, demand, and environmental factors have been considered, a marketer can now set the initial price structure. The price structure takes into account the price to various channel members, such as wholesalers and retailers, as well as the recommended price to final consumers or organizational buyers.

Change Price as Needed

There are many reasons why an initial price structure may need to be changed. Channel members may bargain for greater margins, competitors may lower their prices, or costs may increase with inflation. In the short term, discounts and allowances may have to be larger or more frequent than planned to get greater marketing effort to increase demand to profitable levels. In the long term, price structures tend to increase for most products as production and marketing costs increase.

CONCLUSION

Pricing decisions that integrate the firm's costs with marketing strategy, business conditions, competition, demand, product variables, channels of distribution, and general resources can determine the success or failure of a business. This places a very heavy burden on the price maker. Modern-day marketing managers cannot ignore the complexity or the importance of price management. Pricing strategies must be continually reviewed and must take into account that the firm is a dynamic entity operating in a very competitive environment. There are many ways for money to flow out of a firm in the form of costs, but often there is only one way to bring in revenues and that is by the price-product mechanism.

Additional Readings

Dolan, Robert J., and Hermann Simon. *Power Pricing.* New York: Free Press, 1996.
Monroe, Kent B. *Pricing: Making Profitable Decisions.* 2d ed. New York: McGraw-Hill, 1990.
Nagle, Thomas T., and Reed K. Holden. *The Strategy and Tactics of Pricing.* 2d ed. Englewood Cliffs, NJ: Prentice Hall, 1995.
Simon, Hermann, and Robert J. Dolan. "Price Customization." *Marketing Management,* Fall 1998, pp. 11–17.

Marketing in Special Fields

Part D

12 The Marketing of Services

13 Global Marketing

Section I Essentials of Marketing Management

The Marketing of Services

Over the course of the past 25 years, the fastest growing segment of the American economy has not been the production of tangibles but the performance of services. Spending on services has increased to such an extent that today it captures more than 50 cents of the consumer's dollar. In addition, the service sector in the United States produces a balance-of-trade surplus and is expected to be responsible for all net job growth through the year 2005.[1] And the dominance of the service sector is not limited to the United States. The service sector accounts for more than half the GNP and employs more than half the labor force in most Latin American and Caribbean countries. Over the course of the next decade, the service sector will spawn whole new legions of doctors, nurses, medical technologists, physical therapists, home health aids, and social workers to administer to the needs of an aging population, along with armies of food servers, child care providers, and cleaning people to cater to the wants of two-income families. Also rising to the forefront will be a swelling class of technical workers, including computer engineers, systems analysts, and paralegals.

Many marketing textbooks still devote little attention to program development for the marketing of services, especially those in the rapidly changing areas of health care, finance, and travel. This omission is usually based on the assumption that the marketing of products and services is basically the same, and, therefore, the techniques discussed under products apply as well to the marketing of services. Basically, this assumption is true. Whether selling goods or services, the marketer must be concerned with developing a marketing strategy centered on the four controllable decision variables that comprise the marketing mix: the product (or service), the price, the distribution system, and promotion. In addition, the use of marketing research is as valuable to service marketers as it is to product marketers. However, because services possess certain distinguishing characteristics, the task of determining the marketing mix ingredients for a service marketing strategy may raise different and more difficult problems than those encountered in marketing products.

The purpose of this chapter is fourfold. First, the reader will become acquainted with the special characteristics of services and their strategy implications. Second, key concepts associated with providing quality services will be discussed. Third, obstacles will be described that in the past impeded and still continue to impede development of services marketing. Finally, current trends and strategies of innovation in services marketing will be explored. Using this approach, the material in the other chapters of the book can be integrated to give a better understanding of the marketing of services.

Before proceeding, some attention must be given to what we refer to when using the term *services*. Probably the most frustrating aspect of the available literature on services is that the definition of what constitutes a service remains unclear. The fact is that no common definition and boundaries have been developed to delimit the field of services. The American Marketing Association has defined services as follows:[2]

1. *Service products,* such as a bank loan or home security, that are intangible, or at least substantially so. If totally intangible, they are exchanged directly from producer to user, cannot be transported or stored, and are almost instantly perishable. Service products are often difficult to identify, since they come into existence at the same time they are bought and consumed. They are composed of intangible elements that are inseparable; they usually involve customer participation in some important way, cannot be sold in the sense of ownership transfer, and have no title. Today, however, most products are partly tangible and partly intangible, and the dominant form is used to classify them as either goods or services (all are products). These common, hybrid forms, whatever they are called, may or may not have the attributes just given for totally intangible services.

2. *Services,* as a term, is also used to describe activities performed by sellers and others that accompany the sale of a product and that aid in its exchange or its utilization (e.g., shoe fitting, financing, an 800 number). Such services are either presale or postsale and supplement the product but do not comprise it.

The first definition includes what can be considered almost pure services such as insurance, banking, entertainment, airlines, health care, telecommunications, and hotels; the second definition includes such services as wrapping, financing an automobile, providing warranties on computer equipment, and the like, because these services exist in connection with the sale of a product or another service. This suggests that marketers of goods are also marketers of services. For example, one could argue that McDonald's is not in the hamburger business. Its hamburgers are actually not very different from those of the competition. McDonald's is in the service business.

More and more manufacturers are also exploiting their service capabilities as stand-alone revenue producers. For example, General Motors, Ford, and Chrysler all offer financing services. Ford and General Motors have extended their financial services offerings to include a MasterCard, which offers discounts on purchases of their automobiles.

The reader can imagine from his or her own experience that some purchases are very tangible (a coffeemaker) while others are very much intangible (a course in marketing). Others have elements of both (lunch on a flight from New York to Chicago). In other words, in reality there is a goods-service continuum, with many purchases including both tangible goods and intangible services. Figure 12–1 illustrates such a continuum. On the goods side of the continuum, the buyer owns an object after the purchase. On the services side of the continuum, when the transaction is over, the buyer leaves with an experience and a feeling. When the course in marketing is over or the flight from New York to Chicago is completed, the student or passenger leaves with a feeling.

The examples of services on the right side of Figure 12–1 are mostly or entirely intangible. They do not exist in the physical realm. They cannot appeal to the five senses.

IMPORTANT CHARACTERISTICS OF SERVICES

Services possess several unique characteristics that often have a significant impact on marketing program development. These special features of services may cause unique problems and often result in marketing mix decisions that are substantially different from those found in connection with the marketing of goods. Some of the more im-

FIGURE 12–1
The Goods-Service
Continuum

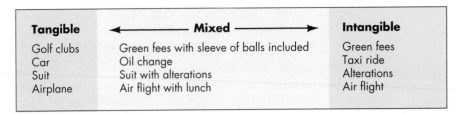

Source: Adapted from G. A. Churchill, Jr. and J. Paul Peter, *Marketing: Creating Value for Customers* (Burr Ridge, IL: Irwin: McGraw-Hill, 1998), p. 290.

portant of these characteristics are intangibility, inseparability, perishability and fluctuating demand, highly differentiated marketing systems, and a client relationship.

Intangibility

The obvious basic difference between goods and services is the intangibility of services, and many of the problems encountered in the marketing of services are due to intangibility. To illustrate, how does an airline make tangible a trip from Philadelphia to San Francisco? These problems are unique to service marketing.

The fact that many services cannot appeal to a buyer's sense of touch, taste, smell, sight, or hearing before purchase places a burden on the marketing organization. For example, hotels that promise a good night's sleep to their customers cannot actually show this service in a tangible way. Obviously, this burden is most heavily felt in a firm's promotional program, but, as will be discussed later, it may affect other areas. Depending on the type of service, the intangibility factor may dictate use of direct channels because of the need for personal contact between the buyer and seller. Since a service firm is actually selling an idea or experience, not a product, it must tell the buyer what the service will do because it is often difficult to illustrate, demonstrate, or display the service in use. For example, the hotel must somehow describe to the consumer how a stay at the hotel will leave the customer feeling well rested and ready to begin a new day.

The above discussion alludes to two strategy elements firms should employ when trying to overcome the problems associated with service intangibility. First, tangible aspects associated with the service should be stressed. For example, advertisements for airlines should emphasize (through text and visuals) the newness of the aircraft, the roominess of the cabin, and the friendliness of the flight attendants. Second, end benefits resulting from completion of the service encounter should be accentuated. In the case of air travel, an individual's ability to make an important meeting or arrive home in time for a special occasion could be the derived benefit.

Inseparability

In many cases, a service cannot be separated from the person of the seller. In other words, the service must often be produced and marketed simultaneously. Because of the simultaneous production and marketing of most services, the main concern of the marketer is usually the creation of time and place utility. For example, the bank teller produces the service of receiving a deposit and markets other appropriate bank services at the same time. Many services, therefore, are tailored and not mass produced. Often, because a company's employees are "the company" at the point of contact, they must be given wide latitude and assistance in determining how best to tailor a specific service to meet customer needs.

The implication of inseparability on issues dealing with the selection of channels of distribution and service quality is quite important. Inseparable services cannot be inventoried, and thus direct sale is the only feasible channel of distribution. Service

Marketing Highlight   Ten of the Most Critical Differences between Products and Services

PRODUCTS

1. The customer owns an object.
2. The goal of producing a product is uniformity—all widgets are alike.
3. A product can be put into inventory; a sample can be sent in advance for the customer to review.
4. The customer is an end user who is not involved in the production process.
5. One conducts quality control by comparing output to specifications.
6. If improperly produced, the product can be pulled off the line or recalled.
7. The morale of production employees is important.
8. Customer can determine level of quality by comparing product to other products.
9. There is a low level of collaboration between the buyer and the seller.
10. Greater number and variety of product brands are available to customer.

SERVICES

1. The customer owns a memory. The experience cannot be sold or passed on to a third party.
2. The goal of service is uniqueness; each customer and each contact is special.
3. A service happens at the moment. It cannot be stockpiled or saved to be used at a later date.
4. The customer is a coproducer who is a partner in creating the service.
5. Customer conducts quality control by comparing expectations to experience.
6. If improperly performed, apologies and reparations are the only means of recourse.
7. The morale of service employees is critical.
8. Customer can determine level of quality throughout the delivery of the service.
9. There is a high level of collaboration between the buyer and the seller.
10. Fewer brands of services are available to customer.

Sources: Ron Zemke, "The Emerging Art of Service Management," *Training*, January 1992, pp. 36–42; and Ralph W. Jackson, Lester A. Neidell, and Dale A. Lunsford, "An Empirical Investigation of the Differences in Goods and Services as Perceived by Organizational Buyers," *Industrial Marketing Management* 24 (1995), pp. 99–108.

quality is sometimes unable to be completely standardized due to the inability to completely mechanize the service encounter. However, some industries, through innovative uses of technology, have been able to overcome or, at least, alleviate challenges associated with the inseparability characteristic.

For example, in the financial services industry, automated teller machines (ATMs) and home banking, through use of computers and telephones, have contributed greatly to eliminating the need for the customer to directly interact with a bank teller. Further, many banks are developing computer applications to allow tellers and other service representatives to think like expert problem solvers. These applications allow for platform banking, a means of enabling bank representatives in any location to bring up on a screen all the information the bank has about the customer. Every face-to-face contact with a customer can mean an opportunity to make a sale and, more important, further the relationship with the customer. Of course, the bank representative is still of critical importance as the one who might recognize by the customer's expression or words that this visit is not the appropriate time to be marketing additional services.

In addition to technology, tangible representations of the service can serve to overcome the inseparability problem. For example, in the insurance industry, a contract serves as the tangible representation of the service. The service itself remains inseparable from the seller (insurance provider), but the buyer has a tangible representation of the service in the form of a policy. This enables the use of intermediaries (agents) in the marketing of insurance. Another example would be in the use of a credit card—the card itself is a tangible representation of the service that is being produced and consumed each time the card is being used.

Perishability and Fluctuating Demand

Services are perishable and markets for most services fluctuate either by season (tourism), days (airlines), or time of day (movie theaters). Unused telephone capacity and electrical power; vacant seats on planes, trains, buses, and in stadiums; and time spent by catalog service representatives waiting for customers to reach them all represent business that is lost forever.

The combination of perishability and fluctuating demand has created many problems for marketers of services. Specifically, in the areas of staffing and distribution, avenues must be found to have the services available for peak periods, and new strategies need to be developed to make use of the service during slack periods. Some organizations are attempting to cope with these problems through the use of pricing strategy. *Off-peak pricing* consists of charging different prices during different times or days in order to stimulate demand during slow periods. Discounts given for weekend calling, Saturday night stay-overs, early-bird dinners, or winter cruises are all examples of efforts made by service providers to redistribute demand.

Other organizations are dealing with issues related to peak period demand through the use of technology. To illustrate, a well-designed voice mail system allows companies and callers to cut down on missed phone calls, eliminates long waits on hold, and delivers clear, consistent messages. In the catalog industry, automated call routing (ACR) is used to route incoming calls to available service representatives in the order in which they were received. Finally, in the utilities industry, many electric utilities no longer have to generate capacity that will meet peak electrical demand. Instead, they rely on buying unused power from other utilities in other regions of the country.

Highly Differentiated Marketing Systems

Although the marketer of a tangible product is not compelled to use an established marketing system, such systems are often available and may be the most efficient. If an established system is not available, the marketer can at least obtain guidelines from the systems used for similar products. In the case of services, however, there may be little similarity between the marketing systems needed and those used for other services. To illustrate, the marketing of banking and other financial services bears little resemblance to the marketing of computer services or telecommunications. The entire area of services marketing, therefore, demands creativity and ingenuity on the part of marketing management. For example, trucking companies are now making arrangements with railways to combine forces on some routes. This form of intermodal transportation allows the trucking companies' customers to take advantage of the cheaper fuel and labor associated with rail transport, coupled with the faster, more reliable service offered by trucks. Likewise, the U.S. Postal Service, due to the heavy volume of mail processed, knows that some of its staff is at work every day of the week. As a result, they instituted Sunday delivery on Express Mail packages to gain an advantage over Federal Express and other private carriers that shut down on Sundays. Conversely, Federal Express, as a result of its efficient delivery processes, is able to now provide same day delivery of packages on Mondays through Fridays.

Marketing Highlight   Expectations of Service Customers in Selected Industries

Type of Service	Type of Customer	Principal Expectations
Automobile repair	Consumers	*Be competent.* Fix it right the first time. *Explain things.* Explain why the customer needs the suggested repairs—provide an itemized list. *Be respectful.* "Don't treat me like an idiot."
Automobile insurance	Consumers	*Keep me informed.* "I shouldn't have to learn about insurance law changes from the newspaper." *Be on my side.* "I don't want them to treat me like I am a criminal just because I have a claim." *Play fair.* "Don't drop me when something goes wrong." *Protect me from catastrophe.* "Make sure my estate is covered in the event of a major accident." *Provide prompt service.* "I want fast settlement of my claims."
Hotel	Consumers	*Provide a clean room.* "Don't have a deep-pile carpet that can't be completely cleaned . . . You can literally see germs down there." *Provide a secure room.* Good bolts and a peephole on the door. *Treat me like a guest.* "It is almost like they're looking you over to decide whether or not they're going to let you have a room." *Keep your promise.* "They said the room would be ready at the promised time, but it wasn't."
Property and casualty insurance	Business customers	*Fulfill obligations.* Pay up. *Learn my business and work with me.* "I expect them to know me and my company." *Protect me from catastrophe.* Cover risk exposure so there is no single big loss. *Provide prompt service.* Fast claim service.
Equipment repair	Business customers	*Share my sense of urgency.* Speed of response. "One time I had to buy a second piece of equipment because of the huge downtime with the first piece." *Be prepared.* Have all the parts ready.
Truck and tractor rental/leasing	Business customers	*Keep the equipment running.* Have equipment working all the time—that is the key. *Be flexible.* "The leasing company should have the leasing flexibility to rent us equipment when we need it." *Provide full service.* Get rid of all the paperwork and headaches.

Source: A. Parasuraman, Leonard L. Berry, and Valarie A. Zeithaml, "Understanding Customer Expectations of Service," *Sloan Management Review,* Spring 1991, pp. 39–48.

Client Relationship

In the marketing of a great many services, a client relationship, as opposed to a customer relationship, exists between the buyer and the seller. In other words, the buyer views the seller as someone who has knowledge that is of value. Examples of this type of relationship are the physician-patient, college professor–student, accountant–small business owner, and broker-investor. The buyer, many times, abides by the advice offered or suggestions provided by the seller, and these relationships may be of an ongoing nature. Also, since many service firms are client-serving organizations, they may approach the marketing function in a more professional manner, as seen in health care, finance, and legal, governmental, and educational services.

There appear to be at least two marketing challenges that professionals face. First, in many cases, fear or hostility is brought to the transaction because the customer is uncertain about how genuine the professional's concern for his or her satisfaction is. For example, many unpleasant reasons exist for consulting doctors, lawyers, bankers, or even visiting a college professor. These could include having surgery, being sued, having to take out a loan, or doing poorly on an exam. Second, even high-quality service delivery by the professional can lead to dissatisfied customers. For a physician, the ability to provide high-quality medical care may be overshadowed by a brusque, unfriendly personality. For a college professor, the demand on students to only contact or visit him or her during office hours, coupled with students' own hectic work schedules, can diminish the impact of the professor's classroom presentations. It is vitally important that the professional service provider strive to build long-term positive relationships with clients. Marketing Highlight 12–3 illustrates the use of unconditional guarantees, which are one way to help build such a relationship.

PROVIDING QUALITY SERVICES

In today's increasingly competitive environment, quality service is critical to organizational success. Unlike products where quality is often measured against standards, service quality is measured against performance.[3] Since services are frequently produced in the presence of a customer, are labor intensive, and are not able to be stored or objectively examined, the definition of what constitutes good service quality can be difficult and, in fact, continually changes in the face of choices.[4] Customers determine the value of service quality in relation to available alternatives and their particular needs. In general, problems in the determination of good service quality are attributable to differences in the expectations, perceptions, and experiences regarding the encounter between the service provider and consumer. These gaps can be classified as

1. The gap between consumer expectations and management perceptions of consumer expectations.
2. The gap between management perceptions of consumer expectations and the firm's service quality specifications.
3. The gap between service quality specifications and actual service quality.
4. The gap between actual service delivery and external communications about the service.

In essence, the customer perceives the level of service quality as being a function of the magnitude and direction of the gap between expected service and perceived

1. *Prices are high.* Fees for management consulting, legal, advertising, and many other types of professional services often run into six figures. By offering compensation for a service failure, the guarantee reduces perceived risk and creates value for clients.

2. *The negative consequences of unsolved problems are high.* Bad service from a restaurant can ruin someone's evening; bad service from a medical center or law firm can ruin someone's life. The greater the client's expected aggravation, expense, and time lost, the greater the guarantee's power.

3. *Services are highly customized.* The professional service firm's past performance with other buyers typically does not provide a reliable indication of how the firm will do with a new product, since different customers are often served in entirely different ways. A guarantee can provide a strong indication of a firm's reliability.

4. *Brand name recognition isn't easily achieved through conventional means.* Marketing opportunities and differentiating characteristics tend to be restricted for professional service firms. An unconditional guarantee can provide such a differentiator, making the firm stand out in potential clients' minds.

5. *Buyer resistance is high.* Clients tend to purchase professional services very cautiously, which sends the firm on long and often fruitless sales efforts. An unconditional guarantee can effectively overcome resistance and close the sale.

Source: Christopher W. L. Hart, Leonard A. Schlessinger, and Dan Maher, "Guarantees Come to Professional Service Firms," *Sloan Management Review*, Spring 1992, pp. 19–29.

service. Management of a company may not even realize that they are delivering poor-quality service due to differences in the way managers and consumers view acceptable quality levels. To overcome this problem and to avoid losing customers, firms must be aware of the determinants of service quality. A brief description of these determinants follows.

1. *Tangibles* include the physical evidence of the service. For example, employees are always visible in a hotel lobby dusting, emptying ash trays, or otherwise cleaning up. Likewise, clean, shiny, up-to-date medical equipment or aircraft are examples of tangible elements.

2. *Reliability* involves the consistency and dependability of the service performance. For example, does a bank or phone company always send out accurate customer statements? Likewise, does the plumber always fix the problem on his or her first visit?

3. *Responsiveness* concerns the willingness or readiness of employees or professionals to provide service. For example, will a physician see patients on the same day they call in to say they are ill? Will a college professor return a student's call the same day?

4. *Assurance* refers to the knowledge and competence of service providers and the ability to convey trust and confidence. This determinant encompasses the provider's name and reputation; possession of necessary skills; and trustworthiness, believability, and honesty. For example, a bank will guarantee same-day loan processing; a doctor is highly trained in a particular specialty.

5. *Empathy* refers to the service provider's efforts to understand the customer's needs and then to provide, as best as possible, individualized service delivery. For example, flight attendants on a customer's regular route learn what type of beverages the customer drinks and what magazines the customer reads.

Each of the determinants on the previous page plays an important role in how the customer views the service quality of a firm. Turning service quality into a powerful competitive weapon requires continuously striving for service superiority—consistently performing above the adequate service level and capitalizing on opportunities for exceeding the desired service level. Relentless efforts to continually improve service performance may well be rewarded by improvements in customer attitudes toward the firm: from customer frustration to customer preference to customer loyalty. What should be obvious is that to be successful, a service firm must have both an effective means to measure customer satisfaction and dedicated employees to provide high-quality service.

Customer Satisfaction Measurement

As mentioned above, satisfied customers can become loyal customers. Service quality and customer satisfaction are of growing concern to business organizations throughout the world, and research on these topics generally focuses on two key issues: (1) understanding the expectations and requirements of the customer; and (2) determining how well a company and its major competitors are succeeding in satisfying these expectations and requirements.[5]

As such, an organization's approach to measuring service quality through customer satisfaction measurement (CSM) and effectively implementing programs derived from results of such studies can spell the difference between success and failure. Research on market leaders' CSMs found they had the following aspects in common:

1. Marketing and sales employees were primarily responsible (with customer input) for designing CSM programs and questionnaires.
2. Top management and the marketing function championed the programs.
3. Measurement involved a combination of qualitative and quantitative research methods that primarily included mail questionnaires, telephone surveys, and focus groups.
4. Evaluations included both the company's and competitors' satisfaction performance.
5. Results of all research were made available to employees, but not necessarily to customers.
6. Research was performed on a continual basis.
7. Customer satisfaction was incorporated into the strategic focus of the company via the mission statement.
8. There was a commitment to increasing service quality and customer satisfaction from employees at all levels within the organization.

The Importance of Internal Marketing

Properly performed customer satisfaction research can yield a wealth of strategic information about customers, the sponsoring company, and competitors. However, service quality goes beyond the relationship between a customer and company. Rather, as shown by the last aspect listed, it is the personal relationship between a customer and the particular employee that the customer happens to be dealing with at the time of the service encounter that ultimately determines service quality. The importance of having customer-oriented, frontline people cannot be overstated.[6] If frontline service personnel are unfriendly, unhelpful, uncooperative, or uninterested in the customer, the customer will tend to project that same attitude to the company as a whole. The character and personality of an organization reflects the character and personality of its top management. Management must develop programs that will stimulate employee commitment to customer service. To be successful, these programs must contain five critical components:

1. *A careful selection process in hiring frontline employees.* To do this, management has to clearly define the skills the service person must bring to the job.[7] For example, Fairfield Inn often considers as many as 25 candidates for each housekeeping or front-desk position.[8]

2. *A clear, concrete message* that conveys a particular service strategy that frontline people can begin to act on. People delivering service need to know how their work fits in the broader scheme of business operations.[9] They need to have a cause because servicing others is just too demanding and frustrating to be done well each day without one.[10]

3. *Significant modeling by managers,* that is, managers demonstrating the behavior that they intend to reward employees for performing. For example, some airline executives regularly travel economy class to talk to customers and solicit ideas for improvement.[11]

4. *An energetic follow-through process,* in which managers provide the training, support, and incentives necessary to give the employees the capability and willingness to provide quality service. For example, AT&T Universal Card Services has set up an umbrella organization, aptly called Universal Card University, to give all of its employees a single point of reference in their training.[12]

5. *An emphasis on teaching employees to have good attitudes.* This type of training usually focuses on specific social techniques, such as eye contact, smiling, tone of voice, and standards of dress.

However, organizing and implementing such programs will only lead to temporary results unless managers practice a strategy of internal marketing. We define *internal marketing* as the continual process by which managers actively encourage, stimulate, and support employee commitment to the company, the company's goods and services, and the company's customers. Emphasis should be placed on the word *continual*. Managers who consistently pitch in to help when needed, constantly provide encouragement and words of praise to employees, strive to help employees understand the benefits of performing their jobs well, and emphasize the importance of employee actions on both company and employee results are practitioners of internal marketing. In service marketing, successful internal marketing efforts, leading to employee commitment to service quality, are a key to success.

Federal Express serves as a prime example of the benefits accruing to a company that successfully practices internal marketing.[13] Federal Express is the first service organization to win the Malcolm Baldrige National Quality Award. The company's motto is "people, service, and profits." Behind its purple, white, and orange planes and uniforms are self-managing work teams, gainsharing plans, and empowered employees seemingly consumed with providing flexible and creative services to customers with varying needs. Federal Express is a high-involvement, horizontally coordinated organization that encourages employees to use their judgment above and beyond the rulebook.

OVERCOMING THE OBSTACLES IN SERVICE MARKETING

The factors of intangibility and inseparability, as well as difficulties in coming up with objective definitions of acceptable service quality, make comprehension of service marketing difficult. However, in view of the size and importance of services in our economy, considerable innovation and ingenuity are needed to make high-quality services available at convenient locations for consumers as well as businesspeople. In fact, the area of service marketing probably offers more opportunities for imagination and creative innovation than does goods marketing. Unfortunately, many service firms still lag in the area of creative marketing. Even today, those service firms that have done a relatively good job have been slow in recognizing opportunities in all aspects of their marketing programs. Four reasons, connected to past practices, can be given for the lack of innovative marketing on the part of service marketers: (1) a limited view of marketing, (2) a lack of strong competition, (3) a lack of creative management, and (4) no obsolescence.

Limited View of Marketing

Because of the nature of their service, many firms depended to a great degree on population growth to expand sales. A popular example here is the telephone company, which did not establish a marketing department until 1955. It was then that the company realized it had to be concerned not only with population growth but also with meeting the needs of a growing population. Increases in educational levels and the standard of living also bring about the need for new and diversified services.

Service firms must meet these changing needs by developing new services and new channels and altering existing channels to meet the changing composition and needs of the population. For many service industries, growth has come as a result of finding new channels of distribution. For example, some banks and other financial service companies were able to grow and tap into new markets by establishing limited-service kiosks in malls and supermarkets. Airlines have successfully brought in a whole new class of travelers by offering advance-purchase discounted fares. Traditionally, users of these fares either drove or used other means of transportation in order to reach their destination.

While many service firms have succeeded in adopting a marketing perspective, others have been slow to respond. It was not until deregulation of the telecommunications industry took place in 1984 that the telephone companies began taking a broadened view of marketing. Even today, critics point to the obsession with inventing new technology versus using current technology in meeting customer needs as a weakness of these companies.

Limited Competition

A second major cause of the lack of innovative marketing in many service industries was the lack of competition. Many service industries like banking, railroads, and public utilities have, throughout most of their histories, faced very little competition; some have even been regulated monopolies. Obviously, in an environment characterized by little competition, there was not likely to be a great deal of innovative marketing. However, two major forces have changed this situation. First, in the past two decades the banking, financial services, railroad, cable, airline, telecommunications industries, and utilities have all been deregulated in varying degrees. With deregulation has come a need to be able to compete effectively. For example, AT&T was once the sole provider of long-distance telephone service. Now, AT&T has to compete not only against such companies as MCI and Sprint but also against the regional Bell operating companies such as

On the Internet, you cannot have a more convenient location than your competition. Everyone is just a click away. It is critical that it is easy to do business with your company in order to attract and retain customers. Following are some ways to improve e-service.

1. A customer should be able to buy something in seven clicks or less beginning from the home page. Many experts believe the ideal should be four clicks.
2. Shorten the time it takes for images to load. Research shows that eight seconds is the longest people will wait before they move on to another site.
3. From a product section of your site, customers should be able to get from your home page to a product page in that section in one click.
4. Shopping should be easy. Searching, browsing, checking out, returning items, and getting assistance from a live person must be easy.
5. Customers should have the choice to register their personal information (e.g., address and credit card information) or to enter this informaiton each time they purchase.
6. A customer should be able to check out in no more than three steps.
7. Delivery should be on time.

Source: Ron Zemke, *E-Service: 24 Ways to Keep Your Customers—When the Competition Is Just a Click Away* (New York: Amacon, 2001).

Ameritech and US West, which once were part of AT&T. Second, service marketing has taken on an international focus. Today, many foreign companies are competing in domestic service markets. Foreign interests own several banks, many hotels (including Holiday Inn), and shares in major airlines (including Northwest and US Airways). Likewise, American companies are expanding overseas as markets open up. For example, Merrill Lynch & Co. purchased Smith New Court PLC, a large British security firm, to become the world's largest brokerage firm.

Noncreative Management

For many years, the managements of service industries have been criticized for not being progressive and creative. Railroad management was criticized for many years for being slow to innovate. More recently, however, railroads have become leading innovators in the field of freight transportation, introducing such innovations as piggyback service and containerization, and in passenger service, introducing luxury overnight accommodations on trains with exotic names such as the Zephyr. Some other service industries, however, have been slow to develop new services or to innovate in the marketing of their existing services. In fact, as a whole, U.S. firms lag behind their Japanese and German competitors not only in collecting customer satisfaction data but also in designing services that address customers' needs.[14]

No Obsolescence

A great advantage for many service industries is the fact that many services, because of their intangibility, are less subject to obsolescence than goods. While this is an obvious advantage, it has also led some service firms to be sluggish in their approach to marketing. Manufacturers of goods may constantly change their marketing plans and seek new and more efficient ways to produce and distribute their products. Since service firms are often not faced with obsolescence, they often failed to recognize the need for change. This failure has led to wholesale changes in many industries as new operators, who possessed marketing skills, revolutionized the manner in which the service is performed and provided. Many a barbershop and hair dresser have gone out of business due to an inability to compete against hairstyling salons. Many accountants have lost clients to tax preparation services, such as H&R Block, that specialize in doing one task well and have used technology, including computerized filing services, to their advantage. Likewise, the old, big movie house has become a relic of the past as entrepreneurs realized the advantages to be gained from building and operating theater complexes that contain several minitheaters in or near suburban malls.

THE SERVICE CHALLENGE

Despite traditional thinking and practices on the part of many marketing managers and writers concerning the similarities between the operation of manufacturing and services organizations, the past decade has seen the growth of many innovative ways of meeting the service challenge. The service challenge is the quest to (1) constantly develop new services that will better meet customer needs, (2) improve on the quality and variety of existing services, and (3) provide and distribute these services in a manner that best serves the customer. This next section illustrates the challenges facing companies in various service industries and examples of marketing strategies employed by them to meet the service challenge.

Banking

"Banking is vital to a healthy economy. Banks are not." This is the message that a banking expert delivered to a group of his peers.[15] Needless to say, the days when banking was considered a dead-end career, but one that offered stable employment for marketers, are long gone. Perhaps banking best exemplifies the changes that are taking place as service organizations strive to become practitioners of the "marketing concept." Buy or be bought is the new watchword in the banking industry, which is experiencing the biggest wave of consolidation in its history.

Banking is becoming an increasingly technology-driven business. The main reason is that more and more financial services, from loans to credit cards, are being marketed through computers and telephones instead of through branches. Banks large enough to afford big technology investments can reach customers nationwide even though their physical franchise may be limited. For example, most consumers possess credit cards from banks they have never physically visited. Further, the advent of new electronic delivery systems (via computer) for consumer and small-business banking could, within the next decade, greatly reduce the number of branch banks needed. To prevent a loss of a large portion of their customer base, many of the leading banks, such as Chase Manhattan and Citibank, are aligning themselves with software and hardware manufacturers to develop home banking systems.

Banks have also learned the value of bundling services. Many now offer an account that combines checking, savings, credit card, and auto loan features. Benefits to the customer include free ATM transactions, interest-bearing checking accounts, no-fee credit cards, and the convenience of one-stop banking. In addition, they offer preapproved auto loans and cash-flow statements. Most banks also target some marketing activities toward senior citizens, which may include discount coupons for entertainment, travel newsletters, and lower monthly minimum required balances.

Competition between banks and other financial institutions will continue to intensify. The survivors will be those that have best mastered the art of services marketing.

Health Care

The distribution of health care services is of vital concern. In health care delivery, the inseparability characteristic presents more of a handicap than in other service industries because users (patients) literally place themselves in the hands of the seller. Although direct personal contact between producer and user is often necessary, new and more efficient means of distribution seem to be evolving.

Up until the past few decades, medical care has been traditionally associated with the solo practice, fee-for-service system. Recently, several alternative delivery systems have been developed, most notably the health maintenance organization (HMO). This type of delivery system stresses the creation of group health care clinics using teams of salaried health practitioners (physicians, pharmacists, technicians, and so forth) that serve a specified, enrolled membership on a prepaid basis. The primary benefits to the customer (patient) from membership in an HMO are (1) the ability to have all ailments treated at one facility, (2) payment of a fixed fee for services, and (3) the encouragement of preventive versus remedial treatments. The success of the HMO concept in traditional medical care has inspired similar programs to be developed for dental and eye care.

In the pharmaceutical field, Chronimed of Minnetonka, Minnesota, has focused on providing great customer service as its avenue to success.[16] The company supplies 100,000 patients across the United States with specialized medications that local pharmacies can't afford to stock. Chronimed's skill is twofold. First, it provides needed drugs by mail to organ transplant recipients and patients with diabetes or AIDS. Second, it employs a team of 50 pharmacists and assistants who provide much-needed information about the medications they dispense, such as details about drug interaction and side effects. As evidenced by the above examples, health care companies, regardless of what specific area in which they compete, are becoming more and more market oriented as they try to differentiate their offerings from those of the competition.

Insurance

In recent years, the insurance industry has exploded with new product and service offerings. Not too long ago, customers were faced with limited options in choosing life, hospital, or auto insurance. Now, there is a wide array of insurance policies to choose from, including universal life policies, which double as retirement savings; nursing care insurance; reversible mortgages, which allow people to take equity from their house while still living in it; and other offerings aimed at serving an aging population. To illustrate, Prudential Insurance Company offers a program whereby terminally ill policyholders are allowed to withdraw funds against the face value of their policy while still alive. In addition to insurance services, most insurance companies now offer a full range of financial services, including auto loans, mortgages, mutual funds, and certificates of deposit.

Distribution of insurance services has also been growing. The vending machines found in airports for flight insurance have been finding their way into other areas. Travel auto insurance is now available in many motel chains and through the AAA. Group insurance written through employers and labor unions also has been extremely successful. In each instance, the insurance industry has used intermediaries to distribute its services.

Travel

The travel industry, most notably the airlines, has been a leader in the use of technology. Computerized reservation systems allow customers to book plane tickets from home or work. Nearly all airlines are using Internet sites to dispense flight and fare information. Airlines are in the midst of implementing ticketless travel programs in

1. Customers do not buy your services—they buy solutions to their problems.

2. There are only two conditions under which customers will change their behavior: (*a*) when it's a matter of life and death (and then not in every case), and (*b*) if they want to—if they are given a reason to change.

3. The most important parts of employees' contributions to the goals of your organization are being made at their discretion.

4. Management and leadership are exercised outside, not inside the office.

5. Quality service means never having to say "that's not my job."

6. How your employees feel is eventually how your customers will feel.

7. Customers should never be required to restate their request or complain to several employees before having it resolved.

8. If you establish negative expectations for your customers, you will always meet them.

9. The delivery of quality service is never the customer's job.

10. If you are an underdog, only compete in market segments where you have or can develop strengths, avoid head-to-head competition with dominant competitors, emphasize profits rather than volume, and focus on specialization rather than diversification.

Source: Adapted from James H. Donnelly, Jr., *25 Management Lessons from the Customer's Side of the Counter* (Burr Ridge, IL: McGraw-Hill, 1996).

which passengers purchase tickets, select their seats, and pick up boarding passes and luggage tags at machines resembling ATMs.[17] Technology has also allowed airlines to make strategic pricing decisions through the use of yield management. In yield management, certain seats on aircraft are discounted and certain ones aren't. Through the use of elaborate computer programs, managers are able to determine who their customer segments are and who is likely to purchase airline tickets when and to where.

Despite its success in employing technology to attract additional customers and offer added convenience, the airline industry has operated in somewhat dire straits, plagued by problems associated with over-capacity, high labor costs, and low perceived service quality. The decade of the 90s could be considered the most turbulent ever encountered by U.S. commercial airlines.[18] During this time, some airlines either went out of business (Midway, Eastern, and Pan Am) or were in and out of bankruptcy proceedings (Continental, America West, and TWA); and most others operated at a loss. Fortunately, in recent years, good news came to the industry in the form of decreased fuel prices, the abandoning of some hub-and-spoke operations, and other events leading to cost decreases.

A notable exception to the fate that befell most carriers is Southwest Airlines, which has finally convinced its peers that a carrier can be consistently profitable by offering cheap fares on short-distance routes. Now, big carriers such as Continental and United have created their own Southwest look-alikes to supplement their long-haul, full-service, high-fare operations. Southwest's secret to success (which other airlines may or may not be able to imitate) is the high level of employee morale exhibited by everyone associated with the company. This has come as a direct result of upper management's internal marketing efforts.

Implications for Service Marketers

The preceding sections emphasized the use of all components of the marketing mix. Many service industries have been criticized for an overdependence on advertising. The overdependence on one or two elements of the marketing mix is a mistake that service marketers cannot afford. The sum total of the marketing mix elements represents the total impact of the firm's marketing strategy. The slack created by severely restricting one element cannot be compensated by heavier emphasis on another, since each element in the marketing mix is designed to address specific problems and achieve specific objectives.

Services must be made available to prospective users, which implies distribution in the marketing sense of the word. The revised concept of the distribution of services points out that service marketers must distinguish conceptually between the production and distribution of services. The problem of making services more widely available must not be ignored.

The above sections also pointed out the critical role of new service development. In several of the examples described, indirect distribution of the service was made possible because "products" were developed that included a tangible representation of the service. This development facilitates the use of intermediaries, because the service can now be separated from the producer. In addition, the development of new services paves the way for companies to expand and segment their markets. With the use of varying service bundles, new technology, and alternative means of distributing the service, companies are now able to practice targeted marketing.

CONCLUSION

This chapter has dealt with the complex topic of service marketing. While the marketing of services has much in common with the marketing of products, unique problems in the area require highly creative marketing management skills. Many of the problems in the service area can be traced to the intangible and inseparable nature of services and the difficulties involved in measuring service quality. However, considerable progress has been made in understanding and reacting to these difficult problems, particularly in the area of distribution. In view of the major role services play in our economy, it is important for marketing practitioners to better understand and appreciate the unique problems of service marketing.

Additional Readings

Berry, Leonard T. *Discovering the Soul of Service.* New York: The Free Press, 2000.

Brown, Stephen W. "The Move to Solutions Providers." *Marketing Management,* Spring 2000, pp. 10–11.

Burton, Richard, and Dennis Howard. "Recovery Strategies for Sports Marketers." *Marketing Management,* Spring 2000, pp. 42–50.

Price, B. Joseph, III, and James Gilmore. "Welcome to the Experience Economy." *Harvard Business Review,* July–August 1998, pp. 97–105.

Shank, Matthew D. *Sports Marketing.* Upper Saddle River, NJ: Prentice Hall, 1999.

Wood, Stephen D. "Getting More and Better Business from Service Customers." *Marketing Management,* Fall 2000, pp. 10–11.

Chapter 13

Global Marketing

A growing number of U.S. corporations have transversed geographical boundaries and become truly multinational in nature. For most other domestic companies, the question is no longer, Should we go international? Instead, the questions relate to when, how, and where the companies should enter the international marketplace. The past 15 years have seen the reality of a truly world market unfold.

Firms invest in foreign countries for the same basic reasons they invest in their own country. These reasons vary from firm to firm but fall under the categories of achieving offensive or defensive goals. Offensive goals are to (1) increase long-term growth and profit prospects; (2) maximize total sales revenue; (3) take advantage of economies of scale; and (4) improve overall market position. As many American markets reach saturation, American firms look to foreign markets as outlets for surplus production capacity, sources of new customers, increased profit margins, and improved returns on investment. For example, the ability to expand the number of locations of McDonald's restaurants in the United States is becoming severely limited. Yet, on any given day, only 0.5 percent of the world's population visits McDonald's. Indeed, in the recent past, of the 50 most profitable McDonald's outlets, 25 were located in Hong Kong. For PepsiCo, the results are similar. Its restaurant division operates over 10,000 Kentucky Fried Chicken, Pizza Hut, and Taco Bell outlets abroad.

Multinational firms also invest in other countries to achieve defensive goals. Chief among these goals are the desire to (1) compete with foreign companies on their own turf instead of in the United States, (2) have access to technological innovations that are developed in other countries, (3) take advantage of significant differences in operating costs between countries, (4) preempt competitors' global moves, and (5) not be locked out of future markets by arriving too late.

Such well-known companies as Zenith, Pillsbury, A&P, Shell Oil, CBS Records, and Firestone Tire & Rubber are now owned by non-U.S. interests. Since 1980, the share of the U.S. high-tech market held by foreign products has grown from less than 8 percent to over 25 percent. In such diverse industries as power tools, tractors, television, and banking, U.S. companies have lost the dominant position they once held. By investing solely in domestic operations or not being willing to adapt products to foreign markets, U.S. companies are more susceptible to foreign incursions. For example, there has been a great uproar over Japan's practice of not opening up its domestic automobile market to U.S. companies. However, as of the end of the 90s, a great majority of the American cars shipped to Japan still had the steering wheel located on the left side of the vehicle—the opposite of where it should be for the Japanese market.

In many ways, marketing globally is the same as marketing at home. Regardless of which part of the world the firm sells in, the marketing program must still be built around a sound product or service that is properly priced, promoted, and distributed to a carefully analyzed target market. In other words, the marketing manager has the same controllable decision variables in both domestic and nondomestic markets.

Although the development of a marketing program may be the same in either domestic or nondomestic markets, special problems may be involved in the implementation of marketing programs in nondomestic markets. These problems often arise because of the environmental differences that exist among various countries that marketing managers may be unfamiliar with.

In this chapter, marketing management in a global context will be examined. Methods of organizing global versus domestic markets, global market research tasks, methods of entry strategies into global markets, and potential marketing strategies for a multinational firm will be discussed. In examining each of these areas, the reader will find a common thread—knowledge of the local cultural environment—that appears to be a major prerequisite for success in each area.

With the proper adaptations, many companies have the capabilities and resources needed to compete successfully in the global marketplace. To illustrate, companies as diverse as Kellogg's, Avon, Eli Lilly, and Sun Microsystems each generate a large percentage of their sales from foreign operations. Smaller companies can also be successful. For example, Nemix, Inc., of Bell Gardens, California, is a franchisee of Church's Fried Chicken. Small by world standards, this company has succeeded in developing a fully vertical operation in Poland, doing everything from raising chickens to operating restaurants.[1]

ORGANIZING FOR GLOBAL MARKETING

When compared with the tasks it faces at home, a firm attempting to establish a global marketing organization faces a much higher degree of risk and uncertainty. In a foreign market, management is often less familiar with the cultural, political, and economic situation. Many of these problems arise as a result of conditions specific to the foreign country. Managers are also faced with the decisions concerning how to organize the multinational company.

Problems with Entering Foreign Markets

While numerous problems could be cited, attention here will focus on those firms most often face when entering foreign markets.

Cultural Misunderstanding

Differences in the cultural environment of foreign countries may be misunderstood or not even recognized because of the tendency for marketing managers to use their own cultural values and priorities as a frame of reference. Some of the most common areas of difference lie in the way dissimilar cultures perceive time, thought patterns, personal space, material possessions, family roles and relationships, personal achievement, competitiveness, individuality, social behavior, and other interrelated issues.[2] Another important source of misunderstandings is in the perceptions of managers about the people with whom they are dealing. Feelings of superiority can lead to changed communication mannerisms.

American managers must make the necessary efforts to learn, understand, and adapt to the cultural norms of the managers and customers they deal with in other parts of the world. Failure to do so will result in missed market opportunities. Marketing Highlight 13–1 provides further examples of cultural differences that could lead to marketing problems.

On the other hand, companies should not shy away from attempting to enter global markets because conventional wisdom says that products and service will not succeed in some regions purely due to cultural reasons. For example, PepsiCo's Pepsi division entered into a $500 million offensive to try to grab a larger share of

Marketing Highlight Examples of Cultural Differences That Could Lead to Marketing Problems

BODY LANGUAGE

- Standing with your hands on your hips is a gesture of defiance in Indonesia.
- Carrying on a conversation with your hands in your pockets makes a poor impression in France, Belgium, Finland, and Sweden.
- Shaking your head from side to side means yes in Bulgaria and Sri Lanka.
- Crossing your legs to expose the sole of your shoe is really taboo in Muslim countries. In fact, to call a person a "shoe" is a deep insult.

PHYSICAL CONTACT

- Patting a child on the head is a grave offense in Thailand or Singapore, since the head is revered as the location of the soul.
- In an Oriental culture, touching another person is considered an invasion of privacy; in Southern European and Arabic countries, it is a sign of warmth and friendship.

PROMPTNESS

- Be on time when invited for dinner in Denmark or in China.

- In Latin countries, your host or business associate would be surprised if you arrived at the appointed hour.

EATING AND COOKING

- It is rude to leave anything on your plate when eating in Norway, Malaysia, or Singapore.
- In Egypt, it is rude *not* to leave something.
- In Italy and Spain, cooking is done with oil.
- In Germany and Great Britain, margarine and butter are used.

OTHER SOCIAL CUSTOMS

- In Sweden, nudity and sexual permissiveness are quite all right, but drinking is really frowned on.
- In Spain, there is a very negative attitude toward life insurance. By receiving insurance benefits, a wife feels that she is profiting from her husband's death.
- In Western European countries, many consumers still are reluctant to buy anything (other than a house) on credit. Even for an automobile, they will pay cash.

Source: William J. Stanton, Michael J. Etzel, and Bruce J. Walker, *Fundamentals of Marketing,* 11th ed. © 1997. New York, McGraw-Hill, Inc., p. 544. Reproduced by permission of The McGraw-Hill Companies.

the $6 billion Brazilian soft-drink market.[3] Understanding the dramatic changes that had taken place in Brazil, Pepsi repositioned itself as the choice of a new Brazil. Advertisements for the Pepsi brand feature young people enumerating recent changes in Brazil, such as perhaps the devaluation of its currency in 1999. Does this campaign sound familiar? It should since it's a takeoff on the popular "Pepsi, the choice of a new generation" theme used in the United States. Actions taken by PepsiCo's Frito-Lay unit serve as another example of a successful adaptation to cultural differences.[4] In China, Frito-Lay recently introduced its popular Cheetos snack food. The twist to this effort lies in the fact that the Chinese are not big consumers of dairy products. In China, Cheetos are cheeseless, instead consisting of flavors such as "Savory American Cream" and "Zesty Japanese Steak." As a result of these and other adaptations, it's no wonder that PepsiCo ranks among the leaders in the global food and beverage industry.

Political Uncertainty

Governments are unstable in many countries, and social unrest and even armed conflict must sometimes be reckoned with. Other nations are newly emerging and anxious to seek their independence. These and similar problems can greatly hinder a firm seeking to establish its position in foreign markets. For example, at the turn of the century, firms scaled back their investment plans in Russia due to, among other reasons, (1) a business environment plagued by mobsters, (2) politics badly corrupted by the botched invasion of Chechnya, and (3) an economy troubled by runaway inflation and a plummeting ruble.[5] This is not to say investment in Russia is a poor choice. Rather, in situations like this, caution must be used and companies must have a keen understanding of the risks involved in undertaking sizable investments.

Import Restrictions

Tariffs, import quotas, and other types of import restrictions hinder global business. These are usually established to promote self-sufficiency and can be a huge roadblock for the multinational firm. For example, a number of countries, including South Korea, Taiwan, Thailand, and Japan, have placed import restrictions on a variety of goods produced in America, including telecommunications equipment, rice, wood products, automobiles, and produce. In other cases, governments may not impose restrictions that are commonly adhered to in the United States. For example, Chrysler pulled out of a proposed investment deal in China, worth billions of dollars, because the Chinese government refused to protect its right to limit access to technological information.

Exchange Controls and Ownership Restrictions

Some nations establish limits on the amount of earned and invested funds that can be withdrawn from it. These exchange controls are usually established by nations that are experiencing balance-of-payment problems. In addition, many nations have a requirement that the majority ownership of a company operating there be held by nationals. These and other types of currency and ownership regulations are important considerations in the decision to expand into a foreign market. For example, up until a few years ago, foreign holdings in business ventures in India were limited to a maximum of 40 percent. Once this ban was lifted, numerous global companies such as Sony, Whirlpool, JVC, Grundig, Panasonic, Kellogg's, Levi Strauss, Pizza Hut, and Domino's rushed to invest in this market.[6]

Economic Conditions

As noted earlier, nations' economics are becoming increasingly intertwined, and business cycles tend to follow similar patterns. However, there are differences, mainly due to political upheaval or social changes, and these may be significant. In determining whether to invest, marketers need to perform in-depth analyses of a country's stage of economic development, the buying power of its populace, and the strength of its currency. For example, when the North American Free Trade Agreement (NAFTA) was signed, many American companies rushed to invest in Mexico, building production facilities and retail outlets. These companies assumed that the signing of the agreement would stabilize Mexico's economy. In the long term, these investments may pay off. However, many companies lost millions of dollars there due to the devaluation of the peso. Indeed, the crash of the peso caused the retail giant Wal-Mart to scale back a $1 billion investment project to open stores throughout Mexico.

Organizing the Multinational Company

There are two kinds of global companies—the multidomestic corporation and the global corporation.[7] The *multidomestic company* pursues different strategies in each of its foreign markets. They could have as many different product variations, brand names, and advertising campaigns as countries in which they operate. Each overseas subsidiary is autonomous. Local managers are given the authority to make the necessary decisions and are held accountable for results. In effect, the company competes on a market-by-market basis. Honeywell and General Foods are U.S. firms that have operated this way.

The *global company*, on the other hand, views the world as one market and pits its resources against the competition in an integrated fashion. It emphasizes cultural similarities across countries and universal consumer needs and wants rather than differences. It standardizes marketing activities when there are cultural similarities and adapts them when the cultures are different. Since there is no one clear-cut way to organize a global company, three alternative structures are normally used: (1) worldwide product divisions, each responsible for selling its own products throughout the world; (2) divisions responsible for all products sold within a geographic region; and (3) a matrix system that combines elements of both of these arrangements. Many organizations, such as IBM, Caterpillar, Timex, General Electric, Siemens, and Mitsubishi, are structured in a global fashion.

Most companies are realizing the need to take a global approach to managing their businesses. However, recognizing the need and actually implementing a truly global approach are two different tasks. For some companies, industry conditions dictate that they take a global perspective. The ability to actually implement a global approach to managing international operations, however, largely depends on factors unique to the company. Globalization, as a competitive strategy, is inherently more vulnerable to risk than a multidomestic or domestic strategy, due to the relative permanence of the organizational structure once established.

In determining whether or not to globalize a particular business, managers should look first at their industry.[8] Market, economic, environmental, and competitive factors all influence the potential gains to be realized by following a global strategy. Factors constituting the external environment that are conducive to a global strategy are

1. *Market factors.* Homogeneous market needs, global customers, shortening product life cycles, transferable brands and advertising, and the ability to globalize distribution channels.
2. *Economic factors.* Worldwide economies of scale in manufacturing and distribution, steep learning curves, worldwide sourcing efficiencies, rising product development costs, and significant differences in host-country costs.
3. *Environmental factors.* Improving communications, favorable government policies, and the increasing speed of technological change.
4. *Competitive factors.* Competitive interdependencies among countries, global moves of competitors, and opportunities to preempt a competitor's global moves.[9]

Many of the reasons given in the first part of the chapter as to why a domestic company should become a multinational can also be used to support the argument that a firm should take a global perspective. This is because the integration of markets is forcing companies that wish to remain successful not only to become multinationals but also to take a global perspective in doing so. In the past, companies had the option of remaining domestic or going multinational due to the separation of markets. This is no longer the case.

There are several internal factors that can either facilitate or impede a company's efforts to undertake a global approach to marketing strategies. These factors and their underlying dimensions are

1. *Structure.* The ease of installing a centralized global authority and the absence of rifts between present domestic and international divisions or operating units.
2. *Management processes.* The capabilities and resources available to perform global planning, budgeting, and coordination activities, coupled with the ability to conduct global performance reviews and implement global compensation plans.
3. *Culture.* The ability to project a global versus national identity, a worldwide versus domestic commitment to employees, and a willingness to tolerate interdependence among business units.
4. *People.* The availability of employable foreign nationals and the willingness of current employees to commit to multicountry careers, frequent travel, and having foreign superiors.

Overall, whether a company should undertake a multidomestic or global approach to organizing its international operations will largely depend on the nature of the company and its products, how different foreign cultures are from the domestic market, and the company's ability to implement a global perspective. Many large brands have failed in their quest to go global. The primary reason for this failure is rushing the process. Successful global brands carefully stake out their markets, allowing plenty of time to develop their overseas marketing efforts and evolve into global brands.

Indeed, in many cases, firms do not undertake either purely multidomestic or global approaches to marketing. Instead, a hybrid approach is developed whereby these global brands carry with them the same visual identity, the same strategic positioning, and the same advertising. In addition, local characteristics are factored in. Regardless of the approach undertaken, management and organizational skills that emphasize the need to handle diversity are the critical factors that determine the long-term success of any company's endeavors in the global marketplace.

PROGRAMMING FOR GLOBAL MARKETING

In this section of the chapter, the major areas in developing a global marketing program will be examined. As was mentioned at the outset, marketing managers must organize the same controllable decision variables that exist in domestic markets. However, many firms that have been extremely successful in marketing in the United States have not been able to duplicate their success in foreign markets.

Global Marketing Research

Because the risks and uncertainties are so high, marketing research is equally important (and probably more so) in foreign markets than in domestic markets. Many companies encounter losing situations abroad because they do not know enough about the market.[10] They don't know how to get the information or find the cost of collecting the information too high. To be successful, organizations must collect and analyze pertinent information to support the basic go/no-go decision before getting to the issues addressed by conventional market research. Toward this end, in attempting to analyze foreign consumers and markets, at least four organizational issues must be considered.

Population Characteristics

Population characteristics are one of the major components of a market, and significant differences exist between and within foreign countries. If data are available, the marketing manager should be familiar with the total population and with the regional, urban, rural, and interurban distribution. Other demographic variables, such as the

Growth in global markets has created opportunities for building global brands. The advantages are many and so are the pitfalls. Here are 10 commandments that marketers can use when planning a global branding campaign.

1. *Understand similarities and differences in the global branding landscape.* The best brands retain consistency of theme and alter specific elements to suit each country.

2. *Don't take shortcuts in brand building.* Build brands in new markets from the "bottom up."

3. *Establish marketing infrastructure.* Most often, firms adopt or invest in foreign partners for manufacturing and distribution.

4. *Embrace integrated marketing communications.* Because advertising opportunities may be more limited, marketers must use other forms of communication such as sponsorship and public relations.

5. *Establish brand partnerships.* Most global brands have marketing partners ranging from joint venture partners, franchisees, and distributors who provide access to distribution.

6. *Balance standardization and customization.* Know what to standardize and what to customize.

7. *Balance global and local control.* This is very important in the following areas: organization structure, entry strategies, coordination processes, and mechanisms.

8. *Establish operable guidelines.* Set the rules as to how the brand will be positioned and marketed.

9. *Implement a global brand equity measurement system.* The ideal measurement system provides complete, up-to-date information on the brand and on all its competitors to the appropriate decision makers.

10. *Leverage brand elements.* If the meanings of the brand name and all related trademarked identifiers are clear, they can be an invaluable source of brand equity worldwide.

Source: Kevin Lane Keller, "The Ten Commandments of Global Branding," *MBA Bullet Point,* October 3–16, 2000, p. 3.

---

number and size of families, education, occupation, and religion, are also important. In many markets, these variables can have a significant impact on the success of a firm's marketing program. For example, in the United States, a cosmetics firm can be reasonably sure of the desire to use cosmetics being common among women of all income classes. However, in Latin America the same firm may be forced to segment its market by upper-, middle-, and lower-income groups, as well as by urban and rural areas. This is because upper-income women want high-quality cosmetics promoted in prestige media and sold through exclusive outlets. In some rural and less prosperous areas, cosmetics must be inexpensive; in other rural areas, women do not accept cosmetics.

Ability to Buy

To assess the ability of consumers in a foreign market to buy, four broad measures should be examined: (1) gross national product or per capita national income, (2) distribution of income, (3) rate of growth in buying power, and (4) extent of available financing. Since each of these vary in different areas of the world, the marketing opportunities available must be examined closely.

Willingness to Buy

The cultural framework of consumer motives and behavior is integral to the understanding of the foreign consumer. If data are available, cultural values and attitudes toward the material culture, social organizations, the supernatural, aesthetics, and

Marketing Highlight   Tips for Global Consumer Marketing Research

Many consumer goods companies have sought growth by expanding into global markets. For U.S. companies, this is sound strategy since 95 percent of the world's population and two-thirds of its purchasing power are located outside their country. The potential for success in global markets is enhanced when companies carefully research and analyze consumers in foreign countries, just as it is in domestic markets. Below are some suggestions for companies seeking to successfully market to global consumers.

- Research the cultural nuances and customs of the market. Be sure that the company and brand name translate favorably in the language of the target country, and if not, consider using an abbreviation or entirely different brand name for the market. Consider using marketing research firms or ad agencies that have detailed knowledge of the culture.

- Determine whether the product can be exported to the foreign country as is or whether it has to be modified to be useful and appealing to targeted consumers. Also, determine what changes need to be made to packaging and labeling to make the product appealing to the market.

- Research the prices of similar products in the target country or region. Determine the necessary retail price to make marketing it profitable in the country,

and research whether a sufficient number of consumers would be willing to pay that price. Also, determine what the product has to offer that should make consumers willing to pay a higher price.

- On the basis of research, decide whether the targeted country or region will require a unique marketing strategy or whether the same general strategy can be used in all geographic areas.

- Research the ways consumers purchase similar products in the targeted country or region and whether the company's product can be sold effectively using this method of distribution. Also, determine if a method of distribution not currently being used in the country could create a competitive advantage for the product.

- Pretest integrated marketing communication efforts in the targeted country to ensure not only that messages are translated accurately but also that subtle differences in meaning are not problematic. Also, research the effectiveness of planned communication efforts.

Marketing consumer goods successfully in global markets requires a long-term commitment as it may take time to establish an identity in new markets. However, with improving technology and the evolution of a global economy, both large and small companies have found global marketing both feasible and profitable.

Source: Dom Del Prete, "Winning Strategies Lead to Global Marketing Success," *Marketing News,* August 18, 1997, pp. 1, 2.

language should be analyzed for their possible influence on each of the elements in the firm's marketing program. It is easy to see that such factors as the group's values concerning acquisition of material goods, the role of the family, the positions of men and women in society, and the various age groups and social classes can have an effect on marketing, because each can influence consumer behavior.

In some areas there appears to be a convergence of tastes and habits, with different cultures becoming more and more integrated into one homogeneous culture, although still separated by national boundaries. This appears to be the case in Western Europe, where consumers are developing into a mass market. This obviously will simplify the task for a marketer in this region. However, cultural differences still prevail among many areas of the world and strongly influence consumer behavior. Marketing organizations may have to do primary research in many foreign markets to obtain usable information about these issues.

Differences in Research Tasks and Processes

In addition to the dimensions mentioned above, the processes and tasks associated with carrying out the market research program may also differ from country to country. Many market researchers count on census data for in-depth demographic information. However, in foreign countries there are a variety of problems the market researcher is likely to encounter in using census data. These include[11]

1. *Language.* Some nations publish their census reports in English. Other countries offer census reports only in their native language; some do not take a census.

2. *Data content.* Data contained in a census will vary from country to country and often omit items of interest to researchers. For example, most foreign nations do not include an income question on their census. Others do not include such items as marital status or education levels.

3. *Timeliness.* The United States takes a census every 10 years. Japan and Canada conduct one every 5 years. However, some northern European nations are abandoning the census as a data-collection tool and instead are relying on population registers to account for births, deaths, and changes in marital status or place of residence.

4. *Availability in the United States.* If a researcher requires detailed household demographics on foreign markets, the cost and time required to obtain the data will be significant. Unfortunately, census data for many countries do not exist. For some it will be difficult to obtain, although others can be found on the Internet.

Global Product Strategy

Global marketing research can help determine whether (1) there is an unsatisfied need for which a new product could be developed to serve a foreign market or (2) there is an unsatisfied need that could be met with an existing domestic product, either as is or adapted to the foreign market. In either case, product planning is necessary to determine the type of product to be offered and whether there is sufficient demand to warrant entry into a foreign market.

Most U.S. firms would not think of entering a domestic market without extensive product planning. However, some marketers have failed to do adequate product planning when entering foreign markets. An example of such a problem occurred when American manufacturers began to export refrigerators to Europe. The firms exported essentially the same models sold in the United States. However, the refrigerators were the wrong size, shape, and temperature range for some areas and had weak appeal in others—thus failing miserably. Although adaptation of the product to local conditions may have eliminated this failure, this adaptation is easier said than done. For example, even in the domestic market, overproliferation of product varieties and options can dilute economies of scale. This dilution results in higher production costs, which may make the price of serving each market segment with an adapted product prohibitive.

The solution to this problem is not easy. In some cases, changes need not be made at all or, if so, can be accomplished rather inexpensively. In other cases, the sales potential of the particular market may not warrant expensive product changes. For example, Pepsi's Radical Fruit line of juice drinks was introduced without adaptation on three continents. On the other hand, U.S. companies wishing to market software in foreign countries must undertake painstaking and costly efforts to convert the embedded code from English to foreign languages. This undertaking severely limits the potential markets where individual software products can be profitably marketed. In any case, management must examine these product-related problems carefully prior to making foreign market entry decisions.

Global Distribution Strategy

The role of the distribution network in facilitating the transfer of goods and titles and in the demand stimulation process is as important in foreign markets as it is at home. Figure 13–1 illustrates some of the most common channel arrangements in global marketing. The continuum ranges from no control to almost complete control of the distribution system by manufacturers.

The channel arrangement where manufacturers have the least control is shown at the left in Figure 13–1. These are the most indirect channels of distribution. Here manufacturers sell to resident buyers, export agents, or export merchants located in the United States. In reality, these are similar to some domestic sales, since all of the marketing functions are assumed by intermediaries.

Manufacturers become more directly involved and, hence, have greater control over distribution when agents and distributors located in foreign markets are selected. Both perform similar functions, except that agents do not assume title to the manufacturers' products, while distributors do. If manufacturers should assume the functions of foreign agents or distributors and establish their own foreign branch, they greatly increase control over their global distribution system. Manufacturers' effectiveness will then depend on their own administrative organization rather than on independent intermediaries. If the foreign branch sells to other intermediaries, such as wholesalers and retailers, as is the case with most consumer goods, manufacturers again relinquish some control. However, since the manufacturers are located in the market area, they have greater potential to influence these intermediaries. For example, Volkswagen, General Motors, Anheuser-Busch, and Procter & Gamble have each made substantial investments in building manufacturing facilities in Brazil. These investments allow the companies to begin making direct sales to dealers and retailers in the country.

The channel arrangement that enables manufacturers to exercise a great deal of control is shown at the right in Figure 13–1. Here, manufacturers sell directly to organizational buyers or ultimate consumers. Although this arrangement is most common in the sale of organizational goods, some consumer goods companies have also pursued this arrangement.

FIGURE 13–1
Common Distribution Channels for Global Marketing

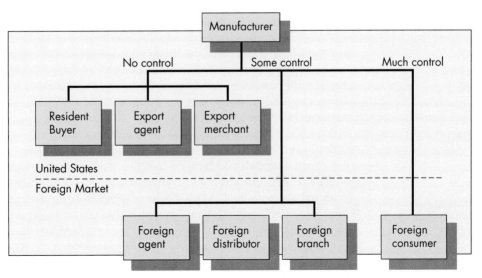

Global Pricing Strategy

In domestic markets, pricing is a complex task. The basic approaches used in price determination in foreign markets are the same as those discussed earlier in the chapter on pricing. However, the pricing task is often more complicated in foreign markets because of additional problems associated with tariffs, antidumping laws, taxes, inflation, and currency conversion.

Import duties are probably the major constraint for global marketers and are encountered in many markets. Management must decide whether import duties will be paid by the firm, by the foreign consumer, or shared by both. This and similar constraints may force the firm to abandon an otherwise desirable pricing strategy or may force the firm out of a market altogether.

Another pricing problem arises because of the rigidity in price structures found in many foreign markets. Many foreign intermediaries are not aggressive in their pricing policies. They often prefer to maintain high unit margins at the expense of low sales volume rather than develop large sales volume by means of lower prices and smaller margins per unit. Many times this rigidity is encouraged by legislation that prevents retailers from cutting prices substantially at their own discretion. These are only a few of the pricing problems encountered by foreign marketers.

Global Advertising and Sales Promotion Strategy

When expanding their operations into the world marketplace, most firms are aware of the language barriers that exist and realize the importance of translating their messages into the proper idiom. However, there are numerous other issues that must be resolved, such as selecting appropriate media and advertising agencies in foreign markets.

There are many problems in selecting media in foreign markets. Often the media that are traditionally used in the domestic market are not available. For example, it was not until recently that national commercial TV became a reality in the former Soviet Union. If media are available, they may be so only on a limited basis or they may not reach the potential buyers. In addition to the problem of availability, other difficulties arise from the lack of accurate media information. There is no rate and data service or media directory that covers all the media available throughout the world. Where data are available, their accuracy is often questionable.

Another important promotion decision that must be made is the type of agency used to prepare and place the firm's advertisements. Along with the growth in multinational product companies, more multinational advertising agencies are available. Among the top 15 global advertising agencies, less than half are U.S. owned. Alliances and takeovers have served to stimulate growth in the formation of global agencies. For the U.S. company, there are two major approaches to choosing an agency. The first is to use a purely local agency in each area where the advertisement is to appear. The rationale for this approach is that a purely local agency employing only local nationals can better adapt the firm's message to the local culture.

The other approach is to use either a U.S.–based multinational agency or a multinational agency with U.S. offices to develop and implement the ad campaign. For example, the Coca-Cola Company uses one agency to create ads for the 80 nations in which Diet Coke is marketed. The use of these so-called super agencies is increasing (annual growth rates averaging over 30 percent in the last decade). By using global advertising agencies, companies are able to take advantage of economies of scale and other efficiencies. However, global agencies are not without their critics. Many managers believe that small, local agencies in emerging markets take a

Marketing Highlight   Checklist of Country Selection Criteria for Companies Considering Investment in Eastern Europe

OVERALL ECONOMIC AND POLITICAL CONDITIONS

- What is the foreign debt service expense as a percentage of hard currency foreign exchange earnings?

- What is the inflation rate? If hyperinflation exists, are appropriate fiscal and monetary policies being implemented to bring it under control?

- How substantial are raw material reserves that can be converted to hard currency?

- Are state subsidies, cheap credits, and tax concessions for state enterprises being phased out?

- Does the government intend to sell stakes in state enterprises to foreign investors?

- Is there an emerging capital market based on real interest rates?

- What progress is being made toward developing a code of company law?

- Is political decision-making authority centralized or fragmented?

- How rapid and sustainable is continued progress toward democracy and a free market economy? Is there any historical tradition to support such trends?

CLIMATE FOR FOREIGN INVESTMENT

- What percentage ownership may foreign companies have in joint ventures? Is government approval required, and if so, how long does it take to obtain?

- Is private ownership of property recognized?

- Are intellectual property rights upheld?

- Can foreign investors obtain premises easily? Can they own real estate?

- Can an initial capital investment by a foreign company be held in hard currency?

- Can a foreign investor sell its stake in a joint venture?

- Can hard currency be used to pay for imported raw materials or to repatriate profits?

- What is the tax rate on business enterprise profits?

MARKET ATTRACTIVENESS

- What is the sales potential in this country?

- Do the country's geographical location and political relations permit it to serve as a gateway to other East European markets?

- How well developed are the necessary managerial and technical skills?

- How skilled is the labor pool? What are labor costs?

- Can continued supply of the raw materials required for production be assured?

- What is the quality of the transportation and telecommunications infrastructure?

- Will Western executives accept being located in the country?

- To what degree have government officials developed a familiarity with Western business practices?

Source: John A. Quelch, Erich Joachimsthaler, and Jose Luis Nueno, "After the Wall: Marketing Guidelines for Eastern Europe," *Sloan Management Review*, Winter 1991, p. 85.

more entrepreneurial and fresher approach to advertising than do global agencies. Much discussion has developed over which approach is best, and it appears that both approaches can be used successfully by particular firms.

The use of sales promotion can also lead to opportunities and problems for marketers in foreign markets. Sales promotions often contain certain characteristics that are more attractive than other elements of the promotion mix.[12] In less-wealthy countries, consumers tend to be even more interested in saving money through price discounts, sampling, or premiums. Sales promotion can also be used as a strategy for bypassing restrictions on advertising placed by some foreign governments.

In addition, sales promotion can be an effective means for reaching people who live in rural locations where media support for advertising is virtually nonexistent.

ENTRY AND GROWTH STRATEGIES FOR GLOBAL MARKETING

A major decision facing companies that desire either to enter a foreign market or pursue growth within a specific market relates to the choice of entry or growth strategy. What type of strategy to employ depends on many factors, including the analysis of market opportunities, company capabilities, the degree of marketing involvement and commitment the company is willing to make, and the amount of risk that the company is able to tolerate.[13] A company can decide to (1) make minimal investments of funds and resources by limiting its efforts to exporting; (2) make large initial investments of resources and management effort to try to establish a long-term share of global markets; or (3) take an incremental approach whereby the company starts with a low-risk mode of entry that requires the least financial and other resource commitment and gradually increases its commitment over time. All three approaches can be profitable. In general, there are six ways by which a company can initially enter a global market and, subsequently, pursue growth in the global marketplace:

1. *Exporting.* Exporting occurs when a company produces the product outside the final destination and then ships it there for sale. It is the easiest and most common approach for a company making its first international move. Exporting has two distinct advantages. First, it avoids the cost of establishing manufacturing operations in the host country; second, it may help a firm achieve experience-curve and location economies. By manufacturing the product in a centralized location and exporting it to other national markets, the firm may be able to realize substantial scale economies from its global sales volume. This method is what allowed Sony to dominate the global TV market. The major disadvantages related to exporting include (1) the sometimes higher cost associated with the process, (2) the necessity of the exporting firm to pay import duties or face trade barriers, and (3) the delegation of marketing responsibility for the product to foreign agents who may or may not be dependable.

2. *Licensing.* Companies can grant patent rights, trademark rights, and the right to use technological processes to foreign companies. This is the most common strategy for small and medium-size companies. The major advantage to licensing is that the firm does not have to bear the development costs and risks associated with opening up a foreign market. In addition, licensing can be an attractive option in unfamiliar or politically volatile markets. The major disadvantages are that (1) the firm does not have tight control over manufacturing, marketing, and strategy that is required for realizing economies of scale; and (2) there is the risk that the licensed technology may be capitalized on by foreign companies. RCA Corporation, for example, once licensed its color TV technology to a number of Japanese firms. These firms quickly assimilated the technology and used it to enter the U.S. market.

3. *Franchising.* Franchising is similar to licensing but tends to involve longer-term commitments. Also, franchising is commonly employed by service firms, as opposed to manufacturing firms. In a franchising agreement, the franchisor sells limited rights to use its brand name in return for a lump sum and share of the franchisee's future profits. In contrast to licensing agreements, the franchisee agrees to abide by strict operating procedures. Advantages and disadvantages associated with franchising are primarily the same as with licensing except to a lesser degree. In many cases, franchising offers an effective mix of centralized and decentralized decision making.

4. *Joint ventures.* A company may decide to share management with one or more collaborating foreign firms. Joint ventures are especially popular in industries that call for large investments, such as natural gas exploration and automobile manufacturing. Control of the joint venture may be split equally, or one party may control decision making. Joint ventures hold several advantages. First, a firm may be able to benefit from a partner's knowledge of the host country's competitive position, culture, language, political systems, and so forth. Second, the firm gains by sharing costs and risks of operating in a foreign market. Third, in many countries, political considerations make joint ventures the only feasible entry mode. Finally, joint ventures allow firms to take advantage of a partner's distribution system, technological know-how, or marketing skills. For example, General Mills teamed up with CPC International in an operation called International Dessert Partners to develop a major baking and dessert-mix business in Latin America. The venture combines General Mills' technology and Betty Crocker dessert products with CPC's marketing and distribution capabilities in Latin America. The major disadvantages associated with joint ventures are that (1) a firm may risk giving up control of proprietary knowledge to its partner; and (2) the firm may lose the tight control over a foreign subsidiary needed to engage in coordinated global attacks against rivals.

5. *Strategic alliances.* Although considered by some to be a form of joint venture, we consider strategic alliances to be a distinct entity for two reasons. First, strategic alliances are normally partnerships entered into by two or more firms to gain a competitive advantage on a worldwide versus local basis. Second, strategic alliances are usually of a much longer-term nature than are joint ventures. In strategic alliances, the partners share long-term goals and pledge almost total cooperation. Strategic alliances can be used to reduce manufacturing costs, accelerate technological diffusion and new product development, and overcome legal and trade barriers.[14] The major disadvantage associated with formation of a strategic alliance is the increased risk of competitive conflict between the partners.

6. *Direct ownership.* Some companies prefer to enter or grow in markets either through establishment of a wholly owned subsidiary or through acquisition. In either case, the firm owns 100 percent of the stock. The advantages to direct ownership are that the firm has (1) complete control over its technology and operations, (2) immediate access to foreign markets, (3) instant credibility and gains in the foreign country when acquisitions are the mode of entry or growth, and (4) the ability to install its own management team. Of course, the primary disadvantages of direct ownership are the huge costs and significant risks associated with this strategy. These problems may more than offset the advantages depending upon the country entered.

Regardless of the choice of methods used to gain entry into and grow within a foreign marketplace, companies must somehow integrate their operations. The complexities involved in operating on a worldwide basis dictate that firms decide on operating strategies. A critical decision that marketing managers must make relates to the extent of adaptation of the marketing mix elements for the foreign country in which the company operates. Depending on the area of the world under consideration and the particular product mix, different degrees of standardization/adaptation of the marketing mix elements may take place. As a guideline, standardization of one or more parts of the marketing mix is a function of many factors that individually and collectively affect companies in their decision making.[15] It is more likely to succeed under the following conditions:

- When markets are economically similar.
- When worldwide customers, not countries, are the basis for segmenting markets.
- When customer behavior and lifestyles are similar.

- When the product is culturally compatible across the host country.
- When a firm's competitive position is similar in different markets.
- When competing against the same competitors, with similar market shares, in different countries, rather than competing against purely local companies.
- When the product is an organizational and high-technology product rather than a consumer product.
- When there are similarities in the physical, political, and legal environments of home and host countries.
- When the marketing infrastructure in the home and host countries is similar.

The decision to adapt or standardize marketing should be made only after a thorough analysis of the product-market mix has been undertaken. The company's end goal is to develop, manufacture, and market the products best suited to the actual and potential needs of the local (wherever that may be) customer and to the social and economic conditions of the marketplace. There can be subtle differences from country to country and from region to region in the ways a product is used and what customers expect from it.

CONCLUSION

The world is truly becoming a global market. Many companies that avoid operating in the global arena are destined for failure. For those willing to undertake the challenges and risks necessary to become multinational corporations, long-term survival and growth are likely outcomes. The purpose of this chapter was to introduce the reader to the opportunities, problems, and challenges involved in global marketing.

Additional Readings

Aaker, David, and Erich Joachimsthaler. "The Lure of Global Branding." *Harvard Business Review,* November–December 1999, pp. 137–144.

Bartlett, Christopher A., and Sumuntra Ghoshal. "Going Global: Lessons from Late Movers." *Harvard Business Review,* March–April 2001, pp. 132–142.

Burnstein, Daniel, and Arne de Keigzer. *Big Dragon China's Future: What It Means for Business, the Economy, and the Global Order.* New York: Simon & Schuster, 1998.

Hise, Richard T. "Overcoming Exporting Barriers to Mexico." *Marketing Management,* Spring 2001, pp. 52–54.

Ho, Suk-ching. "The Emergence of Consumer Power in China." *Business Horizons,* September–October 1997, pp. 15–21.

Mahajan, Vijay; Marcos V. Pratini De Moraes; and Jerry Wind. "The Invisible Global Market." *Marketing Management,* Winter 2000, pp. 30–35.

Montgomery, David B., and George S. Yip. "The Challenge of Global Customer Management." *Marketing Management,* Winter 2000, pp. 22–29.

Section II

Analyzing Marketing Problems and Cases

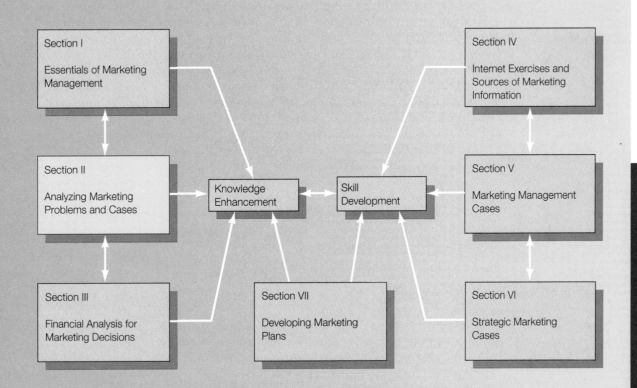

Cases assist in bridging the gap between classroom learning and the so-called real world of marketing management. They provide us with an opportunity to develop, sharpen, and test our analytical skills at

- Assessing situations.
- Sorting out and organizing key information.
- Asking the right questions.
- Defining opportunities and problems.

- Identifying and evaluating alternative courses of action.
- Interpreting data.
- Evaluating the results of past strategies.
- Developing and defending new strategies.
- Interacting with other managers.
- Making decisions under conditions of uncertainty.
- Critically evaluating the work of others.
- Responding to criticism.

Source: David W. Cravens and Charles W Lamb, Jr., *Strategic Marketing: Cases and Applications,* 4th ed. (Burr Ridge, IL: Irwin/McGraw-Hill, 1993), p. 95.

The use of business cases was developed by faculty members of the Harvard Graduate School of Business Administration in the 1920s. Case studies have been widely accepted as one effective way of exposing students to strategic marketing processes.

Basically, cases represent detailed descriptions or reports of business problems. They are often written by a trained observer who was actually involved in the firm or organization and had some dealings with the problems under consideration. Cases generally entail both qualitative and quantitative data, which the student must analyze to determine appropriate alternatives and solutions.

The primary purpose of the case method is to introduce a measure of realism into marketing management education. Rather than emphasizing the teaching of concepts, the case method focuses on application of concepts and sound logic to real-world business problems. In this way, students learn to bridge the gap between abstraction and application and to appreciate the value of both.

The primary purpose of this section is to offer a logical format for the analysis of case problems. Although there is no one format that can be successfully applied to all cases, the following framework is intended to be a logical sequence from which to develop sound analyses. This framework is presented for analysis of comprehensive marketing cases; however, the process should also be useful for shorter marketing cases, incidents, and problems.

A CASE ANALYSIS FRAMEWORK

A basic approach to case analysis involves a four-step process. First, the problem is defined. Second, alternative courses of action are formulated to solve the problem. Third, the alternatives are analyzed in terms of their strengths and weaknesses. And fourth, an alternative is accepted, and a course of action is recommended. This basic approach is quite useful for students well versed in case analysis, particularly for shorter cases or incidents. However, for the newcomer, this framework may be oversimplified. Thus, the following expanded framework and checklists are intended to aid students in becoming proficient in case and problem analysis.

1. Analyze and Record the Current Situation

Whether the analysis of a firm's problems is done by a manager, student, or paid business consultant, the first step is to analyze the current situation. This does not mean writing up a history of the firm but entails the type of analysis described below. This approach is useful not only for getting a better grip on the situation but also for discovering both real and potential problems—central concerns of any case analysis.

Phase 1: The Environment

The first phase in analyzing a marketing problem or case is to consider the environment in which the firm is operating. The environment can be broken down into a number of different components such as the economic, social, political, and legal areas. Any of these may contain threats to a firm's success or opportunities for improving a firm's situation.

Phase 2: The Industry

The second phase involves analyzing the industry in which the firm operates. A framework provided by Michael Porter includes five competitive forces that need to be considered to do a complete industry analysis.[1] The framework is shown in Figure 1 and includes rivalry among existing competitors, threat of new entrants, and threat of substitute products. In addition, in this framework, buyers and suppliers are included as competitors since they can threaten the profitability of an industry or firm.

While rivalry among existing competitors is an issue in most cases, analysis and strategies for dealing with the other forces can also be critical. This is particularly so when a firm is considering entering a new industry and wants to forecast its potential success. Each of the five competitive forces is discussed below.

Rivalry among Existing Competitors   In most cases and business situations a firm needs to consider the current competitors in its industry in order to develop successful strategies. Strategies such as price competition, advertising battles, sales promotion offers, new product introductions, and increased customer service are commonly used to attract customers from competitors.

FIGURE 1   **Competitive Forces in an Industry**

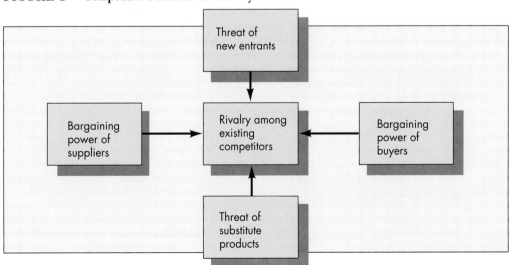

Source: Adapted from Michael E. Porter, "Industry Structure and Competitive Strategy: Keys to Profitability," *Financial Analysts Journal*, July–August 1980, p. 33.

To fully analyze existing rivalry, it is important to determine which firms are the major competitors and what are their annual sales, market share, growth profile, and strengths and weaknesses. Also, it is useful to analyze their current and past marketing strategies to try to forecast their likely reactions to a change in a competitive firm's strategy. Finally, it is important to consider any trends or changes in government regulation of an industry or changes in technology that could affect the success of a firm's strategy.

Threat of New Entrants   It is always possible for firms in other industries to try to compete in a new industry. New entrants are more likely in industries that have low entry barriers. *Entry barriers* include such things as a need for large financial resources, high brand equity for existing brands in an industry, or economies of scale obtained by existing firms in an industry. Also, existing firms in an industry may benefit from experience curves; that is, their cumulative experience in producing and marketing a product may reduce their per-unit costs below those of inexperienced firms. In general, the higher the entry barriers, the less likely outside firms are to enter an industry. For example, the entry barriers for starting up a new car company are much higher than for starting up an online software company.

Threat of Substitute Products   In a broad sense, all firms in an industry compete with industries producing substitute products. For example, in cultures where bicycles are the major means of transportation, bicycle manufacturers compete with substitute products such as motor scooters and automobiles. Substitutes limit the potential return in an industry by placing a ceiling on the prices a firm in the industry can profitably charge. The more attractive the price-performance alternative offered by substitutes, the tighter the lid on industry profits. For example, the price of candy, such as Raisinets chocolate-covered raisins, may limit the price that can be charged for granola bars.

Bargaining Power of Suppliers   Suppliers can be a competitive threat in an industry because they can raise the price of raw materials or reduce their quality. Powerful suppliers can reduce the profitability of an industry or firm if companies cannot raise their prices to cover price increases by suppliers. Also, suppliers may be a threat because they may forward integrate into an industry by purchasing a firm that they supply or other firms in the industry.

Bargaining Power of Buyers   Buyers can compete with an industry by forcing prices down, bargaining for higher quality or more services, and playing competitors off against each other. All of these tactics can lower the profitability of a firm or industry. For example, because Wal-Mart sells such a large percentage of many companies' products, it can negotiate for lower prices than smaller retailers can. Also, buyers may be a threat because they may backward integrate into an industry by purchasing firms that supply them or other firms in the industry.

Phase 3: The Firm

The third phase involves analysis of the firm itself not only in comparison with the industry and industry averages but also internally in terms of both quantitative and qualitative data. Key areas of concern at this stage are such factors as objectives, constraints, management philosophy, financial condition, and the organizational structure and culture of the firm.

Phase 4: The Marketing Strategy

Although there may be internal personnel or structural problems in the marketing department that need examination, typically an analysis of the current marketing strategy is the next phase. In this phase, the objectives of the marketing department are analyzed in comparison with those of the firm in terms of agreement, soundness, and attainability. Each element of the marketing mix as well as other areas, like marketing research and information systems, is analyzed in terms of whether it is internally consistent, synchronized with the goals of the department and firm, and focused on specific target markets. Although cases often are labeled in terms of their primary emphasis, such as "pricing" or "advertising," it is important to analyze the marketing strategy and entire marketing mix, since a change in one element will usually affect the entire marketing program.

In performing the analysis of the current situation, the data should be analyzed carefully to extract the relevant from the superfluous. Many cases contain information that is not relevant to the problem; it is the analyst's job to discard this information to get a clearer picture of the current situation. As the analysis proceeds, a watchful eye must be kept on each phase to determine (1) symptoms of problems, (2) current problems, and (3) potential problems. Symptoms of problems are indicators of a problem but are not problems in and of themselves. For example, a symptom of a problem may be a decline in sales in a particular sales territory. However, the problem is the root cause of the decline in sales—perhaps the field representative quit making sales calls and is relying on phone orders only.

The following is a checklist of the types of questions that should be asked when performing the analysis of the current situation.

Checklist for Analyzing the Current Situation

Phase 1: The Environment

1. What is the state of the economy and are there any trends that could affect the industry, firm, or marketing strategy?
2. What are current trends in cultural and social values and how do these affect the industry, firm, or marketing strategy?
3. What are current political values and trends and how do they affect the industry, firm, or marketing strategy?
4. Is there any current or pending federal, state, or local legislation that could change the industry, firm, or marketing strategy?
5. Overall, are there any threats or opportunities in the environment that could influence the industry, firm, or marketing strategy?

Phase 2: The Industry

1. What industry is the firm in?
2. Which firms are the major competitors in the industry and what are their annual sales, market share, and growth profile?
3. What strategies have competitors in the industry been using and what has been their success with them?
4. What are the relative strengths and weaknesses of competitors in the industry?
5. Is there a threat of new competitors coming into the industry and what are the major entry barriers?
6. Are there any substitute products for the industry and what are their advantages and disadvantages compared to this industry's products?
7. How much bargaining power do suppliers have in this industry and what is its impact on the firm and industry profits?
8. How much bargaining power do buyers have in this industry and what is its impact on the firm and industry profits?

Phase 3: The Firm

1. What are the objectives of the firm? Are they clearly stated? Attainable?
2. What are the strengths of the firm? Managerial expertise? Financial? Copyrights or patents?

A common criticism of prepared cases goes something like this: "You repeated an awful lot of case material, but you really didn't analyze the case." Yet, at the same time, it is difficult to verbalize exactly what *analysis* means—that is, "I can't explain exactly what it is, but I know it when I see it!"

This is a common problem since the term *analysis* has many definitions and means different things in different contexts. In terms of case analysis, one thing that is clear is that analysis means going beyond simply describing the case information. It includes determining the implications of the case information for developing strategy. This determination may involve careful financial analysis of sales and profit data or thoughtful interpretation of the text of the case.

One way of thinking about analysis involves a series of three steps: synthesis, generalizations, and implications. A brief example of this process follows.

The high growth rate of frozen pizza sales has attracted a number of large food processors, including Pillsbury (Totino's), Quaker Oats (Celeste), American Home Products (Chef Boy-ar-dee), Nestlé (Stouffer's), General Mills (Saluto), and H. J. Heinz (La Pizzeria). The major independents are Jeno's, Tony's, and John's. Jeno's and Totino's are the market leaders, with market shares of about 19 percent each. Celeste and Tony's have about 8 to 9 percent each, and the others have about 5 percent or less.

The frozen pizza market is a highly competitive and highly fragmented market.

In markets such as this, attempts to gain market share through lower consumer prices or heavy advertising are likely to be quickly copied by competitors and thus not be very effective.

Lowering consumer prices and spending more on advertising are likely to be poor strategies. Perhaps increasing freezer space in retail outlets could be effective (this might be obtained through trade discounts). A superior product, for example, better-tasting pizza, microwave pizza, or increasing geographic coverage of the market, may be better strategies for obtaining market share.

Note that none of the three analysis steps includes any repetition of the case material. Rather, they involve abstracting a meaning of the information and, by pairing it with marketing principles, coming up with the strategic implications of the information.

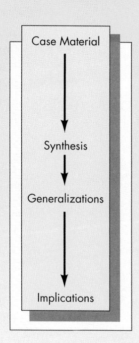

Case Material

Synthesis

Generalizations

Implications

3. What are the constraints and weaknesses of the firm?

4. Are there any real or potential sources of dysfunctional conflict in the structure of the firm?

5. How is the marketing department structured in the firm?

Phase 4: The Marketing Strategy

1. What are the objectives of the marketing strategy? Are they clearly stated? Are they consistent with the objectives of the firm? Is the entire marketing mix structured to meet these objectives?

2. What marketing concepts are at issue in the current strategy? Is the marketing strategy well planned and laid out? Is the strategy consistent with sound marketing principles? If the strategy takes exception to marketing principles, is there a good reason for it?

3. To what target market is the strategy directed? Is it well defined? Is the market large enough to be profitably served? Does the market have long-run potential?

4. What competitive advantage does the marketing strategy offer? If none, what can be done to gain a competitive advantage in the marketplace?

5. What products are being sold? What are the width, depth, and consistency of the firm's product lines? Does the firm need new products to fill out its product line? Should any product be deleted? What is the profitability of the various products?

6. What promotion mix is being used? Is promotion consistent with the products and product images? What could be done to improve the promotion mix?

7. What channels of distribution are being used? Do they deliver the product at the right time and right place to meet customer needs? Are the channels typical of those used in the industry? Could channels be made more efficient?

8. What pricing strategies are being used? How do prices compare with similar products of other firms? How are prices determined?

9. Are marketing research and information systematically integrated into the marketing strategy? Is the overall marketing strategy internally consistent?

The relevant information from this preliminary analysis is now formalized and recorded. At this point the analyst must be mindful of the difference between facts and opinions. Facts are objective statements, such as financial data, whereas opinions are subjective interpretations of facts or situations. The analyst must make certain not to place too much emphasis on opinions and to carefully consider any variables that may bias such opinions.

Regardless of how much information is contained in the case or how much additional information is collected, the analyst usually finds that it is impossible to specify a complete framework for the current situation. At this point, assumptions must be made. Clearly, since each analyst may make different assumptions, it is critical that assumptions be explicitly stated. When presenting a case, the analyst may wish to distribute copies of the assumption list to all class members. In this way, confusion is avoided in terms of how the analyst perceives the current situation, and others can evaluate the reasonableness and necessity of the assumptions.

2. Analyze and Record Problems and Their Core Elements

After careful analysis, problems and their core elements should be explicitly stated and listed in order of importance. Finding and recording problems and their core elements can be difficult. It is not uncommon on reading a case for the first time for the student to view the case as a description of a situation in which there are no problems. However, careful analysis should reveal symptoms, which lead to problem recognition.

Recognizing and recording problems and their core elements is most critical for a meaningful case analysis. Obviously, if the root problems are not explicitly stated and understood, the remainder of the case analysis has little merit, since the true issues are not being dealt with. The following checklist of questions is designed to assist in performing this step of the analysis.

Checklist for Analyzing Problems and Their Core Elements

1. What is the primary problem in the case? What are the secondary problems?
2. What proof exists that these are the central issues? How much of this proof is based on facts? On opinions? On assumptions?
3. What symptoms are there that suggest these are the real problems in the case?
4. How are the problems, as defined, related? Are they independent, or are they the result of a deeper problem?
5. What are the ramifications of these problems in the short run? In the long run?

3. Formulate, Evaluate, and Record Alternative Courses of Action

This step is concerned with the question of what can be done to resolve the problem defined in the previous step. Generally, a number of alternative courses of action are available that could potentially help alleviate the problem condition. Three to seven is usually a reasonable number of alternatives to work with. Another approach is to brainstorm as many alternatives as possible initially and then reduce the list to a workable number.

Sound logic and reasoning are very important in this step. It is critical to avoid alternatives that could potentially alleviate the problem, but would create a greater new problem or require greater resources than the firm has at its disposal.

After serious analysis and listing of a number of alternatives, the next task is to evaluate them in terms of their costs and benefits. Costs are any output or effort the firm must exert to implement the alternative. Benefits are any input or value received by the firm. Costs to be considered are time, money, other resources, and opportunity costs; benefits are such things as sales, profits, brand equity, and customer satisfaction. The following checklist provides a guideline of questions to be used when performing this phase of the analysis.

Checklist for Formulating and Evaluating Alternative Courses of Action

1. What possible alternatives exist for solving the firm's problems?
2. What limits are there on the possible alternatives? Competence? Resources? Management preference? Ethical responsibility? Legal restrictions?
3. What major alternatives are now available to the firm? What marketing concepts are involved that affect these alternatives?
4. Are the listed alternatives reasonable, given the firm's situation? Are they logical? Are the alternatives consistent with the goals of the marketing program? Are they consistent with the firm's objectives?
5. What are the financial and other costs of each alternative? What are the benefits? What are the advantages and disadvantages of each alternative?
6. Which alternative best solves the problem and minimizes the creation of new problems, given the above constraints?

4. Select and Record the Chosen Alternative and Implementation Details

In light of the previous analysis, the alternative is now selected that best solves the problem with a minimum creation of new problems. It is important to record the logic and reasoning that precipitated the selection of a particular alternative. This includes articulating not only why the alternative was selected but also why the other alternatives were not selected.

No analysis is complete without an action-oriented decision and plan for implementing the decision. The accompanying checklist indicates the type of questions that should be answered in this stage of analysis.

Checklist for Selecting and Implementing the Chosen Alternative

1. What must be done to implement the alternative?
2. What personnel will be involved? What are the responsibilities of each?
3. When and where will the alternative be implemented?
4. What will be the probable outcome?
5. How will the success or failure of the alternative be measured?

PITFALLS TO AVOID IN CASE ANALYSIS

Below is a summary of some of the most common errors analysts make when analyzing cases. When evaluating your analysis or those of others, this list provides a useful guide for spotting potential shortcomings.

1. *Inadequate definition of the problem.* By far the most common error made in case analysis is attempting to recommend courses of action without first adequately defining or understanding the core problems. Whether presented orally or in a written report, a case analysis must begin with a focus on the central issues and problems represented in the case situation. Closely related is the error of analyzing symptoms without determining the root problem.

2. *The search for "the answer."* In case analysis, there are usually no clear-cut solutions. Keep in mind that the objective of case studies is learning through discussion and exploration. There is usually no one "official" or "correct" answer to a case. Rather, there are usually several reasonable alternative solutions.

3. *Not enough information.* Analysts often complain there is not enough information in some cases to make a good decision. However, there is justification for not presenting *all* of the information in a case. As in real life, a marketing manager or consultant seldom has all the information necessary to make an optimal decision. Thus, reasonable assumptions have to be made, and the challenge is to find intelligent solutions in spite of the limited information.

4. *Use of generalities.* In analyzing cases, specific recommendations are necessarily not generalities. For example, a suggestion to increase the price is a generality; a suggestion to increase the price by $1.07 is a specific.

5. *A different situation.* Considerable time and effort are sometimes exerted by analysts contending that "If the situation were different, I'd know what course of action to take" or "If the marketing manager hadn't already fouled things up so badly, the firm wouldn't have a problem." Such reasoning ignores the fact that the events in the case have already happened and cannot be changed. Even though analysis or criticism of past events is necessary in diagnosing the problem, in the end, the present situation must be addressed and decisions must be made based on the given situations.

6. *Narrow vision analysis.* Although cases are often labeled as a specific type of case, such as "pricing," "product," and so forth, this does not mean that other marketing variables should be ignored. Too often analysts ignore the effects that a change in one marketing element will have on the others.

7. *Realism.* Too often analysts become so focused on solving a particular problem that their solutions become totally unrealistic. For instance, suggesting a

Marketing Highlight   Understanding the Current Situation through SWOT Analysis

A useful approach to gaining an understanding of the situation an organization is facing at a particular time is called *SWOT analysis*. SWOT stands for the organization's **s**trengths and **w**eaknesses and the **o**pportunities and **t**hreats it faces in the environment. Below are some issues an analyst should address in performing a SWOT analysis.

POTENTIAL INTERNAL STRENGTHS

- Core competencies in key areas.
- Adequate financial resources.
- Well thought of by buyers.
- An acknowledged market leader.
- Well-conceived functional area strategies.
- Access to economies of scale.
- Insulated (at least somewhat) from strong competitive pressures.
- Proprietary technology.
- Cost advantages.
- Better advertising campaigns.
- Product innovation skills.
- Proven management.
- Ahead on experience curve.
- Better manufacturing capability.
- Superior technological skills.
- Other?

POTENTIAL EXTERNAL OPPORTUNITIES

- Serve additional customer groups.
- Enter new markets or segments.
- Expand product line to meet broader range of customer needs.
- Diversify into related products.
- Vertical integration (forward or backward).
- Falling trade barriers in attractive foreign markets.
- Complacency among rival firms.
- Faster market growth.
- Other?

POTENTIAL INTERNAL WEAKNESSES

- No clear strategic direction.
- Obsolete facilities.
- Subpar profitability because . . .
- Lack of managerial depth and talent.
- Missing some key skills or competencies.
- Poor track record in implementing strategy.
- Plagued with internal operating problems.
- Falling behind in R&D.
- Too narrow a product line.
- Weak market image.
- Weak distribution network.
- Below-average marketing skills.
- Unable to finance needed changes in strategy.
- Higher overall unit costs relative to key competitors.
- Other?

POTENTIAL EXTERNAL THREATS

- Entry of lower-cost foreign competitors.
- Rising sales of substitute products.
- Slower market growth.
- Adverse shifts in foreign exchange rates and trade policies of foreign governments.
- Costly regulatory requirements.
- Vulnerability to recession and business cycle.
- Growing bargaining power of customers or suppliers.
- Changing buyer needs and tastes.
- Adverse demographic changes.
- Other?

Source: Adapted from Arthur A. Thompson, Jr. and A. J. Strickland III, *Strategic Management: Concepts and Cases,* 6th ed. (Burr Ridge, IL: Irwin/McGraw-Hill, 1992), p. 88. Reprinted by permission.

$1 million advertising program for a firm with a capital structure of $50,000 is an unrealistic solution.

8. *The marketing research solution.* A quite common but unsatisfactory solution to case problems is marketing research; for example, "The firm should do this or that type of marketing research to find a solution to its problem." Although marketing research may be helpful as an intermediary step in some cases, marketing research does not solve problems or make decisions. In cases where marketing research is recommended, the cost and potential benefits should be fully specified in the case analysis.

9. *Rehashing the case material.* Analysts sometimes spend considerable effort rewriting a two- or three-page history of the firm as presented in the case. This is unnecessary since the instructor and other analysts are already familiar with this information.

10. *Premature conclusions.* Analysts sometimes jump to premature conclusions instead of waiting until their analysis is completed. Too many analysts jump to conclusions upon first reading the case and then proceed to interpret everything in the case as justifying their conclusions, even factors logically against it.

COMMUNICATING CASE ANALYSES

The final concern in case analysis deals with communicating the results of the analysis. The most comprehensive analysis has little value if it is not communicated effectively. There are two primary media through which case analyses are communicated—the written report and the oral presentation.

The Written Report

Since the structure of the written report will vary by the type of case analyzed, the purpose of this section is not to present a "one and only" way of writing up a case. The purpose of this section is to present some useful generalizations to aid analysts in case write-ups.

A good written report starts with an outline that organizes the structure of the analysis in a logical manner. The following is a general outline for a marketing case report.

   I. Title Page
   II. Table of Contents
   III. Executive Summary (one- to two-page summary of the analysis and recommendations)
   IV. Situation Analysis
       A. *Environment*
           1. Economic conditions and trends
           2. Cultural and social values and trends
           3. Political and legal issues
           4. Summary of environmental opportunities and threats
           5. Implications for strategy development
       B. *Industry*
           1. Classification and definition of industry
           2. Analysis of existing competitors
           3. Analysis of potential new entrants
           4. Analysis of substitute products
           5. Analysis of suppliers
           6. Analysis of buyers
           7. Summary of industry opportunities and threats
           8. Implications for strategy development

Marketing Highlight An Operational Approach to Case and Problem Analysis

1. Read the case quickly to get an overview of the situation.
2. Read the case again thoroughly. Underline relevant information and take notes on potential areas of concern.
3. Review outside sources of information on the environment and the industry. Record relevant information and the source of this information.
4. Perform comparative analysis of the firm with the industry and industry averages.
5. Analyze the firm.
6. Analyze the marketing program.
7. Record the current situation in terms of relevant environmental, industry, firm, and marketing strategy parameters.
8. Make and record necessary assumptions to complete the situational framework.
9. Determine and record the major issues, problems, and their core elements.
10. Record proof that these are the major issues.
11. Record potential courses of action.
12. Evaluate each initially to determine constraints that preclude acceptability.
13. Evaluate remaining alternatives in terms of costs and benefits.
14. Record analysis of alternatives.
15. Select an alternative.
16. Record alternative and defense of its selection.
17. Record the who, what, when, where, how, and why of the alternative and its implementation.

C. *Firm*
   1. Objectives and constraints
   2. Financial condition
   3. Management philosophy
   4. Organizational structure
   5. Organizational culture
   6. Summary of the firm's strengths and weaknesses
   7. Implications for strategy development
D. *Marketing strategy*
   1. Objectives and constraints
   2. Analysis of sales, profits, and market share
   3. Analysis of target market(s)
   4. Analysis of marketing mix variables
   5. Summary of marketing strategy's strengths and weaknesses
   6. Implications for strategy development

V. Problems Found in Situation Analysis
  A. *Statement of primary problem(s)*
    1. Evidence of problem(s)
    2. Effects of problem(s)
  B. *Statement of secondary problem(s)*
    1. Evidence of problem(s)
    2. Effects of problem(s)

VI. Strategic Alternatives for Solving Problems
  A. *Description of strategic alternative 1*
    1. Benefits of alternative 1
    2. Costs of alternative 1

      B. *Description of strategic alternative 2*
         1. Benefits of alternative 2
         2. Costs of alternative 2
      C. *Description of strategic alternative 3*
         1. Benefits of alternative 3
         2. Costs of alternative 3
VII. Selection of Strategic Alternative and Implementation
      A. *Statement of selected strategy*
      B. *Justification for selection of strategy*
      C. *Description of implementation of strategy*
VIII. Summary
  IX. Appendices
      A. *Financial analysis*
      B. *Technical analysis*

Writing the case report entails filling out the details of the outline in prose form. Of course, not every case report requires all the headings listed above, and different headings may be required for some cases. Like any other skill, it takes practice to determine the appropriate headings and approach for writing up particular cases. However, good case reports flow logically from topic to topic, are clearly written, are based on solid situation analysis, and demonstrate sound strategic thinking.

The Oral Presentation

Case analyses are often presented by an individual or team. As with the written report, a good outline is critical, and it is often useful to hand out the outline to each class member. Although there is no best way to present a case or to divide responsibility between team members, simply reading the written report is unacceptable since it encourages boredom and interferes with all-important class discussion.

The use of visual aids can be quite helpful in presenting class analyses. However, simply presenting financial statements contained in the case is a poor use of visual media. On the other hand, graphs of sales and profit curves can be more easily interpreted and can be quite useful for making specific points.

Oral presentation of cases is particularly helpful to analysts for learning the skill of speaking to a group. In particular, the ability to handle objections and disagreements without antagonizing others is a skill worth developing.

CONCLUSION

From the discussion it should be obvious that good case analyses require a major commitment of time and effort. Individuals must be highly motivated and willing to get involved in the analysis and discussion if they expect to learn and succeed in a course where cases are used. Persons with only passive interest who perform "night before" analyses cheat themselves out of valuable learning experiences that can aid them in their careers.

Additional Readings

Cravens, David W. *Strategic Marketing*. 6th ed. Burr Ridge, IL: Irwin/McGraw-Hill, 2000.
Kevin, Roger A., and Robert A. Peterson. *Strategic Marketing Problems*. 9th ed. Upper Saddle River, NJ: Prentice Hall, 2001, pp. 693–708.

Section III

Financial Analysis for Marketing Decisions

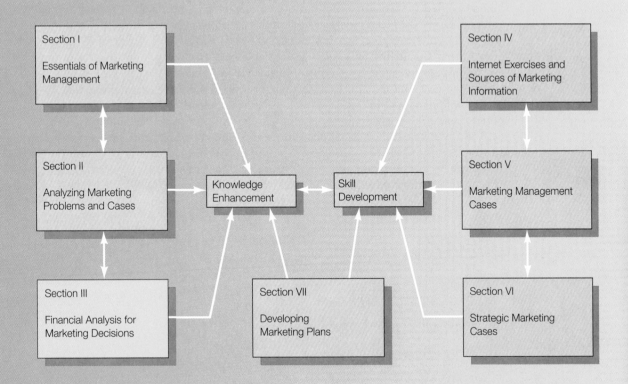

Section I

Essentials of Marketing Management

Section II

Analyzing Marketing Problems and Cases

Section III

Financial Analysis for Marketing Decisions

Knowledge Enhancement

Section VII

Developing Marketing Plans

Skill Development

Section IV

Internet Exercises and Sources of Marketing Information

Section V

Marketing Management Cases

Section VI

Strategic Marketing Cases

FINANCIAL ANALYSIS

Financial analysis is an important aspect of strategic marketing planning and should be an integral part of marketing problem and case analysis. In this section, we present several financial tools that are useful for analyzing marketing problems and cases. First, we investigate break-even analysis, which is concerned with determining the number of units or dollar sales, or both, necessary to break even on a project or to obtain a given level of profits. Second, we illustrate net present value analysis, which is a somewhat more sophisticated tool for analyzing marketing alternatives. Finally, we investigate ratio analysis, which can be a useful tool for determining the financial condition of the firm, including its ability to invest in a new or modified marketing program.

Break-Even Analysis

Break-even analysis is a common tool for investigating the potential profitability of a marketing alternative. The *break-even point* is that level of sales in either units or sales dollars at which a firm covers all of its costs. In other words, it is the level at which total sales revenue just equals the total costs necessary to achieve these sales.

To compute the break-even point, an analyst must have or be able to obtain three values. First, the analyst needs to know the selling price per unit of the product (SP). For example, suppose the Ajax Company plans to sell its new electric car through its own dealerships at a retail price of $5,000. Second, the analyst needs to know the level of fixed costs (FC). Fixed costs are all costs relevant to the project that do not change regardless of how many units are produced or sold. For instance, whether Ajax produces and sells 1 or 100,000 cars, Ajax executives will receive their salaries, land must be purchased for a plant, a plant must be constructed, and machinery must be purchased. Other fixed costs include such things as interest, lease payments, and sinking fund payments. Suppose Ajax has totaled all of its fixed costs and the sum is $1.5 million. Third, the analyst must know the variable costs per unit produced (VC). As the name implies, variable costs are those that vary directly with the number of units produced. For example, for each car Ajax produces, there are costs for raw materials and components to build the car, such as batteries, electric motors, steel bodies, and tires; there are labor costs for operating employees; there are machine costs, such as electricity and welding rods. Suppose these are totaled by Ajax, and the variable costs for each car produced equal $3,500. With this information, the analyst can now determine the break-even point, which is the number of units that must be sold to just cover the cost of producing the cars. The break-even point is determined by dividing total fixed costs by the *contribution margin*. The contribution margin is simply the difference between the selling price per unit (SP) and variable costs per unit (VC). Algebraically,

$$BEP_{(in\ units)} = \frac{\text{Total fixed costs}}{\text{Contribution margin}}$$

$$= \frac{FC}{SP - VC}$$

Substituting the Ajax estimates,

$$BEP_{(in\ units)} = \frac{1,500,000}{5,000 - 3,500}$$

$$= \frac{1,500,000}{1,500}$$

$$= 1,000 \text{ units}$$

In other words, the Ajax Company must sell 1,000 cars to just break even (i.e., for total sales revenue to cover total costs).

Alternatively, the analyst may want to know the break-even point in terms of dollar sales volume. Of course, if the preceding analysis has been done, one could simply multiply the $BEP_{\text{(in units)}}$ times the selling price to determine the break-even sales volume (i.e., 1,000 units × \$5,000/unit = \$5 million). However, the $BEP_{\text{(in dollars)}}$ can be computed directly, using the formula below:

$$BEP_{\text{(in dollars)}} = \frac{FC}{1 - \dfrac{VC}{SP}}$$

$$= \frac{1,500,000}{1 - \dfrac{3,500}{5,000}}$$

$$= \frac{1,500,000}{1 - .7}$$

$$= \$5,000,000$$

Thus, Ajax must produce and sell 1,000 cars, which equals \$5 million sales, to break even. Of course, firms do not want to just break even but want to make a profit. The logic of break-even analysis can easily be extended to include profits (P). Suppose Ajax decided that a 20 percent return on fixed costs would make the project worth the investment. Thus, Ajax would need 20% × \$1,500,000 = \$300,000 before-tax profit. To calculate how many units Ajax must sell to achieve this level of profits, the profit figure (P) is added to fixed costs in the above formulas. (We will label the break-even point as BEP' to show that we are now computing unit and sales levels to obtain a given profit level.) In the Ajax example:

$$BEP'_{\text{(in units)}} = \frac{FC + P}{SP - VC}$$

$$= \frac{1,500,000 + 300,000}{5,000 - 3,500}$$

$$= \frac{1,800,000}{1,500}$$

$$= 1,200 \text{ units}$$

In terms of dollars,

$$BEP'_{\text{(in dollars)}} = \frac{FC + P}{1 - \dfrac{VC}{SP}}$$

$$= \frac{1,500,000 + 300,000}{1 - \dfrac{3,500}{5,000}}$$

$$= \frac{1,800,000}{1 - .7}$$

$$= \$6,000,000$$

Thus, Ajax must produce and sell 1,200 cars (sales volume of $6 million) to obtain a 20 percent return on fixed costs. Analysis must now be directed at determining whether a given marketing plan can be expected to produce sales of at least this level. If the answer is yes, the project would appear to be worth investing in. If not, Ajax should seek other opportunities.

Net Present Value Analysis

The profit-oriented marketing manager must understand that the capital invested in new products has a cost. It is a basic principle in business that whoever wishes to use capital must pay for its use. Dollars invested in new products could be diverted to other uses—to pay off debts, pay dividends to stockholders, or buy U.S. Treasury bonds that would yield economic benefits to the corporation. If, on the other hand, all of the dollars used to finance a new product have to be borrowed from lenders outside the corporation, interest has to be paid on the loan.

One of the best ways to analyze the financial aspects of a marketing alternative is *net present value* analysis. This method employs a discounted cash flow, which takes into account the time value of money and its price to the borrower. The following example will illustrate this method.

To compute the net present value of an investment proposal, the cost of capital must be estimated. The cost of capital can be defined as the required rate of return on an investment that would leave the owners of the firm as well off as if the project was not undertaken. Thus, it is the minimum percentage return on investment that a project must make to be worth undertaking. There are many methods of estimating the cost of capital. However, since these methods are not the concern of this text, we will simply assume that the cost of capital for the Ajax Corporation has been determined to be 10 percent.[1] Again, it should be noted that once the cost of capital is determined, it becomes the minimum rate of return required for an investment—a type of cutoff point. However, some firms in selecting their new product investments select a minimum rate of return that is above the cost of capital figure to allow for errors in judgment or measurement.

The Ajax Corporation is considering a proposal to market instant-developing movie film. After conducting considerable marketing research, sales were projected to be $1 million per year. In addition, the finance department compiled the following information concerning the projects:

New equipment needed	$700,000
Useful life of equipment	10 years
Depreciation	10% per year
Salvage value	$100,000
Cost of goods and expenses	$700,000 per year
Cost of capital	10%
Tax rate	50%

To compute the net present value of this project, the net cash flow for each year of the project must first be determined. This can be done in four steps:

1. Sales – Cost of goods and expenses = Gross income or

$$\$1,000,000 - 700,000 = \$300,000$$

2. Gross income – Depreciation = Taxable income or

$$\$300,000 - (10\% \times 600,000) = \$240,000$$

3. Taxable income – Tax = Net income or

$$\$240,000 - (50\% \times 240,000) = \$120,000$$

4. Net income + Depreciation = Net cash flow or

$$\$120,000 + 60,000 = \$180,000 \text{ per year}$$

Since the cost of capital is 10 percent, this figure is used to discount the net cash flows for each year. To illustrate, the $180,000 received at the end of the first year would be discounted by the factor $1/(1 + 0.10)$, which would be $180,000 \times 0.9091 = \$163,638$; the $180,000 received at the end of the second year would be discounted by the factor $1/(1 + 0.10)^2$ which would be $180,000 \times 0.8264 = \$148,752$, and so on. (Most finance textbooks have present value tables that can be used to simplify the computations.) The table that follows shows the present value computations for the 10-year project. It should be noted that the net cash flow for year 10 is $280,000 since there is an additional $100,000 inflow from salvage value.

Year	Net Cash Flow	0.10 Discount Factor	Present Value
1	$ 180,000	0.9091	$ 163,638
2	180,000	0.8264	148,752
3	180,000	0.7513	135,234
4	180,000	0.6830	122,940
5	180,000	0.6209	111,762
6	180,000	0.5645	101,610
7	180,000	0.5132	92,376
8	180,000	0.4665	83,970
9	180,000	0.4241	76,338
10	280,000	0.3855	107,940
Total	$1,900,000		$1,144,560

Thus, at a discount rate of 10 percent, the present value of the net cash flow from new product investment is greater than the $700,000 outlay required, and so the decision can be considered profitable by this standard. Here the net present value is $444,560, which is the difference between the $700,000 investment outlay and the $1,144,560 discounted cash flow. The *present value ratio* is nothing more than the present value of the net cash flow divided by the cash investment. If this ratio is 1 or larger than 1, the project would be profitable for the firm to invest in.

There are many other measures of investment worth, but only one additional method will be discussed. It is the very popular and easily understood payback method. *Payback* refers to the amount of time required to pay back the original outlay from the cash flows. Staying with the example, the project is expected to produce a stream of cash proceeds that is constant from year to year, so the payback period can be determined by dividing the investment outlay by this annual cash flow. Dividing $700,000 by $180,000, the payback period is approximately 3.9 years. Firms often set a maximum payback period before a project will be accepted. For example, many firms refuse to take on a project if the payback period exceeds three years.

This example should illustrate the difficulty in evaluating marketing investments from a profitability or economic worth standpoint. The most challenging problem is that of developing accurate cash flow estimates because there are many possible alternatives, such as price of the product and channels of distribution, and the consequences of each alternative must be forecast in terms of sales volumes, selling costs, and other expenses. In spite of all the problems, management must evaluate

Years	8%	10%	12%	14%	16%	18%
1	.9259	.9091	.8929	.8772	.8621	.8475
2	.8573	.8264	.7972	.7695	.7432	.7182
3	.7938	.7513	.7118	.6750	.6407	.6086
4	.7350	.6830	.6355	.5921	.5523	.5158
5	.6806	.6209	.5674	.5194	.4761	.4371
6	.6302	.5645	.5066	.4556	.4104	.3704
7	.5835	.5132	.4523	.3996	.3538	.3139
8	.5403	.4665	.4039	.3506	.3050	.2660
9	.5002	.4241	.3606	.3075	.2630	.2255
10	.4632	.3855	.3220	.2697	.2267	.1911

the economic worth of new product and other decisions, not only to reduce some of the guesswork and ambiguity surrounding marketing strategy development but also to reinforce the objective of making profits.

Ratio Analysis

Firms' income statements and balance sheets provide a wealth of information that is useful for developing marketing strategies. Frequently, this information is included in marketing cases, yet analysts often have no convenient way of interpreting the financial position of the firm to make sound marketing decisions. Ratio analysis provides the analyst an easy and efficient method for investigating a firm's financial position by comparing the firm's ratios across time or with ratios of similar firms in the industry or with industry averages.

Ratio analysis involves four basic steps:

1. Choose the appropriate ratios.
2. Compute the ratios.
3. Compare the ratios.
4. Check for problems or opportunities.

1. Choose the Appropriate Ratios

The five basic types of financial ratios are (1) liquidity ratios, (2) asset management ratios, (3) profitability ratios, (4) debt management ratios, and (5) market value ratios.[2] While calculating ratios of all five types is useful, liquidity, asset management, and profitability ratios provide information that is most directly relevant for marketing decision making. Although many ratios can be calculated in each of these groups, we have selected two of the most commonly used and readily available ratios in each group to illustrate the process.

Liquidity Ratios   One of the first considerations in analyzing a marketing problem is the liquidity of the firm. *Liquidity* refers to the ability of the firm to pay its short-term obligations. If a firm cannot meet its short-term obligations, there is little that can be done until this problem is resolved. Simply stated, recommendations to increase advertising, to do marketing research, or to develop new products are of little value if the firm is about to go bankrupt.

1. *Annual Statement Studies.* Published by Robert Morris Associates, this work includes 11 financial ratios computed annually for over 150 lines of business. Each line of business is divided into four size categories.

2. *Industry Norms and Key Business Ratios.* Published by Dun & Bradstreet, this work provides a variety of industry ratios.

3. *Almanac of Business and Industrial Financial Ratios.* The almanac, published by Prentice Hall, Inc., lists industry averages for 22 financial ratios. Approximately 170 businesses and industries are listed.

4. *Quarterly Financial Report for Manufacturing Corporations.* This work, published jointly by the Federal Trade Commission and the Securities and Exchange Commission, contains balance-sheet and income-statement information by industry groupings and by asset-size categories.

5. Trade associations and individual companies often compute ratios for their industries and make them available to analysts.

The two most commonly used ratios for investigating liquidity are the *current ratio* and the *quick ratio* (or "acid test"). The current ratio is determined by dividing current assets by current liabilities and is a measure of the overall ability of the firm to meet its current obligations. A common rule of thumb is that current ratio should be about 2:1.

The quick ratio is determined by subtracting inventory from current assets and dividing the remainder by current liabilities. Since inventory is the least liquid current asset, the quick ratio deals with assets that are most readily available for meeting short-term (one-year) obligations. A common rule of thumb is that the quick ratio should be at least 1:1.

Asset Management Ratios   Asset management ratios investigate how well the firm handles its assets. For marketing problems, two of the most useful asset management ratios are concerned with *inventory turnover* and *total asset utilization*. The inventory turnover ratio is determined by dividing sales by inventories.[3] If the firm is not turning its inventory over as rapidly as other firms, it suggests that too much money is being tied up in unproductive or obsolete inventory. In addition, if the firm's turnover ratio is decreasing over time, it suggests that there may be a problem in the marketing plan, since inventory is not being sold as rapidly as it had been in the past. One problem with this ratio is that, since sales usually are recorded at market prices and inventory usually is recorded at cost, the ratio may overstate turnover. Thus, some analysts prefer to use cost of sales rather than sales in computing turnover. We will use cost of sales in our analysis.

A second useful asset management ratio is total asset utilization. It is calculated by dividing sales by total assets and is a measure of how productively the firm's assets have been used to generate sales. If this ratio is well below industry figures, it suggests that the firm's marketing strategies are less effective than those of competitors or that some unproductive assets need to be eliminated.

Profitability Ratios   Profitability is a major goal of marketing and is an important measure of the quality of a firm's marketing strategies. Two key profitability ratios are *profit margin on sales* and *return on total assets.* Profit margin on sales is determined by dividing profit before tax by sales. Serious questions about the firm and marketing plan should be raised if profit margin on sales is declining across time or is well below other firms in the industry. Return on total assets is determined by dividing profit before tax by total assets. This ratio is the return on the investment for the entire firm.

2. Compute the Ratios

The next step in ratio analysis is to compute the ratios. Figure 1 presents the balance sheet and income statement for the Ajax Home Computer Company. These six ratios can be calculated from the Ajax balance sheet and income statement as follows:

Liquidity ratios:

$$\text{Current ratio} = \frac{\text{Current assets}}{\text{Current liabilities}} = \frac{700}{315} = 2.2$$

$$\text{Quick ratio} = \frac{\text{Current assets} - \text{Inventory}}{\text{Current liabilities}} = \frac{270}{315} = .86$$

Asset management ratios:

$$\text{Inventory turnover} = \frac{\text{Cost of sales}}{\text{Inventory}} = \frac{2,780}{430} = 6.5$$

$$\text{Total asset utilization} = \frac{\text{Sales}}{\text{Total assets}} = \frac{3,600}{2,400} = 1.5$$

Profitability ratios:

$$\text{Profit margin on sales} = \frac{\text{Profit before tax}}{\text{Sales}} = \frac{300}{3,600} = 8.3\%$$

$$\text{Return on total assests} = \frac{\text{Profit before tax}}{\text{Total assets}} = \frac{300}{2,400} = 12.5\%$$

3. Compare the Ratios

While rules of thumb are useful for analyzing ratios, it cannot be overstated that comparison of ratios is always the preferred approach. The ratios computed for a firm can be compared in at least three ways. First, they can be compared over time to see if there are any favorable or unfavorable trends in the firm's financial position. Second, they can be compared with the ratios of other firms of similar size in the industry. Third, they can be compared with industry averages to get an overall idea of the firm's relative financial position in the industry.

Figure 2 provides a summary of the ratio analysis. The ratios computed for Ajax are presented along with the median ratios for firms of similar size in the industry and the industry median. The median is often reported in financial sources, rather than the mean, to avoid the strong effect of outliers.[4]

4. Check for Problems or Opportunities

The ratio comparison in Figure 2 suggests that Ajax is in reasonably good shape financially. The current ratio is above the industry figures, although the quick ratio is slightly below them. However, the high inventory turnover ratio suggests that the slightly low quick ratio should not be a problem, since inventory turns over relatively quickly. Total asset utilization is slightly below industry averages and should be monitored closely. This, coupled with the slightly lower return on total assets, suggests that some unproductive assets should be eliminated or that the production process needs to be made

FIGURE 1   Balance Sheet and Income Statement for Ajax Home Computer Company

Ajax Home Computer Company
Balance Sheet
March 31, 2001
(in thousands)

Assets		Liabilities and Stockholders' Equity	
Cash.............................. $ 30		Trade accounts payable................. $ 150	
Marketable securities..................... 40		Accrued................................. 25	
Accounts receivable.................... 200		Notes payable......................... 100	
Inventory........................... 430		Accrued income tax.................... 40	
Total current assets.................. 700		Total current liabilities............... 315	
Plant and equipment................. 1,000		Bonds................................. 500	
Land................................ 500		Debentures............................ 85	
Other investments.................... 200		Stockholders' equity................. 1,500	
Total assets........................ $2,400		Total liabilities and stockholders' equity... $2,400	

Ajax Home Computer Company
Income Statement
for the 12-Month Period Ending March 31, 2001
(in thousands)

Sales.. $3,600	
Cost of sales	
Labor and materials... 2,000	
Depreciation.. 200	
Selling expenses... 500	
General and administrative expenses......................... 80	
Total cost.. 2,780	
Net operating income.. 820	
Less interest expense	
Interest on notes.. 20	
Interest on debentures...................................... 200	
Interest on bonds... 300	
Total interest.. 520	
Profit before tax.. 300	
Federal income tax (@40%)................................. 120	
Net profit after tax.. $ 180	

FIGURE 2
Ratio Comparison for Ajax Home Computer Company

	Ajax	Industry Firms Median ($1–10 Million in Assets)	Overall Industry Median
Liquidity ratios			
Current ratio	2.2	1.8	1.8
Quick ratio	.86	.9	1.0
Asset management ratios			
Inventory turnover	6.5	3.2	2.8
Total assets utilization	1.5	1.7	1.6
Profitability ratios			
Profit margin	8.3%	6.7%	8.2%
Return on total assets	12.5%	15.0%	14.7%

more efficient. While the problem could be ineffective marketing, the high profit margin on sales suggests that marketing effort is probably not the problem.

CONCLUSION

This section has focused on several aspects of financial analysis that are useful for marketing decision making. The first, break-even analysis, is commonly used in marketing problem and case analysis. The second, net present value analysis, is quite useful for investigating the financial impact of marketing alternatives, such as new product introductions or other long-term strategic changes. The third, ratio analysis, is a useful tool sometimes overlooked in marketing problem solving. Performing a ratio analysis as a regular part of marketing problem and case analysis can increase the understanding of the firm and its problems and opportunities.

Additional Readings

Brealey, Richard A., and Stewart C. Myers. *Principles of Corporate Finance.* 5th ed. New York: McGraw-Hill, 1996.

Day, George, and Liam Fahay. "Valuing Market Strategies." *Journal of Marketing,* July 1988, pp. 45–57.

Ross, Stephen A.; Randolph W. Westerfield; and Jeffrey F. Jaffe. *Corporate Finance.* 5th ed. Burr Ridge, IL: Irwin/McGraw-Hill, 1999.

Ross, Stephen A.; Randolph W. Westerfield; and Bradford D. Jordan. *Fundamentals of Corporate Finance.* 4th ed. Burr Ridge, IL: Irwin/McGraw-Hill, 1998.

Section IV

Internet Exercises and Sources of Marketing Information

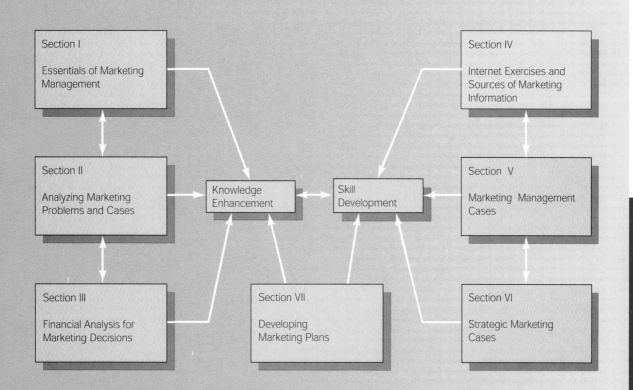

Internet Exercises

Part A

Charles Heath
Xavier University

Exercise 1: Corporate Websites

Every major corporation has a corporate website. For the most part, the primary purpose of the corporate website is to communicate with their current and potential customers, investors, and channel partners. Because they are used to attract new business, corporate websites are a good place to determine what they see as their mission and primary purpose.

IBM [www.ibm.com]   Cisco Systems [www.cisco.com]

Microsoft [www.microsoft.com]   Ben and Jerry's [www.benjerry.com]

For this assignment, visit the corporate websites listed above and look for the following pieces of business information.

1. Look for a statement of mission.
2. Investigate their history and changes.
3. Look for what they claim to be strengths (what are they selling to their investors) and distinctive competencies.
4. Organizational objectives—do they make statements resembling those in Figure 1–2, page 10?
5. Look at their product lines and business units.

Exercise 2: Online vs. Offline Retail Experiences

The growth of e-commerce has brought about a whole new shopping experience. It is easy to see that shopping online is different from shopping at a traditional "brick and mortar" store. But how is it different? What are companies doing to make the shopping experience similar and/or different?

Find two retail sites on the World Wide Web (WWW) that have famous "real world" counterparts.

For example:

Barnes and Noble [www.bn.com]   Macy's [www.macys.com]

Best Buy [www.bestbuy.com]   Nordstroms [www.nordstrom.com/Shop/]

Bloomingdales   Robinsons–May [www.shopmay.com]
[www.bloomingdales.com]   Sears [www.sears.com]

Circuit City [www.circuitcity.com]   Target Stores [www.target.com]

CVS Pharmacy [www.cvs.com]   Toys R Us [www.toysrus.com]

Eddie Bauer [www.eddiebauer.com]   Victoria's Secret [www.victoriassecret.com]

The Gap Online [www.gap.com]   Wal-Mart [www.wal-mart.com]

Longs Drugs [www.longs.com]

1. Compare shopping at the virtual retailer to the physical version. What about the shopping experience is similar?
2. Now, contrast the two experiences. What does the online store offer that the "brick and mortar" store cannot? What does the "brick and mortar" store offer that the virtual store cannot?
3. What value does the online site add to the retailer as a corporation?
4. Will the online site ever completely replace the "brick and mortar" store? Why or why not?

Exercise 3: Consumer Decision-Making Process

When consumers make a purchase, they progress through a series of behaviors. The consumer decision-making process describes those behaviors and the activities that take place at each stage. In order to increase sales, marketers are looking at the five stages and trying to find ways to influence the consumer as they progress through the CDM process.

The Internet is the most recent tool that marketers are using to influence consumers. Discuss the impact of the Internet on the five stages of the CDM process. What happens differently, or how does the Internet use these processes to sell more efficiently?

Need Recognition—During the first stage, the consumer recognizes a need that can be satisfied by a purchase. What are ways that Internet marketers are attempting to trigger consumers' recognition of needs? What are some things that Amazon.com [www.amazon.com] is doing to activate need recognition?

Alternative Search—Once the consumer realizes a need they begin to search for potential ways to satisfy that need that provides details about the alternatives. There are five primary sources of information: internal, group, marketing, public, and experimental sources. How can the Internet provide information for consumers? Which of the sources can the Internet influence? What impact does the information available at Edmunds [www.edmunds.com] have on consumers' alternative search?

Alternative Evaluation—All the viable alternatives that can satisfy the need are evaluated and compared against each other. The consumer selects the brand which best satisfies the need as their intended purchase. Many times comparing products is difficult because of complex product features, numerous available choices, and physical distance between products in stores. Visit iQVC [www.iqvc.com] and select any product category of your choice. How does this website help consumers compare product alternatives?

Purchase Decision—The consumer decides to make a purchase of the intended brand, purchase a different brand, or postpone the purchase. The Internet plays a major role in consumers' purchase decisions. What are some Internet features that influence the purchase decisions? Revisit Amazon.com and discuss some of the ways they influence the consumer's purchase decision. What role does UPS [www.ups.com] play in the purchase decision? Visit the site of Paypal [www.paypal.com] and discuss the role of digital cash, credit cards, cash, and checking accounts on the purchase decision.

Postpurchase Evaluation—The consumer reviews the purchase and the entire purchase process of the product. If a consumer has doubts or second thoughts about a purchase, they experience postpurchase dissonance. What are Internet marketers doing online to help customers avoid dissonance? Go to the Ford website [www.ford.com]. If you had a problem with the purchase of a Ford Explorer what does the site do to help you alleviate or avoid dissonance? How does EBay.com [www.ebay.com] allow consumers to review the purchase process?

Exercise 4: Discovering Product Assortments Online

Most companies manufacture a wide range of products that they then offer to consumers. How companies that offer multiple products and product lines manage those offerings is of extreme importance to the overall success of the company.

Procter & Gamble [www.pg.com]

Kraft Foods [www.kraft.com]

Gillette.com [www.gillette.com]

General Motors [www.gm.com]

General Mills [www.generalmills.com]

Using the Internet, visit one of the corporate sites listed above. Browse through the site and find where they discuss their product offerings. How have they defined their product mix? How many different product lines do they offer? Discuss both the breadth and depth of the product mix. Pick three of their products and tell which type of product they are (convenience, shopping, or specialty) and why the company produces that type of product.

Exercise 5: Brand Equity on the Internet

Branding issues are of extreme importance to manufacturers, traditional retailers, and customers. The growth of the Internet has led to the increased importance of a strong product brand name. The brand name is used to differentiate products in both traditional and online retail situations. Online, there is increased importance because of trust and security issues. Pick a company from the list below and write a few words that describe your thoughts about the company whose website you are about to visit.

Baldwin Pianos [www.baldwin.com]	McDonald's [www.mcdonalds.com]
Ben and Jerry's [www.benjerry.com]	Metropolitan Museum of Art
CD-Now [www.cdnow.com]	[www.metmuseum.org]
Coke [www.coke.com]	MTV [www.mtv.com]
Fender Guitars [www.fender.com]	Ragu [www.eat.com]
IBM [www.ibm.com]	Reebok [www.reebok.com]
L. L. Bean [www.llbean.com]	Target [www.target.com]

Now, browse the company's website and get a good feeling for what information is presented at the site, how the site is organized, how the designers have chosen the theme, color scheme, images, etc.

1. What is the main purpose for the website?
2. Briefly discuss what messages the website is trying to convey.
3. Compare what you thought about the company before visiting the website to the message that was conveyed by the material on the website. Does the Web material match what you thought or is it different?
4. What is it about the company's website that is helping them build brand equity?

Exercise 6: The Impact of Communities on Marketing

Communities are areas online where consumers who share interests gather and interact. There are a number of virtual areas that function as community including discussion lists, chat rooms, and message boards. The unique properties of online communities offer marketers a number of opportunities to reach their customers in ways that never existed before.

1. Go to the Amazon.com [www.amazon.com] homepage and click on the "Friends & Favorites" button (especially the purchase circles section). Discuss how Amazon uses reference groups to influence consumers at their website.

2. Go to one of the sections of the following sites: either message boards or chat at iVillage.com [www.ivillage.com] or "Girl Talk" at Women.com [www.women.com]. How can a sponsor benefit by being associated with a community?

3. Take a tour of GM's Owner Center at the GM website [www.gm.com] by clicking on the Owner Center link on the navigation bar at the top of the page. What are some ways that a company can use community to develop new products or change existing ones?

Exercise 7: Branding for Pure Plays

Barnes & Noble.com (BN.com) entered the e-commerce arena in 1997 and has grown to become the fifth largest online retailer. When it began to operate online, Barnes & Noble already had an established brand name while Amazon.com, a pure play (a company that exists only in an online form), did not.

Brand Equity is determined by the consumer and is the sum of all of the consumer's assessment of the product. Visit both Amazon.com [www.amazon.com] and BN.com [www.bn.com]. Describe the different elements of each of their brand equity (see p. 101, Figure 6–1 for help). How did Amazon develop such a strong brand name? What issues will B & N have to deal with that Amazon did not?

"Brick and Mortar" Retailer		"Pure Play" Retailer
Sam Goody	VS.	CDNow
[www.samgoody.com]		[www.cdnow.com]
Joseph-Beth	VS.	Amazon.com
[www.josephbeth.com]		[www.amazon.com]
Blockbuster Video	VS.	Reel.com
[www.blockbuster.com]		[www.reel.com]

Pick a pair of retailers from the list above and answer the following questions.

1. Compare the purpose of the two sites. How are they similar/different?
2. Which of the two do you think has the advantage in the future and why?
3. What strategic advantage does the "brick and mortar" retailer have that the "pure play" retailer does not?
4. Does the "pure play" retailer have any strategic advantages that the "brick and mortar" retailer does not?

Exercise 8: Pricing Issues on the Internet

One of the easiest places to see the impact of the Internet on marketing is by looking at its effect on pricing decisions and consumers' perceptions of prices. Over just the last five years, the World Wide Web (WWW) has developed the reputation as being *the* place to shop to get the lowest prices.

1. Why has this reputation developed?
2. Why might it be possible to charge lower prices online?
3. Are products really cheaper?

To answer this last question, choose two products and find them for sale online (books, CDs, and software work very well). Calculate the total price that would be charged to your credit card, then go to a "brick and mortar" retailer and find prices for the same product there. Make your comparisons.

1. Where is the cheapest place to buy the products that you have selected?
2. What costs go into determining which place you buy your product?
3. Are there any non-financial costs to shopping online? To offline shopping?

Exercise 9: Selecting the Internet as a Distribution Channel

One very important decision that marketers need to make is which channel of distribution to use for its products or services. Four primary considerations need to be analyzed before making the distribution choice.

Distribution coverage required

Degree of control desired

Total distribution cost

Channel flexibility

Discuss the implications of using the Internet on these four considerations. To help analyze the possible implications of the Internet on these elements, visit the following sites and consider how they distribute their products differently than traditional manufacturers.

Dell Computers [www.dell.com]	Peapod Groceries [www.peapod.com]
Gateway Computers [www.gateway.com]	Amazon.com [www.amazon.com]

Also visit these sites and think about the role that they play in the new breed of channel intermediaries.

Federal Express (FedEx) [www.fedex.com]	Yahoo.com [www.yahoo.com]
United Parcel Service (UPS) [www.ups.com]	IBM eBusiness [www.ibm.com/ebusiness/]
Roadway Express [www.roadway.com]	

Exercise 10: Internet Advertising

Marketers need to decide the best possible way to get the message about their products to those consumers who would be interested in making a purchase. Advertising is one of the most popular methods for companies to use to deliver their product messages. However, not only must the marketing communications manager decide where to advertise but also how to communicate that message. There are four primary objectives that marketers wish to accomplish with advertising.

Awareness

Comprehension

Conviction

Ordering

Discuss how Internet advertising can be used to accomplish these four objectives.

Awareness—Visit both StoreRunner.com [www.storerunner.com] and Amazon.com [www.amazon.com]. What features of their homepages are attempting to trigger awareness in the consumer?

Comprehension—Go to the Sony website [www.sony.com], select electronics, electronics again, then choose televisions from the drop-down list. How does this site help comprehension of the product offering?

Conviction—Go to Cdnow.com [www.cdnow.com] and select the artist and title of your choice. What does CDnow do to try to convince customers to purchase a CD?

Ordering—Go to Yahoo.com [www.yahoo.com] and select computers and internet. At the top of the page, click on the banner ad. How is this banner ad different from TV ads and magazine ads for a consumer that wants to order the product?

Exercise 11: The Adaptation of Services to the Internet

The way that services are offered to consumers is changing drastically because of the impact of the Internet. How have the following industries had to change to adapt to this technological change?

Banking—Go to the US Bank homepage [www.usbank.com] and select internet banking then click on "what is internet banking". Take a look at Citibank [www.citibank.com], eMortgages.com [www.emortgages.com], and Lending Tree [www.lendingtree.com].

Healthcare—Visit one of the following prescription drug sites: Viagra [www.viagra.com], Rogaine [www.rogaine.com], or Prozac [www.prozac.com]. Try one of these sites: Dentists.com [www.dentists.com], Ask a Nurse [www.askanurse.com], or CoolMD.com [www.coolmd.com].

Insurance—Log on to Instant Quote [www.instantquote.com] and click on "how it works." How does this compare to the "old" way of buying insurance?

Travel—Visit one of the following travel sites: Trip.com [www.trip.com], Travelocity.com [www.travelocity.com], Expedia [www.expedia.com]. How have the growth of these online reservation sites affected the travel agencies? What role do Travel agencies *now* play in the marketplace?

Internet Sources of Marketing Information

Part **B**

Charles Heath
Xavier University

When doing research on a company, there are thousands of sites on the World Wide Web (WWW) that can contain information about your company of choice. For example, a search conducted on Google in July of 2002 found over 31,600,000 web pages that contain the word Microsoft on their page! A similar search found 402,000 pages for Monsanto, a life sciences company, and just over 30,000 for Monsanto + strategy. Though far fewer results would occur, it would be impossible to search 30,000 websites for information about the company you are writing your marketing plan about. In fact, a very small percentage of those pages found would contain information that would be of any use!

This section is designed to provide you with a list of sources that would be helpful when uncovering the information necessary to write an insightful marketing plan. The list is not in any order and each company will have different levels of information available at some of these sites. In addition, there are plenty of business resources that are not listed here. Please look beyond this list during your research as well as utilizing these sources. Hopefully this list will help you save hours of time and eliminate the frustration sometimes associated with searching the Internet!

Search Engines and Directories

The enormous growth of the Web has placed a growing strain on the ability of search engines to adequately represent the total number of web pages. In fact, search engines only cover 42% of the Web pages that exist online and the best search engines retrieve information from only about 16 percent of them![1] Despite all this, the search engine can be your friend if you use very specific queries. For help don't hesitate to visit the help section that each search site offers!

www.yahoo.com	Best directory with categorized and indexed results
www.altavista.com	Provides tons of possible results and has a new easy-to-use search tool
www.northernlight.com	Very good for research purposes and covers the greatest percentage of websites
www.hotbot.com	Relevance related results that are usually very relevant!
www.google.com	Started as a project at Stanford, now it keeps producing relevant results!

Corporate Web Sites

When looking for information, you have to look at the company's own website! It can provide a wealth of information about what they are currently doing in the marketplace. Remember that corporate websites are also designed to lure investors and often provide a great deal of investment-level information just for that purpose. Don't expect to find any company secrets though!

The vast majority of corporate sites have bought their own corporation domain name [**www.microsoft.com, www.abc.com, www.ibm.com**].

Others use abbreviated versions of their company name [Procter & Gamble is **www.pg.com** and Ben and Jerry's is **www.benjerry.com**].

[1] Sirapyan, Nancy. Search Sites. ZDNet.com, September 6, 1999.

Government

The government, both federal and state levels, collects a great deal of information about companies and industries. This information has always been available in the government references section of your university library. Now, the government has done an admirable job of creating access to this information via Internet sources! Here are a few of the useful government sites.

www.doc.gov	The Commerce Department website contains useful legislative information pertinent to the external environment.
www.sec.gov	Access to the EDGAR database of quarterly and annual financial reports that must be filed with the SEC.
www.odci.gov	The CIA World Factbook is an excellent resource for international information.
www.census.gov	The Census Bureau details economic and social descriptors.
www.fedstats.gov	Fedstats offers statistics from over 70 federal agencies at one location!
www.loc.gov	The Library of Congress is a vault of information about a great many subjects.
www.dol.gov	The Department of Labor homepage links to labor information including the Bureau of Labor Statistics.

Business Publications

Since business publications focus their reporting eyes on the business world, they are an excellent source for information about companies and today's marketplace. Almost all of the major business publications have websites that include stories from the current issue as well as some archives that can be searched. A few of the sites do require a membership to search their archives.

www.adage.com	The world of advertising is at your mouse click with *Advertising Age's* website.
www.adweek.com	Home of *Adweek* and linked to its partners *Brandweek* and *Mediaweek.*
www.barrons.com	*Barrons* online presents some market information for free and full text versions of the print version to subscribers.
www.business2.com	Internet related issues are featured in the Web version of the E-commerce magazine.
www.businessweek.com	Some of the articles are subscription only, but there is some good free information as well.
www.demographics.com	*American Demographics* magazine and its wealth of statistical data can be found here.
www.dowjones.com	The publishers of *The Wall Street Journal* bring you business news in the WSJ tradition.
www.forbes.com	Access to the type of news, articles, and information that *Forbes* is known for!
www.pathfinder.com	Links to the *Time* magazine homepage, but also links to the Fortune.com and Money.com homepages.

www.salesandmarketing.com	The popular sales publication offers articles online. However, a magazine subscription is needed to search the archieves.
www.thomasregister.com	Information about thousands of U.S. companies including contact information.
www.usnews.com	More than just college rankings, the online version of *US News & World Report* is a wealth of information!

Newspapers

Major newspapers have also made their presence known on the World Wide Web. Since they focus exclusively on news, they are an excellent online source of business information. While the major newspapers carry a good deal of national information, more regionalized newspapers focus on the business news in their immediate geographic region. Matching a company's headquarters with its local newspaper may result in more information than looking only at the large national papers.

National Papers

www.usatoday.com	America's newspaper has a user-friendly site that contains all the major business news.
www.wsj.com	THE business newspaper is a subscription-based service that has archives of its articles online. It might be a good idea to subscribe while you are in college.
www.newsindex.com	This news only search engine looks through more than 250 newspapers online and retrieves all matches to your search request.

Large City Papers

www.nyt.com	The *New York Times* maintains its class and informative content online.
www.chicagotribune.com	The windy city's newspaper makes it easy to search and find corporate information.
www.washingtonpost.com	From the nation's capital, the *Washington Post* is rich in politically based business news.

International Papers

www.sunday-times.co.uk	Get an international flavor by searching through London's source of business information.
www.financialtimes	If you want international business information you must look at the *Financial Times*.

Regional Papers

http://dir.yahoo.com/News_and_Media/Newspapers/By_Region/U_S_States/	Regional newspapers are listed by the state in which they are published.

General Business Sites

In addition to print media and newspapers, there are a number of websites that provide researchers and investors with very timely and in-depth business information. These sites provide news headlines and also allow the researcher to search the site using keywords.

cbsmarketwatch.com	CBS provides business and investment-based news.
www.cnnmoney.com	The financial branch of the news network provides up-to-the-minute information about the marketplace and companies.
www.dailystocks.com	The Web's first and largest stock research site! Tons of additional links that track stock movements and news. A great way to get a feel for a company and its activities.
www.hoovers.com	Possibly the best business information site on the Web. Great information from the business search function plus a business directory that links the researcher to even more business information!
www.msnbc.com	This joint venture between Microsoft and NBC Television has both event news and business information.
www.reuters.com	Reuters is a leading source of business information with a market focus.
www.wsrn.com	Wall Street Research Net is the most comprehensive resource for investors on the Web, mobilizing the best free, for-sale, and in-depth information into one comprehensive, easy-to-use site. Or so THEY say.

Internet Marketing Reference Sites

This collection of sites provides information about Internet marketing or e-commerce issues both B-to-B (business to business) and B-to-C (business to consumer).

www.ClickZ.com	ClickZ has numerous articles that focus on business use of the Internet.
www.cnet.com	CNET central is an online information paradise. Information includes personal technology reviews, corporate news stories, downloads, and more.
cyberatlas.internet.com	Cyberatlas is a great source of Internet-based research including information about cybergraphics and Internet markets.
www.ecommercetimes.com	Information on this site covers most of the areas of e-commerce from CRM issues to technology to small business issues.
www.emarketer.com	eMarketer.com offers tons of good e-commerce focused information.
www.fastcompany.com	Fast Company and its magazine counterpart focus on the e-commerce field.
www.interactiveage.com	Interactive Age provides information about the technical side of the Internet.

www.internet.com	Internet.com is made up of 16 channels of information sources about technology, development, wireless, e-commerce and more.
www.netb2b.com	Business to business based information for marketing and e-commerce strategists.
www.websense.com	Websense analyzes the use of the Internet in the workplace and offers consultative solutions.
wired.com/news/	Wired News contains information about business, culture, politics, and technology.
www.zdnet.com	ZDNet provides business information that focuses on technology firms and advances.

Compilation Sites

The following are sites that have been created and maintained as resources for business-based research.

http://globaledge.msu.edu/ ibrd/ibrd.asp	The Michigan State University Center for International Business Education and Research (CIBER) maintains a directory of international Web resources called globalEDGE.
http://www.lib.umich.edu/ libhome/Documents.center/ stats.html	The University of Michigan's Document Center maintains a listing of Web-based statistical resources.

Section V

Marketing Management Cases

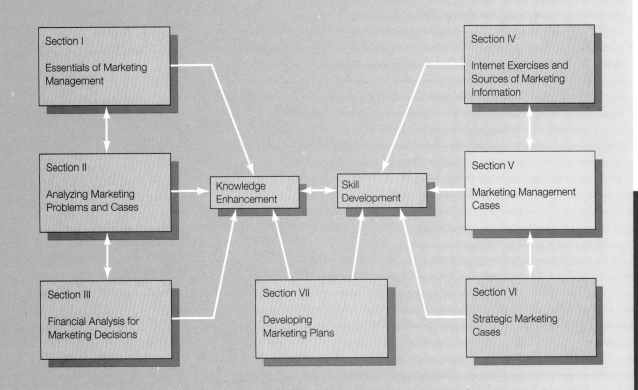

Section I
Essentials of Marketing Management

Section II
Analyzing Marketing Problems and Cases

Section III
Financial Analysis for Marketing Decisions

Knowledge Enhancement

Section VII
Developing Marketing Plans

Skill Development

Section IV
Internet Exercises and Sources of Marketing Information

Section V
Marketing Management Cases

Section VI
Strategic Marketing Cases

Note to the Student

The primary emphasis of the 34 cases in this section is on marketing as a functional business or organizational area. As such, much of the analysis in these cases involves research and selection of appropriate target markets and the development and management of marketing mix variables.

We have divided these cases into six groups to help focus your analysis. These six groups include cases dealing with market opportunity analysis, product strategy, promotion strategy, distribution strategy, pricing strategy, and selected issues in marketing management. However, keep in mind that regardless of how the case is classified, you should not become too focused on a single issue or marketing mix variable and ignore other elements of marketing strategy.

Marketing Opportunity Analysis

1

Abercrombie & Fitch

Jerry C. Olson
Pennsylvania State University

As you stroll into the store you are greeted by blaring music, racy photos, and a cooler-than-cool "sales force" that doesn't actually try to sell you anything. And if you're over 25, there is a decent chance you are the oldest person in the place. To borrow a phrase from another company's marketing compaign, Abercrombie & Fitch is definitely not your father's clothing store. Although, interestingly, it may have been your grandfather's.

A&F is one of a handful of retail chains that has done a masterful job of appealing to fashion conscious teens and college students. The challenge for A&F, Gap, J. Crew, and others is how to remain relevant to the notoriously fickle youth subculture.

Founded in 1892, A&F was originally an outlet for camping gear. Early in its history, in fact, it outfitted former U.S. President Theodore Roosevelt's African safaris. Later it established a niche selling conservative menswear to an older clientele, but eventually sales plummeted and A&F filed for bankruptcy. The Limited purchased the chain in 1988 and four years later hired Michael Jeffries to oversee A&F operations. Jeffries wanted to shift the company's focus away from, as he describes it, the "70 to death" demographic toward a much younger and faster-growing group—consumers between the ages of 14 and 24. The tweed suits came off the racks, replaced by jeans and T-shirts. It worked. By the time The Limited spun off A&F in 1998, the company was already a hit. Sales exploded from $165 million in 1994 to $1.06 billion in 1999. The number of stores jumped from 36 in 1992 to 230 in 2000. A 1999 survey showed A&F to be the sixth coolest brand in the world among kids, outranking Levi's and Nintendo. In the summer of 1999, A&F's spot in the pantheon of youth culture was solidified in a hit pop song by the group LFO, who sang about how much they liked girls who "look like Abercrombie and Fitch."

A&F and its direct competitors are appealing to the so-called "echo boom" generation—people born between 1977 and 1994. By 2010 it is estimated that in the United States there will be 34 million people between the ages of 12 and 19. And,

Jerry C. Olson is the Earl P. Strong Executive Education Professor of Marketing at Pennsylvania State University.

unlike previous generations, most of these youths have money to spend. In 1998 the average teen earned almost $80 per week, and because most of them live at home and have few financial responsibilities, much of that money goes toward clothing.

At an A&F store there is no such thing as a minor detail. According to an analyst at Goldman, Sachs, & Co, "they are very single-minded and very driven. Everything they do is directed to making sure they are truly representative of the lifestyle of their core college-age consumer." A&F unabashedly admits it hires employees based less on skill than on how they look and act. In fact, because A&F believes young people don't like being told what to buy, the sales staff doesn't actually offer sales help. Their job is to greet customers, walk around, and look beautiful. "We're not interested in salespeople or clerks," declared Lonnie Fogel, the director of investor relations. "We're interested in finding people who represent the brand's lifestyle . . . who portray the image of the brand." And management makes certain employees don't deviate from that image. For example, employees can wear only certain kinds of shirts with certain styles of pants. And black shoes are completely forbidden because the company believes they project an undesirable urban street image.

A&F's reach is not limited to its storefront. It is one of only a handful of clothing companies that have successfully targeted young buyers via catalogs. Alloy and the very-hip Delia's also have a large catalog customer base. But A&F's publication, the Quarterly, is more than just a catalog. It has become required reading for people who consider themselves cool. The catalog is filled with erotic photographs of scantily clad co-eds and buff frat boys cavorting on the beach or caught in compromising positions. The Christmas 1999 catalog included a fake interview with a mall Santa purported to be a pedophile along with sexual advice from a renowned porn star. Older folks—including the Michigan attorney general—expressed their concern and A&F agreed to distribute the publication only to those over 18. But one can assume the controversy and eatablishment outrage probably made the catalog (and the brand) all the more appealing to A&F's younger clientele.

How does any company remain popular and keep up with what fashions young people consider cool? It's not easy. Thanks to the Internet and MTV the concept of "fashionable" has become a constantly moving target. Wet Seal is a company that specializes in "club" clothing. Its president Ed Thomas says, "The market is all about change. You have to constantly reinvent yourself to attract people to your store and that's constantly a challenge." The Limited, A&F's former sister chain, was once hailed for its skill at keeping pace with youth fashion trends. But somewhere along the line it lost its touch. In 1998 a $40 million operating loss forced The Limited to close stores. A&F is trying to keep pace with its customers by filling its merchandising and design staffs with people right out of college—young people who already live the A&F lifestyle. Plus, the company employs a team of "field editors"—college students from all over the United States who provide weekly reports on the latest fashion and lifestyle trends.

Despite A&F's success, it is wrong to assume it has a monopoly on the youth market. Some elements of that subculture don't find the A&F lifestyle or clothing to be very appealing. "A lot of my friends think Abercrombie's kind of silly, between the way they advertise with magazines and their high prices," says Erik Lappinen, a high school senior from New Jersey. Another New Jersey high school student, Kristen Ricciardi, agrees. "I'd rather buy the same clothes from The Gap or American Eagle and not have the company's name on my shirt." Gap, Inc.'s Old Navy stores—with their $8 T-shirts and $25 cargo pants—appeal to those who want to keep pace with fashion, but who won't pay A&F's prices. Of course, there are some young people who want to get as far away as possible from the A&F lifestyle and sense of fashion. At the 270-store Hot Topic chain you can buy patent leather military boots, hair dye, vinyl pants, and even jewelry for your pierced tongue.

Why have A&F and other companies been so successful marketing to teens and college students? It is largely because they appeal to a sense of belonging that is especially important to people in this age group. "These young people want to be with one another," says the 55-year-old Jeffries. "That is totally different. My generation grew up as loners." So while the definition of what is fashionable may vary from person to person, most young people do feel social pressure to wear clothes and live a lifestyle that others in their peer group consider to be cool.

Of course, there is a catch-22. How cool is too cool? Airwalk initially marketed its shoes to teens who were part of a more alternative subculture. But eventually so many people were wearing Airwalks that the brand was perceived as being mainstream and therefore not appropriate footwear for someone truly avant-garde. Now the company is trying to reshape its image to become more relevant to those in its original target market. So, somewhat paradoxically, while young people seek social acceptance, they also want to retain some sense of individuality. As one teen said about A&F, "No one wants to admit they shop at a store because it's cool."

In sum, it is a never-ending battle for companies like A&F. Cultural tastes change, fashions change, established competitors redouble their efforts, and new competitors spring up seemingly out of nowhere. To remain a major player in the youth clothing market for the long haul requires an intelligent marketing strategy and an accurate feel for the ever-changing lifestyles of young consumers.

Discussion Questions

1. Companies like J. Crew (**http://www.jcrew.com**) and Banana Republic (**http://www.bananarepublic.com**) are targeting many of the same consumers as Abercrombie & Fitch. Visit their websites and discuss how their marketing strategies are different from those of A&F. Would you suggest any changes in these strategies that would allow these two companies to better position themselves in the minds of consumers?

2. The success of specialty clothing stores has come at the expense of large department stores like Sears and J.C. Penney. What can department stores do to make themselves more relevant to the youth subculture?

3. Check out the Hot Topic website (**http://www.hottopic.com**). Compare the submarkets (subsubcultures) Hot Topic is aiming for with those of Abercrombie & Fitch. Identify the behaviors, affective responses, and cognitions most important in shopping at each store.

4. How can A&F guard against becoming too mainstream and experiencing a customer backlash? Do you believe it is possible for A&F to remain popular with young shoppers for a span of many years?

5. Both A&F and The Gap are trying to use their brand names to market clothing to different age groups. For example, A&F has opened a chain of children's stores called abercrombie (lowercase "a"), while Gap, Inc. has had success with GapKids and BabyGap. Discuss the advantages and potential disadvantages of such a diversification strategy.

Sources: Lauren Goldstein, "The Alpha Teenager," *Fortune,* December 20, 1999, pp. 201–204; Rebecca Quick, "Is Ever-So-Hip Abercrombie & Fitch Losing Its Edge With Teens?" *The Wall Street Journal,* February 22, 2000, pp. B1, B4; Abigail Goldman, "Store Most Likely to Succeed: A&F," *Los Angeles Times,* April 3, 1999, p. 3; Stephanie Stoughton, "Listening to the 'Echo Boom,'" *Washington Post,* March 6, 1999, pp. E1, E3.

2

McDonald's Corporation in the New Millennium

J. Paul Peter and Ashish Gokhale
University of Wisconsin—Madison

Jack Greenberg, CEO of McDonald's Corporation, stared into the clear September skies thinking about the "Big Mac Attack." At one time, the term was an advertising slogan referring to a craving for a McDonald's Big Mac burger. However, "Big Mac Attack" now referred to McDonald's earnings declines in the late 1990s and early 2000s. Dynamic market expansion, new products, and special promotional strategies had made McDonald's Corporation a leader of the fast-food industry. However, sales growth in the United States had slowed to below the industry average in recent years. Jack Greenberg was trying to decide on a set of appropriate strategies for the future in order to reverse the declines and to stay ahead of competition.

The Fast-Food Industry

Years of profit drains and flat sales are driving fast-food chains to find new marketing strategies to compete in a mature market. While McDonald's and most other hamburger chains continue discounting and offering a variety of new products to attract customers, they also seek to shed their "cheap and greasy" image with new store designs. Major competitors in the hamburger segment of the fast-food industry in order of annual sales are McDonalds, Burger King, Wendy's, and Hardees.

Since these chains recognize the importance of drive-through customers (65 percent of sales), they are all trying to increase the speed of drive-through delivery. Strategies include using timers to encourage employees to prepare and deliver food faster, training employees in faster food preparation methods, having separate kitchens and food preparation facilities for drive-through customers, and even windshield responders that automatically bill customers. Drive-through sales are expected

J. Paul Peter is James R. McManus–Bascom Professor in Marketing and Ashish Gokhale is a Project Assistant at the University of Wisconsin–Madison.

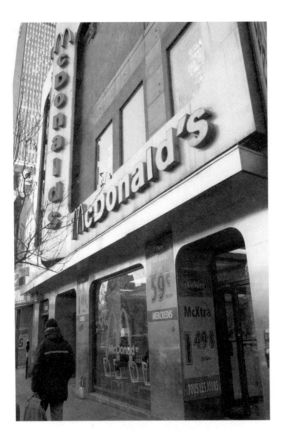

to grow three times faster than on-premise sales. It is estimated that increasing drive-through efficiency by 10 percent increases average fast-food restaurant sales by $54,000. The average fast-food restaurant has sales of about $560,000 per year.

Another segment of the fast-food industry is comprised of a number of non-hamburger fast-food restaurants. Major players in this segment include Pizza Hut, KFC (Kentucky Fried Chicken), and Taco Bell. Sales in these restaurants have grown faster than hamburger chains in recent years. A growing trend is the move by customers to non-hamburger sandwiches. Subway dominates the market with more than 13,200 U.S. outlets. Prepared meals and sandwiches available in super-markets, convenience stores, and gas stations are competitors as are the variety of microwave meals available to consumers.

Another trend is the recognition of the importance of heavy users of fast-food restaurants. It is estimated that heavy users comprise 20 percent of customers but account for 60 percent of all visits. Some of these customers visit fast-food restaurants 20 times per month and spend up to $40 per day in them. Heavy users have been described as single males, under 30 years of age, who have working class jobs, love loud music, don't read much and hang out with friends.

A major change in the fast-food industry is the increase in the fast-casual segment that includes restaurants like Boston Market, Panera Bread Company and Atlanta Bread Company. These chains offer deli sandwiches and meals that are more upscale than traditional fast food, served in nicer restaurants with more comfortable surroundings, but faster than in traditional restaurants. It is estimated that the fast-casual sector is growing from 15 to 20 percent per year, while growth in the quick service sector is only about 2 percent a year. "People are willing to pay a couple dollars more for a better dining experience, yet don't want to sacrifice the convenience of quick service. Fast-casual combines all the elements for what the on-the-go consumer—which seems to be almost everyone these days—is looking for," said one analyst.[1]

Americans are eating out less often compared to previous years and eating habits are changing.[2] Though the recession is a major reason why folks aren't eating out as much at upscale restaurants, it's another story at fast-food restaurants. Many younger consumers are getting tired of fast food and are thinking about their health. There seems to be a growing dissatisfaction with the quality aspect of the McDonald's and Burger Kings of the world. It's not just young adults who are turning away from fast food. Baby boomers are also looking for "better" alternatives and fast food is not as appealing to this large group who frequently eat out.

McDonald's Corporation

McDonald's systemwide sales for 2001 were over $40 billion, but net income shrunk 17 percent to $1.64 billion, as shown in the exhibit. McDonald's U.S. market share remained above that of competitors, but grew more slowly. Its share was up 2.2 percent in 2000 compared to 2.7 percent growth for Burger King Corp. and 2.5 percent for Wendy's International.[3]

Looking for hits to reverse earnings declines, McDonald's accelerated plans for "New Tastes Menu" items.[4] Products for limited-time offers included a fried chicken sandwich of tenderloin strips under the Chicken Selects name, a new grilled chicken sandwich, a brownie, a pork tenderloin sandwich, and a Philly cheese steak sand-

EXHIBIT　McDonald's Corporation Summary of Financial Data 1997–2001

Dollars in Millions, Except per Share Data	2001	2000	1999	1998	1997
Franchised sales	$ 24,838	24,463	23,830	22,330	20,863
Company-operated sales	$ 11,040	10,467	9,512	8,895	8,136
Affiliated sales	$ 4,752	5,251	5,149	4,754	4,639
Total Systemwide Sales	$ 40,630	40,181	38,491	35,979	33,638
Total revenues	$ 14,870	14,243	13,259	12,421	11,409
Operating Income	$ 2,697	3,330	3,320	2,762	2,808
Income before taxes	$ 2,330	2,882	2,884	2,307	2,407
Net income	$ 1,637	1,977	1,948	1,550	1,642
Cash provided by operations	$ 2,688	2,751	3,009	2,766	2,442
Capital expenditures	$ 1,906	1,945	1,868	1,879	2,111
Free cash flow	$ 782	806	1,141	887	331
Treasury stock purchases	$ 1,090	2,002	933	1,162	765
Financial position at year end					
Total assets	$ 22,535	21,684	20,983	19,784	18,242
Total debt	$ 8,918	8,474	7,252	7,043	6,463
Total shareholders' equity	$ 9,488	9,204	9,639	9,465	8,852
Shares outstanding IN MILLIONS	1,280.7	1,304.9	1,350.8	1,356.2	1,371.4
Total Systemwide Restaurants	30,093	28,707	26,309	24,513	22,928

[1]Mitchell Speiser, analyst at Lehman Brothers

[2]Harris Interactive, December 2001

[3]*Advertising Age;* Chicago; Mar 18, 2002; Kate MacArthur

[4]*Brandweek;* New York; Mar 11, 2002; Bob Sperber

wich. Facing competitors' chicken sandwiches, like Wendy's Spicy Chicken Filet and Burger King's Chicken Whopper, McDonald's put chicken menu items at the forefront of its offerings. The chain also added a chicken-honey biscuit item to its menu. Other entries included a breakfast steak burrito similar to an existing sausage version, hot dog McNuggets for kids, and an Italian-style burger similar to the Chicken Parmesan. The McRib sandwich was reintroduced.

McDonald's advertising message focused on tasty and nutritious food, friendly folks, and fun. The company invested heavily in advertising its product and improving its public image. McDonald's annual Charity Christmas Parade in Chicago and its Ronald McDonald House charity provide the company with a positive corporate image. Much of its promotional budget was spent on games, giveaways and deals, including Monopoly II, Scrabble, a Kraft salad dressing give-away, happy meals, Plush toys, in-store kid videos, and various Big Mac-related deals.

McDonald's opened its first domestic McCafe with the expectation that the gourmet coffee shop would move it closer to its goal of doubling sales at existing U.S. restaurants over the next decade.[5] The 32-seat McCafe occupies a 900-square-foot space that shares an entrance with a traditional McDonald's restaurant. The menu features a selection of specialty drinks, including cappuccinos, lattes, teas and fruit smoothies served via a limited service front counter. Enhancing the coffee bar is a glass display case filled with a variety of high-end cakes, pastries, cookies and soft pretzels. Customers can place carryout orders that are packaged in disposable containers. If patrons opt to dine in the cafe, all drinks and food items are served on china with stainless steel flatware. McCafe originated in Australia in 1993 and has grown to more than 300 units in 17 countries. The gourmet coffee concept was created to be placed within or adjacent to existing McDonald's restaurants. McDonald's estimates that the new concept will boost sales by 15 percent. At McCafe, cappuccino drinks start at $2.49 featuring a coffee imported from Italy. The drink menu includes specialty coffees, listed as "Caramel Cream Steamer," "French Vanilla" and "Milky Way." The pastries, including tiramisu, cheesecake, apple tart and muffins, range in price from $1.59 to $2.59. Many of the items are baked on-site and the others are prepared daily by various local suppliers. In addition to three on-premise bakers, the cafe has a staff of 15 with about six employees working each shift. Created to enhance an upscale coffee shop environment, the cafe's decor features lace curtains, mahogany accents, a leather couch, an antique mirror, wall sconces and fresh flowers.

Major Competitors in the Hamburger Segment

McDonald's has three major competitors in the hamburger segment. These include Burger King, Hardee's and Wendy's. Both Burger King and Wendy's have had small gains in market share while Hardee's lost share.

BURGER KING CORP.

Burger King Corp., in its ongoing effort to increase sales and market share, offered a new salad line and a permanent array of value-priced offerings, endeavors already under way at its fast-food competitors. The nation's No. 2 burger chain, hoping to show signs of a turnaround in order to expedite its pending separation from parent Diageo PLC of London, debuted more than 10 new or improved products, including the the Chicken Whopper, which officials said stimulated sales growth. The

---

[5]*Nation's Restaurant News;* New York; May 14, 2001

menu overhaul is one part of a major turnaround strategy engineered by Burger King's chairman and chief executive, John Dasburg, who joined the chain in 2000.

As part of BK's sweeping transformation program, restaurant operators had to make extensive kitchen and drive-through upgrades. The Chicken Whopper, which debuted in 2001, generated "an enormous amount of trial" that led to double-digit same-store-sales growth at restaurants. Burger King is developing a more permanent marketing strategy and moving away from its previous tactical approach, which revolved around the monthly changes in menu items and deals.

HARDEE'S

Hardee's parent, CKE Restaurants Inc., owns or franchises 2,784 Hardee's and 112 Taco Bueno restaurants and showed a 15-percent decline in net income in a recent quarter. The chain posted year-to-year quarterly declines of 4.8 percent in company-owned same-store sales. The efforts to reverse slowing but continuing sales erosion at Hardee's, the industry's No. 4 burger chain, had dominated management's attention in its conversion of Hardee's to a format called "Star Hardee's."

The company attempted to reverse sliding sales by introducing new items on the menu and joining the price-promotion burger wars. The company tested individual item discounts at most of Hardee's company-owned units. Franchisees in selected markets offered sandwiches bundled with regular-sized French fries and a soft drink for $2.99. Other new Hardee's sales-spiking tactics included its mid-priced sandwich option, the Famous Bacon Cheeseburger for $1.59, and a new Croissant Sunrise breakfast sandwich for $1.79. The chain hoped to increase breakfast sales by at least 2 percent; currently breakfast items account for approximately 10 percent of Hardee's sales.

CKE also owns or franchises 878 upscale fast-food chains, Carl's Jr. It rolled out a premium sandwich product that had first debuted on the Hardee's menu in 1994 and recently was second only to the Carl's Jr.'s $3.99 sirloin steak sandwich in trial markets.

WENDY'S INTERNATIONAL

Wendy's has had the strongest same-store-sales gains of the major burger chains in recent years. Chain officials and Wall Street analysts attributed at least part of the growth to Wendy's line of four upscale salads called "Garden Sensations." The nation's No. 3 burger chain holds an enviable position—analysts consistently rank it ahead of chief rivals in quality, customer satisfaction, innovation, and unit-level sales. Citing Wendy's planned 30 percent boost in media outlays to an estimated $308 million in 2002 and its strong focus on in-store operations, one analyst stated, "This one-two punch looks like a formidable foe for rival chains to face this year."[6] Wendy's same-store sales were expected to grow 3 percent in 2002, eclipsing the 2 percent projections for Tricon Global Restaurants' Taco Bell and KFC, and a 1 percent to 2 percent projection for McDonald's Corp.

Wendy's product line includes four core menu items: burgers, chicken sandwiches, its value menu, and its Garden Sensations salads. The salad line is designed to provide custom taste comparable to salads offered by casual-dining chains and includes the $3.99 Chicken BLT, Taco Supremo, Mandarin Chicken and $2.99 Spring Mix salads. The Garden Sensations line was expected to contribute 5 percent to total Wendy's sales.[7]

[6] Mark Kalinowski, restaurant analyst for Salomon Smith Barney
[7] Merrill Lynch analyst Peter Oakes, January 2002

Major Competition in the Non-Hamburger Segment

The gradual shift of consumer preference toward hamburger substitutes has created strong competitors for McDonald's. Three of the major competitors offering non-hamburger fast foods are Pizza Hut, Kentucky Fried Chicken and Taco Bell.

PIZZA HUT

Pizza Hut dominates the pizza segment with 22 percent of all restaurant pizza sales in the country, with Domino's lagging far behind with about 11 percent of sales. Papa John's has steadily expanded to the point where it is the country's 4th largest pizza chain behind Little Caesars.

Pizza Hut is owned by Tricon Global Restaurants, which also owns KFC and Taco Bell. It scored a major success with its P'Zone, a portable, calzone-like item that company officials call "the pizza that actually sold out in test market."[8] The $70 million national product launch featured the P'Zone for $5.99, or two for $10.99. Each pie is made with a 12-inch traditional crust, a layer of sliced mozzarella cheese and a choice of three different ingredient combinations: pepperoni; a mixture of meats that includes pepperoni, sausage, beef and ham; or sausage with green peppers and red onions. The P'Zone exceeded expectations and drove same-store sales up 7 percent to 8 percent. Pizza Hut's latest effort was called "a well-executed, differentiated, yet value-oriented product that would drive traffic and sales over the next several periods"[9] by one industry analyst.

KFC

KFC (Kentucky Fried Chicken) operates 11,000 global outlets of which 5,400 are in the U.S. Its recent strategies included a "Kids Lap Top Pack" meal program, to attract more kids and families to its food offerings. KFC planned to introduce the meals as part of its new product lineup for 2002.[10] Roughly 80 percent of KFC's domestic stores signed up to offer the kids' meals, which featured more food and variety of choices. The meals are priced at $2.99 and offer 18 different food combinations. The kids' meal containers, designed to open as a laptop computer, featured colorfully illustrated interactive puzzles and games. The idea builds upon the latest batch of kids' meals launched previously, which introduced an education theme with crossword puzzles, word searches and mazes. KFC took away the staple of most kids meals—the plastic toy—after company research found that children, especially older ones, were not interested in them. Instead, the new meals included stickers or a paper-based prize. The chain doesn't expect the new meal to generate substantial returns immediately. "This is about brand building; it's not about building sales today,"[11] said a company spokesperson.

Other new products at KFC for 2002 included a meal of three spicy Blazin' Crispy Strips with a choice of side and a biscuit priced at $2.99 and the Blazin' Buffalo Twister sandwich and a beverage in the price range of $2.29 to $2.79. In fiscal 2001, KFC led its sister brands, Pizza Hut and Taco Bell, in same-store sales at U.S. company-owned stores, posting growth of 3 percent.

---

[8] *Nation's Restaurant News;* New York; Feb 11, 2002; Amy Zuber

[9] John Ivankoe of J. P Morgan Securities in New York

[10] Cynthia Koplos, KFC's director of marketing.

[11] Cynthia Koplos, KFC's director of marketing.

TACO BELL

The dramatic rebound in sales at Taco Bell and a 19 percent increase in 2001 profits were due to a strategy shift to higher-priced products, like the Grilled Stuft Burrito and Chicken Quesadilla.[12] Taco Bell's success with high-priced offerings proved that the brand could leverage its strengths to bring up the average meal price, as well as appeal to light and medium users.[13] Taco Bell planned to add more grilled extensions with higher quality tortillas, beef and beans, and sell them at non-discounted prices. Officials said Taco Bell would continue to experiment with ingredients, such as fish and pork, that are unique to fast food.

McDonald's Future

Jack Greenberg recognized the difficult task the company faced in trying to grow sales, market share and profits in a fiercely competitive industry. He recognized the strengths of competitors in the burger segment but also knew that other providers of fast food and other meals were quick to take advantage of changes in customer preferences and tastes. He knew he had to counter attack the "Big Mac Attack" and find market opportunities for McDonald's.

Discussion Questions

1. How are customer tastes changing in the fast-food industry? What impact do these changes have on McDonald's?
2. How well are these changes in customer tastes and preferences being reflected in competitive strategies in the industry?
3. What are McDonald's strengths and weaknesses and what conclusions do you draw about its future?
4. Should McDonald's develop a separate strategy for the heavy user segment of the fast food industry?
5. What should Jack Greenberg do to grow sales, profits, and market share at McDonald's?

---

[12] *Nation's Restaurant News;* New York; Feb 25, 2002; Amy Zuber
[13] Salomon Smith Barney analyst Mark Kalinowski

3

Campus Calendar

William R. Wynd
Eastern Washington University

Eastern Washington University is one of four regional universities in Washington State. Operated on a quarter system, enrollment is around 8,200 students, most of whom are residents of Spokane County. Academic programs at Eastern feature liberal arts, education, business, and science.

Spokane, Washington's second largest city, is 16 miles east. The county is a metro area with over 356,000 people. It is a banking, health care, and distribution center for a portion of three states designated as the "Inland Empire."

As part of a class in basic marketing, eight junior students became so interested in marketing that they banded together for the purpose of applying what they were learning. With the help of their instructor they formed a partnership called CI (Collegiate Images). They sought to develop and market a product for the express purpose of making enough money to fund their senior year tuition of $500 per quarter and gain some practical experience in business.

Over a period of several weeks in the fall quarter they sought to narrow a list of potential products. Three limitations helped purge their list almost immediately. First, each could raise no more than $500 for start-up capital. Second, the venture could require no more than an average of about 15 hours per week per student. Third, if they were to market a product the following fall, only nine months remained for planning and production. Applying these criteria they screened a list and determined that a calendar featuring Eastern students posed in campus settings would be a likely candidate.

The idea of a campus calendar is not new. Several other schools in the Pacific Northwest had produced calendars at one time or another. Since the marketing research section of their beginning course had taught them to start by finding out what others had done, they developed a questionnaire and conducted a telephone survey; the results of that survey are in Table 1. Based on the results of the survey, the students concluded that quality was particularly important. Visual inspection of sample calendars sent by the survey respondents emphasized that the quality of printing, paper, and photography contributed greatly to the product image. The size of the calendar varied from a folded size of $8\frac{1}{2}'' \times 11''$, which was considered small, to $12'' \times 12''$, which was considered large. The large size calendar produced at USC

This case was prepared by William R. Wynd of Eastern Washington University as a basis for class discussion rather than to illustrate either effective or ineffective handling of a managerial situation.

TABLE 1   Comparison of Calendars

Questions	U of M	OSU	U of O	USC
1. Size of market	18,000	15,000	18,000	International Market
2. What type of calendar did you produce? M—Male F—Female B—Both on same page.	F	F	F	M & F
3. Was it a: B—full-body shot S—swimsuit M—mixed	M	M	M	F—swimsuit M—head
4. Did you produce in: B/W—blk/white C—color	C	C	B/W	C
5. Who did your photography? T—themselves C—contracted out	C	C	T	C
6. What calendar year did you use? S—school year C—calendar year	C	C	C	C
7. Did you put advertising on the calendar?	Yes	No	Yes	No
8. What was your unit price?	$3–$4	$6.95	$5–$6	$7.95 $8.95–$9.95
9. How many did you sell?	3,300	6,500	1,000	International Market
10. How did you sell them? R—retail W—wholesale B—both	W	W	W	B
11. Sponsor?	Miller Beer	Several Businesses	Coors Beer	No sponsor

on heavyweight stock was the most attractive. But the survey left many unanswered questions about what was wanted in a product and what information was needed to develop strategies for pricing, promotion, and distribution.

Several focus groups were held to determine how students use a calendar and what they wanted in terms of quality, price, and character of poses. The focus groups revealed that students need a place to write notes and reminders. Normally they try to find a calendar with a date page that is large enough for this purpose. However, most students receive free calendars and so may not specifically purchase a calendar with a large date page. In addition most students, particularly full-time students living on campus or off campus in Cheney, said they would be interested in a calendar featuring Eastern students indicating some school spirit. Older students and many of those who commuted, however, were not interested. They came to Eastern for an education, worked in their spare time, and did not come to the campus except for their classes.

Women said they would like a calendar featuring men, and men said they would like a calendar featuring women in swimsuits. Most said they would prefer a fairly large calendar, especially if it featured attractive pictures.

Information from the focus groups was used to generate a measurement instrument. This one-page questionnaire was administered to 329 students in classes selected at random at a time and on a day when most students attended classes. Results of the survey are shown in Exhibit 1. A check with records in the Office of the Reg-

EXHIBIT 1 Questionnaire

We are students in a marketing class at Eastern Washington University. We are conducting a survey to decide the possibility of a campus calendar. We would appreciate your answer to the following questions. Please answer fully and honestly; all information is anonymous. Thank you for your time and trouble.

1. We would like to produce a quality E.W.U. campus calendar for the year 1989–1990. We plan to use students from the campus as models. Would you be interested in a calendar with only E.W.U. students in it?
   253 (a) yes   76 (b) no

2. What kind of models would you prefer in a single calendar?
   49 (a) all male   62 (c) alternating males and females
   110 (b) all female   108 (d) male & female on the same page

3. What kind of photo poses would you prefer? (Check all that apply):
   107 (a) fully clothed body shot   36 (c) face and chest shot
   12 (b) swimsuit body shot   86 (d) partially clothed

4. What starting date would you prefer?
   132 (a) a calendar year, starting in January
   181 (b) school year, starting in September

5. Would you buy the calendar?
   105 (a) for yourself   32 (b) as a gift   192 (c) not at all

6. If we produce a calendar which is pleasing to you what is the most you would be willing to pay?
   0 (a) $12   19 (b) $10   48 (c) $8   70 (d) $6

7. What is your age?
   135 (a) 18–21   80 (b) 22–24   54 (c) 25–29   60 (d) over 29

8. What is your sex?
   150 (a) male   179 (b) female

9. Where do you reside?
   161 (a) off campus, commute   61 (b) on campus
   107 (c) off campus (Cheney)

10. What is your class standing?
    41 (a) freshman   55 (b) sophomore   82 (c) junior   151 (d) senior

istrar indicated that the proportion of sexes, ages, and class standings in the sample closely matched that of the student body. Ninety-three percent of the student body was classified as full time.

Several cross tabulations were run on the data. These revealed that 54 percent of the students who expressed interest in the calendar were male. In addition, 68 percent of those who said they were interested lived on campus or in Cheney. Seniors were less interested than underclassmen. Student preferences for poses are shown in Table 2. Most males preferred females in swimsuits, whereas most females preferred males with their clothes on.

Several printers were contacted to obtain quotes. There were variations in both price and quality. Production quotes for the best quality and price combination are shown in Table 3.

There was a minimum order of 2,000, and 15 percent for each additional 500. Production costs included paper, printing, and binding. Typesetting was an extra $1,000.

Since the pictures were the central part of the product they had to be of good quality. A number of professional photographers were asked to submit their portfolios. The best work was far ahead of the rest. Their charge was $250 per setting with a minimum of 12 settings. This price included travel, set-up charges, several negatives, and a final camera-ready print.

TABLE 2   **Student Preferences for Poses**

Pose	Male	Female
Fully clothed body shot	42	63
Swimsuit body shot	70	52
Face and chest shot	21	14
Partially clothed shot	45	38

TABLE 3   **Production Costs**

	Size of Calendar	
Weight of Cover Stock	**Small**	**Large**
Light	$6,920	$ 9,829
Heavy	8,000	12,040

Selecting the students to pose for the pictures was a problem. One idea was to have students nominate whom they wanted in the pictures. One of the student partners in Collegiate Images was an amateur photographer and agreed to take the preliminary snapshots that would later be screened by another group of students. Film and developing costs were estimated at $75.

Distribution was also a problem. The campus bookstore offered to take 1,000 calendars at a markup on the cost of 40 percent. A booth in a high traffic area of the Student Union Building could be rented for $2 per day as long as it was connected with a student project. A booth could also be set up in the stadium at the homecoming football game. There were other possibilities but a strategy decision would have to be made about intensive, selective, or exclusive distribution before outlets could be selected.

Promotion possibilities included interviews with the local student newspaper and announcements in the *FOCUS,* a daily flyer available to all students in all buildings on campus. A member of Collegiate Images could also appear as a guest on a talk show aired by the student radio station. None of these activities cost money. On the other hand, an ad in the student newspaper about the size of the date page of the large-size calendar would cost $140. The *Easterner* is published weekly with a press run of 6,000. Flyers about the same size were estimated to cost about $2.50 in quantities of 100.

By this time it was evident that there was not enough money available to meet start-up costs even at the minimum order of 2,000. Someone suggested that an advertiser might be interested in sponsoring a portion of the calendar. Three of the other universities surveyed had sponsors. Advertising consisted of a corporate logo in the background of the date page. Students felt that if accepted, advertisements should be tasteful.

There was a lot of work to be done before attempting to secure sponsorship. A business plan would have to be made on how many calendars to produce, the exact composition of poses, the calendar start date, price, distribution, and promotion strategy. A price for advertising sponsorship for all or a portion of the calendar would have to be established. Everyone knew that the success of the project depended on the amount of creativity used in developing and implementing a marketing strategy.

Case 4

3DV-LS[1]: Assessing Market Opportunity in the Computer Visualization Market

Robin Habeger
Iowa State University

Kay M. Palan
Iowa State University

As Pat Patterson, director of the 3DV Litigation Services business unit, was reviewing the second quarter sales numbers, he sighed heavily and rubbed his temples in an attempt to avert an impending migraine blooming behind his eyes. The sales numbers were disappointing, to say the least. In fact, sales had been low over the last four quarters. Sales had dried up on the east and west coasts because of increased competition, resulting in an alarming 16% average sales decline each of the last four quarters. 3DV had recently reorganized several of its business units, closing some and combining others. To avoid a similar fate, it was imperative that Litigation Services post increasing sales and profits. The decline in sales, Pat knew, put the business unit in jeopardy.

Pat sighed again as his mind ran through the available options. He could give the marketing and sales efforts more time to increase sales. A new Web page, giving the unit improved Internet presence, would soon be implemented, which might spark some sales activity. But, as he pondered the situation, Pat believed that it would take more than this to reverse the declining sales trend. When he joined the company in the mid-1990s as a salesman, he shared a cubicle with three other people. He remembered the lean days when it was touch and go as to whether or not he would even get a paycheck. Now, in December 2000, he had his own corner office. He had

[1]The name of the company and the principal players in this case were disguised to protect the competitive interests of 3DV-LS.

Reprinted by permission from the *Case Research Journal,* volume 22, issue 1. Copyright 2002 by Robin Habeger, Kay M. Palan, and the North American Research Association. All rights reserved.

helped build the Litigation Services unit into the nationwide competitor it now was. Pat was determined to overcome the recent sales decline. He had invested too much of his own time and energy into the business unit to let it fail now.

Just then, Pat heard a knock on his door. Glancing up, he saw Lance Wolffe, one of 3DV-LS's project managers. Lance had an air of excitement about him. "Pat, I've got to show you this magazine article I came across last night!" He tossed the magazine into Pat's hands and continued, "The article discusses how some construction and transportation projects are beginning to use computer-generated models to help clients visualize finished projects—that's something we could be doing, only better!"

Pat briefly looked at the civil engineering trade magazine turned to the article Lance had marked. Pat, too, could see that the kind of computer visualization process used by 3DV might be transferable to other industries such as the construction and transportation industries illustrated in the article. But any enthusiasm Pat shared with Lance was tempered by the realization that entering a new market would take time and resources, and, in the end, might not be any more fruitful than improving the unit's marketing efforts.

To Lance, he said, "It certainly does look like there's some potential for us to expand our efforts into other markets, but there's a lot of information we need to know before we make such a decision. Let's make a list of questions we need to answer."

Pat and Lance created a list of questions to answer regarding this new market opportunity. The list addressed issues such as quantifying market potential, determining 3DV-LS's competitive advantage, and identifying threats and weaknesses to market entry.

As the list grew longer, Lance observed, "What we essentially need to do is a cost/benefit analysis."

Pat agreed, but added, "We need to focus our analysis just on the construction and transportation industries, but we also need to compare the results of the cost/benefit analysis to maintaining the status quo. If we can't demonstrate that entry into this new market will be profitable in a reasonable period of time, then we just won't be able to do it."

Lance felt his bubble burst. He really felt in his gut that expanding 3DV-LS's technological capabilities to the construction and transportation industries was the right thing to do. He grew quiet for a few minutes, trying to settle his desire for immediate market entry.

Finally he said, "We do need to go into this with our eyes open and that means finding as much information as we can. Where do you want me to start?"

"At the beginning," Pat replied. "Find out everything you can about the customers and competitors in the construction and transportation industries, the costs and profits, the attractiveness of the market. You should probably ask Sandy to help you. Since she is in charge of marketing she will have some idea where to find the information you need. Let's plan to meet again in a couple of weeks to review the situation."

As Lance turned to leave, Pat allowed himself a momentary glimmer of hope—could this be the break 3DV-LS needed to improve sales and profitability?

3DV: History of the Company

3DV, founded in 1988 for the purpose of accurately creating 3-D accident reconstructions, used a revolutionary programming code developed by the founders. Attorneys, representing automobile manufacturers, hired 3DV to construct visual animations of automobile accidents. These visualizations were used in court cases to demonstrate how an automobile accident had most likely occurred.

Although the company's primary focus in the early years was accident reconstruction for automobile manufacturers, by 1999 3DV had several distinct products and services, each targeting a select market. For example, using the basis of the original programming code, 3DV developed several different types of software packages that allowed manufacturing companies to use the Internet for project collaboration and visualization. That is, the software enabled employees in different locations to view, modify, and work with the same 3-D model simultaneously, while at the same time maintaining secure online access. Another product helped companies in various industries improve the ergonomics of product designs and workplace tasks. Companies could use still other 3DV software to cost-effectively model and view an entire 2-D/3-D manufacturing facility by designing optimal factory floor plans and testing efficiency through virtual simulation. 3DV provided software support and training and implementation services for all of its software products.

3DV's software had revolutionized the visualization industry. Relative to other companies that provided computer visualization, 3DV produced animation and 3-D models that were the highest quality visualizations available. Consequently, although 3DV had once been fairly unknown, it now enjoyed an international reputation, having served such customers as General Motors, Ford, Toyota, Honda, Eastman Kodak, Lockheed Martin, Johnson & Johnson, Dow Chemical Company, and Motorola. Moreover, 3DV had benefited from the public trading frenzy accorded to high-tech companies in the mid-90s.

But 3DV's fortunes in the last few years had not been good. The stock price had reached a high of $72, but it was currently trading under $20, and the company as a whole had reported a net operating loss of over $40 million in 1999. As a result, 3DV had gone through two major restructurings within the last two years. It closed several business units that fell outside of its core competencies. A second reduction in support staff (human resources, technical support, etc.) followed the first by approximately six to eight months. Although 3DV still employed approximately 600 people worldwide, managers were aware that additional staff reductions were possible in unprofitable business units.

3DV: The Litigation Services Business Unit

From the outset, 3DV had created a specialized business unit, known as 3DV Litigation Services, to focus specifically on litigation visualization services. 3DV Litigation Services (3DV-LS) specialized in animation and 3-D models for attorneys to use as displays or demonstrative evidence in court cases. 3DV-LS offered some additional visualization services, including secure on-line project management workspace, DVD presentation systems, digitally altered photographs for use as before versus after displays, videotape production, and visuals needed for presentation materials. 3DV-LS differentiated itself from other visualization providers by using computers to hardware render the frames (individual pictures) used to make an animation (see Exhibit 1). This method, relative to the more commonly used software rendering, created customized animations faster and with more precision and greater detail. For clients, the primary advantage of hardware rendered animations was the ability to make changes to animations within days, whereas software rendering processes required weeks to make similar changes. In particular, in the litigation industry, attorneys sometimes requested changes right up to the day before the animations were used in a trial. Hardware rendering, unlike software rendering, accommodated these last-minute changes.

However, the process, and, consequently, the advantage of hardware rendering was not well understood by potential clients. Simply put, hardware rendered visualizations

EXHIBIT 1   Definitions for Computer Visualization Terms

Term	Definition
Animation	A group of computer-rendered frames shown in a sequential manner to portray movement or show a specific angle. It takes 1,800 frames to make one minute of animation.
3-D model	A computer-generated picture of a virtual 3-D object usually created in a CAD package that contains all the spatial information (x, y, z, and scale) of a real object.
Rendered frame	A 3-dimensional photograph of the subject material created by a computer, i.e., a picture of a building from a specific angle.
Software render	A computer image rendered using a software program. The speed is restricted by the central processing unit (CPU) processing speed and available RAM. The rendering of one frame is completed in several minutes to several days depending on image complexity. Ongoing programming throughout the development of a visualization is required.
Hardware render	A computer image rendered directly by computer hardware with preprogrammed construction sets. The rendering of an average frame can be completed in approximately 5 to 10 seconds using this process. Some highly complex images may take up to 30 seconds to render. Visualizations take less time to develop because ongoing programming with software is not required.

were created directly by computer hardware, while software rendered visualizations were created from software packages. Pat liked to explain the difference between hardware and software rendering to clients as analogous to how the brain functioned in humans. The brain (the "hardware") was programmed to tell the lungs when to breathe, the eyes to blink, or the heart to beat. It did not require any conscious thought to do these functions and, therefore, no conscious thought ("processing power") was required to complete the tasks. In contrast, Pat would continue, a human activity such as playing chess required a great deal of concentration and conscious thought, thereby slowing down or replacing all brain functions except the preprogrammed tasks like breathing. Software rendering was, therefore, similar to playing chess in that it required the computer to perform higher level processing that required more time and effort than did hardware coded functions. Software rendering required ongoing programming throughout the development of a visualization, but hardware rendering was preprogrammed.

Despite the advantages of hardware rendering, more and more firms were using software rendering to create computer visualizations. As one salesperson had reported to Pat, "We've been losing lots of cases to small mom and pop shops that are located in the same cities as the law firms. The law firms seem to think that it's important for the visualization firm to be geographically close, so they use local firms that do software rendering. They don't seem to 'get it' that our animation and modeling process is more precise and faster." This was directly impacting 3DV-LS's sales.

FINANCIAL POSITION

By 1999, 3DV-LS had created visualizations and reconstructions for thousands of cases involving patent infringement, product liability, medical malpractice, insurance defense, and aviation and automobile accident reconstruction. In 1998 alone, it produced more than 10,000 minutes of litigation animation. 3DV-LS was the giant in the litigation visualization services market. Despite this success, however, the litigation services unit had slowly lost its place of importance within the company as 3DV developed other areas of specialization. The unit's financial position was also worrisome. While sales were decreasing, operating expenses remained the same, including the annual $10,000 marketing budget. At the current level of operations, Pat calculated that 3DV-LS needed to generate at least $2.4 million in yearly sales for the unit to break even. If 3DV-LS entered a new market, there was the possibility of additional costs, such as the training and hiring of salespeople. The cost of hiring just one salesperson was $50,000. Revenues in FY2000 (January 1–December 31) were expected to be $2.7 million.

Contracts for litigation visualizations varied greatly based on the depth and breadth of the case. For example, the animations created for biomedical cases tended to be longer than those created for ground/vehicle accident projects because the information was less common and harder to understand. On average, though, the typical project required approximately 6 to 12 minutes of animation at an average cost of $26,000 to $60,000. For smaller projects, such as still models or storyboards that did not require animation, the cost of the project averaged $5,000 to $15,000. Prices were set at rates that covered variable costs plus a 25–30% profit margin.

ORGANIZATION STRUCTURE AND CULTURE

3DV-LS had 33 employees, most of whom worked on-site. Nearly all of the employees on-site had engineering or technical backgrounds. Pat Patterson, who reported directly to a 3DV vice-president, had a Ph.D. in construction engineering and a law degree. Five project managers reported directly to Pat. Two managers had Ph.D.'s in mechanical engineering, one had a Ph.D. in biological medicine, one had a master's degree in engineering mechanics, and one had a degree in architecture. The qualifications of the project managers gave 3DV-LS an advantage in the litigation market because attorneys preferred dealing with doctorate-prepared managers.

Underneath the project managers were production crews. These employees were either engineers with bachelor's degrees or "technical animators" who had either a two- or four-year degree in graphics art design. Rounding out the on-site group was an administrative assistant who did secretarial tasks and a marketing coordinator who performed a variety of marketing functions. However, most of the marketing efforts required by the unit were performed or controlled by 3DV, which also handled 3DV-LS's accounting and human resource management needs.

3DV-LS employed five field salespeople. These people were dispersed across the country in large metropolitan centers (two in Chicago and one each in New York, Texas, and California). None of the salespeople had backgrounds in the computer or technology industries, but they all had extensive experience in working with and selling to attorneys. The salespeople reported directly to Pat.

The litigation services unit was different from the rest of the company. Whereas 3DV's culture was formal, 3DV-LS's was markedly informal. There were frequent informal meetings among the production staff and project managers to exchange ideas on individual projects. The project managers also talked informally with Pat on a daily basis and kept him apprised of progress on the various projects. Project managers met weekly to allocate the production staff. Every two weeks, the entire business unit met informally over lunch. Nicknamed 'Lit Lunch' (for 'Litigation Lunch'), it was a time to catch up on personal news as well as to informally discuss projects.

In sharp contrast, however, to this free-flowing exchange of technical and creative ideas was the lack of communication between the production section of the business and the marketing coordinator. The marketing coordinator, Sandy Clarke, had been relocated to headquarters from a remote office during one of the reorganizations about two years earlier. The 3DV-LS director tightly controlled and supervised her activities and did not promote interaction with the other employees. About a year later, when Pat Patterson became the 3DV-LS director, his attempts to integrate marketing activities with production failed. Neither the project managers nor the sales staff knew what Sandy did and rarely talked to her about projects. Salespeople independently made decisions about what kind of marketing efforts to use in their region—only rarely would they ask Sandy for help or ideas. Even Sandy, who had extensive experience marketing in the legal industry, was confused about her job responsibilities. Any efforts she made to influence the unit's marketing decisions were ignored.

MARKETING COMMUNICATIONS

Salespeople generally used either e-mail or direct mail campaigns to generate sales leads. Qualified sales leads then received personal sales calls at which the salesperson showed product demos. The marketing coordinator also maintained a customer database and identified sales leads by staying current with various industry publications.

3DV-LS was dependent on 3DV for publicity, advertising, and marketing support. Publication of marketing materials, which had been designed by Sandy Clarke, had to be approved by and contracted by 3DV. News releases were submitted to 3DV's publicity department for release. Unfortunately, as 3DV-LS's favored status within the company declined, so did the marketing support it received.

A recent addition to 3DV-LS's communications package was development of a Web site, which potential clients could access to view all its products. In addition, the site included a feature that allowed viewers to contact a project manager via the Web site. Other than including information about the Web site in all client contacts, 3DV-LS did not develop any specific strategy detailing how to use the site to develop new business.

Assessing the Market Opportunity

Lance hurried to his desk to start compiling the information he would need to complete the analysis. He had worked at 3DV-LS as a project manager for two years, but had yet to complete a task such as this. His usual duties included discussing project-specific concepts and issues with the attorneys that hired 3DV-LS, monitoring the progress of the modeling and animations, and dealing with the production crew. Completing an analysis of the construction and transportation industries in a two-week period would be difficult considering that some of his projects were reaching drop-dead dates.[2]

Lance decided that this was definitely a situation that required more help. He grabbed his list and went to see Sandy Clarke, the marketing coordinator. Lance knew Sandy, but had never worked with her on a project. Because the market and this type of technology were so new, finding accurate and relevant information would be difficult; he was hopeful that Sandy would be able to help. After Lance shared his list with her, Sandy took a deep breath.

"Whew," Sandy said, when Lance finished, "that's a lot of information to find and make sense of in two weeks."

"But is it possible?" Lance queried. "If it helps," he continued, "I've been doing some research on my own, so I already know a little about what's happening in the construction and transportation industries."

"Well, that's a start," Sandy replied, "tell me what you know."

[2]A drop-dead date was the date that visualizations and materials were due to attorneys. Material that did not arrive by the drop-dead date could not legally be admitted into evidence.

THE CONSTRUCTION AND TRANSPORTATION INDUSTRIES

The transportation and construction industries utilized hand-drawn renderings (pictures) of buildings and landscapes in the development of projects. These hand-drawn renderings provided general concept ideas in a washed-out, two-dimensional picture, but they did not allow stakeholders and the public to grasp how the finished project would look in the surrounding environment. Several companies released computer applications that created computer-generated two-dimensional pictures conveying aesthetics and design concepts. However, because many of these computer software programs relied on software rendering, they were not capable of creating complicated or highly detailed pictures in a short period of time. Using the software required high-end computer equipment and an experienced user who was familiar with Computer Aided Drafting (CAD).

Lance learned that certain aspects of construction and transportation projects differed depending on whether or not they were publicly or privately funded. Both types of funded projects used a bidding process, starting with RFPs (Requests for Proposals), to select project consultants. In turn, consultants were responsible for hiring subcontractors, such as 3DV-LS. Any firm could submit bids in response to an RFP, but for public agencies, contracts would only be awarded to firms that had been preapproved by the governing agency. Moreover, the pre-approval process extended to subcontractors. In contrast, privately funded large-scale construction projects did not require a pre-approval process.

Publicly funded and privately funded projects also differed in the project design phase. Publicly funded designs had to go through a public participation process, while privately funded designs used a marketing process. The public participation process, required by all government agencies for any type of construction project, consisted of several meetings at which the public asked questions and provided input to the governing agency. Frequently, the public had very strong opinions concerning these projects, especially those dealing with land acquisition or condemnation. The government agency's role was often to educate the public about the necessity and value of the project.

In contrast, private large-scale development projects were promoted to governing agencies, the public, and investors. This process was mainly concerned with convincing officials and the public that the project was beneficial to the community and would not have any negative impact. For investors, the promotion process centered on the project design issues and associated costs. For either process, accurate visualization of the finished project enhanced the participants' ability to understand the proposed project, and, consequently, could be very important to securing project approval.

In addition to needing computer visualizations of construction and transportation projects, the construction and transportation industries also needed to study human factors in the design of construction and transportation projects. For example, human reaction time to construction zone signing was a concern, as were potential weather effects. The merging of 3-D visualization with Geographical Information Systems (GIS) was a hot topic in many trade publications. GIS was a mapping technology that was the norm in the transportation industry. Light Detection and Ranging (LIDAR) technology, a revolutionary laser scanning system, could also revolutionize the industry. In fact, Lance had been looking into purchasing LIDAR technology for 3DV-LS, but with a price tag of $250,000 he thought it was cost prohibitive. However, purchase of the technology might be justified if 3DV-LS expanded into the transportation industry.

After Lance briefed Sandy on what he knew, they decided to spend the next several days contacting and questioning firms that had won construction and transportation consulting contracts. As Sandy put it, "We need to know more about the size of the market, whether or not it's growing, and more specific information on the use of computer visualization."

USE OF COMPUTER VISUALIZATION IN CONSTRUCTION AND TRANSPORTATION PROJECTS

Firms reported that computer-generated pictures were beginning to replace the hand-rendered sketches that had been the industry standard. However, after talking with several consultants, Lance and Sandy found that only large consultants were heavy users (there was a reluctance to use animations for anything but large-scale projects, i.e., those involving hundreds of millions of dollars) because acquiring the hardware, software, and personnel capable of creating quality models or pictures was extremely expensive. Even those consultants who subcontracted for visualization services were concerned about the cost of computer-generated pictures. "Unless computer visualizations are required, I avoid using them because they add unnecessary expense to an already expensive project," one consultant observed.

Nonetheless, some of the consultants Lance and Sandy talked to mentioned that the benefit of computer visualizations, though not immediately obvious, was still significant. As one consultant put it, "I can show a group of investors a hand-drawn sketch of how a building will look like when it's done, or I can show them a computer-generated picture of the finished building that's about as close to a real picture of the finished building as possible without actually erecting the building. They're always much more impressed with the computer-generated pictures. It saves a lot of time in securing final project approval. I figure the time I save by using computer-generated pictures more than outweighs the expense of creating the pictures." Another consultant stated that computer visualizations made it easier to respond to "what if" scenarios frequently requested by customers.

GROWTH IN CONSTRUCTION AND TRANSPORTATION INDUSTRIES

As Sandy delved deeper into the market trends she found a report released by the American Institute of Architects (AIA). In this report, she found several pieces of interesting information. The AIA projected:

- 1% increase in building activity paralleling population growth, as compared to levels in the first half of the 1990s.
- A 13.91% increase in the average annual volume of contract awards (see Exhibit 2).
- An emphasis on growth in construction spending in the commercial and industrial categories, especially for office buildings.
- A growing share of construction spending for building renovations over the next fifteen years. By 2010, building renovations would exceed new building construction.

The AIA report also reported preliminary results indicating that approximately $24 billion was billed for architectural services in 1999. Roughly one-third of that amount related to the commercial/industrial sector, whereas institutional billings accounted for almost one-half of the billed services.

From a contact in the Department of Transportation, Lance learned that transportation projects would also continue to become available due to the federal government's commitment to rehabilitating the nation's road infrastructure. Billions of dollars were allocated annually for road enhancement projects and large-scale interstate construction.

EXHIBIT 2   Average Volume of Contract Awards (in billions of 2000 dollars)

Source: American Institute of Architects 2000 Firm Survey. Originally given in 1987 dollars, converted to 2000 dollars.

	1991 to 1995	1996 to 2010	% Change
Educational Facilities	$24.3	$24.1	−1%
Health Care Facilities	13.3	13.3	0
Public Buildings	7.1	7.9	10%
Retail Facilities	23.2	22.7	−2%
Office Buildings	16.4	28.1	42%
Industrial Facilities	19.1	21.7	12%
Total	$103.5	$117.9	

PERCEPTIONS OF COMPUTER VISUALIZATION

Next, Sandy put together a list of questions and spent several hours on the phone talking to potential clients. Sandy found that consultants networked through a variety of conferences, most held in conjunction with trade organizations. Consultants usually worked on projects in teams, with the same three or four consultants completing several different types of projects for the same government agency or private developer. Often, the consultants who designed projects for government-initiated projects were the same consultants who designed large-scale commercial projects. The designated primary consultant changed depending on the project but had the same subcontractors. Most consultants decided who to work with based on experience, quality, past working relationship, availability, and price.

The consultants Sandy talked to also shared with her some of their perceptions of 3DV-LS. For example, one consultant told her that 3DV-LS had a reputation of charging high fees for standard services. Another reported a concern that 3DV-LS's prices were too high, since it did not provide any expertise concerning design issues. Sandy was surprised by this, because her research showed 3DV-LS's prices, even with a 25–30% profit margin, to be competitive in the litigation market. She was afraid that the perception of high prices derived from the early years in computer visualization when any type of computer-generated models or animation had been extremely expensive.

Sandy also queried the consultants on whether or not the visualizations they contracted for were software or hardware rendered. Most were uncertain. "I didn't know that there was more than one way to get pictures," was a typical response.

PRICING

The consultants were reluctant to share what they were paying for visualization services in the construction and transportation industries. However, after some digging, Lance was able to identify the going rates for animation and photo simulations in the transportation industry. The rates did not specify what kind of process was used (i.e., hardware or software rendering) to create the visualizations. But, because Lance knew of no other companies who did hardware rendering besides 3DV-LS, he assumed the prices reflected software rendered visualizations.

- Animation—$3,000 to $6,000 per minute
- Digitally altered photographs—$5,000 to $7,000 per image
- Photo-images or 3D models—$800 to $1,500 per image

In the transportation industry, most of the projects were large-scale transportation projects funded by government agencies. The government agency often specified the amount of money to be spent on visualizations. For example, the allowable costs for visualization on a recently approved $500 million transportation project ranged from $70,000 to $150,000.

Neither Sandy nor Lance was able to find a range of prices in the construction industry, but assumed that the rates were most likely comparable to those in the transportation industry. Moreover, because many construction projects were also funded by the government, Lance and Sandy surmised that the government would specify the computer visualization budgets for those projects, also.

COMPETITION

After talking to several consultants, Sandy looked into how competitive the market was. She identified two types of competitors and profiled each of these.

The first competitor was typically a large firm that provided a full complement of services desired by the construction and transportation industries. These firms had the ability to design a project, conduct marketing campaigns and public participation workshops, and manage the implementation or construction of the project. Competitors in this group, such as Howard, Needles, Tammen, and Bergendoff (HNTB), the 8th largest architecture firm nationwide and 4th largest in transportation design, had national brand recognition and many years of extensive and varied experience. Not surprisingly, these firms rarely hired subcontractors, relying, instead, on in-house technology departments for their visualization needs. For example, HNTB's Technology Group employed content planners, media designers, 3-D animators, and networking and programming professionals to provide high-tech communication and information solutions to the architecture, transportation, environmental engineering, and construction services industries. However, HNTB relied on software rendering for its visualization projects.

Another firm that fit this competitor profile was Parsons Brinckerhoff, Inc., a global engineering giant. This firm provided planning, engineering, construction management, and operations and maintenance services to a wide variety of clients around the world. Similar to HNTB, Parsons Brinckerhoff had started Parsons and Brinckerhoff 4D Imaging (PB4D) in 1988 as an advanced computer visual simulation business unit. While PB4D was the industry leader for the visualization of transportation projects, it was also a large-scale multimedia and Internet business unit. Like HNTB, PB4D also relied on software rendering.

The second type of competitor was characterized as firms specializing in design visualization services. Typically, these firms were smaller than 3DV and had regional brand recognition. Although these firms' staffs were small, they also had specific experience with architects, landscape architects, planners, and civil engineers. Consequently, these competitors knew how to communicate with these professionals using industry jargon. Interestingly, most of these firms also relied on software rendering and did not provide extensive product or service lines. One firm typical of this type of competitor was Newlands & Co., a consulting firm located in Portland, Oregon that specialized in design visualization, 3D animation and Web development services. Newlands & Company, Inc. produced high-quality visual simulations, animations, Web and multimedia presentations for transportation, urban design and architecture. Its mission was to employ the best in art and technology to facilitate communication between designers and their clients. Its services included photography, 3-D modeling, photo simulation, animation, multimedia presentation creation, Web development, and training.

The Future

Lance met with Pat two weeks later to present the information he and Sandy had uncovered about the construction and transportation industries. When Lance finished the brief overview, he handed over a complete written report of the findings to Pat. "So," Pat said, "based on what you've learned, what do you think we should do?"

Lance, expecting this question, carefully formulated his response. "I think there's an excellent opportunity for 3DV-LS in this new market. The construction and transportation industries are growing, and there's increasing use of computer visualizations on projects. Plus, I think the advantage of hardware rendering—that is, being able to quickly create and change visualizations—will be just as important to the construction and transportation industries as it has proven to be in the litigation industry. But we'll have to convince consultants of this fact and at the same time compete against companies that are already firmly established in this market. It won't be easy."

Pat thanked Lance for all his hard work. Left alone with his thoughts, Pat pondered his options. One option was to hire and train one to two new salespeople to focus on developing business in the construction and transportation industries. This would require some investment, but would allow the current salesforce to stay focused on the litigation industry. Another option was to allocate the time and efforts of one or two current salespeople to developing small scale bids for regional projects in the construction and transportation industries. This option was less risky financially, but might further affect sales in the litigation industry.

Pat couldn't help but speculate. What if the sales decline in the last year was just temporary? What if the Web site proved to be an effective tool in cultivating sales? Several times over the last few months, Pat had wondered whether the declining sales were a direct effect of poorly communicating the advantages of hardware rendering relative to software rendering. At especially low moments, he worried that, to the average client, the advantages of hardware rendering were not tangible enough to clearly differentiate it from software rendering.

With respect to the new market opportunity, Pat had other nagging questions. Did 3DV-LS have the necessary skills and resources to enter the construction and transportation market while at the same time maintaining its litigation business? In particular, could the current five salespeople adapt their skills, honed in the litigation market, to the construction and transportation market? Could 3DV-LS successfully differentiate its hardware rendering visualization method from the more commonly used software rendering in the new market? Would entry into the new market pull necessary attention from the litigation industry? While Pat appreciated Lance's opinion, he knew that whether or not 3DV-LS should enter the construction and transportation market depended on the answers to these questions.

Case **5**

South Delaware Coors, Inc.

James E. Nelson and Eric J. Karson
University of Colorado

Larry Brownlow was just beginning to realize the problem was more complex than he thought. The problem, of course, was giving direction to Manson and Associates regarding which research should be completed by February 20, 1989, to determine market potential of a Coors beer distributorship for a two-county area in southern Delaware. With data from this research, Larry would be able to estimate the feasibility of such an operation before the March 5 application deadline. Larry knew his decision on whether or not to apply for the distributorship was the most important career choice he had ever faced.

Larry Brownlow

Larry was just completing his M.B.A. and, from his standpoint, the Coors announcement of expansion into Delaware could hardly have been better timed. He had long ago decided the best opportunities and rewards were in smaller, self-owned businesses and not in the jungles of corporate giants. Because of a family tragedy some three years ago, Larry found himself in a position to consider small business opportunities such as the Coors distributorship. Approximately $500,000 was held in trust for Larry, to be dispersed when he reached age thirty. Until then, Larry and his family lived on an annual trust income of about $40,000. It was on this income that Larry decided to leave his sales engineering job and return to graduate school for his M.B.A.

The decision to complete a graduate program and operate his own business had been easy to make. While he could have retired and lived off investment income, Larry knew such a life would not be to his liking. Working with people and the challenge of making it on his own, Larry thought, were far more preferable to enduring an early retirement.

This case was written by Professor James E. Nelson and doctoral student Eric J. Karson, University of Colorado. This case is intended for use as a basis for class discussion rather than to illustrate either effective or ineffective administrative decision making. Some data are disguised. © 1989 by the Business Research Division, College of Business and Administration and the Graduate School of Business Administration, University of Colorado, Boulder, Colorado 80309–0419.

Larry would be thirty in July, about the time money would actually be needed to start the business. In the meantime, he had access to about $15,000 for feasibility research. While there certainly were other places to spend the money, Larry and his wife agreed the opportunity to acquire the distributorship could not be overlooked.

Coors, Inc.

Coors's history dates back to 1873, when Adolph Coors built a small brewery in Golden, Colorado. Since then, the brewery has prospered and become the fourth-largest seller of beer in the country. Coors's operating philosophy could be summed up as "hard work, saving money, devotion to the quality of the product, caring about the environment, and giving people something to believe in." Company operation is consistent with this philosophy. Headquarters and most production facilities are still located in Golden, Colorado, with a new Shenandoah, Virginia, facility aiding in nationwide distribution. Coors is still family operated and controlled. The company issued its first public stock, $127 million worth of nonvoting shares, in 1975. The issue was received enthusiastically by the financial community despite its being offered during a recession.

Coors's unwillingness to compromise on the high quality of its product is well known both to its suppliers and to its consuming public. Coors beer requires constant refrigeration to maintain this quality, and wholesalers' facilities are closely controlled to ensure proper temperatures are maintained. Wholesalers are also required to install and use aluminum can recycling equipment. Coors was one of the first breweries in the industry to recycle its cans.

Larry was aware of Coors's popularity with many consumers in adjacent states. However, Coors's corporate management was seen by some consumers to hold antiunion beliefs (because of a labor disagreement at the brewery some ten years ago and the brewery's current use of a nonunion labor force). Some other consumers perceived the brewery to be somewhat insensitive to minority issues, primarily in employment and distribution. The result of these attitudes—plus many other aspects of consumer behavior—meant that Coors's sales in Delaware would depend greatly on the efforts of the two wholesalers planned for the state.

Manson Research Proposal

Because of the press of his studies, Larry had contacted Manson and Associates in January for their assistance. The firm was a Wilmington-based general research supplier that had conducted other feasibility studies in the south Atlantic region. Manson was well known for the quality of its work, particularly with respect to computer modeling. The firm had developed special expertise in modeling population and employment levels for cities, counties, and other units of area for periods of up to ten years into the future.

Larry had met John Rome, senior research analyst for Manson, and discussed the Coors opportunity and appropriate research extensively in the January meeting. Rome promised a formal research proposal (Exhibits 1 and 2) for the project, which Larry now held in his hand. It certainly was extensive, Larry thought, and reflected the professionalism he expected. Now came the hard part, choosing the more relevant research from the proposal, because he certainly couldn't afford to pay for it all. Rome had suggested a meeting for Friday, giving Larry only two more days to decide.

Larry was at first overwhelmed. All the research would certainly be useful. He was sure he needed estimates of sales and costs in a form allowing managerial analysis, but

EXHIBIT 1   **Manson and Associates Research Proposal**

Mr. Larry Brownlow   January 16, 1989
1198 West Lamar
Chester, PA 12345

Dear Larry:
    It was a pleasure meeting you last week and discussing your business and research interests in Coors
wholesaling. After further thought and discussion with my colleagues, the Coors opportunity appears even
more attractive than when we met.
    Appearances can be deceiving, as you know, and I fully agree some formal research is needed before you
make application. Research that we recommend would proceed in two distinct stages and is described below:

Stage One Research Based on Secondary Data and Manson Computer Models:

Study A: National and Delaware per Capita Beer Consumption for 1988–1992.
              Description: Per capita annual consumption of beer for the total population and population aged
                  21 and over is provided in gallons.
              Source: Various publications, Manson computer model
              Cost: $1,000

Study B: Population Estimates for 1985–1995 for Two Delaware Counties in Market Area.
              Description: Annual estimates of total population and population aged 21 and over is provided for
                  the period 1985–1995.
              Source: U.S. Bureau of Census, Sales Management Annual Survey of Buying Power, Manson
          computer model
              Cost: $1,500

Study C: Coors Market Share Estimates for 1990–1995.
              Description: Coors market share for the two-county market area based on total gallons consumed
                  is estimated for each year in the period 1990–1995. This data will be projected from Coors's
                  nationwide experience.
              Source: Various publications, Manson computer model
              Cost: $2,000

Study D: Estimated Liquor and Beer Licenses for the Market Area, 1990–1995.
              Description: Projections of the number of on-premise sale operations and off-premise sale
                  operations is provided.
              Source: Delaware Department of Revenue, Manson computer model
              Cost: $1,000

Study E: Beer Taxes Paid by Delaware Wholesalers for 1987 and 1988 in the Market Area.
              Description: Beer taxes paid by each of the six presently operating competing beer wholesalers is
                  provided. This can be converted to gallons sold by applying the state gallonage tax rate (6 cents
                  per gallon).
              Source: Delaware Department of Revenue
              Cost: $200

Study F: Financial Statement Summary of Wine, Liquor, and Beer Wholesalers for Fiscal Year 1986.
              Description: Composite balance sheets, income statements, and relevant measures of performance
                  provided for 510 similar wholesaling operations in the United States is provided.
              Source: Robert Morris Associates Annual Statement Studies 1987 ed.
              Cost: $49.50

(continued)

EXHIBIT 1   **Manson and Associates Research Proposal**   (*concluded*)

Stage Two Research Based on Primary Data:

Study G: Consumer Study

> *Description:* Study G involves focus group interviews and a mail questionnaire to determine consumer past experience, acceptance, and intention to buy Coors beer. Three focus group interviews would be conducted in the two counties in the market area. From these data, a mail questionnaire would be developed and sent to 300 adult residents in the market area, utilizing direct questions and semantic differential scale to measure attitudes toward Coors beer, competing beers, and an ideal beer.
>
> *Source:* Manson and Associates
>
> *Cost:* $6,000

Study H: Retailer Study

> *Description:* Group interviews would be conducted with six potential retailers of Coors beer in one county in the market area to determine their past beer sales and experience and their intention to stock and sell Coors. From these data, a personal interview questionnaire would be developed and executed at all appropriate retailers in the market area to determine similar data.
>
> *Source:* Manson and Associates
>
> *Cost:* $4,800

Study I: Survey of Retail and Wholesale Beer Prices

> *Description:* Study I involves in-store interviews with a sample of 50 retailers in the market area to estimate retail and wholesale prices for Budweiser, Miller Lite, Miller, Busch, Bud Light, Old Milwaukee, and Michelob.
>
> *Source:* Manson and Associates
>
> *Cost:* $2,000

Examples of the form of final report tables are attached [Exhibit 2]. This should give you a better idea of the data you will receive.

As you can see, the research is extensive and, I might add, not cheap. However, the research as outlined will supply you with sufficient information to make an estimate of the feasibility of a Coors distributorship, the investment for which is substantial.

I have scheduled 9:00 next Friday as a time to meet with you to discuss the proposal in more detail. Time is short, but we firmly feel the study can be completed by February 20, 1989. If you need more information in the meantime, please feel free to call.

Sincerely,

John

John Rome

Senior Research Analyst

EXHIBIT 2 Examples of Final Research Report Tables

(A) National and Delaware Resident Annual Beer Consumption per Capita, 1988–1992 (Gallons)

	U.S. Consumption		Delaware Consumption	
Year	Based on Entire Population	Based on Population over Age 21	Based on Entire Population	Based on Population over Age 21
1988				
1989				
1990				
1991				
1992				

Source: Study A.

(B) Population Estimates for 1986–1996 for Two Delaware Counties in Market Area

	Entire Population					
County	1986	1988	1990	1992	1994	1996
Kent						
Sussex						

	Population Age 21 and Over					
County	1986	1988	1990	1992	1994	1996
Kent						
Sussex						

Source: Study B.

(C) Coors Market Share Estimates for 1990–1995

Year	Market Share (%)
1990	
1991	
1992	
1993	
1994	
1995	

Source: Study C.

(D) Liquor and Beer License Estimates for Market Area for 1990–1995

Type of License	1990	1991	1992	1993	1994	1995
All beverages						
Retail beer and wine						
Off-premises beer only						
Veterans beer and liquor						
Fraternal						
Resort beer and liquor						

Source: Study D.

(E) Beer Taxes Paid by Beer Wholesalers in the Market Area, 1987 and 1988

Wholesaler	1987 Tax Paid ($)	1988 Tax Paid ($)
A		
B		
C		
D		
E		
F		

Source: Study E.

Note: Delaware beer tax is 6 cents per gallon.

(continued)

EXHIBIT 2 Examples of Final Research Report Tables *(continued)*

(F) Financial Statement Summary for 510 Wholesalers of Wine, Liquor, and Beer in Fiscal Year 1986

Assets	Percentage
Cash and equivalents	
Accounts and notes receivable net	
Inventory	
All other current	
Total current	
Fixed assets net	
Intangibles net	
All other noncurrent	_____
Total	100.0

Ratios
Quick
Current
Debts/worth

Liabilities	Percentage
Notes payable—short-term	
Current maturity long-term debt	
Accounts and notes payable—trade	
Accrued expenses	
All other current	
Total current	
Long-term debt	
All other noncurrent	
Net worth	_____
Total liabilities and net worth	100.0
Income Data	
Net sales	100.0
Cost of sales	
Gross profit	
Operating expenses	
Operating profit	
All other expenses net	_____
Profit before taxes	

Sales/receivables
Cost sales/inventory
Percentage profit before taxes
   based on total assets

Source: Study F (Robert Morris Associates, © 1987)

Interpretation of Statement Studies Figures

RMA recommends that Statement Studies data be regarded only as general guidelines and not as absolute industry norms. There are several reasons why the data may not be fully representative of a given industry:

1. The financial statements used in the *Statement Studies* are not selected by any random or statistically reliable method. RMA member banks voluntarily submit the raw data they have available each year, with these being the only constraints: (a) The fiscal year-ends of the companies reported may not be from April 1 through June 29, and (b) their total assets must be less than $100 million.

2. Many companies have varied product lines; however, the *Statement Studies* categorize them by their primary product Standard Industrial Classification (SIC) number only.

3. Some of our industry samples are rather small in relation to the total number of firms in a given industry. A relatively small sample can increase the chances that some of our composites do not fully represent an industry.

4. There is the chance that an extreme statement can be present in a sample, causing a disproportionate influence on the industry composite. This is particularly true in a relatively small sample.

5. Companies within the same industry may differ in their method of operations which in turn can directly influence their financial statements. Since they are included in our sample, too, these statements can significantly affect our composite calculations.

6. Other considerations that can result in variations among different companies engaged in the same general line of business are different labor markets; geographical location; different accounting methods; quality of products handled; sources and methods of financing; and terms of sale.

For these reasons, RMA does not recommend the Statement Studies figures be considered as absolute norms for a given industry. Rather the figures should be used only as general guidelines and in addition to the other methods of financial analysis. RMA makes no claim as to the representativeness of the figures printed in this book.

(continued)

EXHIBIT 2   **Examples of Final Research Report Tables**   (*continued*)

(G) Consumer Questionnaire Results

	Yes	No			Yes	No
Consumed Coors in the Past:	%	%	**Usually Buy Beer at:**			%
Attitudes toward Coors:	%					

Strongly like		Liquor stores	
Like		Taverns and bars	
Indifferent/no opinion		Supermarkets	
Dislike		Corner grocery	
Strongly dislike		Total	100.0
Total	100.0		

Features Considered Important

Weekly Beer Consumption:	%	**When Buying Beer:**	%
Less than 1 can		Taste	
1–2 cans		Brand Name	
3–4 cans		Price	
5–6 cans		Store location	
7–8 cans		Advertising	
9 cans and over		Carbonation	
Total	100.0	Other	
		Total	100.0

Intention to Buy Coors:	%
Certainly will	
Maybe will	
Not sure	
Maybe will not	
Certainly will not	
Total	100.0

Semantic Differential Scale—Consumers*

	Extremely	Very	Somewhat	Somewhat	Very	Extremely	
Masculine	___	___	___	___	___	___	Feminine
Healthful	___	___	___	___	___	___	Unhealthful
Cheap	___	___	___	___	___	___	Expensive
Strong	___	___	___	___	___	___	Weak
Old-fashioned	___	___	___	___	___	___	New
Upper-class	___	___	___	___	___	___	Lower-class
Good taste	___	___	___	___	___	___	Bad taste

Source: Study G.
*Profiles would be provided for Coors, three competing beers, and an ideal beer.

(H) Retailer Questionnaire Results

Brands of Beer Carried:	%	**Beer Sales:**	%
Budweiser		Budweiser	
Miller Lite		Miller Lite	
Miller		Miller	
Busch		Busch	
Bud Light		Bud Light	
Old Milwaukee		Old Milwaukee	
Michelob		Michelob	
		Others	
		Total	100.0

(*continued*)

EXHIBIT 2 **Examples of Final Research Report Tables** (*concluded*)

Semantic Differential Scale—Retailers*

	Extremely	Very	Somewhat	Somewhat	Very	Extremely	
Masculine	____	____	____	____	____	____	Feminine
Healthful	____	____	____	____	____	____	Unhealthful
Cheap	____	____	____	____	____	____	Expensive
Strong	____	____	____	____	____	____	Weak
Old-fashioned	____	____	____	____	____	____	New
Upper-class	____	____	____	____	____	____	Lower-class
Good taste	____	____	____	____	____	____	Bad taste

Intention to Sell Coors: ____ %

Certainly will
Maybe will
Not sure
Maybe will not
Certainly will not   _____
     Total   100.0

Source: Study G.
*Profiles would be provided for Coors, three competing beers, and an ideal beer.

(I) Retail and Wholesale Prices for Selected Beers in the Market Area

Beer	Wholesale* Six-Pack Price (dollars)	Retail† Six-Pack Price (dollars)
Budweiser		
Miller Lite		
Miller		
Busch		
Bud Light		
Old Milwaukee		
Michelob		

Source: Study I.
*Price that the wholesaler sold to retailers.
†Price that the retailer sold to consumers.

what data in what form? Knowledge of competing operations' experience, retailer support, and consumer acceptance also seemed important for feasibility analysis. For example, what if consumers were excited about Coors and retailers indifferent or the other way around? Finally, several of the studies would provide information that could be useful in later months of operation in the areas of promotion and pricing, for example. The problem now appeared more difficult than before!

It would have been nice, Larry thought, to have had some time to perform part of the suggested research himself. However, there was just too much in the way of class assignments and other matters to allow him that luxury. Besides, using Manson and Associates would give him research results from an unbiased source.

Investing and Operating Data

Larry was not completely in the dark regarding investment and operating data for the distributorship. In the past two weeks he had visited two beer wholesalers in his hometown of Chester, Pennsylvania, who handled Anheuser-Busch and Miller beer, to get a feel for their operations and marketing experience. It would have been nice to interview a Coors wholesaler, but Coors management had strictly informed all of their distributors to provide no information to prospective applicants.

While no specific financial data was discussed, general information had been provided in a cordial fashion because of the noncompetitive nature of Larry's plans. Based on his conversations, Larry made the following estimates:

Inventory		$240,000
Equipment		
Delivery trucks	$150,000	
Forklift	20,000	
Recycling and miscellaneous equipment	20,000	
Office equipment	10,000	
Total equipment		200,000
Warehouse		320,000
Land		40,000
Total investment		$800,000

A local banker had reviewed Larry's financial capabilities and saw no problem in extending a line of credit on the order of $400,000. Other sources also might loan as much as $400,000 to the business.

As a rough estimate of fixed expenses, Larry planned on having four route salespeople, a secretary, and a warehouse manager. Salaries for these people and himself would run about $160,000 annually plus some form of incentive compensation he had yet to determine. Other fixed or semifixed expenses were estimated at:

Equipment depreciation	$35,000
Warehouse depreciation	15,000
Utilities and telephone	12,000
Insurance	10,000
Personal property taxes	10,000
Maintenance and janitorial	5,600
Miscellaneous	2,400
	$90,000

According to the wholesalers, beer in bottles and cans outsold keg beer by a three-to-one margin. Keg beer prices at the wholesale level were about 45 percent of prices for beer in bottles and cans.

Meeting

The entire matter deserved much thought. Maybe it was a golden opportunity, maybe not. The only thing certain was that research was needed, Manson and Associates was ready, and Larry needed time to think. Today is Tuesday, Larry thought—only three days until he and John Rome would get together for direction.

6

Claritas Inc.: Using Compass and PRIZM

Valerie Walsh and J. Paul Peter
University of Wisconsin–Madison

Introduction

Managers are often faced with the task of making tough decisions regarding their marketing strategies. To make effective decisions, they need to understand their markets. In order to do so, they rely on marketing research. Some firms have their own marketing research departments while other firms rely on companies that specialize in analyzing markets. Many firms have found it useful to use technology-driven, desktop marketing information systems, such as Claritas's Compass and PRIZM systems.

Industry Background

The modern marketing information analysis industry was born in the 1970s, after the completion of the first computer-accessible census. Electronic census access made it possible to tabulate demographic data by geographic boundaries. During the 1970s, data (including demographics) were stored on large mainframes as opposed to personal computers. Marketers who wanted to analyze census data either needed a mainframe nearby or a connection to a mainframe via a modem, which used a commercial time-sharing service. Either way, data access was relatively slow and expensive.

One solution to the problem was to reduce the amount of data being analyzed by focusing on neighborhoods rather than individual census households. To accomplish this, a Harvard-educated social scientist named Jonathan Robbin developed the first "geodemographic" segmentation system, PRIZM (Potential Ranking Index

This case was prepared by Valerie Walsh, Nielsen Scholar at the University of Wisconsin–Madison, under the supervision of J. Paul Peter. Information provided by Claritas Inc. Special thanks to Jeremy Schwarz of Claritas Inc. Copyright by J. Paul Peter.

by ZIP Market), in 1974. By analyzing neighborhoods, Robbin was able to convey a great deal about their character and market potential without using a large set of descriptive variables. "Geodemography" was the term given to the linking of demographic data and local neighborhood geography (such as ZIP codes, ZIP + 4 codes, Census Tracts and Block Groups) to create classifications of actual, addressable, mappable neighborhoods where people live and shop.

IMPLEMENTING GEODEMOGRAPHIC ANALYSIS

There are two main types of geography used for marketing applications of data: Census and Postal. The specifications for census geography were created by the U.S. Department of the Census to aid the collection of census data. The specifications for postal geography are developed and maintained by the U.S. Postal Service to aid the delivery of U.S. mail. Exhibit 1 describes the different levels of census and postal geography from the largest to the smallest geographic area for which PRIZM and other data systems are available.

It was not long before census data and geodemography were married to a wealth of survey data. Independent research organizations, such as A. C. Nielsen, R. L. Polk, and Mediamark Research Inc. (MRI) collect and sell television rating data, vehicle registration data, and consumer product consumption and media habit data, respectively. Data can be purchased in raw electronic format or in a prespecified report format.

The system that Robbin developed in 1974 ran on a mainframe, and it was not until 1984 that PRIZM was used on a personal computer. A geodemographic segmen-

EXHIBIT 1   **Geography Definitions**

Census Geography Definitions

- USA: The United States is comprised of the 50 states and the District of Columbia.
- State: A two-digit Federal Information Processing Standards (FIPS) code uniquely identifies each state; codes follow the alphabetic sequence of the states.
- MSA: Metropolitan Statistical Areas consist of one or more entire counties that meet specified standards pertaining to population, commuting ties and metropolitan character. The total population is at least 100,000 and includes a city of 50,000+. MSAs are designated and defined by the federal Office of Management and Budget (OMB) and do not cover the entire United States. There are 358 MSAs in the United States.
- County: The primary political and administrative subdivision of a state. There are 3,141 counties in the United States.
- Census Tract: A subdivision of a county that is designed to be a relatively homogeneous area of 1,200–2,500 people. As of the 1990 census, the entire country is tracted, and there are 61,258 tracts in the United States.
- Block Group: A subdivision of a census tract that is approximately four blocks or 400–800 individuals. There are approximately 226,399 block groups in the United States.
- Block: Blocks are the smallest census geographic entity, usually bounded by prominent physical features such as streets, roads, streams, railroad tracks, and the like. A block generally contains 18–22 households, and there are 6,961,697 blocks in the United States.

Postal Geography Definitions

- ZIP Codes: Established by the U.S. Postal Service for the distribution of mail, ZIP code boundaries do not follow census boundaries and are subject to constant change. Each ZIP code is assigned to one county; actual ZIP boundaries can cross county and state lines.
- ZIP+4: A subdivision of a ZIP code, but not every ZIP code is divided. ZIP+4s are used for more detailed mail routing definition and do not cover the entire United States. Some ZIP+4s are a street block, while others are a floor in a city office building.
- Carrier Route: A three-digit code used by the U.S. Postal Service to specify mail delivery routes. Routes vary in size and cross over ZIP and ZIP+4 boundaries.

tation system links vast amounts of demographic and lifestyle data to actual, mappable neighborhoods. Every U.S. neighborhood is classified into a segment based on demographic characteristics of the people who live there. For an example of how a company would use a segmentation system, consider Jane Smith as one of its best customers. By knowing Jane's ZIP+4 code, the company can find out the demographic and lifestyle profile of Jane's neighborhood. The company can then find out where other neighborhoods like Jane's are located by searching for neighborhoods with Jane's same segment assignment, and can then target those neighborhoods through direct mail or other types of promotion.

In 1987, National Decision Systems (NDS) combined independent survey data and census data with geographic boundaries to create the first desktop marketing information system, Infomark, for the personal computer. This revolutionized the marketing information industry, and other companies quickly followed with their own systems. A desktop marketing information system is a software and data package which allows the users to create reports (see Exhibit 2) and maps (see Exhibit 3) that are used to understand markets and make effective marketing decisions. Today's systems have been enhanced by a greater amount of data, industry-specific geographic boundaries (such as telephone system boundaries), and availability of roads and landmarks for map enhancement. Claritas's Compass and NDS's Infomark are examples of desktop marketing information systems.

Marketing information and segmentation systems are used in many different industries to solve industry specific marketing problems. Some of the main industries using marketing information analysis are financial services, retail, advertising, telecommunications, and print media. As the use of marketing information services increases, companies are demanding that client service representatives have indepth industry knowledge to help solve their problems. Some of the cross-industry uses of marketing information are:

- **Target selection:** Through the use of demographic and lifestyle data, clients can determine who their best prospects are.
- **Direct marketing:** Use of lifestyle data tied to geography can help clients create a promotional mail campaign to target their best prospects.
- **Site selection:** A profile of customers who frequent clients' most profitable stores or branches can be created, and then more customers of the same demographic and lifestyle makeup can be located. This can help clients determine where to open a new retail store or bank branch.
- **Media selection:** Once clients have identified their best prospects, independent survey data can help determine which magazines or television shows to advertise in/on to reach these consumers.
- **Market potential:** Based on past sales, clients can map the sales potential of a specific product within any given market in the United States. This can help them forecast whether the product will be profitable within given markets.

COMPETITIVE ENVIRONMENT

Claritas and NDS are the two main competitors in the desktop marketing information analysis industry. Both companies sell desktop marketing information systems, segmentation systems, and industry specific applications, and both systems operate in an IBM-compatible Windows environment. A third competitor, Strategic Mapping Inc. (SMI), was purchased by Claritas in 1996. With the acquisition of SMI, Claritas gained SMI's Windows-based desktop marketing information system along with a variety of other products. Exhibit 4 lists the systems of the two main competitors.

EXHIBIT 2   Market Potential Index (MPI) Report for Alternative Rock Music in the District of Columbia

Source: Claritas, Inc.

ZIP Code & Post Office Name	Households	MPI	Median Household Income
20050- Washington	880	316	$30,563
20006- Twentieth Street	772	316	26,979
20336- Bolling AFB Quarter	1,144	247	42,409
MPI of 200+	2,796*	288**	
20037- Watergate	5,422	185	44,446
20038- Washington	1,058	175	35,754
20088- Washington	228	165	98,214
20033- Washington	287	161	39,028
20036- Twentieth Street	3,164	160	40,095
20015- Northwest	5,522	155	82,879
20035- Washington	1,046	151	51,129
20016- Eagle	11,397	146	67,081
20007- Calvert	10,639	146	58,292
20057- Georgetown Univ	63	141	41,821
20012- Walter Reed	4,785	138	54,038
20008- Cleveland Park	13,817	137	57,602
20009- Kalorama	19,854	125	36,398
MPI of 200–120	77,282*	143**	
20026- Washington	1,731	118	39,391
20024- L'Enfant Plaza	5,264	114	43,155
20013- Washington	3,364	114	53,045
20017- Brookland	6,036	110	47,453
20005- Central	4,787	107	29,308
20003- Southeast	8,103	102	48,313
20011- Brightwood	20,657	91	37,658
20004- Benjamin Franklin	628	84	11,623
MPI of 120–80	50,570*	101**	
20002- Kendall Green	19,923	72	32,360
20056- Washington	1,292	69	27,101
20010- Columbia Heights	9,194	68	30,338
20018- Customs House	6,553	67	30,771
20020- Anacostia	17,197	67	30,038
20090- Washington	2,606	55	33,839
20001- Le Droit Park	9,594	51	24,373
20032- Congress Heights	12,036	46	26,016
20019- Benning	19,920	45	27,578
20039- Washington	648	40	40,089
20077- Washington	8	40	20,000
20044- Washington	2,396	40	8,013
20515- Washington	8	40	16,250
20043- Washington	345	40	26,289
20091- Washington	736	36	28,188
20030- Washington	943	36	26,477
20029- Washington	1,521	33	35,819
20064- Catholic Univ	0	0	0
20301- Dept of Defense	0	0	0
20059- Howard Univ	0	0	0
MPI of < 80	104,920*	58**	

*Total number of households in each of these ZIP code groups.
**Weighted average MPI for each of these ZIP code groups.

NOTE: Any MPI above 100 is considered to be above average.

A market potential index (MPI) is used to identify geographic areas with high usage potential for a given product. The example above shows that the ZIP code 20050 has the highest market potential index for alternative rock music. In addition, the above report lists the number of households and the median household income in each ZIP code.

EXHIBIT 3   Market Potential for Alternative Rock Music in the District of Columbia

SOURCE: Claritas, Inc.

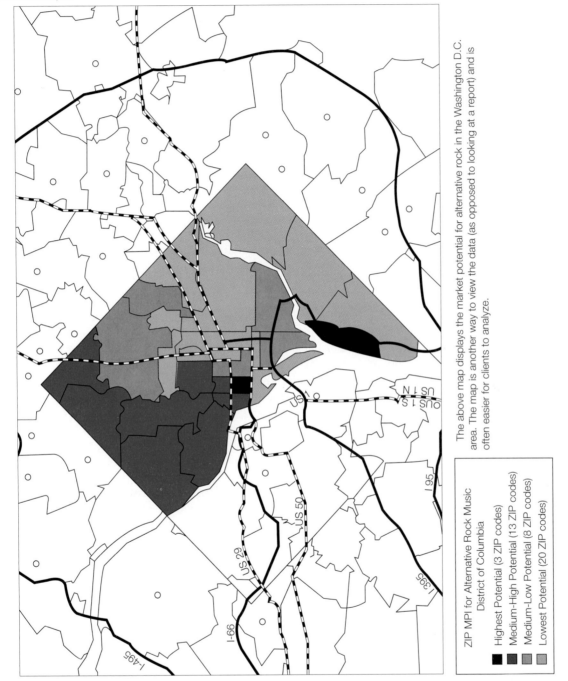

The above map displays the market potential for alternative rock in the Washington D.C. area. The map is another way to view the data (as opposed to looking at a report) and is often easier for clients to analyze.

ZIP MPI for Alternative Rock Music
District of Columbia

■ Highest Potential (3 ZIP codes)
■ Medium-High Potential (13 ZIP codes)
■ Medium-Low Potential (8 ZIP codes)
■ Lowest Potential (20 ZIP codes)

In addition to the three main players in the market, secondary competition comes from geographic information system (GIS) companies. These companies include MapInfo, ESRI, and Tactician. The GIS companies produce and sell mapping software that is used in many industries, including law enforcement, emergency services, and marketing. The problem with GIS software is that data are not

EXHIBIT 4   **Products of Major Competitors in the Desktop Marketing Information Industry**

Products	Claritas	NDS
Desktop Marketing Information System	Compass Conquest (an acquired SMI product)	Infomark
Segmentation System	PRIZM ClusterPLUS 2000 (an acquired SMI product)	MicroVision

conveniently bundled with the software, forcing marketers to build their own system. The advantage to GIS systems is that they have more detailed mapping capabilities, which are useful for activities that involve in-depth mapping of a geographic area. The desktop marketing systems in Exhibit 4 all use one of the main GIS systems for their mapping engine. Claritas uses MapInfo's MapInfo, while NDS uses ESRI's ArcView. Although a GIS system is used for the mapping engine, the geographic detail is greater in a GIS system alone than in a desktop marketing information system.

Company Overview

Claritas was founded in 1971 by Jonathan Robbin, a computer scientist. The word "claritas" is Latin for clarity and it inspired Robbin through a James Joyce book, *A Portrait of the Artist as a Young Man,* in which claritas is cited as one of the three essential elements of great art.

The 1970s were a decade of growth for Claritas, as the company introduced its first version of PRIZM, the segmentation system that would become the backbone of the company. The initial marketing challenge was to create an awareness and acceptance of the new marketing information analysis industry. The company had to convince the business world of the inherent value of purchasing market segmentation information for making marketing decisions, as opposed to the traditional use of primary research.

Claritas is owned by VNU Business Information Services (VNU BIS) which is owned by VNU United Dutch Publishing Companies, a $1.6 billion publishing and information services company based in the Netherlands. Approximately 2,000 people are employed by VNU BIS and the company has annual revenues of more than $150 million. In addition to Claritas, VNU owns seven other U.S. marketing companies. The companies complement each other in many ways, but do not work together very often. The company that is most similar to Claritas is Spectra Marketing. An agreement between Claritas and Spectra grants Spectra the right to sell Claritas's products; however, Spectra customizes the Claritas core segmentation and software products to focus on the packaged goods industry.

PRODUCTS

Claritas's two main areas of business are: (1) nonlicensed data sales and projects, and (2) licensed data and software. Nonlicensed data are typically smaller in quantity and lower in price (under $5,000) and are mostly sold via telephone through Claritas's Data Services Group. These data include demographic market area reports, ZIP code reports, and various other forms of ad-hoc data. Nonlicensed projects are often sold through the consultative field sales force as a stepping stone toward licensing a full software system.

The majority of Claritas's business is licensed data and software sold to clients for a period of one to three years. Selling of these products is the main focus of Claritas's sales and client service staff, and their responsibilities include sales and consulting support of client applications using Claritas data.

PRIZM

PRIZM is a market segmentation system that classifies every U.S. neighborhood into one of 62 distinct types or "clusters." Each PRIZM cluster combines detailed demographics with product, media, and lifestyle preferences to create a profile of the people in these neighborhoods (see the three cluster profiles in Exhibits 5–7). The PRIZM system uses the following assumptions to help identify target markets:

1. **Birds of a feather flock together:** meaning that people living in the same types of neighborhoods tend to be more similar to each other than people in different types of neighborhoods.

2. **The best customers for your product are existing customers:** describing the people who already use your product or a similar one, or other people like your existing customers, as the best prospects.

Marketers use PRIZM to segment customers into groups to better understand customer lifestyles and behavior and then target their best prospects. PRIZM cluster reports can be run to identify clusters with heaviest product usage for specific products (see Exhibit 8). As seen in Exhibits 5–7, different PRIZM clusters contain different types of people. With the identification of which clusters to target comes an identification of what type of person to target. For example, people in the Hispanic Mix cluster have different backgrounds and culture than people in the Blue Blood Estates cluster, hence different marketing strategies might be needed to reach each group. The PRIZM system is rarely licensed alone, but is licensed as an integrated part of Claritas's Compass system.

Compass

Compass is a PC-based marketing workstation used to integrate, analyze, and map demographic, consumer demand and usage, site, and geographic data. Industry-specific applications, such as Compass/Agency (for advertising agencies), Compass/Banking (for banking and insurance companies), and Compass/Cable (for Cable TV companies) are used to address the unique marketing needs of individual industries. Compass also includes dozens of demographic, product usage, media, business, and site databases. Many clients use Compass to help understand their customers by answering the following questions:

- **Who are my target consumers?** The different databases available in Compass allow clients to link their own customer data with neighborhood demographics, PRIZM lifestyle segments, syndicated data, or survey research data. By linking customer data with Compass data, clients can understand exactly what type of consumer is most likely to use their product or service.

- **What are they like?** Once clients have identified their consumer targets, a thorough lifestyle profile can be created. A profile will answer questions like: How do best prospects spend their leisure time? What products do they buy? Where do they travel? How do they invest their money?

- **Where do they live?** Since Compass links demographics and PRIZM clusters to geography, clients can find out where their best customers or prospects live and find more people like them. Once geographic areas of interest are identified, Compass allows the client to print a detailed, full-color map shaded by demographic characteristic or product potential.

EXHIBIT 5   Sample Cluster Profile from the PRIZM System (Cluster 01— Blue Blood Estates)

The **Blue Blood Estates** cluster contains America's wealthiest suburbs, populated by super-upper established executives, professionals, and heirs to "old money" who are accustomed to privilege and live in luxury, supported by servants. One in ten residents is a multi-millionaire, and there is a sharp drop from these heights to the next level of affluence.

Predominant Characteristics

- Households (%U.S.):   729,500 (0.8%)
- Population: 2,181,400
- Demographic caption: Elite super-rich families
- Ethnic diversity: Dominant White, High Asian
- Family type: Married couples w/children
- Predominant age ranges: 35–54
- Education: College graduates
- Employment level: Professional
- Housing type: Owners/Single Unit
- Density centile: 66 (1= sparse, 99=dense)

More Likely To:

Lifestyle	*Products and Services*
Belong to a country club	Purchase a car phone
Travel to Japan/Asia	Eat pita bread
Contract home improvement	Drink imported wine
Go sailing	Own a Lexus
Use maid/housekeeper	Spend 250+ on business suit
Lease car for personal use	Buy Montblanc/Waterman pen
Radio/TV	*Print*
Watch Arts & Entertainment	Read *National Geographic Travel*
Listen to news/talk radio	Read newspaper business section
Watch "Seinfeld"	Read *Elle*
Listen to soft contemp radio	Read *Food & Wine*
Watch Masters (Golf)	Read *Fortune*

EXHIBIT 6   Sample Cluster Profile from the PRIZM System (Cluster 36—Towns and Gowns)

The **Towns and Gowns** cluster describes most of our college towns and university campus neighborhoods. With a typical mix of half locals (Towns) and half students (Gowns), it is wholly unique, with thousands of penniless 18–24-year-old kids, plus highly educated professionals, all with a taste for prestige products beyond their evident means.

Predominant Characteristics

- Households (%U.S.):   1,290,200 (1.4%)
- Population: 3,542,500
- Demographic caption: College town singles
- Ethnic diversity: Dominant White, High Asian
- Family type: Singles
- Predominant age ranges: Under 24, 25–34
- Education: College graduates
- Employment level: White-Collar/Service
- Housing type: Renters/Multi-Unit 10+
- Density centile: 58 (1=sparse, 99=dense)

More Likely To:

Lifestyle	Products and Services
Go to college football games	Have a personal education loan
Play racquetball	Use an ATM card
Go skiing	Own a Honda
Play billiards/pool	Buy 3+ pairs of jeans annually
Use cigarette rolling paper	Drink Coca-Cola Classic
Use a charter/tour bus	Eat Kraft Macaroni and Cheese
Radio/TV	*Print*
Watch VH1	Read *Self*
Listen to alternative rock music	Read newspaper comics section
Watch "Jeopardy"	Read *Rolling Stone*
Listen to variety radio	Read *GQ*
Watch "The Simpsons"	

EXHIBIT 7   **Sample Cluster Profile from the PRIZM System (Cluster 46—Hispanic Mix)**

The **Hispanic Mix** cluster collects the nation's bilingual, Hispanic barrios, which are chiefly concentrated in the Atlantic metro corridor, Chicago, Miami, Texas, Los Angeles, and the Southwest. The neighborhoods are populated by large families with many small children. They rank second in percent foreign-born, first in transient immigration.

Predominant Characteristics:

- Households (%U.S.):   1,420,100 (1.5%)
- Population: 4,473,100
- Demographic caption: Urban Hispanic singles & families
- Ethnic diversity: Dominant Hispanic
- Family type: Singles, parents, married couples
- Predominant age ranges: Under 24, 25–34
- Education: Grade school
- Employment level: Blue-Collar/Service
- Housing type: Renters/Multi-Unit 10+
- Density centile: 91 (1=sparse, 99=dense)

Likely To:

Lifestyle	Products and Services
Go to pro basketball games	Use postal money orders
Go roller skating	Buy stereo equipment
Go to truck & tractor pull races	Own a Mazda
Buy dance music	Eat canned hashes
Smoke regular cigarettes	Eat children's frozen dinners
Rent foreign videos	Drink imported beer often
Radio/TV	*Print*
Watch "Cops"	Read *Jet*
Listen to Spanish radio	Read newspaper classified section
Watch "Geraldo"	Read *Weight Watchers*
Listen to urban contemp radio	Read the *National Enquirer*
Watch "Married with Children"	Read *Motor Trend*

EXHIBIT 8   **1995 Clusters Ranked by Propensity to Listen to Alternative Rock Music**

Source: Claritas, Inc.

Cluster #	Cluster Nickname	Propensity to Listen Index
36	Towns & Gowns	317
40	Military Quarters	247
01	Blue Blood Estates	182
18	Young Influentials	173
46	Hispanic Mix	168
27	Urban Achievers	161
10	Bohemian Mix	161
31	Latino America	157
22	Blue-Chip Blues	149
08	Young Literati	141
07	Money & Brains	134
23	Upstarts & Seniors	132
24	New Beginnings	131
33	Boomtown Singles	129
17	Greenbelt Families	128
28	Big City Blend	126
11	Second City Elite	126
02	Winner's Circle	125
06	Urban Gold Coast	124
12	Upward Bound	124
38	Middle America	123
35	Sunset City Blues	121
04	Pools & Patios	120
42	New Eco-topia	120
13	Gray Power	120
05	Kids & Cul-de-Sacs	119
03	Executive Suites	117
16	Big Fish, Small Pond	115
60	Back Country Folks	111
21	Suburban Sprawl	108
55	Mines & Mills	104
43	River City, USA	104
26	Gray Collars	104
50	Family Scramble	102
37	New Homesteaders	95
09	American Dreams	94
15	God's Country	92
61	Scrub Pine Flats	82
19	New Empty Nests	82
49	Hometown Retired	81
20	Boomers & Babies	79
39	Red, White & Blues	76
62	Hard Scrabble	74

(continued)

EXHIBIT 8   *(concluded)*

Cluster #	Cluster Nickname	Propensity to Listen Index
25	Mobility Blues	73
14	Country Squires	72
32	Middleburg Managers	71
52	Golden Ponds	69
45	Single City Blues	65
56	Agri-Business	65
51	Southside City	63
29	Old Yankee Rows	63
41	Big Sky Families	63
34	Starter Families	59
54	Norma Rae-ville	58
59	Rustic Elders	57
48	Smalltown Downtown	45
58	Blue Highways	43
53	Rural Industrial	41
47	Inner Cities	40
44	Shotguns & Pickups	38
57	Grain Belt	35
30	Mid-City Mix	29

The above report is used to identify PRIZM clusters with high propensity to listen to alternative rock music. A propensity score above 100 is considered to be above average.

- **How can I reach them?** With their best customer targets in mind, clients can use Compass to evaluate the best ways to reach those customers. Clients can find out what magazines and newspapers their target consumers read and what TV, cable, or radio shows they tune in. Compass information is also used to plan in-store promotions and merchandise mixes.

PRICING

Pricing of Claritas licensed products is very complex and is determined by:

- Requested market coverage (national, regional, or market level).
- Requested geographic level (ZIP code, block group, etc.).
- Requested databases (MRI, Nielsen, R. L. Polk, etc.).
- Requested segmentation systems (PRIZM or P$YCLE, a segmentation system for the financial industry).
- Requested length of the license (one to three years).

CUSTOMER SATISFACTION

Claritas has a long list of satisfied customers who have used Compass and PRIZM to make effective marketing decisions in a variety of areas. Reasons for such satisfaction include positive results such as increased response rates from targeted direct mail campaigns, profitable placement of new store sites, and increased sales of consumer products in various markets. Quotes from satisfied customers include:

- "Before using the Claritas system, we were ordering basic reports from a vendor, pulling out Rand McNally maps and photocopying them. We would mark stores and trace ZIP Code areas by hand. By mapping and using more specialized data from Claritas, we are making educated decisions on where to locate our stores and how to better serve our customers. This allows us to be more professional—and profitable."—Rob Groscup, Eddie Bauer Sportswear.

- "This (segmentation) program helps Perdue Farms and our retailers clear out the less desirable products and put in the fast-moving products, but what's less desirable and what's fast-moving varies from store to store. We've never been able to identify that on a per-store basis, and PRIZM has allowed us to do that."—James Mendelsohn, Perdue Farms.

- "The response rates (to our direct mail program) have improved dramatically since implementing the Claritas program and the cost per loan, which had risen as high as $550–$800 variance based on market and time of year, dropped to a consistent $295–$350 per loan, and is headed even lower."—Clare Erlander, Security Pacific Financial Services.

- "We feel we'd be remiss to not use a tool like PRIZM to go after additional ad dollars. The difference it has made is significant."—Walter Rodgers, The Eagle—Tribune.

Discussion Questions

1. What is geodemography and why is it useful?
2. Using Exhibits 2 and 3 in the case, answer the following questions:
   a. What information do the market potential index (MPI) scores in Exhibit 2 provide, how is this information useful, and who would use it?
   b. Who should be targeted based on the alternative rock music MPI?
   c. What is the relationship between median household income and potential alternative rock listeners in Exhibit 2?
   d. How would marketers use the map in Exhibit 3 to target alternative rock listeners?
3. Name three products or services that you think would vary in demand across the three clusters in Exhibits 5, 6, and 7. How would you change the marketing mix for these products or services to appeal to each cluster?
4. Using Exhibits 5, 6, 7, and 8, answer the following questions:
   a. From Exhibit 8, which cluster has the highest index? What is the meaning of the index?
   b. What additional information do Exhibits 5, 6, and 7 provide that would help market an alternative rock music magazine?
   c. How could the report in Exhibit 8 be used for a direct mailing?
5. Suppose you own a chain of computer stores in the state of Massachusetts. Recently you have noticed an increase in sales and a high demand for your products. Your industry is forecasted to continue growing for the next ten years. You decide that you want to expand your business and open more stores. Unfortunately, you are unsure of where to locate them. How could Claritas's Compass system help you?
6. What are the strengths of Claritas's PRIZM segmentation system?
7. Based on information given about the marketing information analysis industry, how should Claritas organize its internal sales and client-service staff to best sell its Compass and PRIZM software? Discuss the advantages and disadvantages of organizing geographically, by industry group, or by product.

Product Strategy

7

Starbucks

Ashish Gokhale and J. Paul Peter
University of Wisconsin–Madison:

Starbucks Coffee Houses were started in Seattle, Washington, in 1971 when three young men, Gerald Baldwin, Gordon Bowker, and Zev Siegl, decided to try their hand at selling gourmet coffee. They were betting that consumers would pay $1.50 for a cup of their coffee compared to 40 cents for generic coffee offered elsewhere. By 2002, there were more than 3,400 Starbucks Coffee Houses throughout the world. Over 10 million coffee lovers spent an average of $3.60 there weekly and 10 percent of them visited twice a day.[1]

Ashish Gokhale is a Project Assistant and J. Paul Peter is James R. Mc Manus–Bascom Professor in Marketing at the University of Wisconsin–Madison.

[1]Source: *www.starbucks.com,* Company facts Jan 2002

The retail value of all U.S. coffee sales in 2001 was $18.5 billion,[2] a one-third increase from 1995. In 2002, the coffee market in the U.S. was comprised of 79 percent of adults over age 18 (161 million) including both daily and occasional drinkers. Daily drinkers comprise 54 percent (110 million adults), while 25 percent (51 million) are occasional drinkers.[3] The largest growth was in occasional drinkers, which can be attributed to the boom in gourmet coffeehouses.[4] Out-of-home coffee consumption was 39 percent of total consumption.[5]

Starbucks made coffee drinking a social phenomenon that draws consumers out of their homes to enjoy a premium beverage in a social atmosphere. During the late '90s, the number of gourmet coffee houses grew from fewer than 500 to more than 8,000. However, only 5 percent of coffee consumption in the United States is done in coffee houses leaving ample room for growth.

Initially opened in areas of the country with cooler climates, coffee houses are now located in most U.S. geographic locations. Starbucks introduced an entirely new social dimension to drinking coffee out of the home. Starbucks entices people to spend a little more money for a great beverage, while offering lots of comfortable seating and personal space, ambient lighting and background music, often with free reading material. In essence it is marketed as an extension of a consumers' living room—a safe place where they can sit down and enjoy coffee at leisure either alone or with friends.

Starbucks introduced a variety of coffee types and roast selections. It has up to 15 different varieties to choose from, including espresso, cappuccino, lattes, frauppucino, and café mochas. Starbucks' evening sales are higher in warmer climates. Iced beverages, which offer larger profit margins than regular drip coffee, are also big sellers in the South and Southwest. Starbucks introduced the concept of cold and iced coffee beverages to coffee houses. Coffee is traditionally hot and black, but Starbucks offers products that use coffee as an ingredient in beverages with milk, ice, whipped cream and chocolate syrup.

The success of Starbucks brought other coffee chains into the market including Millstone Coffee and Borders' Café. However, Starbucks dominates the market with 30 percent market share. Howard Schultz, chairman and CEO of Starbucks Corporation, attributes the company's success to the experience created within the coffee houses and the unsurpassed quality of Starbucks coffee. A steaming café au lait should be perfectly replicated whether the coffeehouse is in Seattle or in New York. In a world filled with people leading busy stressful lives, he believes that Starbucks has created a "third place" between home and work where people can go for personal time out or to relax with friends.

Schultz also attributes his company's success to the 10,000 employees working worldwide.[6] Starbucks' employee training program churns out "baristas" by educating 300 to 400 hires per month in courses such as "Brewing the Perfect Cup at Home" and "Coffee Knowledge." They are taught to remind customers to purchase new beans weekly and that tap water might not be sufficient for brewing really good coffee. They are also encouraged to share their feelings about coffee selling and working with Starbucks. Employees are given guidelines for maintaining and enhancing self-esteem, learning how to listen and acknowledge customer comments, and knowing when to ask for help. If the annual barista turnover of 60 percent compared with

[2]Source: National Coffee Association (NCA), New York. Year:2001

[3]Source: National Coffee Association (NCA), New York Year:2001

[4]Source: National Coffee Association (NCA), New York, Year:2001

[5]Source: National Coffee Association, New York, Year 2001

[6]*www.starbucks.com*

140 percent for hourly wages in the fast food industry is any indication of the quality of its training programs, Starbucks seems to have a handle on how to gain and maintain employee loyalty. About 80 percent of Starbucks employees are white, 85 percent have some education beyond high school, and their average age is 26.

Starbucks has expanded into Europe and Asia. However, one question remains regarding the success of the company in countries already known for their coffee excellence: Will they care for Starbucks Coffee Houses? Continued expansion and visibility has been created domestically as Starbucks has created partnerships with companies such as United Airlines and Barnes & Noble Booksellers, both of which draw from the same type of knowledgeable customer.

The coffee company has opened several full-service dining establishments (Café Starbucks) in response to customers who wanted complete lunches and dinners. The menu offers full meals, breads, pastries, alcohol, and of course, coffee. The company has an Internet site (http://*www.starbucks.com*) that sells not only expensive coffee but also expensive kitchenware, home furnishings, and gourmet food. Starbucks is tying online efforts to its central mission of building customer loyalty around cappuccinos, lattes, and other fancy beverages.[7] Starbucks now runs a simple, easy to use Internet store that sells coffee beans, mugs, brewing machines and not much else. The company has moved away from the idea of merchandizing everything ranging from furniture to video cassettes.[8]

Starbucks has decided to stick to its knitting, understand its core competencies, know what the value proposition is for the customer, and do everything possible to get close to the customer. Starbucks has succeeded in maintaining its competitive advantage by providing an "experience" to the customer and locating in every nook and corner in major cities. Its strategy seems to be working. Revenue for the month of January 2002 rose by 24% to $229 million dollars.[9] A summary of the company's financial highlights is shown in the figure.

Discussion Questions

1. What is Starbucks' product?
2. What changes in society have helped Starbucks be successful?
3. What strategic factors account for Starbucks' success in developing brand equity?
4. What opportunities and threats face Starbucks?
5. What do you think of the inclusion of selling online coffee in Starbucks strategy?
6. What should Starbucks do to continue growing its sales and profits?

---

[7]Source: *www.starbucks.com*
[8]Source: Fast Company Magazine; Boston; August 2001; George Sanders
[9]Source: Dow Jones News Service, Dow Jones Newswires; Tel: 201-938-5388

STARBUCKS FINANCIAL HIGHLIGHTS

NET REVENUES (in millions)

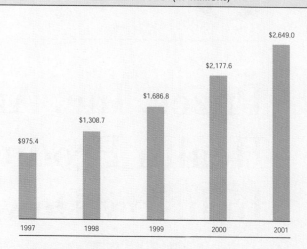

1997	1998	1999	2000	2001
$975.4	$1,308.7	$1,686.8	$2,177.6	$2,649.0

NORTH AMERICAN AND INTERNATIONAL STORES

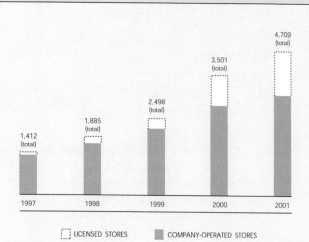

1997	1998	1999	2000	2001
1,412 (total)	1,885 (total)	2,498 (total)	3,501 (total)	4,709 (total)

LICENSED STORES   COMPANY-OPERATED STORES

OPERATING INCOME (in millions)

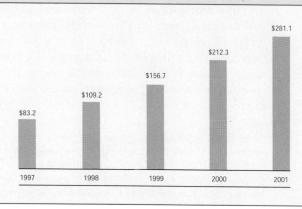

1997	1998	1999	2000	2001
$83.2	$109.2	$156.7	$212.3	$281.1

Case 8

Pfizer, Inc. Animal Health Products[1]— Industry Downturns and Marketing Strategy

Jakki Mohr
University of Montana

Sara Streeter, MBA
University of Montana

Gail Oss, Territory Manager of Pfizer, Inc., Animal Health Group in western Montana and southeastern Idaho, was driving back to her home office after a day of visiting cattle ranchers in her territory. The combination of the spring sunshine warming the air and the snow-capped peaks of the Bitterroot Mountains provided a stunningly beautiful backdrop for her drive. But the majestic beauty provided little relief to her troubled thoughts.

The NAFTA agreement with Canada and Mexico had hit local ranchers particularly hard. The influx of beef cattle into the U.S. market from these countries, as well as beef from other countries (e.g., Australia) that entered the U.S. via more lenient import restrictions in Mexico, had wreaked havoc over the past year. Prices of beef had declined precipitously from the prior year. Ranchers in the past had retained sufficient reserves to come back from a bad year, but this year, things were particularly bad. The prices being offered for the calves by the feedlot operators were, in many cases, less than the costs of raising those calves. Ranchers' objectives had changed from making some modest income off their cattle operations to minimizing their losses.

[1]Some of the information in this case has been modified to protect the proprietary nature of firms' marketing strategies. The case is intended to be used as a basis for class discussion rather than to illustrate either effective or ineffective marketing strategies.

© Copyright Jakki J. Mohr, 1999, All Rights Reserved. Support from The Institute for the Study of Business Markets, Pennsylvania State University, is greatly appreciated.

In this environment, ranchers were actively seeking ways to cut costs. Gail sold high-quality animal health products, oftentimes at a premium price. One way in which ranchers could cut costs was either to scrimp on animal healthcare products, such as vaccines and antibiotics, or to switch to a lower-cost alternative. The current environment posed a particularly severe threat, not only to Gail's company, but also to her very livelihood. Gail had spent a substantial amount of time and effort cultivating long-term relationships with many of these ranchers—many of whom she had had to convince of her credibility, given her gender. Given the time and effort she had spent cultivating these relationships, as well as the camaraderie she felt with her customers, she did not want to see the ranchers in her territory go under. Ranching was an important part of the history of Montana; many ranchers had ties to the land going back generations. They took pride in producing the food for many tables in the U.S. and other areas of the world. Gail felt that Pfizer could use its fairly significant resources in a very influential manner to help these ranchers. Merely lowering the price on her products (if that was even possible) was merely a band-aid solution to the problem.

As part of Gail's weekly responsibilities, she communicated via an automated computer system to her sales manager, Tom Brooks, (also in Montana) and to the marketing managers at headquarters (in Exton, Pennsylvania). She knew she needed to report the severity of the situation, but more importantly, she wanted to encourage headquarters to take the bull by the horns, so to speak. So, she was pondering the message she would write that evening from her kitchen table.

Industry Background

The supply chain (Exhibit 1) for beef begins with the cow/calf producer (the commercial rancher). Commercial ranchers are in the business of breeding and raising cattle for the purpose of selling them to feedlots. Ranchers keep a herd of cows that are bred yearly. The calves are generally born in the early spring, weaned in October, and shipped to feedlots generally in late October/early November. The ranchers' objectives are to minimize death loss in their herd and to breed cows that give birth to low birth-weight calves (for calving ease), produce beef that will grade low choice by having a good amount of marbling, and produce calves that gain weight quickly. Success measures include conception rate of cows exposed to bulls, live birth rates, birth weights, weaning weights, death loss, and profitability. By the time a rancher sells his calves to the feedlot, the name of the game is pounds. The rancher generally wants the biggest calves possible by that time.

Within a commodity market, basic laws of supply and demand are influenced by those in a position to control access to the markets. Four meatpackers controlled roughly 80% of the industry. Meatpackers have acted as an intermediary between the meat consumer and the meat producer. This situation has not facilitated a free flow of information throughout the supply chain, and therefore, the industry has not been strongly consumer focused.

EXHIBIT 1 **Supply Chain for Beef**

Cow/Calf Producers → Feedlot → Meat Packer → Customers (food service, retail, etc.)

EXHIBIT 2   **Per Capita Meat Consumption % Market Share (Retail Weight)**

Source: USDA & NCBA.

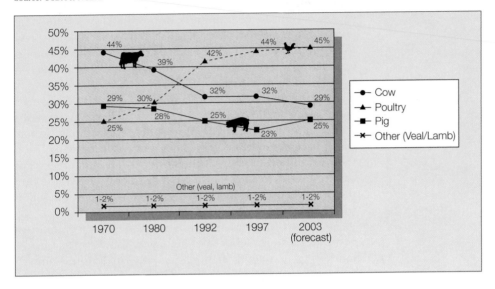

Exhibit 2 traces the market share for beef, pork, and poultry from 1970–1997 and projects changes in the market through 2003. The market share for beef has fallen from 44% in 1970 to 32% in 1997, a 27% drop.

Some of the reasons for the decline included

- Changes in consumer lifestyles (less time spent in preparing home-cooked meals); an interesting statistic is that two-thirds of all dinner decisions are made on the same day and of those, three-quarters don't know what they're going to make at 4:30 PM.
- Health/nutritional issues (dietary considerations involving cholesterol, fat content, food-borne diseases, etc.).
- Switching to alternative meat products.

In addition, the pork and poultry industries had done a better job of marketing their products. During 1997, the number of new poultry products (for example, stuffed chicken entrees, gourmet home meal replacements) introduced to the market increased 13% from the prior year, compared to an increase of only 3.5% for new beef products. And, retail pricing for beef remained stubbornly high (although this high price did not translate into higher prices of the calves on a per-weight basis to the ranchers, as discussed subsequently).

Based upon historical data, shown in Exhibit 3, the beef production cycle spans a twelve-year period in which production levels expand and contract. As Exhibit 3 shows, the amount of beef produced (bars in the chart, millions of pounds on the left-hand scale) increased through the mid-90s—despite the declining beef consumption in the U.S. shown in the prior figure. This relationship between production and consumption is consistent with other commodity markets, where there exists an inverse relationship between supply and demand.

Some of the reasons for increased beef production in the mid-90s included

- Herd liquidation: low cattle prices, coupled with the high cost of feed, drove some producers out of business.

EXHIBIT 3   Beef Production and Price

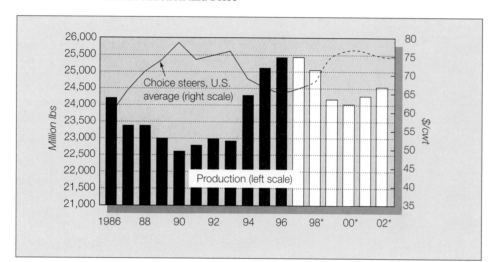

- Improved genetics and animal health/nutrition increased production yields; indeed, although cow numbers had decreased by 10% since 1985 (as noted by Exhibit 4), productivity per cow increased by 29%.
- Export of beef increased sevenfold since 1985 (to 2 billion pounds); key markets include Japan (54% of export volume); Canada (16%); Korea (11%), and Mexico (9%).

Exhibit 3 also shows that the price the ranchers received for their beef cattle varied inversely with production (right-hand scale). Although calf prices were expected to rise slightly through the late 90s/early 2000s, the prices paid were still far below the relatively high prices consumers paid at retail. One of the reasons given for the relatively low prices paid to ranchers on a per-pound basis for their calves was the high degree of concentration at the meat packer level of the supply chain. As noted previously, four packing houses controlled access to the market. Some ranchers believed this gave the packing houses near-monopoly power in setting prices (both for what they would pay feedlot operators for the calves, and in charging prices to their downstream customers (e.g., the grocery store chains). Although the U.S. government had investigated the possibility of collusion among packers, the evidence was not sufficient to draw any firm conclusions.

To further complicate matters, the NAFTA agreement passed in 1989 had given open access to the U.S. markets from Mexican and Canadian ranchers. The lowering of trade barriers, coupled with weakness in the Canadian dollar and the Mexican peso, made imported livestock cheap, compared to U.S.-grown animals. As a result, thousands of head of cattle came streaming across the borders. The flow was heaviest from Canada.

During the summer of 1998, ranchers had been quite vocal in drawing attention to the influx of cattle from Canada. Local governments were somewhat responsive to their concerns. Indeed, trucks carrying Canadian cattle had been turned back at the U.S./Canadian border for minor infractions, such as licensing. In addition, the trucks were consistently pulled over for inspections. A private coalition of ranchers, calling itself the Ranchers-Cattlemen Action Legal Foundation (R-CALF) filed three separate petitions with the U.S. International Trade Commission (ITC) on October 1, 1998, two against Canada and one against Mexico, asking for U.S. government

EXHIBIT 4   Total U.S. Inventory

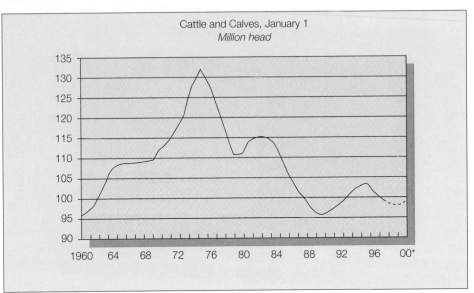

trade investigations. The group requested that anti-dumping duties be levied on meat or livestock imports from the two countries. The Montana Stockgrowers Association had been an early and steadfast supporter of R-CALF.

The ITC determined that there was evidence to support the charge that Canadian cattle imports are causing material injury to U.S. domestic cattle producers. The Department of Commerce began to collect information on Canadian subsidies and prices at which Canadian cattle are sold in Canada and in the United States. In the case against Mexico, the ITC determined that there was no indication that imports of live cattle from Mexico were causing "material injury" to the domestic industry in the U.S. Dissatisfied with the response, R-CALF decided to appeal the case to the Court of International Trade.

Ranchers were doing what they could to minimize the impact of the NAFTA agreement on their livelihoods; however, some could not sustain their operations in light of the lower cattle prices. The number of cattle operations was declining. In many cases, smaller ranchers were selling out to their larger neighbors. This reality was reflected in the cattle inventory statistics, shown in Exhibit 4. The number of cattle kept by U.S. ranchers had declined from a high of approximately 132 million head in 1975, to just under 100 million head in 1998. As noted previously, improvements in genetics and animal health and nutrition allowed ranchers to increase production yields, even with fewer head.

Additional Industry Changes

Some of the changes that had occurred in the poultry and pork industries, including more ready-to-eat products and branded products, were expected to diffuse into the cattle industry. Industry analysts believed that the beef industry would need to develop products that could be more easily prepared, and to develop branded products that consumers could recognize and rely upon for quality and convenience. In addition, industry analysts believed that the beef industry would need to improve the quality of its products (in terms of more consistent taste and tenderness), as currently only 25% of the beef produced met quality targets.

The development of branded beef would require a tracking system from "birth-to-beef" in the supply chain. Such tracking would allow standardized health, quality, and management protocols, as well as improved feedback through the entire production model. This change would also necessitate the producers being more closely linked to the feedlots to improve the quality of the beef. Branded beef production would move the industry from a cost-based (production) model to a value-added model. Better coordination along the supply chain would insure an increased flow of information from the consumer to the producer. Alliances between the cow/calf producer and the feedlots would allow ranchers to better track the success of their calves (based on health and weight gain). Such data could allow the ranchers to further improve the genetics of their herd by tracking which cow/bull combinations had delivered the higher-yield calves. As part of these trends, some degree of integration or vertical coordination will occur in the beef industry. Ranchers will need to participate in order to ensure market access for their product. Ranchers will have to think beyond the boundaries of their own ranches.

Pfizer Animal Health Group

Pfizer Inc. is a research-based, diversified health care company with global operations. Pfizer Animal Health is one of the corporation's three major business groups (the other two being the Consumer Health Care Group and U.S. Pharmaceuticals). The Animal Health Products Group accounted for roughly 12% of the company's revenues in 1998 (Pfizer Annual Report).

Pfizer Animal Health products are sold to veterinarians and animal health distributors in more than 140 countries around the world for use by livestock producers and horse and pet owners; the products are used in more than 30 animal species. Pfizer Animal Health is committed to providing high-quality, research-based health products for livestock and companion animals. The company continues to invest significant dollars for research and development. As a result, Pfizer has many new animal health products in its research pipeline, a number of which have already been introduced in some international markets and will become available in the United States in the next several years.

As Exhibit 5 shows, the Animal Health Group is divided into a North America Region with a U.S. Livestock Division, a U.S. Companion Animal Division (cats, dogs, etc.), and Canada. The Cow/Calf Division falls under the Cattle Business Unit within

EXHIBIT 5   **Pfizer Animal Health Organization**

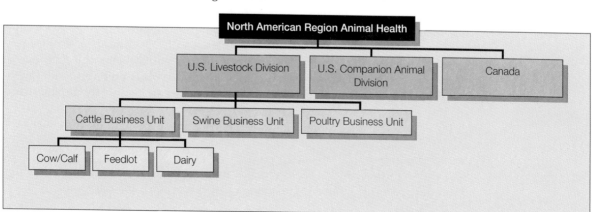

the Livestock Division. That Division is organized further by product type (Wood Mackenzie Report).

The marketing managers for each cattle market segment work closely with product managers and sales managers to ensure timely, accurate information back from the field. Territory managers responsible for all sales activities report to an Area Sales Manager, who in turn reports to the national sales and marketing manager. Territory managers are typically compensated on a roughly 80% salary/20% commission basis. This percentage would vary by salesperson by year: in a good year the commission might be a much higher percentage of overall earnings, while in a bad year, the salary component might be a greater percentage of the salesperson's overall earnings.

Marketing Strategy

Pfizer's Cow/Calf Division offers a full range of products to cattle ranchers, including vaccines for both newborn calves and their mothers, medications (for example, de-wormers, anti-diarrheals), and antibiotics (for pneumonia and other diseases). Pfizer's sophisticated research-and-development system resulted in a number of new and useful products for the market. For example, Pfizer developed a long-lasting de-wormer that was simply poured along the cow's back. This technology was a significant time-saver to the rancher, eliminating the need to administer either an oral medication or an injection. Moreover, Pfizer had been the first company to come up with a modified-live and killed virus vaccine, a significant technological breakthrough which provided safety in pregnant animals and the efficacy of a modified-live virus.

Pfizer offered a diverse product line to cow/calf ranchers. Some of Pfizer's key product lines are compared to those of competitors in Exhibit 6.

Pfizer segmented ranchers in the cow/calf business on the basis of herd size, as shown in Exhibit 7.

"Hobbyists" are so called because in many cases, these ranchers run their cattle as a sideline to some other job held. "Traditionalists'" main livelihood is their cattle operation. The "Business" segment operations are large ranches, owned either by a family or a corporation.

Pfizer's extensive network of field sales representatives visits the ranchers to inform them about new and existing products. Time spent with accounts was typically allocated on the basis of volume of product purchased.

Pfizer positioned its products on the combination of superior science (resulting from its significant R&D efforts) and high-quality production/quality control techniques. For example, although other companies in the market (particularly generics) used similar formulations in their products, on occasion they did not have good quality control in the production line, resulting in batches of ineffective vaccines and recalls. Pfizer backed its products completely with a Technical Services Department. If ranchers had any kind of health or nutritional problem with their herds, they could call on a team of Pfizer technical specialists who would work with the local veterinarian, utilizing blood and other diagnostics to identify the problem and suggest a solution.

Pfizer also was very involved in the cattle industry itself. Each territory manager was given an annual budget that included discretionary funds to be spent in his/her territory to sponsor industry activities such as seminars on herd health, stock shows, 4-H, and so forth. Gail Oss, for example, chose to spend a significant portion of her discretionary funds sponsoring meetings and conferences for the Montana Stock-

EXHIBIT 6 **Comparison of Product Lines***

Company	Pfizer	American Home Products (Fort Dodge)	Bayer	Merial
Sales and Profitability	10-year average annual sales growth increase of 3.8%; average for global veterinary market is 6.9%. Profit rate in 1997 was 8.4%. Market share in 1997 was 15.3%	10-year average annual sales growth increase of 7.8%; average for global veterinary market is 6.9%. Profit rate in 1997 was 11.0%; market share was 9.0%	10-year average annual sales growth increase of 10.2%; average for global veterinary market is 6.9%. Profit rate in 1997 was 16.8%; market share was 10.9%.	10-year average annual sales growth increase of 11.9%; average for global veterinary market is 6.9%. Profit rate in 1997 was 22.8%; market share was 16.4%.
Bovine Diseases Covered by Product Range	IBR; P1–3; BVD; BRSV; leptospira; rotavirus; coronavirus; campylobacter; clostridia; E.Coli; pasteurellosis; haemophilus.	Pasteurellosis; enterotoxaemia; chlamydia; salmonella; IBR; P1–3; brucellosis; rabies; E.Coli; anaplasmosis; tetanus; BVD; BRSV; leptospirosis; trichomonas; campylobacter; papilloma; haemophilus	IBR; FMD; IPV; P1–3; balanoposthitis; clostridia; haemophilus; BRSV; BVD; leptospira; E.Coli; rhinotracheitis; campylobacter.	Foot and mouth; rabies; brucellosis; paratuberculosis; rhinotracheitis; rotavirus; coronavirus; colibacillosis; parainfluenza; BVD; aglactia; foot rot; black leg; IBR; leptospira; clostridia; pasteurella; BRSV; E.Coli.
Significant Products for Cattle	Comprehensive product line; anti-infectives have formed basis of product line for many years; vaccine businesses also very important; also sells a performance enhancer, virginiamycin; parasiticides, led by Dectomax, starting to make significant impact on sales; Valbazen anthelmintic; broad range of general pharmaceuticals.	Predominantly a vaccine company; antibiotics centered on anti-mastitis products; anti-infectives based on penicillins, tetracyclines, sulphonamides and quinolones; parasiticides led by Cydectin; main products in general pharmaceuticals are anabolic implants for muscle growth.	Product range biased towards parasiticides, particularly ectoparasiticides, and antibiotics; overall product range is diverse; some mastitis anti-microbials; wide range of pharmaceuticals, but sales value of each product is limited; focus is more towards companion animal market.	Most important product sector is parasiticides, with product range dominated by Ivermectin, which was the first endectocide to reach the market; success of Ivermectin has drawn strong competition; remainder of product range made up primarily of anthelmintics and a range of general pharmaceuticals and vaccines.
Strengths	Strong manufacturing capabilities based on fermentation expertise and capacity; global marketing coverage supported by strategic local manufacture;	Leading global vaccine business; good international exposure; comprehensive vaccine product range; potential for growth through Cydectin.	Growing market in expanding companion animal sector; solid in-house manufacturing supported by global distribution capability;	Leading veterinary vaccine company with broad product portfolio; strong line of new product introductions; good companion animal

(continued)

EXHIBIT 6 *(concluded)*

Company	Pfizer	American Home Products (Fort Dodge)	Bayer	Merial
			business focused on key market areas.	business; global distribution network; strength in parasiticides and vaccines sectors.
Weaknesses	North America still dominates turnover; high proportion of sales due to off-patent products; heavily dependent on performance of livestock markets.	Business with disparate parts requiring strong central focus; except for vaccines, product range is dominated by commodity products; R&D likely to be reduced.	Underweight in USA; lack of critical mass in biologicals; no blockbuster product in North American market; narrow anti-infectives product portfolio; current R&D emphasis away from new product discovery.	Specialist pharmaceutical product line, not significantly involved in livestock sectors; aging anti-infectives portfolio; Ivermectin subject to intense competition.
% of R&D to Sales*	5	3	3	2
Position on Quality vs. Price**	5	3.5	3	3
Price Support of Distibution Channel***	2	4	3	3

*This information is taken from the Wood MacKenzie Animal Health Market Review and its Veterinary Company Profiles, both done on a worldwide basis.

* Specific ratios are considered proprietary. Hence, a general rating scale is used where 5 means a higher percentage of R&D/Sales and 1 is a lower percentage.

** 5 = Focus on Quality only; 1 = Focus on Low Price only

*** 5 = Strong emphasis on SPIFs (Special Promotional Incentive Funds) and price-related trade promotions; 1 = low emphasis

EXHIBIT 7   Pfizer Market Segments, 1998

Segment	# of Cattle	# of Operations	% of National Cattle Inventory
Hobbyist	<100	808,000	50%
Traditionalist	100–499	69,000	36%
Business	500+	5,900	14%

grower's Association, which might include a veterinarian or a professor from the Extension Office of a state university speaking on issues pertinent to ranchers.

The majority of Pfizer's trade advertising was focused on specific products and appeared in cattle industry publications, such as *Beef Magazine* and *Bovine Veterinarian.* One ad read, "More veterinarians are satisfied with [Pfizer's] Dectomax Pour-On," and went on to describe veterinarians' superior satisfaction and greater likelihood of recommending Dectomax compared to a key competitor, Ivomec:

> Eighty-four percent of veterinarians who recommended Dectomax Pour-On said they were satisfied or very satisfied with its performance—compared to only 51% who were satisfied or very satisfied with Ivomec Eprinex Pour-On. . . . If choosing only between Dectomax and Ivomec, over three out of four veterinarians would choose to recommend Dectomax Pour-On.

Another ad read, "Calf Health Program Boosts Prices by Up to $21 More per Head." The data in the copy-intensive ad highlighted that "cow-calf producers enrolled in value-added programs like Pfizer Select Vaccine programs are being rewarded for their efforts with top-of-the-market prices." Such programs are based on a consistent program of vaccinating animals with specific products, and they provide optimal disease protection. The programs result in cattle that perform more consistently and predictably in terms of weight gain and beef quality—resulting in higher prices at sale time.

Although the territory managers called on ranchers (as well as the veterinarians, distributors, and dealers) in their territories, they sold no product directly to ranchers. Ranchers could buy their animal health products from either a local veterinarian or a distributor or dealer (such as a feed-and-seed store). The percentage of product flowing through vets or distributors and dealers varied significantly by region. In areas where feedlots (versus cow/calf ranchers) were the predominant customers, 95% of the product might flow through distributors. In areas where ranchers are the predominant customers, vets might sell 50% of the product, depending upon customer preferences.

Vets were particularly important given that the overwhelming majority of ranchers said that the person they trusted the most when it came to managing the health of their herd was their veterinarian. Pfizer capitalizes on this trust in the vet in its marketing program. When the vet consults and recommends a Pfizer product to a rancher, the vet gives the rancher a coded coupon which may be redeemed at either a vet clinic or supply house. When the coupon is sent back to Pfizer for reimbursement, the vet is credited for servicing that product, regardless of where the product is purchased.

Pfizer offers some trade promotions to vets and distributors, including volume rebate programs, price promotions on certain products during busy seasonal periods, and so forth. However, Pfizer's competitors oftentimes gave much more significant discounts and SPIFs to distributors. As a result, when a rancher went to a distributor to buy a product the vet had recommended, the distributor might switch the rancher to a similar product for which the distributor was making more profit. If it was a Pfizer product the vet had recommended, the distributor might switch the rancher to a competitor's product. Pfizer had historically avoided competing on the basis of such promotional tactics, feeling instead that redirecting such funds back into R&D resulted in better long-term benefits for its customers.

So, as Gail pondered these various facets of the company's market position and strategies, she decided to take a strong stance in her weekly memo. It was time to cut the bull.

Discussion Questions

1. Evaluate the trends affecting the cattle ranching industry.

2. To what degree is a high quality/premium price position a strength or a liability during an industry downturn? What are the various ways Pfizer could handle this situation?

3. Evaluate the various dimensions of Pfizer's marketing strategy: Market segmentation and positioning; product/price; distribution; trade advertising and trade promotion; personal selling; public relations and sponsorships. What makes sense and what doesn't? Why or why not?

4. Would Pfizer benefit from a relationship marketing focus? How would its marketing strategy need to be modified to take such a focus?

5. When an industry is in decline, to what extent should a supplier be involved in ensuring its customers' livelihoods?

Snacks to Go

JoAnn K. Linrud
Central Michigan University

Jill Harms' half-year tenure as Assistant Category Manager for the Nuts, Natural Snacks and Cookies Category at Sathers, Inc. had been exciting. The variety of tasks in her category had been a challenge partly because Sathers management had targeted the Nuts, Natural Snacks and Cookies Category for growth, and partly because she had been given full responsibility for the category from the first day she had started at Sathers. That meant that she had direct responsibility to Mike Halverson, Director of Marketing.

Her focus on this Friday in mid-July of 1995 was the recommendation she would make to Mike on Monday concerning Snacks to Go, the snack nuts product line introduced earlier in the year. After a fast start, sales had lagged. Now, with lackluster market-monitoring reports on her desk, Jill was being asked to decide the line's fate. As she thought about possible alternatives for the product line, she knew she could commission a new round of research. But pressures were mounting to improve the line's performance—soon—or drop the line completely.

Background

HISTORY

As if the economic woes of the Great Depression weren't enough, in 1936 John Sather's grocery store in Round Lake, Minnesota, burned to the ground. With a tenacity of spirit that wouldn't allow him to give up, he instead began to distribute cookies in bulk to area grocers, adding other products as time passed. Ten years later, his son Kenneth joined the business, after serving as a bomber pilot in WWII. Kenneth implemented the philosophy of value by selling packages of cookies and other products such as almond bark, four packages for $1.00, to grocers in a five-county area. Sathers serviced their accounts with a sales force that personally took orders, delivered product, and stocked shelves. A turning point came when a number of salesmen left the organization, leaving Sathers shorthanded. As a stop-gap measure, Sathers management offered discounts to the customers who would order by telephone and stock their own shelves. Consequently, Sathers became an early entrant in the field of telephone marketing.

In the 1960s Kenneth Sather initiated the "pegboard" display: hanging cellophane bags with paper headers. Distributing product in ten states by this time, Sathers candy caught the eye of some regional Kmart managers, who were at that time responsible for making buying decisions for their own stores. Kenneth convinced these Kmarts to carry two bags of candy for $1.00, Sathers' original "Two for One." Success in these stores led to the capture of the entire Kmart account by 1972. So began national distribution of the Sathers line of packaged candy.

Still emphasizing repackaging (called "rebagging" by some in the trade), Sathers purchased a nut roasting operation in the 1960s, expanding the product line beyond cookies and candy. Further acquisitions included a New Orleans manufacturing plant from American Candy Company in 1985, and an additional candy manufacturing operation in the later 1980s. Sathers acquired Powell's Inc., a Hopkins, Minnesota, candy manufacturer and distributor with over 340 employees and revenues of about $30 million in 1991, bringing the company's total employees to 1,500 and its in-house production to fifty percent, well toward its goal of eighty percent. The Powell's acquisition also netted Sathers a film-printing business, Flex-o-Print, which would increase their packaging capabilities.

In 1992, Sathers upgraded its Round Lake packaging facility with a robotics operation. By 1993, Sathers' $135 million in sales marked the tenth straight year of sales gains. In 1994, Sathers broadened the product line produced in the Hopkins operation. That year also brought the acquisition of the assets of North Star Candy Company, a Wisconsin-based niche candy marketer.

To manage the change from distributor to manufacturer, Sathers hired a professional management team, headed by Howard Kosel, who came to Sathers as President in 1980. He assumed the CEO duties when William S. Bradfield joined the organization as Executive Vice President in 1989. Bradfield became COO and President in 1991, positions he continued to hold. Michael Halverson was brought in as Director of Marketing, a newly created position, in 1992. Mr. Halverson instituted the Category Manager organizational design for his department; some Category Managers' positions were unfilled. (See Marketing organizational chart, Exhibit 1.) Over the years, ownership had passed to four grandsons of John Sather. Although their management style was "hands-off," a family atmosphere pervaded the Round Lake facility.

OPERATIONS

In 1995, Sathers manufactured and distributed bag candy, nuts, natural snacks, and cookies, sold through over 50,000 drug, convenience, grocery, variety, and discount stores worldwide. Sathers grouped its products into six categories: general candy, seasonal candy, nuts and natural snacks, cookies, international, and private label candy. (See Exhibit 2 for a description of each category.)

Hanging bag candy was Sathers' mainstay; the "Two for $1.00" Value Line generated up to fifty percent of the vertically integrated company's $150 million in revenues. Sathers employed approximately 1,500 people in its manufacturing plants in Hopkins, a Minneapolis suburb, and New Orleans, and in its distribution centers in Chattanooga, Pittston, Pennsylvania, and Round Lake, and at Flex-o-Print, at Rogers, just north of Minneapolis.

The 350,000 square foot facility at Round Lake (population 463, in the southwestern part of Minnesota) was command central for all operations, including the

EXHIBIT 1   Marketing Organizational Chart

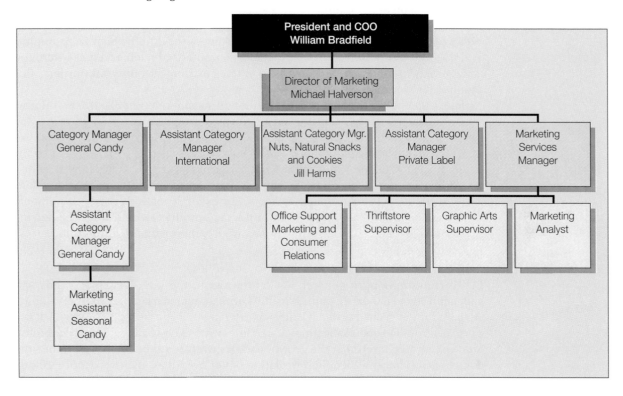

EXHIBIT 2   Sathers Product Categories

Category	Description
General Candy	• 119 items in the 2/$1.00 line (chocolate candy, licorice, jelly/gummy candy, mint candy, kiddie candy, coconut candy, hard candy, caramel candy, traditional candy, sugar-free candy, Hispanic candy); • 70 items in the profit-advantage line; • 25 items in the 2/$3.00 line in the traditional "peg board" hanging bags; • 85 different candy products offered in bulk; • other package alternatives including prepacked shippers and large lay-down bag candy.
Seasonal Candy	• Many products in the general candy lines, offered in special packages and priced for seasonal product movement.
Nuts and Natural Snacks	• 24 items in the 2/$1.00 line (such as Salted-in-the-shell, Sunflower Seeds and Peanuts, Spanish Peanuts, Banana Chips, Mixed Nuts, Aloha Mix, Trail Mix, Pineapple Tidbits, Red and Natural Pistachios, etc.); • 23 items in the profit-advantage line; • over 30 items offered in bulk.
Cookies	• 16 items in the 2/$1.00 line (such as Chocolate Covered Regal Graham Cookies, Coco Chip Cookies, Oatmeal Raisin Cookies, Fig Bars, Striped Shortbread Cookies, sandwich crèmes, etc.); • sugar-free wafers in four flavors with separate counter and floor displays.
International	• Sales of candy, nuts, and natural snacks to thirty accounts in countries such as Mexico, Canada, Saudi Arabia, Panama, Uruguay, and countries in the Caribbean.
Private Label Candy	• Sales of candy, nuts, and natural snacks to twelve accounts of national and regional drug and discount stores.

telemarketing arm and the fleet of trucks used for distribution in the U.S. and Canada. The plant was equipped with a $5 million robotics packaging operation, to run ten lines using the latest robotics and vision inspection system, ending with robotics palletization. The system gave Sathers state-of-the-art efficiency in packaging and quality control. Round Lake also had a computerized telemarketing system for calling each customer every three weeks to track existing accounts, take orders, and monitor new business efforts.

The Sathers truck fleet capped its distribution system with over 300 trucks running at almost 100 percent efficiency, carrying finished product out and supplies in. The system enabled Sathers to complete delivery in about half the time of typical truck delivery, allowing customers to minimize inventory. Sales were to confections distributors, retail chain distribution centers, and some direct store-door delivery accounts. And, while Sathers did very little consumer promotions, it heavily supported retailers and distributors' efforts to sell to retailers. For example, Sathers provided point-of-purchase signage and racks, product reorder tags, product samples, and detailed instructions for product display, order and reorder. Sathers paid no slotting allowances.

CANDY MARKET

Candy consumption, in general, was on the rise in the U.S., from 16 pounds per capita in 1986 to almost 22 pounds in 1994, with a retail market of $12 to $15 billion. Reasons for the growth varied. Candy was often treated as a reward, even in (and because of) troubled economic times. Value lines were likely to do better in recessions. Some experts believed that the growth had occurred at a time of increasing health-consciousness because people were eating better overall, so they were more willing to reward themselves. About eighty percent of consumer candy decisions were made at the retail store.

The candy market could be divided into two parts: chocolate and nonchocolate. Since chocolate candy made up sixty percent of all confection sales, Sathers competed with other nonchocolate producers for the remaining shelf space. "[The nonchocolate category] is a tough game," according to Jan Kitt, a sales and marketing consultant who specializes in candy. "Good hard candy tastes the same no matter who makes it. It's very difficult to get a point of difference . . . Since candy is a commodity business, distribution is the name of the game. If the product is out there, it will be purchased. The more it's available, the more people will buy it. That stands more true for confection than for any other category" (1). Of all suppliers of confections, gum, and snacks to U.S. convenience stores in 1991, Sathers ranked twelfth, according to the *ICC/Accutracks Convenience Store Report,* ahead of Cornnuts, Inc., and E. J. Brach Corp. And, Sathers ranked seventh of all nonchocolate brands, ahead of Tootsie Roll. After-tax profit margins in the candy industry ranged from two to five percent.

SATHERS' STRATEGY FOR SUCCESS

Competitors and the trade recognized Sathers' competitive advantages. "There are a lot of rebaggers, but Sathers' strength is in distributing the product," according to Kenneth McCarley, of the Winona Division of Brock Candy Company of Chattanooga, a competitor. Another competitor, Ron Meyer of Shari Candies, Inc. (Mankato, Minnesota) recognized Sathers as a "very well-run company whose business has been built on service." Keith Canning of Pine State Tobacco and Candy (Augusta, Maine) called Sathers "the single most successful company we've brought on in the last five years. The penetration they've had in the East has been nothing short of phenomenal. You can't go into a store in this area and not see it." And Dave

McElhatten, a candy buyer for Kmart, pointed to Sathers' creativity: "They're always looking for new products. They're very good at innovation."[1]

Sathers' strategy for success was built on offering a price point, exemplified by the "Two for $1.00" Value Line, and building a distribution network based on service. Sathers President William Bradfield pointed out that value, to Sathers, "doesn't only mean more product for the money. It includes product quality, variety, availability, price, packaging, and quantity. . . . The consumer value is the driving force of the company. We have a very real mindset that whatever we do has to add value for the customer."[2]

Vice President of Operations Charlie Mayer echoed the idea. "The path we've taken has been a tremendous advantage because we control the product from start to finish. Everything in this company revolves around service to the customer first because that's what distribution is. That has been the cornerstone of the development of this company."[3]

Building on that cornerstone, William Bradfield identified Sathers' goals. "We have a very simple formula—be profitable, continue to grow, with a focus on candy." Sathers' strategy for the twenty-first century will be to "continue to develop our position in nuts, natural snacks and cookies, but we will dominantly be a candy manufacturer."

The Snacks to Go Product Line

DEVELOPMENT OF SNACKS TO GO

When Jill arrived at Sathers as an Assistant Category Manager and was given responsibility for the Snacks to Go line in January of 1995, progress in developing the line was well underway. The idea for a snack nuts product in a ziplock package for "on the go" consumers was initiated in early 1994. The aim in developing the line was to become one of the first in the industry to introduce a ziplock package filled with nuts and natural snacks, while achieving Sathers' company objective of developing the nuts and natural snacks category.

To explore the feasibility of using a ziplock bag closing for snack nuts, Sathers had contacted Zip-Pak, the originator of the ziplock zipper bag closing, to learn more about ziplock zippers. Zip-Pak provided information from a 1989 Food Packaging Research Study of 300 food shoppers in four U.S. cities conducted by an independent research firm. The study revealed that most consumers who preferred resealable packaging would switch brands and pay more for the food protection, convenience, and freshness that resealable packaging offered. Over half of the respondents preferred nuts in resealable packaging, and of those who ate nuts often, most believed that it was important to preserve the freshness of the food, to keep it from drying out and becoming stale, and that the package should be easy to open and close.

In general, consumers appeared to have positive responses to the idea of resealable packages. With that information, the next step was to gain knowledge of consumers' snack nuts consumption. To do that, Sathers commissioned a nationally recognized marketing research firm to conduct focus groups and personal interviews. Sathers believed such analysis would offer greater depth about usage patterns than other research types, such as mail or telephone surveys, for instance.

[1]Fink, Laurie (1992), "Sweet Success," *Corporate Report—Minnesota,* (March), pp. 28–32.

[2]"It's in the bag: hanging bag candy manufacturer Sathers, Inc." (1994), *U.S. Distribution Journal,* (July 15), pp. 42–43.

[3]Tiffany, Susan (1995), "Sathers secures niche as manufacturer," *Candy Industry,* (July), pp. 51–57.

1. Focus Groups—Phase 1   The firm conducted two focus groups in June, 1994, to explore positioning and package themes. Qualifying participants for these focus groups, conducted in Chicago, had purchased nuts for snacking within the past three months, at a drug, convenience, or discount store, from a stand-up display, pouch, or hanging bag, jar or can, and were between 18 and 44 years old. Objectives of the research included determining attitudes toward snacking and the role of nuts in snacking; attitudes toward and usage of packaged nuts; awareness, attitudes, and imagery of packaged nut brands; opinions regarding packaging formats; reactions to the ziplock concept and execution; reactions to three selected positionings: "freshness," "convenience," and "health"; reactions to three package designs; and interest in a microwaveable snack nut product sold in convenience stores.

Results revealed that these focus group participants snacked every day, eating both salty and sweet snacks. While snacking, for them, was often solitary, nuts were associated with parties, as well as with routine snacking, and were chosen for their taste, convenience, and protein. Disadvantages of nuts as a snack included being fattening, greasy, more expensive, and containing harmful oils. There was no "right time" for snacking on nuts; purchase was often driven by mood and a coupon or sale, and included a variety of nut types, rather than just one type. Snack nuts were purchased in discount, grocery, and convenience stores, as planned and impulse purchases.

In terms of package format, the advantage of cans and jars was their resealability, while bags were more portable, more appropriate for one or several snacks, and more easily disposed when finished. However, they were often easy to spill and not resealable. A ziplock closing for snack nuts was seen as a clear advantage, with a primary benefit of preventing spilling. A larger bag that could be resealed for a later snack could also yield a cost savings. The "convenience" positioning, therefore, captured the essence of the portability concept. While "freshness" was an appealing concept, most of these respondents did not have problems with stale nuts. Because of their high fat content, snack nuts were not seen as being "healthy." Consequently, the ideal packaged snack nuts product would be convenient, easy to open and seal, fresh, portable, and a healthier alternative to "typical" snacks. A microwaveable snack nut product was not appealing to these consumers.

Packaging designs viewed by these focus groups corresponded with the three positioning alternatives, "freshness," "convenience," and "health." These packages were larger and more colorful than the traditional Sathers "Two for $1.00" header package. Participants seemed to prefer the new lively package, considering it to be more eye-catching, communicating a better quality, fresher product, and perhaps more successful at upgrading the image of the "Two for $1.00" package.

While Planters, Fisher and Evon's were the most recognized, better quality brands, the respondents exhibited little brand loyalty within the snack nuts category. Purchase of an unknown brand was more likely, however, if the consumer could see the product through a film or cellophane "window." The participants' attitudes towards brands revealed that Sathers was either not well recognized or was known for candy. Respondents' perceptions were drawn from the Sathers' "Two for $1.00" package, Planters' Mr. Peanut, and Fisher's colorful foil packages and advertising. A projective technique used to ascertain brand impressions resulted in the following profiles.

Sathers: unsophisticated, plain, common, not necessarily downscale, but thrifty/frugal;

Planters: conservative/traditional/classic, stable, ranging between affluent and middle class, aged 50s;

Fisher: trendy, sophisticated, affluent, aged 30s to 40s.

2. Focus Groups—Phase 2   The research firm conducted a second set of two focus groups in Tampa in August, 1994, to gauge reactions to revised positioning and packaging designs and to assess ziplock packaging for Sathers. The qualifying characteristics for these participants were the same as before; the purposes were the same, except for the addition of an objective about attitudes toward salt, and the omission of the "microwaveable" objective.

Tampa participants' responses about snacking in general and snack nuts in particular were very similar to the Chicago groups' responses. However, brand was more important for these consumers. They purchased from a small set of "known" brands (Planters, Eagle, and Fisher, most often) partly because of their confidence that better-known brands were fresher, a concern in the hot, humid Florida climate. Planters' quality image was favored for its duration in the marketplace, availability, and advertisements. Brand impressions resulting from a projective technique included:

> Sathers (based on the traditional "Two for $1.00" package): Younger group members suggested a teenaged, downscale male. Older members suggested a 20–40 year old male or female, unsophisticated and nondescript;
>
> Planters: older gentleman who enjoys the finer things in life and has finances to pay for them;
>
> Fisher: upscale, young, trendy male or female.

Members of these groups were also more particular about package format features. Determination of freshness came from a package with evidence of air in the bag (vacuum sealed) and a clear product-viewing area (more important for unknown brands). Flashy, brightly colored packages appealed more to younger respondents. Reactions to the concept and execution of a ziplock package closing were universally favorable.

Tampa respondents preferred the "freshness" positioning concept over the "convenience" concept. Ideal positioning, however, would include both, plus being easy to open and close, economical, and a healthier alternative to "typical" snacks.

The Tampa residents viewed somewhat different package executions than the Chicago groups, since the designs were modified on the basis of the Chicago groups' responses. Of four executions, all larger and more brightly colored than the traditional Sathers "Two for $1.00" package, more preferred a lively white and green Snacks to Go package with nut cartoon characters, a design that they believed to be more attention-getting and that upgraded the image of the brand. Some expressed concern that the window didn't reveal enough of the product within.

While the presence of salt was a concern, particularly among the 35–44 year old consumers, most agreed that salt was an important ingredient in snack nuts. "Lightly salted" nuts were viewed favorably; most group members did not purchase "salt substitute" products.

3. Personal Interviews   To enhance and crystallize these findings, an additional research effort was conducted in September, 1994, by the same research firm. In this investigation, seventy-six respondents completed personal interviews at two locations in Chicago. Respondent qualifications were identical to the earlier studies, with the exception of extending the upper age limit to 54. These respondents answered questions about the ziplock features and the Snacks to Go name, and they rated three different package executions:

> green package with red letters;
>
> blue package with graduated darkening of the blue;
>
> green package with yellow letters.

The blue package rated highest on a 5-point like-dislike scale. In addition, it was also chosen as the best at gaining attention, conveying a quality product, and conveying a premium-priced product. Again, the ziplock was overwhelmingly rated as a good idea. Over eighty percent liked the Snacks to Go name. In a comparison of the blue Snacks to Go package with competitive brands' packages, Planters outperformed Sathers, but Sathers was rated higher than the Fisher package.

THE SNACKS TO GO PROGRAM

With these three research reports to guide their decision making, Jill and Mike Halverson developed the program for introducing Snacks to Go in the spring of 1995.

PRODUCTS

Products chosen for the Snacks to Go line were the top two items in the Sathers snack nuts line (Salted-in-the-shell Sunflower Seeds and Shelled Roasted Sunflower Nuts) and the top two items in their Natural Snacks line (Trail Mix and California Mix). The main selling point would be the ziplock package closing feature, which would appeal to active 18–44 year olds. To accommodate their on-the-go lifestyle, the product would be available in convenience stores. To ensure freshness, a "nitrogen flushing" procedure would be used before sealing the packages. Some products, particularly Shelled Roasted Sunflower Nuts, had a tendency to spoil when exposed to oxygen. In packaging, "nitrogen flushing" would remove the oxygen from the package, preserving freshness and ensuring a longer shelf life. The process would not be necessary for nonroasted products, such as Trail Mix, California Mix, and Salted-in-the-shell Sunflower Seeds.

Packaging for the four items, identical but for the item names, consisted of a 9.5″ by 6″ film package, bright blue in the center graduated to dark blue at the bottom. (See Exhibit 3.) A bright yellow band crossed the upper portion of the package; "Snacks to Go" was printed in large yellow letters across the center blue portion. Below the letters, on the left side were two cashew nut cartoon characters wearing helmets, one driving a sporty red cartoon car, the other on in-line skates, depicting "on the go" activities. To the right of the characters was a clear window, approximately 2″ by 1.5″ to display the contents, above which read the item name in a half-inch band, black letters on white background.

The brand name "Sathers" was emblazoned in half-inch red letters on the yellow band near the package top, beside a red banner proclaiming "NEW! Resealable Package." At the very top, a red stripe crossed the package, with the words "ZIP-PAK" and "Resealable Packaging" identifying the closing feature in white letters. The package backside contained directions for opening and resealing the zipper, nutrition facts, ingredients, distribution information, a guarantee and thank you message from Sathers, a bar code and a repeat of the cashew character in the red sports car.

These packages were designed to hang on a state-of-the-art tubular blue metal display rack approximately 5′ high by 18″ wide, in a three-by-four format: three facings of an item in a row with four rows, approximately six bags deep. The top of the display repeated the yellow-on-blue "Snacks to Go" name and art, with "Sathers" and "ZIP-PAK" in somewhat smaller letters. The rack would hold six cases of product (72 packages, 18 of each product).

PRICING

Because the ziplock closing feature required a minimum package size, the price points for the four items were chosen to remain competitive. Expected retailer and distributor combined margins for all items were around thirty percent. Suggested

EXHIBIT 3   The Snacks to Go Product Line

retail price for California Mix (6.25 oz.), Trail Mix (7.0 oz.), and Shelled Roasted Sunflower Nuts (9.0 oz.) would be $1.49, while Salted-in-the-shell Sunflower Seeds (6.25 oz.), would be sold at $.89. A $.99 price point was considered for all four packages, but it was not profitable to produce the smaller package with a ziplock closing that the $.99 price point would have required. Suggested retail prices were not printed on the packages.

PROMOTION AND DISTRIBUTION

Sathers account executives would be responsible for introducing the Snacks to Go program to convenience store distributors and large retailers with their own warehouses. Incentives included a $3.00 per rack spiff for all distributor salespeople who gained placement in stores. There was a $.20 per case allowance for distributors who met their quota, established by Sathers. The blue tubular rack (at a cost of approximately $60 each to Sathers) would be supplied free to the retailer.

Sales incentives for the account executives were designed to successfully motivate the sales force during the roll-out period of the new program. As such, both individual and regional performance would be rewarded. Each salesperson participating in the program would be provided with realistic sales quotas by his or her Regional Sales Manager. Over the four-month duration of the program, case sales by salesperson (as a percent of quota) and regional sales would be posted on a tally board. At the end of the fourth month, all salespersons achieving quota would earn a choice of a Sony Watchman TV or a Sony portable CD player. The salesperson with the highest sales, as a percentage over quota, would receive a weekend getaway package worth $500. For an entire region achieving quota, a special event, such as a team outing at an Atlanta Braves baseball game, would be offered.

To assist the sales force, supplementary support materials and a direct mail kit were provided. The printed support materials included a brochure outlining the key features of the program and the bold graphics of the packaging. In addition, a sell sheet, line art (an artist's rendering of what the display rack would look like), a planogram (a diagram of product packages to be displayed on the rack, per the contract), and a contract were designed to aid in the selling effort to distributors (see Exhibits 4a–4d). The contract was binding between Sathers and the retailer; among other specifications, it stated that the rack would be used exclusively for Snacks to Go product. The direct mail kit included a large sample of the Snacks to Go ziplock package, a sales flier, and an introduction letter to the distributor's buyer to familiarize each account with the program and prepare them for the salesperson's visit. No consumer promotions were planned.

THE ROLL-OUT

While convenience stores throughout the nation were the eventual outlet through which Sathers would market Snacks to Go, convenience stores in the Southeast region were targeted for the March to June program roll-out. Specifically, this included Oklahoma, Arkansas, Louisiana, Mississippi, Tennessee, Alabama, Georgia, North and South Carolina, Virginia, Florida, and part of Texas. Although the entire snack nut category's heaviest concentration of sales was in the Northeast, the Southeast was a stronger area for the Sathers brand. Competition in the Southeast would come mostly from Planters (with 1994 market share of 35.2 percent), Fisher (3.8 percent), and Eagle (2.6 percent). Private labels accounted for 19.2 percent market share. The remainder of the market was composed of many small, regional brands. David and Sons was known in the sunflower seeds and sunflower nuts categories. The Snacks to Go line would be competitively priced (see Exhibit 5). There was

EXHIBIT 4A   Snacks to Go Sell Sheet

Introducing...

SATHERS,   has created a brand new innovation in the nut and snack market. **SATHERS**,   line of fresh roasted nuts are now available in convenient resealable zip lock packages. Eat some now ... save some for later!

- Your customers will love the convenience of a resealable and spill-proof package.
- Your impulse sales will soar with the colorful and bold graphics.
- The unique and dynamic floorstand will attract consumers to the Snacks to Go‰ display.
- The Snacks to Go‰ zip lock package will provide a fresh snack every time you use it!
- We offer a variety of four different items: California Mix, Trail Mix, Salted-in-Shell Sunflower Seeds and Sunflower Nuts

Item Code	Description	Case Pack	SRP
5200	Shelled Roasted Sunflower Nuts	12	$1.49
5201	Trail Mix	12	$1.49
5202	California Mix	12	$1.49
5203	Salted-in-Shell Sunflower Seeds	12	$ .89
3420	Floorstand (Provided by Sathers with program participation)		

SATHERS   Round Lake, Minnesota 56167

F-191-A

(895)

The National Value Line,

some seasonality in the snack food market. Generally, presentations to distributors were made six months in advance to obtain seasonally-appropriate distribution. Snack food presentations often began in January.

One hundred ten distributor accounts in the southeast region were selected, to be sold by seven account executives and a Regional Sales Manager. The goal for this region was to have 10,000 cases and 1,200 display racks placed by June 30, with sales of $650,000 by December 1, 1995. The initial presentation to the Sathers sales force occurred February 27, at the American Wholesale Marketers Association trade show. Through March and April the sales force introduced the Snacks to Go program to

EXHIBIT 4B   Snacks to Go Line Art

SNACKS TO GO LINE ART

their targeted accounts. All accounts had been presented by the end of May, with product completely placed by the end of June.

PERFORMANCE

Beginning with initial placement, the sales force tracked sales of the targeted accounts with weekly performance checks, usually on Monday. The Snacks to Go line had achieved good distributor placement at the outset, building upon the strength of the Sathers distribution network. Of the 110 targeted accounts, fifty percent took initial placement. And while weekly case sales showed slow movement in March and into April, by mid-April sales picked up and showed dramatic increases through May.

EXHIBIT 4C   Snacks to Go Planogram

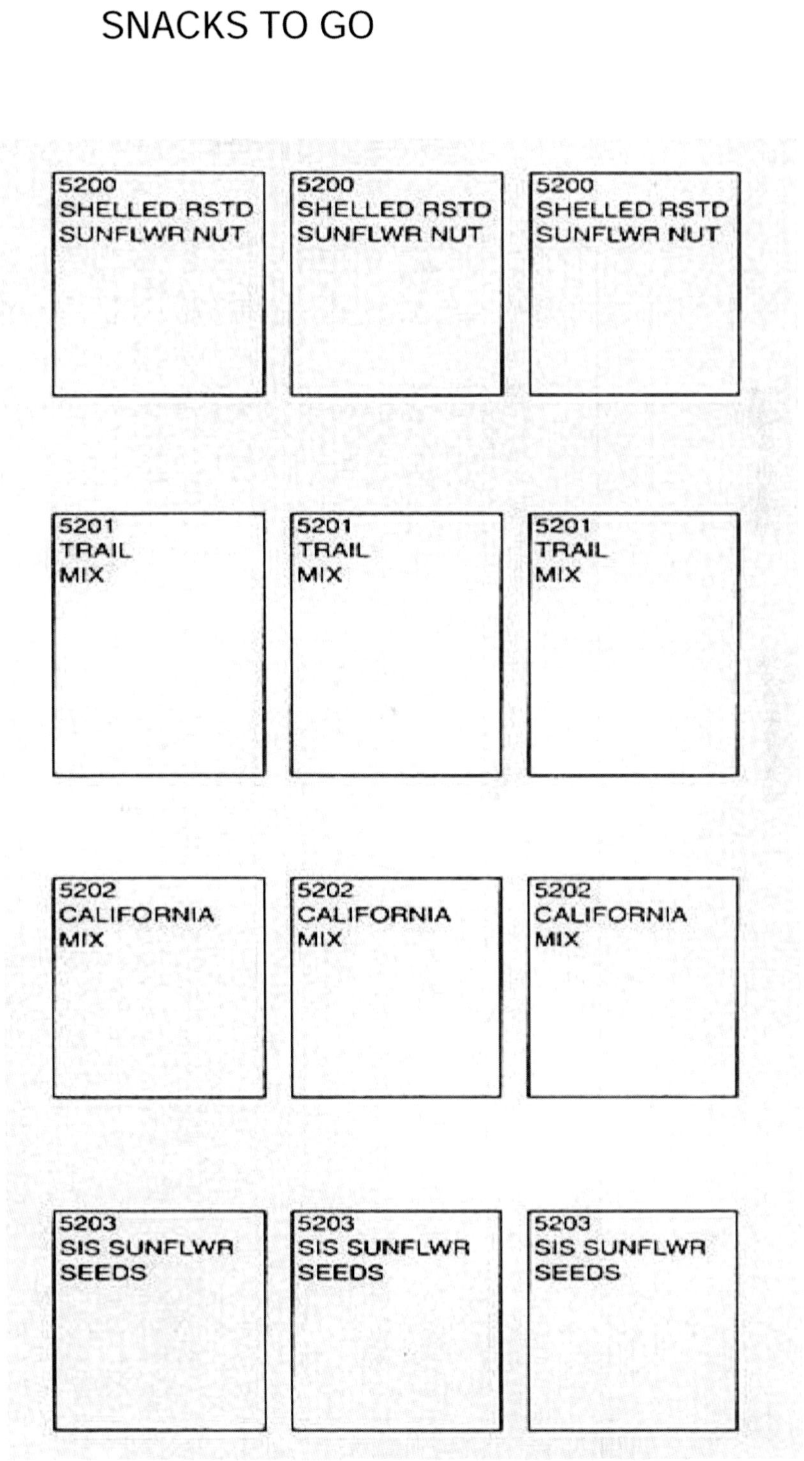

SNACKS TO GO

5200 SHELLED RSTD SUNFLWR NUT	5200 SHELLED RSTD SUNFLWR NUT	5200 SHELLED RSTD SUNFLWR NUT
5201 TRAIL MIX	5201 TRAIL MIX	5201 TRAIL MIX
5202 CALIFORNIA MIX	5202 CALIFORNIA MIX	5202 CALIFORNIA MIX
5203 SIS SUNFLWR SEEDS	5203 SIS SUNFLWR SEEDS	5203 SIS SUNFLWR SEEDS

EXHIBIT 4D   **Snacks to Go Contract**

SATHERS® SNACKS TO GO PROGRAM

Sathers Inc. (hereinafter referred to as "Sathers") and _____
_____, the participating customer (hereinafter referred to as the "Participant"), agree to the
following:

1. Sathers will supply Participant with the merchandising floorstand attached as Exhibit A as
   specified below at no charge to the Participant.

2. Participant will order sufficient quantities of open stock Sathers Snacks to Go™ (zip lock bags) on
   an ongoing basis to fill and maintain distribution of Sathers Snacks to Go™ (zip lock bags) on the
   floorstands.

3. Participant will display only Sathers Snacks to Go™ (zip lock bags) products on the floorstand.
   The merchandising floorstands remain the property of Sathers Inc.

4. If the floorstand becomes damaged or additional stands are needed, Participant agrees to contact
   their Sathers sales representative immediately.

5. Floorstands will be set to a planogram agreed to by Participant and Sathers.

This contract becomes effective on the day signed and will remain in effect until cancelled by either the
Participant or Sathers.

Participant:
Number of stands per store:

Number of stores:

Total floorstands requested:

Signature:

Date:

Sathers Inc.

Signature:

Title:

Date:

By June, however, case sales had slowed again. While initial placement with distributors had been good, none of the distributors took the program for all their stores.
Just twenty-six distributors placed reorders.

The June sales report showed that sales had slowed to five to six packages per week
per store, very slow movement indeed compared to about twenty-five packages per
week for Sathers "Two for $1.00" brand. Fewer than 8,000 cases had been sold, and
fewer than 800 racks had been placed. (See Exhibit 6 for sales charts.) In consultation
with Mike Halverson, Jill had extended the promotional program for another month.

June's slow sales were doubly disappointing when added to the packaging problem
Jill had faced. In April, she had been alerted to a problem with the Shelled Roasted

EXHIBIT 5   Price Comparisons

Brand	Weight in Oz.	Price	Price per Oz.
Sunflower Seeds			
Planters	2.0	.33	.11
SATHERS	6.25	.89	.1424
David & Son*	6.25	.89	.1424
Evons	2.75	.50	.1818
Fisher	3.25	.69	.212
Sunflower Kernels			
SATHERS	9.0	1.49	.1655
David & Son*	10.0	1.99	.199
Planters	3.75	.75	.20
Trail Mix			
SATHERS	7.0	1.49	.2128
Evons	2.0	.50	.25
Planters (Fruit & Nut)*	3.0	1.09	.3633
California Mix			
Golden Stream	12.0	2.59	.2158
SATHERS	6.25	1.49	.2384
Harmony	4.0	.99	.2475
Evons*	2.0	.50	.25
Fisher	2.5	.97	.388

*Dominant brand in category, nationwide.

Sunflower Nuts package. After carefully inspecting the packages, she'd discovered that the film package had air leaks, which allowed oxygen to mix with the product, causing the product to spoil and the shelf life, which had originally been one year, to deteriorate. While all new product had been packaged with a new, more resilient film, and distributed, about 2,000 cases of the old product had already been sold.

So, at the end of June, seeking specific reasons for the declining sales, Jill had asked for a quick internal study of snack nuts consumers in convenience stores where Snacks to Go had been distributed, and a poll of distributors in the Southeast region. The results, which she'd just reviewed, were not encouraging (see Exhibits 7 and 8).

Mike Halverson was anticipating her review and recommendation. What would she tell him? She could commission a new round of research, which should include store tests at grocery and drug stores, in addition to convenience stores, to monitor case sales by product type. But this would take ten weeks, at a minimum, and cost approximately $30,000. Or, she could suggest a different approach to marketing the product. She'd have to give more thought to exactly what she would change: additional trade promotions? price changes? additional design changes? How about a product change—a switch to candy? But, would that be consistent with the Snacks to Go concept and William Bradfield's charge to develop the snack nuts category? Finally, she knew she could recommend dropping the line completely. That would be a tough decision; would it be giving up too soon?

It was a mixed blessing that the company was closing at 2:30 this Friday, Jill thought, as she packed the sales and research study reports into her briefcase. It was going to be a long weekend of careful thinking about what she'd recommend to Mike on Monday morning for the future of the Snacks to Go product line.

EXHIBIT 6   Weekly Case Sales Patterns for Snacks to Go Products

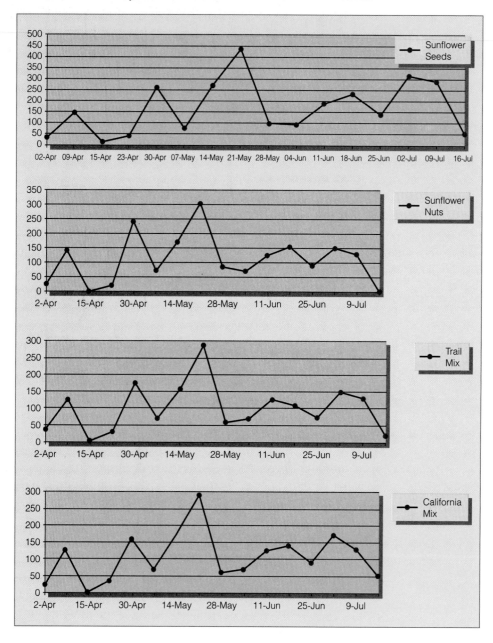

EXHIBIT 7   Convenience Store Survey Results*

Demographics: (Of 57 labeled surveys)

	White male	White female	Black male	Black female	Hispanic female
Teenager	6	3			
20s and 30s	14	7	6		3
40s+	9	6	1	2	

Results: (Of 72 total respondents)

Percent who did not recognize the ziplock closing feature: 69%
Percent who wanted a change in the variety of products: 21
Percent who thought the ziplock was worth paying more money for: 65

EXHIBIT 7 *(concluded)*

Interviewer's Comments:

It seems to be the teenagers and the travelers who are most likely to buy this package.
Everyone liked the colorful graphics and were attracted mostly by the bright colors.
A lot of people mentioned that they would like to see candy in a ziplock bag.
It was mentioned several times that the top of the package was sort of boring.
The product in the window seems to be drowning out the characters, hard to see them.

*This was a mall-intercept survey of consumers in one convenience store where the Snacks to Go line was sold.

EXHIBIT 8 **Comments from Distributors' Surveys***

Positive comments:

- Packaging, nice rack system.
- Likes package, likes rack.
- Rack and packaging looked very good at spring show.
- The rack was very nice, packaging was nice, looked good.
- Ziplock/unpriced.
- Ziplocks, rack system.
- Graphics/rack and unpriced.
- Good concept, but not sure if its niche is drug outlets, perhaps better in food stores.
- New concept.
- All the items are top selling items.
- Ziplock bag.
- Package stands out, is attractive.
- Love the package.
- Rack was easy to put together, and had all contents needed.
- Love the ziplock feature; attraction is the graphics and design of the display; very bright graphics is eye catching.
- Chain retailers feel ziplock differentiates program from others and helps sales.

Negative comments:

- Too many facings on racks, because it is selling so slow retailers are putting other items on the rack. Need more items to fill rack.
- $1.49 too high, $1.29 better. Rack too large for 4 items.
- Consumer doesn't realize it is a resealable bag. Resealable needs to be more prominent.
- It is not selling.
- Market is very competitive, thus hard to get good selling numbers. Program is average selling at best.
- Add pistachios.
- If Sathers were a guaranteed product everyone would order more when a new product is introduced, and avoid running out of a good selling item.
- $.89 OK, $1.49 too high, should be $.99.
- Package geared towards kids, but good package.
- $.89 OK, $1.49 too high, recommend $.99.
- Would like one retail price; would like to see different variety, some candy in the bags; already so many nut/snack competitors. Other suggestions: banana chips, sesame sticks, chocolates.
- Add ziplock gummies to mix.

*These comments were offered by the twenty-one distributors who returned the survey. Additionally, they reported that some convenience stores utilized the rack, while others placed the Snacks to Go products "in line," on the shelf with other snack products. Of those that did use the rack, some placed it near the front of the store, some near the back, some near the pop cooler, and some in other locations within the store.

Case 10

Salomon: The Monocoque Ski

Francis Bidault
International Management Development Institute

> Yes, it's excellent . . . I really love this prototype. You have all done a truly superb job! But, we are still only half way into this venture. There is a lot more work to do. . . . I would say you will probably need another four years before we can see Salomon skis, as well as boots and bindings, on the slopes. But, it is time to discuss an action plan and I would like to present it at next month's New Product Committee meeting! So, I'd appreciate it if you could let us have your plan a few days beforehand.

Georges Salomon, the 62-year-old president of Salomon S.A., was stroking, with visible excitement, the new prototype that the development team had just presented during one of his regular meetings with them. It was November 15, 1987, and he was glad to see the progress made by the team on this truly strategic project which he had initiated in July 1984: to design a Salomon ski as an addition to the company's successful product portfolio.

As Georges Salomon was making his concluding comments, the project team had mixed feelings. They were happy that their work had gained such positive recognition from the president, but they also felt under pressure, knowing what remained to be done. Until now, the development of the first Salomon ski had been a very exciting adventure: unlimited creativity, daring solutions, and generous support. That was the easy part. Now, the time had come to try and make the "dream" come true: They would have to work hard to complete the development and prepare a commercial launch. The real challenge was still ahead.

As they were leaving the meeting room, each member of the team was recollecting the key events that had led to this development and considering the significance of this project for the company and for the overall ski market.

Salomon S.A.

Salomon, a fast-growing company with headquarters in Annecy in the French Rhône-Alpes region, was proud of being the world leader (based on its sales) in winter sports equipment (refer to Exhibits 1–3). The company, always aiming for the top, had regularly improved its position in each of its market areas: number one in ski bindings with a 46 percent market share; number one in cross-country ski boot-bindings with a 30 percent market share; and number two in alpine ski boots where it was just a few percentage points behind Nordica. A line of accessories—clothes, bags, caps, and such ("Club-Line")—completed its winter sports offerings. In addition, Salomon owned Taylor-Made, a successful firm in the golf equipment business (clubs and accessories).

Salomon's sales were distributed around the globe: 30 percent in North America, 22 percent in Japan, 40 percent in Europe, and 8 percent in the rest of the world. Salomon had fully owned subsidiaries in 12 countries, including Japan, which was the largest in terms of sales.

The company was heavily involved in competitive events in winter sports as well as in golf. Success in competition was considered very important for establishing the credibility and reputation of Salomon and Taylor-Made products. The company invested a significant amount of money (some FF 50 million annually) in amateur and professional sporting events.

Salomon's management philosophy revolved around three basic principles:

- Partnership with employees.
- Cooperation with suppliers and distributors.
- Innovation for customers.

EXHIBIT 1   **Salomon S.A. Sales and Profits (FF Million)**

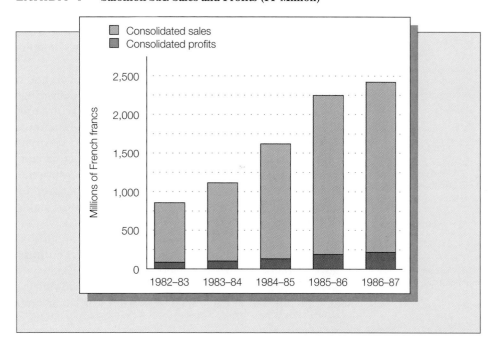

EXHIBIT 2   **Growth of Sales and R&D Expenditures**

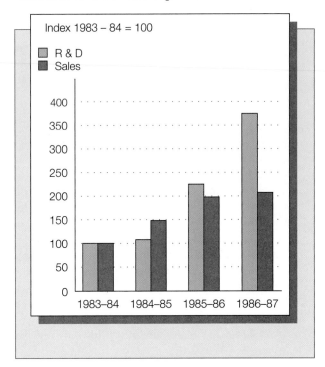

The partnership with the company's workforce was founded on the premise that success could only come if the employees were competent and felt associated with the future of the firm. Therefore, training was regarded as a key driver in the company's effectiveness, with over 5 percent of the payroll "invested" in this activity. In addition, employees benefited from the company's success by receiving bonuses, based on annual results, and a regular distribution of shares. The 1986–1987 annual report[1] mentioned that 3 percent of the company's common stock was held by its employees.

Salomon recognized that cooperation with suppliers and distributors was needed in order to have effective high-quality support for delivering its products. The company relied on numerous subcontractors to manufacture up to 60 percent of its production of bindings and boots, and all of its "Club-Line" products. There was also a worldwide network of retailers offering the necessary service to the customer (advice, testing, adjustments, etc.). For both the subcontractors and the retailers, Salomon provided continuous information and training to ensure the quality of their contribution. Recently, the company had taken a further step by introducing the concept of the "Salomon Authorized Dealer," whereby the rights and duties of retailers vis-à-vis the company were specified.

The third principle was no less essential: ongoing innovation and investment in new technology that would serve the needs of sports enthusiasts in increasingly better ways! Salomon spent some 4 percent of its consolidated sales on research and development, and registered around 100 patents worldwide every year. From the very beginning, innovation had always been a key word at Salomon.

---

[1]Salomon's annual report covered the time period from April 1 to March 31 of the following year.

EXHIBIT 3   Salomon S.A. Five-Year Financial Summary, 1983–1987 (Thousands of French francs)

Source: Company annual report for 1987.

			Year Ended March 31		
Operations	1983	1984	1985	1986	1987
Net sales	FF817,170	FF1,109,263	FF1,666,277	FF2,220,686	FF2,241,700
Other revenues	8,656	22,182	19,462	25,200	21,307
Total revenues	825,826	1,131,445	1,685,739	2,245,886	2,443,077
Cost of sales—materials	(271,272)	(351,540)	(578,712)	(772,247)	(869,233)
Payroll expenses	(165,757)	(209,256)	(250,565)	(303,253)	(346,977)
Depreciation charge	(33,870)	(49,553)	(66,354)	(108,338)	(128,585)
Other operating expenses	(188,466)	(274,867)	(379,315)	(526,268)	(569,116)
Operating profit	166,461	246,229	410,793	535,780	529,166
Interest expense, net	(36,965)	(38,385)	(47,368)	(84,361)	(90,959)
Nonoperating items	(10,383)	(10,487)	(38,124)	(38,759)	(79,407)
Pretax net income	119,113	197,357	325,301	414,660	358,800
Provision for income taxes	(53,700)	(96,651)	(156,655)	(197,625)	(135,637)
Net income	FF 65,143	FF100,706	FF168,646	FF217,035	FF223,163
Financial Position					
Cash and marketable securities	FF169,037	FF263,258	FF363,854	FF830,126	FF656,544
Accounts receivable	174,527	185,191	279,927	350,293	414,537
Inventories	158,951	260,536	381,093	562,221	601,505
Other current assets	37,382	157,758	58,414	77,719	195,184
Total current assets	539,897	866,743	1,083,288	1,820,359	1,877,770
Property, plant and equipment, net	94,666	145,575	197,614	364,432	445,694
Other noncurrent assets	5,993	5,493	47,100	13,645	12,134
Total assets	640,556	1,017,811	1,328,002	2,196,436	2,325,598
Loans payable	108,893	300,230	302,329	646,597*	532,222*
Accounts payable and accrued expenses	326,462	300,943	381,830	496,495	568,546
Other liabilities	13,055	4,231	49,144	55,634	42,067
Shareholders' equity	192,146	412,407	594,699	97,710	1,182,763
Total liabilities and shareholders' equity	FF640,556	FF1,017,811	FF1,328,002	FF2,196,436	FF2,325,598

*Including capital lease obligations.

Salomon: The First Forty Years

In 1947, François Salomon and his wife, Jeanne, set up a small firm that performed metal processing activities. Initially, it made saw blades and steel edges for skis, a technology for which François owned a patent. At that time, the edges were attached to the wooden skis by the retailers.

The Salomons' son Georges decided to give up his job as a schoolmaster and to join the family firm. Soon afterward, Georges invented a machine to improve the processing of steel for ski edges.[2] However, in only a few years, the Salomons realized that the ski manufacturers were integrating this process and that they needed to look for other activities to prepare for the future.

[2]Salomon S.A., Case Study, Jim Whyte, Department of Management, Napier College, Edinburgh, 1986.

In the early '50s, Georges was approached by a Parisian inventor with a new type of ski binding that no manufacturer was interested in. Georges immediately saw its potential and decided to buy the technology. This innovative device filled a real need at a time when the market was developing quickly. Orders came soon and sales grew fast, particularly in North America. Thus, the firm was able to benefit from the post-World War II growth of skiing as a major leisure activity, at an international level right from the beginning. In 1962, Georges realized that the growth of his company needed to address the world market. From then on, the commercial development of Salomon S.A. was based on two pillars: new products and international presence.

Georges, however, did not become complacent with success and systematically continued to look for ways to improve the protection of skiers against accidents. In 1967, he introduced the first ski binding without a cable. This innovation was a real breakthrough, one that radically changed skiing safety and comfort, and also resulted in a profound restructuring of the bindings industry. Such an accomplishment had only occurred because Georges was determined to concentrate on product innovation, devoting much of his time to it—as he preferred that activity to administrative tasks.

By 1972, Salomon had gained a real presence in foreign markets, surpassing Tyrolia and Marker to become the world leader in bindings—a position the company has since maintained.

In the early '70s, Salomon began to look for new products beyond ski bindings. Several options were studied, among them the markets for ski boots and skis. In 1974, the decision was made to pursue the former. Georges Salomon had a clear objective: to come up with a boot that was not only better but would also offer a significant and visible improvement. In 1979, Salomon introduced a truly innovative boot design—the rear-entry boot—which addressed a key frustration for skiers: lack of comfort. This "revolutionary" ski boot concept was reasonably well accepted. However, in spite of success with Giradelli, the industry (racers, journalists, ski instructors, etc.) gave it a lukewarm welcome. They claimed that it was not tight enough on the foot and gave it the uncomplimentary nickname, "*la pantoufle*."[3] Even though sales were significant, they did not develop as quickly as expected. Salomon gradually adapted its design, keeping rear entry for only one part of the line and, in this way, eventually was able to gain a steady market share. By 1987, the company held second place, close behind Nordica (of Italy).

During this same time period, starting in 1978, Salomon undertook to enter the cross-country ski market. Again, the ambition was to offer a clearly superior product. In 1980, Salomon made the headlines when it introduced a unique system: a cross-country boot and binding combination. This was definitely a superior concept, which took off very quickly and put Salomon at the top with an amazing 30 percent of the market in 1987.

Meanwhile, being dependent on winter sports had become a major concern for Salomon's management. The company considered several activities that could provide a counterbalance. One option was windsurfing, which was turned down because it did not offer enough potential and was already suffering from a huge overcapacity. Eventually, the golfing business was chosen, an industry twice as big as winter sports: about FF 12 billion. In 1984, Salomon purchased the entire shareholdings of the American company, Taylor-Made, which manufactured and sold upmarket golf clubs. The choice of Taylor-Made was based on its similarity to Salomon: the philosophy of providing excellence through innovation.

---

[3]"The slipper."

Over the years, Salomon's progressive product diversification reflected ambitious goals for each market entry, which had its roots in the corporate culture and, especially, in the personality of the president.

Management, Structure, and Culture

In the mid-'80s, Salomon had become a mini-multinational with subsidiaries in 12 countries. The headquarters in the suburb of Annecy also had a definite international feeling, with managers coming from around the world (Canada, Norway, the United States). Like Philips and Bosch, Salomon had a matrix organization that was structured around its products (bindings, shoes, cross-country equipment, etc.) and their respective markets (using national sales organizations). The company had come a long way from the little workshop that made ski edges to become a multi-line sports equipment firm.

At Salomon S.A., recruitment was considered a particularly important task. The company was very demanding and therefore selective, and could afford to be so because its sporty and dynamic image made it a very attractive employer. Early on, it had recruited engineers and technicians from the best schools. It also was able to attract the most senior managers from top companies. The majority of the people working at Salomon had a double profile: highly skilled in their discipline and expert in a sport. Indeed, several of them were former ski champions. Consequently, Salomon was managed with state-of-the-art technology and highly skilled motivated teams who, literally, "loved" their products.

The personality of Georges Salomon as an individual had a big impact on the culture of the company. Even though he did not have a technical education, he spent a lot of his time looking for ways that new technology could bring value to products. He had personally developed several products, which gave him credibility with his team. He was the one mainly responsible for the goal to launch only products that were clearly and visibly superior. Also essential to the company's successful product development record was its impeccable use of extreme caution in all decision making. This prudence came, in large part, from Georges's anxiety about the outcome of each company product. Everyone who managed a major project knew that he must be thoroughly prepared with an answer for all of Georges's concerns. Above all, Georges was a mountaineer and a careful climber who was aware that "rushing tends to be dangerous."

Georges Salomon's daily behavior also carried some messages to his organization; he made no secret about where his priorities were. Even though he had received countless awards in Paris for the company's performance (in design, innovation, exports), Georges avoided personal publicity. He did not care much about pleasing the establishment, either. He much preferred walking around the company's workshops discussing new products, contributing ideas, even occasionally drawing a quick sketch. When he had to meet with bankers or high-ranking officials, he would insist on inviting them to the company canteen.

Georges's personal life-style reflected his passion for his job and dedication to the company. In his dress, he was informal and casual—preferring mountaineer clothing. For a long time, he drove a rusty Renault 5, which was a frequent topic of discussion. His chalet, on a slope overlooking Annecy, was considered spacious but not luxurious.

He played a central role in company strategy, particularly when it came to market entry decisions. Georges was very demanding, systematically wanting to ensure that every product would really make a difference and that the strategy concerning its development and launch was optimal. He often reminded the project team that he would "pull the plug" at any time if he had any doubts about the project's success. And he meant it; indeed, he had actually canceled some projects a few weeks before their official launch.

The Decision to Enter the Ski Market

By 1984, Georges Salomon had come to the conclusion that it was time to enter the ski market. In his view, Salomon, the world's largest company in the winter sports industry, could no longer ignore such an essential piece of equipment for skiers.

Skis, as a product, had several characteristics that made them attractive to Salomon. First of all, they were the most visible piece of equipment. In practical terms, in a photograph of a skier in action, it was the skis that one could see most clearly; the boot and the binding were usually not so easily distinguishable. Hence, from a communication point of view, skis offered better support to the brand name. Secondly, skis were the most expensive item bought by skiers and, therefore, the market size was bigger (about twice the amount of the bindings market). Finally, skis were the piece of equipment most talked about by skiers, the focus of an enthusiast's passion, in a way that boots and bindings could not equal. Consequently, skis were a powerful contributor to brand awareness. As Georges Salomon explained to his staff: "Ski companies that are much smaller than Salomon in terms of sales enjoy a greater brand recognition by the public . . . which is why this ski development challenge is so important for our firm."

Salomon's management felt that it had the capability to enter the ski market successfully. The company had adequate experience, it was argued, to take on this new activity, given its track record and current situation. For example, Salomon had:

- A **mastery of innovation,** thanks to the most advanced design tools, and databases on skiers' needs and desires and on the behavior and reaction of various materials.
- A **know-how in automation,** which allowed it to achieve higher quality levels and competitive production costs.
- A **financially healthy situation,** which made it possible for the corporation to afford the high R&D expenditures and the necessary financial investment at the manufacturing stage.
- A **strong brand image and distribution network,** which could quickly promote sales of this new ski and generate economies of scale at the same time.

In a survey conducted in 1984 to learn about Salomon's brand image, it appeared that the market was definitely anticipating such a move: in fact, a significant proportion of interviewees believed that Salomon was already making skis! This surprising piece of information provided even more motivation to enter this market, in spite of the risks.

Salomon's management was conscious that moving into skis was not a risk-free operation. After all, the company's bindings were being mounted on other manufacturers' skis. Even though the ski-binding assembly was done at the retail level, some feared that large ski competitors might try to retaliate by joining forces with some other bindings producers—for example, "ski X prefers bindings Y." Also, this move could prompt a countermove into Salomon's own territory, with other ski manufacturers deciding to compete in bindings and boots. Finally, the issue of branding was also raised. Salomon was planning to offer all three products (skis, bindings, and boots) under its own brand name. It would be the first company to make such an offering. Clearly, there were some risks associated with this strategy—that is, if a customer had a bad experience with one of the products, the other products could be affected as well.

These concerns, however, did not prevent the company from going ahead with the diversification. By 1985, Salomon's top management had set up ambitious objectives for the ski business:

1. To become a world leader, in five or six years, in the medium to top segments of the market.
2. To reach, at "cruising speed," a net profitability of the same order of magnitude as bindings and boots (around 9 percent of sales).

In order to pursue these demanding objectives, the following strategic principles were established:

- To give skiers a piece of equipment with a "plus," based on some visible innovation that would be identified through market surveys and technical research.
- To emphasize partnership with distributors in order to provide optimal quality service.
- To gain recognition through success in competition, with the Winter Olympics in Albertville (Winter 1992) being used to enhance the impact.

The Ski Market in 1987

There were some 55 million skiers in the world in 1987. Most of them were in Western Europe (around 30 million), North America (9 million), and Japan (the single largest national market with over 12 million skiers). There were also some minor markets in Eastern Europe (particularly Yugoslavia, Poland, Czechoslovakia, and the USSR) and in Australia. The proportion of skiers to the total population varied tremendously from country to country and was partly a function of local skiing possibilities. Switzerland was clearly the highest (with a ratio of 30.4 percent), followed by Austria (27.7 percent) and Sweden (23.8 percent), then Germany, Italy, and France (in the 10–12 percent range). The United States, although a large market of 5.4 million skiers, had a very low ratio (2.2 percent) compared to Japan (9.9 percent).

Skiing as a sport was being influenced by several important trends. First of all, skiing had become affordable and accessible to an increasing number of consumers, but the relative time spent participating in winter sports had been diminishing. Secondly, skiers tended to be less "fanatic" than in the past, especially as the competitive pressure of other leisure activities (golfing, cruising, tourism in exotic countries) grew stronger. Thirdly, skiing had become an increasingly diversified sport—with "off-piste" (off the official groomed trails), mogul, freestyle, acrobatic, and speed skiing, as well as the introduction of new types of equipment (monoskis and surfboards). The final factor was fashion: Colors in equipment and clothing were becoming brighter and more dramatic, and styles and shapes were ever changing.

THE MARKET

The international ski market was already mature. It was expected to plateau at around 6.5 million pairs (refer to Exhibit 4) with possible ups and downs following business cycles and the amount of snowfall. The world market was estimated at FF 4.5 billion, compared to FF 3.5 billion for ski boots and FF 2 billion for bindings. The largest national markets were (in rank order) Japan, the United States, Germany, and France (refer to Exhibit 5). Some markets still seemed to be growing (North America), while others were flattening (Japan, Western Europe) or even declining (Scandinavia) over the short to medium term.

EXHIBIT 4   Ski Sales in the 1980s

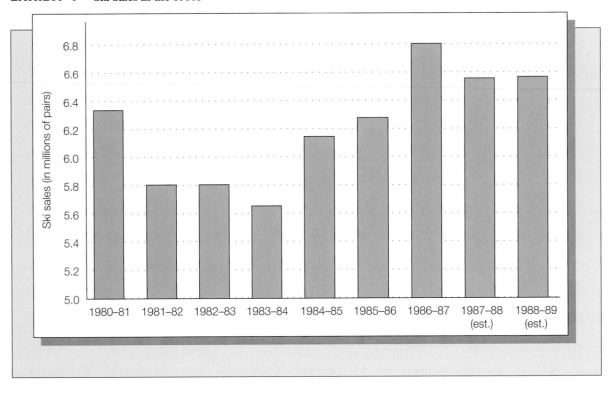

EXHIBIT 5   Sales of Skis, by Country, 1986–1987 Winter Season

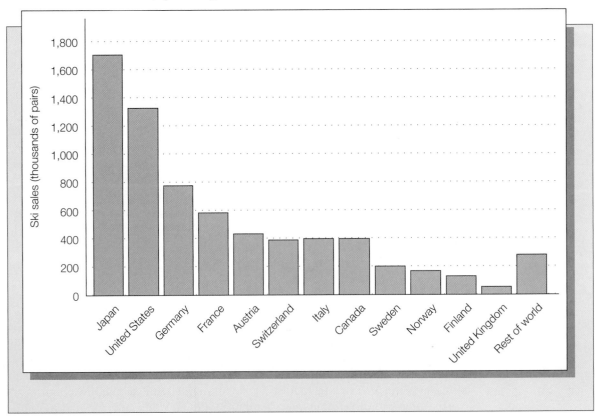

EXHIBIT 6   **The Market Price Structure in the Ski Market**

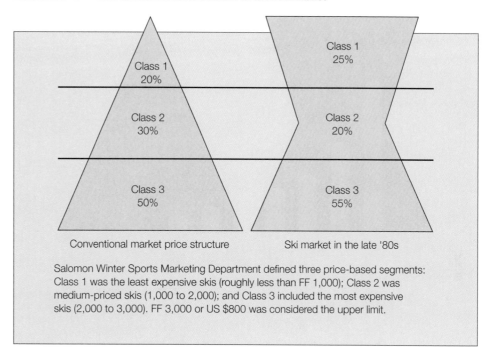

Salomon Winter Sports Marketing Department defined three price-based segments: Class 1 was the least expensive skis (roughly less than FF 1,000); Class 2 was medium-priced skis (1,000 to 2,000); and Class 3 included the most expensive skis (2,000 to 3,000). FF 3,000 or US $800 was considered the upper limit.

The price structure of the market was somewhat peculiar. In most markets, the distribution of sales along the price range could be seen as a pyramid, with sales of the most expensive segment being the smallest. The ski market, however, presented a different pattern, as the most expensive products sold more than the medium-priced ones (refer to Exhibit 6).

The traditional market segmentation made a first distinction between rental (10 percent of the volume), junior (another 20 percent) and adult (the remainder). Within the adult segment, there were three types of users: leisure (55 percent of the volume), sport (20 percent) and performance (25 percent). Leisure skiers tended to be people who skied for recreation and to have fun, not for "records." The second segment included skiers that were more "aggressive" on the slopes, but not competing in any way. The last segment was those skiers who were involved in some form of competition. The last two segments (sport and performance), sometimes called "medium" and "top," represented around 2 million pairs of skis.

THE COMPETITORS

The number of competitors was much higher in skis than in bindings or boots. Some 80 different brands were competing worldwide (21 in Japan, 15 in the United States, 12 in Austria, 6 in France, and 20 more in other countries). Most companies owned one brand, except large players like the world leader Rossignol (France) which controlled Dynastar (also in France). On the average, the number of brands present in each country was about twice as large as in bindings.

In addition, skis were sold under private label. The estimate was that, worldwide, this represented around 50 percent of volume, with the proportion varying considerably from country to country.

The market was dominated by Rossignol (France), Atomic (Austria), Elan (Yugoslavia), Head (United States), Dynastar (France), and Blizzard (Austria),

EXHIBIT 7 **Sales by Manufacturers**

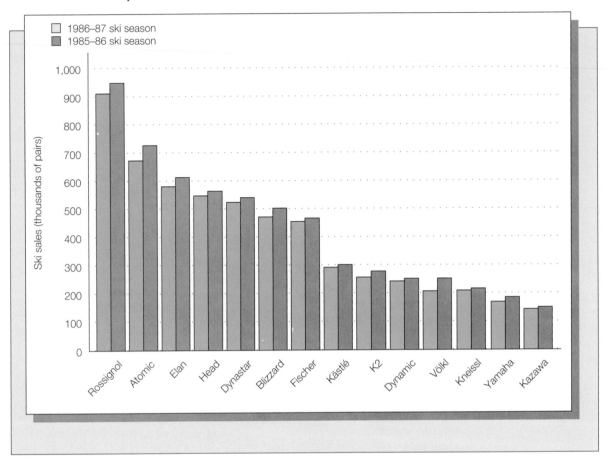

which all sold more than half a million pairs every year (refer to Exhibit 7). Most Japanese manufacturers were relatively small (100 to 150,000 pairs), except for Yamaha, which barely passed the 200,000 pair threshold. While the Western brands were present in Europe, the Japanese producers were virtually nonexistent outside Japan.

Competitors differed in their approach to the ski market in many ways. A few strategic dimensions seemed to be critical in discriminating among industry players. The first dimension was overall product positioning. Some companies, such as Rossignol and Atomic, offered skis for all levels—from beginners to racers— while others focused on a specific market niche (the upmarket: Völkl, Fischer, K2; the low to medium end: Head, Elan). Participation in ski competition also affected a company's positioning. Brands that addressed the top end of the market (Rossignol, Völkl, K2) sponsored ski racers in an effort to enhance the visibility of their products, while companies focusing on the lower niches did not pursue this activity. Another important dimension was the scope of market presence. Most of the 80 ski manufacturers around the world were only local players that marketed their products in their own country. This situation was particularly true for the Japanese brands. Among the companies that had "gone international," the scope of market coverage differed. The leaders (Rossignol, Atomic, Elan, Head, Dynastar) were present in all significant markets; other companies (like

EXHIBIT 8   **Types of Ski Structures**

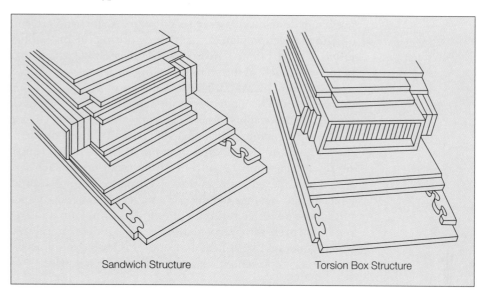

Sandwich Structure   Torsion Box Structure

Blizzard) had substantial international sales, but were not represented in all national markets.

THE MANUFACTURING OF SKIS

Skis, which had been in existence for at least 5,000 years, only were considered "sports equipment" at the beginning of the 20th century, when they were brought to Switzerland by British tourists. The first skis were very simple, made out of ordinary wood. In order to achieve a more solidly constructed ski, one of the first innovations was to use laminates of wood that were glued together, thus gaining greater flexibility and a longer ski. Metal edges were introduced later in order to reduce deterioration of the sole of the ski and provide a better grip. After World War II, plastic soles were added to enhance the ski's sliding capability. In 1950, Head introduced the metal sandwich ski, which irreversibly changed ski technology. Metal was later replaced by the various plastic and composite materials that dominated the market in the '80s.

At this point in time, several types of design were used in the construction of skis. The most common structures were the sandwich ski and the torsion box ski (refer to Exhibit 8). A sandwich ski was essentially made of various materials arranged in layers, with the more rigid and resistant layers on the top and the bottom of the ski. This technology, which increased resistance to flexion and shock absorption, was the most widely used (75 percent of skis). In a torsion box ski, the resistance was obtained from a box located in the core of the ski. It gave a better grip in the snow, as well as a quicker reaction. Together, the sandwich and torsion box technologies represented 90 percent of the skis manufactured. There were a few other technologies—for example, the "omega" structure—but most of them had only a very limited production.

THE PRODUCTION CYCLE

The production of skis started a full year before the winter season, in November. For instance, skis sold by retailers between November 1985 and March 1986 had been produced between November 1984 and November 1985. This production phase had been preceded by development work on shape, materials, and art work. The duration of the development phase depended on the importance of the work involved, from four years for a major ski innovation to a few months for a cosmetic change, which was being done every year in recent years (colors and art work).

The production plan, initially made during the preceding summer, could be adjusted at three points. The first occasion was ISPO, the annual sports industry exhibition in Munich, in the second part of February every year when distributors started to order. Later, in May, when the number of orders was better known, a second adjustment would be made. Lastly, in September–October, as orders were being completed, it was possible to fine-tune production to market demand (volume and mix).

Over time, manufacturing had become a complex process. In the '80s, it involved the assembly of several kinds of material (steel, fibers, resins, plastic sheets) which represented around 13 percent of the retail price. Each material was carefully selected, as it played a role in the performance of the ski. Production workers would typically put together the different materials needed (the sole, the edges, the various layers, polyester resin, the upper platform) into a mold, which would then be put into a press with warm plates. Because of the material and equipment involved, which generated both heat and odor, working conditions were difficult. Manufacturing costs represented 19.5 percent of the retail price.

DISTRIBUTION

Skis were sold through a network of wholesalers and retailers, which was organized by the manufacturers. Small brands tended to rely on local independent distributors (one per country), while large manufacturers often had their own sales organization for major countries. It was estimated that the cost of the wholesale function amounted to 17.5 percent of the retail price.

Retailing was shared between independent outlets and distribution chains. In ski resorts, independent retailers—usually also managing a large rental activity—were dominant. In major towns and cities, large retail chains (such as Intersport in Germany and Decathlon in France) represented the major portion of the market. Nonspecialized chains (hypermarkets) had a limited participation, mostly selling inexpensive products. On average, the retailers' margin was 50 percent of the final price, including sales tax.

Depending on the country, retailers offered 5 to 10 different brands,[4] with 4–5 models in each one. There were some real technical differences, in terms of materials, structure, and shape, that needed to be evaluated in the selection process, along with more superficial considerations. Consumers thus had an enormous choice. The selection of a ski was often made through the recommendation of a salesperson, on the basis of physical characteristics, skiing style, ability, and budget (refer to Exhibit 9).

Therefore, the sales process required having capable, often technical, explanations by the retail staff, a situation which called for training. Although makers of the best-selling brands made a genuine effort to provide technical information to their network, product descriptions and performance data provided to retailers sometimes tended to be unclear, with an overemphasis on jargon. Ill-founded rumors and myths were not uncommon.

Communication with the consumer was done through advertising in specialized magazines and point-of-sale material (catalogs, leaflets). In addition, magazines published articles appraising new products coming onto the market and were another channel of information, mostly for the high end of the market.

---

[4]Except in Japan, where retailers typically stored 25 different brands.

EXHIBIT 9   **The Ski Purchasing Process**

The following table presents the distribution of answers to the question below asked to a sample of ski buyers. "What do you think is the best way to choose skis when buying them?" Respondents could give more than one answer so the percentages do not add to 100%.

	Total	France	Germany	United States	Japan
1. Pick a brand with a good reputation.	26%	27%	21%	31%	25%
2. Select a brand you have already used.	17	16	27	15	9
3. Listen to other people's advice.	44	35	45	39	56
4. Be guided by a ski salesman.	26	31	30	15	28
5. It is a personal decision. Choose the ski you like.	16	12	5	19	26
6. Gather information, read reviews, study technical tests.	20	14	23	23	18
7. Follow advice from ski instructors.	8	12	8	4	7
8. Rent a ski and test it before buying.	16	16	23	18	6
9. Pick the brand a champion uses.	2%	*%	2%	5%	*%
Sample size (total respondents)	n=1,444	n=350	n=373	n=361	n=360

*Negligible.

The Monocoque Project

The origin of the monocoque[5] project could be traced to early 1984 when Georges Salomon entered the office of Roger Pascal, the director of the Bindings Division, and said: "Pascal, you have to make me a ski!"

Roger Pascal, then 46 years old, had worked with Salomon since 1969. He was an engineer by training (INSA, Lyon), but he was also an expert skier, having been a ski instructor (École du Ski Français) while he was a student. He had started in the engineering department and eventually had become manager, before heading the ski boot engineering department.

INITIAL STEPS

Georges Salomon and Roger Pascal agreed that there could be no meaningful entry into the ski business without an in-depth knowledge of the ski market and industry. They reckoned that, even though Salomon was selling in related markets, its information on consumers' needs, technological solutions, and marketing processes was not sufficient to make a difference in the ski market.

The ski project got underway with the appointment of Jean-Luc Diard in July 1984. Jean-Luc had just completed his studies at the ESC Paris, one of the top business schools in France. He was also an excellent skier, having won the annual French student ski championship. Recruited as a special kind of trainee,[6] he was sent to Salomon's Austrian subsidiary to study the ski market and industry. He focused on making an international study of the best products available at the time, and traveled extensively to meet and interview the world's experts. The information he gathered was encouraging for Salomon: There were still ways to improve on existing ski technologies.

---

[5]Pronounced *mon-oh-caulk.*

[6]A program that allowed a graduate to be a trainee in a French firm or public organization outside of France, as a replacement for military service.

At the same time, a series of market surveys was launched in order to appraise the level of satisfaction among skiers. The first results came as a surprise. While Salomon had detected significant frustration with ski boots in earlier surveys, it seemed that consumers were generally satisfied with skis. These results renewed Georges Salomon's conviction that the new ski must be radically better if it were to make a difference in the marketplace. In order to have a specific goal and objective for the team, Georges and Roger agreed that the ski should be able to sell at a 15 percent premium above the market price.

THE PROJECT TEAM

In the summer of 1985, Georges Salomon was able to convince two technology experts—Maurice Legrand and Yves Gagneux—to join the ski development team. Maurice Legrand, the former head of Rossignol's engineering department, was in charge of product technology. Yves Gagneux, the former head of manufacturing at Dynamic, was made responsible for process technology.

The team—Roger, Jean-Luc, Maurice, and Yves—functioned like a "commando operation"—that is, a group of highly skilled volunteers who were totally devoted to their "secret mission." The team was maintained out of the normal organization, in an effort to preserve confidentiality as long as possible. Their work was kept secret, even to insiders, as Salomon did not want its competitors to know about it. Also, like a commando group, there was a sense of close community among the members, with each one knowing what the others were doing. Indeed, the competence of all the team members was truly exceptional: each individual was outstanding in his field and all were excellent skiers as well. In addition, the interaction was so interconnected that their disciplinary boundaries were blurred. Thus, Jean-Luc, in charge of marketing, also contributed technical solutions, while Maurice came up with marketing ideas.

PROJECT MANAGEMENT

The activity of the ski development team was characterized by a high energy level, thanks to the enthusiasm and the sense of challenge that surrounded their mission. This project, however, was not a "skunk works" operation.[7] Quite the contrary. Yves Gagneux explained: "Maurice Legrand and myself were able to bring the technical knowledge that Salomon was lacking. But, Salomon provided us with a superb project management approach without which our expertise, as good as it was, would have been a lot less effective. Clearly, that was a strong point at Salomon!"

The management of the project actually used the whole gamut of modern techniques. At the very beginning, Georges Salomon had set the goal: to introduce a ski in five or six years, with excellent and visible advantages over existing products. The team translated this objective into a very detailed action plan, specifying the milestones, the resources needed, the tools used—Quality Function Deployment, Design to Manufacturing, Consumer Clinics. Early on, the team had worked on a business plan that outlined expenditures and income on a yearly basis, from the project's inception to the "cruising speed" period in the mid-'90s.

The team reported regularly to the Executive Committee for major investment or expenditure decisions. It also presented a progress report to the New Model Committee on implementation issues. However, more important than the formal reporting were the team's meetings, which Georges Salomon personally attended. In summing up his style, one individual commented: "Georges Salomon isn't usually

[7]A "skunk works" project typically operated with a minimum budget and no real facilities.

found behind his desk . . . he is more likely to be in the product development lab . . . clomping around in ski boots and baggy sweater . . . doing what he likes best . . . devising ways to frustrate his competition."[8] In order to answer all the probing questions that an anxious Georges Salomon inevitably asked, the team had to be well prepared—an exercise that obviously took time. "*Se hâter lentement*"[9] could have been the motto for this project.

THE CONCEPT DEVELOPMENT

Between July 1985 and January 1987, Roger Pascal asked the team, which over time had progressively been enlarged, to systematically study all aspects of ski technology: measurements, the core, the sole, printing techniques, the spatula, edges, polishing, wax. The mandate was for each team member to come up with two or three ideas for improving every aspect studied. The team leaders would meet regularly to review these ideas and seek ways to incorporate them into a concept. In fact, they succeeded in producing the first plaster model by the second semester of 1985.

The shape of the ski gradually emerged as a result of these systematic experiments. The team realized early on that little could be done to the shape of the sole, which had been already optimized over time to the point where skiers were accustomed to it. However, alternatives for the walls on both sides and for the surface of the ski could be considered. The team started to challenge the verticality of the side walls. Were they optimum? Could other settings be better? In a very creative fashion, they explored the various options: from being slanted outward to slanted inward. A close examination revealed that the best solution was actually a progressive profile, with nearly vertical walls under the ski boots to provide an optimum grip where it was most needed, and side walls slanted inward to ensure optimum cutting into the snow at both extremes. These changes, in addition, had the required characteristics of being visible, one of the conditions set clearly by Georges Salomon (refer to Exhibit 10).

This initial idea naturally led to another important discovery: the side walls and surface of the ski should be made of a unique shell that would carry a major part of the stress. In conventional skis, the action of the skier passed from the steel edges through a succession of layers, particularly in the sandwich ski. This method of transmission was more indirect and resulted in less precision. The monocoque structure (the unique piece linking the surface to the edges) would thus provide a better control of the ski.

EXHIBIT 10   **The Ski Concept: Progressive Profile**

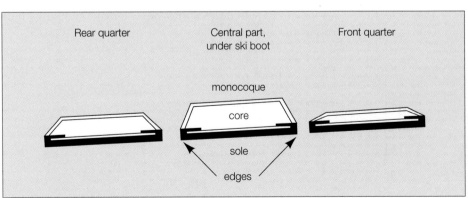

The team was supplied with the best computer-assisted design (CAD) system available in the industry at the time (ComputerVision and Sun Microsystems). The ideas were quickly converted into drawings in the engineering lab. Molds for prototypes were machined directly from the CAD system, which allowed them to create a large number of shapes for testing. By the middle of 1986, the first prototypes were available. They were tested in labs as well as on the snow, with test engineers and expert skiers hired as consultants with a confidentiality agreement. The team at that time comprised around 35 people.

Several ideas for improving the manufacturing process were conceived. While most ski manufacturers applied composite material in a tacky state, the team found a new way to handle this step more satisfactorily. Yves Gagneux explored the "dry process," which consisted of using fibers that had already been impregnated with resin and dried, which were therefore not only much easier to manipulate but had the additional advantage of not smelling strongly, as the "wet process" did. It was expected that these enhanced working conditions would produce a much higher level of quality as well.

By November 1987, the engineering studies were providing interesting results. The team had developed a detailed understanding of the ski market. It knew the strengths and weaknesses of the best competitors. It had identified a long list of possible improvement areas. It had even singled out the particular areas where it wanted the new ski to make a difference. The prototypes that had been developed, through numerous trials and tests, were showing very promising potential.

The Decision

There were, of course, still a number of issues that needed to be clarified. In one sense, it was obvious that the team had done a good job, considering that the project had started from scratch in 1984. They had gone a long way toward the development of a radically new ski. Some of the detailed engineering still needed for the ski's final development was clearly going to be even more demanding. In order to proceed, the New Product Committee would have to release a budget for engineering work, testing, and for the construction of a new plant. Given the technology required, some of it actually calling for custom-made equipment, the budget would amount to some FF 300 million. Additionally, using a full-time team that would be expanded to 50 people would increase the operating costs.

The team's next challenge was to prepare a clear action plan for finalizing the development of Salomon's monocoque ski and launching it into the already crowded and mature ski market.

11

Cannondale Corporation

Romuald A. Stone
Keller Graduate School of Management

John E. Gamble
University of South Alabama

In early 2000 Cannondale Corporation was the world's leading manufacturer and marketer of high-performance aluminum bicycles. The company also marketed CODA bicycle components, HeadShok suspension forks, and a line of bicycle accessories including such items as clothing, packs, and bags. The company's bicycles, which carried its "Handmade in the USA" logo, were known for their innovative designs, light weight, exceptional performance, and durable construction and were sold in the United States and in more than 60 other countries. Since the company's founding in 1971, Cannondale's products had been recognized for their innovation by such publications as *USA Today*, *Sports Illustrated*, *Popular Science*, *Popular Mechanics*, and *Design News*. Cannondale's newest bicycle model, the Jekyll, had been named *Mountain Biking* magazine's "Bike of the Year" for 2000 and dubbed "a manufacturing masterpiece," "a masterful work of art," and "an outstanding achievement in lightweight, dual-suspension performance."[1]

Cannondale achieved success quickly after its founding, recording annual revenues of approximately $8 million by the late 1970s. However, the company's emergence as a major bicycle producer came about only in 1983, when it developed and produced the first affordable aluminum-frame bicycle. Cannondale's aluminum road bikes and its aluminum-frame mountain bike, introduced in 1984, were instant hits and allowed the company's revenues to grow at an annual rate of 30 percent between 1983 and 1985. The company's growth continued at a dramatic rate as the popularity of mountain biking grew exponentially during the late 1980s and early 1990s. In 1982, two years before Cannondale's introduction of its SM 500 mountain bike, there were approximately 200,000 mountain bikers in the United States. By 1992, the number of U.S. mountain bikers had grown to more than 8 million and mountain bikes accounted for 54 percent of U.S. bicycle sales. By 1996 Cannondale

[1] Cannondale press release, PR Newswire, January 31, 2000.

had become the leader of the high-performance mountain bike segment and its stock price had appreciated at an annual rate of 32 percent since its initial public offering in 1994.

In early 2000 the company's prospects for spectacular growth appeared to hinge not on the success of its mountain bikes but on its soon-to-be-introduced MX400 off-road motorcycle. The highly innovative aluminum-frame motorcycle was eagerly awaited by motocross enthusiasts and had been described by *Dirt Rider* magazine as "a monumental bike" that had forced "other manufacturers to rethink their current technology."[2] Cannondale remained a leader in the high-performance segment of the mountain bike industry with innovative products like the Jekyll, but its growth during the late 1990s had been severely restricted as the bicycle industry reached maturity during the mid-1990s and grew at an approximate annual rate of 2 percent during the late 1990s. Cannondale's revenue growth had slowed to an annual rate of 9.7 percent between 1995 and 1999 after growing at a compounded annual rate of 22.3 percent between 1991 and 1995. The company's decelerated growth rate was reflected in its stock price, which had steadily declined since its peak of $27 in 1997. As the company prepared to begin shipping the new MX400 in the spring of 2000, Cannondale's founder and CEO Joseph Montgomery hoped that the new motorcycle would be the strategic spark that the company needed to restart the share price growth it had experienced in earlier years. A summary of Cannondale Corporation's financial performance between 1991 and 1999 is shown in Exhibit 1. Exhibit 2 presents a graph of Cannondale's stock performance between 1995 and early 2000.

The Global Bicycle Market

With over 1 billion bicycles existing in the world, usage varied considerably, with about 70 percent of all bicycles used as a means of transportation, 29 percent used for recreational purposes, and about 1 percent used solely in racing events. In many countries bicycling was the primary means of land transportation for distances that made walking impractical. In China, for example, traffic controllers saw an average of 10,000 cyclists per hour pass the busiest urban intersections. In the city of Tianjin, with more than 4 million people, there were up to 50,000 cyclists per hour passing through high-traffic intersections. In countries with more developed economies, bicycling was more likely to be a secondary mode of transportation or restricted to recreational use.

Among the world's industrialized nations, Western Europeans were the biggest users of bicycles, with an estimated 115 million bicycle owners. Communities in the Netherlands, Denmark, and Germany were called bicycle-friendly because of their balanced use of bicycles for transport, recreation, and sport. Cycling facilities such as bike lanes and parking sites, along with traffic calming and intermodal transit links, encouraged people to use bicycles for as much as 20 to 50 percent of all urban trips.

In the United States, bicycles were employed mainly for recreation, with only about 5 percent of the country's 100 million bicycles used for transportation. Cycling was the fifth most popular recreational activity in the United States, behind exercise walking, swimming, exercising with equipment, and camping.

In some African and Latin American countries bicycle use was heavy, but governments in those geographic regions tended to stigmatize bicycles as "Third World"

[2]Ibid.

means of mobility. While many leaders in government enjoyed the prestige of cars and new highways, their people often relied on walking instead of cycling for essential transport. In countries with developing economies but well-established mass transit systems, such as Russia, bicycles were rare. However, in Eastern European nations such as Hungary, where mass transit was less available and economic conditions made automobile ownership difficult for most, bicycles were used widely and accounted for roughly half of all trips to work.

Most of the world's bicycles were made and used in Asia. Seventy-five percent of the world's bicycles were produced in China, India, Taiwan, Japan, and Thailand. With an average annual production of 30 million units, China produced more bicycles than any other nation in the world. In 1999 there were almost 1,000 bicycle parts makers and assembly plants in China, employing approximately 350,000 workers. About 20 million bicycles were produced each year for sale within China, while more than 10 million units were produced each year for export to other countries. The China Bicycle Company (CBC) of Guangzhou was one of the dominant Chinese bike manufacturers. The company was founded by Jerome Sze, a Hong Kong businessman, and began making bicycles for Western firms such as Schwinn in the 1970s. In 1992, CBC was rated as one of the top 10 foreign investment enterprises in China. Taiwan was the world's second largest producer and world's largest exporter of bicycles. During the late 1990s, over 70 percent of the bikes sold in the United States were made in Taiwan. The biggest Taiwanese bikemakers, Giant Manufacturing Company and Merida Industry Company, manufactured bicycles sold in the United States under brand names that included Trek, Schwinn, and Specialized.

The U.S. Bicycle Industry

In 1999 the U.S. bicycle industry was approximately a $5 billion per year industry, counting the retail value of bicycles, related parts, and accessories through all channels of distribution. There were over 100 brands of bicycles sold in the United States and an estimated 2,000 companies involved in either manufacturing or distributing cycling products. Bicycles were sold at nearly all full-line discount stores and sporting goods superstores, at many department stores, and at approximately 6,800 specialty bicycle stores. The annual U.S. sales of bicycles peaked in 1973 at 15.2 million units and averaged nearly 11.5 million units during the 1990s. Exhibit 3 presents annual U.S. bicycle sales between 1981 and 1998.

MARKET SEGMENTATION BY BICYCLE CATEGORY

There were an estimated 54.5 million active adult cyclists in the United States in 1999 who used their bicycles at least once weekly. Adult bicycles fell into five broad categories: mountain, road-racing, multisport, recreational, and specialty. Mountain bikes combined elements from classic balloon-tire bikes with the lightweight alloy components of quality road-racing bikes. These bikes also featured suspension systems, low gears, beefed-up frames, and straight handlebars (allowing a more upright cycling position than road racing or recreational bikes) and were designed for reliable on-road transportation and heavy-duty touring over rugged terrain. Mountain bikes, the largest segment of the adult market, accounted for 63 percent of all bicycles sold in the United States in 1997.

Road-racing bikes were lightweight, with thin tires and drop (curved) handlebars. Multisport bikes, designed for triathlons and other multisport races, were very aerodynamic and typically had smaller diameter wheels than traditional road racers. Recreational bikes, also known as comfort bikes, hybrids, or cross bikes, were typically

EXHIBIT 1   Consolidated Financial Data for Cannondale Corporation, 1991–99 (In Thousands of Dollars, Except Per Share Data)

Source: Annual reports.

	Twelve Months Ended		
	July 3, 1999	June 27, 1998	June 28, 1997
Statement of operations data			
Net sales	$176,819	$171,496	$162,496
Cost of sales	114,627	110,113	101,334
Gross profit	62,192	61,383	61,162
Expenses			
Selling, general and administrative	40,599	39,361	35,707
Research and development	10,222	6,750	3,576
Stock option compensation	—	—	—
Agent and distributor termination costs	—	—	—
Total operating expenses	50,821	46,111	39,283
Operating income (loss)	11,371	15,272	21,879
Other income (expense):			
Interest expense	(4,557)	(1,995)	(1,574)
Foreign exchange and other	1,160	653	843
Total other income (expense)	(3,397)	(1,342)	(731)
Income (loss) before income taxes, minority interest and extraordinary item	7,974	13,930	21,148
Income tax benefit (expense)	(2,051)	(4,578)	(7,642)
Minority interest in net loss (income) of consolidated subsidiary	—	—	—
Income (loss) before extraordinary item	5,923	9,352	13,506
Extraordinary item, net of income taxes[a]	—	—	—
Net income (loss)	5,923	9,352	13,506
Accumulated preferred stock dividends[b]	—	—	—
Income (loss) applicable to common shares and equivalents	$5,923	$9,352	$13,506
Per common share			
Income (loss) before extraordinary item[c]	$0.79	$1.11	$1.56
Income (loss)	$0.79	$1.11	$1.56
Weighted average common and common equivalent shares outstanding[d]	7,518	8,442	8,638
Balance sheet data			
Working capital	$74,894	$78,975	$77,196
Total assets	162,379	152,277	127,284
Total long-term debt, excluding current portion	55,997	40,352	20,319
Total stockholders' equity	75,010	78,238	81,621

[a]Extraordinary items consist of the costs relating to early extinguishment of debt, net of applicable tax benefit, if any.

[b]Reflects preferred stock dividends accumulated during the fiscal period. All cumulative preferred stock dividends were paid in 1995 at the time of the redemption of the preferred stock in connection with the company's initial public offering.

[c]No cash dividends were declared or paid on the common stock during any of these periods.

Twelve Months Ended		Ten Months Ended		Twelve Months Ended	
June 29, 1996	July 1, 1995	July 2, 1994	July 3, 1993	September 4, 1992	August 31, 1991
$145,976	$122,081	$102,084	$80,835	$76,911	$54,544
92,804	79,816	72,083	59,429	58,927	37,623
53,172	42,265	30,001	21,406	17,984	16,921
32,577	27,023	22,290	19,615	18,527	11,993
2,837	1,751	1,317	1,105	1,314	907
—		2,046	—	—	—
—		—	271	1,196	—
35,414	28,774	25,653	20,991	21,037	12,900
17,758	13,491	4,348	415	(3,053)	4,021
(2,224)	(3,929)	(4,460)	(4,177)	(2,990)	(1,976)
414	24	324	828	(868)	419
(1,810)	(3,905)	(4,136)	(3,349)	(3,858)	(1,557)
15,948	9,586	212	(2,934)	(6,911)	2,464
(5,802)	(1,353)	(791)	(179)	1,422	(959)
—		—	—	850	(343)
10,146	8,233	(579)	(3,113)	(4,639)	1,162
—	(685)	—	(464)	—	—
10,146	7,548	(579)	(3,577)	(4,639)	1,162
—	(400)	(1,008)	—	—	—
$ 10,146	$ 7,148	$ (1,587)	$(3,577)	$(4,639)	$ 1,162
$1.23	$1.18	$(.37)	$(.73)	$(1.08)	$0.28
$1.23	$1.08	$(.37)	$(.83)	$(1.08)	$0.28
8,216	6,606	4,246	4,291	4,296	4,179
$ 62,032	$ 22,313	$ 6,366	$ 6,107	$ 3,615	$ 1,903
109,945	84,008	67,870	65,245	57,877	35,617
13,114	5,602	6,995	7,872	7,484	6,183
68,294	36,088	9,640	8,220	4,525	6,893

[d] Shares underlying options granted during fiscal 1994 are treated as outstanding for fiscal 1994 and all prior periods, using the treasury stock method. Weighted average number of shares outstanding in 1995 reflects the issuance of 2,300,000 shares of common stock in connection with the company's initial public offering. Weighted average number of shares outstanding in 1995 reflects the issuance of 1,366,666 shares of common stock in connection with a public offering in fiscal 1996.

EXHIBIT 2   Monthly Trading Range and Price-Earnings Ratio of Cannondale's
Common Stock, 1995–January 2000

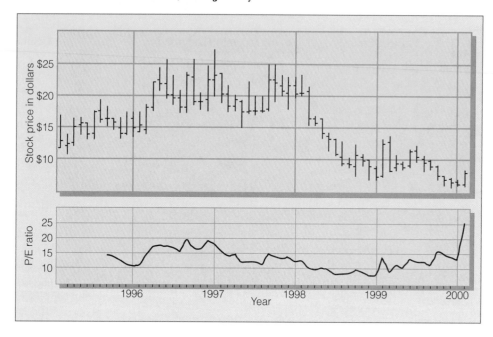

EXHIBIT 3   U.S. Unit Sales of Bicycles (20-Inch and Larger Wheel Sizes), 1981–98
(In Millions)

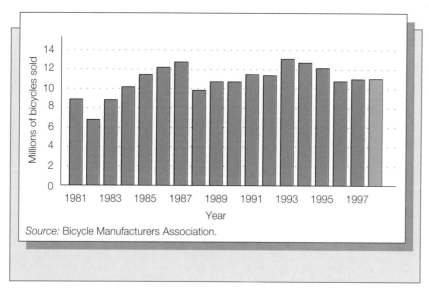

Source: Bicycle Manufacturers Association.

more comfortable versions of mountain bikes. The specialty bicycle market encompassed various niche products, including tandem bikes, cruisers, and bicycle motocross (BMX) bikes. Cruisers were styled similarly to the venerable Schwinn of the 1950s, with big balloon tires, huge cushy saddles, and swept-back handlebars. BMX bikes, which featured 20-inch wheels, a relatively short but very strong and light frame, and no gears, were originally designed for short races over dirt tracks but were more commonly used by children and adolescents for everyday recreational use.

FACTORS AFFECTING INDUSTRY DEMAND

Federal Legislation

During the 1990s the U.S. government enacted legislation that required communities to include cycling in local transit infrastructure planning. For example, the 1990 Clean Air Act set standards for air quality and required some metropolitan areas to develop methods to reach compliance. One of the recommended approaches involved taking steps to make bicycling a more viable transportation alternative. In addition, the Intermodal Surface Transportation Efficiency Act (ISTEA) of 1991 recognized the transportation value of bicycling and walking and offered mechanisms to increase consideration of bicyclists' and pedestrians' needs within the nation's intermodal transportation system. Federal funding was available from a number of programs, and planning requirements for bicycling were established for states and metropolitan planning organizations. Other provisions of the act included the requirement that states establish and fund a bicycle and pedestrian coordinator in their departments of transportation, and that bicyclist and pedestrian safety continue to be priority areas for highway safety program funding.

However, the provisions of the 1990 Clean Air Act and the 1991 Intermodal Surface Transportation Efficiency Act had done little to create a boom in cycling. Most industry growth during the 1990s was attributable to a growing interest in physical fitness and the popularity of the mountain bike, rather than U.S. government mandates to make cycling an integral part of a balanced intermodal transportation system. There was some belief by industry participants that the 1998 Transportation Equity Act for the 21st Century (TEA-21) would better integrate cycling into mainstream transportation in the United States. TEA-21 would provide as much as $500 million between 1999 and 2003 to create walkable and bicycle-friendly communities that would make cycling and walking safe and practical alternatives to traveling by automobile.

The Appeal of Mountain Biking

The phenomenal growth in mountain biking had been a major factor in the overall growth of the domestic bicycle market during the mid-1980s and early 1990s. The number of mountain bikers in the United States grew from 200,000 in 1982 to approximately 8.5 million in 1997. Only in-line roller skating had grown faster than mountain biking among outdoor recreational and fitness activities between 1987 and 1998. However, by 1999 the mountain bike industry was mature; it remained among the most popular outdoor recreational activities, but its growth rate had slowed considerably (see Exhibit 4).

Three factors contributed to the popularity of mountain bikes: (1) They were more comfortable to ride than typical touring or racing models; (2) the bikes themselves greatly increased the terrain available to bicycles; and (3) more adults were turning toward outdoor activities in their leisure time. The introduction of mountain

EXHIBIT 4   U.S. Participation Rates of Selected Fitness and Sports Activities, 1998

Source: Sporting Goods Manufacturers Association, "Sports Participation Trends Report, 1998."

Activity	Number of U.S. Participation	Annual Change (1997–98)	11-Year Change (1987–98)
Aerobics	21,017,000	−7.9%	−1.0%
Fitness bicycling	13,556,000	n.a.	n.a.
Running/jogging	34,962,000	−4.2	−5.9
Stationary cycling	30,791,000	−3.9	0.1
Treadmill exercise	37,073,000	2.6	743.3
Stair-climbing machine exercise	18,609,000	3.9	777.5
Baseball	12,318,000	−7.2	−18.4
Basketball	42,417,000	−5.9	18.7
In-line roller skating	32,010,000	1.0	581.8
Recreational bicycling	54,575,000	n.a.	n.a.
Golf	29,961,000	−3.4	14.1
Mountain biking	8,612,000	2.1	469.5
Snowboarding	5,461,000	10.5	158.1
Scuba diving	3,448,000	27.7	41.7

n.a. = not available.

bike racing as an Olympic sport in 1996 reflected the growth of mountain bike racing as both a participant and spectator sport and created additional exposure for mountain biking. In addition, downhill racing proved to be increasingly popular with spectators, combining high speed and technically advanced equipment with the celebrity of professional athletes and emerging personalities in the sport. During the 1990s the ski resort industry increasingly promoted summer use of ski mountains for biking, with many ski resorts equipping ski lifts to carry bikes and riders uphill.

FACTORS INFLUENCING DEMAND FOR MOUNTAIN BIKES IN THE LATE 1990S

Environmental Regulation

The coverage of racing events in mountain bike magazines and the use of racing photos in mountain bike manufacturer advertisements had created a backlash against the industry by hikers and others wishing to preserve the environment. Opponents of mountain biking attempted to portray mountain bikers as crazed, out-of-control cyclists who destroyed trails and made it unsafe for hikers to enjoy national parks and other government lands. In response to the critics, the U.S. Forest Service had commissioned a survey in 1996 that looked at the impact of bicycles on public lands. The survey found that 98 percent of National Forests reported mountain biking activity that ranged from 50 to 376,000 cyclists per year. Fifty percent of national parks reported annual mountain bike usage by fewer than 4,500 visitors, while 25 percent of national parks reported more than 15,000 mountain bike riders per year. Seventy percent of forest managers reported conflicts between cyclists and hikers, 59 percent were concerned that mountain bikes contributed to park safety problems, 58 percent believed that mountain bikes damaged park resources, and 48 percent witnessed or knew of accidents in the park related to mountain bike usage.

The International Mountain Bike Association (IMBA) noted to its manufacturing and retailing members that industry sales were directly tied to open biking trails. It developed a mantra of "No trails, no sales" and encouraged manufacturers to discontinue ads that depicted racing photographs. The association also encouraged both manufacturers and retailers to take a proactive position in regard to safe and responsible cycling. The IMBA struck an agreement with the Sierra Club that called for wilderness protection, socially responsible mountain biking, restricted trail access, trail user education, and open communication between local mountain biking groups and Sierra Club entities. Additionally, the association maintained an active lobbying effort to ensure that lands regulated by the Bureau of Land Management and the U.S. Forest Service remained open to cycling.

Technological Innovation

Technological innovations became increasingly important in the industry as rival mountain bike manufacturers attempted to outpace the modest industry growth rate by introducing technological innovations in frames, components, and suspension systems. Innovations diffused quickly throughout the industry as manufacturers kept adding features in attempts to maintain their historical growth rates. Cannondale was the first to offer affordable large-diameter aluminum-tube bicycles in the early 1980s, but by 1999 aluminum-frame bikes were produced by almost all bike manufacturers, including companies that manufactured inexpensive bicycles sold in discount stores. In 1999, aluminum frames were still found on high-end bikes, but other materials (such as carbon composites and titanium) were also used on more technologically advanced mountain bikes. The appeal of titanium frames was the material's light weight combined with strength. Like titanium frames, carbon composite frames were popular because they were light and strong but also because they could be molded into aerodynamic shapes. Steel- or aluminum-frame bicycle designs were typically bound to the traditional double-triangle shape. Other innovations that had become popular with cycling enthusiasts during the late 1990s included clipless pedals, disc brakes, automatic shifting, and suspension systems.

Front- and full-suspension systems were introduced during the early 1990s and quickly became a popular addition to high-end mountain bikes. The suspension systems provided greater comfort and control than what was available on nonsuspension bikes, and by 1999 suspension systems were found on most mountain bikes at midrange price points over $500. Suspension systems were also available on mountain bikes priced between $200 and $300 in discount stores. However, these lower-priced suspension bikes typically used poorer quality suspension systems and did not offer performance equal to that of higher-end suspension bikes. High-end mountain bike manufacturers sought out innovative features on a regular basis to maintain a comfortable level of differentiation over not only other high-end brands but also lower-priced bicycles that incorporated previous-generation mountain bike technology. K2's computer-chip-activated Smart Shock was an example of a technological innovation that could provide a bicycle manufacturer with the level of differentiation necessary to support premium pricing. The Smart Shock technology sampled the ground conditions and sent damping instructions to the shock 1,000 times per second to maximize tire-to-ground contact. K2 models equipped with the Smart Shock sold at prices between $900 and $2,200.

MARKET SEGMENTATION BY CHANNEL OF DISTRIBUTION

Two primary distribution systems existed in the U.S. bicycle industry—large discount retailers and independent specialty bicycle shops. Department stores, discount stores, and toy stores accounted for about 70 percent of all units sold and about half of the total spent on bikes in 1997. Most of the bikes sold by mass merchandise retailers were offered at prices below $200 and tended to be heavy, without the precision machining or reliable components demanded by cycling enthusiasts.

These low-end bikes were fine for cycling around the neighborhood but lacked the durability, reliability, and performance needed for serious biking. The discounters' advantages were price and convenience; their clientele consisted mainly of buyers looking for low-end, low-performance models.

Huffy Corporation, Murray Ohio Manufacturing, and Brunswick Corporation (producer of Roadmaster and Mongoose brands) were the three leading producers of bikes sold by large discounters, department stores, and discount sporting goods superstores. Other brands sold by large discounters were Magna, Pacific, Rand, and Kent. Discount store customers were not particularly brand-loyal and usually made their purchasing decisions based on price and some modest product preferences like bicycle type, color, and size. Competition among manufacturers of less-expensive bicycles, although always strong, had intensified during the 1990s as the discount retail industry had consolidated and low-priced imports from China and Taiwan had fueled a growing price war. Both domestic and Asian bicycle manufacturers were forced to add features and compete more aggressively on price to consistently win contracts with large retailers like Wal-Mart, Target, and Toys "R" Us. During the mid-1990s as little as 40 percent of the bicycles sold by discount retailers were produced outside the United States, but the growing price competition in the industry had compelled low-end manufacturers to abandon bicycle production in the United States. In 1999 both Huffy and Brunswick anticipated losses from their bicycle operations and closed their remaining U.S. production facilities. Both companies had announced that, following those closings, they would source 100 percent of their frames from Asian contract manufacturers.

About 30 percent of the 11 million bicycles sold in the United States during 1998 were sold by small specialty retailers with annual sales averaging about $500,000. These dealers, numbering about 6,800, typically had one location, were family owned, carried four to six brands of midrange to high-end bicycles, and sold about 500 to 600 bikes per year. The sales of parts, accessories, and service accounted for about 50 percent of specialty retailers' gross sales. About 80 percent of bicycles sold by specialty retailers were imported. High-performance bicycle manufacturers like Trek, Schwinn, Giant, Raleigh, Specialized, Cannondale, and Diamondback marketed their bikes exclusively through independent specialty dealers who could provide after-the-sale service for their products.

Specialty bicycle shops accounted for 30 percent of the industry's unit sales and about 50 percent of total dollar sales. Bicycle dealer brands generally started at prices above $200. The average price of a bicycle sold at a bicycle shop was about $350, though prices could range into the thousands. The independent bicycle dealer's ability to offer light, durable, properly assembled bicycles matched to the individual rider's needs worked to the dealer's advantage. In addition, specialty bike dealers commanded a vast majority of parts and accessories sales and virtually 100 percent of the service market. Dealers dominated the market for bicycles selling for $250 and higher. The growing interest in a total fitness lifestyle had also caught the attention of specialty bicycle dealers. Roughly 25 percent of the bicycle stores in the United States sold some kind of indoor exercise equipment (exercise bikes, weight machines, and all associated accessories).

Mountain bikes (26-inch wheel size) represented 55 percent of the bikes sold through the specialty channel in 1997. Mountain bikes had accounted for as much as 63 percent of independent dealer sales as recently as 1995. Children's bikes (20-inch wheels) were the fastest-growing bicycle category sold by specialty dealers, accounting for 33 percent of sales in 1997 versus 20 percent of specialty dealer unit sales in 1994. Recreational bikes were another rapidly growing category and accounted for 10 percent of dealer sales in 1997. It was expected that recreational comfort bikes would become a larger segment of the market as baby boomers aged and the over-40 age category grew. Most dealers had found that comfort bikes were gaining market share directly at the expense of low-end mountain bikes. Road racers accounted for only 2 percent of specialty retailer sales in 1997.

Cannondale's Rivals in the Mountain Bike Segment

Cannondale experienced little competition from the large manufacturers—such as Brunswick Corporation, Huffy Corporation, and Murray Ohio—that sold bicycles to discount retailers. For the most part, discount store brands were not sold by independent dealers and dealer brands were not carried in discount stores. The only exception was Mongoose, which had been a dealer brand until its acquisition by Brunswick in 1997. After the acquisition, Brunswick developed lower-priced Mongoose models for discounters as well as maintaining higher-priced models for its independent dealers. Once Mongoose became available at discount stores, many dealers chose to drop the Mongoose brand because of the difficulty in convincing consumers that the dealers' higher-priced Mongoose models, although similar in appearance, were of better quality than Mongoose models found in discount stores.

The high-performance segment of the bicycle industry was highly competitive in the United States and in many other countries. Competition was based primarily on perceived value, brand image, performance features, product innovation, and price. Competition in foreign markets was affected by duties, tariffs, foreign exchange fluctuations, taxes and the effect of various trade agreements and import restrictions. In 2000 there were several key competing brands in the industry.

In some instances competing brands were actually owned by the same parent corporation or holding company. As growth in the mountain bike segment had slowed during the 1990s and as bicycle manufacturers sought continued growth, a number of mergers and acquisitions involving key brands occurred. Owning more than one brand allowed manufacturers to gain greater coverage in specific geographic locations and communities even though dealers were frequently given some modest assurance of an exclusive territory. For example, Intrepid, Inc. (the parent of Trek bicycles), had acquired two high-end mountain bike manufacturers, Gary Fisher and Klein, which allowed the company to increase its network of retail dealers without alienating its Trek dealers. In addition, even though Trek, Klein, and Gary Fisher manufactured similarly equipped models, Intrepid's dealers were not exposed to the consumer price shopping that was seen by Mongoose dealers after Mongoose became available at discount stores. Other brands involved in mergers or acquisitions included Raleigh, Diamondback, Univega, Mishiski, GT, Dyno, Powerlite, and Robinson.

Cannondale's key competitors in 1999 are discussed in the following sections.

SCHWINN CYCLING & FITNESS

Schwinn was founded in 1895 in Chicago by German bikemaker Ignaz Schwinn. At one time, Schwinn was the most prestigious bicycle company in the industry, with as much as 25 percent of the market and sales of 1.6 million units a year. During its first 100 years, Schwinn sold more than 40 million bicycles. Beginning in the 1970s changing consumer tastes and tough new competitors with lighter, more high-tech products began to slowly erode Schwinn's dominant position.

Rather than innovate, Schwinn became obsessed with cutting costs by moving production overseas. Initially, the company outsourced its bicycles from Japan. But by 1978 Taiwanese manufacturers were beating the Japanese on price. Schwinn shifted gears and began importing Taiwanese-made Giant bikes, on which Schwinn put its nameplate. When Giant became a competitor, Schwinn formed an alliance with the China Bicycle Company, but after a few years CBC also used the knowledge gained through collaborating with Schwinn to launch its own brand in the United States and compete against Schwinn.

To make matters worse, Schwinn made the strategic mistake of ignoring the mountain bike craze for most of the 1980s. By 1992, two-thirds of all bikes sold were mountain bikes. Schwinn managers were not alone in their complacency; many Schwinn retailers failed to notice key market trends or keep up with the technological changes sweeping the industry. The proverbial writing was on the wall, and Schwinn filed for Chapter 11 bankruptcy protection in 1992.

In 1993, what was left of Schwinn was purchased by an investor group for $43 million. Schwinn's new owners moved quickly to rebuild the Schwinn brand. The new owners immediately relocated the company to Boulder, home of the University of Colorado and thousands of outdoor enthusiasts. Historically, Schwinn was viewed as a maker of sturdy low-cost bikes, which was contrary to the 1990s consumer preference for the trendier high-performance mountain bikes. The Boulder culture helped Schwinn designers develop new models that included technological features and performance that better appealed to hardcore cyclists, who often influenced the purchases of less-avid cyclists. Even though Schwinn introduced better-styled and more technologically advanced bikes, its image was a major obstacle in turning around the company. As Greg Bagni, Schwinn's new vice president of marketing and product development, noted, the hardcore cyclists who were key to changing the public's perceptions of Schwinn's performance and quality "wouldn't be caught dead on a Schwinn."[3]

Schwinn's efforts to change its image required what Bagni said was a fundamental shift in strategy. "We've evolved from a marketing-driven company to a market-driven company. A marketing-driven company will try to sell a warehouse full of yellow bikes . . . a market-driven company will determine what the consumer wants first."[4] In addition to determining what features consumers wanted, Schwinn also began showing up on the racing circuit, using cross-promotions with such well-known brands as Old Navy, Toyota, and MCI to promote Schwinn bikes and study what features appealed to hardcore cyclists.

Once Schwinn's turnaround was well under way, the company was sold again in 1997. The new owners retained Schwinn's management team and acquired GT Bicycles in 1998 to add complementary models to Schwinn's line and increase Schwinn's network of dealers. GT Bicycle was a leading designer, manufacturer, and marketer of mid- to premium-priced bicycles sold under the company's GT, Powerlite, Robinson, and Dyno brand names. GT Bicycles sold a full line of more than 40 bicycle models but was best known for its popular juvenile bikes. Like other manufacturers, GT promoted its brand through focused promotional efforts such as sponsorship of professional BMX racing teams and national, regional, and local bicycle races, as well as cooperative advertising programs with independent bicycle dealers.

Schwinn's turnaround and its addition of GT bikes put it into contention for a leadership position in the U.S. specialty retail channel. Schwinn and GT were strongest at low-end price points between $250 and $500 and together commanded an estimated market share of 18.8 percent at year-end 1999.

[3]Nancy Brumback, "Schwinn Cycles Fast to Finish First," *Brandmarketing,* December 1999, p. 6.

[4]L. Loro, "Schwinn Aims to Be a Big Wheel Again," *Advertising Age,* January 1995.

INTREPID, INC.

Intrepid, Inc., was a privately held company that owned the Trek, Gary Fisher, and Klein mountain bike brands and LeMond road-racing bikes. The combined sales of the company's brands made it among the market share leaders in the specialty retailer channel. Trek was Intrepid's best-selling brand and was a pioneer in carbon-fiber frames. The Waterloo, Wisconsin, firm recorded revenues of about $400 million in 1997. Approximately 35 percent of its total revenue came from international sales. The company employed 1,800 people worldwide to build and distribute its five bicycle lines, which included over 100 mountain bike, road-racing, touring, tandem, BMX, and children's models.

Trek began in 1976 by hand-building steel frames in a rented facility in Waterloo, Wisconsin. Pursuing high-quality workmanship, the firm expanded quickly, generating $750,000 in sales after just three years. It soon gained a reputation for quality American-made bicycles. By 1986, sales hit $16 million, but the company's rapid growth did not come without problems. The company sustained losses and accumulated unsold inventory, and employee morale was low. In stepped the founder of Trek, Dick Burke, who quickly took charge and articulated a back-to-basics philosophy that rallied employees and reenergized the company with a new mission statement: "Build a quality product; offer a competitive value; deliver it on time; and create a positive work environment."[5] In addition, Burke revised Trek's marketing strategy, developed new and innovative road bikes, and introduced a new line of mountain bikes. He emphasized quality and efficiency in his plant operations and pushed service excellence as the cornerstone of the sales department. As a result of these initiatives, Trek introduced a number of award-winning bicycles and steadily increased sales every year after 1987. Trek's Y-shaped carbon composite frame was one of the company's more innovative and popular products during the late 1990s and was available on many of its high-end bikes. In 1995, the designers working on Trek's Y-frame mountain bike project were named "Design Engineers of the Year" by *Popular Mechanics* and the Trek 970 Y-frame model was named *Mountain Bike* magazine's "Bike of the Year."

Trek's Y-frame was also available in an aluminum construction and could be outfitted with full suspension or in a hardtail configuration that included front suspension only. Trek's suspension could be adjusted to three positions that matched cross-country, downhill, or general riding or racing conditions. Trek also offered a women's frame with modified geometric proportions to better fit a female rider. Trek cosponsored racing teams with Volkswagen and the U.S. Postal Service and independently sponsored a triathlete team to race-test the company's upcoming generations of products. All three cycling teams won a number of prestigious events during 1999. Trek's most popular models sold at low-end and midrange price points between $250 and $1,200.

Intrepid's Gary Fisher and Klein lines of mountain bikes included a greater proportion of high-end models than its Trek line. The company acquired the Gary Fisher brand in 1993 to help it expand its dealer network further into communities that already carried Trek. Intrepid could offer a new dealer the ability to carry Gary Fisher models without offending its existing Trek dealers. Gary Fisher was a premier brand because of the line's award-winning design and performance and because of the notoriety of the company's founder and namesake. Gary Fisher was an accomplished road racer during the 1960s and 1970s who created the first mountain bike

---

[5]Taken from "Reinventing the Wheel: A Brief History of the Trek Bicycle Corporation," company document.

in 1974. In 1994 *Smithsonian Magazine* proclaimed Gary Fisher the "Founding Father of Mountain Bikes." Gary Fisher's mountain bike racing teams were cosponsored with Saab and boasted a number of Olympic gold medal winners among its members. Gary Fisher models were priced comparably to Trek models although Gary Fisher had fewer low-end models between $250 and $500 than Trek.

While Fisher had fewer low-end models than Trek, Klein was Intrepid's high-end mountain bike brand, with prices beginning at over $1,200. Klein Bicycles began in 1974 as an official MIT Innovation Center project when founder Gary Klein, a competition road racer, was enrolled in the university as an engineering graduate student. Gary Klein, along with three of his classmates and their MIT engineering professor, used a $20,000 grant from the university to develop one of the first aluminum-frame bicycles. The students and their professor built a number of prototypes in 1974 and displayed their refined bikes at an international cycle show in 1975. Upon graduation from MIT, Gary and one of the three classmates moved the operation from MIT to Gary's hometown of Chehalis, Washington, where the company's bicycles were still produced in 2000.

Klein Bicycles was known for its technological innovation and craftsmanship. The company was relatively weak in the midrange category but was among the leaders in high-end mountain bikes. Each Klein bicycle was built by hand, and every component was tested under a stringent quality control process. Klein used only certified aerospace-grade aluminum and custom-made, proprietary production equipment to assemble frames at alignment tolerances as exacting as ±.0002 inches. Klein also produced carbon composite frames that were used on some of its four basic road-racing and mountain bike series, which came in multiple configurations. All Klein mountain bike models were available with either hardtail frames or full-suspension systems. Klein Bicycles and Cadillac jointly sponsored the Team Catera racing team, which included such well-known cyclists as Golden Brainard, the fourth highest ranked American in world rankings.

SPECIALIZED BICYCLES

Specialized Bicycles was a private firm founded by Mike Sinyard in 1974 in Morgan Hill, California, that got its start importing Italian-made bicycle components. In 1981 the company launched the first mass-produced mountain bike—the Stumpjumper (the original model is at the Smithsonian Institution in Washington, D.C.). Specialized also created the first professional mountain bike racing team in 1983, which Mountain Dew began sponsoring in 1996. The company also created and sponsored the Cactus Cup race series that allowed amateurs to race in events similar to professional races but at a level nonthreatening enough for first-time racers to have plenty of fun. During 1998 and 1999 Specialized Cactus Cup races were held in Canada, France, Japan, Brazil, and various locations throughout the United States.

Specialized's slogan was "Innovate or die," and it had been recognized for developing a number of technologically advanced bicycle materials and components used in the production of its mountain bikes. In 1988 Specialized's Stumpjumper Epic became the first mountain bike with a carbon-fiber frame, and in 1989 the company introduced the first composite-material bicycle wheel through a joint venture with DuPont. In 1990 Specialized began producing frames from its M2 metal matrix composite material of aluminum, silicon, copper, and magnesium. The company introduced advanced full-suspension bikes in 1993, and added an improved M4 metal matrix composite frame material in 1998. Specialized also produced a number of models that were equipped with aluminum frames. Other noteworthy innovations developed by Specialized included its S-works wheel sets, which a German university rated the industry's best in terms of rigidity and weight, and its Ground Control suspension systems, which helped keep the rear wheel on the ground even under bumpy surface conditions.

Specialized management believed that its culture was a key contributor to its success in designing innovative new mountain bikes. The company made a practice of hiring avid cyclists as engineers and managers and invited all of its employees along on its daily Specialized Lunch Rides. Each day Specialized employees at its Morgan Hill plant biked over off-road trails and winding roads with the latest Specialized equipment to relieve stress and test the company's newest products. After an hour or so of riding, the employees would take quick showers and head back to their desks to eat a sandwich and return to their work. The company also created a special S-Works R&D team that was allowed to build "dream bikes" without regard to a budget. Mike Sinyard said that the company had "never been satisfied with existing bicycle technology and S-Works allows us to push the edges of the design envelope. Once we perfect new designs for S-Works bikes we begin seeking ways to make those innovations trickle down to consumer price points, which allows us to offer elite design techniques at non-elite prices."[6]

Specialized also believed that its dealers should be knowledgeable about the latest technological innovations in the bicycle industry. The company's Specialized University offered the company's 5,000 dealers in 35 countries courses on the latest frame materials, frame design geometries, and other technological innovations. Specialized University also offered courses that educated dealers and their staffs on proper bicycle sizing and fitting and repair techniques. Specialized dealers carried a full line of 55 models of bicycles that each came in multiple configurations. Specialized's basic classes of bicycles included a BMX line; a juvenile line; two road bike models; and six low-end, midrange, and high-end mountain bike lines.

GIANT GLOBAL GROUP

Giant, which began as a small Taiwanese exporter of bicycles in 1972, was the world's largest bicycle exporter in 1999, with 93 percent of its bicycles sold outside of Taiwan. In 1999 Giant bicycles were sold in 60 countries by more than 10,000 retail dealers across seven continents. The company's 1999 revenues were estimated at approximately $400 million. Giant's growth was made possible in large part by an early alliance with Schwinn, which gave Giant the market savvy and production know-how it needed to be a major competitive force in the industry.

Schwinn began importing a small quantity of bikes from Giant in 1978 when it began looking for a source of low-cost bicycles. Schwinn's sourcing from Giant increased in 1981 when Schwinn's Chicago plant went on strike. Deciding against negotiating a settlement with labor, Schwinn's management closed the plant and moved all its engineers and equipment to Giant's factory in Taiwan. As part of the deal with Giant, Schwinn management handed over everything—technology, engineering, volume—that Giant needed to become a dominant bikemaker. In return Schwinn imported the bikes and marketed them under the Schwinn name. By 1984, Giant was shipping 700,000 bicycles to Schwinn, representing 70 percent of the contract manufacturer's sales. By 1987, Giant was selling its own brand-name bikes in Europe and the United States. To gain market share, Giant told dealers its bikes were Schwinn clones and 10 to 15 percent cheaper. Giant also hired several Schwinn executives to help build up its U.S. distribution capabilities.

[6]Specialized press release, www.specialized.com.

Giant's move to establish a brand name and move away from contract manufacturing continued throughout the 1990s, with the company dedicating 2 percent of its annual revenues to research and development and hiring 65 designers to develop features and performance that cycling enthusiasts demanded. Giant's R&D efforts paid off in the late 1990s as its image in the industry soared and it won numerous awards for design innovation. The company's MCR carbon composite bicycle was named the "Best New Product of 1998" by *Business Week,* and in 1999 its XtC SE1 mountain bike was named *Mountain Biking* magazine's "Bike of the Year." In praising Giant's race-ready mountain bike, the magazine's associate editor commented "I couldn't say enough great things about this bike. First and foremost, we were drawn to every aspect of the bike. A quick glance told us this bike was well thought out and was definitely going to be a contender."[7]

Giant began a racing program to promote the company's name among avid cyclists and signed top mountain bike racers to endorse the company's products. In 1998 the company's race teams were ranked numbers two and three worldwide in road racing, numbers three and four in cross-country mountain bike racing, and numbers two and three in downhill racing. Giant also entered into an agreement with outdoor retailer Eddie Bauer to build special edition bicycles that would be sold by Giant retailers. In 1999 Giant's reliance on contract manufacturing had been reduced to 30 percent of its production. Seventy percent of the bikes produced by the company were sold under the Giant brand at prices that typically ranged between $250 and $800 but went as high as $4,000. The company emphasized a "total best value" design and production approach that attempted to match rivals in terms of frame design, component quality, and finish while beating competing brands on price. Giant's 2000 model year product line included 43 models in the mountain bike, road-racing, BMX, hybrid, and juvenile classes.

The company added two plants in China during 1993 and built a plant in the Netherlands in 1997 to keep up with the increased demand for its bicycles. In 1999 the company produced about 2.5 million bicycles with about 1 million produced in Taiwan, 100,000 produced in the Netherlands, and about 1.4 million produced in China. Giant was expected to increase its production in the Netherlands to 400,000 units per year by 2001 and had discussed building production capacity in North America.

DERBY CYCLE CORPORATION

Nottingham, England–based Derby Cycle was among the world's largest designers, manufacturers, and marketers of bicycles, with 1997 sales exceeding $500 million. The company was established in 1986 with the acquisition of Raleigh, Gazelle, and Sturmey-Archer bicycles from Britain's TI Group. Throughout the late 1980s and 1990s Derby continued to add to its portfolio with acquisitions of popular brands like Nishiki, Univega, and Diamondback. The company sold more than 2.1 million bicycles in 1997 and was the largest seller of bicycles in the United Kingdom, the Netherlands, Germany, Canada, Ireland, and South Africa. Derby Bicycle operated manufacturing facilities in the United Kingdom, the Netherlands, Germany, Canada, and the United States. Derby was one of the top five producers of bicycles sold through the U.S. specialty retailer channel of distribution and targeted the low-end market with retail prices ranging from $250 to $500.

Diamondback, Derby Cycle's most popular brand of mountain bike sold in the United States, was among the leading brands in the low-end category and was known

---

[7]Giant Manufacturing Company press release, www.giant-bicycle.com/aboutgiant/whatsnew.asp.

for incorporating innovative features at moderate prices. The company's 49 basic models of mountain bikes were equipped with either steel or aluminum frames and various suspension options that ranged from a rigid frame to full suspension. Diamondback also offered bikes in the youth, BMX, hybrid, road-racer, cruiser, and fitness equipment segments. Diamondback and other Derby brands had lost some dealer orders in 1999 and 2000 because of consistently poor dealer service.

Cannondale's History and Background

Joseph Montgomery, who grew up on an Ohio peach farm and later dropped out of college three times, began Cannondale Corporation in 1971 after having abandoned careers as a charter boat captain and a securities analyst. Joe Montgomery's first career change occurred after his charter boat sank under his command in shark-infested waters. Montgomery took a less life-threatening but more mundane position as a securities analyst in 1964, but after seven years on Wall Street changed careers again to start Cannondale. Joe Montgomery began Cannondale with the vision of making it the best cycling company in the world. His vision inspired 10 principles that made up the Cannondale philosophy:

1. We care about each other, our shareholders, our customers, and our vendors.
2. We produce a stream of innovative, quality products.
3. We devise flexible manufacturing processes that enable us to deliver those innovative, quality products to the market quickly and then back them with excellent customer service.
4. We limit our distribution to the best specialty retailers in the world.
5. We stay lean, remain competitive and entrepreneurial.
6. We put 90 percent of our profits back into the company to underwrite future growth; the balance we share with all of our employees.
7. We promote from within whenever possible.
8. We concentrate on detail, because the last 5 percent is often the difference between success and failure.
9. We continuously improve everything.
10. We govern our every deed by what is "just and right."

As of 2000 Joseph Montgomery had been Cannondale's only chairperson, president, and chief executive officer. The birth and early history of Cannondale was aptly captured in a 1986 article in *New England Business,* excerpted below.

> "I always wanted to start my own business," says the 46-year-old [Joe] Montgomery; he began the search for opportunities when he started working on Wall Street as an analyst in the 1960s for companies such as Prudential-Bache. His employers were looking for fast-track companies in leisure-time industries such as snowmobiles, but he was looking for less obvious opportunities.
>
> "The bike industry was a sleepy industry," Montgomery said. "The industry had old ideas and designs. Anyone who was really aggressive and designed a functional, quality product could make a go. It was a field ripe for new ideas." In 1972 he had one—a mini-trailer that bike campers could use to tow their gear. He quit his job and on the strength of a contract with a distributor, got a $60,000 loan to finance production.
>
> Sales for the trailer started soft and, working in improvised company offices above a pickle store in Cannondale, Conn., he developed bicycle accessories to expand the line. The timing was good. The 1973 Arab fuel embargo hit, sparking a two-year bike

boom, and his sales leapt ahead to $2.3 million by 1974. Then, in 1975, recession hit and the boom ended. The speed and degree of the drop in bike sales was terrifying. In 1974, 14.1 million units sold. In 1975, 7 million sold. Bike shops all over America closed.

"It was a big washout. A lot of people who were tired of some rat race and figured they'd open a bike shop went under. Our sales were cut in half, and we were stuck with $250,000 in bad debts." Having just gotten started, he wasn't about to file for bankruptcy protection.

"The worst thing you can do in this situation is put your head in the sand. You've got to call the guy and say, 'Look, I know what I owe. Here's my business plan, my cash flow analysis. Not only will I pay you what I owe you, I'll continue to buy from you.'"

His creditors liked his approach, and their cooperation helped the company out of trouble. But Montgomery acknowledges it was a sweat. "Very scary," he said. "Very scary."

Through the 1970s and early 80s, Cannondale quietly achieved steady annual sales at around $8 million and became known for an expanding line of quality bike camping equipment. Montgomery wanted to make a bicycle, though. In 1982, he got a letter from a 25-year-old engineer named David Graham, who felt he was stagnating in the Electric Boat facility in Groton, Conn.

"David wrote, 'I'm an engineer and I want to build an aluminum bike,'" Montgomery remembered. "We'd been working on bikes way back in the 70s, and I was pretty sure I wanted to make an aluminum one. Graham took a 50 percent pay cut to come here."

The first Cannondale aluminum bike came out in 1983. It hadn't been easy. There had been production problems: All the fabrication equipment for the aluminum frame had to be custom designed, and they had trouble getting components that would fit the unusually fat tubing. (Like almost all bike manufacturers, Cannondale makes practically nothing on their own bike except the frame. Gears, shifters, and other components are obtained from outside suppliers. Most of these are from the Far East, which somewhat dilutes current company efforts to position itself as an "American-made" bike.)

Finally, the bike hit dealers' floors. It was weird-looking, expensive at $600, and had a number of bugs still to be worked out. But the equipment nuts, the "spoke sniffers" who permeate the bicycling world and are ever on the lookout for something new, embraced it.

For them, the prime attractions were the technical advantages of aluminum. Aluminum, of course, is light, and in premium bikes, light weight is a vital sales point. Yet Cannondale bikes are not appreciably lighter than comparable steel frame bikes, because Graham took advantage of aluminum and used more of it, making the frame tubing thicker and making the bike structurally stiffer.

Ted Constantino, editor of Bicycle Guide, a Boston-based consumer specialty magazine, explains that a stiff frame without any "give" makes for a more efficient bike. "There's a feeling you get on a Cannondale that every kilowatt of energy you put into the pedal comes out the rear wheel."

As important to sales as what the frame does is its distinctive look. "It doesn't hurt," Montgomery ingenuously acknowledges. "If I'm a spoke sniffer, I am proud you can see that I ride something different."

. . . Cannondale as an American company is bucking prevailing trends in the bike industry. The majority of premium bikes sold in the United States are made in the Far East. European and American companies used to dominate until the mid-70s, when the now familiar one-two punch of high quality and low price from Japan hit the market. During the next ten years, old names such as Raleigh, Motobecane, and Puch ran into deep trouble.

But Cannondale saw sales explode right out to the gate; from 1983 to 1985 it grew at a 30 percent annual rate. They expanded their line from one model to 15. In 1984,

Cannondale netted a lucrative contract making private-label bikes for L. L. Bean. Market demand and publicity within the industry helped it to expand its dealer network through North America, and then to Europe. It found itself continually expanding its headquarters in Georgetown, which now employs 80, and its production facility in Bedford, Penn., which now employs 175.

. . . If not the largest, it certainly may be the most talked about bike company. In that great consumer undercurrent of hearsay that can make or break a product, Cannondale has been designated as the "best" bike around. That means it's trendy. Trendy is transitory, and Montgomery knows he'll have to work hard to get beyond it. For now, though, trendy is OK. Trendy is something Joe Montgomery can take to the bank.[8]

Cannondale in 2000

In 2000 Cannondale was a leading manufacturer and marketer of high-performance bicycles and high-performance bicycle components, with an estimated 20 percent share of the U.S. high-performance bicycle market. The company also provided its dealers with a full line of bicycle components, accessories, and men's and women's cycling apparel. The company had also set a spring 2000 launch date for its MX400 motocross motorcycle. Even though Cannondale management expected the MX400 to be an important contributor to its revenue growth in future years, the company's main business was high-performance bicycles. Cannondale was a leader in the use of lightweight aluminum as a material for bicycle frames and was the only bicycle manufacturer not to build bicycles from steel. With the exception of its carbon-fiber Raven model, all of Cannondale's bicycle models offered for the 2000 model year were constructed with hand-welded aluminum frames. The company's bicycles, marketed under the Cannondale brand name and carrying its "Handmade in the USA" logo, were sold through specialty bicycle retailers in the United States and in more than 60 other countries.

Cannondale's corporate headquarters was located in Georgetown, Connecticut, and its manufacturing facilities for bicycles, motorcycles, bicycle components, accessories, and clothing were located in Bedford, Pennsylvania. At the end of July 1999, Cannondale employed a total of 779 full-time workers in the United States, 115 in its European subsidiary, 16 in its Japanese subsidiary, and 6 in its Cannondale Australia subsidiary.

CANNONDALE'S BUSINESS STRATEGY

Cannondale's overall business strategy had a significant vertical integration component. The company manufactured its own frames in the United States, whereas most of its competitors imported their frames from Asia. Cannondale was one of the first companies to concentrate on aluminum frames and enjoyed the premier position in this category, as bicyclists continued to gravitate toward lighter, sturdier high-performance bicycles. In addition, Cannondale developed a proprietary component line under the Cannondale Original Design Application (CODA) brand that was used in a growing portion of its product mix and was becoming more important in the aftermarket. With components such as handlebars, brakes, cranks, and derailleurs comprising a significant portion of a bike's value, Cannondale hoped to gain a competitive advantage over manufacturers who relied on outside component suppliers such as Shimano, SunTour, and Campionolo.

[8]R. E. Charm, "Like the Company's Sales, Aluminum Bike of Cannondale Stands Out from the Pack," *New England Business* 8, no. 3 (November 3, 1986), p. 41.

Product Innovation

Cannondale's products were designed for cyclists who wanted high-performance, high-quality bicycles. It differentiated its bicycles through technological innovations that made its bicycles lighter, stronger, faster, and more comfortable than those of rivals. The company had an ongoing commitment to R&D and had continued to expand and develop its aluminum bicycle line with a series of innovations, focusing on proprietary frame designs, suspension systems, and components. Each new frame or component innovation went through a two-month battery of tests in the company's $1 million-plus Q-Lab that included fatigue testing, impact testing, finite element analysis, computerized field testing, and brittle-coat testing. Cannondale's know-how and manufacturing skills enabled the company to be a first-mover and trendsetter. Its original product, the Bugger bicycle trailer, was an industry first that pioneered an entire product category. Cannondale produced the first-ever large-diameter, aluminum-tube bicycles in 1983. It introduced its first mountain bike in 1984. In 1990, the company led the industry in introducing suspension systems in bicycles and in 1996 created a lightweight thermoplastic carbon-skin frame that was bonded to a magnesium spine for its new Raven mountain bike. In 2000 the second-generation Raven frame was honored as one of the "Best of What's New" products by *Popular Science*. Joe Montgomery described his philosophy toward innovation: "We approach everything we do—and I mean everything—with an eye toward innovation. And to a large extent, it's the innovations we've developed on the design and manufacturing side that allow us to continually bring these exciting new products to market."[9] Exhibit 5 shows a time line of Cannondale's growth and key innovations since 1971.

Manufacturing

The centerpiece of Cannondale's manufacturing strategy was its flexible manufacturing system. The strengths of the system included reduced production time, simultaneous production of various models and small batch sizes without high tooling changeover costs. A patented process employed lasers and other devices to cut the uniquely configured joints of various bicycle models without individual setup or changeover. Patented self-fixturing joint designs and hold devices allowed the parts to interlock without special tools as they were readied for welding. The manufacturing system enabled the cost-effective production of a wide product line and a broad range of models in a single day in order to respond to consumer demands. Cannondale's proprietary manufacturing system had allowed the company to reduce the time to completed bike from 17 days to only 3. Further efficiencies in the development process for other parts were realized through a new prototyping and tooling center with computer-aided design and manufacturing (CAD/CAM) technology. The company was committed to maintaining its competitive position by supporting research into further improvements in its manufacturing process and drastically reducing the time required to design and produce new bike models.

Cannondale's CAD/CAM system, which automatically calculated specific tube lengths, and its computer-guided laser tube cutters allowed the company to offer custom-fitted bicycles. The company had built custom-fitted bikes since 1994 for its professional racing staff, and began to offer consumers in Japan, Europe, Australia, Canada, and the United States custom-fitted bikes in 1999. Cannondale was expected to introduce custom fitting in the remainder of the 60-plus international markets where its bicycles were sold in 2000. Cannondale charged a $400 custom fitting fee and could deliver the custom-made bike to the consumer within six weeks.

---

[9]M. Sloane, "Cannondale: A Company Built on Innovation," *The Journal of Competitive Cycling* 1 (1995), pp. 7–10.

EXHIBIT 5 25 Years of Connondale Innovations

1971
Joe Montgomery starts Cannondale at the Cannondale train station in Wilton, Connecticut. Cannondale gets its name when employee Peter Meyers, ordering the company's first telephone from a pay phone at the station, is asked how the new company should be listed. Unsure of what to say, Peter notices the train station's sign and says, "Cannondale."

1972
The Bugger, the world's first bicycle-towed trailer, is introduced by Cannondale.

1974
The Toot seat bag, with a revolutionary flexible internal liner, helps Cannondale on its way to becoming the industry's leading bag manufacturer.

1977
Cannondale's Bedford, Pennsylvania, factory opens in a refurbished truck terminal. Total work force: 7.

1983
The ST500 — Cannondale's first bicycle, and the world's first affordable aluminum bike with large-diameter tubes — is introduced. Despite widespread industry skepticism, sales are strong.

1984
Cannondale produces its first mountain bike, the SM500, and its first road racing bike, the SR900.

1988
Cannondale bicycles make their Olympic debut at the Summer Games in Seoul, South Korea.

1989
Cannondale Europe is established in the Netherlands, European response to American-made Cannondales is enthusiastic, and sales quickly grow to 35% of total revenues.

1990
Patented Seat Cleat seat bag attachment system is introduced, immediately obsoleting all other mounting systems.

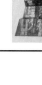

1991
Cannondale begins operations in Japan. The company ignores conventional wisdom by establishing a subsidiary and bypassing Japanese trading companies. Despite widespread industry skepticism, sales are strong.

EXHIBIT 5 25 Years of Connondale Innovations *(concluded)*

1994
Super V named one of the year's best products by *Business Week* magazine, and wins Design and Engineering Award from *Popular Mechanics* magazine.

1994
C-Style apparel introduced, pioneering the move towards performance cycling garments made with natural fabrics and comfortable, relaxed fit.

1996
Super V Active and Super V DH Active full-suspension models introduced.

1997
Cannondale introduces an aluminum full-suspension off-road wheel chair for disabled athletes.

1999
Cannondale introduces its "Custom Cannondale" fitting program that allows cyclists to order custom fitted bikes with more than 8 million possible combinations.

1999
Cannondale's first motorcycle named *Dirt Rider's* "Bike of the year."

2000
Cannondale's full-suspension Jekyll model named *Mountain Biking's* "Bike of the Year."

1994
Volvo/Cannondale Mountain Bike Racing Team riders win seven World Championship medals (including four gold) and one National Championship

1995
Silk Road suspension road bike — another industry first — debuts.

1996
Cannondale introduces the light-as-titanium CAAD3 mountain bike and Slice monocuque carbon fiber road bike.

1998
Cannondale is selected by Tommy Hilfiger to produce Hilfiger Sport special edition bicycle.

1999
Cannondale's Raven model equipped with a HeadShok Lefty forkset is chosen as one of *Popular Science's* "Best of What's New" awards.

1999
Cannondale named as one of the "Top 12 Road Bikes of All Time" by *Cycle Sport.*

Cannondale considered its domestic manufacturing base a key competitive advantage. Whereas the majority of bike companies purchased most, if not all, of their models from huge Far Eastern manufacturers, Cannondale made its bike frames in Pennsylvania. As Montgomery explained, "When you go to Asia to get a new frame design manufactured, the manufacturer makes three bikes for each one you order; one for you, one to sell to another bike company, and one to sell under their own brand name. By the time your new bike finally makes it into bike shops, the market is flooded with similar designs." He went on to describe the advantage of operating his own factories:

> First off, our factories don't have other customers ahead of us in line. When we make an improvement, or add a model, the reaction is instantaneous. Also, our proprietary designs remain proprietary. And of course, our product doesn't spend an extra six months on the water or stuck in customs, before finally becoming available to customers.[10]

Even though Cannondale's U.S.-based manufacturing facilities were a valuable competitive resource, various equipment problems in its Bedford, Pennsylvania, plant had resulted in unfilled dealer orders during the fall of 1999 and had delayed the introduction of some 2000 models.

Purchasing

Aluminum tubing was the primary material used to manufacture bicycles. Cannondale entered into purchasing agreements with various aluminum suppliers to ensure favorable pricing and delivery terms and certain technical assistance, but believed that termination of its contracts would not have a significant impact on its costs because of aluminum's wide availability. Most of its bicycle components were purchased from Japanese, Taiwanese, and U.S. original equipment manufacturers (OEMs). Its largest component supplier was Shimano, which was the source of approximately 19 percent of total inventory purchases in 1999. Cannondale concentrated buying power among fewer suppliers, which allowed the company to secure higher-volume purchase discounts.

Marketing

The goal of Cannondale's sales and marketing program was to establish the company as the leading high-performance bicycle brand in the specialty bicycle retail channel. The marketing effort focused on promotion of the firm's product innovation, performance, and quality leadership; publicity generated from the Volvo/Cannondale mountain bike racing team; and a media campaign designed to attract consumers to specialty bicycle retailers. Cannondale also maintained an innovative Web site (www.cannondale.com) that averaged more than 25 million hits each month.

Promotion

In 1994, Cannondale formed the Volvo/Cannondale racing team. The team generated considerable publicity in both the cycling press and the general press and through television coverage. Cannondale leveraged the success of its racing team by using photo images of the athletes in print media, point-of-sale literature, banners, product packaging, and product catalogs. Since its inception in 1994, the Volvo/Cannondale team had won four World Championships, six World Cup titles, 28 top finishes in World Cup events, nine National Championships, two Pan Am Games gold medals, and a silver medal at the 1996 Summer Olympic Games in Atlanta, Georgia. In addition, Cannondale supported racing teams in other cycling

[10]Ibid.

areas, such as its road-racing team that was cosponsored with Saeco, an Italian firm that was the world's largest manufacturer of espresso machines and its SoBe/Head-Shok grassroots squad that provided technical assistance to team riders and held instructional clinics for Cannondale retailers and their staff. SoBe, the leading maker of wellness beverages, also agreed to cosponsor Cannondale's planned MX400 motocross racing team.

Cannondale's print advertising focused on magazines for cycling enthusiasts and general lifestyle magazines to reach upscale adults with an interest in outdoor and leisure activities. In addition, Cannondale entered into a licensing agreement with Tommy Hilfiger in 1998 to produce a special Hilfiger Sport mountain bike that would be sold by Cannondale retailers. Cannondale management believed that the new Hilfiger bikes would draw customers who normally wouldn't shop in a bicycle store.

Sales and Distribution

Cannondale's distribution strategy was to sell its bicycles through specialty bicycle retailers who it believed could provide knowledgeable sales assistance regarding the technical and performance characteristics of its products and offer an ongoing commitment to service. Cannondale bicycles were not available through mass merchandisers, which generally carried lower-priced products and did not have the expertise to sell and support high-performance bikes. The company had not awarded exclusive rights to retailers in any territory. In 2000 the company sold its bicycles through 1,150 specialty retailer locations in the United States and Canada. Cannondale accessories were carried by an additional 500 retail locations in the United States and Canada. Before establishing a new dealer, the company considered such factors as market density in terms of competition, population, and demographics; ability of the retailer to optimize market penetration; commitment to service and the high-performance segment of the market; and dealer creditworthiness.

Research and Development

Cannondale's product development strategy was directed at continually making bicycles lighter, stronger, faster, and more comfortable. Its Volvo/Cannondale mountain bike racing team was closely tied to its R&D process, thus allowing regular testing of both prototypes and finished production models. Cannondale's vice president of R&D explained the company's view of the R&D function and team sponsorships as follows: "Most bike companies view racing as a marketing tool, and while we enjoy the exposure the team provides, for us it's primarily a research and development tool. That's why we continue to support racing so aggressively. We make high-end, high-performance bicycles and we use the athletes' feedback to bring fresh innovations to our bikes. That's why we partially fund the team from our R&D budget, and why you'll always find more Cannondale engineers than marketing people at the races."[11] This collaboration, combined with the racing experience of its engineering staff, produced revisions, new designs, and new product ideas. The company had spent more than $20 million on research and development between 1997 and 1999 and held 35 U.S. patents related to various products, processes, and designs.

Cannondale had developed several proprietary suspension systems and enhancements. Its HeadShok incorporated the suspension and steering mechanisms into one unit built into the head tube of the bicycle. This design provided more accurate steering control than other front-suspension models and also allowed easy

---

[11]Cannondale press release, www.cannondale.com/bikepres/19981204.html.

adjustability while riding. Cannondale's HeadShok line included 14 models in 2000 and was highlighted by its new Lefty fork, which featured a telescoping blade that reduced weight while delivering 100 millimeters of travel. The Lefty had a distinctive look because of its single fork, which extended down the left side of the bicycle's front wheel.

To ensure structural integrity of its designs, an experimental stress and analysis laboratory was used to collect data on stresses placed on products during actual riding conditions. This information was analyzed and incorporated into the design of new products through its computer-aided design system. In addition, stress analysis testing was conducted during production to verify conformance to design specifications.

International Operations

Cannondale entered the international market in 1989 when it established a European subsidiary, Cannondale Europe, in the Netherlands. Although Cannondale Europe assembled bikes, using imported parts and frames from Cannondale's U.S. facility, it was primarily a selling and distribution organization that reached all of Western Europe directly and served Eastern Europe through distributors. The company sold its bicycles and accessories directly to approximately 1,400 dealers in Austria, Belgium, Denmark, Finland, Germany, Italy, Ireland, Luxembourg, the Netherlands, Norway, Spain, Sweden, Switzerland, and the United Kingdom. Sales growth in Europe, where cycling was second only to soccer in popularity among sports, had averaged a compound growth rate of 12.4 percent between 1993 and 1999.

Cannondale Japan was established in 1992. This subsidiary imported fully assembled bikes and was primarily a selling organization. The company sold bicycles and accessories directly to 300 retailers in Japan and sold accessories only to an additional 27 Japanese retailers. Cannondale's penetration of the Japanese market was estimated to be below 1 percent.

Cannondale Australia was established in 1996 when Cannondale purchased the assets of Beaushan Trading Party Limited. Cannondale's Australian subsidiary imported fully assembled bicycles and a full line of accessories and sold them in Australia and New Zealand to approximately 200 retailers. Exhibit 6 presents Cannondale's net sales contribution and value of identifiable assets by geographic area.

EXHIBIT 6   Selected Financial Data for Cannondale Corporation, by Geographic Area, 1997–99 (In Millions)

Source: Cannondale Corporation 1999 10-K.

	1999	1998	1997
Net sales			
United States	$ 72,413	$ 75,193	$ 80,542
Germany	26,639	25,382	23,569
Other European countries	59,008	52,603	43,478
All other countries	18,759	18,318	14,907
	$176,819	$171,496	$162,496
Identifiable assets			
United States	$54,798	$37,937	$21,905
Netherlands	2,886	3,141	2,949
All other countries	449	380	522
	$58,133	$41,458	$25,376

CANNONDALE'S PRODUCT LINE

Bicycles

In 2000, Cannondale offered 71 models of bicycles, all of which except its carbon-fiber Raven model featured aluminum frames. Cannondale's full-suspension mountain bikes (Super V Raven, Super V, Freeride, and Jekyll) featured front and rear suspension to allow for greater control and comfort at high speeds without sacrificing light frame weight. Cannondale's new Jekyll models included a distinctly different frame design that allowed the geometry of the bike to be customized to the rider's preference by dialing in the head angle and the bottom bracket height. The Jekyll also used the company's new HeadShok Lefty fork that had three times the torsional stiffness of other top forks and weighed just 3.7 pounds. The Jekyll was chosen as *Mountain Biking* magazine's 2000 "Bike of the Year" in its March 2000 issue.

Cannondale's Raven mountain bike was equally innovative. The Raven's frame was made from a carbon composite skin that was stretched over a magnesium spine. The bare frame weighed only 4.7 pounds yet was as rigid as Cannondale's aluminum-frame bicycles. The bike was equipped with Cannondale's HeadShok Lefty fork set and CODA hubs, crank, pedals, saddle, and brakes. The Raven was listed among the four most innovative products, discoveries, or technologies of 1999 by *Popular Science*. The company also offered a variety of front-suspension and rigid-frame mountain bikes among its product line. Cannondale's Smooth Riding Bicycle (SRB) line of mountain bikes was introduced in 1998 and used a mountain bike frame but was outfitted with a wider saddle and tires that were suitable for on-road or off-road use. The SRB also had a more upright riding position that made casual riding more comfortable than a typical mountain bike position. In describing the SRB's place in Cannondale's product line, the company's bicycle product manager said, "Not everyone wants to thrash singletrack or dice it up in the pelotron. But just because a customer wants a more recreational-style bike doesn't mean they want it to be heavy or of poor quality."[12]

Cannondale offered a number of hybrid and comfort bikes to appeal to the cyclist who wanted to cruise around town, get aerobic exercise, commute to work, or occasionally ride off-road trails. Cannondale's comfort bikes were available in full-suspension, front-suspension, or rigid-frame models. Hybrid models were equipped with either front-suspension or rigid frames. Cannondale offered cyclocross bikes for competition in mixed off-road and obstacle races and multisport bikes designed for triathlon and duathlon events.

Cannondale's high-performance road-racing bikes had steep frame angles and a short wheelbase for nimble handling and were equipped with either a front-suspension or rigid frame. In 1999 Cannondale was selected as one of the "Top 12 Road Bikes of All Time" by *Cycle Sport*, a magazine devoted to European road racing. The company's touring bikes included many of the performance features of its other models, but with a longer wheelbase that provided stability when riders were carrying additional gear for camping and touring. Cannondale's flexible manufacturing techniques allowed for small production runs of specialty bicycles such as tandem bikes, which were produced in both mountain bike and road-racing models. Cannondale's product line by category for 2000 is shown in Exhibit 7.

Bicycle Accessories

The accessory line helped the company to capitalize more fully on its distribution channels' capability and, at the same time, build brand-name recognition. As with bicycles, Cannondale sought to differentiate its accessories through innovation.

---

[12]Ibid.

EXHIBIT 7   **Cannondale's Number of Models in Each Bicycle Category for 2000**

Source: Cannondale Corporation 1999 10-K.

Bicycle Category	Number of Models
Mountain bikes	
Full suspension	11
Front suspension	13
Nonsuspended	3
Road bikes	
Front suspension	3
Nonsuspended	15
Multisport recreational	2
Hybrid	7
Comfort	7
Specialty	
Tandem	5
Touring	3
Cyclocross	2
Total	71

- *Packs and bags*—Cannondale offered a variety of bags and panniers (bags mounted on the sides of the wheels for touring): mountain bike bags; lightweight, moderate-capacity road bike bags; and large capacity touring bags. The company also made fanny packs, duffels, and a backpack designed specifically for cyclists. The patented Seat Cleat bag attachment was honored by *Industrial Design* magazine for its design innovation.

- *Apparel and footwear*—Cannondale offered a complete line of men's and women's cycling apparel, including such garments as shorts, jerseys, jackets, and skinsuits. The company's line consisted of four lines: Vertex, a high-performance, competition-level line; HpX, a versatile line of performance-oriented apparel for riders of all abilities; Terra, a more loosely cut line for off-road riding; and a women's Sport line of tailored, form-fitting garments. Some Cannondale apparel was made from its proprietary Micro-C fabric that forced moisture away from the body. Cannondale's Arago clipless compatible mountain biking shoe was very lightweight and contoured to the foot yet stiff enough to efficiently transfer leg energy to the pedal and crank.

- *Components*—Cannondale's proprietary HeadShok front-suspension forks were an important point of differentiation from other bicycle manufacturers, which virtually all used the same brand of forks produced by one of two independent suppliers. Most of the company's HeadShok forks functioned with the bicycle's frame as part of an integrated system, but the 2000 model HeadShok Lefty was a single-legged suspension system that could be mounted on Cannondale frames or other brands of frames. The Lefty had been recognized for its innovative design by such publications as *Design News, Popular Mechanics,* and the *New York Times.*

In 1994 Cannondale began sales of CODA components—featuring brakes, handlebars, bar-ends, seat binders, grips, cranksets, and hubs—and began using these components on certain models of its bikes. The company focused its R&D efforts on developing products superior to or more cost-effective than those available from other parts manufacturers. Cannondale's proprietary components like its CODA Competition suspension seatpost not only helped differentiate the company's bikes from brands that used similar components but also provided an additional source of revenue from aftermarket retail sales.

- *Other accessories*—Cannondale's other accessories included tools, pumps, water bottles, and bicycle trailers manufactured by third parties and sold under the Cannondale brand name.

CANNONDALE'S DIVERSIFICATION INTO MOTORCYCLES

In February 1998 Cannondale founder and CEO Joe Montgomery announced that the company would transfer its bicycle frame design and production skills to the off-road motorcycle industry. Cannondale said that it would bring at least three design innovations to the $700 million market for dirt bikes. Cannondale's new motorcycle would have a radical new engine design, include a unique single-pivot swingarm rear suspension, and be constructed of large-diameter aluminum tubing that would provide greater frame stiffness and lighter weight than a steel frame. Many motorcycle industry observers believed that Cannondale could deliver on its promise to bring innovations to the industry. The publisher of *Motocross Action Magazine* cautioned skeptics, "Don't discount the bicycle manufacturer's ability to compete in the motorcycle world. Today's mountain bikes far exceed motorcycles in the use of creative metallurgy, CAD-CAM frame design, innovative suspension systems, in the case of Cannondale, an American production facility that can easily produce a high-end product."[13]

MX400 engine innovations included a liquid-cooled, reversed cylinder head and innovative air intake design, an electric starter, and fuel injection. Cannondale designers said that the reverse cylinder head allowed the engine to have a more upright placement and a lower center of gravity that would aid in the motorcycle's off-road handling. Also, the reverse head allowed the air intake to face the front of the bike and the exhaust to face the rear, away from the water-cooled engine's radiator. The MX400's forward air intake was built into the steering head of the motorcycle's frame and helped supply a flow of debris-free cool air needed for greater power output and a wider powerband. The long air intake also improved low-speed throttle response. The electric starter feature was already available on almost all street bikes but was not usually found on dirt bikes. Cannondale management believed that the electric starter would be a convenience feature that motocrossers would appreciate—starting a dirt bike often took a considerable amount of strenuous kicking because of the very high compression single-cylinder engine designs. The MX400's fuel injection system that provided better throttle response and less maintenance than a carburetor was expected to take much of the engine-failure-related frustration out of motocross.

The MX400's use of fuel injection also allowed Cannondale's design team to create a rear suspension where the shock absorber was positioned at the optimal angle because there was no carburetor blocking the way. The rear suspension was a unique single-pivot linkless design that required less maintenance and provided greater rigidity than traditional motorcycle rear-suspension systems. The entire MX400 frame was built from Cannondale's trademark large-diameter stiff aluminum tubing and was designed to keep the motorcycle's center of gravity low. Commenting on the company's use of large-diameter aluminum tubing and a single-pivot swingarm, Can-

---

[13]"Bicycle-Maker Cannondale to Unveil New Motorcycle at Indianapolis Trade Show," PR Newswire, February 12, 1999.

nondale's director of marketing said, "Flex resistance is every bit as critical to the performance of a motorcycle frame as it is to the performance of a bicycle frame. Whether it's a bicycle or a motorcycle, you want to minimize side-to-side flex in order to preserve steering precision and stability. Wimpy frames and rear suspensions with long, flexible, linkages can't deliver the kind of handling you need in a high-performance vehicle."[14]

By summer 1998 Cannondale began testing 11 different prototypes of the MX400's new engine and frame. The MX400's final test came in November 1999 when the motorcycle took first place in its racing debut. The MX400 won two 5-lap races on a small 1.25-mile track located near Cannondale's Bedford, Pennsylvania, production facility. The MX400 won both races by more than a minute. The MX400 was named *Dirt Rider* magazine's "Bike of the Year" in late 1999. In reviewing the bike's design innovations, the magazine's editor said, "The MX400 looks more like a high-dollar project from a secret division of a major automobile manufacturer than a first attempt from a leader in the pedal power industry."[15] A *Dirt Action* writer concurred with *Dirt Rider*'s assessment of the new Cannondale motorcycle: "The MX400 contains enough innovation to make everything else with knobbies appear quaintly antique. The other manufacturers are going to hate this bike, because it forces them to move motocross machines into a new technological era."[16] The motorcycle was scheduled for a summer 1999 launch, but unforeseen production problems had delayed the MX400's shipment to Cannondale's network of 159 independent motorcycle dealers in 38 states to the spring of 2000. In January 2000 Cannondale's orders for its new MX400 had exceeded its projected sales forecast by more than 80 percent. Cannondale management planned to capitalize on the initial success of the MX400 with the unveiling of several additional motorcycles at the motorcycle industry's 2000 trade show held in Indianapolis, Indiana.

[14]Cannondale press release, www.cannondalemotorcycle.com/press/19980501.html.
[15]As quoted in Cannondale's 1999 annual report.
[16]Ibid.

Case **12**

Callaway Golf Company

John E. Gamble
University of South Alabama

As Ely Callaway walked through the sea of drivers, irons, putters, golf apparel, golf bags, and training devices displayed at the 2000 PGA Merchandise Show in Orlando, Florida, and toward Callaway Golf Company's booth, he noted that the eyes cast toward him seemed to express a greater sense of anticipation and curiosity than usual. As one of the most recognizable figures in the golf equipment industry, he had grown accustomed to his celebrity status among the golfing world and was aware that both rivals and retailers alike anxiously awaited the new products his company typically launched at the industry's premier annual trade show. However, the drama and suspense surrounding Callaway's new products at the February 2000 show were very different from usual. Callaway had gone ahead and introduced its innovative Big Bertha X-14 irons and Big Bertha Steelhead Plus metal woods in January. The PGA Merchandise Show had been saved for the introduction of the company's highly touted and much-anticipated Callaway golf ball.

Callaway Golf Company had become the leader in the golf equipment industry by developing technologically advanced golf clubs that compensated for the poor swing characteristics of most amateur golfers. During a golf swing, the clubhead travels in an arc around the golfer's body, making contact with the ball for 300 to 500 milliseconds. During this very brief period of contact, inertia is transferred from the clubhead to the ball, and the ball is propelled forward at a speed of up to 150 miles per hour. There are an infinite number of variations in a golfer's swing that can alter the swing path, causing the clubhead to strike the ball not squarely but somewhat off-center, at an angle. The more that a golfer's swing path deviates from square contact with the ball, the greater the loss of accuracy and distance. A golfer loses approximately 12.5 yards of distance for every millimeter that the ball is struck off the clubhead's center.

Ely Callaway, the founder of Callaway Golf Company, understood the importance of the physics of golf, so much so that he made the phrase, "You can't argue with physics," an early company slogan. Callaway Golf revolutionized the golf industry in 1990 by introducing an oversized clubhead called the Big Bertha that was more forgiving of golfers' swing imperfections. A Callaway executive stated in a 1995 *Fortune* interview that the company's objective was to design a club that would allow golfers to "miss [the center of the clubhead] by an inch" and still achieve distance and accuracy.

The company's high-tech golf clubs became so popular with golfers in the 1990s that Callaway Golf's revenues and profits grew by 1,239 percent and 1,907 percent, respectively, between 1991 and year-end 1996. With the company's competitive position securely rooted and a line of innovative new clubs ready for a 1997 launch, Ely Callaway retired as CEO in mid-1996 and turned to Callaway Golf Company president Donald Dye to become the new CEO. Soon after Ely Callaway's retirement, Callaway Golf Company's fortunes reversed due to a variety of factors, including the Asian financial crisis, poor global weather conditions, strategic miscues on the part of Callaway's executives, and the introduction of innovative clubs by rivals. The reversal led to nearly an 18 percent sales decline in 1998. Callaway Golf also broke its string of 24 consecutive quarters of growth in net income in early 1998 and went on to record a net loss of $26.5 million for the entire 1998 fiscal year.

Ely Callaway returned as CEO in November 1998 to launch a vast turnaround effort that included the development of new models of golf clubs and a $54.2 million restructuring program, which brought a number of operational improvements and cost-reduction initiatives. Callaway Golf Company returned to profitability and recaptured a great deal of its lost market share in 1999, but on February 4, 2000, the entire golf industry watched intently as Ely Callaway launched the company's new Rule 35 golf ball. Callaway's entry into the golf ball market had been vigilantly anticipated since mid-1996 when Ely Callaway announced the formation of the Callaway Golf Ball Company, and was considered by many industry participants to be the biggest event in the golf equipment industry since the debut of the Big Bertha. Callaway's managers and investors expected the entry to become a catalyst for the company's future growth. Exhibit 1 presents a summary of Callaway Golf Company's financial performance between 1989 and 1999.

Company History

When Ely (rhymes with *feely*) Reeves Callaway Jr. graduated from Emory University in Atlanta, his father said, "Don't go to work for the family."[1] Ely Callaway Sr. and almost everyone else in La Grange, Georgia, worked for the younger Callaway's uncle, Fuller Callaway. Fuller Callaway owned a number of farms, 23 cotton mills, the local bank, and the local department store. Heeding his father's advice, Ely Callaway Jr. decided to join the army just prior to World War II. By the age of 24, he had achieved the rank of major and had become one of the army's top five procurement officers responsible for purchasing cotton clothing for the U.S. armed forces. At the peak of World War II, Callaway's apparel procurement division of the U.S. Army purchased 70 percent of all cotton clothing manufactured by the U.S. apparel industry.

After the war, Callaway was hired as a sales representative with textile manufacturer Deering, Millikin & Company. He rose quickly through the company's ranks by selling textiles to the manufacturers from which he had purchased apparel while in the Army. Callaway was later hired away from Deering, Millikin by Textron, which subsequently sold its textile business to Burlington Industries—at that time the largest textile manufacturer in the world. Ely Callaway was promoted to president and director of Burlington Industries, but he left the company in 1973 after losing a bid to become its chief executive officer.

Callaway had long believed that Burlington Industries' success was a result of its ability to provide customers with unique, superior-quality products. When Callaway left Burlington and the textile industry, he decided to launch his own business

---

[1] *Inc.*, December 1994, p. 62.

374

EXHIBIT 1 Callaway Golf Company, Financial Summary, 1989–96 (In thousands, except per share amounts)

Source: Callaway Golf Company annual reports.

	1999	1998	1997	1996	1995	1994	1993	1992	1991	1990	1989
Net sales	$714,471	$697,621	$842,927	$678,512	$553,287	$448,729	$254,645	$132,058	$54,753	$21,518	$10,380
Pretax income	$85,497	($38,899)	$213,765	$195,595	$158,401	$129,405	$69,600	$33,175	$10,771	$2,185	$329
Estimated ranking within industry—sales	1st	1st	1st	1st	1st	1st	1st	2nd	6th	14th	23rd
Pretax income as a percent of sales	12%	–6%	25%	29%	29%	29%	27%	25%	20%	10%	3%
Net income	$55,322	($25,564)	$132,704	$122,337	$97,736	$78,022	$42,862[a]	$19,280	$6,416	$1,842	$329
Net income as a percent of sales	8%	–4%	16%	18%	18%	17%	17%[a]	15%	12%	9%	3%
Fully diluted earnings per share[c]	$0.78	($0.38)	$1.85	$1.73	$1.40	$1.07	$0.62	$0.32	$0.11	$0.04	$0.01
Shareholders' equity	$499,934	$453,096	$481,425	$362,267	$224,934	$186,414	$116,577	$49,750	$15,227	$8,718	$6,424
Market capitalization at Dec. 31	$1,349,595	$769,725	$2,120,813	$2,094,588	$1,604,741	$1,127,823	$901,910	$245,254	—[b]	—[b]	—[b]

[a]Includes cumulative effect of an accounting change of $1,658,000.

[b]The company's stock was not publicly traded until February 1992.

[c]Adjusted for all stock splits through February 10, 1995, not adjusted for February 10, 1995, stock split.

founded on that same philosophy. In 1974 he established Callaway Vineyard and Winery outside of San Diego. The well-known northern California vineyards scoffed at Callaway's entry into the industry and predicted a rapid failure of the venture. Not only did Callaway have no experience running a winery but, additionally, no vineyard had ever been successful in the San Diego area. Ely Callaway understood the risks involved and was much better prepared to run a start-up vineyard than skeptics believed. He began by transplanting the very best grape vines from Italy to California and hired winemaking experts to manage the day-to-day operations of the vineyard. Callaway's strategy was to focus on a narrow segment of the wine market where competition with the established wineries was not as strong and barriers to entry were relatively low. Callaway Vineyard and Winery limited distribution of its products to exclusive restaurants that chose to stock only the highest-quality wines. The company made no attempt to distribute its high-quality wines through traditional retail channels. In 1981, Ely Callaway sold the company to Hiram Walker & Sons, Inc., for a $14 million profit.

In late 1982, Ely Callaway decided to enter the golf club industry and, once again, apply his concept of "providing a product that is demonstrably superior to what's available in significant ways and, most importantly, pleasingly different."[2] Callaway purchased Hickory Stick USA, a manufacturer and marketer of replicas of old-fashioned hickory-shafted clubs, for $400,000. From the outset, Callaway grasped the limitations of the company's hickory-shafted product line and realized that the company would have to extend its offerings beyond replicas of antique golf clubs to provide an acceptable return on his investment.

Callaway noticed that most golf equipment had changed very little since the 1920s and believed that many golfers would purchase technologically advanced golf equipment if it would improve their game. Ely Callaway and Richard C. Helmstetter—Callaway Golf's senior executive vice president and chief club designer—put together a team of five aerospace and metallurgical engineers to develop the S2H2 (short, straight, hollow hosel) line of irons. The S2H2 line was introduced in 1988 and was well received by golfers. The following year the company introduced S2H2 traditional-sized metal woods, and in 1990 it introduced the Big Bertha driver—named after the World War I German long-distance cannon. The Big Bertha was revolutionary in that it was much larger than conventional woods and lacked a hosel so that the weight could be better distributed throughout the clubhead. This innovative design gave the clubhead a larger sweet spot, which allowed a player to mis-hit or strike the golf ball off-center of the clubhead and not suffer much loss of distance or accuracy. By 1992 Big Bertha drivers were number one on the Senior PGA, the LPGA, and Hogan Tours. Callaway Golf Company became a public company on February 28, 1992. By year-end 1992 its annual revenues had doubled to $132 million, and by 1996 Callaway Golf had become the world's largest manufacturer and marketer of golf clubs, with annual sales of more than $678 million.

ELY CALLAWAY'S 1996 RETIREMENT AND THE FORMATION OF THE CALLAWAY GOLF BALL COMPANY

Callaway Golf continued to lead the golf equipment industry through the mid-1990s with innovative new lines of clubs. The company also introduced a line of golf apparel in 1996 that was available to golfers through an exclusive licensing agreement with Nordstrom. In May 1996, Ely Callaway announced that even though he would remain involved in the promotion of the Callaway Golf products, he was transferring

---

[2]*Business Week*, September 16, 1991, p. 71.

his position as chief executive officer to the company's president, Donald Dye. Dye had been a business associate of Ely Callaway since 1974, when Callaway was in the wine business. Ely Callaway simultaneously announced that he and Charles Yash, Taylor Made Golf Company's CEO and president, would launch Callaway Golf Ball Company as a subsidiary of Callaway Golf. "We believe that there is a good and reasonable opportunity for Callaway Golf Ball Company, in due time, to create, produce and merchandise a golf ball that will be demonstrably superior to, and pleasingly different from, any other golf ball we know of," said Callaway.[3] Yash, who had been the general manager of Spalding's golf ball business and who turned around Taylor Made with the introduction of the Burner Bubble driver, resigned his post at Taylor Made to become president and CEO of the new venture. Upon announcing his decision to work with Callaway, Yash commented, "This is an exciting and most unusual opportunity to develop a new and important golf ball franchise with Ely Callaway for Callaway Golf Company. As a competitor, I have been in awe of Callaway's accomplishments. As his partner, I look forward to the exciting opportunities and challenges Ely and I are sure to find in this new venture."[4]

CALLAWAY GOLF COMPANY'S 1998 PERFORMANCE AND THE RETURN OF ELY CALLAWAY AS CEO

A variety of events occurred shortly after Ely Callaway's retirement that resulted in Callaway Golf's loss of market share in fairway woods and its poor financial and market performance in 1998. The U.S. and international markets for golf clubs moved from rapid growth to maturity during 1997 and 1998 after a large percentage of avid golfers purchased titanium drivers and saw little reason to upgrade again until dramatic innovations were available. Global market maturity was compounded by the Asian financial crisis that began in late 1997 and made the export of U.S.-made products, especially expensive luxury goods like Callaway golf clubs, unaffordable for many Asians. Also, heavy global rainfall caused by El Niño contributed to an overall decline in the number of rounds played around the world in 1998. In addition, many club manufacturers believed that the United States Golf Association's (USGA) discussions during 1998 to limit innovations in golf club design caused many golfers to postpone club purchases. The USGA had considered a number of limitations on club design, but ultimately decided to bar only a "spring-like effect" in golf clubs. The USGA advised Callaway Golf that none of its products violated the new regulation.

The emergence of shallow-faced fairway woods had as much to do with Callaway's downturn as any other single event. Callaway had dominated the market for fairway woods since the early 1990s, when the Big Bertha line gained in popularity. By 1996 no other manufacturer came close to Callaway in building a loyal following among fairway woods customers. Even when Callaway users experimented with a rival's new driver, they frequently stayed with Callaway for their fairway woods. However, Callaway's dominance in fairway woods was severely challenged in 1997 when relatively unknown golf manufacturers Adams Golf and Orlimar Golf each heavily promoted a line of shallow-faced fairway woods that they claimed made it easier for golfers to hit a ball off the fairway or from a poor lie. The two challengers each ran a series of highly successful infomercials that demonstrated the clubs' performance and led to phenomenal sales growth for both companies. Adams' and Orlimar's success came more

---

[3]"Donald H. Dye Given CEO Duties at Callaway Golf Company." *Two-Ten Communications, Ltd.,* 1996. www.twoten.press.net:80/stories/96/05/13/headlines/appointments_callaway.html, February 6, 1997.

[4]"Keeping His Eye on the Ball," *ParValu Stock Update,* 1996. www.golfweb.com:80/gi/parvalu/updates/03.html, February 6, 1997.

or less directly at the expense of Callaway. No other golf club manufacturer sold large volumes of fairway woods, so when golfers purchased the new clubs offered by Adams and Orlimar, it was typically Callaway that lost sales and market share.

Callaway CEO Donald Dye took much of the blame for Callaway's failure to predict the popularity of shallow-faced woods and was also ultimately responsible for initiatives that took management's focus off of golf clubs. Under Dye, Callaway Golf began new ventures in golf course and driving range management, opened interactive golf sites, created a new player development project, and launched a golf publishing business with Nicholas Callaway, the youngest son of Ely Callaway and a successful publisher of tabletop books. After a record year in 1997, the company's financial and market performance suffered immensely during 1998. In October 1998, Donald Dye resigned as Callaway's CEO and Ely Callaway returned to rebuild the company.

Ely Callaway's first efforts on his return to active management at Callaway Golf were to "direct [the company's] resources—talent, energy, and money—in an ever-increasing degree toward the creation, design, production, sale and service of new and better products."[5] As part of his turnaround strategy, Ely Callaway also initiated a $54.2 million restructuring program that involved a number of cost-reduction actions and operational improvements. During 1997 and 1998 the company had built up a large inventory of older model clubs that were not sold before the latest clubs were shipped to retailers. Callaway management liquidated the inventory of older generation clubs to generate cash flow and improve the company's financial position. In addition, the company divested its interest in noncore businesses began under Dye and combined the administrative and manufacturing functions of Odyssey Golf and Callaway Golf. Callaway's business restructuring eliminated a variety of job responsibilities and thus resulted in the loss of 750 positions from all functional areas of the company. Callaway Golf Company's income statements for 1993 through 1999 are presented in Exhibit 2. Exhibit 3 presents the company's balance sheets for 1993–99. The company's market performance is graphed in Exhibit 4.

The Golf Equipment Industry

In 1999, more than 26 million Americans played golf. Of these, 5.4 million were considered avid golfers, playing more than 25 rounds of golf annually. The number of U.S. golfers was expected to grow 1 to 2 percent annually through 2010 as the baby boom generation aged and had more free time and disposable income. In 1999 the typical golfer was a 39-year-old male with a household income of $66,000 who played golf about twice a month. Many women, juniors, and senior citizens also enjoyed the sport. In 1999 there were 5.7 million women and 2.1 million junior golfers aged 12 to 17 in the United States. Seniors accounted for 25 percent of all U.S. golfers in 1999. The average golf score was 97 for men and 114 for women. Only 6 percent of men and 1 percent of women golfers regularly broke a score of 80. Exhibit 5 provides the number of U.S. golfers during various years between 1986 and 1999.

Golf was popular in developed countries worldwide—especially so in Asia, where there were over 3,500 courses and 16 million golfers. Most of Europe's 2 million-plus golfers resided in England, France, Germany, Scotland, Ireland, and Sweden. The sport was becoming popular in former Soviet-bloc countries—such as Croatia, Slovenia, the Czech Republic, Poland, and Russia—but was not expected to grow dramatically until the economies of those countries stabilized. Russia's first country club opened in Moscow in 1993; by 2000, it had 550 members, who had each paid a $28,000

[5]Callaway Golf Company 1998 annual report.

EXHIBIT 2 Callaway Golf Company, Income Statements, 1993–99 ($000, except per share amounts)

Source: Callaway Golf Company annual reports.

	1999	1998	1997	1996	1995	1994	1993
Net sales	$714,471	$697,621	$842,927	$678,512	$553,287	$448,729	$254,645
Cost of goods sold	376,405	401,607	400,127	317,353	270,125	208,906	115,458
Gross profit	338,086	296,014	442,800	361,159	283,162	239,823	139,187
Selling, general, and administrative expenses	224,336	245,070	191,313	155,177	120,201	106,913	
Research and development costs	34,002	36,848	30,298	16,154	8,577	6,380	3,653
Restructuring and transition costs	(181)	54,235	—	—	—	—	—
Litigation settlement	—	—	12,000	—	—	—	—
Income (loss) from operations	79,909	(40,139)	209,189	189,828	154,384	126,530	68,416
Interest & other income, net	9,182	3,911	4,586	5,804	4,038	2,879	1,184
Interest expense	(3,594)	(2,671)	(10)	(37)	(21)	(4)	—
Income before income taxes and cumulative effect of accounting change	85,497	(38,899)	213,765	195,595	158,401	129,405	69,600
Provision for income taxes (benefit)	30,175	(12,335)	81,061	73,258	60,665	51,383	28,396
Cumulative effect of accounting change	n/a	n/a	n/a	n/a	n/a	n/a	(1,658)
Net income	$55,322	($26,564)	$132,704	$122,337	$97,736	$78,022	$42,862
Primary earnings per share	$0.79	($0.38)	$1.94	$1.83	$1.47	$1.14	$0.62
Fully diluted earnings per share	$0.78	($0.38)	$1.85	$1.73	$1.40	$1.07	$0.60
Common equivalent shares	71,214	69,463	71,698	70,661	69,855	73,104	68,964

EXHIBIT 3 **Callaway Golf Company, Balance Sheets, 1993–99 ($000)**

Source: Callaway Golf Company annual reports.

	1999	1998	1997	1996	1995	1994	1993
Assets							
Current assets							
Cash and cash equivalents	$ 112,602	$ 45,618	$ 26,204	$ 108,457	$ 59,157	$ 54,356	$ 48,996
Accounts receivable, net	54,525	73,466	124,470	74,477	73,906	30,052	17,546
Inventories, net	97,938	149,192	97,094	98,333	51,584	74,151	29,029
Deferred taxes	32,558	51,029	23,810	25,948	22,688	25,596	13,859
Other current assets	13,122	4,310	10,208	4,298	2,370	3,235	2,036
Total current assets	310,472	323,606	281,786	311,513	209,705	187,390	111,466
Property, plant, and equipment, net	142,214	172,794	142,503	91,346	69,034	50,619	30,661
Other assets	120,143	127,779	112,141	25,569	11,236	5,613	2,233
Total assets	$ 616,783	$ 665,827	$ 561,714	$ 428,428	$ 289,975	$ 243,622	$ 144,360
Liabilities and shareholders' equity							
Current liabilities							
Accounts payable and accrued expenses	$ 46,664	$ 35,928	$ 30,063	$ 14,996	$ 26,894	$ 17,678	$ 11,949
Accrued employee compensation and benefits	21,126	11,083	14,262	16,195	10,680	9,364	6,104
Accrued warranty expense	36,105	35,815	28,059	27,303	23,769	18,182	9,730
Accrued restructuring cost	1,379	7,389	—	—	—	—	—
Income taxes payable	—	9,903	—	2,558	1,491	11,374	n/a
Total current liabilities	105,274	184,008	72,384	61,052	62,834	56,598	27,783
Long-term liabilities	11,575	18,823	7,905	5,109	2,207	610	n/a
Shareholders' equity							
Common stock	763	751	743	729	709	680	676
Paid-in-capital	307,329	258,015	337,403	278,669	214,846	75,022	60,398
Unearned compensation	(2,784)	(5,653)	(3,575)	(3,105)	(2,420)	(3,670)	(2,591)
Retained earnings	288,090	252,528	298,728	238,349	131,712	114,402	58,094
Less grantor stock trust*	(93,744)	(54,325)	(151,315)	(152,375)	(119,913)	—	—
Total shareholders' equity	499,934	453,096	481,425	362,267	224,934	186,414	116,577
Total liabilities and shareholders' equity	$616,783	$ 655,827	$ 561,714	$ 428,428	$ 289,975	$ 243,622	$ 144,360

*The sale of 5,300,000 shares to the grantor stock trust had no net impact to shareholders' equity. The shares in the GST may be used to fund the company's obligations with respect to one or more of the company's nonqualified employee benefit plans.

379

EXHIBIT 4 Monthly Performance of Callaway Golf Company's Stock Price,
1992–March 2000

(a) Trend in Callaway Golf Company's Common Stock Price

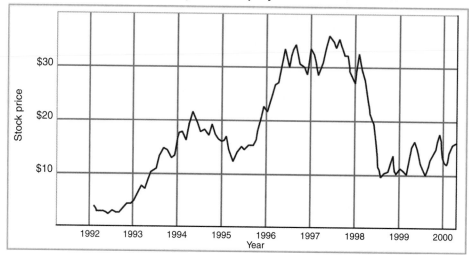

(b) Performance of Callaway Golf Company's Stock Price versus the S&P 500 Index

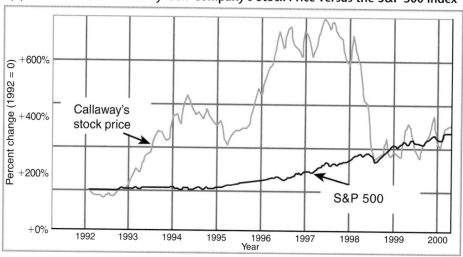

EXHIBIT 5 Number of U.S. Golfers, 1986, 1991, 1993, 1995, 1997, 1999

Source: National Golf Foundation.

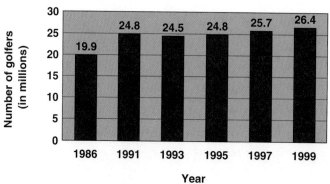

membership fee for the privilege to play the Robert Trent Jones–designed course. However, only 70 of the club's members were Russian. Some teaching professionals working in Russia projected that there could be 100,000 golfers in Russia by 2025, but in 2000 there were fewer than 500 Russians who could be called avid golfers.

The wholesale value of golf equipment sales in the United States had increased from $740 million in 1986 to over $2.7 billion in 1999. In 1999 the U.S. market for golf balls accounted for about 25 percent of the industry's wholesale sales. The wholesale value of the international golf ball market was estimated at $1.5 billion. Exhibit 6 provides wholesale sporting goods equipment sales for selected years during the 1986–99 period. The growth in golf equipment sales during the early 1990s was attributable not so much to an increase in the number of golfers as to the introduction of technologically advanced equipment offered by Callaway Golf and other manufacturers like Ping and Taylor Made. Many of these technological advances made the game much easier for beginners to learn than was possible with older equipment. Additionally, experienced players frequently looked for equipment that could help them improve their game. However, it was expected that in the early 2000s the sales of golf equipment would grow only modestly since most avid golfers had already upgraded their equipment and were unlikely to do so again unless major new innovations came about.

KEY TECHNOLOGICAL INNOVATIONS

The golfing industry had come up with four major innovations that made it easier for golfers to hit better shots and improve their scores: (1) perimeter weighting in the late 1960s, (2) metal woods in the early 1980s, (3) graphite shafts in the late 1980s, and (4) oversized clubheads in the early 1990s. Perimeter weighting came about due to the poor putting of Karsten Solheim, a General Electric mechanical engineer, who took up golf at the age of 47 in 1954. Solheim designed a putter for himself that he found provided more "feel" when he struck the ball. Solheim moved much of the clubhead weight to the heel and toe, leaving a cavity at the rear and center of the club. Perimeter-weighted or cavity-back clubs had a larger "sweet spot" because of a higher moment of inertia or resistance to twisting. The resistance to twisting reduced the gear effect of the clubhead and resulted in straighter, longer shots with irons. In addition to perimeter weighting, Karsten Solheim also developed the investment-casting manufacturing process. This process allowed clubheads to be formed from molds, rather than forged from steel—the traditional manufacturing process.

Solheim made his putters by hand from 1959 until 1967, when he left GE and founded Karsten Manufacturing. By the 1970s, Karsten was manufacturing a full line of perimeter-weighted putters and irons that carried the Ping brand name. Solheim

EXHIBIT 6 Wholesale Sales of Sporting Goods Equipment, 1986, 1993–99 (In millions of dollars)

Source: Sporting Goods Manufacturers Association, 1997–1999 State of the Industry Reports.

Type of Equipment	1999*	1998	1997	1996	1995	1994	1993	1986
Exercise	$ 3,635	$ 3,400	$ 3,180	$ 2,890	$ 2,510	$ 1,825	$ 1,755	$ 680
Golf	2,770	2,800	2,749	2,463	2,130	1,793	1,490	740
Camping	1,700	1,620	1,590	1,500	1,508	1,275	1,225	580
Baseball/softball	340	340	338	350	349	348	328	240
Soccer	230	220	208	200	185	175	155	90
Tennis	220	215	235	240	235	259	380	255
Total sports equipment	$17,805	$17,350	$17,064	$16,395	$15,379	$13,877	$12,433	$8,250

*Estimated

chose this name because of the sound the cavity-back clubhead made when it struck the ball. Karsten Manufacturing's line of Ping putters and irons was thought to be among the most technologically advanced throughout the 1980s and reigned as the market leader. Karsten Manufacturing was renamed Ping, Inc., in 1999. In 2000, over 95 percent of all irons and putters sold worldwide were perimeter-weighted.

Ping's investment-casting manufacturing process also made the manufacture of perimeter-weighted "metal woods" possible. Taylor Made designed the first metal wood which, like the perimeter-weighted irons, had the advantage of a larger sweet spot than traditional clubs. Although they actually had no wood components, metal woods were so named because it had been traditional to use wooden clubs for driving from the tee and for long fairway shots. The hollow metal head made it possible to move the weight to the heel and toe of the clubhead, as was done with perimeter-weighted irons. Conventional wood heads were made of solid persimmon and had a uniform weight distribution.

The characteristics of the golf club shaft affected a club's performance almost as much as the clubhead did. Distance and accuracy were largely a function of shaft characteristics. Weak or overly flexible shafts could torque as a result of the swinging action and the weight of the clubhead. The torquing of the shaft created a gear effect that resulted in a mis-hit golf ball. Additionally, the flex of the shaft had the ability to increase clubhead speed and improve accuracy. Shafts with greater flex at the tip or clubhead end were advantageous to high handicappers because they helped produce greater clubhead speed at the point of contact with the golf ball, caused the ball to have a higher trajectory, and promoted greater distance. Professional and low-handicap golfers preferred shafts that flexed a few inches higher or nearer the grip because a higher flex point produced added control of the shot.

Graphite shafts were introduced in 1969 by Shakespeare, but were not accepted by golfers because they flexed too much and overly dampened the feel of the club striking the ball. By the early 1990s, technological advances in graphite materials, shaft design, and production had eliminated the previous torsion problems, and graphite shafts quickly gained acceptance by both amateur and professional golfers. Shaft manufacturers were using aerospace technology to improve graphite shafts that had as many as 14 to 16 layers of composite materials (carbon fibers, Kevlar, boron, glass-fiber-reinforced epoxy resins, and synthetic fibers). In 1998, graphite shafts were used in 86 percent of drivers, 77 percent of fairway woods, and 46 percent of irons. Because of the higher prices commanded by graphite, the dollar volume of graphite shaft sales exceeded that of steel alloy shafts by a greater margin than the unit volume differential.

Callaway Golf was the first golf club manufacturer to actually increase the size of the hollow metal wood and make the size of the sweet spot bigger. The larger the clubhead, the bigger the sweet spot, but weight was the primary constraint in increasing clubhead size. If oversized clubheads were too heavy, golfers could not achieve as much speed as they could with lighter clubheads. Slower clubhead speeds resulted in shorter flight distances. The vice president of research and development for a golf club manufacturer described the challenge of trying to increase the size of metal wood clubheads as follows:

> The problem with a big driver is that you have to keep the total weight about the same as a normal-sized driver in order to give the same feel to the golfer. You can't build an overweight club or one that you can't swing at the same speed. A slightly bigger head pulls a little more drag through the air, but it's negligible. Making a bigger head is like blowing bubble gum. You have the same amount of gum but you've got to make a bigger bubble, so the metal walls will be thinner.[6]

[6]*Machine Design*, April 23, 1992, p. 32.

Companies experimented with a number of materials, including stainless steel, titanium, silicon aluminum carbide, and thermoplastics, to find a way of increasing clubhead size without adding weight to the clubhead or diminishing its structural integrity. By 1992, most manufacturers had discovered that titanium was the best material for oversized drivers because the material was 20 percent lighter and 40 percent stronger than stainless steel. By using titanium, club manufacturers were able to increase the size of oversized drivers by about 30 percent. A golf club design engineer explained why material selection was vital to the structural integrity of the clubhead:

> Keeping weight to a minimum is the single biggest aggravation. Once you have a shape you're comfortable with, the challenge is to design a driver that will meet your weight standards. Everybody wants to go bigger, bigger, and bigger in drivers, but as you go bigger, your wall gets thinner. You could make a driver three times the normal size, but it would be like tinfoil. It would fold up and crush on impact.[7]

During the late 1990s, innovators like Callaway Golf and Taylor Made began to use combinations of metals in the design of oversized metal woods and irons. In 1997 Callaway introduced a line of irons that were 85 percent titanium and 15 percent tungsten. A tungsten insert was placed directly at the center of the enlarged sweet spot of the titanium clubface to add weight to the portion of the clubhead that should actually strike the ball. The addition of tungsten to the clubhead concentrated 40 percent of the clubhead weight directly at the sweet spot and made it possible to create an oversized clubhead with a weight concentration designed to maximize the energy transfer from the clubhead to the ball. Taylor Made introduced tungsten-titanium oversized clubs shortly after Callaway's introduction of its tungsten-titanium Great Big Bertha irons. In 1998 Callaway and Taylor Made introduced tungsten-titanium woods and Orlimar boasted clubheads that were made from three different metals. Cleveland Golf introduced a four-metal oversized clubhead design in 1999. In 2000 all major golf club manufacturers had at least one oversized exotic metal driver with a graphite shaft in its product line.

COMPETITIVE RIVALRY IN THE GOLF EQUIPMENT INDUSTRY

For decades, the golf equipment industry had been dominated by Wilson Sporting Goods, MacGregor Golf, Inc., and Spalding Sporting Goods. All three companies were very conservative in their approach to new product development, sticking to lines of the standard steel-shafted, forged-steel clubs that had been popular since the 1920s. They were caught completely off guard by the success of companies like Ping, Taylor Made, and Callaway Golf. Amateur golfers readily accepted the technological advances offered by the new golf companies and the market shares of the established brands of the three traditional industry leaders quickly eroded. An executive for one of the new manufacturers stated that Wilson's inability to introduce innovative products of its own had resulted in the company's market share diminishing to a "rounding error."[8]

In the late 1980s as many as 20 manufacturers accounted for about 80 percent of all golf equipment sales, but by 1997 the industry had already consolidated to the point where 6 companies commanded over 80 percent of the market for golf equipment. It was estimated that, of the more than 350 manufacturers in existence, only those 6 were profitable. During the late 1990s industry consolidation stimulated attrition as many smaller club manufacturers exited the industry. Even

[7]Ibid.

[8]*Fortune,* June 12, 1995, p. 110.

though longtime industry participants like Wilson, MacGregor, and Spalding were still in business and had attempted to introduce technologically advanced lines of clubs, they had all largely failed in regaining lost market share.

Manufacturing

Most club makers' manufacturing activities were restricted to club assembly, since clubhead production was contracted out to investment casting houses and shafts and grips were usually purchased from third-party suppliers. Most golf club companies offered two to four general models of irons and woods built around proprietary heads that were internally developed. Each clubhead model line was equipped with shafts of varying flex that were either proprietary designs or standard models purchased from shaft manufacturers. Grip manufacturers such as Eaton/Golf Pride and Lamkin offered a number of models, but club manufacturers usually chose to purchase a limited variety of grips from a single source, since most golfers did not have strong preferences for one brand of grip over another. Some club manufacturers used custom grips bearing the company name and logo, while others used standard grips.

The brand and type of shaft had a relatively important influence over golfers' perceptions of club quality and performance. Most golfers had a strong preference for either steel or graphite and some preference for certain manufacturers. True Temper had one of the best reputations in steel shafts and had dominated that segment of the industry ever since it introduced the steel shaft in 1924. Most club manufacturers purchased standard steel shafts from a sole supplier rather than developing proprietary steel shafts or using a multiple sourcing strategy.

As the 1990s progressed, a larger and larger percentage of golfers' preferences shifted to graphite shafts for both drivers and irons. Graphite shaft manufacturers could easily produce a broad line of shafts with varying degrees of flex at a number of flexpoints. Many golfers were persuaded that the unique characteristics of graphite contributed to game improvement. Companies such as Aldila, United Sports Technologies, HST, Unifiber, and Graman USA were competent manufacturers of high-quality graphite shafts and had made it difficult for True Temper to build a dominant market share in the graphite segment as it had done in steel.

Some companies such as Callaway Golf independently designed their shafts, while others collaborated with shaft manufacturers to develop proprietary graphite shafts. Taylor Made's innovative "bubble shaft" was co-designed and manufactured by respected graphite shaft producer HST. Cobra Golf was the only golf manufacturer to vertically integrate into shaft production and produce 100 percent of its shafts in-house. Cobra Golf was acquired by American Brands (renamed Fortune Brands in 1998 when its cigarette business was divested), which also owned Foot-Joy (a leading maker of golf shoes) and Titleist (the maker of the most popular brand of golf balls and also a producer of golf clubs and other golf equipment). Cobra's golf club shaft facilities were used to produce a portion of the shafts needed for Fortune's Titleist golf clubs.

Marketing

As television networks aired increasing numbers of professional golf tournaments, endorsements by professional golfers started to play a major role in the marketing of golf equipment. The dollar volume of player endorsements was estimated to be three times greater than the projected total Professional Golfers Association (PGA) year 2000 prize money payout of $132 million.

Professional golfer endorsements had been instrumental in the success of some fledgling companies. In 1990, Cobra Golf offered Greg Norman shares of stock and

Australian distribution rights to the new company's products in return for the golfer's use and endorsement of Cobra equipment. Norman accepted the offer and, after the company went public, sold 450,000 Cobra shares for $12 million. Norman received an additional $30 million from the sale of his remaining Cobra Golf shares when American Brands acquired Cobra in 1996. Norman's endorsement of Cobra golf clubs helped make Cobra Golf an almost immediately identifiable brand in the golf equipment industry and an attractive acquisition target. Fortune Brand's belief in endorsements led the company to offer Tiger Woods a $20 million five-year contract upon his professional debut in 1996 to endorse Titleist drivers, irons, and balls. Woods's endorsement of the company's newly designed lines of clubs resurrected the brand's presence in clubs, particularly so in woods, where its new 975D driver became one of the top-selling clubs of 1999. Prior to Woods's endorsement of Titleist clubs, the company was primarily thought of as a golf ball company.

Tiger Woods's entry into the PGA set a new standard for endorsement contracts—the $20 million Woods received in 1996 for endorsing Titleist golf clubs and balls was surpassed by the $40 million he received for endorsing Nike apparel and footwear for a five-year period. In 1999 Woods signed a five-year renewal with Nike for $90 million. Tiger Woods also signed a two-year, $10 to 15 million deal with Buick to appear in Buick ads and carry the Buick logo on his golf bag. Woods's five-year renewal with Titleist provided a $2 million annual fee to use Titleist balls and clubs in PGA tournaments; this contract was primarily a defensive measure for Fortune Brands since Woods's Nike and Buick contracts prevented him from appearing in Titleist advertisements or displaying the Titleist logo on his golf bag. Tiger Woods's success in landing large endorsement contracts had spilled over to other professional golfers to some degree, but in 2000 no other golfer had been able to garner contracts in the same range as those signed by Woods.

Most pro-line or high-quality golf equipment manufacturers distributed their products through on-course pro shops and a select number of off-course pro shops, such as Edwin Watts and Nevada Bob's. The off-course pro shops were quickly accounting for the largest portion of retail golf club sales because they carried a wider variety of brands and marketed more aggressively than on-course shops. Most on-course pro shops sold only to members and carried few clubs since their members purchased golf clubs less frequently than apparel and footwear. In 1997 on-course pro shops carried, on average, 4 brands of drivers, 4 brands of irons, and 6 brands of putters, while off-course pro shops carried, on average, 12 brands of drivers, 18 brands of irons, and 17 brands of putters.

Pro-line manufacturers chose to limit their channels of distribution to on-course and off-course pro shops because they believed that PGA professionals had the training necessary to properly match equipment to the customer. Manufacturers such as Taylor Made, Callaway, and Ping all provided the pro shops with inexpensive devices that gave an estimate of the golfer's swing characteristics. The pro could take the readings from these devices and then custom-fit the golfer with the proper clubs. Custom fitting could be done more precisely with more expensive, specialized computer equipment, but most pro shops had not invested in the new technology. The Sportech Swing Analyzer aided in custom fitting by recording 12 swing variables, such as clubhead speed and path, club face angle at impact, ball position, the golfer's weight distribution, ball flight pattern, and ball flight distance. The pro could use the fit data provided by the Swing Analyzer to select the appropriate club for the customer. Golf equipment manufacturers expected a larger percentage of golfers to demand more precise custom fitting from retailers in the future.

Pro shops generally chose to stock only pro-line equipment and did not carry less expensive, less technologically advanced equipment. Low-end manufacturers such as Spalding, MacGregor, and Dunlop sold their products mainly through discounters, mass merchandisers, and large sporting goods stores. These retailers had no custom-fitting capabilities and rarely had sales personnel who were knowledgeable about the performance features of the different brands and models of golf equipment carried in the store. The appeal of such retail outlets was low price, and they mainly attracted beginning golfers and occasional golfers who were unwilling to invest in more expensive equipment.

Callaway Golf Company

Callaway Golf Company's competitive strategy was rooted in Ely Callaway's philosophy that true long-term success comes from innovative products that are "demonstrably superior to, and pleasingly different from" the products offered by industry rivals. Ely Callaway believed that due to the difficulty of the game of golf (there was tremendous room for variation in *each* swing of the club and for off-center contact with the ball), serious golfers would be willing to invest in high-quality, premium-priced equipment, like the Big Bertha driver and the titanium Great Big Bertha driver, if such clubs could improve their game by being more forgiving of a less-than-optimum swing. Since the introduction of Callaway's S2H2 line of irons in 1988, the company had sought to develop, manufacture, and market the most technologically advanced golf clubs available. In addition, Richard Helmstetter and his team of engineers sought quantum leaps in club performance, rather than incremental improvements, with each new line of clubs introduced by the company.

CALLAWAY'S "DEMONSTRABLY SUPERIOR AND PLEASINGLY DIFFERENT" VALUE CHAIN

Callaway Golf Company's ability to develop "demonstrably superior and pleasingly different" golf clubs was a result of activities performed by the company throughout its value chain. Callaway's differentiation was achieved through both its unique value chain and through its ability to out-execute its rivals where value chain similarities existed.

Product Development and the Helmstetter Test Center

When Ely Callaway purchased Hickory Stick USA he believed strongly that developing "demonstrably superior and pleasingly different" golf clubs would be more closely related to the company's physics-oriented R&D than would a focus on cosmetics. Richard Helmstetter and his engineering team were critical to the execution of Callaway's competitive strategy. As of 2000 Callaway Golf had consistently outspent its rivals on R&D. In 1999 alone, the company spent $27 million on research and development related to its golf club business—more than most of its key rivals' combined R&D budgets. The company's R&D efforts allowed it to continually beat its competitors to the market with new innovations. Callaway's engineers developed the first oversize driver in 1990, were the first to make clubheads even larger by using titanium, and were the first to use a combination of materials (titanium and tungsten) in clubhead design.

Callaway Golf opened the Richard C. Helmstetter Test Center in 1994 to support its research and product development efforts. The test center was located about a mile from Callaway's main campus and included a laboratory and a golfing area. The test center laboratory was home to Helmstetter's engineers, who worked both on teams and individually to develop new models of clubheads and shafts. Callaway's products were designed on powerful workstations running computer-aided design (CAD) software similar to that used in the aerospace industry. The CAD software allowed engineers not only to design new clubheads and shafts but also to conduct aerodynamic and strength testing in a simulated environment. Actual physical models could be created from the computer-generated images through the use of numerically controlled systems. The center's "destruction and durability" laboratory used robots and air cannons to establish minimum thresholds of strength and durability for prototypes of new models of clubheads and shafts.

The club-fitting and specifications area of the test center used the company's Callaway Performance Analysis System to match equipment to a golfer's swing characteristics. The internally developed proprietary video and computer system used stereo imaging techniques to capture a sequence of eight multiple exposures of the clubhead and ball at various time intervals immediately before and after a golfer hit the ball into a net approximately 10 feet from where it was struck. Callaway's proprietary computer software analyzed the video images of the clubhead's approach to the ball and the ball's rotational patterns over its first few feet of flight to make a variety of calculations needed to project the ball's ultimate path. The projected path was displayed on a six-foot video screen that showed the ball's flight along the 18th fairway at Pebble Beach. The computer system also recorded the clubhead speed, ball velocity, side spin, back spin, attack angle, and launch angle to calculate the efficiency rating, carry, roll, total distance, and dispersion (deviation from a straight path). All of these statistics were projected on the screen, along with the image of ball's flight down the fairway. The equipment allowed the company to build a set of clubs for the touring professional that had the perfect swing weight, frequency, loft, lie, and length to maximize distance and accuracy.

The Helmstetter Test Center's golfing area was an 8.1-acre outdoor testing facility that included three putting and chipping greens, a deep pot bunker, a shallow fairway bunker, and a 310-yard fairway that was 80 yards wide at its narrowest point. Sensors located along the fairway recorded the distance and dispersion of any ball landing in the test area. Atmospheric conditions, such as wind speed, direction, temperature, barometric pressure, humidity, and dew point were recorded by three weather stations located around the test site. The facility also included an artificial tee box and green that accurately simulated a real green. Ball reaction on the simulated green was almost identical to that on the other three greens and allowed the company to continue testing while the natural test site was being irrigated or mowed.

The Helmstetter Test Center had two primary uses: It provided an ideal place to custom-fit clubs for the touring pros who used Callaway equipment, and it allowed Callaway R&D staff to test new products during their developmental stage. Once a professional's new clubs were fitted using the video and computer capabilities of the Callaway Performance Analysis System, the touring pro could then use the golfing area to hit balls and fine-tune his or her clubs by requesting minor modifications to the clubhead or shaft. Callaway included nontouring professionals in addition to engineers among its R&D staff. The golfing staff was critical to the product development process since engineers were able to refine new prototypes based on the feedback and recommendations of Callaway's R&D staff golfers. Callaway's engineers also tested prototypes with robots to evaluate the distance and accuracy of the club, but only a human could evaluate the feel of a golf club striking a ball.

Callaway's Purchasing and Production Processes

Once its clubheads were designed on a CAD system and tested in the Helmstetter Center, stainless-steel master plates were cut by Callaway to the exact specifications called for by the system. Each clubhead mold was made by pouring liquid wax between the stainless-steel master plates. The wax clubheads were removed from the master plates and sprayed with a mixture of highly heat resistant material. The wax was melted out of these heat-resistant molds, leaving a hollow core. The hollow molds were then sent to an investment casting house, where either stainless steel or titanium was poured into the molds. The casting house then broke away the mold and welded, sanded, and painted the clubheads before sending them to Callaway for further assembly.

Callaway Golf used five investment casting houses, all of which underwent extensive screening and were closely monitored during the casting process. Callaway management believed that it was particularly important to supervise the casting process since poor casting could produce clubhead inconsistencies that could lead to poor performance or product failures. Callaway had entered into a joint venture with Sturm, Ruger & Company in 1995 to produce its clubheads but had since recognized that quality clubheads could be obtained through outsourcing. Even though Callaway Golf was certain it would obtain high-quality clubheads through its sourcing agreements, it made daily inspections of incoming clubhead shipments using the materials analysis and durability-testing capabilities of the Helmstetter Center.

Like Callaway's clubheads, all of its shafts were designed and tested at the Helmstetter Center. Callaway manufactured all prototype shafts by hand at the testing center but contracted shaft production out to independent shaft manufacturers once specifications were established for the various graphite shafts used in its product line. As with clubheads, shafts were drawn from incoming shipments and tested at the company's R&D facility. Steel shafts were contracted out and inspected in a similar fashion. Callaway had produced as much as 50 percent of its graphite shafts internally during the late 1990s but outsourced 100 percent of its shaft requirements in 2000.

Callaway Golf's cell manufacturing process allowed the company to include quality control inspections throughout each club's assembly. In addition, the assembly plant was highly automated, with all processes requiring very tight tolerances performed by computer-controlled machinery. For example, the drilling necessary to produce Callaway's tapered bore-thru hosels was done by a series of precision drill presses that ensured that each hosel was drilled at the correct angle. Once the hosel had been drilled through, the clubhead moved to a production station that checked the lie and loft angles of the club and made any necessary corrections by slightly bending the clubhead to the proper angle.

Each shaft was inspected for fractures prior to insertion into the clubhead, and then the entire assembled club was weighed to assess the swing weight. Callaway production workers could choose between medallions of four different weights to bring a finished iron to the exact specified swing weight. The chosen medallion was permanently affixed to the back of the clubhead with a press. Swing weights for assembled woods were brought to their specifications by inserting epoxy through a small hole in the rear of the clubhead.

After undergoing a baking process that dried the glue used to attach the shaft to the clubhead, each club was fitted with a grip using a laser alignment device, airbrushed with details like the club number and Callaway trademarks, and then visually inspected for blemishes or other imperfections. Each finished club was wrapped by hand to protect its finish during shipping.

Sales and Customer Service

New product development at Callaway Golf Company was a cross-functional effort that included not only the R&D staff but also the company's sales and advertising staffs. Callaway sales and advertising personnel would evaluate new designs created by the company's aerospace engineers and recommend design changes based on their knowledge of the market. Once a new design was settled on, Callaway's sales force and internal advertising staff would create a name for the new product line, an advertising campaign, and promotional materials that would accompany the product launch in parallel with the R&D staff's developmental and testing processes.

Callaway's customer service department was viewed as a critical component of the company's overall level of differentiation. The customer service staff was made up of experienced employees who were offered a generous compensation package that included commissions for superior performance in meeting the needs of Callaway's retailers and consumers. Many of Callaway's rivals viewed customer service as a low-value-adding activity and typically made customer service a place for entry-level employees to become acquainted with the business. Each of Callaway Golf's customer service representatives received eight weeks of training before being allowed to handle a customer service inquiry. No other company in the industry provided more than three weeks of training to its customer service personnel. In addition to providing extensive training, Callaway promoted a team-oriented atmosphere that allowed the company's knowledge base to expand through the mentoring of newer employees by longtime customer service employees.

The entire customer service staff was empowered to make a final decision regarding a consumer or retailer complaint or warranty claim. Callaway customer service personnel were allowed to make decisions that might be pushed to the CEO at some other golf equipment companies. For example, if a golfer was vacationing and had a problem with a club, a customer service staff member could instruct the consumer to visit a local retailer to pick up a replacement club. If the consumer was out of the country and was not near a Callaway retailer, the Callaway employee was allowed to send a new club to the customer via Federal Express. Callaway customer service staff members were also known to send a gift to club owners who had experienced problems with Callaway equipment. Callaway's two-year warranty on all of its products entitled the owner to replace any defective product with a new product rather than return the product for a repair. In addition, Callaway generally chose to replace defective or broken clubs for the life of the club rather than stick to its two-year warranty period. A Callaway sales executive remarked, "A bad experience with a Callaway product usually winds up making someone a Callaway customer for life."

CALLAWAY GOLF'S PRODUCT LINE

Metal Woods

Callaway Golf's Big Bertha driver was the most innovative club in the industry when it was introduced in 1990. Its key features were a bigger clubhead, a bigger sweet spot, and a longer shaft, all of which helped to improve the consistency with which a golfer could drive the ball off the tee. Callaway wasted no time in capitalizing on the explosive popularity of its new driver; company managers understood that once a driver developed a following among golfers, these golfers usually wanted other woods to match it. The company subsequently introduced a series of fairway woods—a 2 wood, a 3 wood, a 5 wood, two styles of 7 woods, a 9 wood, and an 11 wood—to complement the Big Bertha driver. Many golfers rushed to buy not only the Big Bertha driver but also the company's other Big Bertha metal woods; it was common for Big Bertha enthusiasts to have three or four of the Big Bertha fairway woods in their bag.

Four years later, the company again moved to set itself apart from rival equipment makers (most of whom had by then come out with imitative versions of the Big Bertha line) by introducing the Great Big Bertha driver, made out of strong, lightweight titanium. The driver had a clubhead 30 percent larger than the original Big

Bertha driver but was still just as light because of the substitution of titanium for stainless steel in the clubhead and the use of a graphite shaft; the Great Big Bertha (GBB) was the industry's most technologically advanced golf club and retailed for $500 (a heretofore unheard-of price for a single golf club).

Callaway's introduction of its titanium Biggest Big Bertha in 1997 again caught industry rivals off guard as they moved to match the size of the GBB. The Biggest Big Bertha (BBB) was 15 percent larger than the titanium Great Big Bertha (and the titanium clubs produced by Callaway's rivals) and was equipped with a 46-inch lightweight shaft. The total weight of the BBB was less than the total weight of the titanium GBB and the stainless steel Big Bertha drivers, which had 45- and 44-inch shafts, respectively.

The size of Callaway woods began to decrease with the introduction of its Big Bertha (BB) Steelhead metal woods in 1998 and Hawk Eye titanium metal woods in 1999. The BB Steelhead line was created in response to the popularity of the shallow-faced woods introduced by Orlimar and Adams in 1998. BB Steelhead drivers and fairway woods had a lower center of gravity than GBB and BBB woods, but had a higher profile than Adams and Orlimar woods. The BB Steelhead line incorporated the best features of both competing club designs by maintaining a very low center of gravity but having a larger clubface, which prevented the golfer from hitting below the ball, as was frequently done by amateur golfers using shallow-faced woods.

The BB Steelhead Plus was introduced in January 2000 as an improvement to the BB Steelhead line of drivers and fairway woods. Like the BB Steelhead line, the BB Steelhead Plus included a precision-cast steel chip to lower the club's center of gravity but featured variable clubface thickness that optimized energy transfer between the clubhead and the ball. Callaway's Variable Face Thickness Technology, developed through computer modeling and player testing, allowed the company to vary the clubface thickness to maximize perimeter weighting while keeping an elliptical area near the center of the clubface relatively thick. This thickness directly at the sweet spot of the clubface provided more energy transfer when a ball was well struck, while the perimeter weighting and thin walls near the outside edges of the clubface provided more forgiveness if a ball was mis-hit. Callaway's BB Steelhead Plus metal woods and its Variable Face Thickness Technology are described in the Callaway print ad shown in Exhibit 7. Callaway's Great Big Bertha Hawk Eye titanium drivers and fairway woods featured a titanium body and crown plate and Callaway's exclusive tungsten gravity screw, which accounted for only 2 percent of the clubhead volume but 25 percent of its overall weight. The lightweight titanium clubhead body and crown plate allowed Callaway to increase the overall size of the driver and the sweet spot, while the tungsten screw performed a number of functions. First, the use of tungsten low in the club created a low center of gravity, which helped the golfer produce a high trajectory. The tungsten screw also was strategically positioned in the sole of the clubhead to create Callaway's Draw Bias Technology, which drew the clubhead square at impact and reduced the likelihood of a slice. The tungsten screw also increased backspin, which helped produce greater distance. Exhibit 8 presents a print ad for Callaway's line of GBB Hawk Eye metal woods.

Irons

To capitalize on the initial popularity of the Big Bertha metal woods, Callaway Golf introduced lines of stainless-steel and graphite-shafted Big Bertha irons in 1994. In 1997 the company introduced Great Big Bertha tungsten-titanium irons, which included a tungsten insert located in the sole of the club that lowered the clubhead's center of gravity. The use of titanium allowed Callaway to increase the overall size of the clubface, creating a larger sweet spot, while the tungsten insert allowed Callaway

EXHIBIT 7   Sample Ad for Callaway Golf's New Big Bertha Steelhead Plus Metal Woods

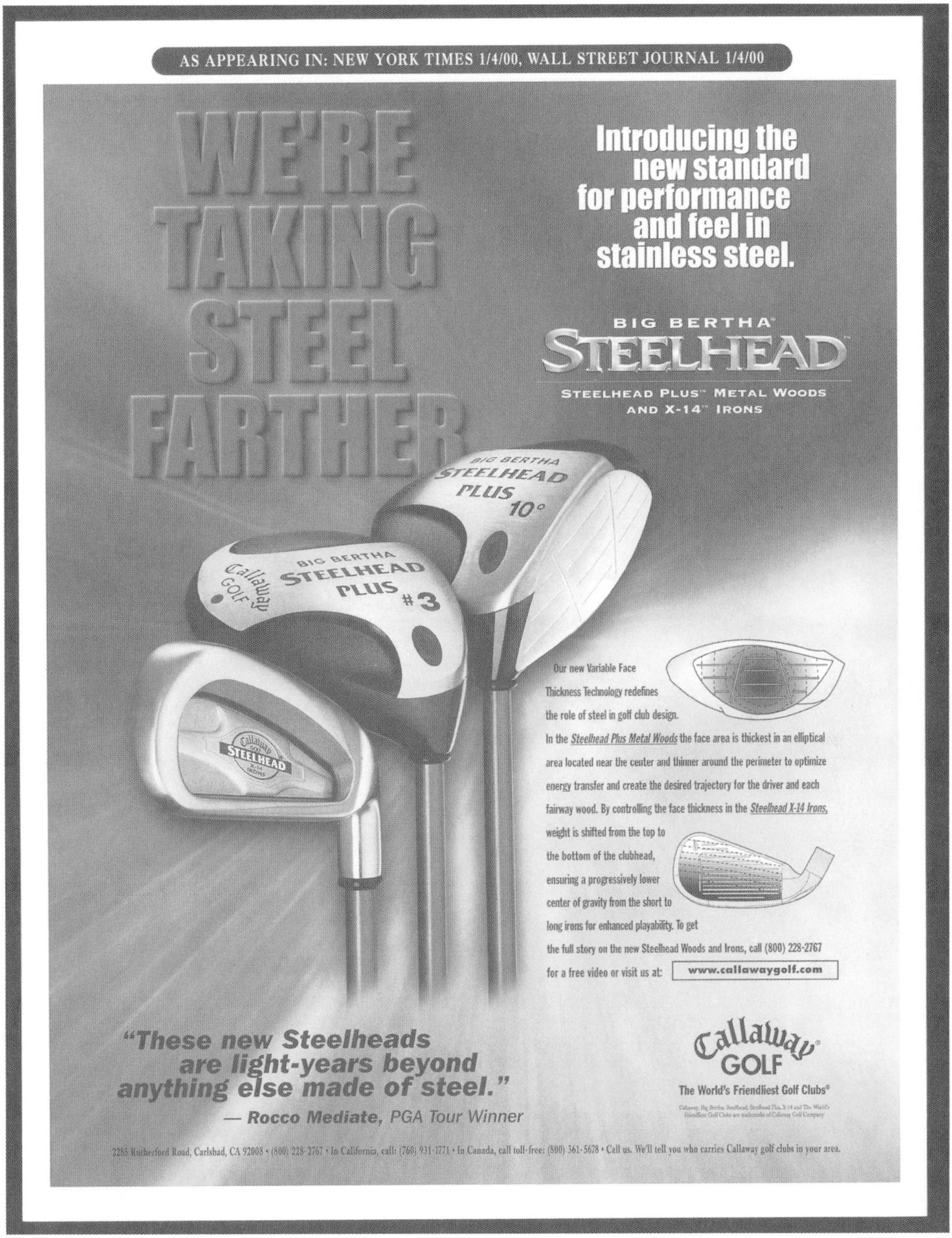

391

EXHIBIT 8   Sample Ad for Callaway Golf's New Hawk Eye Metal Woods

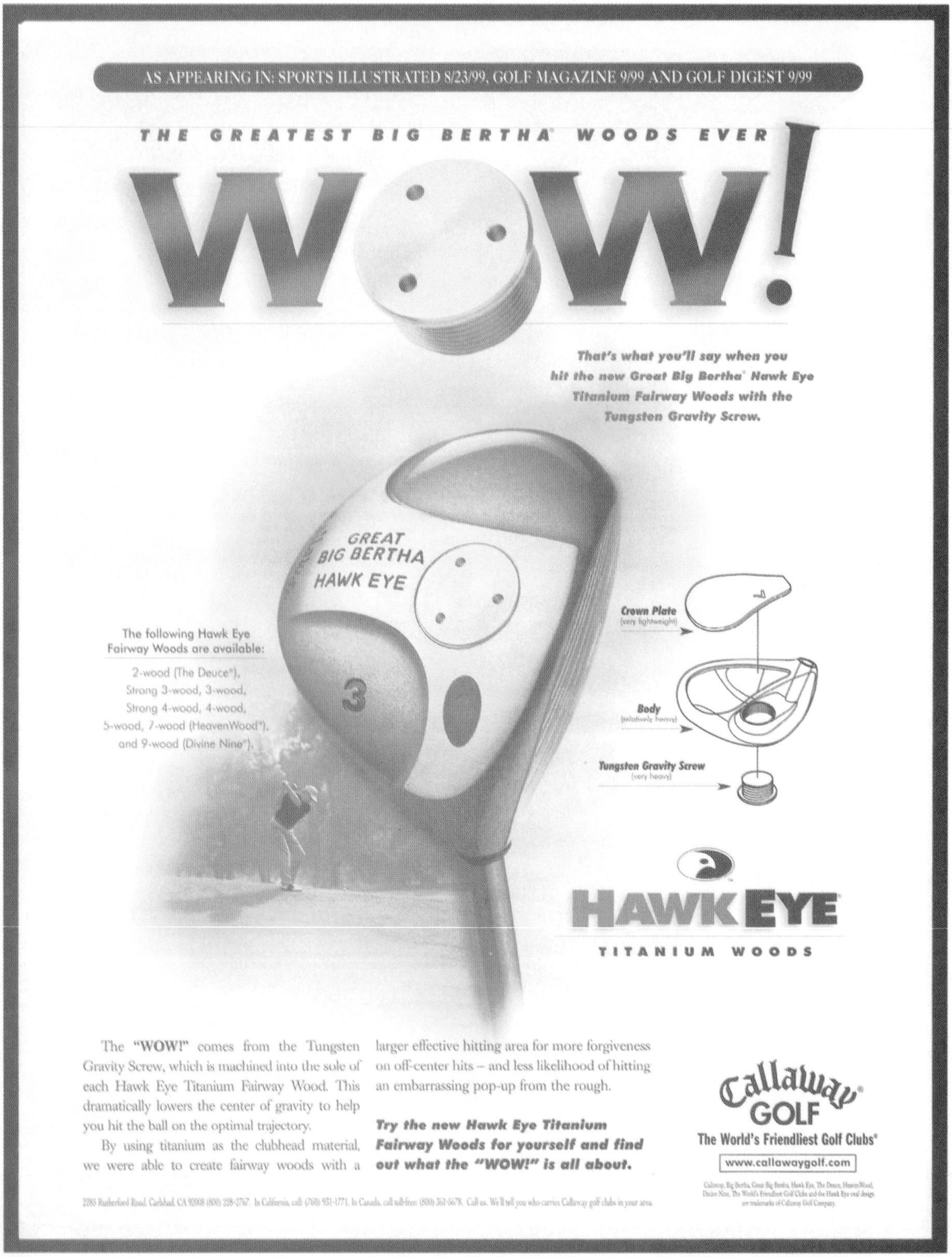

392

to keep the center of gravity low and add weight to the sweet spot. This low center of gravity and concentration of weight in the sweet spot allowed the irons to hit higher, straighter shots.

Callaway's Hawk Eye tungsten-injected titanium irons, introduced in 1999, included innovative design improvements over the original GBB tungsten-titanium irons. The Hawk Eye titanium irons included a hidden cavity that ran the length of the clubhead and extended upward behind the hitting area. Small, uniform tungsten spheres were added by a computer weigh station to the cavity through a port and then covered with a dense molten metal to permanently lock them into place. Each iron contained a different number of spheres depending on the optimal center of gravity for the loft of the club. Once the appropriate number of tungsten spheres and the molten metal were added to the clubhead, the weight port was hidden by a Hawk Eye medallion. The Tungsten Weight Matrix that resulted from the addition of the spheres occupied only 27 percent of the volume of a Callaway Hawk Eye 5-iron yet accounted for 45 percent of the clubhead's weight. The weight matrix created a low center of gravity that acted much like the gravity screw used in Hawk Eye metal woods and allowed golfers to create a high shot likely to maintain a straight path.

Callaway Golf replaced its stainless-steel Big Bertha irons in 1998 with its Big Bertha X-12 irons. The X-12 line of irons included a number of improvements over the Big Bertha irons and became the best-selling iron in the company's history. The X-12 line featured a narrower sole than Big Bertha irons, which made it easier to hit shots out of the rough. Big Bertha X-12 irons also had a multilayer design effect on the back of the clubface that allowed Callaway designers to locate the center of gravity at the ideal location for each length iron. The introduction of a variable 360-degree undercut channel also aided Callaway engineers in placing the center of gravity at the best possible location on the clubhead.

Callaway replaced the X-12 line of irons in 2000 with the Big Bertha X-14 Steelhead line. The X-14 featured Callaway's Variable Face Thickness Technology, which tapered the clubface from top to bottom and from heel to toe to create better perimeter weighting than previous generations of Callaway irons. The technology also allowed Callaway engineers to move the center of gravity to the ideal location on each iron. For example, the X-14 short irons had a higher center of gravity to provide extra control on approach shots, while the midlength irons and long irons had a lower center of gravity to produce a higher ball flight. Exhibit 9 shows a sample ad for Callaway Golf's X-14 irons.

Putters

Callaway Golf Company manufactured and marketed Bobby Jones, Carlsbad, and Tuttle lines of putters and the Odyssey brand of putters. Callaway had moderate success with its own Callaway putter lines, but its acquisition of Odyssey in 1997 made it the leading producer of putters in 2000. The 12 Bobby Jones putters and four Carlsbad putters were all made from stainless steel and came in blade and mallet styles. The Tuttle putter came in one model, which was unique in that it actually resembled a Big Bertha driver but was the size of a putter. Odyssey became known as an innovator in putters when it became one of the first companies to introduce polymer clubface inserts. Many golfers preferred putters with an insert since the soft material created a softer noise and provided more feel when putting a ball. Callaway's Odyssey putter was one of the two leading brands of putter in 2000 (Ping and Odyssey regularly exchanged the number one title) and was available in 26 different blade and mallet designs. Each of Odyssey's 26 models of putters featured its Stronomic polymer insert, available in three degrees of softness. In early 2000, Odyssey introduced its White Hot line of putters, which used Callaway's golf ball material as a clubface insert.

EXHIBIT 9 Sample Ad for Callaway Golf's New Big Bertha Steelhead X-14 Irons

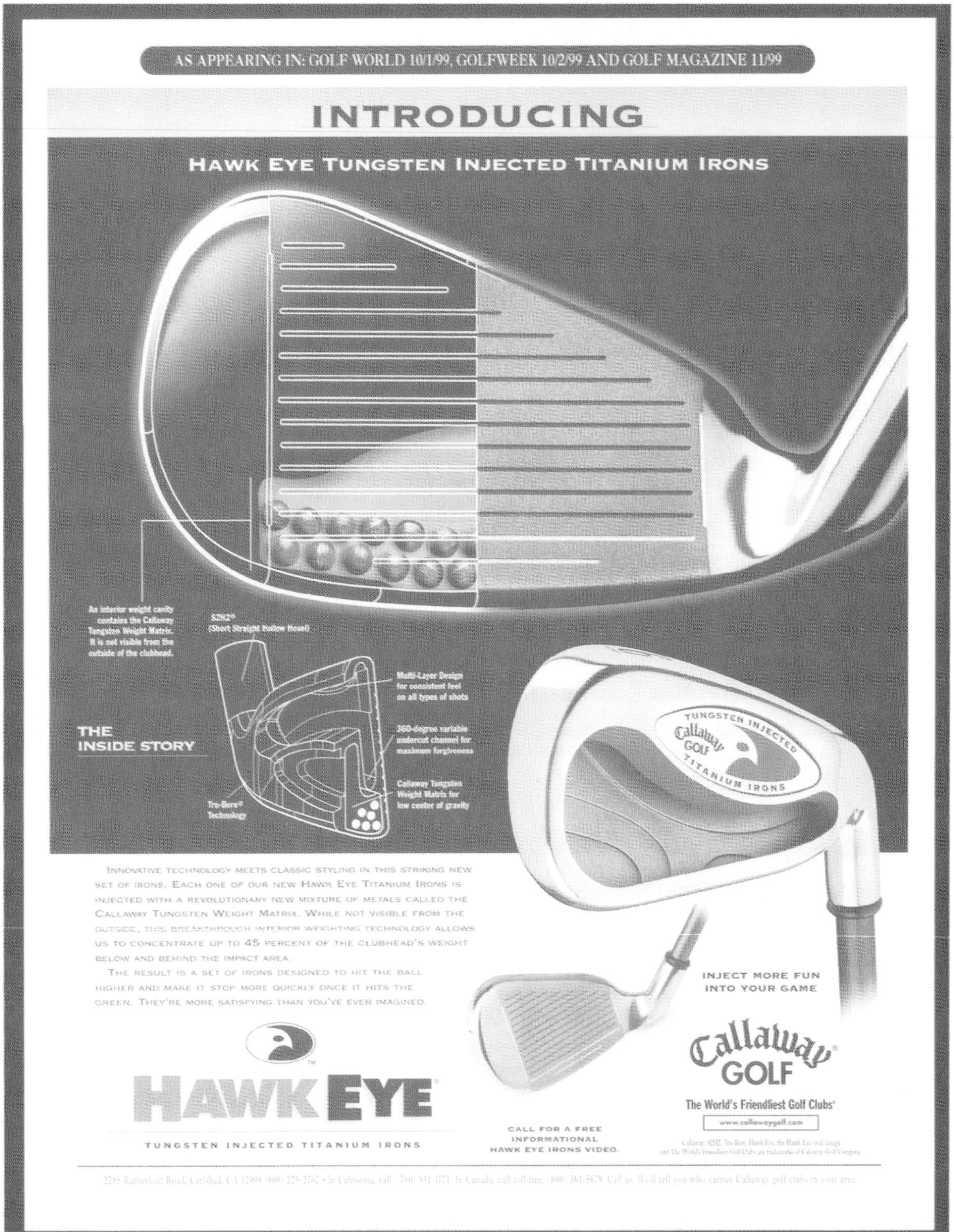

CALLAWAY'S BATTLE AGAINST PATENT AND TRADEMARK INFRINGEMENT

Ever since the Big Bertha driver had gained mass acceptance by professional and amateur golfers, Callaway Golf had been attacked by small golf companies offering clubs that were so similar in design and appearance that they infringed on Callaway's patents and trademarks. Although they looked like the branded clubs, the knockoff clubs were of inferior quality and typically sold for as much as 75 percent less than name-brand clubs. Some knockoff brands outsold the brands offered by such well-known makers as Hogan, Cleveland, and MacGregor. Callaway Golf was extremely committed to battling the makers of knockoff and counterfeit clubs. The company hired a retired U.S. Army counterintelligence expert to investigate trademark infringement cases and also worked in this area with private investigators, U.S. Customs, and U.S. marshals. In early 2000, Callaway Golf carried out a four-state sweep against illegal club makers that netted $65,000 worth of Callaway golf clubs that had been stolen and were being sold over the Internet; officials seized 5,800 golf clubs, including Canterbury Big Bursar V-17 irons and Connection Golf Big Bernard Steel-clad metal woods. However, even when patent infringers and counterfeiters were caught and convicted, it was difficult to collect damages because such companies usually had minimal assets to seize.

Callaway Golf also aggressively protected its legal rights when it believed that a branded rival infringed on its patents or made false claims about either its own products or Callaway's products. In 1998 Callaway brought a suit against Spalding Sports Worldwide for trademark violation after Spalding created a line of System C golf balls and claimed they were specifically designed for Callaway clubs. The two parties settled in 1999, with Spalding agreeing to pull the line of golf balls. In addition, after a legal challenge from Callaway, Orlimar Golf was ordered by the court to retract advertisements falsely claiming that it was the number one metal wood used on the PGA tour. In 1999 Callaway Golf saw that the vice president of Callaway Golf Ball Company could in no way be involved with Taylor Made's golf ball operations after the Callaway employee left with company trade secrets to become Taylor Made's president and CEO. Callaway Golf also forced an apology from the CEO of La Jolla Golf after Callaway found that La Jolla's chief executive had used a fictitious name to make untrue and disparaging remarks about Callaway golf clubs on the Internet.

ENDORSEMENTS AND USE OF CALLAWAY PRODUCTS BY GOLF PROFESSIONALS

Callaway golf clubs were popular with both professionals and amateurs alike. Callaway drivers were endorsed by the professional golfers listed in Exhibit 10. However, many professional golfers used Callaway equipment even though they were not paid to endorse the company's products. In 1999 Callaway drivers were used in 61 wins, Callaway irons were used in 37 wins, and Odyssey putters produced 36 wins in a total of 186 PGA, LPGA, Senior PGA, Nike, and European PGA professional tournaments. A comparison of clubs used by professionals in all five tournaments is presented in Exhibit 11.

Callaway Golf's Major Competitors

Callaway management considered its strongest competitive rivals to be Ping and Taylor Made because of those companies' track records in product innovation and their strong brand-name recognition: Ping irons had dominated the industry during

EXHIBIT 10   Callaway Golf Company Staff Professionals, 2000

Source: Callaway Golf 2000 catalog.

Tour	Staff Players
Professional Golfers Association	Stephen Ames
	Paul Azinger
	Oline Browne
	Carlos Franco
	Brian Henninger
	Rocco Mediate
	Jesper Parnevik
	Paul Stankowski
Senior Professional Golfers Association	Bob Charles
	Jim Colbert
	Jim Dent
	Dave Eichelberger
	Bruce Fleisher
	David Graham
	Orville Moody
	Walter Morgan
	Bob Murphy
Ladies Professional Golfers Association	Jane Geddes
	Rachel Hetherington
	Rosie Jones
	Emilee Klein
	Leta Lindley
	Cindy McCurdy
	Liselotte Neumann
	Alison Nicholas
	Annika Sorenstam
European Professional Golfers Association	Mark McNulty
	Colin Montgomerie
	Eduardo Romero

much of the 1980s and 1990s (the perimeter-weighting feature pioneered by Karsten was a major technological breakthrough and had since become the industry standard in designing irons), while Taylor Made's distinctive bubble shaft was also considered to be a high-tech innovation. Other key rivals of Callaway Golf Company were Titleist, Adams Golf, and Orlimar Golf. Exhibit 12 presents a price comparison of golf equipment produced by Callaway Golf Company and its key rivals.

PING

Ping had not been well known for its drivers but had been one of the industry's premier manufacturers of irons since its Ping Eye 2-irons were introduced in the mid-1980s. The company's Ping Eye 3-irons that were introduced in 1999 were among the most popular irons with both professionals and amateurs. Ping Eye 3-irons were one of the two leading brands of irons sold in the United States and were frequently the most-used iron in various professional tournaments. Ping Eye 3s were available with a compact blade-style clubhead designed for low-handicap golfers and with an oversized clubhead that had greater perimeter weighting for more forgiveness. All Ping Eye 3-irons featured a custom tuning port that was very similar in appearance to Callaway's tungsten weight matrix port, but functioned differently. Rather than acting as a port to add tungsten weights, Ping's custom tuning port allowed the company to make minor adjustments to the loft and lie of the club during custom fitting.

EXHIBIT 11   Golf Club Use Comparison among Professional Golfers (All tours combined), 1998–99

Source: Callaway Golf Company annual reports and Darrell Survey.

	1999	1998
Drivers		
Callaway	38.5%	55.2%
Titleist	24.2	16.9
Ping	13.4	n.a.
Taylor Made	5.3	8.0
Orlimar	3.0	0.1
All others	15.6	17.5
Total drivers	100.0%	100.0%
Fairway woods		
Callaway	52.1%	48.3%
Orlimar	17.9	10.5
Taylor Made	8.8	13.3
Titleist	4.5	5.1
Cleveland	3.1	n.a.
All others	13.6	20.3
Total fairway woods	100.0%	100.0%
Irons		
Callaway	18.3%	19.4%
Ping	15.0	15.3
Mizuno	15.0	14.1
Titleist	14.5	12.6
Taylor Made	4.4	4.7
All others	32.8	33.9
Total irons	100.0%	100.0%
Putters		
Odyssey	28.9%	31.0%
Ping	21.8	24.8
Titleist	19.8	18.7
Never Compromise	11.2	3.7
Tear Drop	4.0	n.a.
All others	14.3	16.0
Total putters	100.0%	100.0%

n.a. = Not available.

EXHIBIT 12   Retail Price Comparison of Equipment Produced by Leading Golf Equipment Companies, March 2000

Source: Edwin Watts Golf Shops and International Golf Discount, March 11, 2000.

Brand	Titanium Drivers	Graphite-Shafted Stainless-Steel Irons (Set of 8)	Putters (Price Range of Most Popular Models)	Golf Balls (Price per Ball—Based on Single Sleeve)
Callaway Golf/Odyssey	$400	$900	$90–$200	$3.60
Ping	$400	$850	$80–$140	n.a.
Taylor Made	$300	$750	$100	$3.33
Titleist	$400	$870	$270	$3.33
Adams Golf	$300	Not carried	n.a.	n.a.
Orlimar Golf	$300	$800	n.a.	n.a.

n.a. = Not applicable.

Ping had elected not to introduce a titanium driver until 1998, because the company's engineers believed that the material provided no advantage over stainless steel. However, in 2000 its 323-cc displacement TiSI titanium driver was actually the largest custom-fit driver available. Ping also offered Ti3 titanium fairway woods that featured a zirconium soleplate and a tungsten bottom weight that were both intended to lower the club's center of gravity. Ping also offered an i3 line of stainless-steel fairway woods in five different lofts.

Ping's greatest strength was in putters, where it alternated every quarter or so with Odyssey as the number one brand of putters in the U.S. and international markets. Depending on the tournament, Ping putters were often used by professional golfers more than any other brand. Ping had 46 models of putters that were made from either antiqued manganese bronze, stainless steel, or laminated maple. Certain Ping putters featured inserts made from an elastomer compound, aluminum pixels, or copper pixels. Ping began offering custom-fit clubs in the 1960s, and in 2000 all Ping metal woods, irons, and putters could be custom-fitted to golfers who desired that service.

TAYLOR MADE–ADIDAS GOLF

Taylor Made was founded in 1979 by Gary Adams, who mortgaged his home and began production of his metal woods in an abandoned car dealership building in McHenry, Illinois. Both touring pros and golf retailers were skeptical of the new club design until they found that the metal woods actually hit the ball higher and farther than persimmon woods. By 1984, Taylor Made metal woods were the number one wood on the PGA tour and the company had grown to be the third largest golf equipment company in the United States. In 1984 the company was acquired by France-based Salomon SA, which provided the capital necessary for the company to continue to develop innovative new lines of clubs. The company's sales had stalled during the late 1980s and early 1990s until it introduced its Burner Bubble drivers in 1994. The bubble shaft design allowed some of the shaft weight to be moved from underneath the grip to just below the grip. Taylor Made management claimed that this weight relocation decreased the club's inertia, which resulted in faster clubhead acceleration. The bubble shaft also featured a reinforced midsection, said to minimize any twisting of the clubhead during the swing.

Many of the company's innovations in drivers and fairway woods mirrored those of Callaway Golf. In 1996, shortly after Callaway's introduction of the Great Big Bertha, Taylor Made had come out with an oversized titanium driver that had its differentiating bubble shaft and copper-colored clubhead. Taylor Made also produced and marketed a line of irons with its patented bubble shafts and introduced a line of bubble-shafted tungsten-titanium irons and a new titanium bubble-shafted T2 driver in 1997. The T2 and Taylor Made's tungsten-titanium irons appeared in retail locations at approximately the same time that the Biggest Big Bertha and the Big Bertha tungsten-titanium irons made their debut. Also in 1997, Taylor Made and its parent were both acquired by the Germany-based sports conglomerate Adidas.

In 2000 Taylor Made offered titanium FireSole metal woods and irons that featured a tungsten sole plug and SuperSteel stainless-steel metal woods and irons. The FireSole was Taylor Made's answer to Callaway's Hawk Eye lines of metal woods and irons, while its promotion of its SuperSteel line touted many of the same benefits as Callaway's BB SteelHead Plus metal woods and X-14 irons. Taylor Made also offered FireSole Rescue clubs, which had a large tungsten sole attached to a reduced-size titanium clubhead that placed 75 percent of the clubhead's weight below the equator of the ball. The rescue woods had an ultralow center of gravity and could be used on either the fairway or the rough. In early 2000 Taylor Made's Rescue fairway woods were unique; no products of similar appearance were offered by other major club manufacturers. Taylor Made also had a line of putters that featured a polymer club-face. Taylor Made introduced its InterGel line of golf balls in 1999.

FORTUNE BRANDS/ACUSHNET (TITLEIST AND COBRA GOLF)

The Acushnet Company was a rubber deresinating company founded in 1910 in Acushnet, Massachusetts. The company opened a golf ball division in 1932 when founder Phil Young believed that a bad putt during a round of golf he was playing was a result of a faulty ball rather than his poor putting. Young took the ball to a dentist's office to have it X-rayed and found that the core of the ball was indeed off-center. Young believed that Acushnet could develop and manufacture high-quality golf balls and teamed with a fellow MIT graduate, Fred Bommer, to create the Titleist line of balls. Young and Bommer introduced their first Titleist golf ball in 1935, and by 1949 Titleist had become the most-played ball on the PGA. In 2000, Titleist was still the number one golf ball on the PGA, being used by more than 75 percent of all professional golfers in tournament play. Acushnet also manufactured and marketed a Pinnacle line of golf balls, developed in 1980 as a lower-priced alternative to Titleist branded golf balls.

Acushnet's acquisition of John Reuter, Jr., Inc., in 1958 and Golfcraft, Inc., in 1969 put Titleist into the golf club business. Titleist's Reuter Bull's Eye putter became a favorite on the PGA tour during the 1960s, and its AC-108 heel-toe weighted irons were among the most popular brands of irons during the early 1970s. In 1996 the Acushnet Company was acquired by American Brands, which had increased its presence in the golf equipment industry in 1985 when it acquired Foot-Joy, the number one seller of golf gloves and shoes. Also in 1996 American Brands acquired Cobra Golf for $715 million. The company's golf and leisure products division had an operating profit of $147 million on sales of $965 million in 1999.

Acushnet's two golf club brands maintained separate sales forces, but every other value chain activity was combined for overall cost savings whenever possible. The Titleist brand of clubs had achieved only moderate success after Ping's perimeter-weighted clubs became popular in the 1980s, but Titleist had become much more successful during the late 1990s due to Tiger Woods's endorsement of the company's irons and metal woods. In 2000 Titleist's 975D driver, used by Tiger Woods, was among the more popular drivers with both professionals and amateurs. The 975D was an oversized titanium driver designed for a flatter ball flight to help a golfer achieve greater roll once the ball hit the ground. The Titleist titanium 975R was a variation of the 975D, which had a more shallow face and a slightly smaller clubhead. Titleist also offered a line of 975F stainless-steel fairway woods in 2000.

Titleist had two lines of stainless steel irons: the DCI 990 and DCI 981. The DCI 990 was intended for low-handicap golfers and had a reduced clubface offset and more weight toward the lower portion of the heel, where better golfers were more prone to mis-hit a golf ball. The DCI 981 line, designed for higher-handicap golfers, had an offset clubface, a low center of gravity, and more weight toward the toe of the clubface of short irons. The overall design objectives of the 981 line were to produce higher trajectories and more forgiveness. The DCI 981 also was available in an SL series intended for seniors or other golfers with less clubhead speed. All Titleist irons and metal woods were available with either steel or graphite shafts. Titleist also marketed a line of 17 different Scotty Cameron putters in stainless steel, teryllium, or platinum finishes. Some Scotty Cameron putters included an elastomer membrane covering the clubface.

In 1996, Cobra Golf held the industry's number two spot in irons and was number three in drivers and fairway woods (behind Callaway and Taylor Made). Cobra's popularity was a result of Greg Norman's endorsement of the clubs and the company's strategy of reducing the loft of its irons. The reduced loft added considerable distance to each club. For example, a golfer switching to King Cobra irons might pick up 20 yards or more on each club. Cobra Golf's King Cobra drivers were also considered a long-distance club.

After its acquisition by Acushnet, Cobra began to rapidly lose market share in both irons and metal woods. The company was forced to change its marketing approach since its high-profile, aggressive marketing practices clashed with the wishes of Acushnet's managers, who preferred a conservative approach to marketing. In addition, Acushnet management believed that Cobra should redesign its clubs to promote forgiveness at the expense of distance. Loyal Cobra customers were disappointed when they found that Cobra new models of clubs did not offer any greater distance than other brands. The decline in demand forced Cobra into a practice of deep discounting, which encouraged golfers to wait for the company to cut prices before they purchased the latest Cobra products. Cobra Golf also lost a considerable number of retailers during the later 1990s. The combination of missteps by Acushnet and Cobra Golf managers had all but made Cobra an afterthought by 1999.

Cobra struggled to rebuild its image and market presence after its strategic gaffes of the late 1990s. In 1999 the company launched a Web site and print ads that promoted its products as hip, nonconformist alternatives to the more technology-based golf clubs on the market. In early 2000 Cobra had abandoned this new image and recast itself as a more mainstream golf company.

Cobra's new products for 2000 included its Gravity Back drivers and fairway metal woods, which featured a titanium clubhead with a bronze alloy backweight placed at the rear of the clubhead. The bronze alloy backweight was designed to give the club a lower center of gravity. The Gravity Back fairway woods also featured a copper-tungsten sole weight to further lower the center of gravity. Cobra's CXI stainless-steel irons featured an X-like design on the backside of the clubface to more evenly disperse weight throughout the rear of the cavity back club. In 1999 Cobra Golf introduced Cobra Dista golf balls, which came in four models.

ADAMS GOLF

Barney Adams founded Adams Golf in 1987 in Plano, Texas, as a golf club components supplier and contract manufacturer. In 1995 the company introduced its Tight Lies line of fairway woods, which featured an innovative low-profile clubface with a very low center of gravity. The shallow clubface and low center of gravity enlarged the effective hitting area of the clubface and created shots with a higher trajectory than shots with traditional-sized metal woods of the same loft. Tight Lies fairway woods were named the "Breakthrough Product of the Year" in 1997 by the Golf Market Research Institute and were rated the "Best of the Best" fairway woods in an independent real-golfer comparison in 1998. Adams Golf went public in July 1998 at an initial offering price of $16.00. The company recorded 1998 sales and earnings of $85 million and $13 million, respectively. In 1997 Adams had revenues of $37 million and a net loss of $5 million.

Adams's success became more difficult to maintain after other leading golf club manufacturers offered new lines of fairway woods with a shallower face than their previous models. In 1999 Adams Golf's revenues had declined to $54 million and the company recorded a net loss of $11 million. The company's stock traded below $2.00 during the first three months of 2000. Adams Golf's product line for 2000 included its Tight Lies² fairway woods, which had a deeper clubface than the original Tight Lies fairway woods. The new Tight Lies² retained the key features of the original Tight Lies line, but its deeper clubface made it easier to hit from the rough. In

1999 Adams introduced a line of SC series drivers, which were available in four different clubface curvatures designed to correct either a slice, a fade, or a hook. One SC driver featured a neutral clubface curvature for golfers without swing path problems. Adams also offered Assault VMI (variable moment of inertia) irons, which were heavier than most other brands of irons and used a patented mathematical formula to determine the ideal weight of the club based on the overall club length, shaft length, grip weight, and shaft weight.

ORLIMAR GOLF COMPANY

Orlimar Golf Company was founded in 1960 by Lou Ortiz in the basement of a converted stable in San Francisco. The company was a little-known maker of custom clubs primarily used by professionals and had annual sales of under $1 million in 1996. The company exploded onto the broad market for golf clubs in 1998 when it introduced its Tri-Metal fairway woods. Orlimar's Tri-Metal woods were made of stainless steel, copper, and tungsten and featured a low center of gravity and a shallower clubface than Callaway's GBB fairway woods. The combination of three metals and the low profile made the Tri-Metal instantly popular with professionals and amateurs alike. By year-end 1998 the company's sales had grown to more than $50 million and it was named as the fastest-growing private company in the San Francisco Bay area.

The company added drivers and irons to its product line in 1999 as its sales of fairway woods began to decline after Callaway's fairway woods began to recapture market share lost in 1997 and 1998. Orlimar's 2000 lineup of new products included its Tri-Metal Plus fairway woods and drivers and Tri-Metal irons. Like Orlimar's original Tri-Metal woods, Tri-Metal Plus fairway woods and drivers were made from stainless steel and included a copper tungsten sole plate to lower their center of gravity, but the Plus line had a deeper clubface than the original Tri-Metals. The clubface of the Tri-Metal Plus metal woods was coated with an Alpha Maraging Face material that the company claimed was harder than titanium. Orlimar's Tri-Metal irons were made from the same materials as the company's metal woods and were designed to produce high trajectories and longer distance than competing clubs.

CALLAWAY'S PROSPECTS FOR GROWTH AND THE FEBRUARY 2000 LAUNCH OF THE CALLAWAY GOLF BALL

Callaway's introduction of its new Rule 35 golf ball had been eagerly awaited since mid-1996, when Ely Callaway announced the formation of Callaway Golf Ball Company and the move of Charles Yash from Taylor Made to the new company. Whereas Nike had entered the golf ball industry in 1999 by outsourcing its production to Bridgestone and Taylor Made chose its mode of entry by purchasing an existing plant from a competitor, Ely Callaway had chosen a more time-consuming route to enter the market for golf balls by electing to construct a new golf ball facility and internally develop an all-new ball. He noted: "This is the first time in the modern history of the industry, to our knowledge, that anyone has built a major-production golf ball business from scratch. After analyzing all of our other options, which included buying an existing company, buying an existing plant or buying a golf ball from another manufacturer and merely stamping our name on it, we decided this was the best way to go in order to create a superior product now and for the future."[9]

Callaway Golf spent three years developing in parallel its new golf ball and its state-of-the-art production facility. The company's entry into the market represented a

[9]"Play Ball: Callaway Introduces the Rule 35," www.pgatour.com.

$170 million investment in the research and development of the ball, construction of the 225,000-square-foot production facility, and development and purchase of special manufacturing equipment. Callaway's manufacturing facility and its equipment were designed specifically for the unique production requirements for the new ball.

Ely Callaway believed that the company's custom-designed manufacturing equipment and facility would contribute to the company's competitive strength and the ball's success: "No one else has the collection of late 90s equipment that we have, everything you need to make a better ball. No one has put it together and purchased it all the way we have. Some of the companies, because of the age of some of their equipment, just can't utilize the latest equipment without going outside."[10] Callaway's competitors were so interested in the company's new golf ball facility that they took aerial photographs of the plant's foundation as it was under construction.

Callaway Golf Ball Company engineers, recruited from Du Pont and Boeing, used aerodynamic computer programs (first used by Boeing and General Electric) to evaluate more than 300 dimple patterns and more than 1,000 variations of ball cores, boundary layers, and cover materials to create the new Rule 35 ball. Callaway engineers designed only two models of the Rule 35 ball—choosing to develop a "complete-performance" ball rather than separate balls developed for spin, control, distance, and durability. Ely Callaway explained the company's product development objectives as follows: "We have combined all of the performance benefits into one ball so players no longer need to sacrifice control for distance, or feel, or durability. Each Rule 35 ball contains a unique synergy of distance, control, spin, feel and durability characteristics. This eliminates confusion and guesswork in trying to identify the golf ball that is right for each individual golfer."[11]

Callaway's production process used computers to mill the rubber core, control injection molding of a boundary layer, and deposit a proprietary urethane coating to golf balls as they were assembled. The golf balls then moved through a transparent tube to a battery of diagnostic machines that ensured that each ball was exactly the same. A laser was then used to twice measure the depth of each of the ball's 382 dimples, and an electrical process was used to bond paint to the ball securely and evenly. Each ball was then X-rayed and machine-inspected before being packed or rejected. Callaway's production process included 16,000 quality assurance checkpoints, and Callaway employees were allowed to stop the flow of balls at the first sign of defects.

Callaway's Rule 35 balls were differentiated from competing brands in a large number of ways. The name Rule 35 was a play on the 34 long-standing rules of golf published by the USGA and the Royal & Ancient Golf Club of St. Andrews. Ely Callaway suggested that there should be a 35th rule of golf—"Enjoy the game."[12] The complete-performance balls came in only two variations, whereas the golf balls offered by competitors came in as many as 10 models. The blue-logo Callaway ball was called the Softfeel and had all of the same characteristics as its red-logo Firmfeel ball but had a slightly softer feel. Ely Callaway believed the availability of only two complete-performance balls and the avoidance of a discussion of the technical aspects of the balls' design and construction would make it easier for golfers to purchase golf balls: "We know there is a lot of complex science that goes into making a golf ball, but we don't think there should be a lot of complexity to buying one."[13] Callaway later commented, "We've come up with two balls. That's it. We're not gonna tell you much

[10]"Long on Promises, Short on Explanation," *Golfweek,* February 5, 2000.

[11]"Callaway Enters the Ball Game," *Show News,* February 5, 2000.

[12]"Play Ball: Callaway Introduces the Rule 35."

[13]"Callaway Enters the Ball Game."

about them. We have only two, you make the choice. If you like a soft feel, you try this one (blue). If you like a firm feel, you try this one (red). We don't say a damn thing about how far they go. We don't say a word about compression or the construction or the details of the cover. We just say, 'Try them.' We believe that either one of them will give you more of what you've been looking for in one ball than anything else."[14]

Callaway Golf Ball Company's CEO, Chuck Yash, discussed the company's philosophy behind offering only two models of the Rule 35 and why the company refused to comment on the ball's technology: "Our basic aim in this process was to make a ball that reflects the parent company's philosophy and vision of creating a 'demonstrably superior and pleasingly different' product. We also set out to cut through the noise regarding the performance claims by most of the competitors' products, and all of the techno-babble about various polymers and compressions and dimple patterns and claims regarding the longest distance balls. What we have in Rule 35 is a very clear message. If you prefer a firm feel, our Firmfeel ball has everything you need in performance. If you prefer a softer feel, our Softfeel ball is the choice. It's that easy."[15]

Callaway golf balls were further differentiated by their logo and packaging. The Callaway name used a stylized script rather than the Old English script used on Callaway golf clubs, and the company's logo was comprised of a letter *C* created from a rendering of the bottom of a golf cup. The balls were also packaged in sleeves of 5 and packs of 10 rather than sleeves of 3 or packs of 12 like other brands. Callaway Golf Ball Company's national sales manager explained why Callaway chose unique packaging for its golf balls: "When we were doing our research, we couldn't find a single person who could tell us why golf balls were packaged in sleeves of three or in dozens. When we discovered that the average golfer uses 4.5 balls per round, we decided the five-ball sleeve was the right way to go with packaging."[16] In addition, unlike the packaging of other brands of balls, Callaway's packaging included only the name and logo printed on a translucent plastic box rather than the name and product performance characteristics printed on a cardboard box. Callaway's use of a five-ball sleeve also allowed its golf balls to be placed away from other brands of balls since most retailers' display cases were designed for three-ball sleeves.

Even though the industry had long been dominated by Titleist and Spalding (see Exhibit 13), many analysts believed that Callaway's ability to develop technologically advanced products, its marketing expertise, and its established retailer network would allow the company to quickly gain a 2 to 3 percent share of the market and achieve $60 to $70 million in sales during 2000. Analysts also speculated that Callaway Golf Ball Company could hit sales of over $200 million within two years of the ball's launch. It was expected that Callaway's golf ball operations would considerably impact the company's net profit since profit margins in the premium segment of the golf ball market ranged between 60 and 75 percent. In addition, golf ball sales were less seasonal since they were consumable items that were purchased throughout the year. Also, unlike a $500 driver, golfers could not delay the purchase of golf balls until they felt financially ready to make a large purchase. The company's objective was for the Rule 35 to capture a 10 percent share of the market within two years and ultimately become one of the two top brands of golf balls. "We have 7 million people out there playing our products, and 80 percent of them think they're the best clubs

[14]"Long on Promises, Short on Explanation."

[15]Callaway press release, February 4, 2000.

[16]"Callaway Enters the Ball Game."

EXHIBIT 13   **Estimated Manufacturing Shares of the Leading Producers of Golf Balls, 12 Months Ending September 30, 1999**

Source: Callaway Golf Company.

	Dollars	Units
Titleist	36%	29%
Top-Flite/Spalding	23	27
Pinnacle	11	14
Maxfli	8	7
Wilson	7	8
Slazenger	5	3
Precept	3	2
Dunlop	2	3
Taylor Made	1	1
All others	4	6
Total	100%	100%

in the world," said Ely Callaway. "We have almost a guaranteed 'try' on our new products."[17] Callaway further commented, "We're going to sell a lot of balls."[18] An advertisement for the Rule 35 golf ball is shown in Exhibit 14.

In February 2000 a survey of golf equipment company executives voted Callaway's Big Bertha driver the best golf product of the century by a 2-to-1 margin. The same group of executives called Ely Callaway the most influential golf trade person of the 1990s. As he approached his 81st birthday, Ely Callaway had vowed to retire by December 31, 2000, and make Chuck Yash the new CEO and president of Callaway Golf Company as well as Callaway Golf Ball Company. Just prior to the PGA Merchandise Show, Chuck Yash commented on his growing responsibility at Callaway Golf Company and the importance of its golf ball operations to the company's future growth: "The trust and faith Ely and the board of directors and the shareholders have shown in us is extraordinary. It has allowed me to use my 20 years of golf experience to build an organization and a team that, we believe, can have a significant impact. That is the way we are looking at things now, as a long-term commitment. It will take years before we feel we can compete with the leading companies in the golf ball market. But that is our objective. If we do that right, we have the potential to continue to grow."[19]

[17]"Rule 35 Tees Off," *San Diego Union-Tribune,* February 4, 2000.
[18]"Play Ball: Callaway Introduces the Rule 35."
[19]"On the Spot: Chuck Yash," *Golf Product News,* January/February 2000.

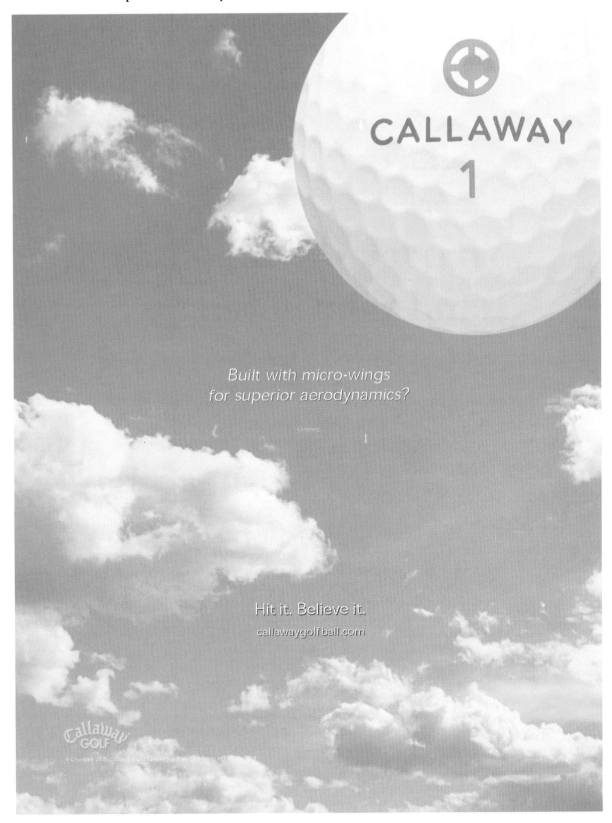

Promotion Strategy

13

harley-davidson.com and the Global Motorcycle Industry

J. Paul Peter
University of Wisconsin–Madison

Harley-Davidson, Inc., achieved its thirteenth consecutive year of record revenue and earnings and a 74 percent increase in the value of the firm in 1998. The company had previously divested interests in other industries and focused its efforts exclusively on the motorcycle industry, including accessories and financing. It strengthened its presence in the industry by obtaining full ownership in Buell Motorcycle Company, a manufacturer of sport motorcycles based on Harley-Davidson components and previously established Eaglemark Financial Services, Inc., to provide financial services to dealers and customers.

The company completed a new 479,200-square-foot facility near Milwaukee in 1998 which manufactures engines and transmissions and finished a 330,000-square-foot facility in Kansas City, Missouri, which produces all six models of Sportsters, Harley's 833cc and 1200cc bikes. The company also introduced a new engine, the Twin Cam 88, a more powerful one to compete with the larger engines in some competitive motorcycles. Overall, it sold 157,152 motorcycles in 1998, a 15 percent increase over the previous year, achieved net sales of over $2 billion, a 17 percent increase over 1997, and gross profits of $104.5 million, a 17.8 percent increase over the previous year.

Chairman and CEO Jeffrey L. Bleustein believed that the phenomenal success of Harley could be attributed to four major factors:

- A powerful and much admired brand centered around the experiences of motorcycling; its attributes of freedom, adventure, and individuality that appeal to people across a wide variety of demographic segments.

- Strong relationships with all of its stakeholders including dealers, customers, employees, suppliers, governments, society, and shareholders.

- A proven management team and empowered employees committed to sustaining steady, manageable growth in a worldwide motorcycle market.
- Harley-Davidson's mystique . . . the ability of the brand to bring together in unique and surprising ways seemingly disparate combinations of products, people, processes, and experiences.

A final measure of the success of Harley-Davidson can be seen in the growth of its Harley Owners Group or H.O.G., started in 1983 with 33,000 members, all in the U.S. In 1997, it had 380,000 members in 105 countries and grew to 430,000 members in 115 countries by 1998. Clearly, the company had made a number of excellent management decisions and had built a large group of satisfied, involved, loyal customers around the world.

Global Competition

Exhibit 1 presents motorcycle registrations in three major regions where Harley competes. All three areas show solid growth which demonstrates, in part, the success of motorcycle manufacturers in generating demand for their products.

Exhibit 2 presents a breakdown of market shares by competitors in three regions. While Harley-Davidson dominates the market in North America, it has the smallest market share of major competitors in Europe and is fourth in the Asia/Pacific region which is dominated by Japanese brands. Part of the reason for Harley's smaller market share in Europe and the Asia/Pacific region is that the company cannot produce enough motorcycles to meet demand and its prices tend to be higher than competitive models. Overall, Harley-Davidson and Buell together achieved 25.2 percent of the global heavyweight motorcycle market.

Product quality for Harley and its major competitors is excellent although competitive bikes are often more technologically advanced. Competition in the industry

EXHIBIT 1 New Heavyweight Motorcycle (651 cc+) Registrations in Three Global Regions (in 000's)

Source: Adapted from Harley-Davidson, Inc., *1998 Annual Report*, p. 52.

Year	North America[1]	Europe[2]	Asia/Pacific[3]	Total
1998	246.2	270.5	69.2	585.6
1997	205.4	250.3	58.9	514.6
1996	178.5	224.7	37.4	440.6
1995	163.1	207.2	39.4	409.7
1994	150.4	201.9	39.1	391.4

[1]Includes United States and Canada.
[2]Includes Austria, Belgium, France, Germany, Italy, Netherlands, Spain, Switzerland and United Kingdom.
[3]Includes Japan and Australia.

EXHIBIT 2 1998 Heavyweight Motorcycle (651 cc+) Market Shares by Global Regions

Source: Adapted from Harley-Davidson, Inc., *1998 Annual Report*, p. 52.

Company	North America	Europe	Asia/Pacific
BMW	2.7%	13.4%	4.3%
Harley-Davidson/Buell	48.5	6.4	15.6
Honda	20.5	24.1	28.0
Kawasaki	10.2	10.7	22.1
Suzuki	10.3	17.2	7.9
Yamaha	4.8	16.3	16.6
Other	3.0	11.9	5.5

Note: Regions defined as in Exhibit 1.

is based on such things as styling, engine displacement (power), features (e.g., cruise control, fuel injection), availability, brand equity and price. Shortages of Harleys lead many consumers to purchase competitive bikes as there are two-year waiting lists for some Harley models.

All of the major competitors produce touring and custom (cruiser) motorcycles that compete directly with Harley and sport bikes that compete with Buell's offerings. BMW's R and K series of bikes; Honda's Gold Wing, ST1100, Shadow, Valkyrie, and Pacific Coast; Kawasaki's Vulcan series and Concours; Yamaha's Venture, Road Star, Royal Star, Virago, and Vstar; and Suzuki's Marauder and Intruder series are some of the major models competing with Harley-Davidson. In addition, most of the major competitors have full lines of smaller motorcycles with engine displacements of less than 651 ccs, a market in which Harley does not compete.

New Competition

In addition to established competitors, there are a number of new competitors entering the market. Polaris, the snowmobile manufacturer, converted an assembly line in its Spirit Lake, Iowa, facility to produce the Polaris Victory Y9ZC, a retro-look, V-twin cruiser. This bike is targeted to Polaris's existing snowmobile customers, 30 percent of whom are also motorcycle enthusiasts. Excelsior-Henderson, once one of the big three motorcycle manufacturers (along with Harley and Indian), has been resurrected in Belle Plaine, Minnesota, to produce the Super X, a direct Harley competitor. A California company purchased the Indian trademark and plans to build a limited edition Indian Chief motorcycle. All of these companies are seeking to capitalize on the demand for heavyweight bikes, particularly Harleys.

Competitive Remakes and Accessories

Big Dog Motorcycles of Sun Valley, Idaho, produces the Big Dog Aerosport Cruiser, a customized Harley selling for thousands over the stock Harley price. A variety of other companies, such as Titan, Ultra Kustom, Illusion, and California Motorcycle Co., make non-Harley Harleys with their own parts. S&S Cycle produces performance parts that compete directly with Harley parts as do other manufacturers who produce seats, exhaust pipes, saddlebags, and windshields that some customers prefer over Harley offerings.

Motorcycle Buyers

The demographic profile of motorcycle buyers has changed over the years. According to the Motorcycle Industry Council, 61 percent of buyers are over 35 years old whereas in 1980, only 27 percent had reached this age. In 1980, only 2.4 percent of motorcycle buyers had incomes of $50,000 or higher, whereas in 1998, over one third were in this income group. White-collar professionals are the largest group of new bike riders, accounting for 36 percent. Many are former riders now stepping up to their dream machines and state that motorcycle riding helps reduce stress in their lives.

Motorcycle Company Websites

Harley-Davidson's management believes that the Internet is a powerful marketing tool. Its website is affectionately called the "anti-website" since it encourages visitors to get off-line and onto their Harleys. The website includes detailed information on the company and its products and had nearly 1.5 million visitors in 1997 alone.

All of Harley's major competitors have products other than motorcycles on their websites including cars (Honda, Acura, Suzuki, BMW), outboard motors (Honda, Yamaha, Suzuki), jet skis (Kawasaki), snowmobiles (Yamaha), boats (Yamaha), generators and power equipment (Honda, Yamaha). However, Harley-Davidson's website is devoted exclusively to motorcycle-related information about Harley's products, experience, and the company itself, including financial data. This may be a competitive advantage for Harley because it illustrates that the company is focused only in the motorcycle industry.

Discussion Questions

1. Why is the Internet a particularly good promotion medium for Harley-Davidson?
2. What different roles could Harley-Davidson's website play for Harley owners, for people shopping for a motorcycle, and for people just interested in motorcycles in general?
3. Visit Harley-Davidson's website (www.harley-davidson.com) and evaluate it on the following criteria:
   a. Home page quality
   b. Site map quality
   c. Ease of browsing
   d. Image speed
   e. Attractiveness
   f. Product information
   g. Dealer information
   h. Company information
   i. Ease of exiting
   j. Overall evaluation (sum of above)

Rate each dimension on a scale from one (poor) to five (excellent). What do you conclude about the quality of Harley's website as a marketing tool?

4. Evaluate Harley-Davidson's website from a promotion strategy point of view. What role does it play in Harley's promotion mix?
5. Compare Harley-Davidson's website with those of its major competitors on the criteria listed in Question 3 above. Focus only on the motorcycle portion of these websites:

   www.bmw.com

   www.honda.com

   www.kawasaki.com

   www.suzuki.com

   www.yamaha-motor.com

   Overall, what are the strengths and weaknesses of each website?

6. Visit the Polaris website at www.victory-usa.com. What is your evaluation of this website and the Polaris Victory Y9ZC?
7. Why do you think the heavyweight motorcycle market has grown so much in recent years?
8. How many motorcycles did each company sell globally in 1998? What accounts for Honda's success?

References

Brown, Stuart F., "The Company That Out-Harleys Harley," *Fortune,* September 28, 1998, pp. 56–57.

della Cava, Marco R., "Motorcycle Maker Caters to the Continent," *USA Today,* April 22, 1998, p. 8B.

Eldridge, Earle, "Motorcycling Passion Climbs the Corporate Ladder," *USA Today,* May 7, 1999, pp. B1–B2.

Harley-Davidson, Inc., 1997 *Annual Report.*

Harley-Davidson, Inc., 1998 *Annual Report.*

Machan, Dyan, "Is the Hog Going Soft?" *Forbes,* March 10, 1997, pp. 114–119.

Melcher, Richard A., "Tune-Up Time for Harley," *Business Week,* April 8, 1996, pp. 90–94.

Motorcycle Cruiser, Los Angeles, CA: Peterson Publishing Company, April 1999.

Stevens, Karen, and Dale Kurschner, "That Vroom! You Hear May Not Be a Harley," *Business Week,* October 1997, pp. 159–160.

14

Wind Technology

Ken Manning
University of South Carolina

Jakki J. Mohr
University of Montana

Kevin Cage, general manager of Wind Technology, sat in his office on a Friday afternoon watching the snow fall outside his window. It was January 1991 and he knew that during the month ahead he would have to make some difficult decisions regarding the future of his firm, Wind Technology. The market for the wind profiling radar systems that his company designed had been developing at a much slower rate than he had anticipated.

The Situation

During Wind Technology's 10-year history, the company had produced a variety of weather-related radar and instrumentation. In 1986, the company condensed its product mix to include only wind-profiling radar systems. Commonly referred to as wind profilers, these products measure wind and atmospheric turbulence for weather forecasting, detection of wind direction at NASA launch sites, and other meteorological applications (i.e., at universities and other scientific monitoring stations). Kevin had felt that this consolidation would position the company as a leader in what he anticipated to be a high-growth market with little competition.

Wind Technology's advantages over Unisys, the only other key player in the wind-profiling market, included the following: (1) The company adhered stringently to specifications and quality production; (2) Wind Technology had the technical expertise to provide full system integration. This allowed customers to order either basic components or a full system including software support; (3) Wind Technology's staff of meteorologists and atmospheric scientists provided the customer with sophisticated support, including operation and maintenance training and field assistance; (4) Finally, Wind Technology had devoted all of its resources to its wind-profiling business. Kevin believed that the market would perceive this as an advantage over a large conglomerate like Unisys.

Wind Technology customized each product for individual customers as the need arose; the total system could cost a customer from $400,000 to $5 million. Various governmental entities, such as the Department of Defense, NASA, and state universities had consistently accounted for about 90 percent of Wind Technology's sales. In lieu of a field sales force, Wind Technology relied on top management and a team of engineers to call on prospective and current customers. Approximately $105,000 of their annual salaries was charged to a direct selling expense.

THE PROBLEM

The consolidation strategy that the company had undertaken in 1986 was partly due to the company being purchased by Vaitra, a high-technology European firm. Wind Technology's ability to focus on the wind-profiling business had been made possible by Vaitra's financial support. However, since 1986 Wind Technology had shown little commercial success, and due to low sales levels, the company was experiencing severe cash-flow problems. Kevin knew that Wind Technology could not continue to meet payroll much longer. Also, he had been informed that Vaitra was not willing to pour more money into Wind Technology. Kevin estimated that he had from 9 to 12 months (until the end of 1991) in which to implement a new strategy with the potential to improve the company's cash flow. The new strategy was necessary to enable Wind Technology to survive until the wind-profiler market matured. Kevin and other industry experts anticipated that it would be two years until the wind-profiling market achieved the high growth levels that the company had initially anticipated.

One survival strategy that Kevin had in mind was to spin off and market component parts used in making wind profilers. Initial research indicated that, of all the wind-profiling system's component parts, the high-voltage power supply (HVPS) had the greatest potential for commercial success. Furthermore, Kevin's staff on the HVPS product had demonstrated knowledge of the market. Kevin felt that by marketing the HVPS, Wind Technology could reap incremental revenues, with very little addition to fixed costs. (Variable costs would include the costs of making and marketing the HVPS. The accounting department had estimated that production costs would run approximately 70 percent of the selling price, and that 10 percent of other expenses—such as top management direct-selling expenses—should be charged to the HVPS.)

HIGH-VOLTAGE POWER SUPPLIES

For a vast number of consumer and industrial products that require electricity, the available voltage level must be transformed to different levels and types of output. The three primary types of power supplies include linears, switchers, and converters. Each type manipulates electrical current in terms of the type of current (AC or DC) and/or the level of output (voltage). Some HVPS manufacturers focus on producing a standardized line of power supplies, while others specialize in customizing power supplies to the user's specifications.

High-voltage power supplies vary significantly in size and level of output. Small power supplies with relatively low levels of output (under 3 kV[1]) are used in communications equipment. Medium-sized power supplies that produce an output between 3 and 10 kV are used in a wide range of products including radars and lasers. Power supplies that produce output greater than 10 kV are used in a variety of applications, such as high-powered X rays and plasma-etching systems.

[1]kV (kilovolt): 1,000 volts.

BACKGROUND ON WIND TECHNOLOGY'S HVPS

One of Wind Technology's corporate strategies was to control the critical technology (major component parts) of its wind-profiling products. Management felt that this control was important since the company was part of a high-technology industry in which confidentiality and innovation were critical to each competitor's success. This strategy also gave Wind Technology a differential advantage over its major competitors, all of whom depended on a variety of manufacturers for component parts. Wind Technology had successfully developed almost all of the major component parts and the software for the wind profiler, yet the development of the power supply had been problematic.

To adhere to the policy of controlling critical technology in product design (rather than purchasing an HVPS from an outside supplier), Wind Technology management had hired Anne Ladwig and her staff of HVPS technicians to develop a power supply for the company's wind-profiling systems. Within six months of joining Wind Technology, Anne and her staff had completed development of a versatile power supply which could be adapted for use with a wide variety of equipment. Some of the company's wind-profiling systems required up to ten power supplies, each modified slightly to carry out its role in the system.

Kevin Cage had delegated the responsibility of investigating the sales potential of the company's HVPS to Anne Ladwig since she was very familiar with the technical aspects of the product and had received formal business training while pursuing an MBA. Anne had determined that Wind Technology's HVPS could be modified to produce levels of output between 3 and 10 kV. Thus, it seemed natural that if the product was brought to market, Wind Technology should focus on applications in this range of output. Wind Technology also did not have the production capabilities to compete in the high-volume, low-voltage segment of the market, nor did the company have the resources and technical expertise to compete in the high-output (10 kV +) segment.

THE POTENTIAL CUSTOMER

Power supplies in the 3–10 kV range could be used to conduct research, to produce other products, or to place as a component into other products such as lasers. Thus, potential customers could include research labs, large end-users, OEMs, or distributors. Research labs each used an average of three power supplies; other types of customers ordered a widely varying quantity.

HVPS users were demanding increasing levels of reliability, quality, customization, and system integration. *System integration* refers to the degree to which other parts of a system are dependent upon the HVPS for proper functioning, and the extent to which these parts are combined into a single unit or piece of machinery.

Anne had considered entering several HVPS market segments in which Wind Technology could reasonably compete. She had estimated the domestic market potential of these segments at $237 million. To evaluate these segments, Anne had compiled growth forecasts for the year ahead and had evaluated each segment in terms of the anticipated level of customization and system integration demanded by the market. Anne felt that the level of synergy between Wind Technology and the various segments was also an important consideration in selecting a target market. Exhibit 1 summarizes this information. Anne believed that if the product was produced, Wind Technology's interests would be best served by selecting only one target market on which to concentrate initially.

COMPETITION

To gather competitive information, Anne contacted five HVPS manufacturers. She found that the manufacturers varied significantly in terms of size and marketing

EXHIBIT 1   HVPS Market Segments in the 3–10 kV Range

Application	Forecasted Annual Growth (%)	Level of Customization/ Level of System Integration*	Synergy Rating**	Percent of $237 Million Power Supply Market***
General/univ. laboratory	5.40	Medium/medium	3	8
Lasers	11.00	Low/medium	4	10
Medical equipment	10.00	Medium/medium	3	5
Microwave	12.00	Medium/high	4	7
Power modulators	3.00	Low/low	4	25
Radar systems	11.70	Low/medium	5	12
Semiconductor	10.10	Low/low	3	23
X-ray systems	8.60	Medium/high	3	10

* The level of customization and system integration generally in demand within each of the applications is defined as low, medium, or high.
** Synergy ratings are based on a scale of 1 to 5; 1 is equivalent to a very low level of synergy and 5 is equivalent to a very high level of synergy. These subjective ratings are based on the amount of similarities between the wind-profiling industry and each application.
*** Percentages total 100 percent of the $237 million market in which Wind Technology anticipated it could compete.
Note: This list of applications is not all-inclusive.

EXHIBIT 2   Competitor Profile (3–10 kV range)

Company	Gamma	Glassman	Kaiser	Maxwell*	Spellman
Approximate annual sales	$2 million	$7.5 million	$3 million		$7 million
Market share	1.00%	3.00%	1.50%		2.90%
Price**	$5,830	$5,590	$6,210	$5,000–$6,000	$6,360
Delivery	12 weeks	10 weeks	10 weeks	8 weeks	12 weeks
Product customization	No	Medium	Low	Medium	Low
System integration experience	Low	Low	Low	Medium	Low
Customer targets	Gen. lab.	Laser	Laser	Radar	Capacitors
	Space	Medical	Medical	Power mod.	Gen. lab.
	Univ. lab.	X ray	Microwave	X ray	Microwave
			Semiconductor	Medical equip.	X ray

*Maxwell was in the final stages of product development and stated that the product would be available in the spring. Maxwell anticipated that the product would sell in the $5,000–$6,000 range.
** Price quoted for an HVPS with the same specifications as the "standard" model developed by Wind Technology.

strategy (see Exhibit 2). Each listed a price in the $5,500–$6,500 range on power supplies with the same features and output levels as the HVPS that had been developed for Wind Technology. After she spoke with these firms, Anne had the feeling that Wind Technology could offer the HVPS market superior levels of quality, reliability, technical expertise, and customer support. She optimistically believed that a one-half percent market share objective could be achieved the first year.

PROMOTION

If Wind Technology entered the HVPS market, they would require a hard-hitting, thorough promotional campaign to reach the selected target market. Three factors made the selection of elements in the promotion mix especially important to Wind Technology: (1) Wind Technology's poor cash flow, (2) the lack of a well-developed marketing department, and (3) the need to generate incremental revenue from sales of the HVPS at a minimum cost. In fact, a rule of thumb used by Wind Technology was that all marketing expenditures should be about 9 to 10 percent of sales. Kevin and Anne were contemplating the use of the following elements:

1. Collateral Material   Sales literature, brochures, and data sheets are necessary to communicate the product benefits and features to potential customers. These materials are designed to be (1) mailed to customers as part of direct-mail campaigns or in response to customer requests, (2) given away at trade shows, and (3) left behind after sales presentations.

Because no one in Wind Technology was an experienced copywriter, Anne and Kevin considered hiring a marketing communications agency to write the copy and to design the layout of the brochures. This agency would also complete the graphics (photographs and artwork) for the collateral material. The cost for 5,000 pieces (including the 10 percent markup for the agency) was estimated to be $5.50 each.

2. Public Relations   Kevin and Anne realized that one very cost-efficient tool of promotion is publicity. They contemplated sending out new product announcements to a variety of trade journals whose readers were part of Wind Technology's new target market. By using this tool, interested readers could call or write to Wind Technology, and the company could then send the prospective customers collateral material. The drawback of relying too heavily on this element was very obvious to Kevin and Anne—the editors of the trade journals could choose not to print Wind Technology's product announcements if their new product was not deemed newsworthy.

The cost of using this tool would include the time necessary to write the press release and the expense of mailing the release to the editors. Direct costs were estimated by Wind Technology to be $500.

3. Direct Mail   Kevin and Anne were also contemplating a direct-mail campaign. The major expenditure for this option would be buying a list of prospects to whom the collateral material would be mailed. Such lists usually cost around $5,000, depending upon the number of names and the list quality. Other costs would include postage and the materials mailed. These costs were estimated to be $7,500 for a mailing of 1,500.

4. Trade Shows   The electronics industry had several annual trade shows. If they chose to exhibit at one of these trade shows, Wind Technology would incur the cost of a booth, the space at the show, and the travel and incidental costs of the people attending the show to staff the booth. Kevin and Anne estimated these costs at approximately $50,000 for the exhibit, space, and materials, and $50,000 for a staff of five people to attend.

5. Trade Journal Advertising   Kevin and Anne also contemplated running a series of ads in trade journals. Several journals they considered are listed in Exhibit 3, along with circulation, readership, and cost information.

6. Personal Selling

(a) *Telemarketing* (Inbound/Inside Sales).[2] Kevin and Anne also considered hiring a technical salesperson to respond to HVPS product inquiries generated by product announcements, direct mail, and advertising. This person's responsibilities would include answering phone calls, prospecting, sending out collateral material, and following up with potential customers. The salary and benefits for one individual would be about $50,000.

(b) *Field Sales.* The closing of sales for the HVPS might require some personal selling at the customer's location, especially if Wind Technology pursued the customized option. Kevin and Anne realized that potentially this would provide them

---

[2]"Inbound" refers to calls that potential customers make to Wind Technology, rather than "outbound," in which Wind Technology calls potential customers (i.e., solicits sales).

EXHIBIT 3   Trade Publications

Trade Publication	Editorial	Cost per Color Insertion (1 page)	Circulation
Electrical Manufacturing	For purchasers and users of power supplies, transformers, and other electrical products.	$4,077	35,168 nonpaid
Electronic Component News	For electronics OEM's. Products addressed include work stations, power sources, chips, etc.	$6,395	110,151 nonpaid
Electronic Manufacturing News	For OEM's in the industry of providing manufacturing and contracting of components, circuits, and systems.	$5,075	25,000 nonpaid
Design News	For design OEM's covering components, systems, and materials.	$8,120	170,033 nonpaid
Weatherwise	For meteorologists covering imaging, radar, etc.	$1,040	10,186 paid

Note: This is a partial list of applicable trade publications. Standard Rate and Data Service lists other possible publications.

with the most incremental revenue, but it also had the potential to be the most costly tool. Issues such as how many salespeople to hire, where to position them in the field (geographically), and so on, were major concerns. Salary plus expenses and benefits for an outside salesperson were estimated to be about $80,000.

DECISIONS

As Kevin sat in his office and perused the various facts and figures, he knew that he would have to make some quick decisions. He sensed that the decision about whether or not to proceed with the HVPS spin-off was risky, but he felt that to not do something to improve the firm's cash flow was equally risky. Kevin also knew that if he decided to proceed with the HVPS, there were a number of segments in that market in which Wind Technology could position its HVPS. He mulled over which segment appeared to be a good fit for Wind Technology's abilities (given Anne's recommendation that a choice of one segment would be best). Finally, Kevin was concerned that if they entered the HVPS market, promotion for their product would be costly, further exacerbating the cash flow situation. He knew that promotion would be necessary, but the exact mix of elements would have to be designed with financial constraints in mind.

Case 15

Lady Foot Locker: The Lobo Launch

Andrew J. Rohm
Northeastern University

David W. Rosenthal
Miami University

Thomas C. Boyd
Cal State Fullerton

As he walked briskly down Broadway to the Lady Foot Locker (LFL) offices in Manhattan, Bill Wyatt recalled the newspaper headline he had seen a month ago, in early January 1997, declaring "*Lobo Signs with the WNBA's New York Liberty.*" Rebecca Lobo had played center on the University of Connecticut women's basketball team and was a member of the U.S. Women's Olympic team that had won the gold medal at the 1996 Olympic Games. Wyatt, the General Merchandise Manager responsible for overseeing footwear and apparel buying and merchandise assortment for all 650 Lady Foot Locker stores, had watched Lobo and her teammates as they played for the gold in Atlanta.

That newspaper headline had motivated Wyatt to initiate discussions with Reebok, one of LFL's primary vendors and one of Lobo's sponsors, regarding the commercial potential in a Rebecca Lobo "signature" shoe. Wyatt believed there was great potential in a signature basketball shoe and apparel collection targeting female basketball players and consumers. Lobo was about to enter the inaugural Women's National Basketball Association (WNBA) season in 1997 as one of the league's most popular athletes, particularly among 12 to 17 year-old girls.

This case is based on personal interviews and field research and was written solely as a basis for class discussion rather than to illustrate either effective or ineffective retail and marketing strategy practices. The decisions, organizations, individuals, and information are real. Thus, the information presented in the case is the same information used by the decision makers. The authors acknowledge the valuable comments of three anonymous reviewers and the editor of the *Case Research Journal*, Linda Swayne. The quality of this case was greatly improved as a result of their efforts.

Wyatt quickened his step. He was running late for an important merchandise meeting he held weekly with his buying staff. This morning they were going to discuss the potential Lobo product launch. In the four weeks since Wyatt had proposed the Lobo idea to Reebok management, a series of negotiations had resulted in a launch plan on which Wyatt and his buying staff had to make a decision soon.

The purpose of this week's merchandise meeting with two of his footwear buyers, Mike Tilbrook and Al Ellerbroek, was to decide whether or not to move ahead with the Lobo launch. While Lobo's popularity was an advantage, LFL faced significant risks in taking a large inventory position in a product, basketball shoes designed specifically for women, targeted to a relatively underdeveloped market segment.

The Athletic Footwear Industry

During the 1970s and 1980s the athletic footwear industry focused on a few core categories—basketball, tennis, running, and fitness. As the industry grew in the early 1990s, the level of product segmentation and number of footwear categories grew as well. However, total sales were falling, so the choice of segments in which to compete was becoming more critical. Exhibits 1 and 2 illustrate dollar and unit sales in the U.S. athletic footwear industry between 1995 and 1997.

INDUSTRY SUPPLIERS

Nike

Nike was the U.S. market share leader in both women's and men's athletic footwear. Its 1996 share of the overall U.S. athletic footwear market was 34.7%. Nike's strengths included product design and development, its Air technology, promotions of its footwear products with well-known athletes such as Michael Jordan, stand-out advertising communications, and operations. Its Swoosh icon and the Just Do It! tagline were recognized worldwide as symbols of performance and quality. In 1996, Nike's global revenues were $7.1 billion (a 35% increase from 1995), and U.S. footwear revenues were estimated at $3.1 billion, a 22% increase from 1995.

EXHIBIT 1   Total U.S. Athletic Footwear Market (wholesale)

Source: Footwear Market Index 1997 (FMI)

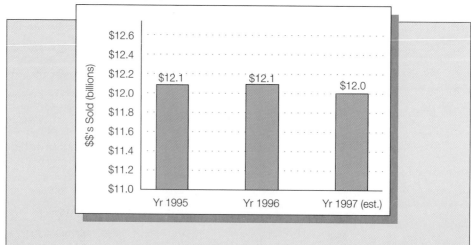

EXHIBIT 2 Total U.S. Athletic Footwear Market

Source: Footwear Market Index 1997 (FMI)

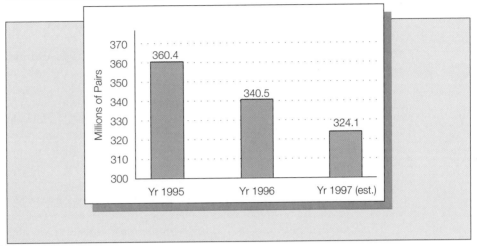

Reebok

Reebok International consisted of three principal operating units: The Reebok Division, The Rockport Company, and the Greg Norman Collection (golf apparel). Reebok designed, marketed, and distributed sports, fitness, and casual footwear, apparel, and equipment. Although Reebok products were sold in approximately 170 countries, the U.S. was Reebok's single largest market.

Reebok's share of the U.S. athletic footwear market in 1996 declined to 17.7% from 18.9%. Reebok's strengths included a category of casual and comfort-based shoes called "Classics" as well as shoes targeting the 25–44 year-old female in the walking, women's fitness, and aerobic categories. In the early 1990s, however, in response to Nike's growing share of the performance footwear segment in the basketball, running, and cross-training categories, Reebok began to target the male-oriented footwear categories. The company renewed product development efforts in the basketball category and signed young, up-and-coming players such as Shaquille O'Neal. In 1996, Reebok's global revenues were $3.5 billion (flat versus 1995 levels); its U.S. footwear revenues declined to $1.2 billion from $1.4 billion in 1995.

Fila

Fila's business grew during the early 1990s amongst the 12–24 year-old urban consumer. In 1996, Fila's share of the global footwear market was 5.4% and its share of the U.S. footwear market was 8.5%. Fila also began signing high-profile endorsers such as Grant Hill of the National Basketball Association (NBA) in order to promote its performance-based basketball shoes. Fila also believed that this strategy would help protect its revenue stream from the vagaries of the fashion market and a relatively fickle young consumer. In 1996, Fila's global revenues were $3.1 billion (a 59% increase from 1995), and U.S. footwear revenues were estimated at $1.3 billion (a 22% increase from 1995).

adidas

Adidas had an 11.3% share of the global footwear market and 5.4% of the overall U.S. athletic footwear market in 1996. For many years prior, however, adidas had been the leader in global athletic footwear sales. Because of this, U.S. retailers viewed adidas as a "sleeping giant" because of its relative market under-performance. In 1996, adidas' global revenues were $1.7 billion, and U.S. footwear revenues were estimated at $400 million, a 13% increase from 1995 levels.

SUBSTITUTE BRANDS

Surf and skate footwear from the more "edgy" alternative brands like Airwalk and Vans, however, had begun to cut into the market share of the core athletic brands. Also, several new, non-traditional competitors entered the athletic footwear and apparel market in 1996. Ralph Lauren licensed its entire Polo footwear business to Rockport, a division of Reebok International, and it was expected to introduce an athletic footwear line in 1998. Nautica had also launched its Nautica Competition athletic footwear and apparel line. Nautica distributed this line through its traditional department-store channel as well as select Foot Locker and Lady Foot Locker stores. Tommy Hilfiger's new athletic footwear line was slated for 1997 exclusive distribution within its department store accounts. Donna Karan had launched its DKNY Active line of athletic footwear and apparel within select department stores as well as Foot Locker, Lady Foot Locker, and Champs. Exhibit 3 highlights the recent unit sales trends within the U.S. athletic footwear market as a percentage of the total U.S. footwear market.

PRIVATE LABEL TRENDS

By 1997, private labels and house brands were gaining momentum within the specialty athletic retail channel. Private-label products provided greater retailer profitability and greater control of the store merchandise mix. Third-party sourcing agents produced private-label brands specifically for the retailer. By buying direct from a factory agent, the retailer was potentially able to increase selling margins from 45% to as much as 65%. Foot Locker had recently developed its In The Zone (ITZ) line of store-brand basketball footwear, signing the NBA's Bobby Hurley as ITZ spokesperson; and JC Penney was planning a line of private-label Olympic footwear displaying the trademarked Olympic rings as part of its U.S. Olympic Committee sponsorship.

INDUSTRY COMPETITION-MARKETING MIX

Product

Economies of scale and purchasing power within the channel provided advantages to companies with broad lines. Nike led the industry with breakthrough product design and technical innovations. Whereas Reebok, adidas, Fila and smaller niche brands

EXHIBIT 3   Total U.S. Athletic Footwear Market (as % of total footwear units sold)

Source: Footwear Market Index 1997 (FMI)

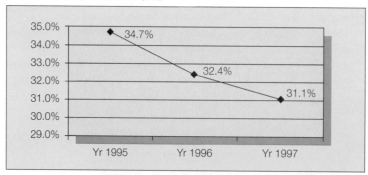

possessed specific category strengths, none were able to match Nike's market share across multiple footwear categories. Larger brands such as Nike, Reebok, adidas, and Fila developed numerous product lines ranging from basketball and tennis to soccer and hiking/outdoor shoes. Smaller, more focused brands such as Saucony or Ryka tended to concentrate on fewer categories; for example, Ryka focused exclusively on categories with greater women's participation, such as aerobics, fitness, and walking.

Several athletic footwear brands offered proprietary technologies designed to enhance their products' performance. Technologies such as Nike Air went through frequent (annual and even bi-annual) evolutions, such as rearfoot and forefoot Air, and varying volume of Air units depending on the specific shoe and price level. Exhibit 4 highlights some of these proprietary footwear technologies.

Air seemed to be the most widely recognized technology among both retailers and end-consumers. Reebok's DMX technology was slated for an April 1997 launch in Reebok's running category, with additional DMX product launches scheduled for later in 1997 in the cross-training and basketball categories. Reebok was confident of DMX's prospects and positioned it directly against Nike Air as a superior cushioning technology system.

Investing in the development and marketing of these technologies helped to build brand credibility and differentiation. Brand managers believed that technology delivered an important point-of-difference between the emerging fashion, or sport casual, brands and the performance brands.

As a result of growing consumer demand, consumer segmentation, and increased competition, manufacturers frequently introduced new products and shortened product life cycles. Product cycles, particularly in the more fashion-dependent basketball category, had evolved from yearly introductions to quarterly and even

EXHIBIT 4   Technology Attributes by Brand

Source: prepared by authors based on various trade publications and discussions with industry personnel

Brand	Technology	Features/Benefits	Price Range (retail)
Nike	Nike Air (introduced 1979)	Pressurized air units in heel and/or forefoot for cushioning	$60–$150
	Zoom Air (due 1997)	Lower profile, lightweight version of Nike Air	$75+
Reebok	Hexalite Viz Hex Suspended Hex Radial Hex (introduced and evolved during the 1980s/1990s)	Lightweight, honeycomb material in heel for cushioning	$50–$70 (regular Hex) $75–$90 (Viz-Hex, Suspended Hex, Radial Hex)
	DMX (due April 1997)	Ten-chambered air unit for dynamic air movement and cushioning	$110+
Asics	Gel (introduced in the mid-1980s)	Lightweight material in heel and/or forefoot for cushioning	$55 +
Fila	Fila 2A (due 1997)	Lightweight cushioning unit	$75+
adidas	Feet You Wear (due 1997)	Shoe outsole designed to mimic the human foot	$100+

EXHIBIT 5   Total U.S. Athletic Footwear Market (% of total pairs sold by top 10 retailers)

Source: Footwear Market Index 1997 (FMI)

Retailer	1995	1996	1997 (est.)
Payless	11.5%	12.1%	12.4%
Wal-Mart	8.2	9.0	9.9
Foot Locker/Lady Foot Locker	**10.1**	**10.5**	**9.2**
Kmart	6.9	6.8	7.4
JC Penney	5.9	5.7	6.3
Sears	3.1	2.6	2.7
Famous Footwear	2.0	2.6	2.5
Target	2.2	2.6	2.4
Kohl's	1.2	1.4	1.9
Sports Authority	0.9	1.0	1.6

monthly introductions. This shift put pressure on the footwear suppliers, such as Reebok, to shorten their design and development timelines.

Pricing

Consumers paid premium prices for athletic shoes with advanced technology because they believed these products enhanced performance. Nike was the industry's product leader, in large part because of its stable of sponsored athletes, such as Michael Jordan, Scottie Pippen, and Andre Agassi, and also due to its well-known Air technology. Nike priced its Air shoes between $60 and $150 at retail, while Reebok priced its Hexalite shoes between $50 and $90. No other footwear brands were able to match Nike's ability to command premium prices for its top-end products. Pricing in the athletic footwear industry was typically based upon 30% to 55% supplier gross margins on wholesale selling price and 45% retailer markups on retail selling price.

Retail Channels

Retail competition within the athletic footwear market was based upon several factors, including target consumer segment, price, merchandise assortment, store or chain reputation, store location, advertising, and customer service. For years, Foot Locker and Lady Foot Locker experienced little direct competition. Few national chains specialized in athletic footwear and even fewer specialized in women's-specific athletic footwear. Exhibit 5 shows the market shares of the ten largest athletic shoe retailers.

Although no other national retailer besides LFL concentrated solely on the women's athletic market, indirect competitors to LFL included national athletic specialty stores such as Footaction and Finish Line as well as "big box" stores such as The Sports Authority, Sneaker Stadium, and Just For Feet. Athletic footwear and apparel departments within regional and national department stores (such as JC Penney's Simply For Sports concept) also competed indirectly with LFL. The department store channel tended to focus on the female consumer. Exhibit 6 details the total U.S. women's athletic footwear market by percent of total pairs sold within the primary retail channels.

Promotion

Companies such as Reebok and Nike depended on promotions to grow market share. Promotions included celebrity endorsements and national brand and image campaigns. Industry sources estimated that adidas spent 12.5 % of its revenues on promotional activity, with much of that spending going to celebrity endorsements.

EXHIBIT 6   Women's U.S. Athletic Footwear Market* (% of total pairs sold by distribution channel)

Source: Footwear Market Index 1997 (FMI)

Distribution Channel	1995	1996	1997 (est.)
High-Priced			
Department Stores	10.7%	9.9%	9.2%
Apparel Specialty Shops	1.1	1.4	1.4
Sporting Goods Shops	8.0	5.9	7.7
Mail Order	2.7	2.4	2.2
Shoe Stores	7.6	7.4	6.2
Athletic Specialty Stores*	11.2	12.7	13.9
Moderate-Priced			
Sears, JC Penney, Wards	9.4	9.6	11.0
Shoe Stores	5.2	4.8	4.3
Factory Outlets	3.3	2.6	4.2
All Other	3.2	2.9	1.8
Low-Priced			
Discount Stores	24.4	26.7	25.8
Self-Service Stores	12.9	13.6	12.3
All Other	0.3	0.2	0.1
	100.0%	100.0%	100.0%

*Lady Foot Locker falls under the Athletic Specialty Store category

The company had recently signed basketball star Kobe Bryant for $10 million, and the entire New York Yankee baseball team at a cost of $100 million.

However, Nike was the industry leader in celebrity endorsements, and its stable of athletes included Michael Jordan, Tiger Woods, and many others. Reebok spent heavily in celebrity endorsements as well, having recently signed basketball player Shaquille O'Neal for $3 million per year. Advertising expenditures for the top ten athletic shoe brands are shown in Exhibit 7. It is important to note that the costs of celebrity endorsements are not included in these figures. "Unmeasured" promotional expenditures (which would include the costs of celebrity endorsements) for Nike totaled $290 million in 1997 (est.) and $160 million in 1996. Reebok's figures were $68.1 million in 1997 (est.) and $68.2 million in 1996.

INDUSTRY TRENDS

As the industry matured and competition intensified, athletic footwear companies attempted to capture sales and market share through market segmentation (often by type of sport or usage category), differentiation, and branding. It was now possible to find a "sneaker" for every conceivable sport or activity, in categories such as cross-training and walking to sub-categories such as Versatraining (Reebok) and Total Body Conditioning (Nike).

The athletic footwear market had been declining for the past two years. Industry sources believed this trend resulted from a shift to alternative footwear, such as sandals and casual shoes, that they expected to continue into 1997. Total market revenue had remained flat at about $12 billion over the same time period, reflecting increasing shoe prices. Exhibit 8 shows sales by category.

EXHIBIT 7   Total Advertising Expenditures of the Top 10 Athletic Footwear Brands: 1996–1997

Source: Ad Age Dataplace
Reprinted by permission from the Advertising Age Data Center at www.AdAge.com. Copyright Crain Communications Inc.

Rank	Brand	Measured Advertising 1997 (in millions)	Measured Advertising 1996 (in millions)
1	Nike	$159.0	$149.0
2	Reebok	55.0	84.0
3	adidas	21.0	14.0
4	Fila	15.0	13.0
5	Converse	8.0	5.0
6	New Balance	4.0	3.0
7	Keds	3.0	3.0
8	Airwalk	2.0	9.0
9	Asics	2.0	2.0
10	Foot-Joy	2.0	2.0

EXHIBIT 8   Total U.S. Retail Athletic Footwear Market (% of total pairs sold by footwear category)

Source: Footwear Market Index 1997 (FMI)

Footwear Category	1995	1996
Aerobic	2.3%	2.9%
Cross Training	9.9	10.0
Basketball	9.1	13.8
Tennis/Court	4.5	6.4
Running	10.4	6.3
Casual Sneakers	25.3	34.6
Walking	17.2	16.6
Infant	7.9	6.0
Other	13.3	3.3
	100.0%	100.0%

THE EMERGING WOMEN'S ATHLETIC MARKET

Both the 1972 Title IX ruling that helped to bring sex parity to intercollegiate sports and the related emergence of sports participation among pre-teen and teen-age girls had recently influenced the women's sport market. According to the Women's Sports Foundation, one in 27 girls participated in high school sports in 1971. By 1997, that figure was one in three. Also, over 13 million women aged six and over played basketball in the U.S. by 1997, compared with 11 million in 1987.

Even with the increase in women's sports participation, Wyatt observed that LFL's average sales volume was still well below that of Foot Locker and Kids Foot Locker, due to relatively greater demand for men's and children's shoes. Wyatt explained that "we're profitable and we maintain a very good sales per square foot, but nothing like Kids (Kids Foot Locker) and nothing like Foot (Foot Locker)." Exhibits 9 and 10 detail the U.S. women's athletic footwear market growth and average retail price per pair. Exhibit 11 also provides information on the primary brands competing within the women's athletic footwear market.

EXHIBIT 9   Women's Athletic Market Size (wholesale)

Source: Footwear Market Index 1997 (FMI)

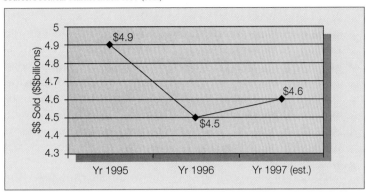

EXHIBIT 10   Women's U.S. Athletic Footwear Market

Source: Footwear Market Index 1997 (FMI)

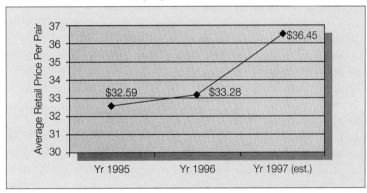

EXHIBIT 11   Women's U.S. Retail Athletic Footwear Market (top brand market shares by % pairs sold)

Source: Footwear Market Index 1997 (FMI)

Brand	1995	1996	1997 (est.)
Nike	17.0%	27.1%	26.8%
Reebok	17.5	16.8	17.0
Keds	8.0	5.6	5.0
Fila	1.8	3.3	4.0
Easy Spirit	1.8	2.3	2.4
adidas	2.5	1.5	2.2
New Balance	1.2	1.6	2.0
Avia	2.0	1.8	1.7
Rockport	1.4	1.1	0.9
Dr. Scholl's	0.8	1.1	0.6

LFL's Background

WOOLWORTH CORPORATION

Woolworth Corporation's Athletic Group included LFL, Foot Locker, World Foot Locker, Kids Foot Locker, Champs Sports, Going To The Game!, and the Eastbay mail order catalogue (acquired by Woolworth in January 1997). The Athletic Group, Woolworth's largest and most profitable business unit, operated 3,588 stores in North America, Europe, Asia, and Australia and led the industry in sales of branded athletic footwear and apparel in the U.S., with 1996 domestic sales of $3.6 billion. In the U.S., the Athletic Group operated 3,083 stores, primarily located in shopping malls. Comparable 1996 U.S. same-store sales growth (versus 1995) within the Athletic Group was 5%.

As part of its growth strategy, the Athletic Group had continually introduced new store designs that combined trend-setting product assortments with exciting retail environments. Historically, its largest proportion of sales and net income were generated during the Back-To-School (BTS) season in August.

LADY FOOT LOCKER

LFL's first retail store opened in 1982 in Joliet, Illinois. As of 1997, LFL operated approximately 650 stores across the United States and in Puerto Rico, primarily in shopping malls. LFL was the premier retailer of athletic footwear, apparel, and related products for women, carrying major brands of athletic footwear and apparel for a variety of sports and fitness activities, including running, fitness, and basketball. LFL prided itself on providing the best in woman-to-woman service and product selection. Its stores typically ranged from 800–1,200 square feet of selling space. Besides operating retail store sales, LFL had recently initiated a mail-order catalogue. The LFL organization chart in Exhibit 12 summarizes the retailer's management structure in early 1997.

THE LFL CONSUMER

LFL targeted the 18–34 year-old active female. According to management, this woman was active in sports, fitness, and family life. The 12–17 year-old teen female represented an important secondary market. Management believed that sales oc-

EXHIBIT 12   **Lady Foot Locker Management Structure**

Source: Lady Foot Locker

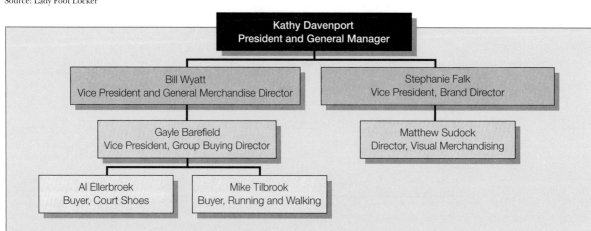

EXHIBIT 13   Total U.S. Athletic Footwear Market (% of total pairs sold by consumer segment)

Source: Footwear Market Index 1997 (FMI)

Segment	1995	1996
Men (17 + years)	33.0%	35.3%
Women (17 + years)	**41.8**	**39.8**
Boys	10.2	11.2
Girls	**7.1**	**7.7**
Infants	7.9	6.0
	100.0%	100.0%

EXHIBIT 14   Women's U.S. Athletic Footwear Market (% of total pairs sold by footwear category)

Source: Footwear Market Index 1997 (FMI)

Footwear Category	1995	1996	1997 (est.)
Aerobic	5.0%	5.8%	5.4%
Cross Training	11.4	10.3	10.5
Basketball	2.8	9.7	9.2
Tennis / Court	4.1	5.1	4.5
Running	10.1	8.5	8.7
Casual Sneakers	25.5	33.4	34.5
Walking	26.1	24.9	25.2
Other	15.0	2.3	2.0
	100.0%	100.0%	100.0%

curred across broad age segments, and thus considered the LFL customer to be "ageless." Exhibit 13 details the U.S. athletic footwear market by percent of total pairs sold within specific age segments and Exhibit 14 highlights the percentage of pairs sold across certain women's athletic footwear categories.

SUPPLIER RELATIONSHIPS

Maintaining relationships with key suppliers was critical for athletic specialty retailers such as LFL. Close supplier relationships and partnerships benefited the retailer in many ways, including the ability to:

- ensure that the retailer had the most current merchandise in stock;
- provide special make-up product[1] that offered the retailer a competitive product point-of-difference;
- increase the level of advertising or in-store marketing support from the supplier.

Until recently, the women's footwear and apparel market had been an afterthought to many LFL suppliers. Other than in categories such as walking and aerobics, women's

---

[1] Special make-up products were custom footwear or apparel products particularly designed for accounts that desired special colors or styles not featured in the suppliers' regular in-line collections. Typically, special make-ups were offered as semi-exclusive products to small groups of retailers or as account-exclusive products to accounts that could afford significant inventory commitments.

sport-specific products constituted a small percentage of new product development. Wyatt commented:

> . . .(in the past) the desire on the retailer's part for women's product was almost nonexistent. Women were buying Ked's and canvas shoes as their leisure footwear, and other than that they were wearing regular shoes. It wasn't until Lady Foot Locker started to develop their stores that women started becoming interested in athletic shoes. Reebok was the one that really kicked off the women's business, when they developed the Princess and Freestyle with the real soft leather uppers . . . then L.A. Gear came along and they were really a major partner with Lady Foot Locker when Lady Foot Locker was going through its growth phase, because nobody really concentrated on that kind of product. L.A. Gear had a fashion twist . . . just basic basketball shoes with a couple of feminine little treatments. Nike didn't really come on board until a few years ago . . . quite honestly, there was so much growth in the men's business that it was challenging enough for most people to concentrate on that market . . . also, many of the tests in the women's market early on were failures.

LFL management believed that its position as a national 650-store chain dedicated to the women's athletic market strengthened its relationships with its vendors such as Reebok. Marketing funds from vendors (typically around 2–3% of account sales, yet sometimes ranging as high as 10%) for advertising, in-store displays, sales associate education, and athlete and event sponsorships were critical to supporting store sales. Negotiations for marketing funds with suppliers such as Reebok and Nike were important to gaining additional merchandising and marketing resources needed to drive store sales.

Several factors determined the success or failure of a product launch. During quarterly meetings called *pre-lines*, LFL buyers, including Tilbrook and Ellerbroek, met with suppliers on issues such as shoe design, product introductions, pricing, inventory commitments, and product delivery dates. Particularly with regards to special make-up product, negotiations between LFL and its vendors centered around shoe design, materials and colors, pricing, product minimums required for account exclusivity (typically between 30,000 and 50,000 total pairs), matching apparel, marketing support such as advertising, and athlete and event tie-ins.

RECENT LADY FOOT LOCKER PRODUCT LAUNCHES

New product successes at LFL were typically measured by weekly sell-through—the inventory of a particular shoe that was sold in a given week. Successful product launches such as the Air Jordan typically resulted in 50% or more product liquidation in a single day at chains such as Foot Locker and approached 20% daily sell-through at LFL.

Recent LFL product launches included the Nike Air Jordan as well as Nike's Sheryl Swoopes (the former Texas Tech basketball star) shoe, launched in 1995 with an update introduced in 1996. Sell-through expectations at LFL for the Swoopes and similar new women's products were closer to 15% weekly "pushes" or sell-through.

The two Swoopes launches featured the industry's first marquee women's basketball product, offered at a suggested retail price of between $100 and $110. Even though Wyatt considered the initial Swoopes launch during Fall 1995 a success, LFL had bought a total of only 7,200 pairs; further, the shoe was not an LFL exclusive. According to Wyatt, it was "a very strong shoe and Lady Foot Locker sold every pair we bought."

However, the second Swoopes launch in 1996 was a different story. Sell-through of the Swoopes II ranged between 3–4% per week and the shoe was marked down after 10 weeks to liquidate the remaining inventory. Due to product quality and design issues and poor sell-through, LFL considered the 1996 Swoopes launch a failure.

PRICING STRATEGY

LFL typically held new footwear products at full suggested retail price for the first two weeks. Although sell-through expectations depended on the brand and type of shoe, LFL buyers typically did not begin to mark down footwear products until they fell below a 10% weekly push. Shoes were marked down in sequential 10% increments in order to liquidate remaining inventory. The number of subsequent mark-downs depended on the weekly sell-through rates, which were monitored by the buyers.

LFL's average footwear retail price per pair was approximately $60 in 1996. Its average gross margin per pair of shoes sold, before vendor discounts, was approximately 45%. LFL planned for and expected vendor discounts averaging 9%, which helped to increase its net gross margins.

PERFORMANCE MEASURES

LFL continually evaluated its product assortment in the context of its *open-to-buy* budget (the money available for new inventory). LFL management used a metric called Gross Margin Return on Investment (GMROI) to make buying decisions and evaluate financial performance. LFL buyers considered gross margin percentage (gross margin dollars/net sales) times the sales-to-stock ratio (net sales/average inventory at cost) in their calculation of GMROI. A GMROI of 140 was typically used as a benchmark for specialty footwear retailers such as LFL, where a GMROI above 140 was considered desirable.

The WNBA and Rebecca Lobo

THE WNBA

The concept of a women's professional basketball league was not a new one. The Liberty Basketball Association, which featured shorter courts, lower rims, and unitard uniforms for the players, opened in 1991 but folded after one exhibition game. The Women's World Basketball Association (WWBA) opened in 1992 with six teams, primarily in the Midwest; however, it soon folded as well.

On April 24, 1996, the National Basketball Association (NBA) Board of Governors approved the concept of a Women's National Basketball Association (WNBA). Shortly after the U.S. women's basketball team won the gold medal in Atlanta, the WNBA signed its first two players, Olympians Rebecca Lobo and Sheryl Swoopes. The WNBA was slated to begin its inaugural season in June 1997. The league selected eight cities to host the charter teams: Charlotte, Cleveland, Houston, Los Angeles, New York, Phoenix, Sacramento, and Salt Lake City. Approximately 155 LFL stores were located in these eight cities. Prior to the WNBA's planned 1997 season, the American Basketball League (ABL), another women's professional league, began its first season in October 1996 with eight teams across the U.S.

WNBA Promotional Partners

WNBA broadcast partners included NBC, ESPN, and Lifetime. Analysts projected that these network partners would reach up to 50 million people over 34 scheduled broadcasts during the WNBA's first season. WNBA marketing partners included Champion, Spalding, Nike, Kellogg USA, and McDonald's. Spalding planned to design and supply the official WNBA game ball, and Nike planned to produce WNBA-themed television commercials featuring its marquee players, including Sheryl Swoopes. Nike planned to conduct basketball leagues, clinics, and camps for young girls. Nike had also received the right to include Nike-sponsored WNBA players in

EXHIBIT 15   **Rebecca Lobo playing for the WNBA's New York Liberty**

Source: www.wnba.com

their team uniforms in advertising and promotional programs. Kellogg planned to promote top WNBA players on cereal boxes and trading card packs available with proof-of-purchase. Total league promotional spending among the WNBA's marketing partners for 1997 was estimated to be between $25–$30 million.

REBECCA LOBO

Rebecca Lobo attended the University of Connecticut between 1992–1995 as a Political Science major. At Connecticut, she became the school's all-time leader in rebounding and blocked shots, while averaging 16.9 points per game. Playing center at Connecticut, Lobo was named the 1994 and 1995 Big East Conference Player of the Year as well as an Academic All-American. In 1995, she led Connecticut to a 35–0 record and the NCAA Championship and was named the Final Four Most Valuable Player. Lobo also received the Wade trophy in 1995 as consensus National Player of the Year. As the youngest member of the 1996 USA Women's Olympic Team, she won a gold medal at the Atlanta Games and played on the 1996 USA Basketball Women's National Team that played 52 games around the world in preparation for the Olympics. Exhibit 15 features Lobo playing with the New York Liberty.

REEBOK'S LOBO ENDORSEMENT

Rebecca Lobo's contract with Reebok enabled Reebok to involve her in product endorsements and advertisements, store appearances, and speaking engagements. However, because Nike (in footwear) and Champion (in apparel) were primary sponsors of the WNBA, Lobo could not appear in WNBA games with Reebok footwear unless the Reebok logo was masked on her shoes. Further, Reebok could not feature Lobo in its advertisements or in-store displays wearing her New York Liberty uniform.

The Current Situation

As their weekly merchandise meeting progressed, Wyatt, Tilbrook, and Ellerbroek outlined the key elements negotiated thus far with Reebok regarding the Lobo launch.

THE TARGET CONSUMER

LFL executives believed that 12–17 year-old female consumers were increasingly critical to reach because of their present and future buying power. Traditionally, Reebok held a relatively low share of this segment compared to other brands such as Nike and adidas. How could Reebok ensure that its Lobo shoe would appeal to the young female consumer? In the past, this segment primarily bought shoes based upon fashion, styling, and brand appeal rather than performance.

Exhibits 16, 17, 18, and 19 provide information on the behavior of teen consumers, including where they shopped, what brands were cool, their sports participation, and their familiarity with and opinions of athletes.

PRODUCT PRICING

Reebok management believed that the Lobo shoe should incorporate Reebok's soon-to-be-introduced DMX technology. Reebok's DMX shoes were slated for $110 suggested retail. LFL, on the other hand, had seen Nike struggle with a $100-plus product in the Swoopes shoe. Both Tilbrook and Ellerbroek thought that a women's-specific basketball shoe from Reebok might command at most $80–85. They proposed that Reebok produce a Lobo product with a version of Hexalite technology, an existing and lower-priced Reebok footwear technology. Reebok had agreed to offer LFL the Lobo shoe with Hexalite cushioning at an $85 suggested retail price, based upon a 45% selling margin.

EXHIBIT 16   Teen Retail Outlet Preferences

Source: 2002 Teenage Research Unlimited, Inc.

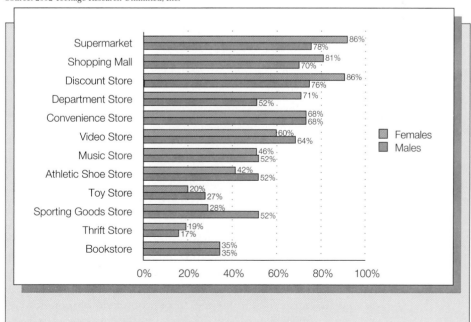

EXHIBIT 17 Coolest Brands According to Teens

Source: 2002 Teenage Research Unlimited, Inc.

The "Coolest" Brands Brands receiving a mention of 3% or more			
	Total	Male	Female
Nike	24%	28%	19%
Sony	16%	26%	6%
Abercrombie & Fitch	11%	8%	13%
adidas	11%	10%	11%
Pepsi	9%	8%	8%
American Eagle	8%	6%	9%
Old Navy	7%	6%	9%
Coke	7%	8%	5%
Chevrolet	8%	8%	4%
Tommy Hilfiger	6%	5%	6%
Ford	5%	6%	5%
Nintendo	5%	8%	2%
Gap	5%	3%	7%
Cover Girl	4%	0%	8%
Mudd	4%	-	7%
Honda	3%	4%	3%
FUBU	3%	5%	2%
L.E.I.	3%	-	6%
Mountain Dew	3%	4%	3%

EXHIBIT 18 Sports Participation among Teens

Source: 2002 Teenage Research Unlimited, Inc.

Males		Females	
1. Basketball	66%	1. Swimming	59%
2. Football	53%	2. Exercise/Aerobics	49%
3. Swimming	47%	3. Running/Jogging	41%
4. Baseball	43%	4. Basketball	46%
5. Bicycling	39%	5. Bicycling	32%
6. Running/Jogging	36%	6. Bowling	38%
7. Billiards/Pool	37%	7. Volleyball	33%
8. Bowling	39%	8. Softball	29%
9. Weight Training	40%	9. Billiards/Pool	27%
10. Fishing	33%	10. Soccer	23%

PRODUCT TIMING AND THE COMMERCIALIZATION PROCESS

LFL and Reebok considered two launch windows if they were to introduce a Lobo shoe: (1) introduce it in June at the start of the inaugural WNBA season, which ran from June to late August 1997, or (2) in October 1997 when school basketball seasons typically began. Men's signature models, such as the Air Jordan, were typically launched during November/December for the holiday selling season.

An eighteen-month cycle, from product development to retail launch, was typical for the athletic footwear industry. In other words, it usually took 18 months to com-

EXHIBIT 19   TRU*Score™ Athlete Ranking

	TRU*			TRU*	
Name	Score	Sport	Name	Score	Sport
Michael Jordan	49	Basketball	Ichiro Suzuki	30	Baseball
Vince Carter	47	Basketball	Grant Hill	30	Basketball
Kobe Bryant	45	Basketball	Bob Burnquist	30	Skateboarding
Tony Hawk	44	Skateboarding	Barry Bonds	30	Baseball
Allen Iverson	42	Basketball	Sheryl Swoopes	29	Basketball
Jason Kidd	39	Basketball	Lisa Leslie	29	Basketball
Tracy McGrady	39	Basketball	Dirk Nowitzki	29	Basketball
Jay Williams	39	Basketball	Apolo Ono	29	Speed skating
Marshall Faulk	38	Football	Ray Lewis	28	Football
Eddie George	37	Football	Steve Nash	28	Basketball
Kevin Garnett	37	Basketball	Mario Lermieux	27	Hockey
Shaquille O'Neal	37	Basketball	Dale Earnhardt, Jr.	27	NASCAR
Sammy Sosa	36	Baseball	Antoine Walker	26	Basketball
Tiger Woods	34	Golf	Brian Urlacher	25	Football
Tim Duncan	34	Basketball	Jaromir Jagr	23	Hockey
Donovan McNabb	34	Football	Alex Rodriguez	23	Baseball
Randy Moss	33	Football	Ben Wallace	20	Basketball
Venus Williams*	33	Tennis	Antawn Jamison	20	Basketball
Mat Hoffman	33	Extreme Biking	Jeff Gordon	20	NASCAR
Serena Williams*	33	Tennis	Jennifer Capriati	19	Tennis
Derek Jeter	32	Baseball	Jay Miron	16	Extreme Biking
Anna Kournikova	32	Tennis	Bode Miller	15	Skiing
Nomar Garciapana	32	Baseball	Pau Gasol	13	Basketball
Dave Mirra	32	Extreme Biking	Anthony Thomas	12	Football
Travis Pastrana	31	Motocross	Brian Deegan	12	Motocross
Michael Vick	31	Football	David Carr	11	Football
Emmitt Smith	30	Football	Claudio Reyna	10	Soccer

Fielded in a Supplemental Sample—August '02

mercialize or introduce a new product at retail from the time the product first appeared as a two-dimensional drawing. The product commercialization process entailed several steps, including translating the designer's drawing to a workable blueprint and sending the blueprint to manufacturers in Asia for tooling and prototyping. After the prototype was developed, the product went through a four-step "tech" process that examined manufacturability, costing, fit-testing, and wear-testing.

Even though Wyatt preferred a June launch in order to capitalize on the hype surrounding the WNBA, he estimated that the earliest possible window in which to launch a Lobo shoe might be October '97. LFL and Reebok agreed that at this stage of the game (February 1997) a June 1997 target would be impossible because of product development and production timing. Since initial designs and blueprints of a women's basketball shoe had been drawn up earlier in 1996, Reebok managers believed that they could accelerate the development process in order to allow for an October 1997 delivery.

RETAIL EXCLUSIVITY

LFL desired retail exclusivity if it were to carry and promote a Lobo shoe and apparel collection. Even though LFL might benefit from a broad national distribution of Lobo product at additional national retailers, Wyatt believed that an exclusivity agreement would help differentiate LFL.

Reebok's management considered the opportunity costs of selling exclusively to LFL. Based upon the potential demand for the shoe at other competing retailers (estimated as high as 50,000 pairs), the companies agreed to 15,000 pairs as the inventory to which LFL would have to commit for Lobo exclusivity. Because the retailer was typically not able to return unsold inventory, inventory cost was treated as a fixed cost in the athletic footwear industry. In the past, LFL had only purchased between 5,000 and 10,000 pairs of similar women's-specific basketball products from Nike; but these products were not LFL exclusives.

MARKETING SUPPORT

Wyatt and his managers had also discussed the marketing support needed behind the Lobo product if the launch were to become a reality. In LFL's view, it would provide the stores and the distribution; it was up to its partners such as Reebok to provide the launch plans and marketing funds. Manufacturers typically provided 2–10% of annual account sales for retailer-specific marketing support and merchandise funds. Promotional and launch support for past basketball products depended on the product. A national launch for a Jordan or Grant Hill product might cost several million dollars due to advertising production and media (television, print, and outdoor) costs as well as in-store merchandise displays. Television commercial production costs alone could run $500,000 and higher, while a print ad might cost as much as $50,000 to $75,000 to produce.

Every two weeks, LFL designated space in its stores for specific vendor supported merchandising (VSM) programs. Thus, Reebok could potentially support a Lobo launch with a two-week VSM within all 650 LFL stores. LFL and Reebok had agreed that if the Lobo launch were to happen, Reebok would fund the following marketing elements: a national television ad featuring the Lobo footwear and apparel as available only at LFL; Lobo/LFL "Go-cards" (postcards) distributed at retailers such as Tower Records; Lobo in-store displays; and store promotions such as an appearance by Rebecca Lobo at specially chosen LFL stores. Additionally, Reebok would conduct salesclerk training at key LFL stores. Wyatt estimated Reebok's total cost for this marketing program would be $1 million. Reebok was willing to commit this level of support as an investment in the LFL account relationship and by extension, the relationship with the entire Athletic Group.

The Decision

Wyatt played devil's advocate with his merchandise team as he thought about their decision. Wyatt began the meeting by discussing how associating a marquee athlete with an athletic shoe had proved effective in the past, particularly on the men's side of the business. "Even though the recent success of the [Nike's] Air Jordan shows the potential of a product connected to an athlete, Jordan is . . . well, Jordan is Jordan," Wyatt mused, "one-of-a-kind." Wyatt could recall only a few instances in which women's-specific shoes had been introduced that were similar to the proposed Lobo launch. "Remember the Swoopes launches . . . the first launch in 1995 was good but the 1996 launch failed miserably compared with what we've achieved on the men's side."

"You really can't compare this Lobo shoe to an Air Jordan. This isn't going to be a Jordan. You can't measure anything against a Jordan!" Ellerbroek countered.

"Yes, but the question is still whether a female athlete can drive product sales or at least create demand," Wyatt responded. "Historically, this hasn't even worked in tennis, with probably some of the most recognizable athletes such as Chris Everett and Martina [Navratilova].”

“It would be great to launch the Lobo at the start of the WNBA season this coming June to capitalize on the excitement around the league, although basketball shoes traditionally do not sell in the summer, outside of the Air Jordan,” Wyatt continued. “But Reebok’s development timelines won’t allow us to get the product in time.”

“[Well] . . . kids really don’t start buying basketball shoes until September and playing hoops until October,” Ellerbroek noted.

Regarding exclusivity, Tilbrook observed, “Reebok has offered us exclusivity on the Lobo shoe, and I know they could place it elsewhere if they wanted to.”

“Exclusivity is a good thing but there are two sides to that coin,” Wyatt countered. “We have to remember that it helps everybody, including us, if there is more exposure to the product, more exposure to the athlete, and more exposure to the Reebok brand, which would come from other retailers carrying the product as well. But, you’re right, in the end we could really benefit from Lady Foot Locker exclusivity with the Lobo product.”

Based upon these critical issues, Wyatt wondered if LFL should consider bringing a Lobo shoe to market in partnership with Reebok. Was there retail potential in a signature product built around an emerging professional women’s player such as Lobo? Could such a product deliver a true point-of-difference for LFL? Did it make sense financially? Wyatt, Tilbrook, and Ellerbroek faced an important decision.

Was there a big enough market for another signature women’s basketball shoe? Nike had both success *and* failure in this arena. Granted, Rebecca Lobo was one of the more popular players to enter the WNBA and seemed to have quite a following of young fans. Would she appeal to the young 12–17 year-old female? Should LFL try to hit an October ’97 delivery or should it wait until June ’98 and the start of the *next* WNBA season in order to launch the Lobo shoe?

Most important were the financial considerations LFL faced with the Lobo launch decision. Would LFL be able to liquidate the approximately 15,000 pairs it would carry, without significant markdowns? Wyatt still harbored concerns that a women’s-specific product such as a Lobo signature model was a tremendous risk. Moreover, Wyatt felt that the sales in the basketball category were trending down. With these questions and more in mind, Wyatt knew they had a difficult decision on their hands—whether or not to launch a Lobo shoe with Reebok.

16

Longevity Healthcare Systems, Inc.

Lawrence M. Lamont and Elizabeth W. Storey
both of Washington and Lee University

Introduction

Kathryn Hamilton, President of Longevity Healthcare Systems, Inc., located in Grand Rapids, Michigan, was reviewing the 1993 annual statements. "We concluded another terrific year," she commented. "Our sales and earnings exceeded expectations, but I'm concerned about the next few years." Although Longevity was successful, it was beginning to experience competition and the uncertainty of health care reform. In February, 1994, a large hospital in Grand Rapids, Michigan had converted an entire wing to a long-term care facility. The hospital also initiated an aggressive sales and advertising campaign and was competing with Longevity for new nursing home residents.

Longevity's recent acquisition of seven nursing homes in Toledo, Ohio, was also proving to be an unprofitable venture. Many of the residents were on Medicare and Medicaid and these health insurance programs generally did not reimburse the full costs of care. Additionally, the families of the Toledo residents were becoming value conscious and they frequently commented about the quality and cost of nursing care. Kathryn realized that to improve the profitability, attention would have to be given to customer satisfaction and attracting more profitable private-pay residents. Health care reform was also a source of concern. It was her belief that reform of the health care industry would be comprehensive with increased emphasis on cost control, competitive pricing and quality of care. She wondered what effect reform would have on Longevity and what the timetable for legislative action would be.

While increased competition and health care reform seemed certain, the most profitable path for future growth was not clear because several marketing opportunities existed. An aging population had created a strong demand for long-term care in nursing homes. Alzheimer's disease was also becoming more common and Longevity had recently lost some nursing home residents to Alzheimer's treatment centers because the company did not offer a specialized facility. Kathryn had to decide whether offering Alzheimer's treatment would be desirable.

Opportunities to expand existing businesses were also an option. The Grand Rapids pharmacy acquired in 1992 had been successfully phased into Longevity and Kathryn was wondering if a similar acquisition would work in Toledo. However, she was concerned about the impact of reform on the pricing of prescription drugs and medical supplies. To date, the pharmacy had been very profitable, but what would the future hold?

Geographic expansion of the firm's nursing and subacute care facilities might also be a profitable avenue for growth. Industry consolidation was making it possible to acquire nursing homes and unprofitable hospitals that could be converted to health care facilities. However, Kathryn envisioned that a future industry trend might be toward vertical integration of health care services. If so, it might make sense to further integrate Longevity's business in the Grand Rapids and Toledo markets before committing to additional geographic expansion.

Beyond decisions on the future direction of Longevity, Kathryn wondered if it was time to begin thinking about a more formal approach to marketing. "I really need to get some ideas about marketing in our different businesses down on paper so I can see how they fit with my views on an overall corporate marketing strategy," she remarked.

History of Longevity Healthcare Systems, Inc.

In 1972, Kathryn Hamilton, R.N., was searching for a nursing home for her mother in Grand Rapids, Michigan. Discouraged by a six-month wait for admission, she decided to move her into the home she occupied with her husband, Richard Hamilton, M.D., who enjoyed a medical practice in Grand Rapids specializing in care for older adults.

A NURSING HOME BUSINESS

In 1974, Richard's mother and father joined the household, and Kathryn and Richard continued to learn how to care for older adults. In 1976, the Hamiltons leased a small, outdated 40-bed hospital in a nearby suburb and converted it into a long-term care facility. Following certification, the facility was opened in 1977 as the Longevity Nursing Home. In addition to their parents, 10 other adults over 65 entered the home during the year. All were "private pay," meaning they paid directly for services with personal assets, but without government assistance. By 1979, the nursing facility was fully occupied with private-pay residents. Longevity was incorporated and Kathryn Hamilton became the President and its Director of Nursing, while her husband, Richard, provided medical services and continued his practice. The leased facility was purchased in 1979.

NEW NURSING SERVICES

By 1980, Longevity found it necessary to add additional nursing services for aging residents. Two levels of care were added and professional nurses were hired to provide the services. The new services were favorably received and the referrals from residents and physicians kept the facility filled.

EXPANSION BY ACQUISITION, 1980–85

The demand for nursing care was strong in the early 1980s and Longevity expanded. Eight unprofitable nursing homes with a total of 480 beds were acquired in Grand

Rapids and nearby communities. All of the homes were licensed, certified by Medicare and Medicaid, and occupied by residents requiring a variety of nursing services. Shortly after the acquisition, Dr. Hamilton left his medical practice to join Longevity full-time as its Medical Director. He added skilled nursing care for residents requiring 24-hour-a-day care and rehabilitation services for those needing physical, speech, and occupational therapy.

NURSING HOME CONSTRUCTION

From 1986–1988, Longevity expanded by constructing three 70-bed nursing homes in nearby communities.[1] Each provided the full range of nursing and rehabilitation services and was licensed for Medicare and Medicaid patients. The homes were quickly filled, and by the end of 1988 Longevity operated 12 nursing homes with a total of 730 beds. Employment had grown to 1,200 full-time and part-time employees.

NEW BUSINESS OPPORTUNITIES

During a medical convention in 1990, Kathryn Hamilton noted a growing concern over the escalating costs of hospital care and the desire of insurance providers to shorten the hospitalization of patients requiring medical supervision, but not the other services traditionally provided by hospitals. Sensing an opportunity, the Hamiltons converted a 30-bed wing of one of the Grand Rapids nursing homes to a subacute care facility for patients that did not need the full services of a licensed acute care hospital. For patients moved from a hospital to the Longevity facility, the needed care was provided for about half the cost. The subacute care facility was licensed in 1991, and it quickly filled with referrals from hospitals, physicians and health care insurers.

The growing recognition that treating patients requiring subacute care in low overhead nursing facilities was a cost effective alternative, substantially increased the demand for Longevity's subacute care.[2] In 1992, following marketing research, Longevity constructed a 50-bed subacute care facility near one of its nursing homes. It was completed in 1993 and, within a few months, operated at capacity with patients referred from insurance companies, physicians, and Longevity nursing homes.

As the demand for specialized nursing and medical care expanded, it became apparent that profitability could be improved by operating a pharmacy. In 1992, Longevity acquired a retail pharmacy in Grand Rapids from a retiring pharmacist. It was converted into an institutional pharmacy to provide prescriptions, medical equipment and supplies, and consulting services to Longevity facilities.

GEOGRAPHIC EXPANSION

Late in 1992, what appeared to be an exceptional business opportunity came to the attention of Kathryn and Richard Hamilton. A few hundred miles away, in Toledo,

---

[1]By 1988, all Longevity nursing homes were certified to receive Medicare and Medicaid patients. Medicare is a federally funded and administered health insurance program that reimburses health care facilities for nursing and medical services. Medicaid is a state-administered reimbursement program that covers skilled and intermediate long-term care for the medically indigent. The benefits paid by Medicaid programs vary from state to state.

[2]Medical services fall along a continuum from intensive care, acute care, subacute care, nursing care and home health care. Hospitals offer intensive and acute care for patients with complex medical conditions. They have fully equipped operating and recovery rooms, radiology services, intensive and coronary care units, pharmacies, clinical laboratories, therapy services and emergency services. Subacute care facilities owned by nursing homes serve the needs of patients who require nursing and medical care, but not many of the specialized services and equipment provided by an acute care hospital.

EXHIBIT 1   Longevity Healthcare Systems, Inc., Historical Development, 1972–1993

Date	Activity
1972–75	Nursing care for parents.
1976–77	Leased a 40-bed hospital and converted it to a nursing home.
1979	Business incorporated as Longevity Nursing Home.
1979	Corporation purchased leased nursing home.
1980–85	Acquired 8 nursing homes in Grand Rapids area, 480 beds.
1986–88	Constructed 3 nursing homes in Grand Rapids area, 210 beds.
1990–91	Converted a 30-bed wing of Grand Rapids nursing home into subacute care.
1992–93	Constructed a 50-bed subacute care facility in Grand Rapids area.
1992	Acquired a retail pharmacy in Grand Rapids.
1992–93	Acquired 7 nursing homes in Toledo area, 280 beds.
1993	Corporation name changed to Longevity Healthcare Systems, Inc.

Ohio, a large health care company was selling seven unprofitable nursing homes with a total of 280 beds for $12,000,000. The homes were occupied primarily by Medicare and Medicaid patients and operated at 70 percent of capacity. The Hamiltons decided to take a one year option on the facilities while they raised the money to complete the purchase. Eventually, 40 percent of Longevity's common stock was sold to a large insurance company and some of the proceeds were used to exercise the purchase option. Kathryn Hamilton hired an experienced administrator and assigned him the task of returning the nursing homes to profitability. To reflect the company's broadening scope in the health care industry, the Hamiltons decided to change its name to Longevity Healthcare Systems, Inc. As shown in Exhibits 1 and 2, Longevity ended 1993 with 12 nursing homes, two subacute care facilities and a pharmacy located in Michigan, and 7 nursing homes located in Ohio. Exhibits 3 and 4 contain the financial statements for the year ending December 31, 1993. Exhibit 5 presents a five-year sales and earnings history, while Exhibit 6 provides some financial information for the pharmacy.

Longevity Marketing

Marketing was used to promote high occupancy in Longevity facilities, expand the percentage of private-pay residents, and increase the profits of its institutional pharmacy.[3] Operating information for the health care facilities is shown in Exhibit 7 and the products and services marketed by Longevity are summarized in Exhibit 8.

Nursing care was marketed locally. The administrator and admissions director of each facility designed a marketing strategy to increase awareness of the nursing home and its services in the market it served. Personal selling using telemarketing and direct contact was targeted to referral sources such as physicians, hospital administrators, home health agencies, community organizations and churches, senior citizens groups, retirement communities, and the families of prospective residents. Longevity

[3]Managed care organizations provide health care products that integrate financing and management with the delivery of health care services through a network of providers (such as nursing homes and hospitals) who share financial risk or who have incentives to deliver cost-effective services. An HMO (Health Maintenance Organization) provides prepaid health care services to its members through physicians employed by the HMO at facilities owned by the HMO or through a network of independent physicians and facilities. They actively manage patient care to maximize quality and cost effectiveness.

EXHIBIT 2   Longevity Healthcare Systems, Inc., Geographic Location of Longevity Healthcare Facilities

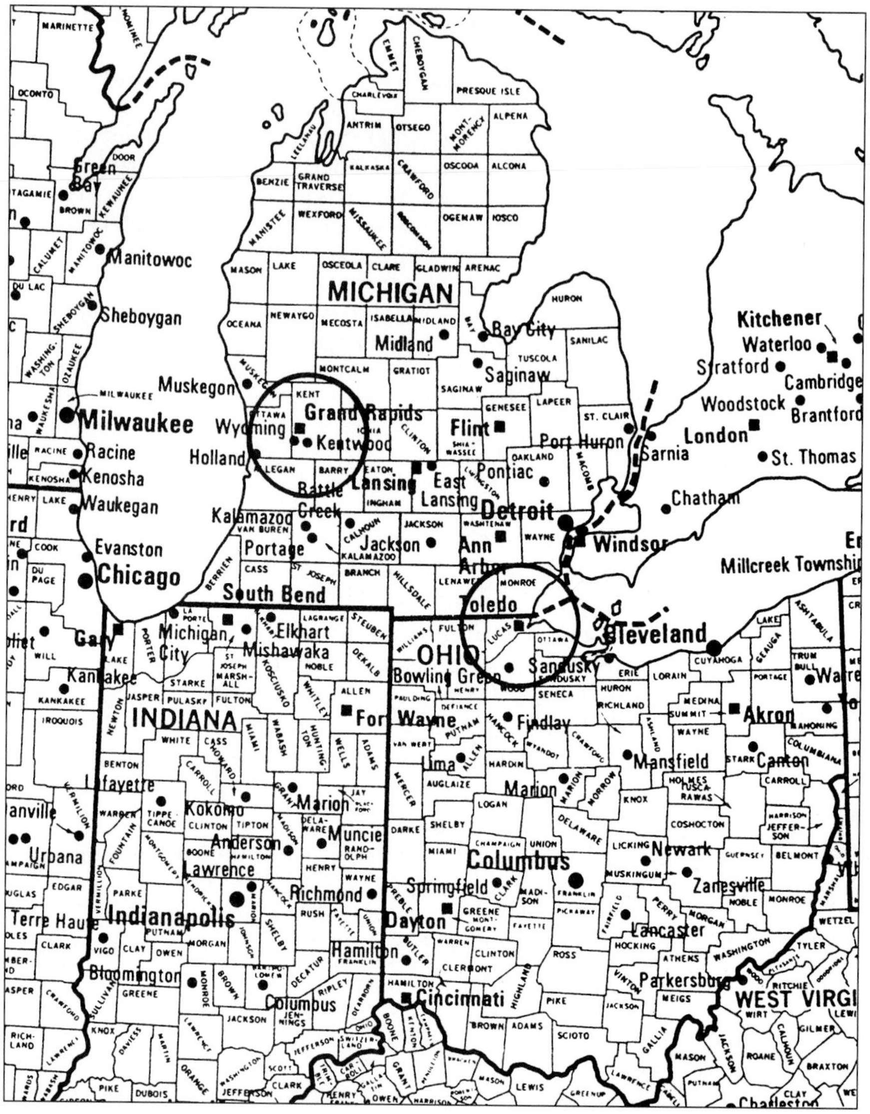

also distributed promotional literature discussing its philosophy of care, services, and quality standards. Frequently the literature was provided to prospective residents and their families when they inquired about nursing or toured the facilities.

Marketing for subacute care was directed by Kathryn Hamilton, who contacted insurance companies, managed care organizations such as HMOs, hospital administrators, and other third-party payors to promote Longevity's services. Kathryn also attended professional meetings where she maintained contact with the various referral sources.

The products and services of the institutional pharmacy were marketed by the pharmacy manager and his assistant by direct contact with Longevity facilities, other nursing homes, hospitals, clinics and home health agencies. In addition to drugs and medical supplies, management also provided consulting services to help ensure quality patient care. These services were especially valuable because they enabled

EXHIBIT 3 Longevity Healthcare Systems, Inc., Income Statement (Year Ending 12–31–93)

Net Revenues

Basic LTC services	$45,500,000
Subacute medical services	9,000,000
Pharmacy services	3,000,000
Total revenues	$57,500,000

Operating Expenses

Salaries, wages and benefits	$20,125,000
Patient services	21,275,000
Administrative and general	3,450,000
Depreciation and amortization	575,000
Total costs and expenses	$45,425,000
Income from operations	$12,075,000
Interest expense	1,726,111
Earnings before taxes	$10,348,889
Income taxes	4,139,555
Net income	$ 6,209,334
Net income per share	$ 0.78

EXHIBIT 4 Longevity Healthcare Systems, Inc., Balance Sheet (Years Ending 12–31–93 and 12–31–92)

Assets	1993	1992
Current Assets		
Cash and equivalents	$ 841,770	$ 501,120
Accounts receivable	3,265,584	2,702,552
Inventory	2,262,816	1,624,399
Property, Plant and Equipment		
Land	$ 9,959,051	$ 7,690,249
Buildings and improvements	27,002,416	13,622,079
Equipment	2,917,136	2,179,842
Accumulated depreciation	(4,028,149)	(2,464,535)
Other Assets		
Goodwill	$ 791,794	$ 655,278
Other long-term assets	5,163,275	4,063,190
Total Assets	$45,175,693	$30,574,174
Liabilities and Shareholders' Equity		
Current Liabilities		
Accounts payable	$ 1,250,201	$ 1,043,648
Accrued expenses	708,447	586,301
Accrued compensation	416,734	344,883
Current portion of long-term debt	2,041,995	2,700,120
Accrued interest	196,694	203,954
Long-term debt (net)	$10,506,622	$12,871,452
Shareholders' Equity		
Common stock, $.01 par value	$ 50,000	$ 50,000
Additional paid-in capital	17,870,666	3,848,816
Retained earnings	15,134,334	8,925,000
Total Liabilities and Shareholders' Equity	$45,175,693	$30,574,174

EXHIBIT 5 Longevity Healthcare Systems Inc., Historical Revenues and Net Income

Year	Revenues	Net Income
1993	$57,500,000	$6,209,334
1992	46,575,000	5,029,560
1991	37,260,000	3,017,736
1990	26,715,420	2,987,692
1989	21,799,783	1,334,147

EXHIBIT 6 Longevity Healthcare Systems Inc., Selected Pharmacy Information (Year Ending 12–31–93)

Income Statement	1993
Net revenue	$3,000,000
Operating expenses	2,430,000
Operating income	570,000
Net income	390,000
Financial ratios	
Current ratio	1.94
Inventory turnover	4.20
Profit margin (%)	13.00
Return on assets (%)	9.29

EXHIBIT 7 Longevity Healthcare Systems Inc., Operating Information for Longevity Healthcare Facilities (Year Ending 12–31–93)

Payor Mix	Grand Rapids	Toledo	Total
Private and other	69.7%	18.7%	44.2%
Medicare	8.4	17.8	13.1
Medicaid	21.9	63.5	42.7
Occupancy	96.4%	81.2%	88.8%
No. of beds	780	280	1,060

EXHIBIT 8 Longevity Healthcare Systems Inc., Products and Services

Business	Products/Services
Nursing care	Custodial care
	Assisted living
	Intermediate nursing care
	Skilled nursing care
Subacute care for	Lung and heart disease
	Coma, pain, and wound care
	Spinal cord injuries
	Head injuries
	Intravenous therapy
	Joint replacements
Rehabilitation services	Occupational therapy
	Physical therapy
	Speech therapy
Institutional pharmacy	Prescription drugs
	Nonprescription drugs
	Medical supplies
	Medical equipment
	Consulting services

the nursing homes to admit patients that required more complex and profitable medical services.

NURSING HOME SERVICES

Longevity nursing homes provided room and board, dietary services, recreation and social activities, housekeeping and laundry services, four levels of nursing care, and numerous specialized services. Custodial care was provided to residents needing minimal care. Assisted living was used by persons needing some assistance with personal care such as bathing and eating. Intermediate care was provided to residents needing more nursing and attention, but not continual access to nurses. Finally, skilled nursing care was available to residents requiring the professional services of a nurse on a 24-hour-a-day basis. Rehabilitation therapy was also available for residents who had disabilities or were returning from hospitalization for surgery or illness. Rehabilitation was an important part of Longevity's care because it helped residents improve their quality of life.

Most of the residents in Longevity nursing homes were female and over 65. Although rates depended on accommodations and the services used, a typical nursing home bed generated monthly revenues of $4,415. It was common for residents to initially enter the nursing home needing only custodial care or assisted living and to progress to higher levels of nursing care as they aged. Exhibit 9 provides a typical schedule of monthly charges for a resident in a semiprivate room with seven hours of therapy.

All of the Longevity nursing homes were licensed in their respective states. Generally, the licenses had to be renewed annually. For renewal, state health care agencies considered the physical condition of the facility, the qualifications of the administrative and medical staff, the quality of care, and the facility's compliance with the applicable laws and regulations.

SUBACUTE CARE

Longevity marketed subacute care for patients with more complex medical needs that required constant medical supervision, but not the expensive equipment and services of an acute care hospital. Subacute care generated higher profit margins than nursing care, although patient stays in the facility were usually shorter.[4] Daily patient rates varied from $250 to $750 depending on the services and equipment required. Longevity's services included care for patients with lung and heart disease,

---

[4]Longevity profit margins for subacute care facilities were about 25 percent higher than for nursing care facilities. The length of stay was usually 20 to 45 days versus 8 months for private-pay nursing care and 2 years for Medicaid patients.

EXHIBIT 9   **Longevity Healthcare Systems Inc., Example Resident Statement for Nursing Care**

Semi-private room, $105.00 per day	$3,150.00 per month[1]
Basic telephone service	15.00
Rehabilitation therapy, 7.0 hours per month	840.00
Pharmacy and other specialized services	360.00
Miscellaneous personal expenses	50.00
Total	$4,415.00
Per day	147.17

[1]Based on private pay. Includes room and board, 24-hour professional nursing care, meals, housekeeping and linen services. Social and recreational activity programs are also included.

spinal cord and head injuries, joint replacements, coma, pain and wound care, and intravenous therapy. Services at the subacute care facilities were not limited to the elderly. Younger patients discharged from hospitals were attractive because of their longer life expectancy and eventual need for nursing and rehabilitation. Based on an average rate of $1,000 per day charged by acute care hospitals, Longevity knew that its prices were substantially lower for comparable services. Like the nursing homes, the subacute care facilities were subject to licensing by the state health care agencies and certification by Medicare. All Longevity subacute care facilities were licensed and certified.

PHARMACY PRODUCTS AND SERVICES

Longevity provided pharmacy products and services to nursing homes, retirement communities, and other health care organizations. The pharmacy's products were frequently customized with special packaging and dispensing systems and delivered daily. The pharmacy also consulted on medications and long-term care regulations and provided computerized tracking of medications, medical records processing, and 24-hour emergency services.

The Market for Long-Term Health Care

Long-term health care includes basic health care (such as that provided in nursing homes), rehabilitation therapy and Alzheimer's care, institutional pharmacy services, subacute care, and home health care. In recent years, spending for these and other health care services has increased significantly. For example, in 1993, one out of every seven dollars that Americans spent went to purchase health care. Total expenditures are projected to increase from $585.3 billion in 1990 to $3,457.7 billion in 2010; an annual growth rate of over 9 percent.

Nursing homes are important providers of long-term health care. Expenditures for nursing home care are expected to increase at a comparable rate, from $53.1 billion in 1990 to $310.1 billion in 2010. This industry consists of about 16,000 licensed facilities with a total of 1,700,000 beds. It includes a large number of small, locally owned nursing homes and a growing number of regional and national companies. The industry is undergoing restructuring in response to stricter regulation, increasing complexity of medical services, and competitive pressures. Smaller, local operators who lack sophisticated management and financial resources are being acquired by larger, more established companies. At present, the 20 largest firms operate about 18 percent of the nursing facilities. Consolidation is expected to continue, but the long-term outlook is extremely positive for the businesses that survive. Nursing home revenues increased by about 12 percent in 1993 and they are expected to experience similar gains in 1994. Several factors account for the optimistic outlook:

FAVORABLE DEMOGRAPHIC TRENDS

Demographic trends, namely growth in the elderly segment of the population, are increasing the demand for health care and the services of nursing homes. Most of the market for nursing care consists of men and women 65 years of age and older. Their number was approximately 25 million in 1980 and is projected to increase to 35 million by 2000 and to 40 million by the year 2010. The 65-and-over segment suffers from a greater incidence of chronic illnesses and disabilities and currently accounts for about two thirds of the health care expenditures in the United States.

PRESSURES TO CONTROL COSTS

Government and private payers have adopted cost control measures to encourage reduced hospital stays. In addition, private insurers have begun to limit reimbursement to "reasonable" charges, while managed care organizations are limiting hospitalization costs by monitoring utilization and negotiating discounted rates. As a result, hospital stays have been shortened and many patients are discharged with a continuing need for care. Because nursing homes are able to provide services at lower prices, the cost pressures have increased the demand for nursing home services and subacute care following hospital discharge.

ADVANCES IN MEDICAL TECHNOLOGY

Advances in technology leading to improved medications and surgical procedures have increased life expectancies. Adults over age 85 are now the fastest growing segment of the population and their numbers are expected to double over the next 20 years. Many require skilled care and the medical equipment traditionally available only in hospitals. Nursing homes are acquiring some of the specialty medical equipment and providing skilled nursing care to older adults through subacute care facilities.

LIMITED SUPPLY OF NURSING BEDS

The supply of nursing home beds has been limited by the availability of financing and high construction and start-up expenses. Additionally, the supply has been constrained by legislation limiting licenses for new nursing beds in states that require a demonstration of need. The effect has been to create a barrier to market entry and conditions where demand for nursing home services exceeds the available supply in many states.

National Health Care Reform

The next decade will be a period of reform for the health care system. Although it is not clear how comprehensive the reform will be and how it will be financed, the focus will be to control costs and provide universal access to quality health care. The most likely plan will probably reform the health insurance industry, build on the current employer-financed approach and call for market incentives to control costs. To ensure universal access, insurance and managed care companies will be prohibited from dropping, rejecting, or pricing out of the market anyone with an expensive medical condition.

Reform will affect long-term care providers, such as nursing homes, in several ways. It will regulate the insurance companies to make health insurance more price competitive and affordable. This change will favorably impact long-term health care providers by increasing the number of residents paying with insurance benefits. Reform may also extend Medicare coverage for home health care. A change such as this would encourage more older adults to receive health care at home instead of at a nursing facility, resulting in an unfavorable impact.

Employers will also have incentives to control costs and deliver quality care. Increasingly they will rely on managed care organizations, such as HMO's, who are likely to contract lower cost providers, such as nursing homes, for subacute care and other cost effective services. Companies capable of providing a variety of health care services at attractive prices should see opportunities to expand demand.

Institutional pharmacies will also be impacted by health care reform. President Clinton's Health Security Act called for the addition of prescription drug coverage to the Medicare program. If adopted, this provision would probably decrease prices of prescription drugs by regulation of pharmaceutical manufacturers. Price decreases, either legislated or achieved through managed care and the market system, may allow institutional pharmacies to enjoy higher profit margins while still providing medications at affordable prices to patients.

Regulation and Competition

Health care providers are regulated at the state and federal levels. Regulation impacts financial management and the quality and safety of care. Ensuring that health care facilities are in compliance with regulatory standards is an important aspect of managing a health care business. In addition, management is increasingly confronted with competition. Nursing homes and subacute care facilities compete for patients who are able to select from a variety of alternatives to meet their needs. Managed care and insurance organizations also negotiate aggressively with health care providers to ensure quality care at attractive prices.

FINANCIAL REGULATION

The Health Care Financing Administration (HCFA) is the federal regulatory agency for Medicare and Medicaid. Both programs are cost-based and use a per-diem payment schedule that reimburses the provider for a portion of the costs of care. Each facility must apply to participate in the Medicare and Medicaid programs and then have its beds certified to provide skilled nursing, intermediate, or other levels of care. A nursing home may have a mix of beds at any time, but it must match patient services to each bed. A facility cannot place a Medicare patient requiring skilled nursing care in a bed certified for intermediate care without recertifying the bed for skilled care. Recertification often required a month or more.

QUALITY AND SAFETY OF CARE

Much of the current regulation facing nursing homes was developed in the Omnibus Budget Reconciliation Act of 1987 (OBRA 87). Facilities that participate in Medicare and Medicaid must be regularly inspected by state survey teams under contract with HCFA to ensure safety and quality of care. OBRA 87 also established a resident "bill of rights" that essentially converted nursing homes from merely custodial facilities into centers for rehabilitation. Nursing homes are now required to establish a care plan for patients and conduct assessments to ensure that the facility achieves the highest practical well-being for each resident.

COMPETITION

Longevity competes with acute care and rehabilitation hospitals, other nursing and subacute care facilities, home health care agencies, and institutional pharmacies. Some offer services and prices which are comparable to those offered by Longevity.

Nursing homes compete on the basis of their reputation in the community, the ability to meet particular needs, the location and appearance of the facility, and the price of services. When a nursing facility is being selected, members of a prospective resident's family usually participate by visiting and evaluating nursing homes over a period of several weeks.

Some of the competing nursing homes in Grand Rapids and Toledo are operated by nonprofit organizations (churches and fraternal organizations) that can finance capital expenditures on a tax-exempt basis or receive charitable contributions to subsidize their operations. They compete with Longevity on the basis of price for private-pay residents.

Longevity competes for subacute care patients with acute care and rehabilitation hospitals, nursing homes, and home health agencies. The competition is generally local or regional and the competitive factors are similar to those for nursing care, although more emphasis is placed on support services such as third-party reimbursement, information management, and patient record keeping. Insurance and managed care organizations exert considerable influence on the decision and increase the competition by negotiating with several health care providers.

The institutional pharmacy market has no dominant competitor in the markets served by Longevity. Twenty percent of the market is accounted for by the institutional pharmacies owned by nursing homes. Independent institutional pharmacies control about 35 percent of the market and retail pharmacies supply the remainder. Retail pharmacies are steadily being acquired by nursing homes and independents to gain market share and achieve economies of scale in purchasing prescriptions and medical supplies. Institutional pharmacies compete on the basis of fast, customer-oriented service, price, and the ability to provide consulting and information management services to customers.

Marketing Issues and Opportunities

Kathryn Hamilton believed that Longevity could improve its marketing. She was concerned about the efforts of individual nursing homes and the need to improve the marketing of subacute care to managed care providers. Finally, she believed that customer satisfaction would become an important competitive factor and Longevity would need to assess the reactions of nursing home residents and their families to the quality of its services.

Continued growth was also on Kathryn's mind. Population demographics and health care reform would create outstanding opportunities for businesses that could design and implement successful marketing strategies. For some time, she had been thinking about expanding into Alzheimer's treatment because of the demographics and the growing need for facilities in the Grand Rapids area. Additionally, she saw an opportunity to further integrate Longevity by establishing a pharmacy in Toledo or by acquiring nursing homes in a new market such as South Bend, Indiana. Each marketing opportunity seemed to make sense, so the final choices would be difficult.

LOCAL MARKETING OF HEALTH CARE SERVICES

Although local marketing had worked well, duplication of effort and overlapping market areas were becoming problems as the number of nursing homes in a market increased. Kathryn wondered what the marketing strategy for nursing home services should be and whether the marketing efforts of the Grand Rapids and Toledo nursing homes could be coordinated in each area to eliminate duplication and preserve local identity. One approach she was considering was to hire a marketing specialist to work with the nursing homes to attract more private-pay customers. Advertising was a related issue because it had not been used, and Kathryn questioned whether it should be part of the marketing strategy. Should an advertising campaign be created for all of the nursing homes in a market, or should it be left to nursing home administrators to decide if advertising was appropriate in their strategy? If advertising was to be used, then a decision would have to be made on the type of advertising, the creative strategy, and the appropriate media.

MARKETING SUBACUTE CARE

Subacute care was viewed as an attractive marketing opportunity because of the profit margins. However, to further penetrate the market, a marketing strategy would have to be developed. Kathryn noted that managed care organizations and other referral sources were like organizational buyers as they made decisions on subacute care for the cases they managed. Instead of marketing the service to physicians and patient families, Longevity would negotiate directly with HMOs and insurance companies to determine services and a rate structure based on the patient's medical needs. Personal selling would be used to build a relationship with the case managers for both the insurance company and the hospital. The marketing objective was to convince the insurance companies that the subacute unit could achieve the same patient outcomes at a lower cost than a hospital. If a marketing strategy could be developed along with appropriate staffing, it might be desirable to expand this part of Longevity's business. Economics favored conversion of a wing of an existing nursing home into a subacute care facility at a cost of $25,000 per bed. One possibility existed in Toledo where an unprofitable 80-bed facility was operating at 60 percent of capacity. If part of the facility was upgraded to subacute care, she expected that within a short time, it would operate at capacity.

CUSTOMER SATISFACTION

Occasional complaints from nursing home residents about the price and quality of care were of concern to management. Since Longevity depended on referrals, customer satisfaction was an important element of a successful marketing strategy. In thinking about the issue, Kathryn noted that the license renewal process generally assured the maintenance of high standards in each facility, but it focused heavily on the inputs necessary to provide quality nursing care and not on customer satisfaction. Kathryn needed to decide what should be done to monitor individual nursing homes to assure customer satisfaction with Longevity's services.

ACQUISITION OF A TOLEDO PHARMACY

One marketing opportunity being considered was the acquisition of a Toledo pharmacy. From management's perspective, an acquisition was interesting because it further integrated the existing health care operations and provided an incremental source of earnings from the Toledo market.

Management had identified an institutional pharmacy serving 15 nursing homes with 700 beds. It was offered at a cash price of $1,050,000 and generated annual revenues of approximately $1,450 per bed served. The pharmacy was quite profitable, with an average profit margin of 12.5 percent over the past five years. To consider the profitability of the acquisition, Kathryn believed it was reasonable to assume that the pharmacy would be able to support the Longevity facilities in Toledo and retain 60 percent of the nursing home beds it presently served if it was staffed with appropriate marketing support.

One concern was the impact of health care reform. Most of the nursing homes served by the pharmacy had a high percentage of Medicare and Medicaid patients. If the reimbursement rates for prescription drugs and medical supplies were to decline, then what seemed to be an attractive opportunity could quickly change.

ALZHEIMER'S TREATMENT

Alzheimer's treatment was being considered because the demand for care was not being met and the development of a cure or drug therapy for the disease was progressing slowly. Kathryn believed that the demand for Alzheimer's treatment would grow at least as fast as the over-65 population. Projections from the U.S. Department of Health and Human Services indicated that by the year 2000, the Alzheimer's care market would increase by 50 percent from the present base of 4,000,000 presently suffering from the disease.

Longevity was considering establishing an Alzheimer's wing in two of the Grand Rapids nursing homes that served areas near older community residents. Each unit would serve 30 patients, and it would be self-contained and secured to protect residents against their wandering habits. The furniture and fixtures would also be renovated to meet the needs of the Alzheimer's patient, including softer colors, more subdued lighting, a separate nurses' station and a secured entrance. If an existing facility was converted, about six nursing rooms would have to be taken out of service to provide a separate activity and dining space. However, management reasoned that the revenue loss would be offset by average monthly revenues of $3,400 per patient and 15 percent lower costs than those for the average nursing home resident. Alzheimer's patients frequently required less costly care because of their younger age, better health, and a tendency to use fewer services. Longevity management had secured cost estimates that indicated the conversion costs would be $2,000 to $3,000 per bed.

In thinking about the opportunity Kathryn also recalled that Alzheimer's units typically had occupancy levels above 95 percent. Patients averaged a three-year length of stay and were almost always private pay. The marketing for Alzheimer's units focused on Alzheimer's associations, Alzheimer support groups, and church groups. Kathryn would have to decide how to position and market the Alzheimer's units so they would not appear to conflict with or be confused with the nursing home services. This would be a difficult but important marketing challenge because nursing homes that were known to operate Alzheimer's units tended to have better relationships with referral sources. Apparently they were perceived as providing an important community service.

Toward a Comprehensive Marketing Strategy

As Kathryn Hamilton completed her review of the financial statements, she was reminded of the need to make improvements in Longevity's marketing strategies. "I wish I could just write a one-paragraph statement of the corporate marketing strategy for this company. Then I could address each of the marketing issues and opportunities using my corporate strategy as a guide," she remarked.

Certainly one issue was improving existing marketing efforts. Marketing of nursing care, subacute care and the institutional pharmacy had been reasonably successful, but Kathryn felt uneasy about going another year without making needed changes. Since most of Kathryn's time was now needed to manage the business, additional marketing personnel would be necessary to develop and implement the marketing strategies for the various services. How many people would be needed and how the marketing effort would be organized also had to be decided.

Because Longevity was still evolving as a company with an uncertain marketing strategy, the most profitable direction for future growth was also important. Selecting attractive marketing opportunities was complicated because the choice depended on financial resources. Should Longevity expand the institutional pharmacy business, the subacute care business, or would resources be better utilized by offering Alzheimer's care? Each would bring Longevity closer to becoming an integrated health care provider:

EXHIBIT 10   **Longevity Healthcare Systems, Inc., Selected Demographic Information**

SOURCE: The Lifestyle Market Analyst, 1993. Health Care Financing Administration, 1991.

	Grand Rapids[1]		Toledo		South Bend[2]	
Retired	235,513	18.9%	161,630	19.9%	119,401	20.0%
Age, Household Head						
55–64	77,383	12.4	54,421	13.2	40,661	13.4
65–74	71,142	11.4	52,772	12.8	39,448	13.0
75 and older	56,165	9.0	40,816	9.9	30,951	10.2
Median age		44.5		46.1		46.7
Lifecycle Stage						
Married, 45–64	87,992	14.1	58,544	14.2	44,910	14.8
Married, 65 +	61,157	9.8	42,053	10.2	34,289	11.3
Single, 45–64	44,932	7.2	31,746	7.7	23,365	7.7
Single, 65 +	56,789	9.1	43,702	10.6	30,951	10.2
Median income	$ 32,928		$ 32,194		$ 31,264	
Adult population	1,246,101		812,212		597,003	
Nursing facilities[3]	439		988		590	
Total nursing beds	49,927		92,518		64,263	

[1]Includes Kalamazoo and Battle Creek, Michigan.
[2]Includes Elkhart, Indiana.
[3]Statewide statistics for certified Medicare and Medicaid facilities and beds.

Just as Kathryn moved to turn her personal computer off for the day, she noticed an electronic mail message from the administrator of the Toledo nursing homes. It said that for the first quarter of 1994, the seven nursing homes were breaking even at 81 percent occupancy and 25 percent private-pay residents. When she arrived home that evening, she was greeted by her husband, Richard, who mentioned that she had received a telephone call from a commercial real estate broker in South Bend, Indiana. The broker had located five nursing homes with a total of 450 beds that were being sold in a bankruptcy proceeding for $5,000,000. During dinner that evening, Richard mentioned that they needed to discuss the South Bend opportunity because the homes were attractively priced in a desirable market. It was his belief that in the future, the most profitable health care businesses would be vertically integrated and geographically diversified. Kathryn nodded in agreement as he handed her the summary information provided in Exhibit 10 and mentioned that a decision would have to be made in five days. She thought to herself, I wonder if it's financially possible?

Distribution Strategy

17

Amazon.com

J. Paul Peter
University of Wisconsin–Madison

In 1994, a young senior vice president at a Wall Street investment firm, Jeff Bezos, decided that he wanted to be a part of the Internet revolution. He decided to try and sell books via the World Wide Web. Why books? Because there were about 1.3 million books in print at the time. And because he thought he would be able to provide the customer discounted prices, the opportunity to get any book wanted, and convenience. Bezos initially came up with a list of possible items he might be able to sell online, including books, music, PC hardware and software, and magazines. After eliminating all but books and music, he realized that only 250,000 music CDs were available at any one time compared to 1.5 million English book titles (3 million titles if all languages are considered). So, Bezos decided to go with books and drew up a business plan as he and his wife drove westward in search of their new home. He subsequently decided to start his new business in Seattle, and sold his first book in July 1995. And with that, **Amazon.com** began its rapid ascent toward becoming one of the most recognized businesses in the world.

While it still hasn't turned a profit, **Amazon.com** has succeeded where so many other fledgling Internet companies have failed. Bezos, who was recently named *Time* magazine's "Person of the Year" and *Advertising Age*'s 1999 "Marketer of the Year," is the first to admit that first mover advantage was instrumental in the growth of his company. He also credits the company's success to the comprehensive selection of books available. "There's no way to have a physical bookstore with 1.1 million titles," he says. "Our catalog, if you were to print it, would be the size of seven New York City phone books." In addition, **Amazon.com** is known for its ability to fulfill and deliver, thanks to large investments in nationwide warehouse distribution centers.

If you are worried that your local Barnes & Noble bookstore might be forced out of business any time soon however, don't be. **Amazon.com** cannot compete when customers want the physical presence of a bookstore. The online book behemoth cannot provide soft, comfortable couches, music, and gourmet coffee. Nor does it allow consumers the opportunity to page through a book before purchasing it, savoring the crisp new pages and the creaking of the binding when it is first opened.

The company does, however, offer several advantages in the way of customer-to-customer and customer-to-author interaction. Customers can log on to the site, post a review on any book they have read, and have it permanently associated with that book's entry in the online catalog. Authors are also able to answer a variety of stock interview questions, which are then posted on the site associated with all of their books. Authors are also able to leave their e-mail addresses so that readers may e-mail their own opinions or comments. Bezos believes that his is the world's most "customer-centric" company.

Another unique feature that the company offers readers who have their own Web sites is the opportunity to set up their own specialized bookstores. For example, suppose that someone is an expert on investing. She may list several investment strategy books on her Web site and then link them from her site directly into the **Amazon.com** catalog. The company is able to track books that are purchased in this manner and gives the individual a commission on all sales. What else can customers expect when they try to purchase a book from **Amazon.com?** Discounts. But don't be fooled. Only roughly 30 percent of the book titles are discounted by 10 to 30 percent. The others are sold at list price.

The company's strategy of providing consumers with a sense of community within their Web site seems to be working. In December 1999, 15.8 million unique visitors logged on. And as the online bookselling market is projected to be worth $4.9 billion by 2003 (compared to $1.3 billion in 1999), **Amazon.com** stands to gain many more loyal customers. In the fourth quarter of 1999 alone, 73 percent of sales were from repeat buyers.

Recently, the mammoth bookseller has moved into other areas. You can now purchase books as well as toys, home improvement products, software, videos, and DVDs online. With this push into selling other products, the company faces increasing competition from traditional retailers and e-commerce startups. Some believe that the company risks diluting its brand name by expanding its business to too many lines, too quickly. But Bezos begs to differ. He says, "I get asked a lot, 'Are you trying to be the Wal-Mart of the Web?' The truth is, we're not trying to be the Anything of the Web. We're genetically pioneers." The company's former UK managing director, Simon Murdoch, adds, "It's a great name. 'Amazon' is not tied to any product category. The brand is extendible; it stands for delivery." Time will tell if the company will continue to deliver. For now, Amazon is one of the few, Internet brands recognized around the world. It is the most frequented Web site in America, and one of the top few in France, Britain, Germany and Japan. Jeff Bezos' vision has certainly become one of the great entrepreneurial success stories.

Discussion Questions

1. Why are books and CDs sold successfully online while many other products haven't sold well?
2. Do you think that consumers who buy from **Amazon.com** also shop at other Web sites for books and CDs and buy from the site that offers the lowest price?
3. What aspects of customer service have helped **Amazon.com** be successful?
4. Why do you think **Amazon.com** isn't profitable even though it generates high sales dollars?
5. What are the differences in the purchasing experience between buying a book at **Amazon.com** versus at a Barnes & Noble brick-and-mortar store?
6. What problems arise as **Amazon.com** expands its offerings to products other than books?

Sources: K. J. Bannan, "Book Battle," *Adweek,* February 28, 2000, pp. 90–94; Anonymous, "Survey: E-Commerce: Amazon's Amazing Ambition," *The Economist,* February 26, 2000, p. S24; B. Rosier, "Amazon Leads Race to Expand Web Services," *Marketing,* February 24, 2000, pp. 19–20; D. A. Williamson, "Marketer of the Year: Amazon.com—Dot-Commerce: Worlds' Biggest E-tail Brand Writes Book on Marketing Savvy," *Advertising Age,* December 13, 1999, pp. 1, 36–40; K. Brooker, "Amazon vs. Everybody," *Fortune,* November 8, 1999, pp. 120–128; M. H. Martin, "The Next Big Thing: A Bookstore?" *Fortune,* December 9, 1996, pp. 168–170; K. Southwick, "An Interview: Jeff Bezos, Amazon.com," *Upside,* October 1996, pp. 29–33.

Tupperware

J. Paul Peter
University of Wisconsin–Madison

In 1958 Justin Dart purchased Tupperware from former DuPont chemist Earl Tupper for $10 million. From that time until 1980 Tupperware earned an estimated $1.5 billion pretax and had a phenomenal 25-year record of doubling sales and earnings every 5 years. In 1983, Tupperware sales slipped 7 percent and operating profits sank 15 percent. In 1992, sales for the second quarter fell 33 percent from the same period a year before. That quarter also saw a 20 percent decline in the number of active U.S. dealers. As shown in Exhibit 1, changes in families and households contributed to the loss of business.

Traditionally, Tupperware plastic products were sold at in-home parties. These parties now are held not only in homes but also in offices and other locations convenient for people going home from work. These parties consist of a part-time salesperson inviting friends and acquaintances to the location and displaying the many varieties of plastic products. The parties typically include refreshments, a free sample of Tupperware, casual conversation, games in which participants can win pieces of Tupperware, and formal offering of Tupperware products. Customers order at the party and pay for the products on delivery by the salesperson.

In order to try to curb the decline, Tupperware offered a variety of new products. These included Modular Mates, which defend against cabinet clutter; TupperWave, which microwaves an entire dinner in 30 minutes; and the Earth Pack, a set of containers in a washable green lunch bag. Many consumers resisted the Earth Pack since they prefer a Ziploc bag to washing it out.

Selling Tupperware might be a lot easier except that most women (55 percent by Tupperware's estimate) either have no idea how to find Tupperware or no desire to go to a Tupperware party. Some 40 percent of Tupperware's sales are from people who skip the parties but send orders along with friends who attend.

Tupperware relies heavily on overseas markets to generate sales growth. However, its sales were brutalized by the economic downturns in Asia and Latin America in the late 1990s and revenues dropped by more than one third. In the U.S., the com-

This case was prepared by J. Paul Peter, James R. McManus-Bascom Professor in Marketing at the University of Wisconsin–Madison.

Sources: Peter Spiegel, "Party On," *Forbes,* May 3, 1999, p. 76; Laurie M. Grossman, "Families Have Changed but Tupperware Keeps Holdings Its Parties," *The Wall Street Journal,* July 21, 1992, pp. A1, A13; Kerry Hannon, "Party Animal," *Forbes,* November 16, 1987, pp. 262–68.

EXHIBIT 1 Changing U.S. Lifestyles Have Hurt Tupperware

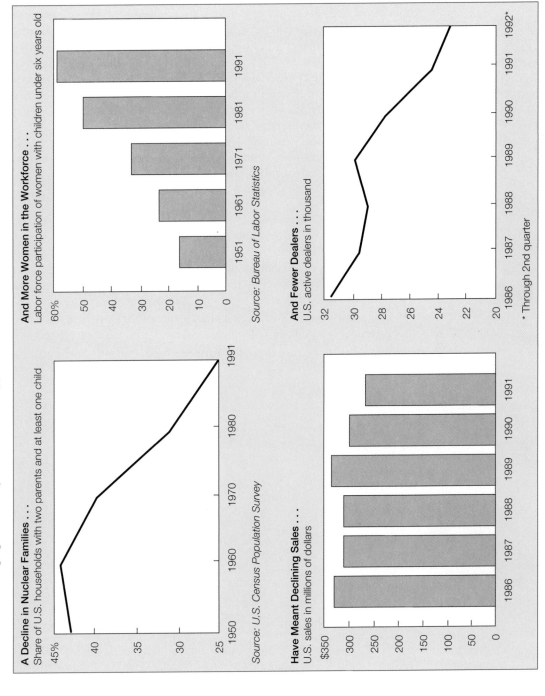

A Decline in Nuclear Families . . .
Share of U.S. households with two parents and at least one child

Source: U.S. Census Population Survey

And More Women in the Workforce . . .
Labor force participation of women with children under six years old

Source: Bureau of Labor Statistics

Have Meant Declining Sales . . .
U.S. sales in millions of dollars

And Fewer Dealers . . .
U.S. active dealers in thousand

*Through 2nd quarter

pany sold only $166 million worth of containers and cookware in 1998. However, its gross margin on these sales was over 60 percent.

Tupperware's major competitor, Rubbermaid, reaches consumers by selling in discount stores and supermarkets. Rubbermaid's products sell at substantially lower prices. For example, a two-quart Tupperware pitcher sells for $10.50 while one from Rubbermaid sells for about one fourth that amount. Lower prices and the convenience of having its products readily available in stores has led Rubbermaid to sales of $1.9 billion annually.

Tupperware's plans for 1999 include two new strategies. First, it plans to sell Tupperware on cart-like kiosks in malls across the country. It tested the idea in five malls and the results were promising. Second, it plans to sell products on the Internet. While the company does not expect this channel to improve sales substantially, it does expect some incremental sales.

In-home parties will continue to be a major part of Tupperware's strategy. The company insists that the in-home party is not an outdated concept since its products are of such high quality that a trained Tupperware lady (the party-givers are almost all women) is needed to explain product advantages.

Discussion Questions

1. Why has direct selling using in-home parties been such an effective channel for Tupperware historically?
2. The data shown in the exhibit suggest a number of social changes that took place in the 1990s. What impact do they have on Tupperware's strategy to use in-home parties to sell its products?
3. Evaluate Tupperware's strategies of using kiosks in malls and the Internet to sell its products.
4. What opportunities are there for Tupperware to curb the decline and increase its sales and profits?

Blockbuster Entertainment Corporation

James A. Kidney
Southern Connecticut State University

Introduction

Seated at his desk in a rented two-story stucco executive office building in downtown Fort Lauderdale, Florida, H. Wayne Huizenga prepared to announce record revenues and net income for his chain of Blockbuster Video stores. His mid-April 1992 announcement would attribute those results to "increasing market penetration, gains in same-store revenue, and continued emphasis on cost control and increased productivity."[1] As Blockbuster Entertainment Corporation's Chairman of the Board and Chief Executive Officer, he also prepared to announce that it was now possible to pay a cash dividend to the company's 8,000 stockholders—something that had not been done before.

At the end of 1991, having achieved a 13 percent share of market, the company announced that its goal was to reach a 20 percent share of the U.S. home video market and have 3,000 Blockbuster Video stores operating in North America by 1995.[2] In some of its most mature markets, such as Atlanta, Chicago, Dallas, Detroit, and South Florida, that would mean market shares well in excess of 30 percent. Such a high share of market has been rare in specialty retailing. However, Blockbuster was the only U.S. video rental chain operating on a nationwide basis. Its next largest competitor was a regional chain, less than one-tenth its size.

This case was prepared by Dr. James A. Kidney, Management Department, School of Business, Southern Connecticut State University, New Haven, CT 06515.

[1]Corporate news release dated April 21, 1992.

[2]The total population of video rental stores operating throughout the U.S. ranged between 25,000 and 29,000, and turnover of individual store locations was quite high during the late 1980s and early 1990s.

External Challenges and Opportunities

As Huizenga optimistically pondered the company's strategic situation over the next five to seven years, there were several interesting external challenges and opportunities lurking on the horizon:

- With a higher market share than all of its 300 closest competitors combined, how much further could the company's market penetration grow?
- Could any significant technological changes in home entertainment alter the video rental industry's attractiveness?
- What were the future implications of Philips Electronics N.V.'s recent investment in Blockbuster stock?

Company History

David P. Cook, a 31-year-old Texas entrepreneur, founded the company in December 1982 as Cook Data Services, Inc., a provider of software and computer services to the oil and gas industries. Facing a sagging market for such services, Cook decided to switch over to a new, rapidly growing niche in specialty retailing—video rental stores. Cook's first store was opened during 1985, and the present corporate name was adopted one year later. From the outset, Cook recognized that an innovative superstore concept would draw many customers away from typical mom-and-pop rental stores and that well-designed computerized information systems would be advantageous for inventory planning and control as well as for customer information.

The typical mom-and-pop store had a spartan, nondescript atmosphere; short hours; a selection of fewer than 3,000 titles stressing recent hits; and empty boxes to be brought to a clerk who would have to find appropriate tapes—provided they were then in stock. Many mom-and-pops obtained significant rental revenues from X-rated videos, and that occasionally created an unwholesome image.

In comparison, Cook's idea was to have a family-oriented atmosphere with an extensive selection of children's videos, longer, more convenient hours, improved layout, quality service, faster check-in/check-out, state-of-the-art real time computer information systems, and a thoroughly trained professional staff.

Attracting Huizenga's Attention

After only two years of operation, Blockbuster's latent potential attracted the attention of Huizenga. By that time, Cook owned 8 stores and franchised 11 more in the Dallas area. Huizenga, then 48 years old, was restless, looking for a way to come back from early retirement, after having successfully made a small fortune from several companies.

Huizenga's previous experience had been in building up businesses in a variety of dissimilar industries, such as trash bin rentals and garbage hauling, dry cleaning, lawn care, portable toilet rentals, water cooler rentals and sale of bottled water. His most notable success was Waste Management, Inc., which he had honed into the world's largest waste collection and disposal company.

There was a common denominator running throughout his past entrepreneurial ventures. Each had rendered relatively basic services, had repeat customers, required little employee training, earned a steady cash flow, and was able to expand within an industry filled with small, undercapitalized competitors. Usually, the fragmented industries he entered were ripe for consolidation, because greater firm size led to economies of scale in marketing, distribution, computerized information systems, and/or potential clout in purchasing products and services.

Expansion and Acquisition of Store Locations

During 1987 Huizenga and a couple of close business associates bought out Blockbuster's founders and franchise holders for $18 million, and soon thereafter began acquiring small regional chains, such as Southern Video Partnership and Movies to Go. To help him run the new business, Huizenga hired several former upper level managers from McDonald's Corporation. His upper management group adopted the view that Blockbuster's target audience should be very similar to McDonald's broad-based restaurant clientele. Thus, Blockbuster's national expansion of its retail business was based upon McDonald's well-established growth philosophy, namely: blitz major markets, add stores quickly, use franchising to speed the process of obtaining managerial talent and operating capital, and never admit that the market is saturated.

Facing a rapid rise in VCR ownership, management tried to combine careful planning with opportunistic risk taking. An aggressive acquisition program was financed by new equity capital, in order to avoid burdensome long-term debt. Over the following four years, additional regional chains, such as Video Library Inc., Major Video Corp., Oklahoma Entertainment Inc., Vector Video Inc., Video Superstores Venture L.P., and Erol's Inc. were eagerly gobbled up.

A major international thrust was launched in early 1992, with the acquisition of Cityvision plc, the largest home video retailer in the U.K. Operating under the "Ritz" name and enjoying a 20 percent share of market, this firm had roughly 800 small stores and was considered to be an underperformer.

Around the same time, several Blockbuster Video stores were opened in Japan in a joint-venture with Fujita & Co., a retailer running over 800 McDonald's restaurants and holding a stake in Toys 'R' Us Japan, Ltd. Jointly they hoped to open 1,000 stores over the next ten years.

Describing the hectic, and occasionally disorganized, rush to add store locations Huizenga explained, "We felt we had to go fast because we had nothing proprietary. We had to get the locations in each area before somebody else moved in. It was a mistake, but it turned out okay. We have the locations, the people are trained, and the customers are ours. Now if somebody else comes in, they have to take it away from us."[3]

Blockbuster Video's Profile as of 1992

Blockbuster Video was a membership only club, serving more than 29 million members worldwide, who rented more than 1 million of the company's videocassettes daily. Without incurring any membership fees, patrons were provided with bar-coded membership cards which allowed for speedy computerized check-out from the issuing store. Cards were sometimes honored at other locations in the chain as well. By requiring personal photo identification and an application for membership, rather than dealing with anonymous walk-ins, the rental store was able to secure an extra measure of control over tapes which left the premises. A major credit card also had to be presented, so that the store could charge members for lost or damaged inventory.

[3] *The New York Times Business World Magazine,* June 9, 1991.

The typical Blockbuster Video store was located in a free-standing building of approximately 6,000 square feet (560 square meters) and was open from 10:00 am to midnight, seven days per week, 365 days per year. The atmosphere was bright and wholesome. Aisles were clearly marked and divided into more than 30 categories to distribute customer traffic and encourage browsing. Video boxes with tapes inside were openly displayed within easy reach. Similar categories were placed adjacent to one another, thereby increasing the potential for increased rentals. Blockbuster's superstores typically carried a comprehensive selection of 10,000 prerecorded videocassettes, consisting of more than 8,000 titles. The strongest months for video store rentals tended to be December through March and June through August, with Hollywood's release schedule being a crucial variable.

Blockbuster Video stores proudly claimed to offer "More Movies Than Anyone In The World." Additionally, their relatively weak, fragmented rivals were seldom able to match Blockbuster's advertising clout and wide array of attractions, such as: computer-driven movie selection aids; a three-evening rental policy; an attractive overnight pricing policy for new hit releases which improved turnover and in-stock positions; a state-of-the-art management information system which tracked rentals and market trends; microwave popcorn and other snack foods; promotional tie-ins with Domino's Pizza, Pepsi-Cola, Pizza Hut, Subway, U.S. Air, and Universal Studios; drop-off boxes for fast returns; and publicity from an annual Blockbuster Bowl football game. Nevertheless, some competitors clearly differentiated themselves from Blockbuster by offering lower prices, reservations, home delivery, or hard core "adult" videos.

As of March 31, 1992, there were 2,829 Blockbuster Video stores, worldwide, up from 19 just five years earlier (Exhibit 1).

Locations and Operations

By the first quarter of 1992, 68 percent of Blockbuster's stores were located in 46 of America's 50 states, with the remaining 32 percent located in Austria, Australia, Canada, Chile, Guam, Japan, Mexico, Puerto Rico, Spain, the United Kingdom, and Venezuela. Nearly all of the company's retail, distribution, and administrative facilities were rented under non-cancellable operating leases, which in most cases contained renewal options. Blockbuster employed approximately 12,500 individuals.

EXHIBIT 1   **Blockbuster Entertainment Corporation (number of Blockbuster video stores, by ownership type)**

Source: Blockbuster's 1991 Annual Report and 1992 press releases.

Date	Company	Franchised	Total
December 31, 1985	1	0	1
December 31, 1986	19	0	19
December 31, 1987	112	126	238
December 31, 1988	341	248	589
December 31, 1989	561	518	1,079
December 31, 1990	787	795	1,582
December 31, 1991	1,025	1,003	2,028
March 31, 1992	1,805	1,024	2,829

Note: The surge in company stores during the first quarter of 1992 is attributable to the Cityvision plc acquisition.

There had historically tended to be a 50–50 balance between company-owned and franchised locations. Although franchising remained beneficial in foreign countries, where local partners made it easier to conduct business, franchising within the U.S. became less essential once the company had an ample cash flow and employed many competent people who could help manage ongoing growth.

The usual initial investment (i.e., franchise fee, inventory, equipment, and start-up capital) for a franchised location ranged from $700,000 to $1,000,000. Annual operating costs per location fell in the $400,000 to $500,000 range. Franchisees were provided extensive guidelines for site selection, store design and product selection, as well as customer service, and management training programs. In addition, the company furnished national and local advertising and promotional programs for the entire system. Franchisees paid royalties and other fees for those services and also routinely paid Blockbuster Entertainment for videocassette inventories, computer hardware and software.

For a typical Blockbuster Video store, cash flow payback on initial store investment occurred rapidly—generally in under three years. The average new store attained monthly revenues of $70,000 within twelve months of opening date.

Systemwide revenues, for company-owned and franchise-owned operations combined, as well as other selected financial data are shown in Exhibit 2.

EXHIBIT 2   **Blockbuster Entertainment Corporation (selected annual financial data)**

Source: Blockbuster's 1991 Annual Report and Standard & Poor's Stock Report.

	1991	1990	1989	1988	1987
Income Data (Million $)					
Systemwide revenue	1,520	1,133	663	284	98
Company revenue	868	633	402	136	43
Operating costs & expenses	714	514	326	110	37
Operating income	154	119	76	26	6
Net income	94	69	44	17	3
Depreciation & amortization	189	124	76	22	5
Cash flow	283	193	120	39	8
Balance Sheet Data (Million $)					
Total assets	804	608	417	235	105
Cash & cash equivalents	48	49	40	9	7
Current assets	163	116	93	39	27
Current liabilities	164	110	83	49	17
Long-term debt	134	169	118	39	22
Shareholders' equity	483	315	208	124	59
Per Share Data ($)					
Earnings per share	.56	.42	.28	.12	.04
Tangible book value	2.35	1.65	1.18	.75	.41
Stock price—high	15.12	13.37	10.81	6.25	2.63
Stock price—low	7.75	6.75	4.87	1.06	.75
Common Stock and Equivalents (Millions)					
Average shares outstanding	168	162	155	142	75

Notes: Systemwide revenues include franchise store revenues, while company revenues do not. Operating costs and expenses include depreciation and amortization. Cash flow is net income plus depreciation and amortization. Tangible book value excludes cost of purchased businesses in excess of market value of tangible assets acquired (unamortized goodwill).

Sources of Revenues

During 1991, 5 percent of company revenues were derived from franchise royalties and fees, 20 percent from product sales mainly to franchisees, and 75 percent from rentals. Other than low-priced used products, outright sales of home videos were never emphasized prior to late 1991, because the largest sellers were highly competitive national discount chains like Wal-Mart and Kmart. As a growing portion of consumer spending went towards videocassette and laser disc purchases, it became logical for video rental stores to begin taking the sell-through market more seriously.

Mr. Joseph Baczko, who headed the highly successful International Division of Toys 'R' Us, Inc. for eight years, was hired in 1991 as Blockbuster's new President and Chief Operating Officer. To carry out a process of "retailing" as well as internationalizing the company, he brought several executives with significant retailing experience into the firm. Promotional and display efforts to stimulate sell-through transactions were given added emphasis under Baczko's direction. Given his background in toys, he was interested in treating child oriented movies, such as *Batman, Bambi, The Little Mermaid,* and *101 Dalmatians,* mainly as sell-through rather than rental products. Blockbuster's stores also began renting Nintendo and Sega Genesis video game products.

Industry Environment

Rentals and sales of home videos in the U.S. amounted to a mere $700 million in 1982. By 1991, domestic revenue for the video rental industry reached $11 billion, and Americans were spending more than twice as much to watch movies at home as they did to watch them in movie theaters. Within the marketplace for prerecorded videocassettes, movies accounted for more than 80 percent of rental revenues and at least 50 percent of dollars spent on purchases. Blockbuster Entertainment estimated that the U.S. video rental market for movies would reach $19.3 billion by the turn of the century (Exhibit 3).

In 1980, the percentage of U.S. households owning at least one television set reached 98 percent and remained at that level thereafter. By 1995, there were expected to be almost 100 million households in the U.S., and 98 percent of them were likely to own at least one color TV set. Blockbuster Entertainment expected 91 percent of those TV owning households also to own VCRs (Exhibit 4), with more than 35 percent of them owning at least two machines.

VCR ownership in Europe also was growing rapidly, with household penetration rates in individual countries lagging behind the U.S. anywhere from two to

EXHIBIT 3   Estimated and Projected Annual U.S. Movie Revenues, by Viewing Method ($ billions)

Source: Blockbuster's 1991 Annual Report.

Viewing Method	1990	1995	2000
Video	10.3	15.2	19.3
Movie theater	5.1	6.9	7.4
Pay cable (premium channels)	5.1	6.2	7.6
Pay-per-view	.01	0.5	2.0
Total	20.6	28.8	36.3

EXHIBIT 4   Estimated and Projected VCR and Cable TV Penetration among U.S. TV Owning Households (millions of TV owning households, percent with VCRs, percent with cable TV, and percent with additional pay-per-view or pay cable services, by year)

Source: Blockbuster's 1991 Annual Report, the Universal Almanac, and author's estimates.

Year	No. of TV Owning Households	Percent with		
		VCR	Cable	Pay Cable
1980	76	1	20	7
1981	78	3	22	10
1982	82	6	30	16
1983	83	10	34	19
1984	84	17	39	24
1985	85	30	43	26
1986	86	42	46	27
1987	87	53	48	26
1988	89	62	49	27
1989	90	68	53	29
1990	92	72	56	29
1991	92	77	58	30
1992	93	82	61	31
1993	95	86	64	32
1994	96	89	67	34
1995	97	91	70	36

Note: From 1982 through 1995, it's assumed that 98 percent of all U.S. households own televisions.

EXHIBIT 5   Estimated Population, Home Video Spending, VCR Penetration and Basic Cable Penetration by Country, as of 1991

Sources: Blockbuster's 1991 Annual Report, *This Business of Television,* and 1992 *World Almanac.*

Country	Population (millions)	Video Spending ($ billions)	VCRs (% of households)	Cable (% of households)
Australia	17	0.7	70	0
Canada	27	1.2	65	69
France	56	0.7	40	10
Germany	79	0.7	46	32
Italy	58	0.6	38	1
Japan	124	2.6	70	20
United Kingdom	57	1.4	70	2
United States	250	11.0	75	57
Others	4,732	2.3	n.a.	n.a.
Worldwide total	5,400	21.2	n.a.	n.a.

Note: n.a. = not available

five years. Total 1991 worldwide spending for home video rental and sales was $21.2 billion (Exhibit 5). Licensing, sale, and rental practices differed from one product/market to another, and in some countries most of the television viewing population remained unaware that movie videos could be rented instead of being purchased.

Movie Production and Distribution

Approximately 390 to 450 new feature films were released annually in the United States. Eight of the largest distributors accounted for more than 90 percent of movie theater film rentals in the United States and Canada. Most of them, such as Paramount, Universal, Warner, Fox, Columbia, and Disney, had been in business for more than 50 years. Leading producers and distributors of videos were usually subsidiaries of large companies which owned other leisure-time businesses. Large distributors also had prime access to international channels for distributing American-made films in foreign countries. Musical, cultural, educational, exercise programs, instructional, and documentary videos tended to be handled by smaller distributors.

The time span from the point when work began on a new movie to the point when its revenue stream was largely realized often was five years or longer. Over that period, producers and distributors attempted to play out their products in a manner which gave them an optimum revenue stream.

By 1991, home video had become a major ancillary source of revenue for movie studios. For example, *Nothing But Trouble* (directed by Dan Aykroyd, 1991) grossed $8.5 million in box office receipts. The studio's share was roughly 50 percent. When released on videocassette, the same movie earned an additional $9.6 million in revenue for the studio.[4]

The sequence of each film's release depended on the nature of individual deals made by the distributor. Domestic release usually occurred somewhat ahead of international release. A typical major studio's United States release tended to be rolled out in the following illustrative manner:

Theatrical showings: January through April, 1992

Home video: Mid-Summer, 1992

Airline: Mid-Summer, 1992

Pay-per-view: Late-Summer or Fall, 1992

Pay cable (premium channels): Winter, 1992–93

If attractively priced, popular movies that were developed for young children were likely to achieve a sell-through market of 1.5 million or more copies. Movies that had been adult hits at the box office within the latest year were the ones most in demand for rentals, and 100,000 to 500,000 copies of them were generally sold, mostly to video rental stores. Assuming a $3 charge per rental, it normally took anywhere from 13 to 19 rentals to recover a store's initial investment in a hit movie tape.

Distributors set high initial suggested retail prices (roughly $80 to $100 on box office hits) for videotaped films they expected consumers to rent and low prices (roughly $20 to $30) for those they expected consumers to buy. Each videocassette cost distributors about $2 to manufacture and $2 to market. Wholesale prices paid by Blockbuster were generally 55 to 65 percent of suggested retail prices.

Wholesalers

Despite the fact that movies were the mainstay of the home video business, Blockbuster Entertainment traditionally purchased its movie rental inventory from wholesalers rather than film distributors. Having achieved nationwide scope, the company

[4]Source: Blockbuster Entertainment 1991 Corp. Annual Report.

could decide to bypass regional wholesalers and purchase its movies more economically directly from motion picture distributors.

Technological Threats

During the decade from 1982 through 1991 Americans purchased 1.2 billion prerecorded and 2.2 billion blank videocassettes. They also built up a $32 billion investment in VCR equipment. This burgeoning consumer commitment to VCR technology seemed to assure long-range demand for videocassettes. Nevertheless, the ease of duplicating and pirating videocassettes was a matter of some concern to movie producers. As laser discs began to attract a modest following, rentals and sales of video discs were being added to many video store's product offerings.

No one knew precisely when new types of home entertainment might begin to undermine home videotape viewing. Cable television was expected to become a more and more serious threat. Even though three out of five TV owning households subscribed to cable service as of 1991, only one third of those subscribers had access to movies on pay cable (e.g. HBO, Showtime, Cinemax, The Disney Channel, The Movie Channel) or pay-per-view channels.

Employing "addressable technology," pay-per-view service allowed customers to call in and have a movie, concert, or sporting event broadcast on their TV for a fee. Being transaction based, pay-per-view depended upon impulse buying. It was sold by direct mailings, advertisements, bill stuffers, and 24 hour "barker" promotional channels.

In 1992, sporting events generated almost twice as much pay-per-view business as other alternatives. As pay-per-view's market potential continued to develop, the Summer of 1992 was regarded as an important psychological turning point. Cable operators were seeking broadcasting rights for live coverage of the Olympic Games in Atlanta, Georgia, hoping that such coverage would significantly boost the number of new subscribers for pay-per-view services.

While viewers had to watch pay-per-view at a scheduled time, this service certainly provided greater convenience than having to make two round trips to a video store. The competitive threat was moderated by the fact that most new movies were released on videocassettes before they appeared on pay-per-view services or pay cable. However, that disparity could disappear rapidly, if movie distributors were enticed by cable's potential for licensing and revenue sharing arrangements.

Interactive Television

Over the long-term, advances in satellite and cable television technology and entry of regional telephone companies into the electronic home delivery arena were other potential concerns within the U.S. market. With new developments in fiber optics and digital signal compression, expansion to 500 channels could become feasible for video delivery systems. Thus, there was a possibility that "video-on-demand" could become a reality on cable or telephone systems by the mid 1990s.

Anticipating major advances in communications, IBM and Time Warner Corp. had begun discussing ways to combine data processing and transmitting expertise with cable TV systems, TV shows, and movies. IBM believed interactive television would eventually encroach upon a wide array of existing entertainment and information product/markets, including catalog shopping, broadcast and cable advertising, home video, information services, theater, video games, electronic messaging, videoconferencing, photography, records, tapes, and CDs. Furthermore, the Federal

Communications Commission (FCC) had allocated a portion of the broadcast spectrum to interactive television and intended to award licenses to investors who could serve large markets.

Nervous Investors

Had the video rental market remained extremely fragmented, it might not have become so large and well-established. Some industry watchers predicted that Blockbuster's success in becoming a high quality specialty retail chain might impair the development of innovative competing technologies for accessing home entertainment.

Recognizing that other forms of retailing were withstanding competition from television, Baczko made the following point, "Home shopping has not taken the store away, and pay-per-view is not going to do so to video. I don't think you can ever beat a retailing environment."[5]

Nevertheless, newspaper reports of questionable depreciation accounting practices, bankruptcy filings by sizable video retailers, and media hype of future electronic home delivery systems, from time to time, stirred predictions of impending disaster for the video rental industry. Consequently, Blockbuster's common stock attracted speculators and short sellers, and the market price per share plunged every so often as frightened investors hastily bailed out to "take profits" or "stop losses." For example, the price per share reached a high of $15.125 and a low of $7.75 on the New York Stock Exchange during the first half of 1991.

Strategic Alliance with Philips Electronics

During 1992, an intriguing strategic alliance began to emerge between Blockbuster Entertainment Corp. and Philips Electronics, N.V. Headquartered in the Netherlands, Philips was the world's second largest consumer electronics company after Japan's Matsushita Electric Industrial Co. Philips' decision to purchase 13 million newly issued common shares (nearly 7.2 percent of outstanding shares) suggested that the two companies might be heading toward a close working relationship.[6]

In 1991 consumer products accounted for 47 percent of Philips' $33 billion in sales revenues. The early 1990s found the U.S., Canada, Australia, the United Kingdom, and Japan all experiencing economic downturns and declining consumer confidence. Stagnant demand and bloody price wars were curbing profits throughout the consumer electronics industry. Battered by stagnant demand and stiff price competition from its Japanese competitors, Philips reported a $3 billion loss in 1990. Philips' new President, Jan D. Timmer, was struggling to slash the payroll, close inefficient plants, and divest unprofitable operations. A streamlining and restructuring process initiated by Timmer provided a $210 million profit on sales of $33 billion in 1991. Recent sales data are shown in Exhibit 6.

Some analysts, suspecting that Huizenga might be ready to move on to another new venture, speculated that Philips might be interested in acquiring a controlling interest in Blockbuster Entertainment Corp. Others expressed doubts that outright ownership and management of a captive group of rental stores would serve Philips' best interest.

Having pioneered such consumer electronics products as the videocassette recorder, audio compact disc, digital compact cassette, and high-definition televi-

---

[5] *The New York Times,* February 21, 1992.

[6] These funds have been used by Blockbuster to help pay for the Cityvision plc acquisition.

EXHIBIT 6   Philips Electronics N.V., Net Sales by Product Sector and Geographical Area (millions of Guilders)

Source: Philips' 1991 Annual Report.

	1991	1990
Product Sector		
Lighting	7,351	7,026
Consumer products	26,861	25,856
Professional products and systems	12,510	12,400
Components and semiconductors	7,844	7,953
Miscellaneous	2,420	2,529
Net sales	56,986	55,764
Geographical Area		
Netherlands	3,206	3,604
Rest of Europe	30,433	30,366
U.S.A. and Canada	12,833	11,819
Latin America	3,142	3,361
Africa	730	772
Asia	5,565	4,770
Australia and New Zealand	1,077	1,072
Net sales	56,986	55,764

Note: On December 31, 1991 and 1990, respectively, one U.S. dollar equaled 1.71 and 1.69 Dutch Guilders.

sion, Philips had long been a superior technological leader. Marketing agility and competitive pricing had never been Philips' strengths. Philips conceivably might be aiming for a reliable international retail base for rapid, broad distribution of future hardware and software products.

Philips owned 51 percent of Super Club Holding & Finance S.A., a poorly performing music and video retail chain. With store locations in Europe and the United States, Super Club might benefit from a tie-in with Blockbuster. Philips also owned 80 percent of Polygram, one of the three largest music publishing, production, marketing, and distribution companies in the world, and a major European manufacturer of compact discs. Recognizing the increasingly complementary natures of the audio and video fields, Polygram had begun producing and distributing filmed entertainment, as part of its strategy to become a multicultural, global entertainment company.

Philips' Multimedia Systems

Potentially even more relevant were Philips' plans for a new Imagination Machine. Philips had developed a new Compact Disk Interactive (CD-I) entertainment system that could turn the family TV into a terminal through which one could play regular music CDs, view photo CD disks, and interact with programs rather than just watch them. Touted as the "VCR of the 21st century," Philips' Imagination Machine was one of the products that Timmer was counting on heavily to revive depressed earnings. Blending text, full-motion video, and stereo-quality sound, it called up sports statistics during live broadcasts, displayed digital snapshots, played karaoke sing-along disks, used Nintendo's new games and played movies and music videos. While CD-I had been promoted primarily to the consumer market, it was also highly suited to the educational market.

Philips utilized a special format for its CD-ROM, which was supported by several other electronics firms as well. Commodore, Apple, Toshiba, and Tandy were offering multimedia equipment with different CD formats. Sony and Panasonic (Matsushita) had not yet revealed the type of standard they might support. Having witnessed the VHS/Beta wars of the late 1970s, Philips recognized the need to insure that its CD-I standard won out over its rivals. Ultimately, the availability of appealing multimedia software would help determine which compact disc standard would dominate.

Potential New Undertakings

As Blockbuster entered numerous foreign markets, its employees started to acquire increasing familiarity with markets for movies and home entertainment within many different cultures and political jurisdictions. Blockbuster's increasing knowledge of ways to formalize and expand global rental markets could help foster widespread acceptance of the rental concept for expensive multimedia CDs, such as encyclopedias, music libraries, and games. Blockbuster could thus become a leading worldwide distributor of a new generation of home entertainment products, perhaps selling and/or renting Philips' Imagination Machines and CDs.

Reacting to investor skepticism a year earlier, Huizenga had optimistically asserted, "We have the best locations in town. We've got a plain vanilla box. We can sell shoes there if we want to. Maybe we'll build a music store that's green and white. We could call it Chartbusters."[7] Such remarks indicate that someday Blockbuster Entertainment Corporation could be attracted to retailing opportunities elsewhere within the diverse, yet more and more intertwined, marketplace for home entertainment products.

[7]*The New York Times Business World Magazine,* June 9, 1991.

Peapod in the Online Grocery Business*

Alan B. Eisner
Lubin School of Business, Pace University

Nicole Belmont
Lubin School of Business, Pace University

Peapod, Inc., co-founded by Andrew B. Parkinson and Thomas L. Parkinson in 1989, was a $68 million online grocery service that used both its own central ware-houses and the retail stores of supermarket partners to fill customers' grocery orders. Peapod was a pioneer of the online grocery industry, getting its start on the Internet well before the Internet became a global phenomenon and well before such competitors as HomeGrocer.com, WebVan, and Netgrocer.com were even organized. However, the company had grown more slowly than first anticipated, revising its "trial and error" strategy several times to find a formula that would attract more customers and make the company profitable. In September 1999, co-founder Andrew Parkinson relinquished the position of CEO and turned the reins over to a new president and CEO, Bill Malloy, who had been recruited from AT&T Wireless to fine-tune and execute Peapod's latest order fulfillment strategy and capitalize on what the co-founders believed was a blossoming opportunity in online grocery sales. Parkinson remained on as chairman of Peapod's board of directors.

Malloy faced three daunting challenges at Peapod. He had to prove that the company's newly revised business model was viable, that the company could be made profitable after six years of mounting losses, and that it could withstand competition from Homegrocer.com, which had recently allied itself with Amazon.com, and from newly formed WebVan, which raised over $350 million in its initial public offering of common stock in the second half of 1999.

Company Background

Founded in 1989 by brothers, Andrew and Thomas Parkinson, Peapod was an early pioneer in e-commerce, inventing an online home-shopping service for grocery

*Many thanks to Arthur A. Thompson, Jr. for his helpful comments, edits, and improvements.

items years ahead of the commercial emergence of the Internet. With its tagline "Smart Shopping for Busy People," the company began providing consumers with a home shopping experience in the early 1990s, going so far as to install modems in their homes to provide an online connection. From its founding in 1989 until 1998, the company's business model involved filling customer orders by forming alliances with traditional grocery retailers. The company chose a retail partner in each geographic area where it operated and used the partner's local network of retail stores to pick and pack orders for delivery to customers. Peapod personnel would cruise the aisles of a partner's stores, selecting the items each customer ordered, pack and load them into Peapod vehicles, and then deliver them to customers at times chosen by customers. Peapod charged customers a fee for its service, and it also collected fees from its retail supply partners for using their products in its online service. Over the next several years, Peapod built delivery capabilities in eight market areas:

Chicago, Illinois

Columbus, Ohio

Houston, Texas

Boston, Massachusetts

San Francisco/San Jose, California

Dallas, Texas

Austin, Texas

Long Island, New York

The company steadily built a base of about 90,000 to 100,000 customers across all eight markets, filling over 700,000 orders annually in 1999. Peapod's revenues rose from $8.0 million in 1994 to $68.4 million in 1998 (see Exhibit 1). Meanwhile, it made improvements in its website (www.peapod.com) and invested in proprietary software technologies to facilitate efficient order fulfillment and delivery routes, accumulate data on customer buying patterns, and better integrate pricing, merchandising, and product promotion. The company went public in June 1997, offering shares at $16. During 1999 and early 2000, Peapod's stock (listed on the Nasdaq National Market under the symbol "PPOD") traded mostly in the $8 to $12 range (for detailed finacials see Exhibits 3 and 4).

In 1997, faced with mounting losses despite growing revenues, Peapod management determined that its original, partner-based business model entailed too high a cost structure for the company to achieve profitable growth. The co-founders opted to shift to a new order fulfillment business model using a local company-owned and operated central distribution warehouse to store, pick, and pack customer orders for delivery. By mid-1999 the company had opened new distribution

EXHIBIT 1   Six-Year Summary of Peapod's Financial Performance, 1994–99

Date	Sales (000$)	Net Income	EPS
1999	73,134	−28,450	−1.62
1998	69,265	−21,565	−1.27
1997	56,943	−12,979	−0.87
1996	27,642	−9,566	−0.82
1995	15,209	−6,592	−0.79
1994	8,005	−4,437	−0.75

centers in three of the eight markets it served—Chicago, Long Island, and Boston; a fourth distribution center was under construction in San Francisco. Peapod stocked its distribution centers with products purchased at wholesale from a variety of food and household products companies, including Kellogg's, Kraft, Colgate-Palmolive, Frito-Lay, Coca-Cola, Clorox, Kimberly-Clark, Procter & Gamble, Nabisco, Ralston Purina, Nestlé, Walgreens, and in some cases, traditional retailers. Peapod management had announced plans to use the centralized distribution model in all eight markets over time and in all new areas it entered. The company was reportedly losing money in five of the markets it served in mid-1999.

Peapod in Early 2000

Going into the new millennium, Peapod was the largest Internet supermarket with over 90,000 customers (based on a count of customers who had placed an order within the past twelve months). It had a 30 percent share of the estimated $235 million market for grocery products sold online.[1] The eight market areas where the company presently operated had an estimated 6.6 million households, representing approximately 7 percent of total U.S. households. Delivery operations in these areas were conducted out of 22 order fulfillment locations. Exhibit 2 shows the company's eight metropolitan markets, the number of households represented in each market, and the company's local retail supermarket partners. Peapod currently processed an average of 2,000 orders daily; average order size was $110–$115 but ran a bit lower in areas where the company utilized central distribution warehouses because Peapod stocked fewer items at its warehouses than were generally available from using the stores of supermarket partners to fill orders. Management believed that Peapod's average order size was about five times the in-store average of supermarkets and convenience stores.

Management's vision for the company was expressed in three statements:

- *Our Dream*—To fundamentally improve people's lives by bringing interactive shopping to a broad consumer market.

EXHIBIT 2 Peapod's Metropolitan Markets, Household Exposure, and Retail Partners, February 2000

Metropolitan Market Area Served	Estimated Number of Area Households, 1998	Retail Partners	Peapod Distribution Center
Chicago, IL	1,732,000	Jewel Food Stores	Yes
Columbus, OH	398,000	Kroger	
Houston, TX	939,000	Randalls Food and Drug	
Boston, MA	1,242,000	Stop and Shop	Yes
San Francisco and San Jose, CA	840,000	Certified Grocers of California, Andronico's, and Walgreens	Yes
Dallas, TX	995,000	Tom Thumb	
Austin, TX	257,000	Randalls Food and Drug	
Long Island, NY	226,000	Giant/Edwards Super Foods Stores	Yes

[1]Peapod, Inc., Investor's Overview, www.peapod.com.

EXHIBIT 3   Peapod's Statements of Income, 1996–98

Source: Company 10-K and 10-Q filings.

	1998	1997	1996
Peapod, Inc.			
Statements of Income			
(in thousands, except per share data)			
Revenues			
Net product sales	57,305	43,487	22,015
Member and retailer	9,650	11,234	4,558
Interactive marketing	1,460	2,222	1,069
Licensing	850		
Total revenues	69,265	56,943	27,642
Costs and expenses			
Cost of goods sold	53,903	40,823	20,485
Fulfillment operations	17,196	14,469	6,889
General and administrative	8,029	5,935	3,785
Marketing and selling	7,545	7,726	4,739
System development and maintenance	3,386	1,696	1,124
Depreciation and amortization	3,264	1,234	651
Total costs and expenses	93,323	71,883	37,673
Operating loss	–24,058	–14,940	–10,031
Other Income (expense)			
Interest income	2,683	2,044	537
Interest expense	–190	–83	–72
Net loss	–21,565	–12,979	–9,566
Net loss per share	–$1.27	–$0.87	–$0.82
Shares to compute loss per share	16,964,439	14,915,734	11,664,956

- *Our Mission*—To be the world's leading and preferred provider of interactive grocery shopping services.
- *Our Passion*—To amaze and delight each one of our customers.

Peapod's recent income statements and balance sheets are shown in Exhibits 3 and 4.

PEAPOD'S CUSTOMERS

Peapod's target market was middle- and upper-income households with PC-savvy adults who were stressed for time and didn't particularly enjoy grocery shopping. This was the basis for its tag line, "Smart Shopping for Busy People." The company's market research indicated that its typical customers were dual income households, households with children, and females between the ages of of 30 and 54. The incomes of customers covered a wide range, with a median annual income exceeding $60,000.

PEAPOD'S STRATEGY

Peapod's strategy was to provide customers with a convenient, user-friendly, and personalized way of shopping for grocery items online 24 hours a day, seven days a week. Its online product offerings consisted of fresh meat, produce, deli, and bakery goods, plus name-brand canned and packaged goods, household items, and health and beauty products—essentially the same perishable and nonperishable name-brand products typically found in local supermarkets or drug stores. Peapod's prices were competitive

EXHIBIT 4   Peapod's Balance Sheets, 1997–1998

Source: Company 10-K and 10-Q filings.

	Peapod, Inc. Balance Sheets (in thousands, except share data)	
	1998	**1997**
Assets		
Current assets		
Cash and cash equivalents	$ 4,341	$54,079
Marketable securities	15,836	8,798
Receivables	2,516	1,195
Prepaid expenses	186	444
Other current assets	974	228
Total current assets	23,853	64,744
Property and equipment		
Computer equipment and software	4,010	4,499
Service equipment and other	2,147	1,053
Property and equipment, at cost	6,157	5,552
Accumulated depreciation	–2,252	–2,301
Net property and equipment	3,905	3,251
Noncurrent marketable securities	15,213	
Capitalized software development costs		998
Goodwill		117
Total assets	$42,971	$69,110
Liabilities and Stockholders' Equity		
Current liabilities		
Accounts payable	$ 3,442	$ 7,514
Accrued compensation	802	1,258
Other accrued liabilities	2,688	926
Deferred revenue	1,000	1,969
Current obligations under capital lease	590	727
Total current liabilities	8,522	12,394
Deferred revenue	448	1,212
Obligations under capital lease, less current portion	395	701
Total liabilities	9,365	14,307
Stockholders' equity		
Common stock, $.01 par value, 50 million shares authorized; 17,245,828 and 16,852,557 shares issued in 1998 and 1997	172	169
Additional paid-in capital	64,319	63,148
Accumulated other comprehensive income		
Unrealized gain on available-for-sale securities	83	—
Accumulated deficit	–30,060	–8,495
Treasury stock	–908	–19
Total stockholders' equity	33,606	54,803
Total liabilities and stockholders' equity	$42,971	$69,110

and it had weekly specials; manufacturer's coupons were accepted. Delivery was available seven days a week and could be scheduled for the same or next day at a time chosen by the customer. Peapod charged a fee for its online order and delivery service that varied by market area. In most markets customers had the option of paying a per-order service charge (about $10 per delivery) or a flat rate for unlimited monthly deliveries.

EXHIBIT 5   Peapod's Welcome Page at www.peapod.com.

Peapod.com   Your Personal Grocer & More.

Local Delivery   **Packages**   **About Peapod**

Welcome | How it works | Prices & Delivery Areas | Questions?

Check it out

New customer? Type your ZIP code below to enter the store and begin shopping. See list of current delivery areas below.

ZIP code [   ]

(go)

Already a Customer?

Please log in to the Local Grocery Delivery store using your username.

username [   ]

password [   ]

(go)

Peapod delivers to these metropolitan areas:
- Austin
- Boston
- Chicago
- Columbus
- Dallas/Fort Worth
- Fairfield County, Conn.
- Houston
- Long Island
- San Francisco/San Jose

Welcome to Peapod

America's #1 online grocer, delivering fresh food to your door.

Now **delivering in Connecticut!**

Top-quality products
- Fresh meat, deli, produce and bakery goods
- Name-brand packaged foods, household items, and health and beauty products

Saving money is easy
- Competitive prices and weekly specials
- No impulse shopping
- Manufacturers' coupons accepted

Convenience, pure and simple
- Shop anytime, night or day
- Choose your delivery time - any day of the week
- No more trips to the grocery store. No more checkout lanes. No more lugging groceries

First-rate customer service
- Trained shoppers hand-pick the freshest and best products - just like you would.
- Friendly drivers deliver your order right to your door.
- Customer Care handles your questions, comments and problems.

$20 in ~~FREE~~ **groceries**
click here

   The company's Welcome Page at its website is shown in Exhibit 5. The site was accessible to anyone using a Web browser, including personal computers, Web-enabled televisions, high-speed cable services, and wireless devices.

Peapod's Multifeatured, Highly Functional Website Technology

Peapod had built an easy-to-navigate website with a variety of highly functional features that management believed helped encourage repeat purchases and differentiated Peapod from other e-tailers and direct competitors. Customers could shop for items in several ways. One was to browse aisles, moving logically from general product categories to individual items (see Exhibit 6). Another was to conduct product searches based on brand or category name, which was particularly useful for coupon redemption or purchasing recipe ingredients. Shoppers could also sort items in any product category alphabetically or based on price, nutritional content (such as fat, grams, calo-

EXHIBIT 6   Ordering Page at Peapod's website

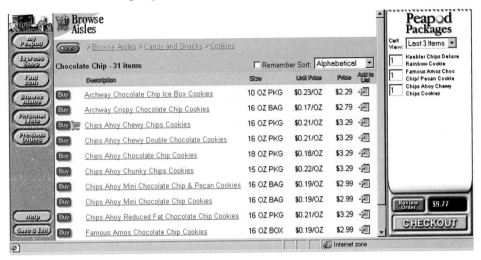

ries, cholesterol, and sodium), sale items, and kosher status. Another feature stored a customer's last three grocery orders, eliminating the need to start a shopping list of frequently purchased items from scratch again. Other features included

- An extensive library of product pictures, nutrition information, and product ingredients.
- An "Express Shop" feature that helped first-time shoppers build their order without having to browse through the aisles or search for items one at a time. For existing customers, Express Shop, in conjunction with the Previous Orders feature, allowed customers to easily add items to their order.
- A "SmartCart" that displayed a list of the items selected for purchase, as well as a running dollar total of the bill.
- The capability to generate Web pages based on a customer's shopping preferences, buying profile, and other variables so as to provide users with a customized shopping experience.
- A "Buddy E-Mail" feature that delivered order confirmations to two different e-mail addresses—something that was useful in households where shopping duties were shared among members.

Gomez Advisors, a leading provider of Internet research and analysis, in September 1999 rated Peapod's website first in terms of Ease of Use among all online grocers.

The company's website technology was designed to capture behavioral information from users—mouse clicks, time spent viewing each page, coupon redemptions, and other factors. The tracking data that was gathered allowed Peapod to generate dozens of metrics to evaluate the quality of its website and to identify opportunities to cross-sell additional goods and services.

Marketing and Advertising

The company's marketing objectives were attracting more users, retaining the business of current users, increasing the frequency with which users placed orders, growing average order size, and enhancing awareness of the Peapod brand. To achieve these objectives, the company used radio and newspaper advertising, direct mail, ads on local mass transit systems, Internet advertising, and branding on delivery trucks and employee uniforms. Company personnel drove attention-getting green Volkswagen "Pod Bugs" with the Peapod insignia to help promote local awareness about Peapod. In 1999, the company's marketing and advertising budget was about $6 million, the majority of which was focused on growing the customer base and helping the company achieve the operating scale needed for profitability.

One Internet marketing effort the company had come up with to attract new customers to Peapod's service was the Peapod Affiliate Program. Peapod started the program in April 1999 as a way of compensating other websites for promoting Peapod and providing links to Peapod from their site. Affiliates could earn a $15 commission for each referred visitor who placed an order with Peapod plus an additional $15 for a customer's third order.

To further promote consumer awareness of Peapod, the company had entered into an agreement with Hearst's HomeArts Network, a premier lifestyle site for women on the Web, whereby Peapod would be the exclusive Internet grocery service promoted on the HomeArts Network. The network provided online programming, as well as features from Hearst's 11 women's magazines, including *Redbook, Good Housekeeping, Cosmopolitan,* and *Country Living.* The HomeArts Network had a user base that strongly matched the target Peapod customer. Peapod had also formed a marketing alliance with Excite, Inc. that made Peapod the exclusive online grocer on Excite's website. The agreement with Excite gave Peapod exposure to an estimated 35 percent of all Internet users.[2]

Peapod Packages

To help build a national presence and awareness of the Peapod brand, the company had begun promoting its "Peapod Packages" for shipment to any location (see Exhibit 7). The company had put together preselected themed product assortments targeting such niche occasions as the Super Bowl, Christmas, Thanksgiving, the arrival of a new baby, or a birthday. There were also care packages for college students and recipe/meal solutions in a box. Shoppers could create their own Peapod Package. Peapod planned to expand the Peapod Package line to include specialty and gourmet foods and gifts.

Distribution Center Operations and Order Fulfillment

Peapod's new $2 million distribution centers each stocked over 12,000 dry grocery, frozen, and dairy products, along with perishable products such as produce, meat,

EXHIBIT 7   **Examples of Peapod Packages**

[2]"Peapod Signs Multi-Year Internet Marketing Deal with Excite," http://www.peapod.com/v5/Html/Press/ press045.html.

and prepared foods. Items were replenished on a just-in-time basis to optimize space utilization and ensure freshness.[3] While Peapod was opening distribution centers in each of its eight markets, it had stated its intention to continue its partnerships with its present retail supermarket allies, albeit on a reduced basis. Until its new central warehousing model was perfected, Peapod was temporarily relying on these partners to stock its central warehouse with perishables, health and beauty aids, and other items it did not currently stock and to fill orders for delivery to cetain addresses not as convenient to its warehouse. Moreover, such alliances gave Peapod an advertising channel for promoting the website at its partners' brick-and-mortar locations.

A major component of Peapod's strategy was to optimize its order fulfillment process from a cost standpoint. As the company began shifting from supermarket partnerships to centralized warehousing, it had reengineered its product distribution and order fulfillment practices to reduce costs, minimize out-of-stock frequencies, improve the accuracy of order picking at warehouses, make it economical to accommodate higher-order volumes, and ensure that orders were delivered within the scheduled time frame. New warehousing, order picking, and delivery routing software and systems had been designed and put in place.

Order fulfillment was managed by a handheld scanning device that contained pick data for a given metropolitan market area and controlled the order selection process in a manner calculated to minimize the labor time for picking and packing orders. The list of items for a particular order was sorted according to the location of each item in the warehouse, thereby requiring only one pass through the warehouse and minimizing the pick time for each order. The handheld unit displayed each item to be picked and provided a variety of features for assuring accuracy and allowing flexibility for handling exceptions. As individual items appeared on the screen, the picker confirmed the proper item by scanning the item's uniform product code and was alerted if the wrong item had been scanned. If an item was out of stock, the device noted the out-of-stock status and, if requested by the customer, automatically directed the picker to the customer-designated substitution. A list of out-of-stock items was automatically transmitted to the manager to generate replacement orders.

Delivery logistics were managed by a sophisticated computer program that provided time management information and point-to-point directions throughout the delivery route. The program accounted for traffic conditions, rush-hour volume, road construction, and other variables that could be predicted within the local area. Peapod drivers delivered the packages to each customer's doorstep or unloaded them in the kitchen (if requested) and obtained feedback from customers on the service. To build customer loyalty, Peapod tried to send the same delivery person to the homes of repeat customers. Peapod management was aggressively pursuing ways to fine-tune and improve all of the new systems it had implemented.

So far, order volume had not reached levels that allowed Peapod's warehouse and order fulfillment operation to realize scale economies. The costs of fulfillment operations were 30 percent of sales revenues during the first nine months of 1999, partly because the company was using both central warehouses and the local stores of its retail supermarket partners to fill orders. However, management expected this percentage to decline as the company moved through the period of getting its warehouses up and operating, as experience with the new systems accumulated, and as order volume increased. For the company to become profitable, order fulfillment costs had to drop to a much smaller percentage of revenues.

---

[3]"Peapod Opens Centralized Operations Center in Chicago," Peapod press release, January 25, 1999.

Nonetheless, Peapod believed that its business model would give it a significant competitive advantage over traditional grocery retailers. By utilizing the Internet to receive orders and central warehouse and distribution facilities to process them, Peapod eliminated the expenses associated with maintaining multiple retail locations in a metropolitan area. Moreover, its use of centralized inventory warehouses, utilizing just-in-time deliveries from suppliers, meant high inventory turns and reduced stock-outs, while at the same time lowering waste and spoilage of perishable goods and reducing the shrinkage associated with store personnel and customer handling of in-store products. Peapod management expected that the efficiencies of its business model would permit competitive pricing and, further, that its sophisticated Web technologies would result in being able to increase sales of higher margin products (private label goods). Thus, over time, it ought to have higher gross margins and better bottom-line profitability than traditional grocery retailers.

Research and Data Partnerships with Suppliers

Peapod was leveraging the database it was accumulating from tracking user behavior and shopping patterns on its website. The company provided advertisers on its website with feedback on the effectiveness of marketing programs, and it provided a forum for consumer goods companies to conduct targeted advertising, test electronic couponing, and gather data on online purchasing behavior. The company had created research panels of users at costs that management believed were well below the costs of consumer panels used by Internet research firms. Peapod linked together users from its eight markets to form a national online network of panelists and users, enabling the company to collect information on user attitudes, purchasing behavior, and demographics. Peapod's database and membership profiles permitted it to deliver highly targeted ads and electronic coupons to users, as well as to measure the number of Web page exposures, click-throughs, coupon redemptions, and sales—all captured in a manner that permitted measuring the impact of a marketing program. Peapod had agreements to provide fee-based online marketing data and research services to a number of national consumer goods companies, resulting in revenues of $1.0 to $1.5 million annually. Management believed that as Peapod's customer base grew in size, consumer goods companies would "increasingly view Peapod as a powerful advertising venue as well as a valuable research tool," thereby generating additional revenues for Peapod. Participating subscribers included Kellogg's, Kraft, Colgate-Palmolive, Frito-Lay, Coca-Cola, Clorox, Kimberly-Clark, Ralston Purina, and Nestle U.S.A.

Growth Strategies

Aside from its efforts to build order volume and add new customers in the eight markets where it already operated, Peapod's strategy to grow its business consisted of two major initiatives: expanding into additional market areas moving beyond groceries and adding altogether new products and services to its lineup of offerings to customers. Peapod management planned to use its central warehouse business model and new systems capabilities as the basis for expanding its service into a total of 40 metropolitan areas with 400,000-plus households. The company planned to keep its investment costs down by building economical $2 million distribution centers. Moreover, by establishing a local order fulfillment network with recurring grocery purchases as a foundation, Peapod management believed it would have a pipeline into customer households through which it could provide an increasingly wide range of goods and services purchased online at little incremental cost. Peapod management believed that its "last mile" delivery network for groceries gave it an unparalleled opportunity to build the Peapod brand and to establish personal relationships with individual customers through regular deliveries. Management planned to transform

Peapod into a one-stop online shopping site offering home delivery of a host of different products and services, thereby dramatically improving profitability.

As one of the first steps to expand Peapod's product offerings, the company had recently formed a strategic product alliance with Walgreens. Under this agreement, Peapod would begin offering health and beauty products, household hardware and small appliances, electrical supplies, audio and videotapes, stationery and art supplies, and seasonal items supplied by Walgreens.[4]

The major impediment to Peapod's growth strategies was a potential shortage of capital. The company had nearly $13 million in cash and marketable securities going into fall of 1999, but the size of the company's losses was creating negative cash flows from operations. The company was depleting its cash reserves to cover the negative cash flow from current operations. Peapod management anticipated that its existing cash and marketable securities would be insufficient to fund the company's operations and capital requirements in 2000 and was currently evaluating financing opportunities. Analysts following the company forecast that Peapod's losses would amount to $17 to $20 million in 2000, equal to a negative $1.10 per share.

MANAGEMENT CHANGES

Peapod's top management team underwent significant change in 1999. Bill Malloy was brought in as president, chief executive officer, and a member of the board of directors. Malloy had established an impressive record of successfully launching new operations and new services while managing rapid growth at AT&T Wireless, and he had been one of the key architects of AT&T's Digital One Rate strategy. Co-founder Andrew Parkinson, while turning over the role of president and CEO to Malloy, remained on as chairman of the board and began devoting his efforts full-time to Peapod's long-term strategy and business development. Malloy made several top-management changes in the months following his appointment. Michael Brennan was promoted to senior vice president of marketing and product management, George F. Douaire was made senior vice president of Peapod Interactive, and Robert P. Ziegler joined Peapod as director of Chicago operations. The top five officers under Malloy collectively had 36 years of experience in the online grocery business, and several officers had previous experience in packaged foods and consumer products at such companies as Kraft Foods and Procter & Gamble. Peapod employed approximately 475 full-time and 370 part-time employees in early 2000.

The Retail Grocery Industry

The U.S. retail grocery industry was a $430 billion business.[5] Sales of health and beauty aids amounted to an additional $200 to $225 billion. Forrester Research estimated that the total sales of grocery and household items, health and beauty items, and beverages in all types of retail outlets amounted to a $720 billion U.S. market.

The top five supermarket chains in 1999 were Kroger, with $43.2 billion in sales; Albertson's, $35.9 billion; Wal-Mart, $27 billion from its grocery operations; Safeway, $26.5 billion; and Ahold, $20 billion.[6] Slow growth and intense competition was driving supermarket industry consolidation. No supermarket chain had an industry

[4]"Peapod and Walgreen Co. Announce Product Alliance," Peapod press release, March 10, 1999.

[5]Ronette King, "Grocery Mergers Are Part of the Growing U.S. Trend," *Times-Picayune*, October 13, 1999, p. A4.

[6] Joan Bergmann, "Food for Thought: Going into the Grocery Industry," *Discount Merchandiser*, May 1999, p. 36.

market share much above 10 percent; the top five had a combined share under 30 percent. Supermarket sales had grown at an average of just 3.4 percent over the past ten years, partly because more consumers were shifting some of their purchases to drug chain, wholesale club, and discount chain "supercenter" formats. Traditional grocers' share of total U.S. food sales had dropped from 42 percent to 40 percent over the last ten years.[7]

Typical supermarkets carried an average of 30,000 items, were from 20,000 to 40,000 square feet in size, and averaged $12 million in sales annually. Consumers tended to be price conscious, and the industry was characterized by fierce price competition.

The supermarket business was a notoriously low-margin business with net profits of only 1 to 2 percent of revenues. Store profits depended heavily on creating a high volume of customer traffic and rapid inventory turnover, especially for perishables such as produce and fresh meat. Competitors had to operate efficiently to make money, and tight control of labor costs and product spoilage was essential. Because capital investment costs were modest, involving mainly the construction of distribution centers and stores, it was not unusual for supermarket chains to realize 15 to 20 percent returns on invested capital.

SUPERMARKET CHAINS AS POTENTIAL COMPETITORS IN THE ONLINE GROCERY SEGMENT

Most supermarket chains were following developments in the online grocery industry carefully. While some observers believed that existing supermarket chains would be slow to enter into online sales for fear of cannibalizing their existing sales and undermining their brick-and-mortar investments, other industry observers expected supermarket chains to enter the online grocery segment, especially if online grocery sales took off. However, other supermarket industry analysts believed some existing supermarket chains would definitely not stand by idly and let online grocery companies steal market share without a fight. These analysts saw existing supermarket chains as potentially formidable competitors in the online segment because they had well-established supply chains, bought in volumes that gave them bargaining power with food and household product suppliers, had well-known brand names, knew local markets, and could use their distribution centers and neighborhood stores as bases from which to make home deliveries. As many as one-third of U.S. grocery chains were said to have experimented with some type of delivery service.[8]

Albertson's had recently begun testing the market by offering online shopping to customers in the Dallas/Fort Worth, Texas area. Albertson's was well established in the Dallas/Fort Worth area with numerous stores and a sizable market share of the supermarket business. If its online venture in the Dallas/Fort Worth area was deemed successful, management indicated that it would expand its online grocery service to other areas.

Clark's Supermarkets, a small family-owned Colorado chain, announced plans in early 2000 to experiment with online grocery sales at its stores. Clark's intended to put the items stocked in its stores online, allowing customers to log on to its website and select the items they wanted. The company had designed a special cart that allowed store personnel to cruise store aisles and pick five orders simultaneously. Clark's strategy was to run the items through its checkout counters, pack them, and

---

[7] Nora Aufretier and Tim McGuire, "Walking Down the Aisles," *Ivey Business Journal*, March–April 1999, p. 49.

[8] Laurent Belise, "A Mouse in the Bakery Aisle," *Christian Science Monitor*, September 8, 1998, p. 11.

have them ready for customer pickup at a time chosen by customers. For the time being, Clark's did not plan to deliver orders to customers' homes. Clark's store in Steamboat Springs was selected to be the pilot for the online experiment; if the service proved popular and successful, Clark's intended to make the service available in other Colorado locations where it had stores. Clark's saw online ordering capabilities as being a time-saving service to customers; management did not expect the service to add substantially to the company's profitability.

The Online Grocery Segment

The online grocery shopping business was in its infancy in 2000. Analysts believed that online grocery sales amounted to about $235 million in 1999, less than 0.25 percent of total supermarket industry sales. There were 45 companies in the online market and none were profitable yet.[9] So far, online grocery shopping had been slow to catch on, and industry newcomers had encountered high start-up and operating costs. Low sales volumes, low profit margins for groceries, and high costs kept online grocers from profitability. The problem, according to industry analysts, was that consumers had been largely disappointed in the service, selection, and prices that they had so far gotten from industry members.

However, some analysts expected online grocery sales to grow at a rapid pace as companies improved their service and selection, PC penetration of households rose, and consumers became more accustomed to making purchases online.[10] Forrester Research forecast that online grocery sales could reach $3 billion by 2003 and as much as $85 billion by 2007. A two-year study by Consumer Direct Cooperative (CDC) concluded that online, consumer-direct grocery sales would account for 8 to 12 percent of the total grocery market share by 2010.[11] CDC had also done a study of the types of online shoppers and which were most likely to shop for groceries online (see Exhibit 8). Most online grocery customers were believed to be either time starved or averse to grocery store visits.

A MARC Group study concluded that "consumers who buy groceries online are likely to be more loyal to their electronic supermarkets, spend more per store 'visit', and take greater advantage of coupons and premiums than traditional customers."[12] Another study found higher demand for produce online. Edward McLaughlin, head of the Food Industry Management Program at Cornell University, found that 12 to 16 percent of grocery expenditures through Peapod were for fresh produce, compared to the supermarket average of about 10 percent.[13] He reasoned that this outcome was because "decisions made through a computer are more rational and choices are for healthier foods."

One of the problems with online grocery shopping was that consumers were extremely price sensitive when it came to buying groceries. The prices of many online grocers were above the prices at supermarkets and shoppers, in many cases, were unwilling to pay online grocers extra for the convenience of home delivery. Consumer price sensitivity meant that online grocers had to achieve a cost structure that would allow them to (1) price competitively, (2) cover the costs of picking and delivering individual grocery orders, and (3) have sufficient margins to earn attractive profits

[9] Sharon Machlis, "Filling Up Grocery Carts Online," *Computerworld*. July 27, 1998, p. 4.

[10] Machlis, "Filling Up Grocery Carts Online," p. 4.

[11] Terry Hennessey, "Sense of Sell," *Progressive Grocer*, August 1998, pp. 107–110.

[12] Bob Woods, "America Online Goes Grocery Shopping for E-Commerce Bargains," *Computer News*, August 10, 1998, p. 42.

[13] "Net Profits: Making the Internet Work for You and Your Business," *Fortune*, Summer 1998, pp. 240–243.

EXHIBIT 8   Types of Online Shoppers and Their Propensity to Be Attracted to Online Grocery Shopping

Source: A study by Consumer Direct Cooperative cited in Michael McGovern, "One Stop Shopping," *Transportation & Distribution* 39 (May 1998).

Types of Online Shoppers	Comments
Shopping avoiders	Dislike going to the grocery; prime candidate for online grocery shopping
Necessity users	Have limited ability to go to the grocery store; strong candidate for using online grocery shopping as a substitute for in-store shopping
New technologists	Young and comfortable with technology; certain to experiment with buying products online; amenable to online grocery shopping if it is a pleasant and satisfying experience
Time-starved shoppers	Insensitive to price, don't mind paying extra to save time
Responsibles	Have available time, get an enhanced sense of self-worth from grocery shopping
Traditional shoppers	Older, may want to avoid technology and buying products online; very likely to prefer "touch and inspect" shopping in a grocery store

and returns on investment. Some analysts estimated that online grocers had to do 10 times the volume of a traditional grocer in order to be successful.[14]

GOMEZ ADVISORS' RATINGS OF ONLINE GROCERS

Gomez Advisors provided user-oriented ratings of numerous types of online companies, ranging from banks to auction sites to travel agents to sellers of sporting goods. Many online shoppers were using the Gomez ratings to help them select which Internet providers to do business with. Gomez evaluated online grocers on five aspects:

- Ease of use—Whether the website had well-integrated features that minimized order time and that gave shoppers product comparison capabilities.

- On-site resources—The breadth of product selection and the quality of information resources provided to users.

- Relationship services—Whether the grocer provided such "extras" as in-home visits with first-time customers, account representatives to answer questions, and willingness to fill unique orders.

- Overall cost—Product costs (based on nonpromoted prices of a market basket of commonly purchased items), delivery charges, length and frequency of price promotions, and membership fees (including whether there were free trial periods for new members).

- Customer confidence—Financial stability, reliability of customer service, and guarantees for what was sold.

Gomez also determined on the basis of its ratings which online grocers were most suitable for selective shoppers, bargain hunting shoppers, time-constrained shoppers, and meal solution shoppers. Exhibit 9 reports the Fall 1999 Gomez ratings of the top 10 online grocers.

[14] Lawrence M. Fisher, "On-Line Grocer is Setting up Delivery System for $1 Billion," *New York Times,* July 10, 1999, p. 1.

EXHIBIT 9 Gomez Ratings of the Top Ten Online Grocers, Fall 1999

Source: www.gomez.com, February 6, 2000.

Company	Ease of Use	Overall Cost	Customer Confidence	Onsite Resources	Relationship Services	Overall Score	Comments
Peapod	9.07	7.96	5.41	7.90	3.75	6.97	Rated third (score of 6.17) for time-short shoppers looking for the best deal with the least hassle.
Homegrocer	7.33	7.41	4.82	7.74	5.00	6.67	Rated second best (score of 7.02) for selective shoppers wanting THE best quality products and delivery service; also rated second best (score of 6.80) for shoppers looking for specific meal solutions (recipes, seasonal foods, and prepared foods).
Webvan	8.22	7.16	2.63	7.32	5.00	6.36	Rated best (score of 7.23) for selective shoppers and best (score of 7.14) for shoppers looking for specific meal solutions.
Streamline	4.62	5.93	5.16	7.47	7.50	6.31	Rated best (score of 6.92) for time-short shoppers.
ShopLink	6.36	6.98	5.33	5.93	6.25	6.26	Rated second best for time-short shoppers (score of 6.70).
HomeRuns	5.56	8.75	4.97	3.41	2.50	5.18	Ranked best (score of 8.68) for bargain shoppers who love to browse and the thrill of shopping for the best deal.
NetGrocer	**8.22**	**3.33**	**2.97**	**5.49**	**3.75**	**4.70**	
Albertson's	4.67	8.16	3.99	0.90	2.50	4.13	Ranked second (score of 7.54) for bargain shoppers.
Grocer Online	5.42	3.46	6.64	0.36	2.50	3.73	
Your Grocer	4.53	3.84	5.91	2.70	5.00	3.68	

Profiles of Selected Peapod Competitors

Peapod management anticipated that the company would experience increasing competitive pressures in the online grocery segment. Competition was expected to come both from supermarket chains adopting "click-and-mortar" strategies and pursuing online sales as a new distribution channel to complement their traditional chain of retail outlets and from the aggressive market expansion efforts of the 45 companies already in the online segment. This section provides a brief look at three of Peapod's competitors in the online grocery business. Exhibit 10 provides a comparison of Peapod's prices for six selected items with those of Webvan, HomeGrocer.com, and Netgrocer.

WEBVAN GROUP, INC.

Webvan's strategic intent was to become the market leader in the full-service online grocery and drugstore business. Louis Borders, a founder of the Borders Group who left the bookstore chain in 1992 to form his own investment firm, launched the Foster City (California) firm, in June 1999 as one of the most ambitious e-commerce enterprises to date. Before going public, Webvan had attracted $122 million in investment capital from CBS, Yahoo, Softbank, Sequoia Capital, Benchmark Capital, and Knight-Ridder and had recruited the head of Andersen Consulting, George Shaheen, to be its president and CEO.[15] Webvan completed an initial public offering of its stock in November 1999, raising $375 million in capital by selling 9 percent of its shares. The shares, initially priced by Goldman Sachs at $13 to $15 a share, rose to as high as $34 per share before ending the first day's trading at $24.875. The company's prospectus forecast that Webvan would post $11.9 million in revenues in 1999, $120 million in 2000, and $518.2 million in 2001. The prospectus also stated that company expectations were for a $73.8 million loss in 1999, a $154.3 million loss in 2000, and a $302 million loss in 2001.[16] The company shares traded in the $15 to $20 range in early 2000.

EXHIBIT 10   **Comparative Prices of Selected Online Grocers, February 2000**

Source: Company websites.

Grocery Item	Peapod's Price	Webvan's Price	Homegrocer.com's Price	NetGrocer's Price
Lea & Perrin's Worcestershire sauce (10 oz.)	$2.19	$2.47	$2.25	$2.39
Campbell's Chunky Classic Chicken Noodle Soup (19 oz.)	$2.45	$2.44	$2.19	$2.29
Bunch of green onions (scallions)	$0.50	$0.50	$0.49	Fresh produce not available
French's mustard squeeze (8 oz.)	$0.97	$0.97	$0.95	$0.99
Maxwell House Instant Crystals (8 oz.)	$4.89	$4.92	$5.49	$5.49
Kraft Macaroni and Cheese Deluxe (14 oz.)	$2.39	$2.47	$2.29	$2.49

[15] Linda Himelstein, "Louis H. Borders," *Business Week,* September 27, 1999, p. 28.

[16] "WebVan Group Files Amended Prospectus for Initial Offering," *The Wall Street Journal,* October 13, 1999, p. A8.

Webvan attracted about 10,000 customers in its first six weeks of operation in the San Francisco Bay area. The company had recruited several executives from Federal Express and was using FedEx's hub-and-spoke delivery system as a model for its own distribution system and delivery service. Webvan was using Wal-Mart as its example of breadth of product selection, Yahoo! as its model for speed, Amazon.com as its model for designing the kind of online shopping experience it wanted to provide, and eBay as its model for "warm-and-fuzzy" feel.[17] It had hired 80 software programmers to create proprietary systems that linked every aspect of its business processes and had recruited managers with expertise in logistics, grocery and drug retailing, and customer service.

Webvan's Strategy and Business Plan

To begin operations, Webvan had constructed a 330,000-square-foot prototype in Oakland to service an area of 40 miles in any direction.[18] The $25 million facility included 4.5 miles of conveyor belts and temperature-controlled rooms to store wine, cigars, produce, meat, and frozen foods. It was designed to serve as many households as 20 to 25 supermarkets. The company planned to eventually stock 50,000 items, including an array of drugstore items, 300 varieties of fresh fruits and vegetables, 750 kinds of cheese, 500 types of cereal, 700 cuts of fresh meat and fish, 700 different wine labels, and chef-prepared meals that could be reheated in the microwave or oven. In the San Francisco market area, Webvan had formed alliances with leading local vendors to provide the freshest produce available; it planned to utilize such alliances in other markets as well. Webvan claimed that its prices were up to 5 percent less than in local grocery stores (see Exhibit 11 for Webvan's home page).

Webvan had entered into an agreement with Bechtel Group, one of the world's largest engineering and construction firms, to build Webvan's distribution centers and delivery systems in 26 markets over the next two years. Webvan's projected investment costs for its distribution centers and delivery systems amounted to $1 billion. The company's second distribution center had recently been built in Atlanta.

Webvan's tracking systems monitored customer orders starting with the time they were placed on the company's website. Orders were directed from the website to the appropriate distribution center. Workers were located at order-picking stations scattered throughout each distribution center; their job was to pick items stocked in their area of the warehouse and put them in color-coded plastic tote bags that signaled whether the items were frozen, refrigerated, or dry. Pickers did not travel up and down aisles but instead moved no more than 20 feet in any direction to reach 8,000 bins of goods that were brought to the picker on rotating carousels. Once pickers completed their portion of a customer's order, the tote was transported on conveyors to other areas of the distribution center where pickers for the remaining items were located. After orders had made the necessary rounds through the warehouse, they were loaded onto trucks refrigerated at 35°F and taken to staging areas located throughout the metropolitan market area. From there totes were loaded onto one of the company's more than 60 vans for delivery to customers' homes. Staging areas were located so that Webvan's couriers did not have to travel more than 10 miles in any direction from the staging area to reach a customer's home. The couriers were trained to be courteous and friendly, and to

---

[17] Linda Himelstein, "Can You Sell Groceries Like Books?" *Business Week,* July 26, 1999, p. EB-44.

[18] Himelstein, "Can You Sell Groceries Like Books?" p. EB 45.

EXHIBIT 11   Webvan's Welcome Page at www.webvan.com

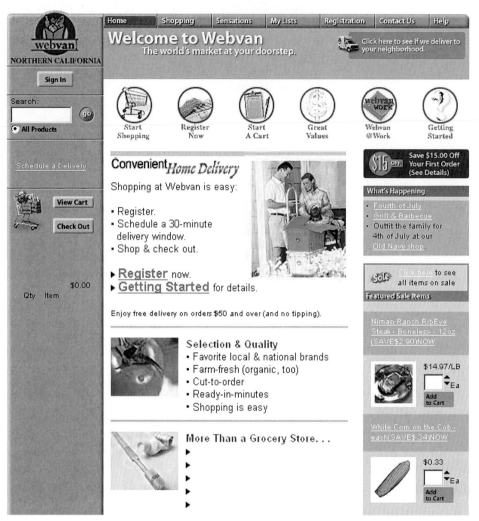

act as customer service professionals and ambassadors for Webvan's service; they were not permitted to accept tips or gratuities. All of the logistics—how many items a tote bag should hold, how far pickers should travel to rotating carousels, how far trucks should travel from staging areas to make deliveries—had been carefully plotted to maximize efficiency.

Webvan management expected that each distribution center would be able to handle 8,000 orders a day (involving more than 225,000 items) and bring in $300 million in annual revenues.[19] Borders, WebVans chairman and founder, predicted that Webvan's business model would be so successful and efficient that the company would be able to charge lower prices than traditional supermarkets as well as rival online grocers.

[19] Himelstein, "Can You Sell Groceries Like Books?" p. EB 46.

Webvan offered free delivery on orders over $50 whereas most other online grocers waived delivery fees on orders over $75. And it did not charge a membership fee. Orders were delivered within a 30-minute window selected by the customer. Webvan's website offered customers recipes and use of a weekly menu planner.

HOMEGROCER.COM

Founded in 1997, HomeGrocer.com provided online grocery ordering and delivery service to customers in Seattle, Washington; Portland, Oregon; Orange County, California; and portions of Los Angeles and San Bernardino County. HomeGrocer offered a broad selection of items, including fresh produce, meats, seafood, dairy products, local specialty foods, health and beauty aids, household items, fresh flowers, pet supplies, best-selling books, video games, and movies. HomeGrocer used a distribution center model also; in early 2000, it had four distribution centers and was adding others in the newly entered Los Angeles area. HomeGrocer.com's signature peach-logo delivery trucks had multiple compartments that permitted products to be stored at their appropriate temperatures without affecting the temperatures of the other products.

Customers could order groceries via the Internet until 11 P.M. and select a 90-minute window for next-day delivery. HomeGrocer.com offered free delivery for all first orders and those $75 or more, in addition to toll-free customer support for its members. To underscore its commitment to quality, the company offered an unconditional 100 percent satisfaction guarantee. HomeGrocer.com had been recognized by Feedback Direct, a leading online customer service authority, as one of the top 50 North American companies to consistently demonstrate superior customer service. Exhibit 12 shows Homegrocer.com's home page.

Although HomeGrocer.com was a fairly small business with fewer than 25,000 customers, it had ambitious plans to expand into 20 other markets in the near future, aided by a $42.5 million investment by Amazon.com.[20] Amazon's investment gave it a 35 percent stake in the company. Amazon had also recently invested in drugstore.com and Pets.com, and there had been speculation that Amazon might start to use HomeGrocer's vans to deliver CDs, books, and prescription drugs to customers' homes. Homegrocer.com had also received funding from the Barksdale Group, an investment firm run by James Barksdale, founder of Netscape, Martha Stewart Living Omnimedia Inc., Hummer Winblad Venture Partners, and Kleiner Perkins Caufield & Byers.[21] The company had filed plans with the Securities and Exchange Commission to issue shares of its common stock to the public in the first half of 2000.

NETGROCER

NetGrocer began operations in 1995 and offered nationwide distribution through a large central warehouse located in New Jersey. NetGrocer's product line included canned and packaged grocery items, paper products, cleaning products, organic and natural foods, international food items, dog and cat foods, laundry items, health and beauty products, dietary supplements, pain relief products, fragrances, baby products, a variety of electronics items (cameras, film, calculators, data organizers,

[20] Andrew Marlatt, "Amazon Diversifies Further with $42M Stake in Grocer," *Internet World,* May 24, 1999.
[21] Rachel Beck, "Online Grocers Work to Build a Market," *Houston Chronicle,* May 30, 1999, p. 7.

EXHIBIT 12   HomeGrocer.com's Welcome Page at www.homegrocer.com

$20 of FREE Groceries!
Try HomeGrocer.com today and we'll give you $20 off your first order of $50 or more — and FREE delivery. Please note: Special offer is for new customers only.

Give Us A Try, Risk-Free!
Farm-fresh produce, restaurant-quality meat and seafood, and all your favorite brands — delivered to your door, at supermarket prices. Plus, your satisfaction is guaranteed, 100%!

Quality, Value, Selection...
And more free time to spend with your family and friends! We'll give you more than you ever hoped for from your grocery store.

About HomeGrocer.com | Jobs | Privacy & Security | Payment Options

audio accessories, batteries, and video games), CDs, and gifts. It generally offered prices of 10 to 20 percent less than supermarkets and free delivery for orders over $75. NetGrocer's orders were delivered by FedEx on the third business day after the order was received.

In 1999 NetGrocer relaunched its website following the removal of CEO Daniel Nissan and the firing of 80 percent of its staff. These changes, which occurred shortly after the company shelved its $38 million IPO, were attributed to market conditions and expense cuts. Since the launch of the new site, NetGrocer's average order size was up 40 percent and time spent on the site had increased dramatically.[22] Exhibit 13 shows NetGrocer.com's home page.

[22]Barry Janoff, "Point, Click, Shop," *Progressive Grocer*, June 1999, p. 31.

EXHIBIT 13   NetGrocer.com's Welcome Page at www.netgrocer.com

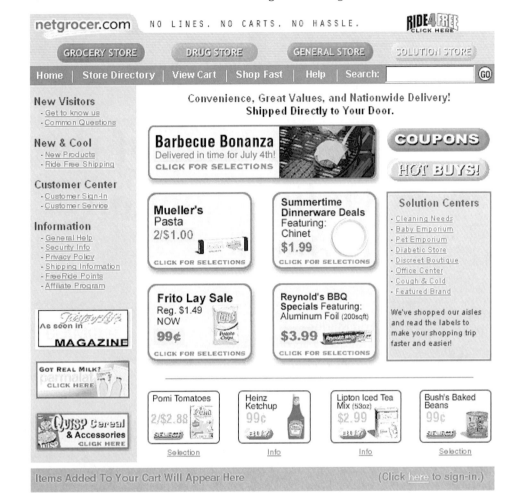

Case 21

eBay: King of the Online Auction Industry

Lou Marino
The University of Alabama

Patrick Kreiser
The University of Alabama

As Pierre Omidyar (pronounced oh-MID-ee-ar), chairman and founder of eBay, set his morning copy of *The Wall Street Journal* down on the desk, he nervously wondered how long eBay would be able to continue its amazing run of success. He had just finished an article detailing the explosion in sales of Amazon.com to $650 million during the fourth quarter of 1999, a number that exceeded the company's entire sales for the year of 1998. Even more disconcerting to Pierre was that online auctions were the fastest growing part of Amazon's business in 1999. Competition from Amazon.com, Yahoo!, and several other enterprising dot-com companies that had started holding auctions at their websites had reduced eBay's dominant market share from 80 percent to 60 percent during 1999. Other outsiders, including Microsoft and Dell, had announced plans to fund new ventures to enter the online auction business.

When Pierre formed eBay in 1995, he had never imagined the company would become so successful. Initially, he had continued to work at his old job even after forming eBay. Soon, however, he realized that the online auction industry business represented a tremendous market opportunity—eBay gave hobbyists and collectors a convenient way to locate items of interest, a way for sellers to generate income, and a means for bargain hunters to pick up a wanted item at less than they might have paid in a retail store. Still, the rapid growth of eBay had surprised almost everyone (see Exhibit 1).

By 1999, when people thought about online auctions, the first name that popped into their heads was "eBay." Going into 2000, eBay had created the world's largest Web-based community of consumer-to-consumer auctions using an entertaining format that allowed people to buy and sell collectibles, automobiles, jewelry, high-end and premium art items, antiques, coins and stamps, dolls and figures, pottery and

EXHIBIT 1   Selected Indicators of eBay's Growth, 1996–1999

	1996	1997	1998	1999
Number of registered users	41,000	341,000	2,181,000	10,006,000
Gross merchandise sales (millions of $s)	$7 million	$95 million	$745 million	$2.8 billion
Number of auctions listed	289,000	4,394,000	33,668,000	129,560,000

glass, sports memorabilia, toys, consumer electronics products, and a host of practical and miscellaneous items. At year-end 1999, the company had listed over 3 million items in over 3,000 categories; browsers and buyers could search listings for specific items or by category, key word, seller name, recently commenced auctions, or auctions about to end. eBay had 7.7 million registered users and, on average, attracted 1.8 million unique visitors daily to its site. eBay members listed more than 375,000 items to the site daily.

However, Pierre Omidyar, Margaret Whitman (eBay's president and CEO), and other eBay executives were well aware that eBay needed to address a myriad of emerging market challenges. The complexion of the online auction industry was changing almost daily. While eBay's management team had met past challenges successfully, it wasn't going to be as easy to hurdle the competitive and market challenges ahead.

The Growth of E-Commerce and Online Auctions

Although the ideas behind the Internet were first conceived in the 1960s, it wasn't until the 1990s that the Internet blossomed into widespread use and truly became a part of everyday life. The real beginning of the Internet economy took place in 1991 when the National Science Foundation (NSF) lifted a restriction on commercial use of the Internet, making electronic commerce, or business conducted over the Internet, a possibility for the first time. By 1996, there were Internet users in almost 150 countries worldwide, and the number of computer hosts was close to 10 million. International Data Corporation (IDC) estimated there would be 320 million Internet users worldwide by 2002 and 500 million by year-end 2003. IDC estimated that commerce over the Internet would increase from approximately $40 billion worldwide in 1998 to approximately $900 billion worldwide in 2003.

The GartnerGroup forecast that business-to-business (B2B) e-commerce would grow from $145 billion in 1999 to $7.29 trillion in 2004 while business-to-consumer (B2C) revenues would climb from $31.2 billion in 1999 to over $380 billion in 2003. Within the B2C segment where eBay operated, B2C e-commerce in the U.S. accounted for over 65 percent of Internet transaction in 1999 but was expected to account for only about 38 percent in 2003.

B2C e-commerce in Europe was projected to grow from $5.4 billion in 1999 (17.3 percent) to over $115 billion (more than 30 percent of the world total) by 2003. As can be seen from Exhibit 2, online auction sales of collectibles and personal merchandise was expected to represent an $18.7 billion market in 2002.

KEY SUCCESS FACTORS IN ONLINE RETAILING

While it was relatively easy to create an Internet website to function as a retail store, the big challenge was for an online retailer to generate traffic to the site in the form of both new and returning customers. Most retailers strived to provide ex-

EXHIBIT 2   Estimated Growth in Global E-Commerce and Online Auction Sales, 1999–2004

	1999	2000	2001	2002	2003	2004
Estimated business-to-business sales	$145 billion	$403 billion	$953 billion	$2.18 trillion	$3.95 trillion	$7.29 trillion

Source: GartnerGroup.

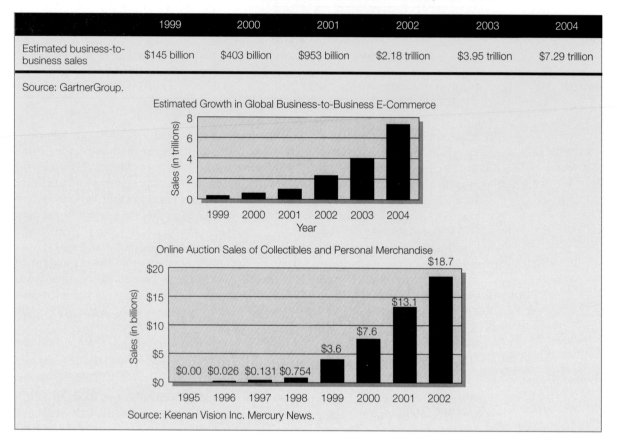

Estimated Growth in Global Business-to-Business E-Commerce

Online Auction Sales of Collectibles and Personal Merchandise

Source: Keenan Vision Inc. Mercury News.

tensive product information, include pictures of the merchandise where possible, make the site easily navigable, and have enough new things happening at the site to keep customers coming back (a site's ability to generate repeat visitors was known as "stickiness"). Retailers also had to overcome users' nervousness of using the Internet itself to shop for items they generally bought at stores and their wariness about entering their credit card number over the Internet. Online retailing had severe limitations in the case of those goods and services where people believed it was important to see the item in person to verify its quality and attributes. From the retailer's perspective, there was the issue of collecting from buyers who wanted to use check or money orders to pay for their online purchases instead of a credit card.

History of Auctions

Auctions are a method of buying and selling goods based on the highest bidder method. A seller offers a particular product or service for sale, and buyers bid on the item until the highest bid is achieved. The buyer who makes the highest offer for the good is considered the auction winner. As the demand for a particular good rises among the buyers (typically due to the scarcity or desirability of the good), the price of the good also rises. Competition among bidders for a desirable good drives up the price. Sometimes, the highest bid will exceed the "generally accepted market value" of the good, a phenomenon known as the "winner's curse." In this situation, the buyer becomes emotionally attached to the good and/or so enamored with placing the highest bid (and thus winning the auction) that he or she ends up bidding more than the good could generally be bought for in a nonauction setting.

The first known auctions were held in Babylon around 500 B.C. In these auctions, women were sold to the highest bidder on the condition that they marry the auction winner. The ancient Romans also auctioned many goods. Roman soldiers would auction the spoils of their victories, and wealthy citizens would auction their expensive belongings and prized possessions. In the year 193 A.D, the entire Roman Empire was put up for auction after the emperor Pertinax was executed. Didius Julianus bid 6,250 drachmas per royal guard, and was immediately named emperor of Rome. However, Julianus was executed only two months later, indicating that he may have been the first-ever victim of the winner's curse!

Since that time, auctions have been conducted in every corner of the globe. The possessions of deceased Buddhist monks were auctioned off as early as the seventh century. In the late sixteenth century, auctions began to be held in taverns and alehouses in Great Britain. Sotheby's was founded in 1744 and Christie's was established in 1766; both have now become world-renowned auction houses for rare and valuable items. Auctions for tobacco, horses, and other domestic animals were commonplace in Colonial America.

Auctions have endured throughout history for several reasons. First, they give sellers a convenient way to find a buyer for something they would like to dispose of. Second, auctions are an excellent way for people to collect difficult-to-find items that have a high value to them personally, such as Beanie Babies or historical memorabilia. Finally, auctions are one of the "purest" markets that exist for goods, in that they bring buyers and sellers into contact to arrive at a mutually agreeable price. Experts estimated that the national market for auctions, garage sales, flea markets, and classified purchases was greater than $100 billion in 1999.

Online Auctions

Online auctions worked in essentially the same way as traditional auctions, the difference being that the auction process occurs over the Internet rather than at a specific geographic location where buyers and sellers are physically present. In 2000, there were three categories of online auctions:

1. Business-to-business auctions, which accounted for $2.5 billion in sales in 1998, and which involved such items as computers, used equipment, and surplus merchandise.
2. Business-to-consumer auctions, where businesses sold goods and services to consumers via the Internet. Many such auctions involved companies interested in selling used or discontinued goods that saw online auctions as a method of liquidating unwanted inventory.
3. Person-to-person auctions, such as those conducted by eBay, that gave interested sellers and buyers the opportunity to use the Internet to meet and engage in competitive bidding.

Since eBay's pioneering of the consumer-to-consumer online auction process in 1995, the number of online auction sites on the Internet had grown to well over 1,600 by the end of 1999. Forrester Research predicted that 6.5 million customers would use online auctions in 2002. In 1999 an estimated 8.2 percent of Internet users registered at an auction site; by 2002 the percentage was expected to be 14.5 percent.

Online auction operators could generate revenue in four principal ways:

1. Charging sellers for listing their good or service.
2. Charging a commission on all sales.
3. Selling advertising on their websites.
4. Selling their own new or used merchandise via the online auction format.

Most sites charged sellers either a fee or a commission and sold advertising to companies interested in promoting their goods or services to users of the auction site.

AUCTION SOFTWARE PACKAGES

In 1996, OpenSite Technologies began to offer packaged software applications to firms that were interested in creating their own online auction websites. Moai Technologies and Trade'ex were other sources for auction software. The ready availability of commercial software packages made it much easier for firms to create and operate online auction sites. OpenSite had marketed over 600 auction packages to such companies as The Sharper Image, CNET, and John Deere. OpenSite claimed that its purpose was to bring together "buyers and sellers, helping businesses dynamically manage inventory, create sales channels, attract customers, and test market new products, to create efficient markets for goods and services."[1]

PROVIDERS OF SITE HOSTING AND ONLINE AUCTION SERVICES

Auction firms could, if they wished, outsource all the hosting functions associated with online auctions from independent site hosting enterprises and could even turn the entire auction process over to an independent online auction specialist. FairMarket, the leader in auction outsourcing in 1999, provided companies such as ZDNet, MicroWarehouse, and CollegeBytes.com with a means of selling their goods at online auction at FairMarket's website. The use of site hosts and independent online auction services was a particularly appealing option for companies that wanted to use online auctions as a distribution channel but preferred to devote only minimal time and energy to site construction and upkeep. By paying FairMarket an annual hosting fee between $2,000 and $10,000, as well as a percentage fee on all transactions, firms were able to have an auction site without having to worry about the hassle of site upkeep.

ONLINE AUCTION USERS

Participants in online auctions could be grouped into three categories: (1) bargain hunting buyers, (2) sellers, and (3) hobbyist/collectors looking to either buy or sell.

Bargain Hunters

Bargain hunters primarily viewed online auctions as a form of entertainment; their primary objective was to find a great deal. One bargain hunter described the eBay experience as follows:

> A friend and I would spend one day a week going flea marketing and auctioning. Since school has started again, time has become a hot commodity. We've found that we can use eBay to fill that flea marketing, auctioning need. We'll call each other, then get on eBay and hunt and find things together even though we can't be together. eBay has definitely been a great way to spend quality time together!

[1]www.opensite.com, April 15, 2000.

Bargain hunters were thought to account for 8 percent of active online users but 52 percent of eBay visitors. To attract repeat visits from bargain hunters, industry observers were of the opinion that sites must appeal to them on both rational and emotional levels, satisfying their need for competitive pricing, the excitement of the "search," and the desire for community.[2]

Hobbyists and Collectors

Hobbyists and collectors used auctions to search for specific goods that had a high level of value to them personally. They were very concerned with both price and quality. Collectors prized eBay for its wide variety of product offerings. One user commented:

> My sister collects Princess House hand-blown ornaments. She needed the first three to complete her series. I posted to the Wanted Board several times, and also put a note on my About Me page. Well, we have now successfully completed her series. We could never have done this without eBay because the first one is so hard to find. Thanks eBay![3]

Sellers

Sellers could be differentiated into at least three types: hobbyists/collectors, casual sellers, and power sellers. Casual sellers included individuals who simply used eBay as a substitute for a classified listing or a garage sale to dispose of items they no longer wanted. While many casual sellers listed only a few items, some of them used eBay to rid themselves of things they no longer used and raise money for some new project. One such seller stated:

> "Thank you! After just starting to use your site less than a month ago, I have increased my earnings by over $1,000. I have not yet received all the cash, but so far the response has been fantastic. This all started with a Kool-Aid container and four cups I had that were collecting dust in a box in the attic. I was "browsing for bargains" and saw someone else had made $29.00 from those plastic things! I was AMAZED! Needless to say, I listed them. I only made $8.00, but I received my first positive feedback. Since then I am listing daily.
>
> My wife and I are scrimping to save for an adoption of a baby. The fees are much more than our modest income can afford, and this extra cash will come in handy. My wife and I sincerely thank you and your company for the opportunity to be a part of eBay."[4]

Sellers who were hobbyists or collectors typically dealt in a limited category of goods and looked to eBay as a way to sell selected items in their collections to others who might want them. Power sellers were typically small to medium-sized businesses that favored eBay as a primary distribution channel for their goods and often sold tens of thousands of dollars worth of goods every month on the site. One estimate suggested that while these power sellers accounted for only 4 percent of eBay's population, they were responsible for 80 percent of eBay's total business.[5]

CONCERNS ABOUT BUYER ADDICTION TO ONLINE AUCTIONS

Some members of the online auction community found the experience so intriguing that they became addicted. According to the Center for Online Addiction, symptoms of online auction addiction ranged from "using online auctions as a way of

---

[2]"Internet Consumer Segments Identified for First Time," *PR Newswire,* April 17, 2000.

[3]www.ebay.com, April 12, 2000.

[4]www.ebay.com, April 15, 2000.

[5]Claire Tristam, " 'AmaZoning' Amazon," www.contextmag.com, November 1999.

escaping from problems or relieve feelings of helplessness, guilt, anxiety, or depression" to "needing to bid with increasing amounts of money in order to achieve the desired excitement."[6] The Center had predicted that "online auction houses will be the next frenzy leading to shopping addiction."[7] The Center had treated online auction addicts that have had to take out a second mortgage or file bankruptcy as a result of their excessive online purchases. One online auction addict told of his experience:[8]

> It became critical [recently], when my boss confronted me. [My employer] had monitored my Internet use, and it was even more than I was aware of. My boss told me he had no choice but to terminate me. I've been at this job almost five years, have achieved recognition at the national level for the program, and have previously been a very capable employee. How can I [justify] throwing all that away? There is no doubt, though, that my productivity had really begun to suffer.

> I was truthful with my boss about how this had become a compulsion I just could not control. I attributed it to some real stresses in my personal life, and kept telling myself that when things settled down, I would get a handle on it. He has put me on admin leave while he thinks things over.

How Does an eBay Auction Work?

It was very simple to buy and sell goods on the eBay website. Exhibits 3 and 4 summarize the process. In order to sell or bid on goods, users first had to register as an eBay user. Once they registered, users selected both a username and a password. Non-registered users also were able to browse the website, but they were not permitted to bid on any goods or list any items for auction. Once on the website, search engines helped customers to determine what goods were currently available. When registered users found an item that they desired, they could choose to enter a single bid or to use automatic bidding. In automatic bidding the customer entered an initial bid that was sufficient to make the user the high bidder and then that bid would be automatically increased as others bid for the same object until either the auction ended and the bidder won, or another bidder surpassed the original customer's maximum specified bid. Regardless of which bidding method was chosen, users could check bids at any time and either bid again, if they had been outbid, or increase their maximum amount specified in the automatic bid. Users could choose to receive e-mail notification if they were outbid. Once the auction had ended, the buyer and seller were each notified of the winning bid and were given each other's e-mail address. The parties to the auction would then privately arrange for payment and delivery of the good.

FEES AND PROCEDURES FOR SELLERS

eBayers were not charged a fee for bidding on items on the site, but sellers were charged mandatory fees including an insertion fee and a final value fee, and they could elect to pay additional fees to promote their listing. Listing, or insertion, fees generally ranged from 25 cents for auctions with opening bids between $0.01 and $9.99, to $2.00 for auctions $50.00 and up. Final value fees ranged from 1.25 percent to 5 percent of the final sale price and were computed based on a graduated

---

[6]http://www.netaddiction.com, April 16, 2000.

[7]Information posted on www.netaddiction.com, April 16, 2000.

[8]Information posted on www.auctionwatch.com, April 16, 2000.

EXHIBIT 3   eBay's Instructions for Becoming a New Bidder

Source: http://pages.eBay.com/help/basics/n-bidding.html

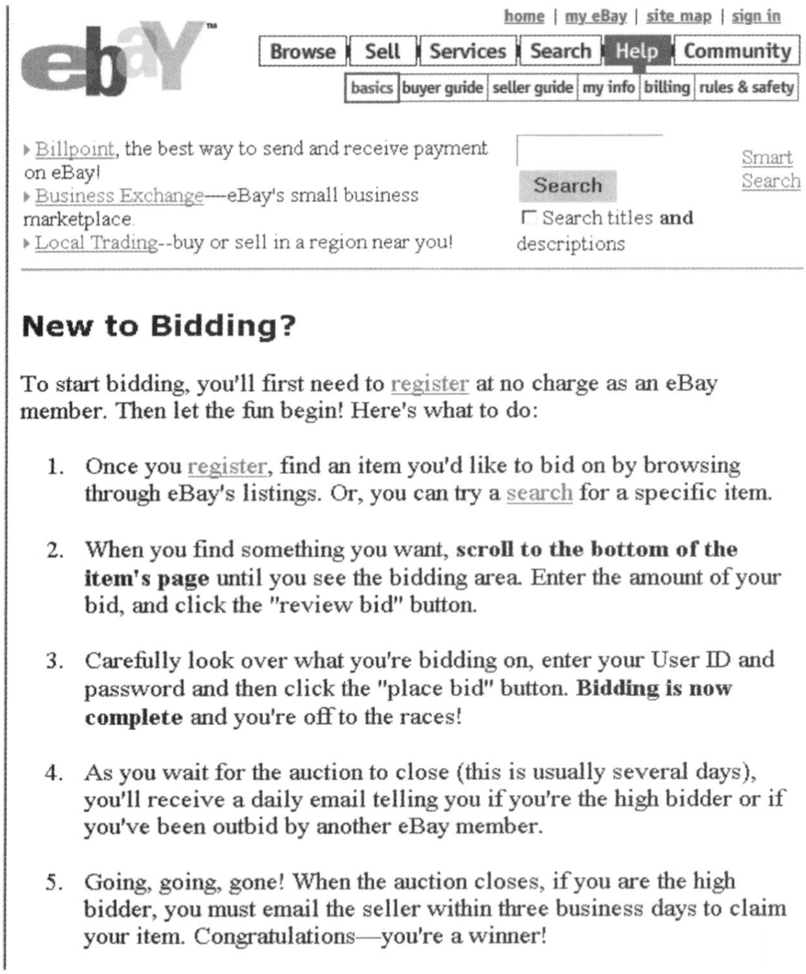

New to Bidding?

To start bidding, you'll first need to register at no charge as an eBay member. Then let the fun begin! Here's what to do:

1. Once you register, find an item you'd like to bid on by browsing through eBay's listings. Or, you can try a search for a specific item.

2. When you find something you want, **scroll to the bottom of the item's page** until you see the bidding area. Enter the amount of your bid, and click the "review bid" button.

3. Carefully look over what you're bidding on, enter your User ID and password and then click the "place bid" button. **Bidding is now complete** and you're off to the races!

4. As you wait for the auction to close (this is usually several days), you'll receive a daily email telling you if you're the high bidder or if you've been outbid by another eBay member.

5. Going, going, gone! When the auction closes, if you are the high bidder, you must email the seller within three business days to claim your item. Congratulations—you're a winner!

fee schedule in which the percentage charged fell as the final sales price rose. As an example, in a basic auction with no promotion enhancing items, if the item had an opening bid of $100.00 and eventually sold for $1,500.00, the total fees paid by the seller would be $32.88 [$2.00 plus $31.88 (5 percent of the first $25.00, 2.5 percent of the additional amount between $25.01 and $1,000.00, and 1.25 percent of the additional amount between $1,000.01 and $1,500.00)].

By paying incremental placement fees, sellers could have items featured in various ways. A seller could highlight his or her item for sale by utilizing a bold font for the item heading for an additional fee of $2.00. A seller with a favorable feedback rating could have his or her auction featured as a "Featured Auction" for $99.95, which allowed the seller's item to be rotated on the eBay home page, or as a "Category Featured Auction" for $14.95, which allowed his or her item to be featured within a particular eBay category. A seller could choose to place a seasonal icon (such as a shamrock in connection with St. Patrick's Day) next to his or her listing for $1.00. A seller could also include a description of the product with links to the seller's website. In addition, a seller could include a photograph in the item's description if the seller

EXHIBIT 4   eBay's Instructions for Becoming New Sellers

Source: http://pages.eBay.com/help/basics/n-selling.html

---

home | my eBay | site map | sign in

eBaY™ | Browse | Sell | Services | Search | **Help** | Community |

| basics | buyer guide | seller guide | my info | billing | rules & safety |

▸ Billpoint, the best way to send and receive payment on eBay!
▸ Business Exchange—eBay's small business marketplace.
▸ Local Trading--buy or sell in a region near you!

[Search]   Smart Search

☐ Search titles and descriptions

New to Selling?

It's so easy—you'll love it! Here's what to do...

1. First, you'll need to register, if you haven't done so already.

2. **Set up your selling account.** Place your credit card on file with eBay and you're ready to sell! If you'd like to accept credit card payments from winning bidders, sign up for Billpoint online payments.

3. **Gather the info** you'll need before you prepare your listing:
   - your item description
   - the URL (web site address) for any photos (see the photo tutorial)
   - the category you'll list under

4. Go to the Sell Your Item form, **fill in the info**, and review your listing. Be sure to check the information carefully, then click on Submit My Listing.

5. You'll see a confirmation page; **jot down the info**, such as your item number. This will be helpful if you want to update your listing, and to keep track of your item's status as your very own auction progresses!

6. When your auction closes, **contact your winning bidder** or bidders within three business days. You'll want to confirm the final cost, including any shipping charges, and tell them where to send payment. When the bidder meets your payment terms, you fulfill your end of the agreement by sending them your item. Your auction forms a binding contract between you and the winning bidder or bidders.

And then that's it—your item is sold!

---

posted the photograph on a website and provided eBay with the appropriate Web address. Items could be showcased in the Gallery section with a catalog of pictures rather than text. A seller who used a photograph in his or her listing could have this photograph included in the Gallery section for $0.25 or featured in the Gallery section for $19.95. The Gallery feature was available in all categories of eBay. Certain categories of items, including real estate, automobiles, and "Great Collections" had different pricing.

New sellers were required to place a credit card on file with eBay for automatic monthly billing while sellers who had opened accounts prior to October 22, 1999, could elect to register a credit card with eBay for monthly billing or to pay-as-you-go. The latter option, however, was relatively unattractive as the accounts of sellers electing this option were blocked anytime their account balance reached $25.00. The block was removed once the fee was paid, or once the seller had registered a credit card with eBay.

HOW TRANSACTIONS ARE COMPLETED

When an auction ended, the eBay system validated if a bid exceeded the minimum price and the reserve price, if one had been set. If the sale was successful, eBay automatically notified the buyer and seller via e-mail; the buyer and seller could then consummate the transaction independent of eBay. At the time of the e-mail notification, eBay generally charged the seller a success fee equal to 5 percent of the first $25 of the purchase price, 2.5 percent of that portion of the purchase price from $25.01 to $1,000, and 1.25 percent of that portion of the purchase price over $1,000. At no point during the process did eBay take possession of either the item being sold or the buyer's payment for the item. Rather, the buyer and seller had to independently arrange for the shipment of and payment for the item, with the buyer typically paying for shipping. A seller could view a buyer's feedback rating (discussed below) and then determine the manner of payment, such as personal check, cashier's check, or credit card, and also whether to ship the item before or after the payment is received. Under the terms of eBay's user agreement, if a seller received one or more bids above the stated minimum or reserve price, the seller was obligated to complete the transaction, although eBay had no power to force the seller or buyer to complete the transaction other than to suspend them from using eBay's service. In the event the buyer and seller were unable to complete the transaction, the seller notified eBay and eBay credited the seller the amount of the success fee. When items carrying a reserve price sold, sellers were credited the $1.00 reserve fee. Invoices for placement fees, additional listing fees, and success fees were sent via e-mail to sellers on a monthly basis.

FEEDBACK FORUM

eBay had pioneered a feature to facilitate the establishment of reputations within its community by encouraging individuals to record comments about their trading partners on each transaction. Every registered eBay user had a feedback profile containing compliments, criticisms, and other comments by users who had conducted business or interacted with the person. eBay users could review a person's feedback profile to check on the person's reputation within the eBay community before deciding to bid on an item listed by that person or in determining how to complete the payment for and delivery of the item. A user who had developed positive reputations over time had a color-coded star symbol displayed next to his or her user name to indicate the amount of positive feedback.

The terms of eBay's user agreement prohibited actions that would undermine the integrity of the Feedback Forum, such as a person's leaving positive feedback about himself or herself through other accounts or leaving multiple negative feedback for others through other accounts. eBay's Feedback Forum system had several automated features designed to detect and prevent some forms of abuse. For example, feedback posting from the same account, positive or negative, could not affect a user's net feedback rating (i.e., the number of positive postings, less the number of negative postings) by more than one point, no matter how many comments an individual made. Furthermore, a user could only give feedback to his or her trading partners in completed transactions. Users who received a sufficiently negative net feedback rating had their registrations suspended and were unable to bid on or list items for sale. The company believed its Feedback Forum was extremely useful in overcoming initial user hesitancy when trading over the Internet, as it reduced the anonymity and uncertainty of dealing with an unknown trading partner.

Pierre Omidyar and the Founding of eBay

Pierre Omidyar was born in Paris, France, and moved to Maryland when his father began a residency at Johns Hopkins University Medical Center. Pierre's passion for computers began at an early age when he would sneak out of gym class in high school to play with computers. While still in high school he took his first computer-related job at age 14 in the school's library where he was hired for $6.00 per hour to write a program to print catalogue cards.[9] After high school Pierre attended Tufts University, where he graduated in 1988 with a B.S. in Computer Science. Upon graduating Pierre entered the computer industry when he joined Claris, an Apple Computer subsidiary in Silicon Valley, and wrote a widely used graphics application, MacDraw. In 1991, Omidyar left Claris and co-founded Ink Development (later renamed eShop), which became a pioneer in online shopping and was eventually sold to Microsoft in 1996. In 1994 Omidyar joined General Magic as a developer services engineer, where he remained until mid-1996 when he left General Magic to pursue fulltime development of eBay.

Traditional Internet folklore has it that eBay was founded solely to allow Pierre's then girlfriend and future wife, Pamela Wesley, to trade and acquire Pez dispensers with other collectors. While Pamela was certainly a driving force in launching the initial website, Pierre had long been interested in how one could establish a marketplace to bring together a fragmented market. Omidyar saw eBay as a way to create a person-to-person trading community based on a democratized, efficient market where everyone could have equal access through the same medium, the Internet. Pierre set out to develop his marketplace and to meet the goals of both he and Pamela in 1995 when he launched the first online auction under the name of Auctionwatch at the domain name of www.ebay.com. The first auctions charged no fees to either buyers or sellers and contained mostly computer equipment, but no Pez dispensers. Omidyar's fledgling venture generated $1,000 in revenue the first month and an additional $2,000 the second.

By February 1996, the traffic at Omidyar's site had grown so much that his Internet service provider informed him that he would have to upgrade his service. When Pierre compensated for this by charging a listing fee for the auction, and saw no decrease in the number of items listed, he knew he was on to something. Although he was still working out of his home, Omidyar began looking for a partner and asked his personal friend, Jeff Skoll, to join him in the venture in May 1996. While Skoll had never cared much about money, his Stanford MBA provided the firm with the business background that Omidyar lacked.[10] With Omidyar as the visionary and Skoll as the strategist, the company embarked on a mission to "help people trade practically anything on earth." Their concept for eBay was to "create a place where people could do business just like in the old days—when everyone got to know each other personally, and we all felt we were dealing on a one-to-one basis with individuals we could trust."

In eBay's early days, Pierre and Jeff ran the operation alone using a single computer to serve all of the pages. Pierre served as CEO, CFO, and president while Skoll functioned as co-president and a director. It was not long until Pierre and Jeff grew the company to a size that forced them to move out of Pierre's living room, due to the objections of Pierre's future wife, and into Skoll's living room. Shortly thereafter, the operations moved into the facilities of a Silicon Valley business incubator for a short period of time until the company settled in its current headquarters facilities in San Jose, California.

Exhibits 5 and 6 present eBay's recent financial statements.

---

[9]http://tbwt.com/interaction/1pomid/1pomid.htm.
[10]Adam Cohen, "1999 Person of the Year, The eBay Revolution," www.time.com.

EXHIBIT 5   eBay's Income Statements, 1996–1999 (in thousands of $, except per-share figures)

Source: Company financial documents. "These materials have been reproduced with the permission of eBay Inc." COPYRIGHT © EBAY INC. ALL RIGHTS RESERVED.

	1996	1997	1998	1999
Net revenues	$32,051	$41,370	$86,129	$224,724
Cost of net revenues	6,803	8,404	16,094	57,588
Gross profit	25,248	32,966	70,035	167,136
Operating expenses				
Sales and marketing	13,139	15,618	35,976	95,956
Product development	28	831	4,640	23,785
General and administrative	5,661	6,534	15,849	43,055
Amortization of acquired intangibles	—	—	805	1,145
Merger related costs		0	—	4,359
Total operating expenses	18,828	22,983	57,270	168,300
Income (loss) from operations	6,420	9,983	12,765	−1,164
Interest and other income (expense), net	−2,607	−1.951	−703	21,377
Income before income taxes	3,813	8,032	12,062	20,213
Provision for income taxes	−475	−971	−4,789	−9,385
Net income	3,338	7061	7,273	10,828
Net income per share				
Basic	.39	0.29	0.14	0.10
Diluted	.07	0.08	0.06	0.08
Weighted average shares				
Basic	8,490	24,428	52,064	108,235
Diluted	45,060	84,775	116,759	135,910

eBay's Transition to Professional Management

From the beginning Omidyar intended to hire a professional manager to serve as the president of eBay so he could "let him or her run the company so . . . [he could] . . .go play."[11] In 1997 both Omidyar and Skoll agreed that it was time to locate an experienced professional to function as CEO and president. In late 1997 eBay's headhunters found Margaret "Meg" Whitman, then General Manager for Hasbro Inc.'s Preschool Division. Whitman received her BA in economics from Princeton and her MBA from the Harvard Business School; her first job was in brand management at Procter & Gamble. Her experience also included serving as the president and CEO of FTD, the president of Stride Rite Corporations Stride Rite Division, and the senior vice president of marketing for the Walt Disney Company's consumer product division.[12]

According to Omidyar, Meg Whitman's experience in global marketing with Hasbro's Teletubbies, Playskool, and Mr. Potato Head brands made her "the ideal choice to build upon eBay's leadership position in the one-to-one online trading market without sacrificing the quality and personal touch our users have grown to expect."[13] When first approached by eBay, Whitman was not especially interested in joining a company that had fewer than forty employees and less than $6 million in revenues

[11]"Billionaires of the Web, The Candyman," *Business2.0,* June 1999.
[12]Company Overview, www.ebay.com.
[13]Press Release, www.ebay.com, May 7, 1998.

EXHIBIT 6   eBay's Consolidated Balance Sheets, 1997–1999 (in thousands of $)

	December 31, 1997	December 31, 1998	December 31, 1999
Assets			
Current assets			
Cash and cash equivalents	$3,723	$37,285	$219,679
Short-term investments	—	40,401	181,086
Accounts receivable, net	1,024	12,425	36,538
Other current assets	220	7,479	22,531
Total current assets	4,967	97,590	459,834
Property and equipment, net	652	44,062	111,806
Investments	—	—	373,988
Deferred tax asset	—	—	5,639
Intangible and other assets, net	—	7,884	12,675
	$5,619	$149,536	$963,942
Liabilities and Stockholders' Equity			
Current liabilities			
Accounts payable	$252	$9,997	$31,538
Accrued expenses and other current liabilities	—	6,577	32,550
Deferred revenue and customer advances	128	973	5,997
Debt and leases, current portion	258	4,047	12,285
Income taxes payable	169	1,380	6,455
Deferred tax liabilities	—	1,682	—
Other current liabilities	128	5,981	7,632
Total current liabilities	1,124	24,656	88,825
Debt and leases, long-term portion	305	18,361	15,018
Other liabilities	157		
Total liabilities	1,586	48,998	111,475
Series B mandatorily redeemable convertible preferred stock and Series B warrants	3,018	—	—
Total stockholders' equity	1,015	100,538	852,467
	$5,619	$149,536	$963,942

the previous year. It was only after repeated pleas that Whitman agreed to meet with Omidyar in Silicon Valley. After a second meeting, Whitman realized the company's enormous growth potential and agreed to give eBay a try. Hiring Margaret Whitman as CEO was seen by many observers as indicative of Omidyar's skill at building a strong management team and a prestigious board of directors (see Exhibit 7). Notable members of eBay's board of directors included Scott Cook, the founder of Intuit, a highly successful financial software company; and Howard Schultz, the founder and CEO of Starbucks.

eBay's Rise to Market Dominance

Whitman assumed the helm of eBay in February 1998 and began acting as the public face of the company. Omidyar stepped back to Chairman of eBay's Board of Directors

EXHIBIT 7   Key Management Personnel and Directors at eBay, 1999

Pierre M. Omidyar founded the company as a sole proprietorship in September 1995. He has been a director and Chairman of the Board since the company's incorporation in May 1996 and also served as its Chief Executive Officer, Chief Financial Officer, and President from inception to February 1998, November 1997, and August 1996, respectively. Prior to founding eBay, Mr. Omidyar held positions at General Magic (a mobile communication platform company), Ink Development Corp., and Claris (a subsidiary of Apple Computer).

Margaret C. Whitman has served as President and Chief Executive Officer of the company since February 1998 and a director since March 1998. From January 1997 to February 1998, she was General Manager of the Preschool Division of Hasbro Inc., a toy company. From February 1995 to December 1997, Ms. Whitman was employed by FTD, Inc. ("FTD"), a floral products company, most recently as President, Chief Executive Officer and a director. From October 1992 to February 1995, Ms. Whitman was employed by The Stride Rite Corporation in various capacities, including President, Stride Rite Children's Group and Executive Vice President, Product Development, Marketing & Merchandising, Keds Division. From May 1989 to October 1992, Ms. Whitman was employed by The Walt Disney Company ("Disney"), an entertainment company, most recently as Senior Vice President, Marketing, Disney Consumer Products. Before joining Disney, Ms. Whitman was at Bain & Co., a consulting firm, most recently as a Vice President. Ms. Whitman holds an AB degree in Economics from Princeton University and an MBA degree from the Harvard Business School.

Gary F. Bengier has served as Chief Financial Officer and Vice President, Operations of the Company, since November 1997. From February 1997 to October 1997, Mr. Bengier was Vice President and Chief Financial Officer of VXtreme, Inc., a developer of Internet video streaming products. Prior to that time, Mr. Bengier was Corporate Controller at Compass Design Automation, a publisher of electronic circuit design software, from February 1993 to February 1997. Mr. Bengier has also held senior financial positions at Kenetech Corp., an energy services company, and Qume Corp., a computer peripherals company, where he participated in numerous debt and equity financing transactions. Prior to joining Qume in 1989, Mr. Bengier spent six years at Bio-Rad Laboratories and held varied financial management roles. Mr. Bengier also spent several years as a management consultant for Touche Ross & Co. Mr. Bengier holds a BBA degree in Computer Science and Operations Research from Kent State University and an MBA degree from the Harvard Business School.

Michael R. Jacobson has served as the Company's Vice President, General Counsel, and Secretary since August 1998. From 1986 to August 1998, Mr. Jacobson was a partner with the law firm of Cooley Godward LLP, specializing in securities law, mergers and acquisitions and other transactions. Mr. Jacobson has an AB degree in Economics from Harvard College and a JD degree from Stanford University.

Jeffrey S. Skoll has served as the company's Vice President, Strategic Planning and Analysis, since February 1998, its president from August 1996 to February 1998 and as a director from December 1996 to March 1998. From July 1995 to July 1996, Mr. Skoll served as Channel Marketing Manager for Knight-Ridder Information Inc., an online information services company and from September 1993 to July 1995 was a student at the Stanford Graduate School of Business. Prior to that time, Mr. Skoll was president of Skoll Engineering, a systems consulting firm that he founded, from September 1987 to August 1993. Mr. Skoll also co-founded Micros on the Move Ltd., a computer rentals company, as an adjunct to Skoll Engineering in 1990. Mr. Skoll has a BaSC degree in Electrical Engineering from the University of Toronto and an MBA degree from the Stanford Graduate School of Business.

Brian T. Swette has served as the Company's Senior Vice President of Marketing since August 1998. From 1981 to June 1998, Mr. Swette was employed by Pepsi-Cola Beverages, a global beverage company, in various capacities including Executive Vice President and Chief Marketing Officer—Global Beverages from March 1996 to June 1998, Executive Vice President Marketing—North America from September 1994 to March 1996, Senior Vice President and General Manager of New Business from February 1992 to September 1994, Senior Vice President Marketing and Strategy—North America from 1990 to 1991, Vice President North Latin America—General Manager from 1986 to 1989, Director of Marketing Planning and Development—Pepsi International from 1984 to 1986 and Country Manager—Brazil from 1981 to 1984. Before joining Pepsi-Cola Beverages, Mr. Swette worked in various capacities for Procter & Gamble from 1977 to 1981. Mr. Swette holds a BS degree in Economics from Arizona State University.

EXHIBIT 7   Concluded

Steven P. Westly has served as the company's Vice President, Marketing and Business Development, since August 1997. From July 1996 to August 1997, Mr. Westly was Vice President, Business Development, of WhoWhere?, an Internet directory and Web-based e-mail company. Prior to that time, Mr. Westly was Director of Sales for Netcom, an Internet service provider, from August 1995 to July 1996 and was Deputy Director of the Office of Economic Development, City of San Jose, California, from April 1991 to August 1995. Before joining the Office of Economic Development, Mr. Westly served as president of Codd and Date International, a relational database consulting firm, from January 1990 to March 1992 and was the managing director of Bridgemere Capital, an investment banking firm, from 1987 to 1990. Mr. Westly holds a BA degree in History from Stanford University and an MBA degree from the Stanford Graduate School of Business.

Michael K. Wilson has served as the company's Vice President, Product Development and Site Operations, since January 1997. From October 1995 to January 1997, Mr. Wilson was Vice President of WELL Engaged, L.L.C., a wholly owned subsidiary of The Well, a software company. Prior to that time, Mr. Wilson was an engineer for daVinci Time and Space, a television company, from February 1995 to October 1995, an engineer for eShop, a software company, from February 1992 to August 1994, and a director of Mainframe Engineering for Neuron Data, an engineering company, from 1987 to 1991. Before joining Neuron Data, Mr. Wilson worked in several capacities at Oracle Corporation from 1982 to 1987, Chevron from 1979 to 1983, and Macy's, a retailer, from 1975 to 1979.

Scott D. Cook has served as a director of the company since June 1998. Mr. Cook is the founder of Intuit Inc. ("Intuit") and has been a director of Intuit, a financial software developer, since March 1984 and its Chairman of the Board since March 1993. From March 1984 to April 1994, Mr. Cook served as President and Chief Executive Officer of Intuit. Mr. Cook also serves on the board of directors of Amazon.com and Broderbund Software, Inc. Mr. Cook holds a Bachelor of Arts degree in Economics and Mathematics from the University of Southern California and an MBA degree from the Harvard Business School.

Robert C. Kagle has served as a director of the company since June 1997. Mr. Kagle has been a member of Benchmark Capital Management Co., L.L.C. ("Benchmark"), the general partner of Benchmark Capital Partners, L.P. and Benchmark Founders' Fund, L.P., since its founding in May 1995. Mr. Kagle also has been a general partner of Technology Venture Investors since January 1984. Mr. Kagle holds a BS degree in Electrical and Mechanical Engineering from the General Motors Institute (renamed Kettering University in January 1998) and an MBA degree from the Stanford Graduate School of Business.

Howard D. Schultz has served as a director of the company since June 1998. Mr. Schultz is the founder of Starbucks Corp ("Starbucks"), a provider of gourmet coffee, and has been its Chairman of the Board and Chief Executive Officer since its inception in 1985. From 1985 to June 1994, Mr. Schultz was also president of Starbucks. Mr. Schultz was the Director of Retail Operations and Marketing for Starbucks Coffee Company, a predecessor to Starbucks from September 1982 to December 1985 and was the Chairman of the Board, Chief Executive Officer and President of Il Giornale Coffee Company, a predecessor to Starbucks, from January 1986 to July 1987. Mr. Schultz is also one of two founding members of Maveron LLC, a company providing advisory services to consumer-based businesses, and is one of two members of a limited liability company that serves as a general partner of its affiliated venture capital fund, Maveron Equity Partners, L.P.

and focused his time and energy on overseeing eBay's strategic direction and growth, business model and site development, and community advocacy. Skoll became the Vice President of Strategic Planning and Analysis where he concentrated on competitive analysis, new business planning and incubation, the development of the organization's overall strategic direction, and supervision of customer support operations.

THE MOVE TO GO PUBLIC

Within months of assuming the presidency of eBay, Whitman took on the challenge of preparing the company to raise capital for expansion through an initial public offering of common stock. Through a series of road shows designed to convince investors of the potential of eBay's business model, Whitman and her team generated significant interest in eBay's initial public offering (IPO). When the shares opened for trading on September 24, 1998, eBay's executives had high hopes for the offering but none of them dreamed that it would close the day at $47, up over 160 percent over the initial offering of $18 per share. The IPO generated $66 million in new capital for the company and was so successful that *Bloomberg Personal Magazine* designated eBay as the Hot IPO of 1998; *Euromoney Magazine* named eBay as the Best IPO in the U.S. market in January 1999. The success of the September 1998 offering led eBay to issue a follow-up offering in April 1999 that raised an additional $600 million. As a qualification to the IPOs, eBay's board of directors retained the right to issue as many as 5 million additional shares of preferred stock with any further input from the current shareholders in case of a hostile takeover attempt.

With the funds received from the IPOs, eBay launched strategic initiatives aimed at six specific objectives:[14]

1. Growing the eBay community and strengthening our brand, both to attract new members and to maintain the vitality of the eBay community;
2. Broadening the company's trading platform by growing existing product categories, promoting new product categories, and offering services for specific regions;
3. Fostering eBay community affinity and increasing community trust and safety through services such as user verification and insurance;
4. Enhancing website features and functionality through the introduction of personalization features such as About Me, which permits users to create their own home page free of charge, and the Gallery, an opportunity for sellers to showcase their items as pictures in a photo catalog;
5. Expanding pre- and post-trade value-added services, such as assistance with scanning and uploading photographs of listed items, third-party escrow services, and arrangements to make shipping of purchased items easier; and
6. Developing international markets by actively marketing and promoting our website in selected countries.

To pursue these objectives, eBay employed three main competitive tactics. First the company sought to build strategic partnerships in all stages of their value chain, creating an impressive portfolio of over 250 strategic alliances with companies such as America Online (AOL), Yahoo, Lycos, Compaq, and Warner Brothers. Second, they actively sought customer feedback and made improvements based on this information. Third, they actively monitored the external environment for developing opportunities.

eBAY'S BUSINESS MODEL

eBay's business model was based on creating and maintaining a person-to-person trading community where buyers and sellers could readily and conveniently exchange information and goods. eBay's role was to function as a value-added facilitator of online buyer-seller transactions by providing a supportive infrastructure that enabled buyers and sellers to come together in an efficient and effective manner. Success depended not only on the quality of eBay's infrastructure but also on the quality and quantity of buyers and sellers attracted to the site; in management's view, this entailed maintaining a compelling trading environment, trust and safety programs, a cost-effective and convenient trading experience, and strong community affinity. By developing the eBay brand name and increasing the customer base, eBay endeavored to attract a sufficient number of high-quality buyers and sellers necessary to meet the organization's goals. The online auction format meant that eBay carried zero inventory and could operate a marketplace without the need for a traditional sales force.

[14]Company S-1 filing with the Securities and Exchange Commission, March 25, 1999, p. 4.

GROWING THE EBAY COMMUNITY AND STRENGTHENING THE BRAND

In developing the eBay brand name and attracting new users, the company initially relied largely on word-of-mouth advertising supplemented by public relations initiatives such as executive interviews and speaking engagements, special online events, and astute management of the public press. Then with funds from the public offerings of common stock, eBay expanded its marketing activities to include online advertising and traditional media advertising that involved placing advertisements in such national magazines as *Parade, People, Entertainment Weekly, Newsweek,* and *Sports Illustrated.* A cornerstone of the strategy to increase eBay's exposure was alliances with a variety of partners including Kinko's, First Auction, and Z Auction as well as Internet portals including AOL, Netscape, and GO.com.

The Alliance with First Auction

In January 1998, eBay entered into a marketing agreement with First Auction, the auction division of the Internet shopping network. The terms of this agreement allowed both companies to advertise their services on each other's sites. Although both organizations offered online auctions, eBay featured person-to-person trading while First Auction engaged in business-to-consumer transactions, which eBay did not consider direct competition. A similar agreement was formed with Z Auction, another vendor-based auction site, in February 1998.

Alliance with America Online

eBay's initial alliance with AOL, announced February 1998, was limited to eBay's providing a person-to-person online auction service in AOL's classifieds section. However, in September 1998 this agreement was expanded. In return for $12 million in payments over three years, AOL made eBay the preferred provider of personal trading services to AOL's 13 million members and the 2 million members of AOL's affiliate CompuServe. In 1998 eBay also became a "distinguished partner" of Netscape's Netcenter. In February 1999, eBay's relationship with Netscape was broadened to include banner ads and bookmarks. In March 1999 eBay's arrangement with AOL was expanded to feature eBay as the preferred provider of personal trading services on all of AOL's proprietary services including Digital Cities, ICQ, Compuserve (both international and domestic), Netscape, and AOL.com. In return for this four-year agreement, eBay agreed to pay Compuserve $75 million and to develop a co-branded version of its services for each of AOL's properties involved in the agreement, with AOL receiving all of the advertising revenues from these co-branded sites.[15]

The Alliance with Kinko's

In February 2000, eBay formed strategic marketing agreements with Kinko's, a global retail provider of document copying and business services, and GO.com, the Internet arm of Walt Disney Company. eBay's alliance with Kinko's allowed eBay in-store signage in Kinko's stores across the country, and eBay users could receive 15 minutes of free computing rental at Kinko's locations. In return, eBay featured Web links to Kinko's Web pages in eBay's computer, business/office, and big ticket categories, and eBay users were encouraged to use Kinko's services such as photo scanning, e-mail, document faxing, and teleconferencing to sell and buy on eBay.

The Alliance with GO.com

The long-term intention for the cooperative agreement with GO.com was for eBay to eventually become the exclusive online trading service across all of Disney's In-

[15]ebay 10k filed 3/30/2000.

ternet properties. In the initial stages of the agreement, however, eBay was only to market and develop co-branded person-to-person sites and merchant-to-person sites on behalf of the Walt Disney company.[16]

BROADENING THE TRADING PLATFORM

Efforts intended to broaden the eBay trading platform concentrated on growing the content within current categories, broadening the range of products offered according to user preferences, and developing regionally targeted offerings. Growth in existing product categories was facilitated by deepening the content within the categories through the use of content-specific chat rooms and bulletin boards as well as targeted advertising at trade-shows and industry-specific publications. Further, in April 1998, custom home pages were created for each category so collectors could search for their next treasured acquisition without having to sort through the entirety of eBay's offerings.

In June 1999 eBay again leveraged its partnering skills and formed a collaborative relationship with the Collecting Channel, a portal owned by ChannelSpace Entertainment, Inc. The Collecting Channel was designed to act as the premier Internet information source for every conceivable category of collectibles. This content was delivered through a variety of resources ranging from original audio/video programming, to live chats, to live video conferencing. Within the terms of this agreement The Collecting Channel would provide deep content to eBay collectors and in return eBay would provide links to the Collecting Channel's home site.

Coupled with the growth in existing product categories, eBay also looked to reach a broader customer base with regional auctions and new product categories and offerings to expand the trading platform and to better meet users' needs. In creating regional auctions, in 1999 eBay focused on the 50 largest metropolitan areas in the United States and launched 53 regional auction sites. Regional markets served by this new service included Atlanta, Baltimore and Washington DC, Boston, Buffalo, Dallas, Indianapolis, Las Vegas, Nashville, New York, Salt Lake City, San Francisco, and Seattle. eBay believed that regional auction sites would encourage the sale of items that were prohibitively expensive to ship, items that tended to have only a local appeal, or items that people preferred to view before purchasing.

Initial efforts intended to increase product offerings were focused on forming broad marketing agreements like those previously discussed with companies such as First Auction and Z Auction and more limited alliances with organizations such as Guernsey and BMW to increase innovative product offerings. In 1998 Guernsey partnered with eBay to conduct a featured eBay auction to sell home run balls hit by Mark McGwire and Sammy Sosa in their 1998 home run race, and in 1999 BMW partnered with eBay to auction the first BMW X5 sports utility vehicle, with the proceeds of the auction going to the Susan G. Komen Breast Cancer Foundation.

Additional efforts to broaden the trading platform involved the development of new product categories and the addition of over 2,000 new categories between 1998 and 2000, expanding the number of categories from the original 10 in 1995 to over 3,000 categories in 2000. While many of these new categories were created to increase ease of navigation on the site, three of the new product categories that represented significant resource commitments on the part of eBay were eBay Great Collections, a new automotive category, and a business-to-business exchange. Each of these new categories was supported by the acquisition of a well-respected organization that had the skills and content knowledge necessary to ensure the new category's success. The establishment of eBay Great Collections, a category devoted to showcasing rare collectibles such as

[16]eBay press release, www.ebay.com, February 8, 2000.

coins, stamps, jewelry, and timepieces as well as fine art and antiques from leading auction houses around the globe was supported by the April 1999 acquisition of Butterfield and Butterfield, one of the world's largest and most prestigious auction houses.

When the rapid increase of automobile trading on the eBay website led to the need for an automotive category, eBay acquired Kruse International, one of the world's most respected organizations in the collector automobile market to support the establishment of the new category. eBay's activities in the automotive category were further expanded in March 2000 through a partnership with AutoTrader.com, the world's largest used car marketplace, that established a co-branded website that would serve as the Internet's largest auction site for consumers and dealers to buy and sell used cars. eBay's entry into the used car marketplace was indicative of a significant shift in eBay's product-category mix to include more practical, as opposed to collectible, items to attract a broader range of customers.

Finally, in March 2000 eBay launched the eBay Business Exchange to serve business-to-business trading needs of companies with fewer than 100 employees. eBay chose the small business market because eBay management perceived that the majority of business-to-business online exchange and trading sites were designed to serve the needs of large businesses and that the needs of smaller companies were going unmet. Specific categories offered in the new eBay business exchange included computer hardware, software, electronics, industrial equipment, office equipment, and professional tools.

FOSTERING eBAY COMMUNITY AFFINITY AND BUILDING TRUST

Since its founding in 1995, developing a loyal, vivacious trading community has always been a cornerstone of the business model. To foster a sense of community among eBay users the company has employed tools and tactics designed to promote both business and personal interactions between consumers, to foster trust between bidders and sellers, and to instill a sense of security and safety among traders.

Interactions between community members were facilitated through the creation of chat rooms based on personal interests. These chat rooms allowed individuals to learn about their chosen collectibles and to exchange information about items they collected. To manage the flow of information in these chat rooms, eBay went to trade shows and conventions to seek out individuals who had both knowledge about and a passion for a specific collectible or a category of goods. These enthusiasts would act as community leaders, or ambassadors (they were never referred to as employees), and they were compensated $1,000 a month to host online discussions with experts.

While personal communication between members fostered a sense of community among traders, as eBay's community grew from "the size of a small village to a large city"[17] additional measures were necessary to ensure a continued sense of trust and honesty among users. One of the earliest efforts in this direction was the creation of the Feedback Forum in February 1996. The Feedback Forum provided a user-policed systematic means for individuals to rate their trading experience with other registered users. This rating embodied a trader's reputation and provided a public record that was open to any registered user (Exhibit 8). At the completion of each auction, both the buyer and seller were allowed to leave positive, negative, or neutral feedback about each other. If any individual disputed the feedback left about them, they could annotate the comment in question and dispute it. By assigning a value of +1 for a positive comment, 0 for a neutral comment, and −1 for a negative comment, the system provided a ranking that was attached to each user name and that traders carry with them

---

[17]Claire Tristam, "'AmaZoning' Amazon" www.contextmag.com, November 1999.

EXHIBIT 8   **An Example of a User Rating from the Feedback Forum**

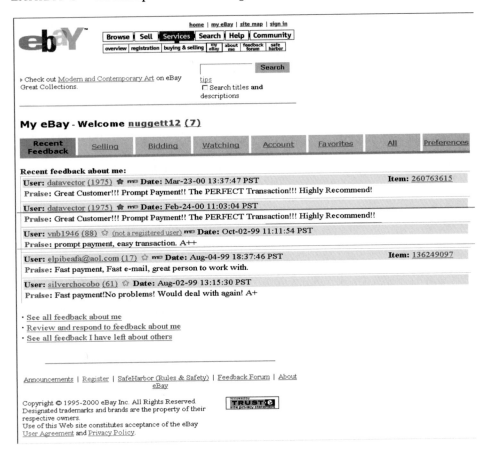

throughout the eBay community. Users who receive four negative comments are automatically suspended from the system; the highest ranking a trader could receive, on the other hand, was a shooting star that indicated a ranking of over 10,000. High volume, well-respected traders could have rankings well into the thousands.

Unfortunately, the Feedback Forum was not sufficient to ensure honesty and integrity among traders. While eBay estimated that less than 1/100 of 1 percent of the millions of transactions involved some sort of fraud or illegal activities, some users such as Clay Monroe, a Seattle-area based trader of computer equipment, estimated that while "Ninety percent of the time everybody is on the up and up . . . (but) . . . Ten percent of the time you get some jerk who wants to cheat you."[18] Fraudulent and illegal activities that traders encountered on eBay originated from both buyers and sellers. Fraudulent or illegal acts perpetrated by sellers included misrepresentation of goods, trading in counterfeit or pirated goods that infringed on others' intellectual property rights, failure to deliver goods paid for by buyers and shill bidding whereby sellers would use a false bidder to artificially drive up the price of a good. Alternately, buyers could manipulate bids by placing an unrealistically high bid on a good to discourage other bidders and then withdraw their bid at the last moment to allow an ally to win the auction at a bargain price. Buyers could also fail to deliver payment on a completed auction.

[18]Stephen Buel, "eBay Inc. Feeling Growing Pains," *San Jose Mercury News,* December 26, 1998.

eBay realized that the threat of fraudulent activities represented a significant danger to eBay's future as its success depended on traders' beliefs that sellers would accurately represent and reliably deliver their listed goods and that buyers would pay the agreed purchase price. As eBay grew, top executives came to the conclusion that a friendly police force would be needed to keep the community thriving.[19]

In response to this need, in February 1998 eBay launched the SafeHarbor program to provide guidelines for trade, provide information to help resolve user disputes and respond to reports of misuse of the eBay service.[20] While the SafeHarbor was relatively limited in its early stages it was greatly expanded in 1999 to actively work with law enforcement agencies and members of the trading community to make eBay more secure. New elements of SafeHarbor included free insurance, with a $25.00 deductible, through Lloyd's of London for transactions under $200.00, an enhanced Feedback Forum, a new class of verified eBay users with an accompanying icon, easy access to escrow services, tougher policies relating to nonpaying bidders and shill bidding, clarification of illegal items that are not permissible for sale, and a strengthened antipiracy and anti-infringement program. The use of verified buyer and seller accounts was viewed as especially significant as it allowed eBay to ensure that suspended users did not open new eBay accounts under different names. User information was verified through Atlanta-based Equifax Inc.

To meet these increased responsibilities between 1999 and 2000 SafeHarbor was expanded from 24 to 182 employees, including full-time employees and independent contractors, and the SafeHarbor department was split into three areas including investigations, community watch, and fraud prevention. The investigations group is responsible for examining reported trading violations and possible misuses of eBay. Alternately, the fraud prevention department acts as a type of mediator in customer disputes and attempts to help resolve disputes over the quality of the goods sold or potentially fraudulent transactions. If a written complaint of fraud is filed with this department against a user, eBay will generally suspend the potential offender's account pending an investigation. Finally, the community watch department works with over 100 industry-leading companies ranging from software publishers to toy manufactures to apparel makers to protect intellectual property rights. To protect intellectual property rights and ensure that illegal items are not being sold, eBay conducts automated daily keyword searches on auction content. Offending auctions are closed and the seller is notified of the violation. Repeated violations result in the suspension of the seller's account.

As eBay expanded its categories to include eBay's Great Collections and the new automobile categories, new safeguards were introduced to meet the unique needs of these areas. In the eBay Great Collections category, the company partnered with Collector's Universe to offer authentication and grading services for specific products such as trading cards, coins, and autographs. In the automobile area, eBay partnered with carclub.com to provide users with access to carclub.com's inspection and warranty service to ensure the quality of automobiles sold through eBay's site.

ENHANCING WEBSITE FEATURES AND FUNCTIONALITY

In designing the website, eBay placed great importance on ensuring that the site was intuitive and easy to use for buyers and sellers, and that the service was reliable.[21] Efforts to ensure ease of use ranged from narrowly defining categories to allow users to quickly locate desired products to introducing services designed to personalize a

[19]Claire Tristam, " 'AmaZoning' Amazon," www.contextmag.com, November 1999.
[20]eBay 10-K filed 7/15/1998.
[21]eBay S-1, filed 3/25/1999.

user's eBay experience. Two specific services developed by eBay to increase personalization were "My eBay" and "About Me."

"My eBay" was launched in May 1998 to allow users to centralize access to confidential, current information regarding their trading activities. From the "My eBay" page members could view information pertaining to their current account balances with eBay, their feedback rating, and the status of any auctions in which they were participating, as either a buyer or a seller, and they could monitor auctions in their favorite categories.

In October of the same year, eBay introduced the "About Me" service that allowed users to create customized home pages that could be viewed by all other eBay members. These pages could include elements from the "My eBay" service such as user ratings or items the user has listed for auction, as well as personal information and pictures. This service not only increased customer ease of use, but also contributed to the sense of community among the traders. One seller stated that the "About Me" service "has made it easier and more rewarding for me to do business with others."[22]

When eBay first initiated service, the only computer resource it had was a single Sun Microsystems setup with no backup capabilities. By 1999 eBay's explosive growth required 200 windows NT servers and a Sun Microsystems server to manage the flow of users on the site, process new members, accept bids, and manage the huge database containing the list of all items sold on the site. The strain of managing these processes while attempting to integrate new product and service offerings proved too much for the system on June 10, 1999, and the eBay site crashed and stayed down for 22 hours. The outage not only seriously shook user confidence in eBay's reliability but also cost the company some $4 million in fees; the company's stock price reacted to the outage by falling from $180 to $136.[23]

Unfortunately, the June 10 site crash proved to be the first in a string of outages the company experienced. While none of them was as significant as the first—most of the additional outages lasted only between one and four hours—confidence in eBay continued to decline in both the online community and on Wall Street as eBay's stock fell to 87 11/16 in August 1999. To counter these problems eBay sought out Maynard Webb, a premier software engineer and troubleshooter who was working at Gateway Computers.

Webb put a moratorium on new features until system stability was restored. Webb believed that it was virtually impossible to completely eliminate outages, so he set a goal of reducing system downtime and limiting outages to one hour.[24] To achieve this goal Webb believed he would need a back-up for the 200 Windows NT servers, another for the Sun Micro-Systems unit, and a better system for managing communications between the Windows NT and Sun systems. In attacking these challenges, eBay acquired seven new Sun servers, each valued at $1 million, and outsourced its technology and website operations to Exodus Communications and Abovenet. These outsourcing agreements were intended to allow Exodus and Abovenet to "manage network capacity and provide a more robust backbone" while eBay focused on its core business.[25] While eBay still experienced minor outages when it changed or expanded services (for example a system crash coincided with the introduction of the 22 regional websites), system downtime decreased. However, the stability of the system under eBay's explosive growth and continuous introduction of new features and services was a major and continuing management concern.

---

[22]Ann Pearson from an eBay press release dated October 15, 1998.

[23]Julie Pita, "Webb Master," *Forbes,* December 13, 1999.

[24]Ibid.

[25]eBay press release, October 8, 1999.

EXPANDING PRE- AND POST-TRADE VALUE-ADDED SERVICES

To make it easier for eBay's sellers and buyers to transact business on the eBay site, in 1998 eBay announced that it would offer an " 'end-to-end' person-to-person trading service . . . [by providing] . . . a variety of pre- and post-trade services to enhance the user experience".[26] Pretrade services that eBay planned to offer included authentication and appraisal services, while planned post-trade services included third-party escrow services, as well as shipping and payment services.

In preparation for Christmas 1998, eBay formed alliances with Parcel Plus, a leading shipping service, and two services, Tradesafe, and I-Escrow, that guaranteed that buyers would get what they paid for. According to eBay's agreement with I-Escrow, monies paid to the seller were held in an escrow account until the buyer received and approved the merchandise they purchased. eBay's arrangement with Tradesafe called for the seller to register a credit card with Tradesafe to guarantee funds up to $1,200; proceeds of a sale were deposited directly into the seller's bank account. If the buyer was not satisfied with the transaction, all or part of the money was refunded. Both I-Escrow and Tradesafe charged a small percentage of the purchase price for their services.

In April 1999, eBay entered into a five-year partnership with Mail Boxes, Etc. (the world's largest franchiser of retail business, communications, and postal service centers) and iShip.com (the leader in multicarrier Web-based shipping services for e-commerce) to offer person-to-person e-commerce shipping solutions.[27] ebay's agreement with iShip gave eBay users access to accurate zip-code to zip-code shipping rates with various shipping services and allowed users to track packages. The agreement with Mail Boxes, Etc. was to promote MBE's retail locations as a place where sellers could pack and ship their goods; eBay and MBE were contemplating expanding their agreement to allow buyers to open and inspect their newly purchased goods at MBE retail stores prior to accepting the shipment.

To facilitate person-to-person credit card payments, eBay acquired Billpoint, a company that had software capability to use credit cards to transfer money from one cardholder to another. Using the newly acquired capabilities of Billpoint, eBay was able to offer sellers the option of accepting credit card payments from other eBay users; for this service, eBay charged sellers a small percentage fee of the transaction. eBay's objective was to make credit card payment a "seamless and integrated part of the trading experience."[28] In March 2000, eBay and Wells Fargo, the owner-operator of the largest Internet bank, entered into an arrangement whereby Wells Fargo would purchase a minority stake in Billpoint and Billpoint would utilize Wells Fargo's extensive customer care and payment processing infrastructure to process credit card payments by eBay buyers to eBay sellers.

In January 2000, eBay entered into an exclusive agreement with E-Stamp that allowed E-Stamp to become the exclusive provider of United States Postal Service Internet postage on eBay's website. In return for being prominently featured on eBay's website, eBay users received easy access to E-Stamp's site, reduced convenience fees for the E-Stamp service, and a significant discount on the E-Stamp Internet postage starter kit. According to sources close to the deal, E-Stamp paid eBay close to $10 million a year for gaining such access to eBay's customers.[29]

---

[26]eBay S-1 filed July 15, 1998, page 46.

[27]eBay press release, April 8, 1999.

[28]eBay press release, May 18, 1999.

[29]Jane Weaver, "eBay: Can It Keep Customers Loyal?" www.zdnet.com, May 13, 2000.

DEVELOPING INTERNATIONAL MARKETS

As competition increased in the online auction industry, eBay began to seek growth opportunities in international markets in an effort to create a global trading community. While international buyers and sellers had been trading on eBay for some time, there were no facilities designed especially for the needs of these community members. In entering international markets, eBay considered three options. It could build a new user community from the ground up, acquire a local organization, or form a partnership with a strong local company. In realizing their goals of international growth, eBay employed all three strategies.

In late 1998 eBay's initial efforts at international expansion into Canada and the U.K. relied on building new user communities. The first step in establishing these communities was creating customized home pages for users in Canada and the U.K. These home pages were designed to provide content and categories locally customized to the needs of users in specific countries, while providing these users with access to a global trading community. Local customization in the U.K. was facilitated through the use of local management, grass roots and online marketing, and participation in local events.[30]

In February 1999 eBay partnered with PBL Online, a leading Internet company in Australia, to offer a customized Australian and New Zealand eBay home page. When the site went live in October 1999, transactions were denominated in Australian dollars and, while buyers could bid on auctions anywhere in the world, they could also search for items located exclusively in Australia. Further, local chat boards were designed to facilitate interaction between Australian users, and country-specific categories and content were offered such as Australian coins and stamps as well as cricket and rugby memorabilia.

To further expand its global reach, eBay acquired Germany's largest online person-to-person trading site, alando.de AG, in June 1999. eBay's management handled the transition of service in a manner calculated to be smooth and painless for alando.de AG's users. While users would have to comply with eBay rules and regulations, the only significant change for alando.de AG's 50,000 registered users was that they would have to go to a new URL to transact their business.

To establish an Asian presence, in February 2000 eBay formed a joint venture with NEC and launched eBay Japan. According to the new CEO of eBay Japan, Merle Okawara, an internationally renowned executive, NEC was pleased to help eBay in leveraging the tried and trusted eBay business model to provide Japanese consumers with access to a global community of active online buyers and sellers, whether they be in Tokyo, Osaka, London or New York. In customizing the site to the needs of Japanese users the content on the site was exclusively in Japanese, users bid in yen and the site had over 800 categories ranging from internationally popular ones such as computers, electronics and Asian antiques to categories with a local flavor including "Hello Kitty," Pokemon, and pottery. The eBay Japan site also debuted a new merchant-to-person concept known as Supershops that allowed consumers to bid on items listed by companies.

HONORS AND AWARDS

As a result of the relentless implementation of its business model, eBay had met with significant success. Not only was the company financially profitable from its first days (Exhibits 5 and 6) it had won many prestigious honors and awards in 1998 and 1999.

---

[30]eBay 10K filed March 30, 2000.

Among the most significant were Best Internet Auction Site (*San Francisco Bay Guardian,* July 1998), Electronic Commerce Excellence (CommerceNet, October 1998), Top E-Commerce Program/Service (*Computer Currents* Readers' Choice Awards, February 1999), Editor's Choice Award (*PC Magazine,* March 1999), and *Worth* magazine's Top 50 CEOs (*Worth* magazine, May 1999).

How eBay's Auction Site Compared with Those of Rivals

Auction sites varied in a number of respects: site design and ease of use, range of items up for auction, number of simultaneous auctions, duration of the bidding process, and the fees charged. Gomez Advisors, a company that helped Internet users select which online enterprises to do business with, had developed rankings for the leading online auction sites as a basis for recommending which sites were best for bargain hunters, hobbyist/collectors, and sellers. To be considered in the Gomez ratings, an auction site had to (1) have more than 500 lots of original content, (2) conduct auctions for items in at least three of the following six categories: collectibles, computers/electronics, jewelry, sports, stamps/coins, and toys, (3) have more than five lots in each qualifying category, and (4) have sustained bidding activity in each category. Exhibit 9 shows the Winter 1999 Gomez ratings of online auction competitors—the latest ratings can be viewed at www.gomez.com.

eBAY'S MAIN COMPETITORS

In the broadest sense, eBay competed with classified advertisements in newspapers, garage sales, flea markets, collectibles shows, and other venues such as local auction houses and liquidators. As eBay's product mix had broadened beyond collectibles to include practical household items, office equipment, toys, and so on, the company's competitors had broadened to include bricks-and-mortar retailers, import/export companies, and catalog and mail order companies. eBay management saw these traditional competitors as inefficient because their fragmented local and regional nature made it expensive and time-consuming for buyers and sellers to meet, exchange information, and complete transactions. Moreover, they suffered from three other deficiencies: (1) they tended to offer limited variety and breadth of selection as compared to the millions of items available on eBay; (2) they often had high transaction costs; and (3) they were information inefficient in the sense that buyers and sellers lacked a reliable and convenient means of setting prices for sales or purchases. eBay's management saw its online auction format as competitively superior to these rivals because (1) it facilitated buyers and sellers meeting, exchanging information, and conducting transactions; (2) it allowed buyers and sellers to bypass traditional intermediaries and trade directly, thus lowering costs; (3) eBay provided global reach to greater selection and a broader base of participants; (4) the eBay format permitted trading at all hours and provided continuously updated information; and (5) it fostered a sense of community among individuals with mutual interests.

From an e-commerce perspective, Amazon.com and Yahoo! Auctions had emerged as eBay's main competitors going into 2000, but FairMarket, AuctionWatch, GO Network Auctions, and Auctions.com were beginning to make market inroads and contribute to erosion of eBay's share of the online auction business. Moreover, the prospects of attractive profitability and low barriers to entry were stimulating more firms to enter the online auction industry and imitate eBay's business model. eBay management saw competition in the online auction industry as revolving around ten factors: the volume and selection of goods, the population of buyers and sellers, community interaction, customer service, reliability of delivery and payment by users, brand image, website construction, fees and prices, and quality of search tools.

EXHIBIT 9   Comparative Ratings of Leading Online Auction Sites

Source: Website for Gomez Advisors, www.gomez.com, March 2, 2000.

A. Ratings Based on Site Characteristics (Rating scale: 0 = lowest; 10 = highest)

Auction Site	Ease of Use*	Customer Confidence**	On-Site Resources***	Relationship Services****	Overall Score
1. eBay	9.07	6.99	8.40	8.40	7.97
2. Amazon.com	9.05	8.49	7.03	6.17	7.67
3. Yahoo! Auctions	8.69	6.91	4.18	8.62	7.11
4. GO Network Auctions	9.14	7.44	6.49	5.89	7.00
5. FairMarket Network	7.97	6.89	6.73	5.17	6.42
6. Auctions.com	8.22	6.78	5.50	5.10	6.41
7. utrade	8.87	4.60	2.43	6.57	5.65
8. Boxlot	7.20	7.83	3.19	4.09	5.63
9. Haggle Online	7.62	4.65	4.80	4.72	5.29
10. edeal	8.05	4.04	2.35	5.83	5.17
11. ehammer	7.59	5.35	4.21	3.15	5.09

* Based on such factors as screen layout, tightly integrated content, functionality, useful demos, and the extensiveness of online help.
** Includes the reliability and security of the online auction site, knowledgeable and accessible customer service, and quality guarantees.
*** Based on the range of products, services, and information offered, information look-up tools, and transactions data.
**** Based on personalization options, programs, and perks that build a sense of community and customer loyalty to the site.

Source: Website for Gomez Advisors, www.gomez.com, March 2, 2000.

B. Ratings Based on Type of Auction Site User* (Rating scale: 0 = lowest; 10 = highest)

Auction Site	Bargain Hunters	Hobbyists/Collectors	Sellers
1. eBay	8.43	7.98	7.94
2. Amazon.com	7.46	7.71	6.87
3. Yahoo! Auctions	7.37	6.67	6.96
4. GO Network Auctions	6.84	6.72	6.54
5. FairMarket Network	6.16	6.44	6.10
6. Auctions.com	5.94	6.31	5.47
7. utrade	5.65	5.01	5.34
8. edeal	5.61	4.83	4.89
9. ehammer	5.05	5.27	4.60
10. Haggle Online	5.00	4.88	5.07
11. Boxlot	4.79	5.57	4.57

* Each of the four criteria in part A above were weighted according to their perceived importance to bargain hunters, hobbyists/collectors, and sellers. These criteria were then averaged together to develop a score for each of the three types of online auction site users.

Exhibit 10 provides selected statistics for the leading competitors in the online auction market. Exhibit 11 provides comparative financial data, and Exhibit 12 provides comparative website traffic.

Amazon.com

At the end of 1999, Gomez.com ranked Amazon as the second best online auction website. Amazon.com was created in July 1995 as an online bookseller and had rapidly transitioned into a full-line, one-stop shopping retailer with a product offering that included books, music, toys, electronics, tools and hardware, lawn and patio products, video games, software, and a mall of boutiques (called zShops)—some 18 million items at last count. Amazon.com was the Internet's number one music, video, and book retailer. The company's 1999 revenues of $1.64 billion were up 169 percent over 1998. As seen in Exhibit 13, despite the company's rapid revenue growth, it was incurring huge losses due to the expenses of establishing an infrastructure to support

EXHIBIT 10   Selected Auction Statistics for eBay, Amazon, and Yahoo! (January 21, 2000)

	eBay	Yahoo! Auctions	Amazon.com
Number of items listed for auction	3.8 million	1.3 million	415,000
Percentage of listed auctions closing with a sale	65%	14%	11%
Average number of bids per item	3.03	0.59	0.33
Average selling price for completed auctions	$65.19	$31.09	$25.77

*Taken from *Individual Investor* "Internet: eBay: Crushing the Competition," January 21, 2000.

EXHIBIT 11   Comparative 1999 Financial Statistics for eBay, Amazon, and Yahoo!*

Source: 1999 Company Financial Statements

	eBay	Amazon.com	Yahoo.com
Net revenues	$224,724,000	$1,639,839,000	$588,608,000
Cost of goods sold	$57,588,000	$1,349,194,000	$92,334,000
Net income	$10,828,000	($719,968,000)	$61,133,000
Net income per share	$0.04	($2.20)	$0.20

* Includes all business areas for Amazon.com and Yahoo!, not just online auctions.

EXHIBIT 12   Number of Unique Visitors during December 1999

Source: www.mediametrix.com

Website	Total Number of Unique Visitors
Yahoo! sites	42,361,000
GO Network	21,348,000
Amazon.com	16,631,000
eBay.com	10,388,000

EXHIBIT 13   Amazon's Net Revenue 1996–1999

Year	Net Loss
1996	$ 6.2 million
1997	31.0 million
1998	124.5 million
1999	720.0 million

its sales (the company expanded its worldwide distribution capacity from 300,000 square feet to over 5 million square feet in 1999) and attracting customers via advertising and online.

While Amazon's management was under mounting pressure to control expenses and prove to investors that its business model and strategy were capable of generating good bottom-line profitability, it was clear that management's decisions and strategy were focused on the long term and on solidifying Amazon's current position as a market leader. Management believed that its business model was inherently capital efficient, citing the fact that going into 2000 the company had achieved annualized sales of $2 billion with just $220 million in inventory and $318 million in fixed assets. The company's customer base rose from 6.2 million to 16.9 million during 1999. The company invested more than $300 million in infrastructure in 1999 and opened two international sites, Amazon.co.uk and Amazon.de. These two sites, along with Amazon.com, were the three most popular online retail domains in Europe. Amazon also entered into a number of strategic alliances. During the fourth quarter of 1999 and the first month of 2000, the company announced partnerships with NextCard, Ashford.com, Greenlight.com, Audible, and living.com, as well as an expanded partnership with drugstore.com. It already had e-commerce partnerships with Gear.com, Homegrocer.com, Della.com (an online service for gift registry, gift advice, and personalized gift suggestions), Pets.com, and Sotheby's (a leading auction house for art, antiques, and collectibles).

With its customer base of almost 17 million users in over 150 countries and a very well-known brand name, Amazon.com was considered an imposing competitive threat to eBay. Amazon.com launched its online auction site in March 1999. The site charged sellers for listing their products and also a commission on sales. Although Amazon's selection of auctions did not match the one offered by eBay, the company reported that online auctions were the fastest growing part of its business in 1999. The number of auctions on Amazon grew from 140,000 to 415,000 during the second half of 1999. Amazon.com offered three major marketplaces for its users: Auctions, zShops, and sothebys.amazon.com. Its auction site formed partnerships with DreamWorks to promote Stuart Little and American Beauty (72 auctions, averaging 27 bids per auction, total gross merchandise sales of over $25,000, yielding an average of over $400 per item) and with Oprah Winfrey (25 auctions, averaging 38 bids per auction, total gross merchandise sales of over $130,000, yielding an average of over $6,000 per item).[31] An example of an auction from the Amazon.com website is shown in Exhibit 14.

Yahoo! Auctions

Yahoo.com, the first online navigational guide to the Web, launched Yahoo! Auctions in 1997. Yahoo.com offered services to nearly 120 million users every month and the Yahoo! Network operated in North America, Europe, Asia, and Latin America. Yahoo! reported net revenues of $588 million in 1999 (up 140 percent from 1998) and net income of $142 million. Yahoo's user base grew from 60 million to 120 million during 1999, and 40 million of these users were outside the United States. In December 1999, Yahoo's traffic increased to an average of 465 million page views per day. Yahoo! had entered into numerous alliances and marketing agreements to generate additional traffic at its site and was investing in new technology to improve the performance and attractiveness of its site.

Its auction services were provided to users free of charge, and the number of auctions listed on Yahoo! increased from 670,000 to 1.3 million during the second half of 1999. Yahoo! Auctions were expanded to include Hong Kong, Taiwan, Korea, Mexico, Brazil, and Denmark at the end of 1999. Localized Yahoo! auctions outside the United States were being conducted in 16 countries in 11 different languages. Yahoo! Japan Auctions was the largest localized online auction service in Japan. At the end of 1999, Yahoo! launched Yahoo! Merchant Auctions and Featured Auctions in order to allow retailers and sellers to promote their auctions. Yahoo! Auctions also offered many extra services to its users. Gomez.com

---

[31]Press Release, www.amazon.com, February 2, 2000.

EXHIBIT 14   An Example of an Auction from Amazon.com

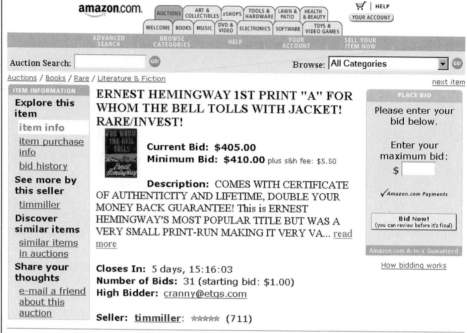

rated Yahoo! Auctions as the number 1 online auction site in the Relationship Services category. An example of an auction from Yahoo! Auctions is shown in Exhibit 15.

FairMarket

FairMarket, a new online auction provider that went online in September 1999, had quickly emerged as one of the leading providers of private-label, outsourced, networked auction services for business clients. It offered a number of formats: hosted auctions, fixed price auctions, declining price or markdown auctions for merchants wishing to dispose of overstocked merchandise, and shopping by request services. The company was formed through an alliance of Microsoft, Dell Computer, Lycos, Excite, CBS Sportsline, CompUSA, and several others. The FairMarket network of

EXHIBIT 15   A Sample Yahoo Auction

Source: Reproduced with permission of Yahoo! Inc. © 2000-2002 by Yahoo! Inc. YAHOO! and the YAHOO! logo are trademarks of Yahoo! Inc.

auctions included Alta Vista Auctions, CityAuction, Excite Auctions, GoAuction, Lycos Auctions, and MSN Auctions. The company went public in early 2000, raising approximately $75 million to support expansion.

Fairmarket managed and maintained online auctions for such customers as JCPenney (which had auctions that allowed customers to purchase new, quality merchandise and auctions that incorporated an automatic markdown format for overstocked merchandise from JCPenney retail store and catalog operations), the Times Digital Company (which conducted local auctions in New York City and other locations), Dell Computer (which held auctions for customers wishing to sell their used computers and for equipment coming off lease), Ritz Camera (which used auctions to sell end-of-life camera equipment), Outpost.com (which auctioned a mix of new and refurbished computer and computer accessory items) and Sporting-Auction (which used FairMarket's network systems to auction an extensive selection of high-quality sporting goods).

FairMarket received a percentage fee of all the items sold on auctions it conducted for its customer-sellers.

AuctionWatch

AuctionWatch.com was formed in July 1998 and incorporated in January 1999 as a privately held company backed by several venture capital firms and private investors. The company, a very small online auction site originally, had raised $10 million in capital to expand both its site and its available features in August 1999. The AuctionWatch site was designed to model eBay, and had many of the same types of offerings. By the end of 1999, AuctionWatch.com was conducting over 25,000 auctions daily, had served over 2 million auction images per day, and received over 20,000 posts each month in its visitor center. AuctionWatch catered to businesses looking to use online auctions as a new distribution channel and to attract new customers. One of the unique features at AuctionWatch was a content service that allowed users to compare and contrast the fee structures of the top consumer-to-consumer, business-to-consumer, and business-to-business auction sites; the information was updated monthly.

As of April 2000, AuctionWatch had over 250,000 registered users and was conducting about 1 million auctions monthly. AuctionWatch attracted 1.7 million unique visitors in March 2000, an increase of over 100 percent from February and over 500 percent from December 1999. In the first quarter of 2000, businesses and auction enthusiasts used AuctionWatch to sell over $120 million worth of merchandise.

GO Network Auctions

GO.com was the result of a November 1999 merger between Walt Disney's online unit, the Buena Vista Internet Group (BVIG), and Infoseek Corporation. The company oversaw ABC.com, ESPN.com, and Disney.com, as well as several other popular websites; its chief activity was serving as the Internet business arm of the Walt Disney Company. The GO.com portal focused on entertainment, leisure, and recreation activities. The online auction section of the GO Network, auction.go.com, was experiencing rapid growth. Go Network Auctions offered over 100 product categories and provided users with a guarantee against fraudulent listings; one of its main features was auctioning Disney products, including movie sets, props, and memorabilia from movies from Walt Disney Studios and from ABC-produced shows. The website was also considered extremely easy to navigate. Gomez.com ranked GO Network Auctions #1 in the Ease of Use category among online auctions.

In February 2000, GO.com and eBay announced a four-year agreement to develop and market online trading and auction experiences in a co-branded person-to-person site and new merchant-to-person sites. According to terms of the agreement, eBay would ultimately become the online trading and auction service for all of Disney's Internet properties, including the GO Network portal, and would collaborate on merchant-to-person auctions for authenticated products, props, and memorabilia from throughout the Walt Disney Company.

Auctions.com

Auctions.com was originally launched as Auction Universe in November 1997. After being acquired by Classified Ventures in 1998, the site was relaunched as Auctions. com on December 13, 1999. The site claimed to be "the world's fastest growing on-line auction network" at the beginning of 2000.[32] Auctions.com had hundreds of categories and several thousand product listings available for users. Not only did the company's website offer 24-hour customer service support, it also had the premiere online transaction security program (Bid$afe). The Federal Trade Commission claimed that Bid$afe was one of the "best fraud protection programs on the Web."[33]

Niche Auctions

Many new competitors had also begun offering auctions targeted at smaller segments of the online auction industry. These auctions primarily specialized in one product or service type, such as computers/electronics, fine art, industrial products, music-related goods, international auctions, and just about any other product or service imaginable. There were sites offering laptop computers (AuctionLaptops.com), guitars (Guitarauction.com), German wines (Koppe and Partner Wine Auctions), and even a site that auctioned nothing but racing pigeons! (ipigeon.com). There were several significant companies conducting niche auctions:

- **Outpost.com** Outpost.com was founded in 1995 to service primarily the small office/home office market. By the end of 1999, the company offered over 170,000 products online, primarily in the computer/electronics area. Bizrate.com rated Outpost.com the number 1 consumer shopping experience on the Web and Forrester Research awarded the company the 1999 number 1 PowerRanking for Computing. The company had half a million customers and 4 million monthly visitors. In 2000, the company announced separate partnerships with Golf Galaxy and Computer.com. Outpost claimed to differentiate itself from other online auction sites "by focusing on the needs of the customer and delivering its services with reliability, fully encrypted secure servers, depth of product selection and building a team of dedicated and knowledgeable professionals that support all efforts of the business."[34]

- **eWanted.com.** eWanted.com pioneered the idea of the "backward auction" in October 1998. These auctions were the opposite of the traditional online auction. Buyers would place ads specifying the item that they wanted, as well as the product's primary characteristics. Then sellers would browse these ads and submit offers to the buyers. The theory was that sellers would compete with each other for a particular buyer, thus driving the auction price down. In return, sellers received a marketplace where they knew that buyers existed for their particular product or service.

[32]www.auctions.com/backgrounder.asp, April 20, 2000.

[33]www.auctions.com/backgrounder.asp, April 20, 2000.

[34]Investor Relations, www.outpost.com, April 20, 2000.

- **eRock.com.** eRock.com specialized in offering rock and roll memorabilia to "serious die hard fans, collectors, and dealers."[35] The site had twelve different categories of music auctions available, and also offered a chat room for users to talk about their musical interests and links to the Web pages of several popular rock groups.

The Future

As eBay headed into the second quarter of 2000 it was enjoying incredible success and looking for new avenues to expand services. According to Brian Swette, eBay was "at the five yard line with their core business,"[36] and the next driver of growth would be international expansion, followed by business-to-business, automobile, and regional sites.[37] Swette predicted that each of these areas could wind up "as large as the core eBay."[38]

In response to the increasing opportunities in the business-to-business segment and the number of small companies that were trading on eBay, the company developed the eBay Business Exchange in March 2000. To avoid major competitors in this market, eBay focused its initial efforts on meeting the needs of businesses with fewer than 100 employees. Brian Swette, Chief Operation Officer of eBay, saw this development as a natural evolution of the eBay business model and expected that larger companies would eventually join the exchange.

To further the strategy of international expansion, eBay announced its intention to enter France, Europe's third largest online commerce market. eBay viewed France as a critical step to capturing the European market. However, well-established competition existed in the French market in the form of QXL.com, the leading British online auctioneer, and the I-Bazar Group, a French-based corporation that began preparations for eBay's arrival in 1998 by purchasing the domain name eBay.fr.

eBay's market dominance was not only being challenged abroad, but also in the United States. Between 1998 and January 2000, the number of concurrently active eBay auctions soared from 1 million to a high of approximately 4.5 million. However, from January 2000 to March 2000 the growth trend faltered and was holding at a relatively constant 4.2–4.4 million. eBay spokesperson Kevin Pursglove dismissed the trends stating "Listings are an interesting thing to look at, but sellers are more interested in selling their merchandise."[39] Wall Street analysts, however, use this number as an indication of future revenues and profits and were concerned that competitors Yahoo! and Amazon might be taking share from eBay.

Omidyar folded his paper to prepare for a meeting with Whitman in which they would discuss two developing situations. The first topic on the list involved the possibility of a strategic alliance based on cross-marketing with competitor Yahoo. The primary benefit of this alliance to eBay would be access to Yahoo's broad customer base. Yet, should eBay partner with a competitor that also offered auction services? The second item on the list involved the possibility of launching storefront opera-

---

[35]www.erock.com, April 20, 2000.

[36]"The One Thing Not for Sale on eBay," www.thestandard.com, April 20, 2000.

[37]Ibid.

[38]Ibid.

[39]"Auction Growth Slows at eBay—Can Earning's Growth Be Far Behind?" Baron's Online, April 17, 2000.

tions where eBay members could purchase goods at a fixed price, much like Amazon. Omidyar began to wonder if eBay's recent product innovations and expansions could be the reason it was slipping in its core market. He recalled a statement that Meg had made in a recent interview: "I have this philosophy that you really need to do things 100 percent. Better to do five things at 100 percent than 10 things at 80 percent. Because the devil in so much of this is in the detail and while we have to move very, very fast, I think you are not well-served by moving incredibly rapidly and not doing things that well."[40] Given recent developments, Pierre was forced to wonder if eBay was operating at 100 percent. If Forrester Research was correct in its prediction that the majority of online retailers would be out of business by the end of 2000,[41] would 100 percent be enough? If not how could eBay exorcise its devils and get back on the road to dominance?

[40]"What's Behind the Boom at eBay?" *Business Week,* May 21, 1999.
[41]Press Release, www.forrester.com, April 11, 2000.

Pricing Strategy

22

Little Caesars

J. Paul Peter
University of Wisconsin–Madison

Pizza is fun food that can also be nutritious if topped with the right ingredients. Consumers have a variety of ways they can obtain this tasty meal; they can make their own pizza favorites from scratch, buy boxed pizza mixes to prepare at home, or buy frozen pizza to have on hand for a present or future meal or snack; microwavable pizza also cuts down preparation time. Consumers can also buy hot, prepared pizza from supermarkets or family restaurants where pizza is a supplement to other foods or products.

The largest segment of the pizza market involves the purchase of hot, prepared pizza which consumers either eat at the pizzeria or take home. One estimate suggests that pizzeria pizza sales are ten times larger than frozen pizza sales. There are over 60,000 pizzerias in the United States. As shown in Exhibit 1 the three largest pizza chains are Pizza Hut, Domino's, and Little Caesars.

PepsiCo-owned Pizza Hut has the largest sales of any pizzeria chain, $4.45 billion, and a market share of 27.8 percent in 1992. A competitive advantage for Pizza Hut is that it offers sit-down dining with a reasonably pleasant atmosphere and a good salad bar. It is more of a family restaurant—a place to eat and chat—than other national pizza chains. It also features a variety of menu items for diners not interested in pizza, important when one in a group who doesn't want pizza could lead the others to a different type of restaurant altogether.

Little Caesars' second largest competitor is Domino's, whose sales in 1992 were $2.36 billion with a market share of 14.8 percent and over 5,000 outlets. The company made millions of dollars in the 1980s when it was the only national pizzeria company that delivered fresh, hot pizza to a buyer's home or office guaranteed to arrive within thirty minutes of an order. While this guarantee helped build Domino's sales, there has been some backlash since delivery drivers may drive too fast or recklessly in order to make the half-hour deadline.

This case prepared by J. Paul Peter, University of Wisconsin–Madison.
Source: Based on Gary Strauss, "Pizza Makers Spice Up War with Value." *USA Today,* May 26, 1993,
pp. 1B, 2B; Julia Produs, "Little Caesars Sets Tone in Pizza War," *Wisconsin State Journal,* May 1993, p. 7C.

EXHIBIT 1 1992 U.S. Pizza Market Shares

Company	Sales	Market Share
Pizza Hut	$ 4.45 billion	27.8%
Domino's	2.36 billion	14.8
Little Caesars	2.16 billion	13.5
Chuck E. Cheese's	343.6 million	2.2
Round Table	315.0 million	2.0
Sbarro	300.6 million	1.9
Godfather's	242.0 million	1.5
Pizza Inn	193.0 million	1.2
All others (includes regional chains and local restaurants)	5.64 billion	35.0

Although it is the third largest company with sales of $2.16 billion in 1992 and a market share of 13.5 percent, Little Caesars has been taking market share from the other competitors. The chain consists of 4,500 restaurants. Its competitive advantage is that it provides larger quantities of pizza at lower prices and has well-located, convenient pick-up counters. Little Caesars is famous for offering two pizzas for the price of one on a regular basis.

The success of Little Caesars has not gone unnoticed by its competitors. In fact, a senior vice president for Domino's commented that "In the past the decision making was based on what Domino's was doing with free delivery. Now, decision making is based on what Little Caesars is doing with inexpensive pizza."

Some of the competitive advantages of these firms have already been diluted. For example, all three now offer free delivery which mitigates Domino's delivery advantage. All three now offer special huge pizzas at reduced prices. For example, backed by a $1 million advertising campaign, Pizza Hut introduced the "Big Foot," a two foot by one foot 21-slice pizza selling for $9 to $11. However, this pizza is only available as a carryout item and could be 15 to 20 percent less profitable than other pizzas. Domino's brought out the "Dominator" for $8.99 to $11.99 (price varies depending on location) which offers 30 slices of pizza (2 by 2 1/2 feet) with one topping. Little Caesars, several months before, began offering the Big Big Cheese pizza, which for $8.88, offers 24 slices of a thick pan cheese pizza.

Competitors are also trying a number of new menu items. Pizza Hut is offering more varieties of pizza and testing items such as chicken platters. Domino's has added salad, submarine sandwiches, and breadsticks. Little Caesars may launch pasta dishes such as lasagna to bolster its menu.

Discussion Questions

1. Considering price, quantity, and quality of the supersize pizzas, how do you think consumers choose among each of these alternatives? In more general terms, what variables are involved in making a purchase decision for pizza?

2. A top executive at Pizza Hut stated that "We aren't targeting people. We are targeting occasions for when people want a lot of pizza for a little money." How important do you think the usage occasion is for pizza purchases?

3. If variable cost for Little Caesar's Big Big Cheese Pizza were $1.88, and fixed cost per store for this product were $7,000, what is the breakeven point for this product per store? What is the breakeven point for the whole pizza chain?

4. What recommendations do you have for Little Caesars management to increase sales, market share, and profits?

Case 23

Schwinn Bicycles

J. Paul Peter
University of Wisconsin–Madison

Inside a plain, brown building in Boulder, Colorado, is a shrine to an American icon: the Schwinn bicycle. Some mud-caked from daily use, some shiny museum pieces—dozens of bikes stand atop file cabinets and lean against cubicles. Amid the spokes and handlebars, a group of zealots is working to pull off the turnaround of the century in the bike business. Brimming with energy, they're determined to resurrect the best known brand on two wheels. But as Schwinn celebrates its 100th anniversary, its management team faces a long uphill climb. Just two years ago, once-mighty Schwinn had a near-death experience in bankruptcy court. Now it's trying to rise to the top of the crowded mountain bike market.

For years, Schwinn was the top U.S. brand, with as much as 25 percent of the market. Now, it has less than 5 percent of the $2.5 billion annual retail bike market. The new Schwinn will sell about 400,000 redesigned bikes—many of them Asian-made models—that sell for $200 to $400 retail, the lower end of the adult bike market. Those models are catching on. But the turnaround won't be a success unless Schwinn persuades cyclists to fork over $700 or more for its newer bikes. Below are market shares of manufacturers for bikes retail-priced $400 and up:

Trek	24%
Cannondale	12%
Specialized	12%
Schwinn	7%
Giant	6%
Diamondback	6%
GT	6%
Scott	4%
Mongoose	3%
Pro Flex	3%

This case prepared by J. Paul Peter of the University of Wisconsin–Madison.
Source: Patrick McGeehan, "Biking Icon Wants to Lose Training Wheels," *USA Today,* August 8, 1995, pp. 1B, 2B; "Hard Pedaling Powers Schwinn Uphill in Sales, Toward Profits," *Chicago Tribune,* June 22, 1995, p. 2N; " 'New Schwinn' Bike Has Gone Full Cycle," *Chicago Tribune,* May 16, 1995, p. 3N.

The mass market for low-priced bikes and those made for children is dominated by three U.S. manufacturers: Huffy, Murray, and Roadmaster. The mass market accounts for about 8.5 million of the 12 million bikes sold in the nation annually.

Schwinn's history as a maker of sturdy, low-cost bikes is no longer the asset it once was. Many under-30 cyclists see Schwinns as the bikes their parents rode. They prefer trendier mountain bikes, with their padded seats, upright handlebars, fat tires and additional gears for climbing.

"We have an image challenge," admits Schwinn Marketing Director Gregg Bagni. That's clear from a walk around the University of Colorado campus a half-mile away. Outside dorms and classrooms, racks are filled with bikes made by Trek Bicycle, Specialized Bicycle Components, Cannondale and Giant. Waterloo, Wisconsin-based Trek is the leader. This year it expects about $300 million in revenue on sales of more than 900,000 bikes.

"When I was a kid, if you had a Schwinn, you were the luckiest kid in the world," says Scott Montgomery, a Cannondale marketing chief. "Ask a college kid now and they'll say, 'Oh, Schwinn? They're toast.'"

For decades, the Schwinn brand, synonymous with durability, ruled the road. Generations of kids clamored for the company's Excelsiors, Phantoms, Sting-Rays and 10-speed Varsitys. "Schwinn used to be number one and you could hardly find number two," says industry consultant Bill Fields. But in the late '70s and early '80s, cyclists veered off the road into the woods and mountains. Schwinn ignored the mountain bike craze for most of the '80s. By 1992, two-thirds of bikes sold were mountain bikes and Schwinn was in bankruptcy court. Unable to pay lenders or suppliers, the descendants of company founder Ignaz Schwinn sold the company to the Zell/Chilmark Investment fund for $43 million. Zell/Chilmark appointed new management and funded the company, Scott Sports Group, with an additional $7 million.

So far, the Schwinn turnaround is being attempted on a shoestring. Schwinn's workforce shrank from 300 employees to about 180 when the company was reorganized and moved from Chicago to Boulder. The move west was calculated to attract young workers plugged into the mountain-biking community. Once assembled, the managers focused on product design. They had inherited a Schwinn line whose only mountain bikes were priced at the low end of the bike-shop range, between $200 and $400.

"Previous management wouldn't believe anybody would buy a $1,500 mountain bike with the Schwinn name on it," one Schwinn executive stated. Now, Schwinn is emblazoned on everything from $100 kids' bikes to $2,500 mountain bikes. Its top-of-the-line, American-made Homegrown model starts at $1,750. One of its hottest products is a decidedly low-tech, retro-style, one-speed Cruiser with a wide seat and balloon tires. It's selling fast in Sunbelt states for up to $250. The Cruiser appeals to retirees and snowbirds in beach communities and to college students who call them "bar bikes" because they are ridden to bars and back.

"They want to position this company as high-end, high-tech," says Cannondale's Montgomery. "And what they've got is this traditional, old-fashioned Harley-Davidson type of product. That's their greatest marketing challenge."

Today's bike business is quite different from the one Schwinn dominated so long ago. Exclusive dealerships like Schwinn uses are disappearing, being replaced by independent bike shops. The typical bike shop carries four brands, so Schwinn bikes are subjected to side-by-side comparisons with competing products. Some of the other brands, such as Trek and Cannondale, have built reputations for cutting-edge technology. Cannondale makes aluminum-frame bikes in U.S. plants, and Trek, a pioneer in carbon fiber frames, is moving production back from Taiwan. All but a few thousand Schwinns are made in Asia.

"Handmade in the USA is a tremendous marketing feature," says Brett Hahn, manager of Yeti Cycles in Durango, Colorado. "Bottom line: Mountain biking is a U.S. sport." Yeti makes hundreds of frames for Schwinn's top-of-the-line Home-grown models. Schwinn is considering buying Yeti or another U.S. manufacturer.

Discussion Questions

1. What are the strengths and weaknesses of Schwinn?
2. What opportunities and threats face the company?
3. How important is it for mountain bikes to be made in America?
4. Evaluate Schwinn's strategy of selling bikes for prices from $100 to $2,500.
5. Evaluate Zell/Chilmark's decision to invest $50 million in Schwinn. What did it get for its money? Calculate the breakeven point and the payback period for this investment given the following assumptions: Schwinn has 4 percent of the retail bike market; Schwinn bikes are marked up an average of 20 percent at retail; Schwinn has a 25 percent profit margin on its bikes.
6. Noting that 80 percent of Trek's sales are for bikes priced $400 and over, how many bikes does Schwinn sell in this category?

Case

24

Cowgirl Chocolates

John J. Lawrence
University of Idaho

Linda J. Morris
University of Idaho

Joseph J. Geiger
University of Idaho

Marilyn looked at the advertisement—a beautiful woman wearing a cowboy hat in a watering trough full of hot and spicy Cowgirl Chocolate truffles (see Exhibit 1). The ad would appear next month in the March/April edition of *Chile Pepper* magazine, the leading magazine for people who liked fiery foods. The ad, the first ever for the business, cost $3,000 to run and Marilyn wondered if it would be her big mistake for 2001. Marilyn allowed herself one $3,000–$6,000 mistake a year in trying to get her now four-year old business to profitability. Two years ago, it was the pursuit of an opportunity to get her product into Great Britain on the recommendation of the owner of a British biscuit company who loved her chocolates. Despite significant effort and expense, she could not convince anyone in Great Britain to carry her chocolates. Last year it was her attempt to use a distributor for the first time. It was a small, regional distributor, and she had provided them with $5,000 worth of product and had never gotten paid. She eventually got half her product back, but by the time she did it had limited remaining shelf life and she already had enough new stock on hand to cover demand. She ended up giving most of what she got back away.

Marilyn knew it took time to make money at something. She was now an internationally celebrated ceramicist, but it had taken 20 years for her ceramic art to turn a profit. She also knew, however, that she could not wait 20 years for her foray into chocolates to make money, especially not at the rate that she was currently losing money. Last year, despite not paying herself a salary and occasionally bartering her art for services, the small business's revenues of $30,000 did not come close to covering her $50,000+ in expenses. While her art for a long time did not make money, it did not lose that kind of money either. Her savings account was slowly being depleted

Reprinted by permission from the *Case Research Journal,* volume 22, issue 1. Copyright 2002 by John L. Lawrence, Linda J. Morris, Joseph J. Geiger, and the North American Case Research Association. All rights reserved.

EXHIBIT 1   Cowgirl Chocolate Ad to Appear in *Chile Pepper* Magazine

spicy chocolate truffles and more • www.cowgirlchocolates.com • toll free 888.882.4098

as she loaned the company money. She knew that the product was excellent—it had won numerous awards from the two main fiery food competitions in the U.S.—and her packaging was also excellent and had won awards itself. She just was not sure how to turn her award winning products into a profitable business.

Company History

Cowgirl Chocolates was started in Moscow, Idaho, in 1997 by Marilyn Lysohir and her husband, Ross Coates. Marilyn and Ross were both artists. Marilyn was an internationally known ceramicist and lecturer; Ross was also a sculptor and a professor of fine arts at a nearby university. They had started publishing a once a year arts magazine in 1995 called *High Ground*. *High Ground* was really a multimedia product—each edition contained more than simply printed words and pictures. For example, past editions had included such things as vials of Mount St. Helen's ash, cassette tapes, seeds, fabric art, and chocolate bunnies in addition to articles and stories. One edition was even packaged in a motion picture canister. With a total production of about 600 copies, however, *High Ground* simply would not pay for itself. But the magazine was a labor of love for Marilyn and Ross, and so they sought creative ways to fund the endeavor. One of the ways they tried was selling hot and spicy chocolate truffles.

The fact that Marilyn and Ross turned to chocolate was no random event. Marilyn's first job, at age 16, was at Daffin's Candies in Sharon, Pennsylvania. The business's owner, Pete Daffin, had been an early mentor of Marilyn's and had encouraged her creativity. He even let her carve a set of animals, including an 8-foot tall chocolate bunny, for display. Her sculptures proved irresistible to visiting youngsters, who would take small bites out of the sculptures. It was at this point that Marilyn realized the power of chocolate.

In addition to loving chocolate, Marilyn loved things hot and spicy. She also was aware that cayenne and other chilies had wonderful health properties for the heart. But it was her brother who originally gave her the idea of combining hot and spicy with chocolate. Marilyn considered her brother's idea for a while, and could see it had possibilities, so she started experimenting in her kitchen. She recruited neighbors, friends and acquaintances to try out her creations. While a few people who tried those early chocolates were not so sure that combining hot and spicy with chocolate made sense, many thought the chocolates were great. Encouraged, and still searching for funding for *High Ground*, Marilyn found a local candy company to produce the chocolates in quantity, and she and her husband established Cowgirl Chocolates.

The name itself came from one friend's reaction the first time she tasted the chocolates—the friend exclaimed "these are cowboy chocolates!" Marilyn agreed that there was a certain ruggedness to the concept of hot and spicy chocolates that matched the cowboy image, but thought that *Cowgirl* Chocolates was a more appropriate name for her company. Marilyn found the picture of May Lillie that would become the Cowgirl Chocolate logo in a book about cowgirls. May Lillie was a turn of the century, pistol-packing cowgirl, and Marilyn loved the picture of May looking down the barrel of a pistol because May looked so tough. And it certainly was not hard to envision May adopting the Cowgirl Chocolate motto—Sissies Stay Away. That motto had come to Marilyn when a group of friends told her that they really did not like her hot and spicy chocolates. Marilyn was a little disappointed and hurt, and thought to herself 'well, sissies stay away, if you don't like them, don't eat them.'

The Product

Cowgirl chocolate sold its hot and spicy creations in three basic forms: individually wrapped truffles, chocolate bars, and a hot caramel dessert sauce. The individually wrapped truffles were available in a variety of packaging options, with most of the packaging designed to set Cowgirl Chocolates apart. The truffles could be purchased in gift boxes, in drawstring muslin bags, and in a collectible tin. According to Marilyn, this packaging made them "more than a candy—they become an idea, an experience, a gift." The truffles were also available in a plain plastic bag over Cowgirl Chocolate's website for customers who just wanted the chocolate and did not care about the fancy packaging. The chocolate bars and truffles were offered in several flavors. The chocolate bars were available in either orange espresso or lime tequila crunch. The truffles were available in plain chocolate, mint, orange, lime tequila, and espresso. The plain chocolate, mint, and orange truffles were packaged in gold wrappers, while the lime tequila truffles were packaged in green wrappers. The espresso truffles were the hottest, about twice as hot as the other varieties, and were wrapped in a special red foil to give customers some clue that these were extra hot. Cowgirl Chocolates' full line of product offerings are described in Exhibit 2 and are shown in Exhibit 3.

Marilyn was also in the process of introducing "mild-mannered" truffles. Mild-mannered truffles were simply the same fine German chocolate that Marilyn started with to produce all of her chocolates, but without the spice. Marilyn had chosen silver as the wrapper color for the mild-mannered truffles. While she took kidding from friends about how this did not fit with the company's motto—Sissies Stay Away—which was integrated into the company's logo and printed on the back of company t-shirts and hats, she had decided that even the sissies deserved excellent chocolate. Further, she thought that having the mild-mannered chocolate might allow her to get her product placed in retail locations that had previously rejected her chocolates as being too spicy. Marilyn was the first to admit that her chocolates packed a pretty good kick that not everybody found to their liking. She had developed the hot and spicy chocolates based primarily on her own tastes and the input of friends and acquaintances. She had observed many peoples' reactions upon trying her hot and spicy chocolates at trade shows and at new retail locations, and while many people liked her chocolates, the majority found at least some of the varieties to be too hot. In general, men tended to like the hotter truffles much more than women did. Marilyn knew her observations were consistent with what information was available on the fiery foods industry—only approximately 15% of American consumers were currently eating hot and spicy foods and men were much more inclined to eat hot and spicy foods than were women. In addition to introducing "mild-mannered" chocolates, Marilyn was also thinking about introducing a chocolate with a calcium supplement aimed at woman concerned about their calcium intake.

All of Cowgirl Chocolate's chocolate products were sourced from Seattle Chocolates, a Seattle-based company that specialized in producing European-style chocolate confections wrapped in an elegant package fit for gift giving. Seattle Chocolates obtained all of its raw chocolate from world-renowned chocolate producer Schokinag of Germany. Seattle Chocolates sold its own retail brand plus provided private label chocolate products for a variety of companies including upscale retailers like Nieman Marcus and Nordstroms. Seattle Chocolates was, at least relative to Cowgirl Chocolates, a large company with annual sales in excess of $5,000,000. Seattle Chocolates took Cowgirl Chocolates on as a private label customer because they liked and were intrigued by the company's product and owners, and they had made

EXHIBIT 2   Cowgirl Chocolate Product Offerings with Price and Cost Figures

Item	Approximate Percentage of Total Revenues	Suggested Retail Price[1]	Wholesale Price[1]	Total Item Cost (a + b)	Cost of Chocolate or Sauce (a)	Cost of Product Packaging[2] (b)
Spicy Chocolate Truffle Bars (available in 2 flavors: orange-espresso or lime tequila crunch)	50%	$2.99	$1.50	$1.16	$1.04	$0.12
1/4 pound Muslin Bag (13 truffles in a drawstring muslin bag—available in 3 flavors: assorted hot, lime-tequila, and mild-mannered)	16%	$6.95	$3.50	$2.35	$1.69	$0.66
1/2 pound Tin (assorted hot & spicy truffles in a collectable tin)	12%	$14.95	$7.50	$4.78[3]	$3.25	$1.53
Hot Caramel Dessert Sauce (9.5 oz. Jar)	10%	$5.95	$3.50	$2.50	$2.00	$0.50
Sampler Bag (4 assorted hot truffles in a small drawstring muslin bag)	7%	$2.95	$1.50	$0.97	$0.52	$0.45
1/4 pound Gift Box (assorted hot truffles or mild-mannered truffles in a fancy gift box with gift card)	~ 1%	$8.95	$4.50	$2.95	$1.69	$1.26
1 pound Gift Box (assorted hot truffles or mild-mannered truffles in a fancy gift box with gift card)	~ 1%	$24.95	$12.95	$9.05	$6.37	$2.68
Gift Bucket (tin bucket containing 1/4 pound gift box, 2 truffle bars and 1 jar of caramel sauce)	~ 1%	$39.95	$20.95	$11.02	$5.77	$5.25
Gift Basket (made of wire and branches and containing 1/2 pound tin, 2 truffle bars, 1 jar of caramel sauce and a T-shirt)	~ 1%	$59.95	$30.95	$23.06	$15.29[3]	$7.77
Nothing Fancy (one pound assorted hot truffles or mild-mannered truffles in a plastic bag)	~ 1%	$19.50	N.A.	$7.42	$6.37	$1.05

[1]Approximately 1/3 of sales were retail over the Cowgirl Chocolate website, the remaining 2/3 of sales were to wholesale accounts (i.e., to other retailers).
[2]Packaging cost includes costs of container (bags, tins, or boxes), labels, and individual truffle wrapping. Packaging cost assumes Marilyn packs the items and does not include the packing & labeling fee charged by Seattle Chocolates if they do the packing ($1.00 per 1/2 pound tin or 1 pound box; $0.75 per 1/4 pound box; $0.25 per 1/4 pound bag; $0.20 per sampler bag).
[3]This cost includes the cost of the T-shirt.

EXHIBIT 3   **Picture of Cowgirl Chocolate Products & Packaging**

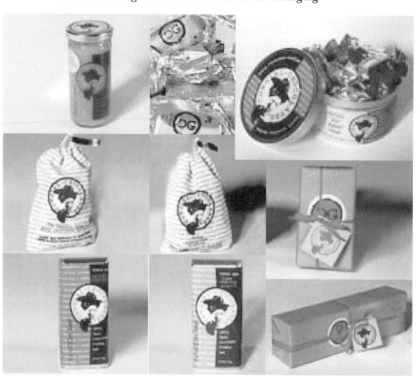

some efforts to help Cowgirl Chocolates along the way. Seattle Chocolates provided Cowgirl Chocolates with a small amount of its table space at several important trade shows and produced in half batches for them. A half batch still consisted of 150 pounds of a given variety of chocolate, which was enough to last Cowgirl Chocolates for six months at 2000 sales rates. Marilyn hoped that she could one day convince Seattle Chocolates to manage the wholesale side of Cowgirl Chocolates, but Seattle Chocolates simply was not interested in taking this on at the present time, at least in part because they were not really sure where the market was for the product. Marilyn also knew she would need to grow sales significantly before Seattle Chocolates would seriously consider such an arrangement, although she was not sure exactly how much she would have to grow sales before such an arrangement would become attractive to Seattle Chocolates.

The chocolate bars themselves cost Cowgirl Chocolates $1.04 per bar while the individual chocolate truffles cost $0.13 per piece. Seattle Chocolates also performed the wrapping and packing of the product. The chocolate bar wrappers cost $0.06 per bar. The wrapper design of the bars had recently been changed to incorporate dietary and nutritional information. While such information was not required, Marilyn felt it helped convey a better image of her chocolates. The change had cost $35 to prepare the new printing plates. Including the materials, wrapping the individual truffles cost $0.02 per piece.

The distinctive muslin bags, collector tins and gift boxes also added to the final product cost. The muslin bags cost $0.35 each for the quarter-pound size and $0.32 each for the sampler size. The tamperproof seals for the bags cost an additional $0.05/bag. The minimum size bag order was 500 bags. As with the chocolate bar wrappers, Cowgirl Chocolate had to buy the printing plates to print the bags. The plates to print the bags, however, cost $250 per plate. Each color of each design required a separate plate. Each of her three quarter-pound bag styles (assorted, lime-tequila, and mild-mannered) had a three-color design. One plate that was used to produce the background design was common to all three styles of bags, but each bag required two additional unique plates. There was also a separate plate for printing the sampler bags. Marilyn was planning to discontinue the separate lime-tequila bag, and just include lime-tequila truffles in the assorted bag as a way to cut packaging costs. The lime-tequila bags had been introduced a year ago, and while they sold reasonably well, they also appeared to mostly cannibalize sales of the assorted bags.

The collectible tins cost $0.80 each, and the labels for these tins cost $0.19 per tin. The tape used to seal the tins cost $0.04 per tin. The minimum order for the tins was for 800 units. The company that produced the tins had recently modified the tin design slightly to reduce the chance that someone might cut themselves on the edge of the can. Unfortunately, this change had resulted in a very small change to the height of the can, which left Cowgirl Chocolate with labels too big for the can. Each label currently had to be trimmed slightly to fit on the can. The alternative to this was to switch to a smaller label. This would require purchasing a new printing plate at a cost of about $35 and might require the purchase of a new printing die (the die holds the label while it is printed), which would cost $360. Marilyn also had hopes of one day being able to get her designs printed directly on the tins. It would make for even nicer tins and save the step of having to adhere the labels to the tins. The minimum order for such tins, however, was 15,000 units.

The gift boxes, including all of the associated wrapping, ribbon, and labels, cost about $1.70 per box. The gift boxes did not sell nearly as well as the tins or bags and were available primarily through Cowgirl Chocolates website. Marilyn was still using and had a reasonable inventory of boxes from a box order she had placed three years ago.

Marilyn currently had more packaging in inventory than she normally would because she had ordered $5,000 worth in anticipation of the possibility of having her product placed in military PX stores at the end of 2000. Seattle Chocolates had been negotiating to get their product into these stores, and there had been some interest on the part of the PX stores in also having Cowgirl Chocolate products. Given the six- to eight-week lead-time on packaging, Marilyn had wanted to be positioned to quickly take advantage of this opportunity if it materialized. While Marilyn was still hopeful this deal might come about, she was less optimistic than she had been at the time she placed the packaging order.

Marilyn was concerned that the actual packing step was not always performed with the care it should be. In particular, she was concerned that not enough or too many truffles ended up in the bags and tins, and that the seals on these containers, which made the packages more tamper resistant, were not always applied correctly. Each quarter-pound bag and gift box was supposed to contain 13 individual truffles, each half-pound tin was supposed to contain 25 individual truffles, and each one-pound gift box was supposed to contain 49 individual truffles. The tins, in particular, had to be packed pretty tightly to get 25 truffles into them. Marilyn had done some of the packing herself at times, and wondered if she would not be better off hiring local college or high school students to do the packing for her to insure that the job was done to her satisfaction. It could also save her some money, as Seattle Chocolates charged her extra for packing the tins and bags. The tins, in particular, were expensive because of the time it took to apply the labels to the top and side of the tin and because of the extra care it took to get all 25 truffles into the tin. Seattle Chocolates charged $1.00 per tin for this step.

Marilyn made the caramel sauce herself with the help of the staff in a commercial kitchen in Sandpoint, Idaho, about a 2½-hour drive north of Moscow. She could make 21 cases of 12 jars each in one day, but including the drive it took all day to do. As with the chocolate, she used only the best ingredients, including fresh cream from a local Moscow dairy. Marilyn figured her costs for the caramel sauce at about $2.50 per jar, which included the cost of the ingredients, the jars, the labeling and the cost of using the Sandpoint kitchen. That figure did not include any allowance for the time it took her to make the sauce or put the labels on the jars. She was considering dropping the caramel sauce from her product line because it was a lot of work to produce and she was not sure she really made any money on it after her own time was factored in. She had sold 70 cases of the sauce in 2000, however, so she knew there was some demand for the product. She was considering the possibility of only offering it at Christmas time as a special seasonal product. She was also looking into the possibility of having a sauce company in Montana make it for her. The company produced caramel, chocolate, and chocolate-caramel sauces that had won awards from the fancy food industry trade association. Marilyn thought the sauces were quite good, although she did not like their caramel sauce as much as her own. The company would sell her 11 oz. jars of any of the sauces, spiced up to Marilyn's standards, for $2.75 per jar. Marilyn would have to provide the labels, for which she would need to have new label designs made to match the jar style the company was set up for, and she would also have to pay a shipping cost of $70–$90 per delivery. The company requested a minimum order size of 72 cases, although the company's owner had hinted that they might be willing to produce in half batches initially.

All of Cowgirl Chocolate's products had won awards, either in the annual Fiery Food Challenges sponsored by *Chile Pepper* magazine or the Scovie Award Competitions sponsored by *Fiery Foods* magazine (the Scovie awards are named after the Scovie measure of heat). All in all, Cowgirl Chocolates had won eleven awards in these two annual competitions. Further, the truffles had won first place in the latest Fiery Food Challenge and the caramel sauce won first place in the latest Scovie competition. The packaging, as distinctive as the chocolate itself, had also won several awards, including the 2000 Award for Excellence for Package Design from American Corporate Identity.

Distribution and Pricing

Marilyn's attempts to get her chocolates into the retail market had met with varying degrees of success. She clearly had been very successful in placing her product in her hometown of Moscow, Idaho. The Moscow Food Co-op was her single best wholesale customer, accounting for 10%–15% of her annual sales. The Co-op sold a wide variety of natural and/or organic products and produce. Many of its products, like Cowgirl Chocolates, were made or grown locally. The Co-op did a nice job of placing her product in a visible shelf location and generally priced her product less than any other retail outlet. The Co-op sold primarily the chocolate bars, which it priced at $2.35, and the quarter-pound muslin bags of truffles, which it priced at $5.50. This compared to the suggested retail prices of $2.99 for the bars and $6.99 for the bags. The product was also available at three other locations in downtown Moscow: Wild Women Traders, a store that described itself as a 'lifestyle outfitter' and that sold high-end women's clothing and antiques; Northwest Showcase, a store that sold locally produced arts and crafts; and Bookpeople, an independent bookstore that catered to customers who liked to spend time browsing an eclectic offering of books and drinking espresso before making a book purchase.

Marilyn was unsure how many of these local sales were to repeat purchasers who really liked the product and how many were to individuals who wanted to buy a locally made product to give as a gift. She was also unsure how much the Co-op's lower prices boosted the sales of her product at that location. At the Co-op, her product was displayed with other premium chocolates from several competitors, including Seattle Chocolates' own branded chocolate bars, which were priced at $2.99. Marilyn knew the Seattle Chocolate bars were clearly comparable in chocolate quality (although without the spice and cowgirl image). Some of the other competitors' comparably sized bars were priced lower, at $1.99, and some smaller bars were priced at $1.49. While these products were clearly higher in quality than the inexpensive chocolate bars sold in vending machines and at the average supermarket checkout aisle, they were made with a less expensive chocolate than she used and were simply not as good as her chocolates. Marilyn wondered how the price and size of the chocolate bar affected the consumer's purchase decision, and how consumers evaluated the quality of each of the competing chocolate bars when making their purchase.

Outside of Moscow, Marilyn had a harder time getting her product placed onto store shelves and getting her product to move through these locations. One other Co-op, the Boise Food Co-op, carried her products, and they sold pretty well there. Boise was the capital of Idaho and the state's largest city. The Boise Museum of Fine Arts gift shop also carried her product in Boise, although the product did not turn over at this location nearly as well as it did at the Boise Co-op. Other fine art museums, gift shops in places like Missoula, Montana, Portland, Oregon, and Columbus, Ohio, carried Cowgirl Chocolates and Marilyn liked having her product in these outlets. She felt that her reputation as an artist helped her get her product placed in such locations, and the product generally sold well in these locations. She thought her biggest distribution coup was getting her product sold in the world-renowned Whitney Museum in New York City. She felt that the fact that it was sold there added to the product's panache. Unfortunately, the product did not sell there particularly well and it was dropped by the museum. The museum buyer had told Marilyn that she simply thought it was too hot for their customers. Another location in New York City, the Kitchen Market, did much better. The Kitchen Market was an upscale restaurant and gourmet food take-out business. The Kitchen Market was probably her steadiest wholesale customer other than the Moscow Co-op. The product also sold pretty well at the few similar gourmet markets where she had gotten her product placed, like Rainbow Groceries in Seattle and the Culinary Institute of America in San Francisco.

Marilyn had also gotten her product placed in a handful of specialty food stores that focused on hot and spicy foods. Surprisingly, she found, the product had never sold well in these locations. Despite the fact that the product had won the major fiery food awards, customers in these shops did not seem to be willing to pay the premium price for her product. She had concluded that if her product was located with similarly priced goods, like at the Kitchen Market in New York City, it would sell, but that if it stood out in price then it did not sell as well. Marilyn was not sure, however, just how similarly her product needed to be priced compared to other products the store sold. It seemed clear to her that her $14.95 half-pound tins were standing out in price too much in the hot and spicy specialty stores that thrived on selling jars of hot sauce that typically retailed for $2.99 to $5.99. Marilyn wondered how her product might do at department stores that often sold half pound boxes of "premium" chocolates for as little as $9.95. She knew her half pound tins contained better chocolate, offered more unique packaging and logo design, and did not give that "empty-feeling" that the competitor's oversized boxes did, but wondered if her product would stand out too much in price in such retail locations.

Several online retailers also carried Cowgirl Chocolates, including companies like Salmon River Specialty Foods and Sam McGee's Hot Sauces, although sales from such sites were not very significant. Marilyn had also had her product available through Amazon.com for a short time, but few customers purchased her product from this site during the time it was listed. Marilyn concluded that customers searching the site for music or books simply were not finding her product, and those who did simply were not shopping for chocolates.

Marilyn also sold her products retail through her own website. The website accounted for about one-third of her sales. She liked Web-based sales, despite the extra work of having to process all the small orders, because she was able to capture both the wholesale and retail profits associated with the sale. She also liked the direct contact with the retail customers, and frequently tossed a few extra truffles into a customer's order and enclosed a note that said "a little extra bonus from the head cowgirl." Marilyn allowed customers to return the chocolate for a full refund if they found it not to their liking. Most of her sales growth from 1999 to 2000 had come from her website.

The website itself was created and maintained for her by a small local Internet service provider. It was a fairly simple site. It had pages that described the company and its products and allowed customers to place orders. It did not have any of the sophisticated features that would allow her to use it to capture information to track customers. Although she did not know for sure, she suspected that many of her Internet sales were from repeat customers who were familiar with her product. She included her website address on all of her packaging and had listed her site on several other sites, like saucemall.com and worldmall.com that would link shoppers at these sites to her site. Listing on some of these sites, like saucemall.com, was free. Listing on some other sites cost a small monthly fee—for the worldmall.com listing, for example, she paid $25/month. Some sites simply provided links to her site on their own. For example, one customer had told her she had found the Cowgirl Chocolate site off of an upscale shopping site called Style365.com. She was not sure how much traffic these various sites were generating on her site, and was unsure how best to attract new customers to her website aside from these efforts.

Marilyn had attempted to get her product into a number of bigger name, upscale retailers, like Dean & Delucca and Coldwater Creek. Dean and Delucca was known for its high-end specialty foods, and the buyers for the company had seemed interested in carrying Cowgirl Chocolates, but the owner had nixed the idea because he found the chocolates too spicy. One of the buyers had also told Marilyn that the owner was more of a chocolate purist or traditionalist who did not really like the idea of adding cayenne pepper to chocolate. Marilyn had also tried hard to get her product sold through Coldwater Creek, one of the largest catalog and online retailers in the country that sold high-end women's apparel and gifts for the home. Coldwater Creek was headquartered just a couple of hours north of Moscow in Sandpoint, Idaho. Like Dean & Delucca, Coldwater Creek had decided that the chocolate was too spicy. Coldwater Creek had also expressed some reservations about carrying food products other than at its retail outlet in Sandpoint. Marilyn hoped that the introduction of mild-mannered Cowgirl Chocolates would help get her product into sites like these two.

Promotion

Marilyn was unsure how best to promote her product to potential customers given her limited resources. The ad that would appear in *Chile Pepper* magazine was her first attempt at really advertising her product. The ad itself was designed to grab readers' attention and pique their curiosity about Cowgirl Chocolates. Most of the ads in the magazine were fairly standard in format. They provided a lot of information and images of the product packed into a fairly small space. Her ad was different—it had very little product information and utilized the single image of the woman in the watering trough. It was to appear in a special section of the magazine that focused on celebrity musicians like Willie Nelson and The Dixie Chicks.

Other than the upcoming ad, Marilyn's promotional efforts were focused on trade shows and creating publicity opportunities. She attended a handful of trade shows each year. Some of these were focused on the hot and spicy food market, and it was at these events that she had won all of her awards. Other trade shows were more in the gourmet food market, and she typically shared table space at these events with Seattle Chocolates. She always gave away a lot of product samples at these trade shows, and had clearly won over some fans to her chocolate. But while these shows occasionally had led to placement of her product in retail locations, at least on a trial basis, they had as yet failed to land her what she would consider to be a really high volume wholesale account.

Marilyn also sought ways to generate publicity for her company and products. Several local newspapers had carried stories on her company in the last couple of years, and each time something like that would happen, she would see a brief jump in sales on her website. The *New York Times* had also carried a short article about her and her company. The day after that article ran, she generated sales of $1,000 through her website. More publicity like the *New York Times* article would clearly help. The recently released movie *Chocolat* about a woman who brings spicy chocolate with somewhat magical powers to a small French town was also generating some interest in her product. A number of customers had inquired if she used the same pepper in her chocolates as was used in the movie. Marilyn wondered how she might best capitalize on the interest the movie was creating in spicy chocolates. She thought that perhaps she could convince specialty magazines like *Art & Antiques* or regional magazines like *Sunset Magazine* or even national magazines like *Good Housekeeping* to run stories on her, her art and her chocolates. But she only had so much time to divide between her various efforts. She had looked into hiring a public relations firm, but had discovered that this would cost something on the order of $2,000/month. She did not expect that any publicity a public relations firm could create would generate sufficient sales to offset this cost, particularly given the limited number of locations where people could buy her chocolates. Marilyn was considering trying to write a cookbook as a way to generate greater publicity for Cowgirl Chocolates. She always talked a little about Cowgirl Chocolates when she gave seminars and presentations about her art, and thought that promoting a cookbook would create similar opportunities. The cookbook would also feature several recipes using Cowgirl Chocolate products.

In addition to being unsure how best to promote her product to potential customers, Marilyn also wondered what she should do to better tap into the seasonal opportunities that presented themselves to sellers of chocolate. Demand for her product was somewhat seasonal, with peak retail demand being at Christmas and Valentine's Day. But she was clearly not seeing the Christmas and Valentine sales of other chocolate companies. Seattle Chocolates, for example, had around three-quarters of its annual sales in the fourth quarter, whereas Cowgirl Chocolate sales in the second half of 2000 were actually less than in the first half. Likewise, while Cowgirl Chocolates experienced a small increase in demand around Valentine's Day, it was nowhere near the increase in demand that other chocolate companies experienced. Marilyn did sell some gift buckets and baskets through her website, and these were more popular at Christmas and Valentine's Day. The Moscow Co-op had also sold some of these gift baskets and buckets during the 2000 Christmas season. Marilyn knew that the gift basket industry in the U.S. was pretty large, and that the industry even had its own trade publication called the *Gift Basket Review*. But she was not sure if gift baskets were the best way to generate sales at these two big holidays and thought that she could probably be doing more. One other approach to spur these seasonal sales that she was planning to try was to buy lists of e-mail addresses, that would allow her to send out several e-mails promoting her products right before Valentine's Day and Christmas. She had talked to the owners of a jewelry store about sharing the expense of this endeavor and they had tentative plans to purchase 10,000 e-mail addresses for $300.

What Next?

Marilyn looked again at the advertisement that would be appearing soon in *Chile Pepper* Magazine. The same friend who had helped her with her award winning package design had helped produce the ad. It would clearly grab people's attention, but would it bring customers to her products in the numbers she needed?

Next to the ad sat the folder with what financial information she had. Despite having little training in small business accounting and financial management, Marilyn knew it was important to keep good records. She had kept track of revenues and expenses for the year, and she had summarized these in a table (see Exhibit 4). Marilyn had shared this revenue and cost information with a friend with some experience in small business financial management, and the result was an estimated income statement for the year 2000 based upon the unaudited information in Exhibit 4. The estimated income statement, shown in Exhibit 5, revealed that Cowgirl had lost approximately $6,175 on operations before taxes. Combining the information in Exhibits 4 and 5, it appeared that the inventory had built up to approximately $16,848 by December 31, 2000. Marilyn had initially guessed she had $10,000 worth of product and packaging inventory, about twice her normal level of inventory, between what was stored in her garage turned art studio turned chocolate warehouse and what was stored for her at Seattle Chocolates. But the financial analysis indicated that she either had more inventory than she thought or that she had given away more product than she originally thought. Either way, this represented a significant additional drain on her resources—in effect cash expended to cover both the operational loss and the inventory buildup was approximately $23,000 in total (see note 5 of Exhibit 4 for a more detailed explanation). When Marilyn looked at the exhibits, she could see better why she had to loan the firm money. She also recognized that the bottom line was that the numbers did not look good, and she wondered if the ad would help turn things around for 2001.

If the ad did not have its desired affect, she wondered what she should do next. She clearly had limited resources to work with. She had already pretty much decided that if this ad did not work, she would not run another one in the near future. She was also pretty wary of working with distributors. In addition to her own bad experience, she knew of others in the industry that had bad experiences with distributors, and she did not think she could afford to take another gamble on a distributor. She wondered if she should focus more attention on her online retail sales or on expanding her wholesale business to include more retailers. If she focused more on her own online sales, what exactly should she do? If she focused on expanding her wholesale business, where should she put her emphasis? Should she continue to pur-

EXHIBIT 4   Summary of 2000 Financial Information (unaudited)

Revenues:

Product Sales	$ 26,000
Revenue from Shipping	4,046 (see Note 1)
Total Revenues	**$ 30,046**

Expenses: (related to cost of sales)

Chocolate (raw material)	$16,508
Caramel (raw material)	2,647
Packaging (bags, boxes, tins)	9,120
Printing (labels, cards, etc)	3,148
Subtotal	$31,423 (see Note 2)

Other Expenses

Shipping and Postage	$ 4,046
Brokers	540
Travel (airfare, lodging, meals, gas)	5,786
Trade shows (promotions, etc.)	6,423
Website	1,390
Phone	981
Office Supplies	759
Photography	356
Insurance, Lawyers, Memberships	437
Charitable Contributions	200
Miscellaneous Other Expenses	1,071
State Taxes	35
Subtotal	$ 22,024
Total Expenses	**$ 53,447**
Cash needed to sustain operations	**$ 23,023** (see Note 3)

Estimated year-end inventory (12/31/00):

Product Inventory	$ 9,848
Extra Packaging and Labels	7,000
Total Inventory	**$16,848**

Notes

(1) The $4,046 Revenue from Shipping represents income received from customers who are charged shipping and postage up front as part of the order. Cowgirl then pays the shipping and postage when the order is delivered. The offsetting operating expense is noted in "Other Expenses."

(2) Of this amount, $14,575 is attributed to product actually sold and shipped. The remaining $16,848 represents leftover inventory and related supplies (i.e., $16848 + $14575 = $31,423).

(3) Marilyn made a personal loan to the firm in the year 2000 for approximately $23,000 to sustain the business's operations.

sue retailers that specialized in hot and spicy foods, try to get her product placed in more Co-ops, expand her efforts to get the product positioned as a gift in museum gift shops and similar outlets, or focus her efforts on large, high-end retailers like Coldwater Creek and Dean & Delucca now that she had a nonspicy chocolate in her product mix? Or should she try to do something else entirely new? And what more should she do to create publicity for her product? Was the cookbook idea worth pursuing? As she thought about it, she began to wonder if things were beginning to spin out of control. Here she was, contemplating writing a cookbook to generate publicity for her chocolate company that she started to raise money to publish her arts magazine. Where would this end?

EXHIBIT 5   Cowgirl Chocolates Income Statement (accountant's unaudited estimate for Year 2000)

			% of Sales
Revenues:			
Product Sales	$26,000		
Miscellaneous Income	$4,046		
Total Net Sales		**$30,046**	100%
Cost of Sales (shipped portion of chocolate, caramel, packaging, and printing)		$14,197	47%
Gross Margin		**$15,849**	53%
Operating Expenses:			
Advertising & Promotions:			
Trade Shows	6,423		
Website	1,390		
Charitable Contributions	200		
Subtotal		8,013	27%
Travel		5,786	19%
Miscellaneous		1,071	4%
Payroll Expense/Benefits @ 20%	(no personnel charges)	—	0%
Depreciation on Plant and Equipment	(no current ownership of PPE)	—	0%
Continuing Inventory (finished and unfinished)	(not included in income statement)	—	
Shipping & Postage		4,046	13%
Insurance, Lawyers, Professional Memberships		437	1.5%
Brokers		540	1.8%
Office Expenses (phone, supplies, photography, taxes)		2,131	7%
Total Operating Expenses		**22,024**	
Grand Total: All expenses		**$36,221**	
Profit before Interest & Taxes		**($6,175) [see note]**	
Interest Expense (short term)		—	
Interest Expense (long term)		—	
Taxes Incurred (Credit @ 18%, approximate tax rate)		($1,124)	
Net Profit After Taxes		**($5,051.15)**	
Net Profit After Taxes/Sales			−17%

Note: The ($6,175) loss plus the $16,848 in inventory build-up approximates the cash needed ($23,023—see Exhibit 4) to cover the total expenses for year 2000.

Case 25

America Online (AOL)

Natalya V. Delcoure, Lawrence R. Jauch, and John L. Scott
Northeast Louisiana University

Introduction

America Online, Inc. (NYSE: AOL) was founded in 1985. This media company, with headquarters in Dulles, Virginia, has more than 10 million members and currently operates in the United States, Canada, the United Kingdom, France and Germany. AOL provides online services including electronic mail, online conferencing, Internet access, news, magazines, sports, weather, stock quotes, mutual fund transactions, software files, games, computing support and online classes.

According to the company, its mission is "to lead the development of a new interactive medium that eliminates traditional boundaries between people and places to create a new kind of interactive global community that holds the potential to change the way people obtain information, communicate with one another, buy products and services, and learn."

To accomplish this mission, the company's strategy is to continue investment in the growth of its subscriber base, pursue related business opportunities often through joint ventures and acquisitions, provide a full range of interactive services, and maintain technological flexibility.

AOL's rapid growth and community orientation have made it the most popular, easiest, and well-known way for consumers to get online. In December 1996, AOL had 8.5 million member sessions a day; 7 million e-mails sent to 12 million recipients a day; and it accounted for approximately $750,000 per day in merchandise transactions.

But AOL has not been trouble-free. On August 7, 1996, AOL threw 6 million subscribers off line for 19 hours due to software problems. America Online revealed that the glitch resulted from an error made by its working subsidiary, ANS Co., in reconfiguring software, and from a bug in router software. The error cost AOL $3 million in rebates. On January 8, 1997, America Online suffered a partial outage that forced it to shut down half of its system for four hours to find a problem. The problem was with an interface in a router device, which manages the flow of data in the network. The outage drew front-page headlines around the world, as millions of users were unable to access electronic mail, the Internet, and a variety of services and publications online for nearly a day.

America Online—Company Profile

America Online emerged from a firm founded in the early 1980s as Control Video Corp., which aimed to create an online service that specialized in games. It failed to meet strong competition from the Apple II and Commodore 64. Control Video was reorganized as Quantum Computer Services and became a custom developer of on-line services for other companies. Over time, Quantum managed to persuade Tandy Corp. and Apple Computers to offer a new service called Applelink Personal Edition. At the last minute, Apple withdrew from the deal and left Quantum holding software it had developed expressly for Applelink. In 1989 Quantum was only scraping by, and it did not have much money for splashy ad campaigns to attract computer users to their new service—America Online. So it came on the market with a unique approach, which was to blanket the countryside with diskettes containing America Online software. As the years went by, the company changed the way it accounted for the costs of acquiring subscribers and its pricing plans, but America Online had never actually made any money in its entire life. At the same time America Online has tried to position itself as the first "digital media company."

AOL Organization

AOL Corporation now oversees the operations of several subsidiaries and three divisions: AOL Networks, ANS Access, and AOL Studios. The Corporate Division comprises the core business functions of Finance, Human Resources, Legal Affairs, Corporate Communications, Corporate Development, and Technology. The Technology group is responsible for delivering research, development, network/data center operations, and member support to the other America Online divisions, technology licensees, and joint venture partners. The group is also responsible for support functions—including technical support, billing, and sales.

AOL Networks is responsible for extending the AOL brand into the market, developing new revenue streams, advertising, and online transactions. AOL Networks is led by Robert Pittman, President, formerly managing partner and CEO of Century 21 and co-founder of MTV Network.

ANS Access is responsible for the telecommunication network. The network consists of more than 160,000 modems connecting 472 cities in the U.S. and 152 cities internationally. Nearly 85 percent of the American population can dial into AOLNet on a local number. For America Online's members who travel, GlobalNet offers access in approximately 230 additional cities in 83 countries. The ANS technical team is responsible for architecture, design, development, installation, management and maintenance of hardware and software for the nationwide corporate data networks and Internet backbone by which communications take place.

AOL Studios runs AOL's innovative chat (iChatco), games (INN), local (Digital City), and independent (Greenhouse) programming properties. AOL Studios is the newest division in AOL. It is working on development of leading-edge technology for broadband and mid-band distribution, interactive brands that can be extended into other media properties such as TV and radio, and managing joint ventures with companies including Time-Warner and CapCities/ABC. Imagination Network Inc. is the provider of computer online entertainment services for AOL.

Digital City provides local programming, news, services, chat rooms, and commerce to AOL members as well as to the Internet at large. To date, Digital City has been launched nationally in Washington DC, Boston, Philadelphia, Atlanta, San Francisco and Los Angeles. Digital City planned to expand to over 40 cities in 1997. Digital City, Inc., is owned by Digital City LP. AOL owns a majority interest in that entity, and the Tribune Company owns the remaining interest.

Advanced CO+RE Systems, Inc., is a wholly owned subsidiary of America Online, which provides network services for AOLnet, together with Sprint Corporation and BBN Corporation. Through this subsidiary, America Online designs, develops, and operates high performance wide-area networks for business, research, education, and government organizations.

In February 1996, AOL merged with the Johnson-Grace Company, a leading developer of compression technology and multimedia development and delivery tools. Using the Johnson-Grace technology, America Online is able to deliver the data-intensive graphics and audio and video capabilities using narrow-band technologies, even over the slower speed modems currently used by most AOL members.

In fiscal 1996 AOL combined its key production areas to form AOL Productions, Inc., a wholly owned subsidiary. AOL Productions has emerged as a leading studio system with expertise in all phases of interactive content development for online, World Wide Web, Internet, and CD-ROM delivery.

2Market, Inc., is a joint venture between America Online, Apple Computer, and Medior. It provides retail catalog shopping CD-ROMs that include online ordering capabilities. In 1997 America Online, along with Netscape Communications and Disney's ABC unit, announced their plans to launch ABCNEWS.com, a 24-hour news service.

Since the beginning of 1995, the company also acquired Advanced Network and Services, Inc., Ubique, Ltd., Navisoft, Inc., Global Network Navigator, Inc., Book-Link Technologies, Inc., and Redgate Communications Corporation. AOL is also planning to go into the bookselling business in a joint venture with Barnes & Noble, but the timing is still uncertain.

AOL Marketing

The goals of the firm's consumer marketing programs are to increase the general visibility of America Online and to make it easy for customers to experiment with and subscribe to its services. AOL attracts new subscribers through independent marketing programs such as direct mail, disk inserts and inserts in publications, advertising, and a variety of co-marketing efforts. The company has entered into co-marketing agreements with numerous personal computer hardware, software, and peripheral production companies, and also with certain of its media partners. These companies bundle America Online software with their products and cater to the needs of a specific audience.

America Online has also been expanding into business-to-business markets, using AOL's network to provide customized network solutions to both individual businesses and to professional communities and industries. These private AOLs (the "PAOLs") offer the ease of use America Online is known for, as well as customized features and functionality accessible only by preauthorized users, access to the fleet of AOL distribution platforms, secure communications and information. The company offers these products using a direct sales force and direct marketing, and through resellers and system integrators.

America Online utilizes specialized retention programs designed to increase customer loyalty and satisfaction and to maximize customer subscription life. These retention programs include regularly scheduled online events and conferences; the regular addition of new content, services, and software programs; and online promotions of upcoming online events and new features. The firm also provides a variety of support mechanisms such as online technical support and telephone support services.

In May 1995 America Online introduced its Web browser, which provides integrated World Wide Web access within the AOL services. The integrated approach allows the user to seamlessly use the full suite of America Online features, including chat room, e-mail gateways and mailing lists, file transfer protocol, USENET Newsgroups, WAIS, and Gopher.

In the summer of 1997 America Online, Inc. planned to offer its 8 million members a three-dimensional gaming world, CyberPark. The company will try to compete with such heavyweights as Microsoft, Internet Gaming Zone site, and MCI, which will launch a service in 1997 that allows computer users to play their favorite CD-ROM games. The projected earnings are expected to reach $127 million in 1997, but there are still some technical problems to overcome and the uncertainty of how much to charge future users.

America Online has included international market expansion in its strategy to gain competitive advantage. In April 1995, AOL entered into a joint venture with Bertelsmann, one of the world's largest media companies, to offer interactive services in Europe: Germany (November 1995), the United Kingdom (January 1996), and France (March 1996). Bertelsmann agreed to contribute up to $100 million to fund the launch of the European services, provided access to its book and music club membership base of over 30 million, and offered its publishing content to the joint venture on a most favored customer basis. In addition, Bertelsmann acquired approximately a 5 percent interest in America Online and was designated a member of the company's Board of Directors. AOL contributed interactive technology and management expertise, proprietary software licenses and development services, staff training, and technical support in order to develop, test, and launch the interactive services in Europe. Subscribers to the European services enjoy access to America Online's services in the United States, and United States subscribers enjoy access to the European services.

AOL Canada, launched in January 1996, features local content and services. In October 1996, AOL Canada offered Canadian members software, thirteen local channels, billing in Canadian dollars, e-mail, message boards, and easy access to the Internet through a Web browser. AOL Canada's key partners include Citytv, an internationally renowned broadcaster and program producer; MuchMusic, Canada's first national music television channel; Shift Magazine, Canada's hottest publication in media; Intuit Canada, makers of the world's leading personal finance software, Quicken; and Southam New Media, a wholly owned subsidiary of Southam Inc., Canada's largest news organization.

In May 1996, America Online announced a partnership with Mitsui & Co., one of the world's largest international trading companies, and Nikkei, one of Japan's leading media companies with respected business and computer publications. The joint venture consists of Mitsui & Co. owning 40 percent, Nikkei 10 percent and AOL 50 percent. Japanese partners contributed more than 120 years of experience and credibility in the Japanese market, a strong management team, and $56 million to fund the launch of the Japanese service. America Online brings to the venture its ability to develop, manage, and execute interactive online services in the U.S., Europe, and Canada.

America Online's wildly successful marketing ploy of flat rate pricing in the U.S. turned out to contribute to AOL's latest problem. About 75 percent of AOL's customers took the flat-rate offer. As a result, total daily AOL customer use soared from 1.6 million hours online in October 1996 to more than 4 million hours in January 1997. (These problems are more fully described later in this case.)

MEETING CUSTOMER NEEDS

The company provides tools to its members so that they can control their child's or teen's experience online without cramping the adults who enjoy using AOL's services to talk to other adults. Parental controls can block or limit the use of chat, Instant Messages, e-mail, binary files, news groups, or the Web. Different online areas support different values. For instance:

- ACLU forum: encourages lively yet responsible debate. Illegal activities (harassment, distribution of illegal materials) are not permitted in this area.
- Womens' Network: is a women-friendly and safe space for chatting, learning, teaching and networking, but men are still welcome to join the communication.
- Christian Chat room: allows fellowship among Christian members. In this space, proselytizing is forbidden.
- Kids Only: gives children their own space online for searching help with homework, sending e-mail, and hanging out in chat rooms. Parental control can be set up in this area.

The average adult spends about an hour per day on line, but the average child spends three. Currently, there are 4.1 million kids surfing the Net. By 2000, it is expected there will be 19.2 million. Kids, who spent $307 million in 1996 on online services, will spend $1.8 billion by 2002, and that is why media and Web giants are scrambling to offer new kid-friendly sites. Fox TV features cartoons and kid shows. Disney gave AOL first crack at hosting Daily Blast, which offers kids games, comics, and stories for $4.95 per month or $39.95 per year. But, says Rob Jennings, vice-president for programming for AOL networks, "we felt we had a good mix already." Yahooligans! offers kids-friendly Web-sites for free. AOL still has partnerships with other media giants such as Disney rival Viacom Inc.'s Nickelodeon unit, for other offerings.

Since 1994, AOL has offered a Kids Only area featuring homework help, games, and online magazines, as well as the usual fare of software, games, and chat rooms. The area gets about 1 million 8- to 12-year-old visitors monthly.

In April 1996, America Online began to see the effect of seasonality in both member acquisitions and in the amount of time spent by customers using its services. The company expects that member acquisition is to be highest in the second and third fiscal quarters, when sales of new computers and computer software are highest due to holiday seasons. Customer usage is expected to be lower in the summer months, due largely to extended daylight hours and competing outdoor leisure activities.

AOL EMPLOYEES

As of June 30, 1996, America Online had 5,828 employees, including 1,058 in software and content development; 3,271 in customer support; 199 in marketing; 1,099 in operations; and 291 in corporate operations. None of AOL's employees is represented by a labor union, and America Online has never experienced a work stoppage.

AOL employs numerous part-time workers around the world known as remote staff. These are volunteer staff who develop content and provide both marketing and operations functions. Remote staff write informational articles, produce graphics, host chat rooms, provide technical assistance, and fulfill various support functions. Remote staff duties vary. Some may work as little as ten hours per week or more than forty hours per week.

AOL's remote staff are compensated for these services with "community leader accounts"—a membership for which the staff members are not charged. Relatively few remote staff are paid as independent contractors.

AOL's flat rate pricing plan had a serious impact on its remote staff. Prior to the flat rate, members paid about $3 per hour of online access. Hence, a "free account" would have a value of approximately $300 for a staff member who spent three hours per day online. After the flat rate pricing plan, this account's value fell to $20. This enormous decrease in incentives led many remote staff to resign their positions. The positions hardest hit were those for which the job pressures were highest. AOL's once touted "Techlive" is now all but invisible.

AOL FINANCE

Exhibits 1 and 2 present the financial statements for fiscal years 1995 and 1996. About 90 percent of the firm's revenues are generated from online subscription fees. AOL's other revenues are generated from sales of merchandise, data network services, online transactions and advertising, marketing and production services and development and licensing fees. The increase of over $600 million in service revenues from 1995 to 1996 was primarily attributed to a 93 percent increase in AOL subscribers.

This is expected to undergo radical change, due to flat rate pricing, with much less revenue coming from subscriber fees, which AOL hopes to make up by increases in the other revenue streams.

Cost of revenue, which includes network-related costs, consists of data and voice communication costs, costs associated with operating the data centers, and providing customer support. These increased almost $400 million from 1995 to 1996. This increase was related to a growth of data communication cost, customer support cost and royalties paid to information and service providers.

EXHIBIT 1   Income Statement, Year Ended June 30 (amounts in thousands, except per share data)

	1996	1995
Revenues:		
Online service revenues	$ 991,656	$344,309
Other revenues	102,198	49,981
Total revenues	1,093,854	394,290
Costs and expenses:		
Cost of revenues	627,372	229,724
Marketing	212,710	77,064
Product development	53,817	14,263
General and administrative	110,653	42,700
Acquired research and development	16,981	50,335
Amortization of goodwill	7,078	1,653
Total costs and expenses	1,028,611	415,739
Income (loss) from operations:	**65,243**	**(21,449)**
Other income (loss) from operations	(2,056)	3,074
Merger expenses	(848)	(2,207)
Income (loss) before provision for income taxes	62,339	(20,582)
Provision for income taxes	(32,523)	(15,169)
Net income (loss)	$ 29,816	$ (35,751)
Earnings (loss) per share:		
Net income (loss)	$ 0.28	$ (0.51)
Weighted average shares outstanding	108,097	69,550

EXHIBIT 2   Consolidated Balance Sheets, June 30 (amounts in thousands, except per share data)

	1996	1995
Assets		
Current assets:		
Cash and cash equivalents	$118,421	$ 45,877
Short-term investments	10,712	18,672
Trade accounts receivable	42,939	32,176
Other receivables	29,674	11,381
Prepaid expenses and other current assets	68,832	25,527
Total current assets	270,578	133,633
Property and equipment at cost, net	101,277	70,919
Other assets:		
Product development costs, net	44,330	18,949
Deferred subscriber acquisition costs, net	314,181	77,229
License rights, net	4,947	5,579
Other assets	35,878	9,121
Deferred income taxes	135,872	35,627
Goodwill, net	51,691	54,356
Total assets	$958,754	$405,413
Liabilities and Stockholders' Equity		
Current liabilities:		
Trade accounts payable	$105,904	$ 84,640
Other accrued expenses and liabilities	127,898	23,509
Deferred revenue	37,950	20,021
Accrued personnel costs	15,719	2,863
Current portion of long-term debt	2,435	2,329
Total current liabilities	289,906	133,362
Long-term liabilities:		
Notes payable	19,306	17,369
Deferred income taxes	135,872	35,627
Other liabilities	1,168	2,243
Total liabilities	$446,252	$188,601
Stockholders' Equity:		
Preferred stock, $.01 par value; 5,000,000 shares authorized; 1,000 shares issued and outstanding at June 30, 1996	1	—
Common stock, $.01 par value; 300,000,000 and 100,000,000 shares authorized, 92,626,000 and 76,728,268 shares issued and outstanding at June 30, 1996 and 1995, respectively	926	767
Additional paid-in capital	519,342	252,668
Accumulated deficit	(7,767)	(36,623)
Total stockholders' equity	512,502	216,812
Total liabilities and equity	$958,754	$405,413

For fiscal 1996, marketing expenses increased 176 percent over fiscal 1995. This was primarily attributed to an increase in the size and number of marketing programs designed to expand the subscriber base.

Product development costs include research and development and the amortization of software. For fiscal 1996, these costs increased 277 percent over fiscal 1995, and increased as a percentage of total revenues from 3.6 percent to 4.9 percent. The increases in product development costs were primarily attributable to an increase in the number of technical employees. Product development costs, before capitalization and amortization, increased by 242 percent.

For fiscal 1996, general and administrative costs increased 159 percent over fiscal 1995 and decreased as a percentage of total revenues from 10.8 percent to 10.1 percent. The increase in general and administrative costs was related to higher personnel, office, and travel expenses related to an increase in the number of employees. The decrease in general and administrative costs as a percentage of total revenues was a result of the substantial growth in revenues, which more than offset the additional general and administrative costs, combined with the semi-variable nature of many of the general and administrative costs.

Acquired research and development costs relate to in-process research and development purchased with the acquisition of Ubique, Ltd., in September 1995. Acquired research and development costs relate to in-process research and development purchased as part of the acquisitions of BookLink Technologies, Inc. ("Booklink"), and Navisoft, Inc. ("Navisoft").

The amortization of goodwill increase relates primarily to America Online's fiscal 1995 acquisitions of Advanced Network & Services, Inc., and Global Network Navigator, Inc., which resulted in approximately $56 million of goodwill. The goodwill related to these acquisitions is being amortized on a straight-line basis over periods ranging from five to ten years. The increase in amortization of goodwill results from a full year of goodwill recognized in fiscal 1996 compared to only a partial year of goodwill recognized in fiscal 1995.

Other income (expenses) consists of interest expense and nonoperating charges net of investment income and nonoperating gains. The change in other income (expense) was attributed to the $8 million settlement of a class action lawsuit partially offset by an increase in investment income.

Nonrecurring merger expenses totaling $848,000 were recognized in fiscal 1996 in connection with the merger of America Online with Johnson-Grace Company. Nonrecurring merger expenses totaling $2,207,000 were recognized in fiscal 1995 in connection with the mergers of AOL with Redgate Communications Corporation, Wide Area Information Servers, Inc., and Medior, Inc.

In December 1993, the company completed a public offering of 8,000,000 shares of common stock, which generated net cash proceeds of approximately $62.7 million. In April 1995, the joint venture with Bertelsmann to offer interactive online services in Europe netted approximately $54 million through the sale of approximately 5 percent of its common stock to Bertelsmann. In October 1995, AOL completed a public offering of 4,963,266 shares of common stock, which generated net cash proceeds of approximately $139.5 million. In May 1996, America Online sold convertible preferred stock to Mitsui in its joint venture with Mitsui & Co., Ltd., and Nohon Keizai Shimbun, Inc., to offer interactive online services in Japan. The preferred stock has an aggregate liquidation preference of approximately $28 million and accrues dividends at a rate of 4 percent per annum. Accrued dividends can be paid in the form of additional shares of preferred stock. Exhibit 3 shows the history of share prices of AOL's common stock.

America Online has financed its operations through cash generated from operations and the sale of its capital stock. AOL has financed its investments in facilities and telecommunications equipment principally through leasing. America Online leases the majority of its facilities and equipment under non-cancelable operating leases. The communication network requires a substantial investment in telecom-

EXHIBIT 3   **Market Price of Common Stock**

For the Quarter Ended	High	Low
September 30, 1994	$10.28	$ 6.88
December 31, 1994	14.63	7.47
March 31, 1995	23.69	12.31
June 30, 1995	24.06	16.75
September 30, 1995	37.25	21.38
December 31, 1995	46.25	28.25
March 31, 1996	60.00	32.75
June 30, 1996	71.00	36.63
September 30, 1996	37.75	34.65
December 31, 1996	33.38	32.25

munications equipment, which America Online plans to finance principally through leasing. The company has never declared, nor has it paid, any cash dividends on its common stock. AOL currently intends to retain its earnings to finance future growth.

The company uses its working capital to finance ongoing operations and to fund marketing and content programs and the development of its products and services. America Online plans to continue to invest in computing and support infrastructure. Additionally, AOL expects to use a portion of its cash for the acquisition and subsequent funding of technologies, products, or businesses complementary to the company's current business. For example, America Online is investing in the development of alternative technologies to deliver its services. AOL has entered into agreements with several manufacturers of PDAs, including Sony, Motorola, Tandy, and Casio, to bundle a palmtop edition of America Online's client software with the PDAs sold by such manufacturers. AOL is participating in early cable trials using cable as the conduit into PCs, and has announced future support of ISDN and wireless. In the paging market, AOL has entered into agreements with AT&T Wireless Services and MobileMedia to provide their paging customers who subscribe to AOL with mobile access to certain America Online services.

AOL's Environment

For a long time such companies as AT&T, Western Union, and RCA dominated the telecommunication industry. The courts deregulated the telephone industry in the 1980s. Although technology and market development made passage of new telecommunications legislation inevitable, it took about ten years to frame it. Even though the Telecommunications Reform Act of 1996 meant to remove many of the regulatory barriers and make it easier for telecom companies to invest in the information superhighway, so far it has made little difference. The Department of Commerce and the U.S. Trade Representative has pushed the World Trade Organization to open up the telecom sector to more service and equipment competition. As the result of trade negotiations in Singapore, tariffs on many telecommunications products and services will be reduced with great potential benefit to U.S. firms. Additional talks were under way in Switzerland in 1997, which may permit U.S. telecommunications companies to compete on equal footing with providers in Europe and elsewhere.

America Online must pay particular attention to changes in the regulatory environment relating to telecommunications and the media. Additional legislative proposals from international, federal, and state government bodies in the areas of content regulations, intellectual property, privacy rights and state tax issues could impose additional regulations and obligations upon all online service providers.

Telephone companies are collecting high revenues as computer and online services expand. One study found that local carriers collected revenues totaling $1.4 billion in 1995 from second phone lines used mainly for Net links, while spending only $245 million to upgrade their networks for the additional usage. Phone companies experienced 8 percent to 9 percent profit growth in 1996 since second phone line installations at homes grew 25 percent. Both local carriers and online service providers agree that there is a necessity to build higher capacity networks to satisfy the increasing demand for public phone networks to meet the growing trend in cybersurfing.

The future of technology is difficult to predict, but can affect AOL's future strategy. Some speculate that interactive TV is going to be replaced by network computers (such as those from Sun). Some argue that Internet connections should be available for people who want to use them, and that public monies should be provided to ensure access for all. There is a growing place for satellite and fiber in the new communication system. Technology trends are sometimes born of social change. Here are some of the most important trends to watch for in the next five years.

- The world phone could be a satellite wireless phone that uses digital technology. A combination of Global System for Mobilization (GSM) and satellite technologies could be the model for the world phone. Pioneers such as Wildfire Communications, Lucent Technologies, Dialogic, and VDOnet are among hundreds of alternative carriers that try to unite PCs, phone, e-mail, fax, and video into a seamless fabric. They are designing software that sends phone calls around the world on the Internet very cheaply. The line dividing computers and telephones, voice and data is blurring. Building on the union of data networks and computers, the Internet has become the new global communications infrastructure for businesses.

- Personal Communication Systems (PCS) could broadside local telecom carriers. Projections are that local exchange carriers must brace for a loss of 35 percent of high-margin business customers and 25 percent or more of their residential shares to PCS providers. Mobile subscribers could represent 17 percent of traditional wireline carrier business by 2010. VocalTec Ltd., leading maker of Internet telephone products, recently broadened the appeal by introducing gateways that connect the Internet to standard phone systems—allowing PC users to call non-PC users on their phones and vice versa. VocalTec claims it saves $10,000 a month on phone bills between the company's New Jersey and Israeli offices.

- Wireless convergence: commercial mobile wireless will include mobile satellite, and satellite communication will overlap coverage and mobility with cellular/PCS. Cordless telephony will play major roles. Several years ago, Microsoft Corp. and Novell Inc. tried to apply computer-telephony integration technology to any desktop by creating competing standards for connecting phone systems to PC networks. But the products, TAPI and TSAPI, which allowed desktop computers to receive and manage phone calls through their PCs, went nowhere. Now, a wave of products built on TAPI and TSAPI that work with standard telecom equipment is hitting the market. Users can select a handful of names from a database and command the phone switch to set up a conference call with all of them. Pacific Bell is testing a sophisticated messaging service on 300 wireless-phone customers in San Diego. It answers incoming phone calls, screens them, and automatically routes them to wherever you are—a conference room, your home office, or a shopping mall. For a richer media experience, many companies are concentrating on desktop videoconferencing products from Intel, C-Phone, and VDOnet, among others. Those products are very cost efficient and price compatible.

- Asynchronous transfer mode: ATM carrier services are still expensive. Originally developed by Bell Laboratories for high-speed voice networks, ATM has now been adapted for data applications. They are able to move data at 155 mbps, whereas advanced modems top out at 56 kbps. The Defense Department uses a fiber-optic ATM network between the U.S. and Germany. The Mayo Clinic in Rochester, Minn., uses ATM for "tele-medicine"—doctors can video conference with patients. ATM switches account for an estimated savings of $200,000 per month for American Petroleum Institution, which uses this tool to transmit drilling-site data over satellite. This technology is moving quickly into the public phone network, which increases the speed of the global communication network.

- Residential gateways: will let customers plug in telecom carriers and cable companies' networks and give users more control.

Increased competition makes it hard to make money on selling unlimited online access. Service providers have to upgrade their equipment to handle higher modem speeds and install separate equipment and phone lines for rival technologies. Sales of new modems are expected to be huge, driven by the Internet boom. AOL signed a deal with U.S. Robotics, which was scheduled to start turning on telephone access numbers on February 27, 1997, to give subscribers log-on access at a faster speed. Currently, the only high speed (56 kbps) modems that America Online customers can use are made by U.S. Robotics, which now controls a quarter of the market. Modems from the Open 56K Forum group—available in March 1997—can't talk to those of U.S. Robotics. Most of the Open 56K group will have modems out in March 1997. The No. 2 modem maker, Hayes Microcomputer Products Inc., registered more than 40,000 people for a deal it offered on the company's Web page: customers can get their high-speed modems for $99 by sending in any brand modem. U.S. Robotics sells its superfast modems for $199 for a version that is installed into the computer, or $239 for an external model.

Use of the Net has dramatically increased the demand for techies. An estimated 760,000 people are working for Net-related companies alone. The Internet is full of companies' ads wanting programmers. A new study by the Information Technology Association of America estimates that 190,000 infotech jobs stand vacant in U.S. companies—half in the information industry. The situation can get worse, because the number of college students in computer science has fallen 43 percent in the past decade. Net-related companies are spending millions of dollars recruiting employees. In 1996, pay for info-tech workers rose by 12 percent to 20 percent, while average annual pay for software architects rose to $85,600.

The online services market is highly competitive. Major direct competitors include Prodigy Services Company, a joint venture of IBM and Sears; e-World, a service of Apple Computer, Inc.; GEnie, a division of General Electric Information Services; Delphi Internet Services Corporation, a division of News Corp.; Interchange, a service of AT&T Corp.; and Microsoft Corp., which launched its online service under the name Microsoft Network. Microsoft has been devoting considerable resources and energy to focus the firm and its products squarely on the Internet. The Internet directory services are another source of competition, including NETCOM On-Line Communication Services, Inc.; Bolt, Beranek & Newman, Inc.; Performance System International, UUNET Technologies with Internet MCI; Yahoo, Inc.; Excite, Inc.; Infoseek Corporation; and Lycos, Inc. Finally, software providers such as Intuit Inc. and Netscape Communication Corporation are another category of competitors.

America Online is, by far, the largest online service, with 10 million American members, as of September 1997. Compuserve was the second largest service prior to AOL acquiring it. The Microsoft Network is now the second largest online service, with 2.3 million subscribers. But a great deal of the competition comes from the small local Internet providers, who were the catalyst that drove AOL to the flat rate pricing plan.

The imperatives for global communications look very promising. Telecom and data networks should become a lifeline for nations, businesses, and individuals. The Internet is pushing world financial markets and the flow of goods and services. The Net has the potential to revolutionize business and human lives, but it also has the danger that the network can be a vehicle of isolation. Communication by fax, modem, wireless handset, video conferencing, or telecommuting can create personal isolation. A high-tech world may need to be counterbalanced by community, family and person-to-person contacts. The Internet and more advanced computing plus training for people to understand and participate in the network have obvious educational potential.

THE FLAT RATE DEBACLE

Through December 31, 1994, the company's standard monthly membership fee for its service, which included five hours of services, was $9.95, with a $3.50 hourly fee for usage in excess of five hours per month. Effective January 1, 1995, the hourly fee for usage in excess of five hours per month decreased from $3.50 to $2.95, while the monthly membership fee remained the same.

In October 1995, AOL launched its Internet Service, Global Network Navigator (GNN), which was aimed at consumers who wanted a full-featured Internet-based service, but without the full service quality of AOL. The monthly fee for GNN was $14.95. This fee included 20 hours of service per month with a $1.95 hourly fee for usage in excess of 20 hours per month. In May 1996, AOL announced an additional pricing plan, which was oriented to its heavier users and called "Value Plan." It became effective July 1, 1996, and included 20 hours of services for $19.95 per month, with a $2.95 hourly fee for usage in excess of 20 hours per month.

AOL usage increased dramatically when the company announced its plans to offer flat rate unlimited pricing in October 1996. AOL switched its more than 7 million members at that time to unlimited access for $19.95 a month. Its network was deluged by subscribers, many of whom could not log onto the system during peak evening hours or on weekends. Exhibit 4 shows comparative data before and after this new pricing policy.

EXHIBIT 4   AOL System Use before and after Flat Rate Pricing

Average AOL	January 1997	September 1996
Member daily usage	32 minutes	14 minutes
Daily sessions	10 million	6 million
Total hours daily	4.2 million	1.5 million
Total hours per month	125 million (est.), (Dec.: 102 million)	45 million
Peak simultaneous usage	260,000	140,000
Avg. minutes per session	26 minutes	16 minutes

Following the second shutdown of its system in January 1997, the company's Chairman and CEO, Steve Case, emphasized that AOL took full responsibility for the "busy signals." "When we decided . . . to introduce unlimited use pricing, we were well aware that usage would increase substantially. We did some consumer testing and operations modeling to generate usage forecast, and we began building extra capacity in advance of the December launch of unlimited pricing. We thought that there would be some problems with busy signals during our peak periods in some cities. . . . But we expected those problems to be modest, and not too long in duration."

AOL has tried to decrease the "busy signal" by increasing the size and the pace of the system capacity expansion, by bringing in new hardware, installing circuits, adding 150,000 new modems, increasing the number of customer service representatives to 4,000, offering a toll-free line, and reducing marketing efforts. Mr. Case even asked the customers for help by moderating their own use of AOL during peak hours.

Even so, AOL became fodder for comics and lawsuits. In one comic strip, the customer is shown on the telephone conversing with "customer service":

Caller: "I am not getting my money's worth with your online service."

Service: "Good news, sir! We have just cut our rates."

Caller: "Your lines are always busy . . . I can't get online!"

Service: "Don't forget you get unlimited time online for no extra charge."

A number of AOL customers filed lawsuits against the company in more than 37 states, charging the firm with civil fraud, breach of contract, negligence, and violation of state consumer-protection statutes. The negative publicity from the "busy signals" allowed other online providers the opportunity to expand their number of subscribers and increase their revenues from advertising and merchandising fees.

America Online began a refund offer to its members, and the Attorneys General in several states agreed to support its proposed plan to members. The plan gives customers a refund policy: customers had a choice of a free month online or up to $39.90—the cost of two months of its unlimited service. In addition, AOL increased customer service staffing to handle member cancellations so that calls were answered within two minutes. Also, AOL gave customers the opportunity to cancel their membership through mail, fax, or toll-free number.

In the meantime America Online was facing another legal problem, this time from its shareholders. On February 24, 1997, shareholders sued in U.S. District Court in Virginia alleging that AOL directors and outside accountants violated securities laws in the way the company did its accounting. The online giant took a $385 million charge in October 1996 for marketing expenses it had capitalized.

The various problems facing America Online raised serious doubts among analysts about its ability to meet its goal to earn $60 million in fiscal year 1998 (ending in June) without more revenues from sources outside of operations. An analyst with Smith, Barney & Company believed that the $1.7 billion company has a cash flow problem which could force AOL to raise cash through bank loans or another stock offering—which would be the company's fourth. "The worst time to go to the market—is when you need to," notes Abe Mastbaum, money manager of American Securities.

Prior to 1997, AOL was able to maintain its positive cash flow through the addition of new members. Due to overload of the system, brought on by flat-rate pricing, new members cannot be added as aggressively as needed. The company will have to develop new sources of revenue, such as online advertising and fees on electronic transfers, or charge additional fees for premium channels. AOL launched its first premium channel in July of 1997. Its premium games channel allows people from around the world to play both traditional games, such as hearts, and new games against each other. It charges $2 per hour for the premium games channel.

Since AOL did not have the infrastructure in place to handle the increased usage that came with the revised pricing structure, America Online planned to hold its membership at 8 million and spend $350 million to expand system capacity and customer support. At least that was the plan before the Compuserve acquisition.

In April 1997, rumors were heard about AOL acquiring CompuServe from H&R Block. America Online declined to comment. CompuServe said the company is in "external discussions" regarding a deal. Buying CompuServe would add much-needed network capacity to AOL's strained system. Those speculations gave a boost to both companies' stock: CompuServe's shares jumped 12 percent to $11; AOL's stock was up 7.6 percent to $45.75. A month before, CompuServe Corp. had quietly cut 500 jobs, or 14 percent of its work force, which was the latest evidence of the online company's troubles as it lost members in an intense competition with America Online and other rivals. The cuts left CompuServe's home office in Columbus, Ohio, with about 3,200 employees who are primarily online content and service specialists. At the same time CompuServe posted a $14 million quarterly loss and three days later the company's president and chief executive, Robert J. Massey, resigned. In September 1997, AOL traded ANS Access from Worldcom for CompuServe's online service.

Sun Microsystems: A High Growth, Loosely Organized Giant in a Constrained, Technology Intensive Environment

Walter E. Greene
University of Texas Pan American
William C. House
University of Arkansas–Fayetteville

Introduction

In 1982, four individuals, who were 27 years old, combined forces to found Sun Microsystems, with the objective of producing and marketing computer workstations to scientists and engineers. Two of the four were Stanford MBA graduates—Michigan born Scott McNealy, and Vinod Khosla, a native of India. They were joined by Andreas Bechtolsheim, a Stanford engineering graduate who had constructed a computer workstation with spare parts in order to perform numerical analysis, and Unix software expert William Joy from the Berkeley campus. Sun's founders believed there was demand for a desktop computer workstation costing between $10,000 and

The research and written case information was prepared by Wm. C. House of the University of Arkansas–Fayetteville, and Walter E. Greene, Professor, University of Texas Pan American for presentation at the North American Case Research Association Symposium (Atlanta, 1991).

$20,000 in a market niche ignored by minicomputer makers IBM, Data General, DEC, and Hewlett-Packard.

Sun Microsystems is the market leader in the fast-growing workstation industry, expecting sales revenue growth of 30 percent annually during the next five years compared to 5 to 10 percent for the personal computer industry. Workstations can be used in standalone fashion or as part of networked configurations. The product lines produced range from low priced diskless units to higher powered graphics oriented stations at the top of the line.

In contrast to personal computers, workstations are characterized by 32-bit instead of 16-bit microprocessors, a strong tendency to use the UNIX operating system instead of MS/DOS, more sophisticated software and graphics capabilities, larger storage capacities, faster processing speeds and the ability to function effectively in a networking environment. The principal users of workstations have been engineers and scientists. However, price reductions and technological improvements have broadened the appeal of workstations so that they are finding use in financial trading, desktop publishing, animation, mapping, and medical imaging applications.

Sun, the fastest growing company in the computer hardware industry, has revenues that are increasing at a five year compounded rate of 85 percent and income increasing at a 67 percent rate from 1985 to 1990.[3] For fiscal year 1991, Sun's revenues were $3.2 billion and net income was $190 million.[13] The company's rapid growth rate has severely drained its cash resources.

Chairman and CEO of Sun Microsystems

Scott McNealy, the current chairman of Sun, is a native of Detroit and grew up on the fringes of the U.S. automobile industry. Originally rejected by both Harvard and Stanford Business Schools, he graduated from Harvard with a major in economics. In 1981, at the age of 26, McNealy became manufacturing director at Onyx systems, a small minicomputer maker. The company was faced with serious quality problems. In two months, the operation showed drastic improvement as McNealy probed work rules and production bottlenecks, encouraging workers to identify problems and overcome obstacles on the way toward improving workplace efficiency.

In 1982, former Stanford classmates Andy Bechtolsheim and Vinod Khosla asked him to join them as Director of Operations in a new company to be called Sun Microsystems. Two years later, McNealy was chosen by the Board of Directors to be CEO over Paul Ely, now executive vice president of Unisys. During the first month after he became CEO, one of the three cofounders resigned, the company lost $500,000 on $2 million in sales, and two-thirds of its computers didn't work.

He is a workaholic, working from daylight to dark, seven days a week, rarely finding time for recreation activities. The frantic pace at Sun engendered by McNealy is sometimes referred to as Sunburn. There is a tendency for Sun executives to take on too many projects at once, thereby creating tremendous internal pressure and organizational chaos.

McNealy's philosophy can be capsuled in these company sayings[9]:

1. On Decision-making—Consensus if possible, but participation for sure.
2. On Management Cooperation—Agree and commit, disagree and commit, or just get the hell out of the way.
3. On Market Response—The right answer is the best answer. The wrong answer is second best. No answer is the worst.
4. On Individual Initiative—To ask permission is to seek denial.

He has stated that the company is trying to achieve four goals—significant increases in revenue and book value, improved product acceptance, and higher profit margins.

Chief Computer Designer

Andreas Bechtolsheim, chief computer designer, was one of Sun's cofounders. At age 35 he has the title of vice president of technology. A native of West Germany, Bechtolsheim designed his first computer in 1980 while still a graduate student at Stanford University. It was a workstation designed for scientists and engineers. However, he was unable to sell the idea to any computer company then in existence. Shortly thereafter, he joined Joy, Khosla, and McNealy in founding Sun Microsystems and the company's first product was based on his machine.

Initially, Bechtolsheim persuaded Sun to use off-the-shelf products to develop its workstations instead of following the usual industry practice of utilizing proprietary components. This meant that company products would be easy for competitors to copy, but it also allowed quick entry into the marketplace. As nonproprietary open systems came to be more widely accepted, competitors such as Apollo, DEC, and IBM encountered problems in keeping pace with product lines that lacked the flexibility and performance of Sun's products. When Steve Jobs formed Next, Inc., and announced the development of a desktop workstation, Bechtolsheim urged Sun officials to build a truly desktop computer. There was considerable resistance to the project, and he almost left the company at that point. Because the company has had a culture based on building bigger boxes, the new sparcstation was widely criticized within the company as being too small. However, Bechtolsheim stubbornly refused to change the specifications and eventually prevailed.

Field Operations Director

Carol Bartz, National Sales Director and the number two executive at Sun Microsystems, has about half of the company's 12,000 employees reporting to her. Bartz attended the University of Wisconsin, receiving a Bachelor of Computer Science degree in 1971. After that, she spent seven years with Digital Equipment Corporation. Since joining Sun in 1983, she has become intimately involved in supervising field support activities and a subdivision that sells to federal governmental agencies. According to Bob Herwick, an investment analyst, Bartz is a very effective problem solver, turning around a sluggish service organization and ensuring that the company fully exploited the market potential in the government market.[5]

Team and Consensus Management at Sun

McNealy, current Sun chairman, attended Cranbrook, a North Detroit prep school. While there, he excelled in a variety of activities including music, tennis, golf, and ice hockey. According to Alan De Clerk, a high school classmate, McNealy developed a strong self-image and competitive spirit as a result of participating in sports activities and competing with two brothers and a sister. Through the years he has approached all activities as if they were team sports.

McNealy's efforts to build consensus among executives before a decision is made have become famous throughout the company. As he has stated, "Give me a draw and I'll make the decision but I won't issue an edict if a large majority is in favor of

EXHIBIT 1   A Comparison of Performance Measures for Major Workstation Makers

Source: J. A. Savage, "Price Takes Backseat with Users," *Computerworld*, September 2, 1991, p. 4.

	Price	Specmarks	Price per Specmark
Hewlett Packard 9000	11,990	55.5	216.00
Sun Sparcstation ELC	4,995	20.1	248.50
IBM RS/6000	13,992	32.8	426.50
Sun Sparcstation IPX	13,495	24.2	557.60

an alternative proposal."[9] A frequently quoted example occurred in 1988 when he stubbornly resisted changing prices at a time when rapidly increasing memory costs were reducing profit margins. With a consensus arrayed against him, he finally agreed to some product price increases which were enacted without reducing sales. In fact, he has a hard time saying no to any project pushed by one or more company groups. He demands complete loyalty within his concept of teamwork and becomes very angry if he believes that individuals or teams have let him down.[9]

Product Line Focus

The Sparcstation I was introduced in April 1989 at a stripped down price of $9,000. A lower priced version was introduced in May of 1990, costing $5,000. The machine processes data at 12 mips and runs about twice as fast as personal computers. Sun expected the lower price to facilitate sales to large companies who base computer purchases on quantity discounts. However, the low end sparcstation does not have disk drives, color monitors, or add-in slots. Therefore, it must be networked and cannot be used as a standalone unit.

An improved version of Sparc I was introduced in the summer of 1990 with an improved graphical interface, a color monitor, and sales price of $10,000. Sun has asserted that a personal computer with the same characteristics as the IPC would cost $15,000 to $20,000 and would have only about one third the processing power of this workstation model. The Sparcstation is now Sun's top seller among all its product lines and Sparcstation products produce 80 to 90 percent of total company revenues.

Exhibit 1 shows prices and specmarks (a measure of processing power and speed) for two Sun models as well as for the latest Hewlett Packard and IBM workstation models. From this table, the relative performance of the Sun computers in terms of computing power per dollar can be compared with its major competitors.

Company Strategy

Early on, Sun executives believed that they only had a short time to focus on growing demand for computer workstations from scientists and engineers before large companies such as IBM, DEC, and Hewlett Packard would aggressively move into that market niche. Therefore, company strategy was designed to emphasize gaining market share, concentrating on all out sales growth, no matter what the cost. At one point, the organization was adding more than 300 employees and a new sales office each month. Company engineers developed a steady stream of innovative but sometimes impractical prototypes. Products were sold largely by word of mouth with virtually no formal sales promotion programs.

As part of the market share focus, in the mid-80s the company began creating autonomous divisions to develop and market its products. This policy allowed rapid movement into such market areas as sales to government agencies, universities, and financial institutions. The autonomous groups did create unnecessary duplication and contributed to development costs that were almost twice the industry average. When attempts were made to consolidate functions, fierce turf battles resulted and top executives were forced to step in and referee the conflicts.

The market share/sales growth emphasis created many unexpected problems. Needed investments in customer service and data processing activities had to be postponed. The existence of independent, autonomous divisions caused numerous difficulties for both sales and manufacturing activities. At one point, the company had more than 10,000 computer and option combinations to keep track of. Three different product lines based on three different microprocessors—Sparc, Motorola 68000, and Intel 386—required excessive investment and extensive coordination to ensure that they all worked on the same network. Overlaps and duplications in marketing and finance made forecasting all but impossible. At its current size the company can no longer scramble madly to meet shipping deadlines at the last minute.

By the summer of 1989, the company was experiencing production bottlenecks as discounted sales of older products mushroomed. Demand for newer products also increased faster than expected. Large backlogs of sales orders were not being entered in the inventory control system, preventing the company from knowing how many or what kinds of products it needed to produce.

In the last quarter of 1989, Sun experienced a $20 million loss due to misjudging consumer demand for its new Sparcstation and incurring parts shortages. A new management information system produced inaccurate parts forecasts which contributed to order snafus and lower earnings. However, it posted a $5 million profit in the first quarter of 1990. Sun produced revenues of $2.5 billion in fiscal 1990 and expected to achieve revenues of $3.3 billion in 1991.[8] Sun is now changing its approach to place more emphasis on profitability and less on growth, on expanding customer service and hiring fewer employees. Sun President McNealy has recently tied executive pay to before tax return on investment. In the 1989 annual report he stated that he desired performance to be judged on the basis of significant increases in revenues, acceptance of new products, improvements in profit margins, and increases in book value.

McNealy was one of the early pioneers pushing open systems which would allow computers of many different manufacturers to be linked together in networks. In fact, Sun has actually encouraged competition with itself through its focus on open systems development and invited the industry to build Sparc based clones in order to expand the position of the workstation industry. As the percentage of total Sparc based computers sold by Sun has begun to decline, Sun appears to be changing its position on clones. Recently, it told its own dealers they would incur Sun's displeasure if they sold Sun clones along with Sun workstations. Many of these dealers are angry at what they perceive to be Sun's arrogance.

Sun has consistently maintained a narrow product line focus. It has gradually phased out all microprocessors except Sparc and has concentrated on low-end workstations with the greatest market share growth possibilities. It has avoided entering markets for higher priced lines and the personal computer segment with emphasis on low price and compactness. However, recently Sun announced plans to move into high end workstation markets where processing speed and power requirements necessitate linking a series of microprocessors and using sophisticated software. Sun may encounter problems in this market similar to those it experienced in product upgrades of its lower level models, since it does not have a good record in managing product introductions.

As workstations become more powerful and less expensive, workstation manufacturers face a serious challenge in maintaining profit margins. Current models now combine high functionality with high volume, in contrast to an earlier focus on producing highly functional units in small quantities. Extensive use of application specific integrated circuits with fewer components reduces system size, increases reliability, and lowers product costs. Sun and other companies increasingly follow the practice of involving manufacturing representatives in the design process as early as possible in order to minimize manufacturing problems. Increased attention is also being paid to maintaining product quality and improving product testing before systems are shipped.

In past years, Sun's strategies have included focusing on lower prices, well developed marketing programs and third party software development. From 1,500 to 2,000 applications are available for the Sun Sparcstation compared to approximately 1,000 for Hewlett Packard and DEC. The company is licensing its Sparc chip to third party clone companies with the desire of expanding the installed RISC computer base. The overall company goal is to deliver a complete processing solution, including graphics, input/output, software, and networking.

Distribution Channels and Customer Service

Workstation makers have traditionally sold their units using manufacturers' sales forces and specialized hardware resellers, who repackage specialized software with other companies' workstations. Sun has about 300 VARS (i.e., value added resellers) compared to more than 500 for Hewlett Packard with Digital and IBM falling somewhere in between. Some authorities think the majority of VARs are not capable of selling workstations.[11] Sun is now considering the possibility of selling some of its models through retailers such as Microage in a manner similar to personal computer sales now made by IBM, COMPAQ, and Apple. Such a move would reduce selling and inventory costs but is meeting initial resistance from dealers unaccustomed to handling complex workstation models.

Sun still sells a large number of workstations through its 1,000 person salesforce. In July 1990, Sun selected 200 dealers from three retail chains and gave them training in selling workstations. The company expects to sell $30 million of workstations through retail dealers in fiscal 1990, but a full-fledged dealer network may require several years to develop. Because of the higher average selling prices and greater product differentiation and uniqueness of workstations compared to personal computers, many PC vendors are expressing interest in handling workstations in spite of the small volumes generated.

One area of concern has been Sun's field service organization, which has not been very effective in supporting customer software. Bartz has stated that the company wants to improve on customer service without making large monetary expenditures or building a dinosaur service group.[2] In line with this, Sun has announced plans to start using company trained, third party service personnel who can be dispatched to customer locations on demand.

Customer Categories

The workstation market for engineers and scientists is rapidly becoming saturated. About one-third of Sun's customers now come from the commercial side, up from only 10 percent several years ago. The company is now concentrating more of its efforts on airlines, banks, insurance and finance companies, trying to persuade users to utilize Sun workstations to solve new problems. Sun Vice-President Eric Schmidt says that Sun tends to get early adopters of new technology.[7] Often, by starting with a pilot program that proves successful, workstations can be expanded to other areas in a customer's operations. Eastman Kodak began using Sun workstations in engineering design and soon expanded their use of marketing databases and mailroom operations.

Sun machines are being used by Wall Street firms Merrill Lynch, Shearson/ Lehman/Hutton and Bear/Sterns on the trading floor. Northwest Airlines uses 500 workstations in Minneapolis to monitor ticket usage, checking the correctness of air fare charges and the impact of flight delays or cancellations on revenues and profits. To increase customer satisfaction, Sun has had to change product designs, to make its machines easier to install, and to improve understandability of product manuals. As Sun has discovered, commercial customers need more help than engineers.

Dataquest says that by 1994, 29.1 percent of workstation sales will be made to commercial users as opposed to scientific/engineering users in a market expected to reach $22 billion.[16] Workstation makers are moving into the personal computer area by offering Unix versions that will run on both workstations and on personal computers. Workstations provide much greater computing power at a lower cost than would be required to enhance a personal computer so that it possessed the equivalent capability of a typical workstation. Workstations seem to be making their biggest inroads into CPU intensive applications formerly done on mainframes (e.g., stock transactions, airline reservations).

Sun's first major TV advertising effort occurred in April 1991 and took the form of a 30-second commercial seen on CNN, ESPN, and the three major TV networks. The commercial was not directed specifically at a consumer audience, but instead was an attempt to get broad exposure for a new message beamed at the business market. Sun expected the advertisement to reach 59 percent of U.S. households and 42 percent of the target market of senior level corporate and computer executives. The campaign also included an eight-page insert in *The Wall Street Journal*.

Sun's advertising budget of approximately $4.6 million in 1990 was spent on computer and general interest business publications. Sun's advertising budget is only about 0.25 percent of sales revenues compared to 1.0 to 1.5 percent spent by its major competitors. Some observers have questioned the cost-effectiveness of a high priced TV advertisement by a company which sells high priced computers to a limited group of customers.

Software Developments

Availability of software still remains a major problem in expanding sales of workstations. Only about 5 to 10 percent of UNIX based software is designed for business and commercial applications. Sun is trying to sign up software developers to produce UNIX based versions of many common personal computer products. It now has UNIX based versions of popular PC software, including Lotus 1–2–3 and DBASE IV. It hopes the increased availability of software plus the narrowing cost gap between low end workstations and high end personal computers will help it penetrate the personal computer market. However, it must sell users on the benefit/cost performance of workstations compared to personal computers and also needs to expand its existing base of software developers.

The type of software to be run is often the determining factor in deciding between a personal computer or workstation. For productivity and business applications, PCs can be more cost efficient. For technical and graphics applications, workstations are more appropriate. Differences in costs are no longer a differentiating factor.

An entrenched personal computer MS/DOS operating system base and lack of commercial workstation software have hampered a switch from high end personal computers to workstations. MS/DOS based computers appear adequate for a majority of user needs, especially with the advent of the Windows operating environment. PC users are more likely to change if complex applications such as multimedia, integrated data base, or windowing become desirable rather than on the basis of price alone. Workstations may become less attractive if 80846-based personal computers with considerably more computing power than today's systems become more widely available.

Product/price performance is no longer as important a differentiating factor as it used to be. Software availability and usability are increasing in importance. In recognition of this, Sun has formed two software subsidiaries—one for application software and one to concentrate on improvements in the Unix operating system. The Open Look Graphical Interface has been added to make Sun products more user friendly. The key to maintaining market position seems to be improving systems software and selling software developers and users on the benefits of workstations over other hardware options.

Sun has announced that it will release a new version of its operating system designed to run on Intel based personal computers. Some analysts say that Sun will face a stiff test in competing with Microsoft's DOS/Windows combination and that it is a defensive move, made in realization that Sun no longer can generate enough revenue from its own machines to meet its growth goals. McNealy denies that the Sun announcement is defensive, saying that high powered PC owners will move to Sun's operating systems to take advantage of advanced capabilities (e.g., running multiple programs simultaneously) which is something that has been vaguely promised by Microsoft's Windows new NT versions.[13] McNealy has sharply criticized Windows NT version, referring to it as illusionary or not there.

Sun's Solaris operating system will not be available until mid-1991, and will work on both Intel's X86 series and Sun's Sparc processors. The new operating system will make it easier for Sun's customers to link Sun workstations with other computers in a network and increase the number of Sun users. Sun hopes that this will encourage independent software houses to write new programs for Sun OS. So far, approximately 3,500 application programs are available for Sun OS compared with more than 20,000 for IBM-compatible personal computers.[12]

Competition in the Marketplace

Although still the market leader, Sun is facing increasing competition from much larger computer companies. Sun shipped 146,000 workstations in 1990 (39 percent of the market) out of a total of 376,000 and is expected to ship 200,000 in 1991.[4] Having fully absorbed Apollo into its organization, Hewlett Packard is selling about two-thirds as many workstations as Sun, with about 20 percent of the market, and DEC, which has completely reworked its product lines, has about 17 percent of the workstation market. Hewlett Packard has also introduced a new workstation model comparable in price to the sparcstation, which runs about twice as fast as Sun's current

EXHIBIT 2   Computer Workstation Market Shares

Company	1989	1990
Sun Microsystems	30.4%	38.8%
Hewlett Packard	26.1	20.1
Digital Equipment	26.6	17.0
Intergraph	7.0	3.8
IBM	1.2	4.5
Silicon Graphics	5.1	2.6
Sony	—	3.3
Next	—	2.6
Other	3.6	7.0
Total	100.0%	100.0%

model. Exhibit 2 shows the 1989 and 1990 market shares for the major firms in the workstation market.

IBM has made a significant comeback in the workstation market with the RS/6000, after its first workstation model proved to be a slow seller. In 1990, IBM shifted more than 25,000 workstations, producing revenue of 1 billion dollars and attaining a market share of 6.6 percent or more than double its 1989 market share.[4] In 1991, some analysts estimate IBM will sell between $2 and $3 billion of workstations. IBM has a stated goal of overtaking Sun by 1993, achieving a 30 percent market share, although some experts predict it is more likely to achieve a 15 percent market share by that date.[14]

With the workstation market expected to exceed 20 billion dollars by the mid-1990s, competition is expected to be fierce. IBM's late entry, entrenched positions of competitors in the market, lack of a low-priced entry level model, and the use of nonstandard operating and graphics environments are likely to hamper its efforts to achieve a market share much above 15 percent.[6] IBM's service and sales reputation, its large reseller base, and strong position in commercial markets should give the company leverage to enter the fast growing markets for network servers and small or branch office multiuser systems. However, if IBM focuses its efforts on penetrating these markets with its RS/6000, it runs a serious risk of undercutting sales of the AS/400.

Cost no longer seems to be the primary factor in decisions to acquire workstations. Workers must become more accustomed to graphic as opposed to character based systems before adoption by current PC users becomes more widespread. Some companies feel that workstations have yet to demonstrate significant productivity advantages over personal computers. The biggest shortcomings of workstations are lack of application software and integration difficulties.

Financial Analysis

Exhibit 3 shows revenues, expenses, and income for the five-year period 1986 to 1990. Revenues have increased at a more rapid rate than net income during the period being considered. Return on sales has declined significantly to 4.5 percent from the peak of almost 7 percent in 1987 with revenue per shipment also declining in 1990 compared to 1989 and 1988. Book value per share and unit shipments have increased significantly during the five years.

EXHIBIT 3   Revenues, Expenses, and Income for Five Years (billions of $)

Source: Adapted from 1990 Annual Report.

	1990	1989	1988	1987	1986
Net revenues	2,466	1,765	1,052	538	210
Cost of sales	1,399	1,010	550	273	102
Gross profit	1,067	755	502	265	108
R&D outlays	302	234	140	70	31
Selling, adm. & general expenses	588	433	250	127	57
Total	890	667	390	197	88
Operating income	177	88	111	68	20
Interest income	(23)	(10)	(302)	834	369
Income taxes	43	17	44	33	9
Net income	111	61	66	36	11
Net income/sales	4.5%	3.4%	6.3%	6.8%	5.3%
Net income/share	1.21	0.76	0.89	0.55	0.21
Book value/share	9.82	7.77	4.75	3.57	2.04
Unit shipment (000'S)	118.3	80.7	48.4	24.6	9.9
Revenue/unit shipped (000'S)	20.8	21.9	21.7	21.8	21.2

EXHIBIT 4   Computer Industry Data for Years 1989 and 1990

Source: *Business Week*, 1000 Companies, 1991, 1990.

Company	Sales Growth		Income Growth		Asset Growth		Net Inc./Sales		Mkt. Value/ Equity	
	1990	1989	1990	1989	1990	1989	1990	1989	1990	1989
Apple	1.07	1.21	1.14	1.05	1.12	1.24	8.7	8.2	4.81	3.21
Compaq	1.25	1.39	1.36	1.31	1.30	1.31	12.6	11.6	3.26	3.31
Dec	1.01	1.05	0.00	0.72	1.03	1.10	−.72	6.8	1.21	1.13
Hew Pck	1.10	1.20	0.95	0.97	1.09	1.31	5.7	6.6	1.83	1.98
Intrgrph	1.21	1.07	0.79	0.80	1.06	0.97	6.0	9.2	1.79	1.73
IBM	1.10	1.05	1.60	0.68	1.30	1.06	8.7	6.0	1.75	1.62
NCR	1.06	0.99	0.90	0.94	1.01	0.95	5.9	6.9	3.54	3.40
Silgrphs	1.41	1.73	1.97	1.94	1.37	0.94	8.3	5.9	3.57	4.30
Sun Mcrs	1.34	1.41	318.	0.40	1.49	1.50	5.5	1.8	2.72	1.41
Wang	0.87	0.90	0.00	0.00	0.72	0.87	−6.7	−13.9	1.27	0.87
Avg.	1.14	1.20	32.7	0.88	1.15	1.12	5.4	4.9	2.58	2.37

Exhibit 4 indicates that Sun's sales, income and asset growth are higher than the industry average in 1990 and 1989 with the market value/equity ratio also above the industry average. However, the net income/sales ratio was below the industry average in 1989 and slightly above the industry average in 1990. As Exhibit 5 indicates, Sun appears to be very close to the industry average in terms of two common productivity measures, sales/assets and sales/employee. In reviewing the common leverage measures, Sun is well above the industry average for R&D expenses/revenues and R&D expenses/employee.

EXHIBIT 5   Computer Industry Data for Years 1989 and 1988

Source: *Business Week* 1000 Companies, 1991; Innovation in America, Special *Business Week* Issues, 1990, 1988.

Company	Sales/ Assets		Sales/ Employee		Adv. Exps./ Sales		R&D Exps./ Sales		R&D Exps./ Employee	
	1990	1989	1989	1988	1989	1988	1989	1988	1989	1988
Apple	1.82	1.91	364	377	7.34	8.30	8.0	6.7	28,937	25,233
Compaq	1.32	1.38	303	289	1.75	2.87	4.6	3.6	13,945	10,849
Dec	1.13	1.15	101	94	1.38	1.01	12.0	11.4	12,123	10,753
Hew Pck	1.22	1.21	125	113	2.69	2.35	10.7	10.4	13,358	11,713
Intrgrph	1.20	1.07	105	110	1.00	1.00	10.6	11.1	11,157	12,216
IBM	0.79	0.81	164	154	1.17	0.44	8.3	7.4	13,572	11,415
NCR	1.38	1.32	106	100	1.06	0.53	7.5	7.0	7,964	6,940
Silgrphs	1.22	1.19	180	105	1.00	1.00	11.9	15.8	21,150	21,908
Sun Mcrs	1.27	1.41	172	148	1.00	0.74	13.3	13.3	22,934	19,733
Wang	1.35	1.12	109	97	1.00	1.02	9.8	8.7	10,543	8,510
Avg.	1.27	1.26	173	159	2.64	1.93	9.7	9.5	15,568	14,027

End Notes

1. Susan E. Fisher, "Vendors Court Reseller Partners as Workstations Go Mainstream," *PC Week,* July 30, 1990.
2. Jonathan B. Levine, "High Noon for Sun," *Business Week,* July 24, 1989, pp. 71, 74.
3. John Markoff, "The Smart Alecs at Sun Are Regrouping," *New York Times,* April 28, 1991.
4. Andrew Ould, "IBM Challenges Sun in Workstation Market," *PC Week,* February 28, 1991.
5. Andrew Ould, "Carol Bartz: Star Is Still Rising for Hard Driving Executive," *PC Week,* September 3, 1990.
6. Andrew Ould, "What's Behind Lower Workstation Prices," *UNIX World,* July 1990.
7. Julie Pitta, "The Trojan Horse Approach," *Forbes,* April 15, 1991.
8. Kathy Rebello, "Sun Microsystems on the Rise Again," *USA Today,* April 20, 1990.
9. "Sun Microsystems Turn on the Afterburners," *Business Week,* July 18, 1988.
10. G. Paschal Zachary, "Sparc-station's Success Is Doubly Sweet for Sun Microsystem's Bechtolsheim," *The Wall Street Journal,* May 29, 1990.
11. Fisher, op. cit.
12. Robert D. Hof, "Why Sun Can't Afford to Shine Alone," *Business Week,* September 9, 1991.
13. G. Paschal Zachary, "Sun Challenges Microsoft's Hold over Software," *The Wall Street Journal,* September 4, 1991.
14. Bob Francis, "Big Blue's Red Hot Workstation," *Datamation,* October 15, 1990.
15. Lawrence Curran, "HP Speeds Up Workstation Race," *Electronics,* April 1991.
16. "Getting Down to Business," *Information Week,* January 14, 1991.

Case
Group F

Social and Ethical Issues in Marketing Management

Case

27

Notetakers Company: Selling Class Notes and Instructional Notes to Students

S. J. Garner and Judy Spain
both of Eastern Kentucky University

Company Background

Kevin and Jennifer own a business called Notetakers which is located in a strip mall near the campus of a major midwestern university. They started their business a year ago with start-up funds of $5,000. The small storefront contains a counter, a price board, a leased copier, a cabinet full of copier paper, a telephone and three file cabinets. Their product? Class notes.

Each semester, Kevin and Jennifer recruit honor students who are enrolled in large auditorium sections of popular general education classes and some business

This case was written by professors Garner and Spain of Eastern Kentucky University, Department of Management and Marketing.

courses such as beginning marketing and beginning management. The honor students are paid to take and transcribe notes of the classes in which they are enrolled. Each student receives $50 for each "module" of class notes which are delivered to Notetakers one week before a course exam is scheduled. Most courses contain three or four modules (each of which is several weeks long). The honor students also receive a royalty of five percent of the gross sales of each module.

Kevin and Jennifer make copies of the class notes and sell them to students enrolled in the classes. Each module sells for six to ten dollars, depending on the length of the notes. Each module is printed with a cover sheet containing the name of the university, the name and section number of the course, room number, professor's name and time that the class meets. Copies are also included of any handouts given by that particular professor in class.

Kevin originally had the idea for this service because he is dyslexic and had difficulty taking coherent notes when he was in school. He had also noticed that students with ADD (attention deficit disorder) had similar problems. Jennifer estimates that thirty to forty percent of the note copies they sell are to disabled students. Students who have missed class due to illness or for other reasons also purchase note modules.

Notetakers offers no guarantee as to the accuracy of the notes they sell. They do place a written notice on each module warning students that they should compare the notes to others taken in class and the textbook materials.

Modules are available for around thirty-six classes currently. But more are added as honor students are recruited and class sizes increase. Currently, each notetaker makes around $300 per course per semester.

The business is open from 8:00 to 5:00 five days a week. Kevin and Jennifer split the counter duties, each spending approximately four and a half hours a day receiving, copying and selling notes. They currently have 20 honor students employed as notetakers.

Business expenses include storefront rental, utilities, supplies, copier lease costs, royalties and base payments to employee notetakers. These expenses total 55 percent of gross receipts. The other 45 percent is split between Kevin and Jennifer.

Notetakers has relied on two promotional methods during its first year of operation. Promotional flyers, designed by Jennifer, are handed out to students visiting the strip center during the first two weeks of class. Kevin and Jennifer merely stand in the door of their shop and hand the flyers to passing students. Secondly, as a condition of their shop lease, they have the strip center's permission to place their flyers on every car parked at the center which has a university parking tag hung on its mirror. So far, these two methods have generated some word-of-mouth among the student population.

Kevin feels that some additional promotion would increase their store traffic and also assist them in recruiting more notetakers to cover more classes. He feels that an advertisement in the student newspaper would be cost-effective and generate maximum exposure to their specific target market without adding waste circulation. Jennifer has designed a six inch by two column ad for use in the newspaper (see Exhibit 1). Kevin has discovered that the base rate for black and white ads is four dollars per column inch for a single insertion. Each insertion will therefore cost $48. (Two columns × six inches × $4 = $48.)

Kevin plans to insert the advertisement four times during the coming semester in the weekly college newspaper. The first two insertions will be during the first two weeks of class, the third insertion will be the week before midterm exams and the fourth the week before final exams take place. He has written a check for the first two insertions and mailed it along with a camera ready copy of the ad to the student newspaper.

EXHIBIT 1   Notetakers Newspaper Ad

Miss a few classes?
Have trouble taking notes?

Let

NOTETAKERS

help!!!

We have notes available for over 36 auditorium section classes. All our notes are taken and transcribed by currently enrolled honor students. Call today for prices and sections available.

NOTETAKERS
31 Oak St. in the Campus Strip Center
8–5 Monday through Friday
555 - 706 - NOTE

Bad News Arrives

A week after mailing the ad to the student newspaper, Notetakers received the following letter in the mail.

> Dear Owners of Notetakers:
>
> I am returning your check and advertisement. It is my feeling that the service you provide has the effect of encouraging students to cut classes and thus miss a large part of their education. I do not feel it is ethical for you to provide this service and I certainly do not feel it would be ethical of me to allow this ad to be run in the student newspaper.
>
> Sincerely,
>
> Bob Richardson
> Retail Advertising Manager

Kevin showed the letter to Jennifer and said, "This isn't fair at all! I've seen ads for beer and adult movies and videos in the newspaper—why are they picking on us? To say our business is unethical is very hypocritical!" Jennifer replied, "It was probably the faculty advisor who rejected the ad. Why don't you call and ask to speak with the advisor. Maybe you can change his mind."

Two days later Kevin told Jennifer that he had spoken to the newspaper's faculty advisor. The advisor told Kevin that he had not banned the ad. He left the decision up to the newspaper advertising manager and told him that he would have to stand behind his own decision. He also said that this was not the first ad to be rejected by the newspaper. Other ads which had been turned down included one from a group that wanted people to appear in a documentary "debunking" the Holocaust as a myth and another for a "stripper" pen featuring a woman who disrobed whenever the pen was tilted.

Kevin went on to say that the advisor also told him that he thought that Notetakers was doing a disservice to students by selling these notes, that it is a well-known fact that students who attend class learn more and make better grades and that Notetakers was encouraging negative behavior. To top it all off, the advisor said he had sent a copy of the Notetakers ad to the university lawyers to see if they could do anything to prevent Notetakers from stealing the intellectual property of the professors teaching these classes and using the name of the university!

More Bad News Arrives

Four weeks after the rejection letter arrived, Jennifer called Kevin at home and said, "You better get down here in a hurry to meet with our lawyer. We're being sued! The university just had us served with papers. As near as I can tell, they are saying we have infringed on their trademarks by having the name of the university, the course numbers, sections and dates on our covers. There is also something about some of the professors who teach the courses we have notes for having contracts with publishers to produce study guides based on their class notes. The publishers hold the copyrights on these materials. What are we going to do?"

Kevin and Jennifer met with their attorney, Steve King. Steve reviewed the advertisement, the cover sheet, and samples of the note packets. He told Kevin and Jennifer that the university was alleging a violation of the Lanham Trade-Mark Act of 1964, 15 U.S.C. sec. 1125(a).

The Lanham Act prohibits anyone from engaging in misrepresentation of origin and deceptive advertising regarding the origin of the notes. Specifically, Steve stated that the university is contending that because Notetakers used the course number, name, etc., on the cover sheet, it created confusion as to the actual source of the notes.

After talking to the attorney, Kevin and Jennifer were really confused. What should they do? Should they stop producing the notes and close their business? Were they really in violation of the law? If not in violation of the law, were they really acting unethically as the Advertising Manager said?

Case 28

Nintendo versus SEGA: Sex, Violence, and Videogames

Romuald A. Stone
James Madison University

Violence in America in 1994 was considered by many people to have reached epidemic proportions. All across the United States—in cities and towns large and small—citizens were increasingly fearful and concerned that violence was out of control. What was causing this violent behavior? There was no easy answer. But many experts said that the pervasive violence in television programming, films, and videogames was one seed that promoted physical aggression in some individuals and helped create a culture tolerant of violence.

Just as television emerged as a powerful social and cultural force in the early 1950s, videogames were said to be emerging as a potentially powerful influence on children's behavior in the 1990s. While the impact of the growing violence in videogames was debatable, the years of research on violence in television programming provided instructive warning. According to Parker Page, president of the Children's Television Resource and Education Center, "years of research indicate that children who watch a steady diet of violent programming increase their chances of becoming more aggressive towards other children, less cooperative and altruistic, more tolerant of real life violence and more afraid of the world outside their homes."[1] The advent of virtual reality technology in videogame programming led Page to express a special concern in his testimony before a joint Senate subcommittee hearing held in December 1993.

> Mortal Kombat is simply the first in a new generation of video games that allows software designers to combine high levels of violence with fully digitalized human images. No more cute hedge hogs or cartoonish Super Mario Brothers—increasingly, the characters that a young player beheads, disembowels or crushes will look more

---

[1]U.S. Senate, Violence in Videogames: Joint Hearing of the Judiciary Subcommittee on Juvenile Justice and Government Affairs Subcommittee on Regulation and Government Information (testimony of Parker Page, PhD.), 103rd Cong., 1993.

and more like the kids at school, the neighbor who lives down the street or the young woman heading for aerobics class.[2]

Alarmed by the violent content of many videogames, parents and concerned citizens started lobbying for a comprehensive, industrywide videogame rating system that would give parents the information they needed to make informed choices. To address these concerns, Senators Lieberman and Kohl sponsored legislation to establish the National Independent Council for Entertainment in Video Devices as an independent agency of the federal government to oversee the development of "voluntary" standards to alert parents to the content of videogames. In his testimony before the hearing, Robert Chase, vice president of the National Education Association, expressed the collective concern of educators, children's advocates, and parents:

> America's children are faced with a bewildering set of messages from television, movies, music, electronic games, and print media. Too often, the almost unrelenting assault on the senses encouraging aggression and irresponsibility are in direct opposition to the values families hope to instill and the mores our society struggles to preserve. Parents, social scientists, and the community at large share deep trepidation about the fruits of this ever widening dispersal of negative images. The explosion of media in the latter half of this century has made the problem all the more pervasive and the challenges for parents and community leaders all the more difficult.[3]

At the same hearing, the Software Publishers Association (SPA) provided a counter argument:

> In our attempt to protect our children from those relatively few video games which contain unacceptable violence, however, we must not lose sight of the fact that the vast majority of videogames are appropriate for children, and have the potential for developing many important and socially desirable skills. As stated so eloquently by Bob Keeshan, otherwise known as Captain Kangaroo, "Video games . . . provide the potential for heretofore unknown opportunities for information, education and delightful entertainment. . . . The technology is to be encouraged because, used appropriately, such games can be a tool for education as well as entertainment."[4]

The SPA indicated in its testimony that the software entertainment industry was committed to moving quickly and decisively on this issue. The SPA was in the process of working with a coalition of concerned parties to establish a rating system that would be easy for consumers to understand and one that the industry could implement. Nintendo and SEGA had also initiated moves toward a rating system.

Nintendo's Position

When Nintendo entered the U.S. videogame industry in 1985, the company established written Game Content Guidelines requiring games marketed under the Nintendo Seal of Quality to meet the following standards:

- No sexually suggestive or explicit content.
- No sexist language or depictions.
- No random, gratuitous, or excessive violence.
- No graphic illustration of death.
- No domestic violence or abuse.

[2]Ibid.
[3]Ibid. (testimony of Robert Chase).
[4]Ibid. (testimony of Ilene Rosenthal).

- No excessive force in sports games.
- No ethnic, racial, religious, or sexual stereotypes.
- No profanity or obscenity.
- No use of drugs, smoking materials, or alcohol.
- No subliminal political messages or overt political statements.

As an example of Nintendo's pledge to control and monitor its game content, the company insisted that one of its largest licensees, Acclaim Entertainment, remove objectionable material from the controversial arcade game "Mortal Kombat." In its original form, the game included scenes in which characters' heads were ripped off, their spines were pulled out, they were impaled on spikes, and they spurted blood when hit. All of these graphics were deemed unacceptable and removed from the Nintendo version of the game. SEGA released the game in its entirety.

Some games had been simply rejected outright, since no amount of modification would make them acceptable to Nintendo. One such game was "Night Trap," which contained full motion videos of young, scantily clad females being attacked by hooded men who drilled holes in their bodies to suck out blood.

Howard Lincoln, Nintendo's then senior vice president (and later chairman), reiterated his company's continued commitment to wholesome family entertainment that was both challenging and exciting to youth while remaining nonoffensive to parents:

> This will remain our philosophy despite the fact we have been criticized by both video game players and others in our industry for taking what we feel is the only responsible approach . . . we believe our game guidelines have served us and our customers well for the past eight years. And we have no intention of abandoning this approach.[5]

However, Nintendo apparently decided to moderate its position following a raft of angry letters from users. Nintendo's 1994 holiday season new version of the "Mortal Kombat" game was just as gruesome as the arcade version.

Sega's Position[6]

In 1993, SEGA established a three-pronged approach designed to help parents determine the age-appropriateness of its stable of interactive video software. It included a rating classification system, a toll-free hotline, and an informational brochure. Building on the motion picture industry model, the SEGA rating system applied one of three classifications to each interactive video program it released:

GAF   For general audiences.
MA-13   For mature audiences age 13 and over.
MA-17   Adult appropriate, not suitable for those under age 17.

SEGA's toll-free hotline was staffed by professionals who could supplement the rating classification by informing parents about the specific content of each SEGA product. SEGA also offered its "Everybody Wins" brochure that provided additional information to shoppers at more than 2,800 retail stores. In addition, SEGA formed an independent Videogame Rating Council consisting of experts in the areas of psychology, sociology, cinema, and education to evaluate games and assign appropriate rating classifications. By the end of 1993, 173 SEGA titles had been rated with the

---

[5]Ibid. (testimony of Howard C. Lincoln).
[6]Ibid. (testimony of William White, vice president, SEGA of America Inc.).

EXHIBIT 1   Rating Guideline

Source: *The Washington Post.*

Interactive Digital Software Association (IDSA) is using five categories by age to rate video game cartridges such as Nintendo, Sega, Atari. They are:

- Early childhood, ages 3 and up
- Kids to adult, ages 6 and up
- Teen, ages 13 and up
- Mature, ages 17 and up
- Adults only

The Software Publishers Association (SPA) is using a label that shows the level of violence, sex, and strong language used in a computer software or CD-ROM game. Games with no offensive material receive a "Suitable for all audiences" label.

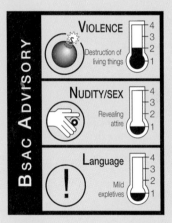

following distribution: 86 percent rated for general audiences (GA); 10 percent earned an MA-13 rating; and only 4 percent were targeted for exclusively adult (MA-17) audiences. To make SEGA's rating system work, the company decided that products bearing the MA-17 label should not be distributed to retail toy stores.

Progress Report[7]

In July 1994, the U.S. Senate subcommittee endorsed rating guidelines issued by an industry trade group, the Interactive Digital Software Association (IDSA)—see Exhibit 1. The IDSA ratings provided age guidance with five categories similar to those used by the Motion Picture Association of America. The ratings were expected to appear on videogame packages by mid-November, in time for the holiday season. Retailers who rent games planned to adhere to the ratings guidelines. Some mass merchants (Sears, Wal-Mart, Toys 'R' Us) had vowed to carry only rated videogames. An informal survey of retailers, however, revealed that large numbers of unrated games were on retailers' shelves for the 1994 seasonal buying rush.[8] Although the IDSA had rated more than 280 titles, the ratings were apparently completed after game packages were printed.

[7]M. Moran, "Retailers See Videogame Ratings as a Helpful Guide," *Video Business* 14, no. 32 (1994), pp. 12, 16.

[8]P. Farhi, "A Waiting Game for Rating Games," *The Washington Post,* December 24, 1994, p. D1.

The SPA encountered similar problems. At the end of 1994, only 40 CD-ROM and other software game titles had been rated. Exhibit 1 depicts SPA rating guidelines. Ken Wasch, executive director of the SPA, commented: "I wish more had been rated, but it took longer than we expected to get products submitted, to get them rated, and to get them out to the stores."[9]

There was no agreement among game producers on an industrywide rating system. Some observers believed the existence of several rating systems would confuse consumers. There also appeared to be a debate emerging whether widespread dissemination of rated products would ultimately hurt or help sales.

[9]Ibid.

Case 29

E. & J. Gallo Winery

A. J. Strickland III and Daniel C. Thurman
both of The University of Alabama

In the mid-1980s, alcohol consumption in the United States had been declining in virtually every category except low-priced wines. A number of producers in the wine industry did not believe they should be producing what they called skid-row wines (wines fortified with additional alcohol and sweetener and sold in screwtop, half-pint bottles). Richard Maher, president of Christian Brothers Winery in St. Helena, California, who once was with E. & J. Gallo Winery, said he didn't think Christian Brothers should market a product to people, including many alcoholics, who were down on their luck. "Fortified wines lack any socially redeeming values," he said.

Major producers of the low-end category of wines, called "dessert" or "fortified" (sweet wines with at least 14 percent alcohol), saw their customers otherwise. Robert Hunington, vice president of strategic planning at Canandiaqua (a national wine producer whose product, Wild Irish Rose, was the number one low-end wine), said 60 percent to 75 percent of its "pure grape" Wild Irish Rose was sold in primarily black, inner-city markets. Hunington described Wild Irish Rose's customer in this $500 million market as "not super-sophisticated," lower middle-class, and low-income blue-collar workers and mostly men. However, Canandiaqua also estimated the annual national market for dessert category wine to be 55 million gallons; low-end brands accounted for 43 million gallons, with as much as 50 percent sold in pints (typically the purchase choice of winos—alcoholics with a dependency on wine). Daniel Solomon, a Gallo spokesman, said Gallo's Thunderbird had lost its former popularity in the black and skid-row areas and was consumed mainly by retired and older people who didn't like the taste of hard distilled products or beer.[1]

Tony Mayes, area sales representative for Montgomery Beverage Company, Montgomery, Alabama, said one-third of the total revenue from wine sales in the state of Alabama was from the sale of one wine product—Gallo's Thunderbird. Sales crossed all demographic lines. According to Mayes, a consumer developed a taste for wine through an education process that usually began with the purchase of sweet wines from the dessert category. He attributed the high sales of Thunderbird to the fact

Prepared by Daniel C. Thurman, doctoral student, under the supervision of A. J. Strickland III, both of The University of Alabama.

[1]Alix M. Freedman, "Misery Market—Winos & Thunderbird Are a Subject Gallo Doesn't Like to Discuss," *The Wall Street Journal,* February 25, 1988, pp. 1, 18.

that the typical wine drinker in Alabama was generally not the sophisticated wine drinker found in California or New York.

Company History and Background

The E. & J. Gallo Winery, America's biggest winery, was founded by Ernest and Julio Gallo in 1933. More than 55 years later, the Gallo Winery was still a privately owned and family-operated corporation actively managed by the two brothers. The Gallo family had been dedicated to both building their brands and the California wine industry.

The Gallos started in the wine business working during their spare time in the vineyard for their father, Joseph Gallo. Joseph Gallo, an immigrant from the Piedmont region in northwest Italy, was a small-time grape grower and shipper. He survived Prohibition because the government permitted wine for medicinal and religious purposes, but his company almost went under during the Depression. During the spring of 1933, Joseph Gallo killed his wife and chased Ernest and Julio with a shotgun. He killed himself following their escape. Prohibition ended that same year, and the Gallos, both in their early '20s and neither knowing how to make wine, decided to switch from growing grapes to making wine. With $5,900 to their names, Ernest and Julio found two thin pamphlets on wine-making in the Modesto Public Library and began making wine.[2]

The Gallos had always been interested in quality and began researching varietal grapes in 1946. They planted more than 400 varieties in experimental vineyards during the 1950s and 1960s, testing each variety in the different growing regions of California for its ability to produce fine table wines. Their greatest difficulty was to persuade growers to convert from common grape varieties to the delicate, thin-skinned varietals because it took at least four years for a vine to begin bearing and perhaps two more years to develop typical, varietal characteristics. As an incentive, in 1967, Gallo offered long-term contracts to growers, guaranteeing the prices for their grapes every year, provided they met Gallo quality standards. With a guaranteed long-term "home" for their crops, growers could borrow the needed capital to finance the costly replanting, and the winery was assured a long-term supply of fine wine grapes. In 1965, Julio established a grower relations staff of skilled viticulturists to aid contract growers. This staff still counsels growers on the latest viticultural techniques.[3]

Private ownership and mass production were the major competitive advantages contributing to Gallo's success. Gallo could get market share from paper-thin margins and absorb occasional losses that stockholders of publicly held companies would not tolerate. Gallo was vertically integrated, and wine was its only business. While Gallo bought about 95 percent of its grapes, it virtually controlled its 1,500 growers through long-term contracts. Gallo's 200 trucks and 500 trailers constantly hauled wine out of Modesto and raw materials in. Gallo was the only winery to make its own bottles (2 million a day) and screw-top caps. Also, while most of the competition concentrated on production, Gallo participated in every aspect of selling its product. Julio was president and oversaw production, while Ernest was chairman and ruled over marketing, sales, and distribution. Gallo owned its distributors in about a dozen markets and probably would have bought many of the more than 300 independents handling its wines if laws in most states had not prohibited it.

---

[2]Jaclyn Fierman, "How Gallo Crushes the Competition," *Fortune,* September 1, 1986, pp. 24–31.
[3]"The Wine Cellars of Ernest & Julio Gallo, a Brief History," a pamphlet produced by Ernest & Julio Gallo, Modesto, Calif.

Gallo's major competitive weakness over the years had been an image associated with screw tops and bottles in paper bags that developed because of its low-end dessert wine, Thunderbird.[4] There were stories, which Gallo denied, that Gallo got the idea for citrus-flavored Thunderbird from reports that liquor stores in Oakland, California, were catering to the tastes of certain customers by attaching packages of lemon Kool-Aid to bottles of white wine to be mixed at home.[5]

Thunderbird became Gallo's first phenomenal success. It was a high-alcohol, lemon-flavored beverage introduced in the late 1950s. A radio jingle sent Thunderbird sales to the top of the charts on skid rows across the country: "What's the word? Thunderbird. How's it sold? Good and cold. What's the jive? Bird's alive. What's the price? Thirty twice." Thunderbird has remained a brand leader in its category ever since. In 1986, Ernest Gallo poured $40 million into advertising aimed at changing Gallo's image to one associated with quality wines.

Information on Gallo's finances was not publicly available, and the brothers maintained a tight lid on financial details. In a 1986 article, *Fortune* estimated that Gallo earned at least $50 million a year on sales of $1 billion. By comparison, the second leading winery, Seagram's (also the nation's largest distillery), had approximately $350 million in 1985 wine revenues and lost money on its best-selling table wines. *Fortune* stated that several of the other major Gallo competitors made money, but not much.[6]

Gallo produced the top-selling red and white table wines in the country. Its Blush Chablis became the best-selling blush-style wine within the first year of its national introduction. Gallo's award-winning varietal wines were among the top sellers in their classification. The company's Carlo Rossi brand outsold all other popular-priced wines. Gallo's André Champagne was by far the country's best-selling champagne, and E & J Brandy has outsold the number two and three brands combined. Gallo's Bartles & Jaymes brand was one of the leaders in the new wine cooler market.[7]

The U.S. Wine Industry

Wine sales in the United States grew from about 72 million gallons in 1940 to over 600 million gallons, accounting for retail sales in excess of $9 billion (see Exhibit 1). This retail sales volume had exceeded such major established grocery categories as detergents, pet foods, paper products, and canned vegetables. While wine consumption had grown at an astonishing rate, trends toward moderation and alcohol-free life-styles made this growth rate impossible to maintain. Nevertheless, annual growth was projected to be 3.2 percent through 1995.

Per capita consumption of wine was low in the late 1950s and early 1960s because wine drinking was perceived as either the domain of the very wealthy or the extreme opposite. "Fortified" dessert wines were the top-selling wines of the period. The first surge in consumption in the late 1960s was the result of the introduction of "pop" wines, such as Boones Farm, Cold Duck, and Sangrias. These wines were bought by baby boomers, who were now young adults. Their palates were unaccustomed to wine drinking and these wines were suited to them. By the mid-1970s, the pop wine drinkers were ready to move up to Lambruscos and white wine "cocktails," and per capita consumption increased (see Exhibit 2). The wine spritzer became the trend, still the alternative to more serious wines for immature palates. Just as this surge

---

[4]Fierman, "How Gallo Crushes the Competition."

[5]Freedman, "Misery Market."

[6]Fierman, "How Gallo Crushes the Competition."

[7]"Gallo Sales Development Program," a pamphlet produced by Ernest & Julio Gallo, Modesto, Calif.

EXHIBIT 1   The National Wine Market (1977–86)

Source: *National Beverage Marketing Directory,* 10th ed., 1988.

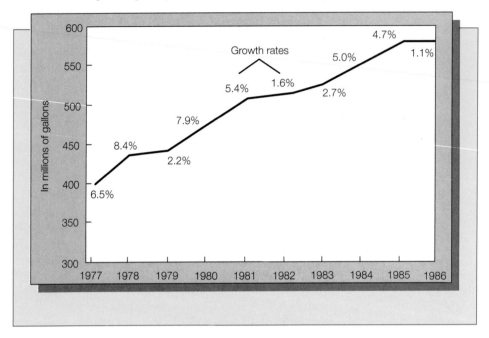

EXHIBIT 2   Per Capita Consumption of Wine in the U.S.

Source: *National Beverage Marketing Directory,* 10th ed., 1988.

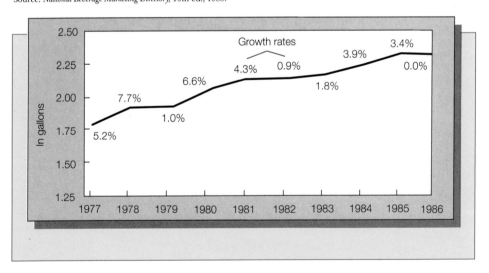

began to wane, wine coolers were introduced in 1982 and exploded on the market in 1983. Wine coolers were responsible for a 5 percent market surge in 1984 and experienced four consecutive years of very high growth rates, rising 6 percent in 1987 to 72.6 million nine-liter cases.

The imported wines category enjoyed an upward growth rate from 6.6 percent of the market in 1960 to a high of 27.6 percent in 1985 (see Exhibits 3 and 4). The category lost market share to 23.1 percent in 1986 primarily because of the shift from

EXHIBIT 3   Wine Production by Place of Origin (millions of nine-liter cases)

Source: *Impact* 17, no. 11 (June 1, 1987), p. 4.

Origin	1970	1975	1980	1985	1986	Average Annual Compound Growth Rate			Percent Change
						1970–75	1975–80	1980–85	1985–86
California	82	115	139.5	133.2	133.3	7.0%	3.9%	−0.9%	−0.1%
Other states*	18	19	18.7	16.9	17.3	1.4	−0.3	−2.0	2.4
United States	100	134	158.2	150.1	150.6	6.1	3.3	−1.0	0.3
Imports	13	21	43.1	57.2	45.3	10.5	15.8	5.8	−20.8

*Includes bulk table wine shipped from California and blended with other state wines.

Note: Addition of columns may not agree because of rounding.

EXHIBIT 4   Market Share Trends in Wine Production

Source: *Impact* 17, no. 11 (June 1, 1987), p. 4.

Place Produced	1970	1975	1980	1985	1986	Share Point Change		
						1970–80*	1980–85	1985–86
California	73%	74%	69.3%	64.3%	68.0%	4	−5.0	3.8
Other states	16	12	9.3	8.2	8.8	−7	1.1	0.7
United States	88	86	78.6	72.4	76.9	−10	−6.2	4.5
Imports	12	14	21.4	27.6	23.1	9	6.2	−4.5
Total†	100%	100%	100.0%	100.0%	100.0%	—	—	—

*1980 based on unrounded data.

†Addition of columns may not agree because of rounding.

EXHIBIT 5   1985 Share of U.S. Wine Market

Source: Jaclyn Fierman, "How Gallo Crushes the Competition," *Fortune*, September 1, 1986, p. 27.

Company	Percent
E. & J. Gallo Winery	26.1%
Seagram & Sons	8.3
Canandiaqua Wine	5.4
Brown-Forman	5.1
National Distillers	4.0
Heublein	3.7
Imports	23.4
All others	24.0
Total	100.0%

Lambruscos to wine coolers. Additional factors were the weakening dollar and an overall improved reputation for domestic wines.

There were about 1,300 wineries in the United States. *Fortune* identified the major market-share holders in the U.S. market in a September 1986 article. It showed Gallo as the clear leader, nearly outdistancing the next five competitors combined (see Exhibit 5).

A number of threats had faced the wine industry, not the least of which had been the national obsession with fitness and the crackdown on drunken driving. Americans drank 6.5 percent less table wine in 1985 than in 1984 (see Exhibits 6 and 7),

EXHIBIT 6   Shipments of Wine Entering U.S. Trade Channels by Type (millions of nine-liter cases)

Source: *Impact* 17, no. 11 (June 1, 1987), p. 3.

Type	1970	1975	1980	1984	1985	1986	Average Annual Compound Growth Rate			Percent Change*
							1970–75	1975–80	1980–85	1985–86
Table	55.9	88.9	150.8	170.9	159.2	147.1	9.9%	11.2%	1.1%	−7.4%
Dessert	31.1	28.2	19.1	15.5	14.3	14.7	−2.0	−7.5	−5.7	3.2
Vermouth	4.2	4.2	3.7	3.0	2.9	2.7	—	−2.5	−4.8	−6.9
Sparkling	9.3	8.4	12.7	19.7	19.4	18.7	−1.9	8.6	8.6	−4.5
Special natural	11.8	24.0	13.6	10.9	10.7	10.9	15.3	−10.7	−4.7	1.9
Imported specialty†	0.3	1.0	1.5	1.0	0.9	1.8	25.4	8.1	−9.7	104.7
Total‡	112.6	154.7	201.3	220.1	207.3	195.9	6.6%	5.4%	0.6%	−5.5%

*Based on unrounded data.
†Imported fruit wines and wine specialties (includes sangria and fruit-flavored wines).
‡Addition of columns may not agree because of rounding.

EXHIBIT 7   Share of Market Trends in Shipments of Wine Entering U.S. Trade Channels, by Type

Source: *Impact* 17, no. 11 (June 1, 1987), p. 3.

Type	1970	1975	1980	1984	1985	1986	Share Point Change		
							1970–80*	1980–85	1985–86
Table	50%	57%	74.9%	77.2%	76.8%	75.1%	25	1.9	−1.7
Dessert	28	18	9.5	7.0	6.9	7.5	−18	−2.6	0.6
Vermouth	4	3	1.8	1.4	1.4	1.4	−2	−0.4	‡
Sparkling	8	5	6.3	9.0	9.4	9.5	−2	3.0	0.2
Special natural	10	16	6.8	5.0	5.2	5.6	−3	−1.6	0.4
Imported specialty	‡	1	0.7	0.5	0.4	0.9	+	−0.3	0.5
Total†	100%	100%	100.0%	100.0%	100.0%	100.0%	—	—	—

*1980 based on unrounded data.
†Addition of columns may not agree because of rounding.
‡Less than 0.05%.

and consumption was projected to be down another 5 percent in 1986. The industry answer to this problem had been introduction of wine coolers. Gallo's Bartles and Jaymes Coolers were number one until they lost the lead by only a slight margin to a Seagram's brand in 1987.

Another trend had been a shift toward a demand for quality premium wines made from the finest grapes. Premium wines increased market share from 8 percent in 1980 to 20 percent in 1986. Again, Gallo had sold more premium wine than any other producer, but Gallo's growth had been limited by its lack of snob appeal.[8]

Although more than 80 percent of the U.S. adult population enjoyed wine occasionally, Gallo's research indicated most Americans were still infrequent wine drinkers by global standards. Only about one in four Americans drank wine as often as once a week. Per capita consumption in the United States was less than 2.5 gallons per year, compared to about 20 gallons in some Western European countries.[9]

[8]Fierman, "How Gallo Crushes the Competition."
[9]"Gallo Sales Development Program."

EXHIBIT 8   Beverage Consumption Patterns

Source: *Impact* 17, no. 18 (September 15, 1987), pp. 3–4.

1986 National Beverage Consumption by Gender (Percent of volume):

Gender	Malt Beverages	Wine	Distilled Spirits	Coolers	Total Nonalcoholic Beverages	Total Beverages
Male	80.8%	51.6%	62.6%	44.9%	51.1%	52.7%
Female	19.2	48.4	37.4	55.1	48.9	47.3
Total	100.0%	100.0%	100.0%	100.0%	100.0%	100.0%

1986 National Alcoholic Beverage Consumption by Household Income (Percent of volume):

Household Income	Malt Beverages	Wine	Distilled Spirits	Coolers	Total Alcoholic Beverages
Under $15,000	26.1%	11.7%	19.7%	22.3%	26.5%
$15,000–$24,999	19.1	13.9	18.1	19.5	21.3
$25,000–$29,999	10.8	14.2	6.6	10.9	12.1
$30,000–$34,999	11.7	9.9	14.7	7.9	10.3
$35,000 & over	32.3	50.3	40.9	39.4	29.8
Total	100.0%	100.0%	100.0%	100.0%	100.0%

1986 National Beverage Consumption by Time of Day (Percent of volume):

Time of Day	Malt Beverages	Wine	Distilled Spirits	Coolers	Total Nonalcoholic Beverages	Total Beverages
Breakfast/morning	2.7%	2.1%	4.6%	1.5%	32.7%	30.6%
Lunch	6.8	5.8	4.2	4.4	20.8	19.8
Snack	27.5	19.0	31.9	27.0	10.9	12.0
Dinner	14.2	45.8	15.5	13.7	22.9	22.6
Evening	48.8	27.3	43.8	53.4	12.7	15.0
Total	100.0%	100.0%	100.0%	100.0%	100.0%	100.0%

1986 National Beverage Consumption by Location of Consumption (Percent of volume):

Location	Malt Beverages	Wine	Distilled Spirits	Coolers	Total Nonalcoholic Beverages	Total Beverages
Total home	64.6%	75.8%	61.4%	76.9%	76.1%	75.5%
Total away from home	35.4%	24.2%	38.6%	23.1%	23.9%	24.5%

Though the health-consciousness and alcohol-awareness of the 1980s had a moderating influence on wine growth patterns as consumers traded up in quality and drank less, long-term growth was expected to be steady but slower than that of the 1970s and early 1980s. Exhibit 8 provides drinking patterns for 1986. Personal disposable income was expected to grow in the United States through 1995; busy lifestyles contributed to more dining out; and sale of wine in restaurants was expected to increase. As the aging baby boomers grew in number and importance, their wine purchases were expected to increase. All these factors contributed to the projected average yearly increase in growth rate of 3.2 percent through 1995.[10]

[10]"Coolers Providing Stable Growth," *Beverage Industry Annual Manual,* 1987.

The Dessert Wine Industry

Dessert wine represented a 55 million-gallon, $500 million industry. The dessert wine category, also called fortified wines, included wines that contained more than 14 percent alcohol, usually 18 percent to 21 percent. They were called fortified because they usually contained added alcohol and additional sugar or sweetener. This category included a group of low-end priced brands that had been the brunt of significant controversy. Canandiaqua's Wild Irish Rose had been the leading seller in this category, with Gallo's Thunderbird claiming second place, followed by Mogen David Wine's MD 20/20.[11]

Dessert wines had shown a decreasing trend both in amount of wine consumed and in market share from 1970 through 1985. However, the trend changed in 1986 when dessert wine's market share rose six-tenths of a share point to 7.5 percent of the total wine market (see Exhibit 7). The rise was attributed in large measure to the 19 percent federal excise tax increase on distilled spirits. An additional factor in the increase in the dessert wine category was the shift to fruit-flavored drinks, which also affected the soft drink industry and wine coolers.[12]

A number of factors indicated that the growth trend would continue for the $500 million dessert wine category. The desire to consume beverages that contained less alcohol than distilled spirits and were less expensive than distilled spirits, the desire for fruit flavor, and the American trend toward eating out at restaurants more often contributed to the trend toward increased consumption of dessert wines. Additionally, the dessert wine category had survived relatively well with virtually no promotion or advertising. This had been possible because, of the category's 55 million gallons, low-end brands accounted for 43 million gallons, approximately 50 percent of which was sold in half pints; and this market had not been accessible by traditional advertising or promotion.

The dessert wine category had been a profitable venture because many of the wines in this category were made with less expensive ingredients, packaged in less expensive containers, and had usually been sold without promotion. Canandiaqua estimated that profit margins in this category were as much as 10 percent higher than those of ordinary table wines. Gallo said this was not true for its products, but it would not reveal the figures.

The low-end dessert wines were a solid business. *The Wall Street Journal* reported that, of all the wine brands sold in America, Wild Irish Rose was the number six best seller, Thunderbird was 10th, and MD 20/20 was 16th. In contrast to the growth expectations of other brands and categories, sales of these low-end brands were expected to be up almost 10 percent. Yet the producers of these top-selling wines distanced themselves from their products by leaving their corporate names off the labels, obscuring any link to their products. Paul Gillette, publisher of the *Wine Investor*, was quoted in a discussion of this unsavory market as saying: "Makers of skid-row wines are the dope pushers of the wine industry."[13]

---

[11]Freedman, "Misery Market."

[12]"U.S. News and Research for the Wine, Spirits and Beer Executive," *IMPACT* 17, no. 11 (June 1, 1987): and *IMPACT* 17, no. 18 (September 15, 1987).

[13]Freedman, "Misery Market."

30

Sarah Norton and Wise Research

Ronald L. Coulter, D. Michael Fields, and Mary K. Coulter
All of Southwest Missouri State University

Rebecca J. Gordon-Runyan
WRG Inc.

When Jeff Baird knocked on the Dallas motel room door on an early August evening in 1995, he expected to see his bubbling and enthusiastic girlfriend. He expected her to be excited, both because it was her birthday and because she was nearing completion of the first week in a two-week training program for the new job she had recently accepted. Instead, the young woman who answered looked troubled and tired.

"Sarah, you don't look very happy," said Jeff.

"I'm not," explained Sarah. "This week has not gone exactly as I expected, and I am seriously questioning whether or not I should even be here."

Although the tone of the meeting had obviously changed dramatically, Jeff was glad he had made the trip. Sarah was extremely troubled and clearly needed to talk to someone about her concerns. Jeff was happy that he was there to listen as Sarah tried to put in perspective the events of the last four days.

Initiating the Job Search

Sarah Norton was nearing the point where she had just one semester remaining before obtaining her MBA degree from a large state university in Hammonsville, Missouri. She was preparing, with some concern, to begin her job search. Sarah had identified at least three factors that would make finding a job in her field difficult. First, from a general perspective, American industry was still in the process of its most substantial downsizing. Much of the downsizing was at the expense of lower levels of management—which had depressed the hiring environment for MBAs across the nation. Second, Sarah's area of specialization was market research. Although many companies expressed a continued dependence on research in order to be effective in the mature markets that dominated the U.S. marketplace, the research industry was not considered to be a growth industry. This situation was further complicated for MBA students because many undergraduates were in competition for the same jobs and could be employed at lower salaries. Finally, Sarah preferred to remain in Hammonsville. The city of 150,000 was close to her parents, and Jeff was there. The location issue might prove to be particularly limiting because a city of 150,000 would generate a smaller market for researchers. Although the situation was less than encouraging, Sarah still felt that she had some advantages in pursuing and getting a job in her field.

Sarah's Background

Sarah was known to her professors and friends as a mature 32-year-old woman who had grown up in central Missouri in a strong family with loving parents. She had a strong religious background that helped to guide her when she had to make tough personal decisions. She was a very pleasant person to be around, and she was both liked and respected by her colleagues and friends. While her personal philosophy was to respect and treat others as she would like to be treated, she never pushed her moral, ethical, or religious views on others. She was genuine and personable in her relationships and was considered to be a fun person to be around.

Sarah had one younger sister with whom she remained very close. Sarah's first job had been with the state of Missouri in the Professional Registration office of the Board of Healing Arts. She enjoyed working there; the office was operated in a very professional manner, and the employees showed a genuine appreciation for each other. After several years in this job, Sarah realized that she wanted to complete her college degree. At the urging of her sister, Sarah transferred to Hammonsville to work in the local state vocational rehabilitation office. Here Sarah assisted several vocational rehabilitation counselors and took classes at the local state university. Sarah was known for her positive work ethic, strong moral values, and intelligence. She received her undergraduate degree in marketing and management (a double major) and graduated with high honors. During her coursework, Sarah was especially taken with the research classes and decided that she wanted to pursue a career in marketing research.

With this sense of direction, Sarah openly sought opportunities in several research projects with her professors in order to develop her research skills. As a result, she was competent and confident of her ability to do all phases of a research project. She could design questionnaires, input data, analyze and interpret statistical tests, and write reports. She was a proficient statistician. Sarah was also very aware of the importance of collecting and reporting unbiased data. The ethical handling of data had been stressed in her research courses, and such an approach was consistent with her personality and personal values. While no industrywide standards existed for the collection and handling of data, Sarah was aware of the code of ethics developed by the Marketing Research Association, Inc. (see Exhibit 1). This organization consisted of approximately 2,100 members from across the United States. Members used the organization for education and training and for networking opportunities in the field of marketing research.

Sarah knew from her professors' lectures, and from her assigned research readings, that corporations annually spend millions of dollars on research. The results of that research are used to influence multimillion-dollar decisions regarding new product lines, manufacturing employment, and promotional strategies. Sarah was also aware that marketing research conducted by outside research suppliers was a

EXHIBIT 1   Code of Ethics of the Marketing Research Association

Source: Used with permission of the Marketing Research Association, Inc., Rocky Hill, CT.

The Code of Professional Ethics and Practices

1. To maintain high standards of competence and integrity in marketing and survey research.
2. To maintain the highest level of business and professional conduct and to comply with federal, state, and local laws, regulations, and ordinances applicable to my business practice and those of my company.
3. To exercise all reasonable care and to observe the best standards of objectivity and accuracy in the development, collection, processing, and reporting of marketing and survey research information.
4. To protect the anonymity of respondents and hold all information concerning an individual respondent privileged, such that this information is used only within the context of the particular study.
5. To thoroughly instruct and supervise all persons for whose work I am responsible in accordance with study specifications and general research techniques.
6. To observe the rights of ownership of all materials received from and/or developed for clients, and to keep in confidence all research techniques, data and other information considered confidential by their owners.
7. To make available to clients such details on the research methods and techniques of an assignment as may be reasonably required for proper interpretation of the data, providing this reporting does not violate the confidence of respondents or clients.
8. To promote the trust of the public for marketing and survey research activities and to avoid any procedure which misrepresents the activities of a respondent, the rewards of cooperation, or the uses of data.
9. To refrain from referring to membership in this organization as proof of competence, since the organization does not so certify any person or organization.
10. To encourage the observance of principles of this code among all people engaged in marketing and survey research.

growing industry concern. Articles she had read on the subject reinforced this concern regarding the ethical collection of marketing research data.

When Sarah completed her undergraduate degree in 1994, the job market was particularly tight. Several of her professors suggested that she consider an MBA degree, so Sarah applied to the graduate school and was accepted into the MBA program. This allowed her to remain in Hammonsville. She also was given a graduate assistantship in the marketing department which paid her tuition and living expenses. While working on her MBA, Sarah continued to develop her marketing research skills. She took 12 hours in her graduate program specifically in research classes and also worked on several special projects for the College of Business for publication and classroom instruction purposes. She also helped acquire secondary data from the library. Sarah had fully expected to return to her assistantship position in the fall of 1995; she had already been offered the head graduate assistant position.

Sarah had agreed to take on the additional responsibilities of head graduate assistant in her final semester of graduate school in the fall—coordinating the schedules and activities of the five graduate assistants who worked in the marketing department. She was confident that the additional time needed would not interfere with either her preparation for classes or what she considered to be her most important activity—finding an entry-level position in the marketing research field. By mid-summer, Sarah had updated her résumé and was ready to begin aggressively pursuing the job market.

Reacting to the Position Announcement

Sarah had been casually looking through the employment section of the Hammonsville *News Monitor* on Sunday, July 9, 1995, when she noticed a position announcement for a market research manager. She eagerly read the balance of the ad copy to get more details about the opportunity. The advertisement did not give any specific job requirements, but the copy did provide a catchy reference to details, dilemmas, and deadlines as they related to an entry-level management position. The advertisement gave a post office box number in Hammonsville and asked potential applicants to send a cover letter with their résumés. No company name was provided in the advertisement.

Sarah thought long and hard about applying for the position. If she applied and was offered the position, she thought she might get to stay in Hammonsville. She liked the city, and very few managerial positions ever became available in her specialized area of marketing research. She would likely have to wait to finish the last nine hours on her MBA degree, but she could still finish the degree at the university. She would also have to give up her head graduate assistant position. She especially wanted her professors to know what she was contemplating so they could hire a replacement before the fall semester began. The local university had been good to her, and she did not want to do anything that would appear improper to her professors or to herself. She discussed the situation with her major professor, who encouraged her to look seriously at the position. If it did not appear to be the type of position she wanted, she could simply withdraw from the interview process. Sarah agreed and mailed in her résumé and cover letter.

The Initial Response and Sarah's Preparation

Within a week of mailing her application letter, Sarah received a phone call from a woman named Katie. Katie said that Mr. Bill Wise, the company's president, would be arriving in Hammonsville from Dallas to do interviews and that he wanted to interview her. Sarah agreed to meet with Mr. Wise on Thursday, July 27. Sarah inquired as to the name of the organization and was told "Wise Research." A follow-up call was to be made by Katie at a later date to verify the interview time.

Sarah tried to get some background information about the organization so that she could intelligently discuss the company and how she might fit into its plans. She found the company listed in the Hammonsville telephone directory under market research firms. Her professor recommended that she call the number to inquire about the operation prior to the interview, but not to indicate why the call was being made. Sarah called the number and spoke with a young man who said he was the office manager. She asked what type of research they conducted and was informed that the company, located in the Westfield Mall, was strictly involved in fieldwork. The company did not generate any questionnaires, nor did it analyze any of the data it collected. The company simply collected data for other marketing research firms that were providing information to their own clients, such as Procter & Gamble, Ragu, or Campbell's. Sarah, remembering her marketing research text, classified the company as a field service organization (see Exhibit 2); this meant that the firm concentrated on collecting data for research projects. The office manager also indicated that the staff at his facility were not college educated.

The manager, who sounded apprehensive, then asked Sarah why she was interested in this information. Sarah truthfully answered that the president of the company was coming to Hammonsville to interview her for a position, but she did not

EXHIBIT 2   Types of Marketing Research Service Suppliers

Customized research services	Companies that work with individual clients from developing the problem/opportunity through the entire research process. They are also referred to as full-service suppliers.
Field research services	These companies concentrate only on collecting data on research projects. They may specialize in various interviewing methodologies such as mail surveys, telephone surveys, personal surveys, focus groups, or mall intercept surveys.
Data analysis research services	These firms specialize in data coding, data editing, and data analysis. They are sometimes referred to as "tab houses," although some specialize in sophisticated data analysis techniques.
Syndicated research services	Companies that routinely collect information to provide to other firms who subscribe to their services.
Branded products research services	These companies have developed specialized data collection and analysis techniques, which are relevant to address specific types of research problems. Their research is branded and marketed like branded products.
Standardized research services	Firms which do marketing research projects conducted in a standard, prespecified manner; the results are then supplied to several different clients.

have any information about the company. The manager seemed upset that the president of the company was coming to Hammonsville and he had not been notified. Sarah specifically indicated that she did not know anything about the position.

The Interview Process

THE INITIAL INTERVIEW

When Katie called several days later to confirm Sarah's interview, she indicated that the interviews were to be held at a local hotel in Hammonsville. Sarah was somewhat surprised because she had expected to be interviewed at the local office in the mall. When she arrived at the hotel, she dialed the extension number Katie had provided. Karen Wise, Bill Wise's wife, answered the phone. She indicated that she also worked at Wise Research. Karen Wise came to the hotel lobby and gave Sarah an application to complete. This was a standard form with a space for annual salary requirement. Sarah responded $25,000–$35,000, knowing that it was a high request for the local market conditions.

After completing the application, Sarah went upstairs to the Wises' hotel room. The interview with Mr. and Mrs. Wise was informal and was held at a small table set in the center of a large room. Mr. Wise sat on one side, his wife sat on his side of the table but more to the end, and Sarah sat on the other side. Mr. Wise was dressed in a lightweight, short-sleeve shirt without a tie or jacket, and Mrs. Wise wore a dress. Sarah did not get the impression from their appearance or the interview process that either of them had much formal education or training. Both were very pleased with the sample paperwork Sarah had brought.

Sarah brought with her a copy of a marketing plan she had done as a student and three questionnaires she had developed to collect data for various projects. During her interview she discussed her data-entry skills and her knowledge of various statistical packages to analyze data. She also discussed her work on several special projects with professors in the College of Business. She explained that for the past year she had been employed as a graduate assistant in the marketing department. She indicated that she had expected to return to this position in the fall since she had already been offered the head graduate assistant position. She also discussed her undergraduate employment at a popular local restaurant where she had been responsible for operations in the absence of the owner. She had often managed the restaurant when the owner was away for several days.

The Wises discussed the deadlines necessary for different projects and how the manager might sometimes have two projects going one day and eight working the next. They gave Sarah a short history of the company. The organization had been in business for about 25 years and operated five mall research offices. Three of the offices were located in Dallas; one was located in Tulsa; and the Hammonsville office was the newest, having been in existence for about 10 years.

Sarah was then told that the local manager was being let go because he was unable to achieve the required production levels. The person the Wises chose would be trained in Dallas for two weeks and then returned to Hammonsville where he or she would be responsible for the Westfield Mall office. The interview was spent primarily discussing the job requirements. Sarah was given the impression that while there would be some contact between the Dallas office and the Hammonsville office, the manager they hired would have direct contact with the clients and autonomy to work with the employees as he or she saw fit.

Sarah's next question was about validating surveys. Survey validation is a procedure where supervisors, or other objective individuals, recontact a small random sample of respondents to check the accuracy of the fieldwork being done. Validation is particularly needed when the temptation for interviewer cheating may be present. Sarah was told that the clients did the validations and that the supervisor also did some. The context of the interview led Sarah to believe that the Wises' organization was contracting to provide valid survey data. Sarah was then told that callbacks for second interviews would be made that afternoon.

THE SECOND INTERVIEW

Karen Wise called and left Sarah a message on her answering machine that Thursday evening. Sarah returned the call later in the evening. Karen told Sarah that the pay was $11 per hour with time and a half paid for any overtime work. Sarah specifically asked if it was 40 hours per week, and Karen replied in the affirmative. Karen Wise said this would come out to be $25,000 per year with benefits that Bill Wise would tell her about the next day. Sarah accepted the second interview and then calculated that it would take about 42.5 hours per week to make $25,000 per year.

The second interview was held in the same hotel and was as casual as the first interview. The Wises told Sarah that they were leaving on vacation as soon as they were done in Hammonsville. Again, no mention was made of touring the local Hammonsville facilities or of meeting the staff. The benefit package presented to Sarah included health insurance premiums paid on a plan of Sarah's choice, up to the amount that the company paid for Dallas employees. This was done because the Wise Research insurance plan did not cover Missouri employees. One week of vacation was offered after one year of employment. A performance review would be scheduled after three months, and then another review would be held nine months later. Mr. Wise stated that it didn't behoove them to give raises in that interim.

In preparation for the second interview, Sarah had compiled a list of 17 questions that she considered to be important. Much of the second interview consisted of Sarah's questions and the corresponding answers (see Exhibit 3), as she sought to gain more information about the research firm.

EXHIBIT 3   **The Second Job Interview: Sarah Norton's Questions and Her Notes on Wise Research's Answers**

1. How is the staff paid?
   The staff was paid on an hourly basis.
2. Is there a budget for incentives?
   No, but they were considering one on a trial basis and would possibly use the Hammonsville office to try out a new program. They felt there were problems with incentives based just on completions of surveys as some people screen potential respondents while others actually do the interviews. The Wises seemed to be concerned with the fairness of this method.
3. Are paychecks distributed from Dallas?
   The paychecks come from Dallas (verified at a later date).
4. Are the staff paid weekly or monthly?
   Twice a month.
5. What are the benefits? Health insurance? Profit sharing? Bonuses for production?
   Insurance was provided by the company; there was no profit sharing plan; and bonuses for production might include a pizza party on the company for all the employees, but no specific program was in place.
6. If the Hammonsville office was extremely busy and needed more production, could the manager help do the fieldwork?
   Yes.
7. How do you support your managers?
   Sarah never specifically asked this question but tried to discern information from her conversations. The Wises seemed supportive of their managers. Frequent communication between offices was discussed. They felt that the open lines for assistance from other mall managers would help. Overall, Sarah felt that they would support their managers regarding decisions and actions as long as they were keeping up production.
8. How often are performance reviews done? 3 months? 6 months?
   Reviews were done after the third month and then again at one year.
9. What is the average overtime for a manager?
   No specific time was given, but the Wises did feel that there would be plenty of overtime opportunities. It was mentioned that if the manager frequently had excessive overtime that they would look for either inefficiencies or the need for an additional assistant. Requests for overtime were required prior to actually working. Approval was mandatory.
10. How are the employees trained? Does the manager have latitude in the content of employee training?
    No specific training program had been designed and Sarah would be responsible for how the Hammonsville employees were trained within some guidelines.
11. How does Wise Research get its referrals?
    Companies come to them, and much of their business is repeat. If a mall office does a good job, the client may again specifically ask for that office. The client and mall manager will be able to communicate directly without going through the Dallas office every time. It was mentioned that Hammonsville had a bad reputation and that many clients did not want to use them. The Wises felt this problem could be overcome with time and a new manager.
12. If Sarah increased production in the Hammonsville office, would Wise Research have enough business to keep the office busy?
    Yes, the Wises did not feel that this would be any problem.
13. Would Sarah have autonomy and authority over her office (to set up an evaluation system, to tie bonuses to performance, to specify dress, approach, etc.)?
    The Wises would not directly answer this question. Sarah did not feel that the Wises were willing to let the manager operate completely and independently. The manager did have the authority over his or her office to a certain extent, with the final word coming from Dallas.

(continued)

EXHIBIT 3   *(Concluded)*

14. Were any promotion dollars budgeted to raise the image of the Hammonsville office?
    In preparing for the interview, Sarah had spoken to a variety of Hammonsville people about being interviewed in the mall. The typical first response she received was always negative toward mall interviewers. They were viewed as interruptive, and most people did not like to talk with them. Sarah felt that some efforts to change people's perceptions about the interviewers' work would enable the Hammonsville office to raise production. The Wises indicated that their organization does not budget for any self-promotion efforts.
15. Where in the mall can interviewers go?
    Interviewers are allowed to go anywhere in the original section of the mall. This is quite a large area, but most interviewers were staying primarily by the research office. Interviewers were typically not going farther into the mall because interviews were typically conducted in the research office and the original section of the mall was so large that it could be a long trip back to the office. The people Sarah talked with often tried to avoid the original mall areas where the interviewers typically stood. The Wises did want to see the interviewers branch out further into the mall.
16. How are focus group participants solicited?
    A file of willing participants was maintained to be used when needed.
17. During the Dallas training what would Sarah be provided with?
    The Wises indicated that the company would provide a room close to the mall, and they would provide a rental car if needed. Airfare would be provided from Hammonsville, and Sarah would also receive reimbursement for her expenses.

After completing the interview, the Wises indicated that they would make their decision later that afternoon. They also told Sarah they would call her either that afternoon or the following Monday.

Karen Wise called Sarah from her car phone later that afternoon and offered Sarah the position. Sarah accepted the position and indicated that she could fly out on Monday, August 7, 1995, for training in Dallas. The following week Sarah withdrew from her fall graduate program courses, informed the marketing department that she would not be returning for the fall semester, wrapped up her summer work as a research assistant, and prepared her personal calendar to be in Dallas from August 7 to August 21, 1995.

The Dallas Training

Sarah arrived at the Dallas Love Field airport around noon on Monday, August 7, and was picked up at the gate by Mark Wise, the son of Mr. and Mrs. Wise. Mark, who was in his early 20s, was very personable and open about the organization. He also spoke very highly of Cindy Brewster, the supervisor with whom Sarah was to train. Mark did bring up the fact that someone had called their Hammonsville office and asked about the position; he was very curious. The first time he discussed it, Sarah let it go without response. He brought the subject up again during the drive and at lunch. He mentioned that they had received a résumé from another employee in the Hammonsville office. They were confused as to how that could have happened because they had just listed a post office box number in the advertisement. Sarah simply commented that Hammonsville was a small town in many respects, even though the population was around 150,000, and that it would not be unusual for word to get around.

Mark also commented that his parents were tired of the Hammonsville situation. They were determined to hire someone who could make the office work, and they wanted to keep that person in Hammonsville no matter what it required. Mark said that the company had received a large number of résumés, and he thought they had interviewed nearly 100 applicants. When Sarah looked at him in disbelief, he quickly added that his statement might not be exactly accurate, but that they had interviewed for two days. He also stated that they felt happy with their decision and excited about her employment.

Sarah and Mark also had a conversation about her educational background. Mark was interested in research and said what he really wanted to know was how to design the questionnaires in order to get the data they wanted. Sarah briefly discussed some of the aspects of questionnaire design and data collection. It seemed very odd to Sarah that Mark had very little understanding of the research process as a whole, but she chalked it up to his being the younger son who did not work full-time at the company.

Mark took Sarah to lunch and then to a car rental agency where the Wises' other son had rented a car for Sarah to use during her two-week training program. Sarah was lodged in a hotel across the parking lot from a shopping mall which housed the research office where she would be training. Mark then took Sarah to the hotel and on to the mall where he gave her an envelope containing $200 in cash and a handwritten note, asking for her signature to indicate that she had received the $200 for expenses.

At the Chesterfield Mall, Sarah was introduced to the office supervisor, Cindy Brewster, and Mark left to return to the main office. Cindy immediately informed Sarah that she had been instructed by the main office not to disclose why Sarah would be in their office for two weeks. Cindy had told the employees that Sarah was an auditor and monitor who would be watching her. Cindy had Sarah complete another standard personnel form, which again requested simple information such as name, address, emergency contact, and salary. Upon completion of the form, Cindy faxed it to the main office.

Cindy then took Sarah on a tour of the facility. It soon struck Sarah that she had seen no evidence of a computer or typewriter. Later she did see a computer sitting on a shelf in the storage room. Sarah asked if they were computerized, and Cindy replied no. Cindy added that only the main office had computers.

In further conversations with Cindy, Sarah discovered that Wise Research considered 37.5 hours as a full-time week. Katie, the office manager at the main office, had sent an envelope for Sarah which Cindy gave to her. Sarah was surprised the front of the envelope was marked For Cindy's Eyes Only and Top Secret. The envelope contained copies of the routine paperwork that supervisors were responsible for completing. Cindy then mentioned that someone had called the Hammonsville office for information about the position. Again, Sarah did not reveal any information, but it seemed very peculiar to Sarah that the organization was so concerned about this incident, particularly if they had interviewed as many people as Mark had indicated.

Sarah and Cindy also discussed the story that Cindy had been ordered to tell her employees concerning Sarah's presence in the office. Cindy said that Wise Research had not yet notified the Hammonsville manager that he was being released, and she asked Sarah if that bothered her. Sarah was vague in her response, and Cindy made it clear that it *did* bother her. Cindy said that if the organization could treat the Hammonsville manager that way, they would also likely do it to her.

DAY TWO

Work began on Tuesday at 9 A.M. Sarah was told to carry her time card in her purse so no one would know that she was clocking in and out. To do this, Sarah arrived before the other employees. Cindy began by showing Sarah the paperwork that was to be completed before 10 A.M. At 10 A.M. Cindy held a briefing where the interviewers were brought up to speed on the outstanding projects and were taken through the steps of preparing for new projects. Cindy introduced Sarah as the auditor and monitor that she had told them about.

As the week progressed, Sarah was shown how to check the completed questionnaires and how to report daily progress to the client. When Wise Research began a project, each interviewer received a sheet that contained (1) an estimate of how many completed questionnaires they should be able to get per hour; (2) what percent of people they would approach (called *net incidence*) who would be eligible to respond based on general criteria, such as age or job; and (3) criteria which were specific (called *category incidence*) to the survey, such as "Do you use body shampoo?" Clients were sent a daily report, and Sarah was told that, in preparing this report, supervisors started with the actual production numbers and worked from them. For example, if interviewers were expected to complete two questionnaires per hour and four were actually completed in one day, the supervisor reported that two hours were worked on the job. This way budgeted hours always matched actual hours. They then took the number four and applied the net incidence and category incidence percentages to come up with a fictional number of people they screened out during the day so the final number showed four completions. This total was then distributed over the categories purely at supervisor discretion. They would just manipulate the data until the numbers totaled those estimated by the client. This report was then faxed to the client. Sarah asked Cindy about this practice, and Cindy said it was the way that everyone did it. She then told Sarah a story about how Karen Wise once was discussing one of the numbers with her and Cindy asked her why it bothered her because the numbers were all fabricated anyway. Karen said she was right, and they both had a good laugh. Cindy indicated that she did feel that it was wrong, though, and Sarah questioned how clients could make good decisions based on potentially biased data.

Sarah learned that the actual jobs each office worked on could vary from a home placement of body shampoo (where the client would use the product and then evaluate it) to a mall taste test of liqueurs. Sarah was concerned by some of these practices, so she asked Cindy what would happen if it appeared that a survey was not going to be completed on time. Cindy replied that first you would call the main office for more time. If that wasn't possible, they were often told to get it done no matter what it takes. This might involve calling uncles, nieces, or anyone demographically acceptable to provide the required data. The main office was also likely to tell the supervisor to write it up. Cindy later told Sarah that some of the other mall offices had interviewers who had been caught so many times with invalidated surveys that they were working under three or four different names so the clients would not recognize them.

DAY THREE

As training continued, another incident occurred that concerned Sarah. Cindy received a call from another mall supervisor. The other mall supervisor heard Sarah's voice in the background and immediately asked if Karen Wise had brought in the new Hammonsville supervisor for training. Cindy immediately denied that Sarah was the new manager, as she had been instructed to do from the main office. The comment from the other mall supervisor seemed strange to Sarah, since each office has four to six, primarily female, interviewers scheduled per day. She realized that there was a high rate of turnover for interviewers, but it seemed suspicious that the other mall supervisor immediately asked if Sarah was a new supervisor instead of an interviewer. Sarah questioned Cindy about this, and they talked about the grapevine that was in place at Wise Research. Sarah asked if the grapevine was used mainly for information or power within the organization. Cindy's reply was "For both."

DAY FOUR

By Thursday of the first week, Sarah was directing the briefings on new projects for the interviewers. Cindy sat back and supervised Sarah's efforts. As they went through the questionnaire, one of the interviewers asked about the coding numbers. This led to a discussion about data entry, and one of the interviewers asked Sarah what would happen if a question was not answered. Sarah indicated they would leave it blank when inputting that response and then continue. Sarah explained that one blank response would not invalidate the entire interview. This seemed very annoying to the interviewers, and again Sarah was surprised at the lack of knowledge the employees had about the whole data collection process.

Throughout the daily training sessions, Cindy and Sarah had discussed the culture of the Wise Research organization and again, on Thursday, they began another conversation. Cindy recounted examples of her experiences. She believed that when she was hired for the supervisor's position, Bill Wise had known that she badly needed the job. She had been out of work for several months and her elderly mother needed care, so an income was imperative. Cindy's background was in psychology, and she had worked for mental health institutions prior to being out of work.

They also discussed many of the things that Cindy's boss had told her to do, such as being dishonest with her employees. Cindy told Sarah that there were things that she had been asked to do that she had refused. Sarah was very concerned about Cindy's comment and asked what those things were. Sarah felt that if Cindy had been asked to do these things then she would probably be asked to do them, too. Sarah was becoming upset at the thought of so much dishonesty in the office. What else could they want? Cindy was not specific in her response to Sarah's direct question and implied other things *were* currently happening, but that she had chosen not to be a part of those activities.

In her supervisory position, which she had held for over eight months, Cindy immediately stood out as a Wise Research leader. She was educated and perceived by the interviewers as a fair supervisor. But Cindy was bothered: although she had received notification of her three-month raise earlier, Wise Research had withheld the monetary rewards until just a few weeks before Sarah's arrival. Cindy had made attempts to gain raises for herself and for her assistant, but her attempts had been ignored. When the main office informed Cindy that she was going to receive a pay increase, she was happy, but she also wondered what the Wises might be wanting from her. When she was told she would be supervising Sarah's training, Cindy felt she understood the timing of her raise.

Cindy was aware of Sarah's training benefits. Sarah had been flown in for two weeks and provided with a car, a nice hotel, and $200 in cash for spending money. When Sarah's personnel records were completed and returned to Cindy, she commented on Sarah's starting pay. Apparently, Sarah's starting pay was more than Cindy was receiving even after having been with the company for more than eight months. Cindy explained that when she was hired, training was provided in Dallas-area malls and that she was responsible for all transportation costs. Every single weekday for what was supposed to be one month and ultimately turned into three, Cindy drove 85 miles round trip for her training. She admitted to feeling slighted by the company when Sarah was being treated so well.

By now Sarah did not have the positive feeling that she had when she first accepted her new position with Wise Research. The final straw came when Sarah and

Cindy were discussing pay, and Cindy shared an experience she'd had on the Monday morning of Sarah's arrival. Apparently Cindy and others had worked the previous Saturday and had been loaned a couple of interviewers from another Dallas-area mall. One of Cindy's interviewers had been befriended by one of these women, and a conversation had ensued about how long each had been with the company and what salary was made per hour. On Monday, the visiting interviewer had gone back to work and complained that Cindy's employee made more money than she did although Cindy's employee had been with the company a shorter time. Cindy had received a phone call from Katie at the main office. Katie told her that she was to fire her interviewer because the interviewer had discussed her salary with another employee. Sarah asked Cindy if the employee had known about this rule or had been shown an employee handbook where this rule was stated. Cindy said that only supervisors and their assistants had employee handbooks and, to her knowledge, her assistant had never seen one. She did say that she felt that discussion of wages was inappropriate, and Sarah stated that she did not feel that way. Sarah said that her salary was hers, it was based on her skills, and that she should be able to discuss it with whomever she wanted.

Cindy had called the employee into the office, told her about the main office's stand, and told the employee that she must be fired. The interviewer began to cry and tried to change Cindy's mind. Cindy explained that it was not her decision and that she had been ordered to do this. The employee asked to talk with someone in the main office; Cindy felt that she should be able to do that, so she placed the call. When she told Katie that the employee wanted to talk with her, Katie responded that she did not know what more could be said but that she would speak to the employee.

The employee was crying and asked to keep her job. Cindy indicated that she literally said, "I beg you for my job." Cindy then heard the employee say that she would talk to Cindy. This surprised Cindy because she'd had no say in the firing. When the employee got off the phone, Cindy told her that she did not have to beg her for her job. She would have to formally write her up, but that she could still work. When Cindy called Katie back to tell her what she had done, she was asked why. Cindy explained that the woman worked several jobs to support a husband who didn't work and three children and that she needed the income. Katie responded that it wasn't their problem. Apparently, however, the interviewer was allowed to remain because she was still working when Sarah was in training.

Sarah had only been in the office for four days, but her winning personality and sincerity had made an impression on other employees. Sarah felt comfortable with Cindy and her staff. Thursday was also Sarah's birthday, and she received a fax from the main office and a card from Cindy. Cindy also said that her brother was making Sarah a handcrafted gift and that it would be done before she left town. One of the interviewers brought Sarah a cupcake, which might not have been so unusual had it not been the employee's day off. However, the kindness shown by the employees of the Chesterfield Mall research office was being overshadowed by concerns that engulfed Sarah.

Sarah's Dilemma

Thursday night was Sarah's chance to evaluate the events of the last four days. After another week of training, Sarah would be returning to her hometown. She would return to Hammonsville to take over the research office in the Westfield Mall. She had already sacrificed her graduate assistantship and would now have to complete her MBA degree at a later time. Even though she felt the new company was pleased with her efforts and knowledge, Sarah wondered if she had made a mistake in accepting the position.

This was Sarah's mindset as she anxiously awaited Jeff's arrival. As she waited, she began to consider her options. Should she resign immediately and return to Hammonsville? Would her concerns likely be alleviated in the second week of her training? Should she complete her training, report to the Hammonsville office, attack her work, and simply refuse to do anything that she considered to be unethical? Or, was she simply overreacting to a normal situation in which a company's culture sometimes conflicts with an individual's personal moral philosophies? Sarah was glad that Jeff was coming to Dallas that evening. He could help her sort through her emotions and decide what action would be in her best interest in the long run. The knot in her stomach signaled a sense of urgency in working through her concerns and arriving at a decision sometime before she reported to work the next morning.

31

Philip Morris Companies

Keith Robbins
George Mason University

Philip Morris (PM) is best known as a manufacturer and marketer of cigarettes. In fact, PM is the largest cigarette company in the United States, with a 42 percent share of the $70 billion industry.[1] However, over the past 30 years the company has been pursuing such a systematic diversification strategy that, in addition to cigarettes, the company now ranks as the second largest beer brewer in the United States and the second largest food processing company in the world.[2] The company's brands include Clark Chewing Gum, Louis Kemp Seafood, Miller, Miller Lite, Lowenbrau, Jell-O, Oscar Mayer, Sealtest, Maxwell House, Oroweat Baked Goods, Light Touch Desserts, and Marlboro, Virginia Slims, Bucks, Benson & Hedges, Merit, and Parliament (see Exhibit 1).

Philip Morris Companies was incorporated in Virginia on March 1, 1985, as the holding company for the diverse businesses of Philip Morris, Inc.[3] Today, the company is the largest private employer in Richmond.[4,5] The company's ambition has been and remains to be the most successful consumer packaged goods company in the world.[6]

This ambition is reflected in the company's mission statement presented in its 1991 annual report to shareholders: "We are a global consumer products company, manufacturing and marketing tobacco, food, and beer brands around the world. Our broad-based operations generate strong and growing returns for investors by answering consumer needs with low-priced, high-volume, quality products. We are committed to the highest standards of ethics and fairness in all of our activities and operations."

This case was prepared by Keith Robbins of the School of Business Administration at George Mason University. Development of this case was made possible by a grant from the Funds for Excellence Program of the State Council of Higher Education in Virginia.

[1]Standard & Poor's, *Industry Survey,* 1992.

[2]P. Sellers, "Can He Keep Philip Morris Growing?" *Fortune* 125, no. 7 (1992), pp. 86–92.

[3]Moody's *Industrial Manual,* 1991.

[4]"The Forbes 500 Ranking," *Forbes* 149, no. 9 (April 29, 1992), pp. 190–396.

[5]"The Fortune 500 Largest Industrial Corporations," *Fortune* 125, no. 8, 1991.

[6]PM, annual report, 1991.

EXHIBIT 1 PM Brands

Cigarettes: *Philip Morris U.S.A., Philip Morris International*
    Marlboro Brands
    Virginia Slims
    Benson & Hedges
    Merit
    Parliament
Beer: *The Miller Brewing Company*
    Miller Lite
    Miller High Life
    Milwaukee's Best
    Lowenbrau
    Sharp's
Food: *Kraft General Foods, Kraft International, General Foods International*
    Kraft Cheeses
    Maxwell House Coffees
    Louis Rich Turkey
    Oscar Mayer Luncheon Meats, Hot Dogs, and Bacon
    Louis Kemp Seafood Products
    Post Cereals
    Jell-O Brand Gelatin
    Kool-Aid
    Sealtest Dairy Products
    Breyers Dairy Products
    Light'n Lively Dairy Products
Financial: *Philip Morris Capital Corporation*
    Major equipment leasing programs for customers and suppliers

Current CEO Michael Miles (the first nonsmoking CEO at Philip Morris in 145 years) describes the company's strategy for meeting its goal as developing new products to meet emerging consumer trends, expanding geographically, and manufacturing and marketing globally.[7] The strategy appears to be working, as PM remains the largest and most profitable consumer products company in the world. In 1990, Philip Morris had risen to seventh on *Fortune*'s list of largest U.S. manufacturers, with sales approaching $50 billion.[8]

A History of Diversification Via Acquisition

The company has a distinct heritage among U.S. tobacco companies; it is the only major company that was not formed when the Supreme Court broke up the James Duke American Tobacco Trust in 1912.[9] Since its inception in England, Philip Morris has emphasized growth through acquisitions (see Exhibit 2). The success of Philip Morris in growing the purchased companies into industry leaders is legendary.

In 1957, Philip Morris was sixth and last in the U.S. cigarette market. Under the leadership of Joseph F. Cullman III and by emphasizing the Marlboro brand, the company climbed to first place by the end of 1983. In 1970, it bought Miller Brewing,

[7] Ibid.
[8] "The Fortune 500."
[9] R. Levering, M. Moskowitz, and M. Katz, *The 100 Best Companies to Work for in America* (Reading, Mass.: Addison-Wesley, 1984).

EXHIBIT 2   PM's History of Acquisitions

Source: Moody's *Industrial Manual*, 1991.

June 1944	Purchased cigarette-producing assets from Axton-Fisher Tobacco Company, Louisville, Kentucky, for $8.9 million cash.
Feb. 1945	Acquired 99% interest in Benson & Hedges through common stock exchange on a share-for-share basis.
Dec. 1959	Acquired an interest in C.A. Tabacalera Nacional Venezuela.
Dec. 1963	Acquired a substantial interest in Fabriques de Tabac Reunies, S.A., Swiss cigarette manufacturer and licensee.
April 1967	Acquired an interest in Kwara Tobacco Company, Ilorin, Nigeria.
June 1969	Purchased 53% interest in Miller Brewing Company for $130 million.
Jan. 1970	Acquired control of Mission Viejo, Cal., new city and land developer for $20 million.
Feb. 1977	Acquired Wisconsin Tissue Mills, Menasha, Wis., for 314,000 shares of common stock.
Feb. 1977	Purchased 97% of common stock of The Seven-Up Company, a soft-drink extract manufacturer, for $520 million.
June 1978	Purchased the international cigarette business of Liggett Group, Inc., (consisting of rights to sell L&M, Lark, Chesterfield, Eve, and Decade outside of United States) for $45 million.
Nov. 1985	Purchased General Foods Corporation for $5.6 billion.
Dec. 1988	Acquired, through merger with a subsidiary, Kraft, Inc., for approximately $12.9 billion.
Aug. 1990	Acquired Swiss-based coffee and confectionery company Jacobs Suchard AG for $4.1 billion.

which at the time ranked seventh among U.S. brewers. By 1977, the company had leapfrogged up to second place behind Anheuser-Busch.[10]

Philip Morris has been able to fund its numerous acquisitions through its high-margin tobacco products, which continue to contribute a disproportionate share of corporate earnings. According to U.S. Labor Department statistics, retail tobacco prices have increased on average 10 percent over the past 11 years. This rate of increase exceeds that of any other product, including hospital rooms and prescription drugs, over this period.[11,12] Cigarette manufacturers have found demand for tobacco to be price inelastic—smokers do not seem to decrease consumption despite price increases.

The acquisition spree has been motivated by the company's desire to lessen its dependence on tobacco. Many senior executives openly express concern about the company's heavy dependence on tobacco.[13] Thus, the central issue facing management at Philip Morris is the careful selection of the correct portfolio of consumer packaged goods that will allow the company to protect and build upon global operations. This mixture of businesses must smooth the transition away from tobacco dependence to avoid adverse consequences in an increasingly hostile environment.

[10]Ibid.

[11]J. Dagnoli, "Philip Morris Keeps Smoking," *Advertising Age* 61, no. 48 (1990), p. 20.

[12]E. Giltenan, "Profits Keep Rollin' in . . . ," *Forbes* 146, no. 1 (1992), pp. 152–53.

[13]Sellers, "Can He Keep."

EXHIBIT 3 Company Income and Revenue Contribution by Industry Segment (in millions of dollars)

	1990	1989	1988
Operating revenues:			
Tobacco	$21,090 (41%)	$17,849 (40%)	$16,576 (53%)
Food	26,085 (51)	22,373 (51)	10,898 (35)
Beer	3,534 (7)	3,342 (7)	3,177 (10)
Financial services	460 (1)	516 (2)	622 (2)
Total operating revenues	$51,169	$44,080	$31,273
Operating profit:			
Tobacco	$ 5,596 (67%)	$ 5,063 (72%)	$ 3,846 (84%)
Food	2,205 (27)	1,580 (23)	392 (9)
Beer	285 (4)	226 (3)	190 (4)
Financial services	196 (2)	172 (2)	162 (3)
Total operating revenues	$ 8,282	$ 7,041	$ 4,590

Industry Segments

Philip Morris's significant industry segments consist of tobacco products, food products, beer, and financial services, including real estate. Operating revenues and operating profits for each of the segments over the past three years are detailed in Exhibit 3.

The company's dependence on tobacco is evidenced by the fact that tobacco revenues account for 41 percent of the company's revenue and 68 percent of its income, though this dependence has lessened somewhat recently. Tobacco's profits represented 72 percent of the company's operating income in 1989. Food products accounted for approximately 27 percent of the company's operating profit in 1990, compared with 23 percent in 1989. In 1990, beer accounted for 7 percent of company revenues and 4 percent of income from operations.[14]

TOBACCO PRODUCTS

Philip Morris U.S.A. is responsible for the manufacture, marketing, and sale of tobacco products in the United States (including military sales), and Philip Morris International is responsible for the manufacture, marketing, and sale of such products outside the United States and for tobacco product exports from the United States.

DOMESTIC TOBACCO

Philip Morris sold 220.5 billion units of cigarettes in 1990, an increase of 1 billion units over 1989. Industry sales decreased 0.3 percent in 1990, compared to 1989. Over the past three years, Philip Morris has increased its sales and market share in the United States even though industry revenues have declined:

Year	Industry (billions of units)	Philip Morris	Market Share (%)
1990	522.1	220.5	42.2%
1989	523.9	219.5	41.9
1988	558.1	219.3	39.3

Source: Wheat, First Securities, Inc.

[14]Moody's *Industrial Manual,* 1990, 1991, and 1992.

The major industry rivals in domestic tobacco are American Brands; RJR Nabisco, Inc.; B.A.T. Industries (parent of Brown and Williamson); Loews Corporation (parent of Lorillard); and the Liggett Group. The tobacco companies typically are operated as a subsidiary of diverse parent corporations. American Brands, in addition to its Pall Mall and Carlton cigarettes, markets Titleist golf balls, Jim Beam whiskey, and Master Locks. RJR Nabisco, in addition to its Winston, Salem, and Camel cigarettes, markets Oreos cookies, Planter's Peanuts, Del Monte Fruits, and Grey Poupon mustard. Loews Corporation, in addition to its Newport, Kent, and True cigarettes, owns CNA Financial Services, Inc.; Loews' theaters and hotels; and the Bulova Watch Company.

Philip Morris is the overwhelming leader in domestic market share, achieving 1.5 times the sales of its closest rival, RJR Nabisco (see Exhibit 4).

The Maxwell Consumer Report issued by Wheat, First Securities, Inc., has ranked Philip Morris U.S.A. as the leading cigarette company in the United States market since 1983. The company's best-selling brands are Marlboro, Benson & Hedges, Merit, Virginia Slims, and Cambridge. Philip Morris produces 4 of the top 10 selling brands in the United States, including best-selling Marlboro, which garnered 26 percent of the market in 1990 (see Exhibit 5).

CIGARETTE INDUSTRY SEGMENTS

Premium and Discount Brands

Philip Morris premium brands consist of top 10 performers Marlboro, Benson & Hedges, Merit, and Virginia Slims. In the summer of 1991, PM spent a record $60

EXHIBIT 4   Domestic Cigarette Producers' Market Shares (percentage of industry units sold)

Source: Standard & Poor's *Industry Surveys*, 1991.

Company	1990	1989	1988	1987
Philip Morris	42.0%	42.2%	39.3%	37.8%
Reynolds	28.9	28.7	31.8	32.5
Brown & Williamson	10.8	11.4	10.9	11.0
Lorillard	7.8	7.1	8.2	8.2
American	6.8	7.0	7.0	6.9
Liggett	3.7	3.4	2.8	3.6

EXHIBIT 5   Top 10 Domestic Cigarette Brands, 1990

Sources: Moody's, Standard & Poor's.

Rank	Brand	Company	Units (billions)	Mkt. Share
1	Marlboro	Philip Morris	135.6	26%
2	Winston	Reynolds	46.4	9
3	Salem	Reynolds	32.0	6
4	Kool	Brown & Williamson	32.0	6
5	Newport	Lorillard	25.1	5
6	Camel	Reynolds	21.2	4
7	Benson & Hedges	Philip Morris	20.5	4
8	Merit	Philip Morris	20.3	4
9	Doral	Reynolds	19.2	4
10	Virginia Slims	Philip Morris	16.8	3

million to advertise Marlboro Medium, the first spinoff from the Marlboro brand in 20 years.[15] According to Marlboro VP Nancy Brennan Lund, the brand's 26 percent domestic market share should increase, though its volume probably will not.

A growing industry segment consists of the discount brands. After initially rejecting the idea of selling less-profitable brands, Philip Morris decided to enter the discount segment in 1985. This was prompted by the realization that many of its customers were switching to cheap cigarettes.[16,17] By 1991, Philip Morris became the market leader in the low-priced segment. Now, 17 percent of PM's U.S.A. sales are discount brands, such as Cambridge, Alpine, Bristol, and Bucks.

Industrywide discount brand sales have risen from 11 percent of sales in 1989 to 25 percent today and are expected to double again over the coming five years. Although Philip Morris is performing well in the discount segment, it is unable to put its formidable advertising might behind these brands for fear of cannibalizing its higher-margin premium brands. Recently tobacco companies have raised prices on the discount brands—for example, PM increased its prices by 20 percent on the discount brands.

According to industry analysts,[18,19,20] William Campbell, CEO of Philip Morris U.S.A., is determined to compete in every major cigarette category. The result is that the company now produces low-profit generic cigarettes. Generics, sometimes referred to as *black and whites*, are sold in places like Wal-Mart bearing such names as Best Buy, Basic, and Gridlock: The Commuter's Cigarette—a California brand. Campbell's predominant goal is to increase PM's domestic market share a point a year.

Low Tar

The low tar segment of the market consists of cigarettes delivering 15 milligrams (mg) or less of "tar" per cigarette. In 1990 and 1989, this market accounted for 57.4 percent and 55.5 percent of U.S. industry sales, respectively.[21,22] Philip Morris's low tar brands comprised 42.1 percent of the low tar market in 1990 and 42.8 percent in 1989. The low tar market includes a subsegment referred to as *ultra-low tar* that consists of brands that deliver 6 mg. or less of tar per cigarette. Ultra-low tar brands accounted for 11.3 percent of industry sales in 1990, compared with 10.8 percent in 1989. Philip Morris's ultra-low tar brands garnered 32.9 percent of this market in 1990 and 33.4 percent in 1989.

The low tar and ultra-low tar segments are growing, whereas the industry is in general decline. Philip Morris must ensure that its brands competing in these segments are able to achieve market share positions at least commensurate with its non-low tar cigarettes. This is currently not the case in the rapidly expanding ultra-low tar category, where Philip Morris lost market share during 1990.

INTERNATIONAL TOBACCO

Worldwide tobacco industry sales have been growing at approximately 2 percent per year for the past several years. The United States exported $5 billion of tobacco

[15]Sellers, "Can He Keep."

[16]C. Leinster, "Is Bigger Better for Philip Morris?" *Fortune* 119, no. 10 (1989), pp. 66–68+ .

[17]A. Farnham, "From Soup to Nuts," *Fortune* 119, no. 1 (1989), pp. 43–47.

[18]S. Chakravraty, "Philip Morris Is Still Hungry," *Forbes* 145, no. 7 (1990).

[19]J. Dagnoli, "CEO Miles Sees International Growth for Philip Morris," *Advertising Age* April 8, 1991.

[20]Sellers, "Can He Keep."

[21]Moody's *Industrial Manual,* 1990 and 1991.

[22]S&P's *Industry Surveys,* 1990 and 1991.

products in 1990.[23] Philip Morris International's share of this market was 7.6 percent in 1990, compared with 6.7 percent in 1989. Marlboro is the leader. Its sales increased 13.2 percent in 1990. Its 206.9 billion units accounted for over 4.3 percent of the non-United States cigarette market. In particular, Philip Morris International has strong market share positions in Argentina, Australia, Finland, France, Germany, Hong Kong, Italy, Mexico, Saudi Arabia, and Switzerland, holding at least a 15 percent market share position in each.

Philip Morris is the leading cigarette exporter. Total cigarette exports to 111 foreign countries in 1990 were valued at $4.75 billion. The leading destinations were Asian (58 percent) and European (38 percent) countries. Two factors were primarily responsible for the growth in international sales: the lowering of trade barriers in Japan, Taiwan, and South Korea, and the weakened dollar.[24]

The market for cigarettes outside the United States in 1980 was 3.9 trillion units, with only 40 percent open to Western companies. Currently, international (non-U.S.) consumption stands at 4.9 trillion cigarettes a year, and Western companies now can deal with 95 percent of this market. PM sold 640 billion, or 11.6 percent of the world's cigarettes last year. That places PM second behind the Chinese government (1.5 trillion) in terms of total cigarette sales.

It is interesting that the company's global perspective largely resulted from its inability to penetrate domestic markets. When it was No. 6 among U.S. tobacco companies during the '50s, PM was the first U.S. manufacturer to begin selling its products in duty-free shops in foreign countries. It focused on those countries most frequented by U.S. travelers. Because many of these markets were closed to imports, the company was forced to license the sale of its cigarettes in the areas. The company reasoned that foreign-domestic managers could best oversee these foreign operations. As a result of this early emphasis on international operations, PM's management is more globally diverse than most: Miles and Mayer are Americans, Maxwell is a Scot, Campbell is Canadian, David Dangoor (PM U.S.A. marketing head) is Iranian. Two of the three bosses Miles vied with for the CEO position are Australian; the third is German.[25]

Though many foreign markets recently have opened access to U.S. firms, many protectionist policies are mitigating penetration. Many governments control prices, levy huge taxes, and even market state-owned brands (Taiwanese government's Long Life cigarettes; Japan's Dean cigarettes). Last year in Hong Kong, a 200 percent tax increase on imported cigarettes effectively doubled the price of a pack of Marlboros and cut PM's sales by 80 percent. The government later cut the tax in half after Philip Morris International employees and friends gathered 75,000 signatures.

In Italy, the company was implicated in a government investigation of cigarette imports that illegally avoided Italian taxes. Consequently, Italy imposed a one-month ban on Marlboro, Merit, and Muratti, a popular local blend.

International tobacco's profit margins are half those of the United States. These margins are improving—they rose 24 percent in 1991 on a 14 percent increase in revenues. In the European community, sales volume has risen 25 percent during the past three years. PM management views Turkey as the "gateway to the east," particularly the former Soviet Union and Central Asia. PM recently broke ground on a $400 million cigarette factory there.[26]

[23]M. Levin, "U.S. Tobacco Firms Push Easily into Asian Markets," *Marketing News* 25, no. 2 (January 21, 1991), pp. 2, 14.

[24]Sellers, "Can He Keep."

[25]Ibid.

[26]Moody's *Industrial Manual,* 1992.

In 1990, PM bought three deteriorating East German factories that churn out the leading local cigarette, F6. In a recent year, PM shipped 22 billion cigarettes to the former Soviet Union.[27]

FOOD

CEO Miles was formerly head of Kraft General Foods (KGF), which was formed after PM bought Kraft. He was instrumental in the successful implementation of Hamish Maxwell's diversification strategy. Miles's promotion to chief executive helped ease the tension between PM and General Foods that had existed since the latter's hostile takeover. Miles's insight into the food business permitted him to ignore pessimistic forecasts for traditionally strong brands, such as Maxwell House and Post. Many insiders felt that these brands could expect, at best, marginal increases in volume. Miles reemphasized growth and, as a consequence, sales of such leading products as Kool-Aid, Jell-O, and Grape Nuts cereal are expanding again.[28,29] Operating profits in General Foods exceeded $700 million in 1991, versus $433 million in 1989.

Kraft's cheese division has not fared as well. Sales have stagnated. Analysts blame this on Miles's continued price hikes in the face of stable prices for private label cheeses. During 1991, Kraft began cutting prices in an attempt to regain lost market share from the private labels. However, the retailers—who profit quite nicely off their own private label brands—were naturally reluctant to pass the cuts on down to the consumers.[30] The division experienced a shortfall of $125 million between anticipated and realized cheese profits. The problems of the cheese division also have resulted from increased health consciousness among consumers. Cheese products are notoriously high in saturated fat and cholesterol. As more consumers become sensitive to nutritional guidelines espoused by leading health agencies, overall demand for cheese likely will continue to decline. Kraft's products in general and cheese products in particular typically are not purchased by health conscious consumers due to their high fat content.

Richard Mayer, president and CEO of KGF, has two primary ideas for stimulating the food division: (1) to get market research and computer people working in teams with brand managers to make better use of scanner-generated sales data and (2) to distribute all KGF products within a particular region from a single warehouse location to serve customers better.[31] Presently, grocers buy 10 percent of all their grocery items from KGF but draw from many warehouses. These strategies should help KGF respond more expeditiously to market trends and competitors' moves.

Philip Morris as an Employer

Philip Morris consistently is ranked as one of the more progressive employers in the United States. Levering, Moskowitz, and Katz included PM among their listing of *The 100 Best Companies to Work for in America.*

According to James Bowling, director of public relations and public affairs, caring about its employees is what distinguishes Philip Morris: "everybody bought tobacco competitively at auction; manufactured cigarettes in Kentucky, Virginia, and

[27]PM, annual reports, 1991 and 1992.

[28]Dagnoli, "CEO Miles Sees."

[29]Sellers, "Can He Keep."

[30]Ibid.

[31]Dagnoli, "CEO Miles Sees."

North Carolina; used essentially the same machinery; paid the same union wages; and sold through the same wholesalers and retailers. Therefore, they said that, if there is going to be a difference, it will have to be in the people. As simplistic and corny as that seems, it has been the guiding principle here since that day. We have always tried to treat our people better—by being the first or among the first with amenities and working pleasantries."

One survey of senior managers conducted by an independent auditor, showed very high satisfaction with the company. The benefits package includes long- and short-term disability compensation. Employees automatically are insured for twice their annual salary, and there is a survivor income benefit that, in the event of employee death, would start paying, after four years, 25 percent of last base pay to surviving spouses every month plus 5 percent of your last base pay to each surviving child. There is an employee stock ownership plan and employees who smoke—and the majority do—are entitled to one free carton of cigarettes per week.[32]

Philip Morris was one of the first companies to employ blacks in sales positions. One out of every four persons who works for the company is a minority-group member—and minorities hold 14 percent of positions classified as "officials and managers."[33]

The Richmond cigarette factory is a futuristic plant completed in 1974 at a cost of over $200 million—at the time the largest capital investment in the company's history. The plant boasts of parquet floors and floor-to-ceiling windows overlooking elaborate ornamental gardens.[34]

1991 Performance and Future Prospects

Philip Morris currently sells more than 3,000 items. The value of the shares of stock outstanding reached $74 billion in December 1991 (trading at $75 per share) exceeding the value of all other U.S. companies except Exxon. Among the 1991 highlights: revenues increased 10 percent to $56.5 billion; operating income grew 14 percent to $9.9 billion; unit sales increased nearly 200 million in the United States over 1990, whereas U.S. industry volume decreased by 13 billion units.

Despite many bright spots, particularly in fat-free products, beverages, and breakfast cereals, overall results in North American food businesses were lower than expected. Volume in the brewing business grew 0.4 percent despite a doubling of the federal excise tax at the beginning of the year. Performance in 1991 allowed the company to increase dividends by 22.1 percent to an annualized rate of $2.10 per share, the 24th consecutive year of dividend increases.[35]

According to Miles, the company will throw off free cash of more than $21 billion. This is the excess after capital expenditures, dividends, and taxes—and Philip Morris can use it either to pay for acquisitions or to buy back stock, or both. The company currently realizes $15 billion annually from international operations (more than Coca-Cola, PepsiCo, and Kellogg combined). Marlboro is especially strong internationally in Asia, Eastern Europe, and the former Soviet Union.[36]

As portrayed in the company's consolidated income statement (Exhibit 6), Philip Morris U.S.A.'s sales went up 9 percent to $9.4 billion in 1991, and operating prof-

[32]Levering et al., *The 100 Best.*
[33]PM, annual report, 1991.
[34]Levering et al., *The 100 Best.*
[35]PM, annual report, 1992.
[36]Sellers, "Can He Keep."

EXHIBIT 6   Philip Morris Companies, Inc: Consolidated Income (in millions of dollars)

	1991	1990	1989	1988	1987
Operating revenues	$56,458	$51,169	$44,080	$31,273	$27,650
Cost of sales	25,612	24,430	21,868	13,565	12,183
Excise taxes on products	8,394	6,846	5,748	5,882	5,416
Gross profit	22,452	19,893	16,464	11,826	10,051
Marketing, admin., & research	13,331	11,499	9,290	7,304	5,956
Amortization of goodwill	499	448	385	125	105
Operating income	8,622	7,946	6,789	4,397	3,990
Interest & other debt expense	1,651	1,635	1,731	670	646
Earnings before income taxes	6,971	6,311	5,058	3,727	3,344
Provision for income taxes	3,044	2,771	2,112	1,663	1,502
Earnings before cumulative effect of acct. change	3,927	3,540	2,946	2,064	1,842
Cumulative effect of acct. change for income taxes	(921)			273	
Net earnings	3,006	3,540	2,946	2,337	1,842
Retained earnings (B.O.Y.)	10,960	9,079	7,833	6,437	5,344
Common dividends	(1,765)	(1,432)	(1,159)	(941)	(749)
Four-for-one stock split			(478)		
Exercise of stock options	(172)	(218)	(63)		
Other	9	(9)			
Retained earnings (E.O.Y.)	12,038	10,960	9,079	7,833	6,437

its rose even faster to reach $4.8 billion. Operating margin rose a fabulous 51 percent, up from 42 percent seven years ago. Philip Morris's gains in market share are impressive, too—43.3 percent of total U.S. cigarette sales today, versus 35.9 percent in 1985.

The primary objective at Philip Morris traditionally has been to achieve 20 percent annual earnings growth. Hamish Maxwell hit the mark each of the last five years, but Miles is facing a more maleficent marketplace.

The company is in a very solid financial position as it remains one of the more liquid U.S. companies. It often is referred to as the "King of Cash" (see Exhibit 7).

Threats To Philip Morris's Traditional Level of Performance

THE DECLINING AMERICAN CIGARETTE INDUSTRY

Domestic cigarettes contributed $4.8 billion in operating income last year, roughly half the corporate total. But the American cigarette industry is declining 2 to 3 percent per year. Additionally, the trend is toward budget brands with smaller profit margins and away from premium products, such as Marlboro, Merit, Virginia Slims, and Benson & Hedges. According to industry analysts, the bargain brands—including those marketed by Philip Morris—pose more of a threat to the 20 percent target than the product liability litigation now pending Supreme Court review.[37]

[37]S&P's *Industry Survey,* 1992.

EXHIBIT 7   Comparative Consolidated Balance Sheet as of December 31 (in millions of dollars)

	1991	1990	1989	1988	1987
Assets					
Consumer products:					
Cash & equivalents	$ 126	$ 146	$ 118	$ 168	$ 90
Receivables, net	4,121	4,101	2,956	2,222	2,065
Inventories	7,445	7,153	5,751	5,384	4,154
Other current assets	902	967	555	377	245
Total current assets	12,594	12,367	9,380	8,151	6,554
Property, plant, & equipment	15,281	14,281	12,357	11,932	9,398
Less accum. depreciation	5,335	4,677	3,400	3,284	2,816
Property account net	9,946	9,604	8,951	8,648	6,582
Other assets	20,306	20,712	17,251	16,992	5,411
Total consumer products assets	42,846	42,683	35,588	33,791	18,547
Total financial & real estate assets	4,538	3,886	3,440	3,169	2,890
Total assets	$47,384	$46,569	$39,028	$36,960	$21,437
Liabilities					
Total current liabilities	11,824	11,360	8,943	7,969	5,164
Total consumer products liabilities	31,344	31,460	26,108	26,664	12,234
Total financial & real estate assets	3,528	3,162	2,849	2,617	2,330
Stockholders' Equity					
Common stock ($1, par)		935	935	240	240
Additional paid-in capital				252	272
Earnings reinvested in business		10,960	9,079	7,833	6,437
Currency translation adj.		561	143	117	146
Net stockholders' equity	12,512	11,344	9,871	8,208	6,803
Total	$47,384	$45,956	$38,828	$37,489	$21,367

SLOWING PROCESSED FOOD SALES

Recession intensifies price elasticity, so shoppers are moving toward less-costly private label brands. Increasing consumer awareness of ingredients has invited comparison between the private labels and national brands, such as Kraft General Foods (KGF). In many cases, there is no substantive difference. KGF's North American revenues rose only 1 percent last year. Excluding special charges, operating income increased a disappointing 8 percent.

ANTISMOKING LITIGATION AND LEGISLATION

Investors remain concerned about tobacco's legal status. This hinged on a Supreme Court ruling expected during the summer of 1992. The court will decide whether the federally mandated warning labels on cigarette packs—required since 1966—insulate tobacco companies from liability claims in state courts.

Smoking and Health Related Issues

Since 1964, the Surgeon General of the United States and the Secretary of Health and Human Services have released reports alleging a correlation between cigarette smoking and numerous physical maladies, including cancer, heart disease, and chronic diseases of the respiratory system. Recent reports continue to emphasize the health warnings from the earlier studies and additionally focus on the addictive nature of smoking and the demographics of smokers. In particular, the prevalence and growth rates of smoking among women and African-Americans have received much publicity.[38]

Federal law requires marketers of cigarettes in the United States to include one of four warnings on a rotating basis on cigarette packages and advertisements:

> SURGEON GENERAL'S WARNING: Smoking Causes Lung Cancer, Heart Disease, Emphysema, and May Complicate Pregnancy.
>
> SURGEON GENERAL'S WARNING: Quitting Smoking Now Greatly Reduces Serious Risk to Your Health.
>
> SURGEON GENERAL'S WARNING: Smoking by Pregnant Women May Result in Fetal Injury, Premature Birth, and Low Birth Weight.
>
> SURGEON GENERAL'S WARNING: Cigarette Smoke Contains Carbon Monoxide.

In addition to the warnings, federal regulations require that cigarettes sold in the United States disclose the average tar and nicotine deliveries per cigarette.

A more recent concern has been the alleged health risks to nonsmokers from what is most often referred to as *passive smoking* or *environmental tobacco smoke* (ETS). In 1986, the U.S. Surgeon General issued a report claiming that nonsmokers were at increased risk of lung cancer and respiratory illness due to ETS. The Environmental Protection Agency is currently at work on a report detailing the risks of ETS. The findings concerning ETS have been instrumental in the passage of legislation that restricts or bans cigarette smoking in public places and places of employment.

Television and radio advertising of cigarettes has been prohibited in the United States since 1971. Since this time, regulatory agencies have acted to further restrict or prohibit smoking in certain public places, on buses, trains, and airplanes, and in places of employment.

Such restrictions are not exclusive to the United States. Many foreign countries have restricted or prohibited cigarette advertising and promotion, increased taxes on cigarettes, and openly campaigned against smoking. Thailand, Hong Kong, France, Italy, and Portugal all have implemented cigarette advertising bans. This virtually precludes successful introduction of new brands in these countries. The European Economic Community (EEC) is contemplating a ban on tobacco advertising in newspapers, magazines, and billboards.[39] More recently, the Asian Consultancy on Tobacco Control, a 14-nation consortium, has been formed to combat smoking in this region. Thus, some countries have tighter restrictions than the United States.

Litigation

Approximately 50 court cases are pending, wherein plaintiffs are seeking damages from leading United States cigarette manufacturers. The litigation involves alleged cancer and other health maladies directly resulting from cigarette smoking. Philip Morris was a defendant in 23 actions pending as of March 1, 1991, compared with 24 at the same point in 1990 and with 32 in 1989. The number of court cases appears to have stabilized.

---

[38]Ibid.

[39]P. Engardio, "Asia: A New Front in the War on Smoking," *Business Week* (Industrial/Technical Edition), no. 3201 (February 25, 1991), p. 66.

Philip Morris's primary defense tactic has been based on seeking a preemption of liability based on the Federal Cigarette Labeling and Advertising Act. Five federal courts have ruled that the cigarette labeling act does protect cigarette manufacturers from some liability claims. Conversely, the Supreme Court of New Jersey and one of the Texas appellate courts ruled that the cigarette labeling act does not limit the liability of the cigarette manufacturers.

As with any court case the outcome is uncertain. A finding in favor of the plaintiff would have the effect of denying preemption of liability on the basis of the existence of the cigarette warning labels. This could entice additional litigation against cigarette manufacturers. Philip Morris remains confident that, even in this worst-case scenario, the lawsuits will not pose a substantive threat to its overall financial health.

The Company's Position

No tobacco company has ever lost a liability case or paid a penny to settle; juries thus far have ruled that smokers have been adequately warned cigarettes can ruin their health. According to John McMillin of Prudential Securities: "A Supreme Court ruling against the industry has limited downside for the stock because worries have already pulled down the price. A tobacco victory could mean the end of major litigation risk and take Philip Morris's stock up 15 to 20 percent."

Tobacco use is one of the most widely discussed health issues around the world. The company's position was stated by CEO Miles in a letter to shareholders in 1992: "Given the general availability of information concerning the health issue, we regard smoking as a voluntary lifestyle decision that need not be subjected to new marketing or use restrictions."

He added: "While we believe that consumers are aware of the claimed health risks of smoking, nonetheless in February 1992 we took actions to begin placing the U.S. Surgeon General's health warning on all our cigarette packages worldwide where warnings are not currently required. This initiative applies to brands manufactured in the United States for export, as well as to those produced overseas by our affiliates and affected licensees. We are taking these steps because the lack of warning on a relatively small number of packages—approximately 10 percent of our volume—has become an issue out of proportion to its importance."

Continuing, Miles stated: "Moreover in the United States we are acting to increase awareness and enforcement of minimum age purchase restrictions on our tobacco products through multimillion-dollar programs involving advertising, trade relations, and family education."

Future Prospects

According to Miles, the company has no plans to diversify outside of packaged goods. Since acquisition opportunities in tobacco are limited, most analysts predict a major food acquisition, probably in Western Europe within the coming year or so. In 1990, PM bought one of Europe's largest coffee and chocolate companies, Jacobs Suchard, well known for Toblerone candy bars. The $4.1 billion deal made PM the third-largest food marketer in Europe, behind Nestlé and Unilever. The company's European revenues today are approaching $10 billion in food. Nestlé has about $15 billion in European sales but, with acquisitions, PM figures it will grow faster.

There is much speculation centered on acquisition targets. One is rumored to be H. J. Heinz, a European powerhouse. PepsiCo is not considered a likely target but

Cadburry Schweppes is. Another suspected target is Paris-based BSN, which would help PM penetrate the lucrative French cheese market with its Velveeta, Cracker Barrel, and Kraft Natural brands.

For Miles to meet the company's goals, PM must reach $85 billion in sales by 1995, with net income of $9 billion.[40] The future of the tobacco industry, particularly domestically, is cloudy. With numerous product liability lawsuits pending and increasing antismoking sentiments, PM must face the increasingly realistic possibility that cigarette smokers will become virtually nonexistent. As pessimistic as this may sound, a more threatening though less-likely scenario exists: cigarette manufacturing could be banned by the FDA. Within the coming five years, Miles must reposition the firm so it may withstand the effects of declining tobacco income.

[40]Sellers, "Can He Keep."

32

Black Diamond Equipment, LTD.

Steven J. Maranville
University of St. Thomas

Madeleine E. Pullman
Colorado State University

Jeff Jamison looked above at the glistening ice and snow of the frozen waterfalls. He had waited three weeks for the ice to get to this perfect condition, thick enough to support his weight, and the correct consistency for holding the picks of the two axes in his hands and the tooth-covered crampons on his feet. On this Saturday in early January of 1993, he was trying out a new axe, the Black Prophet, a state-of-the-art climbing tool with a light weight, composite handle, and innovative head design produced by Black Diamond Equipment, Ltd. Everyone in the mountaineering world was talking about the Black Prophet's novel design and waiting for the tool to enter the stores in the coming months. Jeff was lucky enough to have a connection with one of Black Diamond's sales representatives and thus had access to the new Black Prophet before its formal release to the market.

At the top of the last pitch of the climb, he sank the Black Prophet in the ice and suddenly felt a disconcerting snap. Jeff watched with disbelief as pieces of the broken axe plummeted thousands of feet to the canyon floor. As he fought off panic, Jeff realized that he would be forced to descend with only one axe, a doable but challenging feat. During the long, arduous descent, all Jeff could think about was how a tool like that one could have left Black Diamond's factory.

The following Monday, January 4, 1993, Mellie Abrahamsen, Black Diamond's new quality assurance manager, a recent MBA graduate from the University of Utah, entered her office and turned on her computer to scan her e-mail. The news of the axe incident was echoing throughout the plant. Research and Development, Production, Customer Service, Marketing, and the president were all demanding an explanation and a plan. With all the excitement over the new design, preseason orders for the Black Prophet had exceeded expectations. Although the tool was on back order for many customers, the first production run of the axe had already been shipped to mountaineering stores throughout the world. Highlighted at the top of

Abrahamsen's e-mail listing was a priority message from Peter Metcalf, president of Black Diamond, calling an emergency meeting with all department heads to develop a plan for handling the crisis.

Monday Morning Meeting

By 9:00 A.M. Black Diamond's top management team was huddled around the square butcher-block table that filled the center of Metcalf's congested corner office. As Mellie Abrahamsen approached, she could see into Metcalf's office through the two large windows that faced the shop floor. Because she was new to the company, many of the artifacts peculiar to Black Diamond still caught her attention.

Metcalf's office walls were decorated with framed photographs of mountain-climbing and skiing adventures. The management team members sitting around the table were dressed casually; many were wearing Black Diamond sportswear—T-shirts and sweaters with the Black Diamond insignia. Abrahamsen squeezed through the office and found a seat next to Metcalf, from which she had a view out the windows.

Metcalf spoke anxiously to the group: "This incident is a devastating blow. Thank goodness the guy didn't get hurt; but now every one of our axes out there is suspect. If we have to issue a recall on the product, that will kill our axe business. If we have to discontinue our axe program, all the European competitors will step in and copy the technology that we worked so long to perfect. Yet think of the liability implications of an accident from this tool! How could this have happened? I thought this axe had the latest and greatest technology! We've never had problems like this with our regular mountaineering axes."

Maria Cranor, the marketing manager, added to Metcalf's fervent speech: "If customers see this axe as being of poor quality, we'll be forced to cease the axe program. But worse, if customers think Black Diamond is a company that markets unsafe products, our whole business is in jeopardy! Black Diamond must not lose its leadership image."

"My sales representatives are having a fit," Stan Smith, manager of customer service, proclaimed loudly. "They have huge back orders for the axe, and the retail shops have several customers a day asking about the tool. You folks know how this industry is—rumors about tool failures and accidents get around fast."

In a despondent tone, the designer of the Black Prophet, Chuck Brainard, said, "I can't believe this nightmare. Just as we were sitting on top of the world with the most innovative design to enter the market in years—all the competition taken by surprise, and a good ice-climbing season ahead—a major stroke of bad luck hits."

"I can't help but think," said Stan Brown, the production manager, "that the cause of the axe's failure is in its design. It's great to be innovative, but I think the design is so innovative that it just doesn't work."

"Now wait a minute, Stan," Metcalf interjected. "I don't want this to deteriorate into finger pointing."

Brainard spoke up. "No, no, that's all right, Peter. Stan might be right. Maybe we did go too far."

Metcalf went on: "We don't know all the facts. So let's stay focused and not jump to conclusions. This is a companywide problem."

Trying to refocus the group, Cranor said, "We tried to cut the lead time on this project so that we would have at least a year of sales before the French, Swiss, and other U.S. competitors could copy our concept and steal our market share. We have a reputation as a high-quality and innovative design company. This incident is potentially very damaging to our reputation as the market leader for innovation."

"We've got to nip this one in the bud and find a way to reassure our customer base," contended Smith. "I need an answer as soon as possible."

John Bercaw, manager of research and development, said, "Stan, I appreciate the urgent need that you're feeling with regard to handling customer concerns, but we need more than a quick fix. We need to find out why the failure occurred and to put systems in place to prevent this from happening again."

"I agree," Metcalf said. "As I said, this is a companywide problem."

Brainard attempted to clarify the situation. "As I see it, the possible sources of the failure are design, materials, and/or assembly."

"I can speak about the development phase of the project," stated Bercaw. "We worked hard to develop this axe and cut down on the lead time between the conceptualization and production of the final tool. Peter, you know we've been under tremendous pressure to have this new axe into the production phase and on the market in under two years."

Metcalf nodded. "That's been our strategy," he said, "being the 'firstest with the mostest.'"

Bercaw continued. "This project has been a real struggle: we've been working with all sorts of new technologies, like composite construction and modular tool design. The vendors normally don't make tools for these types of applications. They've had a hard time meeting our specifications, and many of the vendors don't want to work on our products because of potential liability implications."

"What about the assembly?" asked Metcalf.

Brown answered, "Well, the shop worked like crazy to get those axes out for the winter season and I put my best people on the rush assembly. The shop has been really taxed, what with the increasing growth rate for all our climbing and mountaineering products. We're always scrambling to meet the back orders. We need more people and new machines to keep up with this demand and improve our quality."

Metcalf persisted. "Do you know of anything in particular that may have been out of the ordinary during assembly?"

Brown replied, "I'd have to talk to Brian, our lead assembler, to see if he has any clues about why that axe could have failed in the field."

Metcalf turned to his left, where Black Diamond's newest management team member was sitting. "I realize that this is all new to you and that you came in after the fact, so I doubt the Quality Assurance Department can do much about this situation now."

Caught somewhat by surprise, Abrahamsen pulled her thoughts together and said, "Since this job is a newly created position, I wasn't here during the design development and testing phase. I would like to see the procedures and testing information on the production lot of axes. Black Diamond wants to be ISO 9000-certified, and we would need to have all those documents for ISO 9000 certification anyway, so this is a good starting place. Meanwhile, I think we should bring all the field axes back for inspection to reinforce customer confidence and prevent what happened on Saturday from happening again."

Looking out of his office's windows, Metcalf pointed to the shop floor and remarked, "Isn't that Brian walking through the shop? Ask him to come in."

Brian Palmer, the lead assembler, entered Metcalf's office. There was no place to sit, so he remained standing. Metcalf explained to Brian the purpose for bringing him into the meeting. Brian indicated that he had heard about the climbing incident involving the Black Prophet.

Metcalf continued. "Brian, we're not on a witch hunt; we're trying to understand the full range of factors that could have contributed to the tool's failure. What can you tell us about the assembly?"

Brian spoke frankly: "I personally put together all of those axes. We didn't have any procedures, because it was the first time we had made a production lot. Normally when we work on a new product, we go through a learning curve trying to figure out the best assembly method. We make so many different types of products in the shop, it's really like a craft shop. And I'm not even sure if I have the most up-to-date prints right now. The vendor had a lot of trouble casting all those parts to the exact dimensions. But I was able to find enough parts that seemed to fit, and with a little extra elbow grease, I hammered the pieces together. I had to work overtime to meet the deadline and get all the preliminary orders out to the customers. But that's what matters—pleasing the customer."

"But is creating a defective axe really pleasing the customer?" questioned Abrahamsen. "What good is it to be first to market if the product fails in the field? Sure, we have to get to market fast; but we also have to make the axe right the first time. The way we deal in the short term with the Black Prophet situation will have some long-term implications for Black Diamond's strategy. I think we should examine the new-product introduction process as well as the ongoing production processes to see how we can prevent this type of thing from happening in the future."

The Market for Mountaineering Equipment

The established customer for mountaineering products, including mountaineering skis, had traditionally been the serious international mountaineer—professionals as well as expert amateurs. Some dedicated mountaineers worked as professional guides and explorers; nonprofessionals had other jobs, but both professionals and amateurs spent their vacations and weekends climbing in their local areas and traveling throughout the world attempting to conquer remote peaks. This traditional customer base had been primarily in North America, eastern and western Europe, Japan, and Korea, although limited numbers of participants were from other countries.

Mountaineering was as popular in Europe as basketball was in the United States, with mountaineering stars earning high incomes through competitions, product endorsements, and other media exposure. Because of the long history of climbing in Europe, the European market was the biggest segment in the world climbing market, with 10 percent of the market in France alone. Not only did the adult urban European population prefer to spend vacations in mountain villages, but increasingly younger generations of Europeans were forsaking crowded beaches for mountain holidays revolving around mountain sports.

Starting in the 1980s, media exposure had brought mountain sports to previously ignored market segments throughout the world. Rock climbing and mountaineering images had become popular for advertising many types of products and for adding "color" to music videos and movie plots. Because of this exposure, teenage and recreational customers—predominantly in the U.S. market—represented high-growth segments, with the noticeable growth rate in the mid-1980s erupting into an explosive rate of 40 percent in the early 1990s. Customers in this growing market segment had no intention of traveling the world looking for untouched and ever more challenging peaks; instead, they climbed and skied purely for fun in their local and national resort areas.

Customarily, people wishing to learn mountain sports would employ guide services and schools for acquiring the necessary skills. The newer converts, however, were bypassing this conventional route by going to indoor climbing gyms or learning skills from friends. Many industry experts speculated that the breakdown of the conventional training methods would contribute to an increased lack of knowledge regarding mountaineering safety and lead to increased accident rates. In turn, accidents would increase the chances of litigation for all firms involved in the industry. These trends concerned mountain-sports firms worldwide.

Competition in the Mountaineering Equipment Industry

Located in Salt Lake City, Utah, Black Diamond Equipment, Ltd., was a major player in the burgeoning international mountaineering industry, on both domestic and global fronts. Black Diamond manufactured and distributed a full range of products for mountain sports, from rock-climbing gear to mountaineering and backcountry skis, and faced few domestic or global competitors whose business was on a similar scale. (Exhibit 1 offers a company/product profile of the mountaineering industry.)

The industry that served the mountaineering market consisted of three groups: retailers, wholesalers, and manufacturers.

RETAILERS

The retail businesses serving the market's diverse variety of mountaineering customers were one of three types. The first group, the "core" mountaineering shops, were small retail operations specializing in products specific to mountaineering such as ropes, climbing protection, climbing axes, expedition clothing, packs, harnesses, and information guides for local and national sites. Because these shops were usually located in mountain areas such as the Rocky Mountains or the Alps, the shop personnel were experts in the special tools and applications for their regions. In addition, these employees often had personal knowledge of other locations around the world.

Mountaineering shops usually carried products made in their region with specialized products from other countries. The core shops competed on the basis of the expertise of their personnel and their stock of technically appropriate tools. These retailers specialized in high-quality, cutting-edge-technology products. Prices were relatively high. The majority of their customers were highly skilled mountaineers. Black Diamond operated a small retail shop in this category located next to its Salt Lake City manufacturing facility. Black Diamond's full product range sold well in its own shop as well as in other core shops.

Because of their remote locations, many core shops made effective use of catalogs as a direct-marketing tool. Several mail-order companies, including Black Diamond's mail-order division, competed in this core area, selling products both nationally and internationally.

The second group, mom-and-pop stores, were also small retail outlets, but they sold all types of equipment, from camping and backpacking equipment to bikes and skis. The product mix varied depending on the geographical location. Most of these stores carried a limited assortment of climbing products—usually ropes, harnesses, and carabiners (small clips used in all climbing applications to attach the climber to rock or snow). The personnel in mom-and-pop stores usually had limited technical knowledge of the products being sold.

The third group consisted of sporting goods and department store chains, ranging in size from regional chains such as Eastern Mountain Sports (seven stores) to national chains such as Recreational Equipment Inc. (REI) (40 stores). These stores, which were located in major cities with access to mass markets, had extensive outdoor clothing departments, tents, stoves, canoes and kayaks, sleeping bags, bikes, skis, and so on. Products in each category were selected for volume sales. Thus, in the climbing department, the product line covered the needs of entry-level or intermediate recreational climbers. The expertise of department store personnel was, however, generally limited.

EXHIBIT 1 Comparative Market Shares of Mountaineering Industry Competitors, by Product

Source: Estimates of industry representatives.

Product Category	Manufacturers	National Market Share %	International Market Share %
Carabiners	Black Diamond	50	10
	Omega	10	3
	SMC	10	3
	Wild Country	10	20
	DMM	10	20
	Petzl	5	30
	MSR (REI)	5	4
Climbing protections	Black Diamond	50	20
	Metolius	20	10
	Lowe	10	10
	Wild Country	10	25
	DMM	10	25
Harnesses	Black Diamond	45	10
	Petzl	20	50
	REI	20	
	Blue Water	10	10
	Wild Country	5	20
Plastic boots	Scarpa*	40	30
	Merrell	25	5
	Koflach	25	40
	Lowe	15	5
Adjustable ski poles	Black Diamond	60	5
	Life Link	40	5
Mountaineer skis	Rossignol	30	50
	Hagen*	20	10
Climbing accessories	Black Diamond	55	15
	Omega	25	10
	Petzl	20	75
Gloves	Black Diamond	50	5
Axes			
Snow climbing	Charlie Moser	50	10
	Black Diamond	20	5
Ice climbing	Black Diamond	30	10
	Charlie Moser	30	16
	DMM	25	30
	Grivel	15	30
Rock shoes	Scarpa*	25	20
	Sportiva	25	35
	Boreal	25	35
	Five Ten	15	5
Ropes	Mamutt	30	50
	PMI*	20	40
	New England	20	0
	Blue Water	20	10

*European manufacturers producing Black Diamond designs.

In the United States, REI was the dominant firm in this group of retailers. REI operated department stores in Seattle, Boston, Los Angeles, and Washington, DC, with limited national competition on this level. Because of its large size and wide scope, REI could buy in volume for all its stores and could offer very competitive prices. The Canadian retailer Mountain Equipment Co-op (MEC) served a similar market in Canada, with a large store in each of Canada's major cities. In France, Au Vieux Campeur owned multiple department stores in major French cities, serving a broad customer base.

WHOLESALERS

Retail outlets bought their product lines from wholesalers during semiannual outdoor equipment shows held throughout the world. The wholesaler category of firms consisted of (1) companies that either manufactured their own products or subcontracted the manufacturing of their designs and distributed their own product lines, (2) companies licensed to distribute the products of other companies in certain geographic areas, and (3) companies that represented various combinations of the two types. Black Diamond was in this last category. The company distributed equipment designed and manufactured in its Utah plant, equipment manufactured for Black Diamond by other firms, and merchandise designed by Black Diamond and distributed under other manufacturers' names. In all, Black Diamond offered over 250 different items, covering most mountain sports (see Exhibit 2).

REI was Black Diamond's biggest wholesale customer, making up almost 10 percent of Black Diamond's total sales. The next biggest customer, Lost Arrow—Japan, was a Japanese distributor comprising 5 percent of Black Diamond's sales. The other major wholesale customers were North American outdoor sports department store chains, mail-order companies, and Black Diamond's own retail shop and mail-order business. Combined, the top 20 percent of Black Diamond's retail customers— roughly 60 companies—accounted for about 80 percent of total sales.

Domestically, Black Diamond's wholesaling competition came from Omega Pacific, which manufactured and distributed its own metal products, and Blue Water,

---

EXHIBIT 2   **Black Diamond's Product Line**

Climbing Protection	**Ropes and Rope Bags**
Camming devices	**Packs**
Nuts	Hip packs
Stoppers	Backpacks
Pitons	**Tents**
Piton hammers	**Snow and Ice Tools**
Slings	Axes
Runners	Crampons
Daisy chains	Ice screws and hooks
Etriers	**Ski Tools**
Webbing	Skis
Belay devices	Bindings
Carabiners	Poles
Harnesses	**Climbing Clothing**
Sport climbing	T-shirts
Alpine mountaineering	Sweatshirts
Big wall	Shorts
Footwear	Pants
Mountaineering boots	Hats
Ski boots	Belts
Rock-climbing shoes	Chalk bags

which wholesaled its own lines of ropes and harnesses. Neither of these companies, however, carried a product line as extensive as Black Diamond's.

The international wholesaling segment included strong competition from two British firms, Denny Morehouse Mountaineering and Wild Country, and a French company, Petzl. These firms wholesaled a full range of mountaineering products manufactured by companies with strong international reputations. Additional competition came from regional firms. Most countries had several smaller manufacturers of specific products such as carabiners or climbing axes that were successful in wholesaling their own products.

Several issues influenced sales in the international marketplace. First, the International Organization for Standardization had mandated that by 1997 "personal protective equipment" would have to meet ISO 9000 quality certification standards in order to be sold in Europe. Companies that had been granted certification stamped their products with a symbol showing that the product's manufacturer had met the relevant ISO 9000 standards. The certification was intended to give consumers more confidence in a product's quality. Most of the European mountaineering manufacturers had initiated the certification process and were well on their way to obtaining certification. In contrast, very few American companies had even begun the certification process. Black Diamond had begun the process but was not yet near completion. (Exhibit 3 provides an overview of the ISO 9000 standards.)

Second, some European countries had a long history of climbing and mountaineering, and certain manufacturers, Grivel, for example, dated back to the late

EXHIBIT 3   ISO 9000 Standards

The ISO 9000 standards provide the requirements for documenting processes and procedures. The intent of the standards is to ensure that organizations "do what they say and say what they do." The standards offer three quality system models—ISO 9001, ISO 9002, and ISO 9003—with increasing levels of stringency. ISO 9003 covers documentation and procedure requirements for final inspection and testing, ISO 9002 adds production and installation, and ISO 9001 includes design and development. An organization chooses the appropriate standard depending on the strategically important functional areas requiring quality procedures. In most cases, manufacturers use ISO 9001 for covering all areas.

In order to receive ISO 9000 certification, a company will spend several years complying with the requirements in the standards. This compliance usually requires extensive documentation of the company's existing quality program and training for all employees involved in processes related to quality. Individual auditors, who work for the international ISO registration organization, evaluate the company for requirement compliance. The certified companies are reevaluated every two years to ensure continuing compliance.

The following is a brief overview of the ISO 9001 requirements:

- The entire quality system must be defined and documented to ensure that each product meets specifications.
- The contractual requirements for quality between the company and the customer must be defined and documented.
- Procedures are required to ensure that critical processes are under control.
- Procedures are required for inspection at all levels and for identification of nonconforming parts or products.
- Procedures are required to prevent nonconforming parts from getting damaged in storage, delivery, or packing.
- Training is required for all personnel affecting quality.
- The quality system must be audited internally to ensure effectiveness and compliance.

1800s. Although several European companies had well-established worldwide reputations for quality and innovative products, others relied on home-country support, producing relatively low-quality, low-priced products. All mountainous European countries had small factories for carabiners, skis, axes, or shoes that produced, at relatively low cost, simple products in high volume for domestic consumption.

Third, the European market was predominantly ethnocentric in purchasing behavior. French climbers preferred to buy French products, while German climbers preferred German products. Because of the risks involved in climbing and mountaineering, customers chose equipment they knew the most about and had the most confidence in. Usually, these products were from the buyers' respective countries.

MANUFACTURERS

As a manufacturer, Black Diamond faced both domestic and international competition. Domestic manufacturing firms ran the gamut from small garage operations to large machine shops with 50 or more employees, and most produced either "software" or "hardware." The software firms worked with textile products such as ropes and harnesses. The majority of the software firms, including Blue Water, Sterling Rope, and Misty Mountain, were located in the southeastern United States. These more specialized manufacturing firms expanded their market by catering to the needs of nonmountaineering industries, such as construction safety, military applications, and spelunking. The hardware group manufactured or assembled metal products such as carabiners and other climbing tools and protection. This group of manufacturers included Friends, Rock Hardware, and Rock Exotica. These firms had reputations as producers of innovative and high-quality equipment.

REI had recently started up a small manufacturing facility for carabiners. The manager of the facility had many years of engineering experience with Boeing Aircraft and had designed a highly automated manufacturing system capable of both production and quality testing.

Because Black Diamond had begun as a machine shop, the company had strong capabilities in metalworking. Specifically, the Salt Lake City facility manufactured cold-forged metal parts associated with carabiners, axes, and other climbing accessories and protection. Hot-forging and casting were subcontracted by Black Diamond to manufacturers specializing in this area. Black Diamond was beginning to expand into simple soft goods, such as slings and other webbing products, and intended to continue developing its in-house sewing capabilities.

Black Diamond had plans to become vertically integrated. Management believed that in-house performance of operations related to core products would enhance Black Diamond's competitiveness. Consequently, Black Diamond had started reviewing some of its subcontracting practices to determine what functions could be brought in-house. In particular, the company wanted to bring in-house all sewing of climbing gear and some metal treatments such as heat-treating.

Other products, such as skis, ski poles, foot gear, and ropes, required very specific technologies, production skills, and economies of scale for competitive pricing and quality. Black Diamond entered into subcontracting agreements with international manufacturers to design and manufacture such products. The company also subcontracted the production of its harnesses to a technically sophisticated harness manufacturer located next door to the Salt Lake City facility that made the harnesses on a semiautomated assembly line. This process required minimal human involvement, in contrast to a "garment industry" sewing process by which one person sews the complete harness from start to finish.

By the late 1980s, European competition was becoming a more significant factor in the U.S. market. In particular, Petzl, a French company with a full range of products, had taken an aggressive position in the U.S. market. Like several of the European competitors, Petzl had a well-established reputation as a producer of high-quality, innovative products. Petzl had set up a manufacturing facility in the United States within 60 miles of Black Diamond's manufacturing facility and had sponsored several professional U.S. climbers. Black Diamond, of course, was making efforts to sell its own products in Europe, but faced the problem of ISO 9000 certification.

Some international manufacturing activity went on in Korea and Japan. Products produced by these manufacturers were marketed and distributed through other international companies. The majority of these products were low-cost, mass-produced items such as carabiners.

The continuing growth of copyright violations and product piracy—especially prevalent within international markets—added a further dimension to global competition. Several U.S. and European companies had used machine shops in Korea and Japan as subcontractors, supplying dies and other technological know-how. Consequently, unlicensed clones of more expensive items were expected to appear soon in the international market.

Black Diamond's Operations

Black Diamond Equipment, Ltd., opened for business in 1989 after a group of former managers, with employee support, bought the assets of Chouinard Equipment from Lost Arrow Corporation during Chapter 11 bankruptcy proceedings. The bankruptcy resulted from four lawsuits related to climbing equipment accidents during the 1980s. Chouinard Equipment was the first U.S. company to develop and manufacture rock-climbing gear. From its inception and for the following decade, Chouinard Equipment had a reputation for innovation and quality unmatched by any national competitors.

After the purchase, the new owners chose a new name for the company that would reflect its roots yet would project a fresh beginning. Chouinard Equipment's previous logo had been a diamond. The new company decided to keep the diamond image and chose the name Black Diamond because of the different associations the name might evoke: diamond in the rough, rogue, bad boy, unusual. (See Exhibit 4 for the Black Diamond logo.) Furthermore, a black diamond was used to identify the most difficult type of run in ski areas, and the company owners hoped the name would appeal to the "extreme" athlete, their primary targeted customer base. Black Diamond's management believed that "if you target the extremists, the recreational customers will follow."

The mission of Black Diamond was "to design, manufacture, and bring to market, in a profitable and on-time manner, innovative and technical products of high quality, high performance, and exemplary durability that are targeted toward our primary customers—climbers and backcountry skiers." The company was committed to 10 guiding principles:

1. Being the market leader, synonymous with the sports we serve and are absolutely passionate about;
2. Having a truly global presence;
3. Supporting the specialty retailer;
4. Creating long-term partnerships with companies we do business with;
5. Being very easy to do business with;

EXHIBIT4   **Black Diamond Logo**

6. Being a fierce competitor with the highest ethical standards;
7. Developing sustainable, competitive advantage;
8. Sharing the company's success with its employees;
9. Creating a safe, personally fulfilling work environment for all employees;
10. Championing the preservation of and access to our mountain environments.

In 1991, the owner-employees relocated the business from Ventura, California, to Salt Lake City, Utah, where they would be closer to the targeted customer. Black Diamond began operations with a staff of roughly 40, covering all functional areas. (See Exhibit 5 for Black Diamond's organizational structure.) Black Diamond was 50 percent owned by employees; the remaining 50 percent of the stock was held by outside investors, predominantly distributors, customers, and friends and family of the main employee stockholders. Of the 50 percent that was employee owned, 75 percent was held by Peter Metcalf, the CEO; Maria Cranor, head of marketing; and Clark Kawakami, the chief financial officer.

In 1993, Black Diamond's annual sales were expected to be approximately $12 million, with a gross profit margin of about 40 percent (around $4.8 million) and a net profit margin of about 10 percent (around $1.2 million). From 1990 through 1993, the climbing industry had experienced tremendous sales growth of 20 to 40 percent per year. The market demanded more innovative products and faster delivery. Black Diamond struggled to keep up with the exploding customer demand by hiring more employees and upgrading shop machinery to increase productivity. Slowly, the original machinery was being replaced by automated machining centers and testing devices. By 1993, the company employed more than 100 people.

Like other metalworking shops, Black Diamond specialized in certain types of metalworking; its areas of specialization consisted of cold-forging metal parts, stamping and forming, computer numerically controlled (CNC) machining, and assembly or fabrication. Forging, stamping, and forming, along with the assembly processes, had been done for 20 years by the original Chouinard company, and these processes were considered to be Black Diamond's technical core. These core processes used the same multiton presses that forced metal stock into a die or mold to obtain the desired shape.

Since moving to Salt Lake City, the company had expanded into CNC machines—large programmable machine tools capable of producing small-to-medium-sized batches of intricate parts—in an effort to reduce costs and to move more production

EXHIBIT 5 Black Diamond Organizational Structure

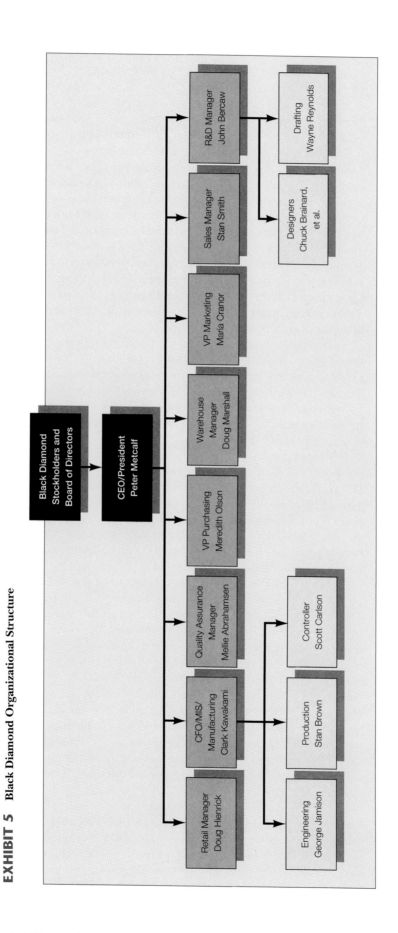

processes in-house. These machines were expensive, but they provided the advantages of capacity and product flexibility. Many of Black Diamond's processes, however, required machinery that was too costly to justify purchase for the manufacturing of a limited number of parts. Consequently, Black Diamond subcontracted with other vendors for aluminum hot-forging, investment casting, laser-cutting steel, preshearing metals, anodizing, heat treating, welding, screw machining, wire forming such as springs, and aluminum extrusion. These processes were subcontracted to achieve economies of scale (e.g., aluminum extrusion) or because the specialized equipment and skills required were beyond Black Diamond's capabilities (e.g., hot-forging).

Black Diamond's production facility was divided into several functional areas: the machine shop, which built prototypes and constructed and maintained tool and die apparatus; the punch press room, where parts were pressed out at a rate of one per second by several multiton presses; a room with assorted machines (including CNC machines), each operated by one person doing drilling, milling, or grinding; a tumbling and polishing room, where large batches of parts were polished; the assembly room, where parts were assembled by individuals or teams; and, finally, a room for materials and shipping.

Supported by a material requirements planning (MRP) system, materials were ordered several months in advance for a full batch of products—for example, 5,000 carabiners or 500 axes. When fairly common parts such as springs and aluminum rod stock were involved, the orders arrived on time and met standard quality requirements. The more complex and customized parts, such as investment-cast axe parts, were difficult for vendors to make to specifications and thus often did not meet the assembly deadline.

When the parts arrived in the materials supply area, one person was responsible for spot-checking the order to see if the parts met specifications. For example, when 500 axe heads arrived, the inspector would randomly select 15 parts and would measure 20 key dimensions on each part to determine if the tolerances met specifications. If one dimension was out of tolerance, the quality manager was summoned for an evaluation. Depending on how much impact the flaw would have on other assembly processes, a larger meeting, involving all potentially affected parties, might be necessary to determine a course of action.

Most of Black Diamond's products began as a sheet of steel or aluminum rod. After receiving the metal, the incoming inspector would pull a sample to check hardness and dimensions. When production on an order was ready to begin, the metal was moved from a hallway to the press room. The press operator would receive an order for 5,000 parts and would set up the press to begin cutting and smashing parts to shape. Once the dies were in place, the operator would smash a few sample parts and check with an inspector for approval.

As the dies wore down, the parts might turn out to have excess metal, or the logo engraving might be substandard. Depending on the demand for the parts, the inspector might feel pressure to pass on cosmetically imperfect parts. Once approval was given, the operator would proceed to press out as many parts as possible in the shortest time. Often chips of metal would settle in the die and become imbedded in many parts before being discovered by the operator. When this occurred, thousands of parts needed to be scrapped.

After the smashing process, the parts were usually sent out for heat-treating to harden the metal. The heat-treatment plant was located in California, so this procedure had a turnaround time of several weeks. When the parts returned, they went to the tumbling and drilling rooms for further processing. When color was needed, the parts would be shipped out again for anodizing, an electrolytic process by which metal is covered with a protective and/or decorative oxide film.

Finally, when the main body of a product was finished, the materials department would issue batches of all the other components needed to finish that product. All of these parts would proceed to a group of assemblers, seated around tables, who were responsible for putting together the final product. The assembly room was the epitome of a craft shop environment. Large and expensive products such as axes were assembled in small batches by one individual, while products such as carabiners were assembled in larger batches by teams of people who often rotated jobs. The finished products would go through individual testing and inspection before passing to the shipping area. One inspector might evaluate thousands of parts in a day.

Originally, the company had one employee who was responsible for quality assurance and several shop employees who performed quality control functions. The quality assurance person worked for the R&D department and focused on testing new products, prototypes, and work in production. As the company grew and ISO 9000 certification loomed in the future, several members of the management team decided that quality issues needed more prominent attention. Black Diamond needed not only testing but also a plantwide program to ensure that defects did not occur in the first place.

Black Diamond's original quality assurance officer had left the company to guide climbing expeditions, after which Black Diamond's management created a stand-alone quality assurance department and hired Mellie Abrahamsen as the manager. At the time of Abrahamsen's hiring, the members of R&D and the shop functioned along craft-shop lines. Product designers built prototypes on the shop floor, iterating between field testing and lab testing until they felt the design was ready. When the new design went into production, the shop personnel used trial and error to develop an assembly procedure. Out-of-tolerance parts were often accepted by shop personnel, who invented creative ways of adapting the parts or the procedures for assembling the products.

Implementing a quality-control program would mean introducing formal testing and assembly procedures for both designers and shop workers. As Andrew McLean, a head designer, said, "We are like artists here, and you just can't restrain or rush creativity and get good results." Chuck Brainard complained, "If we have to write procedures for every step of production, we'll be changing those things a million times."

Like most machine-shop workers, Black Diamond's shop employees labored under comparatively unglamorous working conditions, involving, for example, noise, grease, and monotony. Many shop workers lacked a high school education and some could not read or write in English. Although the shop workers were the lowest-paid employees at Black Diamond, the company offered them a generous profit-sharing bonus and tried to involve them in monthly meetings concerning the financial performance of the company. Despite these measures, the shop had a high rate of employee turnover.

Because quality control programs require procedure writing, blueprint reading, and statistical techniques, the shop employees needed elementary math and language training so that they could learn the more complicated subjects. Stan Brown acknowledged that the workers needed training, but said, "I can't let those people miss too much work for training. We really need everyone working nonstop to get products out the door."

Many of the professional employees at Black Diamond were avid climbers and users of the products, taking great pride in trying to make the very best products available. Marketing was concerned about keeping up the company's innovative image with new products every season. Production worried about vendor costs, delivery of parts, and the shop's ability to meet sales forecasts. R&D attempted to simultaneously develop buildable new products, reduce lead time for new-product development, and improve existing products. Customer service tried to keep retailers pacified with partial deliveries and promises.

Finally, the new quality assurance department was charged with implementing quality control procedures, conducting training, testing products, and resolving problems attributed to parts or products not meeting specifications. All functional areas faced the problems inherent in trying to achieve the simultaneous goals of meeting customer demand and ensuring the highest-quality products, and the different areas often clashed on the best means and methods of achieving these goals.

The Black Prophet

The concept for the Black Prophet axe was originally developed to round out Black Diamond's product line of axes. The product line had two other axes: the Alpamayo, a glacier-walking and snow-climbing axe; and the X-15, a versatile axe for both snow and ice climbing. The Black Prophet was designed specifically for ice climbing and incorporated an innovative ergonomic shape to reduce arm fatigue, a composite, rubber-bounded shaft construction for gripability and weight reduction, and interchangeable modular components that allowed the use of different types of tools—a hammer head, picks, or an adze—for miscellaneous ice applications. (Exhibit 6 is a drawing of the Black Prophet and its component parts.)

Designing and producing the axe entailed several years of working with different vendors to develop the appropriate production process for each component. The axe was designed as a prototype and field-tested with different constructions until R&D agreed on a specific configuration. This configuration was then reviewed by sales representatives considered to be mountaineering experts and by other company members at the quarterly meetings. If the tool did not pass the scrutiny of those examiners, R&D would begin a new phase of prototype development and field tests. This development process would continue until a companywide consensus was reached.

The axe required five parts: shaft, head, hammer, pick, and adze. Three parts were cast metal, requiring a casting subcontractor with the ability to meet strict specifications. The composite shaft was produced by a composite and bonding manufacturer, and the pick was manufactured in Black Diamond's plant. Black Diamond received the parts from each vendor, inspected them for conformance to specifications, and assembled the axes.

The Black Prophet, which cost approximately $80 to produce, sold at retail for $200; the wholesale price was $140. The initial shipment of Black Prophets for the winter season of 1993 comprised approximately 200 axes. Management expected the Black Prophet to be one of Black Diamond's top 10 selling winter products, with yearly sales projected to be at least 2,500 units. The entire company regarded it as a very big image item on the world mountaineering scene. Every competitor in the industry had an axe for glacier walking; axes were especially popular in Europe, where Black Diamond foresaw superb potential for its new offering.

The axe had been well received at the previous year's outdoor product show. At that time, no other axe like it was in the wings, and the climbing industry anticipated the Black Prophet's arrival with great excitement. All of the major U.S. and European industry magazines had published articles about the Black Prophet, and famous mountaineers had called Black Diamond requesting Black Prophets for their upcoming expeditions.

The Dilemma

As the Monday morning meeting continued, Black Diamond's top management team struggled to find answers to the questions raised by the axe crisis. They knew

EXHIBIT 6   **The Black Prophet**

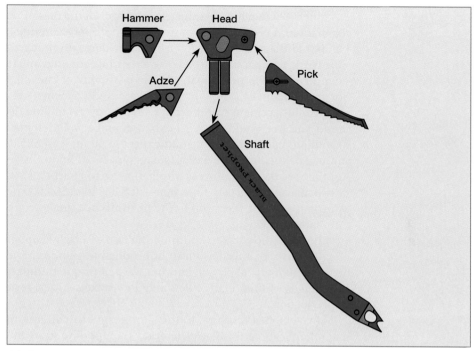

(a) Components Parts

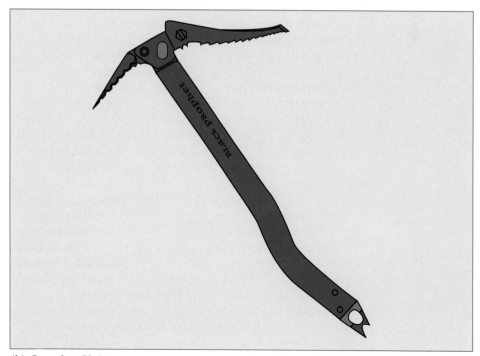

(b) Complete Unit

that the situation required both short- and long-term solutions. In the short term, management needed to address the pressure for immediate delivery confronting customer service. Should management recall all the Black Prophet axes currently on the market? A recall would come with high shipping, testing, and opportunity costs. Or should Black Diamond ignore the incident, assuming the accident was a one-time freak, and continue to sell the axes while refuting any rumors about the product's questionable performance? The possibility of lawsuits had to be considered. For any accident causing injury, legal fees could be expected to run $500,000, and a catastrophic accident could bring a suit for several million dollars. While Black Diamond's insurer would pay legal expenses and any settlement involved, with a cap of $1 million, Black Diamond could expect to pay at least $25,000—the company's insurance deductible—for each legal action. In addition, there would be the costs of lost time for those employees who had to go to court (such costs might involve one or two managers' salaries for a year—at $40,000 to $60,000 per person). Several catastrophic accident cases won by the plaintiffs in a single year could put the company into bankruptcy.

Another option was to continue the sale of Black Prophets—including the axes already released as well as those in production—but to require all units to be sold with a cautionary label. Still another was to just quietly and quickly sell those Black Prophets already in retail outlets and undertake a critical review only of the axes still in production.

Management's response to the short-term issue of customer service would have major implications for Black Diamond's competitive strategy. Would Black Diamond be able to meet the market's rapidly growing demand for all products while improving—or at the very least maintaining—product quality? Would Black Diamond be able to maintain an image as the recognized industry leader in the manufacture of innovative tools and equipment? Would Black Diamond be able to balance the realities of increased risk associated with innovative product design and of increased liability corresponding to the greater potential for accidents, while still establishing a dominant competitive position? Even though various members held strong—and in some cases, divergent—opinions, the management team was willing to consider enterprising alternatives.

Nevertheless, management also knew that a more long-term plan needed to be put into place. "When crises strike," Metcalf said, "there will always be some degree of needing to react to the surprise of the situation. But we need to institute a system of managing crises proactively—that means organizing the business to prevent the preventable crises."

Even though the management team thought the quality assurance department should be a constructive resource in this long-term effort, the department was so new that no one had a clear idea of its role. Abrahamsen also questioned her role: "I was hired to implement a plantwide quality control program and to specifically work on ISO 9000 certification. Representing QA, I'm supposed to improve the efficiency of the company by reducing or eliminating defects in the whole production chain, but I'm not sure that a TQM (total quality management) approach will completely solve Black Diamond's problems. Perhaps the whole process of new-product development and ongoing operations would be more effective if a BPR (business process reengineering) approach were used. Either way, my challenge is to get all these other employees and departments to change the way they do things so they're both more efficient and effective."

(Black Diamond's Web address is www.bdel.com.)

Section VI

Strategic
Marketing Cases

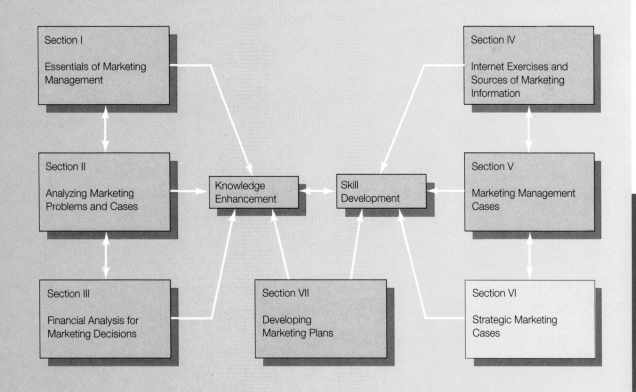

Note to the Student

The 9 cases in this section emphasize the role of marketing in developing successful business or organizational strategies. While marketing is critical in these cases, successful analysis and strategy formulation will often involve other areas in the organization as well.

The knowledge and skills you've developed in the analysis of the cases in the previous section provide a useful foundation for analyzing the cases in this section. However, these cases are intended to broaden your knowledge of marketing and your skills at analyzing various strategic problems.

Case 1

Caterpillar Inc.

Sara L. Pitterle and J. Paul Peter
both of the University of Wisconsin–Madison

After a record year in 1988, Caterpillar's profits declined steadily, culminating in a $404 million loss ($4.00 per share of common stock) in 1991. The loss was attributed to a number of factors, including a prolonged global recession and one-time charges associated with facility closings, consolidation, and employment reductions. These cutbacks were designed to reduce Caterpillar's manufacturing costs over the long term. On April 23, 1992, Caterpillar announced a $132 million loss for the first quarter. Although a strike by the United Auto Workers had disrupted production for the entire quarter, management attributed the loss solely to lower sales. (Appendix A contains a summary of Caterpillar's recent financial performance.)

These losses were incurred by a company which had made unprecedented changes over the past decade in response to the changing industrial equipment market. These changes include a multibillion dollar plant modernization program begun in 1985 and a company reorganization undertaken in 1990. These two changes were designed to ensure Caterpillar's profitability for the 1990s and beyond. However, the 1991 and 1992 profit results led management to wonder whether the changes would be successful.

History

Caterpillar is a multinational corporation headquartered in Peoria, Illinois, that competes in three principal business segments. The company designs, manufactures, and markets engines for a wide range of applications including electrical power generation systems, on-highway trucks, and industrial machinery. The company also designs, manufactures, and markets earthmoving, construction, and materials-handling machinery. (See Appendix B for a complete listing of Caterpillar equipment.) In addition, Caterpillar provides financial products to assist customers in purchasing Caterpillar and noncompetitive related equipment.[1] The company has manufacturing facilities and/or marketing offices in fifteen countries besides the United States.[2]

This case was prepared by Sara L. Pitterle, Nielson Fellow at the University of Wisconsin–Madison, under the supervision of J. Paul Peter.

[1] Caterpillar Inc. Annual Report for 1991.

[2] Taken from speech by Ed Terrel, Manager of Human Resources for Caterpillar Inc., at the University of Wisconsin–Madison, September 23, 1992.

Caterpillar, the largest manufacturer of engines and construction equipment in the world, traces its origins to two inventors, Daniel Best and Benjamin Holt, who in the late 1800s independently developed mechanized agricultural equipment. In February 1889, Daniel Best introduced the first steam-powered harvester, replacing the 40-horse-drawn combine with an 8-man, 11-ton, self-propelled tractor using wheels eight feet in diameter. Around the same time, Benjamin Holt began field testing the first crawler-type equipment, built simply by replacing the wheels on existing equipment with new "track" structures—pairs of treads comprised of wooden slats linked loosely together.

The two companies prospered, driven by increasing demand in agriculture, road building, military equipment, and industrial construction. The introduction of the internal-combustion engine provided yet another boost for the evolving heavy-equipment industry. In 1925, the Holt and Best companies merged to form Caterpillar Tractor Company, setting the stage for several decades of uninterrupted growth through technological leadership and a commitment to total quality.

In 1931, the first Caterpillar diesel tractor was introduced. This product initiated a six-year sales growth from $13 million to $63 million and launched the track-type tractor into prominence as the single largest user of diesel power. Caterpillar's growing reputation for industry leadership and technological superiority was further strengthened during World War II by U.S. government defense contracts. These contracts included demand for both existing equipment (e.g., bulldozers and graders) and special government requests for revolutionary and sophisticated equipment such as air-cooled diesel engines for advanced military operations.

Throughout the postwar years, and into the 1970s, Caterpillar generally concentrated on the development of large industrial-sized machines and engines. During this time the company purchased the Trackson Company of Milwaukee to produce hoists, pipe layers, and hydraulically operated tractor shovels for Caterpillar crawlers. Later, Towmotor Corporation was acquired to continue the company's expansion into heavy equipment with forklift trucks and straddle carriers for a wide range of materials-handling applications. By the early 1970s, Caterpillar had achieved at least foothold positions in a variety of heavy equipment product lines, with the objective of achieving industry leadership in each of the new areas.

In 1977, Caterpillar unveiled the single largest, most technologically advanced tractor in the world—the D-10. Foremost among its advantages were an elevated drive sprocket and modular-designed major components. The elevation of the drive sprocket removed it from high-wear and shock-load areas, reduced overall stress on the undercarriage, and produced a smoother ride. The modular design of major components not only permitted faster and more efficient servicing, but also provided the opportunity to pretest components before final assembly. Modular designs thereby reduced repair and overall downtime in some cases by as much as 80 percent.[3] Caterpillar rapidly introduced other new products which incorporated the modular design concept.

In the early 1980s, after 50 years of uninterrupted profits, Caterpillar appeared to be invincible because of its ability to continually introduce technologically superior machines that became the industry standard. The company built the biggest and the best equipment in the world for which customers were willing to pay hefty premiums. Then, during 1982, in the words of past Caterpillar chairman and chief executive officer George Schaefer, "Almost overnight the world changed for us."[4]

---

[3]Donald Eckrich, "Caterpillar Tractor Company," in J. Paul Peter and James H. Donnelly, Jr., *Marketing Management: Knowledge and Skills,* 3rd ed. (Homewood, IL: Richard D. Irwin, 1991), pp. 702–4.

[4]Ronald Henkoff, "This Cat Is Acting Like a Tiger," *Fortune,* December 19, 1988, p. 72.

The construction industry collapsed. Oil and other commodity prices fell, eliminating demand for Caterpillar equipment in mining, logging, and other heavy equipment markets. The dollar strengthened against the yen, giving Japanese equipment makers, especially Komatsu, an opportunity to aggressively pursue the United States' equipment market with cost advantages of up to 40 percent.[5] If these factors were not enough to disrupt the "profits as usual" pattern at Caterpillar, the United Auto Workers, Caterpillar's largest union, went out on strike for seven months during 1982. After making record profits of $579 million in 1981, the company lost $953 million over the next three years.

Realignment Strategies

Some of Caterpillar's financial problems during the early '80s were a result of management's failure to react to the changing world environment. Caterpillar was increasing its plant capacity at a rate of 5 percent a year as late as 1982, even though expansion in the world heavy-equipment market ended in 1980. In fact, Caterpillar had pursued expansion until less than half of existing capacity was needed. As a result of this overcapacity, the company reduced plant space by one-third, closing 10 plants (8 in the United States) between 1983 and 1987. During this same time period, 28 percent of the company's equity and 40 percent of its labor force, more than 30,000 jobs, were eliminated.[6]

NEW PRODUCTS

With the realization that world demand for large heavy equipment would expand only marginally in the future, the company began to consider other market opportunities. The company recognized that it had been ignoring small contractors who did not need such massive equipment, but who represented a growing market segment. The company responded by introducing new multipurpose products for the owner/operator or small construction contractor. These products included tractor mounted backhoes, front-end loaders, and even farm tractors.[7] While Caterpillar has gained market share in these segments quite successfully (11 percent by 1987), these smaller products also have smaller profit margins and more competition from both domestic manufacturers, such as Deere & Company and Tenneco's J. I. Case, and Japanese companies such as Komatsu, Kawasaki, and Kubota.[8]

PRICE CHANGES

Because of Caterpillar's leadership position in product quality and innovation, the company was able to obtain a premium price for its equipment. However, when Komatsu began offering comparable equipment at a 40 percent lower price in the early 1980s, Caterpillar was forced to cut prices to match those of a competitor for the first time in its history. The company decided to sacrifice profits to protect market share and ensure the company's long-term survival. Even using this strategy, Caterpillar's North American market share dropped 11 points from 1981 to 1986. Most analysts

[5]Allan J. Magrath, "Eight Ways to Avoid Marketing Shock," *Sales & Marketing Management,* April 1989, p. 55.

[6]Robert S. Eckley, "Caterpillar's Ordeal: Foreign Competition in Capital Goods," *Business Horizons,* March–April 1989, p. 80.

[7]Henkoff, p. 73.

[8]Kathleen Deveny, "For Caterpillar, the Metamorphosis Isn't Over," *Business Week,* August 31, 1987, p. 73.

agree the figures would have been worse had the company not slashed prices and profits in response to its competitors.[9]

In addition, Caterpillar recognized that pricing was just one part of the overall revenue-generating strategy for the corporation. Caterpillar pursued other strategies to generate income. For example, the company capitalized on its recognized strength in distribution of products, and sold logistic services to a variety of corporations including Land Rover and Chrysler.[10]

PRODUCTION CHANGES

In response to Japanese competition, Caterpillar also broke with its traditional policy of manufacturing everything it sells. The company's paving equipment, sold under the Cat name, was manufactured by CMI Corp. Caterpillar also began a joint venture with Mitsubishi Heavy Industries Ltd. to make excavation equipment in Japan, as well as light construction equipment and forklifts for the U.S. market. In addition, almost all of the equipment sold with the Caterpillar name in the Pacific Rim was manufactured jointly with Mitsubishi.

PLANT WITH A FUTURE PROGRAM

Although Caterpillar was profitable in 1985, management had no illusions about the company's ability to remain profitable for the long term with its historically high cost structure. For this reason, the company decided to concentrate on driving costs down and improving quality standards. To achieve these objectives, Caterpillar completed a massive six-year, $1.2 billion plant modernization program called *Plant with a Future (PWAF)*. At the heart of PWAF were automation, new factory layouts, and continuous work flow. The program meant a complete remake of Caterpillar's tooling and manufacturing methods, as well as a change to global sourcing to achieve the lowest possible costs on components.

The first priority for the Plant with a Future program was to simplify and integrate assembly-line processes. This objective was accomplished using a cell manufacturing concept in which plants and equipment are arranged to process families of components from start to finish. For example, machining, welding, heat treating, and painting might all be functions within a single cell. Work flow is continuous because all cells feed the assembly line just in time. Thus, the entire plant requires just-in-time (JIT) delivery schedules.

For Caterpillar to integrate just-in-time delivery to each cell, computer integrated manufacturing (CIM) was utilized. CIM links self-contained manufacturing cells (independent islands of automation) to a material tooling and information network. The program allows and enhances electronic communication between engineering, logistics, and the factory floor. At the completion of the modernization program, interplant communication flowed through a corporate information center coupled with global marketing and financial databases. All systems, from the plant's host computer to personal computers on the shop floor, were linked—resulting in unprecedented coordination and optimization of all manufacturing functions.

An example of what Plant with a Future accomplished can be found at the East Peoria, Illinois, transmission factory. Modernization took five years and cost $200 million. While workers put together gears and clutch assemblies, construction crews

---

[9]Henkoff, p. 72.

[10]Allan J. MaGraph, "Ten Timeless Truths about Pricing," *Journal of Consumer Marketing,* Winter 1991, pp. 5–13.

worked to build an underground chamber the size of a high school gymnasium. The chamber became a computer-controlled heat treatment system, just one part of the modernization program that touched every corner of this 20-acre factory. Transmission assembly, formerly performed in five different buildings, has been consolidated under one roof. Nearly every one of the 500 machine tools has been moved or replaced, and all of this modernization was accomplished without slowing down production lines.

Efficiency at the East Peoria plant increased even during modernization. By installing a computerized inventory control system, the time it took to run components through the plant was cut dramatically. The parts for a clutch housing used to take 20 days to assemble and ship under the old system. With the new system, this same process took just four hours. Quality standards were maintained by shifting quality-control responsibilities to the workers themselves. Costs at this plant were expected to drop 19 percent.[11]

COMPANY REORGANIZATION

In addition to the plant modernization program, Caterpillar tried to reduce costs and maintain a competitive advantage by restructuring the entire company. In 1990, the company announced a plan to change the company from its functional structure to a modern product orientation. The new matrix revolves around 13 profit centers spread throughout the world. Each profit center is divided into specific product groups and four service divisions. This new structure has streamlined processes to such an extent that the company has been able to eliminate 1,000 positions that were no longer necessary.[12]

Caterpillar's new structure tied the entire company much more closely to its customers. For example, although Caterpillar has always had an impressive global dealer network, the old structure required countless phone calls to multiple functional areas in order to receive assistance from the company. Under the new structure, customers and dealers are able to contact each product group directly. The ability to effectively communicate with dealers and customers enabled Caterpillar to guarantee delivery of replacement parts in 48 hours or there was no charge.

This enhanced ability to communicate directly with customers and dealers enabled Caterpillar to respond to customer suggestions more rapidly, and allowed the company to exploit product niches. Under the new structure, decisions were pushed down to lower level management throughout the company. This simplification of the decision making chains enabled the company to introduce new models every two years instead of every five as it had under the old system.[13]

LABOR AGREEMENTS

Caterpillar's responses to foreign competitors and sliding market share in the '80s assumed that personnel, both salaried and hourly, would give full support to each new program. The plant-modernization program and the company's reorganization into strategic profit centers required unequivocal labor support to be successful. Caterpillar assumed personnel support through these changes. The company endured a decade of tumultuous relations with its largest union, the United Auto Workers.

The company weathered two prolonged strikes, a seven-month strike in 1982 and a five-month strike beginning in late 1991. In between these strikes, the company

---

[11]Henkoff, p. 74.

[12]Tracy E. Benson, "Caterpillar Wakes Up," *Industry Week,* May 20, 1991, p. 33.

[13]Gary Slutsker, "Cat Claws Back," *Forbes,* February 17, 1992, p. 46.

managed to increase its production flexibility by winning union approval to cut the number of union job classifications from 418 to 150 in 1986.

During the 1991 strike, Caterpillar steadfastly refused to accept another "pattern agreement" with the United Auto Workers as it has done since 1950.* The company maintained that such pattern agreements provided Japanese competitors with a 25 percent wage cost-advantage. While the union never accepted this position, the strike was broken when Caterpillar announced plans to replace all striking workers. The company hoped to gain productivity increases by avoiding job security clauses that were traditionally part of union contracts.

By breaking the union's strike, Caterpillar had an opportunity to negotiate favorable wage and benefit terms but also had to manage a disgruntled and disheartened workforce. The company, at this writing, has not been able to regain workers' trust. In November 1992, the union cancelled all worker involvement programs. These worker involvement programs had been a successful and critical part of both the factory modernization and company reorganization programs. At a single plant in Aurora, Illinois, the worker involvement programs had saved the company in excess of $4 million. Now, many workers view these programs as management's attempt to weaken the influence of the UAW at Caterpillar.[14]

Dealers

While Caterpillar substantially changed its manufacturing systems, philosophy, and corporate structure, the company did not change its distribution system. Caterpillar's channel involved a network of independent dealers. Caterpillar's dealer network handled all sales and service worldwide, with the exception of direct sales to the U.S. government, the Soviet Union, and the People's Republic of China. Caterpillar's 215 independent dealers represented an enterprise almost as large as the company itself; it included operating, sales, parts, and service outlets in more than 140 countries, and employed approximately 72,000 people. A typical dealership sold and serviced Caterpillar equipment exclusively and was likely to be in a second- or third-generation affiliation with the company. Caterpillar's dealer network has long been recognized as the strongest in the industry.

In the early '80s, Caterpillar responded to Komatsu's entrance into the U.S. market by capitalizing on the area where it had a strong competitive advantage—its extensive global dealer network. Caterpillar chose to compete with a total product concept by providing the services that customers deemed most important, which included postsales support and responsiveness to equipment malfunction. Typically, the purchaser of industrial equipment can expect to spend three to four times the original investment on repair and maintenance costs over the life of the machine. While equipment breakdown is a normal part of using this equipment, customers expect quick service and replacement parts for machinery; downtime is extremely costly for them. Caterpillar, through its dealers, has been able to provide unequaled postsales service to the end users.

Caterpillar expects its dealers to be experts in the industry in which they compete. The dealers must know which Caterpillar equipment is required by what market seg-

---

*Pattern bargaining is a potent negotiating tactic for the United Auto Workers, although it was abandoned long ago by unions in other industries like communications and steel. Under pattern bargaining, a union negotiates a new contract with one company and that contract then becomes the pattern for contracts with the company's competitors. In Caterpillar's case, its UAW contract would be patterned on contracts negotiated with both Deere and Tenneco's J. I. Case.

[14]Robert L. Rose and Alex Kotlowitz, "Strife between UAW and Caterpillar Blights Promising Labor Idea," *The Wall Street Journal,* November 23, 1992, Section A: p. 1.

ments and how best to reach these market segments in their own territories. Dealers decide on the best marketing strategy to reach potential customers in their territory. Dealers can elect to reach their customers through direct-mail campaigns, electronic media, trade shows, or some unique combination of the above. The company supports each dealer's marketing plans through merchandising plans, inventory plans, and assistance in pricing and advertising.

Caterpillar recognizes that to sustain its competitive advantage in the industry, it must provide an aggressive program of ongoing training and support for its dealers. Caterpillar provides training for dealership personnel, both sales and service, to make them more responsive to the market and to improve total product image. As the company's product line broadens and deepens, it has to ensure that dealers are aware of each new product and its potential market. In 1985, Caterpillar initiated a program known as the *Sales Team Development System (STDS)*. The aim of the program was to provide professional assistance in utilizing all the resources that are available through Caterpillar. The results from STDS were impressive: 80 percent of the participating dealers felt they significantly improved their planning skills, product/technical knowledge, and general marketing sales skills. Dealers participating in the program increased their net revenues by 102 percent during a time of contraction in global markets.[15]

Caterpillar also increased its support for dealers through improved information flow and communications. The company modernized its communications capabilities with the purchase of advanced computer equipment that allowed for more accurate record and inventory keeping. During the 1991 strike at Caterpillar's U.S. plants, the ability to communicate effectively with dealers enabled Caterpillar to meet the needs of the majority of customers. Equipment was moved between dealers as needed, and some used equipment was leased to customers until new equipment could be made available. Domestic dealers, who normally received most of their inventory from manufacturing plants in the United States, received equipment from Japan, Belgium, and Brazil to meet their customers' orders. Caterpillar management stated repeatedly that they could not identify a single sale lost due to the strike.[16]

Caterpillar's distinct advantage lies not only in its control of the largest market share in the United States, but also in having the most extensive and competent dealership organization in the industry. Its customer offering goes beyond the equipment to a complete package of unique benefits. Caterpillar was able to break away from the competition because of its stronger distribution network. Caterpillar's dealers compete directly and effectively with competitors' dealers, especially Komatsu's and Deere's, by being able to respond to individual customer needs more effectively.

Competition

Caterpillar is striving to remain the dominant manufacturer in a mature industry that has many competitors. One competitor, Japan's Komatsu, has aggressively pursued Caterpillar for the last decade. Its motto has been "Encircle Cat."[17] Long before the crisis in the early 1980s, management had identified Komatsu as deadly serious in its quest to become the new industry leader. While management had

[15]S. Tamer Cavusgil, "The Importance of Distributor Training," *Industrial Marketing Management*, February 1990, p. 5.

[16]Robert L. Rose, "Caterpillar Reports First-Quarter Loss Plays Down Strike," *The Wall Street Journal*, April 23, 1992, Section A: p. 6.

[17]Robert L. Rose and Masayoshi Kanabayashi, "Corporate Focus: Komatsu Throttles Back on Construction Equipment; Japanese Company, Lagging Rival Caterpillar, Eyes Other Areas for Growth," *The Wall Street Journal*, May 13, 1992, Section B: p. 4.

identified the risk, it failed to act upon this information. In 1982, Komatsu began to aggressively pursue market share in the United States. The strong dollar allowed Komatsu to offer prices 40 percent below Caterpillar's prices and still remain profitable.

In 1983, Komatsu continued its aggressive entry into Caterpillar's home market by adding five lines to the crawler tractor and loaders already being sold in the United States. Two years later, the company established a manufacturing plant in Tennessee and bought an old Caterpillar plant in England. In 1988, Komatsu and Dresser formed a 50/50 joint venture for their operations in the United States, Canada, and Latin America. The joint venture combined the two companies' manufacturing, financial, and distribution functions but maintained the companies' separate product lines. The joint venture did not change the dealership network of either company. Komatsu dealers still competed with Dresser dealers in most territories.

Komatsu's surge in the U.S. market slowed in 1987 when it lost its price advantage. Komatsu began to lose market share in the following year, and by 1991 its market share in the United States had fallen from a high of 20 percent to 18 percent. During this same period, Caterpillar increased its market share from 34.5 percent to 36.4 percent.[18]

In addition to losing its price advantage, Komatsu had problems with the Dresser joint venture from the beginning. After the joint venture was established, Dresser executives felt left out of decision making, and most U.S. employees could not understand the work ethic or culture of Japanese personnel. Another major problem for the Komatsu-Dresser venture was that the dealers of both companies struggled against each other for sales, instead of focusing on the major competition from Caterpillar dealers. As a solution to this problem, Komatsu-Dresser began encouraging dealers to combine operations and sell both lines of equipment. Currently, over 50 percent of dealers have combined operations. Komatsu-Dresser's sixty independent U.S. and Canadian dealers have a net worth of $300 million. In comparison, Caterpillar's 65 full-line U.S. dealers have a net worth of $1.72 billion.[19]

Komatsu reported its first annual loss of $14.4 million in 1990. It was followed by a $74 million operating loss in 1991. Both of these losses were attributed to low sales volume as a result of a severe recession. Komatsu began to diversify away from construction equipment, which accounted for 63 percent of the company's total sales. Company executives said publicly that they were no longer trying to overtake Caterpillar as industry leader and that Komatsu's future lies in robotics and machine tools. To underline this shift away from construction equipment, the bulldozer was removed from atop the corporate headquarters in Tokyo.[20]

While Komatsu states that it is no longer going head-to-head with Caterpillar, the companies are still arch rivals in all markets. Although Komatsu has lost many of its competitive advantages, the company has been able to maintain a better relationship with blue-collar workers in its North American factories. In addition, its per unit labor costs are lower than Caterpillar's. In the international market arena, when Caterpillar was constrained by U.S. foreign policy from selling to many former communist countries, Komatsu was able to develop strong trading relationships with them. For example, when Caterpillar was prohibited by the Carter administration from making sales to the Soviet Union, Komatsu was able to provide the necessary equipment.

---

[18]Ibid.

[19]Kevin Kelly, "A Dream Marriage Turns Nightmarish," *Business Week,* April 29, 1991, p. 94.

[20]Robert L. Rose and Masayoshi Kanabayashi, "Corporate Focus: Komatsu Throttles Back on Construction Equipment; Japanese Company, Lagging Rival Caterpillar, Eyes Other Areas for Growth," *The Wall Street Journal,* May 13, 1992, Section B: p. 4.

MAJOR DOMESTIC COMPETITORS

While Caterpillar and Komatsu battle for the number one and two positions in the heavy equipment market around the world, Caterpillar also competes with a number of domestic manufacturers. These include Deere & Company and Tenneco's J. I. Case in selected product lines. While Deere is more commonly known for its major share of the farm equipment market, it does manufacture and market a line of industrial equipment. Caterpillar has met more competition from Deere & Company since introducing backhoes and front-end loaders for smaller construction companies. These are areas that have traditionally been serviced by Deere and others.

Deere & Company has gone through a turbulent decade much the same as Caterpillar. The company has survived strikes by its largest union and a decade-long slump in its farm-equipment markets. Deere responded by trimming its payroll by 29,000 jobs, which included both salaried and hourly positions. The company restructured and modernized its manufacturing facilities to be able to react more quickly and efficiently to changing customer requirements. Deere expects to compete aggressively in all market segments, but sees its best growth potential in the farm equipment segment of its business.

Tenneco's J. I. Case was primarily a manufacturer of tractors and industrial equipment until it acquired International Harvester and Steiger Tractor Company. Case now has a full line of agricultural equipment and has the number two position for the farm equipment market behind Deere & Company. Case competes with Caterpillar primarily in the smaller construction lines and the farm equipment segment.

International Sales

Caterpillar has traditionally sold approximately 50 percent of its products in countries other than the United States. Sales outside of the United States are projected to increase in the future. Many of Caterpillar's greatest opportunities lie in developing countries that are not able to pay for products in hard currency. Caterpillar established the Caterpillar World Trade Corporation in response to these payment difficulties. The World Trade Corporation negotiates payment for Caterpillar equipment in commodities or other finished goods that are then resold to obtain hard currency.

An example of how the World Trade Corporation facilitates Caterpillar's equipment sales can be seen in a recent sale of mining equipment to a Brazilian corporation. Instead of paying for the equipment in an agreed-upon currency, the Brazilian company traded iron ore for it. Caterpillar's World Trade Corporation sold the iron ore to a company in Hungary for men's suits. These suits were then sold in London for hard currency. Although this is a complex means of receiving payment for construction equipment, it allows Caterpillar to take advantage of opportunities in developing countries.[21]

AFRICA

Caterpillar is one of the largest exporters to Africa. The company has been successful on this continent because it has exploited the expertise of its local dealers. In addition, the company has been extremely flexible in arranging sales terms. The company will sell to governments under existing international loans programs, or establish long-term leasing arrangements. Counter-trade options have also been

[21] Taken from speech by Ed Terrel, manager of human resources for Caterpillar Inc., at the University of Wisconsin–Madison, September 23, 1992.

used with success.* The company has met with success on this continent on its own terms. The company, while adopting the local business practices, will not indulge in bribery or other kickbacks, which are a common means of facilitating business exchanges in many parts of this continent. In the future, Africa is expected to be an area of continued growth for mining equipment because of the continent's mineral wealth.

BRAZIL

The decline in the company's overall profits during 1990 was due in large part to difficulties in the Brazilian unit. The unit was profitable through 1989 and the first quarter of 1990, but incurred an operating loss for the year overall. The Brazilian government, in March 1990, introduced austerity programs that curtailed government spending and reduced sales volume for Caterpillar. The Brazilian currency weakened substantially, which meant that sales that were finalized translated into fewer dollars for the parent company.[22] In 1991, due to continuing economic turmoil in Brazil, Caterpillar Brasil S.A. announced the planned closing of its facility in São Paulo and the consolidation of all operations in Piracicaba. Business conditions are expected to continue to be affected by political and economic factors in the short term.

EASTERN EUROPE AND COUNTRIES OF THE FORMER SOVIET UNION

While there are definite opportunities for industrial equipment manufacturers in the countries that made up Eastern Europe and the former Soviet Union, in all these countries some means of payment for imported equipment must be established. Counter-trade arrangements and international loan programs are expected to play a major role in these countries. Caterpillar pursued these opportunities with caution because of continued political instability. The company has tried to extend its distribution network into these countries. However, establishing dealerships in these countries is difficult because most interested parties do not meet Caterpillar's criteria, which include a stable financial position and the ability to do business with Caterpillar in English.

SOUTHEAST ASIA, CHINA, AND PACIFIC RIM COUNTRIES

Caterpillar has been quite successful in pursuing opportunities in these countries. The company has established a special Far East trading company to focus on the opportunities and special problems associated with transacting business in many of these countries. Caterpillar already has a manufacturing plant in Indonesia and has been successful in selling heavy equipment in China. To take advantage of many of these sales, the company has had to establish complex counter-trade arrangements. In the future, there should be additional opportunities in Cambodia if the recently signed peace agreement is successful.

Counter trade has not been necessary when dealing with the developed countries of Australia and New Zealand. Caterpillar had been extremely successful in selling equipment, particularly large mining equipment, in these two countries. Recently, environmental concerns in both these countries have reduced sales. In Australia, large new mining developments in the Northern Territory have been rejected because of environmental concerns and complaints from indigenous people. In addition, the government has been prohibiting the expansion of even existing mining operations in all regions of the country.

---

*Counter-trade options are defined as the selling company accepting commodities in lieu of cash payment. Caterpillar's World Trade Corporation specializes in counter-trade options.

[22]James P. Miller, "Caterpillar Shares Tumble as Firm Says Profit Will Drop Substantially in 1990," *The Wall Street Journal*, June 26, 1990, Section C: p. 15.

Caterpillar's Future

Slow growth in the industrial equipment market is projected for the short term because of continued global recession. In the United States, industrial equipment market growth is closely linked to expansion in the national economy. The need to upgrade and maintain the public infrastructure in older cities is expected to increase and stimulate growth in the construction equipment segment of this market. In addition, highway and bridge repair may continue to provide a major source of market demand, as will the continued construction of new power plants and water supply facilities.

Environmental issues are affecting the demand of industrial equipment. Demand for products used primarily in large mining operations will be most affected by the increased awareness of environmental issues. The world's recent focus on the environment has forced many existing mining operations to downsize, and in some countries, mining projects which would utilize industrial equipment are not being approved.

The equipment market is expected to be stimulated by the growing versatility of products in which attachments are designed to be changed quickly. For example, excavators can now be equipped with bucket or rock-breaker attachments for a wide range of applications. In addition, higher productivity is being achieved through computerized power transmissions that automatically control the engine speed and hydraulic output to maximize productivity and achieve fuel savings. These product improvements promote higher product-replacement rates in the near term.[23]

Caterpillar responded to the challenges of the 1980s better than many other U.S. manufacturers. The company made unprecedented changes and learned from previous mistakes. Even with all these changes, the company still recorded losses in recent years and continues to be troubled by severe labor problems. The company must decide whether there is a profitable future for it as a U.S.–based manufacturer of heavy construction equipment and diesel engines.

[23]1991 U.S. Industrial Outlook.

APPENDIX A Four-Year Financial Summary (Dollars in millions except per share data)

Years Ended December 31

	1991	1990	1989	1988
Sales and revenues	$ 10,182	$ 11,436	$ 11,126	$ 10,435
Sales	9,838	11,103	10,882	10,255
Percent inside U.S.	41%	45%	47%	50%
Percent outside U.S.	59%	55%	53%	50%
Revenues	344	333	244	180
Profit (loss)	(404)	210	497	616
As a percent of sales and revenue	(4.0%)	1.8%	4.5%	5.9%
Profit (loss) per share of common stock	(4.00)	2.07	4.90	6.07
Dividends per share of common stock	1.05	1.20	1.20	.86
Return on average common stock equity	(9.4%)	4.7%	11.6%	16.0%
Capital expenditures:				
Land, buildings, etc.	653	926	984	732
Equipment leased to others	121	113	105	61
Depreciation and amortization	602	533	471	434
R&E expense	441	420	387	334
As a % of sales and revenue	4.3%	3.7%	3.5%	3.2%
Provision (credit) for income taxes	(152)	78	162	262
Wages, salaries, and employee benefits	3,051	3,032	2,888	2,643
Average number of employees	55,950	59,662	60,784	57,954

December 31

	1991	1990	1989	1988
Total receivables:				
Trade and other	2,133	2,361	2,353	2,349
Finance	2,145	1,891	1,498	1,222
Inventories	1,921	2,105	2,120	1,986
Total assets:				
Machinery and engines	9,346	9,626	9,100	8,226
Financial products	2,696	2,325	1,826	1,460
Long-term debt due after one year:				
Machinery and engines	2,676	2,101	2,561	1,428
Financial products	1,216	789	491	525
Total debt:				
Machinery and engines	3,136	2,873	2,561	2,116
Financial products	2,111	1,848	1,433	1,144
Ratios—excluding financial products:				
Ratio of current assets to current liabilities	1.74 to 1	1.67 to 1	1.78 to 1	1.76 to 1
Percent of total debt to total debt and stockholders' equity	43.7%	38.8%	36.4%	34.0%

*Data taken from Caterpillar's 1991 Annual Report, pp. 28–29.

APPENDIX B   Caterpillar Product Line

Source: Tabulated from Caterpillar's 1991 Annual Report.

Type of Equipment	Number of Models
Wheel loaders	10
Integrated tool carriers	4
Backhoe loaders	5
Pavement profilers	4
Asphalt pavers	5
Road reclaimer/soil stabilizer	2
Compaction equipment	15
Wheel tractors	3
Compactors	2
Landfill compactors	4
Track loaders	10
Track-type tractors	22
Motor graders	6
Excavators	18
Pipelayers	4
Scrapers	12
Trucks	6
Tractors	4
Articulated trucks	8
Forest machines	4
Skidders	4
Engines	7
Lift trucks	8

Harley-Davidson, Inc. —Motorcycle Division

J. Paul Peter
University of Wisconsin–Madison

Harley-Davidson, Inc., is a diversified company with corporate headquarters at 3700 Juneau Avenue, Milwaukee, Wisconsin. Its three major business segments include (1) motorcycles and related products, (2) transportation vehicles including both recreational and commercial vehicles, and (3) defense and other businesses. In 1990, the company experienced another record year of growth. In the *Business Week 1,000* ranking of the top U.S. companies, Harley-Davidson, Inc., with a market value of $515 million, moved from the 973rd to the 865th largest U.S. company. Richard F. Teerlink, president and chief executive officer of the company, offered the following introduction to the company's 1990 annual report:

> Fellow Shareholder: I am again pleased to announce a record year at Harley-Davidson, Inc. in terms of revenues, profits and earnings. I'm especially proud this year because we were able to deliver very impressive results despite the fact that 1990—the third and fourth quarters, especially—was tough on most American manufacturers.
>
> Revenues for 1990 totaled $864.6 million, an increase of 9.3 percent over 1989. Net income was $37.8 million, a 14.8 percent increase and net earnings per share increased 11.0 percent to $2.12. Since 1987, revenues, net income, and net earnings per share have increased 33.8, 78.3, and 29.3 percent, respectively. Considering where we were as recently as five years ago, these are tremendous results.

Indeed, these were tremendous results given that the company is the only U.S. motorcycle manufacturer still in business, although there were once more than 140 competitors. In addition, the company had tremendous difficulties surviving the 1970s and early '80s and few analysts thought it would survive. In fact, the company would have gone bankrupt in 1985 had it not gotten refinancing with only days to spare.

Company Background and Operations

Harley-Davidson was established in 1903 and had a virtual monopoly on the heavyweight motorcycle market by the 1960s.[1] In the early '60s Japanese manufacturers entered the marketplace with lightweight motorcycles that did not directly compete with Harley-Davidson. The influx of the Japanese products backed by huge marketing programs caused the demand for motorcycles to expand rapidly.

Recognizing the potential for profitability in the motorcycle market, American Machine and Foundry (AMF, Inc.) purchased Harley-Davidson in 1969. AMF almost tripled production to 75,000 units annually over a four-year period to meet the increases in demand. Unfortunately, product quality deteriorated significantly as over half the cycles came off the assembly line missing parts and dealers had to fix them up in order to make sales. Little money was invested in improving design or engineering. The motorcycles leaked oil, vibrated, and could not match the excellent performance of the Japanese products. While hard-core motorcycle enthusiasts were willing to fix up their Harleys and modify them for better performance, new motorcycle buyers had neither the devotion nor skill to do so. If Harley-Davidson was to remain in business, it desperately needed to improve quality and update its engine designs. Japanese manufacturers also moved into the heavyweight motorcycle market and began selling Harley look-alike motorcycles. Yamaha was the first company to do so and was soon followed by the three other major Japanese manufacturers, Honda, Suzuki, and Kawasaki. Their products looked so similar to Harley's that it was difficult to tell the difference without reading the name on the gas tank. The Japanese companies also copied the style of the Harley advertisements. As one Harley executive put it, "We weren't flattered."

In late 1975, AMF appointed Vaughn Beals in charge of Harley-Davidson. He set up a quality control and inspection program that began to eliminate the worst of the production problems. However, the cost of the program was high. For example, the company had to spend about $1,000 extra per bike to get the first 100 into shape for dealers to sell at around $4,000. Beals along with other senior managers began to develop a long-range product strategy—the first time the company had looked 10 years ahead. They recognized the need to upgrade the quality and performance of their products to compete with the faster, high-performance Japanese bikes. However, they also recognized that such changes would require years to accomplish and a huge capital investment.

In order to stay in business while the necessary changes in design and production were being accomplished, the executives turned to William G. Davidson, Harley's styling vice president. Known as "Willie G." and a grandson of one of the company founders, he frequently mingled with bikers, and with his beard, black leather, and jeans was well accepted by them. Willie G. understood Harley customers and stated that:

> They really know what they want on their bikes: the kind of instrumentation, the style of bars, the cosmetics of the engine, the look of the exhaust pipes, and so on. Every little piece on a Harley is exposed, and it has to look just right. A tube curve or the shape of a timing case can generate enthusiasm or be a total turnoff. It's almost like being in the fashion business.[2]

[1]This section is based on "How Harley Beat Back the Japanese," *Fortune,* September 25, 1989, pp. 155–64.
[2]Ibid., p. 156.

Willie G. designed a number of new models by combining components from existing models. These included the Super Glide, the Electra Glide, the Wide Glide, and the Low Rider. Each model was successful and other Harley executives credit Davidson's skill with saving the company. One senior executive said of Willie G., "The guy is an artistic genius. In the five years before we could bring new engines on-stream, he performed miracles with decals and paint. A line here and a line there and we'd have a new model. It's what enabled us to survive."

Still, Harley-Davidson was losing market share to its Japanese competitors, who continued to pour new bikes into the heavyweight market. By 1980, AMF was losing interest in investing in the recreational market and decided to focus its effort on its industrial product lines. Since AMF could not find a buyer for Harley-Davidson, it sold the company to 13 senior Harley executives in an $81.5 million leveraged buyout financed by Citicorp on June 16, 1981.

In 1982 things turned worse than ever for Harley-Davidson. Overall demand for motorcycles dropped dramatically and Harley's market share of this smaller market also continued to drop. The company had a large inventory of unsold products and could not continue in business with its level of production and expenses. Production was cut drastically, and more than 1,800 of the 4,000 employees were let go.

The Japanese manufacturers continued producing and exporting to the United States at rates well above what the market could endure. Harley-Davidson was able to prove to the International Trade Commission (ITC) that there was an 18-month finished-goods inventory of Japanese motorcycles that fell well below fair market value and asked for protection. The ITC can offer protection to a U.S. industry being threatened by a foreign competitor. In 1983, President Reagan increased the tariffs on large Japanese motorcycles from 4.4 percent to 49.4 percent, but these would decline each year and be effective for only five years. While this did decrease the imports somewhat and gave Harley some protection, Japanese manufacturers found ways to evade most of the tariffs, for example, by assembling more of their heavyweight bikes in their U.S. plants. Harley-Davidson's market share in the 1983 heavyweight motorcycle market slipped to 23 percent, the lowest ever, although it did earn a slight profit. By 1984, it had sales of $294 million and earned $2.9 million; it has continued to increase sales and profits through the early 1990s.

MANUFACTURING CHANGES

From the late 1970s Harley-Davidson executives recognized that the only way to achieve the quality of Japanese motorcycles was to adopt many of the manufacturing techniques used by them. The manufacturing systems changes that were instituted included a just-in-time manufacturing program and a statistical operator control system.[3]

The just-in-time manufacturing program was renamed MAN which stood for Materials As Needed. When the program was discussed with managers and employees at the York, Pennsylvania manufacturing facility, many of them reacted in disbelief. The York plant already had a modern computer-based control system with overhead conveyors and high-rise parts store and the new system would replace all of this with push carts! However, the MAN system eliminates the mountains of costly parts inventory and handling systems, speeds up set-up time, and can solve other manufacturing problems. For example, parts at the York facility were made in large batches for long production runs. They were stored until needed and then loaded on a 3.5 mile conveyor that rattled endlessly around the plant. In some cases, parts couldn't be

[3]This section is based on Thomas Gelb, "Overhauling Corporate Engine Drivers Winning Strategy," *Journal of Business Strategy,* November/December 1989, pp. 8–12.

found, or when they were, they were rusted or damaged. In other cases, there had been engineering changes since the parts were made and they simply no longer fit. The MAN system consists of containers that travel between the place where the parts are made and where they are to be used. The containers serve as a signal at each end to either "feed me" or "empty me." This system is credited with reducing work-in-process inventory by $22 million.

The statistical operator control (SOC) system allows continuous process improvements to reduce costs. The system involves teaching machine operators to use simple statistics to analyze measurements taken from parts to determine dimensional accuracy and quality. The system helps identify problems that occur during production early enough that they can be corrected before many parts are produced.

HUMAN RESOURCE CHANGES

In designing the new manufacturing processes, Harley executives recognized the importance of employee involvement.[4] In 1978 the company was among the first in the United States to institute a companywide employee involvement program. Harley-Davidson was the second U.S. company to begin a quality circles program which permits employees to contribute their ideas, solve problems, and improve the efficiency and quality of their work. Prior to these changes, engineers would figure out how to improve the manufacturing process and then tell operating employees what changes they needed to make. Naturally, the engineering plans were not flawless but the operating employees would not lift a finger to help solve the problems and would simply blame the engineers for screwing up again.

The changes in manufacturing and human resource strategy were credited with a 36 percent reduction in warranty costs; a 46 percent increase in defect-free vehicles received by dealers since 1982; inventory turnover up 500 percent; and productivity per employee up 50 percent.

MARKETING CHANGES

By 1983 Harley executives recognized that they had become too internally-oriented and needed to pay greater attention to customers.[5] They recognized that they would not be able to compete effectively with the Japanese manufacturers by offering a complete product line of motorcycles but rather would have to find a niche and defend it successfully. They decided to focus all of their efforts on the superheavyweight motorcycle market (850cc or greater) and adopted a "close-to-the-customer" philosophy. This involved several unique marketing strategies. First, Harley executives actively sought out and discussed motorcycle improvement issues with customers. Second, it started the Harley Owner Group (HOG) to bring together Harley riders and company management in informal settings to expand the social atmosphere of motorcycling. The club is factory sponsored and is open to all Harley owners. It sponsors national rallies and local events and gives customers a reason to ride a Harley and involves them in a social group whose main activities revolve around the product.

Third, it began a Demo Ride program in which fleets of new Harleys were taken to motorcycle events and rallies and licensed motorcyclists were encouraged to ride them. This program was felt to be critical for convincing potential new customers that Harley-Davidson motorcycles were of excellent quality and not the rattling, leaking bikes of the 1970s. The program was renamed SuperRide and $3 million was

[4]Ibid.
[5]Ibid.

committed to it. A series of TV commercials was purchased to invite bikers to come to any of Harley's over 600 dealers for a ride on a new Harley. Over three weekends, 90,000 rides were given to 40,000 people, half of whom owned other brands. While sales from the program did not immediately cover costs, many of the riders came back a year or two later and purchased a Harley.

Fourth, the company invited several manufacturing publications to visit the plant and publish articles on quality improvement programs. These articles reached the manufacturing trade audience and the national media as well. Finally, recognizing that many dealers viewed their business as a hobby and did not know how to sell, the company increased its sales force by 50 percent to give sales representatives more time to train dealers in how to sell Harleys.

FINANCIAL CHANGES

Although Harley-Davidson was improving its quality, reducing its breakeven point, catching up with competitors in the superheavyweight market, and marketing more aggressively, Citicorp was concerned about the economy and what would happen to Harley-Davidson when the tariffs on Japanese bikes were lifted in 1988.[6] The bank decided it wanted to recover its loans and quit being a source of funds for the company. After a number of negotiations, Citicorp took a $10 million write-off which might have facilitated Harley obtaining new financing. However, other bankers felt that the company must have been in really bad shape if Citicorp took a write-off and refused financial assistance. While lawyers were drawing up a bankruptcy plan, Harley executives continued to seek refinancing. Finally, several banks did agree to pay off Citicorp and refinance the company with $49.5 million.

Harley-Davidson went public with a stock sale on the American Stock Exchange in 1986. The company hoped to raise an additional $65 million and obtained over $90 million with the sale of common stock and high-yielding bonds. It then was in an excellent cash position and purchased Holiday Rambler Corporation, at that time the largest privately held recreational vehicle company in the United States. Holiday Rambler is similar to Harley-Davidson in that it is a niche marketer that produces premium-priced products for customers whose lives revolve around their recreational activities. In 1987 the company moved to the New York Stock Exchange and made two additional stock market offerings. Selected financial data for Harley-Davidson is contained in Exhibits 1 through 4.

By 1987, Harley-Davidson was doing so well that it asked to have the tariffs on Japanese bikes removed a year ahead of schedule. On its 85th birthday in 1988, the company held a huge motorcycle rally involving over 40,000 motorcyclists from as far away as San Francisco and Orlando, Florida. All attenders were asked to donate $10 to the Muscular Dystrophy Association and Harley memorabilia was auctioned off. The event raised over $500,000 for charity. The final ceremonies included over 24,000 bikers whose demonstration of product loyalty is unrivaled for any other product in the world.

Motorcycle Division—Early 1990

Exhibit 5 shows the motorcycle division's growth in unit sales. In 1990, Harley-Davidson dominated the superheavyweight motorcycle market with a 62.3 percent share while Honda had 16.2 percent, Yamaha had 7.2 percent, Kawasaki had 6.7 percent, Suzuki

[6]Ibid.

EXHIBIT 1   Harley-Davidson, Inc., Selected Financial Data (in thousands, except share and per share amounts)

Source: Harley-Davidson, Inc., Annual Report 1990, p. 29.

	1990	1989	1988	1987	1986
Income statement data:					
Net sales	$864,600	$790,967	$709,360	$645,966	$295,322
Cost of goods sold	635,551	596,940	533,448	487,205	219,167
Gross profit	229,049	194,027	175,912	158,761	76,155
Selling, administrative, and engineering	145,674	127,606	111,582	104,672	60,059
Income from operations	83,375	66,421	64,330	54,089	16,096
Other income (expense):					
Interest expense, net	(9,701)	(14,322)	(18,463)	(21,092)	(8,373)
Lawsuit judgment	(7,200)	—	—	—	—
Other	(3,857)	910	165	(2,143)	(388)
	(20,758)	(13,412)	(18,298)	(23,235)	(8,761)
Income from continuing operations before income taxes and extraordinary items	62,617	53,009	46,032	30,854	7,335
Provision for income taxes	24,309	20,399	18,863	13,181	3,028
Income from continuing operations before extraordinary items	38,308	32,610	27,169	17,673	4,307
Discontinued operation, net of tax	—	3,590	(13)	—	—
Income before extraordinary items	38,308	36,200	27,156	17,673	4,307
Extraordinary items	(478)	(3,258)	(3,244)	3,542	564
Net income	$ 37,830	$ 32,942	$ 23,912	$ 21,215	$ 4,871
Weighted average common shares outstanding	17,787,788	17,274,120	15,912,624	12,990,466	10,470,460
Per common share:					
Income from continuing operations	$ 2.15	$ 1.89	$ 1.70	$ 1.36	$ 0.41
Discontinued operation	—	0.21	—	—	—
Extraordinary items	(.03)	(.19)	(.20)	0.28	0.05
Net income	$ 2.12	$ 1.91	$ 1.50	$ 1.64	$ 0.46
Balance sheet data:					
Working capital	$ 50,152	$ 51,313	$ 74,904	$ 64,222	$ 38,552
Total assets	407,467	378,929	401,114	380,872	328,499
Short-term debt, including current maturities of long-term debt	23,859	26,932	33,229	28,335	18,090
Long-term debt, less current maturities	48,339	74,795	135,176	178,762	191,594
Total debt	72,198	101,727	168,405	207,097	209,684
Stockholders' equity	198,775	156,247	121,648	62,913	26,159

In December 1986, the Company acquired Holiday Rambler Corporation. Holiday Rambler Corporation's results of operations are not included in the income statement data for 1986.

had 5.1 percent, and BMW had 2.5 percent. Net sales for the division were $595.3 million with parts and accessories accounting for $110 million of this figure. Production could not keep up with demand for Harley-Davidson motorcycles although a $23 million paint center at the York, Pennsylvania plant was nearing completion and would increase production to 300 bikes per day.[7]

[7]Harley-Davidson, Inc. Annual Report 1990, p. 12.

EXHIBIT 2   Harley-Davidson, Inc., Consolidated Statement of Income (in thousands except per share amounts)

Source: Harley-Davidson, Inc., Annual Report 1990, p. 34.

Years Ended December 31	1990	1989	1988
Net sales	$864,600	$790,967	$709,360
Operating costs and expenses:			
Cost of goods sold	635,551	596,940	533,448
Selling, administrative, and engineering	145,674	127,606	111,582
	781,225	724,546	645,030
Income from operations	83,375	66,421	64,330
Interest income	1,736	3,634	4,149
Interest expense	(11,437)	(17,956)	(22,612)
Lawsuit judgment	(7,200)	—	—
Other-net	(3,857)	910	165
Income from continuing operations before			
provision for income taxes and extraordinary items	62,617	53,009	46,032
Provision for income taxes	24,309	20,399	18,863
Income from continuing operations before extraordinary time	32,610	27,169	38,308
Discontinued operation, net of tax:			
Income (loss) from discontinued operation	—	154	(13)
Gain on disposal of discontinued operation	—	3,436	—
Income before extraordinary items	38,308	36,200	27,156
Extraordinary items:			
Loss on debt repurchases, net of taxes	(478)	(1,434)	(1,468)
Additional cost of 1983 AMF settlement, net of taxes	—	(1,824)	(1,776)
Net income	$ 37,830	$ 32,942	$ 23,912
Earnings per common share:			
Income from continuing operations	$ 2.15	$ 1.89	$ 1.70
Discontinued operation	—	.21	—
Extraordinary items	(.03)	(.19)	(.20)
Net income	$ 2.12	$ 1.91	$ 1.50

Approximately 31 percent of Harley-Davidson's 1990 motorcycle sales were overseas. The company worked hard at developing a number of international markets. For example, anticipating the consolidation of Western European economies in 1992, a European parts and accessories warehouse was established in Frankfurt, Germany, in 1990. After entering a joint venture in 1989 with a Japanese distributor, the company bought out all rights for distribution in Japan in 1990. Revenue from international operations grew from $40.9 million in 1986 to $175.8 million in 1990.

PRODUCT LINE

For 1991, Harley-Davidson offered a line of 20 motorcycles shown in Exhibit 6. Other than the XLH Sportster 883 and XLH Sportster 883 Hugger which had chain drives, all models were belt driven; all models had a five speed transmission. Three of the Sportster models had an 883cc engine and one had a 1200cc engine; all of the remaining models had a 1340cc engine. The first five models listed in Exhibit 6 were touring models while the remaining bikes were standard and cruising types. All of the models exhibited impressive painting and classic styling attributes visually reminiscent of Harley-Davidson motorcycles from the '50s and '60s.

EXHIBIT 3   Harley-Davidson, Inc., Consolidated Balance Sheet (in thousands except share amounts)

Source: Harley-Davidson, Inc., Annual Report 1990, p. 33.

December 31	1990	1989
Assets		
Current assets:		
Cash and cash equivalents	$ 14,001	$ 39,076
Accounts receivable, net of allowance for doubtful accounts	51,897	45,565
Inventories	109,878	87,540
Deferred income taxes	14,447	9,682
Prepaid expenses	6,460	5,811
Total current assets	196,683	187,674
Property, plant and equipment, net	136,052	115,700
Goodwill	63,082	66,190
Other assets	11,650	9,365
	$407,467	$378,929
Liabilities and Stockholders' Equity		
Current liabilities:		
Notes payable	$ 22,351	$ 22,789
Current maturities of long-term debt	1,508	4,143
Accounts payable	50,412	40,095
Accrued expenses and other liabilities	72,260	69,334
Total current liabilities	146,531	136,361
Long-term debt	48,339	74,795
Other long-term liabilities	9,194	5,273
Deferred income taxes	4,628	6,253
Commitments and contingencies (Note 6)		
Stockholders' equity:		
Series A Junior Participating preferred stock, 1,000,000 shares authorized, none issued	—	—
Common stock, 18,310,000 and 9,155,000 shares issued in 1990 and 1989, respectively	183	92
Additional paid-in capital	87,115	79,681
Retained earnings	115,093	77,352
Cumulative foreign currency translation adjustment	995	508
	203,386	157,633
Less:		
Treasury stock (539,694 and 447,091 shares in 1990 and 1989, respectively), at cost	(771)	(112)
Unearned compensation	(3,840)	(1,274)
Total stockholders' equity	198,775	156,247
	$407,467	$378,929

Motorcycle magazine articles commonly were favorable toward Harley-Davidson products but pointed out weaknesses in various models. For example, a review of the XLH Sportster 1200 in the December 1990 edition of *Cycle* reported that

But Harley undeniably has its corporate finger on the pulse of Sportster owners, and knows what they want. All of the complaints—poor suspension, high-effort brakes, awkward riding position, short fuel range, engine vibration, and poor seat—have echoed through the halls of 3700 Juneau Ave. for more than a decade, yet have had

EXHIBIT 4   Harley-Davidson, Inc., Business Segments and Foreign Operations

Source: Harley-Davidson, Inc., Annual Report 1990, p. 43.

A. Business Segments (in thousands)			
	1990	**1989**	**1988**
Net sales:			
Motorcycles and related products	$595,319	$495,961	$397,774
Transportation vehicles	240,573	273,961	303,969
Defense and other businesses	28,708	21,045	7,617
	$864,000	$790,967	$709,360
Income from operations:			
Motorcycles and related products	$ 87,844	$ 60,917	$ 49,688
Transportation vehicles	825	12,791	20,495
Defense and other businesses	2,375	2,236	755
General corporate expenses	(7,699)	(9,523)	(6,608)
	83,375	66,421	64,330
Interest expense, net	(9,701)	(14,322)	(18,463)
Other	(11,057)	910	165
Income from continuing operations before provision for income taxes and extraordinary items	$ 62,617	$ 53,009	$ 46,032

	Motorcycles and Related Products	Transportation Vehicles	Defense and Other Businesses	Corporate	Consolidated
1988					
Identifiable assets	$180,727	$215,592	$2,863	$1,932	$401,114
Depreciation and amortization	10,601	6,958	3	396	17,958
Net capital expenditures	14,121	6,693	66	29	20,909
1989					
Identifiable assets	192,087	176,813	7,018	3,011	378,929
Depreciation and amortization	9,786	7,282	1,125	1,814	20,007
Net capital expenditures	18,705	3,524	1,190	200	23,619
1990					
Identifiable assets	220,656	177,498	7,163	2,150	407,467
Depreciation and amortization	13,722	6,925	1,166	618	22,431
Net capital expenditures	34,099	2,547	1,257	490	38,393

There were no sales between business segments for the years ended December 31, 1990, 1989, and 1988.

B. Foreign Operations			
	1990	**1989**	**1988**
Assets	$25,853	$18,065	$ 6,557
Liabilities	17,717	15,814	3,761
Net sales	82,811	39,653	22,061
Net income	5,555	2,281	1,941

Export sales of domestic subsidiaries to nonaffiliated customers were $93.0 million, $75.4 million and $56.8 million in 1990, 1989, and 1988, respectively.

EXHIBIT 5   **Harley-Davidson Motorcycle Unit Sales 1983–1990**

Source: Adapted from Harley-Davidson, Inc., Annual Report 1990, p. 20.

Year	Total Units	Domestic Units	Exports Units	Export Percentage
1990	62,458	43,138	19,320	30.9
1989	58,925	43,637	15,288	25.9
1988	50,517	38,941	11,576	22.9
1987	43,315	34,729	8,586	19.8
1986	36,735	29,910	6,825	18.6
1985	34,815	29,196	5,619	16.1
1984	39,224	33,141	6,083	15.5
1983	35,885	31,140	4,745	13.2

EXHIBIT 6   **Harley-Davidson, Inc., 1991 Product Line and Suggested Retail Prices**

Source: Adapted from *Cycle World 1991 Motorcycle Buyer's Guide*, pp. 76–82.

Model	Suggested Retail Price
FLTC Tour Glide Ultra Classic	$13,895
FLHTC Electra Glide Ultra Classic	$13,895
FLTC Tour Glide Classic	$11,745
FLHTC Electra Glide Classic	$11,745
FLHS Electra Glide Sport	$10,200
FXDB Sturgis	$11,520
FLSTC Heritage Softail Classic	$11,495
FLSTF Fat Boy	$11,245
FXSTS Springer Softail	$11,335
FXSTC Softail Custom	$10,895
FXLR Low Rider Custom	$10,295
FXRT Sport Glide	$10,595
FXRS Low Rider Convertible	$10,445
FXRS SP Low Rider Sport Edition	$10,295
FXRS Low Rider	$10,195
FXR Super Glide	$ 8,995
XLH Sportster 1200	$ 6,095
XLH Sportster 883 Deluxe	$ 5,395
XLH Sportster 883 Hugger	$ 4,800
XLH Sportster 883	$ 4,395

seemingly little effect on XL sales. H-D sold 24,000 Sportsters over the past two years, and these complaints have been common knowledge to anyone who's cared enough to listen.[8]

The article, however, was very complimentary of the newly designed engine and new five speed transmission and concluded that "This is the best Sportster ever to roll down an assembly line."

A review of the same model in *Cycle World's 1991 Motorcycle Buyer's Guide* pointed out a number of the same problems but concluded that

[8]"Harley-Davidson 1200 Sportster," *Cycle,* December 1990, p. 90.

Yet the bike's appeal is undeniable. A stab at the starter button rumbles it into instant life, and as the engine settles into its characteristically syncopated idle, the bike is transformed into one of the best platforms anywhere from which to Just Cruise. And that means everything from cruising your immediate neighborhood to cruising (with appropriate gas and rest stops) into the next state.

This the bike is more than willing to do, with its premium tires and seemingly bullet-proof reliability. The important thing is to not ask the Sportster 1200 to be something it isn't. What it is, is a Sportster, much as Sportsters always have been.

This is merely the best one yet.[9]

PRICING

The suggested retail prices for 1991 Harley-Davidson motorcycles are also shown in Exhibit 6. These products were premium-priced although the low-end XLH Sportster 883 and XLH Sportster 883 Hugger were less so in order that new motorcyclists could buy them and then trade up at a later time to larger, more expensive models. In fact, in 1987 and 1988, the company offered to take any Sportster sold in trade on a bigger Harley-Davidson at a later time.

The prices for Harleys can be compared with competitive products.[10] For example, the three 1991 Honda Gold Wing touring models with larger 1520cc engines had suggested retail prices of $8,998, $11,998 and $13,998. A Harley look-alike, the Kawasaki Vulcan 88, had a 1470cc engine and a suggested retail selling price of $6,599; a Kawasaki Voyager XII with a 1196cc engine had a suggested retail selling price of $9,099. Another Harley look-alike, the Suzuki Intruder 1400, had a 1360cc engine and a suggested retail selling price of $6,599. The Yamaha Virago 1100, another Harley look-alike, had a 1063cc engine and also had a suggested retail selling price of $6,599.

PROMOTIONAL ACTIVITIES

Kathleen Demitros, vice president of marketing for the Motorcycle Division, discussed a problem in designing advertising for Harley-Davidson motorcycles:

> One of the problems was that we had such a hard-core image out there that it was turning off a lot of people, even though people basically approved of Harley-Davidson. We had to find a way to balance our image more, without turning it into 'white bread' and making it bland. Our goal was to get as close to our Harley riders as possible and communicate with them very personally.[11]

In addition to print advertising in general magazines, and Harley's own quarterly magazine, called *Enthusiast*, Harley has its own catalogs with full color pictures and descriptions of each model and discussions of Harley-Davidson products. For example, following is an excerpt from the 1991 Harley-Davidson catalog:

> To the average citizen, it's a motorcycle. To the average motorcyclist, it's a Harley. To the Harley owner, it's something else entirely, something special. Once you've got your Harley, it's much more than a piece of machinery or a way to get around. In a sense, it actually owns you. It occupies you even when you're not riding it. It's part of your life. And while you might not ever be able to explain it to anyone who doesn't know, you know; the trip certainly doesn't end after the road does. Different? Most wouldn't have it any other way.

---

[9]"Harley-Davidson Sportster 1200—Improving on Tradition," *Cycle World 1991 Motorcycle Buyer's Guide,* April–May 1991, p. 27.

[10]All prices are taken from the same reference as footnote 9.

[11]Kate Fitzgerald, "Kathleen Demitros Helps Spark Comeback at Harley-Davidson," *Advertising Age,* January 8, 1990, p. 3.

In 1990 the Harley Owner Group had 650 chapters and 134,000 members with expected growth in 1991 of 15 percent and an additional 55 chapters.[12] In addition to national, regional, and state rallies and other events, meetings between HOG members and Harley management continued to provide suggestions for product improvements. HOG groups have "adopted" various scenic highways and have taken responsibility for their upkeep. In the 10 years Harley-Davidson and its owner groups have been involved, they have raised over $8.6 million for the Muscular Dystrophy Association.

DEALER IMPROVEMENTS

Several years earlier Harley-Davidson instituted a Designer Store program to improve the appearance, image, and merchandising of its products at the retail level. By the end of 1990, more than 310 of the company's 851 domestic and international motorcycle dealerships had completed major store renovation projects or had agreed to do them in 1991. Some dealers reported receiving full return on the renovation investment within 12 to 18 months due to increased sales brought about by a more inviting shopping environment.

MARKET INFORMATION

The traditional U.S. motorcyclist is an 18- to 24-year-old male.[13] Since 1980, the number of men in this age group has declined from 42.4 million to 35.3 million. By 2000 the number is expected to be only slightly higher, at 36.1 million. Women are buying motorcycles in increasing numbers and sales to them have doubled. However, they still account for only 6 percent of the total motorcycles purchased. Motorcycle manufacturers have responded to this market, however, by designing bikes that are lower slung and easier for women to ride. The Harley-Davidson XLH Sportster 883 Hugger was designed in part for this market.

The sale of motorcycles, including three- and four-wheel off-road vehicles, peaked in 1984 at 1,310,240 units. Five years later sales had dropped to 483,005 units. Sales dropped in all categories, although dirt bikes had the largest sales losses. Sales of larger motorcycles, which tend to be purchased by older buyers for use on highways, represented 12.2 percent of sales in 1984 but increased to 21.3 percent of sales five years later.

As less affluent young men have drifted away from motorcycling, the sport has been taken up by professionals and businesspeople in their 40s and 50s. Likely, the late Malcolm S. Forbes, motorcycle enthusiast and wealthy magazine publisher, influenced this market which is older, more conservative, and often rides long distances with their spouses on luxury vehicles.

There is some evidence that many motorcycle owners do not use their bikes very often, some only for a ride or two in the summer. Although the number of fatal accidents involving motorcycles declined 9 percent in a recent year, this decrease was likely because of decreased usage. The Insurance Institute for Highway Safety reported that in a crash, a person was 17 times more likely to die on a motorcycle than in a car.

COMPETITION

Exhibit 7 shows changes in overall market share percentages for the five major competitors in the U.S. motorcycle market.[14] Honda clearly lost the greatest share and

---

[12]This discussion is based on Harley-Davidson, Inc., Annual Report 1990, pp. 15–26.

[13]This discussion is based on Doron P. Levin, "Motorcycle Makers Shift Tactics," *New York Times,* September 16, 1989.

[14]This discussion is based on "That 'Vroom!' You Hear Is Honda Motorcycles," *Business Week,* September 3, 1990, pp. 74, 76.

EXHIBIT 7   U.S. Motorcycle Market Shares for Major Manufacturers

Source: R. L. Polk & Co., as reported in "That 'Vroom!' You Hear Is Honda Motorcycles," *Business Week*, September 3, 1990, p. 74.

Company	1985	1987	1989
Honda	58.5	50.8	28.9
Yamaha	15.5	19.8	27.7
Kawasaki	10.2	10.2	15.6
Suzuki	9.9	11.6	14.2
Harley-Davidson	4.0	6.3	13.9

its sales decreased from $1.1 billion in fiscal 1985 to $230 million in fiscal 1990. However, motorcycle sales represent less than 1 percent of Honda's worldwide revenues.

Honda's plan to battle its sagging sales involved the introduction of more expensive, technologically-advanced bikes. However, with an increase in the value of the yen from 250 to the dollar in 1987 to 120 by 1988, all Japanese competitors had to raise prices. Honda had to raise their prices even more to cover their new expensive models and became less price competitive. In fact, nearly 600 Honda motorcycle dealers went out of business since 1985, leaving the company with 1,200 dealers in North America. Honda's Maryville, Ohio, plant had so much excess capacity that executives considered transforming much of it to production of auto parts.

Honda's 1990 strategy included cutting back prices and a $75 million advertising campaign to reintroduce the "wholesome" angle of cycling to reach new market segments. Promotional emphasis was also given to encouraging Americans to use motorcycles for commuting as an alternative to cars as is done in Europe and the Far East. High levels of air pollution, increased traffic, and rising fuel costs supported Honda's strategy. The advertising campaign was oriented less to selling individual products than to selling the idea that motorcycling is fun. Honda also offered free rides in shopping malls, sponsors races, and paid for Honda buyers to be trained at Motorcycle Safety Centers throughout the country.

In 1991, Honda's motorcycle product line included 25 models with displacements from 49 to 1520cc's including sportbikes, touring, cruisers, standards, and dual purpose types. It also included four models of 4-wheel all terrain vehicles (ATVs). Kawasaki's line included 23 motorcycle models in a variety of types and four 4-wheel models. Suzuki offered 24 models of motorcycles and 8 4-wheel models. Yamaha offered 25 motorcycle models and 7 4-wheel models. Other smaller competitors in the U.S. market included ATK, BMW, Ducati, Husqvarna, KTM, and Moto Guzzi.

THE FUTURE

Rich Teerlink and the other Harley executives have much to be proud of in bringing back the company to a profitable position. However, they must also plan for the future, a future that is uncertain and fraught with problems. For example, the company faces much larger, well-financed competitors in the industry. The company faces increasing legislation on motorcycle helmet use and noise abatement laws that could decrease industry sales.

The company clearly recognizes the fact that the motorcycle industry has contracted greatly since the mid-1980s. It faces the problem of judging how much to increase supply of Harley-Davidson motorcycles given that it is a mature product whose future is uncertain. It faces decisions concerning how much should be invested in such an uncertain market and what marketing approaches are the most appropriate given this situation.

Case **3**

Nanophase Technologies Corporation

Lawrence M. Lamont
Washington and Lee University

The 2001 business year was finished and **Nanophase Technologies Corporation,** the industry leader in commercializing nanotechnology, had just reported financial results to shareholders. It was a discouraging year for the Romeoville, Illinois, company, with revenues declining to $4.04 million from $4.27 million in 2000. The year was disappointing in other respects as well. Nanophase reported a loss of $5.74 million for 2001, even though management had been optimistic about achieving operating profitability. Reflecting on the Statement of Operations shown in Appendix Table 1 and the Balance Sheet in Appendix Table 2, the company's President and CEO, stated:

> "2001 was disappointing in terms of revenue growth due to the economic recession, especially in the manufacturing sector that represents our primary customer and business development market, and the events in September, which lingered through the end of the year," stated Joseph Cross, President and CEO. "However we believe that the company had several outstanding accomplishments that provide a solid basis for future revenue growth." (Nanophase Technologies Corporation, Press Release, February 20, 2002)

Later, Cross expanded on the operating results and future prospects when Nanophase hosted a quarterly conference call for investors which was broadcast over

Nanophase Technologies Corporation was prepared by Dr. Lawrence M. Lamont, Professor Emeritus of Management, Washington and Lee University. The case is the property of the author and may not be copied or reproduced without written permission. Case material is prepared as a basis for class discussion and not designed to present illustrations of either effective or ineffective handling of administrative problems.

The author gratefully acknowledges Nanophase Technologies Corporation for reviewing the accuracy of the case study and granting permission to reproduce certain materials used in the preparation. Copyright 2002.

the Internet and posted on the company website (www.nanophase.com). In the transcript of his prepared remarks, Cross said:

> Entering 2002, we believe that the company is stronger and better positioned than at any time in its history. We have established the vital delivery capabilities to succeed with our enlarged platform of nanoengineering technologies and delivery capability investments, our market attack is broader and at the same time better focused, the infrastructure-people and equipment are ready to deliver, our processes have been proven demonstrably scalable and robust, and we have strengthened the company's supply chain. (Nanophase Technologies Corporation, Fourth Quarter Conference Call, February 21, 2002)

While Cross was encouraged about the future, there were reasons to be cautious. After all, the company had been in business since 1989 and had not yet earned a profit. Questions arose about 2002, because the U.S. economy was only beginning to emerge from a significant manufacturing recession. Nanophase management remembered that in 2001, after its largest customer had expanded and extended its supply agreement, a weak economy had caused the customer to delay receipt of shipments of zinc oxide powder during the year to adjust inventory. Given the short notice provided by the customer, Cross had indicated that the company would not be able to find additional business to fill the revenue shortfall. Later in 2001, a UK company, Celox, Ltd., failed to fulfill a purchase contract for a catalytic fuel additive which resulted in a substantial loss of revenues and a nonrecurring inventory adjustment. In late November, Nanophase announced a temporary hourly manufacturing furlough until January 7, 2002 to enable the company to reduce existing inventory and lower its cost of operations during the holiday period. (Nanophase Technologies Corporation, Press Releases: October 25 and November 14, 2001 and February 20, 2002)

Transition times from start-up to commercialization exceeding 10 years were not unusual for companies developing emerging technologies. Typically new high-technology firms struggled with product development, experienced set-backs in bringing products to market and were slow to earn profits. Nanophase experienced some of these problems, but the company had managed to achieve a solid record of revenue growth since introducing its first commercial products in 1997. Table 1 summarizes the revenues, profit (loss) and cost of revenues for the 1993–2001 time period.

Nanophase records revenue when products are shipped, when milestones are met regarding development arrangements or when the company licenses its technology and transfers proprietary information. Cost of revenue generally includes

TABLE 1   Revenue, Costs and Profit (Loss), 1993–2001

Source: SEC form 10-K, 1997 and 2002.

Year	Revenues	Net Profit (Loss)	Cost of Revenues
2001	$4,039,469	$(5,740,243)	$4,890,697
2000	4,273,353	(4,518,327)	4,754,485
1999	1,424,847	(5,117,067)	2,610,667
1998	1,303,789	(5,633,880)	3,221,996
1997	3,723,492	(3,072,470)	3,935,766
1996	595,806	(5,557,688)	4,019,484
1995	121,586	(1,959,874)	532,124
1994	95,159	(1,287,772)	167,746
1993	25,625	(729,669)	61,978

costs associated with commercial production, customer development arrangements, the transfer of technology and licensing fees. It does not include all of the costs incurred by the company. Gross margin, a useful indicator of a business's move toward profitability, can be calculated as revenue minus cost of revenue divided by revenue.

What Is Nanotechnology?

Nanotechnology is the science and technology of materials at the nanometer scale—the world of atoms and molecules. It is a multidisciplinary science drawing on chemistry, biology, engineering materials, mathematics and physics. Scientists use nanotechnology to create materials, devices and systems that have unusual properties and functions because of the small scale of their structures. Nanophase uses the technology in its patented manufacturing processes to produce nanocrystalline materials, like microfine zinc oxide powder, sold as a component material to producers of industrial and consumer products, such as cosmetics. See Appendix Table 3 for additional description.

Over the next 20–30 years, it is expected that nanotechnology will find applications in chemicals and engineering materials, optical networking, memory chips for electronic devices, thin film molecular structures and biotechnology. Experts predict that the technology could spawn a new industrial revolution. According to Mihail Roco, senior advisor for nanotechnology at the National Science Foundation's Directorate for Engineering: "This is a technology that promises to change the way we live, the way we combat disease, the way we manufacture products, and even the way we explore the universe. Simply put, nanoscale manufacturing allows us to work with the fundamental building blocks of matter, at the atomic and molecular levels. This enables the creation of systems that are so small that we could only dream about their application years ago." "Because of nanotechnology, we'll see more changes in the next 30 years than we saw in all of the last century." (Roco, 2001)

Because nanotechnology promises to impact so many different industries, the National Nanotechnology Initiative has received the financial support of the United States government. The annual letter sent by the Office of Science and Technology Policy and the Office of Management and Budget to all agencies put nanotechnology at the top of R&D priorities for fiscal year 2001. The expenditures have reflected the priority, and in fiscal 2001 actual federal expenditures for nanotechnology were $463.85 million. In 2002, Congress enacted a fiscal year nanotechnology appropriation of $604.4 million. The 2003 budget request was set at $710.2 million, another substantial increase reflecting the continuing interest and commitment to the commercial potential of the technology. (www.nano.gov)

History of Nanophase Technologies Corporation

Nanophase Technologies Corporation traces its beginnings to the mid-1980s and the research of Richard Siegel, who developed the "physical-vapor synthesis" (PVS) method for producing nanocrystalline materials at the Argonne National Laboratory, southwest of Chicago. Siegel, an internationally known scientist, co-founded the company in 1989 after receiving funding from the Argonne National Laboratory–University of Chicago Development Corporation. The mission of Nanophase was to produce nanostructured materials by developing and applying the PVS process. For several years, the company was located in Burr Ridge, Illinois. In 2000, Nanophase expanded its manufacturing capabilities and moved its headquarters to a facility in Romeoville, Illinois. The original Burr Ridge manufacturing facility was also retained and is currently the main source of PVS production. The Romeoville addition enables the company to increase its manufacturing operations and expand its customer application technology to meet future demand. (Stebbins, 2000; www.nanotechinvesting.com; Nanophase Technologies Corporation, 2000 Annual Report)

DEVELOPING THE TECHNOLOGY

From its beginning as a 1989 start-up, Nanophase emphasized the development of technology, the pursuit of patents and the design of manufacturing processes to transition the company from R&D to a commercial enterprise. Through 1995, the majority of the company's revenues resulted from government research contracts. From this research, the company developed an operating capacity to produce significant quantities of nanocrystalline materials for commercial use. At the same time, Nanophase was involved with potential customers to facilitate the development of products that would utilize the capabilities of the PVS process. During 1996, Nanophase began emerging from product development and in 1997, the first complete year of commercial operations, the company significantly increased its revenues from sales to businesses.

PROTECTING INTELLECTUAL PROPERTY

Nanophase was also successful in protecting its technology, equipment and processes with patents. Early in 2002, the company had 38 U.S. and foreign patents, patent applications, or licenses covering core technologies and manufacturing processes. (Nanophase Technologies Corporation, Fourth Quarter Conference Call, February 21, 2002) Intellectual property such as patents and trade secrets are valuable because they protect many of the scientific and technological aspects of the company's business and result in a competitive advantage.

REDUCING MANUFACTURING COSTS

Nanophase placed importance on research and technology development to reduce manufacturing costs. Although the company de-emphasized the pursuit of revenue from government research contracts in 1995, research was funded by the company to improve manufacturing processes for commercial production. For example, in 2001, Nanophase made expenditures to improve PVS manufacturing technology in product quality and output quantity. Nanophase was successful in reducing variable manufacturing cost by 40 to 65% (including a 25% reduction in manufacturing staff) and increased reactor output by 100 to 200% depending on the material. The company was also successful in commercializing a new, lower-cost manufacturing process, trademarked NanoArc Synthesis™. The new process promises to further cut some production costs by an estimated 50 to 90%, increase production output rates by estimated factors of 2 to 10 times, and permit the use of less expensive raw materials. The process also will allow Nanophase to increase the variety of nanocrystalline products available for sale and address the needs of potential customers who need nanoparticles in liquid solutions and dispersions. (Nanophase Technologies Corporation, Press Release, February 20, 2002; Fourth Quarter Conference Call, February 21, 2002)

FINANCING OPERATIONS

To date, Nanophase has financed operations from a private offering of approximately $19,558,069 of equity securities and an initial public offering in 1997 of 4,000,000 common shares at $8.00 a share to raise $28,837,936 for continued development of the company. (SEC form 10-K405, 1997) In 2000, Nanophase entered into an agreement with BASF (its largest customer) to borrow $1.3 million to finance the purchase and installation of new equipment to meet the customer's requirements during 2001–2002. (Nanophase Technologies Corporation, Press Release, December 8, 2000)

Nanophase will need additional financing to complete another year of operations. At the end of 2001, the balance sheet indicated that about $7.4 million was available from cash and investments. Nanophase has reported cumulative losses of $34,754,188 from inception through December 31, 2001. (Nanophase Technologies Corporation, 2001 Annual Report)

Transition and Changes in Management

To speed the transition to a commercial venture, executives with experience in developing high-technology businesses were hired. According to critics, Nanophase had too many development projects under way and did not have enough products and customers to generate a dependable revenue stream. As a result, the company lost its focus and progress fell behind expectations.

Joseph E. Cross came to Nanophase in November 1998 as a Director and President and Chief Operating Officer. In December 1998, Cross was promoted to CEO and he continues to serve in that capacity. Cross brings a background of directing high-technology start-ups and managing rapid growth and turnaround operations. His biography is in Appendix Table 4.

According to Cross, Nanophase was focused more on pure research than on finding practical applications for nanoengineered materials and making money. Cross stated: "We had a bunch of scientists but didn't have any engineers or a sales distribution or manufacturing system." (Stebbins, 2000) Since his appointment, Cross and his management team have been concentrating on six major areas:

1. Emphasizing new business development to expand revenues.
2. Achieving a positive gross margin on products.
3. Increasing the technology and intellectual property base by developing new manufacturing processes and establishing patents and trademarks.
4. Reducing manufacturing costs by using less expensive raw materials, increasing output rates and yields and reducing supply chain costs.
5. Increasing manufacturing skills and the capability to produce products to address current and new market opportunities.
6. And, strategically positioning the company for economic recovery.

Following his appointment to CEO, Cross moved quickly to expand and strengthen the management team in the areas of marketing, manufacturing, technology and engineering. Table 2 shows the executive officers of the company, including their title,

TABLE 2   **Profile of Executive Officers**

Company Officer	Title	Joined	Previous Experience
Joseph Cross	President and CEO	1998	Senior Management
Daniel Billicki	VP Sales and Marketing	1999	Senior Management
Dr. Richard Brotzman	VP R&D	1994	Research Director
Dr. Donald Freed	VP Business Development	1995	Senior Marketing
Jess Jankowski	VP and Controller	1995	Controller
Dr. Gina Kritchevsky	Chief Technology Officer	1999	Business Development
Robert Haines	VP Operations	2000	Manufacturing

year of appointment and previous business experience. At the end of 2001, Nanophase had approximately 51 full-time employees.

Nanophase also attracted an impressive outside Board of Directors to provide management and technical advice to the company. In addition to Cross, the Board included Donald Perkins, retired Chairman of the Board of Jewel Companies, a Chicago retail supermarket and drug chain; James A. Henderson, former Chairman and CEO of Cummins Engine Company; Richard Siegel, co-founder and internationally known scientist; Jerry Pearlman, retired Chairman of Zenith Electronics Corporation and James McClung, a Senior Vice President and a corporate officer for FMC Corporation. Donald Perkins currently serves as Chairman of the Nanophase Board of Directors. (www.nanophase.com)

The Science of Nanotechnology at Nanophase

Nanotechnology is used to produce nanocrystalline particles in powder form using metallic materials such as aluminum, cerium, copper, iron and zin. The extremely small size of the particles, combined with the properties of surface atoms gives nanoparticles unusual chemical, mechanical, electrical and optical properties that often exceed those of the original raw materials.

Different technologies are used to achieve these results, but two of the most important are Physical Vapor Synthesis (PVS) and Discrete Particle Encapsulation (DPE). Figure 1 illustrates the PVS process patented and used by Nanophase.

The PVS process uses a solid metallic wire or rod which is heated in a reactor to high temperatures (about 3000 F) using jets of thermal energy. The metal atoms boil off, creating a vapor. A reactive gas is introduced to cool the vapor, which condenses into liquid molecular clusters. As the cooling process continues, the molecular clusters are frozen into solid nanoparticles. The metal atoms in the molecular clusters mix with reactive gas (e.g., oxygen atoms), forming metal oxides such as zinc and aluminum oxide. The nanocrystalline particles are near-atomic size. For example, about nine hundred million zinc oxide crystals could be spread across the head of a pin in a single layer. (Nanophase Technologies Corporation, 2000 Annual Report)

Because of the PVS process, Nanophase is able to produce nanoparticles with properties that are highly desirable to customers. These product features include spherical, nonporous particles of uniform size and large surface area, particles vir-

FIGURE 1   Nanopase Patented PVS Process

Source: www.nanophase.com

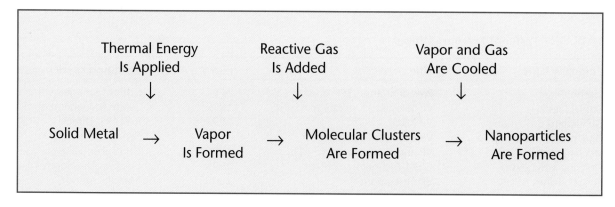

tually free of chemical residues and particles that flow freely without clustering together. The company is also able to use the PVS process and NanoArc Synthesis (TM) to custom-size the particles for a customer's application.

In some applications, the nanoparticles created by the PVS process require additional surface engineering to meet customer requirements. Nanophase has developed a variety of surface treatment technologies to stabilize, alter or enhance the performance of nanocrystalline particles. At the core of these surface treatment technologies is the patented Discrete Particle Encapsulation (DPE) process. DPE uses selected chemicals to form a thin durable coating around nanoparticles produced by the PVS process to provide a specific characteristic such as preventing the particles from sticking together or enabling them to be dispersed in a fluid or polymer to meet specific customer needs. (SEC form 10-K405, 1997)

Product Markets and Customer Applications

Substantial commercial interest has developed in nanotechnology because of its broad application. Although most companies refuse to disclose their work with the technology, it is likely that materials science, biotechnology and electronics will see much of the initial market development. Nanotechnology has already attracted the interest of large companies like IBM (using the technology to develop magnetic sensors for hard disk heads); Hewlett-Packard (using the technology to develop more powerful semiconductors); 3M (producing nanostructured thin film technologies); Mobil Oil (synthesizing nanostructured catalysts for chemical plants) and Merck (producing nanoparticle medicines). In other applications, Toyota has fabricated nanoparticle reinforced polymeric materials for cars in Japan and Samsung Electronics is working on a flat panel display with carbon nanotubes in Korea. (Roco, 2001)

Nanophase is not active in all of the areas. Instead, the company focuses selectively on products and market opportunities in materials science that can be developed within 12–18 months. Longer range product applications in the 18–36 month time frame were also of interest, but they were pursued mainly to give the company a pipeline of new, future opportunities. Nanophase evaluated markets by using criteria such as revenue potential, time-to-market and whether or not a product developed for one application could be successfully modified for sale in other markets.

Dr. Donald Freed, Vice President of Business Development, explained the company's strategy for commercializing nanotechnology: "Opportunities for nanomaterials will mature at different rates, and there are substantial opportunities in the near term—those with a not too demanding level of technical complexity. There are truly different problems in nanotechnology, such as those falling into the realm of human genetics or biotechnology. So we are successfully pursuing a staged approach to developing products for our customers." Freed further explained that this staged approach to developing customer applications enables the company to build product-related revenues while also expanding its foundations for developing more complicated applications. Nanophase was established in six product markets and was developing one potential market that met its time-to-market criteria of 12 to 18 months. (Nanophase Technologies Corporation, Press Release, October 31, 2000; Nanophase Technologies Corporation, 2000 Annual Report; Analyst Presentation, 2000)

HEALTHCARE AND PERSONAL PRODUCTS

The largest product market for Nanophase was zinc-oxide powder used as an inorganic ingredient in sunscreens, cosmetics and other health care products produced by the BASF cosmetic chemicals group. In early 2001, BASF signed an exclusive long-term purchase contract in which Nanophase agreed to supply a product that met technical and FDA regulatory requirements for active cosmetic ingredients. When added to a sunscreen the specially designed particles are small enough to allow harmless light to pass through the sunscreen while the ultraviolet light bounces off the particles and never makes it to the skin. Zinc-oxide formulations also eliminate the white-nose appearance on the user's skin without a loss of effectiveness. BASF Corporation is a diversified $30 billion global corporation and the third largest producer of chemicals and related products in the United States, Mexico and Canada. Sales to this company accounted for 75.5 percent of Nanophase revenues in 2001. (SEC form 10-Q, May 15, 2002)

In another healthcare application, Schering-Plough Corporation uses Nanophase zinc oxide as an ingredient in Dr. Scholl's foot spray to act as a fungicide and prevent the nozzle from clogging. (Stebbins, 2000) The unique properties of nanoparticles have also enabled their use in antifungal ointments and as odor and wetness absorbents. Both customers continue to explore opportunities for Nanophase products in other areas. The company estimated the market potential for its products in the healthcare and cosmetics market at approximately $45 million. (Nanophase Technologies Corporation, Press Release, October 31, 2000; Nanophase Technologies Corporation, 2000 Annual Report; SEC form 10-K, 2000; Stebbins, 2000)

ENVIRONMENTAL AND CHEMICAL CATALYSTS

Nanophase was beginning to sell cerium dioxide to a manufacturing company that supplied one of the three largest automobile companies in the U.S. with catalytic converters for installation on a new car model. The product replaced expensive palladium, which was used in the converters to reduce exhaust emissions. Because a pound of nano-size particles has a surface area of 5.5 acres, less active material was needed to produce comparable emission results saving the customer money and space. Catalysts promised to be a rapidly growing market for Nanophase. Opportunities in industry for new types of nanoparticles to catalyze chemical and petroleum processes and for other environmental applications offered the potential to generate $30–$60 million in revenues. (Nanophase Technologies Corporation, Press Release, October 31, 2000; Nanophase Technologies Corporation, 2000 Annual Report)

CERAMICS AND THERMAL SPRAY APPLICATIONS

Nanoparticles were sold for the fabrication of structural ceramic parts and components used in corrosive and thermal environments. The properties of the company's materials enabled the rapid fabrication of ceramic parts with improved hardness, strength and inertness. Fabrication costs were lower because nanoparticles reduced the need for high temperatures and pressures and costly machining during the manufacturing process. Nanophase worked with parts fabricators to design and develop ceramic parts and components using its technologies and materials. (SEC form 10-K405, 1997)

Nanophase products were also used in thermal spray materials to repair worn or eroded metal parts on naval vessels and replace conventional ceramic coatings where properties such as abrasion and corrosion resistance and tensile strength were needed for longer service life. For example, the U.S. Navy uses thermal sprays incorporating aluminum and titanium oxides to recondition worn steering mechanisms in ships and submarines. With less wear and barnacle growth on the bow planes used to steer, the Navy expects to save $100 million a year when the program is fully implemented. Nanophase sells its products to U.S. Navy approved contractors who formulate the spray with nanoparticles and then apply it to critical parts. In addition to the Navy, Nanophase has several development programs with industrial companies involving similar applications. According to Dr. Donald Freed, Vice President of Business Development, "Our materials are being evaluated in such diverse applications as improving wear resistance in the plastics molding industry and in protective coatings for industrial equipment, gas turbine and aircraft engines." The company estimates the potential market for these and similar applications to be in the range of $25 million. (Nanophase Technologies Corporation, Press Release, October 31, 2000)

TRANSPARENT FUNCTIONAL COATINGS

Nanophase has translated the technology used to make transparent sunscreens into ingredients for coatings designed to improve the scratch resistance of high gloss floor coatings, vinyl flooring and counter tops. Apparently, nanoparticles fit so tightly together that they make vinyl flooring up to five times more scratch resistant than existing products. Additionally, Nanophase is pursuing a number of opportunities for abrasion resistant coatings. Eventually the products may end up in automobile and appliance finishes, eyeglass lense coatings, fabrics and medical products. According to management, the opportunity in transparent functional coatings is estimated at $50–$60 million. (Nanophase Technologies Corporation, Press Release, October 31, 2000; Nanophase Technologies Corporation, 2000 Annual Report)

CONDUCTIVE AND ANTI-STATIC COATINGS

Nanophase produces indium/tin oxide and antimony/tin oxide formulations for use as conductive and anti-static coatings for electronic products. The nanoparticle coatings are stored and used at room temperatures, which is an economic advantage to manufacturers. Indium/tin oxide is used primarily as a conductive coating to shield computer monitors and television screens from electromagnetic radiation. The world market for indium/tin oxide conductive coatings is estimated at $10–$20 million.

Antimony/tin oxide materials are used for transparent anti-static coatings in electronic component packaging. Nanophase replaced coatings based on carbon black and/or evaporated metals. The key advantage of nanoparticles in this market is that the transparent coatings maintained anti-static protection while enabling end-users to see the contents inside a package. (Nanophase Technologies Corporation, 2000 Annual Report)

ULTRAFINE POLISHING

The newest application for Nanophase was the use of nanoparticles to create ultra smooth, high quality polished surfaces on optical components. The company provided NanoTek® metal oxides engineered specifically for polishing semiconductors, memory disks, glass photo masks and optical lenses. The application was made possible because of the 2001 technology advances in the core PVS process, commercialization of the new NanoArc Synthesis™ process, and the improved technology for preparation of stable dispersions of nanocrystalline metal oxides. Nanophase received orders of $100,000 and $200,000 for the materials in early 2002 and expected the application to quickly grow to annual revenues of approximately $500,000. (Nanophase Technologies Corporation, Press Release, February 21, 2002)

NANOFIBERS—A DEVELOPING MARKET

In a developing market called Nanofibers, engineered nanoparticles that could be incorporated directly into fibers for better wear properties and ultraviolet resistance were being developed. It was expected that the customer solution would result in a more stain- and wear-resistant fiber with a high level of permanence. The products were being co-developed with leading companies producing nylon, polyester and polypropylene fibers for industrial carpets and textiles. Nanophase estimated that the applications could be commercialized in about 18 months with a potential market opportunity of several million dollars. (Nanophase Technologies Corporation, Fourth Quarter Conference Call, February 21, 2002)

Business Model and Marketing Strategy

BUSINESS MODEL

For most of its revenues, the Nanophase business model used direct marketing to customers. Teams worked collaboratively with prospective customers to identify an unsatisfied need and apply the company's proprietary technology and products to solve a problem. In most cases, the nanocrystalline materials were custom engineered to the customer's application. International and some domestic sales were made through trained agents and distributors that served selected markets. Nanophase was also engaged in ongoing research, technology licensing and strategic alliances to expand revenues. The markets served were those where the technology and nanocrystalline materials promised to add the most value by improving the functional performance of a customer's product or the economic efficiency of a process.

MARKETING STRATEGY

The marketing strategy used a business development team to work on nanotechnology applications with new customers. Business development activities included evaluation and qualification of potential markets, identification of the lead customers in each market and the development of a strategy to successfully penetrate the market. Nanophase then formed a technical/marketing team to provide an engineered solution to meet the customer's needs. Since one-third of the company staff had a masters or doctorate in materials-related fields, including chemistry, engineering, physics, ceramics and metallurgy, Nanophase had the expertise to understand the customer's problem, determine the functions needed and apply nanocrystalline technology. The team formed a partnership with the customer to create a solution that delivered exceptional value. After a satisfactory solution was achieved, application engineering and customer management staff were moved to a sales team organized along market lines. The sales team was expected to increase revenue by selling product and process solutions and broadening the customer base in the target market. Customers and applications were carefully selected so the science and materials would represent a technology breakthrough thus enabling the customer to add substantial value to its business, while at the same time making Nanophase a profitable long-term supplier. (Nanophase Technologies Corporation, 2001 Annual Report)

Although Nanophase focused its strategy in the markets previously mentioned, applications existed in related markets where the performance of products could be improved using similar technologies without extensive re-engineering. Based on market research, these included applications in fibers, footwear and apparel, plastics and polymers, paper, pigments and other specialty markets. The company strategy in these instances was to pursue only those applications which fit its primary business strategy and were strongly supported by a significant prospective customer.

Nanophase permitted prospective customers to experiment with small research samples of nanoparticles. About eight different products, branded NanoTek®, were available for sale in quantities ranging from 25 grams to 1 kilogram. The samples included aluminum oxide, antimony/tin oxide, cerium oxide, copper oxide, indium/ tin oxide, iron oxide, yttrium oxide and zinc oxide. They were sold by customer inquiry and on the Nanophase website in different particle sizes and physical properties. Prices for research materials ranged from $0.80 to $10.00 per gram depending on the product and the quantity desired. (www.nanophase.com)

Customer inquiries were initiated by a variety of methods including the Nanophase web page, trade journal advertising, telephone inquiries, attendance and participation at trade shows, presentations and published papers, sponsorship of symposia and technical conferences and customer referrals. Management and staff followed up on inquiries from prospective customers to determine their needs and qualify the customer and application as appropriate for a nanotechnology solution. Cross described the process as developing a collaborative relationship with the customer. "Our particular sort of chemistry enables people to do things they can't do any other way. To make that happen, you have to have a close relationship with a customer. You have to make it work in their process or their product. So it is indeed providing a solution; not just the powder that we make, which is nanocrystalline in nature. It's formulating the powder to work in a given application." (CNBC Dow Jones Business Video, 1999)

Using management and staff to build collaborative relationships with customers was time consuming and expensive. Table 3 provides the annual selling, general and administrative expenses for the years 1993–2001. While not all of the expenses can be attributed to personal selling, the expenditures are indicative of the substantial growth of the expense category as Nanophase built the business development and marketing capability to commercialize its business. Management expected that these expenses would decrease or stabilize as the markets for the company's products developed.

In a few instances, Nanophase leveraged its resources through partnerships with organizations and individuals focused on market-specific or geographic-specific areas. For example, licensees and agents were used to increase manufacturing, engineering and sales representation. The agents were specialized by geographic region and the types of products they were permitted to sell. Ian Roberts, Director of U.S. and International Sales stated: "The use of experienced sales agents in selected markets is a fast and cost effective way to multiply the Nanophase sales strategy. The agents bring years of industry experience and contacts to the task of introducing nanoparticles to potential customers. We intend to form close partnerships with selected agents for specific products to speed product introduction and horizontal applications." (Nanophase Technologies Corporation, Press Release, November 27, 2000)

TABLE 3   Selling, General and Administrative Expense, 1993–2001

Source: www.nanophase.com; Nanophase 2001 Annual Report; SEC form 10-K405, 1997.

Year	Expenditures
2001	$3,798,543
2000	3,388,758
1999	3,641,736
1998	3,594,946
1997	2,074,728
1996	1,661,504
1995	1,150,853
1994	799,558
1993	556,616

In November 2000, Nanophase appointed Wise Technical Marketing, specialists in the coatings industry, to represent the line of NanoEngineered Products™ in the Midwest and the Gillen Company LLC to promote the NanoTek® metal oxides in Pennsylvania and surrounding areas. Nanophase also announced the appointment of Macro Materials Inc., specialists in thermal spray materials and technology, as its global, nonexclusive agent for marketing and sales of the company's line of NanoClad™ metal oxides for thermal spray ceramic coatings.

Nanophase retained international representation in Asia through associations with C.I. Kasei Ltd. and Kemco International of Japan. C.I. Kasei was the second largest customer, accounting for 9.4 percent of Nanophase revenues in 2001. Kasei was licensed to manufacture and distribute the Company's NanoTek® nanocrystalline products, while Kemco represented conductive coatings. Nanophase was also working with customers in Europe and intended to expand its European presence as part of its future marketing strategy. (Nanophase Technologies Corporation, Press Release, November 27, 2000; Nanophase Technologies Corporation, 2000 Annual Report; SEC form 10-Q, May 15, 2002)

Competition

Competition in nanomaterials is not well-defined because the technology is new and several potential competitors are start-up businesses. However, the situation is temporary and eventually Nanophase could face competition from large chemical companies, new start-ups and other industry participants. Five types of industry participation seem to exist.

First, there were several large chemical companies located in the United States, Europe and Asia already involved in manufacturing and marketing of silica, carbon black and iron oxide nanoparticles sold as commodities to large volume users. The companies have a global presence and include prestigious names such as Bayer AG, Cabot Corporation, Dupont, DeGusa Corporation, Showa Denka and Sumitoma Corporation. All of these companies are larger and more diversified than Nanophase and pose a significant threat because they have substantially greater financial and technical resources, larger research and development staffs and greater manufacturing and marketing capabilities.

Second, there are OEMs making nanoparticles for use in their proprietary processes and products. For example, Eastman Kodak makes nanoparticles for use in photographic film. Similarly, the technology attracted the interest of other large OEMs like IBM, Intel, Lucent Technologies, Hitachi, Mitsubishi, Samsung, NEC, Thermo Electron, Micron Technology, Dow Chemical, Philips Electronics and Hewlett-Packard. They are pursuing applications that involve optical switching, biotechnology, petroleum and chemical processing, computing and microelectronics. These companies are potential competitors in the sense that they could sell nanoparticles not needed in their own operations to outside customers, putting them into competition with Nanophase.

Third is the group of start-up companies shown in Table 4 that will compete directly with Nanophase. These competitors, funded by venture capital or other private sources, are located in the United States, Canada, Europe and the Middle East. Most were founded in the 1990s after nanotechnology began to gain attention. For example, Oxonica Ltd., Nanopowder Enterprises Inc. and TAL Materials are spin-off firms out of university and government research laboratories. They were founded by scientists and engineers attempting to commercialize a

TABLE 4   **Summary of Potential Nanophase Competitors**

Source: Company Internet Websites.

Company	Location	Year Founded	Public/Private
Lightyear Technologies Inc.	Vancouver	1996	Private
Argonide Corporation	Florida	1994	Private
TAL Materials Inc.	Michigan	1996	Private
Altair Nanotechnologies Inc.	Wyoming	1999	Private
Nanomat	Ireland	1995	Private
Oxonica Ltd.	England	1999	Private
Nanopowders Industries	Israel	1997	Private
Nanopowder Enterprises, Inc.	New Jersey	1997	Private
Nanosource Technologies, Inc.	Oklahoma	Unknown	Private

nanotechnology developed while they were employed in a research organization. Richard Laine, a scientist at the University of Michigan, was a driving force behind the founding of TAL Materials. TAL was incorporated to commercialize the nanotechnologies developed in the Science and Engineering Department at the university. (Spurgeon, 2001) Most of the firms listed in Table 4 have not yet reached commercial production. Nanophase is presently the only firm capable of producing substantial quantities of nanoparticles to rigid quality standards. The company is acknowledged by industry peers as the world leader in the commercialization of nanomaterials.

Fourth, there are firms that hold process patents or supply commercial equipment to nanotechnology firms, but also have the capability to produce nanomaterials in small quantities using an alternative manufacturing process. These companies, while not competitors at present, could enter the nanocrystalline materials market and compete with Nanophase in the future. Plasma Quench Technologies is an example. This company, which holds a process patent, recently spun out two small development companies, NanoBlok and Idaho Titanium Technologies, to produce titanium powders using the company's patented plasma quench manufacturing process.

Finally, Altair Nanotechnologies is an emerging competitor that has a natural resource position in titanium mineral deposits. Altair is developing the technology to produce nanoparticles such as titanium dioxide in commercial quantities. The company is completing a manufacturing plant and offering its products for sale on an Internet website. (www.altairtechnologies.com)

Recent Developments

As the U.S. economy dramatically slowed during 2001, companies around the world delayed the receipt of shipments and rescheduled purchase orders for future delivery. Nanophase was impacted by the slowdown, but the company continued to aggressively pursue applications of nanoparticles with selected customers in each of its product markets. Fortunately, the interest level in nanotechnology remained and some customers continued to move forward on the business development projects already initiated. Despite some setbacks, the results of Nanophase's R&D and intensified business development activities slowly began to show results.

APRIL 24, 2002

On April 24, Joseph Cross, President and Chief Executive Officer, offered some observations about the position of the company:

> Cross said that the company entered 2002 with a wider array of improved technology applications tools than it entered 2001 with, and has significantly increased momentum in business development in several markets. "The improvement in our core PVS Technology, commercialization of our new NanoArc Synthesis™ process technology, and multiple application developments during the last half of 2001 and this far into 2002, provide an integrated platform of nanotechnologies that should allow the company to engineer solutions across more markets," explained Cross. (Nanophase Technologies Corporation, Press Release, April 24, 2002)

MAY 29, 2002

Nanophase completed a private placement of 1.37 million newly issued shares of common stock for a gross equity investment of $6.85 million. Nanophase plans to use the net proceeds to fund the continued development and capacity expansion of its NanoArc Synthesis™ process technology, expand marketing and business development activities, increase process capability and capacity in the PVS process and for general corporate purposes. (Nanophase Technologies Corporation, Press Release, May 29, 2002)

JUNE 26, 2002

Nanophase announced a strategic alliance with Rodel, Inc., a part of the Rohm and Haas Electronic Materials Group. Rodel is a global leader in polishing technology for semiconductors, silicon wafers and electronic storage materials. The company will combine its patented technology with Nanophase's new nanoparticle technology to develop and market new polishing products for the semiconductor industry. The alliance is a five-year partnership and supply agreement with appreciable revenues targeted for 2003 and a planned ramp in volume through 2005 and beyond. Nanophase believes that the revenue opportunities approach the size of the company's personal care and sunscreen markets. Rodel, headquartered in Phoenix, Arizona, has operations throughout the United States, Asia and Europe. (Nanophase Technologies Corporation, Press Releases, June 26 and June 28, 2002)

JULY 24, 2002

Nanophase announced financial results for the first two quarters of 2002. Revenues were $3.07 million compared with first half 2001 revenues of $2.12 million for a revenue growth of 45% year-over-year. Gross margin for the first half of 2002 averaged a positive 12% of revenues versus the annual 2001 average of a negative 21%. The company reported a net loss for the first half of 2002 of $2.72 million, or $0.20 per share, compared with a net loss for the first half of 2001 of $2.38 million, or $0.18 per share. Appendix Table 5 shows the comparative results for the first two quarters of operations.

Commenting on the balance of 2002, President Cross noted:

> While we are somewhat concerned with general market conditions and the normal market slowness that we expect during the summer, we remain cautiously positive about 2002. Based on information from current and prospective customers, we currently believe additional orders will be received during July through September toward our an-

nual revenue target. Although orders are always subject to cancellation or change, and these estimates are based on various product mix, pricing, and other normal assumptions, we are maintaining our 2002 revenue target of $7.00 million or an anticipated revenue growth of approximately 75% compared to 2001. (Nanophase Technologies Corporation, Press Release, July 24, 2002)

Synopsis

The 2001 business year had proven to be difficult for Nanophase. The economic recession in the manufacturing sector of the economy had impacted the company's primary customer base: the manufacturing firms using nanomaterials in their processes and products. While interest continued to remain strong in the potential of nanotechnology, it was still difficult to stimulate interest among prospective customers who were also facing economic challenges and declining business activity. Finally, as the third quarter of 2002 rolled in, a slowly improving economic environment was on the horizon. Maybe 2002 and the years that followed would be the breakout years management was planning for.

Discussion Questions

1. Using the Internet, update the financial information on Nanophase. Construct a statement of operations for the next two unreported fiscal years. What are the assumptions and the risks in your forecast?

Answer the remaining questions using the information in the case study.

2. Review the business model of Nanophase. What are the key elements of the model?
3. Why does a technology such as nanotechnology take so long to commercialize?
4. Summarize the marketing strategy used by Nanophase. What is the role of collaboration and relationship marketing in the strategy? What problems (if any) do you see in the strategy?
5. What strategy do you think a competitor might use to compete against Nanophase? Explain.
6. Is management a strength in this company? Explain.

References

Nanophase Technologies Corporation—Press Releases.

Nanophase Announces Second Quarter and First Half 2002 Results, July 24, 2002. PRNewswire.

Nanophase Technologies Provides Additional Information at Annual Shareholder Meeting, June 28, 2002. PRNewswire.

Rodel Partners with Nanophase Technologies to Develop and Market Nanoparticles in CMP Slurries for Semiconductor Applications, June 26, 2002. PRNewswire.

Nanophase Technologies Completes Private Equity Financing, May 29, 2002. PRNewswire.

Nanophase Technologies Announces First Quarter 2002 Results, April 24, 2002. PRNewswire.

Nanophase Receives Order for Ultrafine Optical Polishing Application, February 21, 2002. PRNewswire.

Nanophase Technologies Announces Fourth Quarter and 2001 Results, February 20, 2002. PRNewswire.

Nanophase Announces Temporary Hourly Manufacturing Furlough, November 14, 2001. PRNewswire.

Nanophase Technologies Announces Third Quarter 2001 Results, October 25, 2001. PRNewswire.

Nanophase Technologies Announces Capital Investment, December 8, 2000. PRNewswire.

Nanophase Technologies Increases Sales Representation, November 27, 2000. PRNewswire.

Experts From Nanophase Elaborate on New Technology Opportunities, October 31, 2000. PRNewswire.

Online Magazine and Newspaper Articles

Spurgeon, Brad, "Nanotechnology Firms Start Small in Building Big Future," January 29, 2001. *International Herald Tribune.* www.iht.com.

CEO Interview with Joseph E. Cross, January 22, 2001. Reprinted from The Wall Street Transcript.

Roco, Mihail C. "A Frontier for Engineering," January, 2001. www.memagazine.org.

Stebbins, John, "Nanophase Expects to Turn Tiniest Particles into Bigger Profits," November 5, 2000. www.bloomberg.com

Transcripts of Online Conference Calls, Analyst Presentations and Personal Interviews

Fourth Quarter Conference Call, February 21, 2002. www.nanophase.com

An Interview with Joseph Cross, President and CEO of Nanophase Technologies Corporation, January 2002. www.nanophase.com.

Analyst Presentation, 2000. www.nanophase.com.

CNBC/Dow Jones Business Video, February 9, 1999.

SEC Documents

SEC form 10-K, 2002.

SEC form 10-Q, May 15, 2002.

SEC form 10-K, 2001.

SEC form 10-K, 2000.

SEC form 10-K405, 1997.

Annual Reports

Nanophase Technologies Corporation, 2001 Annual Report.

Nanophase Technologies Corporation, 2000 Annual Report.

Websites

www.altairtechnologies.com

www.argonide.com

www.ltyr.com

www.nano.gov

www.nanomat.com

www.nanophase.com

www.nanopowders.com

www.nanopowderenterprises.com

www.nanosourcetech.com

www.nanotechinvesting.com

www.oxonica.com

www.plasmachem.de

www.talmaterials.com

APPENDIX TABLE 1 Statements of Operations (years ended December 31)

Source: Nanophase Technologies Corporation, 2001 Annual Report.

	2000	2001
Revenue		
Product revenue	$3,824,159	$3,650,914
Other revenue	449,194	388,555
Total revenue	4,273,353	4,039,469
Operating Expense		
Cost of revenue	4,754,485	4,890,697
R&D expense	1,837,036	1,601,671
Selling, general and administrative expense	3,388,758	3,798,543
Total operating expense	9,980,279	10,290,911
Loss from operations	(5,706,926)	(6,251,442)
Interest Income	1,188,599	511,199
Loss before provision for income taxes	(4,518,327)	(5,740,243)
Provision for income taxes	—	—
Net loss	$(4,518,327)	$(5,740,243)
Net loss per share	$(0.34)	$(0.42)
Common shares outstanding	13,390,741	13,667,062

APPENDIX TABLE 2   Balance Sheets (years ended December 31)

	2000	2001
Assets		
Current Assets:		
Cash and cash equivalents	$473,036	$582,579
Investments	16,831,721	6,842,956
Accounts receivable	1,238,334	1,112,952
Other receivables, net	144,818	67,449
Inventories, net	892,674	956,268
Prepaid expenses and other current assets	770,200	381,696
Total current assets	20,350,783	9,943,900
Equipment and leasehold improvements, net	3,266,245	8,914,745
Other assets, net	213,135	325,743
Total Assets	$23,830,163	$19,184,388
Liabilities and Stockholders' Equity		
Current Liabilities		
Current portion of long-term debts	$285,316	$ 714,135
Current portion of capital lease obligations		48,352
Accounts Payable	824,338	1,233,466
Accrued Expenses	884,780	732,427
Total Current Liabilities	1,994,434	2,728,380
Long-term debt	827,984	758,490
Long-term portion of capital lease obligations		53,900
Stockholders' equity		
Preferred stock, $.01 par value; 24,088 authorized and none issued	—	—
Common stock, $.01 par value; 25,000,000 shares authorized and 13,593,914 shares issued and outstanding at December 31, 2000; 12,764,058 shares issued and outstanding at December 31, 1999	135,939	137,059
Additional paid-in capital	49,885,751	50,260,747
Accumulated deficit	(29,013,945)	(34,754,188)
Total stockholders' equity	21,007,745	15,643,618
Total liabilities and stockholders' equity	$23,830,163	$19,184,388

APPENDIX TABLE 3   Nanocrystalline Materials (Nanoparticles)

Source: SEC form 10-K, 2001.

Nanocrystalline materials generally are made of particles that are less than 100 nanometers (billionths of a meter) in diameter. They contain only 1,000s or 10,000s of atoms, rather than the millions or billions of atoms found in larger size particles. The properties of nanocrystalline materials depend upon the composition, size, shape, structure, and surface of the individual particles. Nanophase's methods for engineering and manufacturing nanocrystalline materials results in particles with a controlled size and shape, and surface characteristics that behave differently from conventionally produced larger-sized materials.

APPENDIX TABLE 4   Biographical Profile of Joseph E. Cross, Chief Executive Officer

Source: The Wall Street Transcript, January 22, 2001.

Joseph E. Cross is CEO of Nanophase Technologies Corporation. Mr. Cross has been a Director since November 1998 when he joined Nanophase as President and Chief Operating Officer. He was promoted to Chief Executive Officer in December 1998. From 1993–1998, Mr. Cross served as President and CEO of APTECH, Inc., an original equipment manufacturer of metering and control devices for the utility industry and as President of Aegis Technologies, an interactive telecommunications company. He holds a BS in Chemistry and attended the MBA program at Southwest Missouri University. He brings a background of successfully directing several high-technology start-ups, rapid growth and turnaround operations.

APPENDIX TABLE 5   Statements of Operations (six months ended June 30)

Source: Nanophase Technologies Corporation, Press Release, July 24, 2002.

	June 30, 2001	June 30, 2002
Revenue		
Product revenue	$1,937,489	$2,829,773
Other revenue	183,815	239,755
Total revenue	2,121,304	3,069,528
Operating Expense		
Cost of revenue	1,857,122	2,696,720
R&D expense	800,189	1,003,726
Selling, general and administrative expense	2,226,949	2,091,319
Total operating expense	4,884,260	5,791,765
Loss from operations	(2,762,956)	(2,722,237)
Interest Income	416,616	61,177
Interest Expense	(17,664)	(56,282)
Other, net	(12,000)	(50)
Loss before provision for income taxes	(2,376,004)	(2,717,392)
Provision for income taxes	(30,000)	(30,000)
Net loss	(2,406,004)	(2,747,392)
Net loss per share	$(0.18)	$(0.20)
Common shares outstanding	13,628,562	13,980,694

Case 4

L. A. Gear, Inc.

A. J. Almaney, S. Green, S. Slotkin, and H. Speer
All of DePaul University

Overview

In February 1989, Robert Y. Greenberg stood on the floor of the New York Stock Exchange and watched as the letters "LA" flashed across the ticker tape for the very first time after L. A. Gear was listed on the Big Board. "It was my proudest moment. It was my dream," Greenberg said. "You see, I always wanted to be the president of a company on the New York Stock Exchange,"[1] he added.

For over 14 years, L. A. Gear promoted the Southern-California lifestyle with attractively styled shoes designed primarily for women. Later, however, the company altered its focus to include products that appealed to the men's performance athletic market. The company continued to produce fashion shoes for women, but its core business became the performance athletic market where sales were not as dependent on swings in consumer tastes. The company achieved its position as the number three brand maker of footwear products when it surpassed Converse, Inc. in 1989. Greenberg set his sights at the number one position in the industry by challenging Nike and Reebok.

However, L. A. Gear began to experience financial difficulties in 1991. Its market share dropped from a high of 12 percent in 1990, to 8 percent in 1991, and to 5 percent in 1992. And its net sales declined from $820 million in 1990, to $619 million in 1991, and to $430 million in 1992. The company incurred losses of $45 million in 1991 and $72 million in 1992. As a result, L. A. Gear was unable to obtain credit from its lenders. To enhance its credit rating, L. A. Gear managed to lure a new investor, Trefoil Capital Investors L.P. who, in September 1991, paid $100 million for a 34 percent stake in the company.

Since the Trefoil deal, L. A. Gear's internal operations underwent major restructuring. As part of the restructuring, the Trefoil team replaced L. A. Gear's top management—including the company's founder, Robert Y. Greenberg. Stanley P. Gold, managing director of Trefoil Capital Investors L. P., and Mark R. Goldston,

Presented and accepted by the refereed Midwest Society for Case Research. All rights reserved to the authors and the MSCR. Copyright © 1993 by A. J. Almaney (312) 362-6785. This case was prepared by A. J. Almaney, S. Green, S. Slotkin, and H. Speer of DePaul University and is intended to be used as a basis for class discussion rather than to illustrate either effective or ineffective handling of the situation. A. J. Almaney is Professor of Management at DePaul University.

former Reebok executive, took over. Gold succeeded Greenberg as the company's new chairman and chief executive officer, and Goldston was appointed president and chief operating officer.

Gold and Goldston developed a survival strategy to nurse the ailing L. A. Gear back to health. At the core of the turnaround strategy was a new advertising campaign built around the theme, "Get in Gear." In an effort to create a clear identity for L. A. Gear, Goldston reorganized product lines into three groups: athletic, lifestyle, and children. The new management also launched a restructuring program aimed at paring the company's costs.

In their letter to the shareholders, Gold and Goldston stated, "We believe that the accomplishments of the past year have laid the groundwork upon which we can build to achieve our ultimate objective—to make L. A. Gear a leader in the footwear industry and one of the most admired companies in America." But, will they be able to accomplish their objective in this highly competitive industry?

History

Robert Y. Greenberg, L. A. Gear's founder, had a knack for selling. First, it was wigs. Later it was roller skates and jeans for the trendy residents of Venice Beach, California. Then it was sneakers. As one analyst described him, "Greenberg is the quintessential salesman."[2]

Greenberg's story is a 1980s financial fairy tale with a 1990s climax: A streetsmart shoemaker who always feared being poor would create a pair of sneakers that brought him fortune. As a kid working in the Brooklyn's family produce business and reading his father's copies of *Forbes* magazine, Greenberg set his sights on starting his own company. He took his first step toward that goal by enrolling in a beauty school. After graduation, he opened a chain of hair salons in Brooklyn in the mid-1960s. Later, he started a wig-importing business. As that venture petered out, Greenberg spotted another trend—fashion jeans—and began importing them from South Korea. By 1979, the jeans business had started to fade, and Greenberg decided to pack up for Southern California.

His next inspiration came soon after his arrival in Los Angeles, as he waited three hours at Venice Beach to rent roller skates for his wife and kids. "I figured the guy must be taking in $4,000 to $5,000 a day," he said. So, Greenberg walked out of that skate shop and immediately plunked $40,000 into his own, which soon expanded to nine locations. Not only did he sell skates through the stores, but he established a skate-manufacturing business. The market for skates quickly soured, though. As a result, Greenberg opened a clothing store on Melrose Avenue which he named L. A. Gear. By 1985, the L. A. Gear store was losing money.

Greenberg started looking for the next trend to ride. Having watched Reebok storm the market a year earlier with its fashionable aerobics shoes, Greenberg went chasing after Reebok with his own candy-colored sneakers, all aimed at a market he knew: trend-conscious teenage girls. In what proved to be a brilliant marketing strategy, he opted to sell his shoes not just to sporting-goods stores but to big department stores like Nordstrom, May Co., and Bullock's. L. A. Gear's big break came the following year, 1987, when Reebok underestimated the demand for its wildly popular black-and-white athletic shoes. Greenberg stepped in to meet the demand by marketing "The Workout," a simple canvas shoe that became the flagship of the company.

During Greenberg's Venice Beach tenure, he had become friends with Sandy Saemann, who was making skating safety equipment while Greenberg was hawking skates. After Saemann launched his own advertising agency, Greenberg brought him into the company to help craft L. A. Gear's frothy image of sun and sex.

The Greenberg-Saemann combination worked. L. A. Gear soon became a highly profitable operation. Sales mushroomed from $200,000 per month at the beginning of 1985 to 1.8 million per month by mid-year. As the company grew to an operation of 51 employees, it needed outside funds for more development and opted for an initial public offering which was completed on July 1, 1986.

The company used the $16.5 million in proceeds from the offering to fund its growing working capital requirements and to fund a hefty advertising and promotion budget. The initial single style of footwear developed into 150 styles, and L. A. Gear's preeminence in the youth market expanded to include footwear for customers of all ages. In 1986, L. A. Gear launched lines for men, children, and infants and expanded its women's line to include athletic shoes for basketball, aerobics, and crosstrainers.

In 1989, sales rocketed to $617 million from $71 million in 1987, and the company surpassed Converse Inc. to become the nation's third-largest seller of athletic shoes. In 1989, L. A. Gear's stock switched from trading in the over-the-counter market to the Big Board. L. A. Gear's stock price in 1988 was $10.94 with $224 million in sales. By early December 1989, L. A. Gear's stock had climbed more than 178 percent, more than any Big Board stock.[3] *The Wall Street Journal, Business Week,* and *Fortune* named L. A. Gear the best performing stock on the New York Stock Exchange in 1989. Greenberg boasted that he would push L. A. Gear past Reebok and Nike by 1991. Mark R. Goldston, L. A. Gear's current president, described the company's early success as a phenomenon achieved by innovative styling and a unique ability to have their ear to the market and respond quickly.

In 1990, however, the company's stock price started to decline, and investors became concerned that L. A. Gear was losing its appeal to fashion-conscious young women. Some analysts marked the beginning of L. A. Gear's troubles with the failure of its Michael Jackson shoes.[4] In 1989, Sandy Saemann, executive vice president, signed a $20 million contract with Michael Jackson for endorsement of a line of black, silver-buckled shoes. But the shoes proved to be a failure. Other signs of trouble included reports of stock selling by insiders as well as the Justice Department's investigation of alleged underpayment of custom duties.[5]

In April 1991, L. A. Gear posted a fiscal first-quarter loss of $12.5 million. Sales fell 8.8 percent to $171 million from $187 million. L. A. Gear posted a tangible net worth of $193 million as of February 28, 1991.[6]

In May 1991, L. A. Gear agreed to sell a 30 percent stake to Roy E. Disney's Trefoil Capital Investors L.P. for $100 million. Under the agreement, Trefoil would also receive three seats on L. A. Gear's board of directors and the opportunity to have first option to buy shares of Greenberg's 3.5 million in common shares should Greenberg decide to sell. L. A. Gear also agreed to hire Disney's Shamrock Capital Advisors Inc. as consultants for three years, paying fees of $500,000 the first year, $600,000 the second year, and $700,000 the third year.

Shortly after the Trefoil agreement was initiated, Sandy Saemann—a flamboyant, gold-chain decked executive vice president—resigned. Saemann was the architect of L. A. Gear's sexy marketing campaign which often featured scantily clad models. He was also credited with gathering celebrity endorsers for L. A. Gear. Saemann agreed to provide consulting services to L. A. Gear for 2.5 years. Analysts said Saemann resigned because his flamboyant personality conflicted with the Trefoil team.[7] Kevin Ventrudo, 32, senior vice president of administration and a board member, also resigned. Mark R. Goldston succeeded Robert Greenberg as president. Greenberg remained chairman and chief executive.

On January 27, 1992, Robert Greenberg, L. A. Gear's founder, was eased out as chairman and chief executive and a director, along with Gil N. Schwartzberg, vice chairman. Stanley P. Gold, 50, managing director of Trefoil, was appointed as the new chairman and chief executive officer of L. A. Gear.

Board of Directors

As shown in Exhibit 1, the board of directors was composed of 11 members. Three of them were insiders, while the others were outsiders. One of the outside directors was a woman, Ann E. Meyers, who worked as a sports commentator. The chairman of the board was Stanley P. Gold who also served as the chief executive officer (CEO) of the firm. The board carried out its duties through the Executive and Nominating Committees. The Executive Committee consisted of Stanley Gold, R. Rudolph Reinfrank, and Mark Goldston. Reinfrank served as chairman of the Executive Committee. The Nominating Committee consisted of Stephen A. Koffler, Robert G. Moskowitz and Mark Goldston. Koffler served as the chairman of the Nominating Committee.

Top Management

L. A. Gear's top management underwent major changes since the consummation of Trefoil's $100 million investment in the company. Below is a profile of each of the key executives.

EXHIBIT 1 L. A. Gear's Board of Directors

Source: L. A. Gear, 1992 Annual Report, p. 29.

Stanley P. Gold
Chairman of the Board and Chief Executive Officer
L. A. Gear, Inc.
President and Managing Director
Trefoil Investors, Inc. and Shamrock Capital Advisors, Inc.

Mark R. Goldston
President and Chief Operating Officer
L. A. Gear, Inc.

Richard W. Schubert
General Counsel and Secretary
L. A. Gear, Inc.

Alan E. Dashling
Chairman of the Board and Chief Executive Officer
Sterling West Bancorp.

Willie D. Davis
President and Chief Executive Officer
All-Pro Broadcasting

Stephen A. Koffler
Executive Vice President and Director of Investment Banking
Sutro & Co., Inc.

Ann E. Meyers
Sports Commentator
KMPC Radio, Prime Ticket, ESPN, Sportschannel, and ABC

Clifford A. Miller
Chairman
The Clifford Group, Inc.

Robert G. Moskowitz
Managing Director
Trefoil Investors, Inc. and Shamrock Capital Advisors, Inc.

R. Rudolph Reinfrank
Executive Vice President
Shamrock Holdings, Inc.

Vappalak A. Ravindran
Chief Executive Officer
Paracor Company
President
Elders Finance, Inc.

Stanley P. Gold   Stanley Gold, 50 years old, succeeded Greenberg as chairman and chief executive officer of L. A. Gear, Inc. Formerly, he was president and chief executive officer of Shamrock Holdings, Inc., a Burbank, California-based company wholly owned by the Roy Disney Family. Gold was considered to be a turnaround expert. He proved himself by helping revive Walt Disney Co., oil driller Enterra, and soybean processor Central Soyal. Prior to assuming his positions at Shamrock, Gold was a managing partner of Gange, Tyre, Ramer & Brown, Inc., a prominent Los Angeles law firm he joined in 1968. For a number of years, he specialized in corporate acquisitions, sales, and financing. Earlier in his legal career, he served as a trial lawyer in major corporate and civil litigation.[8]

A native of Los Angeles, California, Gold first studied at the University of California at Berkeley and subsequently graduated from the University of California at Los Angeles with an A.B. degree in political science. After receiving his J.D. degree from the University of Southern California Law School in 1967, he did postgraduate work at Cambridge University in England.[9] Gold's professional and civic affiliations included the American Bar Association and the Copyright Society. He served as a guest lecturer at the Wharton School at the University of Pennsylvania. He was Chairman of the Board of Governors of Hebrew Union College, a Trustee of the Center Theater Group in Los Angeles, the George C. Marshall Foundation, and a member of the USC Law Center Board of Councilors.

Mark R. Goldston   Mark Goldston, 38 years old, succeeded Robert Y. Greenberg, the company's founder, as president and chief operating officer. Greenberg was also eased out as chairman, chief executive, and a director at a board meeting in an apparent effort by the company's largest investor, Trefoil Capital Investors L.P., to bury the "old" L. A. Gear.[10] Despite Greenberg's assertions that "the company is left in great hands," the ouster capped a four-month battle between the laid-back Greenberg and the buttoned-down Trefoil team for the soul of L. A. Gear.[11]

Goldston was a principal of Odyssey partners, a leverage buyout and investment firm. At Odyssey, Goldston was part of an internal operating unit that supervised the management of certain portfolio companies. His responsibilities included the development, execution, and management of operating plans and the evaluation of strategic alternatives for those portfolio companies. Prior to joining Odyssey, Goldston was senior and chief marketing officer of Reebok International, Ltd. where he spearheaded the marketing effort for "The Pump," a $500 million line of athletic footwear products. As one of the inventors of the Reebok "Visible Energy Return System Technology," Goldston was on the U.S. patent for that technology. Additionally, Goldston was involved in the development of the Hexalite and Energaire product lines for Reebok. Prior to joining Reebok, Goldston was president of Faberge USA, Inc., a cosmetics and personal care products company. During his tenure there, the company's U.S. sales increased about 50 percent.

Goldston was on the J. L. Kellogg Graduate School of Management Dean's Advisory Board at Northwestern University. In addition, he sat on the board of directors of Revel/Monogram, Inc., ABCO Markets, and Collection Clothing Corp. Goldston's book, entitled *The Turnaround Prescription*, detailing a step-by-step blueprint for effecting a corporate marketing turnaround, was published in 1992.[12]

In his new position as president and chief operating officer, Goldston brought in fresh talent by hiring former Reebok employees—Gordie Nye, Robert Apatoff and Christopher Walsh. Gordie Nye, Vice President of Marketing Athletic Footwear, joined the company in December 1991. Previously, he was at Reebok where he was Senior Director of Fitness Marketing, with responsibility for marketing men's and women's fitness products.

Christopher Walsh   Christopher Walsh was 43 years old. He joined L. A. Gear as senior vice president of operations in December 1991. Previously, he was vice president of production at Reebok for three years, where he was in charge of worldwide supply sources. Prior to joining Reebok, he spent two years at Toddler University, a children's shoe manufacturer, as vice president of operations. Prior to that, he worked as a senior consultant for Kurt Satmon Associates for two years, focusing on strategic planning. Earlier in his career, he worked at Nike for ten years in production and sourcing.[13]

William L. Benford   William L. Benford, 50 years old, was appointed chief financial officer in September 1991.[14] Prior to that, he was senior vice president and chief financial officer of Central Soya company. Before that he was vice president and treasurer of Dekalb, Inc. He was also affiliated with Shamrock Holdings, Inc., an investment company for the Roy E. Disney Family. Shamrock Holdings, Inc., bought Central Soya company in 1985, turned it around, and sold the company two years later at a profit of about $125 million.

Mission

L. A. Gear defined its mission as follows:

> The Company's principal business activity involves the design, development, and marketing of a broad range of quality athletic and casual/lifestyle footwear. Since its inception, the Company has expanded its product line from its original concentration on fashionable women's footwear to diversified collections of footwear for men, women, and children. The Company is organized into two primary marketing divisions: Athletic (including men's and women's basketball, fitness, walking, tennis, and aerobics) and Lifestyle (casual footwear styles intended for non-athletic use). All of the Company's footwear products are manufactured to its specifications by independent producers located primarily in South Korea, Indonesia, Taiwan and the People's Republic of China.[15]

Objectives and Strategies

L. A. Gear's short-term objective was to streamline its operations over the next two years. In the long-term, the company would attempt to achieve the following objectives:

- To provide a broad range of quality athletic and casual/lifestyle footwear, primarily in the "mid" price range (i.e., $30 to $65 retail).
- To improve relations with, and increase shelf space at, full-margin retailers.
- To improve production and quality control practices.
- To increase international sales and profitability.

In attaining these objectives, L. A. Gear adopted a retrenchment/turnaround strategy that involved a comprehensive restructuring of its operations. Thus, in 1992 the company's staff was reduced by 613 employees, or about 45 percent. In addition, the company reduced its occupancy of about 200,000 square feet of leased office space in five buildings to about 116,000 square feet in two buildings. Further, the general and administrative expenses were reduced in 1992 by $42.7 million, or 21.2 percent, to $158.7 million from $201.4 million in 1991. The company also discontinued its apparel marketing and design operations which had a pre-tax operating loss of $14.2 million in 1991.

The company's restructuring was augmented with a product development strategy. The product strategy involved developing a broad range of innovative new products for the athletic, lifestyle, and children's line. Grouping products into three well identified divisions was well received by analysts of the footwear industry. Bob McAllister, West Coast market editor for *Footwear News,* said, "In the past, there was no rhyme or reason to L. A. Gear's different styles. Now, the company has introduced new lines that are cleanly divided into athletic, lifestyles and kids."[16]

The company also sought to differentiate its products from its competitors. Goldston was confident that L. A. Gear would increase its market share by using materials in a unique way to carve a specific niche for its products. According to Goldston, "L. A. Gear is committed to designing shoes that do not resemble its competition."[17] While pursuing retrenchment and product development strategies, L. A. Gear launched a marketing campaign that focused on projecting a consistent brand image across varying retail price points and distribution channels.

Production

L. A. Gear's footwear was manufactured to its specifications by independent producers located primarily in The People's Republic of China, Indonesia, South Korea, and Taiwan. In 1992, manufacturers in these countries supplied 34, 32, 30, and 4 percent of total pairs of footwear purchased by the company respectively.

The footwear products imported into the United States by the company were subject to customs duties, ranging from 6 to 48 percent of production costs. Duty rates depended on the construction of the shoe and whether the principal component was leather or some other material.

The use of foreign manufacturing facilities subjected the company to the customary risks of doing business abroad, including fluctuations in the value of currencies, export duties, import controls, trade barriers, restrictions on the transfer of funds, work stoppage, and political instability. Thus far, these factors, however, did not seem to have had an adverse impact on the company's operations.

Products

L. A. Gear's product lines were organized into three marketing categories: Athletic, Lifestyle, and Children's. Athletic footwear included fitness, walking, tennis, crosstraining, and basketball shoes, as well as the recently introduced Light Gear CrossRunner and Dance Training shoes. These products were marketed under two brand names: L. A. Gear, with suggested domestic retail prices under $70; and L.A. Tech, the newly released, which were a higher priced premium brand.

The Lifestyle lines included men's and women's casual footwear styles that included the Street Hiker, Vintage Series, and Fashion Athletic and Casual Collections. The Children's footwear incorporated features from the Athletic and Lifestyle lines plus products specifically developed for children. L. A. Lights, lighted shoes for children introduced in June 1992, became one of the largest selling children's shoes in the company's history. The age of the company's target market for the adult products was 14 to 35 years, and for children 5 to 13.[18] Some of L. A. Gear's products and the technologies incorporated in the Athletic, Lifestyle, and Children's lines are described in Exhibit 2.

Product Quality

In 1990, L. A. Gear committed a grave marketing blunder in the process of launching its new line of basketball shoes. In a scramble to launch the new shoes, the com-

EXHIBIT 2 **L. A. Gear's Products and Their Technologies**

Source: L. A. Gear, 1992 10-K Form, p. 4.

Athletic	Description
Catapult	A midsole system consisting of a carbon graphite spring to provide cushioning and shock absorption
Encapsole Air	A cushioning system which uses air chambers built into the outsole to provide shock absorption
Light Gear	Shoes incorporating battery-powered lights in the outsole that flash upon impact

Lifestyle	Description
Street Hiker	A lightweight casual hiking shoe
Vintage Series	Footwear based on classic athletic styles

Children's	Description
L. A. Gear (Galactica for boys; L. A. Twilight for girls; Nightcrawlers for infants)	Shoes incorporating motion activated battery-powered lights in the outsole that flash with movement
Regulator	Shoes with an adjustable fit and support system using an air inflation device to cushion the foot over the midfoot area
Bendables	Flexible shoes for infants
Clear Gear	Shoes with a clear outsole in flexible plastic with an assortment of designs printed on the midsole

pany outfitted the Marquette University team with handmade pairs, since molds were not completed yet for the large sizes the team members required. As TV cameras zeroed in on one player, the bottom of his sneaker peeled away from the top. This and other cases of poor quality served to seriously tarnish the company's brand image. In an effort to improve quality, L. A. Gear reduced the number of foreign manufacturers from 44 in 1991 to 29 in 1992, retaining only those known for their quality products. The company also engaged a "sourcing" agent with the responsibility of inspecting finished goods prior to shipment by the manufacturer, supervising production management, and facilitating the shipment of goods.

Advertising

Sandy Saemann, Greenberg's second in command, was the architect of L. A. Gear's early advertising campaign. His success in signing such celebrities as Paula Abdul and Kareem Abdul-Jabbar was responsible for the phenomenal increase in the company's sales between 1985 and 1990. Saemann fit the image of the laid-back California executive perfectly—right down to the silver necklace. And his flamboyant vision proved perfect for peddling flashy sneakers. Saemann represented L. A. Gear's brash, entrepreneurial roots by producing virtually all of the company's ads and commercials himself without the help of Madison Avenue. However, L. A. Gear's tumble began, ironically, with its biggest advertising deal ever. In 1989, Saemann was able to sign megastar Michael Jackson in what was described as the largest endorsement contract ever: $20 million. L. A. Gear had hoped to time the release of a new line of shoes to an upcoming Michael Jackson greatest-hits album, but the album never materialized. Teenagers everywhere thumbed their noses at the black, buckle-laden shoes. The company was eventually forced to discontinue the entire line, taking a loss of several million dollars.

Since the failure of the Michael Jackson advertising campaign, L. A. Gear stopped contracting for the endorsement of its products by entertainment celebrities. Instead, the company chose to contract endorsements with athletic stars such as Karl "The Mailman" Malone of the Utah Jazz, Hakeem Olajuwon of the Houston Rockets, and Joe Montana of the San Francisco Forty-Niners. A new slogan, "Get in Gear," was used in the campaign.

Under the new management, L. A. Gear changed the focus of many of its advertising campaigns from promoting a fashionable shoe to promoting a performance shoe. Performance was emphasized with the advertisement tag line for the Catapult performance shoe, "It's not just a shoe, it's a machine."[19] L. A. Gear's most successful commercial was the use of the tag line "Anything else is just hot air" to promote the Catapult shoe, with its high-tech, carbon-fiber soles. The ad was an indirect attack at Nike who made the Air Jordan shoes, endorsed by Chicago Bulls' star Michael Jordan. NBC refused to run the television ads, and the ensuing exposure received by coverage of NBC's refusal was worth millions to L. A. Gear.[20] In promoting the $110 Catapult shoe, the new management decided to drop the L. A. Gear logo, believing that the L. A. Gear name was a liability in performance shoes.

The new management team subdivided the marketing of the company's products on the basis of price. Shoes costing less than $70 per pair retained the L. A. Gear name and logo, and shoes priced over $70 per pair carried the L.A. Tech name. L. A. Gear's management believed that the L.A. Tech name would help establish the line as a high-technology and performance product. The lowest-cost L. A. Gear shoe retailed for approximately $30 per pair, whereas the top of the line L.A. Tech shoe, the Catapult, topped out at about $150 per pair.[21] L. A. Gear's budget amounted to between 10 and 15 percent of total sales.

Research and Development

In designing its products, L. A. Gear conducted comprehensive market research, using a variety of conventional research techniques. Primarily, the company depended on focus groups, product testing, and interviews with consumers and retailers. These methods allowed the company to accurately gauge the image and reputation of L. A. Gear's products and to incorporate changes demanded by the public.

Sales

The phenomenal rise in L. A. Gear's sales between 1985 and 1990 was due to Greenberg's ability to create a clear-cut image for the company with brightly colored shoes and sexy ads aimed at teenage girls. The company's spectacular success led Greenberg to set a higher objective for the company, $1 billion in sales. To achieve this objective, Greenberg tried to challenge Nike and Reebok directly by adding a line of men's performance shoes. The move was too much, too fast. Venturing into men's performance shoes blurred L. A. Gear's image. According to one analyst, "When L. A. Gear moved into the performance side, it lost its way." Greenberg, however, was unwilling to lay the company's problems on the men's shoes. Instead, he maintained that "in any battle you're gonna get a little bruised or battered. And we're playing with a couple of billion-dollar companies that don't need us around."

The rapid growth also placed an enormous strain on the company. Employees had to push hard to attain the new growth objective. As a result, the company's

EXHIBIT 3   Net Sales (dollars in thousands)

Source: L. A. Gear, 1992 10-K Form, p. 5.

	1992		1991		1990	
	$	%	$	%	$	%
Domestic footwear						
Women's	112,990	26	178,481	29	285,709	35
Men's	104,593	24	176,238	28	196,969	24
Children's	90,997	21	134,485	22	174,486	21
Other	2,688	1	2,517	—	4,217	1
Total domestic net sales	311,268	72	491,721	79	661,381	81
International footwear	118,926	28	127,454	21	158,220	19
Total net sales	430,194	100	619,175	100	819,601	100

internal controls got out of hand. A shareholders' class action lawsuit called those controls "chaotic and virtually nonexistent."

As a result of the relentless push for fast growth, product-quality problems, and the attendant bad publicity, L. A. Gear saw its share of the overall athletic shoe market drop from a high of 12 percent in 1990 to 5 percent in 1992. The company net sales, as shown in Exhibit 3, declined from $820 billion in 1990 to $619 billion in 1991 and to $430 in 1992. The 1992 sales figure represented a 31 percent decline from 1991. The company incurred losses of $72 million in 1992 and $45 million in 1991. Net international sales, which accounted for about 28 percent of the company's total net sales, decreased by 6.7 percent from 1991.

According to management, the overall decline in net sales for 1992 was principally due to a drop in the number of pairs sold worldwide resulting from decreased customer demand, and, to a lesser extent, to an average decrease of $1.52 in the selling price per pair. The decline was also due to the continuing effects of the recession and price reductions by the company's principal competitors, which resulted in increased competition at lower prices.

Another factor that contributed to the drop in the 1992 sales volume was delivery delays. As part of its restructuring program in 1992, the company changed the manufacturers from which it purchased products. These changes contributed to the company's difficulties in meeting its delivery deadlines on orders for its back-to-school season.

International Strategy

In recent years, sales of athletic and casual/lifestyle footwear in many international markets grew at a faster rate than in the United States. However, L. A. Gear's own sales in the international market declined from $158 million in 1990, to $127 million in 1991, and to $119 million in 1992.

In an effort to stem this decline in sales, L. A. Gear decided to increase its investment in the international market through joint ventures, acquisitions of distributors, and the creation of wholly owned foreign subsidiaries. By selling its products directly abroad (as opposed to the company's historical reliance on independent distributors in those markets), the company sought to increase sales by adopting more competitive marketing and distribution programs. In March 1992, the company established its first foreign subsidiary to conduct direct sales of its products in France.

L. A. Gear also began to focus on Asia for its potential as a retail sales market. "We see Asia as a huge market. You have basically got two billion pairs of feet out here," said Goldston. Consequently, the company began investigating promotional alliances and equity partnerships with Asian companies.

Distribution

L. A. Gear distributed its products out of a one million square foot warehouse/ distribution center in Ontario, California. The company's products were sold in the U.S. to about 4,000 distributors that included department, sporting goods, athletic footwear and shoe stores, and wholesale distributors.

In recent years, L. A. Gear relied on extensive distribution through wholesale distributors who sold into deep-discount outlets. This policy tarnished the company's image and, as a result, several key retail accounts ceased or reduced their business with the company in 1991. To improve relations with full-margin retailers, the company began to distribute its products through specific channels, using what it called the "Gear Strategy Classification System." In line with this system, distribution channels were grouped in terms of "Image," "Mainstream," "Volume," and "Value." The Image channels were used to market the most technologically advanced and expensive high-performance products such as the L.A. Tech. The Mainstream and Volume channels were used to market "2nd Gear" and "1st Gear" products which incorporated fewer technological and aesthetic features. The Value channels were intended only for the distribution of inventory that could not be sold through the other channels. As part of the Value channels, the company planned to open a limited number of outlet stores.

Under Greenberg, the company maintained a next-day (at once) open stock system, where retailers could order products and have them shipped within 24 hours. This system forced inventory expenses to skyrocket. To mitigate this problem, the company also adopted a "futures" ordering system which provided discounts to retailers who ordered products four to six months in advance of shipment. It was hoped that the new program would enable the company to improve inventory management.

Internationally, L. A. Gear distributed its product in about 60 countries, primarily through agreements with independent distributors. The distribution agreements were intended to maintain a consistent product offering and brand image throughout the world. However, this arrangement afforded the company little or no control over the ultimate retail price of its footwear. It also restricted both profit and growth potential.

Research and Development

L. A. Gear maintained close ties with firms that conducted basic materials research. For example, L. A. Gear had an alliance with U.T.I. Chemicals Corporation of California. U.T.I. developed a new outsole material known as Z-thane which was a patented plastic compound that outlasted similar materials already in the marketplace.[22] L. A. Gear also applied older materials to their shoe lines, such as the innovative use of carbon fiber heel protectors in its performance shoes. With the Catapult, L. A. Gear hoped to challenge the high performance image of Nike and Reebok by luring the performance oriented buyer away from these market leaders.

L. A. Gear, however, lagged behind its competitors in product innovation. For example, the company introduced a "pump" style shoe almost two years after Nike and

Reebok introduced their versions of this technology. Ironically, former CEO Robert Greenberg once boasted that the company spent a fraction of what its competition spent on research and development.[23] The company's "catch-up" R&D practices damaged its relations with retailers. For example, one shoe buyer to a large department-store chain said: "We saw Nike and Reebok 1993 spring lines in May or June of 1992 and started committing for product in July. We didn't see L. A. Gear's product until mid-August."[24]

Human Resources

L. A. Gear employs 753 full-time employees. In 1991, the company embarked on a restructuring program to reduce its workforce. By 1992, 613 employees ceased employment with the company, 152 of whom were associated with the company's discontinued apparel design and marketing operations. This represented a 45 percent reduction in staff and reduced the company's monthly payroll expense from $4.8 million in 1991 to $3.4 million in 1992. The company's employees were not covered by any collective bargaining agreement, but management considered the company's relations with its employees to be satisfactory. The company offered its employees 401(k) retirement savings programs and had an employee stock option plan (ESOP) in place. The ESOP program was instituted as an incentive program for employees and management.

Communication and Corporate Culture

As L. A. Gear grew bigger, it had to hire more employees to handle the new functions. In 1985, 50 people turned out the product; by 1992, that figure swelled to 1,200. As a result, the company which was characterized by an informal communication system and corporate culture, splintered into departmental fiefdoms scattered in several buildings. The new structure eroded the informal relationships that existed among L. A. Gear's management and employees. In the early days, for instance, Greenberg and Saemann worked just across the hall from each other, and their basic form of communication was to yell back and forth. Greenberg, who had a passion for tropical fish and kept a large tank in his office, would often march across the hall to see Saemann with a dripping net in one hand and a new sneaker design in the other.

The new management brought with it buttoned-down seriousness. Coats and ties were now a regular sight at L. A. Gear. Gone were the days when Greenberg would slip each of his employees $100 bills in pink envelopes whenever the company turned a profit. Now, employees carried around black coffee mugs that read ATTACK BUSINESS COSTS.

Legal Issues

In 1990 and 1991, three class action lawsuits were brought against L. A. Gear by shareholders. The shareholders claimed that the company violated the U.S. securities laws by inflating sales by tens of millions of dollars in 1990 when it counted as revenues merchandise that was being stored in L. A. Gear's warehouses and docks. In settling these lawsuits, the company recorded a $23 million pre-tax charge against its 1992 earnings.

In October 1992, L. A. Gear reached an agreement with the U.S. Attorney for the District of Massachusetts regarding the resolution of all customs claims arising from the importation of footwear from Taiwan in 1986 and 1987. Accordingly, L. A. Gear entered a guilty plea with respect to two counts of charging underpayment of duties on such shipments. A sentencing hearing was scheduled in 1993. In addition, the company paid $1.3 million in settlement of all potential civil claims arising from underpayment of duties on the 1986 and 1987 shipments from Taiwan.

In November 1992, L. A. Gear settled a patent infringement lawsuit brought against it by Reebok International Ltd, alleging that certain footwear products marketed by the company infringed on a patent issued to Reebok covering "inflatable bladder" shoe technology. L. A. Gear paid Reebok $1 million to settle the lawsuit. As part of the settlement, L. A. Gear entered into a license agreement under which Reebok granted the company a four-year non-exclusive worldwide license to manufacture, use, and sell footwear utilizing the "inflatable bladder." The license agreement, however, did not grant L. A. Gear access to Reebok's technology.

Another legal issue involved L. A. Gear's relationship with entertainer Michael Jackson. In September 1992, the company filed a complaint against Jackson alleging, among other things, fraud, breach of contract, and breach of good faith. The company's claims arose from contracts between the company and the defendant which granted the company the exclusive right to use Jackson's name and likeness in advertising and promoting the company's shoes and apparel as well as the right to develop and market a Michael Jackson athletic shoe line. Michael Jackson countered with a lawsuit, alleging fraud and breach of good faith on the part of the company. No settlement of this dispute has been reached yet.

Finance and Accounting

L. A. Gear's gross profit declined from $286 million in 1990, to $170 million in 1991, and to $109 million in 1992. While the company earned a net income of $31 million in 1990, it lost $66 million and $72 million in 1991 and 1992 respectively.

Because of an imbalance between inventory purchases and sales, L. A. Gear accumulated inventory greater than that necessary for its business. The introduction of the company's new product lines also resulted in a greater number of styles being discontinued than would otherwise have been the case. As a result, as part of an inventory reduction program, the company sold inventory at significant discounts resulting in lower margins. As was the custom in the footwear industry, substantial changes to the current product lines were made at least twice a year (i.e., for the spring and back-to-school seasons). As a result, a certain number of styles were usually discontinued.

In September 1991, Trefoil Capital Investors, L.P. invested $100 million in L. A. Gear in the form of a new issue of Series A Cumulative Convertible Preferred Stock, the net proceeds of which were used to repay indebtedness. In November 1992, the company had cash and cash equivalent balances of $84 million. In addition, the company expected to receive income tax refunds in 1993 of about $25 million.

Industry

The U.S. general footwear market was valued at about $12 billion. The athletic shoe market comprised about $6 billion. According to *Footwear News*, the domestic retail shoe market was expected to continue to grow at a rate of 5.5 percent at least until the year 2000.[25]

A 1987 Census of Manufacturers conducted by the U.S. Bureau of the Census revealed that over 100 companies participated in the men's and women's footwear industries.[26] During 1992 there were two dozen companies competing in the U.S. branded footwear market.[27] Domestically, the two largest athletic shoe makers were Nike and Reebok with a combined share of the market totaling 50 percent.[28] Although Nike and Reebok, as well as L. A. Gear, were headquartered in the U.S., the majority of their products was manufactured in Asian, European, and South American countries. A shoe that retailed for $100 cost the company between $20 and $25 if manufactured in foreign countries. Markups to the retailer and consumer were nearly 100 percent.

The footwear industry was not cyclical but did show some seasonality with back-to-school sales in August and September. Although profitability and sales for footwear companies fluctuated, these fluctuations were attributable not to economic cycles but to changes in advertising expenditures, price, product quality, and overall market trends such as consumer preferences for fashion versus performance shoes.

Entry into the footwear industry was rather difficult. This was due to the fact that success in this industry depended to a great extent on heavy advertising, brand awareness, and intensive research and development. In the high-performance athletic shoe market, advertising was critical to footwear producers as a means of promoting new styles and creating brand awareness. Footwear companies spent vast sums to get popular athletes to endorse certain shoes. Nike and Reebok, for example, spent $200 million on advertising and promotion in 1992. This medium was cost prohibitive to smaller firms whose revenues were often too small to mount effective marketing campaigns. Another barrier to entry was brand awareness. Consumers purchased shoes based on either how well they perceived a brand to perform or on its fashion characteristics. On the average, when selecting a shoe, men tended to look at sole cushioning and how well an inner structure supported the foot—not fashion or style. Women's purchases, however, were determined more by the design or style of the shoe.[29]

An even greater entry barrier in the footwear industry was the excessive capital required for research and development. Nike, Reebok, and L. A. Gear allocated large budgets toward R&D. Each of the top three competitors had a highly advanced technology. Nike had its Air Jordan; Reebok had the Pump and Insta Pump; and L. A. Gear had its Catapult and Regulator shoes that incorporated high-tech carbon fiber soles.

In the highly competitive discount-athletic footwear market, barriers to entry were less formidable. Volume companies (mass producers) tended to carve out a niche through brands they licensed or created on their own. According to *Footwear News*, "the mass market usually followed where the better-grade merchandise had already beaten a path. Volume sources capitalized on the consumer appetite for branded-athletic footwear generated by the sophisticated marketing of companies such as Nike, Reebok, and L. A. Gear." According to the Sporting Goods Manufacturers Association, discount stores commanded $3.4 billion of the athletic shoe market.[30]

The U.S. footwear industry was maturing and analysts expected that consumers would purchase more non-athletic footwear than athletic footwear. With the domestic market maturing, many footwear companies began expanding overseas where the market was expected to grow at a rate of 23 percent a year in the next decade.[31]

The appeal of overseas markets to U.S. footwear companies stemmed not only from their sheer size but also from the cheap advertising common in such markets. Furthermore, a growing number of consumers overseas were becoming increasingly interested in U.S. sports generally and in basketball in particular. Actually, U.S. basketball was now a close second to soccer in worldwide popularity.[32] As a result, footwear companies discovered that their big endorsers, like Michael Jordan for Nike, translated well across borders.

Competitors

The athletic and athletic-style footwear industry was highly competitive in the United States and on a worldwide basis. L. A. Gear's competitors included both specialized athletic shoe companies and companies with diversified footwear product lines. The company's primary competitors in the domestic athletic and athletic-style markets were Nike and Reebok. These companies were more established than L. A. Gear and had greater financial, distribution, and marketing resources, as well as greater brand awareness, than the company. Internationally, L. A. Gear's major competitor was Adidas. Below is a brief profile of each of L. A. Gear's major competitors.

NIKE

Nike was a publicly held sports and fitness company with a 26 percent share of the domestic market. Nike was the first company in the sports and fitness industry to exceed $2 billion in U.S. revenues and $3 billion worldwide. The company accomplished this in 1991. The diversity of Nike's product lines was far reaching. The company designed and marketed athletic footwear, apparel, and related items for competitive and recreational uses. To promote this breadth of product line, Nike was successful with advertisements that used high-profile athletes. Nike had an impressive stable of endorsers with Michael Jordan, Bo Jackson, David Robinson, and Andre Agassi. The success of these advertising campaigns enabled Nike to command a higher price for its shoes than its competitors.

To add to their image as one of the premier athletic footwear companies, Nike began to open a series of high-tech futuristic looking, company-owned outlets around the world called Nike Town. This outlet was a tribute to Nike's innovative flair and marketing genius.[33] The design concept incorporated sports, fitness, entertainment, history, and product innovation.

Nike spent more than its competitors on research and development. Nike learned the hard way to push its technology. In 1987, Nike was surpassed by rival Reebok as the number one domestic footwear company. At this time, Nike was concentrating on marketing its apparel and fashion shoes instead of promoting its air cushioning system. Within eighteen months of being surpassed by Reebok, Nike regained the number one spot by marketing its Nike Air Jordan shoes. Now, Nike's engineers began to call the shots—not its fashion designers.

REEBOK

Reebok International Ltd. was a designer and marketer of active lifestyle and performance products, including footwear and apparel. Reebok held 24 percent of the domestic footwear market. According to industry sources, Reebok was the company best positioned to take advantage of the developing worldwide sneaker market.[34] Reebok announced in early 1992 that it had established a new worldwide sports marketing unit and that it would spend 25 percent more on advertising. Additionally, international sales soared 75 percent to $832.6 million from $475.2 in 1990. The sports marketing unit worked in conjunction with the fitness and casual units to deliver the best products and programs to consumers and retailers worldwide.

In 1988, Reebok acquired Avia and Rockport—two fast-growing companies. Paul Fireman, chairman and chief executive officer, believed that Avia and Rockport exemplified a "sense of aliveness" which was a characteristic of Reebok.[35] In 1991, Avia's sales rose 4.3 percent to $161 million, and Rockport's sales grew 8.5 percent to $251.3 million. Rockport produced products primarily for the walking shoe market while Avia competed directly with the Reebok brand for the athletic footwear market.

Reebok replaced its ineffective advertising with a cause-related campaign aimed at supporting philanthropic organizations while promoting its own products. In 1990, industry sources noted that Reebok was lacking a winning advertising campaign. In that year, two consecutive advertising campaigns flopped. In 1991 and 1992, Reebok reversed this trend with its cause-related advertising. Practitioners maintained that cause-related advertising could be risky, but when handled carefully, could supply the best of all promotional worlds: higher visibility, a unique image niche resulting from association with worthy projects, and stronger ties to the community.[36] As part of its cause-related marketing, Reebok gave financial support to Amnesty International's Human Rights Now tour. Angel Martinez, vice president of business development at Reebok's Los Angeles office, said that "the tour was an extension of our value system as a company. We believe in freedom of expression and wanted to do something of importance, beyond selling sneakers."[37] Reebok's President, Joseph LaBonte, added: "We both believe very strongly in the freedom to do what you want."

To remain competitive with Nike, Reebok also planned to contract endorsements with high-profile athletes. Even though the Insta-Pump would not be available to consumers until January 1993, Reebok hoped to get a lot of promotional mileage by putting the shoes on several Olympic track-and-field stars at the 1992 summer games in Barcelona, Spain.

ADIDAS AND PUMA

A decade ago, most athletic shoes sold in Europe were made by Adidas or its smaller rival, Puma. For years, the two German companies controlled about 75 percent of Europe's athletic shoe and apparel market, and they were also strong in the U.S. Things changed, however. Now, Nike and Reebok, and to a lesser degree L. A. Gear, made spectacular inroads in Europe. Although Adidas continued to be No. 1 with $1.6 billion in revenues, Nike ranked second with $500 million and Reebok ranked third with $380 million. L. A. Gear's sales were less than $119 million.

Both Nike and Reebok profited from long-term problems at Adidas and Puma. In the past five years, both German companies reported steady streams of losses because of unfocused marketing, high costs, and a glut of products. At Adidas, the confusion was acute: In footwear alone, it had 1,200 different variations and styles. "We had everything," said Michel Perrauding, Adidas' manager for logistics, "even shoes for left-handed bowlers."

Adidas' poorly coordinated marketing in Europe angered many distributors who started to desert to Nike and Reebok. And in the United States where Adidas was once No. 1 in athletic shoes, chronic delivery problems and a failure to spot the trend to more comfortable shoes led to huge losses and a dramatic drop in market share.

Nike and Reebok, however, might have to confront the possibility that Adidas and Puma might fight back. A Swedish company took full control of Puma and planned to pump cash into it. At Adidas, a new French owner slashed its product range in shoes and apparel to several hundred from several thousand, retired hundreds of employees, and started a network of more efficient purchasing and production facilities in Asia. Adidas launched a new line, Equipment, featuring no-frills shoes for such sports as soccer, tennis, and track. There was also a new Adidas series of hiking and outdoors shoes. Nevertheless, Adidas and Puma lacked the deep pockets of Nike and Reebok to enable them to spend as much on advertising as the two U.S. companies.

Customers

L. A. Gear sold to retail stores, specialty shoe stores, and sporting goods stores but their ultimate customer was the individual retail consumer. L. A. Gear's customers historically were young fashion minded girls. Under Greenberg, the company promoted the young Southern-California lifestyle. Its advertisements were of young blondes on the beach in stylish L. A. Gear shoes. Under the new management, the company repositioned itself. Former CEO Robert Greenberg said that they knew that in order to grow they would eventually have to enter the men's market and that meant more technically-oriented footwear.[38] Fashion athletics was now only a part of L. A. Gear.

Government Regulations

In 1990, the U.S. Congress passed the Textile, Apparel, and Footwear Trade Act (the "Textile Act") which would have set highly restrictive global quotas on imported textile, apparel, and footwear products. This legislation was vetoed by President Bush, and the veto was sustained by the House of Representatives.

There was a possibility that a similar legislation would be proposed in the future. If such a legislation was enacted into law, L. A. Gear could face restrictions on its ability to import into the U.S. its footwear products manufactured abroad.

In 1992, the U.S. placed L. A. Gear's suppliers in Taiwan, China, Indonesia, and South Korea on a "priority watch list" for engaging in unfair trade practices. If such countries were proved to be engaged in unfair trade practices, the U.S. might retaliate against them, which could result in increases in the cost, or reductions in the supply, of footwear generally and L. A. Gear's footwear in particular.

Demographics

The U.S. population, which totaled 250 million in 1990, was expected to reach 283 million by the year 2010. That was an increase of about 13 percent. Perhaps more significant to the footwear industry was the rise in the size of the baby boom generation, born between 1946 and 1964. A prime target of footwear companies, this segment, which comprised 18 percent of the population in 1990, was expected to grow by about 9 percent by the year 2010.

Culture

Lifestyle changes in the United States, as well as in many other countries, were propitious for footwear producers. An increasing segment of the population was becoming more health conscious, engaging in athletic activities such as jogging and walking. Because of the increasing popularity of walking, the walking-shoes market was expected to be the largest growth segment of the footwear industry. According to industry sources, 75 percent of the walking-shoes market consisted of women in their mid-30s and up.[39]

Economy

In 1991 and 1992, the Federal Reserve Board laid the groundwork for an economic recovery by keeping prime interest rates low and gradually expanding the money supply. The Fed was able, at the same time, to keep inflation at less than 4 percent. Depressed consumer confidence in economic recovery, however, continued to be a major obstacle to increased consumer and business spending. The slow start of President Clinton's economic program served only to slow a long-awaited growth in the nation's economy.

Technology

Counterfeiting is the perennial enemy of brand-name producers in Asia. Recognizing the danger to his company's technology, Goldston, L. A. Gear's president said, "The major focus of our agreements with new manufacturers is on integrity. Our technology innovation will be protected."[40] However, an L. A. Gear executive said the means available to foreign shoe manufacturers for protecting patents were limited. As a result, athletic-shoe makers could find their most nagging competitors were not each other but the companies who filled their orders. Such companies as L. A. Gear "tend to stumble when faced with competition, and this time it will come from say, . . . a factory in Indonesia that has acquired the technology to make a good jogging shoe."[41]

Politics

With political changes occurring in Eastern Europe and the Soviet Union, markets that were previously closed to Western companies were now fairly wide open.

The enactment of NAFTA (North American Free Trade Agreement) among the U.S., Canada, and Mexico, was likely to strengthen U.S. exports. According to estimates made by the U.S. Trade Representative, the tariff reductions alone, if undertaken by all countries, could raise U.S. real GNP by 3 percent by the year 2000.[42]

Conclusion

As they implement their turnaround strategy, Gold and Goldston have their work cut out for them. What should they do next? And will their strategic moves be sufficient to restore L. A. Gear to its heyday or will they cause the company to disappear?

Endnotes

1. "L. A. Gear," *Los Angeles Magazine,* December 1991, p. 116.
2. "L. A. Gear Calls in a Cobbler," *Business Week,* September 16, 1991, p. 78.
3. "L. A. Gear +184.6%," *Institutional Investor,* March 1990, pp. 52, 53.
4. "L. A. Gear Co-Founder Saemann Quits in Wake of Firm's Deal with Trefoil," *The Wall Street Journal,* June 13, 1991, p. B1.
5. "The Best and Worst Stocks of 1989," *Fortune,* January 29, 1990, p. 114.
6. "L. A. Gear Inc.," *The Wall Street Journal,* April 4, 1991, p. B1.
7. "L. A. Gear Co-Founder Saemann Quits in Wake of Firm's Deal with Trefoil," *The Wall Street Journal,* June 13, 1991, p. B1.
8. "Stanley P. Gold L. A. Gear Chairman & Chief Executive Officer," L. A. Gear Press Release, January 24, 1992.
9. Ibid.
10. "L. A. Gear Inc. Investor Steps in With New Team," *The Wall Street Journal,* January 27, 1992, pp. B1, B5.

APPENDIX A   L. A. Gear, Inc. Consolidated Balance Sheet, as of November 30 (in thousands)

Source: L. A. Gear, 1992 Annual Report, p. 17.

	1992	1991
Assets		
Current assets:		
Cash and cash equivalents	$ 55,027	$ 1,422
Collateralized cash	28,955	—
Accounts receivable, net	56,369	111,470
Inventories	61,923	141,115
Prepaid expenses and other current assets	2,557	8,506
Refundable income taxes	25,269	22,795
Deferred income taxes	—	11,763
Total current assets	230,100	297,071
Property and equipment, net	17,667	26,869
Other assets	1,735	1,631
Total assets	$249,502	$325,571
Liabilities, Mandatorily Redeemable		
Preferred Stock and Shareholders' Equity		
Current liabilities:		
Borrowing under line of credit	$ —	$ 20,000
Accounts payable and accrued liabilities	49,753	55,856
Dividends payable on mandatorily redeemable preferred stock	7,746	—
Costs related to discontinued operations	4,552	18,000
Total current liabilities	62,051	93,856
Mandatorily redeemable preferred stock:		
7.5% Series A Cumulative Convertible Preferred Stock, $100 stated value; 1,000,000 shares authorized, issued and outstanding; redemption value of $100 per share	100,000	100,000
Shareholders' equity:		
Common stock, no par value; 80,000,000 shares authorized; 22,898,182 shares issued and outstanding at November 30, 1992 (19,542,513 shares issued and outstanding at November 30, 1991)	127,714	92,331
Preferred stock, no stated value; 9,000,000 shares authorized; no shares issued	—	—
Retained earnings (accumulated deficit)	(40,263)	39,384
Total shareholders' equity	87,451	131,715
Commitments and contingencies	—	—
	$249,502	$325,571

11. Ibid.

12. "L. A. Gear Inc. Investor Steps in With New Team," *The Wall Street Journal,* January 27, 1992, pp. B1, B5.

13. Ibid.

14. "L. A. Gear, Several Changes at Senior Level," *The Wall Street Journal,* September 17, 1991, p. A22.

15. L. A. Gear, Form 10-K, 1991, p. 2.

APPENDIX B   L. A. Gear, Inc. Consolidated Statements of Cash Flows, as of November 30 (in thousands)

Source: L. A. Gear, 1992 Annual Report, p. 17.

	1992	1991	1990
Operating activities:			
Net income (loss)	$(71,901)	$(66,200)	$31,338
Adjustment to reconcile net income (loss) to net cash provided by (used in) operating activities: Shareholders' litigation settlements	17,075	—	—
Depreciation and amortization	7,107	7,182	3,394
Provision for loss on discontinued operations	—	18,000	—
Loss on sale or abandonment of property and equipment	1,871	4,146	—
Issuance of shares to employee stock savings plan	233	382	—
(Increase) decrease in: Accounts receivable, net	55,101	44,431	(52,969)
Inventories	79,192	19,553	(21,152)
Prepaids and other assets	6,343	1,565	(998)
Refundable and deferred income taxes	8,791	(26,174)	(3,795)
Increase (decrease) in:			
Accounts payable and accrued liabilities	(6,103)	(8,222)	3,143
Costs related to discontinued operations	(8,343)	—	—
Net cash provided by (used in) operating activities	89,366	(5,337)	(41,039)
Investing activities-capital expenditures	(4,881)	(14,188)	(18,939)
Financing activities:			
Net proceeds from issuance of mandatorily redeemable preferred stock	—	92,511	—
Payment of dividends on mandatorily redeemable preferred stock	—	(1,265)	—
Exercise of stock options and warrants	1,986	414	908
Tax benefits arising from the disposition/exercise of incentive stock options	2,089	356	5,408
Proceeds from issuance of common stock	14,000	—	—
Net borrowing (repayment) under line of credit agreement	(20,000)	(74,000)	56,600
Net cash provided by (used in) financing activities	(1,925)	17,656	62,916
Net increase (decrease) in cash and cash equivalents	82,560	(1,869)	2,938
Cash at beginning of year	1,422	3,291	353
Cash and cash equivalents at end of year, including collateralized cash	$83,982	$ 1,422	$ 3,291

16. Ibid.

17. Ibid.

18. L. A. Gear Inc., 1990 Annual Report (Los Angeles, CA: L. A. Gear Inc.), p. 7.

19. B. Horivitz, "Some Companies Find They Get More," *Los Angeles Times,* February 5, 1991, p. D6.

20. "L. A. Gear Says High Inventories May Affect 1992 Earnings," *Bloomberg News,* March 3, 1992.

21. Ibid., p. B5.

22. L. A. Gear Inc., 1990 Annual Report (Los Angeles, CA: L. A. Gear Inc.), p. 8.

23. "The Goldston Prescription," *Footwear News,* January 27, 1992, pp. 11–12.

24. "L. A. Gear Still Looks Like an Also-Ran," *Business Week,* December 21, 1992, p. 37.

25. "Footwear (Men's, Women's, Boys' and Girls')," *Fairchild Fact File,* 1990, pp. 5–9.

26. Ibid., pp. 5–9.

27. F. Meeds, "The Sneaker Game," *Forbes,* October 22, 1990, p. 114.

28. J. Schlax, "The Shoe as Hero," *Forbes,* August 20, 1990, p. 77.

29. K. Kerwin, "L. A. Gear Is Going Where the Boys Are," *Business Week,* June 19, 1989, p. 54.

30. Ibid., p. 52.

31. M. Grimm, "To Munich and Back with Nike and L. A. Gear," *Adweek's Marketing Week,* February 18, 1991, p. 21.

32. Ibid., p. 22.

33. M. Wilson, "Nike Town Goes Back to the Future," *Chain Store Age Executive,* February, 1991, pp. 82–83.

34. M. Tedeschi, "Reebok Splits U.S. Int'l Setups," *Footwear News,* November 26, 1990, p. 12.

35. S. Gannes, "America's Fastest-Growing Companies," *Fortune,* May 23, 1988, p. 37.

36. A. Shell, "Cause-Related Marketing: Big Risks, Big Potential," *Public Relations Journal,* July, 1989, pp. 8, 13.

37. Ibid., p. 8.

38. M. Rottman, "L. A. Gear Catapults into Technology," *Footwear News,* February 18, 1991, pp. 12, 14.

39. D. McKay, "Walk This Way," *Footwear News,* September 9, 1991, pp. 14–15.

40. "L. A. Gear President Says Shoe Maker Will Recover and Will Focus on Asia," *The Wall Street Journal,* October 16, 1992, p. B7.

41. Ibid.

42. OECD Economic Survey, United States, 1990/1991, pp. 60–65.

Case 5

Kikkoman Corporation in the Mid-1990s: Market Maturity, Diversification, and Globalization

Norihito Tanaka
Kanagawa University

Marilyn L. Taylor
University of Missouri at Kansas City

Joyce A. Claterbos
University of Kansas

In early 1996 Mr. Yuzaburo Mogi, president of Kikkoman Corporation, faced a number of challenges. Analysts indicated concern with Kikkoman's slow sales growth and noted that the company's stock had underperformed on the Nikkei Exchange in relation to the market and to its peers for several years. Throughout the world ongoing

Paid-in-full members of NACRA are encouraged to reproduce any case for distribution to their students without charge or written permission. All other rights reserved jointly to the authors and the North American Case Research Association (NACRA).

Reprinted by permission from the Case Research Journal, volume 21, issue 3. Copyright 2001 by Norihito Tanaka, Marilyn Taylor, Joyce A. Claterbos, and the North American Case Research Association. All rights reserved.

The authors express deep appreciation to Kikkoman Corporation, which provided encouragement to this study, including access to the U.S. manufacturing and marketing facilities in addition to time in the corporate offices in Japan. The authors also gratefully acknowledge the support for this study provided by the Japanese Department of Education and the Institute for Training and Development in Tokyo. Quotes and data in this case study were drawn from a variety of personal interviews in the United States and Japan, company documents, and public sources. Documents and public sources appear in the list of references at the conclusion of the case.

changes in taste preferences and dietary needs presented threats to the company's traditional food lines. The company marketed its branded products in 94 countries and had to consider which products and markets to emphasize as well as which new markets to enter. As Mr. Mogi described the company's focus, ". . . we are now concentrating on further enhancing our ability to serve consumers in Japan and overseas. The basic keynotes of this effort are expansion of soy sauce markets, diversification and globalization."

In Japan, Kikkoman had long dominated the soy sauce market, and its mid-1990s market share position of 27 percent was well beyond the 10 percent of its next closest competitor. However, its share of the soy sauce market had continued to decline from its high of 33 percent in 1983, falling from 28 percent in 1993 to 27.2 percent in 1994. Further, although the company's worldwide sales had increased slightly overall from 1994 to 1995, sales of soy sauce in Japan had decreased over 1 percent during that period.

The U.S. market had provided significant opportunity in the post–World War II period. However, the company's U.S. market share for soy and other company products was essentially flat. In addition, three competitors had built plants in the United States beginning in the late 1980s. Mr. Mogi was aware that Kikkoman's choices in the U.S. market would provide an important model for addressing higher income mature markets.

With a market capitalization of nearly ¥160 billion,[1] Kikkoman Corporation was the world's largest soy sauce producer, Japan's nineteenth largest food company, and also Japan's leading soy sauce manufacturer. The company was the oldest continuous enterprise among the 200 largest industrials in Japan. The company began brewing shoyu, or naturally fermented soy sauce, in the seventeenth century and had dominated the Japanese soy industry for at least a century. The company held 50 percent of the U.S. soy sauce market and 30 percent of the world market. Kikkoman had 13 manufacturing facilities in Japan and one each in the United States, Singapore, and Taiwan. The company was one of the few traditional manufacturers to successfully establish a presence worldwide. (Exhibits 1 and 2 have the locations of and information on the company's principal subsidiaries. Exhibits 3 and 4 list the consolidated financial statements.)

Kikkoman in Japan

THE BEGINNINGS IN NODA

In 1615, the widow of a slain samurai warrior fled 300 miles from Osaka to the village of Noda near Edo (now called Tokyo). With her five children the widow Mogi embarked upon rice farming and subsequently began brewing shoyu, or soy sauce. The quality of the Mogi family's shoyu was exceptional almost from its beginnings. At the time, households produced shoyu for their own use, or local farmers made and sold excess shoyu as a side enterprise to farming. As more people moved to the urban areas in the seventeenth and eighteenth centuries, there was increased demand for non-home production. Households developed preferences for the product of a particular brewer. (See Appendix A: The Making of Soy Sauce.)

Shoyu had come to Japan with the arrival of Buddhism in the sixth century. The teachings of Buddhism prohibited eating meat and fish. Residents of the Japanese islands turned from meat-based to vegetable-based flavorings. One of the favorites became a flavorful seasoning made from fermented soy beans. A Japanese Zen Buddist priest who had studied in China brought the recipe to Japan. The Japanese discovered that adding wheat gave the sauce a richer, more mellow flavor.

EXHIBIT 1 **Locations of Principal Subsidiaries**

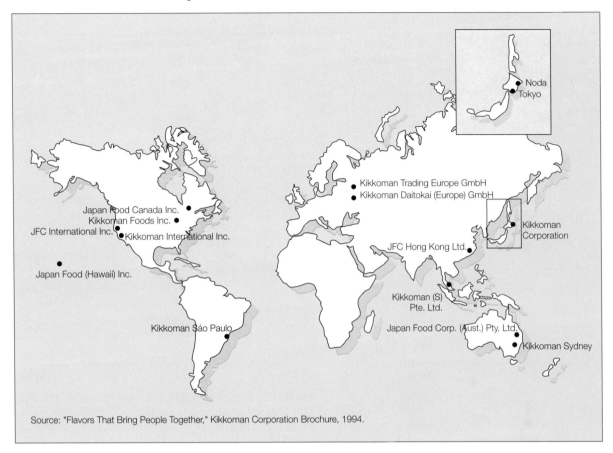

Source: "Flavors That Bring People Together," Kikkoman Corporation Brochure, 1994.

Over the eighteenth century, Noda became a major center for shoyu manufacturing in Japan. Shoyu's major ingredients, soybeans and wheat, grew readily in the rich agricultural Kanto plain that surrounded Noda. The trip to the major market of Edo took only one day on the Edo River. The various shoyu-producing families in the Noda area actively shared their knowledge of fermentation. The Mogi family and another Noda area family, the Takanashi family, were especially active in the industry. By the late eighteenth century, the two families had become interrelated through marriage. Their various enterprises made considerable investment in breweries, and family members began ancillary enterprises such as grain brokering, keg manufacture, and transportation.

JAPAN'S SHOYU DISTRIBUTION SYSTEM AND INDUSTRY STRUCTURE

Japan's neophyte and fragmented shoyu industry had two distribution systems during this time. In the rural areas the shoyu breweries sold their products directly to households. In the cities, urban wholesalers distributed shoyu, vinegar, and sake. The wholesalers purchased bulk shoyu and established their own brands. The wholesalers controlled pricing, inventory, distribution, and marketing knowledge. They would distribute branded shoyu only on consignment. During the 1800s, the whole-

EXHIBIT 2   Consolidated Subsidiaries as of FY 1995

Source: Table 4: Consolidated Subsidiaries, UBS Securities Limited, May 28, 1996, as reported by *Investext*.

Subsidiary	Country	Paid-In Capital ((Y)m/$m)	Kikkoman Equity (%)
Japan Del Monte	Japan	900	99.7
Mann's Wine	Japan	900	100
Pacific Trading	Japan	72	66.7
Morishin	Japan	30	66.7
Kikkoman Foods, Inc.	US	US$6	100
Kikkoman International	US	US$3.5	92.6
JFC International	US	US$1.2	98
Kikkoman Trading Europe	Germany	DM1.5	75
Kikkoman Pte	Singapore	S$7.5	100
Kikkoman Trading Pte	Singapore	S$.4	100
Tokyo Food Processing	US	US$.02	100
Hapi Products	US	US$.05	100
Rex Pacific	US	US$1.5	100

EXHIBIT 3   Consolidated Profit and Loss Statement ((Y) m)

Sources: Table 9: UBS Securities Limited, May 28, 1996; *The World Almanac*, 1998 (original source: IMF).

	1989	1990	1991	1992	1993	1994	1995
Sales	195,851	196,925	206,861	211,671	203,491	200,976	203,286
COGS	117,062	118,808	122,872	124,882	118,504	117,809	119,656
Gross Profit	78,789	78,117	83,989	86,789	84,987	83,167	83,629
Gross Profit Margin (%)	40.2	39.7	40.6	41	41.8	41.4	41.1
SG&A Expenses	71,227	71,876	74,181	76,019	74,320	72,689	72,836
SG&A Exp. (%)	36.4	36.5	35.9	35.9	36.5	36.2	35.8
Operating Profit	7,562	6,240	9,807	10,769	10,666	10,477	10,792
Operating Margin (%)	3.9	3.2	4.7	5.1	5.2	5.2	5.3
Net Non-Op. Income	−572	−1,042	−1,564	−1,895	−2,282	−2,197	−2,305
Recurring Profit	6,990	5,197	8,243	8,873	8,384	8,280	8,487
Recurring Margin (%)	3.6	2.6	4	4.2	4.1	4.1	4.2
Net Extraordinary Income	181	1,165	1,317	59	108	1,434	−1,177
Pretax Profit	7,170	6,363	9,559	8,932	8,493	9,714	7,310
Tax	3,327	3,299	4,726	5,178	4,597	4,157	3,569
Tax Rate (%)	46.4	50.7	49.4	58	54.1	42.8	48.8
Minority Interest	56	78	37	34	1	−52	46
Amortization of Consol. Dif.	0	0	−35	1	5	0	−314
Equity in Earnings	1,097	1,464	1,188	1,245	887	1,002	996
Net Profit	4,697	4,694	6,166	4,928	4,688	6,614	4,447
Shares Outstanding (m)	169.08	169.71	169.97	178.61	187.62	187.77	197.2
EPS	27.8	27.7	31.3	25	23.8	33.5	22.6
EPS Change (%_)	80	−0.4	13.3	−20.2	−4.9	41	−32.8
Cash Flow per Share	20.8	46.5	48	41.9	44.4	58.5	46.8
Average Exchange Rate (yen/USD)	137.96	144.79	134.71	126.65	111.20	102.21	94.06

EXHIBIT 4   Consolidated Balance Sheet ((Y) m)

Source: Nikkei Needs as reported in Table 12: Consolidated Balance Sheet, UBS Securities Limited, May 28, 1996.

	1990	1991	1992	1993	1994	1995
Current Assets	81,611	88,092	89,705	103,152	105,220	107,339
Cash and Deposits	13,254	17,570	18,261	28,826	36,381	37,366
Accounts Receivable	43,579	44,661	44,503	46,009	44,246	44,439
Securities	315	1,012	1,316	3,310	3,306	3,307
Inventories	21,769	21,300	22,484	21,469	18,579	19,258
Fixed Assets	94,631	97,999	105,231	113,940	112,183	119,411
Tangible Assets	52,087	53,254	59,276	67,649	65,795	72,684
Land	11,768	12,011	11,910	15,156	15,613	11,540
Investments	26,371	29,597	31,771	33,051	34,083	35,006
Total Assets	177,583	187,316	195,955	218,561	218,805	228,308
Liabilities and Owner's Equity						
Current Liabilities	48,040	52,626	54,014	50,272	46,663	63,400
Short-Term Borrowings	18,846	18,908	19,046	17,462	14,838	15,741
Fixed Liabilities	58,374	58,850	62,351	85,532	85,143	71,710
Long-Term Borrowings	4,457	4,549	4,723	3,274	3,091	2,312
Bonds and CBs*	26,565	26,346	26,231	46,170	44,776	29,921
Minority Interest	1,223	1,166	1,157	1,103	1,024	427
Total Liabilities	107,638	112,643	117,522	136,909	132,832	135,538
Shareholders' Equity	69,945	74,673	78,434	81,651	85,973	92,770
Total Liabilities and Equity	177,583	187,316	195,955	218,561	218,805	228,308

*There were two CBs issued Jan. 90 exercisable at (Y) 1,522. The other two were issued July 93 and were exercisable at (Y) 969. With the share price at approximately (Y) 100, the total dilution factor was about 18 percent, with 80 percent of that dependent on the two CBs exercisable at (Y) 969. Of 228 ((Y) m) in 1995, about 170 belonged to the parent (i.e., Japan corporation) company.

salers formed alliances that gave them near monopolistic power over the Tokyo market. As the shoyu manufacturers became more efficient, they found it impossible to lower prices or make other adjustments to increase their market share.

The Mogi and Takanashi families took several steps to counteract the wholesalers' dominance. The Takanashi family had diversified into wholesaling some years prior and were part of the wholesalers' alliance. One Mogi family intermarried with a wholesaler's family—a traditional strategy in Japan for cementing strategic alliances. In addition, the Mogi and Takanashi families worked to increase brand recognition and dominance. In 1838, Mogi Saheiji applied for and received the shogunate's recognition of his family's premier brand, named Kikkoman. He aggressively promoted the brand by sponsoring professional storytellers and sumo wrestlers, embossing paper lanterns and umbrellas with the Kikkoman trademark, and putting ornate gold labels from Paris on his Kikkoman shoyu kegs. In the latter part of the nineteenth century, Kikkoman shoyu won recognition in several world's fairs.

In reaction to depressed market prices and fluctuating costs of inputs, a number of the Noda shoyu brewers formed the Noda Shoyu Brewers' Association in 1887. The association purchased raw materials, standardized wages, and regulated output quality. The members' combined efforts resulted in the largest market share at the time, 5 to 10 percent of the Tokyo market, and widespread recognition of the high quality of Noda shoyu.

Noda brewers, and especially the Mogi and Takanashi families, began research and development activities early. The Japanese government encouraged the Noda shoyu brewers to conduct research in the recovery and processing of the two by-products of shoyu manufacture, shoyu oil and shoyu cake. In the early 1900s, the association began to fund a joint research and development laboratory.

THE SHOYU INDUSTRY IN THE TWENTIETH CENTURY

In 1910, there were still 14,000 known makers of shoyu in Japan. However, a number of changes led to consolidation. Manufacturing shifted from a small-batch, brewmaster-controlled production process to a large-batch, technology-controlled process. Mogi families in Noda invested in modernized plants, and a fifth-grade Japanese geography reader featured a state-of-the-art Kikkoman facility. A national market also developed, thanks to the development of a railway system throughout most of the country. In addition, consumer tastes shifted to the Tokyo-style shoyu produced by eastern manufacturers such as the Noda Shoyu Brewers' Association.

Consumers also began to purchase shoyu in smaller glass bottles rather than in the traditional large wooden barrels that sometimes leaked and were expensive to build and difficult to store. Raw materials also became more expensive as the brewers increasingly sought higher quality imported soybeans (from Manchuria, China, and Korea) and salt (from England, Germany, and China). The association members controlled costs by purchasing in bulk and demanding high-quality materials from suppliers.

THE NODA SHOYU COMPANY: 1918–1945—A FAMILY ZAIBATSU[2]

In 1918, seven Mogi families and a related Takanashi family combined their various enterprises into a joint stock holding company called the Noda Shoyu Company. The merger was in reaction to the market upheaval caused by World War I. The new company was a small zaibatsu with nearly a dozen companies in manufacturing fermented grain-based products, transportation, and finance. Unlike early shoyu manufacturing where ownership, management, and operations were clearly separated, the Mogi and Takanashi families owned, managed, and operated their firm. Initially the family produced 34 different brands of shoyu at various price points. The Kikkoman brand had a history of heavy promotion for over 40 years, greater Tokyo market share, and a higher margin than the company's other brands. The Kikkoman brand became the company's flagship brand. The new corporation continued its long-standing emphasis on research and development and aggressively pursued new manufacturing processes, increased integration, and acquired other shoyu companies.

After the Mogi Takanashi coalition, the company aggressively pursued a strong nationwide sole agent system and direct distribution. The combined company also continued Kikkoman's well-known advertising activities. Kikkoman had carried out the first newspaper advertising in 1878. In 1922, the company carried out the firm's first advertising on the movie screen.

During the 1920s, the company aggressively modernized with machines such as hydraulic presses, boilers, conveyors, and elevators. The company's modernization efforts were emulated by competitors, and the results were increased supply and heightened industry competition. The changes brought about by increased automation led to severe labor unrest. One particularly long strike against the Kikkoman company in the late 1920s almost destroyed the participating labor union. After the strike ended, Kikkoman rehired about a third of the striking employees. The company centralized and reorganized the work processes to accommodate improved technology, restructured work practices, and established methods to monitor and reward workers for their performance. However, the company also established efforts to improve the identity of the workers with the company. Internal communications carried the message that all employees were members of one family, or ikka, united in a common purpose, i.e., the production of shoyu. The Noda Shoyu Company was also heavily involved in the city of Noda and supported many of its cultural and charitable activities as well as the local railroad, bank, town hall, cultural center, library, fire station, elementary school, hospital, recreation facilities and association, and much of the city's water system.

KIKKOMAN'S INTERNATIONAL ACTIVITIES

Kikkoman's initial export activities began in the late seventeenth century with Dutch and Chinese traders. The Dutch began to export shoyu to Holland and the rest of Europe, while the Chinese served the southeast Asian markets. The shoyu brewers relied on agents for these early export transactions. During the nineteenth century, one Mogi patriarch opened a factory in Inchon, Korea. Demand for the increasing export, marketing, and direct investment continued to come primarily from Japanese and other peoples living abroad whose traditional cuisines called for shoyu. In 1910, the Noda city brewers' international activities were recognized when the Japanese government selected Noda shoyu to appear in a public relations publication introducing Japan's industries overseas.

Noda Shoyu Company continued to expand internationally between World War I and World War II. Acquisition of raw materials from abroad continued. The company added a manufacturing facility for shoyu and miso in Manchuria and two shoyu factories in North America. Other facilities in Japan were expanded or updated to support increasing international sales.

The company established sales offices in China and Korea to market shoyu, miso, and sake. By the late 1930s, the company exported 10 percent of its output, about half to the Asian region—especially Korea, China, and Indonesia—and half to Hawaii and California. Almost all of the exports were the Kikkoman brand and were sold through food import/export firms to the company's traditional customers.

POST–WORLD WAR II KIKKOMAN IN JAPAN

At the end of World War II, Kikkoman operated only in Japan. Activities elsewhere had been closed. To meet the need for capital, Kikkoman issued publicly-traded stock in 1946, reducing family ownership markedly. (Exhibit 5 shows the changes in ownership from 1917 to 1993.) The post–World War II period brought a number of social changes to Japanese society. Japanese families began the change to nuclear rather than extended-family formation. Food tastes changed leading, among other trends,

EXHIBIT 5   Noda Shoyu Company and Kikkoman Corporation Ownership

Sources: W. Mark Fruin, *Kikkoman—Company, Clan, and Community* (Cambridge, MA, Harvard, University Press, 1983), pp. 98, 121, 249, *Japan Company Handbook*, Toyo Keizai, Inc., 1993, p. 207.

Shareholder Name	Holdings (% of total shares or assets)			
	1917	1925	1955	1993
Mogi-Takanashi-Horikiri Brewing Families	100%[a]	34.6%	15.0%[b]	2.3%
Senshusha Holding Company		62.0%	3.1%	3.4%
Insurance and Banking Companies			9.9%[c]	20.5%[c]
All Others		3.6%	71.1%	73.6%

[a]Eight holdings ranging from 1.4 percent to 29.3 percent.
[b]Five holdings ranging from 1.5 percent to 4.4 percent.
[c]In 1955 and 1993, including Meiji Mutual Insurance Co, Mitsubishi Trust Bank; in 1955, including Kofukan Foundation and Noda Institute of Industrial Science; in 1993, including Nitsuit Trust Bank, Nippon Life Insurance, Sumitomo Trust, and Yasuda Trust.

to a decline in per capita consumption of shoyu. Compared with other industries, demand for soy sauce grew very slowly. In 1942, demand for soy sauce in Japan was 1.7 times greater than in 1918. Demand in the 1960s was expected to be 2.2 times greater than that in 1918. However, modernization led to increased output.

Kikkoman had received considerable recognition for its advertising efforts prior to World War II. After the war, the company began to market even more aggressively in Japan. These efforts included establishing the company's strong nationwide distribution system throughout Japan; mounting aggressive activities in marketing research, advertising, and consumer education; and changing to a new and more Western image. As a result of Kikkoman's marketing efforts, the company's market share rose sharply. (Exhibit 6 shows the national output of shoyu and the company's market share from 1893 to 1994.) By 1964 the company officially changed its name to Kikkoman Shoyu and in 1980 became Kikkoman Corporation. The word *Kikkoman* is a combination of "kikko" (the shell of a tortoise) and "man" (10,000). It was taken from an old Japanese saying, "A crane lives a thousand years and a tortoise 10,000 years." (Implying , in other words, "May you live as long!") In essence, the Kikkoman brand connotes a long-lasting living thing. Kikkoman had become well-known for its advertising skill in Japan and had found that the word *Kikkoman* was easy for Americans to pronounce.

The company also diversified its product line using its expertise in shoyu manufacture, fermentation, brewing, and foods marketing. This diversification included a 1963 venture to market Del Monte products in Japan. In 1990, the company bought the Del Monte assets and marketing rights for the Del Monte brand name in the Asia–Pacific region. (Exhibit 7 shows Kikkoman Corporation's product lists as of 1949, 1981, and 1993.) Kikkoman's R&D expertise led to activities in biotechnology and products such as enzymes, diagnostic reagents, and other biologically-active substances used to test for microorganisms in water samples in hospitals, food processing factories, and semiconductor plants. The company also developed a number of patents at home and overseas. The company became involved in both the import and export of wines. It also undertook activities in food processing machinery.

EXHIBIT 6   National Output and Company Market Share of Shoyu (in kiloliters)[a]

Source: W. Mark Fruin, *Kikkoman—Company, Clan, and Community* (Cambridge, MA, Harvard University Press, 1983), pp. 40–41.

Year	National Output (Japan)	Noda Shoyu Share
1893	230,360	3.5%
1903	317,500	4.5%
1913	430,435	6.1%
1923	624,764	5.1%
1933	576,026	10.1%
1943	680,955	12.0%
1953	822,179	14.1%
1963	1,051,730	21.4%
1973	1,277,887	31.4%
1983	n.a.	33.0%
1993	n.a.	28.0%[c]
1994	1,323,529[b]	27.2%[c]

[a]1 kiloliter = 264 gallons.
[b]Derived from Kikkoman's production of 360,000 kl and its 27.2 percent market share. Residents of Japan consumed about 2.6 gallons of soy sauce per capita yearly. In contrast, U.S. citizens consumed about 10 tablespoons.
[c]As reported by UBS Securities Limited, May 28, 1996 in *Investext*. This source also reported that demand for soy sauce was flat in Japan and production between 1984 and 1994 had declined about 5.1 percent.

EXHIBIT 7   **Kikkoman Corporation Products and Product Lines**

Sources: W. Mark Fruin, *Kikkoman—Company, Clan, and Community* (Cambridge, MA, Harvard University Press, 1983), pp. 275–276; "Flavors That Bring People Together," Kikkoman Corporation Brochure, 1994.

1949	1981	1994
Kikkoman Brand soy sauce, sauce, memmi and tsuyu (soup bases)	*Kikkoman Brand* soy sauce, mild soy sauce (lower salt, 8%), light color soy sauce (usu-kuchi), teriyaki barbecue marinade and sauce, Worcestershire sauce, tonkatsu sauce, memmi and tsuyu (soup bases), sukiyaki sauce, instant soy soup mix, instant osumono (clear broth soup mix)	*Kikkoman Brand* soy sauce, mild soy sauce (lower salt, 8%), light color soy sauce (usu-kuchi), teriyaki sauce, Worcestershire sauce, tonkatsu sauce, memmi (soup base), sukiyaki sauce, sashimi soy sauce, lemon flavored soy sauce, mirin (sweet rice wine), Aji-Mirin, plum wine, instant miso (soybean paste) soups, egg flower soup mixes, rice crackers, tofu, neo-genmai (puffed brown rice), genmai soups, oolong tea, tsuyudakono (soup base), ponzu soy sauce, soy sauce dressing, oyster sauce, bonito stock
Manjo Brand mirin (sweet rice wine), sake, shochu, whiskey	*Manjo Brand* mirin (sweet rice wine), shochu, plum wine *Yomonoharu Brand* sake *Del Monte Brand* tomato ketchup, juice, puree, paste, chili sauce, Mandarin orange juice *Disney Brand* fruit juice (orange, pineapple, grape), nectar (peach, orange) *Mann's Brand*[a] wine and sparkling wine, brandy *Higeta Brand* shoyu, tsuyu, Worcestershire sauce *Ragu Brand* spaghetti sauces *Kikko's Brand* tomato ketchup *Monet Brand* cognac	*Manjo Brand* triangle, komaki *Yomonoharu Brand* *Del Monte Brand* tomato ketchup, juice, fruit drinks, Mandarin orange juice *Mann's Brand* koshu, koshu (vintage), zenkoji, blush, brandy *Beyoung* protein powder, wheat germ *Imported wines* aujoux, chateau tatour, borie-manoux, franz reh and sohn, pol roger

*Marketed, not manufactured, by Kikkoman.
[a]The company established it Mann Wine subsidiary in 1964.

In spite of the diversification, Kikkoman's domestic sales were still about 55 percent soy-sauce related.

In the 1990s, soy sauce continued as a perennial favorite in Japan's cuisine, although demand was essentially flat. Among the remaining 3,000 shoyu companies in Japan, Kikkoman produced 360,000 kl in Japan, or about 27 percent of the country's output. (Exhibit 6.) The company faced price pressures especially on its base product of soy sauce, mainly due to the competitive pressures at the retail level in

EXHIBIT 8 **Parent Company Revenues by Product Line ((Y) m)**

Source: Table 5: UBS Securities Limited, May 28, 1996, as available on *Investext.*

	1994	1995	Percent Change	1996E	Percent Change
Soy Sauce	74,666	73,843	−1.1	75,000	1.6
Food	15,091	16,310	8.1	18,500	13.4
Del Monte	24,692	19,857	−19.6	19,000	−4.3
Alcohol	24,993	25,925	3.7	27,000	4.1
Others	4,159	4,285	3	4,500	5
Total	143,601	140,220	−2.4	144,000	2.7

EXHIBIT 9 **Parent Company Balance Sheet ((Y) m)**

Source: UBS Securities Limited, May 28, 1996. Table 11 as reported by *Investext.*

	1993	1994	1995
Current Assets	78,463	81,805	80,749
Fixed Assets	88,007	86,029	89,599
Total	166,802	168,000	170,348
Short-Term Liabilities	33,469	32,033	46,762
Long-Term Liabilities	79,898	79,527	66,567
Equity	53,434	56,440	57,019
Total Liabilities and Equity	166,802	168,000	170,348

Japan and the aggressive introduction of private brands. Sales in the Del Monte line also decreased in the early 1990s. To improve performance, Kikkoman began to reduce its product line from a high of 5,000 items to an expected eventual 2,500. One bright spot was the growth in wines and spirits. In addition, Kikkoman also introduced successful new soy-sauce related products in 1993, 1994, and 1995 in the form of two soup stocks and Steak Soy Sauce. Profit increases in the early 1990s came primarily from higher priced luxury products. (Exhibits 8 and 9 display the parent company financial statements.) The company recognized that continuing success in its mature domestic market would depend on continuous development of new applications and variations of its older products as well as development of new products.

Kikkoman in the United States in the Post–World War II Era

U.S. MARKET POTENTIAL

The various Mogi family branches and Noda Shoyu Company had expanded company efforts beyond Japan since the early 1800s. By the end of World War II, the various family enterprises and the Noda Shoyu Company had ended all activities outside Japan. Japanese expatriates living in various countries and other peoples whose traditional cuisine used shoyu comprised the company's primary pre–World War II markets. In 1949, Kikkoman started to export soy sauce, mainly to the United States. In the 1950s, consumption of soy sauce began to decline in Japan. Noda Shoyu Company made the decision to invest heavily in expanding the international sales of Kikkoman brand shoyu to overseas markets. Prior to World War II, Noda Shoyu's major overseas markets were Asia and Hawaii. After the war, the company decided to focus on the mainland United States because (1) political and economic conditions in Asia were very unstable, (2) the Japanese community in Hawaii had re-learned shoyu brewing during World War II, and there were many small Hawaiian shoyu breweries that would have made competition intense in that market, and (3) the United States had a healthy and rapidly growing economy.

Several changes in the U.S. market made that market attractive to Noda Shoyu Company. First, Americans who had been in Asia during or just after World War II developed a taste for Japanese goods, including food. Second, the company expected that as Asians in the United States became more Americanized, their consumption of traditional foods including soy sauce would decline. Third, American eating habits were shifting to more natural foods and to food that could be prepared quickly. Noda Shoyu Company moved to target both Asians and non-Asians in its marketing efforts.

During the 1956 U.S. presidential elections, Noda Shoyu bought air time to advertise Kikkoman brand products. Yuzaburo Mogi, son of the head of the company's planning department, urged this move to U.S. television advertising.

U.S. DISTRIBUTION ACTIVITIES

During the years immediately after World War II, Japanese companies in general relied on a small group of internationalized and entrepreneurial Japanese and Japanese-American individuals. Sale of food products in the United States involved a complex distribution system with heavy reliance on food brokers as promoters to local wholesalers and retailers. Food brokers required careful training by a knowledgeable sales team in how to use the product, especially where the product was unusual or unfamiliar to consumers. Food brokers marketed the product to wholesalers and large retailers, took orders for the product, and relayed the orders to the manufacturer or, in the case of foreign manufacturers, the manufacturer's agent. The manufacturer or agent then made delivery of the product to the wholesaler or retailer and handled all billing and accounts, paying the broker a commission for his/her marketing representation. The food broker was an important link between the manufacturer and the wholesaler or retailer. Food brokers were evaluated based on their ability to persuade retailers and wholesalers to carry products and to feature them prominently.

In 1957, the company formed Kikkoman International, Inc. (KII), a joint venture between Noda Shoyu Company in Japan and Pacific Trading of California. KII was incorporated in San Francisco to serve as the marketing and distribution center for Kikkoman products in the United States. Most of the products were produced by Noda Shoyu Company, but some were purchased from other manufacturers and sold under the Kikkoman label.

Over the next 10 years, sales grew 20 to 30 percent a year. In 1960, the Safeway grocery store chain agreed to have some of its stores carry Kikkoman Soy Sauce. Noda Shoyu opened regional sales offices for KII in Los Angeles (1958), New York City (1960), Chicago (1965), and Atlanta (1977). Retail marketing activities included in-store demonstrations, advertising campaigns in women's magazines that emphasized soy sauce use in American cuisine, and limited television commercials. The company used brokers as their distribution channels to supermarkets and wholesalers for the small oriental retail stores. The company encouraged food brokers through contests and training. For the food service and industrial market segments, the company carried out industrial magazine ad campaigns and special educational programs. The company also formed partnerships with the American Veal Manufacturers' Association and the Avocado Association to feature Kikkoman Soy Sauce in their product advertisements.

Other major international companies had to modify their products for the United States. However, Kikkoman marketed the same soy sauce in the United States as in Japan. The company's experience in its campaign to "westernize" soy sauce for the Japanese market applied to the campaign in the United States. In the United States Kikkoman provided the traditional, low-sodium preservative-free, and dehydrated soy sauce. The company also marketed tailor-made sauces, other food extracts, and agents.

EXPLORATION OF POTENTIAL U.S. MANUFACTURING CAPACITY

As early as 1965, Kikkoman Corporation began to explore the possibility of manufacturing in the United States. However, the company determined that sales in North America were insufficient to support the economies of scale required for a minimum efficient scale production facility. Instead, in 1968 Kikkoman Corporation contracted with a subsidiary of Leslie Salt Company of Oakland, California, to bottle the Kikkoman soy sauce shipped in bulk from Japan and to blend and bottle teriyaki sauce, a major ingredient of which was soy sauce. These bottling efforts constituted Kikkoman's first post–World War II manufacturing efforts in the United States. Bottling in the United States reduced customs and tariff costs. However, moving goods back and forth from the United States and Japan added considerably to the company's costs. In the mid 1980's Japan imported 95 percent and 88 percent of its soybeans and wheat respectively. The United States was Japan's major source of supply. Transportation of raw materials (e.g., soybeans and wheat) to Japan was between 5 percent and 20 percent of preproduction costs; transportation costs of brewed soy sauce from Japan to the United States was 25 percent of production costs. Various import/export restrictions and tariffs increased the risk and expense of importing raw materials to Japan and exporting finished goods to the United States.

The North American market was potentially much larger than the Japanese market, and Kikkoman had a greater share of the North American market than the company had in Japan. Yuzaburo Mogi hired a Columbia University classmate as a consultant, and the company formed a team to work with him to consider a U.S. plant. By 1970, the analyses, in spite of higher U.S. labor costs, favored construction of a U.S. manufacturing facility. As Yuzaburo Mogi put the company's motivation, "We made a decision to go after the American consumer."

SELECTION OF WALWORTH, WISCONSIN

The team considered over 60 potential sites in the east, west, and midwest. The team chose the midwest because of its central location and crop production. Ultimately, the team selected a 200-acre dairy farm site in Walworth, Wisconsin. Walworth provided the best fit with the five criteria established by the company: (1) access to markets (proximity to Milwaukee and Chicago, as well as the geographic convenience of a midway point between the east and west coasts made shipping relatively efficient); (2) ample supplies of wheat and soybeans (soybeans came from Wisconsin, wheat from North Dakota, and salt from Canada); (3) a dedicated workforce, (4) a strong community spirit; and (5) an impeccable supply of water. Kikkoman also appreciated Wisconsin's emphasis on a clean environment.

Walworth, Wisconsin, was situated about 2 hours northwest of Chicago and about 1 hour west of Milwaukee. A community of about 1,100, Walworth was surrounded by some of the most productive farmland in the United States. The area included a number of other smaller communities whose economies depended primarily on farming and summer vacation home residences. The company hired a local consultant, lawyer Milton Neshek, who ultimately became general counsel of Kikkoman Foods, Inc. Mr. Neshek described the original reaction to Kikkoman's purchase of prime farmland as mixed, "with a small faction on the town board opposed to the company coming in." Yuzaburo Mogi described the opposition as strong. Residents of the small, rural, close-knit farming community expressed concerns about the impact of a large, especially foreign, corporation in a small community, potential inflation of land values, and the possibility of industrial pollution.

One of Neshek's partners, Thomas Godfrey, visited Kikkoman facilities in Noda City, Japan. "When Kikkoman called me in 1971," said Godfrey, "and asked me to create a Wisconsin corporation for them so they could make soy sauce, I didn't even know what the hell soy sauce was. Nobody else around here did either." Walworth's plant manager, Bill Wenger, recalled his introduction to the company. In 1972, he was stationed with the U.S. Marines in Hawaii. His mother sent a newspaper clipping about the soy sauce plant, suggesting that it might be a good place to begin his return to civilian life. Wenger and his wife didn't know what soy sauce was either, but his wife went to the local grocery store and bought a bottle. As Wenger described it, the purchase was ". . .some horrible local Hawaiian brand. She brought it home and opened it. We looked at one another and said, '*@& . . ., this stuff is terrible.' " Another of the three American production managers employed at the plant had a similar tale. The production manager said, "The first year I worked here, we never had any soy sauce in my home. My wife wouldn't buy it, wouldn't even allow it in the house. I finally brought home a bottle and put it on some meatloaf. Now we use it on just about everything. I put it on peaches. And we even have a local minister who puts it on his ice cream . . . I do too. It's good."

No other Japanese-owned manufacturing facility had been constructed in the United States at the time. Neshek's partner, Godfrey, visited Noda because as he put it, "I had to see for myself what it was they were talking about. I had to make sure the factory wasn't going to pollute the air and water and stink up the place." Local Kikkoman representatives met with organizations such as the Local Grange, Farm Bureau groups, church groups, Rotary, and ladies' clubs. Wisconsin's governor, Patrick Lucey, came to one of the seven town meetings held to discuss the plant and explain the state's role and position. Yuzaburo Mogi described the process as "removing the fears of the local people and local council about the building of the new factory." The company was able to convince area residents that Kikkoman would not pollute the environment and would use local labor and other resources. The final vote of the county zoning board was 53 for, 13 against. The town board declined to oppose the zoning board's action. Among other issues, Kikkoman put a great deal of effort into reducing potential pollution. In talking about this process of "nemawashi" or root tending, Mr. Mogi emphasized the importance of a prosperous coexistence between the company and the local community. He said, "We've been doing business in Noda for 360 years. We learned a long time ago that to survive you need to coexist with the surrounding community."

OPENING THE NEW PLANT

In January 1971, Kikkoman executives along with Japanese, Walworth, and Wisconsin officials held a ceremonial groundbreaking on the 200-acre site. A Cleveland, Ohio, design and construction firm built the plant. Other American companies, many located in the region, built many of the critical components. The initial investment in the 10,000 kiloliter facility was $8 million, and the plant was finished just in time to avoid the 1973 American embargo on the sale of soybeans to Japan. Kikkoman's Walworth plant was the first Japanese investment in production capacity in the United States in the post–World War II period and the first plant Kikkoman built outside Japan after World War II. Opening ceremonies included dignitaries and officials from Wisconsin, Kikkoman, Japan, and the United States. The 700 invited guests heard the texts of telegrams from the Japanese Prime Minister and President Richard Nixon. President Nixon referred to the plant as a ". . . visionary step (that) will mean meaningful trade relations and balance of trade and will enhance further friendships between our two countries."

From its opening in 1972 through the mid-1990s, the company expanded the Walworth facility eight times to 500,000 square feet. Kikkoman invested in facilities or equipment every year with production increasing 8 to 10 percent per year. Originally, the plant produced two products, soy sauce and teriyaki sauce. In the mid-1990s, the plant produced 18 products, including regular and light soy sauce, teriyaki steak sauce, sweet and sour sauce, and tempura dip. All but one used a soy base. The company had been very careful about pollution, treating its wastewater carefully so that there was no threat to nearby popular Geneva Lake. The Walworth town clerk said, "There's no noise, no pollution. I live about three-quarters of a mile from them, and once a day, I get a whiff of something that's like a sweet chocolate odor. It's no problem." The company marketed the plant's output in all 50 states plus Canada and Mexico. Soy sauce was shipped in many varieties, including bottles ranging from 5 to 40 ounces, 1- to 5-gallon pails, and sometimes in stainless steel tank trucks for large customers. McDonald's, for example, used soy sauce in one of the Chicken McNuggets condiments.

MANAGEMENT OF THE WALWORTH PLANT

The company maintained a state-of-the-art laboratory at the Walworth facilities. However, plant management pointed out that the most accurate test during production was the human nose. "Our people have worked with the product for so long, a whiff can tell them something is not quite right," said one Kikkoman director. The venture was described as "a prime example of the best combination of Japanese and American business and industrial savvy." As the plant's general manager, Michitaro Nagasawa, a Ph.D in Biochemistry from the University of Wisconsin, put it, "The productivity of this plant is the highest of all our plants. . . . It's an exceptional case in Kikkoman history. We took the sons and daughters of farmers, trained them and taught them about total quality management. They were raw recruits with no experience in making soy sauce. People with farm backgrounds are very diligent workers. They will work seven days a week, 24 hours a day if necessary. They understand what hard work is."

The plant opened with 50 employees. Originally, 14 Japanese Kikkoman employees and their families came to Walworth to train employees and get the plant functioning. The Japanese families scattered in groups of two or three to settle in Walworth and various nearby communities. Local women's community organizations "adopted" the Japanese wives, formed one-to-one friendships, and helped the Japanese wives become acclimated to the communities, including learning to drive, using the local supermarkets, and hiring baby-sitters for their children. The Japanese husbands joined local service clubs. "That helped achieve an understanding between the Americans and Japanese and helped them to assimilate faster. It exposed Japanese people to a farming town that had had no Asian people before," noted Bill Nelson, Kikkoman Foods Vice President. Kikkoman established the practice of rotating its Japanese employees back to Japan after an average of 5 years in the United

States. In the mid-1990s, only seven Japanese families remained in the Walworth area, still spread throughout the local communities.

COMMUNITY CONTRIBUTIONS

Kikkoman Foods, Inc., was an active and contributing member of the community. The company donated time and funds on three levels. At the local level the company established Kikkoman Foods Foundation in 1993. The foundation, which was to be ultimately funded at the $3 million level, was formed to support area charitable activities. The company supported as many as 30 local projects a year, including college scholarships for area students, local hospital activities, a vocational program that assisted people in developing employment-related skills, and a nearby facility that preserved circus-related items. As Walworth's town clerk put it, "They sponsor just about everything—Community Chest (an organization similar to the United Way), Boy Scouts, Girls Scouts, all the way down the line. They're very good neighbors." The clerk treasurer from a nearby town said, "You see their name in the paper almost every week helping out some organization."

At the state level, Kikkoman Foods, Inc., supported the University of Wisconsin educational system, established up to four Beloit College scholarships to honor Governor Lucey at his alma mater, and funded a Mogi Keizaburo scholarship at the Milwaukee School of Engineering. Members of the board of directors served on several public service boards and commissions. At the national level, Kikkoman Corporation, through its U.S. subsidiary Kikkoman Foods, Inc., supported Youth for Understanding exchange programs. At the fifth anniversary celebration, Kikkoman's chairman reported that the plant had developed better than had been anticipated. At the tenth anniversary celebration of the Kikkoman plant, the local Walworth paper reported, "In the 10 years that Kikkoman Foods, Inc., has been located here, it has become an integrated part of the community. The company has truly become a part of the Walworth community, and not only in a business sense." In 1987, reflecting Kikkoman's contributions, Wisconsin's governor appointed Yuzaburo Mogi as Wisconsin's honorary ambassador to Japan.

KIKKOMAN'S JAPANESE–AMERICAN MANAGEMENT IN THE UNITED STATES

In the mid-1990s, Kikkoman operated its U.S. activities through two subsidiaries, Kikkoman Foods, Inc. (KFI), and Kikkoman International, Inc. (KII). KFI owned and operated the Walworth manufacturing plant. KII in San Francisco, California, undertook marketing responsibilities, including wholesaler and distributor activities throughout the United States. The boards of directors for both subsidiaries had several members from the parent corporation but were primarily Americans from among local operations officers or local Walworth citizens (for KFI) or the broader U.S. community (for KII). The KFI board met as a whole once a year and rotated the site of its annual stockholders' meeting between Japan and Wisconsin. An executive committee met monthly to consider operational decisions. The executive committee included Yuzaburo Mogi, who attended two to three meetings in the United States every year, and the head of Kikkoman Corporation's International Division. The remaining members of the executive committee included American and Japanese officers from the U.S. corporation. The KII Board operated in a similar manner but met only in the United States.

Yuzaburo Mogi believed that a long-term commitment was essential for international success. A 1961 alumnus of Columbia University's Graduate School of Business, Mr. Mogi was the first Japanese to graduate from a U.S. university with an MBA degree. In the years following graduation, he worked in various departments in Kikkoman, including accounting, finance, computers, long-range planning, and new product development. In time, he took on other roles, including member of Kikkoman's board of directors (1979), managing director of the company (1982), executive management director (1989), and executive vice president (1994). The seventeenth generation of his family to brew soy sauce, Mr. Mogi had become Kikkoman's president in early 1995. He explained his view regarding the necessity of a long-term perspective: "We should do business from a longer range viewpoint. It will be very difficult to expect fruitful results in the short run under different and difficult circumstances. Failure will be inevitable in foreign countries if one proceeds with a short-range view. In fact, it took Kikkoman 16 years to become established in the United States."

Of the five senior managers at the Walworth facility, three were Japanese and two were American. The plant manager, the finance manager, and the laboratory manager were Japanese. It was expected that these three positions would continue to be Japanese appointments. One American manager described the situation, "We know we will only attain a certain level, but that's OK, though. I can accept that. Soy sauce has been made in Japan for centuries. It's their product, their technology. They have the history, the research."

The general manager, i.e., plant manager, was the most senior person in authority at the plant and was responsible directly to headquarters in Japan. The appointment would be a person who had been with the company for many years. The finance manager's position required someone who was familiar with Japanese accounting systems and who was steeped in the Japanese emphasis on long-range profits. Japanese corporate headquarters controlled their foreign branches through their accounting and finance sections.

Mr. Mogi explained the Japanese appointment to the position of laboratory manager, "The production of soy sauce is very sophisticated. Normally, we recruit graduates with a master's degree in Japan who have gone to universities that have specialized programs in soy sauce production. In America, there is no university that teaches soy sauce production techniques, so it is difficult to promote Americans into general manager positions." As Dr. Magasawa, general manager at the Walworth plant, put it in explaining the discriminating tastes the Japanese have developed since childhood, "The sensory system, passion, feeling, or sensitivity can't transfer. That is based on just experience. Our vice president is a kind of god in this plant because he recognizes (even) a slight difference . . . I don't have that. That's why I can't be manufacturing vice president. I am a general manager—nothing special. I am a biochemist (with) 39 years in Kikkoman, mostly in research."

Decisions at the Walworth plant, when possible, were made by consensus. KFI vice president Bill Nelson described the plant management as American in content and Japanese in style, with decisions arrived at from the bottom up and most matters of importance needing a consensus of employees. "It's hard, really, to get at because of the fact that nothing . . . here should run in an American style or a Japanese style or what have you. It was just simply—let's see what happens when you have both parties participate," he said. Nelson gave the example of an idea for changing summer working hours to start at 7 A.M. instead of 8 A.M. so that workers could leave earlier and enjoy more daylight. It was, Nelson, pointed out, unusual for a company to even entertain the idea. Nelson explained the process: "Instead of simply exploring it on a management level, here we started the process of asking individual employees what personal inconvenience would be experienced if the hours were changed."

Milton Neshek observed that Japanese management and the middle management at the Walworth plant worked well together with long-range budgeting and strategic planning carried out by the Japanese executive team. He described the situation, "Our 30 employees feel like part of our family. That makes management more responsive to employees. Decisions, whenever possible, are made by consensus." The fact that the plant has no labor union was no surprise to Nelson. As he put it, a union "has never been an issue here."

Yuzaburo Mogi summarized Kikkoman's approach to its U.S. operations and, in particular, its Walworth plant as a five-point approach:

> Kikkoman has been successful doing business in the United States by adapting to American laws, customers, and most importantly, its culture . . . (An) important matter to consider, especially when establishing a manufacturing plant in a foreign country, is the maintenance of what has come to be called "harmony" with society and the local community. A foreign concern should try to prosper *together* with society and the local community. . . . It is important to try to localize the operation. . . . (Our). . . first commitment is the employment of as many local people as possible. Second we try to participate in local activities . . . trying to be a good corporate citizen (in Wisconsin) and contributing to society through our business activities. Third, we have been trying to avoid the so-called "Japanese-village" . . . by advising our people from Japan not to live together in one single community, but to spread out and live in several separate communities in order to become more families with the local people. Fourth, we try to do business with American companies. The fifth commitment is our practice of delegating most authority to local management in order to better reflect local circumstances. Through this process we are better able to make the most responsible decision. If we have an opinion, for example, we discuss it with other members at a local meeting in our American plant before reaching a decision. Kikkoman attempts to avoid a remote-control situation with letters or telephone calls from Japan. . . . If we have an opinion, we discuss it with other members at a local meeting in our American plant before reaching a decision.

The plant did encounter intercultural issues, however. For example, plant manager Bill Wenger pointed out "Communication can be a problem sometimes. The language barrier is one reason. Then there's the problem of saving face. If a mistake is made, the Japanese tend to cover up for one another so the person who made the mistakes doesn't lose face."

The company was a popular local employer in Walworth. Local unemployment was phenomenally low at 2 percent, but the Walworth plant had over 1,000 active applications on file for the plant's total 136 positions. However, turnover among plant employees was negligible. "No one quits unless it is a move by a spouse. Our absenteeism is minimal and as for tardiness—we just don't have it. We offer competitive wages and good benefits . . . employees feel like part of our family," said general counsel Neshek. Company officials stated that they paid about 10 percent more than the state average of $9.71 per hour, and employees did not have to contribute to the cost of their health insurance. As the company's vice president Shin Ichi Sugiyama put it, "In management, our primary concern is always the employee." The employees reported, "We feel like they listen to us. Our opinion counts, and we have the ability to make change, to better the company."

Mr. Sugiyama pointed out that the Walworth plant's productivity and quality had been about equal to that of Japanese plants. Productivity improved following the plant opening and by 1993 was actually the best of all the company's plants.

The U.S. Market in the 1990s[3]

U.S. DEMAND IN THE 1990s

After the opening of the Walworth plant, Kikkoman's U.S. sales growth slowed somewhat. However, Ken Saito, Kikkoman's brand manager for the midwest, summarized the company's hopes: "Americans are more adventurous than Japanese when it comes to trying new foods. That's why we have developed some products only for the American market. But most Americans still are not familiar with how to use soy sauce." Thus, the company developed a number of non-oriental recipes that call for soy sauce and other Kikkoman products, for example, teriyaki chicken wings and Pacific Rim pizza with sweet and sour sauce, beef and chicken fajitas, and grilled salmon with confetti salsa flavored with "lite" soy sauce. Kikkoman clearly expected Americans to increasingly use soy sauce for applications beyond oriental foods and expected significant growth in the company's base product in the United.States. According to Saito, "We figure the market in the United States will increase 100 times in the next decade." Kikkoman marketing coordinator, Trisha MacLeod, articulated the goal as ". . . to get consumers to realize soy sauce is the oldest man-made condiment, and that it can also be used in meatloaf, barbecue—across the spectrum."

MacLeod pointed out, "Americans eat a lot more soy sauce than they realize." However, America's per capita consumption was barely 10 tablespoons, translating into $300 million in North American sales. In contrast, Japanese per capita consumption was about 10.5 quarts per person, which translated into about $1.4 billion in annual sales in Japan.

The population of Asian immigrants and families of Asian descent was projected to grow significantly in the United States. The California population increased 127 percent to 2.8 million during the 1980s. The total population of Asian-Americans in the United States was estimated at 7.3 million in 1990, up 108 percent over the 1980s. Asian peoples represented the traditional mainstay market for oriental foods. Asians had higher income and educational levels than any other ethnic groups in the United States. However, each country represented a different cuisine, and the different Asian ethnic groups required different marketing approaches. Asian populations had spread throughout many parts of the United States, and retail outlets were learning how to highlight and display oriental foods to spur sales. Restaurants greatly influenced American food-buying habits. One industry executive observed that almost all U.S. restaurant kitchens in the 1990s had soy sauce. A 1996 National Restaurant Association study indicated that ethnic foods were increasing in popularity. Thus, oriental food manufacturers and distributors expected that oriental food sales would increase sharply.

Some information in the mid-1990s suggested strong and increasing popularity for oriental foods. U.S. sales of oriental foods had slowed considerably. The most recent aggregate information regarding the demand for oriental food in the United States in the mid-1990s is shown in Exhibit 10.

By the late 1980s consumers began to indicate dissatisfaction with canned entrees, at $81 million in sales the second largest subcategory of oriental foods. Sales of this subcategory had declined as much as 10 percent (1991 to 1992) and showed no signs of abating. Competition was intense, with a third of all products sold on the basis of feature, price, and/or display promotion.

U.S. MAJOR COMPETITORS

Kikkoman's two major competitors in the United States were Chun King and LaChoy. Both companies made soy sauce by hydrolyzing vegetable protein. This European

EXHIBIT 10   **U.S. Oriental Food Sales ($000,000)**

Source: Information Resources, Inc., Chicago, IL.

Year	1992	1993	1994
Sales	$275	$305	$301

derived method was faster and less expensive than the six-month fermentation process Kikkoman used. By 1971, Kikkoman had surpassed Chun King in supermarket sales of soy sauce, becoming #2 in the American marketplace. In 1976, Kikkoman outsold LaChoy brand soy sauce and became the #1 retailer of soy sauce in the United States, a position it continued to hold in the mid-1990s. However, the company faced strong competitors in the oriental foods category and in the sauces and condiments subcategory.

The new consumer focus was on oriental food ingredients that individuals could add to home-cooked dishes. "People are cooking more oriental foods at home," said Chun King's vice president of marketing, "Over 40 percent of U.S. households stir-fry at least once a month. Sauces are an opportunity to get away from the canned image." Indeed, sauces were the only growth area on the oriental food category, with 1992 sales rising 11 percent over the previous year. Rivals Chun King and LaChoy were flooding the oriental foods aisle in American supermarkets with new products. LaChoy had about 40 percent of the shelf products in oriental foods and Chun King had about 20 percent.

However, there were more changes than just new products. In the early 1990s, LaChoy and Chun King had revved up their marketing efforts under new ownership. LaChoy was owned by ConAgra's Hunt-Wesson division. Among other initiatives, ConAgra, a major U.S. food company, hired a new advertising firm for LaChoy.

A Singapore-based firm purchased Chun King in 1989 and brought in a new management team. As one observer put it, "The brand had really been neglected as part of Nabisco (its previous owner). It was just a small piece of a big pie." The new management team introduced a line of seasoned chow mein noodles and another of hot soy sauces. The firm's marketing plan included consumer promotions and a print ad campaign in women's magazines. Chun King's 1992 oriental food sales were estimated at $30 million. In mid-1995, ConAgra purchased Chun King from the Singapore company and added the brand to its Hunt-Wesson division. ConAgra was no stranger to the Chun King brand. The large U.S. competitor had purchased Chun King's frozen food line in 1986 from Del Monte. It was expected that Hunt-Wesson would eventually consolidate manufacturing but continue to aggressively advertise the two brands separately. As a Hunt-Wesson executive put it, "They're both established leaders in their field, and they both have brand strength."

LaChoy advertised itself as "the world's largest producer of oriental foods created for American tastes." The company led the oriental foods category with sales (excluding frozen) of $87 million in 1992 and $104.4 million in 1994. Its products included chow mein noodles, bamboo shoots, sauces, and miscellaneous foods. About $28 million of the 1992 sales came from sauce and marinade sales. LaChoy's manager of corporate communications indicated that the Chicago-based firm planned no increase in marketing spending in reaction to the new Chun King initiatives. However, the company did plan to advertise two new lines—Noodle Entrees and Stir-Fry Vegetables 'N Sauce. The company expected to expend most of its marketing support for the latter product line, a set of vegetables in four sauces formulated for consumers to stir-fry with their choice of meat.

KIKKOMAN AND OTHER COMPETITORS

Kikkoman remained the one bright spot in the oriental food category of sauces and marinades. Kikkoman controlled $63 million of the $160 million sauces/marinades segment and supported its position with a moderate amount of advertising—$3.2 million in 1992, about the same as 1991. In its major product lines, Kikkoman controlled about two-thirds of the California market and had about one-third market share in other major U.S. sales regions. The company was test-marketing a new line of sauces for addition to the consumer's own vegetables and meat.

Kikkoman also had to consider recent moves by several other competitors. Yamasa Shoyu Co., Ltd., Japan's second-largest soy sauce maker, had announced plans to build a factory in Oregon in mid-1994. This multigenerational company was founded in 1645 in Choshi City, Japan. Estimates on the cost of the Oregon factory ranged from $15 million to $20 million, and the plant was expected to eventually employ 50 workers. Yamasa intended to produce soy sauce for the U.S. market by using soybeans shipped from the midwest. It took Yamasa 4 years to select the final site for its new plant. The company produced a number of products in addition to soy sauce, including other food and drugs made from biological raw materials such as soybean protein and wheat starch.

Hong Kong–based Lee Kum Kee was a producer and importer of Chinese-oriented sauces and condiments. Lee Kum Kee had opened a sauce manufacturing plant in Los Angeles in 1991 to keep up with rising U.S. demand and to reduce dependence on imports thus avoiding payment of import duties, which could be as high as 20 percent. The company was a Hong Kong subsidiary of one of Japan's leading soy sauce brewers. Lee Kum Kee retailed its sauces in big supermarket chains in all 50 states. Historically, the company imported its soy sauce through an independent U.S.-based importer of the same name. The U.S. importer also imported about 40 other food products, mostly marinades, curries, and sauces from the East. Lee Kum Kee found its sales propelled by the population doubling of Americans of Asian or Pacific Island descent.

Competitor San-J International of the San-Jirushi Corporation of Kuwana, Japan, built a soy sauce plant in Richmond, Virginia in 1988. Hawaiian competitor Noh Foods of Hawaii innovated a line of oriental dried seasonings and powdered mixes. In reaction, other manufacturers, including Kikkoman, produced copycat products. Noh Foods distributed its products in the United States, Europe, and Australia through distributors and trade show activities.

Kikkoman's International Position

THE KIKKOMAN VISION

In the mid-1990s, Kikkoman manufactured in four countries and marketed its brand products in over 90 countries. (Exhibit 11 shows the comparison of domestic and non-Japan sales and operating profits.) Of the company's 3,200 employees, over 1,000 were in international subsidiaries, and only 5 percent of those were Japanese. The company saw at least part of its mission as contributing to international cultural exchange. Yuzaburo Mogi explained,

EXHIBIT 11   **Consolidated Results FY 1995 ((Y) m)**

Source: UBS Securities Limited, May 28, 1996. Table 7 as reported by *Investext*.

	Domestic	Non-Japan
Sales	162,426	40,860
Operating Profit	6,640	4,152
Operating Margin	4.0	10.1

Kikkoman believes that soy sauce marketing is the promotion of the international exchange of food culture. In order to create a friendlier world, I believe we need many types of cultural exchanges. Among these, there is one that is most closely related to our daily lives—the eating of food. Soy sauce is one of the most important food cultures in Japan. Hence, the overseas marketing of soy sauce means the propagation of Japanese food culture throughout the world.

As one U.S. scholar who had studied the company extensively in the 1980s put it, "There is an evident willingness on the part of Kikkoman to experiment with new products, production techniques, management styles, and operational forms in the international arena." Yuzaburo Mogi put it similarly when he said, "It should be understood that adjustment to different laws, customs, and regulations is imperative, instead of complaining about those differences."

KIKKOMAN IN EUROPE

Kikkoman began its marketing activities in Europe in 1972. Kikkoman found Europeans more conservative and slower to try new tastes than Americans. The firm found Germany the least conservative and opened restaurants there in 1973. By the early 1990s, the company had opened six Japanese steak houses in Germany. The restaurants gave their customers, over 90 percent of whom were non-Asian, the opportunity to try new cuisine. The Kikkoman trading subsidiary in Germany was the company's European marketing arm. Said the managing director for Kikkoman's European marketing subsidiary located in Germany, "Germany and Holland are big business for us, as both countries are very much into interesting sauces and marinades." Kikkoman's managing director of Europe made it clear that he had aggressive plans to grow sales both by increasing the sales of soy sauce as well as extending the markets in which the company operated. The massive ready-made meal business in both the United States and Europe had huge potential for Kikkoman. The firm would need to market to end consumers at the retail level as well as to food manufacturers.

The company established its second overseas manufacturing facility in 1983. This facility supplied soy sauce to Australian and European markets. By the early 1990s, Kikkoman had about 50 percent of the Australian soy sauce market. The United Kingdom brand debut occurred in 1986, and the 1992 U.K. market was estimated at 1 billion pounds. In 1993, the firm opened a 25,000-square-foot warehouse in London. With $1.66 billion (U.S.) in sales, Kikkoman had come a long way with "just" soy sauce. Overall, analysts noted that the United States had experienced about 10 percent annual growth in soy sauce demand and expected Europe to expand similarly.

KIKKOMAN IN ASIA

In Asia, the company opened a production facility in Singapore in 1983 and incorporated a trading company in 1990. Industry observers expected the company to enter the soy sauce market in China in the near future. In addition, other Asian countries offered various opportunities in sauces, condiments, and foods.

KIKKOMAN—THE CHALLENGES

The company the Mogi family had headed for nearly 400 years confronted a number of challenges on the global stage in the latter part of the 1990s. Kikkoman executives realized that the company's future could depend primarily on its mature domestic market. The multigeneration family firm would have to change its image as a maker of a mature product. As Mr. Mogi stated "We . . . take pride in our ability to contribute to the exchange of cultures by using some of the world's most familiar flavors. We are now concentrating on further enhancing our ability to serve consumers in Japan and overseas. Kikkoman continues as a company that is proud of its heritage, but nevertheless willing and able to adapt to the constantly evolving requirements of our customers and markets."

Endnotes

1. In early 1996, the exchange rate was about 95 yen per U.S. dollar. Thus, in U.S. dollars, Kikkoman's market value was about $1.7 billion. Sales at year end 1995 for the consolidated company were 203 billion yen, or slightly less than $2 billion (See Exhibits 2 and 3 for consolidated financial data and Exhibits 8, 9, and 11 for parent company and domestic versus non-Japan revenues plus other selected financial information.)

2. *Zaibatsu:* Industrial and financial combines dissolved by occupation fiat after World War II, but which have reemerged as somewhat weaker entities. Some of these *zaibatsu* have developed into large conglomerates such as Mitsubishi. However, they should be distinguished from *keiretsu* (of which Mitsubishi is also one of the largest). *Keiretsu* are informal enterprise group-based associations of banks, industrials, and so forth.

3. Information on the market and competitors was drawn primarily from InfoScan.

References

Allen, Sara Clark. "Kikkoman, a Good Neighbor in Wisconsin," *Business,* Tuesday, June 11, 1996.

Bergsman, Steve. "Patience and Perseverance in Japan," *Global Trade,* Vol. 109, Issue 8 (August 1989), pp. 10, 12.

Campbell, Dee Ann. "Del Monte Foods to See European Foods Business," *Business Wire,* April 17, 1990.

Demestrakakes, Pan. "Quality for the Ages," *Food Processing,* Vol. 70, No. 6 (September 1996).

"Fireflies Help Kill Germs," *Times Net Asia,* January 1, 1996.

Forbish, Lynn. "Grand Oriental Celebration Held for Opening of Kikkoman Foods," *Janesville Gazette,* June 18, 1973.

Forrest, Tracy. "Kikkoman: a Way of Life," *Super Marketing,* January 28, 1994.

Fruin, W. Mark. *Kikkoman: Company, Clan, and Community* (Cambridge, Massachusetts: Harvard University Press, 1983).

Hewitt, Lynda. "Liquid Spice," *Food Manufacture,* February, 1993, p. 23.

Hostveldt, John. "Japan's Kikkoman Corp. Brews Success Story in Walworth," *Business Dateline: The Business Journal—Milwaukee,* Vol. 3, No. 31, Sec. 3 (May 19, 1986), p. 17.

"In-Store: Happy New Year's Feast," (Article on Kikkoman's In-Store Promotion), *Brandsweek,* Vol. 37 (January 1, 1996), pp. 14–15.

Jensen, Debra. "Kikkoman Executive Lauds Wisconsin, Lucey," *Gazette,* January 13, 1989, p. 1B.

Jensen, Don. "A Stainless Success Story," *Kenosha News,* Business Section, August 1, 1993.

Jensen, Leah. "Kikkoman Spices Up Walworth's Quality of Life," *Janesville Gazette,* January 21, 1984.

Kikkoman Corporation: Flavors That Bring People Together (Company Brochure).

Kinugasa, Dean. "Kikkoman Corporation," 1979 (Private Translation by Norihito Tanaka and Marilyn Taylor, 1994).

LaChoy's Homepage (www.hunt-wesson.com/lachoy/main/mission/).

LaGrange, Maria L. "RJR Sells Del Monte Operations for $1.4 Billion," *Los Angeles Times,* Vol. 108, Issue 297, September 26, 1989, p. 2.

Mogi, Yuzaburo. *"Masatsunaki Kokusai Senryaku,"* (Tokyo, Japan: Selnate Publishing Co., Ltd., 1988—in English Translation).

Mogi, Yuzaburo. "The Conduct of International Business: One Company's Credo—Kikkoman, Soy Sauce and the U.S. Market," (Available from Company).

Ostrander, Kathleen. "Kikkoman's Success Tied to Proper Blend," *Business Datelines (Wisconsin State Journal),* March 1, 1992, p. 29.

Plett, Edith. "Kikkoman Foods Marks Fifth Year," *Janesville Gazette,* January 26, 1979.

Redman, Russell. "Hunt-Wesson Acquires Chun King," *Supermarket News,* Vol. 45, No. 19 (May 8, 1995), p. 101.

SBA Homepage, Wisconsin Gallery.

Schoenburg, Lorraine. "Governor Supports Kikkoman," *Janesville Gazette,* September 14, 1989.

Shima, Takeshi. "Kikkoman's Thousand-Year History," *Business JAPAN,* January, 1989, p. 65.

"The Joy of Soy: How a Japanese Sauce Company Found a Happy Home in Walworth, Wisc.," *Chicago Tribune Magazine,* January 31, 1993, p. 13.

Wilkins, Mira. "Japanese Multinational in the United States: Continuity and Change, 1879–1990," *Business History Review,* Vol. 64, Issue 4 (Winter 1990), pp. 585–629.

Yates, Ronald E. "Wisconsin's Other Brew," *Chicago Tribune Magazine,* January 31, 1993, p. 14.

In addition to personal interviews in Tokyo, Walworth, Wisconsin, and San Francisco, information and quotations were also drawn from these references. This list is part of a much broader set of sources that the authors consulted.

Appendix A

The Making of Soy Sauce

The Chinese began making jiang, a precursor of soy sauce, about 2,500 years ago. The most likely story of soy sauce's origins relates how Kakushin, a Japanese Zen priest who studied in China, returned to Japan in the middle of the thirteenth century and began preparing a type of miso, or soybean paste produced through fermentation, that became a specialty of the area. By the end of the thirteenth century, the liquid was called *tamari* and sold commercially along with the miso. Experimentation with the raw ingredients and methods of fermentation began. Vegetarianism also became popular in Japan during this time, and people were eager for condiments to flavor their rather bland diet. Soldiers also found the transportability of the seasonings useful.

Soy sauce evolved from tamari and miso by adding wheat to the soybean fermentation mash. The Japanese modified the shoyu to include wheat to gentle the taste so that it did not overwhelm the delicate flavors of Japanese cuisine. Most households made their shoyu during the slack time in agricultural cycles. Families harvested grains in the fall and processed them into mash. The mash fermented beginning in October–December to January–March when the shoyu was pressed from the mash.

Regional differences among the soy sauces developed depending upon the mix of soybean, wheat, and fermentation techniques. Even in the last decade of the twentieth century, there were hundreds of local varieties of soy sauce available commercially in Japan.

Produced in the traditional way, soy sauce was a natural flavor enhancer. In the latter part of the twentieth century, ingredient-conscious consumers shied away from artificial flavor enhancers. Soy sauce responded to the challenge of finding ingredients to flavor foods. For vegetarian manufacturers, the "beefy" taste provided by the soy sauce without any meat extract was highly desirable.

There were two methods of manufacturing soy sauce—the traditional fermentation process used by Kikkoman and the chemical method.

SOY SAUCE THROUGH FERMENTATION—KIKKOMAN'S TRADITIONAL METHOD

Kikkoman's process was the traditional one and involved processing soy and wheat to a mash. Kikkoman had developed an innoculum of seed mold that the company added. The seed mold produced a growth, the development of which was controlled by temperature and humidity. The resulting mash (koji) was discharged into fermentation tanks where selected microorganism cultures and brine were added. The product (moromi mash) was aerated and mixed, then aged. During this process, enzymes formed in the cells of the koji and provided the characteristics of the brewed sauce. The soybean protein changed to amino acid, and the enzymatic reaction that occurred between the sugar and amino acids produced the taste and color. Enzymes changed the wheat starch to sugars for sweetness, and a special yeast developed changing some of the sugars to alcohol. Fermentation changed other parts of the sugars to alcohol that produced tartness. The brewing process determined flavor, color, taste, and aroma. The brine added to the koji mixture stimulated the enzymes and produced the reddish brown liquid mash. This process resulted in umami—or flavor-enhancing—abilities, as well as the brewed flavor components. The final mash was pressed between layers of cloth under constant pressure. After a pasteurization process to intensify color and aromas, the shoyu was filtered again and bottled. There were no flavorings, coloring, additives, or artificial ingredients in the product. According to produce developers, these complex flavors were not present in brewed soy sauce.

CHEMICALLY PRODUCED SOY SAUCE

Nonbrewed soy sauce could be made in hours. Soybeans were boiled with hydrochloric acid for 15 to 20 hours. When the maximum amount of amino acid was removed from the soybeans, the mixture was cooled to end the hydrolysis action. The amino acid liquid was then neutralized, mixed with charcoal, and finally purified through filtration. Color and flavor were introduced via varying amounts of corn syrup, salt, and caramel coloring. The resulting soy sauce was then refined and bottled.

6

Kentucky Fried Chicken and the Global Fast-Food Industry in 1998

Jeffrey A. Krug
University of Illinois at Urbana–Champaign

In 1998, Kentucky Fried Chicken Corporation (KFC) was the world's largest chicken restaurant chain and third largest fast-food chain. KFC held over 55 percent of the U.S. market and operated over 10,200 restaurants worldwide. It opened 376 new restaurants (more than one restaurant a day) and operated in 79 countries.

One of the first fast-food chains to go international during the late 1960s, KFC developed one of the world's most recognizable brands. Japan, Australia, and the United Kingdom accounted for the greatest share of KFC's international expansion during the 1970s and 1980s. During the 1990s, KFC turned its attention to other international markets that offered significant opportunities for growth: China, with a population of over 1 billion, and Europe, with a population roughly equal to that of the United States. Latin America offered a unique growth opportunity because of the size of its markets, its common language and culture, and its geographical proximity to the United States. Mexico was of particular interest because of the North American Free Trade Agreement (NAFTA), which went into effect in 1994.

Prior to 1990, KFC expanded into Latin America primarily through company-owned restaurants in Mexico and Puerto Rico. By 1995, KFC had also established company-owned restaurants in Venezuela and Brazil, as well as franchised units in numerous Caribbean countries. During the early 1990s, KFC shifted to a two-tiered strategy in Latin America. First, it established 29 franchised restaurants in Mexico following the enactment of Mexico's new franchise law in 1990. This allowed KFC to expand outside of its company restaurant base in Mexico City, Guadalajara, and

This case was prepared by Jeffrey A. Krug, University of Illinois at Urbana–Champaign.

Monterrey. KFC was one of many U.S. fast-food, retail, and hotel chains to begin franchising in Mexico following the new franchise law. Second, KFC began an aggressive franchise-building program in South America. By 1998, it was operating franchised restaurants in 32 Latin American countries. Much of this growth was in Brazil, Chile, Colombia, Ecuador, and Peru.

Company History

Fast-food franchising was still in its infancy in 1952 when Harland Sanders began his travels across the United States to speak with prospective franchisees about his Colonel Sanders Recipe Kentucky Fried Chicken. By 1960, "Colonel" Sanders had granted KFC franchises to over 200 take-home retail outlets and restaurants across the United States. He had also succeeded in establishing a number of franchises in Canada. By 1963, the number of KFC franchises had risen to over 300 and revenues had reached $500 million.

By 1964, at the age of 74, the Colonel had grown tired of running the day-to-day operations of his business and was eager to concentrate on public relations issues. Therefore, he sought out potential buyers, eventually deciding to sell the business to two Louisville businessmen—Jack Massey and John Young Brown Jr.—for $2 million. The Colonel stayed on as a public relations representative and goodwill ambassador for the company.

During the next five years, Massey and Brown concentrated on growing KFC's franchise system across the United States. In 1966, after being taken public, KFC was listed on the New York Stock Exchange. By the late 1960s, the company had gained a strong foothold in the United States, and Massey and Brown turned their attention to international markets. In 1969, KFC signed a joint venture with Japan's Mitsuoishi Shoji Kaisha, Ltd., and acquired the rights to operate 14 existing KFC franchises in England. Subsidiaries were also established in Hong Kong, South Africa, Australia, New Zealand, and Mexico. By 1971, KFC had 2,450 franchises and 600 company-owned restaurants worldwide, and was operating in 48 countries.

HEUBLEIN, INC.

In 1971, KFC entered negotiations with Heublein, Inc., to discuss a possible merger. The decision to seek a merger candidate was partially driven by Brown's desire to pursue other interests, including a political career (Brown was elected governor of Kentucky in 1977). Several months later, Heublein acquired KFC. Heublein was in the business of producing vodka, mixed cocktails, dry gin, cordials, beer, and other alcoholic beverages. However, Heublein had little experience in the restaurant business. Conflicts quickly erupted between Colonel Sanders, who continued to act in a public relations capacity, and Heublein management. Sanders became increasingly distraught over quality control issues and restaurant cleanliness. By 1977, new restaurant openings had slowed to about 20 per year; few restaurants were being remodeled, and service quality had declined.

In 1977, Heublein sent in a new management team to redirect KFC's strategy. The team immediately implemented a back-to-the-basics strategy and discontinued new-unit construction until existing restaurants could be upgraded and operating problems eliminated. KFC then refurbished restaurants, placed emphasis on cleanliness and service, cut out marginal products, and reestablished product consistency. By 1982, KFC's strategic focus had proved successful and the company was again aggressively building new units.

R. J. REYNOLDS INDUSTRIES, INC.

In 1982, R. J. Reynolds Industries, Inc. (RJR), merged Heublein into a wholly owned subsidiary. The merger with Heublein represented part of RJR's overall corporate strategy of diversifying into unrelated businesses, including energy, transportation, food, and restaurants. RJR's objective was to reduce its dependence on the tobacco industry, which had driven RJR sales since the company's founding in North Carolina in 1875. Sales of cigarettes and tobacco products, while profitable, were declining because of reduced consumption in the United States. This was mainly the result of an increased awareness among Americans about the negative health consequences of smoking.

RJR had no more experience in the restaurant business than did Heublein. However, it decided to take a hands-off approach to managing KFC. Whereas Heublein had installed its own top management at KFC headquarters, RJR left KFC management largely intact, believing that existing KFC managers were better qualified to operate KFC's businesses than its own managers were. In doing so, RJR avoided many of the operating problems that plagued Heublein. This strategy paid off as KFC continued to expand aggressively and profitably under RJR ownership. In 1985, RJR acquired Nabisco Corporation for $4.9 billion. Nabisco sold a variety of well-known cookies, crackers, cereals, confectioneries, snacks, and other grocery products. The merger with Nabisco represented a decision by RJR to concentrate its diversification efforts on the consumer foods industry. It subsequently divested many of its non-consumer food businesses. RJR sold KFC to PepsiCo, Inc., one year later.

PepsiCo, Inc.

CORPORATE STRATEGY

In 1965 the merger of the Pepsi-Cola Company and Frito-Lay, Inc., created one of the largest consumer products companies in the United States: PepsiCo, Inc. Pepsi-Cola's traditional business was the sale of soft drink concentrates to licensed independent and company-owned bottlers that manufactured, sold, and distributed Pepsi-Cola soft drinks. Pepsi-Cola's best known trademarks were Pepsi-Cola, Diet Pepsi, Mountain Dew, and Slice. Frito-Lay manufactured and sold a variety of snack foods, including Fritos corn chips, Lay's potato chips, Ruffles potato chips, Doritos, Tostitos tortilla chips, and Chee-tos cheese-flavored snacks. PepsiCo quickly embarked on an aggressive acquisition program similar to that pursued by RJR during the 1980s, buying a number of companies in areas unrelated to its major businesses. Acquisitions included North American Van Lines, Wilson Sporting Goods, and Lee Way Motor Freight. However, these businesses failed to live up to expectations, mainly because the management skills required to operate them lay outside of PepsiCo's area of expertise.

Poor performance in these businesses led then-chairman and chief executive officer Don Kendall to restructure PepsiCo's operations in 1984. First, the company divested itself of businesses that did not support PepsiCo's consumer product orientation, such as North American Van Lines, Wilson Sporting Goods, and Lee Way Motor Freight. Second, PepsiCo sold its foreign bottling operations to local businesspeople who better understood the culture and business environment in their respective countries. Third, Kendall reorganized PepsiCo along three lines: soft drinks, snack foods, and restaurants.

RESTAURANT BUSINESS AND ACQUISITION OF KENTUCKY FRIED CHICKEN

PepsiCo first entered the restaurant business in 1977 when it acquired Pizza Hut's 3,200-unit restaurant system. Taco Bell was merged into a division of PepsiCo in 1978. The restaurant business complemented PepsiCo's consumer product orientation. The marketing of fast-food followed many of the same patterns as the marketing of soft drinks and snack foods. PepsiCo therefore believed that its management skills could be easily transferred among its three business segments. This was compatible with PepsiCo's practice of frequently moving managers among its business units as a way of developing future top executives. PepsiCo's restaurant chains also provided an additional outlet for the sale of Pepsi soft drinks. Pepsi-Cola soft drinks and fast-food products could also be marketed together in the same television and radio segments, thereby providing higher returns for each advertising dollar. To complete its diversification into the restaurant segment, PepsiCo acquired Kentucky Fried Chicken Corporation from RJR-Nabisco for $841 million in 1986. The acquisition of KFC gave PepsiCo the leading market share in chicken (KFC), pizza (Pizza Hut), and Mexican food (Taco Bell), three of the four largest and fastest-growing segments within the U.S. fast-food industry.

MANAGEMENT

Following the acquisition by PepsiCo, KFC's relationship with its parent company underwent dramatic changes. Whereas RJR had operated KFC as a semi-autonomous unit, satisfied that KFC management understood the fast-food business better than its own management did, PepsiCo acquired KFC in order to complement its already strong presence in the fast-food market. Rather than allowing KFC to operate independently, PepsiCo undertook sweeping changes: negotiating a new franchise contract to give PepsiCo more control over its franchisees, reducing staff in order to cut costs, and replacing KFC managers with its own. In 1987, a rumor spread through KFC's headquarters in Louisville that the new personnel manager, who had just relocated from PepsiCo's headquarters in New York, had said "There will be no more home-grown tomatoes in this organization."

Such rumors indicated a more serious morale problem, created by several restructurings that led to layoffs throughout the KFC organization, the replacement of KFC personnel with PepsiCo managers, and conflicts between KFC and PepsiCo's corporate cultures. KFC's culture was built largely on Colonel Sanders's laid-back approach to management, under which employees enjoyed relatively good job stability and security. Over the years, a strong loyalty had been created among KFC employees and franchisees, mainly because of Colonel Sanders's efforts to meet his employees' benefits, pension, and other non-income needs. In addition, the friendly, relaxed atmosphere at KFC's corporate offices in Louisville had mirrored the company's corporate culture, which had been left essentially unchanged during the Heublein and RJR years.

In stark contrast, PepsiCo's corporate culture was characterized by a strong emphasis on performance. Top performers expected to move up through the ranks quickly. PepsiCo used its KFC, Pizza Hut, Taco Bell, Frito Lay, and Pepsi-Cola divisions as training grounds for its top managers, rotating its best managers through its five divisions on average every two years. This practice created immense pressure on managers to continuously demonstrate their prowess within short periods, in order to maximize their potential for promotion. This practice also left many KFC managers with the feeling that they had few career opportunities with the new company. One PepsiCo manager commented, "You may have performed well last year, but if you don't perform well this year, you're gone, and there are 100 ambitious guys with Ivy League MBAs at PepsiCo who would love to take your position." An unwanted effect of this performance-driven culture was that employee loyalty was often lost and turnover became higher than in other companies.

When asked about KFC's relationship with its corporate parent, Kyle Craig, president of KFC's U.S. operations, commented:

> The KFC culture is an interesting one because I think it was dominated by a lot of KFC folks, many of whom have been around since the days of the Colonel. Many of those people were very intimidated by the PepsiCo culture, which is a very high-performance, high-accountability, highly driven culture. People were concerned about whether they would succeed in the new culture. Like many companies, we have had a couple of downsizings, which further made people nervous. Today, there are fewer old KFC people around and I think to some degree people have seen that the PepsiCo culture can drive some pretty positive results. I also think the PepsiCo people who have worked with KFC have modified their cultural values somewhat and they can see that there were a lot of benefits in the old KFC culture.
>
> PepsiCo pushes its companies to perform strongly, but whenever there is a slip in performance, it increases the culture gap between PepsiCo and KFC. I have been involved in two downsizings over which I have been the chief architect. They have been probably the two most gut-wrenching experiences of my career. Because you know you're dealing with peoples' lives and their families, these changes can be emotional if you care about the people in your organization. However, I do fundamentally believe that your first obligation is to the entire organization.

A second problem for PepsiCo was its poor relationship with KFC franchisees. A month after becoming president and chief executive officer in 1989, John Cranor addressed KFC's franchisees in Louisville, in order to explain the details of the first contract change in 13 years. The new contract gave PepsiCo greater power to take over weak franchises, relocate restaurants, and make changes in existing restaurants. In addition, it no longer protected existing restaurants from competition with new KFC units, and it gave PepsiCo the right to raise royalty fees as contracts came up for renewal. After Cranor finished his address, the attending franchisees jumped to their feet to protest the changes. The franchisees had long been accustomed to relatively little interference from management in their day-to-day operations (a policy begun by Colonel Sanders). Interference, of course, was a strong part of PepsiCo's philosophy of demanding change. KFC's franchise association later sued PepsiCo over the new contract. The dispute remained unresolved until 1996, when the most objectionable parts of the contract were removed by KFC's new president and CEO, David Novak. A new contract was ratified by KFC's franchisees in 1997.

PEPSICO'S DIVESTITURE OF KFC, PIZZA HUT, AND TACO BELL

PepsiCo's strategy of diversifying into three distinct but related markets—soft drinks, snack foods, and fast-food restaurants—created not only one of the world's largest consumer products companies but also a portfolio of some of the world's most recognizable brands. Between 1990 and 1996, PepsiCo grew at an annual rate of over 10 percent, surpassing $31 billion in sales in 1996. However, this sales growth masked troubles in PepsiCo's fast-food businesses. Operating margins (profit as a percentage of sales) at Pepsi-Cola and Frito Lay averaged 12 and 17 percent, respectively, between 1990 and 1996. During the same period, margins at KFC, Pizza Hut, and Taco Bell fell from an average of over 8 percent in 1990 to a little more than 4 percent in 1996. Declining margins in the fast-food chains reflected increasing maturity in the U.S. fast-food industry, more intense competition, and the aging of KFC and Pizza Hut's restaurant base. As a result, PepsiCo's restaurant chains

EXHIBIT 1   Tricon Global Restaurants, Inc., Organization, Chart, 1998

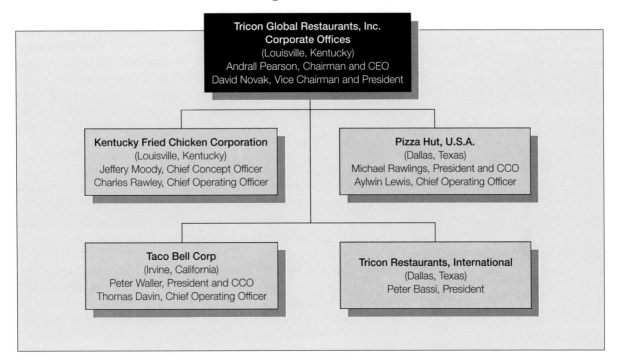

absorbed nearly one-half of the company's annual capital spending during the 1990s while generating less than one-third of PepsiCo's cash flows. Therefore, cash was diverted from PepsiCo's soft drink and snack food businesses to its restaurant businesses. This reduced PepsiCo's return on assets and its stock price, and made effective competition with Coca-Cola (PepsiCo's leading rival) more difficult. In 1997, PepsiCo spun off its restaurant businesses into a new company called Tricon Global Restaurants, Inc. (see Exhibit 1). The new company was based in KFC's Louisville headquarters. PepsiCo's objectives were to reposition itself as a packaged goods company, to strengthen its balance sheet, and to create more consistent earnings growth. PepsiCo received a one-time distribution from Tricon of $4.7 billion, $3.7 billion of which was used to pay off short-term debt. The balance was earmarked for stock repurchases.

Fast-Food Industry

According to the National Restaurant Association (NRA), food-service sales topped $320 billion for the approximately 500,000 restaurants and other food outlets making up the U.S. restaurant industry in 1997. The NRA estimated that sales in the fast-food segment of the food-service industry grew 5.2 percent, to $104 billion, up from $98 billion in 1996. This marked the fourth consecutive year that fast-food sales either matched or exceeded sales in full-service restaurants, which in 1997 grew 4.1 percent, to $104 billion. The growth in fast-food sales reflected the gradual change in the restaurant industry, in which independently operated sit-down restaurants were becoming dominated by fast-food restaurant chains. The U.S. restaurant industry as a whole grew by approximately 4.2 percent in 1997.

MAJOR FAST-FOOD SEGMENTS

Six major business segments made up the fast-food segment of the food-service industry. Sales data for the leading restaurant chains in each segment are shown in Exhibit 2. Most striking is the dominance of McDonald's, which had sales of over $16 billion in 1996. This represented 16.6 percent of U.S. fast-food sales, or nearly 22 percent of sales among the nation's top 30 fast-food chains. Sales at an average McDonald's restaurant totaled $1.3 million per year, compared to about $820,000 for the average U.S. fast-food restaurant. Tricon Global Restaurants (KFC, Pizza Hut, and Taco Bell) had U.S. sales of $13.4 billion in 1996. This represented 13.6 percent of U.S. fast-food sales and 17.9 percent of the top 30 fast-food chains.

Sandwich chains made up the largest segment of the fast-food market. McDonald's controlled 35 percent of the sandwich segment, while Burger King ran a distant second, with a 15.6 percent market share. Competition had become particularly intense within the sandwich segment as the U.S. fast-food market became more saturated. In order to increase sales, chains turned to new products to win customers away from other sandwich chains, introduced products traditionally offered by other types of chains (such as pizza, fried chicken, and tacos), streamlined their menus, and upgraded product quality. Burger King recently introduced its Big King, a direct clone of the Big Mac. McDonald's quickly retaliated by introducing its Big 'n Tasty, a direct clone of the Whopper. Wendy's introduced chicken pita sandwiches, and Taco Bell introduced sandwiches called wraps, breads stuffed with various fillings. Hardee's successfully introduced fried chicken in most of its restaurants. In addition to offering new products, chains lowered prices, improved customer service, co-branded with other fast-food chains, and established restaurants in nontraditional locations (e.g., McDonald's installed restaurants in Wal-Mart stores across the country).

The second largest fast-food segment was dinner houses, dominated by Red Lobster, Applebee's, Olive Garden, and Chili's. Between 1988 and 1996, dinner houses increased their share of the fast-food market from 8 to over 13 percent. This increase came mainly at the expense of grilled buffet chains, such as Ponderosa, Sizzler, and Western Sizzlin'. The market share of such chains (also known as steak houses) fell from 6 percent in 1988 to under 4 percent in 1996. The rise of dinner houses during the 1990s was partially the result of an aging and wealthier population that increasingly demanded higher quality food and more upscale settings than those of sandwich chains. However, rapid construction of new restaurants, especially among relative newcomers—such as Romano's Macaroni Grill, Lone Star Steakhouse, and Outback Steakhouse—resulted in overcapacity within the dinner house segment. This reduced average restaurant sales and further intensified competition. In 1996, 8 of the 16 largest dinner houses posted growth rates in excess of 10 percent. Romano's Macaroni Grill, Lone Star Steakhouse, Chili's, Outback Steakhouse, Applebee's, Red Robin, Fuddruckers, and Ruby Tuesday grew at rates of 82, 41, 32, 27, 23, 14, 11, and 10 percent, respectively.

The third largest fast-food segment was pizza, long dominated by Pizza Hut. While Pizza Hut controlled over 46 percent of the pizza segment in 1996, its market share slowly eroded thereafter because of intense competition and its aging restaurant base. Domino's Pizza and Papa John's Pizza have been particularly successful. Little Caesars is the only pizza chain to remain predominantly a take-out chain, though it recently began home delivery. However, its policy of charging $1 per delivery damaged its reputation among consumers as a high-value pizza chain. Home delivery, successfully introduced by Domino's and Pizza Hut, was a driving force for success among the market leaders during the 1970s and 1980s. However, the success of home delivery drove competitors to look for new methods of increasing their

EXHIBIT 2 Leading U.S. Fast-Food Chains (ranked by 1996 sales, $ millions)

Source: *Nation's Restaurant News.*

Sandwich Chains	Sales	Share
McDonald's	$16,370	35.0%
Burger King	7,300	15.6
Taco Bell	4,575	9.8
Wendy's	4,360	9.3
Hardee's	3,055	6.5
Subway	2,700	5.8
Arby's	1,867	4.0
Dairy Queen	1,225	2.6
Jack in the Box	1,207	2.6
Sonic Drive-In	985	2.1
Carl's Jr.	648	1.4
Other chains	2,454	5.2
Total	$46,745	100.0%

Dinner Houses		
Red Lobster	$ 1,810	15.7%
Applebee's	1,523	13.2
Olive Garden	1,280	11.1
Chili's	1,242	10.7
Outback Steakhouse	1,017	8.8
T.G.I. Friday's	935	8.1
Ruby Tuesday	545	4.7
Lone Star Steakhouse	460	4.0
Bennigan's	458	4.0
Romano's Macaroni Grill	344	3.0
Other dinner houses	1,942	16.8
Total	$11,557	100.0%

Grilled Buffet Chains		
Golden Corral	$ 711	22.8%
Ponderosa	680	21.8
Ryan's	604	19.4
Sizzler	540	17.3
Western Sizzlin'	332	10.3
Quincy's	259	8.3
Total	$3,116	100.0%

Family Restaurants		
Denny's	$1,850	21.2%
Shoney's	1,220	14.0
Big Boy	945	10.8
International House of Pancakes	797	9.1
Cracker Barrel	734	8.4
Perkins	678	7.8
Friendly's	597	6.8
Bob Evans	575	6.6
Waffle House	525	6.0
Coco's	278	3.2
Steak 'n Shake	275	3.2
Village Inn	246	2.8
Total	$8,719	100.0%

(continued)

EXHIBIT 2   *(concluded)*

Pizza Chains	Sales	Share
Pizza Hut	$ 4,927	46.4%
Domino's Pizza	2,300	21.7
Little Caesars Pizza	1,425	13.4
Papa John's Pizza	619	5.8
Sbarro	400	3.8
Round Table Pizza	385	3.6
Chuck E. Cheese's	293	2.8
Godfather's Pizza	266	2.5
Total	$10,614	100.0%
Chicken Chains		
KFC	$ 3,900	57.1%
Boston Market	1,167	17.1
Popeye's Chicken	666	9.7
Chick-fil-A	570	8.3
Church's Chicken	529	7.7
Total	$ 6,832	100.0%

customer bases. Pizza chains diversified into nonpizza items (e.g., chicken wings at Domino's and Italian cheese bread at Little Caesars), developed nontraditional units (e.g., airport kiosks and college campuses), offered special promotions, and offered new pizza variations with an emphasis on high-quality ingredients (e.g., Roma Herb and Garlic Crunch pizza at Domino's and Buffalo Chicken Pizza at Round Table Pizza).

CHICKEN SEGMENT

KFC continued to dominate the chicken segment, with 1997 sales of $4 billion (see Exhibit 3). However, rather than building new restaurants in the already saturated U.S. market, KFC focused on building restaurants abroad. (In fact, the number of KFC restaurants in the United States declined slightly, from 5,128 in 1993 to 5,120 in 1998.) In the United States, KFC focused on closing unprofitable restaurants, upgrading existing restaurants with new exterior signage, and improving product quality. The strategy paid off. While overall U.S. sales during the 10 years up to 1998 remained flat, annual sales per unit increased steadily in 8 of the 9 years up to 1998.

Despite KFC's continued dominance within the chicken segment, it lost market share to Boston Market, which by 1997 had become KFC's nearest competitor, with $1.2 billion in sales. Emphasizing roasted chicken rather than fried, Boston Market successfully created the image of an upscale deli offering healthy, home-style alternatives to fast foods. It has broadened its menu beyond rotisserie chicken to include ham, turkey, meat loaf, chicken pot pie, and deli sandwiches. In order to minimize its image as a fast-food restaurant, Boston Market had refused to put drive-thrus in its restaurants and had established most of its units in outside shopping malls rather than in the freestanding units at intersections so characteristic of other fast-food restaurants.

In 1993, KFC introduced its own rotisserie chicken, called Rotisserie Gold, to combat Boston Market. However, it quickly learned that its customer base was considerably different from that of Boston Market's. KFC's customers liked KFC chicken despite the fact that it was fried. In addition, customers did not respond well to the

EXHIBIT 3   Top U.S. Chicken Chains

Source: Tricon Global Restaurants, Inc., 1997 annual report; Boston Chicken, Inc., 1997 annual report; Chick-fil-A, corporate headquarters, Atlanta; AFC Enterprises, Inc., 1997 annual report.

U.S. Sales ($ millions)	1992	1993	1994	1995	1996	1997	Annual Growth Rate
KFC	$3,400	$3,400	$3,500	$3,700	$3,900	$4,000	3.3%
Boston Market	43	147	371	754	1,100	1,197	94.5
Popeye's Chicken	545	569	614	660	677	727	5.9
Chick-fil-A	356	396	451	502	570	671	11.9
Church's Chicken	414	440	465	501	526	574	6.8
Total	$4,758	$4,952	$5,401	$6,118	$6,772	$7,170	8.5%
Number of U.S. Restaurants							
KFC	5,089	5,128	5,149	5,142	5,108	5,120	0.1%
Boston Market	83	217	534	829	1,087	1,166	69.6
Popeye's Chicken	769	769	853	889	894	949	4.3
Chick-fil-A	487	545	534	825	717	762	9.0
Church's Chicken	944	932	937	953	989	1,070	2.5
Total	7,372	7,591	8,007	8,638	8,795	9,067	4.2%
Sales per Unit ($ 000s)							
KFC	$ 668	$ 663	$ 680	$ 720	$ 764	$ 781	3.2%
Boston Market	518	677	695	910	1,012	1,027	14.7
Popeye's Chicken	709	740	720	743	757	767	1.6
Chick-fil-A	731	727	845	608	795	881	3.8
Church's Chicken	439	472	496	526	531	537	4.1
Average	$ 645	$ 782	$ 782	$ 782	$ 782	$ 782	3.9%

concept of buying whole chickens for take-out. They preferred instead to buy chicken by the piece. KFC withdrew its rotisserie chicken in 1996 and introduced a new line of roasted chicken called Tender Roast, which could be sold by the piece and mixed with its Original Recipe and Extra Crispy Chicken.

Other major competitors within the chicken segment included Popeye's Chicken and Church's Chicken (both subsidiaries of AFC Enterprises in Atlanta), Chick-fil-A, Bojangle's, El Pollo Loco, Grandy's, Kenny Rogers Roasters, Mrs. Winner's, and Pudgie's. Both Church's and Popeye's had similar strategies—to compete head-on with other "fried chicken" chains. Unlike KFC, neither chain offered rotisserie chicken, and both chains limited non-fried-chicken products. Chick-fil-A focused exclusively on pressure-cooked and char-grilled skinless chicken breast sandwiches, which it served to customers in sit-down restaurants located predominantly in shopping malls. As many malls added food courts, often consisting of up to 15 fast-food units competing side-by-side, shopping malls became less enthusiastic about allocating separate store space to food chains. Therefore, in order to complement its existing restaurant base in shopping malls, Chick-fil-A began to open smaller units in shopping mall food courts, hospitals, and colleges. It also opened freestanding units in selected locations.

DEMOGRAPHIC TRENDS

A number of demographic and societal trends in the United States contributed to increased demand for food prepared away from home. Because of the high divorce rate and the fact that people married later in life, single-person households represented about 25 percent of all U.S. households in 1998, up from 17 percent in 1970. This increased the number of individuals choosing to eat out rather than eat at home. The number of married women working outside of the home also increased dramatically during the 25 years up to 1998. About 59 percent of all married women had careers. According to the Conference Board, 64 percent of all married households will be double-income families by 2000. About 80 percent of households headed by individuals between the ages of 25 and 44 (both married and unmarried) will be double-income. Greater numbers of working women increased family incomes. According to *Restaurants & Institutions* magazine, more than one-third of all households had incomes of at least $50,000 in 1996, and about 8 percent of all households had annual incomes over $100,000. The combination of higher numbers of dual-career families and rising incomes meant that fewer families had time to prepare food at home. According to Standard & Poor's *Industry Surveys,* Americans spent 55 percent of their food dollars at restaurants in 1995, up from 34 percent in 1970.

Fast-food restaurant chains responded to these demographic and societal changes by expanding their restaurant bases. However, by the early 1990s, the growth of traditional free-standing restaurants slowed as the U.S. market became saturated. The major exception was dinner houses, which continued to proliferate in response to Americans' passion for beef. Since 1990, the U.S. population has grown at an average annual rate of about 1 percent; the total reached 270 million people in 1997. Rising immigration in the 1990s dramatically altered the ethnic makeup of the U.S. population. According to the Bureau of the Census, Americans born outside of the United States made up 10 percent of the population in 1997. About 40 percent of that number were Hispanic, while 24 percent were Asian. Nearly 30 percent of Americans born outside of the United States arrived since 1990. As a result of these trends, restaurant chains expanded their menus to appeal to the different ethnic tastes of consumers, expanded into nontraditional locations such as department stores and airports, and made food more available through home delivery and take-out service.

INDUSTRY CONSOLIDATION AND MERGERS AND ACQUISITIONS

The slowdown in growth in the U.S. fast-food market intensified competition for market share among restaurant chains and led to consolidation, primarily through mergers and acquisitions, during the mid-1990s. Many restaurant chains found that market share could be increased quicker and more cheaply by acquiring an existing company rather than building new units. In addition, fixed costs could be spread across a larger number of restaurants. This raised operating margins and gave companies an opportunity to build market share by lowering prices. An expanded restaurant base also gave companies greater purchasing power over suppliers. In 1990, Grand Metropolitan, a British company, purchased Pillsbury for $5.7 billion. Included in the purchase was Pillsbury's Burger King chain. Grand Met (which in 1988 had purchased Wienerwald, a West German chicken chain, and the Spaghetti Factory, a Swiss chain) strengthened the franchise by upgrading existing restaurants and eliminating several levels of management in order to cut costs. This gave Burger King a long-needed boost in improving its position against McDonald's, its largest competitor.

Perhaps most important to KFC was Hardee's acquisition of 600 Roy Rogers restaurants from Marriott Corporation in 1990. Hardee's converted a large number of these restaurants to Hardee's units and introduced Roy Rogers fried chicken to its menu. By 1993, Hardee's had introduced fried chicken into most of its U.S. restaurants. Hardee's was unlikely to destroy the customer loyalty that KFC long enjoyed. However, it did cut into KFC's sales, because it was able to offer consumers a widened menu selection that appealed to a variety of family eating preferences. In 1997, Hardee's parent company, Imasco Ltd., sold Hardee's to CKE Restaurants, Inc. CKE owned Carl's Jr., Rally's Hamburgers, and Checker's Drive-In. Boston Chicken, Inc., acquired Harry's Farmers Market, an Atlanta grocer that sold prepared meals. The acquisition was designed to help Boston Chicken develop distribution beyond its Boston Market restaurants. AFC Enterprises, which operated Popeye's and Church's, acquired Chesapeake Bagel Bakery of McLean, Virginia, in order to diversify away from fried chicken and to strengthen its balance sheet.

The effect of these and other recent mergers and acquisitions on the industry was powerful. The top 10 restaurant companies controlled almost 60 percent of fast-food sales in the United States. The consolidation of a number of fast-food chains within larger, financially more powerful parent companies gave restaurant chains strong financial and managerial resources that could be used to compete against smaller chains in the industry.

INTERNATIONAL QUICK-SERVICE MARKET

Because of the aggressive pace of new restaurant construction in the United States during the 1970s and 1980s, opportunities to continue such expansion in the 1990s were limited. Restaurant chains that did build new restaurants found that the higher cost of purchasing prime locations resulted in immense pressure to increase annual sales per restaurant. Many restaurants began to expand into international markets as an alternative to continued domestic expansion. In contrast to the U.S. market, international markets offered large customer bases with comparatively little competition. However, only a few U.S. restaurant chains had defined aggressive strategies for penetrating international markets by 1998; key among these were McDonald's, KFC, Pizza Hut, and Taco Bell.

McDonald's operated the largest number of restaurants. In 1998 it operated 23,132 restaurants in 109 countries (10,409 restaurants were located outside the United States). In comparison, KFC, Pizza Hut, and Taco Bell together operated 29,712 restaurants in 79, 88, and 17 countries, respectively (9,126 restaurants were located outside the United States). Of these four chains, KFC operated the greatest percentage of its restaurants (50 percent) outside of the United States. McDonald's, Pizza Hut, and Taco Bell operated 45, 31, and 2 percent of their units outside the United States, respectively. KFC opened its first restaurant outside the United States in the late 1960s. By the time of its acquisition by PepsiCo in 1986, KFC was already operating restaurants in 55 countries. KFC's early expansion abroad, strong brand name, and managerial experience in international markets gave it a strong competitive advantage vis-à-vis other fast-food chains that were investing abroad for the first time.

Exhibit 4 shows *Hotels'* list of the world's 30 largest fast-food restaurant chains at year-end 1993 (*Hotels* discontinued reporting these data after 1994). Seventeen of these chains (ranked by number of units) were headquartered in the United States. There were a number of possible explanations for the relative scarcity of fast-food restaurant chains outside the United States. First, the United States represented the largest consumer market in the world, accounting for over one-fifth of the world's gross domestic product. Therefore, the United States was the strategic focus of the largest restaurant chains. Second, Americans were quick to accept the fast-food concept, whereas many other cultures had strong culinary traditions that were difficult to break down. Europeans, for example, had long preferred to frequent more mid-

EXHIBIT 4   **The World's 30 Most Global Fast-Food Chains (year-end 1993, ranked by number of countries)**

Source: *Hotels*, May 1994; 1994 PepsiCo, Inc., annual report.

Rank	Franchise	Location	Units	Countries
1	Pizza Hut	Dallas, Texas	10,433	80
2	McDonald's	Oakbrook, Illinois	23,132	70
3	KFC	Louisville, Kentucky	9,033	68
4	Burger King	Miami, Florida	7,121	50
5	Baskin-Robbins	Glendale, California	3,557	49
6	Wendy's	Dublin, Ohio	4,168	38
7	Domino's Pizza	Ann Arbor, Michigan	5,238	36
8	TCBY	Little Rock, Arkansas	7,474	22
9	Dairy Queen	Minneapolis, Minnesota	5,471	21
10	Dunkin' Donuts	Randolph, Massachusetts	3,691	21
11	Taco Bell	Irvine, California	4,921	20
12	Arby's	Fort Lauderdale, Florida	2,670	18
13	Subway	Milford, Connecticut	8,477	15
14	Sizzler International	Los Angeles, California	681	14
15	Hardee's	Rocky Mount, North Carolina	4,060	12
16	Little Caesars	Detroit, Michigan	4,600	12
17	Popeye's Chicken	Atlanta, Georgia	813	12
18	Denny's	Spartanburg, South Carolina	1,515	10
19	A&W Restaurants	Livonia, Michigan	707	9
20	T.G.I. Friday's	Minneapolis, Minnesota	273	8
21	Orange Julius	Minneapolis, Minnesota	480	7
22	Church's Chicken	Atlanta, Georgia	1,079	6
23	Long John Silver's	Lexington, Kentucky	1,464	5
24	Carl's Jr.	Anaheim, California	649	4
25	Loterria	Tokyo, Japan	795	4
26	Mos Burger	Tokyo, Japan	1,263	4
27	Skylark	Tokyo, Japan	1,000	4
28	Jack in the Box	San Diego, California	1,172	3
29	Quick Restaurants	Berchem, Belgium	876	3
30	Taco Time	Eugene, Oregon	300	3

scale restaurants, where they spent several hours in a formal setting enjoying native dishes and beverages. While KFC was again building restaurants in Germany by the late 1980s, it previously failed to penetrate the German market because Germans were not accustomed to take-out food or to ordering food over the counter. McDonald's had greater success penetrating the German market, because it made a number of changes in its menu and operating procedures in order to better appeal to German culture. For example, German beer was served in all of McDonald's German restaurants. KFC had more success in Asia and Latin America, where chicken was a traditional dish.

Aside from cultural factors, international business carried risks not present in the U.S. market. Long distances between headquarters and foreign franchises often made it difficult to control the quality of individual restaurants, as well as to solve servicing and support problems. Transportation and other resource costs were higher than in the domestic market. In addition, time, cultural, and language differences increased communication and operational problems. Therefore, it was reasonable to expect U.S. restaurant chains to expand domestically as long as they achieved corporate profit and growth objectives. As the U.S. market became saturated and companies gained expertise in international markets, however, more companies could be expected to turn to profitable international markets as a means of expanding restaurant bases and increasing sales, profits, and market share.

Kentucky Fried Chicken Corporation (www.kfc.com)

KFC's worldwide sales, which included totals from both company-owned and franchised restaurants, grew to $8 billion in 1997. U.S. sales grew 2.6 percent over 1996 and accounted for about one-half of KFC's sales worldwide. KFC's U.S. share of the chicken segment fell 1.8 points, to 55.8 percent (see Exhibit 5). This marked the sixth consecutive year that KFC sustained a decline in market share. In 1998, KFC's market share had fallen by 16.3 points since 1988, when it held a 72.1 percent market share. Boston Market, which established its first restaurant in 1992, increased its market share from 0 to 16.7 in the same period. On the surface, it appeared as though Boston Market achieved its market share gain by taking customers away from KFC. However, KFC's sales growth had remained fairly stable and constant over the previous 10 years. Boston Market's success was largely a function of its appeal to consumers who did not regularly patronize KFC or other fried-chicken chains. By appealing to a market niche that was previously unsatisfied, Boston Market was able to expand the existing consumer base within the chicken segment of the fast-food industry.

REFRANCHISING STRATEGY

The relatively low growth rate in sales in KFC's domestic restaurants during the 1992–97 period was largely the result of KFC's decision in 1993 to begin selling company-owned restaurants to franchisees. When Colonel Sanders began to expand the Kentucky Fried Chicken system in the late 1950s, he established KFC as a system of independent franchisees. This was done in order to minimize his involvement in the operations of individual restaurants and to concentrate on the things he enjoyed the most—cooking, product development, and public relations. This resulted in a fiercely loyal and independent group of franchisees. As explained earlier, when PepsiCo acquired KFC in 1986, PepsiCo's strategy demanded increased involvement in

EXHIBIT 5   **Market Shares of Top U.S. Chicken Chains, 1988–1997**

Source: *Nation's Restaurant News.*

	KFC	Boston Market	Popeye's	Chick-fil-A	Church's	Total
1988	72.1%	0.0%	12.0%	5.8%	10.1%	100.0%
1989	70.8	0.0	12.0	6.2	11.0	100.0
1990	71.3	0.0	12.3	6.6	9.8	100.0
1991	72.7	0.0	11.4	7.0	8.9	100.0
1992	71.5	0.9	11.4	7.5	8.7	100.0
1993	68.7	3.0	11.4	8.0	8.9	100.0
1994	64.8	6.9	11.3	8.4	8.6	100.0
1995	60.5	12.3	10.8	8.2	8.2	100.0
1996	57.6	16.2	10.0	8.4	7.8	100.0
1997	55.8	16.7	10.1	9.4	8.0	100.0
Change 1988–1997	(16.3)%	+16.7%	(1.9)%	+3.6%	(2.1)%	

EXHIBIT 6   KFC Restaurant Count (U.S. Restaurants), 1986–1997

Source: Tricon Global Restaurants, Inc., 1997 annual report; PepsiCo, Inc., annual report, 1994, 1995, 1996, 1997.

	Company-Owned	Percent of Total	Franchised/Licensed	Percent of Total	Total
1986	1,246	26.4%	3,474	73.6%	4,720
1987	1,250	26.0	3,564	74.0	4,814
1988	1,262	25.8	3,637	74.2	4,899
1989	1,364	27.5	3,597	72.5	4,961
1990	1,389	27.7	3,617	72.3	5,006
1991	1,836	36.6	3,186	63.4	5,022
1992	1,960	38.8	3,095	61.2	5,055
1993	2,014	39.5	3,080	60.5	5,094
1994	2,005	39.2	3,110	60.8	5,115
1995	2,026	39.4	3,111	60.6	5,137
1996	1,932	37.8	3,176	62.2	5,108
1997	1,850	36.1	3,270	63.9	5,120

1986–93 Compound Annual Growth Rate

7.1%		(1.7%)		1.1%

1993–97 Compounded Annual Growth Rate

(2.1%)		1.5%		0.1%

decisions over franchise operations, menu offerings, restaurant management, finance, and marketing. KFC franchisees were fiercely opposed to increased control by the corporate parent. One method for PepsiCo to deal with this conflict was to expand through company-owned restaurants rather than through franchising. PepsiCo also used its strong cash flows to buy back unprofitable franchised restaurants, which could then be converted into company-owned restaurants. In 1986, company-owned restaurants made up 26 percent of KFC's U.S. restaurant base. By 1993, they made up about 40 percent (see Exhibit 6).

While company-owned restaurants were relatively easier to control compared to franchised outlets, they also required higher levels of investment. This meant that high levels of cash were diverted from PepsiCo's soft drink and snack food businesses into its restaurant businesses. However, the fast-food industry delivered lower returns than the soft drink and snack foods industries. Consequently, increased investment in KFC, Pizza Hut, and Taco Bell had a negative effect on PepsiCo's consolidated return on assets. By 1993, investors became concerned that PepsiCo's return on assets did not match returns delivered by Coca-Cola. In order to shore up its return on assets, PepsiCo decided to reduce the number of company-owned restaurants by selling them back to franchisees. This strategy lowered overall company sales, but it also reduced the amount of cash tied up in fixed assets, provided PepsiCo with one-time cash flow benefits from initial fees charged to franchisees, and generated an annual stream of franchise royalties. Tricon Global continued this strategy after the spinoff in 1997.

MARKETING STRATEGY

During the 1980s, consumers began to demand healthier foods, greater variety, and better service in a variety of nontraditional locations such as grocery stores, restaurants, airports, and outdoor events. This forced fast-food chains to expand menu offerings and to investigate nontraditional distribution channels and restaurant designs. Families also demanded greater value in the food they bought away from home. This increased pressure on fast-food chains to reduce prices and to lower operating costs in order to maintain profit margins.

Many of KFC's problems during the late 1980s surrounded its limited menu and inability to quickly bring new products to market. The popularity of its Original Recipe Chicken had allowed KFC to expand without significant competition from other chicken competitors through the 1980s. As a result, new-product introductions were never an important element of KFC's overall strategy. One of the most serious setbacks came in 1989 as KFC prepared to add a chicken sandwich to its menu. While KFC was still experimenting with its chicken sandwich, McDonald's test-marketed its McChicken sandwich in the Louisville area. Shortly thereafter, it rolled out the McChicken sandwich nationally. By beating KFC to the market, McDonald's was able to develop strong consumer awareness for its sandwich. This significantly increased KFC's cost of developing awareness for its own sandwich, which KFC introduced several months later. KFC eventually withdrew its sandwich because of low sales.

In 1991, KFC changed its logo in the United States from Kentucky Fried Chicken to KFC, in order to reduce its image as a fried chicken chain. (It continued to use the Kentucky Fried Chicken name internationally, however.) It then responded to consumer demands for greater variety by introducing several products that would serve as alternatives to its Original Recipe Chicken. These included Oriental Wings, Popcorn Chicken, and Honey BBQ Chicken. It also introduced a dessert menu that included a variety of pies and cookies. In 1993, it rolled out Rotisserie Chicken and began to promote its lunch and dinner buffet. The buffet, which included 30 items, was introduced into almost 1,600 KFC restaurants in 27 states by year-end. In 1998, KFC sold three types of chicken—Original Recipe and Extra Crispy (fried chicken) and Tender Roast (roasted chicken).

One of KFC's most aggressive strategies was the introduction of its Neighborhood Program. By mid-1993, almost 500 company-owned restaurants in New York, Chicago, Philadelphia, Washington, D.C., St. Louis, Los Angeles, Houston, and Dallas had been outfitted with special menu offerings to appeal exclusively to the black community. Menus were beefed up with side dishes such as greens, macaroni and cheese, peach cobbler, sweet-potato pie, and red beans and rice. In addition, restaurant employees wore African-inspired uniforms. The introduction of the Neighborhood Program increased sales by 5 to 30 percent in restaurants appealing directly to the black community. KFC followed by testing Hispanic-oriented restaurants in the Miami area, offering such side dishes as fried plantains, flan, and tres leches.

One of KFC's most significant problems in the U.S. market was that overcapacity made expansion of freestanding restaurants difficult. Fewer sites were available for new construction and those sites, because of their increased cost, were driving profit margins down. Therefore, KFC initiated a three-pronged distribution strategy. First, it focused on building smaller restaurants in nontraditional outlets such as airports, shopping malls, universities, and hospitals. Second, it experimented with home delivery, beginning in the Nashville and Albuquerque markets in 1994. By 1998, home delivery was offered in 365 of KFC's U.S. restaurants. Other nontraditional distribution outlets being tested included units offering drive-thru and carry-out service only, snack shops in cafeterias, scaled-down outlets for supermarkets, and mobile units that could be transported to outdoor concerts and fairs.

A third focus of KFC's distribution strategy was restaurant co-branding, primarily with its sister chain, Taco Bell. By 1997, 349 KFC restaurants had added Taco Bell items to their menus and displayed both the KFC and Taco Bell logos outside their restaurants. Co-branding gave KFC the opportunity to expand its business dayparts.

While about two-thirds of KFC's business was dinner, Taco Bell's primary business occurred at lunch. By combining the two concepts in the same unit, sales at individual restaurants could be increased significantly. KFC believed that there were opportunities to sell the Taco Bell concept in over 3,900 of its U.S. restaurants.

OPERATING EFFICIENCIES

As pressure continued to build from price-conscious consumers, restaurant chains searched for ways to reduce overhead and other operating costs in order to improve profit margins. In 1989, KFC reorganized its U.S. operations in order to eliminate overhead costs and to increase efficiency. Included in this reorganization was a revision of KFC's crew training programs and operating standards. A renewed emphasis was placed on clean restaurants, fast and friendly service, and product quality. In 1992, KFC reorganized its middle-management ranks, eliminating 250 of the 1,500 management positions at KFC's corporate headquarters. More responsibility was assigned to restaurant franchisees and marketing managers, and pay was more closely aligned with customer service and restaurant performance. In 1997, Tricon Global signed a five-year agreement with PepsiCo Food Systems (which was later sold by PepsiCo to AmeriServe Food Distributors) to distribute food and supplies to Tricon's 29,712 KFC, Pizza Hut, and Taco Bell units. This provided KFC with significant opportunities to benefit from economies of scale in distribution.

International Operations

Much of the early success of the top 10 fast-food chains was the result of aggressive building strategies. Chains were able to discourage competition by building in low-population areas that could only support a single fast-food chain. McDonald's was particularly successful at quickly expanding into small towns across the United States, thereby preempting other fast-food chains. It was equally important to beat a competitor into more densely populated areas where location was of prime importance. KFC's early entry into international markets placed it in a strong position to benefit from international expansion as the U.S. market became saturated. In 1997, 50 percent of KFC's restaurants were located outside of the United States. While 364 new restaurants were opened outside the United States in 1997, only 12 new restaurants were added to the U.S. system. Most of KFC's international expansion was through franchises, though some restaurants were licensed to operators or jointly operated with a local partner. Expansion through franchising was an important strategy for penetrating international markets, because franchises were owned and operated by local entrepreneurs who understood local language, culture, and customs, as well as local law, financial markets, and marketing characteristics. Franchising was particularly important for expansion into smaller countries such as the Dominican Republic, Grenada, Bermuda, and Suriname, which could only support a single restaurant. Costs of operating company-owned restaurants in these smaller markets were prohibitively high. Of the 5,117 KFC restaurants located outside the United States in 1997, 68 percent were franchised, while 22 percent were company-owned and 10 percent were licensed restaurants or joint ventures.

In larger markets such as Japan, China, and Mexico, there was a stronger emphasis on building company-owned restaurants. By coordinating purchasing, recruiting and training, financing, and advertising, KFC could spread fixed costs over a large number of restaurants and negotiate lower prices on products and services. KFC was also better able to control product and service quality. In order to take advantage of economies of scale, Tricon Global Restaurants managed all of the international units of its KFC, Pizza Hut, and Taco Bell chains through its Tricon International division, located in Dallas, Texas. This enabled Tricon Global Restaurants to leverage its strong advertising expertise, international experience, and restaurant management experience across all three chains.

LATIN AMERICAN STRATEGY

KFC's primary market presence in Latin America during the 1980s was in Mexico, Puerto Rico, and the Caribbean. KFC established subsidiaries in Mexico and Puerto Rico, from which it coordinated the construction and operation of company-owned restaurants. A third subsidiary in Venezuela was closed because of its high fixed costs. Franchises were used to penetrate countries in the Caribbean whose market size prevented KFC from profitably operating company restaurants. In Mexico, KFC, like most other fast-food chains there, relied exclusively on the operation of company-owned restaurants through 1989. While franchising was popular in the United States, it was virtually unknown in Mexico until 1990, mainly because of the absence of a law protecting patents, information, and technology transferred to the Mexican franchise. In addition, royalties were limited.

In 1990, Mexico enacted a new law that provided for the protection of technology transferred into the country. Under the new legislation, the franchisor and franchisee were free to set their own terms and to collect royalties. Royalties were taxed at 15 percent on technology assistance and know-how, and at 35 percent for other royalty categories. The advent of the new franchise law resulted in an explosion of franchises in fast-food, services, hotels, and retail outlets. In 1992, franchises had an estimated $750 million in sales in over 1,200 outlets throughout Mexico. Prior to passage of Mexico's franchise law, KFC limited its Mexican operations primarily to Mexico City, Guadalajara, and Monterrey, in order to better coordinate operations and minimize costs of distribution to individual restaurants. The new franchise law gave KFC and other fast-food chains the opportunity to expand their restaurant bases into rural regions of Mexico, where responsibility for management could be handled by local franchisees.

After 1990, KFC altered its Latin American strategy in a number of ways. First, it opened 29 franchises in Mexico to complement its company-owned restaurant base. It then expanded its company-owned restaurants into the Virgin Islands and reestablished a subsidiary in Venezuela. Third, it expanded its franchise operations into South America. In 1990 a franchise was opened in Chile, and in 1993 one was opened in Brazil. Franchises were subsequently established in Colombia, Ecuador, Panama, and Peru, among other South American countries. A fourth subsidiary was established in Brazil, in order to develop company-owned restaurants. Brazil was Latin America's largest economy and McDonald's primary Latin American investment location. By June 1998, KFC operated 438 restaurants in 32 Latin American countries. By comparison, McDonald's operated 1,091 restaurants in 28 countries in Latin America.

Exhibit 7 shows the number of KFC and McDonald's operations in Latin America. KFC's early entry into Latin America during the 1970s gave it a leadership position in Mexico and the Caribbean. It had also gained an edge in Ecuador and Peru, countries where McDonald's had not yet developed a strong presence. McDonald's focused its Latin American investment in Brazil, Argentina, and Uruguay, countries where KFC had little or no presence. McDonald's was also strong in Venezuela. Both KFC and McDonald's were strong in Chile, Colombia, Panama, and Puerto Rico.

ECONOMIC ENVIRONMENT AND THE MEXICAN MARKET

Mexico was KFC's strongest market in Latin America. While McDonald's had aggressively established restaurants in Mexico since 1990, KFC retained the leading

EXHIBIT 7   Latin America Restaurant Count—KFC and McDonald's (as of December 31, 1997)

Source: Tricon Global Restaurants, Inc.; McDonald's, 1997 annual report.

	KFC Company Restaurants	KFC Franchised Restaurants	KFC Total Restaurants	McDonald's
Argentina	—	—	—	131
Bahamas	—	10	10	3
Barbados	—	7	7	—
Brazil	6	2	8	480
Chile	—	29	29	27
Colombia	—	19	19	18
Costa Rica	—	5	5	19
Ecuador	—	18	18	2
Jamaica	—	17	17	7
Mexico	128	29	157	131
Panama	—	21	21	20
Peru	—	17	17	5
Puerto Rico and Virgin Islands	67	—	67	115
Trinidad and Tobago	—	27	27	3
Uruguay	—	—	—	18
Venezuela	6	—	6	53
Other	—	30	30	59
Total	207	231	438	1,091

market share. Because of its proximity to the United States, Mexico was an attractive location for U.S. trade and investment. Mexico's population of 98 million people was approximately one-third that of the United States and represented a large market for U.S. companies. In comparison, Canada's population of 30.3 million people was only one-third as large as Mexico's. Mexico's proximity to the United States meant that transportation costs between the two were significantly lower than those between the United States and Europe or Asia. This increased the competitiveness of U.S. goods in comparison to European and Asian goods, which had to be transported to Mexico across the Atlantic or Pacific Ocean at substantial cost. The United States was, in fact, Mexico's largest trading partner. Over 75 percent of Mexico's imports came from the United States, while 84 percent of its exports went to the United States (see Exhibit 8). Many U.S. firms invested in Mexico in order to take advantage of lower wage rates, which meant that goods produced in Mexico could be shipped back into the United States or to third markets and sold at lower cost.

While the U.S. market was critically important to Mexico, Mexico still represented a small percentage of overall U.S. trade and investment. Since the early 1900s, the portion of U.S. exports to Latin America had declined. Instead, U.S. exports to Canada and Asia, where economic growth outpaced growth in Mexico, increased more quickly. Canada was the largest importer of U.S. goods. Japan was the largest exporter of goods to the United States, with Canada a close second. U.S. investment in Mexico was also small, mainly because of past government restrictions on foreign investment. Most U.S. foreign investment was in Europe, Canada, and Asia.

The lack of U.S. investment in and trade with Mexico during this century was mainly the result of Mexico's long history of restricting trade and foreign direct investment. The Institutional Revolutionary Party (PRI), which came to power in Mex-

EXHIBIT 8   Mexico's Major Trading Partners, 1992, 1994, and 1996

Source: International Monetary Fund, Direction of Trade Statistics Yearbook, 1997.

	1992		1994		1996	
	Exports	Imports	Exports	Imports	Exports	Imports
U.S.	81.1%	71.3%	85.3%	71.8%	84.0%	75.6%
Japan	1.7	4.9	1.6	4.8	1.4	4.4
Germany	1.1	4.0	0.6	3.9	0.7	3.5
Canada	2.2	1.7	2.4	2.0	1.2	1.9
Italy	0.3	1.6	0.1	1.3	1.2	1.1
Brazil	0.9	1.8	0.6	1.5	0.9	0.8
Spain	2.7	1.4	1.4	1.7	1.0	0.7
Other	10.0	13.3	8.0	13.0	9.6	12.0
Total	100.0%	100.0%	100.0%	100.0%	100.0%	100.0%
Value (in millions)	$46,196	$62,129	$60,882	$79,346	$95,991	$89,464

ico during the 1930s, had historically pursued protectionist economic policies in order to shield Mexico's economy from foreign competition. Many industries were government-owned or controlled, and many Mexican companies focused on producing goods for the domestic market without much attention to building export markets. High tariffs and other trade barriers restricted imports into Mexico, and the Mexican government prohibited or heavily restricted foreign ownership of assets in Mexico.

Additionally, a dictatorial and entrenched government bureaucracy, corrupt labor unions, and a long tradition of anti-Americanism among many government officials and intellectuals reduced the motivation of U.S. firms to invest in Mexico. The nationalization of Mexico's banks in 1982 led to higher real interest rates and lower investor confidence. Afterward, the Mexican government battled high inflation, labor unrest, and lost consumer purchasing power. However, investor confidence in Mexico improved after 1988, when Carlos Salinas de Gortari was elected president. Following his election, Salinas embarked on an ambitious restructuring of the Mexican economy. He initiated policies to strengthen the free-market components of the economy, lowered top marginal tax rates to 36 percent (down from 60 percent in 1986), and eliminated many restrictions on foreign investment. Foreign firms can now buy up to 100 percent of the equity in many Mexican firms, instead of the previous limit of 49 percent.

PRIVATIZATION

The privatization of government-owned companies came to symbolize the restructuring of Mexico's economy. In 1990, legislation was passed to privatize all government-run banks. By the end of 1992, over 800 of some 1,200 government-owned companies had been sold, including Mexicana and AeroMexico, the two largest airline companies in Mexico, as well as Mexico's 18 major banks. However, more than 350 companies remained under government ownership. These represented a significant portion of the assets owned by the state at the start of 1988. Therefore, the sale of government-owned companies, in terms of asset value, was moderate. A large number of the remaining government-owned assets were controlled by government-run companies in certain strategic industries such as steel, electricity, and petroleum. These industries had long been protected by government ownership. As a result, additional privatization of government-owned enterprises until 1993 was limited. However, in 1993, when President Salinas opened up the electricity sector to independent power producers, Petroleos Mexicanos (Pemex), the state-run petrochemical monopoly, initiated a program to sell off many of its nonstrategic assets to private and foreign buyers.

NORTH AMERICAN FREE TRADE AGREEMENT (NAFTA)

Prior to 1989, Mexico levied high tariffs on most imported goods. In addition, many other goods were subjected to quotas, licensing requirements, and other nontariff trade barriers. In 1986, Mexico joined the General Agreement on Tariffs and Trade (GATT), a world trade organization designed to eliminate barriers to trade among member nations. As a member of GATT, Mexico was obligated to apply its system of tariffs to all member nations equally and therefore dropped tariff rates on a variety of imported goods. In addition, import license requirements were dropped for all but 300 imported items. During President Salinas's administration, tariffs were reduced from an average of 100 percent on most items to an average of 11 percent.

On January 1, 1994, the North American Free Trade Agreement (NAFTA) went into effect. The passage of NAFTA, which included Canada, the United States, and Mexico, created a trading bloc with a larger population and gross domestic product than those of the European Union. All tariffs on goods traded among the three countries were scheduled to be phased out. NAFTA was expected to be particularly beneficial for Mexican exporters because reduced tariffs made their goods more competitive in the United States compared to goods exported to the United States from other countries. In 1995, one year after NAFTA went into effect, Mexico posted its first balance of trade surplus in six years. Part of this surplus was attributed to reduced tariffs resulting from the NAFTA agreement. However, the peso crisis of 1995, which lowered the value of the peso against the dollar, increased the price of goods imported into Mexico and lowered the price of Mexican products exported to the United States. Therefore, it was still too early to assess the full effects of NAFTA.

FOREIGN EXCHANGE AND THE MEXICAN PESO CRISIS OF 1995

Between 1982 and 1991 in Mexico, a two-tiered exchange rate system was in force that consisted of a controlled rate and a free-market rate. The controlled rate was used for imports, foreign debt payments, and conversion of export proceeds. An estimated 70 percent of all foreign transactions were covered by the controlled rate. The free market rate was used for other transactions. In 1989, President Salinas instituted a policy of allowing the peso to depreciate against the dollar by one peso per day. The result was a grossly overvalued peso. This lowered the price of imports and led to an increase in imports of over 23 percent in 1989. At the same time, Mexican exports became less competitive on world markets.

In 1991, the controlled rate was abolished and replaced with an official free rate. In order to limit the range of fluctuations in the value of the peso, the government fixed the rate at which it would buy or sell pesos. A floor (the maximum price at which pesos could be purchased) was established at Ps 3,056.20 and remained fixed. A ceiling (the maximum price at which the peso could be sold) was established at Ps 3,056.40 and allowed to move upward by Ps 0.20 per day. This was later revised to Ps 0.40 per day. In 1993, a new currency, called the new peso, was issued with three fewer zeros. The new currency was designed to simplify transactions and to reduce the cost of printing currency.

When Ernesto Zedillo became Mexico's president in December 1994, one of his objectives was to continue the stability of prices, wages, and exchange rates achieved by Salinas during his five-year tenure as president. However, Salinas had achieved stability largely on the basis of price, wage, and foreign exchange controls. While giving the appearance of stability, an overvalued peso continued to encourage imports, which exacerbated Mexico's balance of trade deficit. Mexico's government continued to use foreign reserves to finance its balance of trade deficits. According to the Banco de Mexico, foreign currency reserves fell from $24 billion in January 1994 to $5.5 billion in January 1995. Anticipating a devaluation of the peso, investors began to move capital into U.S. dollar investments. In order to relieve pressure on the peso, Zedillo announced on December 19, 1994, that the peso would be allowed to depreciate by an additional 15 percent per year against the dollar compared to the maximum allowable depreciation of 4 percent per year established during the Salinas administration. Within two days, continued pressure on the peso forced Zedillo to allow the peso to float freely against the dollar. By mid-January 1995, the peso had lost 35 percent of its value against the dollar and the Mexican stock market plunged 20 percent. By November 1995, the peso had depreciated from 3.1 pesos per dollar to 7.3 pesos per dollar.

The continued devaluation of the peso resulted in higher import prices, higher inflation, destabilization within the stock market, and higher interest rates. (See Exhibit 9 for selected economic data for Canada, the United States and Mexico.) Mexico struggled to pay its dollar-based debts. In order to thwart a possible default by Mexico, the U.S. government, International Monetary Fund, and World Bank pledged $24.9 billion in emergency loans. Zedillo then announced an emergency economic package, called the *pacto*, which reduced government spending, increased sales of government-run businesses, and placed a freeze on wage increases.

LABOR PROBLEMS

One of KFC's primary concerns in Mexico was the stability of labor markets. Labor was relatively plentiful and wages were low. However, much of the workforce was relatively unskilled. KFC benefitted from lower labor costs, but labor unrest, low job

EXHIBIT 9   Selected Economic Data for Canada, the United States, and Mexico

Source: International Monetary Fund, *International Financial Statistics,* 1998.

	Annual Percentage Change (%)				
	1993	**1994**	**1995**	**1996**	**1997**
GDP Growth					
Canada	3.3%	4.8%	5.5%	4.1%	n.a.
United States	4.9	5.8	4.8	5.1	5.9%
Mexico	21.4	13.3	29.4	38.2	n.a.
Real GDP Growth					
Canada	2.2%	4.1%	2.3%	1.2%	n.a.
United States	2.2	3.5	2.0	2.8	3.8
Mexico	2.0	4.5	(6.2)	5.1	n.a.
Inflation Rate					
Canada	1.9%	0.2%	2.2%	1.5%	1.6%
United States	3.0	2.5	2.8	2.9	2.4
Mexico	9.7	6.9	35.0	34.4	20.6
Depreciation (Appreciation) against U.S. Dollar					
Canada (C$)	4.2%	6.0%	(2.7)%	0.3%	4.3%
Mexico (NP)	(0.3)	71.4	43.5	2.7	3.6

retention, high absenteeism, and poor punctuality were significant problems. Absenteeism and poor punctuality were partially cultural. However, problems with worker retention and labor unrest were also the result of workers' frustration over the loss of their purchasing power due to inflation and government controls on wage increases. Absenteeism remained high, at approximately 8 to 14 percent of the labor force, though it was declining because of job security fears. Turnover continued to be a problem and ran at between 5 and 12 percent per month. This made employee screening and internal training important issues for firms investing in Mexico.

Higher inflation and the government's freeze on wage increases led to a dramatic decline in disposable income after 1994. Further, a slowdown in business activity, brought about by higher interest rates and lower government spending, led many businesses to lay off workers. By the end of 1995, an estimated 1 million jobs had been lost as a result of the economic crisis sparked by the peso devaluation. Industry groups within Mexico called for new labor laws giving them more freedom to hire and fire employees and increased flexibility to hire part-time rather than full-time workers.

Risks and Opportunities

The peso crisis of 1995 and resulting recession in Mexico left KFC managers with a great deal of uncertainty regarding Mexico's economic and political future. KFC had benefitted from economic stability between 1988 and 1994. Inflation was brought down, the peso was relatively stable, labor relations were relatively calm, and Mexico's new franchise law had enabled KFC to expand into rural areas using franchises rather than company-owned restaurants. By the end of 1995, KFC had built 29 franchises in Mexico. The foreign exchange crisis of 1995 had severe implications for U.S. firms operating in Mexico. The devaluation of the peso resulted in higher inflation and capital flight out of Mexico. Capital flight reduced the supply of investment funds and led to higher interest rates. In order to reduce inflation, Mexico's government instituted an austerity program that resulted in lower disposable income, higher unemployment, and lower demand for products and services.

Another problem was Mexico's failure to reduce restrictions on U.S. and Canadian investment in a timely fashion. Many U.S. firms had trouble getting approvals for new ventures from the Mexican government. A good example was United Parcel Service (UPS), which sought government approval to use large trucks for deliveries in Mexico. Approvals were delayed, forcing UPS to use smaller trucks and putting the company at a competitive disadvantage vis-à-vis Mexican companies. In many cases, UPS was forced to subcontract delivery work to Mexican companies that were allowed to use larger, more cost-efficient trucks. Other U.S. companies, such as Bell Atlantic and TRW, faced similar problems. TRW, which signed a joint venture agreement with a Mexican partner, had to wait 15 months longer than anticipated before the Mexican government released rules on how it could receive credit data from banks. TRW claimed that the Mexican government slowed the approval process in order to placate several large Mexican banks.

A final area of concern for KFC was increased political turmoil in Mexico during the last several years. On January 1, 1994, the day NAFTA went into effect, rebels (descendants of the Mayans) rioted in the southern Mexican province of Chiapas on the Guatemalan border. After four days of fighting, Mexican troops had driven the rebels out of several occupied towns. Around 150 people—mostly rebels—were killed. The uprising symbolized many of the fears of the poor in Mexico. While President Salinas's economic programs had increased economic growth and wealth in Mexico, many of Mexico's poorest felt that they had not benefitted. Many of Mexico's farmers, faced with lower tariffs on imported agricultural goods from the United States, felt that they might be driven out of business because of lower priced imports. Social unrest among Mexico's Indians, farmers, and the poor could potentially unravel much of the economic success achieved in Mexico during the last five years.

Further, President Salinas's hand-picked successor for president was assassinated in early 1994 while campaigning in Tijuana. The assassin was a 23-year-old mechanic and migrant worker believed to be affiliated with a dissident group upset with the PRI's economic reforms. The possible existence of a dissident group raised fears of political violence in the future. The PRI quickly named Ernesto Zedillo, a 42-year-old economist with little political experience, as their new presidential candidate. Zedillo was elected president in December 1994. Political unrest was not limited to Mexican officials and companies. In October 1994, between 30 and 40 masked men attacked a McDonald's restaurant in the tourist section of Mexico City to show their opposition to California's Proposition 187, which would have curtailed benefits to illegal aliens (primarily from Mexico). The men threw cash registers to the floor, cracked them open, smashed windows, overturned tables, and spray-painted the walls with slogans such as "No to Fascism" and "Yankee Go Home."

KFC thus faced a variety of issues in Mexico and Latin America in 1998. KFC halted openings of franchised restaurants in Mexico; all restaurants opened there since 1995 were company-owned. KFC began aggressively building restaurants in South America, which had remained largely unpenetrated by KFC through 1995. Of greatest importance was Brazil, where McDonald's had already established a strong position. Brazil was Latin America's largest economy and a mostly untapped market for KFC. The danger in KFC's ignoring Mexico was that a conservative investment strategy could jeopardize its lead over McDonald's in a large market where KFC had long enjoyed enormous popularity.

Case

7

The Black & Decker Corporation in 2000

John E. Gamble
University of South Alabama

Arthur A. Thompson
University of Alabama

In 2000 Black & Decker Corporation was still struggling to get out from under the array of financial and strategic problems stemming from the company's $2.8 billion acquisition of Emhart Corporation in 1989. Black & Decker had long been the world's leading producer and marketer of power tools and power tool accessories. But it had begun a program of diversification in the 1980s that had produced mixed results for shareholders. The company's foray into small household appliances had been a success originally, but the small-appliance division acquired from General Electric in the early 1980s had recently been divested because of its drag on B&D's growth. The follow-on acquisition of Emhart, a conglomerate with very diverse business interests, had proved to be a significant impairment to the company's earnings and cash flow as well as a management burden, and during the past 11 years Black & Decker had achieved success in only a few of the businesses it obtained in the Emhart acquisition.

Black & Decker described itself as a diversified global manufacturer and marketer of household, commercial, and industrial products. Going into 2000, the company was the world's largest producer of power tools, power tool accessories, security hardware, and electric lawn and garden products. The company's Price Pfister kitchen and bathroom faucets subsidiary, a business acquired in the Emhart deal, had gained market share for 11 consecutive years to become the third largest brand of plumbing fixtures in North America. Black & Decker was also the worldwide leader in the market for certain types of mechanical fastening systems used in automobile assembly and in other industrial applications—fasteners had been one of Emhart's businesses as well. But while Black & Decker's business portfolio included a lineup of several competitively strong brands, the company's stock price had been a ho-hum performer throughout the unprecedented bull market of the 1990s, substantially lagging behind the performance of well-known indexes like the Dow Jones Industrials Average and the Standard & Poor's 500 Index. A graph of Black & Decker's stock performance between 1985 and January 2000 is presented in Exhibit 1. Exhibit 2 provides an 11-year summary of Black & Decker's financial performance.

EXHIBIT 1   Market Performance of Black & Decker's Common Stock, by Quarter, 1985–January 2000

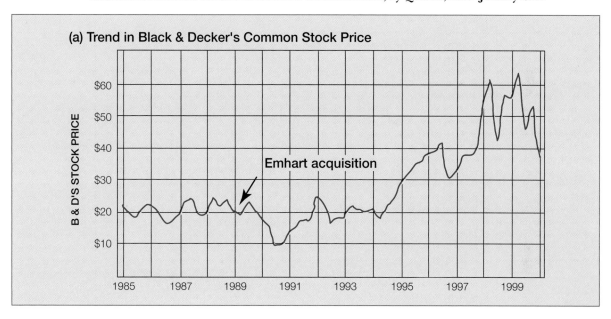

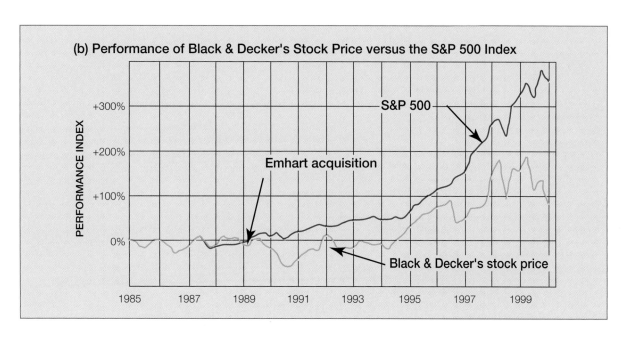

EXHIBIT 2   Summary of Black & Decker's Financial and Operating Performance, 1989–99 (in millions of dollars except per share and employee data)

Source: The Black & Decker Corporation annual reports.

	1999	1998	1997	1996	1995	1994	1993	1992	1991	1990	1989
Sales	$4,520.5	$4,559.9	$4,940.5	$4,914.4	$4,766.1	$4,365.2	$4,121.5	$4,045.7	$3,952.6	$4,313.2	$3,172.5
Operating income	536.3	(466.2)	489.3	356.9	426.1	351.9	302.7	177.1	365.2	458.1	259.2
Operating income excluding restructuring and goodwill amortization*	536.3	509.2	552.6	514.5	494.5	424.9	364.4	391.3	436.0	524.1	284.5
Income taxes	141.0	166.5	122.3	43.5	9.0	62.7	60.7	44.3	54.5	72.4	32.9
Earnings data:											
Earnings (loss) from continuing operations	300.3	(754.8)	227.2	159.2	216.5	89.9	64.1	(95.3)	16.1	19.7	30.0
Discontinued operations	—	—	—	70.4	38.4	37.5	31.1	22.0	36.9	31.4	—
Extraordinary item	—	—	—	—	(30.9)	—	—	(22.7)	—	—	—
Cumulative effects of accounting change	—	—	—	—	—	—	(29.2)	(237.6)			
Net earnings (loss)	300.3	(754.8)	227.2	229.6	224.0	127.4	66.0	(333.6)	53.0	51.1	30.0
Total assets	4,012.7	3,852.5	5,360.7	5,153.5	5,545.3	5,264.3	5,166.8	5,295.0	5,456.8	5,829.7	6,258.1
Long-term debt	847.1	1,148.9	1,623.7	1,415.8	1,704.5	1,723.2	2,069.2	2,108.5	2,625.8	2,754.7	2,629.7
Total debt	1,243.5	1,360.6	1,862.5	1,705.8	2,351.7	2,393.3	2,564.6	2,563.8	2,870.3	3,266.2	4,057.5
Stockholders' equity	801.1	574.0	1,791.4	1,632.4	1,423.2	1,169.4	1,048.9	1,074.0	1,027.1	920.7	720.7
Capital expenditures	171.1	146.0	203.1	196.3	203.1	181.5	190.3	167.7	94.9	103.1	112.1
Depreciation and amortization	160.0	155.2	214.2	214.6	206.7	195.4	182.4	188.3	187.1	197.8	131.0
Number of employees	22,100	21,800	28,600	29,200	29,300	29,200	30,500	32,300	31,900	35,900	38,600
Number of shares outstanding	88.4	91.8	96.5	96.1	94.4	85.3	84.5	76.3	62.6	61.4	59.6
Dividends per share	$0.48	$0.48	$0.48	$0.48	$0.40	$0.40	$0.40	$0.40	$0.40	$0.40	$0.40

*For 1998 this figure also excludes goodwill write-off and gain on sale of businesses.

The Expectation of Better Times for Black & Decker

In late 1998 Black & Decker management celebrated the completion of an almost decade-long effort to divest nonstrategic businesses gained through its 1989 acquisition of Emhart Corporation and expected the company to enter a long-awaited period of growth as its entire management attention was refocused on its core power tools, plumbing, and security hardware businesses. Black & Decker's CEO, Nolan Archibald, told Wall Street analysts in early 1998 that the pending elimination of nonstrategic businesses that manufactured and marketed such products as True Temper golf club shafts and Emhart glass-making machinery would allow the company to position itself for greater growth in 1999 and 2000. "This [portfolio restructuring] will allow us to focus on core operations that can deliver dependable and superior operating and financial results."[1] However, with the exception of a brief run up to $60 per share in mid-1999, the portfolio restructuring had done little to improve the market performance of the company's securities. In January 2000 Black & Decker's common shares traded at a 52-week low and at a price below the high for 1996 and 1997. Nevertheless, management continued to express confidence that the company's streamlined business portfolio would allow Black & Decker to achieve revenue and earnings growth that the market would find impressive. In commenting on the company's year-end 1999 financial performance, Nolan Archibald said, "We are extremely pleased with Black & Decker's performance this past year, which resulted in record earnings and clearly indicates that the strategic repositioning we undertook in 1998 has been successful."[2]

Company Background

Black & Decker was incorporated by Duncan Black and Alonzo Decker in 1910 and initially produced milk cap machines and candy dippers. In 1916 the company introduced its first power tool—a portable half-inch electric drill that was eventually placed on display in the Smithsonian Institution. Over the next 40 years, Duncan Black and Alonzo Decker undertook a number of actions that established the company as the dominant name in power tools and accessories. Black & Decker introduced the first portable screwdriver in 1922, the first electric hammer in 1936, finishing sanders and jigsaws in 1953, and the Dustbuster handheld vacuum in 1978. The company expanded internationally in 1919 when it began sales operations in Russia, Japan, and Australia and opened a production facility in Canada in 1922. The company eventually became known worldwide for its power tools, particularly so in Europe. Black & Decker was managed by the two partners until they died—Black in 1951 and Decker in 1956. As managers, Black and Decker achieved growth by adding to the company's lineup of power tools and accessories and by increasing its penetration of more and more foreign markets. The company maintained a corporate growth strategy tied exclusively to product-line extensions and international expansion until the mid-1980s.

DIVERSIFICATION INTO SMALL HOUSEHOLD APPLIANCES

Black & Decker began to pursue diversification in the 1980s because of growing maturity of its core power tools business. In 1984 Black & Decker acquired General Electric's housewares business for $300 million. GE's brands had about a 25 percent share

---

[1] As quoted in *Knight-Ridder/Tribune Business News,* January 28, 1998.

[2] As quoted in PR Newswire, January 27, 2000.

of the small-appliance market and generated annual revenues of about $500 million. GE sold its small-appliance division, despite its number one market position, because of the division's low profitability. GE's strong suit was in irons and toaster ovens, where its share was close to 50 percent; sales of GE irons alone totaled about $250 million. Among the other 150 GE products acquired by Black & Decker were coffeemakers, hair dryers and hair curlers, food mixers and processors, toasters, electric skillets, can openers, waffle irons, and blenders. Also in 1984, Black & Decker purchased three European tool manufacturers to fill in product gaps and strengthen its manufacturing base; the acquisition involved a Swiss manufacturer of portable electric woodworking tools for professional users, the leading European manufacturer of drill bits, and a German producer of hobby and precision power tools.

The acquisition of GE's housewares division launched Black & Decker on a course to transform the company from a power tools manufacturer into a consumer products company. In early 1985, the firm changed its name from Black & Decker Manufacturing Company to Black & Decker Corporation to reflect its new emphasis on "being more marketing driven" rather than being merely engaged in manufacturing.

BLACK & DECKER'S CEO—NOLAN D. ARCHIBALD

The chief architect of Black & Decker's foray into diversification was Nolan D. Archibald. Black & Decker hired Archibald as president and chief operating officer in 1985, shortly after the acquisition of GE's small household appliance business. Prior to joining Black & Decker, Archibald was president of the $1.7 billion consumer durables group at Beatrice Companies, where he was responsible for such business units as Samsonite luggage, Culligan water treatment products, Del Mar window coverings, Stiffel lamps, and Aristocraft kitchen cabinets. At the time he was hired, Archibald was 42 years old; he was chosen from a pool of some 50 candidates for the position and turned down offers to be president at two other companies to take the B&D job. Archibald had been at Beatrice since 1977 and was successful in engineering turnarounds in three of Beatrice's businesses. Prior to that, he had headed a turnaround of Conroy Inc.'s Sno-Jet Snowmobile business. Archibald spent two years of his youth winning converts as a Mormon missionary, was an All-American basketball player at Utah's Dixie College, became a standout player at Weber State College in Utah, earned his MBA degree at Harvard Business School, and tried out (unsuccessfully) for the Chicago Bulls professional basketball team. Corporate headhunters rated Archibald as a good strategic thinker who was personable, versatile, and sensitive to people.

Archibald's Early Successes at B&D

According to one Black & Decker dealer, prior to when Archibald took over as president in September 1985 "Black & Decker had been coasting along for quite a few years like a ship without a captain."[3] Archibald wasted little time in reorganizing Black & Decker's worldwide manufacturing operations. Within three months, Archibald initiated a restructuring plan to close older, inefficient plants and boost factory utilization rates by consolidating production within B&D's newest and biggest plants. Approximately 3,000 jobs were eliminated, including a number of high-level managerial jobs. In 1985, B&D took a $215 million write-off for plant shutdowns and other cost-saving reorganization efforts.

Prior to 1985, the company had pursued a decentralized, multicountry strategy. Each geographic area had its own production facilities, its own product-design cen-

---

[3]As quoted in *Business Week*, July 13, 1987, p. 90.

ters, and its own marketing and sales organizations to better cater to local market conditions. Over the years, this had resulted in short production runs at scattered production sites, reduced overall manufacturing efficiency, and prevented achievement of scale economies—for example, there were about 100 different motor sizes in B&D's product line. Archibald set the company on a more globalized approach to product design and manufacturing, with much greater communication and coordination between geographic operating units. Production at plants was organized around motor sizes, the number of product variations was reduced, and production runs were lengthened. From 1984 to 1989 seven plants were closed and nearly 3,000 employees were let go. Archibald also insisted more emphasis be put on quality control—during the early 1980s, B&D's reputation in power tools had been tarnished by shoddy product quality.

Meanwhile, Archibald put additional resources into new product development and redesign of the company's power tools and small-appliance lines. Archibald set a goal for the tool division to come up with more than a dozen new products each year—more than B&D had introduced in the five years before his arrival. He also created panels of dealers to suggest new products and features that consumers desired. The company introduced a number of highly successful products such as its Snakelight flashlights; a line of cordless power tools; Macho rotary hammers that could punch holes in stone, brick, and concrete; DeWalt professional power tools; and VersaPak rechargeable batteries that fit both Black & Decker power tools and household appliances.

One of Archibald's biggest marketing challenges was transferring consumers' brand loyalty for GE small appliances over to Black & Decker. Some observers believed Black & Decker would have trouble because B&D's traditional customers were men, and buyers of houseware products were usually women—as a *Wall Street Journal* article headline put it, "Would You Buy a Toaster from a Drillmaker?" B&D executives believed, however, that many women were familiar with the Black & Decker name because they bought power tools as gifts for men and because B&D had pioneered the development of household appliances powered by rechargeable batteries. Black & Decker's handheld DustBuster vacuum cleaner was the market leader, with a 45 percent share. B&D also had been marketing a cordless rotary scrub brush, a cordless rechargeable shoe shiner, and a rechargeable flashlight. Even before acquiring GE's housewares business, B&D had planned to introduce a line of cordless kitchen appliances, but gaining ample retail shelf space was often a hit-or-miss proposition. What made the GE acquisition attractive to B&D was the extra clout that being able to offer retailers a full line of housewares would have in competing for shelf space.

Black & Decker's competitors in small appliances saw the brand-name transition from GE to Black & Decker as an opportunity to gain market share that once was GE's. Sunbeam Appliance quadrupled its 1985 ad budget to $42 million because it wanted to replace GE as the best-known brand in small appliances. Norelco launched a new line of irons and a handheld can opener powered by rechargeable batteries to wrest share away from GE/Black & Decker. Hamilton Beach introduced a battery-operated carving knife. Nearly all small-appliance producers were rumored to be trying to develop cordless adaptations of irons, coffee makers, handheld mixers, and electric carving knives.

Archibald responded to the brand transfer challenge with a series of actions. Since Black & Decker had until 1987 to put its own name on all the GE products it acquired, it led off the transfer process by first putting its name on GE's innovative, expensive, high-margin Spacemaker products, which were designed to be mounted under kitchen cabinets—a line that was not as strongly identified with the GE name. Then B&D introduced a new iron (invented by GE) that shut off automatically when it sat too long or was tipped over; B&D's TV ads for the iron showed an elephant walking away from an iron that had been left on, with a tag line: "Even elephants forget." The brand transfer was accomplished product by product, in each case accompanied by heavy advertising. Under Archibald, Black & Decker spent approximately $100 million during the 1985–87 period to promote the brand transition. The company also organized a large team of brand transition assistants to hang paper tags on display models of newly rebranded products in about 10,000 retail stores across the United States—the tags stated that GE previously sold products now made by Black & Decker. Most analysts regarded Archibald's brand transfer program as successful; a Harvard Business School professor stated, "It is almost a textbook example of how to manage a brand transition."[4]

Archibald was promoted to chairman, president, and chief executive officer in 1986. He was listed among *Fortune* magazine's 10 Most Wanted Executives that year and was named as one of the Six Best Managers of 1987 by *Business Week*. By year-end 1988, Archibald was widely credited with engineering another impressive turnaround, having boosted Black & Decker's profits to $97.1 million—up sharply from the loss of $158.4 million posted in 1985. Archibald was also the recipient of the American Marketing Association's 1996 Edison Achievement Award for his accomplishments as Black & Decker chief executive.

FAILED ACQUISITION ATTEMPTS

In early 1988 Black & Decker began an unsolicited takeover bid for American Standard Inc., a diversified manufacturer of bathroom fixtures, air conditioning products, and braking systems for rail and automotive vehicles. American Standard had revenues of $3.4 billion and earnings of $127 million in 1987 (compared to revenues of $1.9 billion and earnings of almost $70 million for Black & Decker). After several months of negotiations, the takeover effort failed and B&D withdrew from the battle.

In January 1989, Black & Decker negotiated a deal with Allegheny International to purchase its Oster/Sunbeam appliance division for about $260 million. Oster/Sunbeam was a leading manufacturer and marketer of small household appliances—blenders, can openers, food mixers, electric skillets, steam irons, and other kitchen items. However, in February, Allegheny International backed out of the sale and merged with another company instead.

THE EMHART ACQUISITION

A month later, in March 1989, Black & Decker agreed to acquire Emhart Corporation for $2.8 billion, rescuing the firm from a hostile takeover bid. Emhart had 1988 sales of $2.8 billion, earnings of $127 million, assets of $2.4 billion, and shareholders' equity of $971 million. Emhart was a diversified manufacturer of industrial products (1988 sales of $1.6 billion), information and electronic systems (1988 sales of $654 million), and consumer products (1988 sales of $547 million). Approximately 40 percent of Emhart's sales and earnings came from foreign operations, the majority of which were concentrated in Europe. Exhibit 3 provides a profile of Emhart's business portfolio. Exhibit 4 provides data on the financial performance of Emhart's business units.

In the days following the announcement of Black & Decker's friendly plan to acquire Emhart, B&D's stock price dropped about 15 percent. There was considerable skepticism over the wisdom of the acquisition, both from the standpoint of whether

---

[4]Ibid.

EXHIBIT 3   Emhart Corporation's Business Portfolio in 1989 (at the time of the company's acquisition by Black & Decker)

Business and Product Categories	Trademarks/Names	Primary Markets/Customers
Industrial Businesses (1988 sales of $1.6 billion)		
Capacitors, audible signal devices	Emhart, Mallory, Sonalert, Arcotronica	Telecommunications, computer, automotive, and electronic components industries
Electromechanical devices, solid-state control systems, hydrocarbon leak detection systems	Emhart, Mallory, Pollulert	Appliance, automotive, and environmental controls manufacturers
Commercial door hardware, electronic locking systems	Emhart, Carbin, Russwin	Commercial, institutional building construction, and original equipment manufacturers
Footwear materials (insoles, toe puffs, shanks, eyelets, tacks, and nails)	Emhart, Texon, Aquiline	Manufacturers of footwear
Fastening systems (rivets, locknuts, screw anchors, adhesive systems, sealants, and grouts)	Emhart, Molly, Warren, Gripco, Bostik, Kelox, Dodge, Heli-Coil, POP	Appliance, construction, electronics, furniture/woodwork, packaging, automotive, and other transportation industries
Glass container machinery	Emhart, Hartford, Powers, Sundsvalls	Producers of glass containers for beverage, food, household, and pharmaceutical products
Printed circuit board assembling machinery	Emhart, Dynapert	Electronics industry
Information and Electronic Systems (1988 sales of $654 million)		
Technology-based systems and services (including computer-based systems), scientific research services, program management	Emhart, PRC, Planning Research Corp., PRC System Services, PRC Environmental Management, PRC Medic Computer Systems, Nova, Stellar	Governmental units and agencies, real estate multiple listing services, group medical practices, and public utilities
Consumer Products Businesses (1988 sales of $547 million)		
Door hardware, including lock sets, high-security locks, and locking devices	Emhart, Kwikset	Residential construction
Nonpowered lawn and garden equipment, landscape lighting	Garden America, True Temper	Do-it-yourself homeowners
Underground sprinkling and watering systems	Lawn Genie, Drip Mist, Irri-trol	Landscape specialists, do-it-yourself consumers
Golf club shafts, bicycle-frame tubing	True Temper, Dynamic Gold, Black Gold	Golf club manufacturers
Bathroom and kitchen faucets	Price Pfister, The Pfabulous Pfaucet with the Pfunny Name	Residential and commercial construction
Adhesive, sealants	Bostik, Thermogrip	Residential and commercial construction, do-it-yourself consumers
Fasteners, staplers, nailers	Blue-Tack, POP, Molly	Residential and commercial construction

EXHIBIT 4   Financial Performance of Emhart's Business Groups, 1986–88 (in millions of dollars)

Source: Emhart 1988 annual report.

	1988	1987	1986A*	1986B
Revenues				
Industrial				
Components	$ 641.8	$ 671.9		$ 653.9
Fastening systems	640.5	638.8		576.3
Machinery	279.0	291.1		419.2
	$1,561.3	$1,601.8		$1,649.4
Information and electronic systems	653.7	438.3		39.3
Consumer	547.5	414.4		405.6
Total	$2,762.5	$2,454.5		$2,094.3
Operating Income (Loss)				
Industrial				
Components	$ 63.8	$ 65.7	$ 48.2	$ (5.4)
Fastening systems	74.8	78.7	68.3	24.8
Machinery	42.7	34.1	44.4	3.9
	$ 181.3	$ 178.5	$160.9	$ 23.3
Information and electronic systems	37.2	22.3	2.0	2.0
Consumer	84.8	68.3	60.4	51.7
	$ 303.3	$ 269.1	$223.3	$ 77.0
Corporate expense	(35.0)	(32.9)	(30.3)	(34.0)
Total	$ 268.3	$ 236.2	$193.0	$ 43.0
Identifiable Assets				
Industrial				
Components	$ 457.8	$ 472.0		$ 400.3
Fastening systems	428.4	428.2		409.7
Machinery	167.8	164.8		297.2
	$1,054.0	$1,065.0		$1,107.2
Information and electronic systems	546.7	361.3		334.5
Consumer	702.7	225.1		266.1
	$2,303.4	$1,651.4		$1,707.8
Corporate	123.2	378.5		148.9
Total	$2,426.6	$2,029.9	$000.0	$1,856.7

*1986 before provision for restructuring.

Emhart's businesses had attractive strategic fit with B&D's businesses and whether B&D could handle the financial strain of making such a large acquisition. Emhart was significantly larger than Black & Decker:

1988 Financials	Emhart	Black & Decker
Sales revenues	$2.76 billion	$2.28 billion
Net earnings	126.6 million	97.1 million
Assets	2.43 billion	1.83 billion
Stockholders' equity	970.9 million	724.9 million
Long-term debt	$674.3 million	$277.1 million

The acquisition agreement called for Black & Decker to purchase 59.5 million shares (95 percent) of Emhart Corporation common stock at $40 per share—a price almost three times book value per share ($14.32). Altogether, Black & Decker had to secure $2.7 billion in financing to acquire Emhart. To come up with the funds, Black & Decker entered into a credit agreement with a group of banks that consisted of term loans due 1992 through 1997 and an unsecured revolving credit loan of up to $575 million. The loans carried an interest rate of ¼ percent above whatever the prevailing prime rate was. Scheduled principal payments on the term loans were as follows:

1992	$201,217,000
1993	274,287,000
1994	275,221,000
1995	743,923,000
1996	401,318,000

The credit agreement included covenants that required Black & Decker to achieve certain minimum levels of cash flow coverage of its interest obligations and not to exceed specified leverage (debt-to-equity) ratios during the term of the loan:

Fiscal Year	Maximum Leverage Ratio	Minimum Cash Flow Coverage Ratio
1992	3.25	1.35
1993	2.75	1.50
1994	2.25	1.55
1995 and thereafter	1.50	1.60

Note: The leverage ratio was calculated by dividing indebtedness, as defined by the credit agreement, by consolidated net stockholders' equity. The cash flow coverage ratio was calculated by dividing earnings before interest, taxes, depreciation, and amortization of goodwill minus capital expenditures by net interest expense plus cash income tax payments and dividends declared.

Other covenants in the credit agreement limited Black & Decker's ability to incur additional indebtedness and to acquire businesses or sell assets.

Black & Decker also entered into factoring agreements with financial institutions where it sold its receivables at a discounted rate to avoid waiting 30 to 60 days to collect on its invoices. The company ended its sale of receivables program in December 1997 when it became able to meet its liquidity requirements without factoring receivables.

Black & Decker recorded the excess amount of its purchase price for Emhart over the book value of Emhart's net assets as goodwill to be amortized on a straight-line basis over 40 years. This resulted in Black & Decker's having increased depreciation and amortization charges of about $45 million annually.

INITIAL DIVESTITURES OF EMHART BUSINESSES

Senior management at Black & Decker realized early on that as much as $1 billion of Emhart's business assets would have to be sold to reduce B&D's interest expenses and debt obligations and enable it to meet its covenant agreements. According to accounting rules, these assets had to either be sold within a year or be consolidated with the rest of B&D assets—a move that could cause B&D to fail to meet its maximum leverage covenant. The Emhart businesses that were identified for sale within one year from the acquisition date included footwear materials, printed circuit board assembly equipment (Dynapert), capacitors, chemical adhesives (Bostik), and the entire information and electronic systems business unit (PRC). During 1989 and early 1990, Black & Decker sold the Bostik chemical adhesives division to a French company for $345 million, the footwear materials business to the United Machinery Group for approximately $125 million, and its Arcotronics capacitors business to Nissei Electric of Tokyo for about $80 million; the net proceeds from these sales were used to reduce debt. In early 1990, when the one-year period expired, Black & Decker was forced to consolidate about $566 million of the unsold assets, boosting the goodwill on its balance sheet by $560 million, raising annual amortization charges by $14 million. To keep from violating the maximum debt/equity ratio allowed under its credit schedule, Black & Decker was forced to issue $150 million in new preferred stock, $47 million of which was purchased from its 401(K) employee thrift plan when no other buyers came forward.

Throughout 1991 Black & Decker continued to struggle to meet its covenant agreements. The company divested Emhart's Garden America business unit and the Mallory Controls operations in North America and Brazil for a combined total of about $140 million. The company also sold its True Temper Hardware unit, its PRC Medic unit, and its U.S. Capacitors business for a combined total of nearly $110 million. The prices B&D got for the Emhart businesses it sold were generally below management's expectations, partly because oncoming recessionary effects reduced what buyers were willing to pay.

Nonetheless, these divestitures (described by B&D management as "nonstrategic assets") and the sale of $150 million in preferred stock, allowed Black & Decker to reduce its total debt from a peak of $4 billion following the Emhart acquisition in April 1989 to $2.9 billion at year-end 1991. Even so, Black & Decker was still hard pressed to generate enough cash to meet its debt repayment schedule, a problem compounded by the 1990–91 recession, which hit the company's tool and household goods businesses fairly hard. The company's stock price fell from the mid-20s at the time of the Emhart acquisition to a low of $11–$12 in early 1991—many observers believed that the fundamental cause of B&D's financial plight was that it had paid too much for Emhart. There was also concern about whether there was enough strategic fit between Emhart and B&D. By early 1992, the stock price had recovered to the low 20s, partly because a decline in the prime rate from 10 percent to 6.5 percent had lowered B&D's interest burden substantially. (The credit agreement pegged the interest rate B&D paid at ¼ percent above the prevailing prime rate.)

SUBSEQUENT DIVESTITURES: 1993–96

During the next six years, Black & Decker's corporate management sought to find buyers for several nonstrategic businesses acquired as part of the Emhart deal. Three were sold between 1993 and 1996.

Dynapert

The Dynapert business unit provided automated equipment for assembling printed circuit boards to electronics customers around the world. The equipment was among the most complex computer-controlled machinery being used in any industrial application. Dynapert had two manufacturing plants (one in the United States and one in England) and sales and service facilities throughout the world. The unit had launched a total quality program and implemented just-in-time manufacturing techniques.

Sales were made directly to users by an employee sales force and independent sales representatives. Dynapert faced competition from both U.S. and foreign manufacturers. Competition centered on technological and machine performance features, price, delivery terms, and provision of technical services. The Dynapert division, which generated 1991 sales of about $180 million, had been put on the market shortly after the Emhart acquisition, and was sold two years later to Dover Corporation's Universal Instrument division for an undisclosed amount.

Corbin Russwin

Emhart's Corbin Russwin manufactured locks and door hardware for the European commercial security hardware market. The unit employed 550 people at its plant in Berlin, Germany. Yale and Valour, Inc., the British manufacturer of Yale locks, purchased the Corbin Russwin unit from Black & Decker in 1994 for $80 million. Black & Decker recorded a gain of $18 million on the combined sales of the Corbin Russwin and Dynapert units.

PRC Information Systems and Services

This segment consisted of a single business unit known as PRC, Inc., headquartered in McLean, Virginia. PRC and its predecessors had been in business since the mid-1970s. A majority of PRC's business came from contracts with various agencies and units of the federal government. Approximately 40 percent of PRC's 1991 revenues were from contracts with the Department of Defense. In addition, PRC was the leading provider of (1) online printed residential real estate multiple listing systems and (2) computer-aided emergency dispatch systems. The types of services PRC provided were highly competitive, and strategic defense expenditures were expected to decline given the improvement of foreign relations. Many of PRC's competitors were large defense contractors with significantly greater financial resources. As the Department of Defense's expenditures for weapons programs continued to decline, these large contractors were expected to bid more aggressively for the types of contract work done by PRC. PRC had also been put on the market for sale following the Emhart acquisition. In 1991, PRC had sales of $684 million and pretax operating earnings of $32.3 million. In mid-1991 B&D appointed a new person to head PRC; shortly thereafter, PRC launched an initiative to pursue new markets. The objective was to shift PRC's business mix so that half came from U.S. customers and half from overseas customers. However, PRC management had great difficulty developing new nongovernment customers and was only growing at about one-third the rate of its closest competitors under Black & Decker ownership.

Black & Decker had little success in locating interested buyers for the PRC unit until 1995, when PRC Realty Systems and PRC Environmental Management, Inc., were sold for $60 and $35.5 million, respectively. Litton Industries agreed to purchase the remaining PRC operations in 1996 for $425 million. Prior to its sale to Litton, when it appeared that finding a buyer was becoming increasingly unlikely, Black & Decker management had considered a spinoff of the unit in 1992. The spinoff was never finalized because Wall Street showed little interest in a $350 million public offering of PRC stock. PRC's 1995 sales and after-tax earnings were $800 million and $38.4 million, respectively.

BLACK & DECKER'S 1998 DIVESTITURES

Black & Decker again initiated portfolio restructuring in 1998 when it divested its household products business and two businesses gained through the Emhart acquisition.

Household Products

Black & Decker's household products business had established itself as a worldwide leader in products used for home cleaning, garment care, cooking, and food and beverage preparation by 1990. It had the largest market share of any full-line producer of household appliance products in the United States, Canada, Mexico, and

EXHIBIT 5   Unit Volume for Selected Small Appliances and Market Shares of Leading Producers, 1990, 1993, and 1996 (unit volume in thousands)

Source: Compiled by case researchers from data presented in *Appliance,* April 1991 and April 1997.

Product/Leading Brands	1990	1993	1996
Can openers	6,200	6,380	6,910
Rival	33%	27%	26%
Hamilton Beach/Proctor Silex	13	15	24
Black & Decker	26	28	13
Oster/Sunbeam	11	13	13
Coffeemakers	17,740	14,390	15,000
Mr. Coffee	28%	31%	32%
Hamilton Beach/Proctor Silex	19	18	24
West Bend	—	3	9
Black & Decker	20	17	8
Food processors	4,760	1,916	1,525
Hamilton Beach/Proctor Silex	21%	19%	40%
Cuisinart	Unknown	13	18
Black & Decker	25	21	10
Oster/Sunbeam	18	19	8
Hand mixers	4,400	5,060	5,280
Hamilton Beach/Proctor Silex	14%	18%	24%
Black & Decker	34	28	15
Oster/Sunbeam	25	18	13
HPA/Betty Crocker	—	—	11
Irons	16,950	17,460	15,600
Black & Decker	50%	50%	38%
Hamilton Beach/Proctor Silex	24	30	29
Oster/Sunbeam	17	10	17
Rowenta	—	—	7
Toaster ovens	2,800	3,340	3,670
Black & Decker	57%	56%	56%
Toastmaster	13	16	17
Hamilton Beach/Proctor Silex	19	20	11
HPA/Betty Crocker	—	—	6
Toasters	8,900	9,850	10,760
Hamilton Beach/Proctor Silex	35%	50%	37%
Toastmaster	27	31	30
Rival	—	—	17
HPA/Betty Crocker	—	—	5
Black & Decker	16	13	4

Australia and a growing presence in Europe, Southeast Asia, and Latin America. The household products division was using the worldwide distribution network and brand-name recognition that had been established by the tools division to gain greater global penetration in household appliances. However, by 1996, the company had lost substantial market share in almost every housewares product category. Its Toast-R-Ovens and irons were the only remaining Black & Decker products that held leading shares of their respective markets. (See Exhibit 5 for market shares of the major competitors by product category for 1990, 1993, and 1996.)

Like the market for power tools, the market for small household appliances was both mature and cyclical. Growth opportunities existed mainly in the form of creating innovative new products and in increasing market penetration in the countries of Eastern Europe and other developing nations where household appliance saturation rates were low. It was difficult to grow sales in the United States without introducing innovative new products since most small appliances had very high household saturation rates. In 1996 blenders were found in 80 percent of U.S. households, coffeemakers had a 74 percent saturation rate, and toasters were found in 90 percent of U.S. households. Many consumers clearly had both a toaster and toaster oven, since toaster ovens had a 42 percent U.S. household saturation rate.

Black & Decker's housewares business unit had been successful at launching new products that might entice a consumer into replacing an existing small appliance for one offering more features or better performance. The company's SnakeLight flexible flashlight was introduced in 1994 and quickly became one of the most popular small appliances ever developed by the company. In 1996 the company introduced a revamped Quick 'N Easy line of irons with a new Sure Steam system, and in 1998 it improved the glideability of its irons with a new proprietary coated soleplate. The company also introduced cordless products such as the ScumBuster, a submersible scourer and scrubber, and the FloorBuster, an upright vacuum cleaner that achieved rapid sales increases.

In late 1997 the company launched a designer line of small kitchen appliances, Kitchentools, which won five Industrial Design Excellence Awards in 1998. The Kitchentools line carried premium pricing; the stand mixer had a suggested retail price of $289.99, the thermal coffeemaker listed at $159.99, the blender was priced at $139.99, the food processor was priced at $229.99, the hand mixer's retail price was $69.00, and the Kitchentools can opener carried a suggested retail price of $34.99. Even though the Kitchentools line was praised for its quality and innovative styling, it did not sell as well as Black & Decker management had expected. The company also had some difficulty manufacturing the products and getting them to market by the planned launch date.

Black & Decker had lost substantial market share in recent years and had seen its profit margins erode despite its best efforts to maintain efficient operations. Between 1995 and 1997 the company had completely overhauled its supply chain management to reduce finished goods inventory and improve customer service and production planning. The company had eliminated $150 million from logistics costs during that time period but still only averaged about 2 percent profit margins on its housewares products. The business unit was identified for divestiture by Nolan Archibald in January 1998 and was sold to Windmere-Durable in May 1998 for $315 million. The agreement allowed Black & Decker to retain its DustBuster, FloorBuster, ScumBuster, and SnakeLight product lines. In June 1998 Black & Decker announced the sale of its housewares operations in New Zealand and Australia to Gerard Industries, an Australian electrical products manufacturer. The company had also sold its consumer glue gun and stapler business to Longwood Industries for an undisclosed amount in July 1998.

Recreational Outdoor Products

In 1998 B&D's True Temper Sports business unit was the leading global designer, manufacturer, and marketer of steel golf club shafts; with over a 60 percent market share in the steel shaft segment, it was three times as large as its closest rival. True Temper also manufactured graphite shafts but had a very limited market share in that segment since it focused on the premium end of the market. The division supplied more than 800 golf club manufacturers around the world, including such industry leaders as Callaway Golf, Ping, Titleist, and Taylor Made. The sales of this unit had grown at a compounded annual rate of 12 percent between 1995 and 1997. True Temper Sport's growth rate reflected the overall growth in the golf equipment industry. The unit also manufactured specialty tubing for the bicycle and sporting goods industries. Many of the bicycles and kayak paddles used by U.S. Olympians were manufactured from True Temper precision tubing.

Black & Decker sold the business to Cornerstone Equity Investors in June 1998 for $178 million. The new owners stated that they intended for True Temper to remain the leader in golf club shafts and that they intended to expand into new product categories requiring specialty tubing. True Temper's president said that the new company would develop precision tubing products for such sporting goods industries as down-hill skiing and archery.

Glass-Container-Forming Machinery

In 1998 B&D's Emhart glass-container-forming machinery division was considered the global leader and offered the world's most complete line of glass-container-making equipment. Important competitive factors were price, technological and machine performance features, product reliability, and technical and engineering services. An increasing worldwide preference for plastic and other nonglass containers had led to a slowing growth rate for glass-container-forming equipment and inspection equipment. There was little seasonal variation in industry demand. Glass-container-making equipment was in 24-hour use in virtually all plants worldwide, creating a predictable need for servicing and rebuilding; nearly two-thirds of the unit's revenues came from rebuilding and repair services and technology upgrades. In January 1998 the business was identified as a nonstrategic asset that was to be divested; it was sold to Bucher Holding AG of Switzerland in September 1998 for $178 million.

Black & Decker's Business Portfolio in 2000

In 2000 Black & Decker Corporation was a diversified multinational enterprise with a business portfolio consisting of

- Power tools and accessories for both do-it-yourselfers and professional tradespeople.
- Lawn and garden equipment.
- Security hardware for residential markets in the United States and residential and commercial hardware in certain European countries.
- Cleaning and lighting products.
- Plumbing products.
- Commercial fastening systems.

Exhibit 6 provides a detailed listing of the products produced and marketed by B&D in these business areas. Exhibit 7 provides 1997–99 financial performance data by business group. A brief description of each business group follows.

POWER TOOLS AND ACCESSORIES

Black & Decker was the world's largest manufacturer, marketer, and servicer of power tools and accessories. The company's products were available at almost all retail outlets that sold power tools in the United States, Europe, and other developed countries. In fact, Black & Decker products were so popular in the United Kingdom that many British do-it-yourselfers referred to home improvement projects as "Black & Deckering." Black & Decker was named as the top-performing hardware brand by 6 out of every 10 U.S. retailers included in a 1997 survey conducted by *Discount Store*

EXHIBIT 6   Black & Decker's Business Portfolio at Year-End 1999

**Power tools and accessories
(1999 sales: $3.21 billion)**

- Drills
- Screwdrivers
- Saws
- Sanders
- Grinders
- Tabletop saws
- Drill bits
- Screwdriver bit
- Saw blades
- Cleaning and lighting products

**Hardware and home improvement
(1999 sales: $882 million)**

- Lock sets
- Deadbolts
- Master keying systems
- Faucets and fixtures
- Lawn and garden care products

**Fastening and assembly systems
(1999 sales: $498 million)**

- Rivets and riveting tools
- Threaded inserts
- Stud welding fastening systems
- Lock nuts
- Self-drilling screws
- Construction anchors

News. Other brands that were highly rated by hardware retailers were Stanley, General Electric, Skil, Rubbermaid, Makita, and Dutch Boy. Black & Decker's products were also highly rated in terms of performance by consumers, and most of its products carried a two-year warranty.

Industry Growth and Competition

Demand for power tools and accessories was regarded as mature and cyclical. Volume was influenced by residential and commercial construction activity, by consumer expenditures for home improvement, and by the overall level of manufacturing activity. (A number of manufacturers used power tools in performing certain production tasks—automotive and aerospace firms, for example, were heavy users of power tools.) Worldwide sales of power tools were an estimated $10 billion in 1999. The North American market for power tools was estimated at $3.5 billion, European sales were estimated at $4.0 billion, Asia/Pacific sales were an estimated $2.0 billion, and Latin American sales of power tools were approximately $500 million. The global market for power tools failed to grow significantly between 1997 and 1999, but was expected to grow at low- to mid-single-digit annual rates between 2000 and 2002. The industry's worldwide demand plateau during the late 1990s was attributable in large part to Asian financial and economic troubles. During 1998 and 1999 North America was the fastest-growing market for power tools as cordless and professional-grade power tools gained in popularity with consumers. Demand in Europe grew more slowly than in the United States during the late 1990s and was expected to continue to lag behind U.S. demand in the near future. Worldwide, the biggest percentage growth during the early and mid-1990s occurred in emerging Asian countries, where the use of power tools was quickly replacing the use of hand tools. Healthy demand for power tools was expected to return to Asian markets once the region had fully recovered from the effects of financial and economic instability that began in late 1997.

EXHIBIT 7 Black & Decker's Financial Performance by Business Segment, 1997–99

Source: Black & Decker annual reports.

	Power Tools and Accessories	Hardware and Home Improvement	Fastening and Assembly Systems	All Others	Currency Translation Adjustments	Corporate Adjustments and Eliminations	Consolidated
1999							
Sales to unaffiliated customers	$3,209.3	$881.8	$497.7	—	($68.3)	$ —	$4,520.5
Operating income before restructuring and exit costs, write-off of goodwill, and gain on sales of businesses	377.3	124.0	84.3	—	(6.9)	(42.4)	536.3
Depreciation and amortization	87.7	31.1	15.4	—	(1.8)	27.6	160.0
Identifiable assets	1,836.0	508.2	273.2	—	2,617.4	1,395.3	4,012.7
Capital expenditures	$ 109.1	$ 38.3	$ 26.9	—	($ 3.5)	$ 0.3	$ 171.1
1998							
Sales to unaffiliated customers	$2,946.4	$851.1	$463.0	$333.6	($34.2)	$ —	$4,559.9
Operating income before restructuring and exit costs, write-off of goodwill, and gain on sales of businesses	293.4	125.2	76.6	16.5	(4.4)	(23.3)	484.0
Depreciation and amortization	88.2	27.1	13.4	—	(1.1)	27.6	155.2
Identifiable assets	1,631.3	507.8	246.7	—	(4.6)	1,471.3	3,852.5
Capital expenditures	$ 79.1	$ 36.5	$ 16.2	$ 13.3	($ 1.1)	$ 2.0	$ 146.0
1997							
Sales to unaffiliated customers	$2,936.4	$804.8	$451.3	$718.1	$29.9	$ —	$4,940.5
Operating income before restructuring and exit costs, write-off of goodwill, and gain on sales of businesses	290.7	121.3	69.7	61.7	(2.3)	(51.8)	489.3
Depreciation and amortization	87.5	24.7	11.9	24.4	(0.3)	66.0	214.2
Identifiable assets	1,635.4	476.5	248.2	438.6	8.0	2,554.0	5,360.7
Capital expenditures	$ 113.2	$ 47.3	$ 15.4	$ 25.3	($ 0.2)	$ 2.1	$ 203.1

Market Segments

There were two distinct groups of buyers for power tools: professional users and do-it-yourselfers. Professional users included construction workers, electricians, plumbers, repair and maintenance workers, auto mechanics, and manufacturing workers. Professional users were very conscious of quality and features; they tended to buy only those tools that were durable, functional, dependable, and capable of precision. They also tended to be very knowledgeable compared to do-it-yourselfers, many of whom were first-time buyers and used power tools infrequently.

Because the needs of professional users and do-it-yourself consumers tended to be sharply different, some manufacturers had a heavy-duty professional line and a consumer/do-it-yourself line and others catered to just one of the two segments. Professional users tended to purchase their tools through jobbers, contractor supply firms, industrial supply houses, building supply centers, and some home improvement centers. Tools for the consumer segment were sold at home improvement centers, building materials centers, mass merchandisers (Sears), discount chains (Wal-Mart, Kmart), and hardware stores.

Until the late 1980s, the consumer tool segment was growing at a faster clip than the professional segment. But narrowing price differentials and a rising interest on the part of gung-ho do-it-yourselfers in professional-quality tools had, in the U.S. market, spurred demand for heavy-duty professional tools. The sales of both consumer-grade and professional-grade cordless products were also becoming increasingly popular, with a compound annual growth rate of over 10 percent during the mid- and late 1990s.

Competition

Power tool manufacturers competed on such variables as price, quality, product design, product innovation, brand-name reputation, size and strength of retail dealer networks, and after-sale service. All makers were working to bring out new products that were lightweight, compact, cordless, quiet, less prone to vibration, strong, and easy to manipulate. The major manufacturers had sales forces whose main task was to expand and strengthen the network of retail dealers carrying their line of tools. Salespeople signed on new dealers and called on major accounts—wholesale distributors, discount chains, home improvement centers, and other mass merchandisers—to win better access to shelf space in their retail outlets, help with promotion and display activities, and upgrade dealers' product knowledge and sales skills. Some manufacturers offered training seminars and provided training videos to dealers/distributors. Manufacturers that concentrated on the professional segment engaged in limited advertising and promotion activities, spending their dollars for trade magazine ads, trade shows, and in-store displays. Those that concentrated on the consumer segment, like Black & Decker, spent comparatively heavily for TV and magazine ads and also for co-op ad programs with dealers.

Black & Decker's Global Competitive Position in Power Tools

In 2000 Black & Decker was the overall world leader in the world power tool industry, followed by Bosch/Skil Power Tools, a division of Robert Bosch Corporation (one of Germany's leading companies), and Japanese brands Makita and Hitachi. Other competitors were Atlas/Copco, Delta/Porter Cable, Hilti, Ryobi, and Electrolux. For most of the company's history, Black & Decker's greatest strength was in the consumer tools segment (see Exhibit 8); it was the market leader in the United States, Europe (where it had had a presence since the 1920s), and many other countries outside Europe. No other manufacturer came close to matching B&D's global distribution capabilities in the do-it-yourself segment. Makita and Ryobi were the leaders in Japan and several other Asian countries. Bosch was strongest in Europe.

EXHIBIT 8 Estimated U.S. Sales and Market Shares of Power Tool Manufacturers, 1979, 1991, and 1997 ($ millions)

Source: Compiled by the case researchers from a variety of sources, including telephone interviews with company personnel; data for 1979 are based on information in Skil Corporation, Harvard Business School, case #9–389–005.

	1979		1991		1997	
	Dollar Sales	Percent Share	Dollar Sales	Percent Share	Dollar Sales	Percent Share
Consumer Tools						
Black & Decker	$169	44.5%	$325	39.7	$460	43.1%
Sears/Ryobi	107	28.2	280	34.0	305	28.5
Milwaukee	6	1.5	4	0.5	6	0.6
Makita	2	0.5	43	5.2	32	3.0
Porter Cable	—	—	—	—	—	—
Delta	—	—	—	—	—	—
Skil	52	13.7	82	10.0	165	15.4
Others	44	11.6	86	10.6	102	9.4
Total	$380	100.0%	$820	100.0%	$1,070	100.0%
Professional Tools						
Black & Decker	$205	42.1%	$125	17.9%	$918	36.7%
Sears/Ryobi	9	1.8	50	7.1	285	11.4
Milwaukee	89	18.2	145	20.7	436	17.4
Makita	22	4.5	160	22.9	304	12.2
Porter Cable	NA	NA	50	7.1	240	9.6
Delta	NA	NA	40	5.7	209	8.4
Skil	54	11.1	40	5.7	32	1.3
Others	109	22.3	90	12.9	76	3.0
Total	$488	100.0%	$700	100.0%	$2,500	100.0%
Total Tools						
Black & Decker	$374	43.1%	$450	29.6%	$1,378	38.6%
Sears/Ryobi	116	13.4	330	21.7	590	16.5
Milwaukee	95	10.9	149	9.8	442	12.4
Makita	24	2.8	203	13.4	336	9.4
Porter Cable	NA	NA	50	3.3	240	6.7
Delta	NA	NA	40	2.6	209	5.9
Skil	106	12.2	122	8.0	197	5.5
Others	153	17.6	176	11.6	210	9.4
Total	$868	100.0%	$1,520	100.0%	$3,570	100.0%

NA = not available

In consumer tools Black & Decker's strongest U.S. competitor was Sears, which marketed tools under the Sears Craftsman label. Sears's longtime supplier of tools was Ryobi, which supplied Sears with 75 percent of its tool requirements. Skil's strength was in power saws; its 1992 joint venture with Robert Bosch Power Tools was contrived to give the two brands more clout in gaining shelf space and greater global coverage capabilities. Black & Decker's consumer-grade power tools were also carried by Sears, and the company had developed a new Quantum line of power tools sold exclusively by Wal-Mart. Quantum was an intermediate line that was more durable than typical consumer lines but did not meet the performance of the company's professional power tools. Black & Decker's Mouse sander, WoodHawk circular saws, and FireStorm drills, along with its products that used the VersaPak interchangeable battery, were among the company's best-selling consumer tools.

Although surveys showed that consumers associated the Black & Decker name with durable power tools, trade professionals viewed Black & Decker products as products for do-it-yourselfers. During the late 1980s, the company's charcoal-gray professional tools line was not seen by professional users as sufficiently differentiated from B&D's traditional black line of consumer tools. Professionals preferred tools made by Makita, Skil, and Milwaukee (a U.S. tool manufacturer with a reputation for quality, heavy-duty tools). During the 1970s and 1980s, Makita had steadily increased its share of the professional segment and by 1991 had captured 53 percent of the U.S. professional handheld power tool segment.

In 1991 B&D executives formed a team, headed by the president of B&D's power tools division, to come up with a new strategy for the professional market segment. The team elected to create an entirely new line of industrial-grade tools for professional users under the DeWalt brand, a name borrowed from a 65-year-old maker of high-quality stationary saws acquired by B&D in 1960. The team changed the tools' color from gray to industrial yellow because the latter was easy to see, signaled safety, and was distinct from other leading brands of professional power tools. Every product in B&D's professional line was redesigned based on input from professionals, dealers, and B&D engineers. The redesigned versions were all tested by professional users; every item had to meet or beat Makita's tools in user tests before going into production. The new DeWalt line was introduced in March 1992. As part of the introduction of the DeWalt line, B&D created "swarm teams" of 120 young, high-energy marketers that visited construction sites to demonstrate DeWalt tools in their bright yellow-and-black Chevy Blazers. DeWalt swarm teams also promoted DeWalt tools at NASCAR events, vocational clubs, union apprenticeship programs, and retail locations. The company intended to double the number of swarm team members in the United States between 1998 and 1999. In 1996 DeWalt swarm teams invaded Europe with a fleet of yellow-and-black Range Rover Defenders with the charge of making DeWalt a leading brand on that continent. The company also instituted a policy of offering professional users the loan of a DeWalt power tool when waiting for their equipment to be fixed at any of the company's 135 U.S. service centers. There were also DeWalt demonstration booths at each of the service centers.

Initial response to the DeWalt line was excellent. As the brand began to gain in popularity with professional users, Black & Decker developed additional DeWalt tools. In 1997, newly introduced DeWalt products were awarded two Industrial Design Excellence Awards from the Industrial Designers Society of America. The success of the new DeWalt line exceeded Black & Decker management's expectations and surpassed its $200 million sales volume objective for 1995 by over $100 million. In 1999 DeWalt was one of the leading power tool brands for professionals and serious do-it-yourselfers.

Black & Decker was also the world leader in the market for such accessories as drill bits, saw blades, and screwdriver bits. Vermont American, Irwin Hanson/American Tool, Bosch, Freud, and Wolfcraft were B&D's closest competitors in the accessories market, but no other company had as broad a product line or geographic coverage as Black & Decker. Most of the company's growth in accessory sales was accounted for by accessory lines developed for the DeWalt brand and a line of new premium woodworking saw blades. The company intended to maintain its market leadership by expanding into more woodworking supply and industrial/construction distribution channels and continuing to introduce innovative products.

In 1998 Black & Decker launched a series of initiatives intended to strengthen its competitive position in power tools and accessories. First, it introduced a corporatewide six sigma quality program to bring about improvements in costs, defect rates, product quality, and customer satisfaction. Second, the company took a $164 million restructuring charge that involved the elimination of 2,900 positions; worldwide plant rationalization that resulted in plant closings in Canada, Singapore, and Italy; a reorganization of its European operations; and various reengineering projects in all plants. Third, it initiated a restructuring of its supply chain management to improve customer service while reducing inventories. Although Black & Decker's restructuring program cut across all business units, it was primarily focused on its global power tools business and was expected to yield more than $100 million annually in cost savings. Additional cost savings were achieved through the integration of Black & Decker's cleaning and lighting products like its DustBuster vacuum cleaner, Scum-Buster wet scrubber, and SnakeLight flashlight with its power tool businesses after the sale of the housewares division to Windmere in 1998.

The April 21, 1999, exit of Joseph Galli, Black & Decker's president of its Worldwide Power Tools and Accessories group, shocked analysts and investors and caused a one-day 8 percent decline in the company's share price. Galli, age 41, was a rising star at Black & Decker and was thought to be the leading candidate to succeed Archibald as CEO. There was a widely held belief in the power tools industry that much of the DeWalt brand's success was attributable to Galli's strategic leadership and that Galli had been forced out of B&D as a result of his desire to become the company's CEO within the near future. Archibald, who had no immediate retirement plans, commented that Galli had "expressed an interest in advancing his management career to a higher level, and we have agreed it makes sense for him to pursue this goal outside of Black & Decker."[5] In June 1999 Joe Galli become president and chief operating officer of Amazon.com. Even though there was some initial concern by investors over Galli's departure, B&D's Power Tools and Accessories group continued to perform well in his absence; its sales increased by 11 percent and operating profit increased by 27 percent during the fourth quarter of 1999. The business unit's annual sales and operating profits increased by 9 percent and 29 percent, respectively, over 1998 sales and operating profits.

Lawn and Garden Equipment

Black & Decker's lawn and garden tools like Groom 'N' Edge, Vac 'N' Mulch, and LeafBuster were distributed through the same channels as the company's power tools. In addition, the buyers of B&D's hedge trimmers, string trimmers, lawn mowers, edgers, and blower/vacuums could get the items repaired at B&D's 150 company-owned service centers worldwide and several hundred other authorized service centers operated by independent owners. Where feasible, B&D's lawn and garden products had a global design. The company had recently begun to offer cordless electric string trimmers and hedge trimmers in North America and Europe. The cordless hedge trimmer could run continuously for about 30 minutes, and the cordless string trimmer could trim hard-to-reach areas from a half-acre lawn on a single battery charge. As of 2000, Black & Decker marketed its cordless lawn mowers only in Europe.

SECURITY HARDWARE

B&D's security hardware business was the leader in the $2 billion global market for door hardware for homes and businesses. The company had developed good-better-best product lines that covered all major residential price points. The Kwikset brand

[5]As quoted in the *Baltimore Sun,* April 22, 1999.

was positioned as an affordable product targeted to do-it-yourselfers; B&D had boosted Kwikset's sales by providing retailers with a videotape that took the mystery out of changing household locks. Kwikset Plus was a midrange product, and the company's TITAN products were designed for the fine home market. TITAN NightSight handsets and deadbolts featured lighted keyways, and the TITAN AccessOne keyless entry deadbolt and handset systems allowed homeowners to use a remote control to unlock the door from as far away as 30 feet. The TITAN line also included the Society Brass Collection of solid brass designer door hardware. All TITAN products boasted a lifetime finish that was protected against tarnishing, rust, and corrosion.

This business, acquired from Emhart, had achieved significant cost savings by integrating its purchasing, distribution, and marketing activities with B&D's other consumer products businesses. B&D's worldwide distribution network was also providing the hardware group wider geographic sales opportunities. In many instances, door hardware was sold in the same retail channels as B&D's power tools and accessories. Black & Decker's restructuring and six sigma quality initiatives, begun in 1998, also affected its security hardware business—products and facilities were rationalized, high-cost operations were restructured, and automation was used where feasible. Black & Decker's major competitors in the North American security hardware market included Schlage, Weiser, Weslock, and a variety of Asian exporters. Major competitors in Europe included Williams, Assa Abloy, Cisa, Keso, and Abus.

PLUMBING PRODUCTS

B&D's plumbing products business, Price Pfister, had gained market share since the Emhart acquisition to become the third largest manufacturer and marketer of plumbing fixtures in North America by 2000. Price Pfister had benefited from access to B&D's retail distribution network by gaining more shelf space in home improvement centers. Price Pfister had also introduced fashionable, but affordably priced, new designs and new lines that had become popular with plumbing wholesalers and plumbing contractors. Price Pfister had increased its brand recognition through in-store merchandising activities and with TV ads using the theme "The Pfabulous Pfaucet with the Pfunny Name" in the early 1990s and "The Pfabulous Pfaucet. Pforever. No Drips, No Tarnish, No Worries" theme in the late 1990s.

Price Pfister's major competitors in the $1.9 billion North American market for sink, tub, shower, and lavatory plumbing hardware were American Standard, Kohler, Delta, and Moen. The industry had grown at a slow rate of 2 to 3 percent since 1995 and was expected to grow at a comparable rate over the next few years. Plumbing products with new styles and features were in the highest demand. Black & Decker expected new decorative faucets like Price Pfister's Georgetown and Roman lines, introduced during the late 1990s, to account for 20 percent of the unit's annual sales. Price Pfister expected to improve its performance with the addition of innovative and attractive new lines, better in-store merchandising, improved manufacturing efficiency, and better supply chain management.

COMMERCIAL FASTENING SYSTEMS

Black & Decker was among the global leaders in the $2 billion fastening and assembly systems market. This business unit marketed fastening products under 26 different brands and trademarks to automotive, electronics, aerospace, machine tool, and appliance companies in the United States, Europe, and the Far East. The industry's recent growth rate had ranged between 3 and 5 percent, and future growth was expected to remain within that range. Some emerging markets did generate higher growth rates as new industries and companies emerged and plant capacity was added.

Products were sold directly to users and also through distributors and manufacturers' representatives. Competition centered on product quality, performance, reliability, price, delivery, and ability to provide customers with technical and engineering services. Competition came from many manufacturers in several countries. Major competitors included Textron, TRW, Eaton, and such regional companies as Raymond, Gesipa, Huck, and Fukui. Black & Decker was the global leader in commercial blind riveting and automotive stud welding systems, and its other fastening system categories held strong positions in various geographic regions. Black & Decker management intended to maintain its leadership in the automotive stud welding category with new product innovations. More than 30 percent of the unit's 1999 sales were accounted for by products introduced within the past five years. Black & Decker intended to improve the performance of the division through implementation of its six sigma quality initiative, reengineered operations, and plant rationalizations.

Black & Decker's Future Prospects

The year 2000 marked the beginning of Black & Decker's second year of operations with its streamlined portfolio of businesses following the 1998 divestiture of its small-appliance, True Temper recreational products, and Emhart glass-forming machinery businesses. Black & Decker had sold the three businesses for more than management's expected $500 million and was able to reduce operating expenses by more than $100 million annually, primarily as a result of the elimination of 3,000 jobs from its payroll. In addition, the series of divestitures had cut the company's amortization of goodwill associated with the Emhart acquisition by about $30 million annually for the next 30 years.

This last round of divestitures, coupled with the sale of businesses in earlier years, completed the divestiture of the nonstrategic Emhart assets gained in the 1989 acquisition. Price Pfister and Kwikset were two of the Emhart businesses that initially captured the attention of Black & Decker management and were now among the three remaining Emhart businesses still included in Black & Decker's portfolio. So far, the 1998 divestitures had not produced steady increases in the company's stock price, but Nolan Archibald was confident that the company's ability to focus solely on power tools and other closely aligned businesses would allow the company to begin to provide its shareholders with above-average returns.

Campbell Soup Company in 2000

John E. Gamble
University of South Alabama

Arthur A. Thompson, Jr.
University of Alabama

As the new millennium began, Campbell Soup's CEO, Dale Morrison, was wrestling with how to get the company's underperforming business portfolio back on track and satisfy shareholder expectations of a steadily rising stock price. Morrison was the third CEO in recent years to struggle to develop a diversification strategy for Campbell that could produce attractive growth in revenues and profits. Under two prior CEOs, George McGovern and David Johnson, Campbell's business portfolio had been revamped, but the gains in performance had proved temporary and the overall results somewhat disappointing. Now the challenge to restore luster to Campbell's business lineup and build shareholder wealth rested with Dale Morrison.

Going into 2000 Campbell Soup Company was one of the world's leading manufacturers and marketers of branded consumer food products, with approximately 24,500 employees, 1999 revenues of $6.4 billion, 30 manufacturing plants in six nations, and over 2,000 products on the market. Its major brands in the United States were Campbell's flagship red-and-white label canned soups, Prego spaghetti sauces, Godiva chocolates, Pepperidge Farm baked goods, V8 vegetable juices, Swanson broths, Franco-American canned pastas, and Pace Mexican salsas. Arnott's baked goods and Home Pride sauces were the best-selling Campbell brands in various international markets.

Company Background

The company was founded in 1869 by Joseph Campbell, a fruit merchant, and Abram Anderson, an icebox maker, and was originally known for its jams and jellies. In 1891 it was incorporated as the Joseph Campbell Preserve Co. in Camden, New Jersey. John T. Dorrance, a brilliant 24-year-old chemist with a PhD from the Massachusetts

Institute of Technology, was hired by the company in 1894 and three years later developed a process for canning soup in condensed form. The new process took water out of the soup during the canning process and thus dramatically reduced production and distribution costs. Soups made with the new production process were awarded the gold medal at the 1900 Paris Exhibition and by 1905 were selling at the rate of 40,000 cases per week. John T. Dorrance purchased the company in 1900, and it was entirely owned by his family until 1954. It was reincorporated as the Campbell Soup Company in 1922.

When John Dorrance died in 1930, he left an estate of over $115 million—the nation's third largest at that time. He also left a company devoted to engineering, committed to providing good products (in recessions it would rather shave margins than cut back product quality or raise price), and obsessed with secrecy. His successor, John T. Dorrance Jr., headed the company for the next 24 years (1930–54) and few, if any, important decisions were made at Campbell without his approval. In 1954, the company went public, with the Dorrance family retaining majority control. In 1999, the Dorrance family still owned about 50 percent of Campbell's stock and, despite having relinquished direct management control, still exerted considerable shareholder influence. Four of Campbell Soup's 16 board members were grandchildren of John T. Dorrance Sr.

Over the years Campbell had diversified into a number of businesses—Swanson frozen dinners, Pepperidge Farm bakery products, Vlasic pickles, Franco-American spaghetti products, Recipe pet food, various fast-food restaurant chains, Godiva chocolates, and even retail garden centers. However, canned soup had always remained Campbell's core business. The company had had three chief executive officers over the last 20 years, and its corporate strategy had evolved with each change in leadership. The company's diversification strategy and new investment priorities had shifted as each new CEO pursued a course to build value for Campbell Soup Company's shareholders.

The Gordon McGovern Era: 1980–89

Gordon McGovern was in business school when Margaret Rudkin, founder of Pepperidge Farm, spoke to his class. She told how she had built her bread company from scratch in an industry dominated by giants. McGovern was impressed. He wrote to Rudkin for a job, received it in 1956, and began his climb through Pepperidge Farm's ranks. When Campbell acquired Pepperidge Farm in 1961, it had sales of $40 million and had only reached $60 million when McGovern became Pepperidge Farm's president in 1968. When McGovern was named president of Campbell in 1980, Pepperidge Farm's annual sales had grown to $300 million under his leadership. McGovern implemented several key elements of Pepperidge Farm's strategy when he took over at Campbell: creativity and a willingness to experiment, emphasis on new product development, and building strong competencies in marketing.

McGOVERN'S CORPORATE STRATEGY AS CAMPBELL'S CEO

During the McGovern years, Campbell's strategic focus was on the consumer. The consumer's "hot buttons" were identified as nutrition, convenience, low sodium, attractive price, good quality, and unique products—and managers were urged to press those buttons. Business unit managers were expected to be responsive to consumer perceptions, needs, and demands regarding nutrition, safety, flavor, and convenience. Key business unit strategies included (1) improving operating efficiency, (2) developing new products to capitalize on consumer trends, (3) updating advertising for new and established products, and (4) continuing Campbell's long-standing emphasis on high production standards and premium-quality products.

Early in his tenure, McGovern developed a five-year plan that featured four financial performance objectives: a 15 percent annual increase in earnings, a 5 percent increase in volume, a 5 percent increase in sales (plus inflation), and an 18 percent return on equity by 1986. The two cornerstones of McGovern's growth strategy were (1) developing and introducing new products and (2) making acquisitions every two years that would bring in $200 million in annual sales. Campbell's acquisition strategy was to look for small, fast-growing food companies strong in product areas where Campbell had no presence and companies on the fast track that were in rapidly growing product categories or industries. Under McGovern, Campbell made a number of acquisitions:

1982

- Mrs. Paul's Kitchens, Inc., a processor and marketer of frozen prepared seafood and vegetable products, with annual sales of approximately $125 million (acquired at a cost of $55 million).
- Snow King Frozen Foods, Inc., engaged in the production and marketing of a line of uncooked frozen specialty meat products, with annual sales of $32 million.
- Juice Bowl Products, Inc., a Florida producer of fruit juices.
- Win Schuler Foods, Inc., a Michigan-based producer and distributor of specialty cheese spreads, flavored melba rounds, food service salad dressings, party dips, and sauces, with annual sales of $6.5 million.
- Costa Apple Products, Inc., a producer of apple juice retailed primarily in the eastern United States, with annual sales of $6 million.

1983

- Several small domestic operations, at a cost of $26 million, including:
  —Annabelle's restaurant chain of 12 units in the southeastern United States.
  —Triangle Manufacturing Corp., a manufacturer of physical fitness and sports medicine products.

1984

- Mendelson-Zeller Co., Inc., a California distributor of fresh produce.

1985

- Continental Foods Company SA and affiliated companies, which produced sauces, confectioneries, and other food products in Belgium and France; the cost of the acquisition was $17 million.
- A 20 percent ownership interest in Arnott's Ltd., an Australian producer of cookies and crackers.

1988

- Freshbake Foods Group, a British producer of baked goods.

CAMPBELL'S BUSINESS PORTFOLIO UNDER McGOVERN

During the McGovern era, Campbell Soup Company was organized into six business units—Campbell U.S., Pepperidge Farm, Vlasic Foods, Mrs. Paul's Kitchens, Other United States, and International. Sales and profit performance by division are shown in Exhibit 1.

EXHIBIT 1   Performance of Campbell's Divisions under Gordon McGovern, 1980–89 ($ millions)

Source: Campbell's annual reports.

	1989	1988	1987	1986	1985	1984	1983	1982	1981	1980
Campbell U.S.										
Sales	$2,776	$2,584	$2,445	$2,507	$2,500	$2,282	$1,987	$1,773	$1,678	$1,608
Operating earnings	175	272	284	302	292	278	250	211	190	205
Pepperidge Farm										
Sales	548	495	459	420	426	435	433	392	329	283
Operating earnings	54	58	54	46	39	35	43	41	35	29
Vlasic Foods										
Sales	441	353	283	263	199	193	168	149	137	130
Operating earnings	39	30	22	24	16	14	13	12	10	8
Mrs. Paul's Kitchens										
Sales	140	150	153	141	138	126	108	—	—	—
Operating earnings	0.4	(4)	10	8	11	14	10	—	—	—
Other United States*										
Sales	—	—	59	76	81	84	64	56	27	35
Operating earnings	—	—	(2)	(7)	(3)	(2)	(1)	(1)	(1)	1
International										
Sales	1,527	1,037	898	766	716	624	599	643	694	512
Operating earnings	($ 81)	$ 58	$ 69	($ 61)	$ 35	$ 34	$ 33	$ 46	$ 46	$ 33

*Division eliminated in 1988 and replaced with a new division named Campbell Enterprises.

The Campbell U.S. Business Unit

In 1989 the Campbell U.S. division was the company's largest operating unit, accounting for just over 50 percent of corporate revenues. The Campbell U.S. division was divided into eight profit centers: soup, frozen foods, grocery, beverage, food service, poultry, fresh produce, and pet foods. Exhibit 2 shows the brands Campbell had in this division and the major competitors each brand faced during most of the 1980s.

The soup business group alone accounted for more than 25 percent of the company's consolidated sales (as compared to around 50 percent in the 1970s). Campbell's flagship brands of soup accounted for 80 percent of the $1 billion–plus annual canned soup market; in 1989, Campbell offered grocery shoppers over 50 varieties of canned soups. Heinz was the second largest soup producer, with 10 percent of the market. Heinz had earlier withdrawn from producing Heinz-label soups and shifted its production over to making soups for sale under the private labels of grocery chains; Heinz was the leading private-label producer of canned soup, holding almost an 80 percent share of the private-label segment.

Although the soup business was relatively mature (McGovern preferred to call it underworked), Campbell's most ambitious consumer research took place in this unit. McGovern opted to grow Campbell's soup sales by turning out a steady flow of new varieties in convenient packages: "Ethnic, dried, refrigerated, frozen, microwave—you name it, we're going to try it."[1] In 1985, Campbell entered the

---

[1]As quoted in *Business Week*, December 24, 1984, p. 67.

EXHIBIT 2   The Campbell U.S. Division: Products, Rival Brands, and Competitors as of 1985

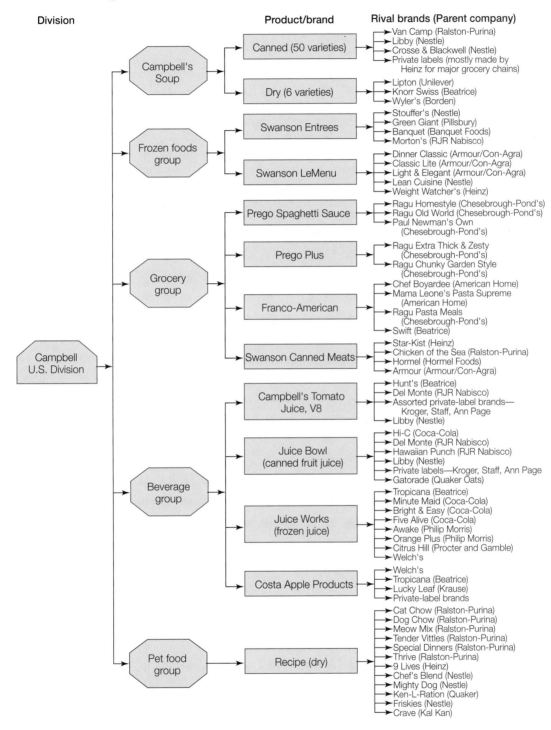

$290 million dry-soup-mix market dominated by Thomas J. Lipton Inc., a business unit of Unilever. Dry-soup sales in the United States were growing faster than sales of canned soup. Lipton's aggressive response to test marketing of an early Campbell dry-soup product resulted in Campbell's rushing a six-flavor line into national distribution ahead of schedule.

In 1982 McGovern caused a stir when he announced publicly that Campbell's Swanson TV-dinner line was "junk food": "It was great in 1950, but in today's world it didn't go into the microwave; it didn't represent any variety or a good eating experience to my palate."[2] Over the past five years, Swanson's sales volume had slipped 16 percent. He maintained that consumers had discovered better-quality options to the TV-dinner concept. Campbell's frozen foods group answered the challenge by creating a new frozen gourmet line, LeMenu. Campbell committed about $50 million in manufacturing, marketing, and trade promotion costs when initial market tests of the LeMenu line proved encouraging.

LeMenu products—packaged on round heatable plates and featuring such selections as chicken cordon bleu, al dente vegetables, and sophisticated wine sauces—produced 21 percent growth in the frozen meal unit, with sales of $150 million during its first year of national distribution (1984), double Campbell's sales projection. In addition, the Swanson line of TV dinners was overhauled to put in less salt and more meat stock in gravies, add new desserts and sauces, and create new packaging and a redesigned logo.

The grocery business unit's star was Prego spaghetti sauce. By 1984 the Prego brand had captured 25 percent of the still-growing spaghetti sauce market, becoming the number two sauce, behind Ragu. A Prego Plus spaghetti sauce line was introduced in 1985.

Pepperidge Farm

Pepperidge Farm was Campbell's third largest division in 1989, with 10 percent of the company's consolidated sales. Although the division was one of Campbell's best performers during the late 1970s (with sales rising at an average compound rate of 14 percent), by the mid-1980s growth had slowed and a number of newly introduced products had produced disappointing results (Star Wars cookies, Vegetables in Pastry). To remedy the division's weak performance, a number of steps were taken:

- The Costa Apple Products unit, acquired in 1982, was transferred to the Campbell U.S. beverage group.
- Pepperidge Farm divested itself of operations that no longer fit into its strategic plan, including Lexington Gardens, Inc., a garden center chain.
- Deli's Vegetables in Pastry went back into research and development to improve quality.
- A new management team was put in place and a comprehensive review of each product was initiated.

Exhibit 3 shows Pepperidge Farm's product portfolio during the 1980s.

Vlasic Foods

Vlasic, Campbell's fourth largest division, was the leading producer and marketer of pickles and relishes in the United States, with a 31 percent market share. During the 1982–84 period, Vlasic also had responsibility for Win Schuler Foods, a Michigan-based maker of cheese spreads, melba rounds, party dips, sauces, and salad dressings. Win Schuler was purchased in 1982, and its products were marketed in several

[2]Ibid.

EXHIBIT 3   The Pepperidge Farm Division: Products, Rival Brands, and Competitors in 1985

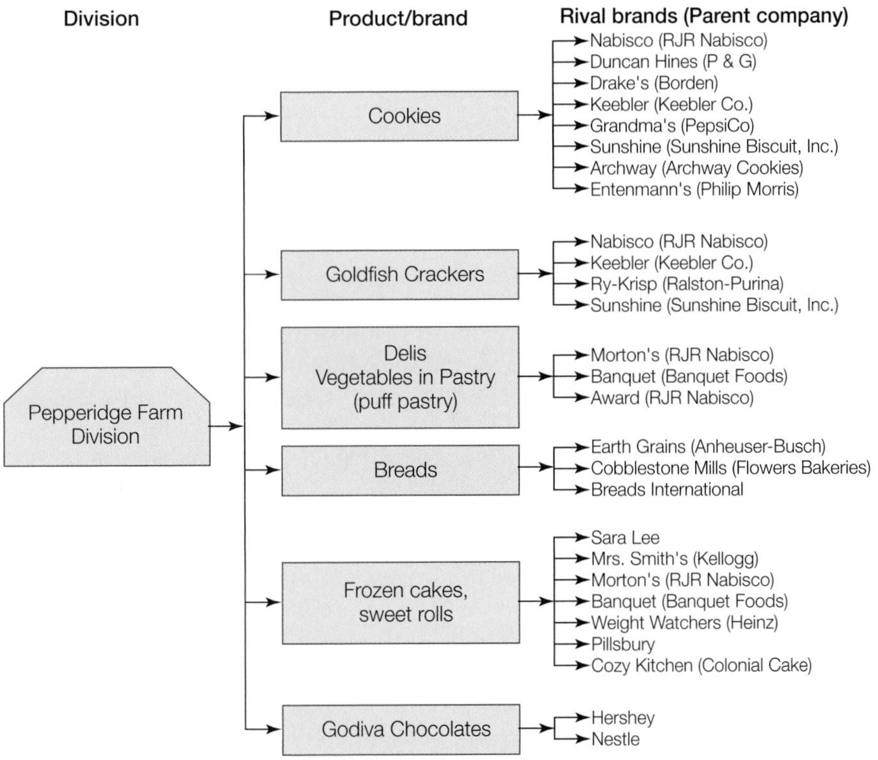

states in the upper Midwest. When sales of the Win Schuler unit flattened in 1984, partly due to a sagging Midwest economy, McGovern transferred the unit to the refrigerated foods group in the Campbell U.S. business division.

In 1985 Vlasic implemented new labels that used color bands and a new flavor scale to help consumers find their favorite tastes quickly on the supermarket shelf. Following up on marketing research indicating consumer desires for new and interesting flavors, Vlasic had introduced Zesty Dills and Bread and Butter Whole Pickle lines in 1985. Heinz was Campbell's leading national competitor in this area, but there were a number of important regional and private-label brands that competed with Heinz and Vlasic for shelf space.

Mrs. Paul's Kitchens

The Mrs. Paul's business unit produced frozen fish entrees, frozen breaded vegetables, and frozen chicken nuggets. When Campbell acquired Mrs. Paul's in 1982, it was rumored that Heinz and Pillsbury, among others, were considering the same acquisition. In 1983, the Mrs. Paul's division responded to consumer preferences for convenience seafood products that were nutritious, low in calories, microwavable, and lightly coated by introducing Light & Natural Fish Fillets. Quality improvements were also made in existing products, and a promising new product line, Light Seafood Entrees, was introduced in 1984. Market share increased about 25 percent over 1983, and Light Seafood Entrees went national in 1985. This line, which featured seven varieties of low-calorie microwavable seafood dishes, accounted for 11 percent of 1985's volume. However, sales of the company's established product lines of breaded seafood items eroded in the years following acquisition because these items had to be fried in cooking oil prior to serving. Revenues had dropped in both 1988 and 1989, and the division was barely profitable in 1989 (see again Exhibit 1).

Campbell's Other United States Business Unit

Grouped into the Other United States business division were Triangle Manufacturing Corporation, a health-and-fitness products manufacturer; Campbell Hospitality, a restaurant unit that operated 59 Pietro's restaurants, 15 Annabelle's restaurants, and 6 H. T. McDoogal's restaurants; and Snow King Frozen Foods, Inc., a manufacturer of frozen specialty meat products. Triangle's best-known product line was The Band wrist and ankle weights, which had the number two position in its market category, with a market share of 14 percent. Triangle was trying to build on its strength by entering the exercise equipment market and by selling its products internationally. The Campbell Hospitality division struggled through most of the 1980s to sustain sales and earnings growth. Snow King was also a weak performer. In 1988, this division was reorganized and renamed Campbell Enterprises; it included Triangle Manufacturing; Godiva International; V8 and Campbell Juices; Campbell Food Services; Snow King Frozen Foods; and Pietro's, Annabelle's, and H. T. McDoogal's restaurant chains. All three restaurant chains were divested in 1989.

Campbell's International Business Unit

The International business unit was Campbell's second largest division throughout the 1980s and accounted for about one-fifth of corporate revenues in 1989. Campbell International had subsidiaries in about 12 foreign countries as of 1989 and had plans to expand further. The division was reorganized in 1985 to build a more solid base for sales and earnings growth. McGovern's goal was for the International division to contribute 25 percent of Campbell's corporate sales and earnings. His strategy was to develop and strengthen Campbell's presence in international markets and to make Campbell a premier international company.

A number of acquisitions were completed in 1989 to strengthen Campbell's international competitive position. The Habitant soup and pickle brands, the Laura Secord brand of jams, and a refrigerated distribution company were all acquired by Campbell's Canadian subsidiary. In Europe, Campbell acquired a German specialty food importer and an Italian producer of institutional foods. Also during 1989, the company increased its ownership in Australia's leading cookie company, Arnott's Ltd., to 32 percent; acquired 50 percent ownership in an Australian juice manufacturer; and obtained complete ownership of Melbourne Mushrooms. The International division's three biggest profit contributors in 1989 were Campbell Soup Canada, the European food and confectionery group, and the operations in Australia.

Even though the company had a number of successes internationally, Campbell management had encountered some difficulties. Campbell's Italian business suffered losses during 1989 as a result of excessive costs brought on by an aggressive and poorly controlled attempt to build market share. Campbell was also having difficulty with making its recently acquired Freshbake Foods unit profitable. The UK food processing company was struggling to absorb a number of acquisitions it had made prior to its acquisition by Campbell in 1988. Campbell management found it necessary to institute an extensive restructuring process at Freshbake, including closing a number of plants.

McGOVERN'S APPROACH TO MANAGING CAMPBELL'S BUSINESS PORTFOLIO

Every Saturday morning McGovern did his family's grocery shopping, stopping to straighten Campbell's displays and inspect those of competitors, studying packages and reading labels, and trying to learn all he could about how and what people were eating. He encouraged his managers to do the same. Several board meetings were held in the backrooms of supermarkets so that afterward directors could roam the store aisles interviewing customers about Campbell products.

McGovern decentralized Campbell management to facilitate entrepreneurial risk taking and new product development, devising a new compensation program to reward these traits. He restructured the company into some 50 autonomous units, each with the leeway to develop new products even if the new product ideas were closely related to another business unit's products. Thus, the Prego spaghetti sauce unit—not the frozen food group—initiated frozen Mexican dinners. And although it wasn't his job, the director of market research created Today's Taste, a line of refrigerated entrees and side dishes. "It's like things are in constant motion," the director said. "We are overloaded but it's fun."[3]

McGovern believed the new structure encouraged managers of business units, who had to compete for corporate funding, to be more creative and venturesome in developing promising products:

> These business divisions allow the company to really get its arms around chunks of the business. The managers are answerable to the bottom line—to their investments, their hiring, their products—and it's a great motivation for performance.[4]

As part of this motivation, Campbell began annually allotting around $30 to $40 million to support new ventures and the creation of new product families; it often took $10 million to develop and test new products. In addition, it took $10 to $15 million in advertising and couponing to launch a new brand. McGovern believed a special new product venture fund was needed to encourage managers to think big in terms of new product development. He emphasized that it was no disgrace to fail if the effort was a good one. High failure rates were common in the industry—only about 20 percent of new products lasted more than one year on the market—but Campbell's failure rate on new product introductions was running even higher. In fact, during the 1980s, only about one out of eight new Campbell products reaching the market was successful.

Every Friday morning McGovern held meetings to discuss new products. The fact-finding sessions were attended by financial, marketing, engineering, and sales personnel. Typical McGovern questions included: "Would you eat something like that?" "Why not?" "Have you tried the competition's product?" "Is there a consumer niche?"[5]

McGOVERN'S NEW PRODUCT DEVELOPMENT AND MARKETING STRATEGIES

McGovern instituted a number of internal changes to make Campbell's product development strategy produce the desired results. Much revolved around efforts to enhance the sophistication of Campbell's corporate marketing strategies and approach to marketing research. Under McGovern, Campbell's market research unearthed several findings and projections that drove the company's product development effort:

- Women comprised 43 percent of the workforce (with a level of 50 percent projected by 1990).
- Two-income marriages represented 60 percent of all U.S. families and accounted for 60 percent of total family income.

[3]As quoted in *The Wall Street Journal,* September 17, 1984, p. A10.

[4]*Advertising Age,* January 3, 1983, p. 38.

[5]*The Wall Street Journal,* September 17, 1984, p. A10.

- Upper-income households would grow 3.5 times faster than the total household formations.
- More than half of all households consisted of only one or two members; 23 percent of all households contained only one person.
- More and more consumers were exhibiting a growing preference for refrigerated and fresh produce over canned and frozen products.
- The percentage of meals eaten at home was declining.
- Nearly half of the adult meal planners in the United States were watching their weight.
- Poultry consumption had increased 26 percent since 1973.
- Ethnic food preparation at home was increasing, with 40 percent, 21 percent, and 14 percent of households preparing Italian, Mexican, and Oriental foods, respectively, at home from scratch.
- There was a growing consumer concern with food avoidance: sugar, salt, calories, chemicals, cholesterol, and additives.
- The "I am what I eat" philosophy had tied food into lifestyles that embraced exercise machines, hot tubs, jogging, racquetball, backpacking, cross-country skiing, and aerobic dancing.

In response to growing ethnic food demand, Campbell began marketing ethnic selections in regions where consumer interests for particular food types were strong. For instance, it marketed spicy Ranchero Beans only in the South and Southwest, and its newly acquired Puerto Rican foods only in New York City and Florida (which had sizable Puerto Rican populations).

Campbell's product-development guidelines emphasized convenience, taste, flavor, and texture. The strategic themes McGovern stressed were these:

- Concentrate on products that represent superior value to consumers and constantly strive to improve those values.
- Develop products that help build markets.
- Develop products that yield a fair profit to Campbell.

In pursuing these guidelines, Campbell adopted several operating practices:

- Using ongoing consumer research to determine eating habits. It included checking home menus, recipes, and food preparation techniques to learn which food items were served together.
- Studying meal and snack occasions to learn which household members participated so that preliminary estimates of volume potential could be made for possible new products and product improvement ideas.
- Testing new or improved products in a large enough number of households across the United States that reliable national sales projections could be made. Once a product met pretest standards, testing in a sample of supermarkets and sales outlets was conducted.
- Rolling out the new products on a regional or national plan and using test-market data to establish the sequence in which area markets should be entered.

By 1983 McGovern's strategy had turned Campbell into the biggest generator of new products in the combined food and health-and-beauty aids categories, with a total of 42 new products. Prego spaghetti sauce, LeMenu frozen dinners, Great Starts breakfasts, and Chunky New England Clam Chowder were among the leading products introduced by Campbell Soup during the early 1980s. Meanwhile Campbell's marketing budget grew from $275 million in 1982, to $488 million in 1985, and to $552 million in 1989. Ad expenditures jumped from $67 million in 1980 to $197 million in 1989. Prior to McGovern, Campbell often trimmed ad spending at the end of a quarter to boost earnings.

In 1982 McGovern was named *Advertising Age*'s Adman of the Year for his efforts in transforming Campbell into "one of the most aggressive market-driven companies in the food industry today."[6] *Advertising Age* cited the company's emphasis on nutrition and fitness as opposed to the former "mmm, mmm, good" emphasis on taste. Print ads featured government studies concerning soup's nutritional values and a new slogan, "Soup is good food."

PRODUCTION, QUALITY, AND COST CONSIDERATIONS DURING THE McGOVERN ERA

Gordon McGovern also stressed the importance of high production quality; a 1984 article in *Savvy* quoted him as saying, "I want zero defects. If we can't produce quality, we'll get out of the business." That same year, Campbell held its first Worldwide Corporate conference dedicated to quality. Hundreds of Campbell managers from all levels and most company locations spent three days at this conference. Management believed that the ultimate test of quality was consumer satisfaction, and the company's goal was to instill a strong quality consciousness among employees in every single operation throughout the company.

Before McGovern took over, Campbell used to adjust the design of new products so that they could be produced with existing equipment and plant facilities. For example, a square omelet was specified for Swanson's breakfasts because it was what the installed machine would make. After McGovern's appointment, although low-cost production was still a strategic factor, market considerations and consumer trends—not existing machinery and production capabilities—were deciding factors in production, packaging, and labeling. Still, the company spent between $150 million and $300 million annually throughout the 1980s for improved equipment, new plants and plant expansions, better packaging technology, and distribution facilities.

Campbell executives believed the company's key strengths during the 1985–89 period were (1) a worldwide system for obtaining ingredients; (2) a broad range of food products that could be used as a launching pad for formulating, producing, and marketing new products; and (3) an emphasis on low-cost production.

CAMPBELL'S PERFORMANCE UNDER GORDON McGOVERN

McGovern's campaign for renewed growth via new product introduction and acquisition produced good results early on. By year-end 1984 sales were up 31 percent—to $3.7 billion—and earnings had risen by 47 percent—to $191 million. During McGovern's 10-year reign as CEO, Campbell introduced 922 new items—more than any other food-processing company. By the late 1980s however, there were signs that Campbell's brand managers had become so involved in new product development that they had neglected the old stand-by products as well as slighting cost-control and profit margin targets. According to one Campbell executive:

> We became fat cats. We said, "We can't fail." We began to throw things against the marketplace that had long paybacks and were in processes, packaging, and distribution that we didn't understand.[7]

---

[6]*Advertising Age,* January 3, 1983, p. 38.

[7]As quoted in *Financial World,* June 11, 1991, p. 53.

Campbell's growth in operating earnings for fiscal years 1985–89 fell short of McGovern's 15 percent target rate, and McGovern in 1989 initiated several internal restructuring moves to eliminate many of the inefficiencies and cost excesses that had crept into the company's operations and new product development efforts. A summary of Campbell Soup's financial performance between 1989 and 1999 is presented in Exhibit 4.

McGovern's Resignation and the Recruitment of a Replacement

Beginning in the late 1980s, the heirs of John T. Dorrance began to show frustration with Campbell Soup's industry-lagging performance and began to openly criticize McGovern's approach to running the company. Quaker Oats management believed that the Dorrance family might be interested in a merger between the two companies and approached Campbell's chairman of the board, Robert Vlasic, in March 1989 to explore the issue. The Dorrance heirs were split on the prospect of a merger, with one faction publicly announcing its intent to sell its shares and another vying to block a merger at all costs. The heirs supporting Campbell Soup's independence successfully prevented a merger but were unable to bring prompt reconciliation among the family.

Disenchanted with the family squabble and stung by outspoken criticism of his performance by family members, Gordon McGovern resigned as CEO and took early retirement in November 1989. Campbell's search for a replacement, spearheaded by Ippy Dorrance and Robert Vlasic, quickly focused on Gerber's CEO, David Johnson, as the best candidate to replace McGovern. A native of Australia, David Johnson had a bachelor's degree in economics from the University of Sydney and an MBA from the University of Chicago. Starting out as a management trainee with the international division of Colgate-Palmolive in Australia, he moved up through the ranks to become managing director of Colgate's South African operations in 1967. In 1973, he moved to Hong Kong as president of Warner-Lambert/Parke Davis Asia; there, exposed to the Orient's fundamentally different customs and approaches, he came to appreciate that if managers were creative enough to look beyond accepted solutions to business problems, it was easy to find innovative answers. Looking back on his Hong Kong experiences, Johnson observed that he gained "an elasticized mind, opened to a greater run of possibilities than I'd ever known before."[8] Warner-Lambert brought Johnson to the United States in 1976 as president of its personal products division; a year later, he was promoted to president of the company's American Chicle division. When Warner-Lambert acquired Entenmann's in 1979, Johnson took over as head; he then moved to General Foods when GF acquired Entenmann's from Warner-Lambert in 1982. As Entenmann's chief executive from 1979 to 1987, he engineered the company's drive from a regional to a national provider of bakery products, more than quadrupling sales and profits. In 1987, Johnson left Entenmann's to become CEO of Gerber Products, a company whose performance had been lackluster for several years. He proceeded to craft a turnaround strategy for Gerber that involved divesting seven business divisions (toys, furniture, trucking) and refocusing Gerber's attention on its core baby-foods business. By 1990, 27 months after Johnson became CEO, Gerber's sales were up 30 percent, profits were up 50 percent, and the stock price had tripled. With the Dorrance family's blessing, Campbell lured Johnson away from Gerber as McGovern's successor.

[8]Jeffrey Zygmont, "In Command at Campbell," *Sky Magazine*, March 1993, p. 60.

EXHIBIT 4   Financial Summary, Campbell Soup Company, 1989–99 (in millions, except per share amounts)

Source: Campbell annual reports.

	1999	1998	1997	1996	1995	1994	1993	1992	1991	1990	1989
Net sales	$6,424	$6,696	$7,964	$7,678	$7,250	$6,664	$6,577	$6,263	$6,204	$6,205	$5,672
Earnings before taxes	1,097	1,073	1,107	1,179	1,042	963	520	779	667	179	107
Earnings before cumulative effect of accounting change	1,097	1,062	713	802	698	630	257	491	402	4	13
Net earnings	724	660	713	802	698	630	8	491	402	4	13
Taxes on earnings	373	384	394	395	344	333	263	309	266	175	93
Interest—net	173	175	165	126	115	64	74	87	90	94	56
Earnings per share	1.63	1.46	1.51	1.61	1.40	1.26	0.02	0.97	0.79	0.01	0.03
Dividends per share	0.89	0.82	0.75	0.67	0.61	0.55	0.46	0.36	0.28	0.25	0.23
Wgt. avg. shares outstanding	445	460	472	498	498	501	504	504	508	518	518
Capital expenditures	297	256	331	416	391	421	371	362	371	397	302
Depreciation and amortization	255	261	328	326	294	255	242	216	209	201	192
Assets	5,522	5,633	6,459	6,632	6,315	4,992	4,897	4,353	4,149	4,115	3,932
Stockholders' equity	$ 235	$ 874	$1,420	$2,742	$2,468	$1,989	$1,704	$2,027	$1,793	$1,691	$1,778

The David Johnson Era: 1990–97

When David Johnson became chairman and CEO of Campbell Soup Company in January 1990, he saw his first priority as crafting a strategy for Campbell that would grow earnings and win the confidence of the Dorrance heirs. While at Gerber, Johnson viewed Campbell, a competitor of Gerber's in some product categories, as an underperforming company that was a likely target for corporate raiders, once even commenting, "Boy, that's a troubled company. I could really run that one."[9] In interviewing for the job at Campbell, Johnson determined that the arguments and differences between the Dorrance family and Campbell's prior management were more a function of "poor results" than of activist family members wanting to meddle in company affairs or the desire of some to sell out their stake and invest their inheritance elsewhere. Johnson deemed the challenge worthy for several reasons:

> It was a company that was founded on incredible strength on which you could build. I knew that it had excellent R&D. I knew it had terrific brands. It had lost its direction, lost its focus, was underperforming, and I knew that it could be refocused and reorganized within six months, and that we could really get it going very quickly.[10]

Johnson immediately embarked on a course of boosting Campbell's performance quickly, not only to pacify disgruntled shareholders but also to get the company's stock price high enough to discourage would-be acquirers from launching a takeover attempt:

> Under those circumstances, when you come in, it's not the pretties of "Here is my vision. Let me explain the principles from the book." When you move in, you've got to do it in an exciting fashion, lay down the challenge—Boom! Strike! Crash! It's short-term focus. You know that dirty word we're all accused of? "Short term." Isn't it terrible? Under those circumstances, if you don't win the first year, if you don't win in the short term, you're dead.[11]

JOHNSON'S TURNAROUND STRATEGY

To spur Campbell's managers and give them something to shoot for in rejuvenating the company's performance, Johnson set financial objectives of 20 percent earnings growth, 20 percent return on equity, and 20 percent cash return on assets: "I used to say, if perfect human vision is 20–20, then perfect business vision is 20–20–20, which was shorthand for earnings, return and cash."[12] This was followed by the establishment of four corporate-level strategic principles to guide the creation of business and functional strategies in each divisional unit:

- The primary purpose of the corporation is to *build shareholder wealth*. It is imperative to provide dividend growth and long-term stock appreciation to reward the stockholders of the corporation.

- Campbell must exploit its *brand power*. Campbell's strong brands have been the basis of the company's strength's over the past 90 years and should be the focal point for the future.

---

[9]As quoted in *Fortune*, September 9, 1991, p. 143.
[10]As quoted in *Sky Magazine*, March 1993, p. 54.
[11]As quoted in *Fortune*, December 14, 1992, p. 112.
[12]Ibid.

- Campbell's ability to sustain its brand power and build on its powerful brands is only possible through *people power.* The company's employees have to be responsible for maintaining the existing brands, for building on these brands, and for finding new markets for these brands. Campbell should encourage individual risk-bearing and teamwork with rewards linked to results.

- It is important to *preserve the company's independence.* Management needs to preserve the heritage of Campbell Soup Company and resist any outside thrust for control through delivery of superior performance on building long-term shareholder wealth.

Johnson disagreed with McGovern's view that Campbell's growth should come primarily from the acquisition of small, fast-growing food companies and from the introduction of new products that served some niche of the food industry. Instead, Johnson believed that Campbell Soup should concentrate on growing sales of its best-known brands—the red-and-white soup line, Prego, Pepperidge Farm, Vlasic, and Swanson—and to increase its U.S. market share in these product categories. During the 1980s, for example, Campbell's tonnage in canned soups had risen a paltry 1 percent annually and Campbell's market share of the U.S. soup market, according to Wall Street estimates, had slipped from a lofty 80 percent in the 1950s and 1960s to 70 percent in the mid-1980s to around 65 percent in 1990. Johnson also decided to press harder and faster than McGovern had to gain increased penetration of foreign markets.

While McGovern had pursued ways to reduce costs and eliminate inefficiencies during his 1989 restructuring, Johnson saw opportunities to achieve further economies and better profit margins, principally by eliminating unprofitable and slow-selling items from Campbell's product lineup and by divesting peripheral lines of businesses that did not complement the company's strengths or bolster the market power of its flagship brands. Consequently, the strategy Johnson crafted to boost Campbell's performance incorporated six major initiatives:

- Divesting poorly performing and nonstrategic business units and reorganizing Campbell's six divisions.
- Eliminating weak items from the company's product lineup.
- Requiring that new product introductions exploit Campbell Soup's strengths, core competencies, and organizational capabilities as well as have the potential to achieve the three 20–20–20 financial performance targets.
- Focusing on the global marketing of the company's competencies and capabilities.
- Installing and expanding low-cost business systems at the corporate level to support the operations of the business divisions.
- Improving utilization of assets to maximize the return to stockholders.

Exhibit 5 shows the business lines that were divested—Johnson saw all of them as either nonstrategic and unrelated to Campbell's core competencies or as chronic money losers or low-return businesses. This pruning of Campbell's portfolio resulted in the sale of 8 plants and the shutdown of 12 plants worldwide plus a workforce reduction of 8,000 people during Johnson's first 18 months as CEO. As the remaining plants bid to absorb the production of the closed plants, overall capacity utilization rose from 60 to 80 percent; Campbell's Maxton, North Carolina, plant was able to increase its output 50 percent and become Campbell's first canned-soup plant to drive manufacturing costs below 50 percent of the retail price of its products. Included among the initial plant closings was the company's 131-year-old Camden, New Jersey, plant with its distinctive water towers painted to look like giant Campbell Soup cans.

EXHIBIT 5   Divested Campbell Soup Company Businesses, 1990–96

Source: Campbell annual reports and 10-Ks.

- Fried chicken plant in Sumpter, South Carolina
- Salmon Farms
- Snow King Frozen Foods—frozen meat products
- Triangle Manufacturing Corporation—a health-and-fitness products manufacturer
- Mushroom farms
- Mendelson-Zeller, Inc.
- Recipe Pet Food
- D. Lazzaroni Cookie Company (Italy)
- Win Schuler Foods, Inc.
- Juice Bowl
- Juice Works
- The fresh produce and frozen vegetable portions of the UK Freshbake Foods Group—the frozen entree portion of Freshbake was retained.
- Campbell Chilled Foods, Ltd. (United Kingdom)
- Mrs. Paul's frozen seafood
- Poultry processing operations
- Marie's salad dressings
- Beeck-Feinkost GmbH chilled foods (Germany)
- Beef farms in Argentina
- Durkee and Early California olives
- Groko BV frozen vegetable processing (Holland)

Johnson's restructuring continued throughout his tenure, with major initiatives approved by the board in 1993 and 1996. The 1993 restructuring program identified six plants and 14 businesses that were to be sold. In 1996 the board approved an additional restructuring that eliminated not only additional plants and businesses but also 2,100 administrative and operational positions at various Campbell Soup facilities. Both restructuring programs were intended to shift production from underutilized or inefficient production facilities to more cost-effective locations and eliminate nonstrategic poor-performing businesses from the portfolio. Under Johnson, Campbell Soup went on to divest a total of 26 businesses that had an average net profit margin of 1 percent. Campbell Soup also closed a total of 10 older and inefficient plants between 1990 and 1997 to boost capacity utilization.

Once Johnson assessed that the turnaround was well under way, he complemented the divestitures with 20 acquisitions of higher-margin business with ample growth potential to complete the portfolio restructuring initiative. In 1996 David Johnson commented on the strategy of moving Campbell from a position of "best in class" to "best in show," the contribution of the newly acquired businesses, and the company's prospects for growth:

> We begin this new attack from a position of great strength. Our balance sheet and cash flow are strong. Since 1990, we have divested non-strategic and low-margin businesses with approximately $800 million in sales and acquired strategic, higher-margin businesses with more than $1.2 billion in sales, including Mexican sauce leader Pace Foods. Our management team has transformed Campbell into a place where results count and where the bar is constantly raised . . . We are poised for breaking away from our competitors in the food industry. This strategic growth plan

EXHIBIT 6   Businesses Acquired by Campbell Soup, 1994–97

1994 (acquisitions totaled $14 million)

- Dandy mushrooms (Australia)
- Fray Bentos canned meats (Australia)

1995 (acquisitions totaled $1.26 billion)

- Pace Foods—the leading salsa brand in the United States, with annual sales of $700 million. The company was purchased for $1.12 billion.
- Increase in share ownership of Arnott's Ltd. to 65 percent.
- Fresh Start Bakeries—maker of buns and English muffins for quick-service restaurants in the United States, Europe, and South America. At the time of the acquisition, the company had approximate annual sales of $75 million, 480 employees, and had been a supplier to McDonald's for more than 30 years. The business was integrated into Campbell's Food Service unit.
- Stratford-upon-Avon Foods—a food-service company operating in the United Kingdom with annual sales of $60 million. The business manufactured, marketed, and distributed canned baked beans, vegetable and fruit products, and branded and private-label pickles.
- Greenfield Healthy Foods—U.S. manufacturer of all-natural, low-fat cakes and cookies. The company provided Pepperidge Farm with new resources to enter the $800 million healthy-snack category.
- Homepride sauces—the best-selling cooking sauce in the United Kingdom. The business, purchased for an estimated $93 million, allowed Campbell to build gravy and sauce sales in the United Kingdom.

1996 (acquisitions totaled $186 million)

- Joint venture began between Arnott's Ltd. and Helios Foods, one of Indonesia's most prominent food companies—thereby providing Arnott's with biscuit manufacturing capability in Asia.
- Joint venture began in Malaysia with Cheong Chan that provided manufacturing facilities for canned soups, ketchup, and soy sauces in Southeast Asia. Campbell Soup also acquired a minority interest in Cheong Chan.
- Joint venture between Godiva and J. Osawa Ltd. to immediately open 33 retail stores and outlets for Godiva chocolates. An additional 20 stores were planned to open by the year 2000.
- Increase in share ownership of Arnott's Ltd. to 70 percent.

1997 (acquisitions totaled $228 million)

- Erasco Group—the leading wet-soup brand in Germany, with annual sales of $223 million and 900 employees. The business was purchased for approximately $210 million. Campbell management believed that the acquisition would accelerate the company's growth throughout Germany and the European Union.
- Kettle Chip Company—salty-snack company operating in Australia and acquired for $18 million.

---

is designed to vault our company into the ranks of the world's renowned consumer goods companies, in terms of financial profile and market multiple.[13]

Exhibit 6 presents a listing and description of business acquisitions initiated by David Johnson. By year-end 1996 the new businesses Johnson had added to Campbell's portfolio achieved an average net profit margin of 12 percent.

---

[13]As quoted in PR Newswire, September 5, 1996.

Many of Johnson's acquisitions were intended to add brands and infrastructure that were necessary for the growth of Campbell's international business. The acquisition of Pace Foods was one of the few acquisitions not specifically aimed at growing international food sales. Pace Foods, the leading U.S. producer and marketer of Mexican salsa, was Campbell's biggest acquisition ever. The $1.12 billion purchase price represented five times Pace's sales and 20 times its earnings. A number of companies, including Heinz and Lea & Perrin, had been attempting to buy Pace for a number of years, but owner Kit Goldsbury was not interested. The chief operating officer of Pace Foods stated that Goldsbury agreed to the sale to Campbell because Goldsbury could identify with and liked Campbell's management team.[14]

As a product category, salsa (a spicy blend of jalapeños, tomatoes, onion, and garlic) surpassed ketchup in 1991 as the nation's best-selling condiment. The salsa category grew at just under a 13 percent compound annual growth rate from 1988 to 1993 as sales increased from $325 million to $700 million. The rapid growth in sales of salsa products was attributed to its spicy flavor and low fat content (a jar of Pace salsa contained no fat and only 70 calories), to the excellent way it complemented such snack foods as tortilla chips, to growing consumer popularity of Mexican dishes, and to a fast-increasing Hispanic population.

JOHNSON'S REVISED NEW PRODUCT DEVELOPMENT AND MARKETING STRATEGIES

David Johnson instituted a more cautious approach to new product development and challenged Campbell marketers to become more aggressive in marketing the company's products. Johnson was quick to comment, "There's no such thing as mature markets, only tired marketers,"[15] when told that low industry growth rates were obstacles to growth. New product ideas were more heavily researched and tested before they were put on the market. Moreover, new products were expected to provide quicker paybacks on investment; potential products that held little promise for near-term profitability and for meeting the 20–20–20 financial performance standards were tabled.

The search for new product ideas was limited to areas where Campbell had production and marketing expertise; as one executive put it, "We want to be in areas we know we are good at and in processes we are good at."[16] Despite the more conservative approach to new product development, Campbell introduced nearly 300 new products during Johnson's first three years as the company's chief executive. Johnson committed between $77 million and $88 million annually to R&D during his last three years as CEO to improve existing products and to develop new products that would be successful in U.S. and international markets. New items included cream of broccoli soup (which became the first new soup since 1935 to rank in the top five best-selling soups), Joseph A. Campbell premium-quality ready-to-serve soups, cheese tortellini soup, Light 'n Tangy V8, Swanson Kids Fun Feast frozen dinners, Vlasic Sandwich Stackers, Prego pizza sauce, and more varieties of Pepperidge Farm products. Johnson suggested that the company's new approach to product development had been successful in developing products that consumers desired and had allowed the company to achieve sales growth in traditionally mature markets: "Innovations and breakthroughs are so simple, but they come only if you're immersed in your field and determined to make the necessary connections. For instance, take our Stackers, which are pickles sliced to lay flat on a sandwich. A simple idea, but it

---

[14]*The Wall Street Journal,* November 29, 1994, p. A3.

[15]As quoted in *Chief Executive,* November 1996.

[16]As quoted in *Financial World,* June 11, 1991, p. 53.

took off: The overall Stackers market grew 55% last year. In addition, we're tapping into growing consumer segments, such as the healthy food category. For example, our new line of cream soups is 98% fat free."[17]

JOHNSON'S CORPORATE REORGANIZATION

Johnson's reorganization effort aimed at capturing strategic-fit benefits among related products and product families. Johnson concluded that McGovern's 50 autonomous units had resulted in lack of communication and cooperation between the different business units. For example, the U.S. soup division once ran a promotion with Nabisco crackers even though Pepperidge Farm produced a competing product. Also, U.S. tomato paste plants did not share technology with Mexican tomato paste plants since the Mexican plants were in a different division. A three-division structure was established during Johnson's first year as Campbell CEO to improve communication and technology sharing between businesses in similar product categories and geographies (see Exhibit 7). This initial structure was modified three times over the next five years. Each shuffling of businesses within the three-division structure was directed at improving the strategic fit within the portfolio of businesses. The series of new alignments also helped Campbell Soup put more emphasis on the company's international businesses.

JOHNSON'S INTERNATIONAL PUSH

Johnson was convinced that a sizable fraction of Campbell Soup's growth should come from international expansion because the world market for processed food products was projected to grow over twice as fast as the 1 percent growth rate projected for the $200 billion U.S. food-processing industry. By 2000, Johnson wanted at least one-third of Campbell's revenues to come from outside of the United States. Johnson saw such companies as Coca-Cola and Gillette, whose international operations contributed 70 to 80 percent of total sales, as prototypes for Campbell Soup's future:

> Clearly, we're not going to be a Coca-Cola or Gillette in two years, but we're inching toward that aim as we go into the next century . . . We're expanding in the United Kingdom, Canada, and Australia, and trying to establish more beachheads in Asia Pacific. Our acquisition of Germany's Erasco increases our total international soup sales to 21 percent of total soup sales. We bought an operation in Malaysia called Cheong Chan, where we're now making the investments that will enable us to produce soup instead of importing it. We're looking for ventures in China and growing in Taiwan.

Campbell marketed its soups in Mexico, Canada, Argentina, Poland, Hong Kong, and China, and its baked goods in Europe and Asia Pacific. In 1993 Campbell increased its 33 percent share of Australia's Arnott's Ltd. to 58 percent to gain an organizational base for increasing its long-term presence in baked goods in the Pacific Rim and Asia. Johnson increased Campbell's ownership of Arnott's further to 65 percent in 1995 and to 70 percent in 1996. To help familiarize himself with Campbell's international operations and to better gauge the company's potential for foreign expansion, Johnson had all of Campbell's top international executives report directly to him for the first 12 months he was at Campbell.

International marketing of prepared foods was not easy. Taste preferences varied significantly from country to country (and sometimes within countries), prompting international producers to employ multicountry strategies to gear product characteristics

---

[17]As quoted in *Chief Executive,* November 1996.

EXHIBIT 7 Comparison of Campbell's Business Unit Structure under Gordon McGovern and David Johnson

Source: Campbell annual reports.

Campbell's Structure under Gordon McGovern		Campbell's Structure under David Johnson		Campbell's Structure under Dale Morrison	
Division	Example Brands/Services	Division	Example Brands/Services	Division	Example Brands/Services
Campbell U.S. • Soup Group	Red-and-white, Healthy Request, Chunky	**U.S.A.** • U.S. Soup Group	Dry and canned soup, Franco-American	Soups and Sauces	All worldwide dry and canned soups, Franco American pastas, V8 Campbell's tomato juice
• Frozen Food Group / Grocery Group	Swanson, LeMenu Prego, Franco-American, Swanson canned meats	• Beverage Group / Meal Enhancement Group	V8, Campbell's tomato juice Open Pit barbecue sauce, Pace salsas, Vlasic, Prego, food service		Prego spaghetti sauces, Pace salsas Swanson broths,
• Beverage Group	Campbell's tomato juice, V8, Juice Bowl, Juice, Works	• Frozen Foods Group	Swanson		Erasco, Cheong Chan, Home Pride, Leibig, Stockpot
• Pet Food Group **Pepperidge Farm**	Recipe Pepperidge Farm breads, cookies, Godiva chocolates, Costa apple juice, Deli's frozen entrees	**Bakery and Confectionery**	Arnott's Ltd., Pepperidge Farm, Delacre, Godiva Chocolatier, Lami Lutti confections, Kettle Chips	Biscuit and Confectionery	Arnott's Ltd., Pepperidge Farm, Godiva Chocolatier, Kettle Chips
Vlasic	Pickles and relishes				
Mrs. Paul's	Frozen fish, frozen chicken, frozen vegetables				
Other U.S.	Triangle Manufacturing Corp.—fitness products Campbell Hospitality—restaurants Snow King Frozen Foods—frozen meats				
Campbell International	Soup—Canada and Mexico Fresh Bake Foods Group (Britain)—baked goods	**International Grocery** • International Soup Group	Red-and-white canned soup, Erasco, Cheong Chan, Home Pride	Away from Home	Distribution and Campbell soups, Pace salsas, and specialty kitchen entrees to food-service markets
		• International Specialty Foods	Stratford-upon-Avon, Fray Bentos, Swift		

EXHIBIT 8   Sales and Earnings of Campbell Soup Company, by Geographic Region, 1991–99 ($ millions)

Source: Campbell annual reports.

	1999	1998	1997	1996	1995	1994	1993	1992	1991
United States									
Net sales	$4,808	$4,850	$5,495	$5,332	$5,012	$4,639	$4,744	$4,649	$4,496
Earnings before taxes	1,196	1,124	1,155	1,123	957	854	715	809	695
Europe									
Net sales	630	859	1,201	1,122	1,143	1,041	1,050	1,043	1,149
Earnings before taxes	32*	36*	50	71	74	64	(170)	45	49
Other countries									
Net sales	1,054	1,044	1,408	1,347	1,179	1,011	917	652	656
Earnings before taxes	$ 121	$ 123	$ 122	$ 172	$ 171	$ 154	$ 99	$ 70	$ 55

*Earnings before interest and taxes.

to local preferences and eating habits. Campbell's 1988 acquisition of Britain's Fresh-bake Foods Group never performed up to expectations partly because Campbell management didn't cater adequately to the taste preferences of British consumers. Also, Campbell's penetration of the European soup market had proved more difficult than originally expected because the predominant forms of store-bought soups on the continent were dry soups and ready-to-serve soups; demand for Campbell's mainstay condensed soups was virtually nonexistent in Europe, and consumers had to be persuaded of the merits of switching to a different preparation technique.

Campbell management opened a Hong Kong taste kitchen as part of the company's effort to ensure that the products it introduced would appeal to Asia's 2 billion consumers, whose average per capita soup consumption averaged six bowls per week. The Hong Kong kitchen proved to be a success, having a role in creating such popular sellers as scallop, watercress, duck-gizzard, and ham soups. The kitchen was experimenting with other soup varieties made from pork, dates, figs, and snake.

Campbell had been successful in Mexico with spicy soups such as Creama de Chile Poblano and had captured 10 percent of Argentina's $50 million soup market within one year of introducing nine varieties of its red-and-white canned soup. A summary of Campbell Soup's geographic performance between 1991 and 1998 is displayed in Exhibit 8.

The Dale Morrison Era Begins: Mid-1997 to Present

When David Johnson's five-year contract expired and he elected to step aside as Campbell Soup Company's CEO in July 1997, the company announced that 48-year-old Dale Morrison would become its new chief executive officer effective July 15, 1997. Morrison joined Campbell Soup in June 1995 as president of Pepperidge Farm, where he was largely responsible for a turnaround of the business that had averaged 2 to 3 percent sales growth between 1990 and 1995. Prior to joining Campbell Soup's management, Morrison spent 14 years with PepsiCo, where he held management positions with both Frito-Lay and Pepsi-Cola. Dale Morrison also coordinated the merger of British snack foods companies while at Frito-Lay. Morrison held a number of positions with General Foods from 1972 to 1981, marketing such brands as Tang, Post cereals, and Kool-Aid.

David Johnson agreed to remain on as chairman of Campbell's board of directors through July 1999 from which he could aid Morrison in an advisory role. Johnson announced, "My priority is to ensure that we continue our relentless commitment to building shareowner wealth. I will assist Dale in exploring the strategies needed to achieve Campbell's vision of becoming the best consumer products company in the world."[18]

MORRISON'S ACCOMPLISHMENTS AT CAMPBELL SOUP PRIOR TO HIS APPOINTMENT AS CEO

When he arrived at Pepperidge Farm, Dale Morrison initiated a number of cost-cutting programs that freed up resources and gave the division enough gross margin leeway to spend additional sums on marketing and product promotion. Such products as Pepperidge Farm Goldfish crackers and Milano cookies benefited from increased advertising and marketing innovations like Goldfish milk-carton-style packaging, which was easier for children to manage than the previous paper-bag-style packaging. Morrison also made a point of visiting all Pepperidge Farm plants and met with the company's independent distributors, whom Morrison reclassified as sales development associates. Morrison's strategies resulted in a 10 percent sales increase in 1996, a 13 percent sales increase in 1997, and a 20 percent earnings increase in both years.

In recognition of his success at Pepperidge Farm, David Johnson gave Morrison added responsibilities at Campbell Soup. Morrison was appointed president of Campbell's International Specialty Foods in November 1996, putting him in charge of Campbell's international grocery, food-service, frozen and specialty foods, and bakery and confectionery businesses.

RECENT TRENDS IN THE PERFORMANCE OF CAMPBELL SOUP'S STOCK PRICE, 1990–2000

Exhibit 9 shows Campbell Soup's market performance relative to the Dow Jones Industrial Index and the Dow Jones composite of other food-processing companies since 1990. The company's stock performance mirrored that of many of its processed food competitors, which averaged a 30 percent decline in their share prices and had collectively seen over $160 billion in market value disappear during 1999. Some of Campbell Soup's share price decline after January 2000 was attributable to a number of class-action lawsuits brought against Campbell Soup that claimed the company misrepresented its revenue from its condensed soup sales between November 1997 and January 1999. The complaints alleged that, in an attempt to meet analysts' quarterly earnings estimates, the company claimed to have sold product to major distributors and resellers when in actuality Campbell never shipped the product to customers. When asked about the suits' allegations by a *Wall Street Journal* reporter, Campbell's chief financial officer retorted, "Campbell Soup does not make and has not made sham shipments of its products. We do not make and have not made false or misleading statements."[19]

MORRISON'S STRATEGY FOR CAMPBELL SOUP

Morrison's strategies to improve Campbell Soup's performance were, for the most part, a continuation and refinement of Johnson's initiatives. Morrison agreed with David Johnson that Campbell Soup should become more like Coca-Cola, with faster sales growth in international markets and a tighter focus on the core business.

[18]As quoted in *Milling & Baking News*, July 8, 1997, p. 14.

[19]As quoted in *The Wall Street Journal Interactive Edition*, February 17, 2000.

EXHIBIT 9   Campbell Soup Company's Stock Performance, 1990–March 2000

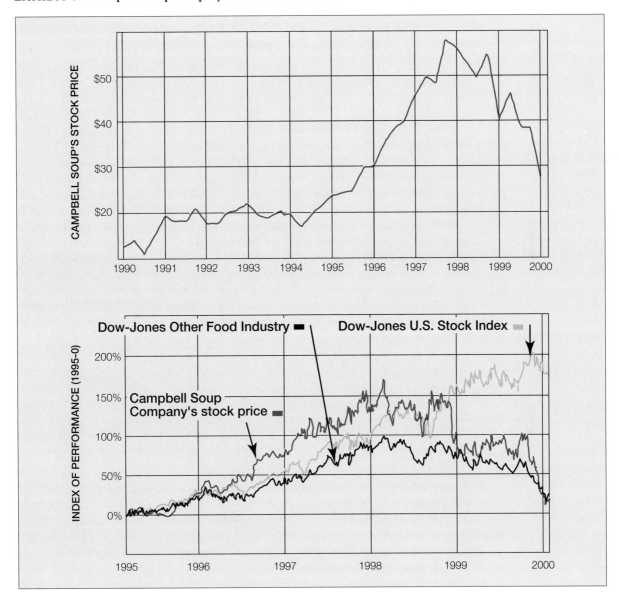

Morrison wanted to increase Campbell Soup Company's annual sales growth to 8 to 10 percent and believed that the company's greatest opportunity for rapid growth lay in focusing on its premium brands, which were differentiated from competing brands in terms of taste, perceived quality, and image. Morrison wanted growth to come more from volume increases rather than price increases and intended to allocate greater resources to advertising some of the company's more highly differentiated brands like Joseph A. Campbell premium-quality ready-to-serve soups, Pepperidge Farm Goldfish crackers, and Milano cookies. The centerpiece of Morrison's plan for boosting unit sales was to increase advertising expenditures from 3.5 percent of sales to 8 percent of sales. Morrison also launched initiatives to enhance Campbell products' differentiated image in international markets. In Japan, for example, the decision was made to upgrade the quality of its soup cans and to re-design the labels on the cans; Japanese consumers were drawn to products with high-quality packaging.

Morrison's Portfolio Restructuring Efforts

In September 1997 Dale Morrison announced the spinoff of seven low-growth businesses with combined sales of $1.4 billion—about 18 percent of Campbell Soup Company's 1997 sales. The spinoff was a carryover of strategic initiatives that David Johnson had announced in September 1996. Under the plan, Vlasic Foods International would become a stand-alone company with operations in the United States, Europe, and South America and over 9,000 employees. The new company's shares would be distributed tax-free to Campbell shareholders, and upon the completion of the spinoff the new company would be ranked 21st among 32 publicly traded food companies. Campbell's Swanson frozen food business in the United States and Canada and its frozen food lines in the United Kingdom would make up Vlasic Foods International's frozen food division. The grocery division would include Campbell's Vlasic retail and food-service products, Swift Armour meats in Argentina, Open Pit barbecue sauces, Stratford-upon-Avon's retail and food-service pickle and canned vegetable businesses in the United Kingdom, Gourmet Specialty Foods in Germany, and the U.S. fresh mushroom business.

Morrison commented at the time of the announced spinoff that shareholders would benefit greatly by a separation of Campbell Soup businesses:

> This is a watershed day for Campbell Soup Company and its shareowners. Spinning off these businesses allows us to focus on our most profitable businesses with the highest growth potential. Our core businesses have gross margins in excess of 45%. Net sales for these businesses grew 10% and earnings grew 15% in fiscal 1997. This is an outstanding platform to drive significant volume growth while continuing to deliver top-quartile earnings. The creation of this new company gives great brands like Vlasic and Swanson tremendous opportunities for growth under a dedicated management team. In both cases, shareowners will reap the rewards of highly focused companies.[20]

Some Wall Street analysts were not as optimistic that the new company would become a strong competitor in the processed-food industry. One portfolio manager suggested that the spinoff would allow Campbell to achieve higher growth rates in terms of sales and earnings, but Vlasic Foods International would find growth difficult: "Whenever a company spins off the crummy parts, it's always good for what's left. What they're spinning off didn't have the value or the growth rate of the other divisions."[21] Another analyst commented on the attractiveness of frozen food, where over the last 10 years the size of the market had declined and margin points were gained only through price cuts: "There is not going to be a mad rush to own this [new] food company. Swanson has been a stagnant brand at best, though I suppose it's a bit better than Schlitz beer."[22]

Even though the frozen foods category was highly competitive and had become commodity-like after the 1980s, Vlasic Foods International did include a number of popular brands and products. Swanson was the originator of the TV dinner in 1954 and continued to maintain category leadership with products like Hungry Man dinners, Great Start breakfasts, and Fun Feast kids' meals. Vlasic was the leader in U.S.

---

[20]Securities and Exchange Commission, Form 8-K, September 9, 1997.

[21]*Knight-Ridder/Tribune Business News,* September 10, 1997.

[22]As quoted in *The New York Times,* September 10, 1997, p. D1.

EXHIBIT 10   Vlasic Foods International's Stock Performance, by Week, March 1998–March 2000

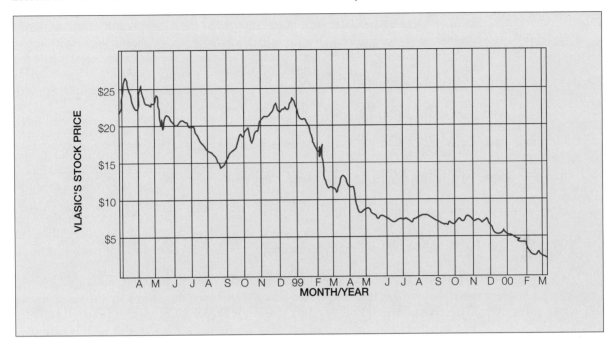

pickle sales, with a 36 percent market share, and approximately 35 percent of Vlasic's sales came from products introduced within the previous five years. In addition, Swift was Argentina's largest exporter of beef, Open Pit was the number one barbecue sauce in the midwestern United States, Gourmet Specialty Foods was Germany's number one specialty foods company, and the company's mushroom business was the largest in the world. The new company's third- and fourth-quarter sales and earnings fell below projections, and sales of pickles and frozen foods were down about 10 percent for the year. The company's stock closed at $22¾ on the first day of trading in March 1998, but was trading in the $13 to $15 range within four months of the spinoff. The market performance of Vlasic Foods' common stock following its spinoff is depicted in Exhibit 10.

Morrison continued to restructure Campbell's portfolio during 1998 and 1999 to allow the company to focus on core brands and activities directly related to either product quality or image. Continental Sweets was sold to a Dutch venture capital fund in 1998. Continental Sweets made and distributed sugar and chocolate confectionery; its facilities were located in France and Belgium. Campbell Soup also sold its European-based Delacre premium biscuit business and Australian-based Melbourne Mushrooms and Spring Valley beverages in 1998.

The company's Fresh Start Bakeries, a supplier of English muffins and buns to quick-service restaurants, was sold to a joint venture between Berkshire Partners and Fresh Start's management in May 1999. Morrison also chose to divest the company's can-making assets to Silgan Holdings—a supplier of food cans with annual sales of approximately $1.5 billion. The can-making operations were sold for $123 million, and the transaction included a 10-year supply agreement between Campbell Soup and Silgan that called for can purchases by Campbell totaling over $200 million each year. The company also took restructuring charges of $262 million and $41 million in 1998 and 1999, respectively, related to streamlining its production and administrative facilities in North America and Europe. The restructuring programs merged certain Canadian and U.S. administrative functions and attempted to maximize capacity utilization among its production facilities by combining operations whenever possible. For example, Campbell closed its Pace salsa plant in San Antonio, Texas, and shifted production of Pace products to Campbell's Paris, Texas, plant, which produced Prego spaghetti sauce, Franco-American gravies, and an assortment of soups. Campbell Soup management expected the restructuring program to reduce the company's operating expenses by $221 million annually.

The spinoff and divestitures allowed Campbell Soup to implement a $2 billion share buyback plan to repurchase 8 percent of the company's 451 million outstanding shares of stock between 1999 and 2001. The strategy to boost earnings per share and return on stockholders' equity was a continuation of an ongoing Johnson strategy of repurchasing 2 percent of the company's outstanding shares annually. Morrison also retained a Johnson-devised strategy of repurchasing shares in addition to the $2 billion buyback plan to offset per share dilution resulting from incentive compensation programs.

To boost Campbell's growth potential, Morrison initiated a number of new acquisitions during 1997 and 1998. In 1997 the company purchased the remaining 30 percent of Arnott's outstanding shares for $290 million, giving Campbell 100 percent ownership of the Australian biscuit company. The company also acquired Leibig soups in 1997 for $180 million. Leibig was France's leading producer of wet soups, with annual sales of approximately $75 million. In June 1998 Campbell Soup acquired privately held Fortun Foods for $105 million. Fortun's Stockpot brand of fresh, chilled soup was distributed to restaurants, supermarkets, and convenience stores in over 20 countries and was the market leader in premium refrigerated soups, with about 50 percent market share of the rapidly growing category and annual sales of $40 million. Campbell Soup had tried unsuccessfully a number of times since the 1980s to develop freshly made chilled soup without preservatives. Fortun's manufacturing process transferred hot soup from the kettle to a vacuum-sealed bag that was then immediately refrigerated. The company's proprietary process allowed Stockpot soups to stay fresh for about 120 days.

Morrison's acquisitions and divestitures prompted a realignment of Campbell Soup divisions and business units. Morrison created a Soups and Sauces division, which included all soup and sauce brands marketed globally. The Biscuit and Confectionery division was reorganized to include all global brands of baked goods, and the makeup of the Away from Home food-service division was adjusted to include all businesses that were dedicated to supplying the growing quick-service restaurant industry. A special division titled Campbell's Other was temporarily formed to handle the details of transferring the divested businesses to the new owners and report the historical performance of divested businesses.

Morrison believed that cross-business skills transfer would be more readily achieved by abandoning Campbell's previous geographically based divisions and placing all businesses sharing common R&D, production, and marketing activities in a common division (see again Exhibit 7, which presents a comparison of business divisions and units under Gordon McGovern, David Johnson, and Dale Morrison). Exhibit 11 provides the sales and operating earnings for Morrison's divisions from 1995 to 1999. The 1995 and 1996 financial data shown in the exhibit have been reorganized to match Campbell Soup Company's divisional structure in 1997–99.

EXHIBIT 11   Sales and Earnings of Campbell Soup Company, by Division, 1995–99 ($ millions)

Source: Campbell annual reports.

	1999	1998	1997	1996	1995
Soups and Sauces					
Sales	$4,423	$4,434	$4,156	$3,742	$3,415
Operating earnings	1,082	1,109	1,012	978	863
Biscuits and Confectionery					
Sales	1,430	1,522	1,546	1,459	1,348
Operating earnings	215	206	154	183	164
Away from Home					
Sales	507	453	459	418	345
Operating earnings	57	53	62	55	40
Other					
Sales	126	334	1,904	2,149	2,204
Operating earnings	(5)	(85)	99	150	135
Interdivision					
Sales	($ 62)	($ 49)	($ 101)	($ 90)	($ 62)

Campbell Soup in 2000

SOUPS AND SAUCES GROUP

The Soups and Sauces division was Campbell's largest operating unit, accounting for about two-thirds of the company's total consolidated sales. The U.S. and international markets for canned soup were mature and possibly entering into a declining stage. The U.S. wet-soup category had grown at low single-digit rates during the late 1990s and was not expected to grow at a faster rate during 2000–2001. The maturity of the U.S. soup segment was attributable to the increased popularity of fresh foods, a 40 percent decrease in the usage of cooking soups in recipes, and an overall reduced tendency of consumers to purchase canned products. The slow growth in international markets was primarily related to the preference for homemade soups in many regions. During most of the 1990s consumption of Campbell's soups grew at 2 to 3 percent annually, but U.S. consumption of Campbell's wet soups declined by about 1 percent in 1998 and by 8 percent in 1999. Campbell's worldwide soup sales grew by 3 percent during 1998, but declined by 4 percent in 1999. The company's 1997 acquisition of Liebig helped Campbell Soup increase its international wet-soup volume by 7 percent in 1999.

Campbell's market share in the condensed soup category had declined from 80 percent in 1993 to 74 percent in 1997. In an attempt to regain lost market share, the company forwent its usual 3 to 7 percent annual price increases in 1998 since much of its lost market share was being captured by lower-priced private-label brands. The level pricing failed to recapture enough lost market share to offset the impact of smaller margins on the division's 1998 revenues. In 1999 the company's U.S. sales of canned soup declined by 8 percent after Campbell management eliminated quarter-end promotions to retailers.

The division implemented a plan to increase advertising spending by 18 percent in 1998 and intended to eventually increase the advertising budget for Campbell soups and sauces from 3.5 percent of sales to 8 percent of sales. Dale Morrison believed that increased advertising was necessary to support new products and newly packaged products and to promote soup in appealing ways to children. Campbell's fastest growing soup and sauce products during the late 1990s were Swanson broths and V8 Splash juices. Swanson's 20 percent annual growth was in large part a result of new 32-ounce recloseable aseptic packaging and its positioning as a 100 percent fat-free seasoning alternative that could be used in a number of recipes. Recent product introduction V8 Splash, a beverage combining carrot and tropical fruit juices, helped the V8 brand grow by more than 10 percent in 1998, and the 1999 introduction of new packaging (e.g., kid-sized juice boxes), new flavors, and a greater availability throughout the world helped V8 Splash become Campbell's most successful new product introduction in more than a decade.

Campbell introduced additional products after Morrison became the company's CEO to improve the sales volumes of products like tomato soup. Its new 32-ounce recloseable plastic ready-to-serve Campbell Tomato Soup allowed consumers to pour a single serving or use what was called for by a recipe and then store the remaining portion in the refrigerator for later use. Campbell marketers believed that having soup in the refrigerator would lead to higher consumption since most people opened the refrigerator more often than the pantry. Campbell Soup added a line of Select Soups, packaged in metal cans, as was the company's Classic line of soups that included tomato, cream of broccoli, and cream of mushroom, but the Select Soups line included more unique varieties of soups. Select Soups used distinctive combinations of ingredients to create flavorful soups like chicken and pasta with roasted garlic—a blend of chicken, penne and rotini pasta, and vegetables with roasted garlic in a chicken broth. Campbell Soup also introduced a Soups-to-Go line of ready-to-serve microwavable single-serving bowls that achieved volume gains in 1999. Joseph A. Campbell premium-quality soups had not experienced the sales gains expected by Campbell management; the line was rebranded Simply Home in 1998 and achieved volume gains in 1999. Campbell's Chunky line was also one of the company's faster-growing lines of canned soup in the late 1990s.

Even though the company had been largely successful with its new product introductions in recent years, Campbell management still believed in David Johnson's commitment to thoroughly assessing a product's potential on the market prior to its launch. Robert Bernstock, president of Campbell's U.S. Grocery division, explained, "In the early 1990s we were launching two new, single SKU products with more than $10 million in sales a year. We're now launching more than 20 a year. Tremendous up-front discipline is the key. We spend 12–18 months in rigorous testing."[23]

BISCUITS AND CONFECTIONERY GROUP

Campbell's Biscuits and Confectionery business unit had 1999 sales of $1.4 billion and operating earnings of $215 million. The division included Pepperidge Farm in North America; Godiva chocolates in North America, Europe, and Asia; Arnott's in the Pacific Rim/Asia; and Kettle Chips in Australia. Such products as Goldfish crackers, Swirl bread, and Milano cookies helped the Biscuits and Confectionery division achieve a sales increase of 5 percent in 1998 prior to the impact of exchange rates. The division had a sales decline of 6 percent in 1999, but Godiva grew its U.S. sales volume by more than 10 percent in 1998 and made some headway in increasing penetration of Euro-

---

[23]As quoted in *Prepared Foods*, September 1997, p. 14.

pean and Asian markets. Campbell management expected the business to continue to increase its strength in Asia as more Godiva retail outlets were opened in the region. The company also opened additional freestanding boutiques in shopping malls and Godiva departments in upscale department stores throughout the United States.

Pepperidge Farm continued the transformation begun by Dale Morrison in 1995 with continued increases in sales volume. The company's increased promotion of Goldfish crackers allowed sales of the product to grow 25 percent in 1996 and 40 percent in 1997. New varieties such as Goldfish Grahams contributed to sales volume increases for Goldfish products in 1999. Other market-leading Pepperidge Farm products included Milano cookies, which grew by 35 percent in 1997, Dessert Classics frozen cakes, and frozen garlic bread, which grew more than 40 percent after being moved adjacent to frozen pasta in grocery freezers. Pepperidge Farm management had established a "2 × 2" program with the objective of doubling sales between 1997 and 2000. The program called for Pepperidge Farm to achieve its growth objective by developing several innovative new products, lowering operating costs by eliminating costs that did not provide value to the customer, and purging waste.

Campbell management believed that a controlling interest in Arnott's Ltd. would yield a competitive advantage in the $3 billion Asian cookie-and-cracker market. The 132-year-old Arnott's was one of Australia's best-known food companies, had access to low-cost ingredients, and had efficient manufacturing processes. Arnott's Australian location also provided a shipping-cost advantage for products exported to the entire Asian/Pacific Rim region. The biscuit and confectionery division introduced popular Pepperidge Farm products to international markets in 1999 when Arnott's Goldfish were launched in Australia.

AWAY FROM HOME GROUP

Dale Morrison, like David Johnson, realized the importance of Campbell's food-service unit, Away from Home, in growing corporate sales and earnings. In 2000, U.S. consumers were projected to eat approximately 46 percent of all meals away from home and spend an estimated $342 billion in restaurants. On an average day, almost 140 million meals were eaten in U.S. restaurants and cafeterias. In addition, nearly 21 percent of U.S. households used some form of takeout or delivery each day. Campbell Soup management intended for the company to make Campbell products readily available to both consumers who purchased food for home preparation and those who chose to dine away from home. Morrison believed that Campbell Soup should position itself to provide soups and other processed foods to consumers in their homes and other locations: "If you look at the U.S. soup business, you could say we have an 80% share of the condensed and ready-to-serve market, and where do we go from there? But if you look at soup consumption in total. . . we really have a 38% share. Under that frame of reference, there's real opportunity."[24]

In 1999 the sales of the Away from Home division reached $507 million—a 12 percent increase over 1998. The division provided pot pies to Kentucky Fried Chicken, soups to roughly one-third of McDonald's restaurants, and a wide variety of Prego entrees and Campbell soups to various restaurants and cafeterias. V8 Splash beverages and Pace Mexican salsas were also distributed to restaurants, delicatessens, and cafeterias. The company had introduced serve-your-own soup vending machines in convenience stores and soup kettles in college cafeterias and had also provided complete meals to supermarket delis and cafeterias that included entrees and side dishes packaged in 5.5- and 2.5-pound aluminum trays. The company also tested the popularity of soup kiosks in airports and sports arenas. Campbell's 1998 acquisition of

[24]Ibid.

Stockpot soups allowed the company to expand its branded soup presence in the food-service market for soups because of Stockpot's proprietary manufacturing process that allowed soups to be shipped fresh and without preservatives.

EVENTS AT CAMPBELL SOUP IN EARLY 2000

Campbell Soup Company was ranked number four among *Fortune* magazine's 1999 and 2000 listings of the most admired food companies; it also was ranked as the third most profitable food company among the Fortune 500. However, Campbell Soup's financial and market performance fell considerably short of being rated "best in show" (a David Johnson objective). In his letter to the stockholders in the company's 1999 annual report, Dale Morrison stated his belief that even though the processed-food industry was confronted by a variety of challenges and Campbell Soup had failed to outperform the overall stock market, it was still feasible for Campbell Soup to deliver an attractive return to its shareholders:

> Campbell Soup Company's primary commitment has been, and always will be, to build shareowner wealth. For many years, we succeeded brilliantly in doing so. Lately, however, much has been said and written about the challenges facing our industry and our company—challenges relating, for example, to changing consumer habits and the pace and prospects for growth. Over the past several years, the food industry has underperformed the overall market. And as we are all aware, this year, in a painful departure from our recent track record, Campbell disappointed our investors as well. Our stock price declined 19 percent in the [1999] fiscal year. So I believe our shareowners today are entitled to ask, "What does the future hold for Campbell Soup Company?"
>
> The answer begins with our central business—soup. For millions of people, the Campbell's name is synonymous with quality, wholesomeness, and the best moments of family life.
>
> Beyond soup, we compete in categories that offer abundant opportunities to grow with changing consumer preferences and lifestyles—sauces, beverages, biscuits and confectionery. Campbell brings significant brand power to these categories with favorites like V8 and V8 Splash, Pace, Prego, Franco-American, Pepperidge Farm, Arnott's and Godiva.[25]

MOUNTING PROBLEMS

Despite Morrison's optimism about the company's growth prospects, Campbell's stock price continued to slide from its all-time high of $63 per share in early 1998. During the first nine months of 1999, the stock price traded mostly in the $40 to $45 per share range. Then in late fall of 1999 it began a steep slide, falling below $30 as the company was hit by (1) a series of shareholder lawsuits alleging that company documents misled shareholders about revenues, (2) a February 2000 recall of 109,000 pounds of canned vegetable soup in 13 states after consumers found long pieces of metal in the soup, and (3) forecasts of slow growth for Campbell's brands by both Wall Street analysts and Campbell's executives. Campbell Soup had reported slightly better-than-expected second-quarter earnings for the period ending December 1999, but several Wall Street analysts expected full-year earnings for fiscal year 2000 (ending July) to be $1.86, rising to perhaps $1.99 at the end of fiscal year 2001.

On March 22, 2000, Dale Morrison resigned as president, CEO, and a director of the company. He was replaced by David Johnson, the company's previous CEO, who agreed to serve while the company's board of directors searched for a permanent replacement. The closing stock price on March 22, 2000, was $29¹¹⁄₁₆, off $1⁷⁄₁₆.

---

[25]Campbell Soup Company 1999 annual report.

Case 9

Dell Computer Corporation: Strategy and Challenges for the 21st Century

Arthur A. Thompson
The University of Alabama

John E. Gamble
University of South Alabama

> You don't ever really know whether you've come up with the right plan until much later—when it either works or it doesn't. What is the right plan? It's the one that helps you identify what you need to do to ensure success. It's the one that rallies your employees around a few common goals—and motivates them to achieve them. It's one that involves your customers' goals and your suppliers' goals and brings them altogether in a unified focus.
> —Michael Dell

In 1984, at the age of 19, Michael Dell founded Dell Computer with a simple vision and business concept—that personal computers could be built to order and sold directly to customers. Michael Dell believed his approach to the PC business had two advantages: (1) Bypassing distributors and retail dealers eliminated the markups of resellers, and (2) building to order greatly reduced the costs and risks associated with carrying large stocks of parts, components, and finished goods. While the company sometimes struggled during its early years trying to refine its strategy, build an adequate infrastructure, and establish market credibility against better-known rivals, Dell's build-to-order, sell-direct approach proved appealing to growing numbers of customers worldwide during the 1990s as global PC sales rose to record levels. And, as Michael Dell had envisioned, the direct-to-the-customer strategy gave the company a substantial cost and profit margin advantage over rivals that manufactured various PC models in volume and kept their distributors and retailers stocked with ample inventories.

Dell Computer's Market Position in Early 2000

Going into 2000, Dell Computer was the U.S. leader in PC sales, with nearly a 17 percent market share, about 1 percentage point ahead of second-place Compaq. Gateway was third with 8.9 percent, followed by Hewlett-Packard with 8.8 percent and IBM with 7.2 percent. Dell overtook Compaq as the U.S. sales leader in the third quarter of 1999, and it had moved ahead of IBM into second place during 1998 (see Exhibit 1). Worldwide, Dell Computer ranked second in market share (10.5 percent) behind Compaq (14.0 percent). IBM ranked third worldwide, with an 8.2 percent share, but this share was eroding. Since 1996, Dell had been gaining market share quickly in all of the world's markets, growing at a rate more than triple the 18 percent average annual increase in global PC sales. Even though Asia's economic woes in 1997–98 and part of 1999 dampened the market for PCs, Dell's PC sales across Asia in 1999 were up a strong 87 percent. Dell was also enjoying strong sales growth in Europe.

Dell's sales at its Web site (www.dell.com) surpassed $35 million a day in early 2000, up from $5 million daily in early 1998 and $15 million daily in early 1999. In its fiscal year ending January 31, 2000, Dell Computer posted revenues of $25.3 billion, up from $3.4 billion in the year ending January 29, 1995—a compound average growth rate of 49.4 percent. Over the same time period, profits were up from $140 million to $1.67 billion—a 64.1 percent compound average growth rate. Since its initial public offering of common stock in June 1988 at $8.50 per share, the company had seen its stock price split seven times and increase 45,000 percent. Dell Computer was one of the top 10 best-performing stocks on the NYSE and the NASDAQ during the 1990s. In recent years, Dell's annual return on invested capital had exceeded 175 percent.

Dell's principal products included desktop PCs, notebook computers, workstations, servers, and storage devices. It also marketed a number of products made by other manufacturers, including CD-ROM drives, modems, monitors, networking hardware, memory cards, speakers, and printers. The company received nearly 3 million visits weekly at its Web site, where it maintained 50 country-specific sites. It was a world leader in migrating its business relationships with both customers and suppliers to the Internet. In 1998 the company expanded its Internet presence with the launch of www.gigabuys.com, an online source for more than 30,000 competitively priced computer-related products. Sales of desktop PCs accounted for about 65 percent of Dell's total systems revenue; sales of notebook computers generated 20–25 percent of revenues, and servers and workstations accounted for 10–15 percent of revenues. Dell products were sold in more than 170 countries. In early 2000, the company had 33,200 employees in 34 countries, up from 16,000 at year-end 1997; approximately one-third of Dell's employees were located in countries outside the United States, and this percentage was growing.

Company Background

When Michael Dell was in the third grade, he responded to a magazine ad with the headline "Earn Your High School Diploma by Passing One Simple Test." At that age, he was both impatient and curious—always willing to try ways to get something done more quickly and easily. Early on, he became fascinated by what he saw as "commercial

EXHIBIT 1 Leading PC Vendors Worldwide and in the United States, Based on Factory Shipments, 1996–99

Source: International Data Corp.

A. Worldwide Market Shares of the Leading PC Vendors*

1999 Rank	Vendor	1999 Market Shipments of PCs	1999 Market Share	1998 Market Shipments of PCs	1998 Market Share	1997 Market Shipments of PCs*	1997 Market Share	1996 Market Shipments of PCs*	1996 Market Share	Compound Growth Rate, 1996–99
1	Compaq Computer	15,732,000	14.0%	13,266,000	14.5%	10,064,000	12.6%	7,211,000	10.4%	29.7%
2	Dell Computer	11,883,000	10.5	7,770,000	8.5	4,648,000	5.8	2,996,000	4.3	58.3
3	IBM	9,287,000	8.2	7,946,000	8.7	7,239,000	9.1	6,176,000	8.9	14.6
4	Hewlett-Packard	7,577,000	6.7	5,743,000	6.3	4,468,000	5.6	2,984,000	4.3	36.4
5	Packard Bell/NEC	5,989,000	5.3	5,976,000	6.5	4,150,000	5.2	4,230,000	6.1	12.1
6	Gateway	4,685,000	4.2	3,540,000	n.a.	n.a.	n.a.	n.a.	n.a.	n.a.
	Others	57,573,000	55.2	50,741,000	55.5	49,369,000	61.8	45,727,000	66.0	10.8
	All vendors	112,726,000	100.0%	91,442,000	100.0%	79,938,000	100.0%	69,324,000	100.0%	17.6%

B. U.S. Market Shares of the Leading PC Vendors, 1998–99

1999 Rank	Vendor	1999 Market Shipments of PCs*	1999 Market Share	1998 Market Shipments of PCs*	1998 Market Share	Percent Growth 1998–99
1	Dell Computer	7,492,000	16.6%	4,799,000	13.2%	56.1%
2	Compaq Computer	7,222,000	16.0	6,052,000	16.7	19.3
3	Gateway	4,001,000	8.9	3,039,000	8.4	31.6
4	Hewlett-Packard	3,955,000	8.8	2,832,000	7.8	39.6
5	IBM	3,274,000	7.2	2,983,000	8.2	9.8
	Others	19,248,000	42.6	16,549,000	45.6	16.3
	All vendors	45,192,000	100.0%	36,254,000	100.0%	24.7%

*Includes branded shipments only and excludes OEM sales for all manufacturers.

opportunities." At age 12, Michael Dell was running a mail-order stamp-trading business, complete with a national catalog, and grossing $2,000 per month. At 16, he was selling subscriptions to the *Houston Post,* and at 17 he bought his first BMW with the more than $18,000 he had earned. He enrolled at the University of Texas in 1983 as a pre-med student (his parents wanted him to become a doctor) but soon became immersed in the commercial opportunities he saw in computer retailing and started selling PC components out of his college dormitory room. He bought random-access memory (RAM) chips and disk drives for IBM PCs at cost from IBM dealers, who often had excess supplies on hand because they were required to order large monthly quotas from IBM. Dell resold the components through newspaper ads (and later through ads in national computer magazines) at 10–15 percent below the regular retail price.

By April 1984 sales were running about $80,000 per month. Michael Dell at age 18 dropped out of college and formed a company, PCs Ltd., to sell both PC components and PCs under the brand PCs Limited. He obtained his PCs by buying retailers' surplus stocks at cost, then powering them up with graphics cards, hard disks, and memory before reselling them. His strategy was to sell directly to end users; by eliminating the retail markup, Dell's new company was able to sell IBM clones (machines that copied the functioning of IBM PCs using the same or similar components) at about 40 percent below the price of an IBM PC. The price-discounting strategy was successful, attracting price-conscious buyers and producing rapid growth. By 1985, with a few people working on six-foot tables, the company was assembling its own PC designs. The company had 40 employees, and Michael Dell worked 18-hour days, often sleeping on a cot in his office. By the end of fiscal 1986, sales had reached $33 million.

During the next several years, however, PCs Limited was hampered by growing pains—a lack of money, people, and resources. Michael Dell sought to refine the company's business model; add needed production capacity; and build a bigger, deeper management staff and corporate infrastructure while at the same time keeping costs low. The company was renamed Dell Computer in 1987, and the first international offices were opened that same year. In 1988 Dell added a sales force to serve large customers, began selling to government agencies, and became a public company—raising $34.2 million in its first offering of common stock. Sales to large customers quickly became the dominant part of Dell's business. By 1990 Dell Computer had sales of $388 million, a market share of 2 to 3 percent, and an R&D staff of over 150 people. Michael Dell's vision was for Dell Computer to become one of the world's top three PC companies.

Thinking its direct-sales business would not grow fast enough, in 1990–93, the company began distributing its computer products through Soft Warehouse Superstores (now CompUSA), Staples (a leading office products chain), Wal-Mart Stores, Sam's Club, and Price Club (now Price/Costco). Dell also sold PCs through Best Buy stores in 16 states and through Xerox in 19 Latin American countries. But when the company learned how thin its margins were in selling through such distribution channels, it realized it had made a mistake and withdrew from selling to retailers and other intermediaries in 1994 to refocus on direct sales. At the time, sales through retailers accounted for only about 2 percent of Dell's revenues.

Further problems emerged in 1993, when Dell reportedly lost $38 million in the second quarter from engaging in a risky foreign-currency hedging strategy; had quality difficulties with certain PC lines made by the company's contract manufacturers; and saw its profit margins decline. Also that year, buyers were turned off by the company's laptop PC models. To get laptop sales back on track, the company took a charge of $40 million to write off its laptop line and suspended sales of those products until it could get redesigned models into the marketplace. The problems resulted in losses of $36 million for the company's fiscal year ending January 30, 1994.

Because of higher costs and unacceptably low profit margins in selling to individuals and households, Dell Computer did not pursue the consumer market aggressively until sales on the company's Internet site took off in 1996 and 1997. Management noticed that while the industry's average selling price to individuals was going down, Dell's was going up—second- and third-time computer buyers who wanted powerful computers with multiple features and did not need much technical support were choosing Dell. It became clear that PC-savvy individuals liked the convenience of buying direct from Dell, ordering exactly what they wanted, and having it delivered to their door within a matter of days. In early 1997, Dell created an internal sales and marketing group dedicated to serving the individual consumer segment and introduced a product line designed especially for individual users.

By late 1997, Dell had become the global industry leader in keeping costs down and wringing efficiency out of its direct-sales, build-to-order business model. Going into 2000, Dell Computer had made further efficiency improvements and was widely regarded as having the most efficient procurement, manufacturing, and distribution process in the global PC industry. The company was a pioneer and acknowledged world leader in incorporating e-commerce technology and use of the Internet into its everyday business practices. The goal was to achieve what Michael Dell called "virtual integration"—a stitching together of Dell's business with its supply partners and customers in real time such that all three appeared to be part of the same organizational team.[1] The company's mission was "to be the most successful computer company in the world at delivering the best customer experience in the markets we serve."[2]

Exhibits 2–5 contain a five-year review of Dell Computer's financial performance and selected financial statements.

MICHAEL DELL

Michael Dell was widely considered one of the mythic heroes of the PC industry, and was labeled "the quintessential American entrepreneur" and "the most innovative guy for marketing computers in this decade." In 1992, at the age of 27, Michael Dell became the youngest CEO ever to head a Fortune 500 company; he was a billionaire at the age of 31. Once pudgy and bespectacled, Michael Dell at the age of 35 was physically fit, considered good-looking, wore contact lenses, ate only health foods, and lived in a three-story 33,000 square-foot home on a 60-acre estate in the Austin, Texas, metropolitan area. In early 2000 Michael Dell owned about 14 percent of Dell Computer's common stock, worth about $12 billion. The company's glass-and-steel headquarters building in Round Rock, Texas (an Austin suburb), had unassuming, utilitarian furniture, abstract art, framed accolades to Michael Dell, laudatory magazine covers, industry awards plaques, bronze copies of the company's patents, and a history wall that contained the hand-soldered guts of the company's first personal computer.[3]

In the company's early days Michael spent a lot of his time with the engineers. He was said to be shy, but those who worked with him closely described him as a likable

---

[1]Michael Dell used the term "virtual integration" in an interview published in the *Harvard Business Review*. See Joan Magretta, "The Power of Virtual Integration: An Interview with Dell Computer's Michael Dell," *Harvard Business Review,* March–April 1998, p. 75.

[2]Information posted on www.dell.com, February 1, 2000.

[3]As described in *Business Week,* March 22, 1993, p. 82.

EXHIBIT 2 Financial Performance Summary, Dell Computer, 1995–2000 (in millions, except per share data)

Source: Dell Computer Corporation 2000 annual report.

	January 28, 2000	January 29, 1999	February 1, 1998	February 2, 1997	January 28, 1996	January 29, 1995
Results of Operations Data						
Net revenue	$25,265	$18,243	$12,327	$7,759	$5,296	$3,475
Gross margin	5,218	4,106	2,722	1,666	1,067	738
Operating income	2,263	2,046	1,316	714	377	249
Income before extraordinary loss	$ 1,666	1,460	944	531	272	149
Net income	$ 1,666	$ 1,460	$ 944	$ 518	$ 272	$ 149
Income before extraordinary loss per common share[ab]						
Basic	$0.66	$0.58	$0.36	$0.19	$0.09	$0.06
Diluted	$0.61	$0.53	$0.32	$0.17	$0.08	$0.05
Number of weighted average shares outstanding[a]						
Basic	2,536	2,531	2,631	2,838	2,863	2,473
Diluted	2,728	2,772	2,952	3,126	3,158	3,000
Balance Sheet Data						
Working capital	—	$ 2,644	$ 1,215	$1,089	$1,018	$ 718
Total assets	$11,471	6,877	4,268	2,993	2,148	1,594
Long-term debt	508	512	17	18	113	113
Total stockholders' equity	5,308	2,321	1,293	806	973	652

[a]All share and per share information has been retroactively restated to reflect the two-for-one splits of common stock.
[b]Excludes extraordinary loss of $0.01 basic per common share for fiscal year 1997.

EXHIBIT 3 Dell Computer's Consolidated Statements of Income, Fiscal Years 1997–2000 (in millions, except per share data)

Source: Dell Computer Corporation's annual reports.

	Fiscal Year Ended			
	January 28, 2000	January 29, 1999	February 1, 1998	February 2, 1997
Net revenue	$25,265	$18,243	$12,327	$7,759
Cost of revenue	20,047	14,137	9,605	6,093
Gross margin	5,218	4,106	2,722	1,666
Operating expenses				
Selling, general and administrative	2,387	1,788	1,202	826
Research, development and engineering	374	272	204	126
Purchased research and development	194	—	—	—
Total operating expenses	2,955	2,060	1,406	952
Operating income	2,263	2,046	1,316	714
Financing and other	188	38	52	33
Income before income taxes and extraordinary loss	2,451	2,084	1,368	747
Provision for income taxes	785	624	424	216
Income before extraordinary loss	1,666	1,460	944	531
Extraordinary loss, net of taxes	—	—	—	(13)
Net income	$ 1,666	$ 1,460	$ 944	$ 518
Basic Earnings per Common Share (in whole dollars)				
Income before extraordinary loss	$ 0.66	$ 0.58	$ 0.36	$ 0.19
Extraordinary loss, net of taxes	—	—	—	(0.01)
Earnings per common share	$ 0.66	$ 0.58	$ 0.36	$ 0.18
Diluted earnings per common share (in whole dollars)	$ 0.61	$ 0.53	$ 0.32	$ 0.17
Weighted average shares outstanding				
Basic	2,536	2,531	2,631	2,838
Diluted	2,728	2,772	2,952	3,126

EXHIBIT 4   Dell Computer's Consolidated Statements of Financial Position, Fiscal Years 1999 and 2000 (in millions of dollars)

Source: Dell Computer Corporation's 2000 annual report.

	January 28, 2000	January 29, 1999
Assets		
Current assets		
Cash and cash equivalents	$ 3,809	$1,726
Short term investments	323	923
Accounts receivable, net	2,608	2,094
Inventories	391	273
Other	550	791
Total current assets	7,681	5,807
Property, plant, and equipment, net	765	523
Other	3,025	547
Total assets	$11,471	$6,877
Liabilities and Stockholders' Equity		
Current liabilities		
Accounts payable	$ 3,538	$2,397
Accrued and other	1,654	1,298
Total current liabilities	5,192	3,695
Long-term debt	508	512
Other	463	349
Commitments and contingent liabilities	—	—
Total liabilities	6,163	4,556
Stockholders' equity		
Preferred stock and capital in excess of $.01 par value; shares issued and outstanding: none	—	—
Common stock and capital in excess of $.01 par value; shares issued and outstanding: 2,543 and 2,575, respectively		1,781
Retained earnings		606
Other		(66)
Total stockholders' equity	5,308	2,321
Total liabilities and stockholders' equity	$11,471	$6,877

young man who was slow to warm up to people.[4] Michael described his experience in getting the company launched as follows:

> There were obviously no classes on learning how to start and run a business in my high school, so I clearly had a lot to learn. And learn I did, mostly by experimenting and making a bunch of mistakes. One of the first things I learned, though, was that there was a relationship between screwing up and learning: The more mistakes I made, the faster I learned.
>
> I tried to surround myself with smart advisors, and I tried not to make the same mistake twice. . . . Since we were growing so quickly, everything was constantly changing. We'd say, "What's the best way to do this?" and come up with an answer. The resulting process would work for a while, then it would stop working and we'd have to adjust it and try something else. . . . The whole thing was one big experiment.

[4]"Michael Dell: On Managing Growth," *MIS Week,* September 5, 1988, p. 1.

EXHIBIT 5   Geographic Area Information, Dell Computer, Fiscal 1998–2000 (in millions of Dollars)

Source: Dell Computer Corporation's 1998 and 2000 annual reports.

	Americas	Europe	Asia Pacific and Japan	Eliminations	Consolidated
Fiscal Year 2000					
Net revenue from unaffiliated customers	$17,879	$5,590	$1,796	—	$25,265
Transfers between geographic segments	48	5	2	(55)	—
Total net revenue	$17,927	$5,595	$1,798	$ (55)	$25,265
Operating income	$ 2,173	$ 403	$ 97	$(194)	$ 2,479
Corporate expenses					(216)
Total operating income					$ 2,263
Depreciation and amortization	$ 82	$ 41	$ 14	—	$ 137
Corporate depreciation and amortization					19
Total depreciation and amortization					$ 156
Identifiable assets	$ 2,456	$1,147	$ 413	—	$ 4,016
General corporate assets					7,455
Total assets					$11,741
Fiscal Year 1999					
Net revenue from unaffiliated customers	$12,420	$4,674	$1,149	—	$18,243
Transfers between geographic segments	33	5	1	–39	—
Total net revenue	$12,453	$4,679	$1,150	($39)	$18,243
Operating income	$ 1,802	$ 446	$ 78	—	$ 2,326
Corporate expenses					–(280)
Total operating income					$ 2,046
Depreciation and amortization	$ 59	$ 29	$ 8	—	$ 96
Corporate depreciation and amortization					7
Total depreciation and amortization					$ 103
Identifiable assets	$ 1,640	$1,017	$ 234	—	$ 2,891
General corporate assets					3,986
Total assets					$ 6,877
Fiscal Year 1998					
Net revenue from unaffiliated customers	$ 8,531	$2,956	$ 840	—	$12,327
Transfers between geographic segments	67	17	—	–84	—
Total net revenue	$ 8,598	$2,973	$ 840	($84)	$12,327
Operating income	$ 1,152	$ 255	$ 33	—	$ 1,440
Corporate expenses					–(124)
Total operating income					$ 1,316
Depreciation and amortization	$ 42	$ 16	$ 5	—	$ 63
Corporate depreciation and amortization					4
Total depreciation and amortization					$ 67
Identifiable assets	$ 1,363	$ 605	$ 172	—	$ 2,140
General corporate assets					2,128
Total assets					$ 4,268

From the beginning, we tended to come at things in a very practical way. I was always asking, "What's the most efficient way to accomplish this?" Consequently, we eliminated the possibility for bureaucracy before it ever cropped up, and that provided opportunities for learning as well.

Constantly questioning conventional thinking became part of our company mentality. And our explosive growth helped to foster a great sense of camaraderie and a real "can-do" attitude among our employees.

We challenged ourselves constantly, to grow more or to provide better service to our customers; and each time we set a new goal, we would make it. Then we would stop for a moment, give each other a few high fives, and get started on tackling the next goal.[5]

In 1986, to provide the company with much-needed managerial and financial experience, Michael Dell brought in Lee Walker, a 51-year-old venture capitalist, as president and chief operating officer. Walker had a fatherly image, came to know company employees by name, and proved to be a very effective internal force in implementing Michael Dell's ideas for growing the company. Walker became Michael Dell's mentor, built up his confidence and managerial skills, helped him learn how to translate his fertile entrepreneurial instincts into effective business plans and actions, and played an active role in grooming him into an able and polished executive.[6] Under Walker's tutelage, Michael Dell became intimately familiar with all parts of the business, overcame his shyness, learned the ins and outs of managing a fast-growing enterprise, and turned into a charismatic executive with an instinct for motivating people and winning their loyalty and respect. Walker also proved instrumental in helping Michael Dell recruit distinguished and able people to serve on the board of directors when the company went public in 1988. When Walker had to leave the company in 1990 because of health reasons, Dell turned for advice to Morton Meyerson, former CEO and president of Electronic Data Systems. Meyerson provided guidance on how to transform Dell Computer from a fast-growing medium-sized company into a billion-dollar enterprise.

Though sometimes given to displays of impatience, Michael Dell usually spoke in a quiet, reflective manner and came across as a person with maturity and seasoned judgment far beyond his age. His prowess was based more on having a pragmatic combination of astute entrepreneurial instincts, good technical knowledge, and marketing savvy rather than on being a pioneering techno-wizard. By the late 1990s, he was a much-sought-after speaker at industry and company conferences. (He received 100 requests to speak in 1997, 800 in 1998, and over 1,200 in 1999.) He was considered an accomplished public speaker and his views and opinions about the future of PCs, the Internet, and e-commerce practices carried considerable weight both in the PC industry and among executives worldwide. His speeches were usually full of usable information about the nuts and bolts of Dell Computer's business model and the compelling advantages of incorporating e-commerce technology and practices into a company's operations. A *USA Today* article labeled him "the guru of choice on e-commerce" because top executives across the world were so anxious to get his take on the business potential of the Internet and possible efficiency gains from integrating e-commerce into daily business operations.[7]

Michael Dell was considered a very accessible CEO and a role model for young executives because he had done what many of them were trying to do. He delegated authority to subordinates, believing that the best results came from "[turning] loose talented people who can be relied upon to do what they're supposed to do." Business

---

[5]Michael Dell, *Direct from Dell* (New York: HarperBusiness, 1999), pp. 17–20.

[6]"The Education of Michael Dell," *Business Week,* March 22, 1993, p. 86.

[7]"E-Commerce's Guru of Choice," *USA Today,* April 15, 1999, p. 3B.

associates viewed Michael Dell as an aggressive personality and an extremely competitive risk-taker who had always played close to the edge. Moreover, the people Dell hired had similar traits, which translated into an aggressive, competitive, intense corporate culture with a strong sense of mission and dedication. Inside Dell, Michael was noted for his obsessive, untiring attention to detail—a trait which employees termed "Michaelmanaging."

Michael Dell's Business Philosophy

In the 15 years since the company's founding, Michael Dell's understanding of what it took to build and operate a successful company in a fast-changing, high-velocity marketplace had matured considerably. His experience at Dell Computer and in working with both customers and suppliers had taught him a number of valuable lessons and shaped his leadership style. The following quotes provide insight into his business philosophy and practices:

> Believe in what you are doing. If you've got an idea that's really powerful, you've just got to ignore the people who tell you it won't work, and hire people who embrace your vision.

> It is as important to figure out what you're not going to do as it is to know what you are going to do.

> We instituted the practice of strong profit and loss management. By demanding a detailed P&L for each business unit, we learned the incredible value of facts and data in managing a complex business. As we have grown, Dell has become a highly data- and P&L- driven company, values that have since become core to almost everything we do.

> For us, growing up meant figuring out a way to combine our signature, informal style and "want to" attitude with the "can do" capabilities that would allow us to develop as a company. It meant incorporating into our everyday structure the valuable lessons we'd begun to learn using P&Ls. It meant focusing our employees to think in terms of shareholder value. It meant respecting the three golden rules at Dell: (1) Disdain inventory, (2) Always listen to the customer, and (3) Never sell indirect.

> I've always tried to surround myself with the best talent I could find. When you're the leader of a company, be it large or small, you can't do everything yourself. The more talented people you have to help you, the better off you and the company will be.

> A company's success should always be defined by its strategy and its ideas—and it should not be limited by the abilities of the people running it . . . When you are trying to grow a new business, you really need the experience of others who have been there and can help you anticipate and plan for things you might have never thought of.

> For any company to succeed, it's critical for top management to share power successfully. You have to be focused on achieving goals for the organization, not on accumulating power for yourself. Hoarding power does not translate into success for shareholders and customers; pursuing the goals of the company does. You also need to respect one another, and communicate so constantly that you're practically of one mind on the most important topics and issues that face the company.

> I have segmented my own job twice. Back in 1993–1994, it was becoming very clear to me that there was far too much to be done and far more opportunities than I could pursue myself . . . That was one of the reasons I asked Mort Topfer to join the company (as vice-chairman) . . . As the company continued to grow, we again segmented the job. In 1997, we promoted Kevin Rollins, who had been a key member of our executive team since 1996, to what we now call the office of the chairman. The three of us together run the company.

> Beyond winning and satisfying your customer, the objective must be to delight your customer—not just once but again and again. I spend about 40 percent of my time with customers . . . Customers know that I am not looking for insincere praise, or an affirmation of our strengths. They know by the quantity of the time

that I spend and the kinds of questions that I ask that I want to hear the truth, and that I want to walk away with a list of ideas about how we can work to make a valued partnership that much more significant . . . When you delight your customers—consistently—by offering better products and better services, you create strong loyalty. When you go beyond that to build a meaningful, memorable total experience, you win customers for life. Our goal, at the end of the day, is for our customers to say, "Dell *is* the smarter way to buy a computer."

The pace of decisions moves too quickly these days to waste time noodling over a decision. And while we strive to always make the right choice, I believe it's better to be first at the risk of being wrong than it is to be 100 percent perfect two years too late. You can't possibly make the quickest or best decisions without data. Information is the key to any competitive advantage. But data doesn't just drop by your office to pay you a visit. You've got to go out and gather it. I do this by roaming around. I don't want my interactions planned; I want anecdotal feedback. I want to hear spontaneous remarks . . . I want to happen upon someone who is stumped by a customer's question—and help answer it if I can . . . I show up at the factory to talk to people unannounced, to talk to people on the shop floor and to see what's really going on. I go to brown-bag lunches two or three times a month, and meet with a cross-section of people from all across the company.[8]

DEVELOPMENTS AT DELL IN EARLY 2000

Dell's unit shipments in the fourth quarter of 1999 were 3.36 million units, compared to 2.3 million units in the fourth quarter of 1998. In laptop PCs, Dell moved into second place in U.S. sales and fourth place worldwide in 1999. In higher-margin products like servers and workstations running on Windows NT, Windows 2000, and Linux, Dell ranked number two in market share in the United States and number three worldwide. In Europe, Dell ranked first in market share in Great Britain, third in market share in France, and second overall behind Compaq Computer. In Asia, Dell's sales were up 87 percent over 1998, despite sluggishness in the economies of several important Asian countries.

In 1999, about half of the industry's PC sales consisted of computers selling for less than $1,000. Dell's average selling price was $2,000 per unit in 1999, down from $2,500 in the first quarter of 1998. The company had recently introduced a line of WebPCs that was intended mainly for browsing the Internet. To counter the decline in the average selling prices of PCs, the company was placing increased emphasis on its line of PowerEdge servers and its Precision line of workstations, where average selling prices were $4,000 and higher, depending on the model.

Market Conditions in the PC Industry in 2000

There were an estimated 350 million PCs in use worldwide in 2000. Annual sales of PCs were approaching 130 million units annually (see Exhibit 6). About 50 million of the world's 350 million PCs were believed to have Intel 486 or older microprocessors with speeds of 75 megahertz or less. The world's population was over 6 billion people. Many industry experts foresaw a time when the installed base of PCs would exceed 1 billion units, and some believed the total would eventually reach 1.5 billion—a ratio of one PC for each four people. Forecasters also predicted that there would be a strong built-in replacement demand as microprocessor speeds continued to escalate past 1,000 megahertz. A microprocessor operating at 450 megahertz could process 600 million instructions per second (MIPS); Intel had forecast that it would be able to produce microprocessors capable of 100,000 MIPS by 2011. Such

[8]Dell, *Direct from Dell*, pp. 29, 57, 50, 59, 60, 64, 65, 69, 139–40, 168–69, and 116.

EXHIBIT 6 Actual and Projected Worldwide Shipments of PCs

Source: International Data Corp.

Year	PC Volume (Millions)
1980	1
1985	11
1990	24
1995	58
1996	69
1997	80
1998	91
1999	113
2000	130 (projected)
2003	190 (projected)

speeds were expected to spawn massive increases in computing functionality and altogether new uses and applications for PCs and computing devices of all types.

At the same time, forecasters expected demand for high-end servers carrying price tags of $5,000 to over $100,000 to continue to be especially strong because of the rush of companies all across the world to expand their Internet and e-commerce presence. Full global build-out of the Internet was expected to entail installing millions of high-speed servers.

DECLINING PC PRICES AND INTENSE COMPETITION

Sharp drops in the prices of a number of PC components (chiefly, disk drives, memory chips, and microprocessors) starting in late 1997 had allowed PC makers to dramatically lower PC prices—sales of PCs priced under $1,500 were booming by early 1998. Compaq, IBM, Hewlett-Packard, and several other PC makers began marketing sub-$1,000 PCs in late 1997. In December 1997, the average purchase price of a desktop computer fell below $1,300 for the first time. It was estimated that about half of all PCs sold in 1998 were computers carrying price tags under $1,500; by 1999, close to half of all PCs sold were units under $1,000. Growth in unit volume was being driven largely by sub-$1,000 PCs. The low prices were attracting first-time buyers into the market and were also causing second- and third-time PC buyers looking to upgrade to more powerful PCs to forgo top-of-the-line machines priced in the traditional $2,000–$3,500 range in favor of lower-priced PCs that were almost as powerful and well-equipped. Powerful, multifeatured notebook computers that had formerly sold for $4,000 to $6,500 in November 1997 were selling for $1,500 to $3,500 in December 1999. The profits at Compaq, IBM, and several other PC makers began sliding in early 1998 and continued under pressure in 1999. Declining PC prices and mounting losses in PCs prompted IBM to withdraw from selling desktop PCs in 1999.

However, unexpected shortages of certain key components (namely, memory chips and screens for notebook computers) drove up prices for these items in late 1999 and moderated the decline in PC prices somewhat. But the shortages were expected to last only until suppliers could gear up production levels.

CONTINUING ECONOMIC PROBLEMS IN PARTS OF ASIA

Economic woes in a number of Asian countries (most notably, Japan, South Korea, Thailand, Indonesia, and to some extent, China) had put a damper on PC sales in Asia starting in 1997 and continuing through much of 1999. Asian sales of PCs in

1998 grew minimally (though sales were fairly robust in China); sales improved in 1999 but remained depressed in Thailand, Indonesia, and several other countries. China began experiencing some economic problems in 1999. In addition, sharp appreciation of the U.S. dollar against Asian currencies had made U.S.-produced PCs more expensive in terms of local currency to Asian buyers. In contrast, sales growth in the United States and Europe in 1999 remained strong, despite all the Y2K fears, mainly because of lower PC prices.

Disk-drive manufacturers and the makers of printed circuit boards, many of which were in Asia, were feeling the pressures of declining prices and skimpy profit margins. Industry observers were predicting that competitive conditions in the Asia-Pacific PC market favored growing market shares by the top four or five players and the likely exit of PC makers that could not compete profitably.

THE UNCERTAIN NEAR-TERM OUTLOOK FOR PC INDUSTRY GROWTH

While few industry observers doubted the long-term market potential for PC sales, there were several troubling signs on the near-term horizon, along with differences of opinion about just how fast the market for PCs would grow. A number of industry observers were warning of a global slowdown in the sales of PCs in 2000 and beyond, partly due to the economic difficulties in several Asian countries and partly due to approaching market maturity for PCs in the United States, Japan, and parts of Europe. Consequently, some analysts were forecasting gradual slowing of the industry growth rates from the 20–25 percent levels that characterized the 1990s down to the 10–12 percent range by 2005. However, U.S. shipments of PCs in the 1997–99 period had grown 20–25 percent annually, a much higher rate than most industry analysts had expected. Some 45 million new PCs were sold in the United States alone in 1999. Sales of servers, along with low-end PCs and workstations, were the fastest-growing segments of the PC industry in 1999 and were expected to be the segment growth leaders in 2000 and beyond.

On the positive side, some analysts expected that worldwide computer hardware sales in the 2000–2003 period would grow at a compound annual rate of 15 to 20 percent, following cautious corporate buying in the second half of 1999 in preparation for meeting Y2K deadlines. Their expectations for 15–20 percent growth were based on (1) the introductions of Windows 2000 and Intel's new 64-bit Itanium microprocessors, (2) rapidly widening corporate use of the Internet and e-commerce technologies, (3) wider availability of high-speed Internet access, and (4) growing home use of PCs—as first-time purchasers succumbed to the lure of reasonably equipped sub-$1,000 PCs and as more parents purchased additional computers for use by their children. The three most influential factors in home ownership of PCs were education, income, and the presence of children in the household.

Competing Value Chain Models in the Global PC Industry

When the personal computer industry first began to take shape in the early 1980s, the founding companies manufactured many of the components themselves—disk drives, memory chips, graphics chips, microprocessors, motherboards, and software. Subscribing to a philosophy of "We have to develop key components in-house," they built expertise in a variety of PC-related technologies and created organizational units to produce components as well as to handle final assembly. While certain "noncritical" items were typically outsourced, if a computer maker was not at least partially vertically integrated and an assembler of some components, then it was not taken seriously as a manufacturer.

But as the industry grew, technology advanced quickly in so many directions on so many parts and components that the early personal computer manufacturers could not keep pace as experts on all fronts. There were too many technological innovations in components to pursue and too many manufacturing intricacies to master for a vertically integrated manufacturer to keep its products on the cutting edge. As a consequence, companies emerged that specialized in making particular components. Specialists could marshal enough R&D capability and resources to either lead the technological developments in their area of specialization or else quickly match the advances made by their competitors. Moreover, specialist firms could mass-produce a component and supply it to several computer manufacturers far cheaper than any one manufacturer could fund the needed component R&D and then make only whatever smaller volume of components it needed for assembling its own brand of PCs.

Thus, in recent years, computer makers had begun to abandon vertical integration in favor of a strategy of outsourcing almost all components from specialists and concentrating on efficient assembly and marketing their brand of computers. Exhibit 7 shows the value chain model that such manufacturers as Compaq Computer, IBM, Hewlett-Packard, and others used in the 1990s. It featured arm's-length transactions between specialist suppliers, manufacturer/assemblers, distributors and retailers, and end users. However, Dell, Gateway, and Micron Electronics employed a shorter value chain model, selling direct to customers and eliminating the time and costs associated with distributing through independent resellers. Building to order avoided (1) having to keep many differently equipped models on retailers' shelves to fill buyer requests for one or another configuration of options and components and (2) having to clear out slow-selling

EXHIBIT 7   **Comparative Value Chains of PC Manufacturers**

Traditional PC industry value chain (utilized by Compaq Computer, IBM, Hewlett-Packard, most others)

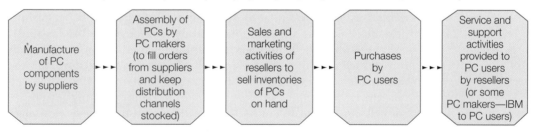

Build-to-order/direct sales value chain (employed by Dell Computer, Gateway, and Micron Electronics)

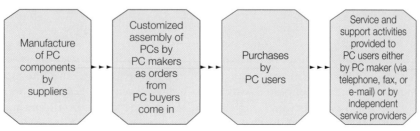

models at a discount before introducing new generations of PCs. Selling direct eliminated retailer costs and markups. (Retail dealer margins were typically in the 4 to 10 percent range.) Dell Computer was far and away the world's largest direct seller to large companies and government institutions, while Gateway was the largest direct seller to individuals and small businesses. Micron Electronics was the only other PC maker that relied on the direct-sales, build-to-order approach for the big majority of its sales.

Dell Computer's Strategy

Dell management believed it had the industry's most efficient business model. The company's strategy was built around a number of core elements: build-to-order manufacturing, partnerships with suppliers, just-in-time components inventories, direct sales to customers, award-winning customer service and technical support, and pioneering use of the Internet and e-commerce technology. Management believed that a strong first-mover advantage accrued to the company from its lead over rivals in making e-commerce a centerpiece in its strategy.

BUILD-TO-ORDER MANUFACTURING

Dell built its computers, workstations, and servers to order; none were produced for inventory. Dell customers could order custom-built servers and workstations based on the needs of their applications. Desktop and laptop customers ordered whatever configuration of microprocessor speed, random access memory (RAM), hard disk capacity, CD-ROM drive, fax/modem, monitor size, speakers, and other accessories they preferred. The orders were directed to the nearest factory. In 2000, Dell had PC assembly plants in Austin, Texas; Nashville/Lebanon, Tennessee; Limerick, Ireland; Xiamen, China; Penang, Malaysia; and El Dorado do Sul, Brazil. All six plants manufactured the company's entire line of products.

Until 1997, Dell operated its assembly lines in traditional fashion, with each worker performing a single operation. An order form accompanied each metal chassis across the production floor; drives, chips, and ancillary items were installed to match customer specifications. As a partly assembled PC arrived at a new workstation, the operator, standing beside a tall steel rack with drawers full of components, was instructed what to do by little red and green lights flashing beside the drawers containing the components the operator needed to install. When the operator was finished, the drawers containing the used components were automatically replenished from the other side, and the PC chassis glided down the line to the next workstation. However, Dell had reorganized its plants in 1997, shifting to "cell manufacturing" techniques whereby a team of workers operating at a group workstation (or cell) assembled an entire PC according to customer specifications. The shift to cell manufacturing reduced Dell's assembly times by 75 percent and doubled productivity per square foot of assembly space. Assembled computers were tested, then loaded with the desired software, shipped, and typically delivered within five to six business days of the order placement.

Dell's build-to-order, sell-direct strategy meant, of course, that Dell had no inhouse stock of finished goods inventories and that, unlike competitors using the traditional value chain model (Exhibit 7), it did not have to wait for resellers to clear out their own inventories before it could push new models into the marketplace—resellers typically operated with 60 to 70 days' inventory. Equally important was the fact that customers who bought from Dell got the satisfaction of having their computers customized to their particular liking and pocketbook.

Quality Control Programs

All assembly plants had the capability to run testing and quality control processes on components, parts, and subassemblies obtained from suppliers, as well as for the finished products Dell assembled. Suppliers were urged to participate in a quality certification program that committed them to achieving defined quality specifications. Quality control activities were undertaken at various stages in the assembly process. In addition, Dell's quality control program included testing of completed units after assembly, ongoing production reliability audits, failure tracking for early identification of problems associated with new models shipped to customers, and information obtained from customers through its service and technical support programs. All of the company's plants had been certified as meeting ISO 9002 quality standards.

PARTNERSHIPS WITH SUPPLIERS AND JUST-IN-TIME INVENTORY PRACTICES

Michael Dell believed it made much better sense for Dell Computer to partner with reputable suppliers of PC parts and components rather than integrate backward and get into parts and components manufacturing on its own. He explained why:

> If you've got a race with 20 players all vying to make the fastest graphics chip in the world, do you want to be the twenty-first horse, or do you want to evaluate the field of 20 and pick the best one?[9]

A central element of Dell Computer's strategy, therefore, was to evaluate the various makers of each component, pick the best one or two as suppliers, and partner with them for as long as they remained leaders in their specialty. Management believed long-term partnerships with reputable suppliers yielded several advantages. First, using name-brand processors, disk drives, modems, speakers, and multimedia components enhanced the quality and performance of Dell's PCs. Because of varying performance of different brands of components, the brand of the components was as important or more important to some end users than the brand of the overall system. Dell's strategy was to partner with as few outside vendors as possible and to stay with them as long as they maintained their leadership in technology, performance, and quality. Second, because Dell's partnership with a supplier was long term and because it committed to purchase a specified percentage of its requirements from that supplier, Dell was assured of getting the volume of components it needed on a timely basis even when overall market demand for a particular component temporarily exceeded the overall market supply. Third, Dell's formal partnerships with key suppliers made it feasible to have some of their engineers assigned to Dell's product design teams and for them to be treated as part of Dell. When new products were launched, suppliers' engineers were stationed in Dell's plant, and if early buyers called with a problem related to design, further assembly and shipments were halted while the supplier's engineers and Dell personnel corrected the flaw on the spot.[10]

Fourth, Dell's long-run commitment to its suppliers laid the basis for just-in-time delivery of suppliers' products to Dell's assembly plants. Many of Dell's vendors had plants or distribution centers within a few miles of Dell assembly plants and could deliver daily or even hourly if needed. To help suppliers meet its just-in-time delivery expectations, Dell openly shared its daily production schedules, sales forecasts,

[9]As quoted in Magretta, "The Power of Virtual Integration," p. 74.
[10]Ibid.

and new-model introduction plans with vendors. Using online communications technology, Dell communicated inventory levels and replenishment needs to vendors on a daily or even hourly basis. Michael Dell explained what delivery capabilities the company expected of its suppliers:

> We tell our suppliers exactly what our daily production requirements are. So it's not, "Well, every two weeks deliver 5,000 to this warehouse, and we'll put them on the shelf, and then we'll take them off the shelf." It's, "Tomorrow morning we need 8,562, and deliver them to door number seven by 7 AM."[11]

Dell also did a three-year plan with each of its key suppliers and worked with suppliers to minimize the number of different stock-keeping units of parts and components in designing its products. Current initiatives included using the Internet to further improve supply chain management and achieve still greater manufacturing and assembly efficiencies.

Why Dell Was Committed to Just-in-Time Inventory Practices

Dell's just-in-time inventory emphasis yielded major cost advantages and shortened the time it took for Dell to get new generations of its computer models into the marketplace. New advances were coming so fast in certain computer parts and components (particularly microprocessors, disk drives, and modems) that any given item in inventory was obsolete in a matter of months, sometimes quicker. Having a couple of months of component inventories meant getting caught in the transition from one generation of components to the next. Moreover, it was not unusual for there to be rapid-fire reductions in the prices of components—in 1997 and early 1998, prices for some components fell as much as 50 percent (an average of 1 percent a week). Intel, for example, regularly cut the prices on its older chips when it introduced newer chips, and it introduced new chip generations about every three months. The prices of hard disk drives with greater and greater memory capacity had dropped sharply in recent years as disk drive makers incorporated new technology that allowed them to add more gigabytes of hard disk memory very inexpensively.

The economics of minimal component inventories were dramatic. Michael Dell explained:

> If I've got 11 days of inventory and my competitor has 80 and Intel comes out with a new 450-megahertz chip, that means I'm going to get to market 69 days sooner.
>
> In the computer industry, inventory can be a pretty massive risk because if the cost of materials is going down 50 percent a year and you have two or three months of inventory versus 11 days, you've got a big cost disadvantage. And you're vulnerable to product transitions, when you can get stuck with obsolete inventory.[12]

Collaboration with suppliers was close enough to allow Dell to operate with only a few days of inventory for some components and a few hours of inventory for others. Dell supplied data on inventories and replenishment needs to its suppliers at least once a day—hourly in the case of components being delivered several times daily from nearby sources. In a couple of instances, Dell's close partnership with vendors allowed it to operate with no inventories. Dell's supplier of monitors was Sony. Because the monitors Sony supplied with the Dell name already imprinted were of dependably high quality (a defect rate of fewer than 1,000 per million), Dell didn't even open up the monitor boxes to test them.[13] Nor did it bother to have them

[11]Ibid.
[12]Ibid.
[13]Ibid.

shipped to Dell's assembly plants to be warehoused for shipment to customers. Instead, using sophisticated data exchange systems, Dell arranged for its shippers (Airborne Express and UPS) to pick up computers at its Austin plant, then pick up the accompanying monitors at the Sony plant in Mexico, match up the customer's computer order with the customer's monitor order, and deliver both to the customer simultaneously. The savings in time, energy, and cost were significant.

The company had, over the years, refined and improved its inventory tracking capabilities, its working relationships with suppliers, and its procedures for operating with smaller inventories. In fiscal year 1995, Dell averaged an inventory turn ratio of 32 days. By the end of fiscal 1997 (January 1997), the average was down to 13 days. The following year, it was 7 days, which compared very favorably with Gateway's 14-day average, Compaq's 23-day average, and the estimated industrywide average of over 50 days. In fiscal year 1999, Dell operated with an average of 6 days' supply in inventory. The company's long-term goal was to get its inventories down to a 3-day average supply.

DIRECT SALES

Selling direct to customers gave Dell firsthand intelligence about customer preferences and needs, as well as immediate feedback on design problems and quality glitches. With thousands of phone and fax orders daily, $35 million in daily Internet sales, and daily contacts between the field sales force and customers of all types, the company kept its finger on the market pulse, quickly detecting shifts in sales trends and getting prompt feedback on any problems with its products. If the company got more than a few of the same complaints, the information was relayed immediately to design engineers, who checked out the problem. When design flaws or components defects were found, the factory was notified and the problem corrected within a matter of days. Management believed Dell's ability to respond quickly gave it a significant advantage over rivals, particularly PC makers in Asia, that operated on the basis of large production runs of standardized products and sold them through retail channels. Dell saw its direct-sales approach as a totally customer-driven system, with the flexibility to change quickly to new generations of components and PC models.

Despite Dell's emphasis on direct sales, industry analysts noted that the company sold perhaps 10 percent of its PCs through a small, select group of resellers.[14] Most of these resellers were systems integrators. It was standard for Dell not to allow returns on orders from resellers or to provide price protection in the event of subsequent declines in market prices. From time to time, Dell offered its resellers incentive promotions at up to a 20 percent discount from its advertised prices on end-of-life models. Dell was said to have no plans to expand its reseller network, which consisted of 50 to 60 dealers.

Dell's Use of Market Segmentation

To make sure that each type of computer user was well served, Dell had made a special effort to segment the buyers of its computers into relevant groups and to place managers in charge of developing sales and service programs appropriate to the needs and expectations of each market segment. Until the early 1990s, Dell had operated with sales and service programs aimed at just two market segments: (1) corporate and governmental buyers who purchased in large volumes and (2) small buyers (individuals and small businesses). But as sales took off in 1995–97, these segments were subdivided into finer, more homogeneous categories (see Exhibit 8).

In 1999, 65 percent of Dell's sales were to large corporations, government agencies, and educational institutions. Many of these large customers typically ordered

---

[14]"Dell Uses Channel to Move System Inventory," *Computer Reseller News*, January 12, 1998.

EXHIBIT 8   Rapid Expansion of Dell Computer's Target Customer Segments, 1994–2000

Source: Joan Magretta, "The Power of Virtual Integration: An Interview with Dell Computer's Michael Dell," *Harvard Business Review*, March–April 1998, p. 78, and www.dell.com, February 1, 2000.

Target Customer Segments			
1994	**1996**	**1997**	**2000**
• Large customers (both corporate and governmental buyers) • Small customers (both small businesses and individuals)	• Large companies • Midsize companies • Government agencies and educational institutions • Small customers (both small businesses and individuals)	• Global enterprise accounts • Large companies • Midsize companies • Federal agencies • State and local government agencies • Educational institutions • Small companies • Individual consumers	• Global enterprise accounts • Large and midsize companies (over 400 employees) • Health care businesses (over 400 employees) • Federal government • State and local government • Education—K–12 and higher education institutions (including special programs for personal-use purchases by faculty, staff, and students) • Small companies (under 400 employees) • Home and home office

thousands of units at a time and bought at least $1 million in PCs annually. Dell had hundreds of sales representatives calling on large corporate and institutional accounts. Its customer list included Shell Oil, Sony, Exxon-Mobil, MCI, Ford Motor, Toyota, Eastman Chemical, Boeing, Goldman Sachs, Oracle, Microsoft, Woolwich (a British bank with $64 billion in assets), Michelin, Unilever, Deutsche Bank, Wal-Mart, and First Union (one of the 10 largest U.S. banks). However, no one customer represented more than 2 percent of total sales.

Dell's sales to individuals and small businesses were made by telephone, fax, and the Internet. It had a call center in the United States with toll-free phone lines; customers could talk with a sales representative about specific models, get information faxed or mailed to them, place an order, and pay by credit card. Internationally, Dell had set up toll-free call centers in Europe and Asia.[15] The call centers were equipped with technology that routed calls from a particular country to a particular call center. Thus, for example, a customer calling from Lisbon, Portugal, was automatically directed to the call center in Montpelier, France, and connected to a Portuguese-speaking sales rep. Dell began Internet sales at its Web site (www.dell.com) in 1995, almost overnight achieving sales of $1 million per day. In 1997 sales reached an average of $3 million daily, hitting $6 million on some days during the Christmas shopping period. Dell's Internet sales averaged nearly $4 million daily in the first quarter of 1997, reached $14 million daily by year-end 1998, and climbed sharply to $35 million daily at the close of 1999. In early 2000, visits to Dell's Web site for information and order placement were approaching 2.5 million weekly, about 20 times more

[15]"Michael Dell Rocks," *Fortune*, May 11, 1998, p. 66.

than the number of phone calls to sales representatives. In early 2000, about 43 percent of Dell's sales were Web-enabled and the percentage was increasing.

Dell in Europe

In fiscal year 1999, $6.6 billion of Dell's $18.2 billion in sales came from foreign customers. Europe, where resellers were strongly entrenched and Dell's direct sales approach was novel, was Dell's biggest foreign market, accounting for sales of $4.7 billion, up from $3.0 billion the prior year. Dell's European revenues were growing over 50 percent annually, and unit volume was increasing at nearly a 35 percent annual rate. Sales of PCs in Europe were 19.7 million units in 1997, 25.4 million units in 1998, and 29.9 million units in 1999. Expectations were for continued growth of 18 to 22 percent for the next several years. Europe's population and economy were roughly the same as those of the United States, but computer usage was only half that of the United States in 1999. Germany led Europe in sales of PCs, with 6.6 million units in 1999 (up 21.6 percent over 1998); Great Britain was second, with unit sales of 5.5 million (up 25.2 percent over 1998); and France was third, with 1999 unit sales of 4.4 million (up 26.7 percent over 1998). According to Dataquest, the top five market leaders in PCs in Europe were as follows:

Company	1999 Shipments	1999 Market Share (%)	1998 Shipments	1998 Market Share (%)	Percent Growth
Compaq	4,675,400	15.6	4,123,900	16.2	13.4
Fujitsu Siemens	3,471,600	11.5	2,615,000	10.3	32.8
Dell	2,612,200	8.7	1,943,600	7.7	34.4
IBM	2,340,300	7.8	2,107,400	8.3	11.1
Hewlett-Packard	1,897,600	6.3	1,482,900	5.8	28.0
Others	14,934,800	49.9	13,128,700	51.7	13.8
Totals	29,931,900	100.0	25,401,500	100.0	17.8

Fujitsu and Siemens had merged their PC operations in 1999 to move ahead of Dell in the ratings in Europe during 1999 (based on the combined market shares of the two brands); based on individual brand, however, Dell ranked second in Europe, ahead of both the Fujitsu brand and the Siemens brand.

Dell in China

Dell Computer entered China in 1998 and by 2000 had achieved a market share close to 2 percent. China was the fifth largest market for PCs in the world, behind the United States, Japan, Germany, and Britain. But with unit volume expanding 30 percent annually and a population of 1.2 billion people, the Chinese market for PCs was expected to become the second largest in the world by 2005 (with annual sales of $25 billion) and to become the world's largest PC market sometime thereafter. The market leader in China was Legend, a local company; other major local PC producers were Founder (ranked fourth) and Great Wall (ranked sixth). IBM, Hewlett-Packard, and Compaq were among the top five market share leaders in China—all three relied on resellers to handle sales and service. Other companies among the top 10 in market share in China included Toshiba, NEC Japan, and Acer (a Taiwan-based company). Dell, ranked eighth in market share in 1999, was the only market contender that employed a direct-sales business model. Dell's sales in China in 1999 were up 87 percent over 1998 levels.

Dell management believed that in China, as in other countries around the world, the company could be very price-competitive by cutting out middlemen and selling direct via the Internet, telephone, and a sales force that called on large customers. Dell's primary market target in China was large corporate accounts. Management believed that many Chinese companies would find the savings from direct sales appealing, that they would like the idea of having Dell build PCs to their requirements and specifications, and that—once they became Dell customers—they would like the convenience of Internet purchases and telephone orders. Dell recognized that its direct-sales approach would temporarily put it at a disadvantage in appealing to small-business customers and individual consumers. According to an executive from rival Legend, "It takes two years of a person's savings to buy a PC in China. And when two years of savings is at stake, the whole family wants to come out to a store to touch and try the machine."[16] But Dell believed that over time, as Chinese consumers became more familiar with PCs and more comfortable with making online purchases, it would be able to attract growing numbers of small-business customers and consumers through Internet and telephone sales.

IBM was the market leader in 1999 in the entire Asia-Pacific region, with an estimated 8.4 percent share, up from 8.1 percent in 1998.[17] Compaq had a second-place 7.3 percent share but was the market leader in a number of individual countries within the region. China-based Legend had a 7.1 percent share, most all of which came from sales in China. Samsung had the fourth largest market share, followed by Hewlett-Packard.

Dell in Latin America

In 2000, PC sales in Latin America were approaching 5 million units annually. Latin America had a population of 450 million people. Dell management believed that in the next few years use of PCs in Latin America would reach 1 for every 30 people (one-tenth the penetration in the United States), pushing annual sales up to 15 million units. The company's new plant in Brazil, the largest market in Latin America, was opened to produce, sell, and provide service and technical support for customers in Brazil, Argentina, Chile, Uruguay, and Paraguay.

CUSTOMER SERVICE AND TECHNICAL SUPPORT

Service became a feature of Dell's strategy in 1986 when the company began providing a year's free on-site service with most of its PCs after users complained about having to ship their PCs back to Austin for repairs. Dell contracted with local service providers to handle customer requests for repairs; on-site service was provided on a next-day basis. Dell also provided its customers with technical support via a toll-free phone number, fax, or e-mail. Dell received close to 40,000 e-mail messages monthly requesting service and support and had 25 technicians to process the requests. Bundled service policies were a major selling point for winning corporate accounts. If a customer preferred to work with its own service provider, Dell supplied that provider with the training and spare parts needed to service the customer's equipment.

Value-Added Services

Selling direct allowed Dell to keep close track of the purchases of its large global customers, country by country and department by department—information that customers found valuable. And its close customer relationships resulted in Dell being quite knowledgeable about what each customer needed and how its PC network functioned. Aside from using this information to help customers plan their PC

---

[16]As quoted in Neel Chowdhury, "Dell Cracks China," *Fortune*, June 21, 1999, p. 121.

[17]According to data compiled by International Data Corporation and provided to the case researchers by IDC.

needs and configure their PC networks, Dell used it to add to the value it delivered to its customers. For example, Dell could load a customer's software at the factory, thereby eliminating the need for the customer's PC personnel to unpack the PC, deliver it to an employee's desk, hook it up, place asset tags on the PC, then load the needed software from an assortment of CD-ROMs and diskettes—a process that could take several hours and cost $200 to $300.[18] Dell's solution was to load the customer's software onto large Dell servers at the factory and, when a particular version of a customer's PC came off the assembly line, to use its high-speed server network to load whatever software the customer had specified onto the PC's hard disk in a few seconds. If the customer so desired, Dell would place the customer's asset tags on the PC at the factory. Dell charged customers only $15 or $20 for the software-loading and asset-tagging services—the savings to customers were thus considerable. One large customer reported savings of $500,000 annually from having Dell load its software and place asset tags on its PCs at the factory.[19] In 1997, about 2 million of the 7 million PCs Dell sold were shipped with customer-specific software already loaded on the PCs.

In late 1997, in another effort to add value for its customers, Dell, following Compaq's lead, created a financial services group to assist customers with financing their PC networks.

Premier Pages

Dell had developed customized, password-protected Web sites (called Premier Pages) for 40,000 corporate, governmental, and institutional customers worldwide. Premier Page sites gave customer personnel online access to information about all Dell products and configurations the company had purchased or that were currently authorized for purchase. Employees of Dell's large customers could use Premier Pages to (1) obtain customer-specific pricing for whatever machines and options they wanted to consider, (2) place an order online that would be electronically routed to higher-level managers for approval and then on to Dell for assembly and delivery, and (3) seek advanced help desk support. Customers could also search and sort all invoices and obtain purchase histories. These features eliminated paper invoices, cut ordering time, and reduced the internal labor customers needed to staff corporate purchasing and accounting functions. A customer's Premier Pages also contained all of the elements of its relationship with Dell, including who the Dell sales and support contacts were in every country where the customer had operations, what software Dell loaded on each of the various types of PCs the customer purchased, and service and warranty records for each machine. So far, customer use of Premier Pages had boosted the productivity of Dell salespeople assigned to these accounts by 50 percent. Dell was providing Premier Page service to thousands of additional customers annually and adding more features to further improve functionality.

www.dell.com

At the company's Web site, which underwent a global redesign in late 1999 and had 50 country-specific sites in local languages and currencies, prospective buyers could review Dell's entire product line in detail, configure and price customized PCs, place orders, and track those orders from manufacturing through shipping. The closing rate on sales coming through www.dell.com were 20 percent higher than sales inquiries received via telephone or fax. The company was adding Web-based

---

[18]Magretta, "The Power of Virtual Integration," p. 79.
[19]"Michael Dell Rocks," p. 61.

customer service and support tools to make a customer's online experience pleasant and satisfying. Already the company had implemented a series of online technical support tools:

- *Support.Dell.com*—This Web-based feature allowed customers to create a customized support home page; review technical specifications for Dell systems; obtain information and answers from an extensive database collected by Dell technicians, service providers, and customers; click on online links to Dell's primary suppliers; and take three online courses on PC usage at no charge. The site enabled customers to select how they received online help, based on their comfort and experience with PC technology. The information available at this part of Dell's Web site was particularly helpful to the internal help-desk groups at large companies. In late 1999, customer visits to support.Dell.com were running at a rate of 19 million per year.

- *E-Support*—Dell had developed advanced technology called "E-Support—Direct from Dell" that helped Dell systems detect, diagnose, and resolve most of their own problems without the need for users to interact with Dell's support personnel. The goal of Dell's E-Support technology was to create computing environments where a PC would be able to maintain itself, thus moving support from a reactive process to a preventive one. Michael Dell saw E-Support as "the beginning of what we call self-healing systems that we think will be the future of online support."[20] Dell expected that by the end of 2000 more than 50 percent of the customers needing technical help would use E-Support—Direct from Dell. Management believed the service would shorten the time it took to fix glitches and problems, reduce the need for service calls, cut customer downtimes, and lower Dell's tech-support costs.

- *Dell Talk*—An online discussion group with 100,000 registered users, Dell Talk brought users and information technology (IT) professionals together to discuss common IT problems and issues.

- *Ask Dudley*—The Ask Dudley tool gave customers instant answers to technical service and support questions. Customers typed in the question in their native language and clicked on "ask."

In February 2000, 40 to 45 percent of Dell's technical support activities were being conducted via the Internet. Dell was aggressively pursuing initiatives to enhance its online technical support tools. Its top priority was the development of tools (as described in the above list) that could tap into a user's computer, make a diagnosis, and if the problem was software related, perform an online fix. Dell expected that such tools would not only make it easier and quicker for customers to resolve technical problems but would also help it reduce the costs of technical support calls (currently running at 8 million calls a year). The company estimated that its online technical support tools had resulted in 25 percent fewer support calls from users, generating savings of between $5 and $10 per call.

Management believed that the enhancements it was making to www.dell.com made it easier and faster for customers to do business with Dell by shrinking transaction and order fulfillment times, increasing accuracy, and providing more personalized content. According to management, a positive Web site experience was a bigger driver of "e-loyalty" than traditional attributes like price and product selection.

---

[20]As quoted in *Austin American-Statesman*, August 26, 1999.

On-Site Service

Corporate customers paid Dell fees to provide support and on-site service. Dell generally contracted with third-party providers to make the necessary on-site service calls. Customers notified Dell when they had PC problems; such notices triggered two electronic dispatches—one to ship replacement parts from Dell's factory to the customer sites and one to notify the contract service provider to prepare to make the needed repairs as soon as the parts arrived.[21] Bad parts were returned to Dell for diagnosis of what went wrong and what could be done to see that the problems wouldn't happen again. Problems relating to faulty components or flawed components design were promptly passed along to the relevant supplier, who was expected to improve quality control procedures or redesign the component. Dell's strategy was to manage the flow of information gleaned from customer service activities to improve product quality and reliability.

On-Site Dell Support

A number of Dell's corporate accounts were large enough to justify dedicated on-site teams of Dell employees. Customers usually welcomed such teams, preferring to focus their time and energy on the core business rather than being distracted by PC purchasing and servicing issues. For example, Boeing, which had 100,000 Dell PCs, was served by a staff of 30 Dell employees who resided on-site at Boeing facilities and were intimately involved in planning Boeing's PC needs and configuring Boeing's network. While Boeing had its own people working on what the company's best answers for using PCs were, there was close collaboration between Dell and Boeing personnel to understand Boeing's needs in depth and to figure out the best solutions.

Migration to New Technology

Dell had opened facilities in both Europe and North America to assist its customers and independent software providers in migrating their systems and applications to Windows 2000, Intel's new 64-bit Itanium computer chip technology, and other next-generation computing and Internet technologies. Dell was partnering with Intel, Microsoft, Computer Associates, and other prominent PC technology providers to help customers make more effective use of the Internet and the latest computing technologies. Dell, which used Intel microprocessors exclusively in its computers, had been a consistent proponent of standardized Intel-based platforms because it believed those platforms provided customers with the best total value and performance. Dell management considered both Intel and Microsoft as long-term strategic partners in mapping out its future.

Customer Forums

In addition to using its sales and support mechanisms to stay close to customers, Dell held regional forums to stimulate the flow of information back and forth with customers. The company formed "Platinum Councils," composed of its largest customers in the United States, Europe, Japan, and the Asia-Pacific area; regional meetings were held every six to nine months.[22] In the larger regions, there were two meetings—one for chief information officers and one for technical personnel. As many as 100 customers and 100 Dell executives and representatives, including Michael Dell, attended the three-day meetings. At the meetings, Dell's senior technologists shared their views on the direction of the latest technological develop-

[21]Kevin Rollins, "Using Information to Speed Execution," *Harvard Business Review,* March–April, 1998, p. 81.
[22]Magretta, "The Power of Virtual Integration," p. 80.

ments, what the flow of technology really meant for customers, and Dell's plans for introducing new and upgraded products over the next two years. There were also breakout sessions on such topics as how to manage the transition to Windows NT, how to manage the use of notebooks by people out in the field, and whether leasing was better than buying. Customers were provided opportunities to share information and learn from one another (many had similar problems) as well as exchange ideas with Dell personnel. Dell found that the information gleaned from customers at these meetings assisted in forecasting demand for the company's products.

PIONEERING LEADERSHIP IN USE OF THE INTERNET AND E-COMMERCE TECHNOLOGY

Michael Dell believed that the Internet had revolutionary business potential, and he was instrumental in making Dell Computer a pioneering first-mover in using the Internet and e-commerce technologies. In a 1999 speech to 1,200 Dell customers, he said:

> The world will be changed forever by the Internet . . . The Internet will be your business. If your business isn't enabled by providing customers and suppliers with more information, you're probably already in trouble. The Internet provides a dramatic reduction in the cost of transactions and the cost of interaction among people and businesses, and it creates dramatic new opportunities and destroys old competitive advantages. The Internet is like a weapon sitting on a table ready to be picked up by either you or your competitors.[23]

Michael Dell believed that for a company to harness the power of the Internet and succeed in revolutionizing the way business was done, it had to observe three rules:

1. Give customers a better experience online than they could get offline.
2. Execute efficiently.
3. Recognize that compressing time and distance in business relationships with suppliers and customers to enhance the velocity of business transactions is the ultimate source of competitive advantage. (Dell was convinced that transacting business with suppliers and customers in real time drove big improvements in business efficiency—requiring fewer people, less inventory, and fewer physical assets and speeding new products to market.)

Dell Computer was rapidly gaining valuable experience and know-how in applying these rules to its business. For example, the company had created valuechain.dell.com, which provided suppliers with secure personalized access to Dell's operations through a single portal. This tool facilitated real-time collaboration on the quality of the items being supplied, helped assure continuity of supply and minimal components inventories, and made it possible for engineers at Dell and its suppliers to jointly develop online designs of next-generation components and products. Dell had also created an online "scorecard" for suppliers showing their performance against the quality standards that had been agreed on and how well they were doing against other suppliers in the same class. Both tools helped the company achieve its strategic objectives of product quality and reliability, rapid inventory turnover, and low costs.

Dell was using the Internet to improve its execution efficiency in several ways. By greatly improving the company's capability to provide order status information quickly and conveniently over the Internet, the company had been able to eliminate tens of thousands of order status inquiries coming in by phone. Order status inquiries

---

[23]Keynote speech given on August 25, 1999, in Austin, Texas, at Dell's "DirectConnect Conference."

handled by phone typically cost the company between $3 and $10; however, the cost could be considerably more if a customer had 100 orders and the status of each one had to checked. Close to 80 percent of Dell's order status inquiries in 2000 were being handled via the Internet at a cost close to zero, saving Dell an estimated $21 million annually and freeing personnel to do higher-value-added activities.

Although Dell was doing a very good job in solving 80 percent of customer issues over the phone (compared to an industry average of 27 percent) and saving money by not having to dispatch an on-site service provider, the company was working to greatly improve its online diagnostic technical support tools—Support.Dell.com, Dell Talk, and Ask Dudley. Management believed that Web-enabled technical support would make it easier and quicker for users to get the technical support they needed, as well as reduce the costs of handling the current total of 8 million technical support calls a year.

In 1998 the company had used technology to tackle the challenge of reducing its infrastructure cost of handling messages from customers. Michael Dell explained:

> The needs for our e-mail structure had grown beyond the support we had internally. We faced a very serious challenge. We were receiving 2.7 million messages per week within Dell's system, 4.3 million per month over the Internet, and our user base was growing at the rate of 50 percent per year. To solve this, we consolidated 200 servers into about 25 PowerEdge servers running Microsoft Exchange. There was a 10 times reduction in the number of servers and the associated management costs. We migrated to Exchange and lowered our user cost by 29 percent.[24]

OTHER ELEMENTS OF DELL'S BUSINESS STRATEGY

Other element of Dell's strategy, in addition to those mentioned above, are discussed below.

Demand Forecasting

Management believed that accurate sales forecasts were key to keeping costs down and minimizing inventories, given the complexity and diversity of the company's product line. Because Dell worked diligently at maintaining a close relationship with its large corporate and institutional customers and because it sold direct to small customers via telephone and the Internet, it was possible to keep a finger on the pulse of demand—what was selling and what was not. Moreover, the company's market segmentation strategy paved the way for in-depth understanding of customers' current needs, evolving requirements, and expectations. Having credible real-time information about what customers were actually buying and having firsthand knowledge of large customers' buying intentions gave Dell strong capability to forecast demand. Furthermore, Dell passed that information on to suppliers so they could plan their production accordingly. The company worked hard at managing the flow of information it got from the marketplace and quickly sending that information to both internal groups and vendors.

Forecasting was viewed as a critical sales skill. Sales-account managers were coached on how to lead large customers through a discussion of their future needs for PCs, workstations, servers, and peripheral equipment. Distinctions were made between purchases that were virtually certain and those that were contingent on some event. Salespeople made note of the contingent events so they could follow up at the appropriate time. With smaller customers, there was real-time information about sales, and direct telephone sales personnel often were able to steer customers

[24]Ibid.

toward configurations that were immediately available to help fine-tune the balance between demand and supply.

Research and Development

Company management believed that it was Dell's job to sort out all the new technology coming into the marketplace and help steer customers to options and solutions most relevant to their needs. The company talked to its customers frequently about "relevant technology," listening carefully to customers' needs and problems and endeavoring to identify the most cost-effective solutions. Dell had about 1,600 engineers working on product development and spent about $250 million annually to improve users' experience with its products—including incorporating the latest and best technologies, making its products easy to use, and devising ways to keep costs down. The company's R&D unit also studied and implemented ways to control quality and to streamline the assembly process. Much time went into tracking all the new developments in components and software to ascertain how they would prove useful to computer users. For instance, it was critical to track vendor progress in making longer-lasting batteries because battery life was very important to the buyers of portable computers. Dell was the first company to put lithium ion batteries with a 5.5- to 6-hour life in all of its laptop models.

Advertising

Michael Dell was a strong believer in the power of advertising and frequently espoused its importance in the company's strategy. His competitive zeal resulted in the company's being the first to use comparative ads, throwing barbs at Compaq's higher prices. Although Compaq won a lawsuit against Dell for making false comparisons, Michael Dell was unapologetic, arguing that the ads were "very effective" and that they allowed the company "to increase customer awareness about value."[25] Dell insisted that the company's ads be communicative and forceful, not soft and fuzzy.

The company regularly had prominent ads describing its products and prices in such leading computer publications as *PC Magazine* and *PC World*, as well as in *USA Today*, *The Wall Street Journal*, and other business publications. In the spring of 1998, the company debuted a major multiyear worldwide TV campaign to strengthen its brand image—the theme for the campaign was "Be Direct." A number of the ads featured Michael Dell talking about the importance of direct customer relationships, the company's attentive and responsive customer service, and the unique value created by the company's direct-sales and build-to-order approaches. One of Dell's tag lines was "Empower Your Business Through the Internet with Dell."

Dell's Increased Emphasis on Servers and Storage Devices

Dell entered the market for low-end PC servers (under $25,000) in the second half of 1996. Its entry strategy included adding 23,000 square feet of production capacity suitable for cell manufacturing techniques and self-contained work teams, training 1,300 telemarketers to sell servers, assigning 160 sales reps with systems know-how to big customer accounts, and recruiting a staff of systems experts to help the sales reps. It also contracted with companies such as Electronic Data Systems, which had in-depth systems and networking expertise, to help provide service to large customers with extensive server networks.

There were several drivers behind Dell's entry into servers. The use of servers by corporate customers was growing rapidly. The margins on servers were large. Moreover, purchase price was not as significant a factor in selecting which brand of server to buy because servers required far more in the way of service, support, and software.

---

[25]"The Education of Michael Dell," p. 85.

Several of Dell's rivals, most notably Compaq Computer, were using their big margins on server sales to subsidize price cuts on desktops and notebooks in an attempt to win corporate PC accounts away from Dell. According to Michael Dell,

> We had to meet the challenge of extending the Dell brand beyond our strong desktop and notebook franchises. The next logical step was servers. Entering the server business was not only a huge opportunity but clearly a competitive necessity. An explosion of networked and internetworked systems was occurring throughout corporations, which meant that our present customers—the techno-savvy, second- or third-time buyers who were our core market—would be looking to make big purchases.
>
> At the same time, the emergence of industry standards for operating systems (Windows NT) and multiprocessor servers meant that Dell could develop its own server systems based on these standards and avoid massive investments in new proprietary technologies that would ultimately become very costly for our customers. It also meant that we did not have to acquire a competitor to enter the server business.
>
> We could profit by offering lower prices through the direct model. We could, in effect, shatter the price premiums customers were paying for proprietary server technologies.
>
> The alternative wasn't pretty. Servers were a force literally big enough to change the operating environment. If we ignored them, the market would consolidate around the top three providers—Compaq, IBM, and HP. We would be seen as a bit player, and would lose our standing with technology providers. And our operating margins would start to thin.
>
> Our large competitors also were using excessively high margins in servers to subsidize the less profitable parts of their business, like desktops and notebooks. If we didn't move into servers, we would be greatly exposed to attack in the desktop and notebook market.
>
> We had the opportunity to do with servers what we had originally done with desktops and then notebooks: rapidly build market share by offering higher performance at a lower price, simultaneously forcing our competitors to lower their server prices and collapse their margins to the point where they couldn't afford to subsidize their other product lines. We couldn't afford not to take such an opportunity.[26]

As Michael Dell predicted, Dell Computer's build-to-order, sell-direct strategy gave it a significant cost and pricing advantage over rival sellers of servers. When Dell launched its new PowerEdge server line, the servers from such competitors as Compaq, IBM, and Hewlett-Packard, all of which relied on networks of resellers, were priced 15 to 20 percent higher than comparable Dell models. To communicate to Dell employees the importance of achieving success in the server market, the company sent out companywide "Message from Michael" e-mails, put up posters in high-traffic areas, and talked through the strategy at numerous brown-bag lunches and company get-togethers.[27] It also staged an event called "The Great Dell Torch Event" for 7,000 employees in a downtown Austin auditorium, opened by Michael Dell running into the auditorium carrying an Olympic-sized torch. In meetings with customers Michael Dell and Dell salespeople told customers to ask their server vendors to meet Dell's pricing so they could at least save money on server purchases if they did not opt to buy from Dell. In the first year that Dell competed in servers, rivals cut prices about 17 percent on their competing models.

Dell's objective was to achieve a double-digit share of the server market by year-end 1998; it achieved that goal in the middle of 1997. By year-end 1997, Dell had

[26]Dell, *Direct from Dell*, pp. 82–83.

[27]Ibid., p. 84.

gone from 10th to 4th in market share worldwide. By the fall of 1998, Dell had passed IBM and Hewlett-Packard in the U.S. market, moving into second place with a 19 percent share; and Dell was the only server provider growing substantially faster than the rest of the market. During the 1997–99 period, Dell expanded its lineup of server products to include more powerful models, added modular features, and boosted its service capabilities for servers. By 2000, the company had captured a sizable share of the market for low-end servers and was a significant competitive force in the server segment.

More recently, Dell had expanded its product line to include storage devices designed to handle a variety of customers' needs for high-speed data storage and retrieval. Dell's PowerVault line of storage products had data protection and recovery features that made it easy for customers to add and manage storage and simplify consolidation. Dell management saw storage devices as a growth opportunity because the computing systems of corporate and institutional customers were making increasing use of storage devices.

Dell's Introduction of a WebPC

In December 1999, Dell unveiled a new line of PCs stripped of fancy features and equipped for easy, quick Internet access by novices. The new line included three models, ranging in price from $999 to $2,349. Each came with a monitor, printer, technical support options, and one-year subscription to Dell's Internet service, Dell-Net. Each of the new WebPCs could be plugged in and made Internet-ready in three steps. The main unit was 6 inches wide, 11 inches high, and 10 inches deep and weighed 10 pounds. Dell believed the new line would help broaden the market for its products and give it a growing presence in the consumer and small-business segments. According to Michael Dell, "If Dell executes in the consumer and small business market alone this could add an additional $10 billion in revenue over the next several years."[28] Two competitors were planning to launch comparable products. Compaq Computer had announced it would begin selling an iPaq PC in early 2000 for $499 without a monitor. Advanced Micro Devices planned to introduce its EasyNow model in late December at prices of $500 to $1,000.

DELL'S EFFORTS TO PROMOTE GOOD STRATEGY EXECUTION

Michael Dell was a strong believer that good planning and good strategy amounted to little without good strategy execution. To promote effective strategy execution, the company had adopted a number of policies and operating practices. The company stressed use of facts and data in daily decision making—"Facts are your friend" was a common phase at Dell and an integral part of the corporate culture. The company had developed detailed profit and loss statements for each part of the business, and managers were expected to make fact-based decisions according to their impact on the bottom line; those who resisted were forced out.

Because much of what had contributed to Dell's success went against the grain of conventional wisdom, Dell Computer made a conscious effort to hire employees who had open, questioning minds and were always ready to learn and try something new.[29] Job applicants were screened carefully; the company looked for people who not only were results-oriented, self-reliant, and intelligent but also expected change to be the norm and liked looking at things from a different angle and coming up

---

[28]As quoted in Connie Mabin, "Dell Focuses on Novice Users with Simple WebPC," *The Associated Press State and Local Wire,* December 1, 1999.

[29]Dell, *Direct from Dell,* pp. 109–11.

with unprecedented, innovative solutions. People were hired not so much for their ability to come in and fill a job opening as for their capacity to grow and develop with the company over the long term. Once hired, Dell employees were encouraged to be innovative, to look for breakthrough ideas, to challenge the status quo, and to experiment with new or better ways of doing things. Self-criticism and acceptance of periodic "course corrections" were ingrained in the Dell culture; everyone could question how things were being done and offer suggestions for improvement. Michael Dell preached against complacency and satisfaction with the status quo:

> We try to avoid being too proud of our accomplishments . . . If we start to think we've made it, we're just setting ourselves up to be eclipsed by someone else . . . It's easy to fall in love with how far you've come and how much you've done. It's definitely harder to see the cracks in the structure you've built yourself, but that's all the more reason to look hard and look often. Even if something seems to be working, it can always be improved.[30]

A substantial part of the work process at Dell was organized around teams. Teams were given objectives and were held accountable for their performance. For example, on the factory floor people worked in teams of two to receive, manufacture, and pack an order for delivery to a customer. Profit-sharing incentives encouraged members to be productive as a team. Hourly metrics for team performance were posted on monitors on the factory floor so that each team could see how it was doing relative to other teams and to performance targets. Ratings of individual performance were based on a 360-degree performance appraisal that involved input from everyone with whom an employee worked rather than just supervisors.

The vast majority of Dell's employees were also stockholders as a result of the company's employee stock purchase plans, stock option grants, and a 401(K) plan in which Dell matched employee contributions with stock rather than cash. The compensation and incentives of Dell employees were tied to the health of Dell's business, measured chiefly by the company's return on invested capital (ROIC) and growth rate. Tying compensation increases and incentive awards to ROIC began in 1995 with a companywide push to educate all employees to the benefits of boosting ROIC that included e-mail "Messages from Michael," articles in the company newsletter, posters, and talks by managers. The company explained how employees could contribute to a higher ROIC by helping reduce cycle times, eliminating scrap and waste, increasing inventory turns, forecasting accurately, boosting sales volumes, controlling operating expenses, collecting accounts receivable more efficiently, and doing things right the first time.[31] Dell executives believed that focusing attention on ROIC mobilized employees around a single company goal. And they believed that treating employees as owners helped employees understand the drivers of the business, fostered a sense of pride, and got them much more involved in the process of questioning procedures, experimenting with new ideas, and learning better ways to do things.

To spur the process of looking for innovations and new opportunities, Dell management made a practice of setting stretch objectives. In 1997, the company set a target of selling 50 percent of its systems at www.dell.com within the next few years. At the time, Web site sales were averaging $1 million per day and annual revenues were $12 billion. The 50 percent target was not picked out of the air but was based on the company's growth, the market potential of the company's products, and the perceived potential of online sales.

---

[30]Ibid., pp. 128–29.
[31]Ibid., pp. 134–35.

Dell management spent a lot of time communicating to employees—explaining what was going on, what the company's strategy was, where the company stood in the market, what its future plans were, and what the organization needed to do to achieve its objectives. Michael Dell conducted "town hall" meetings at various locations annually and spent a lot of time answering questions. Company successes were celebrated at get-togethers and via e-mail communications congratulating teams on big account wins or other special achievements. Best practices in one area were shared with other areas. Much communication took place in real time via extensive use of e-mail and the company intranet.

The company made a concerted effort to avoid hierarchical structure, believing that hierarchy stymied communication and resulted in slower response times. Michael Dell explained:

> We're allergic to hierarchy. Hierarchical structure to me fundamentally implies a loss of speed. It implies that there's congestion in the flow of information. It implies the need for layers of approval and command and control, and signoffs here, there, and everywhere. That's inconsistent with the speed with which we all need to make decisions, both as leaders and as a company, in this fast-paced marketplace . . . Time is everything—the sooner you deal with an issue, the sooner it's resolved.[32]

Recent Changes in the Strategies of PC Makers

Rivalry among the world's makers of PCs was quite strong in 2000. As the CEO of Gateway put it in January, "The environment in which we are operating is tough and getting tougher." Competitive pressures, which had been mounting since 1997, had prompted a number of companies to alter their strategies for competing.

THE ATTEMPTS OF SEVERAL MANUFACTURERS AND RETAILERS TO CLONE DELL'S PC STRATEGY

Dell's competitors—Compaq, IBM, Packard Bell NEC, and Hewlett-Packard—were shifting their business models to build-to-order manufacturing to reduce their inventories and speed new models to market. Compaq launched its build-to-order initiative in July 1997 and hoped to cut costs 10 to 12 percent. Compaq's revamped assembly plants were able to turn out a custom-built PC in three to four hours and could load the desired software in six minutes. Packard Bell NEC's program allowed customers to place orders by phone. But all three were finding that it was hard to duplicate Dell's approach because of the time it took to develop just-in-time delivery schedules with suppliers, to coordinate their mutual production schedules, and to shift smoothly to next-generation parts and components as they appeared on the market. It took extensive collaboration to plan smooth technology transitions. Compaq and Hewlett-Packard had spent 18 months planning their build-to-order strategies and expected it would take another 18 or more months to achieve their inventory- and cost-reduction goals.

At the same time, such computer retailers as Tandy Corporation's Computer City, CompUSA, OfficeMax, and Wal-Mart Stores had gotten into the build-to-order, sell-direct business. CompUSA was offering customers two lines of desktop computers that could be ordered at any of its 134 stores, by phone, at its Web site, or through its corporate sales force; its goal was to undercut Dell's price by $200 on each configuration. Wal-Mart was offering build-to-order PCs made by a contract manufacturer at its Web site.

[32]Ibid., pp. 133, 137.

Dell was seen as having the right strategy to appeal to customers well versed in PC technology who knew what options and features they wanted and who were aware of the price differences among brands. According to one industry analyst, "Dell is everybody's target. No matter who you talk to in the industry, Dell is the brand to beat."[33]

THE MOVES OF PC MAKERS TO BROADEN THEIR BUSINESS

Several leading players in the PC industry made moves in late 1997 and early 1998 to expand into selling more than just PCs in an effort to improve profitability. The sharp declines in the prices of PCs had crimped gross profit margins and prompted such companies as Dell, Compaq, Gateway, Hewlett-Packard, and IBM to view selling PCs as an entrée to providing a bigger lineup of products.

To move beyond simple PC manufacturing, Compaq in late 1997 acquired Digital Equipment Company (DEC), which derived $6 billion in revenues from providing a range of PC services to corporate customers. Both Hewlett-Packard and IBM had always viewed the PC business as part of a larger portfolio of products and services they offered customers. A substantial portion of Hewlett-Packard's revenues and profits came from sales of servers and printers. IBM derived a big portion of its revenues from mainframe computers, software, and technical and support services.

Dell, Gateway, and several other makers of PCs for the home market had begun offering Internet access service to purchasers of their PCs. Gateway's chairman, Ted Waitt, explained, "We're about customer relations a lot more than we are about PCs. If we get a 5 percent margin on a $1,500 PC, we make $75. But if we can make $3 a month on Internet access, that's another $100 over three years. Three years from now, I don't think just selling PC hardware will allow anyone to have a great business."[34] PC makers were also selling printers, scanners, Zip drives, assorted software packages, and other computer-related devices at their Web sites to boost revenues and overall margins. Several PC makers had begun leasing PCs to individuals and households and to finance PCs on low monthly payment plans in hopes of getting the customer to trade in the old PC for a new PC later when the lease expired or the last payment was made.

Profiles of Selected Competitors in the PC Industry

Below are brief profiles of Dell's principal competitors in the global PC market.

COMPAQ COMPUTER

In 1999 Compaq Computer Corporation was the world's largest supplier of personal computer systems and the second largest global computing company (behind IBM), with annual sales of $38.5 billion and profits of $569 million. Compaq became the world's largest seller of PCs in 1995, displacing IBM as the world leader. Compaq acquired Tandem Computer in 1997 and Digital Equipment Corporation in 1998 to give it capabilities, products, and service offerings that allowed it to compete in every sector of the computer industry.[35] When Compaq purchased Digital, Digital was a troubled company with high operating costs, an inability to maintain technological leadership in high-end computing, and a nine-year string of having either lost

[33]As quoted in *Business Week,* September 29, 1997, p. 38.
[34]David Kirkpatrick, "Old PC Dogs Try New Tricks," *Fortune,* July 6, 1998, pp. 186–88.
[35]"Can Compaq Catch Up?" *Business Week,* May 3, 1999, p. 163.

money or barely broken even.[36] The acquisitions gave Compaq a product line that included PCs, servers, workstations, mainframes, peripherals, and such services as business and e-commerce solutions, hardware and software support, systems integration, and technology consulting. Compaq management believed that additional unit volume provided by the Digital acquisition permitted greater economies of scale in production and gave it more leverage in securing favorable pricing from component suppliers.[37] Digital's extensive service and support network allowed Compaq to offer a comprehensive portfolio of professional computing services and technical support through a global network of approximately 27,000 employees as well as 30,000 service delivery partners.[38] Compaq had very strong brand recognition because of its status as the global market share leader in the PC market.

Compaq's Strategy

Compaq's strategy was to sell almost exclusively through resellers—distributors and PC retailers, particularly large computer stores like CompUSA. In 1998 Compaq, responding to mounting competition in PCs, launched internal actions to emulate some of the key elements of Dell Computer's strategy. Compaq began efforts to switch from a build-to-stock to a build-to-order production model and intended to maintain Internet connections with its suppliers and customers to achieve a five-day or less cycle time between the receipt of an order and product shipment.[39] However, as of mid-1999 the company's order-to-delivery time was approximately 12 days (versus an order-to-delivery time of 3.1 days at Dell).[40] Compaq was also striving to improve inventory management and reduce transportation costs, but the results going into 2000 had been modest.[41] Because Compaq had bigger components inventories than Dell and because its resellers sometimes had sizable inventories of Compaq's models on hand, Compaq was slower than Dell in getting new generations of its PCs into the marketplace.

Compaq's extensive network of authorized reseller partners gave it strong distribution capability that covered more than 100 countries across the world. But Compaq's strategy of using reseller partners as its primary distribution channel was a weakness as well as a strength. Reliance on resellers put Compaq at a cost disadvantage relative to Dell, since Dell's direct sales approach entailed lower sales and marketing costs than Compaq's use of resellers. (Resellers had to mark up the factory price they paid Compaq to cover their own selling, general, and administrative costs and realize an adequate return on investment.) Compaq made a push in 1998 to promote direct sales over its Web site, an effort that irritated its 20 distributors and hundreds of reseller partners and may have prompted some resellers to push rival PC/server/workstation brands.[42] Nonetheless, there continued to be much debate

---

[36]Digital's competitive position is discussed in "Compaq-Digital: Let the Slimming Begin," *Business Week,* June 22, 1998.

[37]A discussion of the benefits of the Digital Equipment Corporation acquisition is presented in Compaq Computer Corporation's 1998 annual report; see www.compaq.com/corporate/1998ar/financials/MDA/purchased_nf.html.

[38]Compaq Computer Corporation 1998 10-K.

[39]Compaq Computer Corporation 1998 annual report; see www.compaq.com/corporate/1998ar/letter/english01_nf.html.

[40]"Can Compaq Catch Up?" p. 166.

[41]Compaq was said to have adopted a program that would reduce the number of destinations that the company shipped to by 70 percent by eliminating all but four distributors in North America in a May 10, 1999, *ComputerWorld* online news article; see www.computerworld.com/home/news.nsf/all/9905101compaq2.

[42]"Can Compaq Catch Up?" p. 164. Many distributors and resellers carry more than one brand and can push sales of one brand over another if they are so inclined.

among Compaq investors and Wall Street securities analysts about whether Compaq needed to put considerably more emphasis on direct sales and cut back its number of distributors in North America. Despite the pressures, Compaq management had so far refrained from further attempts to increase direct sales.

Compaq offered a full line of desktop PCs, from sub-$1,000 PCs to top-of-the-line models. It was an aggressive seller of PCs priced under $1,000. It also offered a broad line of laptop PCs. Compaq was also the market leader in PC servers priced under $25,000. Compaq's market strength was greatest among Fortune 1000 companies; it had weaker penetration in the small and medium business segments. To combat the volume discounts that Dell and other direct vendors typically used to help win the accounts of small and medium businesses, Compaq had recently begun working more closely with its resellers on special pricing to make the Compaq brand more competitive in the bidding process for these accounts. To boost its subpar 3 percent share of the Japanese market for PCs, in 1997 Compaq signed a deal that gave Canon Sales Company exclusive distribution and sales rights to Compaq's consumer-oriented Presario models.

Compaq's Acquisition of Digital Equipment Company

In early 1998, Compaq acquired the floundering Digital Equipment Company for $9.6 billion, a move intended to turn Compaq into more of a full-spectrum global supplier of computer hardware and services and put it into better position to challenge IBM as a "global enterprise computing company." Digital had 1997 revenues of $13 billion (versus $14.5 billion in 1996) and net earnings of $141 million (versus a loss of $112 million in 1996). The merged companies would have combined revenues of $37.6 billion, making Compaq the second largest computer company in the world. Following the merger, Compaq set a goal of $50 billion in revenues in 2000.

Digital considered itself a "network solutions company" with strengths in multivendor integration, Internet security, continuous computing, high-availability data, and high-performance networked platforms. Its chief products were large servers (those priced over $1 million), entry servers (those priced under $100,000), large computers and workstations, and personal computers (55 percent of revenues). Services accounted for 45 percent of revenues (about $6 billion); Digital had 25,000 engineers and support people in the field working with customers. (Compaq had 8,000 sales and support people in the field, many of whom spent much of their time servicing retailers of Compaq PCs.) Digital's gross margins on services averaged 34 percent compared to Compaq's 25 percent margins on PC sales. Compaq's corporate customers had been requesting the company to provide more service for years.

In May 1998, Compaq announced plans to cut about 15,000 jobs at Digital when the acquisition was completed; the layoffs were concentrated mainly in Digital's personal computer division, portions of its sales force, and corporate computer operations—where there were significant overlaps with Compaq's business. Digital had a total of 53,500 employees, down from a peak of 130,000 in the 1980s. But despite its recent workforce downsizings, Digital in 1997 employed about 65 percent more people than Compaq to produce about half the volume of sales revenues. Compaq also moved aggressively to reduce Digital's high selling, general, and administrative (SG&A) costs (equal to 24 percent of total 1997 revenues) and bring them more in line with Compaq's SG&A expense ratio of 12 percent of revenues.

Compaq believed that Digital's expertise in networking and information systems integration, coupled with the combined product lines, would give it an advantage with large corporate customers over companies like Dell that offered mainly PC-related services. Compaq also believed that Digital's worldwide service and support capabilities would help it win corporate business for PCs, workstations, and servers away from IBM. (Prior to the Compaq-Digital merger, Dell had contracted with Digital's service organization to maintain its PowerEdge line of servers at a number of corporate accounts; following the merger announcement, Dell replaced Digital as a service provider.)

Problems at Compaq

Despite its status as the world's leading PC manufacturer and the new capabilities seemingly gained from the Tandem and Digital acquisitions, Compaq struggled throughout the 1997–99 period to maintain market share and profitability in the face of mounting price competition and declining PC prices. Furthermore, Compaq management got bogged down in trying to make a success of its acquisition of Digital. While Compaq was described as a company that was "consistently doing the right things and doing them well" at the time of the Digital acquisition, its efforts to get Digital's operations on track and integrated with those of Compaq were behind schedule and not going as well as had been anticipated.[43]

In April 1999, Compaq's board of directors removed CEO Eckhard Pfeiffer because of difficulty with the Digital acquisition and problems in executing the company's plans to copy Dell Computer's build-to-order, just-in-time-inventory, and direct-sales approaches.[44] After a three-month search to find a replacement for Pfeiffer from outside the company, the board chose an insider, Michael Capellas, the company's former chief information officer, to fill the vacant CEO position. Despite the leadership change and aggressive actions initiated by Capellas to return Compaq to profitable growth, Compaq's market share in PCs continued to erode in the United States, Europe, and Asia during the remainder of 1999. Compaq lost its claim to market share leadership to Dell in the U.S. market in the third quarter of 1999 and seemed in danger of losing its global market share leadership to Dell in 2000 if Capellas's turnaround efforts did not produce results. The financial performance of the company's three major business groups was as follows:

Business Group	1999 Revenues	1999 Operating Profit
Enterprise Solutions and Services	$20.1 billion	$2.3 billion
Products	13.5 billion	
Services	6.6 billion	
Commercial Personal Computing	12.2 billion	(448 million)
Consumer PCs	6.0 billion	262 million

Despite the weak 1999 performance, by early 2000 Compaq management believed that the aggressive actions taken in the last six months of 1999 were taking hold and laying the foundation for a comeback in 2000. Capellas said, "During the fourth quarter, we made great strides in defining a clear strategy, realigning for success, getting our cost structure in order, and re-energizing employees . . . We upped the pace in launching innovative new products, signing strategic partnership deals and alliances, and securing major customer wins."[45] Capellas went on to say that the performance of the Enterprise Solutions and Services group indicated "growing market acceptance of Compaq's high-end systems, solutions, and services, which customers are demanding to build nonstop 24 × 7 Internet computing environments."

[43]"Desktop and Mobile Weekly Update," *Dataquest*, February 12, 1998, p. 7.

[44]Compaq's difficulty in making a success of its Digital acquisition is discussed in "Compaq Chief Executive Pfeiffer Ousted," Associated Press Wire, April 19, 1999, and "Can Compaq Catch Up?" pp. 162–66.

[45]Compaq Press Release, January 25, 2000.

In January 2000, Compaq announced that it was spending $370 million to acquire certain assets of Inacom Corporation that would reduce inventories, speed cycle time, and enhance its capabilities to do business with customers via the Internet.

IBM

With 1999 sales of $87.5 billion and earnings of $7.7 billion, IBM was the world's largest seller of computer systems. IBM was considered a "computer solutions" company and operated in more segments of the overall computer industry than Dell. It had the broadest and deepest capabilities in customer service, technical support, and systems integration of any company in the world. The company's slow-growing computer hardware business had total 1999 revenues of over $37 billion from its internal and external sales of mainframe computers, PCs, servers, workstations, display devices, semiconductors, hard disk drives, printer systems, and storage and networking devices. IBM's global services business group, the company's fastest-growing group, was the world's largest information technology services provider, with 1999 sales of nearly $32.2 billion. The company's software business group had 1999 sales of over $12.7 billion and supported more than 29,000 independent software vendors (ISVs) to ensure that the company's software and hardware was included in ISV partner solutions.[46] In 2000, IBM had a lineup of over 40,000 hardware and software products.

IBM's Troubles in PCs

IBM's market share in PCs was in a death spiral—it had lost more market share in the 1990s than any other PC maker. Once the dominant global and U.S. market leader in the late 1980s and early 1990s, with a market share exceeding 50 percent, it was fast becoming an also-ran in PCs, with a global market share under 8 percent. Its last stronghold in PCs was in laptop computers, where its ThinkPad line was a consistent award winner on performance, features, and reliability. The vast majority of IBM's laptop and desktop sales were to corporate customers that had IBM mainframe computers and had been long-standing IBM customers.

Despite its eroding market share, IBM's position as the longtime global leader in mainframe computers and, more recently, as a broad line supplier of computer products and services gave it strong global distribution capability and potent brand-name credibility throughout the world. IBM distributed its PCs, workstations, and servers through reseller partners but relied on its own direct sales force for most corporate customers. IBM competed against its PC rivals by emphasizing confidence in the IBM brand and the company's long-standing strengths in software applications, service, and technical support. IBM had responded to the direct sales inroads Dell had made in the corporate market by allowing some of its resellers to custom-assemble IBM PCs to buyer specifications; it was hoping this effort would cut costs up to 10 percent.

Going into 2000, IBM's personal systems (PCs and workstations) and server businesses accounted for just under 30 percent of corporate revenues, but both groups turned in weak performances in 1998 and 1999 and lost market share to rivals:

	Revenues		Pretax Profit	
	1998	**1999**	**1998**	**1999**
Personal Systems	$12.8 billion	$15.3 billion	($992 million)	($557 million)
Servers	$11.1 billion	$9.0 billion	$2.8 billion	$1.6 billion

[46]IBM 1998 annual report, pp. 84–86.

IBM's PC group had higher costs than rivals, making it virtually impossible to match rivals on price and make a profit. In late 1999, IBM announced that it was discontinuing sales of its Aptiva Desktop PCs through retail channels in North America, although it would continue to sell Aptivas at its Web site. It also announced layoffs of up to 10 percent of its PC workforce and up to 6 percent of its server workforce. Like Dell, IBM was trying to cut technical support costs by getting its customers to use Internet-based support tools; for every service call handled through www.ibm.com, the company estimated it saved 70 to 90 percent of the cost of having a person take the call.[47] In 1999, IBM handled 35 million online service requests, saving an estimated $750 million in customer support costs.

To offset its declining share of PC and server sales, in 1998 and 1999 IBM moved to boost its R&D and manufacturing efforts to become a leading global supplier of computing components (hard drives and storage devices) and microelectronics products. During 1999, for example, it signed a long-term agreement with Dell to supply over $7 billion in components; it was increasing its sales of parts and components to other PC makers as well.

IBM's E-Business Strategy

Throughout the 1990s IBM had struggled to reinvent itself as the growing use of PCs continued to erode corporate dependence on mainframe computers and made mainframe sales and services a stagnating business. (Mainframe prices were falling faster than sales were rising.) While the company added new hardware and software products, revenue growth lagged and lower-cost rivals undercut many of IBM's strategic initiatives to grow. IBM's sales of computer hardware remained flat; revenue growth came chiefly from services and software. IBM's global dominance as a computer hardware systems provider faded. No cohesive new strategic theme really took root at IBM during the 1990s.

However, starting in 1998 and continuing on into 2000, the company's efforts to reinvent itself began to take on a distinct Internet and e-business theme. By early 2000 IBM was directing most of its strategic initiatives toward "e-business services" where it saw explosive growth opportunities. More than 50 percent of IBM's R&D budget was directed to Internet projects. Senior management believed that software and services were the soul of e-business and that the company had a full complement of resources to help corporate customers put integrated e-business capabilities in place. A growing majority of the company's 130,000 consultants were working to provide customers with integrated e-commerce and Internet technology solutions. The company was opening e-business integration centers around the world where customers could meet with IBM specialists to develop next-generation e-business solutions. During the past three years, IBM had handled 18,000 Internet-related jobs for customers, ranging from Web page design to hosting entire online storefronts to hooking corporate databases into new online systems. IBM's revenues from pure e-business projects totaled $3 billion in 1999, but the company estimated that some $20 billion of its revenues was driven by customer demand for e-business solutions, an amount that was expected to grow significantly.

Most observers, as well as IBM executives, seemed to believe that IBM's future success depended far more on becoming the world's leading provider of e-business services than on strengthening its position as a provider of computer hardware. But it faced significant competition in e-business services and software from Intel (which was spending over $1 billion to set up rooms of servers to host Internet sites); Hewlett-Packard (which had a variety of initiatives aimed at do-it-yourself Internet

---

[47]Ira Sager, "Inside IBM: Internet Business Machines," *Business Week*, December 13, 1999, p. EB 34.

technologies that required minimal consulting services and support); Microsoft (which was focusing increasing efforts on Internet-related software and serving e-business customers); Sun Microsystems; and numerous others.

HEWLETT-PACKARD

Going into 2000, Hewlett-Packard (HP) was the world's leading seller of computer printers, the second-ranking seller of workstations, and a top-tier seller of PCs and servers. HP's product line also included scanners, digital cameras, storage devices, and networking software and equipment. The company recorded 1999 revenues and earnings of $42.4 billion and $3.1 billion, respectively.[48] Dell regarded Hewlett-Packard as a strong competitor because of the company's global leadership in printers (a 52 percent market share), HP's strong reputation with corporate customers in almost all parts of the world, and its growing strategic emphasis on PCs, workstations, and servers. HP ranked fourth worldwide in desktop PC sales, first in worldwide sales of workstations, first in worldwide sale of handheld PCs, first in worldwide sales of both midrange and high-end servers running on UNIX operating systems, and among the top five worldwide vendors of servers running on Windows NT and Windows 2000. HP Pavillion PCs were the top-selling PC brand in U.S. retail stores. HP was a co-designer of Intel's new family of 64-bit Itanium microprocessors. HP's partnership with Intel on the Itanium was expected to put HP on the cutting edge of computer technology for the next several years and boost its brand image in PCs, workstations, and servers. The company spent $2.4 billion on R&D in 1998 and the same amount in 1999.

Hewlett-Packard marketed its PC line through resellers. HP's resellers could deliver orders to major corporate accounts within 12 to 24 hours. Hewlett-Packard had the capability to offer after-sale support to PC, workstation, and server purchasers around the world through 600 support offices, 35 response center locations in 110 countries, and a support staff of 17,500 people. The company had won numerous awards for the caliber of its services and technical support. It had 83,200 employees worldwide.

Over the past several years, HP had moved to improve operating efficiencies by outsourcing manufacturing assembly, reducing inventory and field-sales costs, and improving supply chain management. These efforts, combined with lowered component prices, had made HP aggressive in competing on price against its PC, workstation, and server rivals. Nonetheless, Hewlett-Packard's PC division, despite growing unit volume, was thought to be only marginally profitable. However, the company's sales of workstations and servers were major contributors to revenues and profits. In early 2000, the company reported that sales of home PCs and laptops were particularly strong.

Hewlett-Packard's board of directors chose Carly Fiorina, the head of Lucent Technology's Global Service Provider Business, as the company's new CEO in July 1999, to replace the company's retiring CEO. Fiorina had been designated by *Fortune* as the most powerful woman in business in 1998 and 1999. Believing that HP had grown sluggish and lacked entrepreneurial drive, Fiorina had immediately spearheaded initiatives to boost HP's revenue growth and profitability through increased attention to inventiveness and innovation. Fiorina's top priorities were to renew the company's energy and focus and to develop a stream of innovative products

---

[48]Hoover's, Inc., "Hoover's Company Profile Database for Hewlett-Packard," 1998, p. 1. HP's test and measurement business, which accounted for approximately 16 percent of 1998 sales, was spun off as a stand-alone company in March 1999; Hewlett-Packard Company 8-K (filed March 2, 1999), p. 1.

and new types of electronic services aimed at making the Internet "more warm, friendly, pervasive and personal." In late 1999, Fiorina announced a new global brand campaign and a new logo to reflect the reinvented, reenergized Hewlett-Packard.

GATEWAY

Gateway, formerly called Gateway 2000, was a San Diego–based company (recently relocated from South Dakota) with 1999 revenues of $8.6 billion and profits of $428 million. Founder and chairman Ted Waitt, 38, and his brother owned over 40 percent of the company. Waitt had dropped out of college in 1985 to go to work for a computer retailer in Des Moines, Iowa; after nine months, he quit to form his own company. The company, operating out of a barn on his father's cattle ranch, sold add-on parts by phone for Texas Instruments PCs. In 1987, the company, using its own PC design, started selling fully equipped PCs at a price near that of other PC makers. Sales took off, and in 1991 Gateway topped the list of *Inc.* magazine's list of the fastest-growing private companies. The company went public in 1993, achieving sales of $1.7 billion and earnings of $151 million. The company had differentiated itself from rivals with eye-catching ads; some featured cows with black-and-white spots, while others featured company employees (including one with Waitt dressed as Robin Hood). Gateway, like Dell, built to order and sold direct. It had entered the server segment in 1997. To promote the Gateway name in the retail marketplace, the company had opened 280 Gateway Country Stores—227 in the United States, 27 in Europe, and 26 in the Asia-Pacific region—that stocked Gateway PCs and peripheral products and that conducted classes for individuals and businesses on the use of PCs.

Going into 2000, Gateway was the number one seller of PCs to consumers. It was also a major contender in the small-business, educational, and government segments. Despite growing at a rate of nearly 38 percent annually in the 1994–97 period, Gateway saw its profit margins erode steadily from a high of 9.6 percent in 1992 to only 1.7 percent in 1997. Since then, however, company cost-cutting efforts and efficiency improvements had resulted in eight straight quarters of year-over-year margin improvement. Profits in 1999 were at record levels. Nonetheless, Gateway was feeling the pressures of falling PC prices and stiff price competition—although 1999 unit sales were up 32.3 percent over 1998 levels, revenues increased only 15.8 percent. The company's entry-level PC models, which started at $799, accounted for 20 percent of its sales to consumers.

To reduce its reliance on traditional PC sales, Gateway took aggressive steps in 1999 to diversify its revenue stream. In February, Gateway became the first PC maker to bundle its own Internet service with its PCs; at the same time, following Dell, Gateway launched an online software and peripheral Web store with more than 30,000 products. Meanwhile, Gateway increased its service and training offerings to consumers and small businesses at its 280 Country Store locations worldwide. In October, Gateway entered into a wide-ranging strategic alliance with America Online to accelerate distribution of each company's products and services. By the end of 1999, after adding 400,000 new subscribers in less than three months, Gateway's joint Internet service with AOL had more than 1 million subscribers. Gateway management believed its "beyond-the-box" strategy positioned the company extremely well for the future.

Gateway also took aggressive steps in 1999 to boost its sales to small businesses, government agencies, and educational institutions. It established a sales force operating out of its 280 Country Stores that called on area businesses and other organizations. An alliance with GE Capital was formed to promote technology solutions for large enterprises. In Europe, Gateway entered into a two-year partnership with ComputaCenter,

Europe's leading information technology systems and services company, to sell and support Gateway PC products throughout Europe. During 1999, Gateway increased its sales over the Internet by 100 percent over 1998 levels.

To further enhance the Gateway brand with consumers, Gateway committed to sponsorship of the 2002 Winter Olympic Games in Salt Lake City, plus it entered into brand-enhancing alliances with Fidelity Investments and Nickelodeon. Gateway planned to open more than 100 new Country Store locations worldwide during 2000, including 75 in the United States. In early 2000, Gateway introduced a new line of home and small-business desktop PCs powered by Athlon microprocessors made by Advanced Micro Devices (AMD). The new Gateway Select PC line represented an effort to counter the difficulties the company was having in obtaining adequate supplies of Pentium microprocessors from Intel.

TOSHIBA CORPORATION

Toshiba was a $45 billion diversified Japanese electronics and electrical equipment manufacturer with 300 subsidiaries and affiliates worldwide; it ranked as the world's 26th largest corporation in terms of revenues and the world's seventh largest computer and electronics company. Toshiba produced and marketed portable and desktop computers, servers, voice-mail systems, digital business telephone systems, interactive voice-response systems, cable modems, networking systems, and digital, medical, and PC cameras. In the PC arena, Toshiba's biggest strength was in notebook PCs, where it had an 18 percent global share in 1999.

The company's Toshiba America Information System (TAIS) division, headquartered in Irvine, California, had annual sales of approximately $2.5 billion across the United States and Latin America. The TAIS division offered a wide array of portable PCs, selling both direct and through dealers—one of its largest U.S. dealers was Computer Discount Warehouse. In the mid-1990s, TAIS enjoyed a commanding lead over its U.S. laptop rivals in both channels, but its lead had been shrinking in recent years. During the 1996–99 period, TAIS's share of portable computer sales in the United States was in the 15 to 20 percent range. It had a negligible share of the desktop PC market.

PROVIDERS OF HOUSE-LABEL BRANDS

There were about 30,000 resellers of generic, or "house-label," PCs in North America alone and countless thousands more worldwide. The generic segment constituted a $7 to $8 billion market in the United States and Canada, representing shipments of about 7 million units and 25 to 30 percent of sales through resellers. No single generic brand, however, accounted for more than 0.25 percent market share, and most had a lot smaller percentage share. Generic PCs assembled in "screwdriver shops" had been a part of the PC business since its inception—Steve Wozniak and Steve Jobs launched Apple Computer from a garage using components they purchased. Rising technological savvy about how PCs worked and the widespread availability of individual components made it fairly easy for an enterprising operation to assemble a generic PC. Contract manufacturers of PCs, many of whom assembled name brands of PCs for several PC makers, were a major source of house-label PCs marketed by retailers. To keep costs and prices low, the makers of generic PCs typically incorporated components from low-end suppliers. Generic PCs appealed mainly to very price-conscious buyers. The quality and reliability of generic PCs varied from good to poor, depending on the caliber of their components. The makers of generic PCs generally took little responsibility for providing technical support; whatever technical support was available to users typically had to come from resellers.

Michael Dell's View of Dell Computer's Biggest Challenges

Michael Dell believed Dell Computer's biggest challenge in the marketplace was to gain as much acceptance for the company's direct business model outside the United States as it had gained inside the United States. But an even bigger challenge, he believed, was gathering enough talented people to help the company pursue the opportunities in other countries. Dell was active in recruiting foreign nationals graduating from U.S. business schools. Those who hired on with Dell were sent to Austin, Texas, for a couple of years to learn about Dell and the Dell model and to work in various parts of the company's operations. Then they were given assignments to help in Dell's global expansion effort. Michael Dell believed the company needed the expertise of foreigners who knew Dell from the inside and who could help Dell Computer understand different cultures and respond in a sensitive manner to local customs and behaviors.

For the most part, Michael Dell was not particularly concerned about the efforts of competitors to copy many aspects of Dell's build-to-order, sell-direct strategy:

> The competition started copying us seven years ago. That's when we were a $1 billion business. Now we're $25 billion. And they haven't made much progress to be honest with you. The learning curve for them is difficult. It's like going from baseball to soccer . . . We're more challenged by new technologies on the market, some new computing model, something we haven't anticipated.[49]

Michael Dell's near-term vision was for the company to reach $50 billion in annual sales by growing more aggressively in the consumer and small-business segments in computer services, by increasing its market share in foreign countries, and by selling more powerful and more expensive servers to corporate customers.

---

[49]Comments made to students at the University of North Carolina and reported in the *Raleigh News & Observer*, November 16, 1999.

Section VII

Developing Marketing Plans

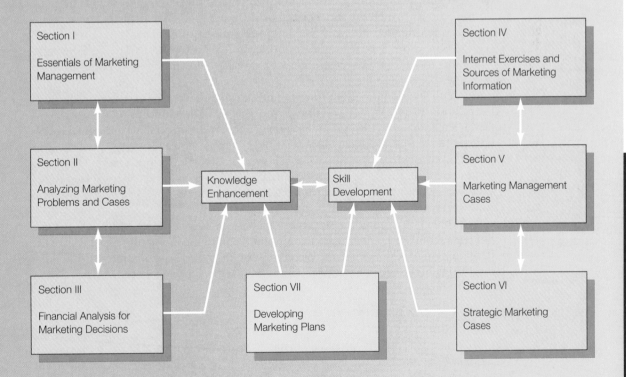

Section I
Essentials of Marketing Management

Section II
Analyzing Marketing Problems and Cases

Section III
Financial Analysis for Marketing Decisions

Knowledge Enhancement

Section VII
Developing Marketing Plans

Skill Development

Section IV
Internet Exercises and Sources of Marketing Information

Section V
Marketing Management Cases

Section VI
Strategic Marketing Cases

Imagine this scenario. After receiving your bachelor's or master's degree in marketing, you are hired by a major consumer goods company. Because you've done well in school, you are confident that you have a lot of marketing knowledge and a lot to offer to the firm. You're highly motivated and are looking forward to a successful career.

After just a few days of work you are called in for a conference with the vice president of marketing. The vice president welcomes you and tells you how glad the firm is that you have joined them. The vice president also says that, since you have done so well in your marketing courses and have had such recent training, he wants you to work on a special project.

He tells you that the company has a new product, which is to be introduced in a few months. He also says, confidentially, that recent new product introductions by the company haven't been too successful. Suggesting that the recent problems are probably because the company has not been doing a very good job of developing marketing plans, the vice president tells you not to look at marketing plans for the company's other products.

Your assignment, then, is to develop a marketing plan for the proposed product in the next six weeks. The vice president explains that a good job here will lead to rapid advancement in the company. You thank the vice president for the assignment and promise that you'll do your best.

How would you feel when you returned to your desk? Surely, you'd be flattered that you had been given this opportunity and be eager to do a good job. However, how confident are you that you could develop a quality marketing plan? Would you even know where to begin?

We suspect that many of you, even those who have an excellent knowledge of marketing principles and are adept at solving marketing cases, may not yet have the skills necessary to develop a marketing plan from scratch. Thus, the purpose of this section is to offer a framework for developing marketing plans. In one sense, this section is no more than a summary of the whole text. In other words, it is an organizational framework based on the text material that can be used to direct the development of marketing plans.

Students should note that we are not presenting this framework and discussion as the only way to develop a marketing plan. While we believe this is a useful framework for logically analyzing the problems involved in developing a marketing plan, other approaches can be used just as successfully.

Often, successful firms prepare much less detailed plans, since much of the background material and current conditions are well known to everyone involved. However, our review of plans used in various firms suggests that something like this framework is not uncommon.

We would like to mention one other qualification before beginning our discussion. Students should remember that one important part of the marketing plan involves the development of a sales forecast. While we have discussed several approaches to sales forecasting in the text, we will detail only one specific approach here.

A MARKETING PLAN FRAMEWORK

Marketing plans have three basic purposes. First, they are used as a tangible record of analysis so the logic involved can be checked. This is done to ensure the feasibility and internal consistency of the project and to evaluate the likely consequences of implementing the plan. Second, they are used as roadmaps or guidelines for directing appropriate actions. A marketing plan is designed to be the best available scenario and rationale for directing the firm's efforts for a particular product or

FIGURE 1
A Marketing Plan
Format

- Title page
- Executive summary
- Table of contents
- Introduction
- Situational analysis
- Marketing planning
- Implementation and control of the marketing plan
- Summary
- Appendix: Financial analysis
- References

brand. Third, they are used as tools to obtain funding for implementation. This funding may come from internal or external sources. For example, a brand manager may have to present a marketing plan to senior executives in a firm to get a budget request filled. This would be an internal source. Similarly, proposals for funding from investors or business loans from banks often require a marketing plan. These would be external sources.

Figure 1 presents a format for preparing marketing plans. Each of the 10 elements will be briefly discussed. We will refer to previous chapters and sections in this text and to other sources where additional information can be obtained when a marketing plan is being prepared. We also will offer additional information for focusing particular sections of the plan as well as for developing financial analysis.

Title Page

The *title page* should contain the following information: (1) the name of the product or brand for which the marketing plan has been prepared—for example, Marketing Plan for Little Friskies Dog Food; (2) the time period for which the plan is designed—for example, 2003–2004; (3) the person(s) and position(s) of those submitting the plan—for example, submitted by Amy Lewis, brand manager; (4) the persons, group, or agency to whom the plan is being submitted—for example, submitted to Lauren Ellis, product group manager; and (5) the date of submission of the plan—for example, June 30, 2003.

While preparing the title page is a simple task, remember that it is the first thing readers see. Thus, a title page that is poorly laid out, is smudged, or contains misspelled words can lead to the inference that the project was developed hurriedly and with little attention to detail. As with the rest of the project, appearances are important and affect what people think about the plan.

Executive Summary

The *executive summary* is a two- to three-page summary of the contents of the report. Its purpose is to provide a quick summary of the marketing plan for executives who need to be informed about the plan but are typically not directly involved in plan approval. For instance, senior executives for firms with a broad product line may not have time to read the entire plan but need an overview to keep informed about operations.

The executive summary should include a brief introduction, the major aspects of the marketing plan, and a budget statement. This is not the place to go into detail about each and every aspect of the marketing plan. Rather, it should focus on the major market opportunity and the key elements of the marketing plan that are designed to capitalize on this opportunity.

It is also useful to state specifically how much money is required to implement the plan. In an ongoing firm, many costs can be estimated from historical data or from discussions with other executives in charge of specific functional areas. However, in many situations (such as a class project), sufficient information is not always available to give exact costs for every aspect of production, promotion, and distribution. In these cases, include a rough estimate of total marketing costs of the plan. In many ongoing firms, marketing cost elements are concentrated in the areas of promotion and marketing research, and these figures are integrated with those from other functional areas as parts of the overall business plan.

Table of Contents

The *table of contents* is a listing of everything contained in the plan and where it is located in the report. Reports that contain a variety of charts and figures may also have a table of exhibits listing their titles and page numbers within the report.

In addition to using the table of contents as a place to find specific information, readers may also review it to see if each section of the report is logically sequenced. For example, situational analysis logically precedes marketing planning as an activity, and this ordering makes sense in presenting the plan.

Introduction

The types of information and amount of detail reported in the *introduction* depend in part on whether the plan is being designed for a new or existing product or brand. If the product is new, the introduction should explain the product concept and the reasons it is expected to be successful. Basically, this part of the report should make the new idea sound attractive to management or investors. In addition, it is useful to offer estimates of expected sales, costs, and return on investment.

If the marketing plan is for an existing brand in an ongoing firm, it is common to begin the report with a brief history of the brand. The major focus here is on the brand's performance in the last three to five years. It is useful to prepare graphs of the brand's performance that show its sales, profits, and market share for previous years and to explain the reasons for any major changes. These exhibits can also be extended to include predicted changes in these variables given the new marketing plan. A brief discussion of the overall strategy followed in previous years also provides understanding of how much change is being proposed in the new marketing plan.

Also useful in the introduction is to offer a precise statement of the purpose of the report as well as a roadmap of the report. In other words, tell readers what this report is, how it is organized, and what will be covered in the following sections.

Situational Analysis

The *situational analysis* is not unlike the analysis discussed in Chapter 1 and Section II of this text. The focus remains on the most critical and relevant environmental conditions (or changes in them) that affect the success or failure of the proposed plan. While any aspect of the economic, social, political, legal, or cooperative environments might deserve considerable attention, there is seldom if ever a marketing plan in which the competitive environment does not require considerable discussion. In fact, the competitive environment may be set off as a separate section called *industry analysis*. The strengths and weaknesses of major competitors, their relative market shares, and the success of various competitive strategies are critical elements of the situation analysis. Section IV of the text offers some sources of information for analyzing the competitive environment.

Marketing Highlight   Some Questions to Consider in Competitive Analysis

Understanding an industry and the actions of competitors is critical to developing successful marketing plans. Below is a list of some questions to consider when performing competitive analysis. Thinking about these questions can aid the marketing planner in developing better marketing strategies.

1. Which firms compete in this industry and what is their financial position and marketing capability?

2. What are the relative market shares of various brands?

3. How many brands and models does each firm offer?

4. What marketing strategies have the market leaders employed?

5. Which brands have gained and which have lost market share in recent years and what factors have led to these changes?

6. Are new competitors likely to enter the market?

7. How quickly do competitive firms react to changes in the market?

8. From which firms or brands might we be able to take market share?

9. What are the particular strengths and weaknesses of competitors in the industry?

10. How do we compare with other firms in the industry in terms of financial strength and marketing skills?

Marketing Planning

Marketing planning is, of course, a critical section of the report. As previously noted, it includes three major elements: marketing objectives, target markets, and the marketing mix.

Marketing Objectives

Marketing objectives are often stated in plans in terms of the percentage of particular outcomes that are to be achieved; for example, 80 percent awareness of the brand in particular markets, increase in trial rate by 30 percent, distribution coverage of 60 percent, or increase in total market share by 3 percent over the life of the plan. Similarly, there may also be objective statements in terms of sales units or dollars or increases in these. Of course, the reasons for selection of the particular objectives and rationale are important points to explain.

Target Markets

The *target markets* discussion explains the customer base and rationale or justification for it. An approach to developing appropriate target markets is contained in Chapter 5 of this text, and a useful source of secondary data for segmenting markets is the *National Purchase Diary Panel.*

This section also includes relevant discussion of changes or important issues in consumer or organizational buyer behavior: for example, what benefits consumers are seeking in this products class, what benefits does the particular brand offer, or what purchasing trends are shaping the market for this product. Discussions of consumer and organizational buyer behavior are contained in Chapters 3 and 4 of this text.

Marketing Mix

The *marketing mix* discussion explains in detail the selected strategy consisting of product, promotion, distribution and price, and the rationale for it. Also, if marketing research has been done on these elements or is planned, it can be discussed in this section.

Product   The *product* section details a description of the product or brand, its packaging, and its attributes. Product life-cycle considerations should be mentioned if they affect the proposed plan.

Of critical importance in this discussion is the competitive advantage of the product or brand. Here it must be carefully considered whether the brand really does anything better than the competition or is purchased primarily on the basis of brand equity or value. For example, many brands of toothpaste have fluoride, yet Crest has the largest market share primarily through promoting this attribute of its brand. Thus, does Crest do anything more than other toothpastes, or is it Crest's image that accounts for sales?

Discussion of product-related issues is contained in Chapters 6 and 7, and services are discussed in Chapter 12 of this text. For discussion of marketing plans for products marketed globally, see Chapter 13.

Promotion   The *promotion* discussion consists of a description and justification of the planned promotion mix. It is useful to explain the theme of the promotion and to include some examples of potential ads as well as the nature of the sales force if one is to be used. For mass-marketed consumer goods, promotion costs can be large and need to be considered explicitly in the marketing plan.

Discussion of promotion-related issues is contained in Chapters 8 and 9 of this text. Secondary sources, such as *Standard Rate and Data, Simmons Media/Market Service, Starch Advertising Readership Service,* and the *Nielsen Television Index,* provide useful information for selecting, budgeting, and justifying media and other promotional decisions.

Distribution   The *distribution* discussion describes and justifies the appropriate channel or channels for the product. This includes types of intermediaries and specifically who they will be. Other important issues concern the level of market coverage desired, cost, and control considerations. In many cases, the channels of distribution used by the firm, as well as competitive firms, are well established. For example, General Motors and Ford distribute their automobiles through independent dealer networks. Thus, unless there is a compelling reason to change channels, the traditional channel will often be the appropriate alternative. However, serious consideration may have to be given to methods of obtaining channel support, for example, trade deals to obtain sufficient shelf space.

Discussion of distribution-related issues is contained in Chapter 10 of this text. Useful retail distribution information can be found in the *Nielsen Retail Index* and the *Audits and Surveys National Total-Market Index.*

Price   The pricing discussion starts with a specific statement of the price of the product. Depending on what type of channel is used, manufacturer price, wholesale price, and suggested retail price need to be listed and justified. In addition, special deals or trade discounts that are to be employed must be considered in terms of their effect on the firm's selling price.

Discussion of price-related issues is contained in Chapter 11. In addition to a variety of other useful information, the *Nielsen Retail Index* provides information on wholesale and retail prices.

Marketing Research.   For any aspect of marketing planning, there may be a need for marketing research. If such research is to be performed, it is important to justify it and explain its costs and benefits. Such costs should also be included in the financial analysis.

Marketing Highlight   Stating Objectives: How to Tell a Good One from a Bad One

For the direction-setting purpose of objectives to be fulfilled, objectives need to meet five specifications:

1. An objective should relate to a single, specific topic. (It should not be stated in the form of a vague abstraction or a pious platitude—"we want to be a leader in our industry" or "our objective is to be more aggressive marketers.")

2. An objective should relate to a result, not to an activity to be performed. (The objective is the result of the activity, not the performance of the activity.)

3. An objective should be measurable (stated in quantitative terms whenever feasible).

4. An objective should contain a time deadline for its achievement.

5. An objective should be challenging but achievable.

Consider the following examples:

1. Poor: Our objective is to maximize profits.

   Remarks: How much is "maximum"? The statement is not subject to measurement. What criterion or yardstick will management use to determine if and when actual profits are equal to maximum profits? No deadline is specified.

   Better: Our total profit target in 2000 is $1 million.

2. Poor: Our objective is to increase sales revenue and unit volume.

   Remarks: How much? Also, because the statement relates to two topics, it may be inconsistent. Increasing unit volume may require a price cut, and if demand is price inelastic, sales revenue would fall as unit volume rises. No time frame for achievement is indicated.

   Better: Our objective this calendar year is to increase sales revenues from $30 million to $35 million; we expect this to be accomplished by selling 1 million units at an average price of $35.

3. Poor: Our objective in 2000 is to boost advertising expenditures by 15 percent.

   Remarks: Advertising is an activity, not a result. The advertising objective should be stated in terms of what result the extra advertising is intended to produce.

   Better: Our objective is to boost our market share from 8 percent to 10 percent in 2000 with the help of a 15 percent increase in advertising expenditures.

4. Poor: Our objective is to be a pioneer in research and development and to be the technological leader in the industry.

   Remarks: Very sweeping and perhaps overly ambitious; implies trying to march in too many directions at once if the industry is one with a wide range of technological frontiers. More a platitude than an action commitment to a specific result.

   Better: During the 2000–2010 decade, our objective is to continue as a leader in introducing new technologies and new devices that will allow buyers of electrically powered equipment to conserve on electric energy usage.

5. Poor: Our objective is to be the most profitable company in our industry.

   Remarks: Not specific enough by what measures of profit—total dollars, or earnings per share, or unit profit margin, or return on equity investment, or all of these? Also, because the objective concerns how well other companies will perform, the objective, while challenging, may not be achievable.

   Better: We will strive to remain atop the industry in terms of rate of return on equity investment by earning a 25 percent after-tax return on equity investment in 2000.

Source: Adapted from Arthur A. Thompson, Jr., and A. J. Strickland, *Strategic Management: Concepts and Cases,* 5th ed. (Burr Ridge, IL: Irwin/McGraw-Hill, 1990), pp. 23–34.

Marketing Highlight Some Questions to Consider in Consumer Analysis

Knowledge of consumers is paramount to developing successful marketing plans. Below is a list of questions that are useful to consider when analyzing consumers. For some of the questions, secondary sources of information or primary marketing research can be employed to aid in decision making. However, a number of them require the analyst to do some serious thinking about the relationship between brands of the product and various consumer groups to better understand the market.

1. How many people purchase and use this product in general?

2. How many people purchase and use each brand of the product?

3. Is there an opportunity to reach nonusers of the product with a unique marketing strategy?

4. What does the product do for consumers functionally and how does this vary by brand?

5. What does the product do for consumers in a social or psychological sense and how does this vary by brand?

6. Where do consumers currently purchase various brands of the product?

7. How much are consumers willing to pay for specific brands and is price a determining factor for purchase?

8. What is the market profile of the heavy user of this product and what percentage of the total market are heavy users?

9. What media reach these consumers?

10. On average, how often is this product purchased?

11. How important is brand equity for consumers of this product?

12. Why do consumers purchase particular brands?

13. How brand loyal are consumers of this product?

If marketing research has already been conducted as part of the marketing plan, it can be reported as needed to justify various decisions that were reached. To illustrate, if research found that two out of three consumers like the taste of a new formula Coke, this information would likely be included in the product portion of the report. However, the details of the research could be placed here in the marketing research section. Discussion of marketing research is contained in Chapter 2.

Implementation and Control of the Marketing Plan

This section contains a discussion and justification of how the marketing plan will be implemented and controlled. It also explains who will be in charge of monitoring and changing the plan should unanticipated events occur and how the success or failure of the plan will be measured. Success or failure of the plan is typically measured by a comparison of the results of implementing the plan with the stated objectives.

For a marketing plan developed within an ongoing firm, this section can be quite explicit, since procedures for implementing plans may be well established. However, for a classroom project, the key issues to be considered are the persons responsible for implementing the plan, a timetable for sequencing the tasks, and a method of measuring and evaluating the success or failure of the plan.

Summary

This *summary* need not be much different than the executive summary stated at the beginning of the document. However, it is usually a bit longer, more detailed, and states more fully the case for financing the plan.

Appendix—Financial Analysis

Financial analysis is a very important part of any marketing plan. While a complete business plan often includes extensive financial analysis, such as a complete cost breakdown and estimated return on investment, marketing planners frequently do not have complete accounting data for computing these figures. For example, decisions concerning how much overhead is to be apportioned to the product are not usually made solely by marketing personnel. However, the marketing plan should contain at least a sales forecast and estimates of relevant marketing costs.

Sales Forecast

As noted, there are a variety of ways to develop sales forecasts. Regardless of the method, however, they all involve trying to predict the future as accurately as possible. It is, of course, necessary to justify the logic for the forecasted figures, rather than offer them with no support.

One basic approach to developing a sales forecast is outlined in Figure 2. This approach begins by estimating the total number of persons in the selected target market. This estimate comes from the market segmentation analysis and may include information from test marketing and from secondary sources, such as *Statistical Abstracts of the United States.* For example, suppose a company is marketing a solar-powered watch that is designed not only to tell time but also to take the pulse of the wearer. The product is targeted at joggers and others interested in aerobic exercise. By reviewing the literature on these activities, the marketing planner, John Murphy, finds that the average estimate of this market on a national level is 60 million persons and is growing by 4 million persons per year. Thus, John might conclude that the total number of people in the target market for next year is 64 million. If he has not further limited the product's target market and has no other information, John might use this number as a basis for starting the forecast analysis.

The second estimate John needs is the annual number of purchases per person in the product's target market. This estimate could be quite large for such products as breakfast cereal or less than one (annual purchase per person) for such products as automobiles. For watches, the estimate is likely to be much less than one since people are likely to buy a new watch only every few years. Thus, John might estimate the annual number of purchases per person in the target market to be .25. Of course, as a careful marketing planner, John would probably carefully research this market to refine this estimate. In any event, multiplying these two numbers gives John an estimate of the *total potential market,* in this case, 64 million times .25

FIGURE 2
A Basic Approach to Sales Forecasting

Total number of people in target markets (*a*)		*a*
Annual number of purchases per person (*b*)	×	*b*
Total potential market (*c*)	=	*c*
Total potential market (*c*)		*c*
Percent of total market coverage (*d*)	×	*d*
Total available market (*e*)	=	*e*
Total available market (*e*)		*e*
Expected market share (*f*)	×	*f*
Sales forecast (in units) (*g*)	=	*g*
Sales forecast (in units) (*g*)		*g*
Price (*h*)	×	*h*
Sales forecast (in dollars)(*i*)	=	*i*

Marketing Highlight Some Questions to Consider in Marketing Planning

Below is a brief list of questions about the marketing planning section of the report. Answering them honestly and recognizing both the strengths and weaknesses of the marketing plan should help to improve it.

1. What are the key assumptions that were made in developing the marketing plan?

2. How badly will the product's market position be hurt if these assumptions turn out to be incorrect?

3. How good is the marketing research?

4. Is the marketing plan consistent? For example, if the plan is to seek a prestige position in the market, is the product priced, promoted, and distributed to create this image?

5. Is the marketing plan feasible? For example, are the financial and other resources (such as a distribution network) available to implement it?

6. How will the marketing plan affect profits and market share and is it consistent with corporate objectives?

7. Will implementing the marketing plan result in competitive retaliation that will end up hurting the firm?

8. Is the marketing mix designed to reach and attract new customers or increase usage among existing users or both?

9. Will the marketing mix help to develop brand-loyal consumers?

10. Will the marketing plan be successful not just in the short run but also contribute to a profitable long-run position?

equals 16 million. In other words, if next year alone John's company could sell a watch to every jogger or aerobic exerciser who is buying a watch, the company could expect sales to be 16 million units.

Of course, the firm cannot expect to sell every jogger a watch for several reasons. First, it is unlikely to obtain 100 percent market coverage in the first year, if ever. Even major consumer goods companies selling convenience goods seldom reach the entire market in the first year and many never achieve even 90 percent distribution. Given the nature of the product and depending on the distribution alternative, John's company might be doing quite well to average 50 percent market coverage in the first year. If John's plans call for this kind of coverage, his estimate of the total available market would be 16 million times .5, which equals 8 million.

A second reason John's plans would not call for dominating the market is that his company does not have the only product available or wanted by this target market. Many of the people who will purchase such a watch will purchase a competitive brand. He must, therefore, estimate the product's likely market share. Of all the estimates made in developing a sales forecast, this one is critical, since it is a reflection of the entire marketing plan. Important factors to consider in developing this estimate include (1) competitive market shares and likely marketing strategies; (2) competitive retaliation should the product do well; (3) competitive advantage of the product, such as lower price; (4) promotion mix and budget relative to competitors; and (5) market shares obtained by similar products in the introductory year.

Overall, suppose John estimates the product's market share to be 5 percent, since other competitive products have beat his company to the market and because the company's competitive advantage is only a slightly more stylish watch. In this case,

Marketing Highlight — Some Questions to Consider in Implementation and Control

Implementation and control of a marketing plan require careful scheduling and attention to detail. While some firms have standard procedures for dealing with many of the questions raised below, thinking through each of the questions should help improve the efficiency of even these firms in this stage of the process.

1. Who is responsible for implementing and controlling the marketing plan?

2. What tasks must be performed to implement the marketing plan?

3. What are the deadlines for implementing the various tasks and how critical are specific deadlines?

4. Has sufficient time been scheduled to implement the various tasks?

5. How long will it take to get the planned market coverage?

6. How will the success or failure of the plan be determined?

7. How long will it take to get the desired results from the plan?

8. How long will the plan be in effect before changes will be made to improve it based on more current information?

9. If an ad agency or other firms are involved in implementing the plan, how much responsibility and authority will they have?

10. How frequently will the progress of the plan be monitored?

---

the sales forecast for year one would be 8 million times .05, which equals 400,000 units. If the manufacturer's selling price was $50, then the sales forecast in dollars would be 400,000 times $50, which equals $20 million.

This approach can also be used to extend the sales forecast for any number of years. Typically, estimates of most of the figures change from year to year, depending on changes in market size, distribution coverage, and expected market shares. The value of this approach is that it forces an analyst to carefully consider and justify each of the estimates offered, rather than simply pulling numbers out of the air.

Estimates of Marketing Costs

A complete delineation of all costs, apportionment of overhead, and other accounting tasks are usually performed by other departments within a firm. All of this information, including expected return on investment from implementing the marketing plan, is part of the overall business plan.

However, the marketing plan should at least contain estimates of major marketing costs. These include such things as advertising, sales force training and compensation, channel development, and marketing research. Estimates may also be included for product development and package design.

For some marketing costs, reasonable estimates are available from sources such as *Standard Rate and Data*. However, some cost figures, such as marketing research, might be obtained from asking various marketing experts for the estimated price of proposed research. Other types of marketing costs might be estimated from financial statements of firms in the industry. For example, Morris's *Annual Statement Studies* offers percentage breakdowns of various income statement information by industry. These might be used to estimate the percentage of the sales-forecast figure that would likely be spent in a particular cost category.

References

The *references* section contains the sources of any secondary information that was used in developing the marketing plan. This information might include company reports and memos, statements of company objectives, and articles or books used for information or support of the marketing plan.

References should be listed alphabetically using a consistent format. One way of preparing references is to use the same approach as is used in marketing journals. For example, the format used for references in *Journal of Marketing* articles is usually acceptable.

CONCLUSION

Suppose you're now back sitting at your desk faced with the task of developing a marketing plan for a new product. Do you believe that you might have the skills to develop a marketing plan? Of course, your ability to develop a quality plan will depend on your learning experiences during your course work and the amount of practice you've had; for example, if you developed a promotion plan in your advertising course, it is likely that you could do a better job on the promotion phase of the marketing plan. Similarly, your experiences in analyzing cases should have sharpened your skills at recognizing problems and developing solutions to them. But inexperience (or experience) aside, hopefully you now feel that you understand the process of developing a marketing plan. You at least know where to start, where to seek information, how to structure the plan, and some of the critical issues that require analysis.

Additional Readings

Cohen, William A. *The Marketing Plan.* New York: John Wiley & Sons, 1995.

Cravens, David W. *Strategic Marketing.* 6th ed. Burr Ridge, IL: Irwin/McGraw-Hill, 2000, pp. 436–59.

Hiebing, Roman G., and Scott W. Cooper. *The Successful Marketing Plan,* 2nd ed. Lincolnwood, IL: NTC Business Books, 1997.

Lehmann, Donald R., and Russell S. Winer. *Analysis for Marketing Planning.* 5th ed. Burr Ridge, IL: McGraw-Hill/Irwin, 2002.

Parmerlee, David. *Preparing the Marketing Plan.* Chicago: NTC Business Books/American Marketing Association, 2000.

Chapter Notes

Chapter 1

1. See Reinhard Angelmar and Christian Pinson, "The Meaning of Marketing," *Philosophy of Science,* June 1975, pp. 208–14.

2. Peter D. Bennett, *Dictionary of Marketing Terms,* 2d ed. (Chicago: American Marketing Association, 1995), p. 166.

3. Much of this section is based on J. H. Donnelly, Jr., J. L. Gibson, and J. M. Ivancevich, *Fundamentals of Management,* 9th ed. (Burr Ridge, IL: Irwin/McGraw-Hill, 1998), chap. 7.

4. The process may differ depending on the type of organization or management approach, or both. For certain types of organizations, one strategic plan will be sufficient. Some manufacturers with similar product lines or limited product lines will develop only one strategic plan. However, organizations with widely diversified product lines and widely diversified markets may develop strategic plans for units or divisions. These plans usually are combined into a master strategic plan.

5. For a discussion of this topic, see Gerald E. Ledford, Jr., Jon R. Wendenhof, and James T. Strahely, "Realizing a Corporate Philosophy," *Organizational Dynamics,* Winter 1995, pp. 4–19; and Stephan Cummings and John Davies, "Mission, Vision, Fusion," *Long Range Planning,* December 1994, pp. 147–50.

6. Philip Kotler and Gary Armstrong, *Principles of Marketing,* 6th ed. (Englewood Cliffs, NJ: Prentice Hall, 1994), chap. 2.

7. Philip Kotler, *Marketing Management: Analysis, Planning, Implementation and Control,* 8th ed. (Englewood Cliffs, NJ: Prentice Hall, 1994), chap. 3.

8. Norton Paley, "A Sign of Intelligence," *Sales & Marketing Management,* March 1995, pp. 30–31.

9. Peter Drucker, *Management: Tasks, Responsibilities, Practices* (New York: Harper & Row, 1974), pp. 77–89; Kotler, *Marketing Management,* chap. 3.

10. Much of the following discussion is based on Drucker, *Management,* pp. 79–87.

11. Noel B. Zabriskie and Alan B. Huellmantel, "Marketing Research as a Strategic Tool," *Long Range Planning,* February 1994, pp. 107–18.

12. Originally discussed in the classic H. Igor Ansoff, *Corporate Strategy* (New York: McGraw-Hill, 1965).

13. For complete coverage of this topic, see Michael E. Porter, *Competitive Advantage: Creating and Sustaining Superior Performance* (New York: The Free Press, 1985). Material in this section is based upon discussions contained in Steven J. Skinner, *Marketing,* 2d ed. (Boston: Houghton Mifflin Co., 1994), pp. 48–50; and Thomas A. Bateman and Carl P. Zeithaml, *Management Function & Strategy,* 2d ed. (Burr Ridge, IL: Irwin/McGraw-Hill, 1993), pp. 152–53.

14. For a complete discussion of this topic, see Michael Treacy and Fred Wiersema, *The Discipline of Market Leaders* (Reading, MA: Addison-Wesley, 1995); and Michael Treacy and Fred Wiersema, "How Market Leaders Keep Their Edge," *Fortune,* February 6, 1995, pp. 88–98.

15. Philip Kotler, *Marketing Management,* p. 13.

16. For a discussion of this issue and other mistakes marketers frequently make, see Kevin J. Clancy and Robert S. Shulman, "Breaking the Mold," *Sales & Marketing Management,* January 1994, pp. 82–84.

17. George S. Day and David B. Montgomery, "Diagnosing the Experience Curve," *Journal of Marketing,* Spring 1983, pp. 44–58.

18. P. Rajan Varadarajan, Terry Clark, and William M. Pride, "Controlling the Uncontrollable: Managing Your Market Environment," *Sloan Management Review,* Winter 1992, pp. 39–47.

19. Reed E. Nelson, "Is There Strategy in Brazil?" *Business Horizons,* July–August 1992, pp. 15–23.

20. Peter S. Davis and Patrick L. Schill, "Addressing the Contingent Effects of Business Unit Strategic Orientation on the Relationship between Organizational Context and Business Unit Performance," *Journal of Business Research,* 1993, pp. 183–200.

21. J. Scott Armstrong and Roderick J. Brodie, "Effects of Portfolio Planning Methods on Decision Making: Experimental Results," *International Journal of Research in Marketing,* January 1994, pp. 73–84.

22. Michel Roberts, "Times Change but Do Business Strategies?" *Journal of Business Strategy,* March–April 1993, pp. 12–15.

23. Donald L. McCabe and V. K. Narayanan, "The Life Cycle of the PIMS and BCG Models," *Industrial Marketing Management,* November 1991, pp. 347–52.

Chapter 2

1. Based on Peter D. Bennett, ed., *Dictionary of Marketing Terms,* 2d ed. (Chicago: American Marketing Association, 1995), p. 77.

2. Gilbert A. Churchill, Jr., and J. Paul Peter, *Marketing: Creating Value for Customers,* 2d ed. (Burr Ridge, IL: Irwin/McGraw-Hill, 1998), p. 116.

3. For a discussion of some general problems in marketing research, see Alan G. Sawyer and J. Paul Peter, "The Significance of Statistical Significance Testing in Marketing Research," *Journal of Marketing Research,* May 1983, pp. 122–33.

4. This section is based on Churchill and Peter, *Marketing,* pp. 114–16.

Chapter 3

1. Richard P. Coleman, "The Continuing Significance of Social Class to Marketing," *Journal of Consumer Research,* December 1983, pp. 265–80.

2. See William O. Bearden and Michael J. Etzel, "Reference Group Influence on Product and Brand Purchase Decisions," *Journal of Consumer Research,* September 1982, pp. 183–94; and Terry L. Childers and Akshay R. Rao, "The Influence of Familial and Peer-Based Reference Groups on Consumer Decisions," *Journal of Consumer Research,* September 1992, pp. 198–211.

3. See Rosann L. Spiro, "Persuasion in Family Decision Making," *Journal of Consumer Research,* March 1983, pp. 393–402.

4. See Janet Wagner and Sherman Hanna, "The Effectiveness of Family Life Cycle Variables in Consumer Expenditure Research," *Journal of Consumer Research,* December 1983, pp. 281–91. Also see Charles M. Schanninger and William D. Danko, "A Conceptual and Empirical Comparison of Alternative Household Life Cycle Models," *Journal of Consumer Research,* March 1993, pp. 580–94.

5. Russell W. Belk, "Situational Variables and Consumer Behavior," *Journal of Consumer Research,* December 1975, pp. 156–64. Also see Jacob Hornik, "Situational Effects on the Consumption of Time," *Journal of Marketing,* Fall 1982, pp. 44–55; C. Whan Park, Easwer S. Iyer, and Daniel C. Smith, "The Effects of Situational Factors on In-Store Grocery Shopping Behavior: The Role of Store Environment and Time Available for Shopping," *Journal of Consumer Research,* March 1989, pp. 422–33; and Mary Jo Bitner, "Service-scapes: The Impact of Physical Surroundings on Customers and Employees," *Journal of Marketing,* April 1992, pp. 57–71.

6. J. Paul Peter and Jerry C. Olson, *Consumer Behavior and Marketing Strategy,* 6th ed. (Burr Ridge, IL: Irwin/McGraw-Hill, 2002), chap. 4.

7. A. H. Maslow, *Motivation and Personality* (New York: Harper & Row, 1954); also see James F. Engel, Roger D. Blackwell, and Paul W. Miniard, *Consumer Behavior,* 8th ed. (Fort Worth, TX: Dryden Press, 1995), chap. 5, for further discussion of need recognition.

8. For a detailed review of research on external search, see Sharon E. Beatty and Scott M. Smith, "External Search Effort: An Investigation across Several Product Categories," *Journal of Consumer Research,* June 1987, pp. 83–95. Also see Narasimhan Srinivasan and Brian T. Ratchford, "An Empirical Test of a Model of External Search for Automobiles," *Journal of Consumer Research,* September 1991, pp. 233–42; and Julie L. Ozanne, Merrie Brucks, and Dhruv Grewal, "A Study of Information Search Behavior during the Categorization of New Products," *Journal of Consumer Research,* March 1992, pp. 452–63.

9. For further discussion of information processing, see J. Paul Peter and Jerry C. Olson, *Consumer Behavior and Marketing Strategy,* 6th ed. (Burr Ridge, IL: Irwin/McGraw-Hill, 2002), chap. 3.

10. For a summary of research on attitude modeling, see Blair H. Sheppard, Jon Hartwick, and Paul R. Warshaw, "The Theory of Reasoned Action: A Meta-Analysis of Past Research with Recommendations for Modification and Future Research," *Journal of Consumer Research,* December 1988, pp. 325–43.

11. For further discussion of postpurchase feelings, see Richard L. Oliver, "Cognitive, Affective, and Attribute Bases of the Satisfaction Response," *Journal of Consumer Research,* December 1993, pp. 418–30; and Haim Mano and Richard L. Oliver, "Assessing the Dimensionality and Structure of the Consumption Experience: Evaluation, Feeling, and Satisfaction," *Journal of Consumer Research,* December 1993, pp. 451–66.

Chapter 4

1. This discussion is based on Gilbert A. Churchill, Jr. and J. Paul Peter, *Marketing: Creating Value for Customers,* 2d ed. (Burr Ridge, IL: Irwin/McGraw-Hill, 1998), pp. 182–84. Also see Michele D. Bunn, "Taxonomy of Buying Decision Approaches," *Journal of Marketing,* January 1993, pp. 38–56.

2. This discussion is based on Eric N. Berkowitz, Roger A. Kerin, Steven W. Hartley, and William Rudelius, *Marketing*, 4th ed. Irwin/McGraw-Hill (Burr Ridge, IL: 1994), p. 184.

3. For research on influence strategies in organizational buying, see Gary L. Frazier and Raymond Rody, "The Use of Influence Strategies in Interfirm Relationships in Industrial Product Channels," *Journal of Marketing,* January 1991, pp. 52–69; and Julia M. Bristor, "Influence Strategies in Organizational Buying," *Journal of Business-to-Business Marketing,* 1993, pp. 63–98.

4. For research on the role of organizational climate in industrial buying, see William J. Qualls and Christopher P. Puto, "Organizational Climate and Decision Framing: An Integrated Approach to Analyzing Industrial Buying Decisions," *Journal of Marketing Research,* May 1989, pp. 179–92.

Chapter 5

1. Russell I. Haley, "Benefit Segmentation: A Decision-Oriented Research Tool," *Journal of Marketing,* July 1968, pp. 30–35; Russell I. Haley, "Benefit Segmentation—20 Years Later," *Journal of Consumer Marketing,* 1983, pp. 5–13; and Russell I. Haley, "Benefit Segments: Backwards and Forwards," *Journal of Advertising Research,* February–March 1984, pp. 19–25.

2. Roger J. Calantone and Alan G. Sawyer, "The Stability of Benefit Segments," *Journal of Marketing Research,* August 1978, pp. 395–404; also see James R. Merrill and William A. Weeks, "Predicting and Identifying Benefit Segments in the Elderly Market," in *AMA Educator's Proceedings,* eds. Patrick Murphy et al. (Chicago: American Marketing Association, 1983), pp. 399–403; Wagner A. Kamakura, "A Least Squares Procedure for Benefit Segmentation with Conjoint Experiments," *Journal of Marketing Research,* May 1988, pp. 157–67; and Michel Wedel and Jan-Benedict E. M. Steenkamp, "A Clusterwise Regression Method for Simultaneous Fuzzy Market Structuring and Benefit Segmentation." *Journal of Marketing Research,* November 1991, pp. 385–96.

3. John L. Lastovicka, John P. Murry, Jr., and Eric Joachimsthaler, "Evaluating the Measurement Validity of Lifestyle Typologies with Qualitative Measures and Multiplicative Factoring," *Journal of Marketing Research,* February 1990, pp. 11–23.

4. This discussion is taken from J. Paul Peter and Jerry C. Olson, *Consumer Behavior and Marketing Strategy,* 5th ed. (Burr Ridge, IL: Irwin/McGraw-Hill, 1999), pp. 361–63.

5. See Al Ries and Jack Trout, *Positioning: The Battle for Your Mind* (New York: Warner Books, 1981); and Al Ries and Jack Trout, *Marketing Warfare* (New York: McGraw-Hill, 1986).

Chapter 6

1. Material for this section is based on discussions contained in Louis E. Boone and David L. Kurtz, *Contemporary Marketing,* 8th ed. (Fort Worth, TX: Dryden, 1995), chap. 2; Gilbert A. Churchill, Jr. and J. Paul Peter, *Marketing: Creating Value for Customers* (Burr Ridge, IL: Irwin/McGraw-Hill, 1995), chap. 1, p. 634; James H. Donnelly, James L. Gibson, and John M. Ivancevich, *Fundamentals of Management,* 9th ed. (Burr Ridge, IL: Irwin/McGraw-Hill 1995), p. 501; Joseph M. Juran, "Made in the U.S.A.: A Renaissance in Quality," *Harvard Business Review,* July–August 1993, pp. 42–47, 50; and Valerie A. Zeithaml, "Consumer Perceptions of Price, Quality, and Value: A Means End Model and Synthesis of Evidence," *Journal of Marketing,* April 1988, pp. 35–48.

2. For a discussion on this topic, see Andrew J. Bergman, "What the Marketing Professional Needs to Know about ISO 9000 Series Registration," *Industrial Marketing Management,* 1994, pp. 367–70.

3. The material for this section comes from Glenn L. Urban and Steven H. Star, *Advanced Marketing Strategy* (Englewood Cliffs, NJ: Prentice Hall, 1991), chap. 16.

4. For a detailed discussion of this topic, see Anne Perkins, "Product Variety beyond Black," *Harvard Business Review,* November–December 1994, pp. 13–14; and "Perspectives: The Logic of Product-Line Extensions," *Harvard Business Review,* November–December 1994, pp. 53–62.

5. Mats Urde, "Brand Orientation—A Strategy for Survival," *Journal of Consumer Marketing,* 1994, pp. 18–32.

6. James Lowry, "Survey Finds Most Powerful Brands," *Advertising Age,* July 11, 1988, p. 31.

7. Peter H. Farquhar, "Strategic Challenges for Branding," *Marketing Management,* 1994, pp. 8–15.

8. Peter D. Bennett, ed., *Dictionary of Marketing Terms,* 2d ed. (Chicago: American Marketing Association, 1995), p. 27.

9. Terance Shimp, *Promotion Management and Marketing Communications,* 2d ed. (Hinsdale, IL: Dryden Press, 1990), p. 67.

10. David A. Aaker and Kevin Lane Keller, "Consumer Evaluations of Brand Extensions," *Journal of Marketing,* January 1990, pp. 27–41.

11. Ibid.

12. For a detailed discussion of brand equity, see David Aaker, *Managing Brand Equity* (New York and London: Free Press, 1991).

13. For a complete discussion of this topic, see Geoffrey L. Gordon, Roger J. Calantone, and C. A. Di Benedetto, "Brand Equity in the Business-to-Business Sector: An Exploratory Study," *Journal of Product & Brand Management*, 1993, pp. 4–16.

14. Jeffrey D. Zbar, "Industry Trends Hold Private-Label Promise," *Advertising Age*, April 3, 1995, p. 31.

15. Karen Benezra, "Frito Bets 'Reduced' Pitch Is in the Chips," *Brandweek*, January 23, 1995, p. 18.

16. Thomas Hine, "Why We Buy," *Worth*, May 1995, pp. 80–83.

17. For a discussion of problems related to this issue, see Geoffrey L. Gordon, Roger J. Calantone, and C. Anthony Di Benedetto, "Mature Markets and Revitalization Strategies: An American Fable," *Business Horizons*, May–June 1991, pp. 39–50.

18. Barry L. Bayus, "Are Product Life Cycles Really Getting Shorter?" *Journal of Product Innovation Management*, September 1994, pp. 300–08.

19. The discussion on benchmarking is based on Stanley Brown, "Don't Innovate—Imitate," *Sales & Marketing Management*, January 1995, pp. 24–25; Charles Goldwasser, "Benchmarking: People Make the Process," *Management Review*, June 1995, pp. 39–43; and L. S. Pryor and S. J. Katz, "How Benchmarking Goes Wrong (and How to Do It Right)," *Planning Review*, January–February 1993, pp. 6–14.

Chapter 7

1. "Face Value: The Mass Production of Ideas, and Other Impossibilities," *The Economist*, March 18, 1995, p. 72.

2. Greg Erickson, "New Package Makes a New Product Complete," *Marketing News*, May 8, 1995, p. 10.

3. Zina Mouhkheiber, "Oversleeping," *Forbes*, June 15, 1995, pp. 78–79.

4. The material on the five categories of new products is from C. Merle Crawford and Anthony Di Benedetto, *New Products Management*, 6th ed. (Burr Ridge, IL: McGraw-Hill/Irwin, 2000), chap. 1.

5. H. Igor Ansoff, *Corporate Strategy* (New York: McGraw-Hill, 1965), pp. 109–10.

6. Richard Stroup, "Growing in a Crowded Market Requires Old and New Strategies," *Brandweek*, August 22, 1994, p. 19.

7. These two examples came from Justin Martin, "Ignore Your Customers," *Fortune*, May 1, 1995, pp. 121–26.

8. "Where Do They Get All Those Ideas?" *Machine Design*, January 26, 1995, p. 40.

9. This section is based on Daryl McKee, "An Organizational Learning Approach to Product Innovation," *Journal of Product Innovation Management*, September 1992, pp. 232–45.

10. The discussion on risk is from Thomas D. Kuczmarski and Arthur G. Middlebrooks, "Innovation Risk and Reward," *Sales & Marketing Management*, February 1993, pp. 44–51.

11. For a more complete discussion on the advantages and disadvantages of strategic alliances, see Richard N. Cardozo, Shannon H. Shipp, and Kenneth J. Roering, "Proactive Strategic Partnerships: A New Business Markets Strategy," *Journal of Business and Industrial Marketing*, Winter 1992, pp. 51–63; and Frank K. Sonnenberg, "Partnering: Entering the Age of Cooperation," *Journal of Business Strategy*, May/June 1992, pp. 49–52.

12. James Quinn, "Managing Innovation: Controlled Chaos," *Harvard Business Review*, May–June 1985, pp. 73–84; and Hirotaka Takeuchi and Ikujiro Nonaka, "The New New Product Development Game," *Harvard Business Review*, January–February 1986, pp. 137–46.

13. For a discussion of this issue, see Eric M. Olson, Orville C. Walker, Jr., and Robert W. Ruekert, "Organizing for Effective New Product Development: The Moderating Role of Product Innovativeness," *Journal of Marketing*, January 1995, pp. 48–62; and Cristopher Meyer, "How the Right Measures Help Teams Excel," *Harvard Business Review*, May–June 1994, pp. 95–97.

14. For a detailed discussion on these stages, see Karl T. Ulrich and Steven D. Eppinger, *Product Design and Development* (New York: McGraw-Hill, 1995); and Glen Rifken, "Product Development: Emphatic Design Helps Understand Users Better," *Harvard Business Review*, March–April 1994, pp. 10–11.

15. Patricia W. Meyers and Gerald A. Athaide, "Strategic Mutual Learning between Producing and Buying Firms during Product Innovation," *Journal of Product Innovation Management*, September 1991, pp. 155–69.

16. For a discussion of this issue, see Christina Brown and James Lattin, "Investigating the Relationship between Time in Market and Pioneering Advantage," *Management Science*, October 1994, pp. 1361–69; Robin Peterson, "Forecasting for New Product Introduction," *Journal of Business Forecasting*, Fall 1994, pp. 21–23; and Tracy Carlson, "The Race Is On," *Brandweek*, May 9, 1994, pp. 22–27.

17. For a discussion of reasons why products fail, see Betsy Spellman, "Big Talk, Little Dollars," *Brandweek,* January 23, 1995, pp. 21–29.

Chapter 8

1. This discussion is adapted from material contained in Gilbert A. Churchill, Jr. and J. Paul Peter, *Marketing: Creating Value for Customers,* 2nd ed., (Burr Ridge, IL: Irwin/McGraw-Hill, 1998), chap. 18.

2. Material for this section is largely based on the discussion of advertising tasks and objectives contained in William Arens and Courtland Bovée, *Contemporary Advertising,* 5th ed. (Burr Ridge, IL: Irwin/McGraw-Hill, 1994), chap. 7.

3. For more comprehensive coverage of this topic, see George E. Belch and Michael A. Belch, *Advertising and Promotion: An Integrated Marketing Communications Perspective,* 5th ed. (Burr Ridge, IL: Irwin/McGraw-Hill, 2001), chap. 12.

4. For a fuller explanation of the pros and cons associated with push marketing strategies, see Betsy Spellman, "Trade Promotion Redefined," *Brandweek,* March 13, 1995, pp. 25–34; and John McManus, "'Lost' Money Redefined as 'Found' Money Won't Connect the Disconnects," *Brandweek,* March 25, 1995, p. 16.

5. This discussion is based on Donald R. Glover, "Distributor Attitudes toward Manufacturer-Sponsored Promotions," *Industrial Marketing Management,* August 1991, pp. 241–49.

6. For a discussion of this topic, see Murray Raphel, "Frequent Shopper Clubs: Supermarkets' Newest Weapon," *Direct Marketing,* May 1995, pp. 18–20; Richard G. Barlow, "Five Mistakes of Frequency Marketing," *Direct Marketing,* March 1995, pp. 16–17; and Alice Cuneo, "Savvy Frequent-Buyer Plans Build on a Loyal Base," *Advertising Age,* March 20, 1995, pp. S10–11.

Chapter 9

1. Warren Keegan, Sandra Moriarty, and Thomas Duncan, *Marketing,* 2d ed. (Englewood Cliffs, NJ: Prentice Hall, 1994), p. 654.

2. Material for this discussion came from Ronald B. Marks, *Personal Selling: An Interactive Approach,* 5th ed. (Boston, MA: Allyn and Bacon, 1994), pp. 12–13.

3. Material for the discussion of objectives is adapted from Joel R. Evans and Barry Berman, *Marketing,* 6th ed. (New York: Macmillan, 1994), pp. 640–42.

4. Unless otherwise noted, the discussion on the relationship-building process is based largely on

material contained in Barton A. Weitz, Stephen B. Castleberry, and John F. Tanner, Jr., *Selling: Building Partnerships,* 3d ed. (Burr Ridge, IL: Irwin/McGraw-Hill, 1998); and Rolph Anderson, *Essentials of Personal Selling: The New Professionalism* (Englewood Cliffs, NJ: Prentice Hall, 1995). For an in-depth discussion of this topic, readers should consult these references.

5. The discussion of aftermarketing is based on the work of Terry Vavra, *Aftermarketing: How to Keep Customers for Life through Relationship Marketing* (Burr Ridge, IL: McGraw-Hill, 1995).

6. Ibid.

7. The discussion on national account management is from James S. Boles, Bruce K. Pilling, and George W. Goodwyn, "Revitalizing Your National Account Marketing Program," *Journal of Business & Industrial Marketing* 9, no. 1 (1994), pp. 24–33.

8. Based on a survey by the National Industrial Conference Board: "Forecasting Sales," *Studies in Business Policy,* no. 106.

9. Much of the discussion in this section is based on material contained in Gilbert A. Churchill, Jr., Neil M. Ford, and Orville C. Walker, Jr., *Sales Force Management,* 4th ed. (Burr Ridge, IL: Irwin/McGraw-Hill, 1993); and William J. Stanton, Richard H. Buskirk, and Rosann L. Spiro, *Management of a Sales Force,* 9th ed. (Burr Ridge, IL: Irwin/McGraw-Hill, 1995), pp. 319–20.

10. For a complete discussion of the skills and policies used by successful sales leaders in motivating salespeople, see David W. Cravens, Thomas N. Ingram, Raymond W. LaForge, and Clifford E. Young, "Hallmarks of Effective Sales Organizations," *Marketing Management,* Winter 1992, pp. 57–66; Thomas R. Wortruba, John S. Mactie, and Jerome A. Colletti, "Effective Sales Force Recognition Programs," *Industrial Marketing Management,* February 1991, pp. 9–15; and Ken Blanchard, "Reward Salespeople Creatively," *Personal Selling Power,* March 1992, p. 24.

Chapter 10

1. Peter D. Bennett, *Dictionary of Marketing Terms,* 2d ed. (Chicago: American Marketing Association, 1995), p. 242.

2. For further discussion of relationship marketing, see Jan B. Heide, "Interorganizational Governance in Marketing Channels," *Journal of Marketing,* January 1994, pp. 71–85; Robert M. Morgan and Shelby D. Hunt, "The Commitment-Trust Theory of Relationship Marketing," *Journal of Marketing,* July 1994, pp. 20–38; and Manohar U. Kalwani and Narakesari Narayandas, "Long-Term Manufacturer-Supplier Relationships: Do

They Pay Off for the Supplier Firm?" *Journal of Marketing,* January 1995, pp. 1–16.

3. This section is based on Donald J. Bowersox and M. Bixby Cooper, *Strategic Marketing Channel Management* (New York: McGraw-Hill, 1992), pp. 104–7; Bert Rosenbloom, *Marketing Channels: A Management View,* 4th ed. (Hinsdale, IL: Dryden Press), pp. 440–65; and Eric N. Berkowitz, Roger A. Kerin, Steven W. Hartley, and William Rudelius, *Marketing,* 3d ed. (Burr Ridge, IL: Irwin/McGraw-Hill, 1992), pp. 387–90.

4. This section is based on Gilbert A. Churchill, Jr. and J. Paul Peter, *Marketing: Creating Value for Customers,* 2d ed. (Burr Ridge, IL: Irwin/McGraw-Hill, 1998), pp. 392–98.

5. This section is based on Churchill and Peter, *Marketing: Creating Value,* pp. 414–18.

6. This classification is taken from Michael Levy and Barton A. Weitz, *Retailing Management,* 3d ed. (Burr Ridge, IL: Irwin/McGraw-Hill, 1998), chap. 3.

7. For an excellent discussion of electronic exchange, see David W. Stewart and Qin Zhao, "Internet Marketing, Business Models, and Public Policy," *Journal of Public Policy & Marketing,* Fall 2000, pp. 287–96.

Chapter 11

1. Kent B. Monroe, "Buyers' Subjective Perceptions of Price," *Journal of Marketing Research,* February 1973, pp. 70–80; also see Donald R. Lichtenstein and Scot Burton, "The Relationship between Perceived and Objective Price—Quality," *Journal of Marketing Research,* November 1989, pp. 429–43.

2. For research concerning the effects of price and several other marketing variables on perceived product quality, see Akshay R. Rao and Kent B. Monroe, "The Effect of Price, Brand Name, and Store Name on Buyers' Perceptions of Product Quality: An Integrative Review," *Journal of Marketing Research,* August 1989, pp. 351–57; and William B. Dodds, Kent B. Monroe, and Dhruv Grewal, "Effects of Price, Brand, and Store Evaluations on Buyers' Product Evaluations," *Journal of Marketing Research,* August 1991, pp. 307–19.

3. For further discussion of price elasticity, see Stephen J. Hoch, Byung-Do Kim, Alan L. Montgomery, and Peter Rosi, "Determinants of Store-Level Price Elasticity," *Journal of Marketing Research,* February 1995, pp. 17–29.

4. For further discussion of legal issues involved in pricing, see Louis W. Stern and Thomas L. Eovaldi, *Legal Aspects of Marketing Strategy* (Englewood Cliffs, NJ: Prentice Hall, 1984), chap. 5.

5. For more detailed discussions, see Frederick E. Webster, *Marketing for Managers* (New York: Harper & Row, 1974), pp. 178–79; also see Thomas T. Nagle and Reed K. Holden, *The Strategy and Tactics of Pricing* (Englewood Cliffs, NJ: Prentice Hall, 1995); and Kent B. Monroe, *Pricing: Making Profitable Decisions,* 2d ed. (New York: McGraw-Hill, 1990).

Chapter 12

1. Much of the material for this introduction came from Ronald Henkoff, "Service Is Everybody's Business," *Fortune,* June 27, 1994, pp. 48–60; and Tim R. Smith, "The Tenth District's Expanding Service Sector," *Economic Review,* Third Quarter 1994, pp. 55–66.

2. Peter D. Bennett, ed., *Dictionary of Marketing Terms,* 2d ed. (Chicago: American Marketing Association, 1995), p. 261.

3. The material in this section draws from research performed by Leonard L. Berry, Valerie A. Zeithaml, and A. Parasuraman, "Quality Counts in Services, Too," *Business Horizons,* May–June 1985, pp. 44–52; A. Parasuraman, Valerie A. Zeithaml, and Leonard L. Berry, "A Conceptual Model of Service Quality and Its Implications for Future Research," *Journal of Marketing,* Fall 1985, pp. 41–50; Leonard L. Berry, A. Parasuraman, and Valerie A. Zeithaml, "The Service-Quality Puzzle," *Business Horizons,* September–October 1988, pp. 35–43; Stephen W. Brown and Teresa A. Swartz, "A Gap Analysis of Professional Service Quality," *Journal of Marketing,* April 1989, pp. 92–98; Leonard L. Berry, Valerie A. Zeithaml, and A. Parasuraman, "Five Imperatives for Improving Service Quality," *Sloan Management Review,* Summer 1990, pp. 29–38; A. Parasuraman, Leonard L. Berry, and Valerie A. Zeithaml, "Understanding Customer Expectations of Service," *Sloan Management Review,* Spring 1991, pp. 39–48; and Leonard L. Berry, *On Great Service: A Framework for Action* (New York: Free Press, 1995).

4. Rick Berry, "Define Service Quality So You Can Deliver It," *Best's Review,* March 1995, p. 68.

5. Material for this section is drawn from John T. Mentzer, Carol C. Bienstock, and Kenneth B. Kahn, "Benchmarking Satisfaction," *Marketing Management,* Summer 1995, pp. 41–46; and Alan Dutka, *AMA Handbook for Customer Satisfaction: A Complete Guide to Research, Planning and Implementation* (Lincolnwood, IL: NTC Books, 1994). For detailed information on this topic, readers are advised to consult these sources.

6. Much of the material for this section was taken from Karl Albrecht and Ron Zemke, *Service America* (Burr Ridge, IL: Irwin/McGraw-Hill, 1985); and Ron Zemke and Dick Schaaf, *The Service Edge 101: Companies That*

Profit from Customer Care (New York: New American Library, 1989).

7. Chip R. Bell and Kristen Anderson, "Selecting Super Service People," *HR Magazine*, February 1992, pp. 52–54.

8. James A. Schlesinger and James L. Heskett, "Breaking the Cycle of Failure in Services," *Sloan Management Review*, Spring 1991, pp. 17–28.

9. Leonard L. Berry and A. Parasuraman, "Services Marketing Starts from Within," *Marketing Management*, Winter 1992, pp. 25–34.

10. Ibid.

11. Leonard L. Berry and A. Parasuraman, "Prescriptions for a Service Quality Revolution in America," *Organizational Dynamics*, Spring 1992, pp. 5–15.

12. Bob O'Neal, "World-Class Service," *Executive Excellence*, September 1994, pp. 11–12.

13. This example is from David E. Bowen and Edward E. Lawler III, "The Empowerment of Service Workers: What, Why, How, and When," *Sloan Management Review*, Spring 1992, pp. 31–39.

14. Howard Schlossberg, "Study: U.S. Firms Lag in Using Customer Satisfaction Data," *Marketing News*, June 1992, p. 14.

15. Andrew E. Serwer, "The Competition Heats Up in Online Banking," *Fortune*, June 26, 1995, pp. 18–19.

16. John Labate, "Chronimed," *Fortune*, February 20, 1995, p. 118.

17. Elaine Underwood, "Airlines Continue Flight to E-Ticketing," *Brandweek*, May 8, 1995, p. 3.

18. Peter L. Ostrowski, Terrence V. O'Brien, and Geoffrey L. Gordon, "Determinants of Service Quality in the Commercial Airline Industry: Differences between Business and Leisure Travelers," *Journal of Travel & Tourism Marketing* 3, no. 1 (1994), pp. 19–47.

Chapter 13

1. Jason Vogel, "Chicken Diplomacy," *Financial World*, March 14, 1995, pp. 46–49.

2. For a full explanation on cultural differences, see Rose Knotts, "Cross-Cultural Management: Transformations and Adaptations," *Business Horizons*, January–February 1989, pp. 29–33.

3. Claudia Penteado, "Pepsi's Brazil Blitz," *Advertising Age*, January 16, 1995, p. 12.

4. Karen Benezra, "Fritos 'Round the World,'" *Brandweek*, March 27, 1995, pp. 32, 35.

5. Material for this section is from Craig Mellow, "Russia: Making Cash from Chaos," *Fortune*, April 17, 1995, pp. 145–51; and Peter Galuszka, "And You Think You've Got Tax Problems," *Business Week*, May 29, 1995, p. 50.

6. Mir Magbool Alam Khan, "Enormity Tempts Marketers to Make a Passage to India," *Advertising Age International*, May 15, 1995, p. 112.

7. This section was taken from James F. Bolt, "Global Competitors: Some Criteria for Success," *Business Horizons*, January–February 1988, pp. 34–41.

8. This section is based on George S. Yip, Pierre M. Loewe, and Michael Y. Yoshino, "How to Take Your Company to the Global Market," *Columbia Journal of World Business*, Winter 1988, pp. 37–48.

9. Ibid.

10. The introductory material on foreign research is based on Michael R. Czintoka, "Take a Shortcut to Low-Cost Global Research," *Marketing News*, March 13, 1995, p. 3.

11. Donald B. Pittenger, "Gathering Foreign Demographics Is No Easy Task," *Marketing News*, January 8, 1990, pp. 23, 25.

12. This discussion is based on John Burnett, *Promotion Management* (Boston: Houghton-Mifflin Co., 1993), chap. 19.

13. The material for this section on market entry and growth approaches is based on Philip R. Cateora, *International Marketing*, 8th ed. (Burr Ridge, IL: Irwin/McGraw-Hill, 1993), pp. 325–34; Charles W. L. Hill, *International Business: Competing in the Global Marketplace* (Burr Ridge, IL: Irwin/McGraw-Hill, 1994), pp. 402–8; and William M. Pride and O. C. Ferrell, *Marketing: Concepts and Strategy*, 9th ed. (Boston: Houghton-Mifflin Co., 1995), pp. 111–14.

14. Bruce A. Walters, Steve Peters, and Gregory G. Dess, "Strategic Alliances and Joint Ventures: Making Them Work," *Business Horizons*, July–August 1994, pp. 5–10.

15. Material in this section is based on Subhash C. Jain, "Standardization of International Marketing Strategy: Some Research Hypotheses," *Journal of Marketing*, January 1989, pp. 70–79.

Section II

1. Michael E. Porter, *Competitive Strategy* (New York: Free Press, 1980). Also see Michael E. Porter, *Competitive Advantage: Creating and Sustaining Superior Performance* (New York: Free Press, 1985); and Michael E. Porter, *The Competitive Advantage of Nations* (New York: Free Press, 1990).

Section III

1. For methods of estimating the cost of capital, see Charles P. Jones, *Introduction to Financial Management* (Burr Ridge, IL: Irwin/McGraw-Hill, 1992), chap. 14.

2. See Eugene F. Brigham, *Fundamentals of Financial Management* (Hinsdale, IL: Dryden Press, 1986).

3. It is useful to use average inventory rather than a single end-of-year estimate if monthly data are available.

4. For a discussion of ratio analysis for retailing, see Joseph B. Mason and Morris L. Mayer, *Modern Retailing: Theory and Practice,* 6th ed. (Burr Ridge, IL: Irwin/McGraw-Hill, 1993), chap. 8.

Index

CASE INDEX

Amazon.com, 451–453
America Online, 543–556

Black and Decker Corporation in 2000, 746–768
Black Diamond Equipment, Ltd., 612–628
Blockbuster Entertainment Corporation, 457–468

Callaway Golf Company, 372–405
Campbell Soup Company in 2000, 769–798
Cannondale Corporation, 343–371
Caterpillar Inc., 631–643
Claritas Inc.: Using Compass and PRIZM, 281–293
Cowgirl Chocolates, 528–543

Dell Computer Corporation: Strategy and Challenges for the 21st Century, 799–840

E. & J. Gallo Winery, 577–584
eBay: King of the Online Auction Industry, 490–523

Harley-Davidson, Inc—Motorcycle Division, 644–656
Harley-Davidson.com and the Global Motorcycle Industry, 406–410

Kentucky Fried Chicken and the Global Fast-Food Industry in 1998, 722–745
Kikkoman Corporation in the Mid-1990s: Market Maturity, Diversification, and Globalization, 697–721

L. A. Gear, Inc., 676–696
Lady Foot Locker: The Lobo Launch, 417–435
Little Caesars, 524–525

Longevity Health Care Systems, Inc, 436–450

Nanophase Technologies Corporation, 657–675
Nintendo versus SEGA: Sex, Violence, and Videogames, 572–576
Notetakers Company Selling Class Notes and Instructional Notes to Students, 568–571

Peapod in the Online Grocery Business, 469–489
Pfizer, Inc.: Animal Health Products, Industry Downturns, and Marketing Strategy, 298–308
Philip Morris Companies, 598–611

Salomon: The Monocoque Ski, 326–342

Sarah Norton and Wise Research, 585–597
Schwinn Bicycles, 526–528
Snacks to Go, 309–325
South Delaware Coors, Inc., 272–280
Starbucks Coffee Houses, 294–297
Sun Microsystems: A High Growth, Loosely Organized Giant in a Constrained Technology Intensive Environment, 557–567

3DV-LS: Assessing Market Opportunity in the Computer Visualization Market, 261–271
Tupperware, 454–456

Wind Technology, 411–416

REFERENCE NAMES INDEX

Aaker, David A., 40, 89, 204, 855n, 856n
Albrecht, Karl, 858n
Allen, Sara Clark, 718
Almaney, A. J., 676
Ambler, Tim, 21
Anderson, Erin, 161
Anderson, James C., 67
Anderson, Kristen, 859n
Anderson, Rolph, 857n
Angelmar, Reinhard, 853n
Ansoff, H. Igor, 853n, 856n
Arens, William, 117, 857n
Armstrong, Gary, 853n
Armstrong, J. Scott, 853n
Assael, Henry, 54
Athaide, Gerald A., 856n
Aufretier, Nora, 480n
Ayers, Douglas, 99

Bannan, K. J., 453
Barlow, Richard G., 857n
Bartlett, Christopher A., 204
Bateman, Thomas A., 853n
Bates, Albert D., 153
Bayus, Barry L., 856n
Bearden, William O., 854n
Beatty, Sharon E., 854n
Beck, Rachel, 487n
Belch, George E., 125, 857n
Belch, Michael A., 125, 857n
Belise, Laurent, 480n
Belk, Russell W., 854n
Bell, Chip R., 859n

Belmont, Nicole, 469
Benezra, Karen, 856n, 859n
Bennett, Peter D., 36, 146, 147, 853n, 854n, 857n, 858n
Benson, Tracy E., 635n
Berenson, Conrad, 95
Bergman, Andrew J., 855n
Bergman, Joan, 479n
Bergsman, Steve, 718
Berkowitz, Eric N., 855n, 858n
Berman, Barry, 161, 857n
Berry, Leonard L., 179, 189, 858n, 859n
Berry, Rick, 858n
Berss, Marcia, 46
Best, Roger, Jr., 53, 54
Bezos, Jeff, 453
Bidault, Francis, 326
Bienstock, Carol C., 858n
Bishop, Bill, 127
Bitner, Mary Jo, 854n
Blackwell, Roger D., 54, 854n
Blanchard, Ken, 857n
Boles, James S., 857n
Bolt, James F., 859n
Boone, Louis E., 855n
Bovée, Courtland, 857n
Bowen, David E., 859n
Bowersox, Donald J., 161, 858n
Boyd, Thomas C., 417
Brealey, Richard A., 228
Brigham, Eugene F., 860n
Bristor, Julia M., 855n
Brodie, Roderick J., 853n

Brooker, K., 453
Brown, Christina, 856n
Brown, Stanley, 856n
Brown, Stephen W., 189, 858n
Brown, Stuart F., 410
Brucks, Merrie, 854n
Brumback, Nancy, 354n
Buel, Stephen, 509n
Bunn, Michele D., 854n
Burnett, John, 859n
Burns, Alvin C., 40
Burnstein, Daniel, 204
Burton, Richard, 189
Burton, Scot, 858n
Bush, Ronald F., 40
Buskirk, Richard H., 857n
Butscher, Stephen A., 110

Calantone, Roger J., 74, 855n, 856n
Calson, Tracy, 856n
Campbell, Dee Ann, 718
Cardozo, Richard N., 856n
Castleberry, Stephen B., 132, 134, 135, 141, 144, 857n
Cateora, Philip R., 859n
Cavusgil, S. Tarner, 637n
Chaigouris, Larry, 97
Chakravarty, S., 603n
Charm, E., 361n
Chaudhuri, Arjun, 97
Childers, Terry L., 854n
Chopra, Sunil, 161
Chowdhury, Neel, 820n

Churchill, Gilbert A., Jr., 10, 35, 36, 39, 40, 66, 78, 93, 144, 176, 854n, 855n, 857n, 858n
Clancy, Kevin J., 853n
Clark, Terry, 853n
Claterbos, Joyce A., 697
Cohen, Adam, 500n
Cohen, William, 852
Coleman, Richard P., 854n
Coney, Kenneth A., 53, 54
Conlan, Ginger, 141
Cooper, M. Bixby, 161, 858n
Cooper, Robert G., 101
Cooper, Scott W., 852
Cooper-Martin, Elizabeth, 80
Coughlin, Anne T., 161
Coulter, Mary K., 585
Coulter, Ronald L., 585
Cox, Jennifer J., 170
Cravens, David W., 206, 217, 852, 857n
Crawford, C. Merle, 107, 110, 856n
Crosby, Lawrence A., 144
Cross, E. Joseph, 672
Cummings, Stephan, 853n
Cuneo, Alice, 857n
Curran, Lawrence, 567n
Czintoka, Michael R., 859n

Dagnoli, J., 600n, 603n, 605n
Danko, William D., 854n
Davies, John, 853n
Davis, Peter S., 853n

Day, George S., 40, 228, 853n
DeBenedetto, Anthony, 110
Delcoure, Natalya V., 543
Dell, Michael, 803n, 806n, 808n, 810n, 828n
Della Cava, Marco R., 410
Demestrakakes, Pan, 718
Dess, Gregory G., 859n
Deveny, Kathleen, 633n
Di Benedetto, C. A., 856n
Dickson, Peter R., 80
Dipak, Jain, 110
Dodds, William B., 858n
Dolan, Robert J., 163, 172
Donnelly, James H., Jr., 77, 188, 632n, 853n, 855n
Drucker, Peter F., 853n
Duncan, Thomas, 114, 127, 857n
Dwyer, F. Robert, 60, 64, 67
Dyan, Machan, 410
Dye, Donald H., 376n

Eckley, Robert S., 633n
Eckrich, Donald, 632n
Eisner, Alan B., 469
El-Ansary, Adel I., 161
Eldridge, Earle, 410
Ellram, Lisa M., 161
Engardio, P., 609n
Engel, James F., 54, 854n
Eovaldi, Thomas L., 858n
Eppinger, Steven D., 856n
Erickson, Greg, 856n
Etzel, Michael J., 86, 151, 192, 854n
Evans, Joel R., 857n

Fahay, Liam, 228
Farhi, P., 575n
Farnham, A., 603n
Farquhar, Peter D., 855n
Ferrell, O. C., 859n
Fields, D. Michael, 585
Fierman, Jaclyn, 578n, 579n, 582n
Fink, Laurie, 313n
Fisher, Lawrence M., 482n
Fisher, Susan E., 567n
Fitzgerald, Kate, 654n
Forbish, Lynn, 718
Ford, Neil M., 144, 857n
Forrest, Tracy, 718
Fram, Eugene H., 144
Francis, Bob, 567n
Frazier, Gary L., 855n
Frazier, Rick, 110
Fredericks, Joan O., 21
Freedman, Alix M., 577n, 579n, 584n
Fruin, W. Mark, 718

Gable, John E., 372
Galuszka, Peter, 859n
Gamble, John E., 343, 746, 769, 799
Gannes, S., 696n
Garner, S. J., 568
Geiger, Joseph J., 529
Gelb, Thomas, 646n

Ghoshal, Sumuntra, 204
Gibson, James L., 853n, 855n
Gilmore, James, 189
Giltenan, E., 600n
Ginter, James L., 80
Glover, Donald R., 857n
Gokhale, Ashish, 250, 294
Goldman, Abigail, 249
Goldstein, Lauren, 249
Goldstine, Jonathan, 97
Goldwasser, Charles, 856n
Goodwyn, George W., 857n
Gordon, Geoffrey L., 99, 131, 856n, 859n
Green, Paul E., 80
Green, S., 676
Greene, Walter E., 557
Grewal, Dhruv, 854n, 858n
Griffin, T., 127
Grimm, M., 696n
Grossman, Laurie M., 454n
Guiltinan, Joseph, 122

Haberger, Robin, 261
Hair, Joseph F, Jr., 19
Haley, Russell I., 73, 855n
Halper, Mark, 159
Hanna, Nessim, 99
Hanna, Sherman, 854n
Hannon, Kerry, 454n
Hart, Christopher W. L., 181
Hartley, Steven W., 855n, 858n
Hartwick, John, 854n
Hawkins, Del I., 53, 54
Heibing, Roman G., 852
Heide, Jan B., 857n
Henkoff, Ronald, 632n, 633n, 634n, 635n, 858n
Hennessey, Terry, 481n
Heskett, James L., 859n
Hewitt, Lynda, 718
Hill, Charles W. L., 859n
Himelstein, Linda, 484n, 485n, 486n
Hine, Thomas, 856n
Hise, Richard T., 204
Ho, Suk-ching, 204
Hoch, J., 858n
Hof, Robert D., 567n
Holbrook, Morris B., 97
Holden, Reed K., 172, 858n
Honeycutt, Earl D., Jr., 62, 67
Horivitz, B., 695n
Hornik, Jacob, 854n
Hostveldt, John, 718
House, William C., 557
Howard, Dennis, 189
Hoyer, Wayne D., 54
Huellmantel, Alan B., 853n
Hunt, Shelby D., 857n
Hyler, Bracey, 110

Iacobucci, Dawn, 21, 35, 36, 39, 40, 127
Ingram, Thomas N., 143, 857n
Ivancevich, John M., 853n, 855n
Ivankoe, John, 255
Iyer, Easwer S., 854n

Jackson, Ralph W., 177
Jaffe, Jeffrey F., 228
Jain, Subhash C., 859n
Janoff, Barry, 488n
Jauch, Lawrence R., 543
Jensen, Debra, 718
Jensen, Don, 718
Jensen, Leah, 718
Joachimsthaler, Erich, 201, 204, 855n
Johnson, Sheree L., 144
Jones, Charles P., 860n
Jordan, Bradford D., 228
Judge, Paul, 71
Juran, Joseph M., 855n

Kahn, Kenneth B., 858n
Kalinowski, Mark, 254, 256
Kalwani, Manohar U., 857n
Kamakura, Wagner A., 855n
Kaminski, Peter, 131
Kanabayashi, Masayoshi, 637n, 638n
Kanuck, Leslie Lazar, 42, 54
Kardes, Frank R., 54
Karson, Eric J., 272
Katz, M., 599n
Katz, S. J., 856n
Keegan, Warren, 857n
Keller, Kevin Lane, 97, 196, 855n
Kelly, Kevin, 638n
Kerin, Roger A., 217, 855n, 858n
Kerwin, K., 696n
Khan, Mir Magbool Alam, 859n
Kidney, James A, 457
Kim, Byung-Do, 858n
King, Robert L., 4
King, Ronette, 479n
Kinugasa, Dean, 719
Kirkpatrick, David, 831n
Kissan, Joseph, 144
Knotts, Rose, 859n
Koplos, Cynthia, 255
Kotler, Philip, 853n
Kotlowitz, Alex, 636n
Kreigzer, Arne de, 204
Kreiser, Patrick, 490
Krieger, Abba M., 80
Krishnamurthy, Sandeep, 127
Krug, Jeffrey A., 722
Kuczmarski, Thomas D., 110, 856n
Kumar, V., 40
Kurschner, Dale, 410
Kurtz, David L., 855n

Labate, John, 859n
LaForge, Raymond W., 143, 857n
LaGrange, Maria L., 719
Laker, Michael, 110
Lamb, Charles W., Jr., 19, 206
Lambert, Douglas M., 161
Lamont, Lawrence M., 436, 657
Lastovicka, John L., 855n
Lattin, James, 856n
Lawler, Edward E., III, 859n
Lawrence, John J., 529
Ledford, Gerald E., Jr., 853n

Lehmann, Donald R., 16, 40, 97, 852
Leinster, C., 603n
Lemon, Katherine N., 144
Levering, R., 599n
Levin, Doron P., 655n
Levin, M., 604n
Levine, Jonathan B., 567n
Levy, Michael, 157, 161, 165, 858n
Lichtenstein, Donald R., 858n
Light, Larry, 97
Liker, Jeffrey K., 110
Linrud, JoAnn K., 309
Loewe, Pierre M., 859n
Loro, L., 354n
Lowry, James, 855n
Lumpkin, James R., 161
Lunsford, Dale A., 177
Lusch, Robert F., 21

Mabin, Connie, 828n
MacArthur, Kate, 252
Machlis, Sharon, 481n
MacInnis, Deborah J., 54
Mactie, John S., 857n
Magrath, Allan J., 633n
Mahajan, Vijay, 110, 204
Maher, Dan, 181
Manning, Ken, 411
Mano, Haim, 854n
Maranville, Steven J., 612
Marconi, Joe, 97
Margretta, Joan, 803n, 815n, 821n, 823n
Marien, Edward J., 161
Marino, Lou, 490
Markoff, John, 567n
Marks, Ronald B., 857n
Marlatt, Andrew, 487n
Martin, Justin, 856n
Maslow, Abraham H., 854n
Mason, Joseph B., 860n
Matanovich, Timothy, 21
Mayer, Morris L., 860n
McArthur, D. N., 127
McCabe, Donald L., 854n
McCarthy, E. Jerome, 123
McCarthy, Michael S., 144
McDaniel, Carl, 19
McGeehan, Patrick, 526n
McGovern, Michael, 482
McGrath, Allan J., 634n
McGuire, Tim, 480n
McKay, D., 696n
McKee, Daryl, 856n
McManus, John, 857n
Meeds, F., 696n
Meindl, Peter, 161
Melcher, Richard A., 410
Mellow, Craig, 859n
Mentzer, John T., 858n
Merrill, James R., 855n
Meyer, Christopher, 856n
Meyers, Patricia W., 856n
Middlebrooks, Arthur G., 856n
Miller, James P., 640n
Miniard, Paul W., 54, 854n
Minor, Michael, 54

Mogi, Yuzaburo, 719
Mohr, Jakki J., 71, 298, 411
Mohr-Jackson, Iris, 95
Monroe, Kent B., 170, 172, 858n
Montgomery, Alan L., 858n
Montgomery, David B., 204, 853n
Moran, M., 575n
Morgan, Robert M., 857n
Moriarty, Sandra, 114, 127, 857n
Morris, Linda J., 529
Morris, Michael H., 62, 67
Moskowitz, M., 599n
Mouhkheiber, Zina, 856n
Mowen, John C., 54
Murphy, Patrick, 855n
Murry, John P., Jr., 855n
Myers, James H., 80
Myers, Stewart C., 228

Nagle, Thomas T., 172, 858n
Narayanan, V. K., 854n
Narayandas, Narakesari, 857n
Narus, James A., 67
Neidell, Lester A., 177
Nelson, James E., 272
Nelson, Reed E., 853n
Nonaka, Ikujiro, 856n
Nueno, Jose Luis, 201

O'Brien, James A., 40
O'Brien, Terrence V., 859n
O'Neal, Bob, 859n
Oakes, Peter, 254
Oliver, Richard L., 854n
Olson, Eric M., 856n
Olson, Jerry C., 54, 247, 854n, 855n
Ostrander, Kathleen, 719
Ostrowksi, Peter L., 859n
Ould, Andrew, 567n
Ozanne, Julie L., 854n

Page, Albert L., 108
Palan, Kay M., 261
Paley, Norton, 853n
Parasuraman, A., 179, 858n, 859n
Park, Whan, 854n
Parmerlee, David, 852
Paul, Gordon, 122
Pearson, Ann, 51ln
Pelton, Lon E., 161
Penteado, Claudia, 859n
Perkins, Anne, 855n
Perreault, William D., Jr, 123
Peter, J. Paul, 10, 40, 54, 66, 77,
    78, 93, 176, 250, 281, 294, 406,
    451, 454, 524, 526, 631, 632n,
    644, 854n, 855n, 857n, 858n
Peterman, John, 127
Peters, Steve, 859n
Peterson, Robert A., 217
Peterson, Robin, 856n
Piett, Edith, 719
Pilling, Bruce K., 857n
Pinson, Christian, 853n
Pita, Julie, 51ln
Pitt, Leyland F., 62, 67
Pitta, Julie, 567n
Pittenger, Donald B., 859n

Pitterle, Dara L., 631
Plank, Richard E., 67
Porter, Michael E., 307, 853n,
    859n
Pratini de Moraes, Marcos V., 204
Prensky, David, 54
Prete, Dom Del, 197
Price, B. Joseph, III, 189
Pride, William M., 853n, 859n
Produs, Julia, 524n
Pryor, L. S., 856n
Pullman, Madeleine E., 612
Punnett, Betsy J., 199
Puto, Christopher P., 855n

Qualls, William J., 855n
Quelch, John A., 201
Quinn, James, 856n

Rao, Akshay R., 854n, 858n
Raphel, Murray, 857n
Ratchford, Brian T., 854n
Rebello, Kathy, 567n
Redman, Russell, 719
Reichheld, Frederick F., 21
Reid, David A., 67
Riche, Martha Farnsworth, 76
Ricks, David A., 199
Ridnour, Rick, 99
Ries, Al, 855n
Rifken, Glen, 856n
Robbins, Keith, 598
Roberts, Michel, 853n
Roco, Mihail C., 672
Rody, Raymond, 855n
Roering, Kenneth J., 856n
Rohm, Andrew J., 417
Rollins, Kevin, 823n
Rose, Robert L., 636n, 637n, 638n
Rosenbloom, Bert, 161, 858n
Rosenthal, David W., 417
Rosi, Peter, 858n
Rosier, B., 453
Ross, Stephen A., 228
Rottman, M., 696n
Rudelius, William, 855n, 858n
Ruekert, Robert W., 856n
Rust, Roland T., 144

Sager, Ira, 836n
Sawyer, Alan G., 74, 854n, 855n
Schaaf, Rick, 858n
Schanninger, Charles M., 854n
Schiffman, Leon G., 42, 54
Schill, Patrick L., 853n
Schlax, J., 696n
Schlesinger, James A., 859n
Schlesinger, Leonard A., 181
Schlossberg, Howard, 859n
Schoenbachler, Denise, 131
Schoenburg, Lorraine, 719
Schwepker, Charles H., Jr., 143
Scott, John L., 543
Sellers, P., 598n, 600n, 603n, 604n,
    605n, 606n
Serwer, Andrew E., 859n
Shane, Scott, 153
Shank, Matthew D., 189

Sheehy, Barry, 110
Shell, A., 696n
Sheppard, Blair H., 854n
Shikhar, Saron, 110
Shima, Takeshi, 719
Shimp, Terance, 855n
Shipp, Shannon H., 856n
Shulman, Robert S., 853n
Shultz, Don E., 97
Simon, Hermann, 163, 172
Sirapyan, Nancy, 240
Skinner, Steven J., 124, 853n
Sloane, M., 362n
Slotkin, S., 676
Slutsker, Gary, 635n
Slywotzky, Adrian J., 21
Smith, Daniel C., 854n
Smith, N. Craig, 80
Smith, Scott M., 854n
Smith, Tim R., 858n
Sobek, Durwood K. H., 110
Solomon, Michael R., 54
Sonnenberg, Frank K., 856n
Southwick, K., 453
Spain, Judy, 568
Speer, H., 676
Speiser, Mitchell, 252
Spell, Chester, 153
Spellman, Betsy, 857n
Sperber, Bob, 252
Spiegel, Peter, 454n
Spiro, Rosann L., 854n, 857n
Spurgeon, Brad, 672
Srinivasan, Narasimhan, 854n
Stanton, William J., 86, 151,
    192, 857n
Stebbins, John, 672
Steckel, Joel H., 40
Steenkamp, Jan-Benedict
    E. M., 855n
Stern, Louis W., 161, 858n
Sternthal, Brian, 127
Stevens, Karen, 410
Stewart, David W., 858n
Stock, James R., 161
Stone, Romuald A., 343, 572
Storey, Elizabeth W., 436
Stoughton, Stephanie, 249
Strahely, James, 853n
Strauss, Gary, 524n
Streeter, Sara, 298
Strickland, A. J., III, 214, 577n, 847
Strom, David, 159
Stroup, Richard, 856n
Strutton, David, 161
Sudman, Seymour, 40
Swartz, Teresa A., 858n

Takeuchi, Hirotaka, 856n
Tanaka, Norihito, 697
Tanner, John F., Jr., 60, 64, 67,
    132, 134, 135, 141, 144, 857n
Taylor, Marilyn L., 697
Taylor, Thayer C., 143
Tedeschi, M., 696n
Terrel, Ed, 631n, 639n
Thompson, Arthur A., Jr., 214,
    746, 769, 799, 847

Thurman, Daniel C., 577n
Tiffany, Susan, 313n
Treacy, Michael, 853n
Tristam, Clare, 495n, 508n, 510n
Trout, Jack, 855n

Ulrich, Karl T., 856n
Underwood, Elaine, 859n
Urban, Glenn L., 855n
Urde, Mats, 855n

Varadarajan, P. Rajan, 853n
Vavra, Terry G., 144, 857n
Vogel, Jason, 859n

Wagner, Janet, 854n
Walker, Bruce J., 86, 151, 192
Walker, Orville C., Jr., 144, 856n,
    857n
Walsh, Valerie, 77, 281
Walters, Bruce A., 859n
Wansley, Brant, 97
Ward, Allen C., 110
Ward, Scott, 97
Warshaw, Paul R., 854n
Weaver, Jane, 512n
Webster, Frederick E., Jr., 4, 15,
    858n
Wedel, Michel, 855n
Weeks, William A., 855n
Weitz, Barton A., 132, 134, 135,
    141, 144, 157, 161, 165, 857n,
    858n
Wells, Melanie, 33
Wells, William D., 54
Wendenhof, Jon R., 853n
Westerfield, Randolph W., 228
White, Philip D., 153
White, William N., 574n
Whyte, Jim, 329n
Wiersema, Fred, 853n
Wilkins, Mira, 719
Williamson, D. A., 453
Wilson, M., 696n
Wind, Jerry, 204
Winer, Russell S., 16, 97, 852
Wood, Stephen D., 189
Woods, Bob, 48ln
Woods, John A., 161
Wortruba, Thomas R., 857n
Wynd, William R., 257

Yates, Ronald E., 719
Yip, George S., 204, 859n
Yoshino, Michael Y., 859n
Young, Clifford E., 857n

Zabriskie, Noel B., 853n
Zachary, G. Paschal, 567n
Zbar, Jeffrey D., 856n
Zeithaml, Carl P., 853n
Zeithaml, Valarie A., 144, 179,
    855n, 858n
Zemke, Ron, 177, 185, 858n
Zhao, Qin, 858n
Zikmund, William G., 40
Zuber, Amy, 255
Zygmont, Jeffrey, 780n

NAME INDEX

Abrahamson, Mellie, 612–615, 625, 628
Adams, Barney, 400–401
Adams, Gary, 398
Agassi, Andre, 422, 690
Ames, Stephen, 396
Ansoff, H. Igor, 100
Apatoff, Robert, 680
Archibald, Nolan D., 749, 750, 751, 752, 766, 768
Armstrong, Mary, 32
Aykroyd, Dan, 464
Azinger, Paul, 396

Baczko, Joseph, 462, 466
Bagni, Gregg, 354, 527
Baird, Jeff, 585, 597
Baldwin, Gerald, 294
Barefield, Gayle, 426
Barksdale, James, 487
Barta, Carol, 558
Bassi, Peter, 727
Bechtolsheim, Andrew, 558, 559
Benford, William L., 681
Bengler, Gary F., 503
Best, Daniel, 63
Bezos, Jeff, 451–452
Billicki, Daniel, 661
Black, Duncan, 749
Bleustein, Jeffrey L., 406
Bommer, Fred, 399
Bonds, Barry, 433
Borders, Louis, 484
Bowker, Gordon, 294
Bowling, James, 605–606
Bradfield, William S., 310, 313, 323
Brainard, Chuck, 613, 623, 625
Brecaw, John, 614
Brennan, Michael, 479
Brewster, Cindy, 593, 594, 595
Brinkerhoff, Parsons, 270
Brooks, Tom, 299
Brotzman, Richard, 661
Brown, John Young, Jr., 723
Brown, Stan, 613, 614, 623
Browne, Oline, 396
Brownlow, Larry, 272–273, 274, 279, 280
Bryant, Kobe, 423, 433
Burke, Dick, 355
Burnquist, Bob, 433

Cage, Kevin, 411, 412, 413, 414–415, 416
Calantone, Roger J., 74
Callaway, Eli, 371–377, 386, 402, 404
Callaway, Fuller, 373
Callaway, Nicholas, 377
Campbell, Joseph, 769
Campbell, William, 603, 604
Capellas, Michael, 834
Capriati, Jennifer, 433
Carlson, Scott, 623
Carr, Dave, 433
Carter, Vince, 433
Case, Steve, 555

Charles, Bob, 396
Cintron, Inez, 33
Clarke, Sandy, 265–266, 267–268, 269, 270
Coates, Ross, 531
Colbert, Jim, 396
Constantino, Ted, 360
Cook, David P., 458
Cook, Scott D., 502, 504
Coors, Adolph, 273
Cranor, Maria, 613, 622, 726
Crawford, C. Merle, 99, 100
Cross, Joseph E., 657–658, 661, 667, 670, 675
Cullman, Joseph F., III, 599–600

Daffin, Pete, 531
Dangoor, David, 604
Dashling, Alan E., 679
Davenport, Kathy, 426
Davidson, William G., 645–646
Davin, Thomas, 727
Davis, Willie D., 679
De Clerk, Alan, 558
Decker, Alonzo, 749
Deegan, Brian, 433
Dell, Michael, 799–803, 806–809, 815–816, 822, 824–830, 837, 840
Demitros, Kathleen, 654
Dent, Jim, 396
Di Benedetto, Anthony, 99, 100
Diard, Jean-Luc, 339, 340
Disney, Roy E., 678, 680
Dorance, Ippy, 780
Dorrance, John T., 769–770, 780
Douaire, George F., 479
Drucker, Peter F., 8
Duncan, Tim, 433
Dye, Donald, 376, 377

Earnhardt, Dale, Jr., 433
Eichelberger, Dave, 396
Ellerbroeck, Al, 418, 426, 428, 431, 434–435
Ely, Paul, 558
Erlander, Clare, 293

Falk, Stephanie, 426
Faulk, Marshall, 433
Ferstandig, Russ, 33
Fields, Bill, 527
Fiorina, Carly, 837
Fleisher, Bruce, 396
Flimin, Mary, 32
Fogel, Lonnie, 248
Franco, Carlos, 396
Freed, Donald, 661, 663

Gagneux, Yves, 340, 342
Galli, Joseph, 766
Gallo, Ernest, 578, 579
Gallo, Joeph, 578
Gallo, Julio, 578
Garciapana, Nomar, 433
Garnett, Kevin, 433
Gasol, Pau, 433

Geddes, Janes, 396
George, Eddie, 433
Gillette, Paul, 584
Godfrey, Thomas, 709
Gold, Stanley P., 676–677, 679, 680, 693
Goldston, Mark R., 676–679, 680, 682, 686, 693
Gordon, Jeff, 433
Graham, David, 360, 396
Greenberg, Robert Y., 676–679, 684, 686–687, 692
Greensberg, Jack, 250, 256
Groscup, Rob, 293

Hahn, Brett, 528
Haines, Robert, 661
Haley, Russell, 72
Halverson, Michael, 309, 310, 316, 323
Hamilton, Kathryn, 436–440, 447–450
Hamilton, Richard, 437, 438, 450
Harms, Jill, 309, 316, 323
Hawk, Tony, 433
Helmstetter, Richard C., 375, 386
Henderson, James A., 662
Henninger, Brian, 396
Herwick, Bob, 558
Hetherington, Rachel, 396
Hill, Grant, 419, 433, 434
Hill, Lauryn, 33
Hoffman, Mat, 433
Holt, Benjamin, 63
Huizenga, H. Wayne, 457–459, 466, 468
Hurley, Bobby, 420

Iverson, Allen, 433

Jackson, Bo, 690
Jackson, Michael, 683, 688
Jacobson, Michael R., 33, 503
Jagr, Jaromir, 433
Jamison, Antawan, 433
Jamison, George, 623
Jamison, Jeff, 612
Jankowski, Jess, 661
Jeffries, Michael, 247, 249
Jeter, Derek, 433
Jobs, Steven, 558, 839
Johnson, David, 769, 780, 782–789, 794
Johnson, Joel, 32
Jones, Robert Trent, 381
Jones, Rosie, 396
Jordan, Michael, 418, 422, 423, 433, 434, 684, 690
Joy, William, 557–559
Joyce, James, 286
Julianius, Didius, 493

Kagle, Robert C., 504
Katz, M., 605
Kawakami, Clark, 622
Kee, Lee Kum, 716

Keechan, Bob, 573
Kendall, Don, 724
Khosla, Vinod, 557–559
Kidd, Jason, 433
Kitt, Jan, 312
Klein, Emilee, 396
Klein, Gary, 356
Koffler, Stephen A., 679
Kohl, Herbert, 573
Kosel, Howard, 310
Kosiur, David, 159
Koumikova, Anna, 433
Kritchevsky, Gina, 661

LaBonte, Joseph, 690
Ladwig, Anne, 413, 414–415
Laine, Richard, 669
Lappinen, Erik, 248
Legrand, Maurice, 340
Lemieux, Mario, 433
Leslie, Lisa, 433
Levering, R., 605
Lewis, Aylwin, 727
Lewis, Ray, 433
Lieberman, Joseph, 573
Lincoln, Howard, 574
Lindley, Leta, 396
Little, May, 531
Lobo, Rebecca, 417, 429, 430, 434, 435
Lysohir, Marilyn, 529–540

MacLeod, Trisha, 714
Malloy, Bill, 469, 479
Malone, Karl, 684
Martinez, Angel, 690
Masagawa, Dr., 711
Maslow, Abraham H., 49
Massey, Jack, 723
Massey, Robert J., 556
Mastbaum, Abe, 555
Maxwell, Hamish, 604, 607
Mayer, Charlie, 313
Mayer, Richard, 605
Mayes, Tony, 577
McAlister, Bob, 682
McCarley, Kenneth, 312
McClung, James, 662
McElhatten, Dave, 312–313
McGovern, George, 769, 770–780, 783
McGovern, Gordon, 794
McGrady, Tracy, 433
McGurdy, Cindy, 396
McLaughlin, Edward, 481
McMillin, John, 610
McNabb, Donovan, 433
McNealy, Scott, 557–559, 561
McNulty, Mark, 396
Mediate, Rocco, 396
Mendelsohn, James, 293
Metcalf, Peter, 613, 614, 622, 623, 628
Meyer, Ron, 312
Meyers, Ann E., 679
Meyers, Peter, 363
Meyerson, Morton, 808

Miles, Michael, 599, 604, 605, 606, 607, 610–611
Miller, Bode, 433
Miller, Clifford A., 679
Miron, Jay, 433
Mirra, Dave, 433
Mogi, Yuzaburo, 697–702, 707, 708, 711–712, 713, 716
Monroe, Clay, 509
Montana, Joe, 684
Montgomerie, Colin, 396
Montgomery, Joseph, 344, 359, 360, 361, 362, 365, 370
Montgomery, Scott, 527
Moody, Jeffrey, 727
Moody, Orville, 396
Morgan, Walter, 396
Morrison, Dale, 769, 789–793, 794, 797, 798
Morton, Sarah, 585–597
Moskowitz, M., 605
Moskowitz, Robert G., 679
Moss, Randy, 433
Murdoch, Simon, 452
Murphy, Bob, 396

Nash, Steve, 433
Nelson, Bill, 710, 711
Neshek, Bill, 713
Neshek, Milton, 711–712
Neumann, Liselotte, 396
Nicholas, Alison, 396
Nielsen, Jakob, 159
Nissan, Daniel, 488
Nixon, Richard M., 710
Norman, Greg, 384–385, 399–400
Novak, David, 726, 727
Nowitzki, Dirk, 433
Nye, Gordie, 680

O'Neal, Shaquille, 419, 423, 433
Olajuwon, Hakeem, 684

Omidyar, Pierre, 490–491, 500–503
Ono, Apolo, 433
Ortiz, Lou, 401
Oss, Gail, 298, 299, 304–307, 308

Page, Parker, 572
Palmer, Brian, 614–615
Parkinson, Andrew B., 469, 479
Parkinson, Thomas L., 469
Parnevik, Jesper, 396
Pascal, Roger, 339, 341
Pastrana, Travis, 433
Patterson, Pat, 261–262, 264, 265, 271
Pearlman, Jerry, 662
Pearson, Andrall, 727
Perkins, Donald, 662
Perrauding, Michel, 690
Pettigrew, Tru, 33
Pfeiffer, Eckhard, 834
Pippen, Scottie, 422
Porter, Michael E., 11–12, 207

Raphael, Sally Jessy, 33
Ravindran, Vappalak A., 679
Rawley, Charles, 727
Rawlings, Michael, 727
Reinfrank, R. Rudolph, 679
Reuter, John, Jr., 399
Reyna, Claudio, 433
Reynolds, Wayne, 623
Ricciardi, Kristen, 248
Robbin, Jonathan, 281–282, 286
Roberts, Ian, 667
Robinson, David, 690
Roco, Mihail, 549
Rodgers, Walter, 293
Rodriguez, Alex, 433
Rome, John, 273, 275
Romero, Eduardo, 396

Roosevelt, Theodore, 247
Rudkin, Margaret, 770

Saemann, Sandy, 677–678, 683
Saito, Ken, 713–714
Salinas de Gortari, Carlos, 741, 742, 745
Salomon, François, 329
Salomon, Georges, 326, 328, 329–330, 331, 332, 339, 340, 341
Salomon, Jeanne, 329
Sanders, Harland, 723, 725, 726
Sathers, John, 309, 310
Sathers, Kenneth, 309–310
Sawyer, Alan G., 74
Schaefer, George, 63
Schubert, Richard W., 679
Schultz, Howard D., 295, 502, 504
Schwartzberg, Gil N., 679
Schwinn, Ignaz, 353–354
Sewte, Brian T., 503
Shaheen, George, 484
Siegel, Richard, 549
Sinyard, Mike, 356–357
Skoll, Jeffrey S., 500, 501, 503
Smith, Emmett, 433
Smith, Stan, 613, 623
Solheim, Karsten, 381
Solomon, Daniel, 577
Sorenstam, Annika, 396
Sosa, Sammy, 433
Stankowski, Paul, 396
Sudeck, Matthew, 426
Suzuki, Ichiro, 433
Swoopes, Sheryl, 428, 429, 433
Sze, Jerome, 345

Takanashi family, 701, 702
Teerlink, Richard F., 644
Thomas, Anthony, 433
Thomas, Ed, 248

Tilbrook, Mike, 418, 426, 428, 431, 435
Timmer, Jan D., 466
Tupper, Earl, 454

Urlacher, Brian, 433

Vavra, Terry, 136
Vick, Michael, 433

Waitt, Ted, 831, 838
Walker, Antoine, 433
Walker, Lee, 808
Wallace, Ben, 433
Waller, Peter, 727
Walsh, Christopher, 680, 681
Wasch, Ken, 576
Wenger, Bill, 709, 713
Wesley, Pamela, 500
Westley, Steven P., 504
Whitman, Margaret, 491, 501–504
Williams, Jay, 433
Williams, Serena, 433
Williams, Venus, 433
Wilson, Michael K., 504
Wise, Bill, 588, 589, 595
Wise, Karen, 589, 590, 592, 594
Wise, Mark, 592, 593
Wolffe, Lance, 262, 266, 267, 268, 271
Woods, Tiger, 385, 399, 423, 433
Wozniak, Steve, 839
Wyatt, Bill, 417, 418, 424, 426, 428, 431, 434–435
Yash, Charles, 376, 401, 403, 404
Young, Phil, 399
Zedillo, Ernesto, 742–743, 745
Ziegel, Zev, 294
Ziegler, Robert P., 479

SUBLECT INDEX

A. C. Nielsen Company, 30, 282
A&P, 190
A&W Root Beer, 88
Abercrombie & Fitch, 247–249
Ability to pay, 196
Achievers, 76
Acid-test ratio, 225
Action commitments, 8
Action-oriented consumers, 74–75
Actualizers, 76
Acura, 409
Acushnet Company, 399–400
Adams, 390
Adams Golf, 376, 396, 400–401
Adidas, 419–420, 691
Administered systems, 152–153
Advertising, 111, 114–122
    all-you-can-afford method, 118
    competitive parity, 118
    and consumers, 120
    in global marketing, 200–202
    on Internet, 236–237
    message strategy, 119–120

objectives, 114–116, 236–237
percent of sales method, 116
per unit expenditure, 116–118
positive-effects theory, 122
procedures for evaluating, 122
regulation of, 128
research approach, 118
revenues produced by, 115
strengths and weaknesses, 113
task approach, 118
Advertising Age, 451
    website, 241
Advertising agencies, 119
    in foreign markets, 200–201
Advertising campaign, 119, 120
Advertising decisions
    allocation question, 118–122
    developing objectives, 117
    expenditure question, 116–118
Advertising media
    average frequency, 122
    cost per thousand, 120–122
    in foreign markets, 200–201

kinds of, 120
mix, 120–122
reach, 122
relative merits of, 121
research on, 118
Adweek, website, 241
Aftermarketing, 136
After-sale service, 131
Agents, 146, 154
Agricultural products, 83
Airborne Express, 12
Airline industry, 187–189
Airwalk, 420
Alcohol and Tobacco Tax Division of Treasury Department, 128
Aldila, 384
Alloy, 248
All-you-can-afford advertising, 118
Almanac of Business and Industrial Financial Ratios, 225
Altavista.com, 240
Alternative courses of action, 212–213

Alternative evaluation, 50, 233
Alternative search, 49–50, 233
Amazon.com, 160, 233, 234, 236, 451–453, 515–517
    brand equity, 235
American Airlines, 126, 136
American Automobile Association, 187
American Basketball League, 429
American Brands, 384, 385, 399
American Candy Company, 310
American cultural values, 42, 43
American Demographics, website, 241
American Eagle, 248
American Home Products, 210, 304, 306
American Marketing Association
    Code of Ethics, 51
    definition of marketing, 3
American Tobacco, 7
American Wholesale Marketers Association, 319
American Yard Products, 74

America Online, 543–556
  company profile, 544
  employees, 547–548
  external environment, 551–554
  finance, 548–551
  flat rate debate, 554–556
  marketing, 545–546
  meeting customer needs, 547
  organizational structure,
    544–545
America West, 188
Ameritech, 185
Analysis of variance (ANOVA), 36
Anheuser-Busch, 199, 279
Annual Statement Studies, 225
Antismoking litigation, 608
Apple Computer, 136, 468, 839
A priori segmentation, 70
Arbitron Company, 30
Arbitron Index, 115
Archway cookies, 88
Arm & Hammer, 11, 100
Ask A Nurse, website, 237
Asset management ratios, 225
Assurance, 181
Athletic footwear industry
  advertising expenditures, 424
  emerging women's market,
    424–425
  marketing mix, 420–423
  private label brands, 420
  substitute brands, 420
  suppliers, 418–420
  technology attributes, 421
  trends, 423
  U. S. market, 422, 424
Atlanta Braves, 318
Atlanta Bread Company, 251
Atomic, 335, 336
AT&T, 94, 184–185
  Universal Card Services, 99, 183
Attitudes toward advertising, 122
Attributes, 94
Auctions
  history of, 492–493
  niche auctions, 521–522
Auctions.com, 521
Auction software packages, 494
AuctionWatch, 520
*Audits and Surveys National Total-
  Market Index,* 846
Auto insurance, 179
Automated call routing, 178
Automated teller machines, 177
Auto repair, 179
Avis, 154
Avon Products, Inc., 158, 191
Awareness, 113, 115
  of advertising, 122

Baby boomers, 43
BabyGap, 249
Bacardi rum, 88
Backward integration, 154
Baldwin Pianos, website, 234
Banking, 186
Bargaining power
  of buyers, 208
  of suppliers, 208

Barnes & Noble, 296, 451
  brand equity, 235
  website, 232
Barriers to entry, 208
Barron's, website, 241
Batteries Plus, 156
Bayer AG, 88, 305, 306
Beaushan Trading Party
  Limited, 367
Beef industry, 293–308
  background, 299–302
  changes in, 302–303
Beef Magazine, 307
Behavioral influences,
  organizational buying
  personal motivations, 61
  role perceptions, 63
Believers, 76
Belongingness needs, 49
Ben & Jerry's, website, 232,
  234, 240
Benchmarking, 94
Benefit segmentation, 72–74
Best Buy, 148
  website, 232
Better Business Bureau, 17
Bicycle Guide, 360
Bicycle industry
  channels of distribution,
    351–353
  demand for mountain bikes,
    350–351
  federal regulation, 349
  global market, 344–345
  market segmentation,
    345–349, 351–353
  mountain biking, 349–350
  United States, 345–353
Big Dog Motorcycles, 408
Bigg's, 156
Black & Decker, 95, 746–768
  business portfolio in 2000,
    760–766
  commercial fastening systems,
    767–768
  company background,
    749–752
  description, 753–754
  divestiture of part businesses,
    755–756
  divestitures in 1998, 757–760
  Emhart acquisition, 752–755
  financial data, 747–748
  future prospects, 768
  lawn and garden equipment,
    766–767
  plumbing products, 767
  subsequent divestitures,
    756–757
Black Diamond Equipment, Ltd.,
  612–628
  Black Prophet, 626–628
  competition, 616–621
  management team, 613–615
  market, 615–616
  operations, 621–626
Blizzard, 335, 337
Blockbuster Entertainment
  Corporation, 457–468
  company history, 458–459

  expansion and
    acquisitions, 459
  industry environment, 462–463
  locations and operations,
    460–461
  nervous investors, 466
  potential new
    undertakings, 468
  profile in 1992, 459–460
  revenue source, 462
  strategic alliance with Philips,
    466–468
  technological threats to, 465
Blockbuster Video, website, 235
Bloomingdale's, website, 232
BMW, 408, 409
Body language, 192
Boeing Company, 402
Borders' Café, 295
Boston Consulting Group, 13, 22
  portfolio model, 23–24
Boston Market, 251
Bovine Veterinarian, 307
Brand equity, 89–90
  on Internet, 234, 235
Branding, 88–90
  global, 196
  and packaging, 90–91
Brand manager system, 95
Brandweek, website, 241
Break-even analysis, 220–222
Break-even formula, 167
Break-even point, 220
Bricks-and-mortar enterprises, 235
Brock Candy Company, 312
Brokers, 146, 154
Brothers Gourmet Coffee, 98
Brown Foreman Distillers, 11
Brunswick Corporation, 352, 353
Buell Motorcycle Company,
  406, 408
Build share, 22
Bundle pricing, 163
Bundling of services, 186
Bureau of Land Management, 351
Burger King, 77, 250, 252
  description, 253–254
Burlington Industries, 373
Business information websites, 243
Business publications websites,
  241–242
Business strength, 25
Business-to-business marketing, 158
Business Week, 358
  website, 241
Buyer motivation, 61
Buyer role perceptions, 63
Buyers, bargaining power, 208
Buying center roles, 59

California Motorcycle Company,
  408
Callaway Golf Ball Company, 373,
  375–376, 401–404
Callaway Golf Company, 372–405
  balance sheet, 379
  company history, 373–374
  growth prospects, 401–404
  income statements, 378

  major competitors, 395–410
  patent and trademark
    infringement, 395
  performance in 1998, 376–377
  product development,
    386–387
  product line, 389–394
  professional endorsements, 395
  purchasing and production,
    387–388
  return of Eli Callaway,
    376–377
  sales and customer service,
    388–389
  staff professionals, 396
  stock performance, 380
  value chain, 386–389
Callaway Performance Analysis
  System, 387
Callaway Vineyard and Winery, 375
Campbell Soup Company,
  77, 769–798
  acquisitions, 785
  business unit structure, 788
  company background,
    769–770
  current status, 795–798
  Dale Morrison era, 789–793
  David Johnson era, 782–789
  divestitures, 784
  financial summary, 781
  Gordon McGovern era,
    770–780
  international business unit, 776
  management changes, 780
  marketing strategies, 777–779
  portfolio restructuring, 792–794
  product development, 777–779
  products, 773
  rival brands and
    competitors, 773
  sales and earnings, 789–795
  stock performance, 790, 791
Campionolo, 361
Candy market, 312
  Cannondale Corporation,
    343–371
  business strategy, 361–367
  diversification into
    motorcycles, 370–371
  financial data, 346–347
  history and background,
    359–361
  international operations, 367
  manufacturing, 362–365
  marketing, 365
  price-earnings ratio, 348
  product innovation, 362
  product line, 368–370
  promotion, 365–366
  purchasing, 365
  research and development,
    366–367
  rivals in motorbikes, 353–359
  sales and distribution, 366
  status in 2000, 361–367
  trading range of stock, 348
Cannondale Original Design
  Application, 361

Career Track, 136
Carl's Jr. restaurants, 254
Case analysis
 case for, 206
 communicating
  oral presentation, 217
  written report, 215–217
 framework, 206–213
  analysis of current
   situation, 207–210
  chosen alternative and
   implementation,
   212–213
  courses of action, 212
  recording problems and
   core elements, 211–212
 meaning of, 210
 operational approach, 216
 pitfalls to avoid, 213–215
 purpose, 206
Cash cows, 23
Catalog sales, 157–158
Category killers, 156
Category management, 95
Caterpillar, Inc., 194, 631–643
 company reorganization, 635
 competition, 637–639
 dealers, 636–637
 financial information, 642
 future, 641
 history, 631–633
 international sales, 639–640
 labor agreement, 635–636
 product line, 643
 realignment strategies, 633–636
CBS, website, 243
CBS Records, 190
CDNow, 237
 website, 234, 235
Census Bureau, website, 241
Census geography definitions, 282
Center for International Business
 Education and Research
 website, 244
Center for Science in the Public
 Interest, 33
Central Intelligence Agency World
 Factbook, 241
Champion, 429, 430
Champs, 420
Channel flexibility, 151
Channel planning, 148
Channels of distribution
 bicycle industry, 351–353
 channel flexibility, 151
 for consumer goods, 147
 coverage required, 149–150
 definition, 145
 degree of control desired, 150
 franchising alternative, 153
 functions performed by, 147
 in global marketing, 199
 kinds of, 146–148
 for organizational goods, 148
 relationship marketing, 152
 selection of, 148–151
 for services, 176–177

total distribution cost, 150–151
 vertical marketing systems,
  152–154
Chase Manhattan, 186
China Bicycle Company, 345, 354
Chronimed, 187
Chrysler Corporation, 103, 175
Chun King, 714–715
Church's Fried Chicken, 191
Cigarette industry, 607
Cinemax, 465
Circuit City, 156
 website, 232
Cisco Systems, website, 232
Citibank, 186
 website, 237
Cityvision plc, 459
CKE Restaurants Inc., 254
Claritas, Inc., 75, 281–293
 company overview, 286
 competitive environment,
  283–286
 customer satisfaction, 292–293
 geodemographic analysis,
  282–283
 industry background, 281–282
 pricing, 292
 product line, 286–292
Clean Air Act of 1990, 349
Cleveland Golf, 395
ClickZ.com, 243
Client relationship, 180
Cluster analysis, 36
CNET.com, 243
Coach Leather Goods, 11
Cobra Golf, 384, 385, 400
Coca-Cola Company, 12, 77, 88,
 94, 116, 123, 200
 website, 234
Code of ethics, organizational
 buyers, 63
Cognitive dissonance, 52–53
Collegiate Images, 257
Columbia Pictures, 464
Commerce Department,
 website, 241
Commercialization, 106
Commercial websites, 159
Commission, 143
Commitment, obtaining, 135
Commodore computer, 468
Communication process, 119
Company research, 34
Companywide managerial
 awareness, 4
Compaq Computer, 103, 830,
 831–835
 acquisition of DEC, 833–834
 problems at, 834–835
 strategy, 832–833
Compass marketing
 workstation, 287
Compensation of sales force,
 142–144
Competition
 effect on pricing, 167–168
 limited in services, 184–185
 in motorcycle industry,
  407–408

in ski market, 335–337
 for 3DV Litigation Services, 270
 for Wind Technology, 413–414
Competitive advantage, 11–12
 sustainable, 12–13
Competitive analysis, 845
Competitive environment, 15
 Claritas Inc., 283–286
Competitive forces, 207–208
 in global strategy
Competitive parity advertising, 118
Competitors, rivalry among,
 207–208
Comprehension, 113, 115
Computer Aided Drafting, 267
ComputerVision, 342
Computer visualization market, 261
ConAgra, 90
Conjoint analysis, 36
Construction industry, 267–269
Consumer behavior
 data sources, 55
 decision making, 233
 marketing influences, 44–45
 social influences on, 41–44
Consumer decision making
 alternative evaluation, 50
 alternative search, 49–50
 extensive, 48
 limited, 48
 need recognition, 48–49
 by organizational buyers, 62
 postpurchase evaluation, 52–54
 psychological influences, 47
 purchase decision, 50–52
 routine, 48
 situational influences, 45–47
Consumer goods, 84
 channels of distribution, 147
 classes of, 86
Consumer promotions, 125
Consumer Reports, 50
Consumers
 action-oriented, 74–75
 and advertising, 120
 awareness, 113
 comprehension, 113
 conviction, 113
 determinants of needs and
  wants, 69
 in foreign markets, 196–197
 marketing research on, 32–33
 and market segmentation, 68
 principle-oriented, 74–75
 status-oriented, 74–75
Continental Airlines, 33, 188
Contract research, 34
Contractual systems, 153–154
Contribution margin, 220–221
Convenience stores, 156
Conviction, 113, 115
Cook Data Services, Inc., 458
CoolMD.com, 237
Cooperative environment, 15
Coors, Inc., 273
Cornnuts, Inc., 312
Corporate systems, 154
Corporate websites, 232, 240
Correlation analysis, 36, 140

Cost considerations in pricing,
 164–166
Cost estimation, 171
Cost leadership strategy, 12
Cost-plus pricing, 164
Cott Corporation, 12
Counterfeit products, 693
Cowgirl Chocolates, 529–542
 company history, 531
 distribution and pricing,
  536–538
 financial data, 541–542
 future of, 540–541
 product, 532–536
 promotion, 538–540
CPC International, 203
Criterion variable, 36
Cross-functional conflict, 10
Cross-functional objectives, 20
Cross-functional sales teams, 137
Cross-functional teams, 105
 skills needed, 109
Cross tabulation, 36
Cub Foods, 156
Cultural differences
 body language, 192
 eating and cooking, 192
 and foreign marketing,
  191–192
 physical contact, 192
 promptness, 192
 social customs, 192
Cultural values, 17
 American, 42, 43
 transmission of, 43
Culture, 43
 in global strategy, 195
Current conditions, 46–47
Current ratio, 225
Customer expectations
 method, 140
Customer migration patterns, 93
Customer orientation, 2
Customers
 ethical conduct toward, 51
 expectations from services, 179
 focus of organizational
  mission, 7–8
 gaps with service provider,
  180–181
 and internal marketing,
  182–183
 organizational buyers, 56–57
 responding to objections by,
  134–135
 service relationship, 180
Customer satisfaction
 measurement, 182
Customer service
 Callaway Golf Company,
  388–389
 critical components, 183
CVS Pharmacy, website, 232
Cyberatlas, 243
Cycle Sport, 368
Cyclical stability, 101

Database management, 38
Data interpretation, 34–35

David and Sons, 318
Decathlon, 338
Deceptive pricing, 168
Deciders, 59
Decision making; *see* Consumer
    decision making
Decision-making skills, 109
Decoding, 119
Deere and Company, 639
Deering, Millikin and
    Company, 373
Deletions, 92–94
Delia's, 248
Dell Computer Corporation, 12,
    56, 799–840
    advertising, 826
    biggest challenges, 840
    build-to-order manufacturing,
        814–815
    business philosophy, 809–810
    in China, 819–820
    company background, 800–803
    competitors, 831–839
    customer service, 820–824
    demand forecasting, 825–826
    direct sales, 817–820
    e-commerce technology,
        824–825
    in Europe, 819
    financial statements, 805–806
    financial summary, 804
    geographic area
        information, 807
    just-in-time systems, 815–817
    in Latin America, 820
    market position in 2000, 800
    market segmentation,
        817–819
    partnership with suppliers,
        815–817
    quality control, 815
    research and development, 826
    servers and storage devices,
        826–828
    strategy execution, 828–830
    technical support, 820–824
    WebPC, 828
    website, 236
Demand fluctuation for
    services, 178
Demand influences on pricing,
    162–164
Demographic factors
    global marketing research,
        195–196
    influences on pricing, 162
Dentists.com, 237
Department of Defense, 412
Department of Justice, 128
Department of Labor, website, 241
Dependent variables, 36
Depth of product mix, 85
Derby Bicycle Corporation,
    358–359
Design News, 343
Dessert wine industry, 584
Diageo PLC, 253
Dialog system, 38
Diamondback, 352, 353

Differentiated marketing
    system, 178
Differentiation strategy, 12
Digital Equipment Corporation,
    833–834
Direct channel, 146
Direct mail, 157–158
Direct mail advertising, 121
Direct marketing, 112, 127, 146
    strengths and weaknesses, 113
Directories, Internet, 240
Direct ownership, 203
Direct sales, 158
Dirt Rider, 344, 371
Disconfirmation paradigm, 54
Discounted cash flow, 222–224
Discriminant analysis, 36
Disney Channel, 465
Distinctive competencies, 7
Distinctiveness, 166
Distribution
    global strategy, 199
    kinds of, 150
    in marketing planning, 846
    by Sathers, Inc., 318
    in ski market, 338–339
    total costs of, 150–151
    by wholesalers, 155–156
Distribution strategy
    Amazon.com, 451–453
    Blockbuster Entertainment,
        457–458
    Internet sales, 236
    Tupperware, 454–456
Distributors
    definition, 146
    function, 148
    trade sales promotions aimed
        at, 123–124
Diversification, 100
Diversification strategy, 11
Divest, 23
Divestitures, 755–760, 784
Document Center, University of
    Michigan, 244
Dogs, 23
Domino's Pizza, 193, 255, 460
Donna Karan, 420
Dow Chemical Company, 263
Dow Jones, website, 241
Dun & Bradstreet, 225
Dunlop, 386
DuPont Corporation, 94, 356, 402,
    454
Dynastar, 335, 336
Dyno, 353

E. and J. Gallo Winery, 577–584
    company history, 578–579
E. J. Brach Corporation, 312
Eagle, 315, 318
Eaglemark Financial Services,
    Inc., 406
Eagle-Tribune, 293
Eastern Airlines, 188
Eastern Europe, foreign
    investment criteria, 201
Eastern Washington University,
    257–260

Eastman Kodak, 94, 95, 263
Eastpak, 33
Eating and cooking, 192
Eaton/Golf Pride, 384
eBay.com, 233, 490–523
    building trust, 508–510
    business model, 505
    competition, 514–521
    enhancing features and
        functionality, 510–511
    feedback forum, 499
    founding of, 500
    future of, 522–523
    honors and awards, 513–514
    international markets, 513
    management, 501–502,
        503–504
    market dominance, 502–505
    operation of, 496–499
    post-trade services, 512
    strengthening the brand,
        506–507
    trading platform, 507–508
E-commerce, 824–825
    growth of, 491–496
E-Commerce magazine, 241
Ecommercetimes.com, 243
Economic conditions, 193
Economic environment, 15–16
Economic factors, in global
    strategy, 194
Eddie Bauer Sportswear, 293, 358
    website, 232
Edmunds, website, 233
Edwin Watts stores, 385
Elan, 335, 336
Electronic exchange, 158–160
    advantages and disadvantages,
        159–160
    recommendations for
        developing, 159
Eli Lilly, 191
eMarketer.com, 243
Emhart Corporation, 752–756
Empathy, 182
Encoding, 119
Encyclopedia of Associations, 31
End users, benefit of
    wholesalers, 155
Entry barriers, 208
Environment
    analysis of, 207
    checklist, 209
    Industry analysis, 207–208
Environmental factors, in global
    strategy, 194
Environmental regulation,
    350–351
Equipment, 179
eRock.com, 522
Erol's Inc., 459
ESRI
Esteem needs, 49
Everyday low pricing, 165
Evon's, 314
eWanted.com, 521
Excelsior-Henderson, 408
Exchange controls, 193
Exclusive distribution, 150

Expedia.com, 237
Expenditures on advertising,
    116–118
Experience curve, 22–23, 208
Experiencers, 76
Experiential research, 33–34
Experiential sources, 50
Exporting strategy, 202
Extended product, 82
External decision making, 438

Facilitating agent, 146
Factor analysis, 36
Fairfield Inn, 183
FairMarket, 518–520
Family branding, 88
Family influence, 55
Family life cycle, 55
Fast Company, 243
Fast-food industry, 722–745
    characteristics, 250–252
    chicken segment, 730–731
    demographic trends, 731–732
    hamburger segment,
        253–254
    industry consolidations,
        732–733
    international quick-service
        market, 733–735
    nonhamburger segment,
        255–256
    sales, 727
    segments, 728–730
Federal Communications
    Commission, 128
Federal Express, 178, 183, 389
    website, 236
Federal Trade Commission,
    128, 225
Fender Guitars, website, 234
Fila, 419, 420
Financial analysis
    break-even analysis, 220–222
    estimates of marketing
        costs, 851
    net present value analysis,
        222–224
    ratio analysis, 224–228
    sales forecasts, 849–851
Financial Times, website, 242
Firms
    checklist, 209–211
    situation analysis, 208
Fischer, 336
Fisher, 314, 315, 316, 318
Fixed costs, 220
Flexible manufacturing, 362–365
Focus groups, 31
Folger's, 47, 98
Food and Drug
    Administration, 128
Food Packaging Research
    Study, 313
Foot-Joy, 399
Foot Locker, 420; *see also* Lady
    Foot Locker
Footwear industry, 688–689
    counterfeit products, 693
Forbes, website, 241

Ford Motor Company, 94, 154, 175, 263, 846
  website, 233
Foreign investment, 190
  country selection criteria, 201
Foreign markets
  advertising media, 200–201
  census data problems, 198
  entry strategies, 202–203
  global marketing research for, 195–198
  growth strategies, 203–204
  import restrictions, 193
  price structure, 200
  problems with entering
    cultural misunderstanding, 191–192
    economic conditions, 193
    exchange controls, 193
    ownership restrictions, 193
    political uncertainty, 193
Foreign ownership of U. S. businesses, 190
Fortune, website, 241
Fortune Brands, 384, 385, 399–400
Forward integration, 154
Fox Studios, 464
Franchise extension, 88
Franchises, 153, 154
  to enter foreign markets, 202
Frequency marketing programs, 126
Frito-Lay, 90, 163, 192
Fujita and Company, 459
Fulfilleds, 76
Functional relationships, 136
Functional skills, 109

Gamma, 414
Gap, Inc., 90, 156, 247, 248
GapKids, 249
Gap Online, 232
Gary Fisher, 353, 355, 356
Gatekeepers, 59
Gateway 2000, 146
Gateway Computer, 146, 838–839
  website, 236
Gazelle, 358
General Electric, 3, 13, 194, 381
General Electric portfolio model, 24–25
General Foods, 98, 194
General Mills, 85, 116, 125–126, 203, 210
  website, 234
General Motors, 175, 199, 235, 263, 846
  website, 234
Generic products, 82, 90
Geodemographic analysis, 282–283
Geodemographic segmentation, 75–76, 77
Geographical information systems, 267
Geography definitions, 282
Giant Corporation, 354
Giant Global Group, 357–358
Giant Manufacturing Company, 345

Gillette Company, 11, 91, 98
  website, 234
Glassman Company, 414
Global bicycle market, 344–345
Global branding, 196
Global company, 194–195
Globalization strategy, 194–195
Global marketing, 190–204
  advertising, 200–202
  distribution strategy, 199
  entry strategies, 202–203
  external environment, 194
  facilitating or impeding factors, 194–195
  growth strategies, 203–204
  hybrid approach, 195
  marketing research, 195–198
  organizing multinational company, 193–195
  pricing strategy, 200
  problems in entering foreign markets, 191–193
  product strategy, 198
  sales promotion, 200–202
Global marketing research, 197
  ability to buy, 196
  population characteristics, 195–196
  task and process differences, 198
  willingness to buy, 196–197
Going-rate pricing, 168
Goldman, Sachs and Company, 248
Golfcraft, Inc., 459
Golf equipment industry, 372–405
  competition in, 383–386
  description, 377–381
  key innovations, 381–383
  major manufacturers, 395–410
  manufacturing, 384
  marketing, 384–386
Golf Market Research Institute, 400
Gomez Advisors, 480–483
GO Network Auctions, 520–521
Goods-service continuum, 176–178
Google.com, 240
Government agencies, 57
Government websites, 243
Grain Division of Agricultural Department, 128
Grainger Corporation, 56
Graman USA, 384
Green zone, 25
Gross national product, 174
Group search sources, 50
Growth strategy, in foreign markets, 203–204
Growth vector matrix, 100
Grundig, 193
GT Bicycles, 353, 354

H. J. Heinz Company, 210
Hallmark Cards, 99
H&R Block, 186
Harbor View Savings and Loan Association, 7
Hardees, 250, 253
  description, 254

Harley-Davidson, Inc., 47, 406–410, 644–656
  company background, 645–646
  competition, 655–656
  dealer improvements, 655
  financial changes, 648
  financial data, 649–653
  future of, 656
  global competition, 407–408
  human resource changes, 647
  manufacturing changes, 646–647
  market information, 655
  marketing changes, 647–648
  motorcycle division in 1990, 648–650
  new competitors, 408
  operations, 645–646
  pricing, 654
  product line, 650–654
  promotion, 654–655
Harley Owners Group, 407
Hartmann Luggage, 11
Harvard University School of Business Administration, 206
Hayes Microcomputer products, 553
HBO, 465
Head skis, 336
Health Care Financing Administration, 446
Health care reform, 445–446
Health care system, 187
  competition, 446–447
  regulation, 446
Health maintenance organizations, 187
Heileman Brewing Company, 80
Hertz, 163
Hewlett-Packard, 103, 830, 837–838
Hickory Stick USA, 375, 386
High/low pricing, 165
High-tech products, 70–71
High-voltage power supplies, 412–416
Hills Brothers, 98
Hiram Walker and Sons, Inc., 375
Hogan, 395
Hold share, 22
Holiday Inn, 154, 185
Homegrocer.com, 487
Home Shopping Network, 158
Honda Motor Company, 12, 88, 171, 263, 408, 409
Honeywell, Inc., 7, 194
Hoovers.com, 243
Horizontal market, 84
Hormel Meats, 7
Hotbot.com, 240
Hotel industry, 179
Hot Topic, 249
Housebrand personal computers, 839
House brands, 90
Howard, Needles, Tammen, and Bergendoff, 270
HST, 384

Huffy Corporation, 352, 353
Hyundai, 77, 171

IBM, 94, 96, 136, 194, 283, 465, 830
  e-business strategy, 836–837
  troubles in PCs, 835–836
  website, 232, 234
IBM eBusiness, 236
ICC/Accutracks Convenience Store Report, 312
Idea generation, 102–103
Idea screening, 104
Illusion, 408
Imitation products, 100
Import restrictions, 193
IMS International, 30
Independent variables, 36
Indirect channels, 148
Industry attractiveness, 24–25
Industry checklist, 209
Industry Norms and Key Business Ratios, 225
Influencers, 59
Information provision, 130
Information sources for consumers, 49–50
Initial price structure, 171
Initiators, 59
Inseparability of services, 176–178
Instant Quote, website, 237
Insurance industry, 177–178, 187
Intangibility of services, 176
Integrated marketing communication, 112–114
  compared to traditional marketing, 113
  in global marketing research, 197
  goal of, 113
Intel Corporation, 56
Intensive distribution, 150
Intention to buy, 122
Interactive Age, 243
Interactive Digital Software Association, 575
Interactive television, 465–466
Intermediaries, 56
Intermodal Surface Transportation Efficiency Act, 349
Internal marketing, 182–183
Internal risk, 104
Internal search sources, 49
International Dessert Partners, 203
International Mountain Bike Association, 350–351
International operations, Cannondale Corporation, 367
Internet
  commercial websites, 159
  direct marketing on, 127
  directories, 240
  retailing on, 158–160
  search engines, 240
  service quality in, 185
Internet advertising, 121
Internet directory advertising, 236–237

brand equity, 234, 235
business publications, 241–242
communities and marketing, 234–235
compilation sites, 244
consumer decision making, 233
corporate websites, 232, 240
distribution channels, 236
general business websites, 243
government websites, 243
marketing reference websites, 243–244
newspaper websites, 242
online/offline retailers, 232
online product assortment, 233–234
pricing issues, 235–236
services, 237
Interpersonal skills, 109
Intersport, 338
Interviews, 31
Intrepid, Inc., 353, 355–356
Inventory turnover, 225
iQVC, website, 233
ISO 9000 standards, 85, 619
ISPO, 338

J. I. Case Company, 639
JC Penney, 90, 159, 249, 420, 422
Jeno's Pizza, 210
Jobber, 146
Job search, 585–597
Johnson & Johnson, 77, 263
Joint ventures, 203
Joseph-Beth, website, 235
Jury of executive opinion, 139
Just For Feet, 422
Just-in-time systems, 58
JVC, 193

Kaiser, 414
Karsten Manufacturing, 381–382
Kawasaki, 408
Keebler, 90
Kellogg's, 88, 116, 191, 193, 429, 430
Kent stores, 352
Kentucky Fried Chicken, 190, 251, 254, 722–745
    acquisition by PepsiCo, 725–726
    company history, 723–724
    description, 255–256
    Heublein, Inc., 723
    international operations, 738–744
    marketing strategy, 736–738
    in Mexico, 739–745
    number of outlets, 736
    operating efficiencies, 738
    R. J. Reynolds Industries, Inc., 724
    refranchising strategy, 735–736
    sold by PepsiCo, 726–727
Kids Foot Locker, 424
Kikkoman Corporation, 697–721
    competitors, 714–716

distribution, 699–702
financial data, 700–701, 706
history, 698–702
international activities, 703
international position, 716–718
management in U.S., 711–713
manufacturing site, 708–711
post-World War II in Japan, 703–706
product lines, 705
U.S. distribution, 707–708
U.S. manufacturing, 708
U.S. market, 713–714
U.S. market potential, 706–707
Klein Bicycles, 353, 356
Klein mountain bike, 355
Kmart, 90, 153, 313, 462
Komatsu, 637–638
Kraft cheese, 11
Kraft General Foods, 605
    website, 234
Kroger, 90, 156
K2 skis, 336

L. A. Gear, 676–696
    advertising, 683–684
    board of directors, 677–679
    communication, 687
    competitors, 690–691
    corporate culture, 687
    and culture, 692
    customers, 692
    demographics, 692
    distribution, 686
    and economy, 692–693
    finance, 688
    financial statements, 694–695
    and footwear industry, 688–689
    history, 677–679
    human resources, 687
    international strategy, 685–686
    legal issues, 687–688
    mission statement, 681
    objectives and strategies, 681–682
    and politics, 693
    production and products, 682–683
    regulations, 692
    research and development, 684, 686–687
    sales, 684–685
    technology, 693
    top management, 679–681
L. L. Bean, 12
    website, 234
LaChoy, 714–715
Lady Foot Locker, 417–435
    background, 426–429
    marketing support, 434
    performance measures, 437
    pricing strategy, 437
    product pricing, 431
    product timing, 432–433
    recent product launches, 430
    retail exclusivity, 433–434
    retail outlets, 431

supplier relationships, 429–430
target customers, 431
Lamkin, 384
Lands' End, 12, 159
Lead generation, 133
Learning curves, 22
Lee jeans, 13
Legal environment, 17
LeMond, 355
Levenger, 158
Lever Brothers, 77
Levi Strauss, 5, 95, 193, 247
Library of Congress, 128
    website, 241
Licensing strategy, 202
Life cycle, and pricing, 166–167
Lifestyle segmentation, 74–75
Light Detection and Ranging, 267
Limited, The, 90, 247, 248
Limited decision making, 438
Limited-line retail chains, 156
Line extension, 88
Liquidity, 224
Liquidity ratios, 224–225
Litigation, tobacco industry, 610–611
Little Caesars, 255, 524–525
Lockheed Martin, 263
Long Drugs, website, 232
Longevity Health Care Systems, Inc., 436–450
    Alzheimer's treatment, 448–449
    comprehensive marketing strategy, 449–450
    history of, 437–439
    marketing, 439–444, 447–448
Long interviews, 31
Long John Silver's, 88
Long-term health care market, 444–445
Long-term relationships, 135–136
Love needs, 49
Lower Americans, 44

MacGregor Golf, Inc., 383, 386, 395
MacManus Group, 33
Macroeconomy, 15–16
Macy's, website, 232
Magazine advertising, 121
Magna stores, 352
Mail Boxes Etc., 136
Major Video Corporation, 459
Makers, 76
Management
    in global strategy, 195
    noncreative, 185
Manson and Associates, 272, 273–279
Manufacturers
    benefit of wholesalers, 155
    in global strategy, 199
    perfect, 151
    rate-of-return target pricing, 166
    selection of retailers, 156–157
    service capabilities, 175
Manufacturers' agent, 146
Manufacturers' representative, 154

Manufacturing, in ski market, 337
MapInfo, 285
Market development, 100
Market development strategy, 11
Market-driven firms, 5–8
Marketers
    cross-functional conflict, 10
    sources of cross-functional conflict, 10
Market factors, in global strategy, 194
Market growth, 24–25
Marketing; see also Global marketing
    Cannondale Corporation, 365
    challenges in service sector, 180, 186–189
    code of ethics, 51
    definition, 3
    general managerial concern, 4
    in golf equipment industry, 384–386
    health care services, 447–450
    internal, 182–183
    limited view of, 184
    personal selling in, 130
    to provide quality services, 180–184
    push vs. pull strategies, 123
    strategic planning for, 3–13
    traditional vs. integrated approach, 114
    unconditional service guarantees, 181
    vertical systems, 152–154
    by wholesalers, 155
Marketing concept, 2–3
    basic elements, 4
Marketing costs, 851
Marketing decision support system, 37–38
Marketing dimensions, 94
Marketing function, 2
Marketing influences on consumers, 44–45
    place, 45
    price, 45
    product, 45
    promotion, 45
Marketing information
    in advertising campaign, 120
    cross-country basis, 283
    factors affecting search for, 53
    sources, 49–50
Marketing information systems, 18, 37–39
    global information sources, 40
Marketing intermediaries, 56
    channels of distribution, 146–154
    classifications and functions, 145–146
    electronic exchange, 158–160
    need for, 145
    nonstore retailing, 157–158
    perfect, 151
Marketing management, 14
    advertising in, 114
    guidelines, 15

implementation and control, 18
marketing information systems, 18
marketing research, 18
product audit, 92–94
and strategic planning, 4–5
Marketing management process, 17–18
situation analysis, 14–17
Marketing-manager system, 95
Marketing mix, 845–846
athletic footwear industry, 420–423
developing, 18
and product life cycle, 92
Marketing mix strategy, 79–80
Marketing myopia, 82
Marketing objectives, 19, 845
Marketing plan
financial analysis, 849–851
framework, 842–848
implementation and control, 848
structure of, 843–845
Marketing planning
consumer analysis, 848
developing marketing mix, 18
distribution, 846
good vs. bad objectives, 847
implementation and control, 18
key issues in, 16
marketing mix, 845–846
marketing research for, 846–848
objectives, 17, 845
price, 846
product, 846
product life cycle in, 92
promotion, 846
questions to consider, 850
related to strategic planning, 21
subsequent to strategic planning, 3
summary on, 19–20
target market, 17–18, 845
Marketing reference websites, 243–244
Marketing research, 18; see also Global marketing research
case, 281–293
company vs. contract, 34
on consumers, 32–33
as customer satisfaction measure, 182
ethical responsibilities, 38–39
in marketing planning, 846–848
role of, 28–29
by Sathers, Inc., 313–316
statistical techniques, 36
types of questions for, 35
value for services, 174
Marketing research process
criteria for evaluating, 37
limitations, 37
performance of research, 34
plan of, 29–34

preparing report, 36–37
primary vs. secondary data, 30–31
processing data, 34–35
purpose, 29
qualitative vs. quantitative, 31–34
Marketing search sources, 50
Marketing strategies
checklist, 211
for global consumers, 46
implications of product life cycle, 93
Pfizer, Inc., 304–308
Sathers, Inc., 312–313
situation analysis, 208–209
Marketing system, for services, 178
Market intermediaries, store retailing, 156–157
Market mix
in banking, 186
in insurance, 187
Market penetration, 100
Market penetration strategies, 10–11
Market potential index, 284
Market pull research, 103
Market risk, 104
Markets, vertical vs. horizontal, 84
Market segmentation, 68–80
bases for, 72–76
bicycle industry, 345–349, 351–353
consumer markets, 72–73
consumer needs and wants, 69
current situation of firm, 68
deciding on strategy, 78–79
definition, 68
dividing markets on relevant dimensions, 69–76
ethics of, 80
for high-tech products, 70–71
logic of, 68
marketability questions, 79
marketing mix strategy, 79–80
meaningfulness questions, 79
measurability questions, 79
organizational buyers, 72–73
a priori vs. post hoc, 70
product positioning, 76–78
relevance of dimensions, 70
target market selection, 79
Market share, 25
Market size, 24–25
Market test, 122
Markup pricing, 164
Marshall Field's, 156
Mary Kay Cosmetics, 158
Massachusetts Institute of Technology Information Center, 356
Mass market, 68
Mass merchandisers, 156
MasterCard, 175
Mathematical modeling research, 34
Matsushita Electric Industrial Company, 466
Maxwell Company, 414

Maxwell House, 47, 98
Maytag, 46
McDonald's Corporation, 11, 49, 77, 154, 175, 190, 250–256, 429, 459
competitors in hamburger segment, 253–254
competitors in nonhamburger segment, 255–256
financial data, 253
future of, 256
website, 234
MCI Communications, 184–185, 354
Mediamark Research Inc., 282
Mediaweek, website, 241
Merchant middleman, 146
Mergers and acquisitions
fast-food industry, 732–733
by Philip Morris Companies, 599–601
Merial, 305, 306
Merida Industry Company, 345
Merrill Lynch, 185
Message strategy, 119–120
Metropolitan Museum of Art, website, 234
Mexican peso crisis, 742–743
Microsoft Corporation, 12, 240
website, 232
Microsoft Network, 554
Middle class, 43–44
Middleman, 146
Midway Airlines, 188
Miliken, 94
Miller Brewing Company, 100, 279
Million Dollar Directory, 31
Millstone Coffee, 98, 295
Mishiki, 353
Mission statement, 6–7
examples, 7
form of, 8
internal and external focus, 8
Mitsubishi, 194
Mobil, 154
Model base management, 38
Modified rebuy, 58
Money magazine, website, 241
Mongoose, 353
Monsanto, 96, 240
Montana Stockgrowers' Association, 304–307
Morgan Stanley Dean Witter, 33
Motivation of sales force, 142–144
Motobecane, 360
Motocross Action Magazine, 370
Motorcycle buyers, 408
Motorcycle industry
Cannondale Corporation, 370–371
global competition, 407–408
Harley-Davidson, Inc., 406–410
new competitors, 408
websites, 408–409
Motorola Inc., 94, 96, 104, 263
Mountain Bike, 355
Mountain bikes
competing firms, 353–359

demand for, 350–351
Mountain Biking, 343
Mountain Dew, 356
Mountaineering equipment industry
manufacturers, 620–621
market, 615–616
retailers, 616–618
wholesalers, 618–620
Movie Channel, 465
Movie production and distribution, 464
Movies to Go, 459
Mrs. Paul's Kitchens, 775–776
MSNBC, website, 243
MTV, website, 234
Multibranding strategy, 88–89
Multidimensional scaling, 36
Multidomestic company, 193–194
Multimedia systems, 467–468
Multinational corporations, 193–195
foreign investment by, 190
Murray Ohio Manufacturing, 352, 353

Nabisco, 90
Nanophase Technologies Corporation, 657–675
business model, 666
competition, 668–669
customer applications, 663–666
financial data, 673–675
history, 659–661
management changes, 661–662
marketing strategy, 666–668
product markets, 663–666
recent developments, 669–671
science at, 662–663
Nanotechnology, 659
National accounting managing programs, 138–139
National Aeronautics and Space Administration, 411–412
National Association of Retail Dealers of America, 31
National Basketball Association, 429
National Cash Register, 7
National Decision systems, 283
National health care reform, 445–446
National Restaurant Association, 727
Nationsbank Visa, 88
Nautica Competition, 420
NBC, 33
Need hierarchy theory, 49
Need recognition, 48–49, 233
by organizational buyers, 65
Nemix, Inc., 191
Nestlé, 98, 210
Netgrocer, 487–489
Net present value analysis, 222–224
Nevada Bob's, 385
New category entries, 99
New England Business, 359
New entrants, threat of, 208

Newlands and Company, 270
New product development, 98–109
  basic questions for, 101–102
  commercialization, 106
  cross-functional teams,
    95–96, 109
  idea generation, 102–103
  idea screening, 104
  importance of time, 106
  misconceptions, 99
  need for research, 108–109
  product development
    stage, 105
  project planning, 104–105
  research for, 103
  strategy, 99–102
  test marketing, 106
  using outsiders, 103
  venture team, 95–96
New products
  categories of, 99–100
  causes of failure, 106–109
  factors associated with
    success, 101
  facts about, 98
  growth vector matrix, 199
  idea sources, 105
  performance
    measurements, 108
  success and failure, 99
  time involved, 98
New product team, 107
News conference, 126
Newspaper advertising, 121
Newspaper websites, 242
News release, 126
New task purchase, 58
New-to-the world products, 99
New York Stock Exchange, 33
New York Times, website, 242
Niche auctions, 521–522
Nielsen Index, 115
Nielsen Retail Index, 846
Nielsen Television Index, 846
Nike, Inc., 12, 170, 385, 395, 418,
  419, 421, 422, 423, 428, 430,
  434, 690
Nintendo, 247, 462, 572–576
Noda Shoyu Company, 702–703
Noncreative management, 185
Nonstore retailing, 157–158
Nordica, 327, 330
Nordstroms, 45
  website, 232
North American Free Trade
  Agreement, 298, 301, 742
Northernlight.com, 240
North Star Candy Company, 310
Northwest Airlines, 185
Notetakers Company, 568–571

Objections, responding to, 134–135
Observational research, 32
Obsolescence, 185–186
Odd pricing, 163
Odyssey Golf, 377
Office Max, 148
Off-peak pricing, 178

Oklahoma Entertainment Inc., 459
Old Navy stores, 33, 248, 354
Omnibus Budget Reconciliation
  Act of 1987, 446
100 Best Companies to Work for in
  America (Levering et al.), 605
Online auctions, 490–523
  buyer addiction, 495–496
  growth of, 491–496
  operation of, 493–494
  success factors, 491–492
  users, 494–495
Online grocery business, 469–489
  Gomez Advisor ratings,
    482–483
Online product assortments,
  233–234
Online retailing, 232
OpenSite Technologies, 494
Opinion tests, 122
Optimists, 71
Ordering, 113, 115
Organizational buyers
  bases for market
    segmentation, 72–73
  code of ethics, 63
  government agencies, 57
  information for sales force, 131
  institutions, 57
  intermediaries
  key differences in marketing
    to, 60
  personal motivations, 61
  potential decisions, 62
  producers, 56
  role perceptions, 63
Organizational buying, 56–67
  behavioral influences, 61–63
  channels of distribution, 148
  differences in types, 59
  functional areas, 67
  key concerns, 67
  post-purchase evaluation,
    66–67
  purchase-type influences,
    57–58
  structural influences, 58–61
Organizational buying process,
  63–67
  organizational need, 65
  purchase activities, 65
  vendor analysis, 65–66
Organizational goods, 84
Organizational growth strategy, 11
Organizational mission, 5–8
  achievable, 8
  focus on markets and
    products, 7–8
  motivational, 8
  specific, 8
Organizational need, 65
Organizational objectives, 8–9
Organizational portfolio plan, 13
Organizational products
  brand equity, 89–90
  classes of, 87
Organizational strategies, 9–12

based on competitive
  advantage, 11–12
based on products and
  markets, 10–11
based on value, 12
choosing, 12–13
Organization history, 7
Organizations
  cross-functional conflict, 10
  environment of, 7
  purchasing policies and
    procedures, 60–61
  purchasing roles, 59
Orlimar Golf Company, 376, 390,
  395, 396, 401
Outdoor advertising, 121
Outpost.com, 521
Out-rotation, 103
Ownership restrictions, 193

Pacific stores, 352
Packaging, 90–91
Packard Bell NEC, 830
Pan Am, 188
Panasonic, 193, 468
Panera Bread Company, 251
Papa John's Pizza, 255
Paramount Studios, 464
Parsons and Brinckerhoff, 270
Partnerships, 136
Patent Office, 128
Payback method, 223
Paypal, website, 233
Peapod, Inc., 469–489
  balance sheet, 473
  company background, 469–471
  competitors, 484–489
  customers, 472
  distribution center, 476–478
  in early 2000, 471–472
  growth strategies, 478–479
  income statement, 472
  management changes, 479
  management vision, 471–472
  marketing and advertising,
    475–476
  metropolitan markets, 471
  order fulfillment, 476–478
  strategy, 472–479
  suppliers, 478
  website, 236
  website technology, 473–474
Penetration pricing, 167
Pepperidge Farm, 90, 774
PepsiCo, 77, 88, 95, 116, 123, 154,
  190, 191–192, 198, 460
  acquisition of KFC, 725–726
  description, 724
Perceived risk, 52
Percent of sales advertising, 116
Perdue Farms, 293
Perishability, 166
  of services, 178
Personal computer industry
  Compaq Computer, 831–835
  competing value chain
    models, 812–814

market conditions in 2000,
  810–812
near-term outlook, 812
recent strategy changes,
  830–831
worldwide vendors, 801
Personal motivation, 61
Personal selling, 112
  evolution of, 135
  importance of, 129–130
  managing sales, 137–144
  relationship building, 137–144
  sales process, 130–137
  strengths and weaknesses, 113
  tasks, 129
Persuasion, 131
Per-unit expenditures on
  advertising, 116–118
Pessimists, 71
Pfizer, Inc., 303
Pfizer, Inc. Animal Health Group,
  293–308
  competitors, 305–306
  description, 303–304
  marketing strategy, 304–308
  product line, 305–306
PGA Merchandise Show, 372
Pharmaceutical industry, 187
Philip Morris Companies, 3, 11,
  98, 598–611
  cigarette industry segments,
    602–603
  company background, 598–599
  diversification by acquisition,
    599–601
  as employer, 605–606
  future prospects, 610–611
  industry segments, 601–602
  international markets, 603–605
  Kraft General Foods, 605
  litigation, 609–610
  performance and prospects,
    606–607
  threats to performance,
    607–609
Philips and Bosch, 331
Philips Electronics, 46, 466–468
Physical contact, 192
Physical features, 45
Physiological needs, 49
Pillsbury, 190, 210
PIMS; see Profit Impact of
  Marketing Strategies
Pine state Tobacco and Candy, 312
Ping, 381, 382, 385, 395–396,
  396–398, 399
Pizza Hut, 190, 193, 251, 460,
  726–727
  description, 255
Pizza sales, 210
Place influences, 45
Planters, 314, 315, 316, 318
Polaris, 408
Polaroid, 96
Political environment, 17
Political uncertainty, 193
Polo footwear, 420
Popular Mechanics, 343, 355

Popular Science, 343, 362, 368
Population characteristics, 195–196
Pork industry, 300
Porsche, 170
Portfolio models, 13
    BCG model, 23–24
    General Electric model, 24–25
    purpose, 22
    review of theory, 22–23
    ROI variables, 23
Portfolio theory, 22–23
Positioning strategies, 76–78
Position map, 77–78
Postal geography definitions, 282
Post cereals, 11
Post hoc segmentation, 70
Postpurchase evaluation, 233
    individual customers, 52–54
    by organizational buyers,
        66–67
Potential Ranking Index by Zip
    Markets, 75–76
Poultry industry, 300
Powell's Inc., 310
Powerlite, 353
Prentice Hall, Inc., 225
Presenting, 134
Present value discount factors, 223
Present value ratio, 223
Prestige pricing, 163
Price changes, 163, 171
Price Club, 156
Price/Costco, 12
Price discrimination, 168
Price elasticity, 164, 170
Price-fixing, 168
Price influences, 45
Price information, 170
Priceline.com, 160
Price structure, 171
Pricing
    athletic footwear
        industry, 422
    break-even formula, 167
    at Claritas Inc., 292
    cost considerations, 164–166
    in global marketing, 200
    in global marketing
        research, 197
    high/low, 165
    on Internet, 235–236
    by Lady Foot Locker, 430
    in marketing planning, 846
    off-peak, 178
    product considerations,
        166–167
    by Sathers, Inc., 316–318
    by 3DV Litigation Services,
        269–270
Pricing decisions
    demand influences
        demographic factors, 162
        price elasticity, 164
        psychological factors,
            162–163
    environmental factors
        competition, 167–168

government regulation,
    168
supply influences
    cost considerations,
        164–166
    pricing objectives, 164
    product considerations,
        166–167
Pricing model, 168–171
    analyze profit potential, 171
    estimating costs and
        limitations, 171
    initial price structure, 171
    price changes, 171
    product-price relationship,
        170–171
    setting objectives, 169
Pricing objectives, 164, 169
Pricing strategy, 524–528
    demand influences,
        162–164
    everyday low pricing, 165
    in retailing, 165
    supply influences on
        decisions, 164–167
    tips for improving, 170
Primary data, 30–31
Principle-oriented consumers,
    74–75
Private label brands/products,
    90, 420
Privatization, in Mexico,
    741–742
PRIZM (Potential Ranking Index
    by Zip Market), 75–76,
    282–283, 287–290
Problem definition
    for case analysis, 211–212
    inadequate, 213
Problem-solving skills, 109
Processed food sales, 608
Procter and Gamble, 7, 88, 89, 98,
    99, 106, 116, 125–126, 199
    website, 234, 240
Producers, 56
Product attributes, 94
Product audit
    deletions, 92–94
    means for controlling
        strategy, 94
    product improvement, 94
Product classification, 83–84
Product definition, 82–83
Product deletions, 92–94
Product development, 100, 105
    Callaway Golf Company,
        386–387
    strategy, 11
Product improvement, 94, 99
Product influences, 45
Product innovation, 362
Product involvement, 47
Production, Callaway Golf
    Company, 387–388
Production cycle, in ski market,
    337–338
Product knowledge, 47
Product life cycle, 91–92

and deletions, 92–93
    rejuvenating products, 95
Product line, 85–88, 99
    additions to, 88
    Callaway Golf Company,
        389–394
    Cannondale Corporation,
        368–370
    by Sathers, Inc., 316
Product line extension, 88
Product management, 96
    branding and brand equity,
        88–90
    organizing for, 94–96
    packaging, 90–91
    product classification, 83–84
    product definition, 82–83
    product line, 85–88
    product mix, 85–88
    product quality and value,
        84–85
Product mix, 85–88
Product orientation, 2
Product planning, 198
Product positioning, 76–78
Product-price relationship, 170–171
Product quality, 84–85
Product rejuvenation, 95
Products
    BCG classification, 23
    branding, 88–90
    considerations in pricing,
        166–167
    contrasted with services, 177
    distinctiveness, 166
    exportable, 197
    high-tech, 70–71
    imitation, 100
    life cycle, 166–167
    in marketing planning, 846
    perishability, 166
    private label, 90
    substitute, 208
Product strategy, 82–96
    elements of, 83
    for global marketing, 198
    product audit, 92–94
    and product life cycle, 91–92
    project management issues,
        82–91
    at Starbucks, 294–297
Product value, 85
Professional pride, 61
Profitability, 24–25
    effect of price changes, 163
Profitability measures
    break-even analysis, 220–222
    net present value analysis,
        222–224
Profitability ratios, 225–226
Profit contribution, 92
Profit Impact of Marketing
    Strategies, 22–23
Profit margin on sales, 226
Profit maximizers, 119–120
Profit potential, 171
Profits
    additional, 101

from advertising, 115–116
Project management, 340–341
Project planning, 104–105
Project teams, 104–105, 340
Promotion
    athletic footwear industry,
        422–423
    Cannondale Corporation,
        365–366
    in marketing planning, 846
    motorcycle industry, 406–409
    by Sathers, Inc., 318
    by Wind Technology, 414–416
Promotional allowances, 171
Promotional pricing, 168
Promotion influences, 45
Promotion mix
    advertising, 114–122
    changes over time, 112
    direct marketing, 127
    elements of, 111–112
    in global marketing, 200–202
    integrated marketing
        communications, 112–114
    public relations, 126
    sales promotion, 123–126
    strengths and weaknesses,
        113
Promptness, 192
Property and casualty
    insurance, 179
Prospecting, 132–133
Prozac, 237
Prudential Insurance Company,
    187
Psychographic segmentation,
    74–75
Psychological influences on
    consumers
    product involvement, 47
    product knowledge, 47
Psychological pricing strategies,
    162–163
Public announcement services, 126
Publicity, 112
    types of, 126
Public relations, 112, 126
    strengths and weaknesses, 113
Public sources, 50
Puch, 360
Pull strategy, 123
Puma, 691
Purchase activities, 65
Purchase decision, 50–52, 233
Purchase-type influences,
    organizational buying
    modified rebuy, 58
    new task purchase, 58
    straight rebuy, 57–58
Purchasing
    Callaway Golf Company,
        387–388
    Cannondale Corporation, 365
Purchasing department, 60–61
Purchasing policies and
    procedures, 60–61
Purex, 95
Push strategy, 123

Quaker Oats, 90, 210
Qualitative research, 31–34
Quality, 84–85
  of services, 180–183
Quality leadership, 25
Quantitative forecasting
  techniques, 140
Quantitative research, 31–34
Quantity discounts, 171
*Quarterly Financial Report for
  Manufacturing
  Corporations,* 225
Question marks, 23
Quick ratio, 225
QVC, 158

R. L. Polk, 282
Radio advertising, 121
Ragu, website, 234
Railroad management, 185
Raleigh, 352, 353, 358, 360
Ralph Lauren, 420
Ranchers-Cattlemen Action Legal
  Foundation, 301
Random lead generation, 133
Rand stores, 352
Rate-of-return target pricing, 166
Ratio analysis
  asset management ratios,
    225
  comparison of ratios, 225–226
  computing ratios, 225
  information sources, 225
  liquidity ratios, 224–225
  opportunities and problems
    from, 226–228
  profitability ratios, 225–226
  steps, 224
Raw materials, 83
RCA Corporation, 202
Recall tests, 122
Recognition tests, 122
Red zone, 25
Reebok International, 419, 420,
  421, 423, 428, 430–435,
  690–691
  Lobo shoe launch, 417–435
  marketing support, 434
  product timing, 432–433
  retail exclusivity, 433–434
  website, 234
Reel.com, 235
Reference groups, 55
Regression analysis, 36
Regulation
  of advertising, 128
  legal environment, 17
  and pricing decisions, 167–168
Relationship-building process,
  131–136
  becoming partnerships, 136
  long-term relationships,
    135–136
  managing, 137–144
  obtaining commitment, 135
  planning sales call, 133–134
  presenting, 134
  prospecting, 132–133

responding to objections,
  134–135
Relationship marketing, 152
Relay approach, 105
Reliability, 181
Remarketing, 92
Repositioning, 100
Research and development,
  366–367
Research approach to
  advertising, 118
Research report, 36–37
Responding to objections, 134–135
Responsiveness, 181
Retailers, 146, 148
  athletic footwear industry, 422
  benefit of wholesalers, 155
  category killers, 156
  trade sales promotions aimed
    at, 123–124
  in vertical marketing
    systems, 154
Retail exclusivity, 433–434
Retail grocery industry, 479–480
  online segments, 481–483
  supermarket chains, 480–481
Retailing
  electronic exchange, 158–160
  everyday low pricing, 165
  nonstore, 157–158
  percent of sales advertising, 116
  store, 156–157
Return on investment, variables, 23
Returns on total assets, 226
Reuters, website, 243
Risk perception, 52
Risks, new product
  development, 104
Risk theorists, 52
Rivalry among competitors,
  207–208
RJ Reynolds Tobacco Company, 80
RJR Nabisco, 95
Roadway Express, 12
  website, 236
Robert Morris Associates, 225
Robinson, 353
Robinsons-May, website, 232
Rockport, 420
Rogaine, 237
Ronald McDonald House, 253
Rossignol, 335, 336
Routine decision making, 438
Royal and Ancient Golf Club of St.
  Andrews, 402
Rubbermaid, 12, 103, 456
Rugby approach, 105
Ryka, 421

Safety needs, 49
Salary, 143
Sales
  from advertising, 115–116
  Callaway Golf Company,
    388–389
  company part of, 138
Sales call, 133–134

Sales expense budget, 142
Sales force
  aftermarketing, 136
  compensation, 142–144
  controlling, 139–140
  evaluation measures, 143
  information from
    organizational
    customers, 131
  motivation, 142–144
  objectives, 130–131
  performance outcomes, 144
  relationship-building process,
    131–136
  support staff, 136–137
  technology for, 141
  types of incentives, 144
Sales force composite method,
  139–140
Sales forecasting, 139, 849–851
  expense budget, 142
  methods, 139–140
Sales leads, 133
Sales management
  analyzing expenses, 142
  establishing quotas, 140–142
  establishing territories, 140–142
  forecasting sales, 139–140
  motivating and compensating
    performance, 142–144
  tasks, 138–139
Sales organization, 138
Salespeople
  evaluation measures, 143
  main link to customers,
    129–130
  salary or commission, 143
  tasks in personal selling, 129
  territories and quotas, 140–142
Sales process, 130–137
  managing, 137–144
Sales promotion, 111, 123–126
  consumer promotions, 125
  in global marketing, 200–202
  objectives, 124
  popularity of, 123
  push or pull, 123
  strengths and weaknesses, 113,
    124–126
  trade sales promotions,
    123–124
Sales quotas, 140–141
Sales territories, 140–141
Sales trends, 92
Sales volume, 221
Salomon S. A., 326–342
  competitors, 335–337
  decision to enter ski market,
    332–333
  description, 327–329
  first forty years, 329–331
  management, structure, and
    culture, 331–332
  Monocoque project, 339–342
  project management, 340–341
  project team, 340
Sam Goody, website, 235

Sara Lee, 11
Sathers, Inc., 309–325
  company history, 309–310
  operations, 310–312
  pricing, 316–318
  product categories, 311
  promotion and
    distribution, 318
  roll-out, 318–320
  Snacks to Go product line,
    313–316
  strategy, 312–313
Saucony, 421
SBU; *see* Strategic business units
Schwinn Bicycles, 352, 357,
  526–528
Schwinn Cycling and Fitness,
  353–354
Screening prospects, 133
Sealed-bid pricing, 168
Sealtest dairy, 11
Search engines, 240
Sears, 153, 249
  website, 232
Secondary data, 30–31
Securities and Exchange
  Commission, 128, 225
  EDGAR database, 241
Security Pacific Financial
  Services, 293
SEGA, 462, 572–576
Selected-lead searching, 133
Selective distribution, 150
Self-actualization needs, 49
Selling orientation, 2
Selling price per unit, 220
Service marketing
  challenges
    banking, 186
    health care, 187
    implications for
      marketers, 189
    insurance, 187–189
    travel, 187
  lessons in, 188
  obstacles to
    limited competition,
      184–185
    limited view of
      marketing, 184
    noncreative
      management, 185
    no obsolescence,
      185–186
  to provide quality, 180–183
Service Merchandise, 156
Service products, 175
Service quality, 180–183
  customer satisfaction
    measurement, 182
  determinants, 181–182
  importance of internal
    marketing, 182–183
  on Internet, 185
Services
  adaptation to Internet, 237
  bundling, 186

channels of distribution,
    176–177
characteristics, 175–180
client relationship, 180
contrasted with products, 177
customer expectation, 179
definitions of, 175
differentiated marketing
    system, 178
fast growth of, 174
fluctuating demand, 178
gaps with customers, 180–181
inseparability, 176–178
intangibility, 176
perishability, 178
unconditional guarantees, 181
Seven-Up, 77
Shakespeare, 382
Shell Oil, 190
Sherman Antitrust Act, 168
Shimano, 361
Showtime, 465
Siemens, 194
Sierra Club, 351
Simmons Media/Market Service, 846
Simmons Reports, 115
Situational influences on business,
    45–47
Situation analysis, 14–17, 68
    checklist, 209–211
    competitive environment, 15
    cooperative environment, 15
    economic environment, 15–16
    environment, 207
    firms, 208
    industry, 207–208
    legal environment, 17
    marketing strategy, 208–209
    political environment, 17
    social environment, 17
    SWOT analysis, 214
Skiing equipment industry,
    326–342
Skunk works, 104–105
Slotting allowances, 171
Smith New Court PLC, 185
Smithsonian Magazine, 356
Smoking and health, 609–610
Snacks to Go
    marketing research for,
        313–316
    performance, 320–325
    pricing, 316–318
    product development, 316–317
    products, 316
    promotion and distribution,
        318
    roll-out, 318–320
Sneaker Stadium, 422
Social class, 43–44
Social customs, 192
Social environment, 17
Social features, 46
Social influences on
    consumers, 41–44
    culture and subculture, 43
    reference groups and
        family, 44

social class, 43–44
Software Publishing Association,
    573, 576
Sole sourcing, 61
Sony Corporation, 193, 202,
    318, 468
    website, 237
South Delaware Coors, Inc.,
    272–280
    investing and operating data,
        279–280
    research proposal, 273–279
Southern Video Partnership, 459
Southwest Airlines, 12, 188
Soy sauce, 720–721
Spalding Sporting Goods, 383,
    386, 403, 429
Spalding Sports Worldwide, 395
Specialized, 352
Specialized Bicycles, 356–357
Specialty stores, 156
Spellman, 414
Sponsorship, 126
Sports Authority, 422
Sports Illustrated, 343
Sprint, 184–185
SRI International, 74
Standard Rate and Data, 846, 851
Starbucks Coffee Houses, 12, 47,
    98, 136, 294–297
*Starch Advertising Readership
    Service,* 846
Starch Reports, 115
Stars, 23
*Statistical Abstract of the United
    States,* 31, 849
Status-oriented consumers, 74–75
Store retailing, 156–157
StoreRunner.com, 236
Straight rebuy, 57–58
Strategic alliances, 104, 136, 203
    Blockbuster and Philips,
        466–468
Strategic business units
    characteristics, 13
    objectives, 23–24
    in portfolio models, 22–25
Strategic Mapping Inc., 283
Strategic plan, 13
Strategic planning, 3–13
    components, 5
    cross-functional objectives, 20
    and marketing management,
        4–5
    related to marketing plan, 21
    summary on, 19–20
Strategic planning process
    choosing appropriate strategy,
        12–13
    organizational mission, 4–8
    organizational objectives, 8–9
    organizational portfolio
        plan, 13
    organizational strategies, 9–12
Strategic risk, 104
Strategies
    cost leadership, 12

differentiation, 12
diversification, 11
    for entering foreign markets,
        202–203
    global, 194–195
    for growth in foreign markets,
        203–204
    of internal marketing, 183
    market development, 11
    marketing mix, 79–80
    market penetration, 10–11
    for market segmentation,
        78–79
    new product development,
        99–102
    organizational growth, 11
    product development, 11
    product positioning, 76–78
    push *vs.* pull, 123
    for service intangibility, 176
Strivers, 76
Structural influences,
    organizational buying
    organization-specific factors,
        59–60
    purchasing policies and
        procedures, 60–61
    purchasing roles, 58–61
Strugglers, 76
Sturmey-Archer bicycles, 358
Sturn, Ruger and Company, 388
Subculture, 43
Substitute products, 208
Subway, 460
Sunday Times of London,
    website, 242
Sun Microsystems, 191, 342,
    557–567
    chairman and CEO, 558
    chief computer designer, 559
    company background, 557–558
    competition, 564–565
    customer categories, 562–563
    customer service, 562
    distribution channels, 562
    field operations director, 559
    financial analysis, 565–567
    product line focus, 560
    software developments,
        563–564
    strategy, 560–562
    team consensus, 559–560
Sunshine Biscuits, 90
SunTour, 361
Super Club Holding and Finance
    S. A., 467
Supermarket chains, 480–481
Suppliers
    bargaining power, 208
    of Lady Foot Locker, 429–430
Supply and demand, 145
Supply influences on pricing,
    164–167
Survey of Current Business, 31
Survey research, 32–33
Sustainable competitive
    advantage, 12–13
Suzuki, 408, 409

SWOT analysis, 214
Systems theory, 150

T. J. Maxx, 156
Taco Bell, 190, 251, 255, 726–727
    description, 256
Tactician
Tandy Corporation, 468, 830
Tangible product, 82
Tangibles, 181
Target market, 845
    definition, 68
    ethics of, 80
    for packaging, 91
    selecting, 17–18, 78–79
Target Stores, 90, 352
    website, 232, 234
Task approach to advertising, 118
Task features, 46
Taylor-Made Golf Company, 330,
    376, 381, 382, 383, 384, 385,
    395–396, 398–399, 401
Technical skills, 109
Technological innovation, 351
Technology
    in banking, 186
    for direct marketing, 127
    for peak period demand, 178
    and sales force, 141
    and travel industry, 187–188
Technology push research, 103
Television advertising, 121
Television home shopping, 158
Tenneco, 639
Test marketing, 106
    limitations, 37
Textron, 373
Theater tests, 122
Thomas J. Lipton Inc., 774
Thomson Electronics, 32
3DV Litigation Services, 261–271
    assessing market
        opportunities, 266–270
    business units, 263–264
    company history, 262–263
    competitors, 270
    construction and
        transportation services,
        267–268
    financial position, 264–265
    future of, 271
    marketing
        communications, 266
    organizational structure and
        culture, 265–266
    perceptions of computer
        visualization, 269
    pricing, 269–270
Time, 46
    factor in new product
        development, 106
Time magazine, website, 241
Time-series analysis, 140
Time to market, 106
Time Warner Corporation, 465
Timex, 194
Timex Group Ltd., 12
Titan, 408

Titleist, 385, 396, 399, 403
Tommy Hilfiger, 366, 420
Tony's Pizza, 210
Tootsie Roll, 312
Toshiba Corporation, 468, 839
Total asset utilization, 225
Total-cost concept, 150–151
Total quality management, 85
Totino's Pizza, 210
Tower Records, 434
Toyota Motors, 77, 88, 263, 354
Toys "R" Us, Inc., 352, 462
    website, 232
Toys "R" Us Japan, Ltd., 459
Trademark, 88
Trade sales promotions, 123–124
Transportation Equity for the 21st
    Century, 349
Transportation industry,
    267–269
Travel industry, 187–189
Travelocity.com, 237
Trek, 352, 353, 355
Tricon Global Restaurants, 254, 255
Trip.com, 237
Triple Dot, 33
Truck and tractor rental/
    leasing, 179
Tupperware, 158, 454–456
TWA, 188

Ultra Kustom, 408
Unifiber, 384
Unisys, 411
United Airlines, 136, 188, 296
United Auto Workers, 635-636
United Parcel Service, 136
    website, 233, 236
United Sports Technologies, 384
United States, bicycle industry,
    345-353
U.S. Air, 460
U.S. Bank, website, 237

United States Forest Service,
    350, 351
United States Gold Association, 376
U.S. International Trade
    Commission, 301
United States Postal Service, 128,
    178, 355
U.S. Robotics, 553
Univega, 353
Universal Studios, 460, 464
University of Michigan, Document
    Center, 244
Upper Americans, 43
Urban Blend, 32
US Airways, 185
USA Today, 343
Users, 59
USNews and World Report
    website, 242
US West, 185

Vaitra, 412
VALS™, 74–75
VALS2™, 74–75
Value, 85
    strategies based on, 12
Value chain
    Callaway Golf Company,
        386–389
    models, 812–814
Values
    American, 42, 43
    cultural, 17
Values and lifestyles, 74
Vans, 420
Variable costs, 220
Vector Video Inc., 459
Vending machines, 158
Vendor analysis, 65, 66
Vendor supported merchandising
    programs, 434
Vertical market, 84
Vertical marketing systems

administered, 152–153
    contractual, 153–154
    corporate, 154
VF Corporation, 12–13
Viagra, 237
Victoria's Secret, website, 232
Video business, 465, 466
Videogame industry, 572–576
Videogame violence
    Nintendo's position, 573–574
    progress report, 575–576
    SEGA's position, 574–575
Video Library Inc., 459
Video Superstores Venture
    L. P., 459
Visa Card, 88
Vlasic Foods, 774–775
VNU Business Information
    Services, 286
VNU United Dutch Publishing
    Companies, 286
Völkl, 336
Volkswagen, 199, 355
Volvo, 77, 365

Walgreens, 90
Wall Street Journal, website, 241
Wall Street Research Net, 243
Wal-Mart, 12, 45, 56, 90, 153, 155,
    156, 158, 159, 193, 208, 352,
    452, 462, 830
    website, 232
Walt Disney Company, 33, 88, 464
Warner Brothers, 464
Washington Post, website, 242
Waste Management, 458
Websense.com, 244
Webvan Group, Inc., 484–487
Wells Fargo, 32
Wendy's International, 250, 253
    description, 254
Whirlpool Corporation, 46, 193
Wholesalers, 56, 146, 148

benefits for channel
        members, 155
    distribution functions,
        155–156
    marketing by, 155
    selection of retailers, 156–157
    video business, 464–465
Width of product mix, 85
Willingness to buy, 196–197
Wilson Sporting Goods, 383
Wind Technology, 411–416
    competition, 413–414
    corporate strategy, 413
    current situation, 411–412
    potential customers, 413
    promotion, 414
    survival strategy, 412
Wine industry, 579–583
Wired News, 244
Women's National Basketball
    Association, 417
Women's Sports Foundation, 424
Women's World Basketball
    Association, 429
Woolworth, 156
Woolworth Corporation's Athletic
    Group, 426
Working class, 44
World Wide Web, 240; see also
    Internet directory
Wrangler jeans, 13

Xerox Corporation, 94, 96

Yahoo! Auction, 517–518
Yahoo.com, 236, 237, 240
Yamaha, 408, 409
Yellow zone, 25

ZDNet, 244
Zenith, 190
ZIP Market, 282
Zip-Pak, 313